FINANCIAL ACCOUNTING

Eleventh Edition

Jan R. Williams
University of Tennessee

Susan F. Haka
Michigan State University

Mark S. Bettner
Bucknell University

Robert F. Meigs
San Diego State University

Boston   Burr Ridge, IL   Dubuque, IA   Madison, WI   New York   San Francisco   St. Louis
Bangkok   Bogotá   Caracas   Kuala Lumpur   Lisbon   London   Madrid   Mexico City
Milan   Montreal   New Delhi   Santiago   Seoul   Singapore   Sydney   Taipei   Toronto

McGraw-Hill Higher Education

*A Division of The **McGraw-Hill** Companies*

FINANCIAL ACCOUNTING

Published by McGraw-Hill/Irwin, a business unit of The McGraw-Hill Companies, Inc., 1221 Avenue of the Americas, New York, NY, 10020. Copyright © 2003, 2001, 1998, 1995, 1992, 1989, 1986, 1983, 1979, 1975, 1970 by The McGraw-Hill Companies, Inc. All rights reserved. No part of this publication may be reproduced or distributed in any form or by any means, or stored in a database or retrieval system, without the prior written consent of The McGraw-Hill Companies, Inc., including, but not limited to, in any network or other electronic storage or transmission, or broadcast for distance learning.

Some ancillaries, including electronic and print components, may not be available to customers outside the United States.

This book is printed on acid-free paper.

domestic   1 2 3 4 5 6 7 8 9 0 VNH/VNH 0 9 8 7 6 5 4 3 2
international 1 2 3 4 5 6 7 8 9 0 VNH/VNH 0 9 8 7 6 5 4 3 2

ISBN   0-07-251668-2

Publisher: *Brent Gordon*
Executive editor: *Stewart Mattson*
Developmental editor I: *Heather Sabo*
Marketing manager: *Ryan Blankenship*
Senior producer, media technology: *Ed Przyzycki*
Project manager: *Catherine R. Schultz*
Lead production supervisor: *Heather D. Burbridge*
Coordinator freelance design: *Artemio Ortiz, Jr.*
Photo research coordinator: *Judy Kausal*
Photo researcher: *Mary Reeg*
Lead supplement producer: *Becky Szura*
Senior digital content specialist: *Brian Nacik*
Cover design: *Artemio Ortiz, Jr.*
Interior design: *Artemio Ortiz, Jr.*
Cover image: *Henryk T. Kaiser, Rex Intstock, PictureQuest*
Typeface: *10.5/12 Times Roman*
Compositor: *Techbooks*
Printer: *Von Hoffmann Press, Inc.*

Library of Congress Cataloging-in-Publication Data

Financial accounting / Jan R. Williams ... [et al.].
    p. cm.
    Includes index.
    ISBN 0-07-251668-2 (alk. paper) — ISBN 0-07-119913-6 (international : alk. paper)
    1. Accounting. I. Williams, Jan R.
HF5635.F5315 2003
657--dc21   2002066018

INTERNATIONAL EDITION ISBN 0-07-119913-6
Copyright © 2003. Exclusive rights by The McGraw-Hill Companies, Inc. for manufacture and export. This book cannot be re-exported from the country to which it is sold by McGraw-Hill.

The International Edition is not available in North America.

www.mhhe.com

To Ben Taylor Wishart and Asher Williams Hunt who have taught me the joys of being a grandfather. — Jan R. Williams

To my parents, Fred and Marjorie. — Mark S. Bettner

For Cliff, Abi, and my mother, Fran.— Susan F. Haka

preface

ABOUT THE AUTHORS

Jan R. Williams Jan R. Williams is Ernst & Young Professor of Accounting and Dean of the College of Business Administration, University of Tennessee. He received a BS degree from George Peabody College, an MBA from Baylor University and a Ph.D. from the University of Arkansas. He was formerly on the faculties of the University of Georgia and Texas Tech University. He is a CPA in Tennessee and Arkansas. Dr. Williams's primary teaching and research interest is corporate finance reporting. He is currently the author or coauthor of four books and more than 70 articles and other publications about financial reporting and accounting education.

Dr. Williams has been extensively involved in professional accounting activities with the American Accounting Association (AAA), the American Institute of CPAs (AICPA), the Tennessee Society of CPAs, and other organizations. In 1999-2000, he served as president of the AAA and in that capacity traveled throughout the world speaking on issues related to accounting education and practice. He has recently served on two task forces of the AICPA to redesign the CPA examination to meet the changing needs of the profession for the 21st century.

Susan F. Haka Currently the Ernst & Young Professor of Accounting in the Department of Accounting and Information Systems at Michigan State University, Sue has received the prestigious All-University Teacher-Scholar Award and has twice received the Department's Outstanding Teaching Award. Sue was chosen to speak at the American Accounting Association's New Faculty Consortium on Teaching. Sue is the editor of *Behavioral Research in Accounting,* has been associate editor of the *Journal of Management Accounting Research, Accounting Horizons,* and *Contemporary Accounting Research,* and is a member of the editorial boards of *The Accounting Review, International Journal of Accounting,* and *Management Accounting Research.* Also active in the American Accounting Association, Sue has served as president of the Management Accounting Section and Director of the Doctoral Consortium.

Mark S. Bettner Associate professor at Bucknell University, Mark Bettner has received numerous teaching and research awards. In addition to his work on the Meigs and Williams titles, he has written many ancillary materials, published in scholarly journals, and presented at numerous academic and practitioner conferences. Mark is also on the editorial advisory boards of several academic journals, including the *International Journal of Accounting and Business Society.*

preface

BRIDGING THE GAP

Financial Accounting: Finally, a text both sides can agree on.

For the last 10 years faculty have debated over the best way to teach financial accounting to all business students. The "preparer-oriented" approach and the "user-oriented" approach differ over issues ranging from financial statement preparation to decision making, yet both face a common problem: how to explain financial accounting to both accounting majors and non-accounting business majors without depriving either group of what they need to succeed in their education and their careers?

Financial Accounting, 11/e, bridges this gap through an integrated learning system that provides both groups with what they need.

preface

BETWEEN PREPARER AND USER.

Balance.
Financial Accounting, 11/e provides students with sufficient technical detail along with insight into why it is relevant. This is accomplished through real-world *vignettes* that open and close each chapter and through our *Case in Point* and *Management Strategy and Financial Reporting* boxes. In addition, the *Your Turn* boxes put students in real-world situations and ask them to apply what they have learned. Finally, a unique global business chapter provides students with an understanding of the issues that impact accounting in the global business environment.

Problem material.
Financial Accounting, 11/e, provides you with a proven, dependable set of problem material. The problems not only help students develop technical accounting skills but the unstructured cases, spreadsheet problems, ethics problems, and Internet exercises build the problem-solving skills necessary in business and for the new Uniform CPA exam. The problem material and supplements have been checked in both the manuscript and page proof stages to ensure the highest accuracy.

Divergent learning styles.
Financial Accounting, 11/e, offers a complete set of tools designed to help students of differing learning styles successfully learn financial accounting. For the audiovisual learners, the My Mentor CD provides a rich, interactive multimedia experience that integrates with the text through icons in the margins. For students with poor math skills, ALEKS Math Prep for Accounting is a Web-based product that provides a user-friendly, self-paced method for getting up to speed. Lastly, our Website provides a wide array of resources for helping students better understand financial accounting.

As you read the rest of this preface you will learn more about the tools available to help you get the most from this textbook. Whether you prefer to focus on financial statement preparation or business decision making, **Financial Accounting, 11/e** will work for you, bridging the gap between two teaching philosophies—and between you and your students.

preface

What makes Financial Accounting such a powerful learning tool?

In-Text Features

Owing to the growing number of service-based companies in business today, the eleventh edition uses a helpful icon to distinguish service-related examples in the text.

- New **chapter openers** feature vignettes that relate real-world companies, such as Intel, to accounting concepts covered in the chapter.

- **Cash Effects** sections show how a transaction or method impacts the cash flow of an organization.

- **Your Turn** boxes put you in the role of decision maker, requiring you to apply chapter concepts to situations faced by investors, creditors, and managers. An ethical icon indicates boxes that require ethical decisions.

preface

Financial Accounting is full of pedagogy designed to make studying productive and hassle-free. On the following pages, you will see the engaging, helpful pedagogical features that enable your students, regardless of academic major or preferred learning style, to master the fundamentals of financial accounting.

- **Case in Point** boxes, retained from the tenth edition, use actual business events to illustrate the relationship between accounting concepts and the real world. An international icon indicates boxes that contain international information.

- **Second Look** boxes at the end of each chapter returns to the real-world company highlighted in the chapter opener. This second look allows students to relate the accounting topics they have just learned to those practiced by actual businesses.

- **Management Strategy and Financial Reporting** boxes link management decision making directly to financial reporting.

preface

What makes Financial Accounting such a powerful learning tool?

Financial Accounting takes a new approach to the accounting cycle. In response to our users, we've expanded the discussion from two to three full chapters: recording entries is covered in Chapter 3, adjusting entries in Chapter 4, and closing entries in Chapter 5. This should make the material much less imposing for your students and improve comprehension and performance as they proceed through the rest of the text.

Students often struggle when learning to record transactions. To help with this challenging topic, the authors have broken the process down into four easy steps.

Step 1: Analysis—shows which accounts were recorded with an increase or decrease.

Step 2: Debit/Credit rules—This helps students remember whether the account should be debited or credited.

Step 3: The Journal Entry is shown to illustrate what has happened in the two previous steps.

Step 4: The ledger T-accounts are shown.

Recording Revenue and Expense Transactions: An Illustration   107

Jan. 31   Paid for utilities used in January, $200.

ANALYSIS	The cost of utilities is an expense. The asset Cash is decreased.
DEBIT–CREDIT RULES	Expenses decrease owners' equity and are recorded by debits; debit Utilities Expense $200. Decreases in assets are recorded by credits; credit Cash $200.
JOURNAL ENTRY	Jan. 31 Utilities Expense . . . . 200 Cash 200
ENTRIES IN LEDGER ACCOUNTS	Cash: 1/27 Bal. 15,800 1/31 1,200; 1/31 2,200 1/31 200 Utilities Expense: 1/31 200

My Notes: Incurred an expense, paying cash

Having analyzed and recorded all of Overnight's January transactions, next we focus upon the company's February activities. Overnight's February transactions are described, analyzed, and recorded as follows:

Feb. 1   Paid *Daily Tribune* $360 cash for newspaper advertising to be run during February.

ANALYSIS	The cost of advertising is an expense. The asset Cash is decreased.
DEBIT–CREDIT RULES	Expenses decrease owners' equity and are recorded by debits; debit Advertising Expense $360. Decreases in assets are recorded by credits; credit Cash $360.
JOURNAL ENTRY	Feb. 1 Advertising Expense . . . . 360 Cash 360
ENTRIES IN LEDGER ACCOUNTS	Cash: 1/31 Bal. 16,600 2/1 360 Advertising Expense: 2/1 360

My Notes: Incurred an expense, paying cash

preface

XI

How does Financial Accounting treat end-of-chapter material?

Defined Key Terms and **Self-Test Questions** review and reinforce chapter material.

Three **Comprehensive Problems,** ranging from two to five pages in length, help students to review and synthesize text material throughout the book.

Demonstration Problems and their solutions allow students to test their knowledge of key points in the chapters.

Cases and Unstructured Problems allow students to think analytically about key concepts from the chapter and apply them to business decisions.

Business Week **Assignments** at the end of each chapter are based on recent articles and require students to answer questions by relating accounting concepts to current events.

The Annual Report from Tootsie Roll Industries, Inc., from 2000 is used throughout the text in exercise and problem material to reveal actual business applications of text material.

Ethics assignments provide a springboard for exploring ethical issues within accounting.

Icons identify exercises involving General Ledger Application Software (GLAS), Excel templates, ethical issues, group activities, and international issues are used throughout the text.

What's new about the Eleventh Edition?

All Chapters:
- Chapter openers
- New Cases-in-Point
- New Your Turn boxes
- New Management Strategy boxes
- New Second Look feature
- New Expanded Financial Analysis sections
- New *Business Week* cases

Chapter 1:

Now includes a brief introduction and definition of the three financial statements, Income Statement, Statement of Financial Position, and Statement of Cash Flows.

Chapter 2

A new chapter opener covers Intel.

Financial highlights material has been moved to Chapter 1.

Updated material.

Chapter 3

Chapter 3 is now the first of three chapters covering the accounting cycle. Chapter 3 begins with transaction analysis and concludes with an introduction of the trial balance.

End-of-chapter changes include:

- New exercise requiring transaction analysis.
- New Internet Assignment involving PC Connection and Apple Computer.

Chapter 4

Chapter 4 is now the second of three chapters covering the accounting cycle and begins with the trial balance introduced in Chapter 3, concluding with the adjusted trial balance. Unlike the previous edition, financial statement preparation and the closing process are deferred to Chapter 5.

End-of-chapter changes include:

- New problem involving the analysis of accruals and deferrals.
- New Internet Assignment involving Hershey.

Chapter 5

Chapter 5 is entirely new and is the third of three chapters covering the accounting cycle. Chapter 5 begins with the adjusted trial balance introduced in Chapter 4 and concludes with the preparation of financial statements, some basic financial analysis, and the closing process.

End-of-chapter changes include:

- Extensively revised exercises and problems involving error corrections, financial statement preparation, basic financial statement analysis, and the closing process
- New real-world problem involving the analysis of Circuit City

Comprehensive Problem 1:

Entirely new comprehensive problem involving the entire accounting cycle.

Chapter 6

Chapter 6 departs from the ongoing Overnight Auto illustration presented in Chapters 2-5. It is our first introduction to merchandising companies.

End-of-chapter changes include:

- New exercise involving perpetual inventory systems
- New real-world exercise contrasting Wal-Mart's profitability to that of Kmart
- New *Business Week* assignment
- New Internet assignment involving Gap, Inc.

Chapter 7

Chapter 7 addresses the financial assets: Cash, Short-Term Investments, and Receivables.

The presentation of bank reconciliation has been revised and updated.

The Financial Analysis section has been revised and improved.

End-of-chapter changes include many new real-world exercises such as:

- Exercise analyzing Microsoft's investment in marketable securities
- Exercise comparing collection performance of Adolph Coors and Anheuser-Busch

preface

Chapter 8

The body of the chapter includes a revised and expanded presentations of the retail estimation method and expanded coverage of financial analysis related to inventory turnover and profitability measures.

End-of-chapter changes include the following exercises:

- Exercise analyzing inventory reporting by Quaker Oats Company
- Exercise analyzing reporting of inventory by Ford Motor Company
- New real-world problem analyzing the financial position of Wal-Mart
- New Internet assignment involving the use of EDGAR.

Chapter 9

The chapter opener now covers Federal Express.

Coverage of goodwill is revised and simplified.

Updated material is consistent with FASB Statement 142 regarding accounting for intangible assets.

Chapter 10

Chapter 10 has been extensively revised by streamlining several issues and presenting them in a Supplemental Topic. These issues include: capital leases, postretirement benefits, and deferred taxes.

Several issues that were formerly presented as Supplemental Topics were revised, expanded significantly, and moved to the body of the text. These issues include: advanced coverage of bonds issued at a discount or a premium, estimated liabilities, loss contingencies, and commitments.

End-of-chapter changes include:

- Revised and new exercises involving accounting for estimated liabilities and contingencies
- New and challenging problems involving accounting for bonds issued at discounts or premiums
- New real-world exercise analyzing DuPont's cost of borrowing

Chapter 11

A new chapter opener covers Sears.

Sources of corporate equity are covered within a new exhibit.

Chapter 12

The chapter opener on Home Depot is revised.

Coverage of stock dividends is coordinated with coverage of stock splits from Chapter 11.

Comprehensive income coverage has been expanded.

Chapter 13

Updated chapter opener (still Harrah's Entertainment).

Indirect method (of computing cash from operating activities) moved from supplemental topic to main body of chapter.

Revised real-world example of direct method (of computing cash from operating activities).

Chapter 14

Updated chapter opener (still Johnson & Johnson).

Updated chapter material.

Chapter 15

A new chapter opener compares Wal-Mart's and Carrefour's international reach.

A discussion of financial reporting differences around the world, including a table that illustrates reporting differences across several countries and regions (European Union).

Appendix A

Updated annual report for Tootsie Roll.

preface

Can technology really help students and professors in the learning process?

Today, nearly 200,000 college instructors use the Internet in their respective courses. Some are just getting started, while others are ready to embrace the very latest advances in educational content delivery and course management.

That's why we at McGraw-Hill/Irwin offer you a complete range of digital solutions. Your students can use **Financial Accounting's** complete Online Learning Center, NetTutor, and PowerWeb on their own, or we can help you create your own course Website using McGraw-Hill's PageOut.

In addition to Web-based assets, **Financial Accounting** boasts My Mentor, a CD-ROM that offers special chapter-by-chapter assistance for the most demanding Financial Accounting topics. With McGraw-Hill's Presentation Manager CD-ROM, instructors have access to nearly every crucial supplement, from the Resource Manual to the Test Bank, in both print and electronic media.

McGraw-Hill is a leader in bringing helpful technology into the classroom. And with **Financial Accounting,** your class gets all the benefits of the digital age.

How can I easily integrate Web resources into my course?

ONLINE LEARNING CENTER (OLC)

More and more students are studying online. That's why we offer an Online Learning Center (OLC) that follows Financial Accounting chapter by chapter. It doesn't require any building or maintenance on your part. It's ready to go the moment you and your students type in the URL.

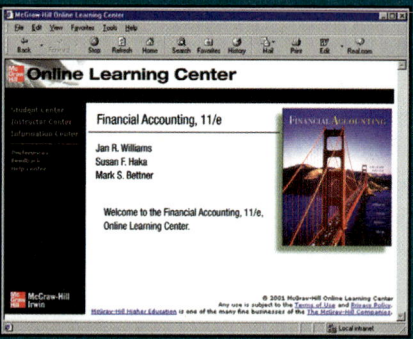

As your students study, they can refer to the OLC Website for such benefits as:

- Links to Professional Resources
- Alternate Problems
- Self-grading Quizzes
- Key Terms
- Chapter Summary
- Text-Related Web Resources
- Business Week Links
- Internet Assignments
- Text Updates
- PowerPoint® Slides
- Link to Financial Accounting PowerWeb
- Excel Templates
- Download of GLAS software
- Help from Net Tutor

A secured Instructor Resource Center stores your essential course materials to save you prep time before class. The Instructor's Manual, Solutions, PowerPoint®, and sample syllabi are now just a couple of clicks away. You will also find useful packaging information and transition notes.

The OLC Website also serves as a doorway to other technology solutions like PageOut which is free to **Financial Accounting** adopters.

preface

Many of my students work or have other obligations outside of class. How can they get book-specific help at their convenience?

NET TUTOR™

NetTutor™ Net Tutor is a breakthrough program that allows one-on-one assistance completely online. Qualified accounting tutors equipped with **Financial Accounting** work online with your students on specific problems or concepts from their text.

NetTutor allows tutors and students to communicate with each other in a variety of ways:

The Live Tutor Center via NetTutor's WWWhiteboard enables a tutor to hold an interactive, online tutorial session with a student or several students. The WWWhiteboard acts as a virtual chalkboard where students can view tutor-created spreadsheets, t-accounts, and written explanations during hours that work with your students' schedules.

The Q&A Center allows students to submit questions at any time and retrieve answers within 24 hours.

The Archive Center allows students to browse for answers to previously asked questions. They can also search for questions pertinent to a particular topic. If they encounter an answer they do not understand, they can ask a follow-up question.

Students are issued five hours of free NetTutor time when they purchase a new copy of Financial Accounting. Additional time may be purchased in five-hour increments. Tutors are available during the week to help students clear those afternoon and evening study hurdles.

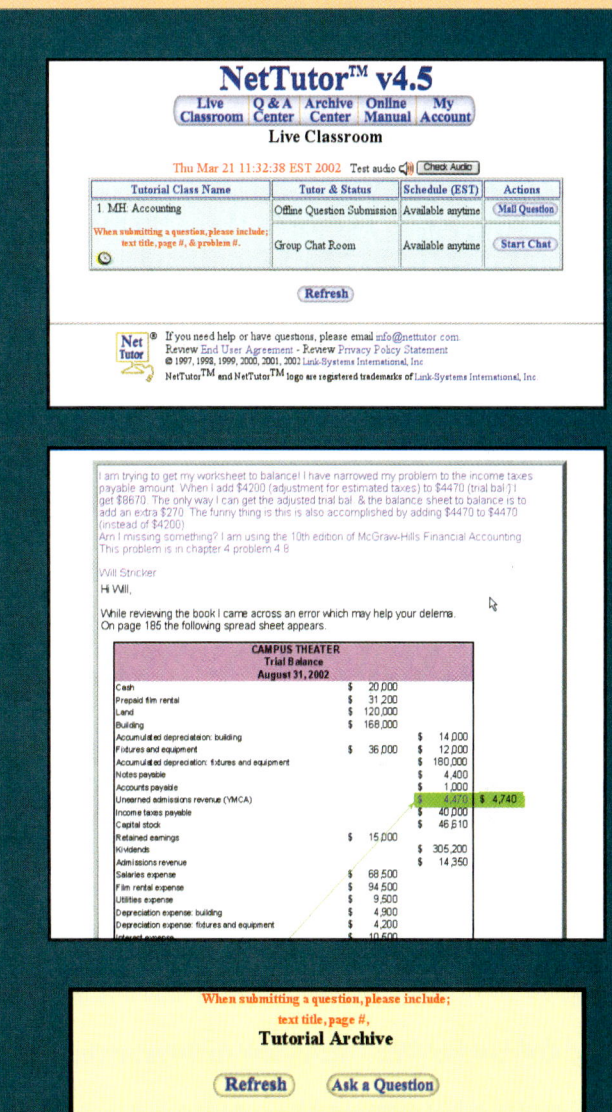

preface

What help can I rely on from McGraw-Hill for setting up my online course?

KNOWLEDGE GATEWAY

Developed with the help of our partner, Eduprise, the McGraw-Hill Knowledge Gateway is an all-purpose service and resource center for instructors teaching online. While training programs from WebCT and Blackboard will help teach you their software, only McGraw-Hill has services to help you actually manage and teach your online course, as well as run and maintain the software. Knowledge Gateway offers an online library full of articles and insights that focus on how online learning differs from a traditional class environment.

The First Level of Knowledge Gateway is available to all professors browsing the McGraw-Hill Higher Education Website, and consists of an introduction to OLC content, access to the first level of the Resource Library, technical support, and information on Instructional Design Services available through Eduprise.

The Second Level is password-protected and provides access to the expanded Resource Library, technical and pedagogical support for WebCT, Blackboard, and TopClass, the online Instructional Design helpdesk and an online discussion forum for users. The Knowledge Gateway provides a considerable advantage for teaching online—and it's only available through McGraw-Hill.

To see how these platforms can assist your online course, visit www.mhhe.com/solutions.

PAGEOUT & SERVICE

PageOut is McGraw-Hill/Irwin's custom Website service. Now you can put your course online without knowing a word of HTML, selecting from a variety of prebuilt Website templates. And if none of our ideas suit you, we'll be happy to work with your ideas.

If you want a custom site but don't have time to build it yourself, we offer a team of product specialists ready to help. Just call 1-800-634-3963, press 0 and ask to speak with a PageOut specialist. You will be asked to send in your course materials and then participate in a brief telephone consultation. Once we have your information, we build your Website for you, from scratch.

INSTRUCTOR ADVANTAGE AND INSTRUCTOR ADVANTAGE PLUS

Instructor Advantage is a special level of service McGraw-Hill offers in conjunction with WebCT and Blackboard. A team of platform specialists is always available, either by toll-free phone or e-mail, to ensure everything runs smoothly through the life of your adoption. Instructor Advantage is available free to all McGraw-Hill customers.

Instructor Advantage Plus is available to qualifying McGraw-Hill adopters (see your representative for details). IA Plus guarantees you a full day of on-site training by a Blackboard or WebCT specialist, for yourself and up to nine colleagues. Thereafter, you will enjoy the benefits of unlimited telephone and e-mail support throughout the life of your adoption. IA Plus users also have the opportunity to access the McGraw-Hill Knowledge Gateway (see above).

preface

How can I easily create an online course?

For the instructor needing to educate students online, we offer **Financial Accounting** content for complete online courses. To make this possible, we have joined forces with the most popular delivery platforms currently available. These platforms are designed for instructors who want complete control over course content and how it is presented to students. You can customize the Financial Accounting Online Learning Center content and author your own course materials. It's entirely up to you.

Products like WebCT, Blackboard, eCollege, and TopClass (a product of WBT) all expand the reach of your course. Online discussion and message boards will now complement your office hours. Thanks to a sophisticated tracking system, you will know which students need more attention—even if they don't ask for help. That's because online testing scores are recorded and automatically placed in your grade book, and if a student is struggling with coursework, a special alert message lets you know.

Remember, **Financial Accounting's** content is flexible enough to use with any platform currently available. If your department or school is already using a platform, we can help. For information on McGraw-Hill/Irwin's course management supplements, including Instructor Advantage and Knowledge Gateway, see "Knowledge Gateway" on the previous page.

PAGEOUT

McGraw-Hill's Course Management System

PageOut is the easiest way to create a Website for your accounting course.

There's no need for HTML coding, graphic design, or a thick how-to book. Just fill in a series of boxes with simple English and click on one of our professional designs. In no time, your course is online with a Website that contains your syllabus!

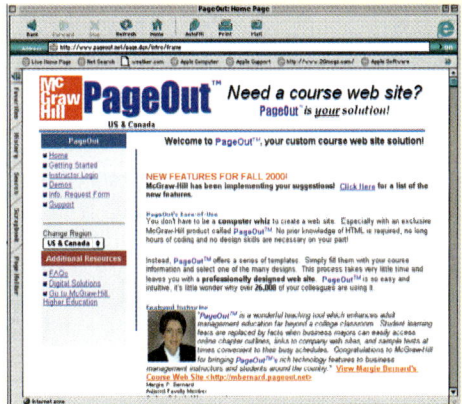

Should you need assistance in preparing your Website, we can help. Our team of product specialists is ready to take your course materials and build a custom Website to your specifications. You simply need to call a McGraw-Hill/Irwin PageOut specialist to start the process. (For information on how to do this, see "PageOut & Service" on the previous page.) Best of all, PageOut is free when you adopt **Financial Accounting**! To learn more, please visit **www.pageout.net**.

preface

How can my students use their study time more effectively?

The online resource GradeSummit tells your students everything they need to know in order to study effectively. And it provides you, the instructor, with valuable insight into which of your students are struggling and which course topics give them the most trouble.

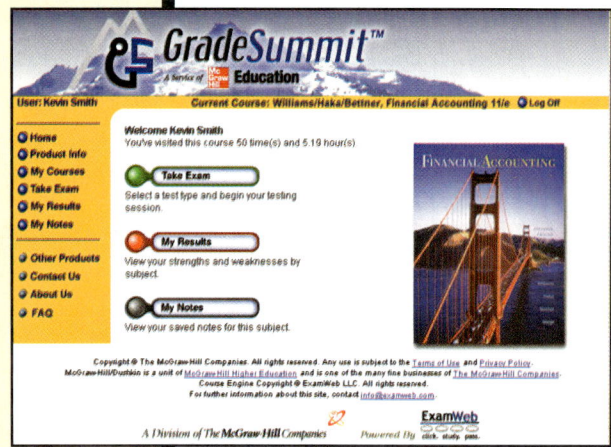

For the student, GradeSummit provides a series of practice tests written to coincide with **Financial Accounting's** coverage. The tests can be taken in various formats according to student preference: practice mode, for instance, displays the correct answer immediately, while exam mode simulates a real classroom exam and displays results at the end. There's even a smart testing engine, SummitExpress, that automatically scales the difficulty level of the questions according to the student's responses.

Once a student has taken a particular test, GradeSummit returns a detailed results page showing exactly where the student did well and where he or she needs to improve. They can compare their results with those of their other classmates, or even with those of every other student using the text nation-wide. With that information, students can plan their studying to focus exclusively on their weak areas, without wasting effort on material they've already mastered. And they can come back to take a re-test on those subjects later, comparing their new score with their previous efforts.

As an instructor, you'll know which students are falling behind simply by consulting GradeSummit's test logs, where results for every student in your course are available for review. Because GradeSummit's results are so detailed, you'll know exactly what topics are causing difficulties—an invaluable aid when it comes to planning lectures and homework.

preface

Can the Internet help me keep my course up to date?

Keeping your course current can be a job in itself, and now McGraw-Hill does that job for you. PowerWeb extends the learning experience beyond the core textbook by offering all of the latest news and developments pertinent to your course, brought to you via the internet without all the clutter and dead links of a typical online search.

PowerWeb is a robust Website that offers these *course-specific* features:

- current articles related to Financial Accounting
- daily and weekly updates with assessment tools
- informative and timely world news culled by a financial accoutant in academia
- referred Web links
- online handbook to researching, evaluating and citing online sources

In addition, PowerWeb provides a trove of helpful learning aids, including self-grading quizzes and interactive glossaries and exercises. Students may also access study tips, conduct online research, and learn about different career paths.

Visit the PowerWeb site at **www.dushkin.com/powerweb** and see firsthand what PowerWeb can mean to your course.

*Through PowerWeb, McGraw-Hill/Irwin has taken the initiative in providing a comprehensive library about the **Enron** accounting controversy. This site will be updated numerous times throughout the semester, insuring your course easy access to the freshest information about this crucial topic.*

preface

Supplements

FOR INSTRUCTORS

Instructor's Resource Manual
ISBN: 0072529210

For each chapter and appendix, you will find:

- A brief topical outline that indicates topics to discuss in class.
- An assignment guide that provides at a glance the topical content of each Exercise, Problem, and Case.
- Comments and observations concerning the chapter content, methods of presentation, and usefulness of specific assignment material.
- Many real-world examples not found in the text, including additional *Business Week* and Internet assignments, sample assignment schedules, and suggestions for using each element of the supplemental package.

Solutions Manual with CD-ROM
ISBN: 0072529229

This comprehensive manual provides solutions to all Discussion Questions, Exercises, Problems, Cases, and Comprehensive Problems. The enclosed CD-ROM contains the manual's electronic files.

Testbank
ISBN: 0072529148

With an abundance of objective questions and short exercises, this supplement is a valuable resource for instructors who prepare their own quizzes and examinations.

Computerized Test Bank
ISBN: 0072529237

This computerized version of the printed testbank is available in Windows® format.

PowerPoint® Slides

This important tool uses PowerPoint software to illustrate chapter concepts. The PowerPoint slides are available on the Instructor CD-ROM and on the Website *www.mhhe.com/williams_financial11e*.

Instructor Excel Templates

Solutions to the students' Excel templates can be found on the Instructor CD-ROM and password protected on the textbook Website *www.mhhe.com/williams_financial11e*.

Instructor CD-ROM
ISBN: 0072529202

Includes PowerPoint Slides, Computerized Test Bank, Instructor's Resource Manual, Solutions Manual, Instructor Excel Templates, General Ledger Applications Template Software, Tutorial Software, and My Mentor Professor Excel Spreadsheets.

Website/Online Learning Center at

www.mhhe.com/williams_financial11e

Case Videos (with Manual)
ISBN: 007561720X

Eight vignettes ranging from 5 to 15 minutes long cover various accounting topics as applied in real-company scenarios. A brief summary, key concepts and topics, suggested homework assignments, students handouts, small group activities, discussion questions, and teaching notes are provided for each vignette. Topical coverage includes external audits, inventory cost flows, ethics and reporting issues, cash versus accrual income, break-even analysis, capital budgeting, corporate bonds, and making investment decisions.

Financial Accounting Video Library
ISBN: 0072376163

This diverse array of videos prepared by Dallas County Community College District Telecourse can be used to stimulate classroom discussion, illustrate key concepts, or review critical material.

FOR STUDENTS

My Mentor Online

This interactive accounting software makes accounting visual and helps students learn key concepts for each chapter of this textbook. It is conveniently located on the textbook Website *(www.mhhe.com/business/accounting/williams_financial11e)* allowing students to access this important tool from anywhere.

Study Guide

ISBN: 0072529172

For each chapter, students can measure their progress through a wealth of self-test material (with solutions) and a summary of the chapter's key points.

Working Papers

ISBN: 0072529180

This softcover booklet is filled with columnar paper for each Problem and Comprehensive Problem in the textbook. Throughout the Working Papers students encounter Checkpoints to ensure they are on the right track.

General Ledger Applications Software (GLAS)

The GLAS accounting program saves time and minimizes errors because it operates as an integrated system. Amounts entered in the general journal or special journals can be posted to the general ledger with a single keystroke. GLAS icons show students where this tool can be used to solve end-of-chapter problems. Available on the textbook Website *(www.mhhe.com/business/accounting/williams_financial11e)*

Excel Templates

This software allows students to develop important spreadsheet skills by using templates to solve selected assignments identified by an icon in the end-of-chapter material. Available on the textbook Website *(www.mhhe.com/business/accounting/williams_financial11e)*

Glas and Excel Templates CD-ROM

ISBN 0072832320

Both the GLAS software and Excel Templates are available on this CD-ROM, which can be packaged with the text for free or purchased alone for a nominal price.

Check Figures

These provide key answers for selected problems and can be found at the end of the text.

Practice Sets

Manual Practice Set

Prepared by William R. Pasewark, Texas Tech University

Understanding Corporate Annual Reports

Instructor ISBN: 0072387165
Student ISBN: 0072387149

Computerized Practice Sets

Prepared by Leland Mansuetti and Keith Weidkamp, Sierra College

Granite Bay Jet Ski Inc., Level 1
Instructor ISBN: 0072426896
Student ISBN: 0072426942

Granite Bay Jet Ski Inc., Level 2
Instructor ISBN: 0072426209
Student ISBN: 0072426950

Wheels Exquisite, Inc., Level 1
Instructor ISBN: 0072427531
Student ISBN: 0072428457

Thunder Mountain Snowmobile
Instructor ISBN: 0072341157
Student ISBN: 0072341149

Gold Run Snowmobile, Inc.
Instructor ISBN: 0072341092
Student ISBN: 0072341076

ALEKS™ Math Prep for Accounting

ALEKS (Assessment and LEarning in Knowledge Spaces) is an artificial intelligence-based system for individualized learning, available from McGraw-Hill over the World Wide Web. ALEKS interacts with the student much as a skilled human tutor would, moving between a student's knowledge state for a given subject, ALEKS can focus clearly on what the student is most ready to learn next. When students focus on exactly what they are ready to learn, they build confidence, and a learning momentum that fuels success. Math Prep for Accounting is a short tutorial that covers basic math concepts such as percentages, ratios, multiplication and division.

Visit the ALEKS Website at *www.business.aleks.com*

ALEKS™ for Financial Accounting

ALEKS for Financial Accounting allows students to learn financial accounting from within the ALEKS framework. **Coming Fall 2003.**

preface

Reviewers

Many of our colleagues throughout the world who have used the prior edition of **Financial Accounting** offered suggestions for improving it. This is vital feedback that we rely on in each edition. Each of those who have offered comments and suggestions has our thanks.

The efforts of many people are needed to develop and improve a text. Among these people are the reviewers who point out areas of concern, cite areas of strength, and make recommendations for change. In this regard, the following professors provided feedback that was enormously helpful in preparing the Eleventh Edition of **Financial Accounting**:

Lisa M. Cole
Pima Community College

Kevin M. Misiewicz
Notre Dame

Craig Bain
Northern Arizona University

Paul M. Buck
Plymouth State College

Frederic S. Bardo
Shippensburg University

Scott N. Cairns
Shippensburg University

David L. Davis
Tallahassee Community College

Joseph M. Hargadon
Widener University

Eugene A. Imhoff
University of Michigan Business School

John A. Marts
The University of North Carolina at Wilmington

Wendy W. Peffley
North Carolina Wesleyan College

Karen N. Russom
North Harris College

E. Daniel Shim
Sacred Heart University

Kenneth Leibham
Columbia Gorge Community Center

Pamela H. Church
Rhodes College

Carolyn E. Clark
St. Joseph's University

Glenn Rechtschaffen
York College of Pennsylvania

We Listened

preface

Reviewer comments for this edition and previous editions have guided us in our revision. We extend our sincere thanks for their efforts to the following people:

Sheila Ammons, *Austin Community College*

Elenito Ayuyao, *Los Angeles City College*

Sharla Bailey, *Southwest Baptist University*

Walter Baggett, *Manhattan College*

Jill Bale, *Doane College*

Scott Barhight, *Northampton County Area Community College*

Glenn S. Barnette, *Gustavus Adolphus College*

William Barze, *St. Petersburg Junior College*

Peter Battelle, *University of Vermont*

Daniel Bayak, *Northampton Community College*

John Bayles, *Oakton Community College*

Janet Becker, *University of Pittsburg*

Jerard Berardino, *Community College of Allegheny*

Teri Bernstein, *Santa Monica College*

Cynthia Bolt-Lee, *The Citadel*

Nancy Boyd, *Middle Tennessee State University*

Sallie Branscom, *Virginia Western Community College*

Russell Bresslauer, *Chabot College*

R.E. Bryson, *University of Alabama*

Paul M. Buck, *Plymouth State College*

Priscilla Burnaby, *Bentley College*

Bryan Burks, *Harding University*

Scott N. Cairns, *Shippensburg University*

Loring Carlson, *Western New England College*

David Chu, *College of the Holy Cross*

Stanley Chu, *Borough Manhattan Community College*

Darlene Coarts, *University of Northern Iowa*

Alice R. Cooperstein, *Central Connecticut State University*

William Cravey, *Jersey City State College*

Marcia Croteau, *University of Maryland—Baltimore County*

Brian Curtis, *Raritan Valley Community College*

Steve Czarsty, *Mary Washington College*

David L. Davis, *Tallahassee Community College*

Larry Davis, *Southwest Virginia County College*

Victoria Doby, *Villa Julie College*

Carlton Donchess, *Bridgewater State College*

Steve Driver, *Horry-Georgetown Tech*

Pamela Druger, *Augustana College*

Anita Ellzey, *Hartford Community College*

Emmanuel Emenyonu, *Sacred Heart University*

David Erlach, *CUNY–Queens College*

Paul Everson, *Northern State University*

Mary Lou Gamma, *East Tennessee State University*

Mary Feifel, *Mira Costa College*

Brother Gerald Fitzgerald, *LaSalle University*

Tom Forehand, *Marist College*

Ralph Fritsch, *Midwestern State University*

Mike Fujita, *Leeward Community College*

Joseph F. Gallo, *Cuyahoga Community College*

Donald Geren, *Northeastern Illinois University*

Don Van Gieson, *Kapiolani Community College*

Peter Gilbert, *Thomas College*

Penny Hanes, *Mercyhurst College*

Joseph M. Hargadon, *Widener University*

Lyle Hicks, *Danville Area Community College*

Richard Hanna, *Ferris State University*

Stephen Hano, *Rockland Community College*

Sara Harris, *Arapahoe Community College*

Medhat Helmi, *University of Alabama—Birmingham*

Paul J. Herz, *Western State College of Colorado*

Jeannelou Hodgens, *Florence-Darlington Technical College*

Patricia H. Holmes, *Des Moines Area Community College*

Michael Holt, *Eastern Nazarene College*

Evelyn Honaker, *Walters State Community College*

Gordon Hosch, *University of New Orleans*

Dave Jensen, *Bucknell University*

Dewey Martin, *Husson College*

Christopher Jones, *George Washington University*

David Junnola, *Eastern Michigan University*

Leo Jubb, *Essex Community College*

Khondkar Karim, *Monmouth University*

James Kennedy, *Texas A&M University*

Rita M. Kingery, *University of Delaware*

Jane Kingston, *Piedmont Virginia Community College*

Ed Knudson, *Linn Benton Community College*

Raymond Krasniewski, *Ohio State University*

Orsay Kucukemiroglu, *Penn State University*

David Lardie, *Tunxis Community College*

Bill Lasher, *Jamestown Community College*

Lawrence Lease, *Shasta College*

Suk Jun Lee, *Chapman University*

Eric Lewis, *Union College*

Philip Little, *Western Carolina University*

J. Thomas Love, *Walters State Community College*

Allie F. Miller, *Drexel University*

Josie Miller, *Mercer Community College*

Cheryl E. Mitchem, *Virginia State University*

Merrill Moore, *Delaware Tech & Community College*

Deborah Most, *Dutchess Community College*

Haim Mozes, *Fordham University*

Frank Olive, *Nicholas College*

Bruce Oliver, *Rochester Institute of Technology*

Ginger Parker, *Creighton University*

Michael Prockton, *Finger Lakes Community College*

Annette M. Leps, *Goucher College*

Gary Reynolds, *Ozard Technical College*

Renee Rigoni, *Monroe Community College*

Earl Roberts, *Delaware Tech & Community College*

Julie Rosenblatt, *Delaware Tech & Community College*

Bob Rothenberg, *SUNY—Oneonta*

Victoria Rymer, *University of Maryland*

Francis A. Sakiey, *Mercer County Community College*

Linda Schain, *Hofstra University*

Mike Schoderbek, *Rutgers University–New Brunswick*

Monica Seiler, *Queensborough Community College*

Janine Sickafuse, *Allegheny College*

Larry Sidwell, *Rend Lake College*

Stan Stanley, *Skagit Valley College*

Jim Stanton, *Mira Costa College*

Carolyn Strickler, *Ohlone College*

Robert Stilson, *CUNY*

Barbara Sturdevant, *SUNY*

Gene Sullivan, *Liberty University and Central Virginia Community College*

Mary Ann Swindlehurst, *Carroll Community College*

Larry Tartaglino, *Cabrillo College*

Martin Taylor, *University of Texas at Arlington*

Anne Tippett, *Tarrant County College South*

Bruce Toews, *Walla Walla College*

Cynthia Tomes, *Des Moines Area Community College*

Grace Tsao, *Colgate University*

Harold Wilson, *Middle Tennessee State University*

Steve Wilts, *Bucknell University*

Teri Yohn, *Georgetown University*

Myung Ho Yoon, *Northeastern Illinois University*

We are grateful . . .

We also want to acknowledge the following individuals, each of whom has authored supplements to accompany the text: Charles W. Caldwell and Richard S. Rand, both of Tennessee Technological University, Susan C. Galbreath of David Lipscomb University, and Jack Terry of Comsource Associates.

Our special thanks goes to Beth Woods, Accuracy Counts, and Barbara Schnathorst, The Write Solution, Inc., for assisting us with detailed reviews of our chapter and assignment material.

The assistance of Robert Zwicker of Pace University and Alice Sineath of Forsyth Technical Community College was invaluable in the preparation of the manuscripts for many supplementary materials.

We appreciate the expert attention given to this project by the staff of McGraw-Hill/Irwin, especially Ryan Blankenship, Heather Burbridge, Brent Gordon, Stewart Mattson, Heather Sabo, Catherine Schultz, Judy Kausal, Artemio Ortiz, Becky Szura, Dan Wiencek, Erwin Llereza, and Ed Przyzycki.

Sincerely,

Jan R. Williams • Susan F. Haka
Mark S. Bettner • Robert F. Meigs

CONTENTS IN BRIEF

1	Accounting: Information for Decision Making	2
2	Basic Financial Statements	40
3	The Accounting Cycle: Capturing Economic Events	88
4	The Accounting Cycle: Accruals and Deferrals	134
5	The Accounting Cycle: Reporting Financial Results	174
	Comprehensive Problem 1—West Branch Rent ALL	**217**
6	Merchandising Activities	220
7	Financial Assets	262
8	Inventories and the Cost of Goods Sold	318
	Comprehensive Problem 2—Guitar Universe, Inc.	**363**
9	Plant and Intangible Assets	366
10	Liabilities	408
11	Stockholders' Equity: Paid-in Capital	460
12	Income and Changes in Retained Earnings	502
13	Statement of Cash Flows	542
14	Financial Statement Analysis	600
	Comprehensive Problem 3—Tootsie Roll Industries, Inc.	**665**
15	Global Business and Accounting	668
	APPENDIX A Annual Report of Tootsie Roll Industries, Inc. 2000	705
	APPENDIX B The Time Value of Money: Future Amounts and Present Values	724
	Index	743
	Check Figures for Problems	751

CONTENTS

1 Accounting: Information for Decision Making 2

Accounting Information: A Means to an End	4
Accounting from a User's Perspective	*4*
Types of Accounting Information	*5*
Accounting Systems	6
Determining Information Needs	*7*
The Cost of Producing Accounting Information	*7*
Basic Functions of an Accounting System	*8*
Who Designs and Installs Accounting Systems?	*8*
Financial Accounting Information	8
External Users of Accounting Information	*8*
Objectives of External Financial Reporting	*9*
Introduction to Financial Statements	11
Characteristics of Externally Reported Information	*13*
Internal Accounting Information	15
Users of Internal Accounting Information	*15*
Objectives of Internal Accounting Systems	*16*
Characteristics of Internal Accounting Information	*17*
Integrity of Accounting Information	19
Institutional Features	*19*
Professional Organizations	*21*
Competence, Judgment, and Ethical Behavior	*22*
Concluding Remarks	25
Supplemental Topic: Careers in Accounting	25
Public Accounting	*26*
Management Accounting	*26*
Governmental Accounting	*27*
Accounting Education	*27*
What About Bookkeeping?	*27*
Accounting as a Stepping-Stone	*28*
End-of-Chapter Review	29
Assignment Material	32

2 Basic Financial Statements 40

Introduction to Financial Statements	42
A Starting Point: Statement of Financial Position	43
Assets	*44*
Liabilities	*47*
Owners' Equity	*47*
The Accounting Equation	*48*
The Effects of Business Transactions: An Illustration	*48*
Effects of These Business Transactions on the Accounting Equation	*53*
Income Statement	55
Statement of Cash Flows	56
Relationships among Financial Statements	58
Financial Analysis	60
Forms of Business Organizations	61
Sole Proprietorships	*61*
Partnerships	*61*
Corporations	*61*
Reporting Ownership Equity in the Statement of Financial Position	*62*
The Use of Financial Statements by Outsiders	63
The Need for Adequate Disclosure	*63*
Management's Interest in Financial Statements	*64*
Concluding Remarks	65
End-of-Chapter Review	67
Assignment Material	71

3 The Accounting Cycle: Capturing Economic Events 88

The Accounting Cycle	90
The Role of Accounting Records	*90*
The Ledger	90
The Use of Accounts	91
Debit and Credit Entries	91
Double-Entry Accounting—The Equality of Debits and Credits	*93*
Recording Transactions in Ledger Accounts: An Illustration	93
The Journal	96
Posting Journal Entries to the Ledger Accounts (and How to "Read" a Journal Entry)	*96*
What Is Net Income?	99
Retained Earnings	*100*
The Income Statement: A Preview	*100*
Revenue	*102*
Expenses	*103*
The Accrual Basis of Accounting	*104*
Debit and Credit Rules for Revenue and Expenses	*104*
Dividends	105
Recording Revenue and Expense Transactions: An Illustration	105
The Journal	*112*

February's Ledger Balances	113
The Trial Balance	115
Uses and Limitations of the Trial Balance	*115*
Concluding Remarks	116
Accounting Cycle in Perspective	*116*
End-of-Chapter Review	117
Assignment Material	123

4 The Accounting Cycle: Accruals and Deferrals 134

Adjusting Entries	136
The Need for Adjusting Entries	*136*
Types of Adjusting Entries	*136*
Characteristics of Adjusting Entries	*137*
Year-End at Overnight Auto Service	*139*
Converting Assets to Expenses	*140*
The Concept of Depreciation	*142*
Converting Liabilities to Revenue	*145*
Accruing Unpaid Expenses	*147*
Accruing Uncollected Revenue	*149*
Accruing Income Taxes Expense: The Final Adjusting Entry	*150*
Adjusting Entries and Accounting Principles	151
The Concept of Materiality	*152*
Effects of Adjusting Entries	*153*
Concluding Remarks	155
End-of-Chapter Review	157
Assignment Material	162

5 The Accounting Cycle: Reporting Financial Results 174

Preparing Financial Statements	176
The Income Statement	*177*
The Statement of Retained Earnings	*179*
The Balance Sheet	*180*
Relationships among Financial Statements	180
Drafting the Notes that Accompany Financial Statements	*181*
What Types of Information Must Be Disclosed?	*181*
Closing the Temporary Equity Accounts	182
Closing Entries for Revenue Accounts	*183*
Closing Entries for Expense Accounts	*184*
Closing the Income Summary Account	*185*
Closing the Dividends Account	*186*
Summary of the Closing Process	187
After-Closing Trial Balance	188
A Last Look at Overnight: Was 2002 a Good Year?	*188*
Preparing Financial Statements Covering Different Periods of Time	*190*
Concluding Remarks	191
Supplemental Topic: The Worksheet	192
Isn't This Really a Spreadsheet?	*194*
How Is a Worksheet Used?	*194*
The Mechanics: How It's Done	*194*
What-If: A Special Application of Worksheet Software	*196*
End-of-Chapter Review	197
Assignment Material	203

Comprehensive Problem 1: West Branch Rent ALL 217

6 Merchandising Activities 220

Merchandising Companies	222
The Operating Cycle of a Merchandising Company	*222*
Income Statement of a Merchandising Company	*223*
What Accounting Information Does a Merchandising Company Need?	*223*
General Ledger Accounts	*224*
Subsidiary Ledger Accounts	*224*
Two Approaches Used in Accounting for Merchandising Transactions	*227*
Perpetual Inventory Systems	227
Taking a Physical Inventory	*229*
Closing Entries in a Perpetual Inventory System	*230*
Periodic Inventory Systems	231
Operation of a Periodic Inventory System	*231*
Closing Process in a Periodic Inventory System	*232*
Comparison of Perpetual and Periodic Inventory Systems	*233*
Selecting an Inventory System	*235*
Modifying an Accounting System	236
Special Journals Provide Speed and Efficiency	*236*
Transactions Relating to Purchases	236
Credit Terms and Cash Discounts	*236*
Returns of Unsatisfactory Merchandise	*238*
Transportation Costs on Purchases	*239*
Transactions Relating to Sales	239
Sales Returns and Allowances	*240*
Sales Discounts	*240*
Delivery Expenses	*241*
Accounting for Sales Taxes	*241*
Evaluating the Performance of a Merchandising Company	242
Net Sales	*242*
Gross Profit Margins	*242*
Concluding Remarks	244
End-of-Chapter Review	245
Assignment Material	249

7 Financial Assets 262

How Much Cash Should a Business Have?	264
The Valuation of Financial Assets	264

Cash 265

Reporting Cash in the Balance Sheet	265
The Statement of Cash Flows	266
Cash Management	266
Internal Control over Cash	267
Cash Disbursements	268
Bank Statements	268
Reconciling a Bank Statement	269
Petty Cash Funds	273
The Cash Budget as a Control Device	273

Short-Term Investments 273

Mark-to-Market: A Principle of Asset Valuation	274

Accounts Receivable 275

Uncollectible Accounts	276
The Allowance for Doubtful Accounts	277
Writing Off an Uncollectible Account Receivable	278
Recovery of an Account Receivable Previously Written Off	279
Monthly Estimates of Credit Losses	279
Direct Write-off Method	282
Income Tax Regulations and Financial Reporting	283
Internal Controls for Receivables	283
Management of Accounts Receivable	283
Factoring Accounts Receivable	284
Credit Card Sales	284
Concentrations of Credit Risk	287
Notes Receivable and Interest Charges	287

Concluding Remarks 288

Supplemental Topic A: Accounting for Marketable Securities 289

Purchases of Marketable Securities	289
Recognition of Investment Revenue	289
Sales of Investments	290
Adjusting Marketable Securities to Market Value	290
Reporting Investment Transactions in the Financial Statements	292

Supplemental Topic B: Notes Receivable and Interest Revenue 292

Nature of Interest	293
Accounting for Notes Receivable	293
The Decision of Whether to Accrue Interest	295

End-of-Chapter Review 297
Assignment Material 302

8 Inventories and the Cost of Goods Sold 318

Inventory Defined	320
The Flow of Inventory Costs	320
Which Unit Did We Sell?	321
Data for an Illustration	321
Specific Identification	322
Cost Flow Assumptions	322
Average-Cost Method	322
First-In, First-Out Method	323
Last-In, First-Out Method	324
Evaluation of the Methods	325
Do Inventory Methods Really Affect Performance?	327
The Principle of Consistency	328
Just-in-Time (JIT) Inventory Systems	328

Taking a Physical Inventory 329

Recording Shrinkage Losses	330
LCM and Other Write-Downs of Inventory	330
The Year-End Cutoff of Transactions	331
Periodic Inventory Systems	332
Importance of an Accurate Valuation of Inventory	335
Techniques for Estimating the Cost of Goods Sold and the Ending Inventory	
The Gross Profit Method	337
The Retail Method	337
"Textbook" Inventory Systems Can Be Modified . . . and They Often Are	338

Financial Analysis 339

Inventory Turnover Rate	339
Accounting Methods Can Affect Financial Ratios	341

Concluding Remarks 341

Supplemental Topic: LIFO Reserves 342

The Significance of a LIFO Reserve	342

End-of-Chapter Review 344
Assignment Material 348

Comprehensive Problem 2: Guitar Universe, Inc. 363

9 Plant and Intangible Assets 366

Plant Assets as a "Stream of Future Services"	368
Major Categories of Plant Assets	368
Accountable Events in the Lives of Plant Assets	368

Acquisitions of Plant Assets 368

Determining Cost: An Example	369
Some Special Considerations	369
Capital Expenditures and Revenue Expenditures	370

Depreciation 371

Allocating the Cost of Plant and Equipment over the Years of Use	371
Causes of Depreciation	372
Methods of Computing Depreciation	373
The Straight-Line Method	374
The Declining-Balance Method	375

Which Depreciation Methods Do Most Businesses Use?	*378*
Financial Statement Disclosures	*379*
The Impairment of Plant Assets	*380*
Disposal of Plant and Equipment	380
Gains and Losses on Disposals of Plant and Equipment	*381*
Trading in Used Assets for New Ones	*382*
Intangible Assets	383
Characteristics	*383*
Operating Expenses versus Intangible Assets	*383*
Amortization	*383*
Goodwill	*383*
Patents	*386*
Trademarks and Trade Names	*386*
Franchises	*386*
Copyrights	*387*
Other Intangibles and Deferred Charges	*387*
Research and Development (R&D) Costs	*388*
Financial Analysis	*388*
Natural Resources	388
Accounting for Natural Resources	*388*
Depreciation, Amortization, and Depletion— A Common Goal	*389*
Plant Transactions and the Statement of Cash Flows	390
Concluding Remarks	390
Supplemental Topic: Other Depreciation Methods	391
The Units-of-Output Method	*391*
MACRS	*391*
Sum-of-the-Years' Digits	*391*
Decelerated Depreciation Methods	*392*
Depreciation Methods in Use: A Survey	*392*
End-of-Chapter Review	393
Assignment Material	397

10 Liabilities 408

The Nature of Liabilities	*410*
Current Liabilities	411
Accounts Payable	*411*
Notes Payable	*411*
The Current Portion of Long-Term Debt	*413*
Accrued Liabilities	*413*
Payroll Liabilities	*413*
Unearned Revenue	*414*
Long-Term Liabilities	415
Maturing Obligations Intended to Be Refinanced	*415*
Installment Notes Payable	*416*
Bonds Payable	*418*
What Are Bonds?	*418*

Tax Advantage of Bond Financing	*420*
Accounting for Bonds Payable	*420*
Bonds Issued at a Discount or Premium	*423*
Accounting for a Bond Discount: An Illustration	*423*
Accounting for a Bond Premium: An Illustration	*426*
Bond Discount and Premium in Perspective	*429*
Concept of Present Value	*429*
Bond Prices after Issuance	*430*
Early Retirement of Bonds Payable	*431*
Estimated Liabilities, Loss Contingencies, and Commitments	432
Estimated Liabilities	*432*
Loss Contingencies	*432*
Commitments	*433*
Evaluating the Safety of Creditor's Claims	434
How Much Debt Should a Business Have?	*435*
Concluding Remarks	436
Supplemental Topic: Special Types of Liabilities	437
Lease Payment Obligations	*437*
Operating Leases	*437*
Capital Leases	*437*
Liabilities for Pensions and Other Postretirement Benefits	*438*
Deferred Income Taxes	*440*
End-of-Chapter Review	442
Assignment Material	447

11 Stockholders' Equity: Paid-in Capital 460

Corporations	462
Why Businesses Incorporate	*463*
Publicly Owned Corporations	*464*
Formation of a Corporation	464
Stockholder Records in a Corporation	*467*
Paid-in Capital of a Corporation	468
Authorization and Issuance of Capital Stock	*468*
Common Stocks and Preferred Stocks	*470*
Characteristics of Preferred Stocks	*471*
Stock Issued for Assets Other Than Cash	*473*
Subscriptions to Capital Stock	*475*
Donated Capital	*475*
Book Value per Share of Common Stock	*475*
Market Value	477
Market Price of Preferred Stock	*478*
Market Price of Common Stock	*478*
Book Value and Market Price	*479*
Stock Splits	*480*
Treasury Stock	*480*
Recording Purchases of Treasury Stock	*481*

Reissuance of Treasury Stock		*481*
Stock Buyback Programs		*483*
Concluding Remarks		484
End-of-Chapter Review		486
Assignment Material		490

12 Income and Changes in Retained Earnings 502

Reporting the Results of Operations	504
Developing Predictive Information	*504*
Reporting Irregular Items: An Illustration	*505*
Continuing Operations	*506*
Discontinued Operations	*506*
Extraordinary Items	*506*
Changes in Accounting Principles	*508*
Earnings per Share (EPS)	*509*
Financial Analysis	*512*
Basic and Diluted Earnings per Share	*512*
Other Transactions Affecting Retained Earnings	513
Cash Dividends	*513*
Dividend Dates	*514*
Liquidating Dividends	*515*
Stock Dividends	*515*
Statement of Retained Earnings	*518*
Prior Period Adjustments	*518*
Comprehensive Income	*519*
Statement of Stockholders' Equity	*520*
Stockholders' Equity Section of the Balance Sheet	*521*
Concluding Remarks	522
End-of-Chapter Review	523
Assignment Material	527

13 Statement of Cash Flows 542

Statement of Cash Flows	544
Purposes of the Statement	*544*
Example of a Statement of Cash Flows	*544*
Classification of Cash Flows	*545*
The Approach to Preparing a Statement of Cash Flows	*547*
Preparing a Statement of Cash Flows: An Illustration	548
Operating Activities	*549*
Investing Activities	*549*
Financing Activities	*551*
Cash and Cash Equivalents	*551*
Cash Flows from Operating Activities	*551*
Cash Payments for Merchandise and for Expenses	*552*
Cash Flows from Investing Activities	*556*
Cash Flows from Financing Activities	*558*
Relationship between the Statement of Cash Flows and the Balance Sheet	*559*
Reporting Operating Cash Flows by the Indirect Method	*559*
Differences between Net Income and Net Cash Flows from Operating Activities	*561*
Reconciling Net Income with Net Cash Flows	*561*
The Indirect Method: A Summary	*563*
The Indirect Method May Be Required in a Supplementary Schedule	*564*
The Statement of Cash Flows: A Second Look	*564*
Financial Analysis	*566*
Annotated Statement of Cash Flows: The Rowe Companies	*567*
Managing Cash Flows	568
Budgeting: The Primary Cash Management Tool	*568*
What Priority Should Managers Give to Increasing Net Cash Flows?	*569*
Some Strategies for Permanent Improvements in Cash Flow	*570*
Concluding Remarks	*572*
Supplemental Topic: A Worksheet for Preparing a Statement of Cash Flows	572
Data for an Illustration	*573*
The Worksheet	*573*
Entry	*574*
End-of-Chapter Review	578
Assignment Material	584

14 Financial Statement Analysis 600

Financial Statements Are Designed for Analysis	*602*
Tools of Analysis	603
Dollar and Percentage Changes	*603*
Trend Percentages	*604*
Component Percentages	*605*
Ratios	*606*
Standards of Comparison	*606*
Quality of Earnings	*607*
Quality of Assets and Relative Amount of Debt	*608*
Measures of Liquidity and Credit Risk	608
A Classified Balance Sheet	*608*
Working Capital	*610*
Current Ratio	*611*
Quick Ratio	*611*
Debt Ratio	*611*
Evaluating Financial Ratios	*612*
Liquidity, Credit Risk, and the Law	*614*
Measures of Profitability	615
Classifications in the Income Statement	*615*
Some Specific Examples of Corporate Earnings and Losses	*616*
Multiple-Step Income Statements	*617*
Earnings per Share	*619*
Price-Earnings Ratio	*620*
Single-Step Income Statements	*620*

Evaluating the Adequacy of Net Income	*621*
Return on Investment (ROI)	*621*
Return on Assets (ROA)	*622*
Return on Equity (ROE)	*622*
Comprehensive Illustration: Seacliff Company	623
Analysis by Common Stockholders	*627*
Return on Investment	*629*
Leverage	*630*
Analysis by Long-Term Creditors	*631*
Analysis by Short-Term Creditors	*632*
Cash Flow Analysis	*636*
Usefulness of Notes to Financial Statements	*637*
Summary of Analytical Measurements	*637*
Concluding Remarks	639
End-of-Chapter Review	641
Assignment Material	645

Comprehensive Problem 3: Tootsie Roll Industries, Inc. 665

15 Global Business and Accounting 668

Globalization	670
Environmental Forces Shaping Globalization	672
Political and Legal Systems	*672*
Economic Systems	*674*
Culture	*674*
Technology and Infrastructure	*676*
Harmonization of Financial Reporting Standards	677
Foreign Currencies and Exchange Rates	678
Exchange Rates	*679*
Accounting for Transactions with Foreign Companies	*680*
Currency Fluctuations—Who Wins and Who Loses?	*684*
Consolidated Financial Statements That Include Foreign Subsidiaries	*686*
Global Sourcing	686
Foreign Corrupt Practices Act	*688*
Concluding Remarks	689

End-of-Chapter Review	691
Assignment Material	694

Appendix A: Annual Report of Tootsie Roll Industries, Inc. 2000 705

Appendix B: The Time Value of Money: Future Amounts and Present Values 724

The Concept	724
Relationships between Present Values and Future Amounts	*724*
Compound Interest	*725*
Applications of the Time Value of Money Concept	*726*
Future Amounts	726
The Tables Approach	*726*
The Future Amount of an Annuity	*728*
Interest Periods of Less Than One Year	*729*
Present Values	730
Using Present Value Tables	*731*
What Is the Appropriate Discount Rate?	*731*
The Present Value of an Annuity	*732*
Discount Periods of Less Than One Year	*733*
Valuation of Financial Instruments	733
Interest-Bearing Receivables and Payables	*734*
"Non-Interest-Bearing" Notes	*734*
Market Prices of Bonds	*735*
Capital Leases	*736*
Obligations for Postretirement Benefits	*737*
Disclosure of Up-to-Date Present Value Information	*738*
Deferred Income Taxes	*738*
Capital Budgeting: Another Application of Present Value	738
Assignment Material	739

Name Index 743

Subject Index 745

Check Figures for Problems 751

FINANCIAL ACCOUNTING

Eleventh Edition

CHAPTER 1

ACCOUNTING:

Information for Decision Making

Learning Objectives

After studying this chapter, you should be able to:

1. Discuss accounting as the language of business and the role of accounting information in making economic decisions.

2. Discuss the significance of accounting systems in generating reliable accounting information.

3. Explain the importance of financial accounting information for external parties—primarily investors and creditors—in terms of the objectives and the characteristics of that information.

4. Explain the importance of accounting information for internal parties—primarily management—in terms of the objectives and the characteristics of that information.

5. Discuss elements of the system of external and internal financial reporting that create integrity in the reported information.

6. Identify and discuss several professional organizations that play important roles in preparing and communicating accounting information.

7. Discuss the importance of personal competence, professional judgment, and ethical behavior on the part of accounting professionals.

8. Describe various career opportunities in accounting.*

---

*Supplemental Topic, "Careers in Accounting."

Terry Wild Studio, Inc., © 2001

America Online, Inc.

Founded in 1985, **AOL** initially offered limited online services for a then miniscule market of personal computer users. Today, **America Online, Inc.**, is a division of **AOL Time Warner**. It serves more than 31 million members. **AOL**'s international division operates localized online services in 16 countries in eight languages.

How does a company as successful and large as **AOL, Inc.**, come under the careful scrutiny of the Securities and Exchange Commission (SEC)? The SEC is the government oversight agency concerned with the protection of investors and creditors who use the financial reports of companies listed on America's stock exchanges. Without admitting or denying any wrongdoing, on May 15, 2000, **AOL** paid a $3.5 million fine assessed by the Securities and Exchange Commission and restated its financial statements to show that previously reported profits were now losses. The payment and the restatement of financial information were required because **AOL**'s management deferred listing significant customer acquisition costs on its financial statements for several years. These costs were related to sending out millions of computer disks to potential customers. By deferring these marketing costs and not classifying them as expenses, the financial statements made **AOL** look more profitable than it really was. As a result, investors who relied on the financial statements might overvalue the stock.

• • •

Source: David Henry, "The Numbers Game," *Business Week*, May 14, 2001. Reprinted by permission, copyright © 2001 by The McGraw-Hill Companies, Inc. and **www.aol.com**.

Determining a company's net income by subtracting its expenses from its revenues is an important part of financial reporting. While this may appear to be a simple process of keeping accounting records, a great deal of judgment is required. For example, when is the cost of acquiring a resource an expense? Or more specifically, when do the costs of goods or services become eligible for recognition in a company's financial statements as expense? The **AOL, Inc.**, opener illustrates that it is critical for managers, who wish to avoid difficulties with the SEC, and for investors, who wish to rely on financial statements, to understand and carefully use accounting information.

Understanding and using accounting information is a prerequisite to any business undertaking. Terms such as sales revenue, profit, cost, and expense have clearly defined meanings and are commonly used in business-related conversations. To be a participant in these conversations and in the business world, you must gain a basic understanding of accounting. The objective of this book is to provide users of financial accounting information with that basic understanding.

ACCOUNTING INFORMATION: A MEANS TO AN END

The primary objective of accounting is to provide information that is useful for decision-making purposes. From the very start, we emphasize that accounting is *not an end,* but rather it is *a means to an end.* The final product of accounting information is the decision that is enhanced by the use of accounting information, whether that decision is made by owners, management, creditors, governmental regulatory bodies, labor unions, or the many other groups that have an interest in the financial performance of an enterprise.

LO 1
Discuss accounting as the language of business and the role of accounting information in making economic decisions.

Because accounting is widely used to describe all types of business activity, it is sometimes referred to as the *language of business*. Costs, prices, sales volume, profits, and return on investment are all accounting measurements. Investors, creditors, managers, and others who have a financial interest in an enterprise need a clear understanding of accounting terms and concepts if they are to understand and communicate about the enterprise. While our primary orientation in this text is the use of accounting information in business, from time to time we emphasize that accounting information is also used by governmental agencies, nonprofit organizations, and individuals in much the same manner as it is by business organizations.

Accounting from a User's Perspective

Many people think of accounting as simply a highly technical field practiced only by professional accountants. In reality, nearly everyone uses accounting information daily. Accounting information is simply the means by which we measure and communicate economic events. Whether you manage a business, make investments, or monitor how you receive and use your money, you are working with accounting concepts and accounting information.

Our primary goal in this book is to develop your ability to understand and use accounting information in making economic decisions. To do this, you need to understand the following:

- The nature of economic activities that accounting information describes.
- The assumptions and measurement techniques involved in developing accounting information.
- The information that is most relevant for making various types of decisions.

Exhibit 1–1 illustrates how economic activities flow into the accounting process. The exhibit shows how the accounting process produces accounting information used by decision makers in making economic decisions and taking specific actions. These decisions and actions result in economic activities, and so on.

Accounting Information: A Means to an End

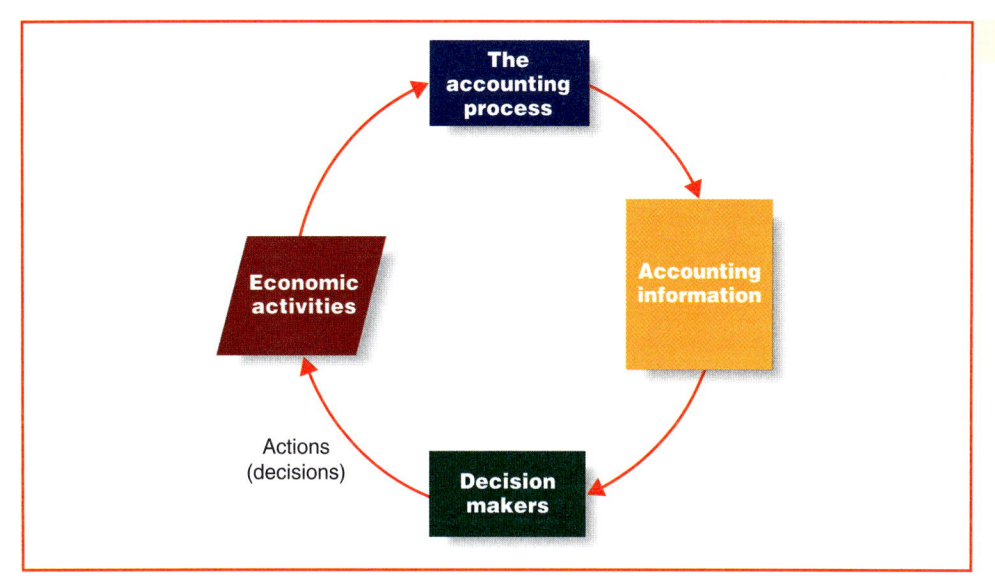

Exhibit 1–1

THE ACCOUNTING PROCESS

Diagram: A circular flow showing "The accounting process" → "Accounting information" → "Decision makers" → Actions (decisions) → "Economic activities" → back to The accounting process.

My Notes

Accounting links decision makers with economic activities—and with the results of their decisions

Types of Accounting Information

Just as there are many types of economic decisions, there are also many types of accounting information. The terms *financial accounting, management accounting,* and *tax accounting* often are used in describing three types of accounting information that are widely used in the business community.

Financial Accounting Financial accounting refers to information describing the financial resources, obligations, and activities of an economic entity (either an organization or an individual). Accountants use the term *financial position* to describe an entity's financial resources and obligations at one point in time and the term *results of operations* to describe its financial activities during the year.

> In **Sony Corporation**'s 2001 financial statements to owners, financial position is presented as consisting of $62,624 million in assets (including cash, inventories, property, and equipment), with obligations against those assets of $44,100 million. This leaves $18,524 million as the owners' interest in those assets. In the same report, results of operations as measured by net income (which measures the excess of revenues over expenses) were $134 million for the year ending March 31, 2001.

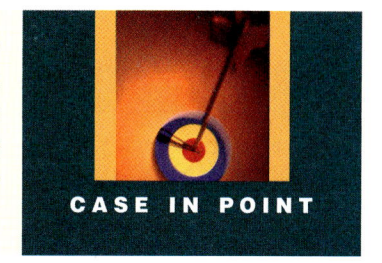

CASE IN POINT

Financial accounting information is designed primarily to assist investors and creditors in deciding where to place their scarce investment resources. Such decisions are important to society, as they determine which companies and industries will receive the financial resources necessary for growth, and which will not.

Financial accounting information also is used by managers and in income tax returns. In fact, financial accounting information is used for so many different purposes that it often is called "general-purpose" accounting information.

Management Accounting Management (or managerial) accounting involves the development and interpretation of accounting information intended *specifically to assist management* in running the business. Managers use this information in setting the company's overall goals, evaluating the performance of departments and individuals, deciding whether to introduce a new line of products, and in making virtually all types of managerial decisions.

A company's managers and employees constantly need such information to run and control daily business operations. For example, they need to know the amount of money in the company's bank accounts; the types, quantities, and dollar amounts of merchandise in the company's warehouse; and the amounts owed to specific creditors. Much management accounting information is financial in nature but has been organized in a manner relating directly to the decision at hand.

Tax Accounting   The preparation of income tax returns is a specialized field within accounting. To a great extent, tax returns are based on financial accounting information. However, the information often is adjusted or reorganized to conform with income tax reporting requirements.

The most challenging aspect of tax accounting is not the preparation of an income tax return, but *tax planning.* Tax planning means anticipating the tax effects of business transactions and structuring these transactions in a manner that will minimize the income tax burden.

Focus of This Text   In this textbook, we introduce the basic concepts of financial accounting. These discussions emphasize the process of *financial reporting* to investors and creditors and the usefulness of financial information to an organization's management and employees. They also cover the preparation and use of accounting information that is specifically intended to support decision-making processes.

Major income tax concepts are discussed at various points throughout the text. Comprehensive coverage of income taxes, however, is deferred to more advanced accounting courses.

Remember that the fields of financial, management, and tax accounting are *closely related.* Thus we often address financial reporting requirements and consider some of management's information needs and income tax issues within a single chapter. Our emphasis throughout this text will be on the accounting information developed in *profit-oriented business organizations.*

ACCOUNTING SYSTEMS

LO 2
Discuss the significance of accounting systems in generating reliable accounting information.

An accounting system consists of the personnel, procedures, devices, and records used by an organization (1) to develop accounting information and (2) to communicate this information to decision makers. The design and capabilities of these systems vary greatly from one organization to the next. In very small businesses, the accounting system may consist of little more than a cash register, a checkbook, and an annual trip to an income tax preparer. In large businesses, an accounting system includes computers, highly trained personnel, and accounting reports that affect the daily operations of every department. But in every case, the basic purpose of the accounting system remains the same: *to meet the organization's needs for accounting information as efficiently as possible.*

Many factors affect the structure of the accounting system within a particular organization. Among the most important are (1) the company's *needs for accounting information* and (2) the *resources available* for operation of the system.

Viewing accounting as an information system focuses attention on the information accounting provides, the users of the information, and the support for financial decisions that is provided by the information. These relationships are depicted in Exhibit 1–2. While some of the terms may not be familiar to you at this early point in your study of accounting, you will be introduced to them more completely as we proceed through this textbook and as you undertake other courses in accounting. Observe, however, that the information system produces the information presented in the middle of the diagram—financial position, profitability, and cash flows. This information meets the needs of users of the information—investors, creditors, managers, and so on—and supports many kinds of financial decisions—performance evaluation and resource allocation, among others. These relationships are consistent with what we have already learned—namely, that accounting information is intended to be useful for decision-making purposes.

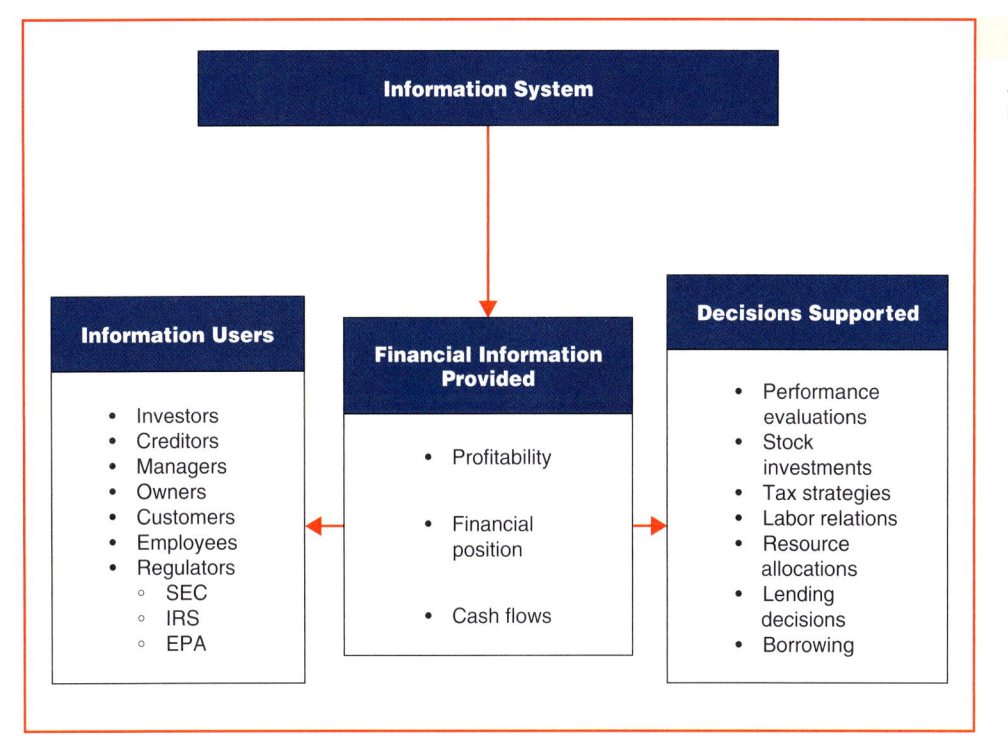

Exhibit 1-2

ACCOUNTING AS AN INFORMATION SYSTEM

Information System

Information Users
- Investors
- Creditors
- Managers
- Owners
- Customers
- Employees
- Regulators
  ○ SEC
  ○ IRS
  ○ EPA

Financial Information Provided
- Profitability
- Financial position
- Cash flows

Decisions Supported
- Performance evaluations
- Stock investments
- Tax strategies
- Labor relations
- Resource allocations
- Lending decisions
- Borrowing

Determining Information Needs

The types of accounting information that a company must develop vary with such factors as the size of the organization, whether it is publicly owned, and the philosophy of management. The need for some types of accounting information may be prescribed by law. For example, income tax regulations require every business to have an accounting system that can measure the company's taxable income and explain the nature and source of every item in the company's income tax return. Federal securities laws require publicly owned companies to prepare financial statements in conformity with generally accepted accounting principles. These statements must be filed with the Securities and Exchange Commission, distributed to stockholders, and made available to the public.

Other types of accounting information are required as matters of practical necessity. For example, every business needs to know the amounts receivable from each customer and the amounts owed to each creditor.

Although much accounting information clearly is essential to business operations, management still has many choices as to the types and amount of accounting information to be developed. For example, should the accounting system of a department store measure separately the sales of each department and of different types of merchandise? The answer to such questions depends on *how useful* management considers the information to be and the *cost* of developing the information.

The Cost of Producing Accounting Information

Accounting systems should be *cost-effective*—that is, the value of the information produced should exceed the cost of producing it. Management has no choice but to produce the types of accounting reports required by law. In other cases, however, management may use *cost-effectiveness* as the criterion for deciding whether or not to produce the information.

In recent years, the development and installation of computer-based accounting systems have increased greatly the types and amount of accounting information that can be produced in a cost-effective manner.

Basic Functions of an Accounting System

In developing information about the financial position of a business and the results of its operations, every accounting system performs the following basic functions:

1. *Interpret and record* the effects of business transactions.
2. *Classify* the effects of similar transactions in a manner that permits determination of the various *totals* and *subtotals* useful to management and used in accounting reports.
3. *Summarize and communicate* the information contained in the system to decision makers.

The differences in accounting systems arise primarily in the manner and speed with which these functions are performed.

In our illustrations, we often assume the use of a simple manual accounting system. Such a system is useful in illustrating basic accounting concepts, but it is too slow and cumbersome to meet the needs of most business organizations. In a large business, transactions may occur at a rate of several hundred or several thousand per hour. To keep pace with such a rapid flow of accounting information, these companies must use accounting systems that are largely computer-based.

Some small businesses that continue to use manual accounting systems modify these systems to meet their needs as efficiently as possible.

Who Designs and Installs Accounting Systems?

The design and installation of large accounting systems is a specialized field. It involves not just accounting, but expertise in management, information systems, marketing, and—in many cases—computer programming. Thus accounting systems generally are designed and installed by a team of people with many specialized talents.

Large businesses have a staff of systems analysts, internal auditors, and other professionals who work full-time in designing and improving the accounting system. Medium-size companies often hire a CPA firm to design or update their systems. Small businesses with limited resources often purchase one of the many packaged accounting systems designed for small companies in their line of business. These packaged systems are available through office supply stores, computer stores, and software manufacturers.

FINANCIAL ACCOUNTING INFORMATION

LO 3
Explain the importance of financial accounting information for external parties—primarily investors and creditors—in terms of the objectives and the characteristics of that information.

Financial accounting is an important subject for students who need only an introduction to the field of accounting, as well as students who will pursue accounting as a major and take many additional accounting courses. Financial accounting provides information about the financial resources, obligations, and activities of an enterprise that is intended for use primarily by external decision makers—investors and creditors.

External Users of Accounting Information

What do we mean by *external users* and who are they? **External users** of accounting information are individuals and other enterprises that have a financial interest in the reporting enterprise, but they are not involved in the day-to-day operations of that enterprise. External users of financial information include the following:

- Owners
- Creditors
- Labor unions
- Governmental agencies
- Suppliers
- Customers

- Trade associations
- General public

Each of these groups of external decision makers requires unique information to be able to make decisions about the reporting enterprise. For example, customers who purchase from the enterprise need information to allow them to assess the quality of the products they buy and the faithfulness of the enterprise in fulfilling warranty obligations. Governmental agencies such as the **Federal Trade Commission** may have an interest in whether the enterprise meets certain governmental regulations that apply. The general public may be interested in the extent to which the reporting enterprise is socially responsible (for example, does not pollute the environment).

Providing information that meets the needs of such a large set of diverse users is difficult, if not impossible, in a single set of financial information. Therefore, external financial reporting is directed toward the information needs of two primary groups—investors and creditors. As you will soon see, investors are individuals and other enterprises that own the reporting enterprise. Creditors, on the other hand, are individuals and other enterprises that have provided credit to the reporting enterprise. For example, a commercial bank may have loaned money to the reporting enterprise, or a supplier may have permitted the reporting enterprise to purchase goods and to pay for those goods later. Our assumption is that by meeting the financial information needs of investors and creditors, we provide information that is also useful to many other users of financial information. In addition, certain external users of financial information, such as government agencies like the **Federal Trade Commission**, can require information that is not generally available to the public. As a result, they are not as dependent on publicly available information as are investors and creditors.

For these reasons, we sometimes refer to investors and creditors as the primary external financial information users. When you see references like these, keep in mind that we are talking about both current investors and creditors and those individuals and other enterprises that may become investors and creditors in the future.

Objectives of External Financial Reporting

If you had invested in a company, or if you had loaned money to a company, what would be your primary financial interest in the company? You probably would be interested in two things, both of which make up the company's **cash flow prospects**. You would be interested in the return to you at some future date of the amount you had invested or loaned. We refer to this as the **return of your investment**. In addition, you would expect the company to pay you something for the use of your funds, either as an owner or a creditor. We refer to this as the **return on your investment**. Information that is useful to you in making judgments about the company's ability to provide you with what you expect in terms of the return of your funds in the future and the return on your funds while you do not have use of them is what we mean by information about *cash flow prospects.*

Assume, for example, that you loan $100,000 to a company that is owned by a friend. Your intent is not to be a long-term investor (owner), but simply to help the company financially through its difficult startup phase. Management of the company agrees to pay you interest at 12% and to repay your loan in one year. Before making this loan, you are interested in seeing information that will allow you to assess the company's ability to provide the following cash flows to you in the future:

Return on investment (that is, interest):	
$100,000 × 12%	$ 12,000
Return of investment:	
$100,000 at maturity	100,000
Total	$112,000

While there is always some risk in entering into a transaction of this type, before making this loan you need to feel reasonably secure that the company will be in a position to pay you these amounts.

Similarly, assume you have an opportunity to invest in a company by becoming one of a large number of owners. As an external owner, rather than an owner-manager, you will not be involved in the daily operations of the company. Before making such an investment, you want to see evidence that the company will be able to pay you a periodic return on your investment (called a *dividend* if the company is organized as a corporation) and that at some future date you can expect to sell your investment to another owner at a favorable price—in other words, that you can expect the return of your investment.

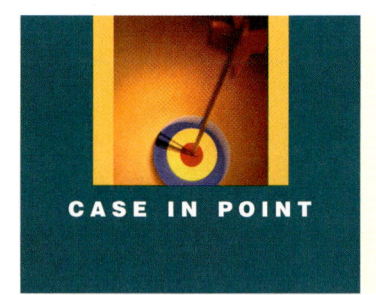

CASE IN POINT

One of the ways companies present information about cash flow prospects to investors and creditors is to provide a statement of cash flows. In 2000, **Intel Corporation** showed in its statement of cash flows how cash was decreased from $3,695 million at the start of the year to $2,976 million at the end of the year as a result of a wide range of business activities that included its ongoing revenue and expense transactions; borrowing and repayment of debt; purchases of land, buildings, and equipment; and payments of dividends to owners.

Providing information about these cash flow prospects essentially is what financial accounting is all about. For the primary external users of financial information—investors and creditors—this information is summarized in the following table:

Information	Investors	Creditors
Return *on* investment	Periodic dividends (for example, annually)	Periodic interest (for example, monthly)
Return *of* investment	Sale of ownership at a future date	Repayment of loan at a future date

The accounting profession has identified certain objectives of external financial reporting to guide its efforts to refine and improve the reporting of information to external decision makers. These general objectives are displayed in Exhibit 1–3 and are best understood if studied from the bottom up—from general to specific.[1]

The first objective is the most general and is to provide information that is useful in making investment and credit decisions. As we indicated earlier, investors and creditors are the primary focus of external financial reporting. We believe that by meeting the information needs of investors and creditors, we provide information that is also useful to many other important financial statement users.

The second objective, which is more specific than the first, is to provide information that is useful in assessing the amount, timing, and uncertainty of future cash flows. As we discussed earlier, investors and creditors are interested in future cash flows to them, so an important objective of financial reporting is to provide information that permits that kind of analysis.

The most specific objective of external financial reporting is to provide information about the enterprise's resources, claims to those resources, and how both the resources and claims to resources change over time. An enterprise's resources are often referred to as *assets,* and the primary claims to those resources are the claims of creditors and owners.

---

[1] FASB, *Statement of Financial Accounting Concepts No. 1,* "Objectives of Financial Reporting by Business Enterprises" (Norwalk, Conn., 1978), p. 4.

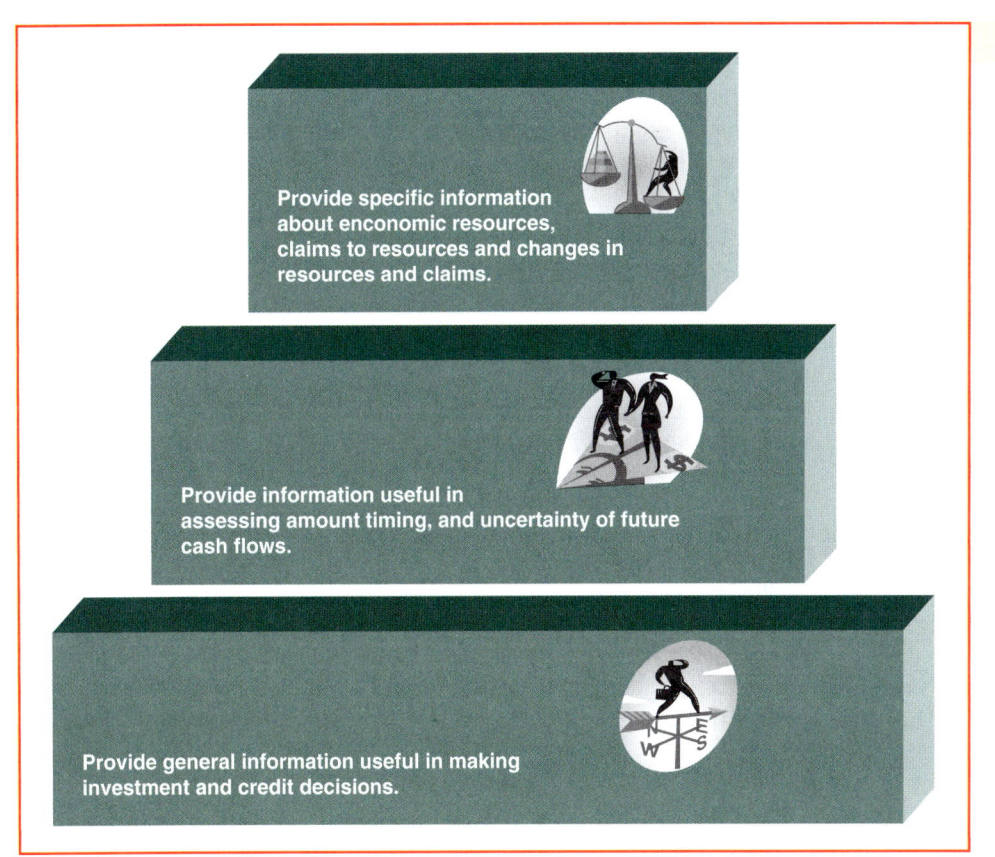

Exhibit 1–3

OBJECTIVES OF FINANCIAL REPORTING: BUILDING FROM THE GENERAL TO THE SPECIFIC

- Provide specific information about enconomic resources, claims to resources and changes in resources and claims.
- Provide information useful in assessing amount timing, and uncertainty of future cash flows.
- Provide general information useful in making investment and credit decisions.

You as an Investor

You have just received a significant inheritance from a favorite uncle who included you in his will. You are considering alternative ways to invest this money to help you pay for your college education and make major purchases in the future, such as a car and a house. What are your primary considerations in choosing an investment for your newly acquired funds? What would cause you to choose to invest in one company over another?

*Our comments appear on page 38.

YOUR TURN

INTRODUCTION TO FINANCIAL STATEMENTS

One of the primary ways investors and creditors assess whether an enterprise will be able to make future cash payments is to examine and analyze the enterprise's financial statements. In the general sense of the word, a statement is simply a declaration of something believed to be true. For example, the statement "This pen is blue" is a declaration concerning the color of the pen that the speaker believes is true. A **financial statement**, therefore, is simply a monetary declaration of what is believed to be true about an enterprise. When accountants prepare financial statements, they are describing in financial terms certain attributes of the enterprise that they believe fairly represent its financial activities.

Time is an important factor in preparing and understanding financial statements. Statements might cover a period as short as a week or as long as a year. *Annual financial statements* of companies include information for a year. See Exhibit 1–4 for some samples of the type of financial information provided in **America Online**'s financial statements. When you examine Exhibit 1–4, notice that the information is provided for the *year* ended June 30.

Financial statements prepared for periods of time shorter than one year (for example, for three months or one month) are referred to as *interim financial statements*. Throughout this text, we use both annual and interim financial statements. As you approach a company's financial statements—either as a user or as a preparer—it is important to establish the time period those statements are intended to cover.

The primary financial statements are the following:

- *Statement of financial position (balance sheet).* The **balance sheet** is a position statement that shows where the company stands in financial terms at a specific date.
- *Income statement.* The **income statement** is an activity statement that shows details and results of the company's profit-related activities for a period of time (for example, a month, quarter [three months], or year).
- *Statement of cash flows.* The **statement of cash flows** is an activity statement that shows the details of the company's activities involving cash during a period of time.

Exhibit 1-4

FINANCIAL HIGHLIGHTS FROM AOL, INC., 2000, 1999, AND 1998 ANNUAL REPORTS*
(amounts in millions)

Years Ended	June 30, 2000	June 30, 2000	June 30, 1998
Sales	$6,886	$4,804	$3,114
Less: expense	5,654	4,050	3,194
Net income (loss)	$1,232	$754	$(80)

Years Ended	June 30, 2000	June 30, 1999	June 30,1998
Assets	$10,673	$5,417	$2,874
Liabilities	4,512	2,322	1,878
Total stockholders' equity	6,161	3,095	996
Cash balance	$2,490	$936	$678

*During the latter part of 2000 AOL, Inc., merged with Time Warner to become AOL Time Warner.

The names of the three primary financial statements are descriptive of the information you find in each. The **statement of financial position**, or balance sheet, for example, is sometimes described as a snapshot of the business in financial or dollar terms (that is, what the enterprise looks like at a specific date). An income statement is an activity statement that depicts the profitability of an enterprise for a designated period of time. The statement of cash flows is particularly important in understanding an enterprise for purposes of investment and credit decisions. As its name implies, the statement of cash flows depicts the ways cash has changed during a designated period. While the interest of investors and creditors is in cash flows to themselves rather than to the enterprise, information about cash activity of the enterprise is considered to be an important signal to investors and creditors.

Financial reporting, and financial statements in particular, can be thought of as a lens through which you can view a business. (See Exhibit 1–5.) A lens allows you to see things from a distance that you would not otherwise be able to see; it also allows you to focus in greater detail on certain aspects of what you are looking at. Financial information, and particularly financial statements, allows you to do just that—focus in on certain financial aspects of the enterprise that are of particular interest to you in making important investing and credit decisions. Because financial statements are only one source of financial accounting information, financial reporting provides a broader view of the business than that provided by financial statements. In other words, financial reporting encompasses financial statements, but it is not limited to financial statements. Precisely how the financial statements identified earlier provide information to external users is introduced in Chapter 2 and is the major subject of several chapters thereafter.

CASH EFFECTS

Reporting information about the cash activities of an enterprise is a particularly important aspect of providing information to both external and internal decision makers. Cash is ultimately what business activity is all about. Despite the importance of cash and information about an enterprise's cash activities, financial reporting is much more than simply displaying the increases and decreases in an enterprise's cash balance. Estimating future cash flows requires a great deal of information about things other than a company's historical record of cash transactions. Many future cash events are impounded today in things other than cash. For example, a company may have many dollars of receivables from its customers as a result of credit sales that have not yet been collected in cash. Those receivables represent expected future cash flows, even though at this moment they are not in cash form. As we develop our knowledge of financial statements, we shall see that this same conclusion can be reached for many items that appear in a company's financial statements.

Characteristics of Externally Reported Information

Financial information that is reported to investors, creditors, and others external to the reporting enterprise has certain qualities that must be understood for the information to have maximum usefulness. Some of these qualities are discussed in the following paragraphs.

Financial Reporting—A Means As we learned in the introduction to this chapter, financial information is a means to an end, not an end in and of itself. The ultimate outcome of providing financial information is to improve the quality of decision making by external parties. Financial statements themselves are simply a means by which that end is achieved.

Financial Reporting versus Financial Statements As our lens diagram in Exhibit 1–5 depicts, financial reporting is broader than financial statements. Stated another way, financial statements are a subset of the total information encompassed by financial reporting. Investors, creditors, and other external users of financial information learn about an enterprise in a variety of ways in addition to its formal financial statements (for example, press releases sent directly to investors and creditors, articles in

Exhibit 1–5

FINANCIAL REPORTING AND FINANCIAL STATEMENTS

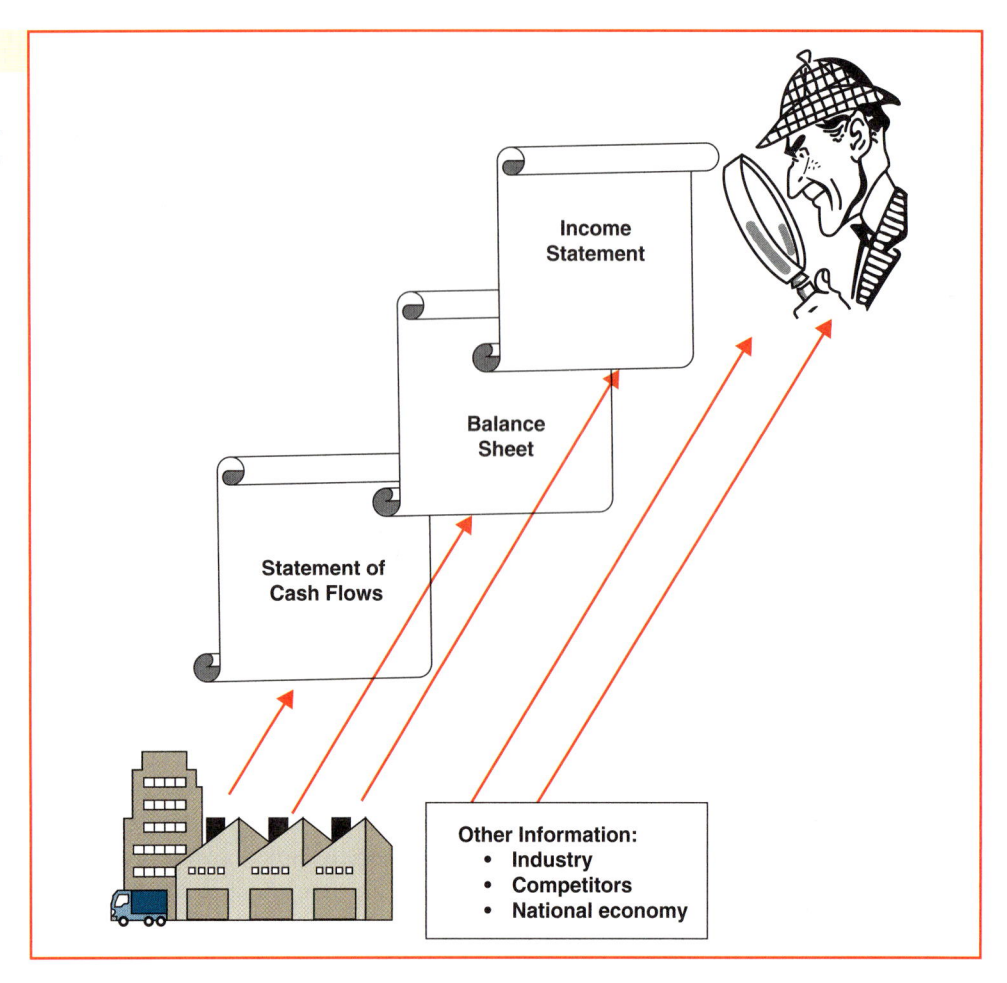

The Wall Street Journal, and more recently open communications via the Internet). Serious investors, creditors, and other external users take advantage of many sources of information that are available to support their economic decisions about an enterprise.

Historical in Nature Externally reported financial information is largely historical in nature. It looks back in time and reports the results of events and transactions that already have occurred. While historical information is very useful in assessing the future, the information itself is more about the past than it is about the future.

Inexact and Approximate Measures Externally reported financial information may have a look of great precision, but in fact much of it is based on estimates, judgments, and assumptions that must be made about both the past and the future. For example, assume a company purchases a piece of equipment for use in its business. To account for that asset and to incorporate the impact of it into the company's externally reported financial information, some assumptions must be made about how long it will be used by the company—how many years it will be used, how many machine-hours it will provide, and so on. The fact that a great deal of judgment underlies most accounting information is a limitation that is sometimes misunderstood.

General-Purpose Assumption As we have already mentioned, we assume that by providing information that meets the needs of investors and creditors, we also meet the information needs of other external parties. We might be able to provide superior information if we treated each potential group of external users separately and prepared different information for each group. This approach is impractical, however, and we instead opt for preparing what is referred to as **general-purpose information** that we believe is useful to multiple user groups (that is, "one size fits all").

Usefulness Enhanced via Explanation The accounting profession believes that the value of externally reported financial information is enhanced by including explanations from management. This information is often nonquantitative and helps to interpret the financial numbers that are presented. For this reason, financial information, including financial statements, is often accompanied by a number of notes and other explanations that help explain and interpret the numerical information.

INTERNAL ACCOUNTING INFORMATION

LO 4
Explain the importance of accounting information for internal parties—primarily management—in terms of the objectives and the characteristics of that information.

Internal decision makers employed by the enterprise create and use internal accounting information not only for exclusive use inside the organization but also to share with external decision makers. For example, in order to meet a production schedule, a producer will design an accounting information system for suppliers detailing its production plans. The producer shares this information with its supplier companies so that they can help the producer meet its objectives. Thus, although the creator and distributor of the accounting information is an internal decision maker, the recipient of the information is, in this case, an external decision maker. Other types of accounting information, however, will not be available to external decision makers. Long-range plans, research and development results, capital budget details, and competitive strategies typically are closely guarded corporate secrets.

Users of Internal Accounting Information

Every employee of the enterprise uses internal accounting information. From basic labor categories to the chief executive officer (CEO), all employees are paid, and their paychecks are generated by the accounting information system. However, the amount of use and, in particular, the involvement in the design of accounting information systems vary considerably. Examples of **internal users** of accounting information systems are as follows:

- Board of directors
- Chief executive officer (CEO)
- Chief financial officer (CFO)
- Vice presidents (information systems, human resources, treasurer, and so forth)
- Business unit managers
- Plant managers
- Store managers
- Line supervisors

Each employee has different specific goals and objectives that are designed to help the enterprise achieve its overall strategies and mission. Looking at the typical, simple organization chart in Exhibit 1–6 you can see that the information created and used by various employees will differ widely. All enterprises follow rules about the design of their accounting information systems to ensure the integrity of accounting information and to protect the enterprise's assets. There are no rules, however, about the type of internal reports or the kind of accounting information that can be generated. A snapshot look inside a firm will demonstrate the diversity of accounting information generated and used in the decision making processes of employees.

Many enterprises use a database warehousing approach for the creation of accounting information systems. This approach, coupled with user-friendly software, allows designated employees access to information to create a variety of accounting reports, including required external financial reports. For example, detailed cost information about a production process is used by the production line supervisor to help control production costs. A process design engineer, when considering the best configuration of equipment and employees, uses the same information to reduce costs or to increase efficiency. Finally, production-related cost information appears in the external financial statements used by investors and creditors.

Exhibit 1–6

TYPICAL SIMPLE ORGANIZATION CHART

[Organization chart showing: Board of Directors (Owners) → Chief Executive Officer (CEO) → Business unit manager, V.P. Human Resources, V.P. Information Services, Chief Financial Officer (CFO). Business unit manager → two Plant managers → Plant accountants, which report to CFO.]

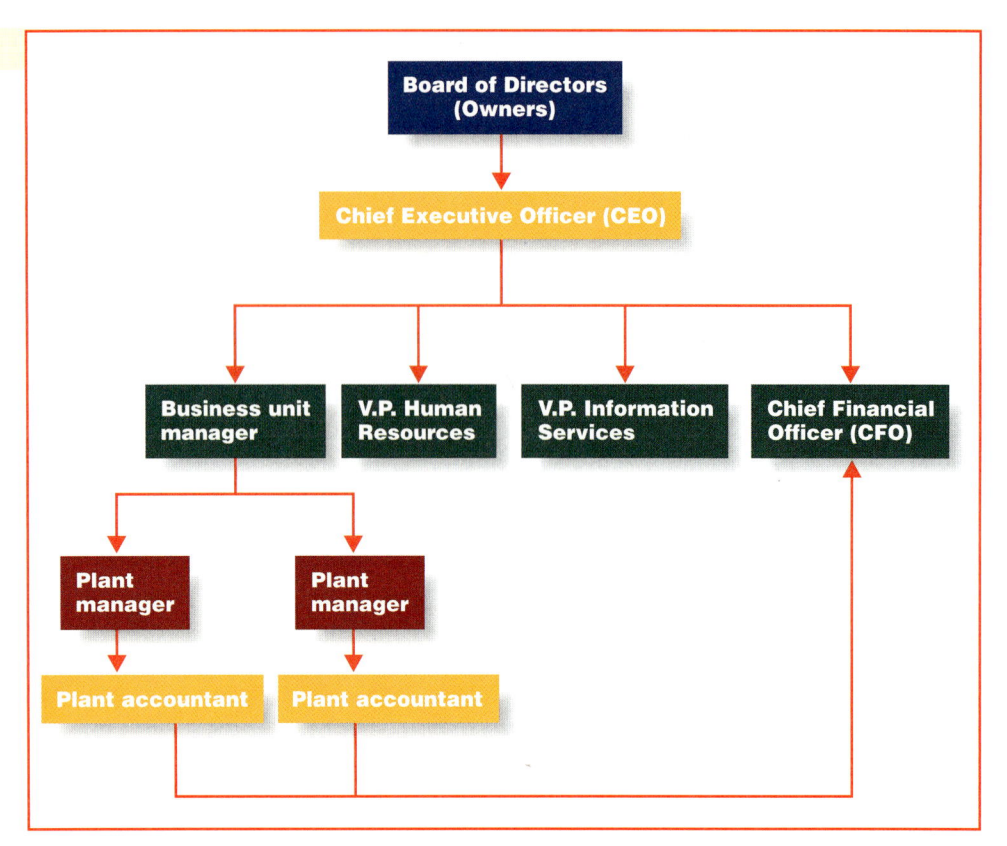

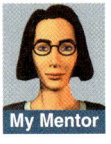

Objectives of Internal Accounting Systems

Each enterprise has implicit and explicit goals and objectives. Many enterprises have a mission statement that describes their goals. These goals can vary widely among enterprises ranging from nonprofit organizations, where goals are aimed at serving specified constituents, to for-profit organizations, where goals are directed toward maximizing the owners' objectives. For example, the **American Cancer Society**, a nonprofit organization, has the following mission:

> The American Cancer Society is the nationwide community-based voluntary health organization dedicated to eliminating cancer as a major health problem by preventing cancer, saving lives and diminishing suffering from cancer through research, education, advocacy, and service.[2]

Procter & Gamble, a for-profit, global producer of consumer products, has the following purpose:

> Our mission as a company is to improve everyone's quality of life every day, everywhere.[3]

Procter & Gamble's annual report to shareholders provides more detail on how the company will achieve its mission. The following goals were identified in P&G's 2001 annual letter to its shareholders:

> Drive costs to best-in-class levels, rationalize our manufacturing capacity and address underperforming businesses.[4]

The constituents of these organizations receive external financial information that helps them assess the progress being made in achieving these goals and objectives. In the case of **Procter & Gamble**, quarterly and annual information is provided to

---
[2] www.cancer.org
[3] Procter & Gamble, 2001 Annual Report, Letter to Shareholders.
[4] Ibid.

shareholders. The **American Cancer Society** is required to report its activities and financial condition to regulators. Providing constituents evaluative information is only one objective of accounting systems.

Enterprises design and use their internal accounting information systems to help them achieve their stated goals and missions. Multiple reports, some as part of the normal reporting process and some that are specially constructed and designed, are produced and distributed regularly. To motivate managers to achieve organizational goals, the internal accounting system is also used to evaluate and reward decision-making performance. When the accounting system compares the plan or budget to the actual outcomes for a period, it creates a signal about the performance of the employee responsible for that part of the budget. In many enterprises management creates a reward system linked to performance as measured by the accounting system.

You as a Manager

You are a plant manager of a facility that manufactures low-cost computers intended primarily for sale to secondary schools and to individual college students. What are some of the decisions you must make and how would management accounting information help you make those decisions?

*Our comments appear on page 38.

YOUR TURN

Thus the objectives of accounting systems begin at the most general level with the objectives and mission of the enterprise. These general organizational goals create a need for information. The enterprise gathers historical and future information from both inside the enterprise and external sources. This information is used by the decision makers who have authority over the firm's resources and who will be evaluated and rewarded based on their decision outcomes.

Characteristics of Internal Accounting Information

The accounting information created and used primarily by decision makers inside the firm is intended above all for planning and control decisions. Because the goal of creating and using internal accounting information differs from the reasons for producing externally reported financial information, its characteristics are different. The following paragraphs identify internal accounting information characteristics.

Importance of Timeliness In order to plan for and control ongoing business processes, accounting information needs to be timely. The competitive environment faced

Both the processes used to create financial accounting reports and the structure of those reports significantly impact management strategy. For example, because external financial reporting standards require companies to include pension-related obligations on their financial statements, management monitors those obligations closely. These pension-related obligations impact labor negotiations and labor-related corporate strategies.

Another example is that the processes necessary to create required external financial reports have historically determined the type of accounting information available inside of companies for internal decision making. Most plants within companies are organized as profit centers where plant-related financial statements mirror those necessary for external reporting purposes.

As you read the chapters of this book, we will remind you about how financial reporting has an impact on and is impacted by management strategies.

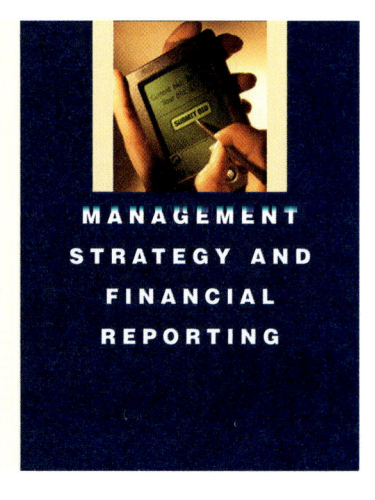

MANAGEMENT STRATEGY AND FINANCIAL REPORTING

by many enterprises demands immediate access to information. Enterprises are responding to this demand by creating computerized databases that link to external forecasts of industry associations, to their suppliers and buyers, and to their constituents. Time lines for development and launch of new products and services are becoming shorter and shorter, making quick access to information a priority.

In addition to needing timely information for planning purposes, enterprises are constantly monitoring and controlling ongoing activities. If a process or activity goes out of control, the enterprise can incur significant costs. For example, recalls of products can be very expensive for a company. If the company can monitor processes and prevent low-quality or defective products from reaching its customers, it can experience significant savings.

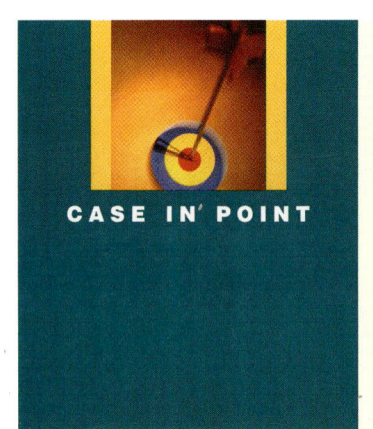

CASE IN POINT

Bridgestone/Firestone, Inc., is still feeling the financial fallout from a product recall in August 2000. The Tokyo-based tire manufacturer recalled about 6.5 million flawed tires. In addition, in 2001 Firestone promised to offer replacements on another 13 million tires in an agreement with the National Highway Traffic Safety Administration. The U.S. division of **Bridgestone/Firestone** expected to lose $200 million in 2001. Experts predict **Firestone** could find itself liable for as much as $3 billion in legal bills associated with the flawed tires.

Jeff Greenberg/PhotoEdit

Identity of Decision Maker Information that is produced to monitor and control processes needs to be provided to those who have decision-making authority to correct problems. Reporting scrap and rework information to line workers without providing them the responsibility for fixing the process is counterproductive. However, a self-directed work team that has been assigned decision-making responsibility over equipment and work-related activities can have a significant impact on rework and scrap if team members control the process causing the problems.

Oriented toward the Future Although some accounting information, like financial accounting information, is historical in nature, the purpose in creating and generating it is to affect the future. The objective is to motivate management to make future decisions that are in the best interest of the enterprise, consistent with its goals, objectives, and mission.

Measures of Efficiency and Effectiveness Accounting information measures the efficiency and effectiveness of resource usage. By comparing the enterprise's resource inputs and outputs with measures of competitors' effectiveness and efficiency, an assessment can be made of how effective management is in achieving the organization's mission. The accounting system uses money as a common unit to achieve these types of comparisons.

Internal Accounting Information—A Means As with financial accounting information, internal accounting information is a means to an end, not an end in and of itself. The ultimate objective is to design and use an accounting system that helps management achieve the goals and objectives of the enterprise.

INTEGRITY OF ACCOUNTING INFORMATION

What enables investors and creditors to rely on financial accounting information without fear that the management of the reporting enterprise has altered the information to make the company's performance look better than it actually was? How can management be sure that internally generated information is free from bias that might favor one outcome over another? The word **integrity** refers to the following qualities: complete, unbroken, unimpaired, sound, honest, and sincere. Accounting information must have these qualities because of the significance of the information to individuals who rely on it in making important financial decisions.

The integrity of accounting information is enhanced in three primary ways. First, certain institutional features add significantly to the integrity of accounting information. These features include standards for the preparation of accounting information, an internal control structure, and audits of financial statements. Second, several professional accounting organizations play unique roles in adding to the integrity of accounting information. Finally, and perhaps most important, is the personal competence, judgment, and ethical behavior of professional accountants. These three elements of the accounting profession come together to ensure that users of accounting information—investors, creditors, managers, and others—can rely on the information to be a fair representation of what it purports to represent.

LO 5
Discuss elements of the system of external and internal financial reporting that create integrity in the reported information.

Institutional Features

Standards for the Preparation of Accounting Information Accounting information that is communicated externally to investors and creditors must be prepared in accordance with standards that are understood by both the preparers and users of that information. We call these standards **generally accepted accounting principles**, often shortened to GAAP. These principles provide the general framework for determining what information is included in financial statements and how this information is to be prepared and presented. GAAP include broad principles of measurement and presentation, as well as detailed rules that are used by professional accountants in preparing accounting information and reports.

Accounting principles are not like physical laws; they do not exist in nature waiting to be discovered. Rather, they are developed by people, in light of what we consider to be the most important objectives of financial reporting. In many ways accounting principles are similar to the rules established for an organized sport, such as baseball or basketball. For example, accounting principles, like sports rules:

- Originate from a combination of tradition, experience, and official decree.
- Require authoritative support and some means of enforcement.
- Are sometimes arbitrary.
- May change over time as shortcomings in the existing rules come to light.
- Must be clearly understood and observed by all participants in the process.

Accounting principles vary somewhat from country to country. The phrase "generally accepted accounting principles" refers to the accounting concepts in use in the United States. However, the principles in use in Canada, Great Britain, and a number of other countries are quite similar. Also, foreign companies that raise capital from American investors usually issue financial statements in conformity with generally accepted accounting principles.

Several international organizations currently are attempting to establish greater uniformity among the accounting principles in use around the world in order to facilitate business activity that increasingly is carried out in more than one country.

In the United States two organizations are particularly important in establishing generally accepted accounting principles—the Financial Accounting Standards Board (FASB) and the Securities and Exchange Commission (SEC).

Financial Accounting Standards Board Today, the most authoritative source of generally accepted accounting principles is the Financial Accounting Standards Board. The FASB is an independent rule-making body, consisting of seven members from the accounting profession, industry, government, and accounting education. Lending support to these members are an advisory council and a large research staff.

The FASB is authorized to issue *Statements of Financial Accounting Standards* (and other authoritative accounting pronouncements), which represent official expressions of generally accepted accounting principles.

In addition to issuing authoritative *Statements,* the FASB has completed a project describing a *conceptual framework* for financial reporting. This conceptual framework sets forth the FASB's views as to the:

- Objectives of financial reporting.
- Desired characteristics of accounting information (such as relevance, reliability, and understandability).
- Elements of financial statements.
- Criteria for deciding what information to include in financial statements.
- Valuation concepts relating to financial statement amounts.

The primary purpose of the conceptual framework is to provide guidance to the FASB in developing new accounting standards. By making each new standard consistent with this framework, the FASB believes that its official *Statements* resolve accounting problems in a logical and consistent manner.

The FASB is part of the private sector of the economy—*it is not a governmental agency.* The development of accounting principles in the United States traditionally has been carried out in the private sector, although the government, acting through the SEC, exercises considerable influence.

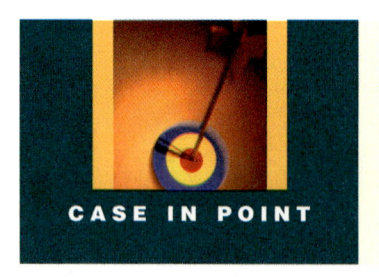

CASE IN POINT

The process for establishing external financial reporting requirements varies significantly from country to country. In some countries like Germany and Japan, the government sets these reporting requirements and as a result financial reporting requirements tend to be very consistent with tax reporting requirements. Because the FASB is independent from the Internal Revenue Service (IRS) in the United States, financial reporting and tax reporting requirements are not always the same.

Securities and Exchange Commission The Securities and Exchange Commission is a governmental agency with the *legal power* to establish accounting principles and financial reporting requirements for publicly owned corporations. In the past, the SEC has generally adopted the recommendations of the FASB, rather than develop its own set of accounting principles. Thus accounting principles continue to be developed in the private sector but are given the *force of law* when they are adopted by the SEC.

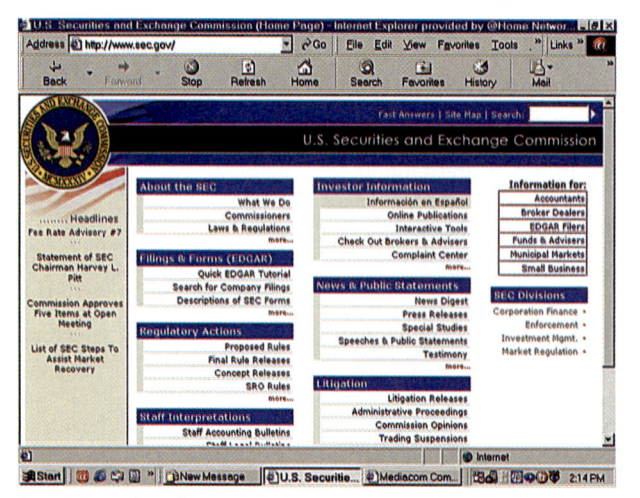

To assure widespread acceptance of new accounting standards, the FASB *needs the support* of the SEC. Therefore, the two organizations work closely together in developing new accounting standards. The SEC also reviews the financial statements of publicly owned corporations to assure compliance with its reporting requirements. In the event that a publicly owned corporation fails to comply with these requirements, the SEC may initiate legal action against the company and the responsible individuals. Thus the SEC enforces compliance with generally accepted accounting principles that are established primarily by the FASB.

Securities and Exchange Commission

Internal Control Structure The decisions made by management are based to a considerable extent on information developed by the accounting system. Therefore, management needs assurance that the accounting information it receives is accurate and reliable. This assurance is provided by the company's *internal control structure.*

A simple example of an internal control procedure is the use of serial numbers on checks issued. Accounting for an unbroken sequence of serial numbers provides assurance that every check issued has been recorded in the accounting records.

The internal control structure includes *all* measures used by an organization to guard against errors, waste, and fraud; to assure the reliability of accounting information; to promote compliance with management policies; and to evaluate the level of performance in all divisions of the company. In short, the internal control structure is intended to ensure that the entire organization *operates according to plan.*

There is a strong *interrelationship* between accounting and internal control. We have stated that the internal control structure includes measures designed to promote the reliability of accounting information. At the same time, one goal of the accounting system is to provide management with information useful in establishing internal control throughout the organization. Thus the topic of internal control goes hand in hand with the study of accounting.

Audits of Financial Statements What assurance do outsiders have that the financial statements issued by management provide a complete and reliable picture of the company's financial position and operating results? In large part, this assurance is provided by an *audit* of the company's financial statements, performed by a firm of *certified public accountants (CPAs).* These auditors are experts in the field of financial reporting and are *independent* of the company issuing the financial statements.

An audit is an *investigation* of a company's financial statements, designed to determine the fairness of these statements. Accountants and auditors use the term *fair* in describing financial statements that are reliable and complete, conform to generally accepted accounting principles, and are *not misleading.*

In auditing financial statements, generally accepted accounting principles are the standard by which those statements are judged. For the auditor to reach the conclusion that the financial statements are fair representations of a company's financial position, results of operations, and cash flows, the statements must comply in all important ways with generally accepted accounting principles.

The 2001 financial statements of **Sony Corporation** are accompanied by a statement issued by **PricewaterhouseCoopers LLP**, the company's auditor and one of the largest public accounting firms in the world. This statement indicates that in the auditor's opinion, the financial statements of the company are in conformity with generally accepted accounting principles and that they present fairly the financial activities of the company for 2001.

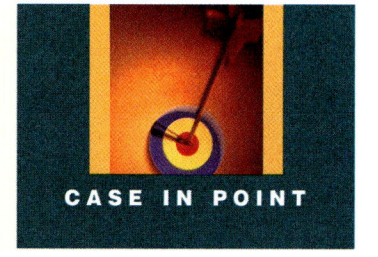

CASE IN POINT

Professional Organizations

Several professional accounting organizations play an active role in improving the quality of accounting information that is used by investors, creditors, management, and others. In addition to the Financial Accounting Standards Board and the Securities and Exchange Commission, discussed earlier, the American Institute of CPAs, the Institute of Management Accountants, the Institute of Internal Auditors, and the American Accounting Association are particularly important.

LO 6
Identify and discuss several professional organizations that play important roles in preparing and communicating accounting information.

American Institute of CPAs (AICPA) The American Institute of CPAs is a professional association of certified public accountants. Its mission is to provide members with the resources, information, and leadership to enable them to provide valuable services in the highest professional manner to benefit the public, employers, and clients. The AICPA participates in many aspects of the accounting profession, including the establishment of auditing standards to be followed by CPAs in the audit of financial statements. The AICPA conducts accounting research and works closely with the FASB in the establishment and interpretation of generally accepted accounting principles. In fact, prior to the establishment of the FASB, the AICPA had primary responsibility for the establishment of accounting principles.

Institute of Management Accountants (IMA) The mission of the Institute of Management Accountants is to provide members personal and professional development opportunities through education, association with business professionals, and certification. The IMA is recognized by the financial community as a respected organization that influences the concepts and ethical practice of management accounting and financial management. The IMA sponsors a number of educational activities for its members, including national seminars and conferences, regional and local programs, self-study courses, and in-house and on-line programs. Two certification programs are available through the IMA—the Certificate in Management Accounting (CMA) and the Certificate in Financial Management (CFM). These designations testify to the individual's competence and expertise in management accounting and financial management.

Institute of Internal Auditors (IIA) With more than 70,000 members in 129 countries, the Institute of Internal Auditors is the primary international professional association dedicated to the promotion and development of the practice of internal auditing. It provides professional development through the Certified Internal Auditor® Program and leading-edge conferences and seminars; research through the IIA Research Foundation on trends, best practices, and other internal auditing issues; guidance through the *Standards for the Professional Practice of Internal Auditing;* and educational products on virtually all aspects of the profession. The IIA also provides audit specialty services and industry-specific auditing programs, as well as quality assurance reviews and benchmarking services.

American Accounting Association (AAA) Membership in the American Accounting Association is made up primarily of accounting educators, although many practicing accountants are members as well. The mission of the AAA includes advancing accounting education and research, as well as influencing accounting practice. The focus of many of the AAA's activities is on improving accounting education by better preparing accounting professors and on advancing knowledge in the accounting discipline through research and publication. An important contribution of the AAA to the integrity of accounting information is its impact through accounting faculty on the many students who study accounting in college and subsequently become professional accountants.

Competence, Judgment, and Ethical Behavior

LO 7
Discuss the importance of personal competence, professional judgment, and ethical behavior on the part of accounting professionals.

Preparing and presenting accounting information is not a mechanical task that can be performed entirely by a computer or even by well-trained clerical personnel. A characteristic common to all recognized professions, including medicine, law, and accounting, is the need for competent individual practitioners to solve problems using their professional judgment and applying strong ethical standards. The problems encountered in the practice of a profession are often complex, and the specific circumstances unique. In many cases, the well-being of others is directly affected by the work of a professional.

To illustrate the importance of competence, professional judgment, and ethical behavior in the preparation of financial statements, consider the following complex issues that must be addressed by the accountant:

- At what point have certain complex transactions actually taken place, thereby making it necessary to include them in financial statements that are sent to investors and creditors?
- At what point should an enterprise account for transactions that continue over a long period of time, such as a long-term contract to construct an interstate highway?
- What constitutes adequate disclosure of information that would be expected by a reasonably informed user of financial statements?

- At what point are a company's financial problems sufficient to question whether it will be able to remain in business for the foreseeable future, and when should that information be communicated to users of its financial statements?
- When have efforts by management to improve (that is, "window dress") its financial statements crossed a line that is inappropriate, making the financial statements actually misleading to investors and creditors?

Judgment always involves some risk of error. Some errors in judgment result from carelessness or inexperience on the part of the preparer of financial information or the decision maker who uses that information. Others occur simply because future events are uncertain and do not work out as expected when the information was prepared.

If the public is to have confidence in the judgment of professional accountants, these accountants first must demonstrate that they possess the characteristic of *competence*. Both the accounting profession and state governments have taken steps to assure the public of the technical competence of **certified public accountants** (CPAs). CPAs are licensed by the states, in much the same manner as states license physicians and attorneys. The licensing requirements vary somewhat from state to state, but in general, an individual must be of good character, have a college education with a major in accounting, pass a rigorous examination, and have several years of accounting experience. In addition, most states require all CPAs to spend at least 40 hours per year in continuing professional education throughout their careers.

Beginning in the year 2000, the AICPA requires its new members to have completed 150 semester hours of college work. This represents about one additional year beyond a bachelor's degree, which usually requires approximately 120–125 semester hours. Most states are changing their licensing requirements to reflect this expectation of better-educated entrants into the accounting profession.

Management accountants are not required to be licensed as CPAs. However, they voluntarily may earn a **Certificate in Management Accounting (CMA)** or a **Certificate in Internal Auditing (CIA)** as evidence of their professional competence. These certificates are issued by the IMA and the IIA, and signify competence in management accounting and internal auditing, respectively. The requirements for becoming a CMA and CIA are similar to those for becoming a CPA.

Integrity in accounting information requires honesty and a strong commitment to ethical conduct—doing the right thing. For a professional accountant, ethical behavior is just as important as competence. However, it is far more difficult to test or enforce.

Many professional organizations have codes of ethics or professional conduct that direct the activities of their members. The AICPA, for example, has a code of professional conduct that expresses the accounting profession's recognition of its responsibilities to the public, to clients, and to colleagues. The principles included in the code guide AICPA members in the performance of their professional responsibilities. This code expresses the basic tenets of ethical and professional behavior and has been codified into law in many states.

You as a Professional Accountant

You are a professional accountant working for a public accounting firm and find yourself in a difficult situation. You have discovered some irregularities in the financial records of your firm's client. You are uncertain whether these irregularities are the result of carelessness on the part of the company's employees or represent intentional steps taken to cover up questionable activities. You approach your superior about this and she indicates that you should ignore it. Her response is "These things happen all of the time and usually are pretty minor. We are on a very tight time schedule to complete this engagement, so let's just keep our eyes on our goal of finishing our work by the end of the month." What would you do?

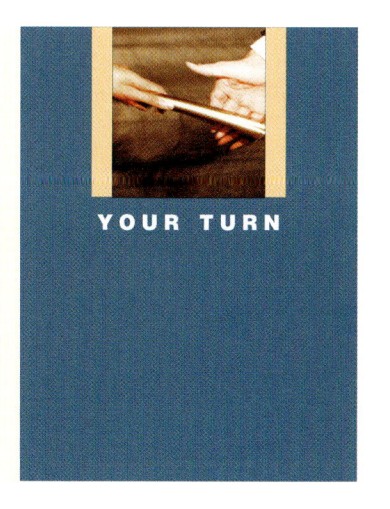

YOUR TURN

*Our comments appear on page 38.

Exhibit 1–7

EXCERPTS FROM THE AICPA CODE OF PROFESSIONAL CONDUCT

Preamble

These Principles of the Code of Professional Conduct of the American Institute of Certified Public Accountants express the profession's recognition of its responsibilities to the public, to clients, and to colleagues. They guide members in the performance of their professional responsibilities and express the basic tenets of ethical and professional conduct. The Principles call for un answering commitment to honorable behavior, even at the sacrifice of personal advantage.

Articles

I. Responsibilities

In carrying out their responsibilities as professionals, members should exercise sensitive professional and moral judgments in all their activities.

II. The Public Interest

Members should accept the obligation to act in a way that will serve the public interest, honor the public trust, and demonstrate commitment to professionalism.

III. Integrity

To maintain and broaden public confidence, members should perform all professional responsibilities with the highest sense of integrity.

IV. Objectivity and Independence

A member should maintain objectivity and be free of conflicts of interest in discharging professional responsibilities. A member in public practice should be independent in fact and appearance when providing auditing and other attestation services.

V. Due Care

A member should observe the profession's technical and ethical standards, strive continually to improve competence and the quality of service, and discharge professional responsibility to the best of the member's ability.

VI. Scope and Nature of Services

A member in public practice should observe the Principles of the Code of Professional Conduct in determining the scope and nature of services to be provided.

Exhibit 1–7 contains excerpts from the AICPA code of professional conduct. One of the principles expressed in the AICPA's code of professional conduct is the commitment of CPAs to the public interest, shown in Article II. The public interest is defined as the collective well-being of the community of people and institutions the profession serves. Other principles emphasize the importance of integrity, objectivity, independence, and due care in the performance of one's duties.

Expectations of ethical conduct are also important for other accountants. The code of ethics of the IMA, for example, includes the following requirements:

- *Competence.* Management accountants should be professionally competent to perform their duties of providing relevant and reliable information in accordance with relevant laws, regulations, and technical standards.

- *Confidentiality.* Management accountants should refrain from disclosing confidential information or using confidential information to their own advantage.

- *Integrity.* Management accountants should avoid conflicts of interest by refusing compromising gifts and favors, by refusing to subvert organizational objectives, by refusing to communicate biased information, and by avoiding activities that could discredit the profession.

- *Objectivity.* Management accountants should communicate information fairly and objectively and disclose all relevant information.

Users of accounting information—both external and internal—recognize that the reliability of the information is affected by the competence, professional judgment, and ethical standards of accountants. While the institutional features and professional organizations that were discussed earlier are important parts of the financial reporting system, the personal attributes of competence, professional judgment, and ethical behavior ultimately ensure the quality and reliability of accounting information.

In this text, we address the topic of ethical conduct primarily through questions, exercises, problems, and cases that emphasize the general concepts of honesty, fairness, and adequate disclosure. Most chapters include assignment material in which you are asked to make judgment calls in applying these concepts. (These assignments are identified by the scales of justice logo appearing in the margin.)

CONCLUDING REMARKS

In this chapter we have established a framework for your study of accounting. You have learned how financial accounting provides information for external users, primarily investors and creditors, and how accounting provides information for internal management. We have established the importance of integrity in accounting information and have learned about several things that build integrity. Looking ahead, in Chapter 2 we begin to look in greater depth at financial accounting and, more specifically, financial statements. You will be introduced to the details of the three primary financial statements that provide information for investors and creditors. As the text progresses, you will learn more about the important information that these financial statements provide and how that information is used to make important financial decisions.

A SECOND LOOK
AMERICA ONLINE INC.

Let's return for a moment to **America Online**, the company we used to introduce this chapter. **AOL** has many investors and creditors who have committed their funds to the company and who expect both a return on their investment and a return of their investment in the future. **AOL** also has extensive management personnel who have an interest in the company. Many decisions are based on the accounting information that is prepared by accountants within **AOL**. That information includes both financial accounting information and other accounting information.

Within **AOL** exist complex accounting systems that are designed to capture information about the company's many transactions. Those systems organize and communicate that information in a manner that facilitates and supports decisions by investors, creditors, managers, and others. It is particularly important that this information have integrity. That is, the information must be properly prepared, complete, and unbiased. For this to be the case, a key element is the integrity of personnel who prepare the information.

Accountants are required to have considerable education and experience to become experts in the design of accounting systems and the preparation of complex financial reports to support decision making. Many people with these qualities work for **America Online** to support the company's need for high-quality financial information.

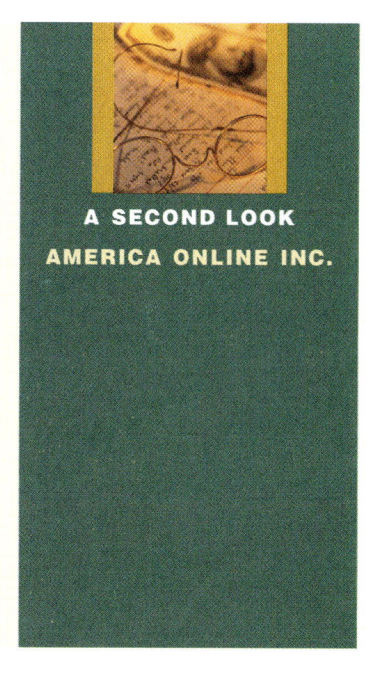

SUPPLEMENTAL TOPIC

CAREERS IN ACCOUNTING

Accounting—along with such fields as architecture, engineering, law, medicine, and theology—is recognized as a profession. What distinguishes a profession from other disciplines? There is no widely recognized definition of a profession, but all of these fields have several characteristics in common.

First, all professions involve a complex and evolving body of knowledge. In accounting, the complexity and the ever-changing nature of the business world, financial reporting requirements, management demands for increasingly complex information, and income tax laws certainly meet this criterion.

LO 8
Describe various career opportunities in accounting.

Second, in all professions, practitioners must use their professional judgment to resolve problems and dilemmas. Throughout this text, we will point out situations requiring accountants to exercise professional judgment.

Of greatest importance, however, is the unique responsibility of professionals *to serve the public's best interest, even at the sacrifice of personal advantage.* This responsibility stems from the fact that the public has little technical knowledge in the professions, yet fair and competent performance by professionals is vital to the public's health, safety, or well-being. The practice of medicine, for example, directly affects public health, while engineering affects public safety. Accounting affects the public's well-being in many ways, because accounting information is used in the allocation of economic resources throughout society. Thus accountants have a basic social contract to avoid being associated with misleading information.

Accountants tend to specialize in specific fields, as do the members of other professions. Career opportunities in accounting may be divided into four broad areas: (1) public accounting, (2) management accounting, (3) governmental accounting, and (4) accounting education.

Public Accounting

Certified public accountants offer a variety of accounting services to the public. These individuals may work in a CPA firm or as sole practitioners.

The work of public accountants consists primarily of auditing financial statements, income tax work, and management advisory services (management consulting).

Providing management advisory services is, perhaps, the fastest-growing area in public accounting. The advisory services extend well beyond tax planning and accounting matters; CPAs advise management on such diverse issues as international mergers, manufacturing processes, and the introduction of new products. The involvement of CPAs in the field of management consulting reflects the fact that *financial considerations enter into almost every business decision.*

A great many CPAs move from public accounting into managerial positions with their client organizations. These "alumni" from public accounting often move directly into such top management positions as controller, treasurer, chief financial officer, or chief executive officer.

Management Accounting

In contrast to the public accountant who serves many clients, the management accountant works for one enterprise. Management accountants develop and interpret accounting information designed specifically to meet the various needs of management.

The chief accounting officer of an organization usually is called the *chief financial officer (CFO)* or *controller.* The term *controller* has been used to emphasize the fact that one basic purpose of accounting data is to aid in controlling business operations. The CFO or controller is part of the top management team, which is responsible for running the business, setting its objectives, and seeing that these objectives are met.

In addition to developing information to assist managers, management accountants are responsible for operating the company's accounting system, including the recording of transactions and the preparation of financial statements, tax returns, and other accounting reports. As the responsibilities of management accountants are so broad, many areas of specialization have developed. Among the more important are the following.

Financial Forecasting A financial forecast (or budget) is a plan of financial operations for some *future* period. Actually, forecasting is much like financial reporting, except that the accountant is estimating future outcomes, rather than reporting past results. A forecast provides each department of a business with financial goals. Comparison of the results actually achieved with these forecast amounts is one widely used means of evaluating performance.

Supplemental Topic

Cost Accounting Knowing the cost of each business operation and of each manufactured product is essential to the efficient management of a business. Determining the per-unit cost of business activities and of manufactured products, and interpreting these cost data, comprise a specialized field called **cost accounting**.

Internal Auditing Large organizations usually maintain a staff of *internal auditors*. **Internal auditing** is the study of the internal control structure and evaluation of efficiency of many different aspects of the company's operations. As employees, internal auditors are not independent of the organization. Therefore, they *do not* perform independent audits of the company's financial statements.

Careers in management accounting often lead to positions in top management—just as do careers in public accounting.

Governmental Accounting

Governmental agencies use accounting information in allocating their resources and in controlling their operations. Therefore, the need for management accountants in governmental agencies is similar to that in business organizations.

The GAO: Who Audits the Government? The **General Accounting Office** (GAO) audits many agencies of the federal government, as well as some private organizations doing business with the government. The GAO reports its findings directly to Congress, which, in turn, often discloses these findings to the public.

GAO investigations may be designed either to evaluate the efficiency of an entity's operations or to determine the fairness of accounting information reported to the government.

The IRS: Audits of Income Tax Returns Another governmental agency that performs extensive auditing work is the **Internal Revenue Service** (IRS). The IRS handles the millions of income tax returns filed annually by individuals and business organizations and frequently performs auditing functions to verify data contained in these returns.

The SEC: The "Watchdog" of Financial Reporting The SEC works closely with the FASB in establishing generally accepted accounting principles. Each year large publicly owned corporations must file audited financial statements with the SEC. If the SEC believes that a company's financial statements are deficient in any way, it conducts an investigation. If the SEC concludes that federal securities laws have been violated, it initiates legal action against the reporting entity and responsible individuals.

Many other governmental agencies, including the FBI, the Treasury Department, and the FDIC (Federal Deposit Insurance Corporation), use accountants to audit compliance with governmental regulations and to investigate suspected criminal activity. People beginning their careers in governmental accounting often move into top administrative positions.

Accounting Education

Some accountants, including your instructor and the authors of this textbook, have chosen to pursue careers in accounting education. A position as an accounting faculty member offers opportunities for teaching, research, consulting, and an unusual degree of freedom in developing individual skills. Accounting educators contribute to the accounting profession in many ways. One, of course, lies in effective teaching; second, in publishing significant research findings; and a third, in influencing top students to pursue careers in accounting.

What About Bookkeeping?

Some people think that the work of professional accountants consists primarily of bookkeeping. Actually, it doesn't. In fact, many professional accountants do *little or no* bookkeeping.

Bookkeeping is the clerical side of accounting—the recording of routine transactions and day-to-day record keeping. Today such tasks are performed primarily by computers and skilled clerical personnel, not by accountants.

Professional accountants are involved more with the *interpretation and use* of accounting information than with its actual preparation. Their work includes evaluating the efficiency of operations, resolving complex financial reporting issues, forecasting the results of future operations, auditing, tax planning, and designing efficient accounting systems. There is very little that is "routine" about the work of a professional accountant.

A person might become a proficient bookkeeper in a few weeks or months. To become a professional accountant, however, is a far greater challenge. It requires years of study, experience, and an ongoing commitment to keeping current.

We will illustrate and explain a number of bookkeeping procedures in this text, particularly in the next several chapters. But teaching bookkeeping skills is *not* our goal; the primary purpose of this text is to develop your abilities to *understand and use* accounting information in today's business world.

Accounting as a Stepping-Stone

We have mentioned that many professional accountants leave their accounting careers for key positions in management or administration. An accounting background is invaluable in such positions, because top management works continuously with issues defined and described in accounting terms and concepts.

An especially useful stepping-stone is experience in public accounting. Public accountants have the unusual opportunity of getting an inside look at many different business organizations, which makes them particularly well suited for top management positions in other organizations.

END-OF-CHAPTER REVIEW

SUMMARY OF LEARNING OBJECTIVES

LO 1
Discuss accounting as the language of business and the role of accounting information in making economic decisions.

Accounting is the means by which information about an enterprise is communicated and, thus, is sometimes called the language of business. Many different users have need for accounting information in order to make important decisions. These users include investors, creditors, management, governmental agencies, labor unions, and others. Because the primary role of accounting information is to provide useful information for decision-making purposes, it is sometimes referred to as a means to an end, with the end being the decision that is helped by the availability of accounting information.

LO 2
Discuss the significance of accounting systems in generating reliable accounting information.

Information systems are critical to the production of quality accounting information on a timely basis and the communication of that information to decision makers. While there are different types of information systems, they all have one characteristic in common—to meet the organization's needs for accounting information as efficiently as possible.

LO 3
Explain the importance of financial accounting information for external parties—primarily investors and creditors—in terms of the objectives and the characteristics of that information.

The primary objectives of financial accounting are to provide information that is useful in making investment and credit decisions; in assessing the amount, timing, and uncertainty of future cash flows; and in learning about the enterprise's economic resources, claims to resources, and changes in claims to resources. Some of the most important characteristics of financial accounting information are it is a means to an end, it is historical in nature, it results from inexact and approximate measures of business activity, and it is based on a general-purpose assumption.

LO 4
Explain the importance of accounting information for internal parties—primarily management—in terms of the objectives and the characteristics of that information.

Accounting information is useful to the enterprise in achieving its goals, objectives, and mission; assessing past performance and future directions; and evaluating and rewarding decision-making performance. Some of the important characteristics of internal accounting information are its timeliness, its relationship to decision-making authority, its future orientation, its relationship to measuring efficiency and effectiveness, and the fact that it is a means to an end.

LO 5
Discuss elements of the system of external and internal financial reporting that create integrity in the reported information.

Integrity of financial reporting is important because of the reliance that is placed on financial information by users both outside and inside the reporting organization. Important dimensions of financial reporting that work together to ensure integrity in information are institutional features (accounting principles, internal structure, and audits); professional organizations (AICPA, IMA, CIA, AAA); and the competence, judgment, and ethical behavior of individual accountants.

LO 6
Identify and discuss several professional organizations that play important roles in preparing and communicating accounting information.

The FASB and SEC are important organizations in terms of standard setting in the United States. The FASB is a private-sector organization that works closely with the SEC, which has legal authority to designate financial reporting standards for publicly held companies. Professional organizations that provide services to individual accountants in various segments of the accounting profession are the AICPA, IMA, IIA, and AAA.

LO 7
Discuss the importance of personal competence, professional judgment, and ethical behavior on the part of accounting professionals.

Personal competence and professional judgment are, perhaps, the most important factors in ensuring the integrity of financial information. Competence is demonstrated by one's education and professional certification (CPA, CMA, CIA). Professional judgment is important because accounting information is often based on inexact measurements and assumptions are required. Ethical behavior refers to the quality of accountants being motivated to "do the right thing" in applying their skills.

LO 8
Describe various career opportunities in accounting.

Accounting opens the door to many diverse career opportunities. Public accounting is the segment of the profession where professionals offer audit, tax, and consulting services to clients. Management, or managerial, accounting refers to that segment of the accounting profession where professional accountants work for individual companies in a wide variety of capacities. Many accountants work for various governmental agencies. Some accountants choose education as a career and work to prepare students for future careers in one of the other segments of the accounting profession. While keeping detailed records (that is, bookkeeping) is a part of accounting, it is not a distinguishing characteristic of a career in accounting; in fact, many accounting careers involve little or no bookkeeping.

KEY TERMS INTRODUCED OR EMPHASIZED IN CHAPTER 1

accounting system (p. 6) The personnel, procedures, devices, and records used by an organization to develop accounting information and communicate that information to decision makers.

American Accounting Association (p. 22) A professional accounting organization consisting primarily of accounting educators that is dedicated to improving accounting education, research, and practice.

American Institute of CPAs (p. 21) A professional accounting organization of certified public accountants that engages in a variety of professional activities, including establishing auditing standards, conducting research, and working closely with the FASB in establishing financial reporting standards.

audit (p. 21) An investigation of financial statements designed to determine their fairness in relation to generally accepted accounting principles.

balance sheet (p. 12) A position statement that shows where the company stands in financial terms at a specific date. (Also called the statement of financial position.)

bookkeeping (p. 28) The clerical dimension of accounting that includes recording the routine transactions and day-to-day record keeping of an enterprise.

cash flow prospects (p. 9) The likelihood that an enterprise will be able to provide an investor with both a return on the investor's investment and the return of that investment.

Certificate in Internal Auditing (p. 23) A professional designation issued by the Institute of Internal Auditors signifying expertise in internal auditing.

Certificate in Management Accounting (p. 23) A professional designation issued by the Institute of Management Accounting signifying expertise in management accounting.

certified public accountant (p. 23) An accountant who is licensed by a state after meeting rigorons education, experience, and examination requirements.

cost accounting (p. 27) Determining the cost of certain business activities and interpreting cost information.

external users (p. 8) Individuals and other enterprises that have a financial interest in the reporting enterprise but that are not involved in the day-to-day operations of that enterprise (e.g., owners, creditors, labor unions, suppliers, customers).

financial accounting (p. 5) Providing information about the financial resources, obligations, and activities of an economic entity that is intended for use primarily by external decision makers—investors and creditors.

Financial Accounting Standards Board (p. 20) A private-sector organization that is responsible for determining generally accepted accounting principles in the United States.

financial forecast (p. 26) A plan of financial operations for some future period.

financial statement (p. 11) A monetary declaration of what is believed to be true about an enterprise.

General Accounting Office (p. 27) A federal government agency that audits many other agencies of the federal government and other organizations that do business with the federal government and reports its findings to Congress.

generally accepted accounting principles (p. 19) Principles that provide the framework for determining what information is to be included in financial statements and how that information is to be presented.

general-purpose information (p. 14) Information that is intended to meet the needs of multiple users that have an interest in the financial activities of an enterprise rather than being tailored to the specific information needs of one user.

income statement (p. 12) An activity statement that shows details and results of the company's profit-related activities for a period of time.

Institute of Internal Auditors (p. 22) A professional accounting organization that is dedicated to the promotion and development of the practice of internal auditing.

Institute of Management Accountants (p. 22) A professional accounting organization that intends to influence the concepts and ethical practice of management accounting and financial management.

integrity (p. 19) The qualities complete, unbroken, unimpaired, sound, honest, and sincere.

internal auditing (p. 27) The study of internal control structure and evaluation of the efficiency of many different aspects of the enterprise's operations.

internal control structure (p. 21) Measures used by an organization to guard against errors, waste, and fraud; to assure the reliability of accounting information; to promote compliance with management policies; and to evaluate the level of performance of all divisions of the company.

Internal Revenue Service (p. 27) A government organization that handles millions of income tax returns filed by individuals and businesses and performs audit functions to verify the data contained in those returns.

internal users (p. 15) Individuals who use accounting information from within an organization (for example, board of directors, chief financial officer, plant managers, store managers).

management accounting (p. 5) Providing information that is intended primarily for use by internal management in decision making required to run the business.

return of investment (p. 9) The repayment to an investor of the amount originally invested in another enterprise.

return on investment (p. 9) The payment of an amount (interest, dividends) for using another's money.

Securities and Exchange Commission (p. 20) A governmental organization that has the legal power to establish accounting principles and financial reporting requirements for publicly held companies in the United States.

statement of cash flows (p. 12) An activity statement that shows the details of the company's activities involving cash during a period of time.

statement of financial position (p. 12) Also called the balance sheet.

tax accounting (p. 6) Preparation of income tax returns and anticipating the tax effects of business transactions and structuring them in such a way as to minimize the income tax burden.

DEMONSTRATION PROBLEM

Find the America Online, Inc., annual report from 2000 at the following Internet address (**www.aoltimewarner.com/investors/financials/annualreports/aol2000.pdf**) to answer the following questions:

a. Name the titles of the financial reports in the AOL, Inc., annual report that provide specific information about economic resources, claims to resources, and changes in resources and claims.
b. Name three other sections from AOL's 2000 annual report that provide information useful in assessing the amount, timing, and uncertainty of future cash flows.
c. Which main categories of other general information are useful in making investment and credit decisions?

Solution to the Demonstration Problem

a.
- America Online, Inc.
  Consolidated Balance Sheets
- America Online, Inc.
  Consolidated Statements of Operations
- America Online, Inc.
  Consolidated Statements of Cash Flows

b.
- Management's Discussion and Analysis of Financial Condition and Results of Operations sections about revenues and advertising costs
- Selected Financial Data
- America Online, Inc., Notes to the Consolidated Financial Statements

c.
- The letter from the chairman and chief executive officer (Steve Case) and the president and chief operating officer (Bob Pittman)
- Management's Discussion and Analysis of Financial Condition and Results of Operations that contains general discussions about competitors, sales and marketing plans, seasonality, inflation, forward-looking statements, and market risk assessments
- Report of the Independent Auditors

SELF-TEST QUESTIONS

Answers to these questions appear on page 39.

1. Which of the following does *not* describe accounting?
   a. Language of business.
   b. Is an end rather than a means to an end.
   c. Useful for decision making.
   d. Used by business, government, nonprofit organizations, and individuals.
2. To understand and use accounting information in making economic decisions, you must understand:
   a. The nature of economic activities that accounting information describes.
   b. The assumptions and measurement techniques involved in developing accounting information.
   c. Which information is relevant for a particular type of decision that is being made.
   d. All of the above.

3. Purposes of an accounting system include all of the following *except:*
   a. Interpret and record the effects of business transactions.
   b. Classify the effects of transactions to facilitate the preparation of reports.
   c. Summarize and communicate information to decision makers.
   d. Dictate the specific types of business transactions that the enterprise may engage in.
4. External users of financial accounting information include all of the following *except:*
   a. Investors.
   b. Labor unions.
   c. Line managers.
   d. General public.
5. Objectives of financial reporting to external investors and creditors include preparing information about all of the following *except:*
   a. Information used to determine which products to produce.
   b. Information about economic resources, claims to those resources, and changes in both resources and claims.
   c. Information that is useful in assessing the amount, timing, and uncertainty of future cash flows.
   d. Information that is useful in making investment and credit decisions.
6. Financial accounting information is characterized by all of the following *except:*
   a. It is historical in nature.
   b. It sometimes results from inexact and approximate measures.
   c. It is factual, so it does not require judgment to prepare.
   d. It is enhanced by management's explanation.
7. Which of the following is *not* a user of internal accounting information?
   a. Store manager.
   b. Chief executive officer.
   c. Creditor.
   d. Chief financial officer.
8. Characteristics of internal accounting information include all of the following *except:*
   a. It is audited by a CPA.
   b. It must be timely.
   c. It is oriented toward the future.
   d. It measures efficiency and effectiveness.
9. Which of the following are important factors in ensuring the integrity of accounting information?
   a. Institutional factors, such as standards for preparing information.
   b. Professional organizations, such as the American Institute of CPAs.
   c. Competence, judgment, and ethical behavior of individual accountants.
   d. All of the above.
10. The code of ethics of the American Institute of Certified Public Accountants includes requirements in which of the following areas?
    a. The Public Interest.
    b. Objectivity.
    c. Independence.
    d. All of the above.

ASSIGNMENT MATERIAL
DISCUSSION QUESTIONS

1. What do we mean when we say that accounting is a means rather than an end?
2. Accounting is sometimes described as the language of business. What is meant by this description?
3. What kinds of organizations, in addition to businesses, use accounting information?

Discussion Questions

4. What is the primary distinction between financial accounting and other accounting?
5. Describe the relationship among the accounting process, accounting information, decision makers, and economic activities.
6. What are some examples of nonfinancial information that is often wanted by users of accounting information?
7. What is an accounting system and what is the primary objective of such a system?
8. What do we mean when we say that an accounting system needs to be cost-effective?
9. What are the three basic functions of every accounting system?
10. Who designs and installs accounting systems?
11. Generally describe and give several examples of external users of accounting information.
12. What are the two primary external groups to which financial accounting information is directed?
13. What do we mean when we say that investors and creditors are interested in a company's cash flow prospects?
14. When you invest your savings in a company, what is the difference between the return *on* your investment and the return *of* your investment?
15. Going from general to specific, what are the three primary objectives of financial accounting information?
16. What are the three primary financial statements with which we communicate financial accounting information?
17. Do the terms *financial reporting* and *financial statements* mean the same thing? Explain.
18. Is externally reported financial information always precise and accurate?
19. What do we mean when we say that financial accounting information is "general-purpose"?
20. How does management's explanation enhance the usefulness of financial accounting information?
21. What are several examples of internal, management-prepared information that ordinarily would not be communicated externally?
22. What are some examples of internal users of accounting information?
23. What is meant by a *database warehousing approach* for the creation of useful accounting information for internal management?
24. What are the three primary ways enterprises use their internal accounting information?
25. Why does internal accounting information need to be timely?
26. Is internal accounting information primarily historical or future oriented? How does that compare with financial accounting information?
27. How does accounting information assist management in measuring efficiency and effectiveness?
28. Why is it important for accounting information to have the quality of integrity?
29. What is meant by *generally accepted accounting principles,* and how do these principles add to the integrity of financial accounting information?
30. What is an *internal control structure,* and how does it add to the integrity of accounting information?
31. What is an *audit,* and how does it add to the integrity of accounting information?
32. What is meant by the professional designations *CPA, CMA,* and *CIA,* and how do these designations add to the integrity of accounting information?
33. What is a *code of ethics,* and how do such codes add to the integrity of accounting information?
34. What is the Financial Accounting Standards Board (FASB), and what is its role in external financial reporting?
35. What is the Securities and Exchange Commission (SEC), and what is its role in external financial reporting?
36. What is the role of the American Institute of Certified Public Accountants in the audit of financial statements?
37. What is the primary mission of the Institute of Management Accountants?
38. What is the mission of the Institute of Internal Auditors, and does the organization have primarily a U.S. or an international focus?
39. Who makes up the majority of the members of the American Accounting Association, and how has this organization affected the practice of accounting?

EXERCISES

EXERCISE 1.1
You as a User of Accounting Information
LO 1

Identify several ways in which *you* currently use accounting information in your life as a student. Also identify several situations in which, while you are still a student, you might be required to supply financial information about yourself to others.

EXERCISE 1.2
Users of Accounting Information
LO 3, 4

Boeing Company is the largest manufacturer of commercial aircraft in the United States and is a major employer in Seattle, Washington. Explain why each of the following individuals or organizations would be interested in financial information about the company.
a. **California Public Employees Retirement System**, one of the world's largest pension funds.
b. **China Airlines**, a rapidly growing airline serving the Pacific Rim.
c. Henry James, a real estate investor considering building apartments in the Seattle area.
d. **Boeing**'s management.
e. **International Aerospace Machinists**, a labor union representing many Boeing employees.

EXERCISE 1.3
What Is Financial Reporting?
LO 3

A major focus of this course is the process of financial reporting.
a. What is meant by the term *financial reporting*?
b. What are the principal accounting reports involved in the financial reporting process? In general terms, what is the purpose of these reports?
c. Do all business entities engage in financial reporting? Explain.
d. How does society benefit from the financial reporting process?

EXERCISE 1.4
Generally Accepted Accounting Principles
LO 6

Generally accepted accounting principles play an important role in financial reporting.
a. What is meant by the phrase *generally accepted accounting principles*?
b. What are the major sources of these principles?
c. Is there a comprehensive list of generally accepted accounting principles? Explain.
d. What types of accounting reports are prepared in conformity with generally accepted accounting principles?

EXERCISE 1.5
Accounting Organizations
LO 6

Describe the roles of the following organizations in establishing generally accepted accounting principles:
a. The FASB
b. The AICPA
c. The SEC

From which of these organizations can you most easily obtain financial information about publicly owned companies?

EXERCISE 1.6
Investment Return
LO 3

You recently invested $10,000 of your savings in a security issued by a large company. The security agreement pays you 8% per year and has a maturity two years from the day you purchased it. What is the total cash flow you expect to receive from this investment, separated into the return on your investment and the return of your investment?

EXERCISE 1.7
Accounting Terminology
LO 3, 4, 5, 7

Match the terms on the left with the descriptions on the right. Each description should be used only once.

Term	Description
_____ Financial accounting	a. The procedural aspect of accounting that involves keeping detailed records of business transactions, much of which is done today by computers.
_____ Management accounting	
_____ Financial reporting	
_____ Financial statements	b. A broad term that describes all information provided to external users, including but not limited to financial statements.
_____ General-purpose assumption	
_____ Integrity	
_____ Internal control	c. An important quality of accounting information that allows investors, creditors, management, and other users to rely on the information.
_____ Public accounting	
_____ Bookkeeping	

Term	Description
	d. The segment of the accounting profession that relates to providing audit, tax, and consulting services to clients.
	e. Procedures and processes within an organization that ensure the integrity of accounting information.
	f. Statement of financial position (balance sheet), income statement, statement of cash flows.
	g. The fact that the same information is provided to various external users, including investors and creditors.
	h. The area of accounting that refers to providing information to support internal management decisions.
	i. The area of accounting that refers to providing information to support external investment and credit decisions.

EXERCISE 1.8

Accounting Organizations

LO 6

Match the organizations on the left with the functions on the right. Each function should be used only once.

Organization	Function
____ Institute of Internal Auditors	a. Government agency responsible for financial reporting by publicly held companies.
____ Securities and Exchange Commission	b. International organization dedicated to the advancement of internal auditing.
____ American Institute of CPAs	c. Private-sector organization that establishes accounting standards.
____ Institute of Management Accountants	d. Organization consisting primarily of accounting educators that encourages improvements in teaching and research.
____ Financial Accounting Standards Board	e. Professional association of Certified Public Accountants.
____ American Accounting Association	f. Organization dedicated to providing members personal and professional development opportunities in the area of management accounting.

EXERCISE 1.9

Financial and Management Accounting

LO 3, 4

The major focus of accounting information is to facilitate decision making.

a. As an investor in a company, what would be your primary objective?
b. As a manager of a company, what would be your primary objective?
c. Is the same accounting information likely to be equally useful to you in these two different roles?

EXERCISE 1.10

Management Accounting Information

LO 4

Internal accounting information is used primarily for internal decision making by an enterprise's management.

a. What are the three primary purposes of internal accounting information?
b. Which of these is the most general and which is the most specific?
c. Give several examples of the kinds of decisions that internal accounting information supports.

EXERCISE 1.11

Accounting Organizations

LO 6

Describe which professional organization(s) would be of greatest value to you if your position involved each of the following independent roles:

a. Accounting educator.
b. Management accountant.
c. Public accountant.

EXERCISE 1.12

Purpose of an Audit

LO 5

Audits of financial statements are an important part of the accounting process to ensure integrity in financial reporting.
a. What is the purpose of an audit?
b. As an external user of accounting information, what meaning would you attach to an audit that concludes that the financial statements are fairly presented in conformity with generally accepted accounting principles?
c. Would your interest in investing in this same company be affected by an auditor's report that concluded the financial statements were *not* fairly presented? Why or why not?

EXERCISE 1.13

Audits of Financial Statements

LO 5

The annual financial statements of all large, publicly owned corporations are audited.
a. What is an audit of financial statements?
b. Who performs audits?
c. What is the purpose of an audit?

EXERCISE 1.14

Ethics and Professional Judgment

LO 7

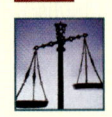

Ethical conduct and professional judgment each play important roles in the accounting process.
a. In general terms, explain why it is important to society that people who prepare accounting information act in an ethical manner.
b. Identify at least three areas in which accountants must exercise *professional judgment,* rather than merely relying on written rules.

*EXERCISE 1.15

Careers in Accounting

LO 8

Four accounting majors, Maria Acosta, Kenzo Nakao, Helen Martin, and Anthony Mandella, recently graduated from Central University and began professional accounting careers. Acosta entered public accounting, Nakao became a management accountant, Martin joined a governmental agency, and Mandella (who had completed a graduate program) became an accounting faculty member.

Assume that each of the four graduates was successful in his or her chosen career. Identify the types of accounting *activities* in which each of these graduates might find themselves specializing several years after graduation.

EXERCISE 1.16

Tootsie Roll Industries, Inc.
General and Specific Information

LO 1, 3, 5

Locate the **Tootsie Roll Industries, Inc.**, annual report in Appendix A of this text. Briefly peruse the annual report and answer the following questions:
a. Name the titles of the financial reports in **Tootsie Roll Industries, Inc.**, annual report that provide specific information about economic resource, claims to resources, and changes in resources and claims?
b. Name three other sections from **Tootsie Roll Industries'** 2000 annual report that provide information useful in assessing the amount, timing, and uncertainty of future cash flows.
c. Which main categories of other general information are useful in making investment and credit decisions?

Due to the introductory nature of this chapter and the conceptual nature of its contents, no items labeled **Problems** are included. In all future chapters you will find a series of Problems that generally include computations, are more complex, and generally require more time to complete than Exercises.

---

* *Supplemental Topic,* "Careers in Accounting."

CASES AND UNSTRUCTURED PROBLEMS

CASE 1.1

Reliability of Financial Statements

LO 5

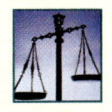

In the early 1980s, **Chrysler Corporation** was in severe financial difficulty and desperately needed large loans for the company to survive. What factors prevented **Chrysler** from simply providing potential lenders with misleading financial statements to make the company look like a risk-free investment?

CASE 1.2

Objectives of Financial Accounting

LO 3

Divide into groups as instructed by your professor and discuss the following:
a. How does the description of accounting as the "language of business" relate to accounting as being useful for investors and creditors?
b. Explain how the decisions you would make might differ if you were an external investor or a member of an enterprise's management team.

CASE 1.3

Accounting Systems

LO 2

You are employed by a business consulting firm as an information systems specialist. You have just begun an assignment with a start-up company and are discussing with the owner her need for an accounting system. How would you respond to the following questions from the owner?
a. What is the meaning of the term *accounting system?*
b. What is the purpose of an accounting system and what are its basic functions?
c. Who is responsible for designing and implementing an accounting system?

CASE 1.4

Codes of Ethics

LO 7

You have recently completed your college degree with a major in accounting and have accepted a position on the accounting staff of a large corporation. In preparing for your first day on the job, your supervisor suggests that you become familiar with the basic principles included in the code of ethics of the Institute of Management Accountants. Briefly explain what you learn as you study the code and how it might affect your behavior on your new job.

BUSINESS WEEK ASSIGNMENT

CASE 1.5

Accounting on Broadway

LO 1, 3, 7

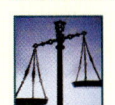

These days the importance of financial statement information for investors and creditors is even evident on Broadway. A popular musical in the 2001 Broadway offerings starring Matthew Broderick has accounting shenanigans as its underlying premise. "It is simply a matter of creative accounting," says Matthew Broderick playing accountant Leopold Bloom in the hit musical **The Producers**. Bloom tells his financially strapped client, Max Bialystock, that "under the right circumstances, a producer could make more money with a flop than he could with a hit." A May 14, 2001, *Business Week* article, "The Numbers Game," by David Henry, outlines the underlying premise of this unethical moneymaking scheme. The objective is to raise as much money as possible from rich widows to finance a proposed Broadway musical called "Springtime for Hitler." In the actual Broadway play, the producer of the proposed musical blows the money on himself under the assumption that "Springtime for Hitler" will bomb so that nobody will ask awkward questions.

Instructions
a. Identify the objectives of external financial reporting discussed in this chapter. How would these objectives help investors make a decision about investing in the musical "Springtime for Hitler" discussed above?
b. How did Leopold Bloom violate the AICPA Code of Professional Conduct described in this chapter?

INTERNET ASSIGNMENTS

INTERNET 1.1

Accessing Information on the Internet

LO 6, 7

The Internet is a good place to get information that is useful to you in your study of accounting. For example, you can find information about current events, professional accounting organizations, and specific companies that may support your study.

Instructions

a. Access the Rutgers University Internet site. Identify eight links to many other sites that provide information about accounting.

   www.rutgers.edu/accounting/raw

b. Look under the category Accounting Resources and then Big-Five. Identify the names of the five largest public accounting firms.

c. Look under the category Publishers and then the sub-category of U.S. Accounting Publishers to locate the publisher of this textbook.

d. Find the Internet sites of the following professional accounting organizations and learn what you can about them from the information provided:

   American Accounting Association
   Financial Accounting Standards Board
   Institute of Internal Auditors
   Institute of Management Accountants

Internet sites are time and date sensitive. It is the purpose of these exercises to have you explore the Internet. You may need to use the Yahoo! search engine http://www.yahoo.com *(or another favorite search engine) to find a company's current Web address.*

OUR COMMENTS ON THE "YOUR TURN" CASES

You as an Investor (p. 11)   Your primary considerations in choosing an investment probably would include the security of your funds and the return you can expect to receive. Concerning security, you would expect to have your investment returned to you at some time in the future. Concerning return on your investment, you would expect a reasonable rate of return on the money you invested. You might have nonfinancial objectives, too. You may be interested in a particular type of company (for example, a car manufacturer, a high-tech organization), or you might be interested in a company that is located in the city where you live.

You as a Manager (p. 17)   Manufacturing a product like computers involves many important decisions. For example: From which suppliers should you purchase the parts you need? How should you sell or market your products? To what extent should you rely on parts and labor from countries other than your own? At what price should you sell your computers? Accounting information is intended to provide internal decision makers information that is useful in answering these and other questions. For example, in pricing your product, what it costs to produce is an important consideration. Internal accounting information may also provide insights into the reliability of suppliers from other countries are compared to those that are closer to your home base.

You as a Professional Accountant (p. 23)   This situation puts you in a very difficult position. On the one hand, you want to do the right thing and, in your opinion, that involves an in-depth study of the problem you have found. On the other hand, you are pulled in the direction of doing what your superior says to do because you may respect her position as your superior and because your responsibility is to take directions from the person with whom you are assigned to work. You might want to discuss with your superior the potential implications of the irregularities that you have found and try to convince her that some additional effort to better understand what is going on may be very important. You may want to discuss this with a peer or another person not directly involved in your engagement but whose opinion you value. You may want to talk with a person higher up in the organization than your superior, although you should be careful to avoid creating a conflict with your superior. You probably should keep a record of steps you have taken to resolve the situation and certainly keep your eyes open for a pattern of similar behavior that may be a signal to you that you need to consider a job elsewhere.

ANSWERS TO SELF-TEST QUESTIONS

1. b 2. d 3. d 4. c 5. a 6. c 7. c 8. a
9. d 10. d

CHAPTER 2
BASIC FINANCIAL STATEMENTS

Learning Objectives

After studying this chapter, you should be able to:

1. Explain the nature and general purpose of financial statements.

2. Explain certain accounting principles that are important for an understanding of financial statements and how professional judgment by accountants may affect the application of those principles.

3. Demonstrate how certain business transactions affect the elements of the accounting equation: Assets = Liabilities + Owners' Equity.

4. Explain how the statement of financial position, often referred to as the balance sheet, is an expansion of the basic accounting equation.

5. Explain how the income statement reports an enterprise's financial performance for a period of time in terms of the relationship of revenues and expenses.

6. Explain how the statement of cash flows presents the change in cash for a period of time in terms of the company's operating, investing, and financing activities.

7. Explain important relationships among the statement of financial position, income statement, and statement of cash flows, and how these statements relate to each other.

8. Explain common forms of business ownership—sole proprietorship, partnership, and corporation—and demonstrate how they differ in terms of their presentation in the statement of financial position.

9. Discuss and illustrate the importance of nonfinancial information to supplement the information in the primary financial statements.

10. Discuss the importance of financial statements to a company and its investors and creditors and why management may take steps to improve the appearance of the company in its financial statements.

Copyright Intel Corporation. All rights reserved.

Intel

Intel supplies the computing and communications industries with chips, boards, and systems building blocks that are the ingredients of computers and servers as well as networking and communications products. These industries use Intel's products to create advanced computing and communications systems. Intel states that its mission is to be the preeminent building block supplier in the worldwide Internet economy.

In **Intel**'s 2000 annual report to stockholders, Chairman Andy Grove indicated that we are in the midst of a transition to a pervasively digital world. He stated:

> In the rise of the Internet, the expansion of e-Commerce and the boom in mobile communications, we are witnessing a fundamental shift in how the world operates. All the daily transactions that a consumer or business undertakes are being repositioned on digital technology. Material is created, transmitted and managed digitally—everything from purchase orders and manufacturing supply lines to checking accounts and art—and this trend will only continue. It's going to touch all endeavors of everyday life all over the world.

Modern-day historians indicate that we are rapidly moving from the industrial age, with an emphasis on heavy manufacturing, to the information age. Companies like **Intel**, **Microsoft**, **Cisco Systems**, and others are major players in this transformation of business. For information-age companies the factors of success are quite different than for industrial-age companies. Information-age companies rely more heavily on intellectual capital, research and development, and other intangibles that played much less of a role for companies whose focus was heavy manufacturing or, even earlier in our history, primarily agricultural.

• • •

If you were a person with considerable wealth who wanted to invest in a forward-looking company as we transition into the information age, how would you know whether Intel or any other company were a wise investment? What information would you seek out to help you decide where to place your investment dollars? A primary source of financial information is a company's financial statements. These statements, which are prepared at least once a year and in many cases more frequently, provide tremendous insight into the current financial status of the company and how successful the company has been in meeting its financial goals. In this chapter you are introduced to the three primary financial statements—the statement of financial position (often referred to as the balance sheet), the income statement, and the statement of cash flows. Combined with information presented in notes and other accompanying discussions, these financial statements provide for investors, creditors, and other interested parties a wealth of useful information. In fact, financial information is what this entire textbook is about, and in this chapter you receive your initial introduction to how financial statements come about and how they may be used to better understand a company.

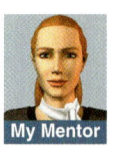

INTRODUCTION TO FINANCIAL STATEMENTS

In Chapter 1 we learned that investors and creditors are particularly interested in cash flows that they expect to receive in the future. Creditors, for example, are interested in the ability of the enterprise, to which they have made loans or sold merchandise on credit, to meet its payment obligations, which may include payment of interest. Similarly, investors are interested in the market value of their stock holdings, as well as dividends that the enterprise will pay while they own the stock.

One of the primary ways investors and creditors assess the probability that an enterprise will be able to make future cash payments is to study, analyze, and understand the enterprise's financial statements. As discussed in Chapter 1, a **financial statement** is simply a declaration of what is believed to be true about an enterprise, communicated in terms of a monetary unit, such as the dollar. When accountants prepare financial statements, they are describing in financial terms certain attributes of the enterprise that they believe fairly represent its financial activities.

In this chapter, we introduce three primary financial statements:

- Statement of financial position (commonly referred to as the balance sheet).
- Income statement.
- Statement of cash flows.

In introducing these statements, we use the form of business ownership referred to as a *corporation*. The corporation is a unique form of organization that allows many owners to combine their resources into a business enterprise that is larger than would be possible based on the financial resources of a single or a small number of owners. While businesses of any size may be organized as corporations, many large businesses are corporations because of their need for the large amount of capital that the corporate form of business organization makes possible. Later in this chapter we introduce two other forms of business organization—the sole proprietorship and the partnership—which are alternatives to the corporate form for some business enterprises.

LO 1
Explain the nature and general purpose of financial statements.

The names of the three primary financial statements describe the information you find in each. The **statement of financial position**, or **balance sheet** is a financial statement that describes where the enterprise stands at a specific date. It is sometimes described as a snapshot of the business in financial or dollar terms (that is, what the enterprise "looks like" at a specific date).

As businesses operate, they engage in transactions that create revenues and incur expenses that are necessary to earn those revenues. An **income statement** is an activity statement that depicts the revenues and expenses for a designated period of time. Revenues are transactions of the enterprise that already have resulted in positive cash flows or that are expected to do so in the near future, meaning that cash will come *into* the enterprise as a result of the transaction. For example, a company might sell a product for $100. This revenue transaction results in an immediate positive cash flow into the enterprise if the transaction is carried out in cash or an expected future cash flow if it is a credit transaction in which payment is to be received later. Expenses have the opposite effect in that they result in an immediate cash flow *out* of the enterprise (if a cash transaction) or an expected future flow of cash out of the enterprise (if a credit transaction). For example, if a company incurs a certain expense of $75 and pays it at that time, an immediate cash outflow takes place. If payment is delayed until some future date, the transaction represents an expected future cash outflow. Revenues result in positive cash flows—either past, present, or future—while expenses result in negative cash flows—either past, present, or future. *Positive* and *negative* indicate the directional impact on cash. The term *net income* (or *net loss*) is simply the difference between revenues and expenses for a designated period of time.

The statement of cash flows is particularly important in understanding an enterprise for purposes of investment and credit decisions. As its name implies, the statement of cash flows depicts the ways cash changed during a designated period—the cash received from revenues and other transactions as well as the cash paid for certain expenses and other acquisitions during the period. While the primary focus of investors and creditors is on cash flows to themselves rather than to the enterprise, information about cash activity of the enterprise is considered to be an important signal to investors and creditors about the prospects of future cash flows to them.

A STARTING POINT: STATEMENT OF FINANCIAL POSITION

All three financial statements contain important information, but each includes different information. For that reason, it is important to understand all three financial statements and how they relate to each other. The way they relate is sometimes referred to as articulation, a term we will say more about later in this chapter.

A logical starting point for understanding financial statements is the statement of financial position, also called the balance sheet. The purpose of this financial statement is to demonstrate where the company stands, in financial terms, at a specific point in time. As we will see later in this chapter, the other financial statements relate to the statement of financial position and show how important aspects of a company's financial position change over time. Beginning with the statement of financial position also allows us to understand certain basic accounting principles and terminologies that are important for understanding all financial statements.

Every business prepares a balance sheet at the end of the year, and many companies prepare one at the end of each month, week, or even day. It consists of a listing of the assets, the liabilities, and the owners' equity of a business. The *date* is important, as the financial position of a business may change quickly. Exhibit 2–1 shows the financial position of Vagabond Travel Agency at December 31, 2002.

VAGABOND TRAVEL AGENCY
Statement of Financial Position
December 31, 2002

Assets		Liabilities & Owners' Equity		
Cash	$ 22,500	Liabilities:		
Notes Receivable	10,000	Notes Payable	$ 41,000	
Accounts Receivable	60,500	Accounts Payable	36,000	
Supplies	2,000	Salaries Payable	3,000	$ 80,000
Land	100,000	Owners' equity:		
Building	90,000	Capital Stock	$150,000	
Office Equipment	15,000	Retained Earnings	70,000	220,000
Total	$300,000	Total		$300,000

Exhibit 2–1

STATEMENT OF FINANCIAL POSITION

My Notes

A balance sheet shows financial position at a specific date

Let us briefly describe several features of the statement of financial position, using Exhibit 2–1 as an example. First, the heading communicates three things: (1) the name of the business, (2) the name of the financial statement, and (3) the date. The body of the balance sheet also consists of three distinct sections: *assets, liabilities,* and *owners' equity.*

Notice that cash is listed first among the assets, followed by notes receivable, accounts receivable, supplies, and any other assets that will *soon be converted into cash or used up in business operations.* Following these assets are the more permanent assets, such as land, buildings, and equipment.

Moving to the right side of the balance sheet, liabilities are shown before owners' equity. Each major type of liability (such as notes payable, accounts payable, and salaries payable) is listed separately, followed by a figure for total liabilities.

Owners' equity is separated into two parts—capital stock and retained earnings. Capital stock represents the amount that owners originally paid into the company to become owners. It consists of individual shares and each owner has a set number of shares. Notice in this illustration that capital stock totals $150,000. This means that the assigned value of the shares held by owners, multiplied by the number of shares, equals $150,000. For example, assuming an assigned value of $10 per share, there would be 15,000 shares ($10 × 15,000 = $150,000). Alternatively, the assigned value might be $5 per share, in which case there would be 30,000 shares ($5 × 30,000 = $150,000). The retained earning part of owners' equity is simply the accumulated earnings of previous years that remain within the enterprise. Retained earnings is considered part of the equity of the owners and serves to enhance their investment in the business.

Finally, notice that the amount of total assets ($300,000) is *equal* to the total amount of liabilities and owners' equity (also $300,000). This relationship *always exists*—in fact, the *equality of these totals* is why this financial statement is frequently called a *balance sheet.*

> **LO 2**
> Explain certain accounting principles that are important for an understanding of financial statements and how professional judgment by accountants may affect the application of those principles.

The Concept of the Business Entity Generally accepted accounting principles require that a set of financial statements describe the affairs of a specific business entity. This concept is called the *entity principle.*

A **business entity** is an economic unit that engages in identifiable business activities. For accounting purposes, the business entity is regarded as *separate from the personal activities of its owners.* For example, Vagabond is a business organization operating as a travel agency. Its owners may have personal bank accounts, homes, cars, and even other businesses. These items are not involved in the operation of the travel agency and should not appear in Vagabond's financial statements.

If the owners were to commingle their personal activities with the transactions of the business, the resulting financial statements would fail to describe clearly the financial activities of the business organization. Distinguishing business from personal activities of the owners may require judgment by the accountant.

Assets

Assets are economic resources that are owned by a business and are expected to benefit future operations. In most cases, the benefit to future operations comes in the form of positive future cash flows. The positive future cash flows may come directly as the asset is converted into cash (collection of a receivable) or indirectly as the asset is used in operating the business to create other assets that result in positive future cash flows (building and land used to manufacture a product for sale). Assets may have definite physical form such as buildings, machinery, or an inventory of merchandise. On the other hand, some assets exist not in physical or tangible form, but in the form of valuable legal claims or rights; examples are amounts due from customers, investments in government bonds, and patent rights.

One of the most basic and at the same time most controversial problems in accounting is determining the dollar amount for the various assets of a business. At present, generally accepted accounting principles call for the valuation of many assets in a balance sheet at *cost,* rather than at their current value. The specific accounting principles supporting cost as the basis for asset valuation are discussed below.

The Cost Principle   Assets such as land, buildings, merchandise, and equipment are typical of the many economic resources that are required in producing revenue for the business. The prevailing accounting view is that such assets should be presented at their cost. When we say that an asset is shown in the balance sheet at its *historical cost,* we mean the original amount the business entity paid to acquire the asset. This amount may be different from what it would cost to purchase the same asset today.

For example, let us assume that a business buys a tract of land for use as a building site, paying $100,000 in cash. The amount to be entered in the accounting records for the asset will be the cost of $100,000. If we assume a booming real estate market, a fair estimate of the market value of the land 10 years later might be $250,000. Although the market price or economic value of the land has risen greatly, the accounting amount as shown in the accounting records and in the balance sheet would continue unchanged at the cost of $100,000. This policy of accounting for many assets at their cost is often referred to as the **cost principle** of accounting.

Exceptions to the cost principle are found in some of the most liquid assets (i.e., assets that are expected to soon become cash). Amounts receivable from customers are generally included in the balance sheet at their *net realizable value,* which is an amount that approximates the cash that will be received when the receivable is collected. Similarly, certain investments in other enterprises are included in the balance sheet at their current market value if management's plan includes conversion into cash in the near future.

In reading a balance sheet, it is important to keep in mind that the dollar amounts listed for most assets do not indicate the prices at which the assets could be sold or the prices at which they could be replaced. A frequently misunderstood feature of a balance sheet is that it *does not* show how much the business currently is worth.

CASE IN POINT

Inflation can undermine the stable currency assumption. Many South American countries that experience prolonged and serious inflation require companies to use current value accounting methods that clarify the impact of inflation on the balance sheet. While not completely abandoning the cost principle, these methods adjust cost data for current price levels. As an illustration, consider the following statement from page 28, note II, part c, in the **Teléfonos de México** 2000 annual report: "The December 31, 2000, restatement factor applied to the financial statements at December 31, 1999, was 8.96%, which corresponds to the applicable inflation from January 1 through December 31, 2000, based on the Mexican National Consumer Price Index (NCPI) published by Banco de México."

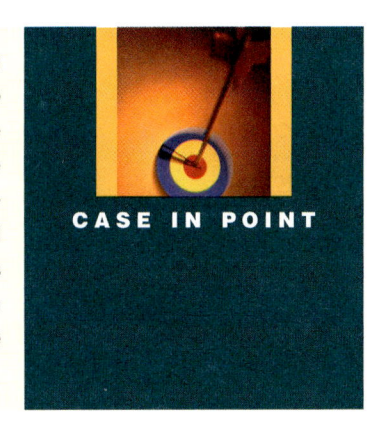

The Going-Concern Assumption   *Why* don't accountants change the recorded amounts of assets to correspond with changing market prices for these properties? One reason is that assets like land and buildings are being used to house the business and were acquired for *use* and not for resale; in fact, these assets usually cannot be sold without disrupting the business. The balance sheet of a business is prepared on the assumption that the business is a continuing enterprise, or a **going concern**. Consequently, the present estimated prices at which assets like land and buildings could be sold are of less importance than if these properties were intended for sale. These are frequently among the largest dollar amounts of a company's assets. Determining that an enterprise is a going concern may require judgment by the accountant.

The Objectivity Principle   Another reason for using cost rather than current market values in accounting for most assets is the need for a definite, factual basis for valua-

YOUR TURN

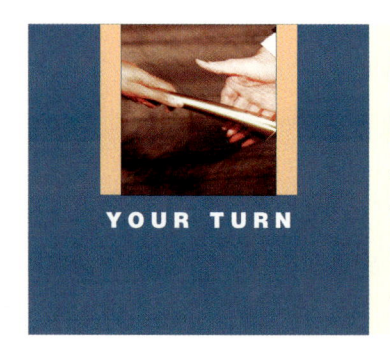

You as a Home Owner

First, assume you have owned your home for 10 years and need to report the value of your home to the city assessor for real estate tax assessment purposes. What information would you provide? Second, assume you are planning to sell your home. What type of information would you provide to potential buyers? What ethical issues arise in these two situations that the objectivity principle helps address?

Our comments appear on page 85.

tion. The cost of land, buildings, and many other assets that have been purchased can be definitely determined. Accountants use the term *objective* to describe asset valuations that are factual and can be verified by independent experts. For example, if land is shown on the balance sheet at cost, any CPA who performed an audit of the business would be able to find objective evidence that the land was actually measured at the cost incurred in acquiring it. On the other hand, estimated market values for assets such as buildings and specialized machinery are not factual and objective. Market values are constantly changing, and estimates of the prices at which assets could be sold are largely a matter of judgment.

At the date an asset is acquired, the cost and market value are usually the same. With the passage of time, however, the current market value of assets is likely to differ considerably from the cost recorded in the owners' accounting records.

The Stable-Dollar Assumption A limitation of measuring assets at historical cost is that the value of the monetary unit or dollar is not always stable. **Inflation** is a term used to describe the situation where the value of the monetary unit decreases, meaning that it will purchase less than it did previously. **Deflation**, on the other hand, is the opposite situation in which the value of the monetary unit increases, meaning that it will purchase more than it did previously. Typically, countries like the United States have experienced inflation rather than deflation. When inflation becomes severe, historical cost amounts for assets lose their relevance as a basis for making business decisions. For this reason, some consideration has been given to the use of balance sheets that would show assets at current appraised values or at replacement costs rather than at historical cost.

Accountants in the United States, by adhering to the cost basis of accounting, are implying that the dollar is a stable unit of measurement, as is the gallon, the acre, or the mile. The cost principle and the **stable-dollar assumption** work well in periods of stable prices but are less satisfactory under conditions of rapid inflation. For example, if a company bought land 20 years ago for $100,000 and purchased a second similar tract of land today for $500,000, the total cost of land shown by the accounting records would be $600,000. This treatment ignores the fact that dollars spent 20 years ago had greater purchasing power than today's dollar. Thus the $600,000 total for the cost of land is a mixture of two "sizes" of dollars with different purchasing power.

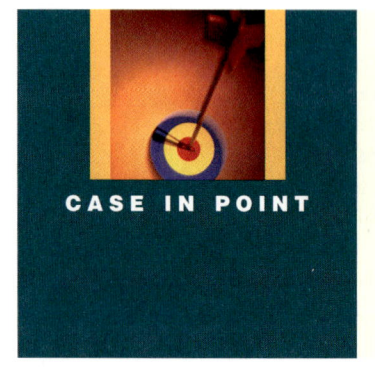

CASE IN POINT

Many countries experience prolonged and serious inflation. Inflation can undermine the stable currency assumption. Several methods have been used in foreign countries to show the impact of inflation on a company's financial position. In the recent past, Brazilian corporate law required companies to adjust their balance sheets to current purchasing power by using indexes provided by the government. The indexes were used to devalue the local currency to provide a more objective representation of the financial condition of the company. During the 1980s and early '90s the United Kingdom asked companies to provide supplementary inflation-adjusted financial statements.

A Starting Point: Statement of Financial Position

After much research into this problem, the FASB required on a trial basis that large corporations annually disclose financial data adjusted for the effects of inflation. But after several years of experimentation, the FASB concluded that the costs of developing this information exceeded its usefulness. At the present time, this disclosure is optional, as judged appropriate by the accountant who prepares the financial statements.

Liabilities

Liabilities are financial obligations or debts. They represent negative future cash flows for the enterprise. The person or organization to whom the debt is owed is called a **creditor**.

All businesses have liabilities; even the largest and most successful companies often purchase merchandise, supplies, and services "on account." The liabilities arising from such purchases are called *accounts payable.* Many businesses borrow money to finance expansion or the purchase of high-cost assets. When obtaining a loan, the borrower usually must sign a formal note payable. A *note payable* is a written promise to repay the amount owed by a particular date and usually calls for the payment of interest as well.

Accounts payable, in contrast to notes payable, involve no written promises and generally do not call for interest payments. In essence, a note payable is a *more formal* arrangement.

When a company has both notes payable and accounts payable, the two types of liabilities are listed separately in the balance sheet. Liabilities are usually listed in the order in which they are expected to be repaid.[1] Liabilities that are similar may be combined to avoid unnecessary detail in the financial statement. For example, if a company had several expenses payable at the end of the year (for example, wages, interest, taxes), it might combine these into a single line called *accrued expenses.* The word *accrued* is an accounting term communicating that the payment of certain expenses has been delayed or deferred.

Liabilities represent claims against the borrower's assets. As we shall see, the owners of a business *also* have claims to the company's assets. But in the eyes of the law, creditors' claims *take priority* over those of the owners. This means that creditors are entitled to be *paid in full,* even if such payment would exhaust the assets of the business and leave nothing for its owners.

Owners' Equity

Owners' equity represents the *owners' claims* on the assets of the business. Because creditors' claims have legal priority over those of the owners, owners' equity is a *residual amount.* If you are the owner of a business, you are entitled to assets that are left after the claims of creditors have been satisfied in full. Therefore, owners' equity is always equal to *total assets minus total liabilities.* For example, using the data from the illustrated balance sheet of Vagabond Travel Agency (Exhibit 2–1):

Vagabond has total assets of	$300,000
And total liabilities of	(80,000)
Therefore, the owners' equity must be	$220,000

Owners' equity does *not* represent a specific claim to cash or any other particular asset. Rather, it is the owners' overall financial interest in the entire company.

---

[1] Short-term liabilities generally are those due within one year. Long-term liabilities are shown separately in the balance sheet, after the listing of all short-term liabilities. Long-term liabilities are addressed in Chapter 10.

Increases in Owners' Equity The owners' equity in a business comes from two sources:

1. *Investments of cash or other assets* by owners.
2. *Earnings* from profitable operation of the business.

Decreases in Owners' Equity Decreases in owners' equity also are caused in two ways:

1. *Payments of cash or transfers of other assets* to owners.
2. *Losses* from unprofitable operation of the business.

Accounting for payments to owners and net losses are addressed in later chapters.

The Accounting Equation

A fundamental characteristic of every statement of financial position is that the total for assets always equals the total of liabilities plus owners' equity. This agreement or balance of total assets with the total of liabilities and owners' equity is the reason for calling this financial statement a *balance sheet*. But *why* do total assets equal the total of liabilities and owners' equity?

The dollar totals on the two sides of the balance sheet are always equal because these two sides are *two views of the same business*. The listing of assets shows us what things the business owns; the listing of liabilities and owners' equity tells us who supplied these resources to the business and how much each group supplied. Everything that a business owns has been supplied to it either by creditors or by the owners. Therefore, the total claims of the creditors plus the claims of the owners equal the total assets of the business.

The equality of assets on the one hand and of the claims of the creditors and the owners on the other hand is expressed in the following **accounting equation**:

$$\text{Assets} = \text{Liabilities} + \text{Owners' Equity}$$
$$\$300,000 = \$80,000 \;\;\;\; + \$220,000$$

The amounts listed in the equation were taken from the balance sheet illustrated in Exhibit 2–1. The balance sheet is simply a detailed statement of this equation. To illustrate this relationship, compare the balance sheet of Vagabond Travel Agency with the above equation.

Every business transaction, no matter how simple or how complex, can be expressed in terms of its effect on the accounting equation. A thorough understanding of the equation and some practice in using it are essential to the student of accounting.

Regardless of whether a business grows or contracts, the equality between the assets and the claims on the assets is always maintained. Any increase in the amount of total assets is necessarily accompanied by an equal increase on the other side of the equation—that is, by an increase in either the liabilities or the owners' equity. Any decrease in total assets is necessarily accompanied by a corresponding decrease in liabilities or owners' equity. The continuing equality of the two sides of the accounting equation can best be illustrated by taking a new business as an example and observing the effects of various transactions.

The Effects of Business Transactions: An Illustration

How does a statement of financial position come about? What has occurred in the past for it to exist at any point in time? The statement of financial position is a picture of the results of past business transactions that has been captured by the company's information system and organized into a concise financial description of where the company stands at a point in time. The specific items and dollar amounts are the direct results of the transactions in which the company has engaged. The balance sheets of two separate companies would almost certainly be different due to the unique nature, timing, and dollar amounts of each company's business transactions.

To illustrate how a balance sheet comes about, and later to show how the income statement and statement of cash flows relate to the balance sheet, we use an example of a small auto repair business, Overnight Auto Service.

The Business Entity   Assume that Michael McBryan, an experienced auto mechanic, opens his own automotive repair business, Overnight Auto Service. A distinctive feature of Overnight's operations is that all repair work is done at night. This strategy offers customers the convenience of dropping off their cars in the evening and picking them up the following morning.

Operating at night also enables Overnight to minimize its labor costs. Instead of hiring full-time employees, Overnight offers part-time work to mechanics who already have day jobs at major automobile dealerships. This eliminates the need for costly employee training programs and for such payroll fringe benefits as group health insurance and employees' pension plans, benefits usually associated with full-time employment.

Overnight's Accounting Policies   McBryan has taken several courses in accounting and maintains Overnight's accounting records himself. He knows that small businesses such as his are not required to prepare formal financial statements, but he prepares them anyway. He believes they will be useful to him in running the business. In addition, if Overnight is successful, McBryan plans to open more locations. He anticipates needing to raise substantial amounts of capital from investors and creditors. He believes that the financial history provided by a series of monthly financial statements will be helpful in obtaining investment capital.

The Company's First Transaction   McBryan officially started Overnight on January 20, 2002. On that day he received a charter from the state to begin a small, closely held corporation whose owners consisted of himself and several family members. Capital stock issued to these investors included 8,000 shares at $10 per share. McBryan opened a bank account in the name of Overnight Auto Service, into which he deposited the $80,000 received from the issuance of the capital stock.

This transaction provided Overnight with its first asset—Cash—and also created the initial owners' equity in the business entity. See the balance sheet showing the company's financial position after this initial transaction in Exhibit 2–2.

Exhibit 2–2

BALANCE SHEET, JAN. 20

OVERNIGHT AUTO SERVICE
Balance Sheet
January 20, 2002

Assets		Owners' Equity	
Cash	$80,000	Capital Stock	$80,000

My Notes

Beginning balance sheet of a new business

Overnight's next two transactions involved the acquisition of a suitable site for its business operations.

Purchase of an Asset for Cash   Representing the business, McBryan negotiated with both the City of Santa Teresa and the Metropolitan Transit Authority (MTA) to purchase an abandoned bus garage. (The MTA owned the garage, but the city owned the land.)

On January 21, Overnight purchased the land from the city for *$52,000 cash*. This transaction had two immediate effects on the company's financial position: first, Overnight's cash was reduced by $52,000; and second, the company acquired a new asset—Land. We show the company's financial position after this transaction in Exhibit 2–3.

Exhibit 2–3

BALANCE SHEET, JAN. 21

My Notes

Balance sheet totals unchanged by purchase of land for cash

OVERNIGHT AUTO SERVICE
Balance Sheet
January 21, 2002

Assets		Owners' Equity	
Cash	$28,000	Capital Stock	$80,000
Land	52,000		
Total	$80,000	Total	$80,000

Purchase of an Asset and Financing Part of the Cost   On January 22, Overnight purchased the old garage building from Metropolitan Transit Authority for *$36,000*. Overnight made a cash down payment of *$6,000* and issued a 90-day non-interest-bearing note payable for the *$30,000* balance owed.

As a result of this transaction, Overnight had (1) $6,000 less cash; (2) a new asset, Building, which cost $36,000; and (3) a new liability, Notes Payable, in the amount of $30,000. This transaction is reflected in Exhibit 2–4.

Exhibit 2–4

BALANCE SHEET, JAN. 22

My Notes

Totals increased equally by debt incurred in acquiring assets

OVERNIGHT AUTO SERVICE
Balance Sheet
January 22, 2002

Assets		Liabilities & Owners' Equity	
Cash	$ 22,000	Liabilities:	
Land	52,000	Notes Payable	$ 30,000
Building	36,000	Owners' equity:	
		Capital Stock	80,000
Total	$110,000	Total	$110,000

Purchase of an Asset On Account   On January 23, Overnight purchased tools and automotive repair equipment from Snappy Tools. The purchase price was *$13,800*, due within 60 days. After this purchase, Overnight's financial position is depicted in Exhibit 2–5.

Exhibit 2–5

BALANCE SHEET, JAN. 23

My Notes

Totals increased equally by debt incurred in acquiring assets

OVERNIGHT AUTO SERVICE
Balance Sheet
January 23, 2002

Assets		Liabilities & Owners' Equity	
Cash	$ 22,000	Liabilities:	
Land	52,000	Notes Payable	$ 30,000
Building	36,000	Accounts Payable	13,800
Tools and Equipment	13,800	Total liabilities	$ 43,800
		Owners' equity:	
		Capital Stock	80,000
Total	$123,800	Total	$123,800

Sale of an Asset   After taking delivery of the new tools and equipment, Overnight found that it had purchased more than it needed. Ace Towing, a neighboring business, offered to buy the excess items. On January 24, Overnight sold some of its new tools to Ace for *$1,800,* a price equal to Overnight's cost.[2] Ace made no down payment but agreed to pay the amount due within 45 days. This transaction reduced Overnight's tools and equipment by $1,800 and created a new asset, Accounts Receivable, for that same amount. A balance sheet as of January 24 appears in Exhibit 2–6.

OVERNIGHT AUTO SERVICE
Balance Sheet
January 24, 2002

Assets		Liabilities & Owners' Equity	
Cash	$ 22,000	Liabilities:	
Accounts Receivable	1,800	Notes Payable	$ 30,000
Land	52,000	Accounts Payable	13,800
Building	36,000	Total liabilities	$ 43,800
Tools and Equipment	12,000	Owners' equity:	
		Capital Stock	80,000
Total	$123,800	Total	$123,800

Exhibit 2–6

BALANCE SHEET, JAN. 24

My Notes

No change in totals by sale of equipment at cost

Collection of an Account Receivable On January 26, Overnight received $600 from Ace Towing as partial settlement of its account receivable from Ace. This transaction caused an increase in Overnight's cash but a decrease of the same amount in accounts receivable. This transaction converts one asset into another of equal value; there is no change in the amount of total assets. After this transaction, Overnight's financial position is summarized in Exhibit 2–7.

OVERNIGHT AUTO SERVICE
Balance Sheet
January 26, 2002

Assets		Liabilities & Owners' Equity	
Cash	$ 22,600	Liabilities:	
Accounts Receivable	1,200	Notes Payable	$ 30,000
Land	52,000	Accounts Payable	13,800
Building	36,000	Total liabilities	$ 43,800
Tools and Equipment	12,000	Owners' equity:	
		Capital Stock	80,000
Total	$123,800	Total	$123,800

Exhibit 2–7

BALANCE SHEET, JAN. 26

My Notes

Totals unchanged by collection of a receivable

Payment of a Liability On January 27, Overnight made a partial payment of $6,800 on its account payable to Snappy Tools. This transaction reduced Overnight's cash and accounts payable by the same amount, leaving total assets and the total of liabilities plus owners' equity in balance. Overnight's balance sheet at January 27 appears in Exhibit 2–8.

---

[2] Sales of assets at prices above or below cost result in gains or losses. Such transactions are discussed in later chapters.

52 Chapter 2 Basic Financial Statements

Exhibit 2–8

BALANCE SHEET, JAN. 27

My Notes

Both totals decreased by paying a liability

OVERNIGHT AUTO SERVICE
Balance Sheet
January 27, 2002

Assets		Liabilities & Owners' Equity	
Cash	$ 15,800	Liabilities:	
Accounts Receivable	1,200	Notes Payable	$ 30,000
Land	52,000	Accounts Payable	7,000
Building	36,000	Total liabilities	$ 37,000
Tools and Equipment	12,000	Owners' equity:	
		Capital Stock	80,000
Total	$117,000	Total	$117,000

Earning of Revenue By the last week in January, McBryan had acquired the assets Overnight needed to start operating, and he began to provide repair services for customers. Rather than recording each individual sale of repair services, he decided to accumulate them and record them at the end of the month. Sales of repair services for the last week of January were $2,200, all of which was received in cash.

Earning of revenue represents the creation of value by Overnight. It also represents an increase in the financial interest of the owners in the company. As a result, cash is increased by $2,200 and owners' equity is increased by the same amount. To distinguish owners' equity that is earned from that which was originally invested by the owners, the account *Retained Earnings* is used in the owners' equity section of the balance sheet. The balance sheet in Exhibit 2–9, as of January 31, reflects the increase in assets (cash) and owners' equity (retained earnings) from the revenue earned and received in cash during the last week of January.

Exhibit 2–9

BALANCE SHEET, JAN. 31

My Notes

Revenues increase assets and owners' equity

OVERNIGHT AUTO SERVICE
Balance Sheet
January 31, 2002

Assets		Liabilities & Owners' Equity		
Cash	$ 18,000	Liabilities:		
Accounts Receivable	1,200	Notes Payable	$ 30,000	
Land	52,000	Accounts Payable	7,000	
Building	36,000	Total liabilities		$ 37,000
Tools and Equipment	12,000	Owners' equity:		
		Capital Stock	$ 80,000	
		Retained Earnings	2,200	$ 82,200
Total	$119,200	Total		$119,200

LO 4

Explain how the statement of financial position, often referred to as the balance sheet, is an expansion of the basic accounting equation.

Payment of Expenses In order to earn the $2,200 of revenue that we have just recorded, Overnight had to pay some operating expenses, namely utilities and wages. McBryan decided to pay all operating expenses at the end of the month. For January, he owed $200 for utilities and $1,200 for wages to his employees, a total of $1,400, which he paid on January 31. Paying expenses has an opposite effect from revenues on the owners' interest in the company—their investment is reduced. Of course, paying expenses also results in a decrease of cash. The January 31 balance sheet, after the payment of utilities and wages, is presented in Exhibit 2–10.

Notice that the expenses of $1,400 ($200 for utilities and $1,200 for wages) reduce the amount of retained earnings in the balance sheet. That balance was formerly $2,200,

Exhibit 2-10

BALANCE SHEET, JAN. 31

OVERNIGHT AUTO SERVICE
Balance Sheet
January 31, 2002

Assets		Liabilities & Owners' Equity		
Cash	$ 16,600	Liabilities:		
Accounts Receivable	1,200	Notes Payable	$ 30,000	
Land	52,000	Accounts Payable	7,000	
Building	36,000	Total liabilities		$ 37,000
Tools and Equipment	12,000	Owners' equity:		
		Capital Stock	$ 80,000	
		Retained Earnings	800	80,800
Total	$117,800	Total		$117,800

My Notes

Expenses reduce assets and owners' equity

representing the revenues for the last week of January. It is now $800, representing the difference between the revenues for the last week of January and the $1,400 of expenses that Overnight incurred during the same period of time. From this illustration we can see that revenues enhance or increase the financial interest of owners while expenses diminish or reduce the interest of owners. In a corporation, the net effect of this activity is reflected in the balance sheet as retained earnings.

Michael Newman/PhotoEdit

The specific assets included in different companies' balance sheets vary considerably and are based primarily on the nature of each company's business. To illustrate, the 2000 balance sheet of **Federal Express** includes over $6.5 billion in property and equipment, the majority of which is flight equipment and package handling equipment, assets critical to the company's operations. Property and equipment constitute over 60% of the company's total assets. **H. J. Heinz**, on the other hand, reports approximately $2.4 billion of property and equipment in its 2000 balance sheet, consisting primarily of land, buildings, and equipment. This amount represents a much smaller portion of Heinz's total assets—approximately 27%.

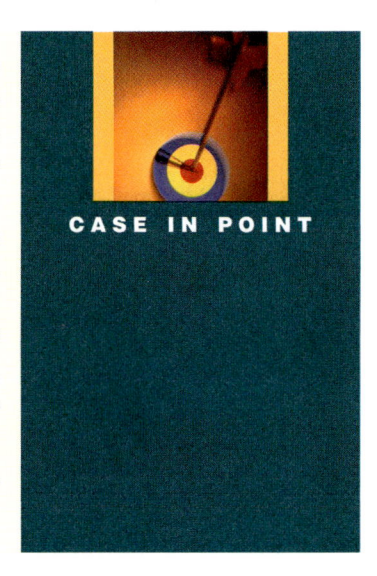

CASE IN POINT

Effects of These Business Transactions on the Accounting Equation

As we learned earlier, the statement of financial position, or balance sheet, is a detailed expression of the accounting equation:

$$\text{Assets} = \text{Liabilities} + \text{Owners' Equity}$$

As we have progressed through a series of business transactions, we have illustrated the effects of Overnight's January transactions on the balance sheet.

To review, Overnight's transactions during January were as follows, with the resulting balance sheet indicated in parentheses:

Jan. 20 Michael McBryan started the business by depositing $80,000 received from the sale of capital stock in a company bank account (Exhibit 2–2).

Jan. 21 Purchased land for $52,000, paying cash (Exhibit 2–3).

Jan. 22 Purchased a building for $36,000, paying $6,000 in cash and issuing a note payable for the remaining $30,000 (Exhibit 2–4).

Jan. 23 Purchased tools and equipment on account, $13,800 (Exhibit 2–5).

Jan. 24 Sold some of the tools at a price equal to their cost, $1,800, collectible within 45 days (Exhibit 2–6).

Jan. 26 Received $600 in partial collection of the account receivable from the sale of tools (Exhibit 2–7).

Jan. 27 Paid $6,800 in partial payment of an account payable (Exhibit 2–8).

Jan. 31 Recorded $2,200 of sales revenue received in cash (Exhibit 2–9).

Jan. 31 Paid $1,400 of operating expenses in cash—$200 for utilities and $1,200 for wages (Exhibit 2–10).

The expanded accounting equation in Exhibit 2–11 shows the effects of these transactions on the accounting equation. The effect of each transaction is shown in red. Notice that the "balances," shown in black, are the amounts appearing in Overnight's balance sheets in Exhibits 2–2 through 2–10. Notice also that the accounting equation is in balance after each transaction.

While this table represents the impact of Overnight's transactions on the accounting equation, and thus on its financial position as shown in its balance sheet, we can now see how the other two financial statements enter the picture. Specifically, the income statement is a separate financial statement that shows how the statement of financial position changed as a result of its revenue and expense transactions, and the statement of cash flows shows how the company's cash increased and decreased during the period. In other words, the income statement is simply a separate financial statement that shows how retained earnings changed because of revenues and expenses during the period (far right column). The statement of cash flows is a separate financial statement that details how the company's cash changed during the period (far left column).

My Notes
Multiple transactions significantly change the enterprise's financial position

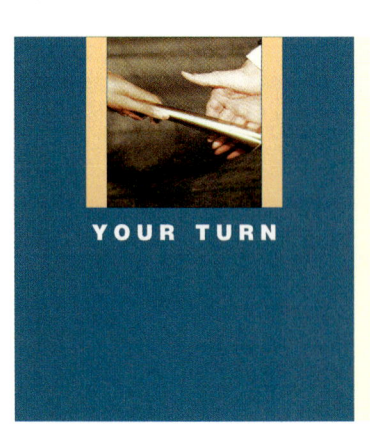

You as a Working College Student

Assume you are out of school for the summer and decide to begin a small business to make money to help cover the cost of school next year and to have spending money this summer. You decide to establish a lawn care service. What assets would you expect to need to start and maintain your business? Assuming you are successful in getting the business started, what revenues and expenses would you expect to incur as you run your business? How would you know if you were doing well in terms of covering your costs and earning money for school next year?

*Our comments appear on page 85.

INCOME STATEMENT

LO 5
Explain how the income statement reports an enterprise's financial performance for a period of time in terms of the relationship of revenues and expenses.

The income statement is a summarization of the company's revenue and expense transactions for a period of time. It is particularly important for the company's owners, creditors, and other interested parties to understand the income statement. Ultimately the company will succeed or fail based on its ability to earn revenues in excess of its expenses. Once the company's assets are acquired and business commences, revenues and expenses are important sources of cash flows for the enterprise. **Revenues** are increases in the company's assets from its profit-directed activities, and they result in positive cash flows. Similarly, **expenses** are decreases in the company's assets from its profit-directed activities, and they result in negative cash flows. *Net income* is the difference between the revenues and expenses for a specified period of time. Should a company find itself in the undesirable situation of having expenses greater than revenues, we call the difference a *net loss*.

Exhibit 2–11

EXPANDED ACCOUNTING EQUATION

OVERNIGHT AUTO SERVICE
Expanded Accounting Equation
January 20–31, 2002

	Assets						=	Liabilities			+	Owners' Equity	
	Cash	+	Accounts Receivable	+	Land	+	Building	+	Tools and Equipment	=	Notes Payable	+	Accounts Payable	+	Capital Stock	Retained Earnings
Jan. 20	+$80,000									=					$80,000	
Balances	$80,000									=					$80,000	
Jan. 21	−52,000				+$52,000					=						
Balances	$28,000				$52,000					=					$80,000	
Jan. 22	−6,000						+$36,000			=						
Balances	$22,000				$52,000		$36,000			=					$80,000	
Jan. 23									+$13,800	=			+$13,800			
Balances	$22,000				$52,000		$36,000		$13,800	=			$13,800		$80,000	
Jan. 24			+$1,800						−1,800	=						
Balances	$22,000		$1,800		$52,000		$36,000		$12,000	=			$13,800		$80,000	
Jan. 26	+600		−600							=						
Balances	$22,600		$1,200		$52,000		$36,000		$12,000	=			$13,800		$80,000	
Jan. 27	−6,800									=			−6,800			
Balances	$15,800		$1,200		$52,000		$36,000		$12,000	=			$7,000		$80,000	
Jan. 31	+2,200									=						+$2,200
Jan. 31	−1,400									=						−1,400
Balances	$16,600		$1,200		$52,000		$36,000		$12,000	=	$30,000		$7,000		$80,000	$ 800

Statement of Cash Flows ← | | | | | | | | | | | | | | | → Income Statement

Overnight's income statement for January is relatively simple because the company did not have a large number of complex revenue and expense transactions.[3] Taking information directly from the Owners' Equity column in Exhibit 2–11, we can prepare the company's income statement as shown in Exhibit 2–12.

Exhibit 2–12

INCOME STATEMENT

My Notes

An income statement displays revenues and expenses for a period of time

OVERNIGHT AUTO SERVICE
Income Statement
For the Period January 20–31, 2002

Sales Revenues		$2,200
Operating expenses:		
Wages	$1,200	
Utilities	200	1,400
Net income		$ 800

Notice that the heading for the income statement refers to a *period* of time rather than a *point* in time, as was the case with the balance sheet. The income statement reports on the financial performance of the company in terms of earning revenue and incurring expenses *over a period of time* and explains, in part, how the company's financial position changed between the beginning and ending of that period.

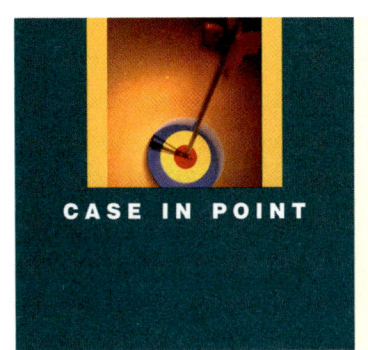

CASE IN POINT

The relationship of net income to revenue or sales varies considerably from company to company. For example, in the 2001 income statement of **Microsoft**, net income ($7,785 million) is reported to be more than 39% of revenue. In contrast, in the 2001 income statement of **Procter & Gamble**, net income ($2,922 million) is a much lower 7.5% of sales.

© The Proctor & Gamble Co., used by permission

STATEMENT OF CASH FLOWS

LO 6

Explain how the statement of cash flows presents the change in cash for a period of time in terms of the company's operating, investing, and financing activities.

We already have established the importance of cash flows to investors and creditors and that the cash flows of the company are an important consideration in investors' and creditors' assessments of cash flows to them. As a result, a second set of information that is particularly important concerning how the financial position changed between two points in time (that is, the beginning and end of a month or year) is cash flow information.

We can use the entire Cash column of the analysis in Exhibit 2–11 to create a statement of cash flows for Overnight Auto Service. The statement classifies the various cash flows into three categories—operating, investing, and financing—and relates these categories to the beginning and ending cash balances. Cash flows from **operating activities** are the cash effects of revenue and expense transactions that are included in

---

[3] In this illustration, only revenue and expense transactions change the amount of owners' equity from the original $80,000 investment of the owner. Examples of other events and transactions that affect the amount of owners' equity, but that are *not included in net income,* are the sale of additional shares of capital stock and the payment of dividends to shareholders. These subjects are covered in later chapters.

the income statement.[4] Cash flows from **investing activities** are the cash effects of purchasing and selling assets. Cash flows from **financing activities** are the cash effects of the owners investing in the company and creditors loaning money to the company and the repayment of either or both.

The statement of cash flows for Overnight Auto Service for the period January 20–31 is presented in Exhibit 2–13.

Exhibit 2–13

STATEMENT OF CASH FLOWS

OVERNIGHT AUTO SERVICE
Statement of Cash Flows
For the Period January 20–31, 2002

Cash flows from operating activities:		
Cash received from revenue transactions	$ 2,200	
Cash paid for expenses	(1,400)	
Net cash provided by operating activities		$ 800
Cash flows from investing activities:		
Purchase of land	$(52,000)	
Purchase of building	(6,000)	
Purchase of tools	(6,800)	
Sale of tools	600	
Net cash used by investing activities		(64,200)
Cash flows from financing activities:		
Sale of capital stock		80,000
Increase in cash for the period		$16,600
Cash balance, January 20, 2002		-0-
Cash balance, January 31, 2002		$16,600

My Notes

A statement of cash flows shows how cash changed during the period

Notice that the operating, investing, and financing categories include both positive and negative cash flows. (The negative cash flows are in parentheses.) Also notice that the combined total of the three categories of the statement (increase of $16,600) explains the total change from the beginning to the end of the month. On January 20, the beginning balance was zero because the company was started on that day. For February, Overnight's beginning cash balance will be $16,600, and the statement of cash flows will explain how that number either increased to a higher balance or was reduced to a lower balance as a result of its cash activities during that month. Notice also that several transactions and parts of transactions had no cash effects and, therefore, are not included in the statement of cash flows. For example, on January 22, Overnight purchased land for $36,000, only $6,000 of which was paid in cash. The remaining $30,000 is not included in the statement of cash flows because it did not affect the amount of cash. Similarly, on January 23, Overnight purchased tools and equipment for $13,800, paying no cash at that time. That transaction has no cash effect on January 23, although the cash payment of $6,800 on January 27, which is a continuation of that transaction, did affect cash and is included in the statement of cash flows. Transactions that did not affect cash are called *noncash investing and financing transactions*. In a formal statement of cash flows, these transactions are required to be noted as we explain later in this text, even though they do not affect the actual flow of cash into and out of the company.

---

[4] In this illustration, net cash amounts provided by operating activities and net income are equal. This is because all revenues and all expenses are cash transactions. This will not always be the case. As we learn more about the accrual method of accounting, you will see that revenues and expenses may be recorded in a different accounting period than the one when cash is received or paid. This will cause net income and net cash from operating activities to be different amounts.

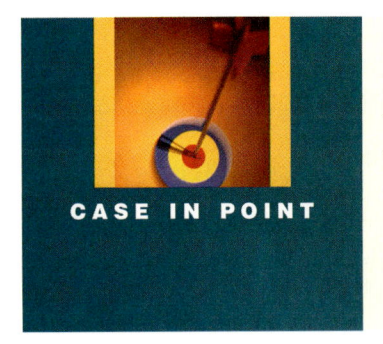

CASE IN POINT

It is not unusual for a company to report an increase in cash from operating activities, but a decrease in the total amount of cash. This outcome results from decreases in cash from investing and/or financing activities. For example, in a recent year **Carnival Corporation**, which owns and operates several cruise lines, reported cash provided by operating activities of almost $1.1 billion but a decrease in total cash of almost $3 million. This was due primarily to large expenditures for property and equipment, such as cruise ships, which are presented as investing activities in the company's statement of cash flows.

RELATIONSHIPS AMONG FINANCIAL STATEMENTS

LO 7
Explain important relationships among the statement of financial position, income statement, and statement of cash flows, and how these statements relate to each other.

As our discussion of Overnight Auto Service indicates, the statement of financial position (balance sheet), the income statement, and the statement of cash flows are all based on the same transactions, but they present different "views" of the company. They should not be thought of as alternatives to each other; rather, all are important in terms of presenting key financial information about the company.

The diagram in Exhibit 2–14 explains how the three financial statements relate to the period of time they cover. The horizontal line represents time (for example, a month or a year). At the beginning and ending points in time, the company prepares a statement of financial position (balance sheet) that gives a static look in financial terms of where the company stands. The other two financial statements—the income statement and the statement of cash flows—cover the intervening *period of time* between the two balance sheets and help explain important changes that occurred during the period.

Exhibit 2–14

FINANCIAL REPORTING TIME LINE

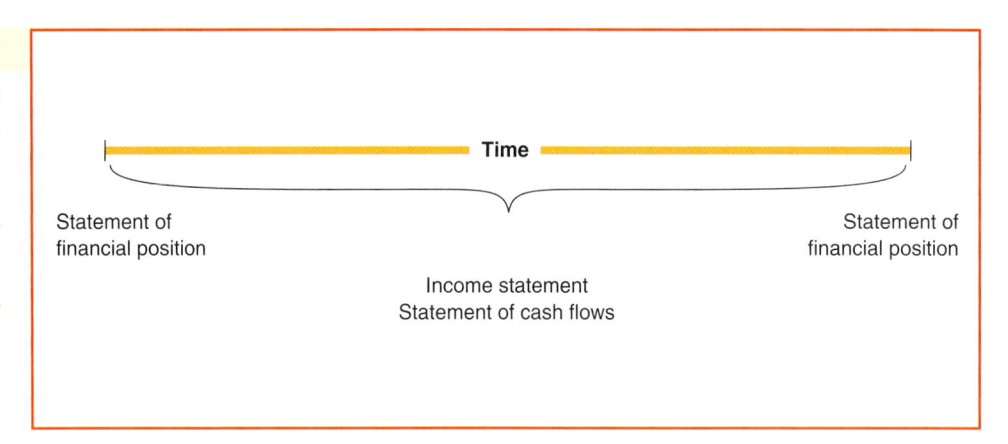

My Notes

Financial statements are closely tied to time periods

```
                              Time
  |---------------------------------------------------------|
Statement of                                        Statement of
financial position                                  financial position
                       Income statement
                   Statement of cash flows
```

If we understand where a company stands financially at two points in time, and if we understand the changes that occurred during the intervening period in terms of the company's profit-seeking activities (income statement) and its cash activities (statement of cash flows), we know a great deal about the company that is valuable in assessing its future cash flows—information that is useful to investors, creditors, management, and others.

Because the balance sheet, income statement, and statement of cash flows are derived from the same underlying financial information, they are said to "articulate," meaning that they relate closely to each other. The diagram in Exhibit 2–15 indicates relationships that we have discussed in this chapter as we have introduced these three important financial statements. The dollar amounts are taken from the Overnight Auto Service example presented earlier in this chapter. In the balance sheet, the property, plant and equipment amount of $100,000 represents the total of land ($52,000), building ($36,000), and tools and equipment ($12,000).

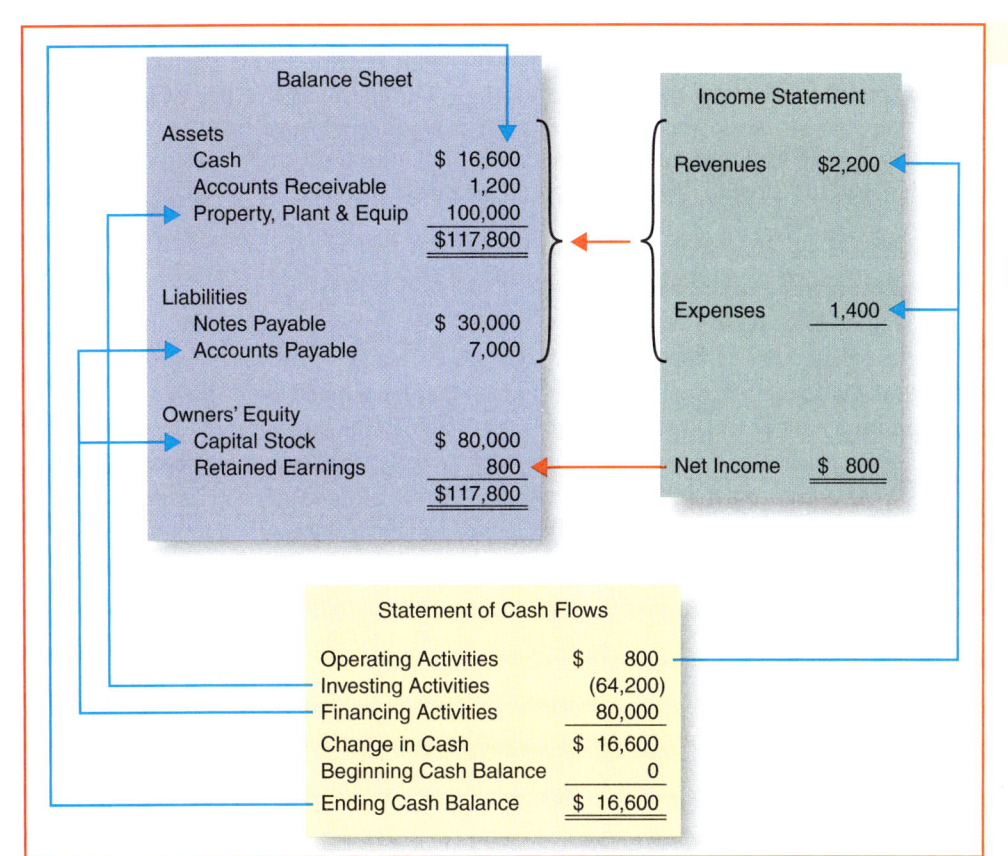

Relationships among Financial Statements

Exhibit 2–15
FINANCIAL STATEMENT ARTICULATION

Balance Sheet

Assets
- Cash . . . . $ 16,600
- Accounts Receivable 1,200
- Property, Plant & Equip 100,000
- $117,800

Liabilities
- Notes Payable . . . . $ 30,000
- Accounts Payable 7,000

Owners' Equity
- Capital Stock . . . . $ 80,000
- Retained Earnings 800
- $117,800

Income Statement

- Revenues $2,200
- Expenses 1,400
- Net Income . . . . $ 800

Statement of Cash Flows

- Operating Activities . . . . $ 800
- Investing Activities . . . . (64,200)
- Financing Activities 80,000
- Change in Cash . . . . $ 16,600
- Beginning Cash Balance 0
- Ending Cash Balance . . . . $ 16,600

My Notes

Financial statements are based on the same underlying transactions

My Mentor

   The balance sheet represents an expansion of the accounting equation and explains the various categories of assets, liabilities, and owners' equity. The income statement explains changes in financial position (that is, assets and liabilities) that result from profit-generating transactions in terms of revenue and expense transactions. The resulting number, net income, represents an addition to the owners' equity in the enterprise. The statement of cash flows explains the ways cash increased and decreased during the period in terms of the enterprise's operating, investing, and financing activities. In this illustration, the cash paid for investing activities ($64,200) represents only part of the property, plant, and equipment balance [$100,000].) These relationships among the financial statements are called articulation.

You as an Investor

Assume you have just inherited a large sum of money and are looking for a company in which to invest. You have obtained financial statements—balance sheets, income statements, and statements of cash flows—from the Internet for three different companies of interest to you. What will be your primary objective in choosing a company in which to invest your money? What key items or relationships will you look for in each financial statement that will help you decide in which company to invest?

*Our comments appear on page 86.

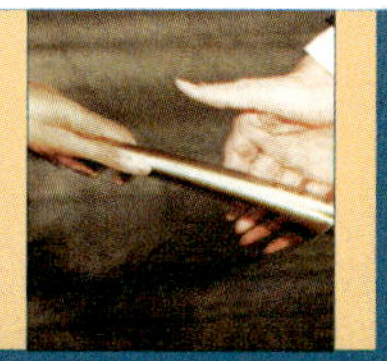

YOUR TURN

   While these three key financial statements include important information, they do not include all possible information that might be presented about a company. For example, look again at Overnight's activities during the latter part of January. We could have prepared a separate financial statement on how liabilities changed or how the Tools and Equipment asset account changed. There is also important nonfinancial information that underlies the statement of financial position, the income statement, and the statement of cash flows that could be presented and that would benefit users of the statements. Accountants have developed methods of dealing with these other types of information, which we will learn about later in this text. At this point, we have focused our attention on the three primary financial statements that companies most often use to describe the activities that are capable of being captured in financial terms.

CASH EFFECTS

We have used the word *cash* extensively in introducing the primary financial statements. As we learned in Chapter 1, ultimately the flow of cash to investors and creditors is very important. These users of financial statements are interested in the cash activities of the enterprise in which they have invested or to which they have made loans or sold on credit. All enterprises are involved in continuous cash-to-cash cycles that vary with the nature of the underlying business. For example, Overnight Auto Service invests in a cash cycle in which it purchased land and a building necessary for its business. These assets, in turn, are used to provide services for customers that result in cash flows back into the company. Another cash cycle is much shorter in terms of time, namely the payment of wages to employees—employees provide services and soon thereafter are paid wages by the company. The underlying purpose, however, is the same as the purchase of land and buildings—namely, to acquire the resources necessary to provide auto repair services that will ultimately result in positive cash flows for Overnight Auto Service. Sometimes the enterprise is able to delay a negative cash flow until it has a positive cash flow to provide the cash for payment. For example, Overnight partially purchased its building on credit, thereby allowing it to use the building to operate and generate positive cash flows, some of which will be used to repay the loan on the building. In other instances, cash payment is required before the positive cash flows from the use of the asset can take place (for example, Overnight's purchase of land for cash). In the final analysis, managing a company's cash flows is an important responsibility of management and may ultimately determine the success or failure of a business.

FINANCIAL ANALYSIS

Relationships among the three primary financial statements provide the opportunity to learn a great deal about a company by bringing pieces of information together in a meaningful way. In fact, some people believe that relationships in the financial statements are more important than the actual dollar figures in those statements.

For example, take another look at the balance sheet in Exhibit 2–10. Notice that the company has $16,600 of cash and $1,200 of accounts receivable, a total of $17,800 in what are sometimes referred to as *current* assets, denoting that they either are cash or will soon become cash. Now look at the liabilities in the balance sheet and notice that the company has notes payable of $30,000 and accounts payable of $7,000 for a total of $37,000 of liabilities. If both types of liabilities are current liabilities, meaning that they will be due in the near future and, therefore, can be expected to require the use of current assets, Overnight Auto Service may have difficulty paying them because they do not have enough liquid assets to cover their liabilities. The relationship of current assets to current liabilities is called the *current ratio*. For Overnight Auto Service it is a low .48 ($17,800 divided by $37,000). This means that Overnight Auto Service has only 48 cents available for every $1 of liabilities that will come due in the near future. On the other hand, if the $30,000 notes payable resulting from the building purchase is not due in the near future, the company's liquidity is much stronger.

While the above refers exclusively to information found in the balance sheet, key information from one financial statement often is combined with information from another financial statement. For example, we may be interested in knowing the amount of cash provided by operations (cash flow statement) relative to the amount of a company's currently maturing liabilities (balance sheet). Or we might want to compare a company's net income (income statement) with the investment in assets (balance sheet) that were used to generate that income.

Many of the chapters in this text introduce you to various types of financial analysis. We build on those introductory discussions in Chapter 14, Financial Statement Analysis, in which we provide a comprehensive treatment of how financial statements are used to inform investors and creditors.

FORMS OF BUSINESS ORGANIZATION

In the United States, most business enterprises are organized as a *sole proprietorship,* a *partnership,* or a *corporation.* Generally accepted accounting principles can be applied to the financial statements of all three forms of organization.

LO 8 Explain common forms of business ownership—sole proprietorship, partnership, and corporation—and demonstrate how they differ in terms of their presentation in the statement of financial position.

Sole Proprietorships

An unincorporated business owned by one person is called a **sole proprietorship**. Often the owner also acts as the manager. This form of business organization is common for small retail stores, farms, service businesses, and professional practices in law, medicine, and accounting. In fact, the sole proprietorship is by far the most common form of business organization in our economy.

From an accounting viewpoint, a sole proprietorship is regarded as a business entity *separate from the other affairs of its owner.* From a legal viewpoint, however, the business and its owner are not regarded as separate entities. Thus, *the owner is personally liable* for the debts of the business. If the business encounters financial difficulties, creditors can force the owner to sell his or her personal assets to pay the business debts. While an advantage of the sole proprietorship form of organization is its simplicity, this *unlimited liability* feature is a disadvantage to the owner.

Partnerships

An unincorporated business owned by two or more persons voluntarily acting as partners (co-owners) is called a **partnership**. Partnerships, like sole proprietorships, are widely used for small businesses. In addition, some very large professional practices, including CPA firms, are organized as partnerships. As in the case of the sole proprietorship, the owners of a partnership are personally responsible for all debts of the business. From an accounting standpoint, a partnership is viewed as a business entity separate from the personal affairs of its owners.[5] A benefit of the partnership form over the sole proprietorship form is the ability to bring together larger amounts of capital investment from multiple owners.

Corporations

A **corporation** is the only type of business organization recognized *under the law* as an entity separate from its owners. Therefore, the owners of a corporation are *not* personally liable for the debts of the business. These owners can lose no more than the amounts they have invested in the business—a concept known as *limited liability.* This concept is the principal reason that corporations are the most attractive form of business organization to many investors. Overnight Auto Service, the company used in our illustrations, is a corporation.

Ownership of a corporation is divided into transferable shares of capital stock, and the owners are called **stockholders** or shareholders. Stock certificates are issued by the corporation to each stockholder showing the number of shares that he or she owns. The stockholders are free to sell some or all of these shares to other investors at any time. This *transferability of ownership* adds to the attractiveness of the corporate form of

---

[5] Creditors of an unincorporated business often ask to see the *personal* financial statements of the business owners, as these owners ultimately are responsible for paying the debts of the business.

organization, because investors can more easily get their money out of the business. Corporations offer an even greater opportunity than partnerships to bring together large amounts of capital from multiple owners.

There are many more sole proprietorships and partnerships than corporations, but most large businesses are organized as corporations. Thus corporations are the dominant form of business organization in terms of the *dollar volume* of business activity. Of the three types of business, corporations are most likely to distribute financial statements to investors and other outsiders.

Reporting Ownership Equity in the Statement of Financial Position

Assets and liabilities are presented in the same manner in the statement of financial position of all three types of business organization. Some differences arise, however, in the presentation of the ownership equity.

Sole Proprietorships A *sole proprietorship* is owned by only one person. Therefore, the owner's equity section of the balance sheet includes only one item—the equity of the owner. If Overnight Auto Service had been organized as a sole proprietorship with Michael McBryan the owner, owner's equity in the January 30 balance sheet would appear as follows:

My Notes

Ownership equity in a sole proprietorship

Owner's equity:	
Michael McBryan, Capital	$80,800

Partnerships A *partnership* has two or more owners. Accountants use the term *partners' equity* instead of owners' equity and usually list separately the amount of each partner's equity in the business. If, for example, Michael McBryan had been in partnership with his sister, Rebecca McBryan, in Overnight Auto Service, and if each had contributed an equal amount of cash ($40,000) and had shared equally in the net income ($400), the partners' equity section of the balance sheet would have been presented as follows:

My Notes

. . . in a partnership

Partners' equity:		
Michael McBryan, Capital	$40,400	
Rebecca McBryan, Capital	40,400	
Total partners' equity		$80,800

Corporations In a business organized as a *corporation,* it is *not* customary to show separately the equity of each stockholder. In the case of large corporations, this clearly would be impossible, as these businesses may have *several million* individual stockholders (owners).

Returning to our original assumption that Overnight Auto Service is organized as a corporation, owners' equity (also referred to as **stockholders' equity** or shareholders' equity) is presented in two amounts—capital stock and retained earnings. This section of the balance sheet appears as follows:

My Notes

. . . and in a corporation

Owners' equity:		
Capital Stock	$80,000	
Retained Earnings	800	
Total stockholders' equity		$80,800

Capital stock represents the amount that the stockholders originally invested in the business in exchange for shares of the company's stock. **Retained earnings**, in contrast, represents the increase in owners' equity that has accumulated over the years as a result of profitable operations.

THE USE OF FINANCIAL STATEMENTS BY OUTSIDERS

As we learned in Chapter 1, investors and creditors use financial statements in making *financial decisions*—that is, in selecting those companies in which they will invest resources or to which they will extend credit. For this reason, financial statements are designed primarily to meet the needs of creditors and investors. Two factors of particular concern to creditors and investors are the *liquidity* and *profitability* of a business organization.

Creditors are interested in **liquidity**—the ability of the business to pay its debts as they come due. Liquidity is critical to the very survival of a business organization—a business that is not liquid may be forced into bankruptcy by its creditors. Once bankrupt, a business may be forced by the courts to stop its operations, sell its assets (for the purpose of paying its creditors), and end its existence.

Investors also are interested in the liquidity of a business organization, but often they are even more interested in its profitability. *Profitable operations increase the value of the owners' equity* in the business. A company that continually operates unprofitably will eventually exhaust its resources and be forced out of existence. Therefore, most users of financial statements study these statements carefully for clues to the company's liquidity and future profitability.

The Short Run versus the Long Run In the short run, liquidity and profitability may be independent of each other. A business may be operating profitably but nevertheless run out of cash needed to meet its obligations. On the other hand, a company may operate unprofitably during a given year yet have enough cash from previous periods to pay its bills and remain liquid.

Over a longer term, however, liquidity and profitability go hand in hand. If a business is to survive, it must remain liquid and, in the long run, it must operate profitably.

Evaluating Short-Term Liquidity As discussed earlier in this chapter, one key indicator of short-term liquidity is the relationship between an entity's *liquid* assets and the liabilities requiring payment *in the near future*. By studying the nature of a company's assets, and the amounts and due dates of its liabilities, users of financial statements often may anticipate whether the company is likely to have difficulty in meeting its upcoming obligations. This simple type of analysis meets the needs of many *short-term* creditors. Evaluating long-term debt-paying ability is a more difficult matter and is discussed in later chapters.

In studying financial statements, users should *always* read the accompanying notes and the auditors' report.

The Need for Adequate Disclosure

The concept of adequate **disclosure** is an important generally accepted accounting principle. Adequate disclosure means that users of financial statements are informed of any facts *necessary for the proper interpretation* of the statements. Adequate disclosure is made in the body of the financial statements and in *notes* accompanying these statements. It is not unusual to find a series of notes to financial statements that are longer than the statements themselves.

Among the events that may require disclosure in notes to the financial statements are occurrences after the date of the financial statements. For example, assume that Overnight Auto Service's building is destroyed by fire on February 2, and that Michael McBryan

LO 9
Discuss and illustrate the importance of nonfinancial information to supplement the information in the primary financial statements.

is using the financial statements to acquire additional financing for the business after that date. Assume also that McBryan has less insurance on the building than will be needed to replace it. Users of the financial statements, such as bankers who might be considering lending money to Overnight, must be informed of this important "subsequent event." This disclosure usually would be done with a note like the following:

Note 7: Events occurring after the financial statement date
On February 2, 2002, the building included in the January 31 statement of financial position at $36,000 was destroyed by fire. While the company has insurance on this facility, management expects to recover only approximately $30,000 of the loss.

In addition to important subsequent events, many other situations may require disclosure in notes to the financial statements. Examples include lawsuits against the company, due dates of major liabilities, assets pledged as collateral to secure loans, amounts receivable from officers or other "insiders," and contractual commitments requiring large future cash outlays.

There is no comprehensive list of the items and events that may require disclosure. As a general rule, a company should disclose any financial facts that a reasonably informed person would consider *necessary to the proper interpretation* of the financial statements. Events that clearly are unimportant *do not* require disclosure. Determining information that should be disclosed in financial statements is another situation that requires significant judgment on the part of the accountant.

Management's Interest in Financial Statements

While we have emphasized the importance of financial statements to investors and creditors, the management of a business organization is vitally concerned with the financial position of the business and with its profitability and cash flows. Therefore, management is anxious to receive financial statements as frequently and as quickly as possible so that it may take action to improve areas of weak performance. Most large organizations provide managers with financial statements on at least a monthly basis. With modern technology, financial statements prepared on a weekly, daily, or even hourly basis are possible.

Managers have a special interest in the *annual* financial statements, as these are the statements most widely used by decision makers outside of the organization. For example, if creditors view the annual financial statements as strong, they will be more willing to extend credit to the business than if they regard the company's financial statements as weak.

A strong statement of financial position is one that shows relatively little debt and large amounts of liquid assets relative to the liabilities due in the near future. A strong income statement is one that shows large revenues relative to the expenses required to earn the revenues. A strong statement of cash flows is one that not only shows a strong cash balance but also indicates that cash is being generated by operations. Demonstrating that these positive characteristics of the company are ongoing and can be seen in a series of financial statements is particularly helpful in creating confidence in the company on the part of investors and creditors. Because of the importance of the financial statements, management may take steps that are specifically intended to improve the company's financial position and financial performance. For example, cash purchases of assets may be delayed until the beginning of the next accounting period so that large amounts of cash will be included in the statement of financial position and the statement of cash flows. On the other hand, if the company is in a particularly strong cash position, liabilities due in the near future may be paid, replaced with longer-term liabilities, or even replaced by additional investments by owners to communicate that future negative cash flows will not be as great as they might otherwise appear.

These actions are sometimes called **window dressing**—measures taken by management to make the company appear as strong as possible in its financial statements. Users of financial statements should realize that, while the statements are fair representations of the financial position at the end of the period and financial performance for the period, they may not necessarily describe the typical financial situation of the business throughout the entire financial reporting period. In its annual financial statements, in particular, management tries to make the company appear as strong as is reasonably possible. As a result, many creditors regard more frequent financial statements (for example, quarterly or even monthly) as providing important additional information beyond that in the annual financial statements. The more frequently financial statements are presented, the less able is management to window dress and make a company look financially stronger than it actually is.

MANAGEMENT STRATEGY AND FINANCIAL REPORTING

Because external stakeholders, particularly creditors, carefully evaluate financial reports, the reports have a significant impact on the strategic choices of management. Suppose Overnight Auto Service was planning to raise more capital in the coming year by selling additional stock. McBryan might delay or accelerate some planned strategic decisions to strengthen the financial position and, as a result, the external financial reports of Overnight Auto Service. For example, the planned purchase of a hydraulic lift might be delayed and the choice to form a partnership with nearby Ace Towing might be accelerated. Delaying ambitious capital expenditures or expediting strategic alliances to ensure the ability to raise additional needed capital are examples of the impact that financial reporting can have on business strategy.

CONCLUDING REMARKS

Throughout this text, we emphasize how accounting information is the basis for business decisions. In this chapter, you have been introduced to business transactions and how they are combined and presented in the form of three basic financial statements—the statement of financial position (balance sheet), the income statement, and the statement of cash flows. These financial statements constitute some of the primary products of the accountant's work, and they provide investors, creditors, and other parties with pertinent information that is useful for decision making.

As you continue your study of financial accounting, in Chapter 3 you will learn how business transactions are actually recorded, how they move through an accounting system, and how they eventually lead to the preparation of financial statements. The foundation you have received in Chapter 2 will be helpful to you as we move into a more sophisticated discussion of business transactions and how they impact a company's financial position, results of operations, and cash flows.

A SECOND LOOK
INTEL

As we began this chapter, we took a brief look at **Intel** and discussed how that company communicates with its owners, creditors and others through its annual report. We have introduced the three primary financial statements—statement of financial position (balance sheet), income statement, and the statement of cash flows—as primary communications tools for valuable information regarding the company's activities for a period of time. These financial statements, along with notes and other disclosures, make up a significant portion of the content of a company's annual report.

While **Intel**'s financial statements are longer and more detailed than those of Overnight Auto Service which we covered in this chapter, they are very similar. The statement of financial position, or balance sheet, describes **Intel**'s financial position at the end of each annual reporting period. The income statement details the company's revenues and expenses, leading to an amount of net income. The statement of cash flows describes cash activity in terms of operating, investing, and financing activities. The three financial statements are based on the same underlying financial information and, thus, are closely related. In other words, they articulate in the same manner as the financial statements of Overnight Auto Service do.

As you progress through this text, you will learn more about these basic financial statements and will eventually reach a point where you are able to gain a great deal of knowledge by analyzing the financial statements of a complex company like **Intel**.

END-OF-CHAPTER REVIEW

SUMMARY OF LEARNING OBJECTIVES

LO 1
Explain the nature and general purpose of financial statements.
Financial statements are presentations of information in financial terms about an enterprise that are believed to be fair and accurate. They describe certain attributes of the enterprise that are important for decision makers, particularly investors (owners) and creditors.

LO 2
Explain certain accounting principles that are important for an understanding of financial statements and how professional judgment by accountants may affect the application of those principles.
Accountants prepare financial statements by applying a set of standards or rules referred to as generally accepted accounting principles. Consistent application of these standards permits comparisons between companies and between years of a single company. Generally accepted accounting principles allow for significant latitude in how certain transactions should be accounted for, meaning that professional judgment is particularly important.

LO 3
Demonstrate how certain business transactions affect the elements of the accounting equation: Assets = Liabilities + Owners' Equity.
Business transactions result in changes in the three elements of the basic accounting equation. A transaction that increases total assets must also increase total liabilities and owners' equity. Similarly, a transaction that decreases total assets must simultaneously decrease total liabilities and owners' equity. Some transactions increase one asset and reduce another. Regardless of the nature of the specific transaction, the accounting equation must stay in balance at all times.

LO 4
Explain how the statement of financial position, often referred to as the balance sheet, is an expansion of the basic accounting equation.
The statement of financial position, or balance sheet, presents in detail the elements of the basic accounting equation. Various types of assets are listed and totaled. The enterprise's liabilities are listed, totaled, and added to the owners' equity. The balancing feature of this financial statement is one of its dominant characteristics because the statement is simply an expansion of the basic accounting equation.

LO 5
Explain how the income statement reports an enterprise's financial performance for a period of time in terms of the relationship of revenues and expenses.
Revenues are created as the enterprise provides goods and services for its customers. Many expenses are required to be able to provide those goods and services. The difference between the revenues and expenses is net income or net loss.

LO 6
Explain how the statement of cash flows presents the change in cash for a period of time in terms of the company's operating, investing, and financing activities.
Cash is one of the most important assets, and the statement of cash flows shows in detail how the enterprise's cash balance changed between the beginning and ending of the accounting period. Operating activities relate to ongoing revenue and expense transactions. Investing activities relate to the purchase and sale of various types of assets (for example, land, buildings, and equipment). Financing activities describe where the enterprise has received its debt and equity financing. The statement of cash flows combines information about all of these activities into a concise statement of changes in cash that reconciles the beginning and ending cash balances.

LO 7
Explain important relationships among the statement of financial position, income statement, and statement of cash flows, and how these statements articulate.
The three primary financial statements are based on the same underlying transactions. They are not alternatives to each other, but rather represent three different ways of looking at the financial activities of the reporting enterprise. Because they are based on the same transactions, they relate, or "articulate," closely with each other.

LO 8
Explain common forms of business ownership—sole proprietorship, partnership, and corporation—and demonstrate how they differ in terms of their presentation in the statement of financial position.
Owners' equity is one of three major elements in the basic accounting equation. Regardless of the form of organization, owners' equity represents the interest of the owners in the assets of the reporting enterprise. For a sole proprietorship, owner's equity consists of the interest of a single owner. For a partnership, the ownership interests of all partners are added together to determine the total owners' equity of the enterprise. For a corporation, which usually has many owners, the total contribution to the enterprise represents its owners' equity. In all cases, the enterprise's net income is added to owners' equity.

LO 9
Discuss and illustrate the importance of nonfinancial information to supplement the information in the primary financial statements.
All important aspects of an enterprise's activities usually cannot be captured in financial terms. Financial statements typically are accompanied by notes that provide qualitative information

LO 10
Discuss the importance of financial statements to a company and its investors and creditors and why management may take steps to improve the appearance of the company in its financial statements.

Financial statements are particularly important for investors and creditors in their attempts to evaluate future cash flows from the enterprise to them. Management is interested in the enterprise looking as positive as possible in its financial statements and may take certain steps to improve the overall appearance of the enterprise. A fine line, however, exists between the steps management can take and the steps that are unethical, or even illegal.

KEY TERMS INTRODUCED OR EMPHASIZED IN CHAPTER 2

accounting equation (p. 48) Assets are equal to the sum of liabilities plus owners' equity.

articulation (p. 43) The close relationship that exists among the financial statements that are prepared on the basis of the same underlying transaction information.

assets (p. 44) Economic resources owned by an entity.

balance sheet (p. 42) The financial statement showing the financial position of an enterprise by summarizing its assets, liabilities, and owners' equity at a point in time. Also called the statement of financial position.

business entity (p. 44) An economic unit that controls resources, incurs obligations, and engages in business activities.

capital stock (p. 63) Transferable units of ownership in a corporation.

corporation (p. 61) A business organized as a separate legal entity and chartered by a state, with ownership divided into transferable shares of capital stock.

cost principle (p. 45) The widely used principle of accounting for assets at their original cost to the current owner.

creditor (p. 47) A person or organization to whom debt is owed.

deflation (p. 46) A decline in the general price level, resulting in an increase in the purchasing power of the monetary unit.

disclosure (p. 63) The accounting principle of providing with financial statements any financial and other facts that are necessary for proper interpretation of those statements.

expenses (p. 54) Past, present, or future reductions in cash required to generate revenues.

financial statement (p. 42) A declaration of information believed to be true and communicated in monetary terms.

financing activities (p. 57) A category in the statement of cash flows that reflects the results of debt and equity financing transactions.

going-concern assumption (p. 45) An assumption by accountants that a business will operate in the foreseeable future unless specific evidence suggests that this is not a reasonable assumption.

income statement (p. 42) An activity statement that subtracts from the enterprise's revenue those expenses required to generate the revenues, resulting in a net income or a net loss.

inflation (p. 46) An increase in the general price level, resulting in a decline in the purchasing power of the monetary unit.

investing activities (p. 57) A category in the statement of cash flows that reflects the results of purchases and sales of assets, such as land, buildings, and equipment.

liabilities (p. 47) Debts or obligations of an entity that resulted from past transactions. They represent the claims of creditors on the enterprise's assets.

liquidity (p. 63) Having the financial ability to pay debts as they become due.

negative cash flows (p. 43) A payment of cash that reduces the enterprise's cash balance.

operating activities (pp. 56–57) A category in the statement of cash flows that includes the cash effects of all revenues and expenses included in the income statement.

owners' equity (p. 47) The excess of assets over liabilities. The amount of the owners' investment in the business, plus profits from successful operations that have been retained in the business.

partnership (p. 61) An unincorporated form of business organization in which two or more persons voluntarily associate for purposes of carrying out business activities.

positive cash flows (p. 43) Increases in cash that add to the enterprise's cash balance.

retained earnings (p. 63) The portion of stockholders' equity that has accumulated as a result of profitable operations.

revenues (p. 54) Increases in the enterprise's assets as a result of profit-oriented activities.

sole proprietorship (p. 61) An unincorporated business owned by a single individual.

stable-dollar assumption (p. 46) An assumption by accountants that the monetary unit used in the preparation of financial statements is stable over time or changes at a sufficiently slow rate that the resulting impact on financial statements does not distort the information.

statement of cash flows (p. 43) An activity statement that explains the enterprise's change in cash in terms of its operating, investing, and financing activities.

statement of financial position (p. 42) Same as balance sheet.

stockholders (p. 61) Owners of capital stock in a corporation.

stockholders' equity (p. 62) The owners' equity of an enterprise organized as a corporation.

window dressing (p. 64) Measures taken by management specifically intended to make a business look as strong as possible in its balance sheet, income statement, and statement of cash flows.

DEMONSTRATION PROBLEM

Account balances for Crystal Auto Wash at September 30, 2002, are shown below. The figure for retained earnings is not given, but it can be determined when all the available information is assembled in the form of a balance sheet.

Accounts Payable	$14,000	Land	$68,000
Accounts Receivable	800	Machinery & Equipment	65,000
Buildings	52,000	Notes Payable (due in 30 days)	29,000
Cash	9,200	Salaries Payable	3,000
Capital Stock	100,000	Supplies	400
Retained Earnings	?		

Instructions
a. Prepare a balance sheet at September 30, 2002.
b. Does this balance sheet indicate that the company is in a strong financial position? Explain briefly.
c. How would an income statement and a statement of cash flows allow you to better respond to part **b**?

Solution to the Demonstration Problem
a.

CRYSTAL AUTO WASH
Balance Sheet
September 30, 2002

Assets		Liabilities & Owners' Equity	
Cash	$ 9,200	Liabilities:	
Accounts Receivable	800	Notes Payable	$ 29,000
Supplies	400	Accounts Payable	14,000
Land	68,000	Salaries Payable	3,000
Buildings	52,000	Total liabilities	$ 46,000
Machinery & Equipment	65,000	Owners' equity:	
		Capital Stock	$100,000
		*Retained Earnings	49,400
Total	$195,400	Total	$195,400

*Computed as $195,400 (total assets) − $46,000 (total liabilities) = $149,400 (owners' equity); $149,400 − $100,000 (capital stock) = $49,400.

b. The balance sheet indicates that Crystal Auto Wash is in a *weak* financial position. The only liquid assets—cash and receivables—total only $10,000, but the company has *$46,000* in debts due in the near future.

c. An income statement for Crystal Auto Wash would show the company's revenues and expenses for the period (month, quarter, or year) ending on the date of the balance sheet,

September 30, 2002. This information would be helpful in determining whether the company was successful in selling its auto wash services at an amount that exceeds its cost of providing those services, something the company must do to remain in business and be successful. The statement of cash flows for the same period as the income statement would show where the company's cash came from and where it went in terms of its operating, investing, and financing activities. This information would be particularly helpful in assessing the strength of the company's ability to satisfy its obligations as they come due in light of the relatively weak balance sheet.

SELF-TEST QUESTIONS

Answers to these questions appear on page 86.

Note: In order to review as many chapter concepts as possible, some self-test questions include *more than one* correct answer. In these cases, you should indicate *all* of the correct answers.

1. A set of financial statements:
   a. Is intended to assist users in evaluating the financial position, profitability, and future prospects of an entity.
   b. Is intended to assist the Internal Revenue Service in determining the amount of income taxes owed by a business organization.
   c. Includes notes disclosing information necessary for the proper interpretation of the statements.
   d. Is intended to assist investors and creditors in making decisions involving the allocation of economic resources.

2. Which of the following statements is *not* consistent with generally accepted accounting principles relating to asset valuation?
   a. Many assets are originally recorded in accounting records at their cost to the business entity.
   b. Subtracting total liabilities from total assets indicates what the owners' equity in the business is worth under current market conditions.
   c. Accountants assume that assets such as office supplies, land, and buildings will be used in business operations rather than sold at current market prices.
   d. Accountants prefer to base the valuation of assets upon objective, verifiable evidence rather than upon appraisals or personal opinion.

3. Arrowhead Boat Shop purchased a truck for $12,000, making a down payment of $5,000 cash and signing a $7,000 note payable due in 60 days. As a result of this transaction:
   a. Total assets increased by $12,000.
   b. Total liabilities increased by $7,000.
   c. From the viewpoint of a short-term creditor, this transaction makes the business more liquid.
   d. This transaction had no immediate effect on the owners' equity in the business.

4. A transaction caused a $10,000 *decrease* in both total assets and total liabilities. This transaction could have been:
   a. Purchase of a delivery truck for $10,000 cash.
   b. An asset with a cost of $10,000 was destroyed by fire.
   c. Repayment of a $10,000 bank loan.
   d. Collection of a $10,000 account receivable.

5. Which of the following is (are) correct about a company's balance sheet?
   a. It displays sources and uses of cash for the period.
   b. It is an expansion of the basic accounting equation: Assets = Liabilities + Owners' Equity.
   c. It is sometimes referred to as a statement of financial position.
   d. It is unnecessary if both an income statement and statement of cash flows are available.

6. Which of the following would you expect to find in a correctly prepared income statement?
   a. Cash balance at the end of the period.
   b. Revenues earned during the period.
   c. Contributions by the owner during the period.
   d. Expenses incurred during the period to earn revenues.
7. What information would you find in a statement of cash flows that you would not be able to get from the other two primary financial statements?
   a. Cash provided by or used in financing activities.
   b. Cash balance at the end of the period.
   c. Total liabilities due to creditors at the end of the period.
   d. Net income.
8. Which of the following statements relating to the role of professional judgment in the financial reporting process is (are) valid?
   a. Different accountants may evaluate similar situations differently.
   b. The determination of which items should be disclosed in notes to financial statements requires professional judgment.
   c. Once a complete list of generally accepted accounting principles is prepared, judgment by accountants will no longer enter into the financial reporting process.
   d. The possibility exists that professional judgment later may prove to have been incorrect.

ASSIGNMENT MATERIAL

DISCUSSION QUESTIONS

1. In broad general terms, what is the purpose of accounting?
2. Why is a knowledge of accounting terms and concepts useful to persons other than professional accountants?
3. In broad terms, what is a financial statement?
4. What is the relationship between time and financial statements?
5. What is the distinction between annual and interim financial statements?
6. What is a business transaction? Give several examples of business transactions and several events that may occur that are not business transactions.
7. Explain briefly why each of the following groups might be interested in the financial statements of a business:
   a. Creditors
   b. Potential investors
   c. Labor unions
8. What is the primary characteristic of the form of business organization called the sole proprietorship?
9. In general terms, what are revenues and expenses? How are they related in the determination of an enterprise's net income or net loss?
10. Why is the statement of financial position, or balance sheet, a logical place to begin a discussion of financial statements?
11. What is the basic accounting equation? Briefly define the three primary elements in the equation.
12. What is meant by the cost principle, and how is that principle related to accounting for assets?
13. Why is the going-concern assumption an important consideration in understanding financial statements?
14. What is meant by the terms *inflation* and *deflation,* and how do they relate to the stable monetary unit assumption underlying financial statements?
15. Can a business transaction cause one asset to increase without affecting any other asset, liability, or owners' equity?

16. Give an example of business transactions that would:
    a. Cause one asset to increase and another asset to decrease, with no effect on either liabilities or owners' equity.
    b. Cause both total assets and liabilities to increase with no effect on owners' equity.
17. What is meant by the terms *positive cash flows* and *negative cash flows*? How do they relate to revenues and expenses?
18. What are the three categories commonly found in a statement of cash flows, and what is included in each category?
19. What is meant by the statement "The financial statements articulate"?
20. What are the major differences in the owners' equity sections of the balance sheet for a sole proprietorship, partnership, and corporation?
21. What is meant by the term *adequate disclosure*, and how do accountants fulfill this requirement in the preparation of financial statements?
22. What is meant by the term *window dressing* when referring to financial statements?
23. What are the characteristics of a strong income statement?
24. What are the characteristics of a strong statement of cash flows?

EXERCISES

EXERCISE 2.1

The Nature of Assets and Liabilities

LO 3

Assets and liabilities are important elements of a company's financial position.
a. Define *assets*. Give three examples of assets other than cash that might appear in the balance sheet of (1) **American Airlines** and (2) a professional sports team, such as the **Boston Celtics**.
b. Define *liabilities*. Give three examples of liabilities that might appear in the balance sheet of (1) **American Airlines** and (2) a professional sports team, such as the **Boston Celtics**.

EXERCISE 2.2

Preparing a Balance Sheet

LO 4

The night manager of Majestic Limousine Service, who had no accounting background, prepared the following balance sheet for the company at February 28, 2002. The dollar amounts were taken directly from the company's accounting records and are correct. However, the balance sheet contains a number of errors in its headings, format, and the classification of assets, liabilities, and owners' equity.

MAJESTIC LIMO
Manager's Report
8 P.M. Thursday

Assets		Owners' Equity	
Capital Stock	$100,000	Accounts Receivable	$ 78,000
Retained Earnings	62,000	Notes Payable	288,000
Cash	69,000	Supplies	14,000
Building	80,000	Land	70,000
Automobiles	165,000	Accounts Payable	26,000
	$476,000		$476,000

Prepare a corrected balance sheet. Include a proper heading.

EXERCISE 2.3

Preparing a Balance Sheet

LO 4

The balance sheet items of the Prosser Company as of December 31, 2002, follow in random order. You are to prepare a balance sheet for the company, using a similar sequence for assets as illustrated in Exhibit 2–9. You must compute the amount for Retained Earnings.

Land $90,000	Office Equipment . . . . $ 12,400
Accounts Payable 43,800	Building 210,000
Accounts Receivable 56,700	Capital Stock 75,000
Cash 36,300	Notes Payable 207,000
	Retained Earnings . . . . ?

EXERCISE 2.4
Accounting Principles and Asset Valuation

LO 2

The following cases relate to the valuation of assets. Consider each case independently.

a. World-Wide Travel Agency has office supplies costing $1,700 on hand at the balance sheet date. These supplies were purchased from a supplier that does not give cash refunds. World-Wide's management believes that the company could sell these supplies for no more than $500 if it were to advertise them for sale. However, the company expects to use these supplies and to purchase more when they are gone. In its balance sheet, the supplies were presented at $500.

b. Perez Corporation purchased land in 1955 for $20,000. In 2002, it purchased a similar parcel of land for $300,000. In its 2002 balance sheet, the company presented these two parcels of land at a combined amount of $320,000.

c. At December 30, 2002, Lenier, Inc., purchased a computer system from a mail-order supplier for $14,000. The retail value of the system—according to the mail-order supplier—was $20,000. On January 7, however, the system was stolen during a burglary. In its December 31, 2002, balance sheet, Lenier showed this computer system at $14,000 and made no reference to its retail value or to the burglary. The December balance sheet was issued in February of 2003.

In each case, indicate the appropriate balance sheet amount of the asset under generally accepted accounting principles. If the amount assigned by the company is incorrect, briefly explain the accounting principles that have been violated. If the amount is correct, identify the accounting principles that justify this amount.

EXERCISE 2.5
Using the Accounting Equation

LO 3

Compute the missing amounts in the following table:

	Assets	=	Liabilities	+	Owners' Equity
a.	$578,000		$342,000		?
b.	?		562,500		$575,000
c.	307,500		?		192,500

EXERCISE 2.6
The Accounting Equation

LO 3

A number of business transactions carried out by Weller Manufacturing Company are as follows:

a. Borrowed money from a bank.
b. Sold land for cash at a price equal to its cost.
c. Paid a liability.
d. Returned for credit some of the office equipment previously purchased on credit but not yet paid for. (Treat this the opposite of a transaction in which you purchased office equipment on credit.)
e. Sold land for cash at a price in excess of cost. (Hint: The difference between cost and sales price represents a gain that will be in the company's income statement.)
f. Purchased a computer on credit.
g. The owner invested cash in the business.
h. Purchased office equipment for cash.
i. Collected an account receivable.

Indicate the effects of each of these transactions on the total amounts of the company's assets, liabilities, and owners' equity. Organize your answer in tabular form, using the following column headings and the code letters **I** for increase, **D** for decrease, and **NE** for no effect. The answer for transaction **a** is provided as an example:

Transaction	Assets	=	Liabilities	+	Owners' Equity
(a)	I		I		NE

EXERCISE 2.7
Effects of Business Transactions
LO 3

For each of the following categories, state concisely a transaction that will have the required effect on the elements of the accounting equation.
a. Increase an asset and increase a liability.
b. Decrease an asset and decrease a liability.
c. Increase one asset and decrease another asset.
d. Increase an asset and increase owners' equity.
e. Increase one asset, decrease another asset, and increase a liability.

EXERCISE 2.8
Forms of Business Organization
LO 8

Felker Software Company has assets of $850,000 and liabilities of $460,000.
a. Prepare the owners' equity section of Felker's balance sheet under each of the following *independent* assumptions:
  1. The business is organized as a sole proprietorship, owned by Johanna Schmidt.
  2. The business is organized as a partnership, owned by Johanna Schmidt and Mikki Yato. Schmidt's equity amounts to $230,000.
  3. The business is a corporation with 25 stockholders, each of whom originally invested $10,000 in exchange for shares of the company's capital stock. The remainder of the stockholders' equity has resulted from profitable operation of the business.
b. Assume that you are a loan officer at Security Bank. Felker has applied to your bank for a large loan to finance the development of new products. Does it matter to you whether Felker is organized as a sole proprietorship, a partnership, or a corporation? Explain.

EXERCISE 2.9
Factors Contributing to Solvency
LO 4

Explain whether each of the following balance sheet items increases, reduces, or has no direct effect on a company's ability to pay its obligations as they come due. Explain your reasoning.
a. Cash
b. Accounts Payable
c. Accounts Receivable
d. Capital Stock

EXERCISE 2.10
Professional Judgment
LO 2

Professional judgment plays a major role in the practice of accounting.
a. In general terms, explain why judgment enters into the accounting process.
b. Identify at least three situations in which accountants must rely on their professional judgment, rather than on official rules.

EXERCISE 2.11
Statement of Cash Flows
LO 6

During the month of October 2002, Oppenheimer Company had the following transactions:
1. Revenues of $10,000 were earned and received in cash.
2. Bank loans of $2,000 were paid off.
3. Equipment of $2,500 was purchased.
4. Expenses of $7,200 were paid.
5. Additional shares of capital stock were sold for $6,000.

Assuming that the cash balance at the beginning of the month was $3,450, prepare a statement of cash flows that displays operating, investing, and financing activities and that reconciles the beginning and ending cash balances.

EXERCISE 2.12
Income Statement
LO 5

Jiminez, Inc., had the following transactions during the month of March 2002. Prepare an income statement based on this information, being careful to include only those items that should appear in that financial statement.
1. Cash received from bank loans was $10,000.
2. Revenues earned and received in cash were $9,500.

3. Dividends of $4,000 were paid to stockholders.
4. Expenses incurred and paid were $6,270.

EXERCISE 2.13

Income Statement

LO 5

An inexperienced accountant for Burdette Company prepared the following income statement for the month of August 2002:

BURDETTE COMPANY August 31, 2002		
Revenues:		
Services provided to customers	$12,000	
Investment by stockholders	5,000	
Loan from bank	15,000	$32,000
Expenses:		
Payments to long-term creditors	$ 9,000	
Expenses required to provide services to customers	7,500	
Purchase of land	16,000	32,500
Net loss		$ 500

Prepare a revised income statement in accordance with generally accepted accounting principles.

EXERCISE 2.14

Statement of Cash Flows

LO 6

Based on the information for Burdette Company in Exercise 2.13, prepare a statement of cash flows in a form consistent with generally accepted accounting principles. You may assume all transactions were in cash and that the beginning cash balance was $7,200.

EXERCISE 2.15

Articulation of Financial Statements

LO 7

John Franklin, sole owner of Franklin Mattress Company, has an ownership interest in the company of $60,000 at the beginning of the year 2002. During that year, he invested an additional $10,000 in the company and the company reported a net income of $25,000. Determine the balance of owners' equity that will appear in the balance sheet at the end of 2002, and explain how the amount of net income articulates with that figure in the balance sheet.

EXERCISE 2.16

Window Dressing Financial Statements

LO 10

Prepare a two-column analysis that illustrates steps management might take to improve the appearance of its company's financial statements. In the left column, briefly identify three steps that might be taken. In the right column, briefly describe for each step the impact on the balance sheet, income statement, and statement of cash flows. If there is no impact on one or more of these financial statements, indicate that.

EXERCISE 2.17

Tootsie Roll Industries, Inc. Financial Statements

LO 4, 5, 6

Locate the balance sheet, income statement, and statement of cash flows of **Tootsie Roll Industries, Inc.** in Appendix A of your text. Review those statements and then respond to the following for the year ended December 31, 2000.
a. Did the company have a net income or net loss for the year? How much?
b. What were the cash balances at the beginning and end of the year? What were the most important causes of the cash decrease during the year? (Treat "cash equivalents" as if they were cash.)
c. What is the largest asset and the largest liability included in the company's balance sheet at the end of the year?

EXERCISE 2.18

Assessing Financial Results

LO 5

Intel's 2000 annual report actually includes income statements for three years—1998, 1999, and 2000. Net income for these three years is presented as follows (all in millions): $6,068 (1998), $7,314 (1999), and $10,535 (2000). As you can see, the amount of net income went up each year when compared with the previous year. Further analysis of the same income statements reveals that revenues were the following amounts for these same years (all in millions): $26,273 (1998), $29,389 (1999), and $33,726 (2000). State each year's net income as a percentage of revenues and comment briefly on the trend over the three-year period.

PROBLEMS

PROBLEM 2.1
Preparing and Evaluating a Balance Sheet

LO 4

Listed below in random order are the items to be included in the balance sheet of Juarez Mountain Lodge at December 31, 2002:

Equipment	$ 39,200	Buildings	$450,000
Land	425,000	Capital Stock	135,000
Accounts Payable	54,800	Cash	21,400
Accounts Receivable	10,600	Furnishings	58,700
Salaries Payable	33,500	Snowmobiles	15,400
Interest Payable	12,000	Notes Payable	620,000
		Retained Earnings	?

Instructions

a. Prepare a balance sheet at December 31, 2002. Include a proper heading and organize your balance sheet similar to Exhibit 2–9. (After "Buildings," you may list the remaining assets in any order.) You will need to compute the amount to be shown for retained earnings.

b. Assume that no payment is due on the notes payable until 2004. Does this balance sheet indicate that the company is in a strong financial position as of December 31, 2002? Explain briefly.

PROBLEM 2.2
Interpreting the Effects of Business Transactions

LO 3

The following six transactions of Max's Moving Company, a corporation, are summarized in equation form, with each of the six transactions identified by a letter. For each of the transactions (a) through (f) write a separate statement explaining the nature of the transaction. For example, the explanation of transaction (a) could be as follows: Purchased equipment for cash at a cost of $3,200.

	Assets					= Liabilities +	Owners' Equity
	Cash +	Accounts Receivable +	Land +	Building +	Equipment =	Accounts Payable +	Capital Stock
Balances	$26,000	$39,000	$45,000	$110,000	$36,000	$42,000	$214,000
(a)	−3,200				+3,200		
Balances	$22,800	$39,000	$45,000	$110,000	$39,200	$42,000	$214,000
(b)	+900	−900					
Balances	$23,700	$38,100	$45,000	$110,000	$39,200	$42,000	$214,000
(c)	−3,500				+13,500	+10,000	
Balances	$20,200	$38,100	$45,000	$110,000	$52,700	$52,000	$214,000
(d)	−14,500					−14,500	
Balances	$ 5,700	$38,100	$45,000	$110,000	$52,700	$37,500	$214,000
(e)	+15,000						+15,000
Balances	$20,700	$38,100	$45,000	$110,000	$52,700	$37,500	$229,000
(f)					+3,500	+3,500	
Balances	$20,700	$38,100	$45,000	$110,000	$56,200	$41,000	$229,000

PROBLEM 2.3
Recording the Effects of Transactions

LO 3

United Communications was organized on December 1 of the current year and had the following account balances at December 31, listed in tabular form:

	Assets				=	Liabilities		+	Owners' Equity
	Cash +	Land +	Building +	Office Equipment	=	Notes Payable +	Accounts Payable	+	Capital Stock
Balances	$37,000	$95,000	$125,000	$51,250		$80,000	$28,250		$200,000

Early in January, the following transactions were carried out by United Communications:

1. Sold capital stock to owners for $35,000.
2. Purchased land and a small office building for a total price of $90,000, of which $35,000 was the value of the land and $55,000 was the value of the building. Paid $22,500 in cash and signed a note payable for the remaining $67,500.
3. Bought several computer systems on credit for $9,500 (30-day open account).
4. Obtained a loan from Capital Bank in the amount of $20,000. Signed a note payable.
5. Paid the $28,250 account payable due as of December 31.

Instructions

a. List the December 31 balances of assets, liabilities, and owners' equity in tabular form as shown.
b. Record the effects of each of the five transactions in the format illustrated in Exhibit 2–11. Show the totals for all columns after each transaction.

PROBLEM 2.4

An Alternate Problem on Recording the Effects of Transactions

LO 3

The items making up the balance sheet of Crabtree Truck Rental at December 31 are listed below in tabular form similar to the illustration of the accounting equation in Exhibit 2–11.

	Assets				=	Liabilities		+	Owners' Equity
	Cash +	Accounts Receivable +	Trucks +	Office Equipment	=	Notes Payable +	Accounts Payable	+	Capital Stock
Balances	$9,500	$13,900	$68,000	$3,800		$20,000	$10,200		$65,000

During a short period after December 31, Crabtree Truck Rental had the following transactions:

1. Bought office equipment at a cost of $2,700. Paid cash.
2. Collected $4,000 of accounts receivable.
3. Paid $3,200 of accounts payable.
4. Borrowed $10,000 from a bank. Signed a note payable for that amount.
5. Purchased two trucks for $30,500. Paid $15,000 cash and signed a note payable for the balance.
6. Sold additional stock to investors for $40,000.

Instructions

a. List the December 31 balances of assets, liabilities, and owners' equity in tabular form as shown above.
b. Record the effects of each of the six transactions in the preceding tabular arrangement. Show the totals for all columns after each transaction.

PROBLEM 2.5
Preparing a Balance Sheet; Effects of a Change in Assets

LO 4

HERE COME THE CLOWNS! is the name of a traveling circus. The ledger accounts of the business at June 30, 2002, are listed here in alphabetical order:

Accounts Payable	$ 26,100	Notes Payable	$180,000
Accounts Receivable	7,450	Notes Receivable	9,500
Animals	189,060	Props and Equipment	89,580
Cages	24,630	Retained Earnings	27,230
Capital Stock	310,000	Salaries Payable	9,750
Cash	?	Tents	63,000
Costumes	31,500	Trucks & Wagons	105,840

Instructions
a. Prepare a balance sheet by using these items and computing the amount of Cash at June 30, 2002. Organize your balance sheet similar to the one illustrated in Exhibit 2–10. (After "Accounts Receivable," you may list the remaining assets in any order.) Include a proper balance sheet heading.

b. Assume that late in the evening of June 30, after your balance sheet had been prepared, a fire destroyed one of the tents, which had cost $14,300. The tent was not insured. Explain what changes would be required in your June 30 balance sheet to reflect the loss of this asset.

PROBLEM 2.6
Preparing a Balance Sheet—a Second Problem

LO 4

The following list of balance sheet items, are in random order, for Rocky Mountain Farms at September 30, 2002:

Land	$590,000	Fences and Gates	$ 33,570
Barns and Sheds	78,300	Irrigation System	20,125
Notes Payable	530,000	Cash	16,710
Accounts Receivable	22,365	Livestock	120,780
Citrus Trees	76,650	Farm Machinery	42,970
Accounts Payable	77,095	Retained Earnings	?
Property Taxes Payable	9,135	Wages Payable	5,820
Capital Stock	290,000		

Instructions
a. Prepare a balance sheet by using these items and computing the amount for retained earnings. Use a sequence of assets similar to that illustrated in Exhibit 2–10. (After "Barns and Sheds" you may list the remaining assets in any order.) Include a proper heading for your balance sheet.

b. Assume that on September 30, immediately after this balance sheet was prepared, a tornado completely destroyed one of the barns. This barn had a cost of $13,700, and was not insured against this type of disaster. Explain what changes would be required in your September 30 balance sheet to reflect the loss of this barn.

PROBLEM 2.7
Preparing a Balance Sheet and Statement of Cash Flows; Effects of Business Transactions

LO 3, 4, 6

The balance sheet items for The Oven Bakery (arranged in alphabetical order) were as follows at August 1, 2002. (You are to compute the missing figure for retained earnings.)

Accounts Payable	$16,200	Capital Stock	$80,000
Accounts Receivable	11,260	Land	67,000
Building	84,000	Notes Payable	74,900
Cash	6,940	Salaries Payable	8,900
Equipment and Fixtures	44,500	Supplies	7,000

During the next two days, the following transactions occurred:

Aug. 2 Additional capital stock was sold for $25,000. The accounts payable were paid in full. (No payment was made on the notes payable or income taxes payable.)

Aug. 3 Equipment was purchased at a cost of $7,200 to be paid within 10 days. Supplies were purchased for $1,250 cash from a restaurant supply center that was going out of business. These supplies would have cost $1,890 if purchased through normal channels.

Instructions

a. Prepare a balance sheet at August 1, 2002.

b. Prepare a balance sheet at August 3, 2002, and a statement of cash flows for August 1–3. Classify the payment of accounts payable and the purchase of supplies as operating activities.

c. Assume the note payable does not come due for several years. Is The Oven Bakery in a stronger financial position on August 1 or on August 3? Explain briefly.

PROBLEM 2.8

Preparing Financial Statements; Effects of Business Transactions

LO 4, 5, 6

The balance sheet items of The Foster Soda Shop (arranged in alphabetical order) were as follows at the close of business on September 30, 2002:

Accounts Payable	$ 8,500	Land	$55,000
Accounts Receivable	1,250	Capital Stock	50,000
Building	45,500	Notes Payable	?
Cash	7,400	Retained Earnings	4,090
Furniture and Fixtures	20,000	Supplies	3,440

The transactions occurring during the first week of October were:

Oct. 3 Additional capital stock was sold for $30,000. The accounts payable were paid in full. (No payment was made on the notes payable.)

Oct. 6 More furniture was purchased on account at a cost of $18,000, to be paid within 30 days. Supplies were purchased for $1,000 cash from a restaurant supply center that was going out of business. These supplies would have cost $1,875 if purchased under normal circumstances.

Oct. 1–6 Revenues of $5,500 were earned and paid in cash. Expenses required to earn the revenues of $4,000 were incurred and paid in cash.

Instructions

a. Prepare a balance sheet at September 30, 2002. (You will need to compute the missing figure for Notes Payable.)

b. Prepare a balance sheet at October 6, 2002. Also prepare an income statement and a statement of cash flows for the period October 1–6, 2002. In your statement of cash flows, treat the purchase of supplies and the payment of accounts payable as operating activities.

c. Assume the note payable does not come due for several years. Is The Foster Soda Shop in a stronger financial position on September 30 or on October 6? Explain briefly.

PROBLEM 2.9

Preparing a Balance Sheet; Discussion of Accounting Principles

LO 4, 8

Helen Berkeley is the founder and manager of Berkeley Playhouse. The business needs to obtain a bank loan to finance the production of its next play. As part of the loan application, Berkeley was asked to prepare a balance sheet for the business. She prepared the following balance sheet, which is arranged correctly but which contains several errors with respect to such concepts as the business entity and the valuation of assets, liabilities, and owner's equity.

BERKELEY PLAYHOUSE
Balance Sheet
September 30, 2002

Assets		Liabilities & Owner's Equity	
Cash	$ 21,900	Liabilities:	
Accounts Receivable	132,200	Accounts Payable	$ 6,000
Props and Costumes	3,000	Salaries Payable	29,200
Theater Building	27,000	Total liabilities	$35,200
Lighting Equipment	9,400	Owner's equity:	
Automobile	15,000	Helen Berkeley, Capital	50,000
Total	$208,500	Total	$85,200

In discussions with Berkeley and by reviewing the accounting records of Berkeley Playhouse, you discover the following facts:

1. The amount of cash, $21,900, includes $15,000 in the company's bank account, $1,900 on hand in the company's safe, and $5,000 in Berkeley's personal savings account.
2. The accounts receivable, listed as $132,200, include $7,200 owed to the business by Artistic Tours. The remaining $125,000 is Berkeley's estimate of future ticket sales from September 30 through the end of the year (December 31).
3. Berkeley explains to you that the props and costumes were purchased several days ago for $18,000. The business paid $3,000 of this amount in cash and issued a note payable to Actors' Supply Co. for the remainder of the purchase price ($15,000). As this note is not due until January of next year, it was not included among the company's liabilities.
4. Berkeley Playhouse rents the theater building from Kievits International at a rate of $3,000 a month. The $27,000 shown in the balance sheet represents the rent paid through September 30 of the current year. Kievits International acquired the building seven years ago at a cost of $135,000.
5. The lighting equipment was purchased on September 26 at a cost of $9,400, but the stage manager says that it isn't worth a dime.
6. The automobile is Berkeley's classic 1978 Jaguar, which she purchased two years ago for $9,000. She recently saw a similar car advertised for sale at $15,000. She does not use the car in the business, but it has a personalized license plate that reads "PLAHOUS."
7. The accounts payable include business debts of $3,900 and the $2,100 balance of Berkeley's personal Visa card.
8. Salaries payable include $25,000 offered to Mario Dane to play the lead role in a new play opening next December and $4,200 still owed to stagehands for work done through September 30.
9. When Berkeley founded Berkeley Playhouse several years ago, she invested $20,000 in the business. However, Live Theatre, Inc., recently offered to buy her business for $50,000. Therefore, she listed this amount as her equity in the above balance sheet.

Instructions

a. Prepare a corrected balance sheet for Berkeley Playhouse at September 30, 2002.
b. For each of the nine numbered items above, explain your reasoning in deciding whether or not to include the items in the balance sheet and in determining the proper dollar valuation.

PROBLEM 2.10
Preparing a Balance Sheet; Discussion of Accounting Principles

LO 2, 4

Hollywood Scripts is a service-type enterprise in the entertainment field, and its manager, William Pippin, has only a limited knowledge of accounting. Pippin prepared the following balance sheet, which, although arranged satisfactorily, contains certain errors with respect to such concepts as the business entity and asset valuation. Pippin owns all of the corporation's outstanding stock.

HOLLYWOOD SCRIPTS
Balance Sheet
November 30, 2002

Assets		Liabilities & Owner's Equity	
Cash	$ 5,150	Liabilities:	
Notes Receivable	2,700	Notes Payable	$ 67,000
Accounts Receivable	2,450	Accounts Payable	35,805
Land	70,000	Total liabilities	$102,805
Building	54,320	Owner's equity:	
Office Furniture	8,850	Capital Stock	5,000
Other Assets	22,400	Retained Earnings	58,065
Total	$165,870	Total	$165,870

In discussion with Pippin and by inspection of the accounting records, you discover the following facts:

1. The amount of cash, $5,150, includes $3,400 in the company's bank account, $540 on hand in the company's safe, and $1,210 in Pippin's personal savings account.
2. One of the notes receivable in the amount of $500 is an IOU that Pippin received in a poker game several years ago. The IOU is signed by "B.K.," whom Pippin met at the game but has not heard from since.
3. Office furniture includes $2,900 for a Persian rug for the office purchased on November 20. The total cost of the rug was $9,400. The business paid $2,900 in cash and issued a note payable to Zoltan Carpet for the balance due ($6,500). As no payment on the note is due until January, this debt is not included in the liabilities above.
4. Also included in the amount for office furniture is a computer that cost $2,525 but is not on hand because Pippin donated it to a local charity.
5. The "Other Assets" of $22,400 represent the total amount of income taxes Pippin has paid the federal government over a period of years. Pippin believes the income tax law to be unconstitutional, and a friend who attends law school has promised to help Pippin recover the taxes paid as soon as he passes the bar exam.
6. The asset "Land" was acquired at a cost of $39,000 but was increased to a valuation of $70,000 when a friend of Pippin offered to pay that much for it if Pippin would move the building off the lot.
7. The accounts payable include business debts of $32,700 and the $3,105 balance owed on Pippin's personal MasterCard.

Instructions

a. Prepare a corrected balance sheet at November 30, 2002.
b. For each of the seven numbered items above, use a separate numbered paragraph to explain whether the treatment followed by Pippin is in accordance with generally accepted accounting principles.

CASES AND UNSTRUCTURED PROBLEMS

CASE 2.1

Content of a Balance Sheet

LO 4

You are to prepare a balance sheet for a *hypothetical* business entity of your choosing (or specified by your instructor). Include in your balance sheet the types of assets and liabilities that you think the entity might have, and show these items at what you believe would be realistic dollar amounts. Make reasonable assumptions with regard to the company's capital stock and retained earnings.

CASE 2.2
Using Financial Statements
LO 4, 5, 6

Note: The purpose of this assignment is to help you visualize the types of assets and liabilities relating to the operations of a specific type of business. You should complete this assignment *without* referring to an actual balance sheet for this type of business.

Obtain from the library the *annual report* of a well-known company (or a company specified by your instructor).

Instructions
From the balance sheet, income statement, statement of cash flows, and notes to the financial statements, answer the following:

a. What are the largest assets included in the company's balance sheet? Why would a company of this type (size and industry) have a large investment in this particular type of asset?

b. In reviewing the company's statement of cash flows:
   1. What are the primary sources and uses of cash from investing activities?
   2. Did investing activities cause the company's cash to increase or decrease?
   3. What are the primary sources and uses of cash from financing activities?
   4. Did financing activities cause the company's cash to increase or decrease?

c. In reviewing the company's income statement, did the company have a net income or a net loss for the most recent year? What percentage of total revenues was that net income or net loss?

d. Select three items in the notes accompanying the financial statements and explain briefly the importance of these items to people making decisions about investing in, or extending credit to, this company.

e. Assume that you are a lender, and this company has asked to borrow an amount of cash equal to 10% of its total assets, to be repaid in 90 days. Would you consider this company to be a good credit risk? Explain.

CASE 2.3
Using a Balance Sheet
LO 4

Moon Corporation and Star Corporation are in the same line of business and both were recently organized, so it may be assumed that the recorded costs for assets are close to current market values. The balance sheets for the two companies are as follows at July 31, 2002:

MOON CORPORATION
Balance Sheet
July 31, 2002

Assets		Liabilities & Owners' Equity		
Cash	$ 18,000	Liabilities:		
Accounts Receivable	26,000	Notes Payable		
Land	37,200	(due in 60 days)		$ 12,400
Building	38,000	Accounts Payable		9,600
Office Equipment	1,200	Total liabilities		$ 22,000
		Stockholders' equity:		
		Capital Stock	$60,000	
		Retained Earnings	38,400	98,400
Total	$120,400	Total		$120,400

STAR CORPORATION
Balance Sheet
July 31, 2002

Assets		Liabilities & Owners' Equity		
Cash	$ 4,800	Liabilities:		
Accounts Receivable	9,600	Notes Payable		
Land	96,000	(due in 60 days)		$ 22,400
Building	60,000	Accounts Payable		43,200
Office Equipment	12,000	Total liabilities		$ 65,600
		Stockholders' equity:		
		Capital Stock	$72,000	
		Retained Earnings	44,800	116,800
Total	$182,400	Total		$182,400

Instructions

a. Assume that you are a banker and that each company has applied to you for a 90-day loan of $12,000. Which would you consider to be the more favorable prospect? Explain your answer fully.

b. Assume that you are an investor considering purchasing all the capital stock of one or both of the companies. For which business would you be willing to pay the higher price? Do you see any indication of a financial crisis that you might face shortly after buying either company? Explain your answer fully. (For either decision, additional information would be useful, but you are to reach your decision on the basis of the information available.)

CASE 2.4

Using Statements of Cash Flows

LO 6

Bill Prince is employed as a bank loan officer for First State Bank. He is comparing two companies that have applied for loans, and he wants your help in evaluating those companies. The two companies—Morris, Inc., and Walker Company—are approximately the same size and had approximately the same cash balance at the beginning of 2001. Because the total cash flows for the three-year period are virtually the same, Bill is inclined to evaluate the two companies as equal in terms of their desirability as loan candidates.

Abbreviated information (in thousands of dollars) from Morris, Inc., and Walker Company is as follows:

	Morris, Inc.			Walker Company		
	2001	2002	2003	2001	2002	2003
Cash flows from:						
Operating activities	$10	$13	$15	$ 8	$3	$(2)
Investing activities	(5)	(8)	(10)	(7)	(5)	8
Financing activities	8	(3)	1	12	4	-0-
Net from all activities	$13	$ 2	$ 6	$13	$2	$6

Instructions

a. Do you agree with Bill's preliminary assessment that the two companies are approximately equal in terms of their strength as loan candidates? Why or why not?

b. What might account for the fact that Walker Company's cash flow from financing activities is zero in 2003?

c. Generally, what would you advise Bill with regard to using statements of cash flows in evaluating loan candidates?

CASE 2.5

Ethics and Window Dressing

LO 10

The date is November 18, 2002. You are the chief executive officer of Omega Software—a publicly owned company that is currently in financial difficulty. Omega needs new large bank loans if it is to survive.

You have been negotiating with several banks, but each has asked to see your 2002 financial statements, which will be dated December 31. These statements will, of course, be audited. You are now meeting with other corporate officers to discuss the situation, and the following suggestions have been made:

1. "We are planning to buy the WordMaster Software Co. for $8 million cash in December. The owners of WordMaster are in no hurry; if we delay this acquisition until January, we'll have $8 million more cash at year-end. That should make us look a lot more solvent."

2. "At year-end, we'll owe accounts payable of about $18 million. If we were to show this liability in our balance sheet at half that amount—say, $9 million—no one would know the difference. We could report the other $9 million as stockholders' equity and our financial position would appear much stronger."

3. "We owe Delta Programming $5 million, due in 90 days. I know some people at Delta. If we were to sign a note and pay them 12% interest, they'd let us postpone this debt for a year or more."

4. "We own land that cost us $2 million, but today is worth at least $6 million. Let's show it at $6 million in our balance sheet, and that will increase our total assets and our stockholders' equity by $4 million."

Instructions

Separately evaluate each of these four proposals to improve Omega Software's financial statements. Your evaluations should consider ethical and legal issues as well as accounting issues.

BUSINESS WEEK ASSIGNMENT

CASE 2.6

LO 1, 2, 6, 10

Cash Burn Rates at Dot-Coms

The importance of financial statement information for investors and creditors is illustrated in the following quote from the January 22, 2001, *Business Week* article, "Dead Companies Walking," by Peter Elstrom.

> A close look at the **financial statements** of about 500 tech and telecom companies show that the crunch is likely to get worse before it gets better. Particularly troubling are the low cash reserves at dozens of money losing players. Nearly 50 tech and telecom companies have 18 months or less of cash, based on conservative estimates of the current rates at which they're burning through their stashes. With investors refusing to pony up more dough, many of these upstarts are likely to close their doors or sell out to rivals . . . remember Theglobe.com? The New York community site saw its stock soar more than 600%, to $31.75, on its first day of trading in 1998. Now it's on life support, with shares at about 50 cents. At the current burn rate, the company's $25 million in cash will last about a year. In a recent financial filing, the company conceded that there is "substantial doubt" that it can continue in business.

Instructions

a. Identify which of the financial statements described in this chapter provide information about the cash burn rate of a company.

b. Describe how a cash burn rate could be calculated.

c. Explain why investors and creditors would be interested in a company's cash balance and its cash burn rate.

d. How does the financial filing of Theglobe.com, discussed in the article above, protect the public interest as described in the AICPA Code of Professional Conduct described in Chapter 1?

INTERNET ASSIGNMENTS

INTERNET 2.1

Gathering Financial Information

LO 4, 5, 9

We'd like to introduce you to EDGAR, the SEC's database of financial information about publicly owned companies. The SEC maintains EDGAR to increase the efficiency of financial reporting in the American economy and also to give the public free access to information about publicly owned companies.

Instructions

Access EDGAR at the following Internet address:

www.sec.gov

Click "Search for Company Filings" and then "Search the EDGAR archives." Then type MCDONALDS CORP into the search box and press the search key. Locate the most recent quarterly (10 Q) balance sheet.

a. What is the street address of McDonald's corporate headquarters?

b. Using the category "Financial Reports." Has the amount of the company's cash (and cash equivalents) increased or decreased since the beginning of the year?

c. Locate the income statement. What was the company's net income for the most recent quarter? Is this amount up or down from the preceding quarter or year?

d. How much cash was provided by operations during the quarter? Where did you find this information?

e. In Form 10Q, notes to the financial statements are called "Financial Comments." Select one of McDonald's financial comments and explain why it would be of interest to investors.

f. While you're in EDGAR, pick a company that interests you and learn more about it. Be prepared to tell the class which company you selected and explain what you learned.

Internet sites are time and date sensitive. It is the purpose of these exercises to have you explore the Internet. You may need to use the Yahoo! search engine http://www.yahoo.com (or another favorite search engine) to find a company's current Web address.

OUR COMMENTS ON THE "YOUR TURN" CASES

You as a Home Owner (p. 46) In both situations, sales of comparable homes in the same location provide information about the value of your home. However, since your home has not been recently sold, the specific home value (asset value) is unknown. The ethical dilemma arises in precisely what objective information to report. For example, if 10 homes in the immediate area have sold within the last three months, which of those sales would you report? If the real estate assessor's office asked for three comparable sales, what information might be provided? The assessor's office will be concerned about the objectivity of the reporting choices made by the home owner.

Because homeowners wish to minimize their tax burden, many municipalities employ city property appraisers to verify the value of real estate. This appraiser operates much like an independent public accountant who assesses whether financial statements are a fair representation of a company's financial position.

Alternatively, because homeowners wish to maximize the sales price of their homes they might choose different comparable home sales prices to report to a buyer than those chosen for the real estate assessor. Thus, although buyers may request comparable home sales information from the seller, they will usually undertake their own investigation (i.e., hire their own appraiser) to verify the value of the home.

The ethical issues are related to objective (not selective) reporting. Having independent parties make an independent assessment of the market price of your home mitigates some of the ethical issues related to objective reporting.

You as a Working College Student (p. 54) The assets you would need include a mower, a trimmer, one or more gas cans, and other similar items. You would also need certain other items, such as oil and gas, that are necessary for the proper functioning of your equipment. Finally, if you plan to work for people who live long distances from your location, you would need a truck or some way to transport your equipment and yourself to the work site. Revenues would consist primarily of amounts paid to you for your services. Expenses would include the cost of your equipment as well as gas, oil, and other necessities to maintain proper functioning of your equipment. You may also incur costs of repair and maintenance on your equipment. Essentially, you would know if you are doing well if you more than cover costs with the amounts you are taking in for your work. This requires detailed record keeping of your revenues and expenses.

You as an Investor (p. 59)   You might have several different objectives, but most people would be primarily interested in the potential for good return on their investment. For that reason, the financial strength of a company in which you invest is particularly important. In the income statement, you would be interested in whether the companies you are considering are profitable—do their revenues exceed their expenses? In the statements of financial position (balance sheets), you may be interested in the amount of their assets in comparison to their liabilities. In the statements of cash flows, you may be particularly interested in how cash is changing and the extent to which the company's operations are generating positive cash flows. Finally, you may find important information in notes to the financial statements and explanations by the management of each company concerning future plans and other aspects of the company that are not included in the primary financial statements.

ANSWERS TO SELF-TEST QUESTIONS

1. a, c, d   **2.** b   **3.** b, d   **4.** c   **5.** b, c   **6.** b, d   **7.** a   **8.** a, b, d

CHAPTER 3

THE ACCOUNTING CYCLE:

Capturing Economic Events

Learning Objectives

After studying this chapter, you should be able to:

1. Identify the steps in the accounting cycle and discuss the role of accounting records in an organization.
2. Describe a ledger account and a ledger.
3. State the rules of debit and credit for balance sheet accounts.
4. Explain the double-entry system of accounting.
5. Explain the purpose of a journal and its relationship to the ledger.
6. Explain the nature of *net income, revenue,* and *expenses.*
7. Apply the *realization* and *matching* principles in recording revenue and expenses.
8. Explain *why* revenues are recorded with credits and expenses are recorded with debits.
9. Prepare a trial balance and explain its uses and limitations.
10. Distinguish between accounting cycle procedures and the *knowledge* of accounting.

Courtesy of Pepsi Company

PepsiCo, Inc.

Capturing the economic events of a lemonade stand is a fairly simple process. In fact, for most lemonade stands, an empty cigar box easily serves as a complete information system.

Capturing the economic events of **PepsiCo, Inc.**, however, is an entirely different matter. This giant corporation generates annual revenue in excess of $20 billion from sales of its soft drink products, its Tropicana juices, and its Frito-Lay snack foods. Employing nearly 120,000 people, and operating hundreds of manufacturing facilities and thousands of warehouses and distribution centers, **PepsiCo, Inc.**, must somehow capture complex business transactions occurring in more than 160 countries worldwide.

From lemonade stands to multinational corporations, being able to efficiently capture the effects of economic events, such as sales orders and raw material purchases, is absolutely essential for survival. Companies like **PepsiCo, Inc.**, rely upon sophisticated computer systems to capture economic activities. Some small enterprises, however, may use paper ledgers and journals to record business transactions.

• • •

LO 1
Identify the steps in the accounting cycle and discuss the role of accounting records in an organization.

Although Overnight Auto Service engaged in several business transactions in the previous chapter, we did not illustrate how these events were captured by Overnight for use by management and other interested parties. This chapter demonstrates how accounting systems record economic events related to a variety of business transactions.

THE ACCOUNTING CYCLE

In Chapter 2, we illustrated several transactions of Overnight Auto Service that occurred during the last week in January 2002. We prepared a complete set of financial statements immediately following our discussion of these transactions. For practical purposes, businesses do not prepare new financial statements after every transaction. Rather, they accumulate the effects of individual transactions in their *accounting records*. Then, at regular intervals, the data in these records are used to prepare financial statements, income tax returns, and other types of reports.

The sequence of accounting procedures used to record, classify, and summarize accounting information in financial reports at regular intervals is often termed the **accounting cycle**. The accounting cycle begins with the initial recording of business transactions and concludes with the preparation of a complete set of formal financial statements. The term *cycle* indicates that these procedures must be repeated continuously to enable the business to prepare new, up-to-date, financial statements at reasonable intervals.

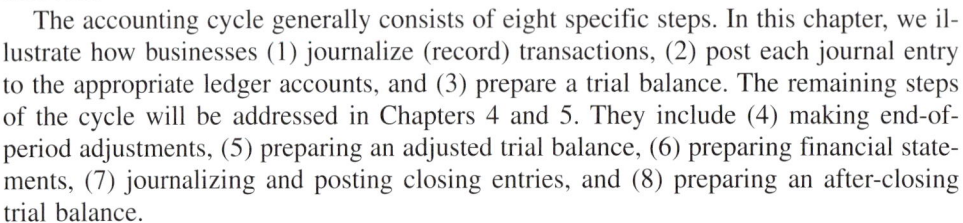

The accounting cycle generally consists of eight specific steps. In this chapter, we illustrate how businesses (1) journalize (record) transactions, (2) post each journal entry to the appropriate ledger accounts, and (3) prepare a trial balance. The remaining steps of the cycle will be addressed in Chapters 4 and 5. They include (4) making end-of-period adjustments, (5) preparing an adjusted trial balance, (6) preparing financial statements, (7) journalizing and posting closing entries, and (8) preparing an after-closing trial balance.

The Role of Accounting Records

The cyclical process of collecting financial information and maintaining accounting records does far more than facilitate the preparation of financial statements. Managers and employees of a business frequently use the information stored in the accounting records for such purposes as:

1. Establishing **accountability** for the assets and/or transactions under an individual's control.
2. Keeping track of routine business activities—such as the amounts of money in company bank accounts, amounts due from credit customers, or amounts owed to suppliers.
3. Obtaining detailed information about a particular transaction.
4. Evaluating the efficiency and performance of various departments within the organization.
5. Maintaining documentary evidence of the company's business activities. (For example, tax laws require companies to maintain accounting records supporting the amounts reported in tax returns.)

THE LEDGER

LO 2
Describe a ledger account and a ledger.

An accounting system includes a separate record for each item that appears in the financial statements. For example, a separate record is kept for the asset cash, showing all increases and decreases in cash resulting from the many transactions in which cash is received or paid. A similar record is kept for every other asset, for every liability, for owners' equity, and for every revenue and expense account appearing in the income statement.

The record used to keep track of the increases and decreases in financial statement items is termed a "ledger account" or, simply, an **account**. The entire group of accounts is kept together in an accounting record called a **ledger**.

THE USE OF ACCOUNTS

An account is a means of accumulating in one place all the information about changes in specific financial statement items, such as a particular asset or liability. For example, the Cash account provides a company's current cash balance, a record of its cash receipts, and a record of its cash disbursements.

In its simplest form, an account has only three elements: (1) a title; (2) a left side, which is called the *debit* side; and (3) a right side, which is called the *credit* side. This form of an account, illustrated below and on the following page, is called a *T account* because of its resemblance to the letter "T." In a computerized system, of course, the elements of each account are stored and formatted electronically. More complete forms of accounts will be illustrated later.

Title of Account

Left or Debit Side	Right or Credit Side

My Notes

A T account—a ledger account in its simplest form

DEBIT AND CREDIT ENTRIES

An amount recorded on the left, or debit, side of an account is called a **debit**, or a debit entry. Likewise, any amount entered on the right, or credit, side is called a **credit**, or a credit entry. In simple terms, debits refer to the left side of an account, and credits refer to the right side of an account.

To illustrate the recording of debits and credits in an account, let us go back to the eight cash transactions of Overnight Auto Service, described in Chapter 2. When these cash transactions are recorded in the Cash account, the receipts are listed on the debit side, and the payments are listed on the credit side. The dates of the transactions may also be listed, as shown in the following illustration:

Cash

1/20	80,000	1/21	52,000
1/26	600	1/22	6,000
1/31	2,200	1/27	6,800
		1/31	200
		1/31	1,200
1/31 Balance	16,600		

My Notes

Cash transactions entered in ledger account

Each debit and credit entry in the Cash account represents a cash receipt or a cash payment. The amount of cash owned by the business at a given date is equal to the *balance* of the account on that date.

Determining the Balance of a T Account The balance of an account is the difference between the debit and credit entries in the account. If the debit total exceeds the credit total, the account has a *debit balance*; if the credit total exceeds the debit total, the account has a *credit balance*.

In our illustrated Cash account, a line has been drawn across the account following the last cash transaction recorded in January. The total cash receipts (debits) recorded in January amount to $82,800, and the total cash payments (credits) amount to $66,200. By subtracting the credit total from the debit total ($82,800 − $66,200), we determine that the Cash account has a debit balance of *$16,600* on January 31.

This debit balance is entered in the debit side of the account just below the line. In effect, the line creates a "fresh start" in the account, with the month-end balance representing the *net result* of all the previous debit and credit entries. The Cash account now shows the amount of cash owned by the business on January 31. In a balance sheet prepared at this date, Cash in the amount of $16,600 would be listed as an asset.

You as a Student

YOUR TURN

You probably do not use debits and credits in accounting for your personal financial activities. Does this mean that the concept of double-entry accounting does not apply to changes in your personal financial position? Explain and provide several examples.

*Our comments appear on page 133.

LO 3
State the rules of debit and credit for balance sheet accounts.

Debit Balances in Asset Accounts In the preceding illustration of a Cash account, increases were recorded on the left, or debit, side of the account and decreases were recorded on the right, or credit, side. The increases were greater than the decreases and the result was a debit balance in the account.

All asset accounts *normally have debit balances*. It is hard to imagine an account for an asset such as land having a credit balance, as this would indicate that the business had disposed of more land than it had ever acquired. (For some assets, such as cash, it is possible to acquire a credit balance—but such balances are only *temporary*.)

The fact that assets are located on the *left* side of the balance sheet is a convenient means of remembering the rule that an increase in an asset is recorded on the *left* (debit) side of the account and an asset account normally has a debit *(left-hand)* balance.

My Notes
Asset accounts normally have debit balances

Any Asset Account	
Debit (representing an increase)	Credit (representing a decrease)

Credit Balances in Liability and Owners' Equity Accounts Increases in liability and owners' equity accounts are recorded by credit entries and decreases in these accounts are recorded by debits. The relationship between entries in these accounts and their position on the balance sheet may be summed up as follows: (1) liabilities and owners' equity belong on the *right* side of the balance sheet, (2) an increase in a liability or an owners' equity account is recorded on the *right* (credit) side of the account, and (3) liability and owners' equity accounts normally have credit *(right-hand)* balances.

My Notes
Liability and owners' equity accounts normally have credit balances

Any Liability Account or Owners' Equity Account	
Debit (representing a decrease)	Credit (representing an increase)

Concise Statement of the Debit and Credit Rules The use of debits and credits to record changes in assets, liabilities, and owners' equity may be summarized as follows:

My Notes
Debit and credit rules

Asset Accounts	Liability & Owners' Equity Accounts
Normally have debit balances. Thus, increases are recorded by debits and decreases are recorded by credits.	Normally have credit balances. Thus, increases are recorded by credits and decreases are recorded by debits.

Double-Entry Accounting—The Equality of Debits and Credits

The rules for debits and credits are designed so that *every transaction is recorded by equal dollar amounts of debits and credits*. The reason for this equality lies in the relationship of the debit and credit rules to the accounting equation:

$$\underbrace{\text{Assets}}_{\text{Debit Balances}} = \underbrace{\text{Liabilities} + \text{Owners' Equity}}_{\text{Credit Balances}}$$

If this equation is to remain in balance, any change in the left side of the equation (assets) *must be accompanied by an equal change* in the right side (either liabilities or owners' equity). According to the debit and credit rules that we have just described, increases in the left side of the equation (assets) are recorded by *debits*, while increases in the right side (liabilities and owners' equity) are recorded by *credits*.

This system is often called **double-entry accounting**. The phrase *double-entry* refers to the need for both *debit entries* and *credit entries,* equal in dollar amount, to record every transaction. Virtually every business organization uses the double-entry system regardless of whether the company's accounting records are maintained manually or by computer. In addition, the double-entry system allows us to measure net income at the same time we record the effects of transactions on the balance sheet accounts.

LO 4
Explain the double-entry system of accounting.

RECORDING TRANSACTIONS IN LEDGER ACCOUNTS: AN ILLUSTRATION

To illustrate how to use debits and credits for recording transactions in accounts we return to the January transactions of Overnight Auto Service. At this point, we discuss only those transactions related to changes in the company's financial position and reported directly in its balance sheet. The revenue and expense transactions that took place on January 31 will be addressed later in the chapter.

Each transaction from January 20 through January 27 is analyzed first in terms of increases in assets, liabilities, and owners' equity. Second, we follow the debit and credit rules for entering these increases and decreases in specific accounts. Asset accounts are shown on the left side of the analysis; liability and owners' equity accounts are shown on the right side. For convenience in the following transactions, both the debit and credit entries for the transaction under discussion are shown in *red*. Entries relating to earlier transactions appear in *black*.

Jan. 20 Michael McBryan and family invested $80,000 cash in exchange for capital stock.

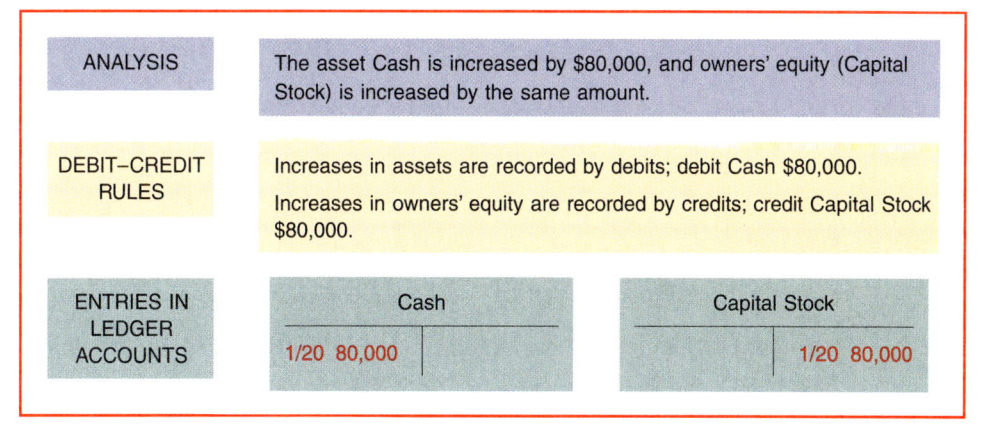

ANALYSIS	The asset Cash is increased by $80,000, and owners' equity (Capital Stock) is increased by the same amount.
DEBIT–CREDIT RULES	Increases in assets are recorded by debits; debit Cash $80,000. Increases in owners' equity are recorded by credits; credit Capital Stock $80,000.
ENTRIES IN LEDGER ACCOUNTS	**Cash** 1/20 80,000 **Capital Stock** 1/20 80,000

My Notes
Owners invest cash in the business

Jan. 21 Representing Overnight, McBryan negotiated with both the City of Santa Teresa and Metropolitan Transit Authority (MTA) to purchase an abandoned bus garage. (The city owned the land, but the MTA owned the building.) On January 21, Overnight Auto Service purchased the land from the city for $52,000 cash.

My Notes

Purchase of an asset for cash

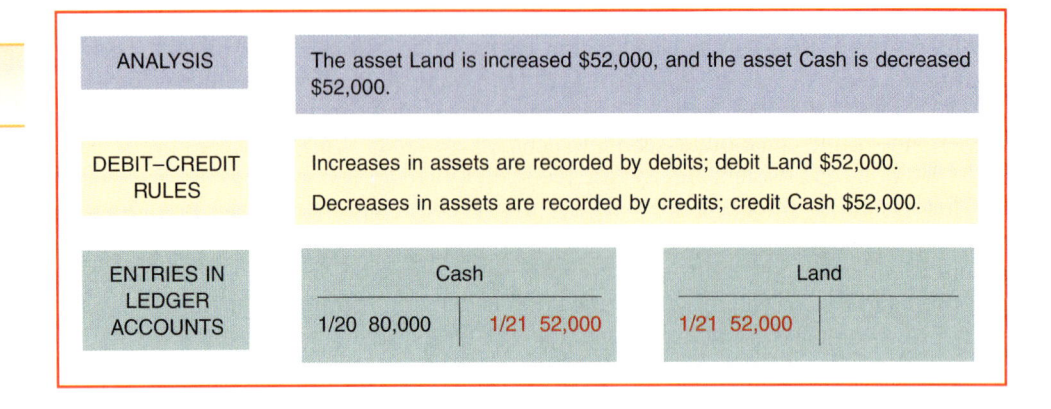

ANALYSIS	The asset Land is increased $52,000, and the asset Cash is decreased $52,000.
DEBIT–CREDIT RULES	Increases in assets are recorded by debits; debit Land $52,000. Decreases in assets are recorded by credits; credit Cash $52,000.
ENTRIES IN LEDGER ACCOUNTS	Cash: 1/20 80,000	1/21 52,000 Land: 1/21 52,000

Jan. 22 Overnight completed the acquisition of its business location by purchasing the abandoned building from the MTA. The purchase price was $36,000; Overnight made a $6,000 cash down payment and issued a 90-day, non-interest-bearing note payable for the remaining $30,000.

My Notes

Purchase of an asset, making a small down payment

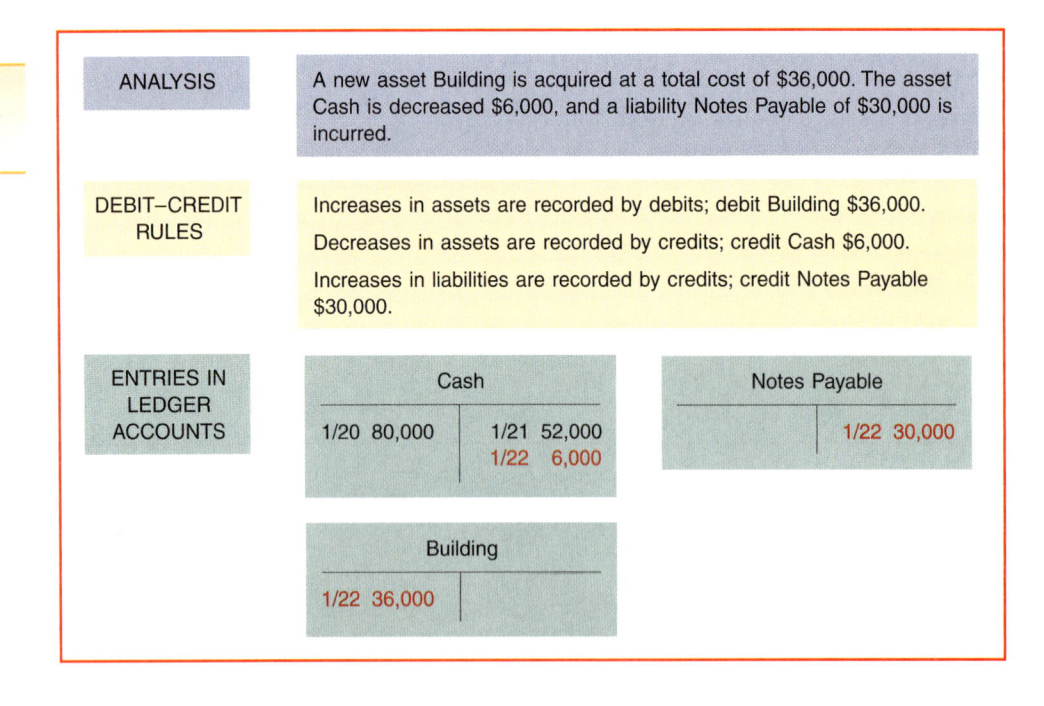

ANALYSIS	A new asset Building is acquired at a total cost of $36,000. The asset Cash is decreased $6,000, and a liability Notes Payable of $30,000 is incurred.
DEBIT–CREDIT RULES	Increases in assets are recorded by debits; debit Building $36,000. Decreases in assets are recorded by credits; credit Cash $6,000. Increases in liabilities are recorded by credits; credit Notes Payable $30,000.
ENTRIES IN LEDGER ACCOUNTS	Cash: 1/20 80,000	1/21 52,000; 1/22 6,000 Notes Payable: 1/22 30,000 Building: 1/22 36,000

Jan. 23 Overnight purchased tools and equipment on account from Snappy Tools. The purchase price was $13,800, due in 60 days.

Recording Transactions in Ledger Accounts: An Illustration

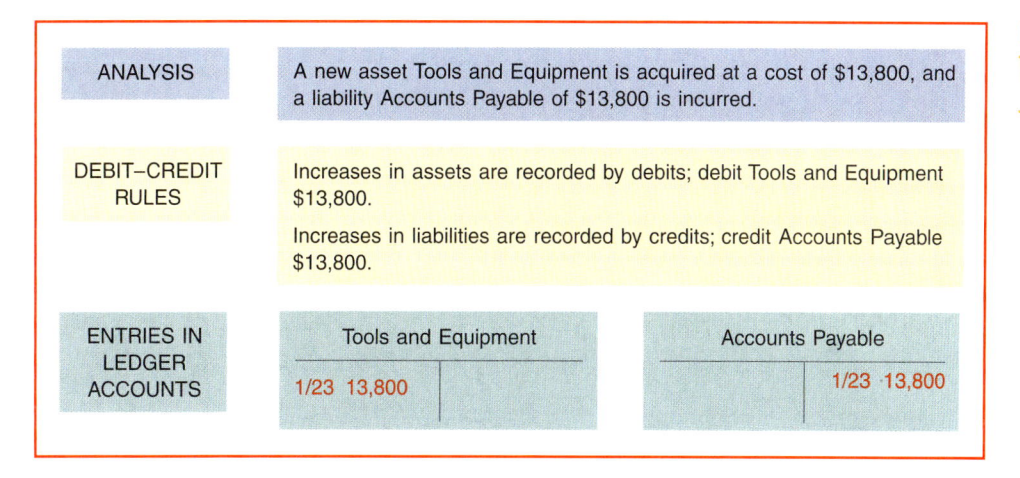

ANALYSIS	A new asset Tools and Equipment is acquired at a cost of $13,800, and a liability Accounts Payable of $13,800 is incurred.
DEBIT–CREDIT RULES	Increases in assets are recorded by debits; debit Tools and Equipment $13,800. Increases in liabilities are recorded by credits; credit Accounts Payable $13,800.
ENTRIES IN LEDGER ACCOUNTS	**Tools and Equipment** 1/23 13,800 **Accounts Payable** 　　　　　1/23 13,800

My Notes
Credit purchase of an asset

Jan. 24 Overnight found that it had purchased more tools than it needed. On January 24, it sold the excess tools on account to Ace Towing at a price of $1,800. The tools were sold at a price equal to their cost, so there was no gain or loss on this transaction.

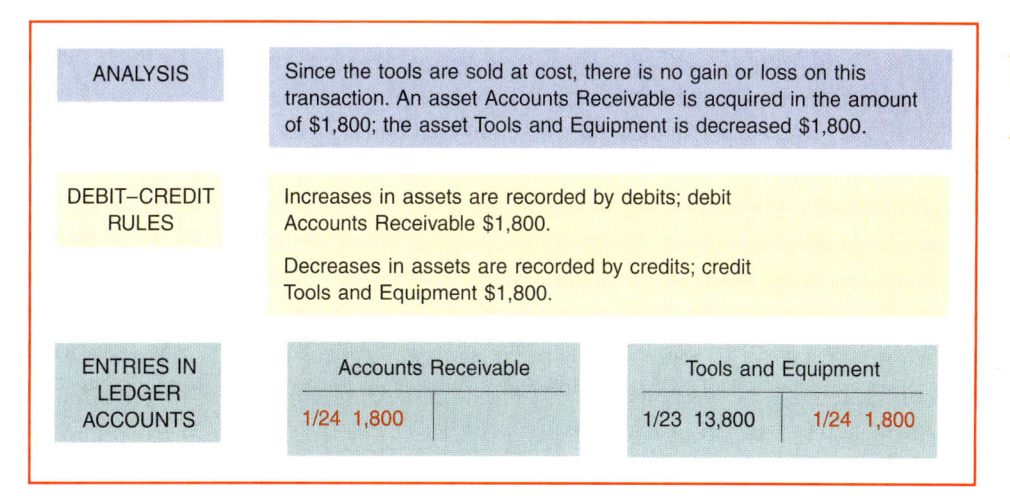

ANALYSIS	Since the tools are sold at cost, there is no gain or loss on this transaction. An asset Accounts Receivable is acquired in the amount of $1,800; the asset Tools and Equipment is decreased $1,800.
DEBIT–CREDIT RULES	Increases in assets are recorded by debits; debit Accounts Receivable $1,800. Decreases in assets are recorded by credits; credit Tools and Equipment $1,800.
ENTRIES IN LEDGER ACCOUNTS	**Accounts Receivable** 1/24 1,800 **Tools and Equipment** 1/23 13,800 | 1/24 1,800

My Notes
Credit sale of an asset (with no gain or loss)

Jan. 26 Overnight received $600 in partial collection of the account receivable from Ace Towing.

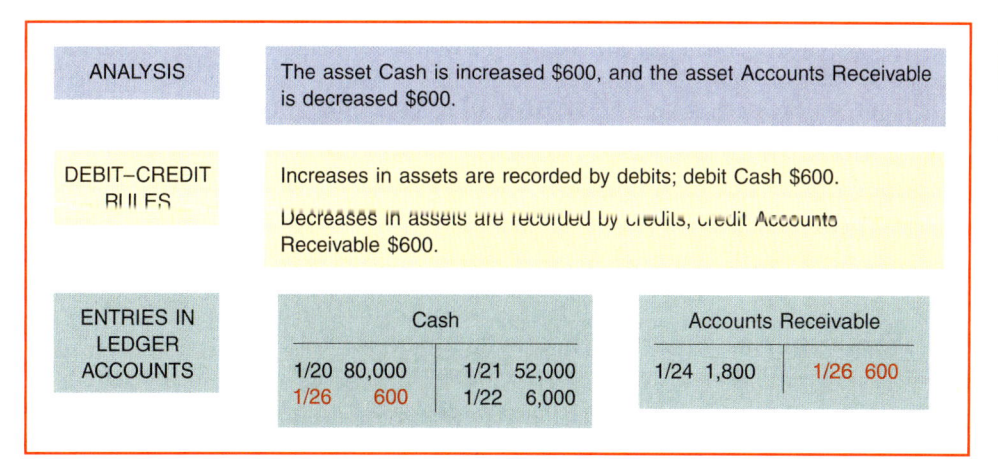

ANALYSIS	The asset Cash is increased $600, and the asset Accounts Receivable is decreased $600.
DEBIT–CREDIT RULES	Increases in assets are recorded by debits; debit Cash $600. Decreases in assets are recorded by credits; credit Accounts Receivable $600.
ENTRIES IN LEDGER ACCOUNTS	**Cash** 1/20 80,000 | 1/21 52,000 1/26 600 | 1/22 6,000 **Accounts Receivable** 1/24 1,800 | 1/26 600

My Notes
Collection of an account receivable

96 Chapter 3 The Accounting Cycle

Jan. 27 Overnight made a $6,800 partial payment of its account payable to Snappy Tools.

My Notes

Payment of an account payable

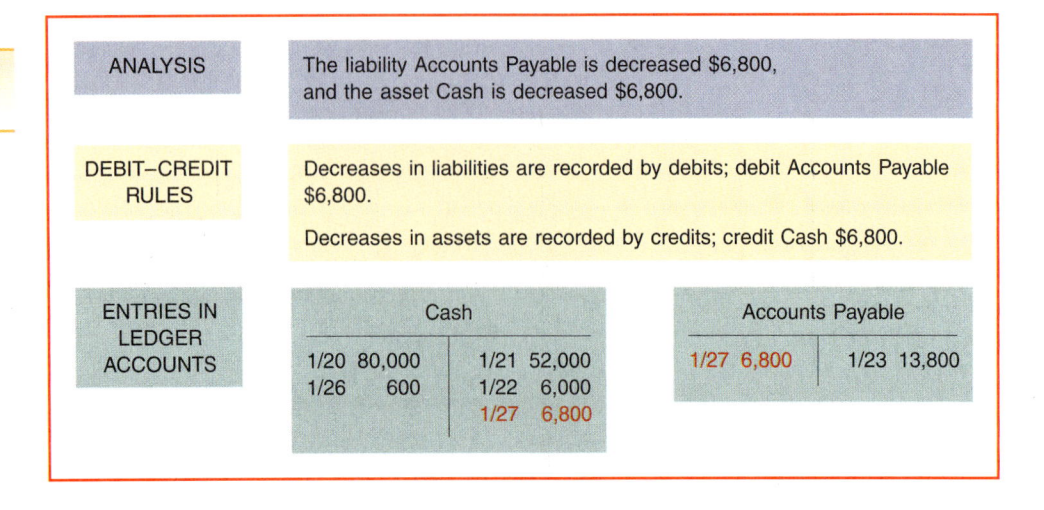

ANALYSIS	The liability Accounts Payable is decreased $6,800, and the asset Cash is decreased $6,800.
DEBIT–CREDIT RULES	Decreases in liabilities are recorded by debits; debit Accounts Payable $6,800.
	Decreases in assets are recorded by credits; credit Cash $6,800.

ENTRIES IN LEDGER ACCOUNTS

Cash		
1/20 80,000	1/21 52,000	
1/26 600	1/22 6,000	
	1/27 6,800	

Accounts Payable	
1/27 6,800	1/23 13,800

THE JOURNAL

LO 5
Explain the purpose of a journal and its relationship to the ledger.

In the preceding discussion, we recorded Overnight Auto Service's transactions in the company's ledger accounts. We did this to stress the effects of business transactions on the individual asset, liability, and owners' equity accounts. In an actual accounting system, however, the information about each business transaction is initially recorded in an accounting record called the **journal**.

The journal is a chronological (day-by-day) record of business transactions. At convenient intervals, the debit and credit amounts recorded in the journal are transferred (posted) to the accounts in the ledger. The updated ledger accounts, in turn, serve as the basis for preparing the company's financial statements.

The simplest type of journal is called a **general journal** as illustrated in Exhibit 3–1. Note the way in which transactions are recorded in the general journal:

1. The name of the account to be debited is written first, and the dollar amount to be debited appears in the left-hand money column.
2. The name of the account credited appears below the account debited and is indented to the right. The dollar amount credited appears in the right-hand money column.
3. A brief description of each transaction appears immediately below each journal entry.

Accounting software packages automate and streamline the way in which transactions are recorded. However, recording transactions manually—without a computer—is an effective way to conceptualize the manner in which economic events are captured by accounting systems and subsequently reported in a company's financial statements.

A familiarity with the general journal form of describing transactions is just as essential to the study of accounting as a familiarity with plus and minus signs is to the study of mathematics. The journal entry is a *tool* for *analyzing* and *describing* the impact of various transactions on a business entity. The ability to describe a transaction in journal entry form requires an understanding of the nature of the transaction and its effect on the financial position of the business.

Posting Journal Entries to the Ledger Accounts (and How to "Read" a Journal Entry)

We have made the point that transactions are recorded *first* in the journal. Ledger accounts are updated *later*, through a process called **posting**. (In a computerized system, postings often occur instantaneously, rather than later.)

The Journal

Exhibit 3–1

GENERAL JOURNAL ENTRIES: JANUARY 20 THROUGH 27

OVERNIGHT AUTO SERVICE
General Journal
January 20–27, 2002

Date	Account Titles and Explanation	Debit	Credit
2002			
Jan. 20	Cash	80,000	
	Capital Stock		80,000
	Owners invest cash in the business.		
21	Land	52,000	
	Cash		52,000
	Purchased land for business site.		
22	Building	36,000	
	Cash		6,000
	Notes Payable		30,000
	Purchased building from MTA. Paid part cash; balance payable within 90 days.		
23	Tools and Equipment	13,800	
	Accounts Payable		13,800
	Purchased tools and equipment on credit from Snappy Tools. Due in 60 days.		
24	Accounts Receivable	1,800	
	Tools and Equipment		1,800
	Sold unused tools and equipment at cost to Ace Towing.		
26	Cash	600	
	Accounts Receivable		600
	Collected part of account receivable from Ace Towing.		
27	Accounts Payable	6,800	
	Cash		6,800
	Made partial payment of the liability to Snappy Tools.		

Posting simply means *updating the ledger accounts* for the effects of the transactions recorded in the journal. Viewed as a mechanical task, posting basically amounts to performing the steps you describe when you "read" a journal entry aloud.

Consider the first entry appearing in Overnight's general journal. If you were to read this entry aloud, you would say: "Debit Cash, $80,000; credit Capital Stock, $80,000." That's precisely what a person posting this entry should do: Debit the Cash account for $80,000, and credit the Capital Stock account for $80,000.

The posting of Overnight's first journal entry is illustrated in Exhibit 3–2. Notice that no new information is recorded during the posting process. Posting involves copying into the ledger accounts information that *already has been recorded in the journal*. In manual accounting systems, this can be a tedious and time-consuming process; but in computer-based systems, it is done instantly and automatically. In addition, computerized posting greatly reduces the risk of errors.

Ledger Accounts after Posting After all the transactions through January 27 have been posted, Overnight's ledger accounts appear as shown in Exhibit 3–3. The accounts are arranged in the same order as in the balance sheet—that is, assets first, followed by liabilities and owners' equity. Each ledger account is presented in what is referred to as a *running balance* format (as opposed to simple T accounts). You will notice that the

Exhibit 3–2

POSTING A TRANSACTION FROM JOURNAL TO LEDGER ACCOUNTS

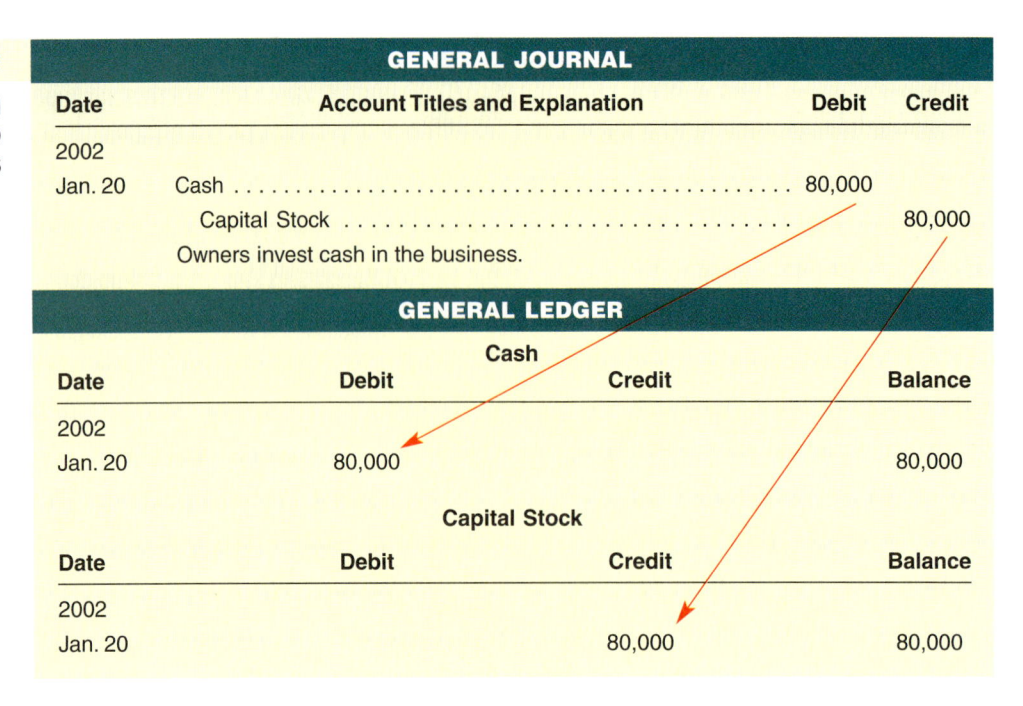

GENERAL JOURNAL

Date	Account Titles and Explanation	Debit	Credit
2002			
Jan. 20	Cash	80,000	
	Capital Stock		80,000
	Owners invest cash in the business.		

GENERAL LEDGER

Cash

Date	Debit	Credit	Balance
2002			
Jan. 20	80,000		80,000

Capital Stock

Date	Debit	Credit	Balance
2002			
Jan. 20		80,000	80,000

running balance format does not indicate specifically whether a particular account has a debit or credit balance. This causes no difficulty, however, because we know that asset accounts normally have debit balances, and liability and owners' equity accounts normally have credit balances.

In the ledger accounts in Exhibit 3–3, we have not yet included any of Overnight's revenue and expense transactions discussed in Chapter 2. All of the company's revenue and expense transactions took place on January 31. Before we can discuss the debit and credit rules for revenue and expense accounts, a more in-depth discussion of *net income* is warranted.

Exhibit 3–3

LEDGER SHOWING TRANSACTIONS

CASH

Date	Debit	Credit	Balance
2002			
Jan. 20	80,000		80,000
21		52,000	28,000
22		6,000	22,000
26	600		22,600
27		6,800	15,800

ACCOUNTS RECEIVABLE

Date	Debit	Credit	Balance
2002			
Jan. 24	1,800		1,800
26		600	1,200

LAND

Date	Debit	Credit	Balance
2002			
Jan. 21	52,000		52,000

BUILDING			
Date	Debit	Credit	Balance
2002			
Jan. 22	36,000		36,000

TOOLS AND EQUIPMENT			
Date	Debit	Credit	Balance
2002			
Jan. 23	13,800		13,800
24		1,800	12,000

NOTES PAYABLE			
Date	Debit	Credit	Balance
2002			
Jan. 22		30,000	30,000

ACCOUNTS PAYABLE			
Date	Debit	Credit	Balance
2002			
Jan. 23		13,800	13,800
27	6,800		7,000

CAPITAL STOCK			
Date	Debit	Credit	Balance
2002			
Jan. 20		80,000	80,000

WHAT IS NET INCOME?

As previously noted, **net income** is *an increase in owners' equity resulting from the profitable operation of the business*. Net income does not consist of any cash or any other specific assets. Rather, net income is a *computation* of the overall effects of many business transactions on *owners' equity*. The effects of net income on the basic accounting equation are illustrated as follows:

Assets = Liabilities + Owners' Equity
Increase = Decrease + Increase

Either (or both) of these effects occur as net income is earned . . .

. . . but **this** is what "net income" really means.

LO 6
Explain the nature of *net income, revenue,* and *expenses*.

My Notes
Net income is not an asset— it's an *increase in owners' equity*

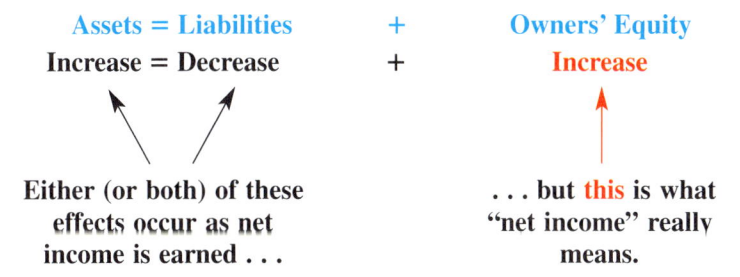

Our point is that net income represents an *increase in owners' equity* and has no direct relationship to the types or amounts of assets on hand. Even a business operating at a profit may run short of cash.

In the balance sheet, the changes in owners' equity resulting from profitable or unprofitable operations are reflected in the balance of the stockholders' equity account, *Retained Earnings*. The assets of the business organization appear in the *assets* section of the balance sheet.

Retained Earnings

As illustrated in Chapter 1, the Retained Earnings account appears in the stockholders' equity section of the balance sheet. Earning net income causes the balance in the Retained Earnings account to increase. However, many corporations follow a policy of distributing to their stockholders some of the resources generated by profitable operations. Distributions of this nature are termed **dividends**, and they reduce both total assets and stockholders' equity. The reduction in stockholders' equity is reflected by decreasing the balance of the Retained Earnings account.

The balance in the **Retained Earnings** account represents the total net income of the corporation over the *entire lifetime* of the business, less all amounts that have been distributed to the stockholders as dividends. In short, retained earnings represent the earnings that have been *retained* by the corporation to finance growth. Some of the largest corporations have become large by consistently retaining in the business most of the resources generated by profitable operations.

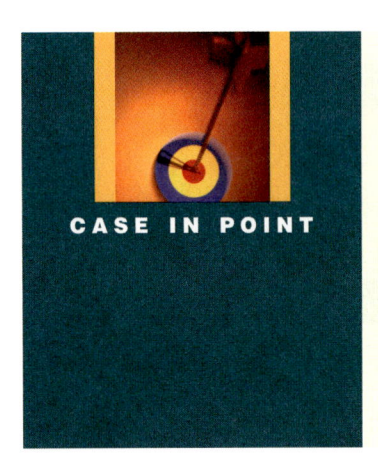

CASE IN POINT

A recent annual report of **Campbell Soup Company** shows total stockholders' equity amounting to nearly $2 billion. Stockholders originally invested only about $71 million—less than 4% of the current equity—in exchange for capital stock. In addition to the original investment, the company has added $1.9 billion to stockholders' equity through profitable operations.

Felicia Martinez/PhotoEdit

The Income Statement: A Preview

An **income statement** is a financial statement that summarizes the profitability of a business entity for a specified period of time. In this statement, net income is determined by comparing *sales prices* of goods or services sold during the period with the *costs* incurred by the business in delivering these goods or services. The technical accounting terms for these components of net income are **revenue** and **expenses**. Therefore, accountants say that net income is equal to *revenue minus expenses*. Should expenses exceed revenue, a **net loss** results.

A sample income statement for Overnight Auto Service for the year ended December 31, 2002, is shown in Exhibit 3–4. In Chapter 5, we show exactly how this income statement was developed from the company's accounting records. For now, however, the illustration will assist us in discussing some of the basic concepts involved in measuring net income.

Income Must Be Related to a Specified Period of Time Notice that our sample income statement covers a *period of time*—namely, the year 2002. A balance sheet shows the financial position of a business at a *particular date*. An income statement, on the other hand, shows the results of business operations over a span of time. We cannot evaluate net income unless it is associated with a specific time period. For example, if an executive says, "My business earns a net income of $10,000," the profitability of the business is unclear. Does it earn $10,000 per week, per month, or per year?

What Is Net Income?

CASE IN POINT

The late J. Paul Getty, one of the world's first billionaires, was once interviewed by a group of business students. One of the students asked Getty to estimate the amount of his income. As the student had not specified a time period, Getty decided to have some fun with his audience and responded, "About $11,000." He paused long enough to allow the group to express surprise over this seemingly low amount, and then completed his sentence, "an hour." (Incidentally, $11,000 per hour, 24 hours per day, amounts to about $100 million per year.)

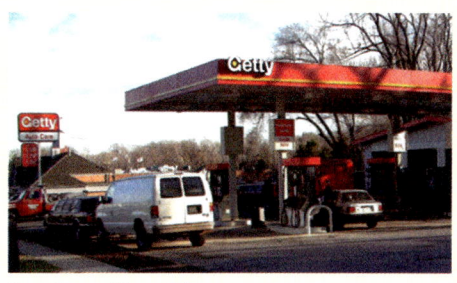

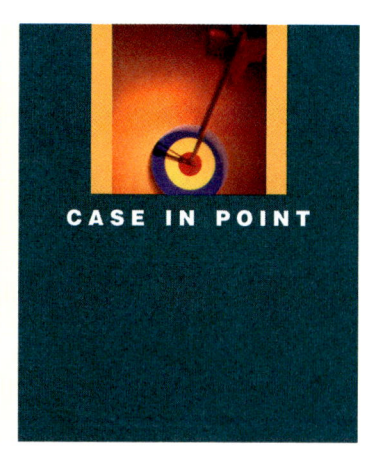

Tom Carter/PhotoEdit

Exhibit 3–4

A PREVIEW OF OVERNIGHT'S INCOME STATEMENT

OVERNIGHT AUTO SERVICE
Income Statement
For the Year Ended December 31, 2002

Revenue:		
Repair service revenue		$172,000
Rent revenue earned		3,000
Total revenue		$175,000
Expenses:		
Advertising	$ 3,900	
Salaries and wages	58,750	
Supplies	7,500	
Depreciation: building	1,650	
Depreciation: tools and equipment	2,200	
Utilities	19,400	
Insurance	15,000	
Interest	30	108,430
Income before income taxes		$ 66,570
Income taxes		26,628
Net income		$ 39,942

Accounting Periods The period of time covered by an income statement is termed the company's **accounting period**. To provide the users of financial statements with timely information, net income is measured for relatively short accounting periods of equal length. This concept, called the **time period principle**, is one of the generally accepted accounting principles that guide the interpretation of financial events and the preparation of financial statements.

The length of a company's accounting period depends on how frequently managers, investors, and other interested people require information about the company's performance. Every business prepares annual income statements, and most businesses prepare quarterly and monthly income statements as well. (Quarterly statements cover a three-month period and are prepared by all large corporations for distribution to their stockholders.)

The 12-month accounting period used by an entity is called its **fiscal year**. The fiscal year used by most companies coincides with the calendar year and ends on December 31. Some businesses, however, elect to use a fiscal year that ends on some other date. It may be convenient for a business to end its fiscal year during a slack season rather than during a time of peak activity.

CASE IN POINT

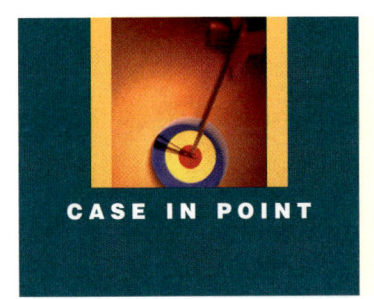

The **Walt Disney Company** ends its fiscal year on September 30. Why? For one reason, September and October are relatively slow months at Disney's theme parks. For another, September financial statements provide timely information about the preceding summer, which is the company's busiest season.

As another example, many department stores, including **Kmart**, **Neiman-Marcus**, **Nordstrom**, and **J. C. Penney**, end their fiscal years on January 31—after the rush of the holiday season.

Let us now explore the meaning of the accounting terms *revenue* and *expenses* in more detail.

Revenue

Revenue is the price of goods sold and services rendered during a given accounting period. Earning revenue causes owners' equity to increase. When a business renders services or sells merchandise to its customers, it usually receives cash or acquires an account receivable from the customer. The inflow of cash and receivables from customers increases the total assets of the company; on the other side of the accounting equation, the liabilities do not change, but owners' equity increases to match the increase in total assets. Thus revenue is the gross *increase in owners' equity* resulting from operation of the business.

Various account titles are used to describe different types of revenue. For example, a business that sells merchandise rather than services, such as **Wal-Mart** or **General Motors**, uses the term *Sales* to describe its revenue. In the professional practices of physicians, CPAs, and attorneys, revenue usually is called *Fees Earned*. A real estate office, however, might call its revenue *Commissions Earned*.

Overnight Auto Service's income statement reveals that the company records its revenue in two separate accounts: (1) *Repair Service Revenue* and (2) *Rent Revenue Earned*. A professional sports team might also have separate revenue accounts for *Ticket Sales, Concessions Revenue,* and *Revenue from Television Contracts.* Another type of revenue common to many businesses is *Interest Revenue* (or Interest Earned), stemming from the interest earned on bank deposits, notes receivable, and interest-bearing investments.

LO 7
Apply the *realization* and *matching* principles in recording revenue and expenses.

The Realization Principle: When to Record Revenue When should revenue be recognized? In most cases, the **realization principle** indicates that revenue should be recognized *at the time goods are sold or services are rendered*. At this point, the business has essentially completed the earnings process and the sales value of the goods or services can be measured objectively. At any time prior to the sale, the ultimate value of the goods or services sold can only be estimated. After the sale, the only step that remains is to collect from the customer, usually a relatively certain event.

CASH EFFECTS

Assume that on July 25 KGPO Radio contracts with Rancho Ford to run 200 one-minute advertisements during August. KGPO runs these ads and receives full payment from Rancho Ford on September 6. In which month should KGPO recognize the advertising revenue earned from Rancho Ford—July, August, or September?

The answer is August, the month in which KGPO *rendered the services* that earned the revenue.[1] In other words, the revenue is recognized when it is *earned,* without regard to when cash payment for goods or services is received.

---

[1] Some readers may wonder what would happen if some of the ads were aired in August and others in September. In this case, KGPO would recognize an *appropriate portion* of the advertising revenue in August and the remainder in September. The accounting procedures for allocating revenue between accounting periods are discussed and illustrated in the next chapter.

Expenses

Expenses are the costs of the goods and services used up in the process of earning revenue. Examples include the cost of employees' salaries, advertising, rent, utilities, and the depreciation of buildings, automobiles, and office equipment. All these costs are necessary to attract and serve customers and thereby earn revenue. Expenses are often called the "costs of doing business," that is, the cost of the various activities necessary to carry on a business.

An expense always causes a *decrease in owners' equity*. The related changes in the accounting equation can be either (1) a decrease in assets or (2) an increase in liabilities. An expense reduces assets if payment occurs at the time that the expense is incurred. If the expense will not be paid until later, as, for example, the purchase of advertising services on account, the recording of the expense will be accompanied by an increase in liabilities.

The Matching Principle: When to Record Expenses A significant relationship exists between revenue and expenses. Expenses are incurred for the *purpose of producing revenue*. In measuring net income for a period, revenue should be offset by *all the expenses incurred in producing that revenue*. This concept of offsetting expenses against revenue on a basis of cause and effect is called the **matching principle**.

Timing is an important factor in matching (offsetting) revenue with the related expenses. For example, in preparing monthly income statements, it is important to offset this month's expenses against this month's revenue. We should not offset this month's expenses against last month's revenue because there is no cause and effect relationship between the two.

CASH EFFECTS

Assume that the salaries earned by sales personnel waiting on customers during July are not paid until early August. In which month should these salaries be regarded as an expense—July or August?

The answer is July, because this is the month in which the sales personnel's services *helped to produce revenue.* Just as revenue and cash receipts are not one and the same, expenses and cash payments are not identical. In fact, the cash payment of an expense may occur before, after, or in the same period that revenue is produced. In deciding when to record an expense, the critical question is "In what period does the cash expenditure help to produce revenue?" *not* "When does the cash payment occur?"

Expenditures Benefiting More Than One Accounting Period Many expenditures made by a business benefit two or more accounting periods. Fire insurance policies, for example, usually cover a period of 12 months. If a company prepares monthly income statements, a portion of the cost of such a policy should be allocated to insurance expense each month that the policy is in force. In this case, apportionment of the cost of the policy by months is an easy matter. If the 12-month policy costs $2,400, for example, the insurance expense for each month amounts to $200 ($2,400 cost ÷ 12 months).

Not all transactions can be divided so precisely by accounting periods. The purchase of a building, furniture and fixtures, machinery, a computer, or an automobile provides benefits to the business over all the years in which such an asset is used. No one can determine in advance exactly how many years of service will be received from such long-lived assets. Nevertheless, in measuring the net income of a business for a period of one year or less, accountants must *estimate* what portion of the cost of the building and other long-lived assets is applicable to the current year. Since the allocations of these costs are estimates rather than precise measurements, it follows that income statements should be regarded as useful *approximations* of net income rather than as absolutely correct measurements.

For some expenditures, such as those for advertising or employee training programs, it is not possible to estimate objectively the number of accounting periods over which revenue is likely to be produced. In such cases, generally accepted accounting principles require that the expenditure be charged *immediately to expense*. This treatment is based upon the accounting principle of **objectivity** and the concept of **conservatism**. Accountants require *objective evidence* that an expenditure will produce revenue in future periods before they will view the expenditure as creating an asset. When this objective evidence does not exist, they follow the conservative practice of recording the expenditure as an expense. *Conservatism,* in this context, means applying the accounting treatment that results in the *lowest* (most conservative) estimate of net income for the current period.

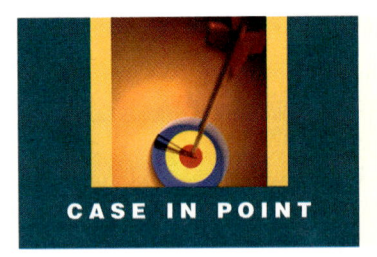

CASE IN POINT

Internationally, there is significant disagreement about whether some business expenditures should be immediately expensed or can be recorded as an asset. In particular, research and development costs, which must be expensed as incurred under U.S. accounting standards, can be either expensed immediately *or* recorded as an asset in Brazil and the Netherlands.

The Accrual Basis of Accounting

The policy of recognizing revenue in the accounting records when it is *earned* and recognizing expenses when the related goods or services are *used* is called the **accrual basis of accounting**. The purpose of accrual accounting is to measure the profitability of the *economic activities conducted* during the accounting period.

The most important concept involved in accrual accounting is the *matching principle*. Revenue is offset with all of the expenses incurred in generating that revenue, thus providing a measure of the overall profitability of the economic activity.

An alternative to the accrual basis is called *cash basis accounting*. Under cash basis accounting, revenue is recognized when cash is collected from the customer, rather than when the company sells goods or renders services. Expenses are recognized when payment is made, rather than when the related goods or services are used in business operations. The cash basis of accounting measures the amounts of cash received and paid out during the period, but it does *not* provide a good measure of the *profitability of activities* undertaken during the period.

CASE IN POINT

Airlines sell many tickets weeks or even months *in advance* of scheduled flights. Yet many expenses relating to a flight—such as salaries of the flight crew and the cost of fuel used—may not be paid until *after* the flight has occurred. Recognizing these events when cash is received or paid would fail to "match" revenues and expenses in the period when flights actually occur.

LO 8
Explain *why* revenues are recorded with credits and expenses are recorded with debits.

Debit and Credit Rules for Revenue and Expenses

We have stressed that revenue increases owners' equity and that expenses decrease owners' equity. The debit and credit rules for recording revenue and expenses in the ledger accounts are a natural extension of the rules for recording changes in owners' equity. The rules previously stated for recording increases and decreases in owners' equity are as follows:

- *Increases* in owners' equity are recorded by *credits*.
- *Decreases* in owners' equity are recorded by *debits*.

This rule is now extended to cover revenue and expense accounts:

- *Revenue* increases owners' equity; therefore, revenue is recorded by *credits*.
- *Expenses* decrease owners' equity; therefore, expenses are recorded by *debits*.

DIVIDENDS

A dividend is a distribution of assets (usually cash) by a corporation to its stockholders. In some respects, dividends are similar to expenses—they reduce both the assets and the owners' equity in the business. However, *dividends are not an expense, and they are not deducted from revenue in the income statement*. The reason why dividends are not viewed as an expense is that these payments do not serve to generate revenue. Rather, they are a *distribution of profits* to the owners of the business.

Since the declaration of a dividend reduces stockholders' equity, the dividend could be recorded by debiting the Retained Earnings account. However, a clearer record is created if a separate Dividends account is debited for all amounts distributed as dividends to stockholders. The disposition of the Dividends account when financial statements are prepared will be illustrated in Chapter 5.

The debit–credit rules for revenue, expenses, and dividends are summarized below:

Owners' Equity

Decreases recorded by Debits	Increases recorded by Credits
Expenses decrease owners' equity	Revenue increases owners' equity
Expenses are recorded by Debits	Revenue is recorded by Credits
Dividends reduce owner's equity	
Dividends are recorded by Debits	

My Notes

Debit–credit rules related to effect on owners' equity

You as a Business Owner

You are the sole owner of a small business. The mortgage payment on your home is due, but you have very little money in your personal checking account. Therefore, you write a check for this payment from the business bank account.

Does it matter whether your business is unincorporated or organized as a corporation?

*Our comments appear on page 133.

RECORDING REVENUE AND EXPENSE TRANSACTIONS: AN ILLUSTRATION

In Chapter 2, we introduced Overnight Auto Service, a small auto repair shop formed on January 20, 2002. Early in this chapter we journalized and posted all of Overnight's balance sheet transactions through January 27. At this point we will illustrate the manner in which Overnight's January income statement transactions were handled, and continue into February with additional transactions.

Three transactions involving revenue and expenses were recorded by Overnight on January 31, 2002. The following illustrations provide an analysis of each transaction.

Jan. 31 Recorded Revenue of $2,200, all of which was received in cash.

My Notes

Revenue earned and collected

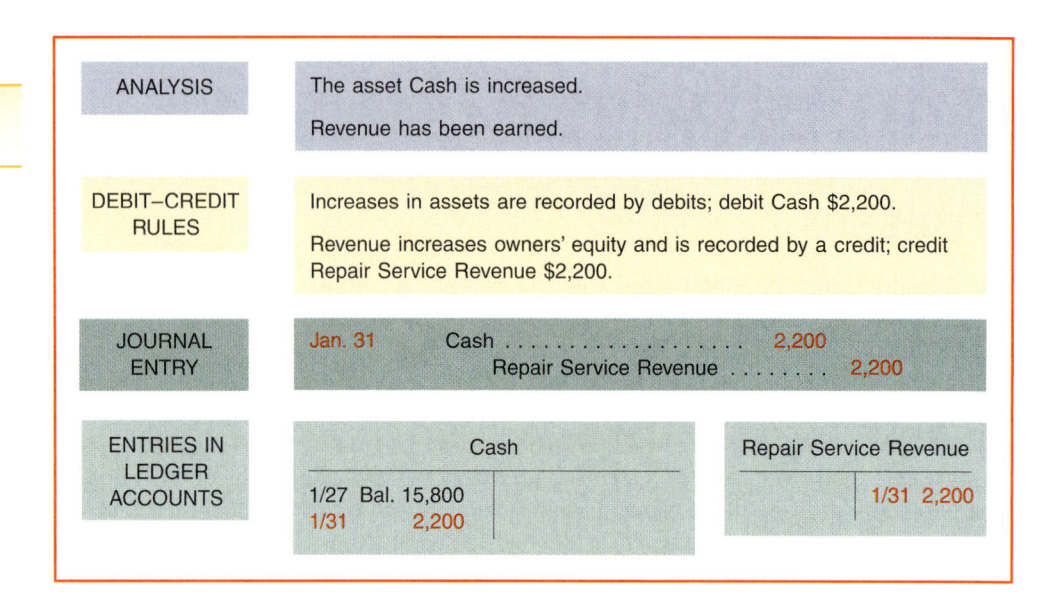

ANALYSIS	The asset Cash is increased. Revenue has been earned.
DEBIT–CREDIT RULES	Increases in assets are recorded by debits; debit Cash $2,200. Revenue increases owners' equity and is recorded by a credit; credit Repair Service Revenue $2,200.
JOURNAL ENTRY	Jan. 31 Cash .... 2,200 Repair Service Revenue 2,200
ENTRIES IN LEDGER ACCOUNTS	**Cash** 1/27 Bal. 15,800 1/31 2,200	**Repair Service Revenue** 1/31 2,200

Jan. 31 Paid employees' wages earned in January, $1,200.

My Notes

Incurred an expense, paying cash

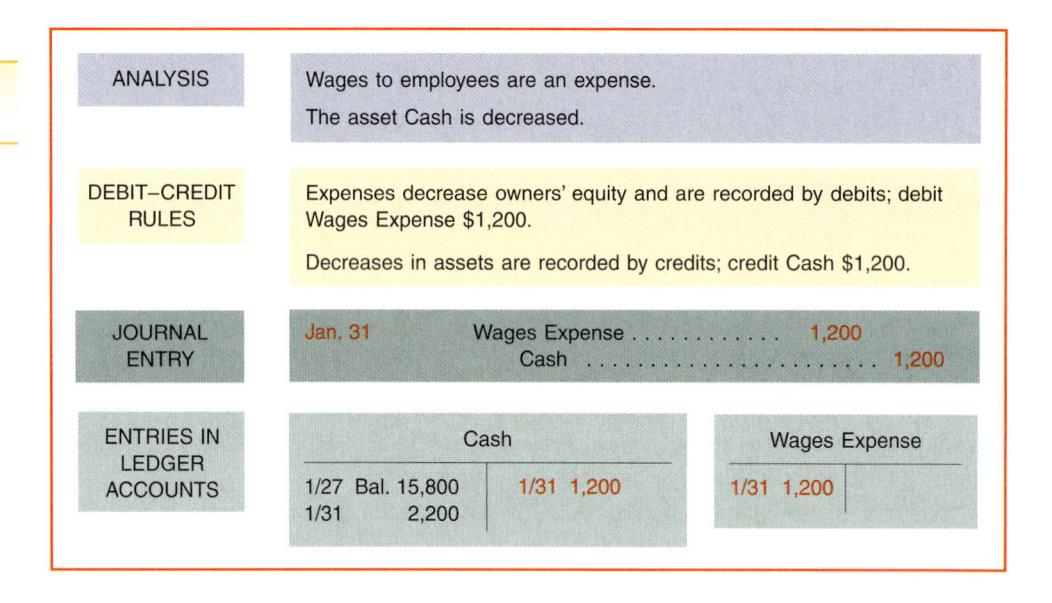

ANALYSIS	Wages to employees are an expense. The asset Cash is decreased.
DEBIT–CREDIT RULES	Expenses decrease owners' equity and are recorded by debits; debit Wages Expense $1,200. Decreases in assets are recorded by credits; credit Cash $1,200.
JOURNAL ENTRY	Jan. 31 Wages Expense .... 1,200 Cash 1,200
ENTRIES IN LEDGER ACCOUNTS	**Cash** 1/27 Bal. 15,800 1/31 1,200 1/31 2,200	**Wages Expense** 1/31 1,200

Recording Revenue and Expense Transactions: An Illustration

Jan. 31 Paid for utilities used in January, $200.

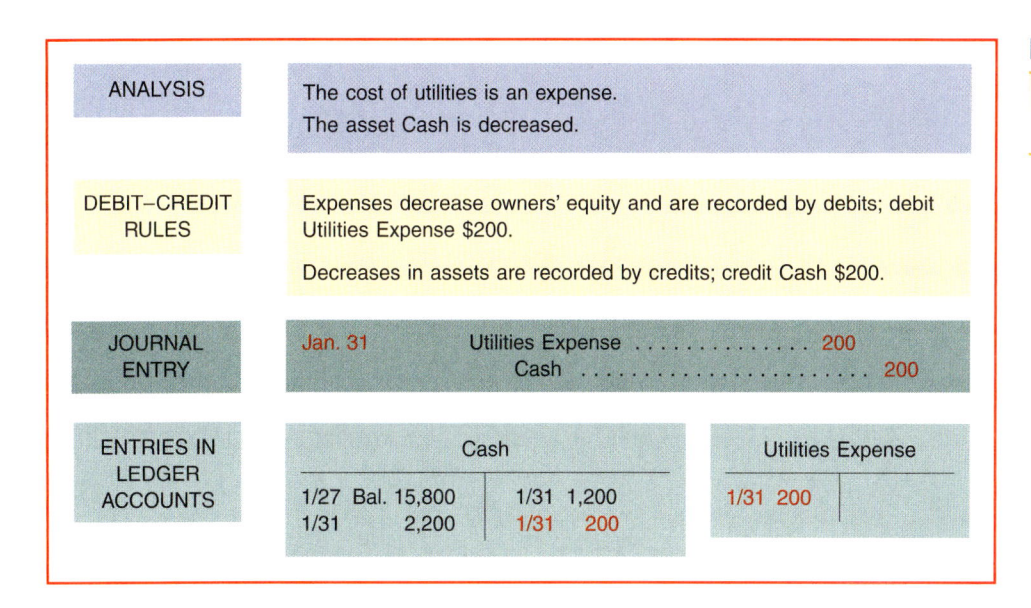

ANALYSIS	The cost of utilities is an expense. The asset Cash is decreased.
DEBIT–CREDIT RULES	Expenses decrease owners' equity and are recorded by debits; debit Utilities Expense $200. Decreases in assets are recorded by credits; credit Cash $200.
JOURNAL ENTRY	Jan. 31 Utilities Expense .... 200 　　　　　　Cash 200
ENTRIES IN LEDGER ACCOUNTS	**Cash** 1/27 Bal. 15,800　│　1/31　1,200 1/31　　　2,200　│　1/31　　200 **Utilities Expense** 1/31　200

My Notes

Incurred an expense, paying cash

Having analyzed and recorded all of Overnight's January transactions, next we focus upon the company's February activities. Overnight's February transactions are described, analyzed, and recorded as follows:

Feb. 1 Paid *Daily Tribune* $360 cash for newspaper advertising to be run during February.

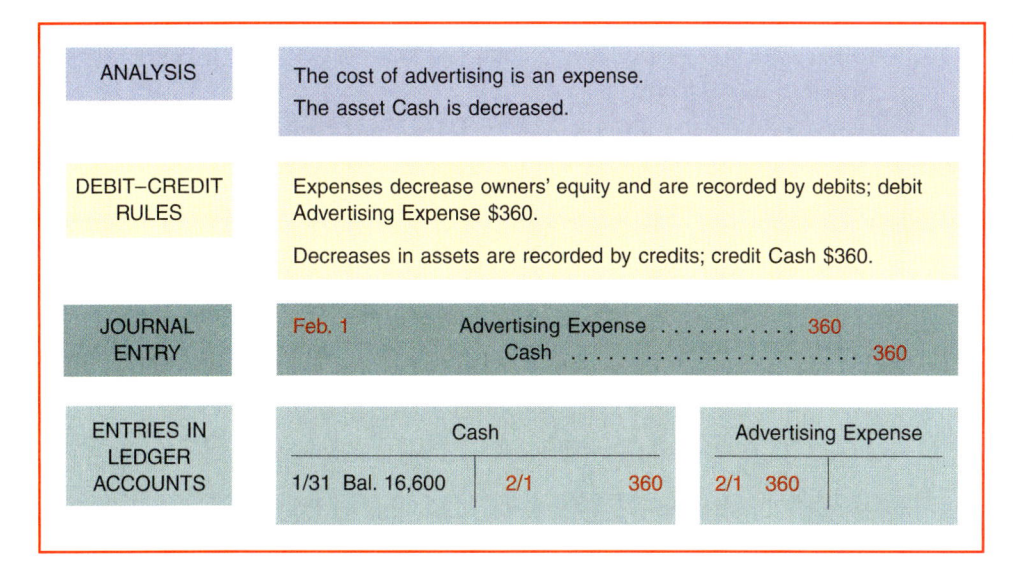

ANALYSIS	The cost of advertising is an expense. The asset Cash is decreased.
DEBIT–CREDIT RULES	Expenses decrease owners' equity and are recorded by debits; debit Advertising Expense $360. Decreases in assets are recorded by credits; credit Cash $360.
JOURNAL ENTRY	Feb. 1 Advertising Expense .... 360 　　　　　Cash 360
ENTRIES IN LEDGER ACCOUNTS	**Cash** 1/31 Bal. 16,600　│　2/1　　　360 **Advertising Expense** 2/1　360

My Notes

Incurred an expense, paying cash

Feb. 2 Purchased radio advertising from KRAM to be aired in February. The cost was $470, payable within 30 days.

My Notes

Incurred an expense to be paid later

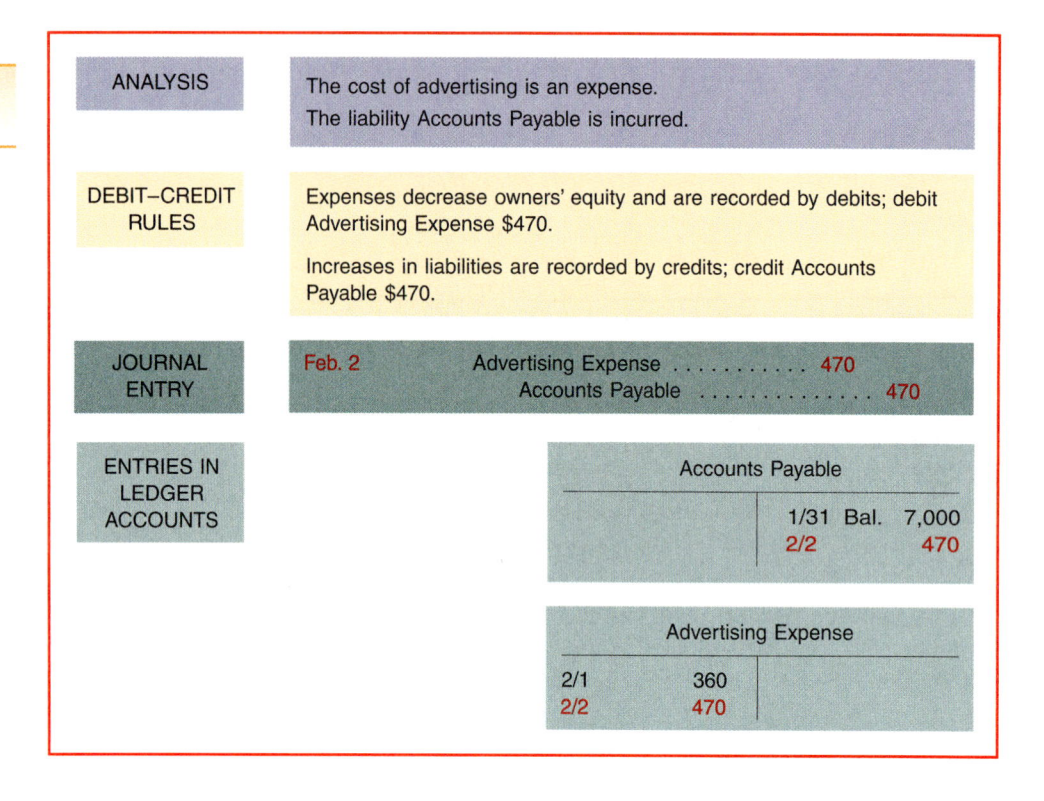

ANALYSIS	The cost of advertising is an expense. The liability Accounts Payable is incurred.
DEBIT–CREDIT RULES	Expenses decrease owners' equity and are recorded by debits; debit Advertising Expense $470. Increases in liabilities are recorded by credits; credit Accounts Payable $470.
JOURNAL ENTRY	Feb. 2 Advertising Expense .... 470 Accounts Payable 470

ENTRIES IN LEDGER ACCOUNTS	Accounts Payable
	  1/31 Bal. 7,000
	  2/2 470
	
	Advertising Expense
	2/1 360
	2/2 470

Feb. 4 Purchased various shop supplies (such as grease, solvents, nuts, and bolts) from CAPA Auto Parts; cost $1,400, due in 30 days. These supplies are expected to meet Overnight's needs for *three or four months*.

My Notes

When a purchase clearly benefits future accounting periods, it's an asset, not an expense

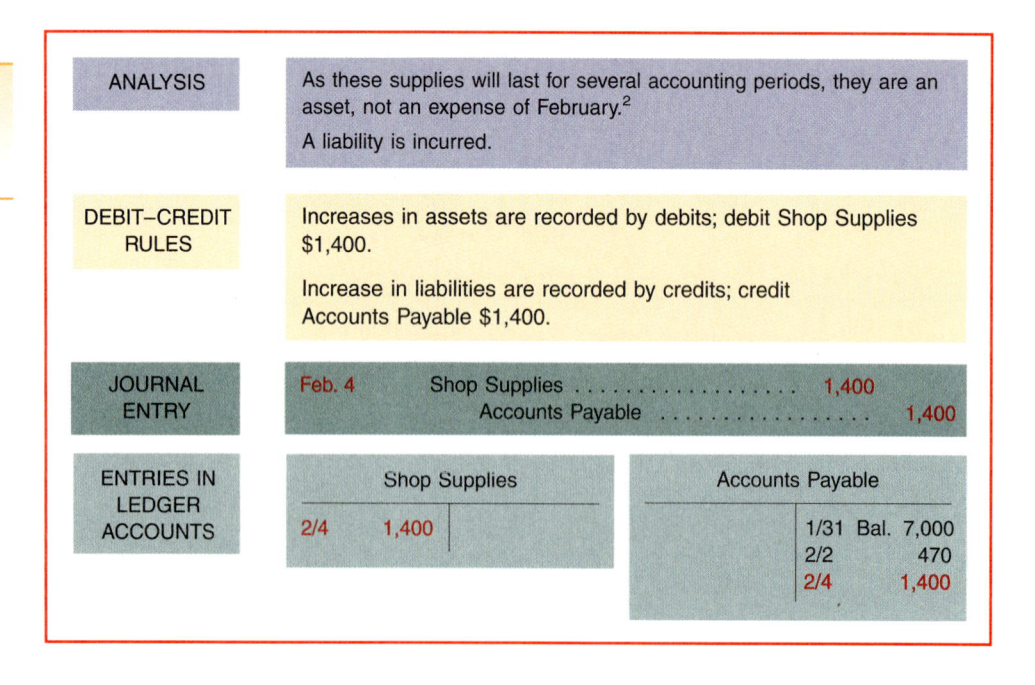

ANALYSIS	As these supplies will last for several accounting periods, they are an asset, not an expense of February.[2] A liability is incurred.
DEBIT–CREDIT RULES	Increases in assets are recorded by debits; debit Shop Supplies $1,400. Increase in liabilities are recorded by credits; credit Accounts Payable $1,400.
JOURNAL ENTRY	Feb. 4 Shop Supplies .... 1,400 Accounts Payable 1,400

ENTRIES IN LEDGER ACCOUNTS	Shop Supplies Accounts Payable
	2/4 1,400 1/31 Bal. 7,000
	                         2/2 470
	                         2/4 1,400

---

[2] If the supplies are expected to be used within the *current* accounting period, their cost is debited directly to the Supplies Expense account, rather than to an asset account.

Recording Revenue and Expense Transactions: An Illustration

Feb. 15 Collected $4,980 cash for repairs made to vehicles of Airport Shuttle Service.

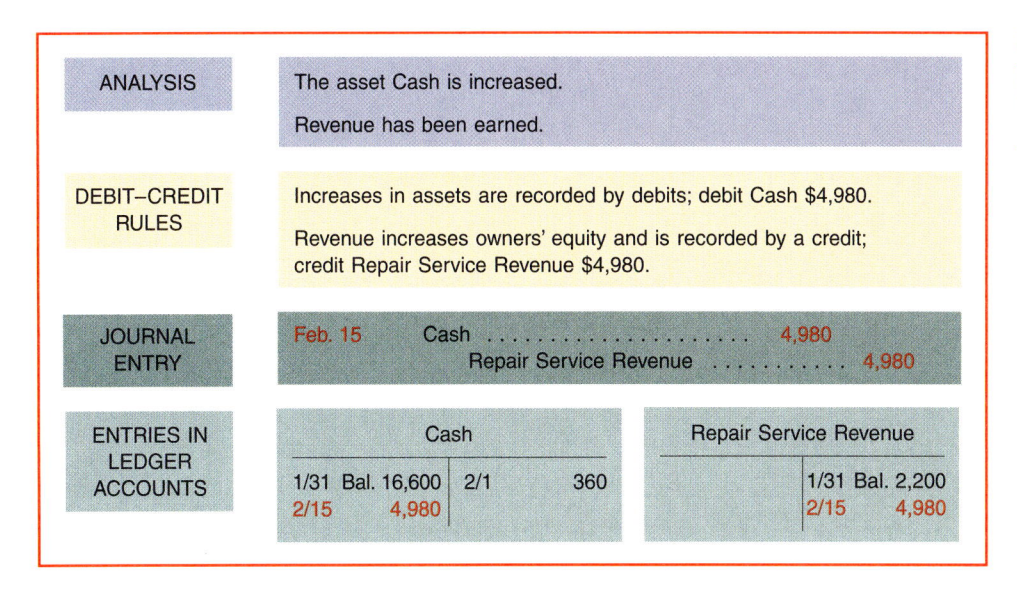

ANALYSIS	The asset Cash is increased. Revenue has been earned.
DEBIT–CREDIT RULES	Increases in assets are recorded by debits; debit Cash $4,980. Revenue increases owners' equity and is recorded by a credit; credit Repair Service Revenue $4,980.
JOURNAL ENTRY	Feb. 15 Cash .... 4,980 Repair Service Revenue 4,980
ENTRIES IN LEDGER ACCOUNTS	Cash 1/31 Bal. 16,600 | 2/1 360 2/15 4,980 Repair Service Revenue | 1/31 Bal. 2,200 | 2/15 4,980

My Notes
Revenue earned and collected

Feb. 28 Billed Harbor Cab Co. $5,400 for maintenance and repair services Overnight provided in February. The agreement with Harbor Cab calls for payment to be received by March 10.

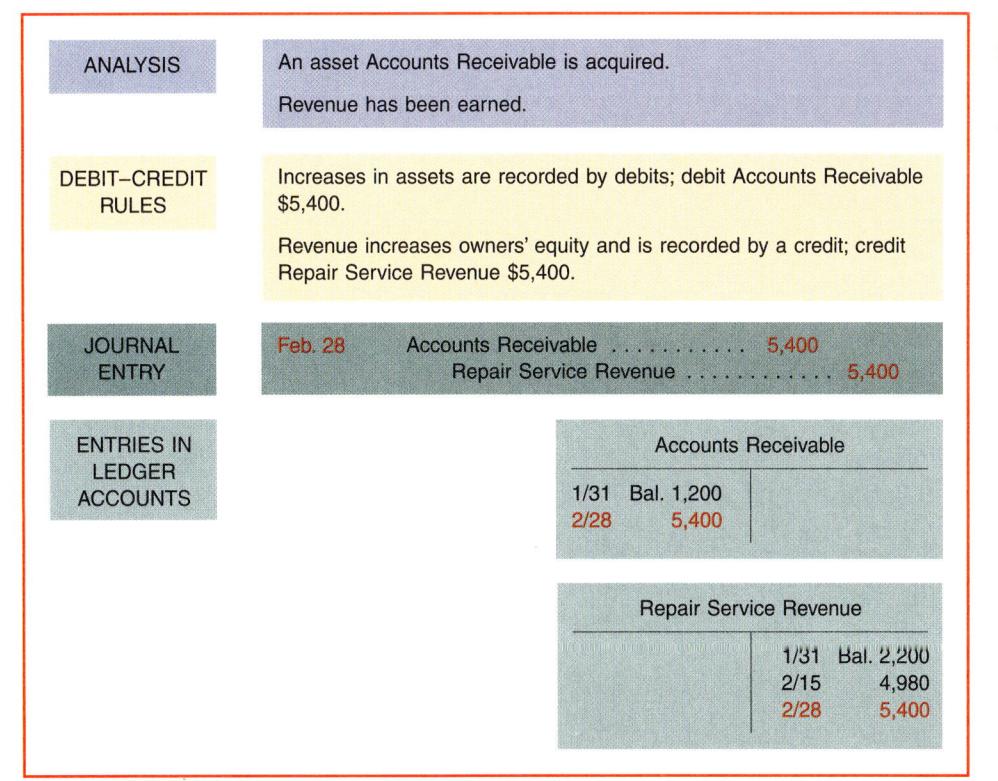

ANALYSIS	An asset Accounts Receivable is acquired. Revenue has been earned.
DEBIT–CREDIT RULES	Increases in assets are recorded by debits; debit Accounts Receivable $5,400. Revenue increases owners' equity and is recorded by a credit; credit Repair Service Revenue $5,400.
JOURNAL ENTRY	Feb. 28 Accounts Receivable .... 5,400 Repair Service Revenue 5,400
ENTRIES IN LEDGER ACCOUNTS	Accounts Receivable 1/31 Bal. 1,200 2/28 5,400 Repair Service Revenue | 1/31 Bal. 2,200 | 2/15 4,980 | 2/28 5,400

My Notes
Revenue earned but not yet collected

Feb. 28 Paid employees' wages earned in February, $4,900.

My Notes

Incurred an expense, paying cash

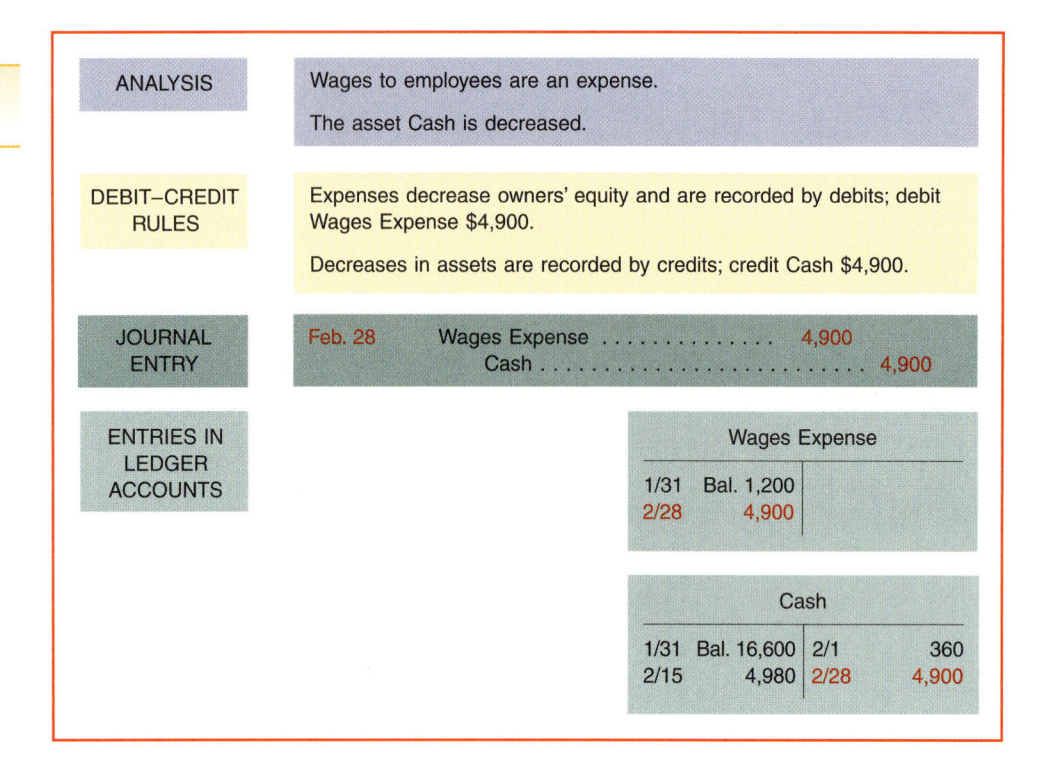

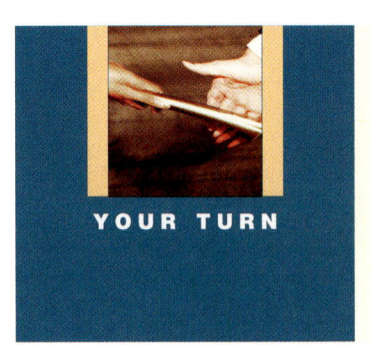

ANALYSIS	Wages to employees are an expense. The asset Cash is decreased.
DEBIT–CREDIT RULES	Expenses decrease owners' equity and are recorded by debits; debit Wages Expense $4,900. Decreases in assets are recorded by credits; credit Cash $4,900.
JOURNAL ENTRY	Feb. 28 Wages Expense .... 4,900 Cash 4,900
ENTRIES IN LEDGER ACCOUNTS	**Wages Expense** 1/31 Bal. 1,200 2/28 4,900 **Cash** 1/31 Bal. 16,600	2/1 360 2/15 4,980	2/28 4,900

YOUR TURN

You as Overnight Auto Service's Accountant

Your good friend, Fred Jonas, is the manager of Harbor Cab Co. Your family and Fred's family meet frequently outside of your respective workplaces for fun. At a recent barbecue, Fred asked you about the amount of repair services rendered by Overnight Auto to Airport Shuttle Services in February. Airport Shuttle Services competes with Harbor Cab Co. for fares to and from the airport. What should you say to Fred?

*Our answer is on page 133.

Recording Revenue and Expense Transactions: An Illustration

Feb. 28 Recorded $1,600 utility bill for February. The entire amount is due March 15.

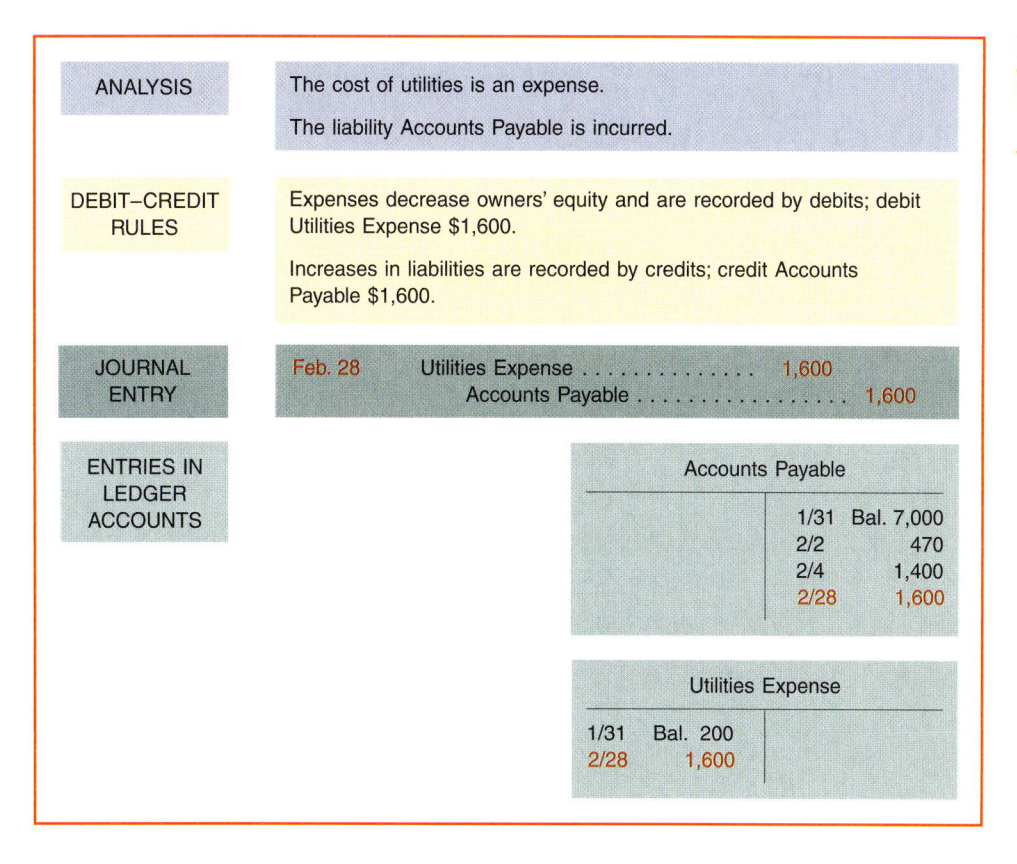

ANALYSIS	The cost of utilities is an expense. The liability Accounts Payable is incurred.	
DEBIT–CREDIT RULES	Expenses decrease owners' equity and are recorded by debits; debit Utilities Expense $1,600. Increases in liabilities are recorded by credits; credit Accounts Payable $1,600.	
JOURNAL ENTRY	Feb. 28 Utilities Expense . . . . 1,600 Accounts Payable 1,600	

ENTRIES IN LEDGER ACCOUNTS	Accounts Payable
	                         1/31 Bal. 7,000
	                         2/2 470
	                         2/4 1,400
	                         2/28 1,600
	
	Utilities Expense
	1/31 Bal. 200
	2/28 1,600	

My Notes
Incurred an expense to be paid later

Feb. 28 Overnight Auto Services declares and pays a dividend of 40 cents per share to the owners of its 8,000 shares of capital stock—a total of $3,200.[3]

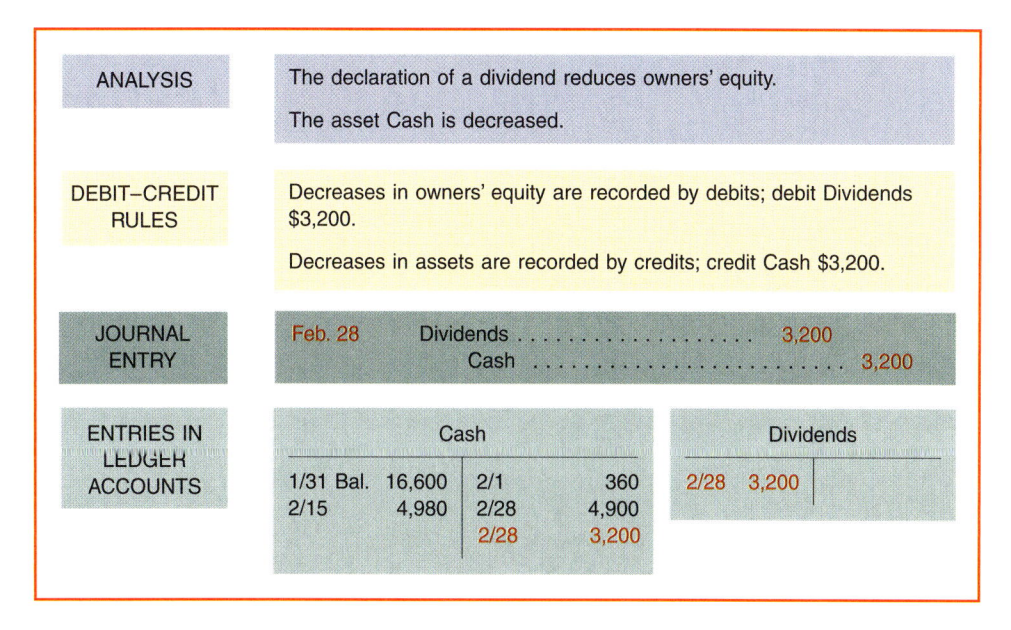

ANALYSIS	The declaration of a dividend reduces owners' equity. The asset Cash is decreased.
DEBIT–CREDIT RULES	Decreases in owners' equity are recorded by debits; debit Dividends $3,200. Decreases in assets are recorded by credits; credit Cash $3,200.
JOURNAL ENTRY	Feb. 28 Dividends . . . . 3,200 Cash 3,200
ENTRIES IN LEDGER ACCOUNTS	Cash 1/31 Bal. 16,600	2/1 360 2/15 4,980	2/28 4,900 	2/28 3,200 Dividends 2/28 3,200

My Notes
A Dividends account signifies a reduction in owners' equity—but it's not an expense

---

[3] As explained earlier, dividends are not an expense. In Chapter 5, we will show how the balance in the Dividends account eventually reduces the amount of retained earnings reported in the owners' equity section of the balance sheet.

The Journal

In our illustration, journal entries were shown in a very abbreviated form. The actual entries made in Overnight's journal appear in Exhibit 3–5. Notice that these formal journal entries include short *explanations* of the transactions, which include such details as the terms of credit transactions and the names of customers and creditors.

Exhibit 3–5

GENERAL JOURNAL ENTRIES: JANUARY 31 THROUGH FEBRUARY 28

My Notes

Journal entries contain more information than just dollar amounts

OVERNIGHT AUTO SERVICE
General Journal
January 31–February 28, 2002

Date	Account Titles and Explanation	Debit	Credit
2002			
Jan. 31	Cash	2,200	
	Repair Service Revenue		2,200
	Repair services rendered to various customers.		
31	Wages Expense	1,200	
	Cash		1,200
	Paid all wages for January.		
31	Utilities Expense	200	
	Cash		200
	Paid all utilities for January.		
Feb. 1	Advertising Expense	360	
	Cash		360
	Purchased newspaper advertising from *Daily Tribune* to run in February.		
2	Advertising Expense	470	
	Accounts Payable		470
	Purchased radio advertising on account from KRAM; payment due in 30 days.		
4	Shop Supplies	1,400	
	Accounts Payable		1,400
	Purchased shop supplies on account from CAPA; payment due in 30 days.		
15	Cash	4,980	
	Repair Service Revenue		4,980
	Repair services rendered to Airport Shuttle Service.		
28	Accounts Receivable	5,400	
	Repair Service Revenue		5,400
	Billed Harbor Cab for services rendered in February.		
28	Wages Expense	4,900	
	Cash		4,900
	Paid all wages for February.		
28	Utilities Expense	1,600	
	Accounts Payable		1,600
	Recorded utility bill for February.		
28	Dividends	3,200	
	Cash		3,200
	Paid cash dividend of 40 cents per share on 8,000 shares of capital stock owned by the McBryan family.		

February's Ledger Balances

MANAGEMENT STRATEGY AND FINANCIAL REPORTING

The accounting records of an enterprise reflect the business strategies being pursued by managers. For example, Overnight Auto appears to be pursuing a business strategy of acquiring other companies as customers (e.g., Airport Shuttle Service and Harbor Cab Co.) rather than individual car owners. If Overnight Auto's accounts receivable records included receivables from individuals (i.e., Betty Brown and Joe Smith), then it would be pursuing a very different type of business strategy.

FEBRUARY'S LEDGER BALANCES

After posting all of the January and February transactions, Overnight's ledger accounts appear as shown in Exhibit 3–6. To conserve space, we have illustrated the ledger in T account form and have carried forward each account's summary balance from January 31. For convenience, we show in *red* the *February 28 balance* of each account (debit balances appear to the left of the account; credit balances appear to the right).

The accounts in this illustration appear in *financial statement order*—that is, balance sheet accounts first (assets, liabilities, and owners' equity), followed by the income statement accounts (revenue and expenses).

Exhibit 3-6

OVERNIGHT AUTO SERVICE'S LEDGER ACCOUNTS

OVERNIGHT AUTO SERVICE
The Ledger

Asset Accounts

Cash

1/31 Bal.	16,600	2/1	360	
2/15	4,980	2/28	4,900	
		2/28	3,200	

Bal. $13,120

Accounts Receivable

1/31	1,200
2/28	5,400

Bal. $6,600

Shop Supplies

1/31 Bal.	0
2/4	1,400

Bal. $1,400

Land

1/31 Bal.	52,000

Bal. $52,000

Building

1/31 Bal.	36,000

Bal. $36,000

Tools and Equipment

1/31 Bal.	12,000

Bal. $12,000

Liability and Owners' Equity Accounts

Notes Payable

	1/31 Bal.	30,000

Bal. $30,000

Accounts Payable

	1/31 Bal.	7,000
	2/2	470
	2/4	1,400
	2/28	1,600

Bal. $10,470

Capital Stock

	1/31 Bal.	80,000

Bal. $80,000

Dividends

1/31 Bal.	0
2/28	3,200

Bal. $3,200

Repair Service Revenue

	1/31 Bal.	2,200
	2/15	4,980
	2/28	5,400

Bal. $12,580

Advertising Expense

2/1	360
2/2	470

Bal. $830

Wages Expense

1/31 Bal.	1,200
2/28	4,900

Bal. $6,100

Utilities Expense

1/31 Bal.	200
2/28	1,600

Bal. $1,800

THE TRIAL BALANCE

Since equal dollar amounts of debits and credits are entered in the accounts for every transaction recorded, the sum of all the debits in the ledger must be equal to the sum of all the credits. If the computation of account balances has been accurate, it follows that the total of the accounts with debit balances must be equal to the total of the accounts with credit balances.

Before using the account balances to prepare a balance sheet, it is desirable to *prove* that the total of accounts with debit balances is in fact equal to the total of accounts with credit balances. This proof of the equality of debit and credit balances is called a **trial balance**. A trial balance is a two-column schedule listing the names and balances of all the accounts *in the order in which they appear in the ledger*; the debit balances are listed in the left-hand column and the credit balances in the right-hand column. The totals of the two columns should agree. A trial balance taken from Overnight Auto's ledger accounts on page 114 is shown in Exhibit 3–7.

LO 9 Prepare a trial balance and explain its uses and limitations.

Exhibit 3–7

OVERNIGHT AUTO SERVICE'S TRIAL BALANCE

My Notes

A trial balance proves the equality of debits and credits—but it also gives you a feel for how the business stands; but wait—there's more to consider

OVERNIGHT AUTO SERVICE
Trial Balance
February 28, 2002

	Debit	Credit
Cash	$ 13,120	
Accounts receivable	6,600	
Shop supplies	1,400	
Land	52,000	
Building	36,000	
Tools and equipment	12,000	
Notes payable		$ 30,000
Accounts payable		10,470
Capital stock		80,000
Retained earnings		0
Dividends	3,200	
Repair service revenue		12,580
Advertising expense	830	
Wages expense	6,100	
Utilities expense	1,800	
	$133,050	$133,050

This trial balance proves the equality of the debit and credit entries in the company's accounting system. Notice that the trial balance contains both balance sheet and income statement accounts. Note also that the Retained Earnings balance is *zero*. It is zero because *no debit or credit entries were made to the Retained Earnings account in January or February*. Overnight, like most companies, updates its Retained Earnings balance only *once each year*. In Chapter 5, we show how the Retained Earnings account is updated to its proper balance at year-end on December 31.[4]

Uses and Limitations of the Trial Balance

The trial balance provides proof that the ledger is in balance. The agreement of the debit and credit totals of the trial balance gives assurance that:

---

[4] The balance of $0 in the Retained Earnings account is a highly unusual situation. Because the company is still in its first year of operations, no entries have ever been made to update the account's balance. In any Trial Balance prepared after the first year of business activity, the Retained Earnings account may be expected to have a balance other than $0.

1. Equal debits and credits have been recorded for all transactions.
2. The addition of the account balances in the trial balance has been performed correctly.

Suppose that the debit and credit totals of the trial balance do not agree. This situation indicates that one or more errors have been made. Typical of such errors are (1) the posting of a debit as a credit, or vice versa; (2) arithmetic mistakes in determining account balances; (3) clerical errors in copying account balances into the trial balance; (4) listing a debit balance in the credit column of the trial balance, or vice versa; and (5) errors in addition of the trial balance.

The preparation of a trial balance does *not* prove that transactions have been correctly analyzed and recorded in the proper accounts. If, for example, a receipt of cash were erroneously recorded by debiting the Land account instead of the Cash account, the trial balance would still balance. Also, if a transaction were completely omitted from the ledger, the error would not be disclosed by the trial balance. In brief, *the trial balance proves only one aspect of the ledger, and that is the equality of debits and credits.*

CONCLUDING REMARKS

The Accounting Cycle in Perspective

In this chapter we have (1) journalized (recorded) transactions, (2) posted each journal entry to the appropriate ledger accounts, and (3) prepared a trial balance. The steps to be covered in Chapters 4 and 5 include (4) making end-of-period adjustments, (5) preparing an adjusted trial balance, (6) preparing financial statements, (7) journalizing and posting closing entries, and (8) preparing an after-closing trial balance.

LO 10
Distinguish between accounting cycle procedures and the *knowledge* of accounting.

We view the accounting cycle as an efficient means of introducing basic accounting terms, concepts, processes, and reports. This is why we introduce it early in the course. As we conclude the accounting cycle in Chapters 4 and 5, please don't confuse your familiarity with this sequence of procedures with a knowledge of *accounting*. The accounting cycle is but one accounting process—and a relatively simple one at that.

Computers now free accountants to focus upon the more *analytical* aspects of their discipline. These include, for example:

- Determining the information needs of decision makers.
- Designing systems to provide the information quickly and efficiently.
- Evaluating the efficiency of operations throughout the organization.
- Assisting decision makers in interpreting accounting information.
- Auditing (confirming the reliability of accounting information).
- Forecasting the probable results of future operations.
- Tax planning.

We will emphasize such topics in later chapters of this text. But let us first repeat a very basic point from Chapter 1: The need for some familiarity with accounting concepts and processes is not limited to individuals planning careers in accounting. Today, an understanding of accounting information and of the business world go hand in hand. You cannot know much about one without understanding quite a bit about the other.

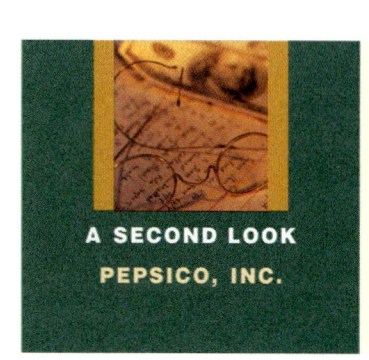

A SECOND LOOK
PEPSICO, INC.

In this chapter, we illustrated how Overnight Auto Service's accounting system captured numerous economic events. While a far more complex set of circumstances exist for **PepsiCo, Inc.**, the general accounting concepts that underlie revenue and expense recognition are pretty much the same for a multinational soft drink giant as they are for Overnight Auto Service.

In the following chapter, we examine certain adjustments to revenue and expense accounts required of most companies—both large and small—to comply with generally accepted principles of the accrual-based accounting method.

END-OF-CHAPTER REVIEW

SUMMARY OF LEARNING OBJECTIVES

LO 1
Identify the steps in the accounting cycle and discuss the role of accounting records in an organization.
The accounting cycle generally consists of eight specific steps: (1) journalizing (recording) transactions, (2) posting each journal entry to the appropriate ledger accounts, (3) preparing a trial balance, (4) making end-of-period adjustments, (5) preparing an adjusted trial balance, (6) preparing financial statements, (7) journalizing and posting closing entries, and (8) preparing an after-closing trial balance.

Accounting records provide the information that is summarized in financial statements, income tax returns, and other accounting reports. In addition, these records are used by the company's management and employees for such purposes as:

- Establishing accountability for assets and transactions.
- Keeping track of routine business activities.
- Obtaining details about specific transactions.
- Evaluating the performance of units within the business.
- Maintaining a documentary record of the business's activities. (Such a record is required by tax laws and is useful for many purposes, including audits.)

LO 2
Describe a ledger account and a ledger.
A ledger account is a device for recording the increases or decreases in one financial statement item, such as a particular asset, a type of liability, or owners' equity. The general ledger is an accounting record that includes all the ledger accounts—that is, a separate account for each item included in the company's financial statements.

LO 3
State the rules of debit and credit for balance sheet accounts.
Increases in assets are recorded by debits and decreases are recorded by credits. Increases in liabilities and in owners' equity are recorded by credits and decreases are recorded by debits. Notice that the debit and credit rules are related to an account's *location in the balance sheet*. If the account appears on the *left side* of the balance sheet (asset accounts), increases in the account balance are recorded by *left-side entries* (debits). If the account appears on the *right side* of the balance sheet (liability and owners' equity accounts), increases are recorded by *right-side entries* (credits).

LO 4
Explain the double-entry system of accounting.
The double-entry system of accounting takes its name from the fact that every business transaction is recorded by *two types of entries*: (1) debit entries to one or more accounts and (2) credit entries to one or more accounts. In recording any transaction, the total dollar amount of the debit entries must equal the total dollar amount of the credit entries.

LO 5
Explain the purpose of a journal and its relationship to the ledger.
The journal is the accounting record in which business transactions are initially recorded. The entry in the journal shows which ledger accounts have increased as a result of the transaction, and which have decreased. After the effects of the transaction have been recorded in the journal, the changes in the individual ledger accounts are then posted to the ledger.

LO 6
Explain the nature of *net income, revenue,* and *expenses*.
Net income is an increase in owners' equity that results from the profitable operation of a business during an accounting period. Net income also may be defined as revenue minus expenses. Revenue is the price of goods sold and services rendered to customers during the period, and expenses are the costs of the goods and services used up in the process of earning revenue.

LO 7
Apply the *realization* and *matching* principles in recording revenue and expenses.
The realization principle indicates that revenue should be recorded in the accounting records when it is *earned*—that is, when goods are sold or services are rendered to customers. The matching principle indicates that expenses should be offset against revenue on the basis of *cause and effect*. Thus, an expense should be recorded in the period in which the related good or service is consumed in the process of earning revenue.

LO 8
Explain *why* revenues are recorded with credits and expenses are recorded with debits.
The debit and credit rules for recording revenue and expenses are based on the rules for recording *changes in owners' equity*. Earning revenue *increases* owners' equity; therefore, revenues are recorded with credit entries. Expenses *reduce* owners' equity and are recorded with debit entries.

LO 9
Prepare a trial balance and explain its uses and limitations.
In a trial balance, separate debit and credit columns are used to list the balances of the individual ledger accounts. The two columns are then totaled to prove the equality of the debit and credit balances. This process provides assurance that (1) the total of the debits posted to the ledger was equal to the total of the credits and (2) the balances of the individual ledger accounts were correctly computed. While a trial balance proves the equality of debit and credit entries in the ledger, it does *not* detect

such errors as failure to record a business transaction, improper analysis of the accounts affected by the transaction, or the posting of debit or credit entries to the wrong accounts.

LO 10

Distinguish between accounting cycle procedures and the *knowledge* of accounting.

Accounting procedures involve the steps and processes necessary to *prepare* accounting information. A knowledge of the discipline enables one to *use* accounting information in evaluating performance, forecasting operations, and making complex business decisions.

KEY TERMS INTRODUCED OR EMPHASIZED IN CHAPTER 3

account (p. 91)   A record used to summarize all increases and decreases in a particular asset, such as cash, or any other type of asset, liability, owners' equity, revenue, or expense.

accountability (p. 90)   The condition of being held responsible for one's actions by the existence of an independent record of those actions. Establishing accountability is a major goal of accounting records and of internal control procedures.

accounting cycle (p. 90)   The sequence of accounting procedures used to record, classify, and summarize accounting information. The cycle begins with the initial recording of business transactions and concludes with the preparation of formal financial statements.

accounting period (p. 101)   The span of time covered by an income statement. One year is the accounting period for much financial reporting, but financial statements are also prepared by companies for each quarter of the year and for each month.

accrual basis of accounting (p. 104)   Calls for recording revenue in the period in which it is earned and recording expenses in the period in which they are incurred. The effect of events on the business is recognized as services are rendered or consumed rather than when cash is received or paid.

conservatism (p. 104)   The traditional accounting practice of resolving uncertainty by choosing the solution that leads to the lower (more conservative) amount of income being recognized in the current accounting period. This concept is designed to avoid overstatement of financial strength or earnings.

credit (p. 91)   An amount entered on the right side of a ledger account. A credit is used to record a decrease in an asset or an increase in a liability or in owners' equity.

debit (p. 91)   An amount entered on the left side of a ledger account. A debit is used to record an increase in an asset or a decrease in a liability or in owners' equity.

dividends (p. 100)   A distribution of resources by a corporation to its stockholders. The resource most often distributed is cash.

double-entry accounting (p. 93)   A system of recording every business transaction with equal dollar amounts of both debit and credit entries. As a result of this system, the accounting equation always remains in balance; in addition, the system makes possible the measurement of net income and also the use of error-detecting devices such as a trial balance.

expenses (p. 100)   The costs of the goods and services used up in the process of obtaining revenue.

fiscal year (p. 101)   Any 12-month accounting period adopted by a business.

general journal (p. 96)   The simplest type of journal, it has only two money columns—one for credits and one for debits. This journal may be used for all types of transactions, which are later posted to the appropriate ledger accounts.

income statement (p. 100)   A financial statement summarizing the results of operations of a business by matching its revenue and related expenses for a particular accounting period. Shows the net income or net loss.

journal (p. 96)   A chronological record of transactions, showing for each transaction the debits and credits to be entered in specific ledger accounts. The simplest type of journal is called a general journal.

ledger (p. 91)   An accounting system includes a separate record for each item that appears in the financial statements. Collectively, these records are referred to as a company's ledger. Individually, these records are often referred to as ledger accounts.

matching principle (p. 103)   The generally accepted accounting principle that determines when expenses should be recorded in the accounting records. The revenue earned during an accounting period is matched (offset) with the expenses incurred in generating this revenue.

net income (p. 99)   An increase in owners' equity resulting from profitable operations. Also, the excess of revenue earned over the related expenses for a given period.

net loss (p. 100)   A decrease in owners' equity resulting from unprofitable operations.

objectivity (p. 104)   Accountants' preference for using dollar amounts that are relatively factual—as opposed to merely matters of personal opinion. Objective measurements can be verified.

posting (p. 96)   The process of transferring information from the journal to individual accounts in the ledger.

realization principle (p. 102)   The generally accepted accounting principle that determines when revenue should be recorded in the accounting records. Revenue is realized when services are rendered to customers or when goods sold are delivered to customers.

retained earnings (p. 100)   That portion of stockholders' (owners') equity resulting from profits earned and retained in the business.

revenue (p. 100)   The price of goods and services charged to customers for goods and services rendered by a business.

time period principle (p. 101) To provide the users of financial statements with timely information, net income is measured for relatively short accounting periods of equal length. The period of time covered by an income statement is termed the company's accounting period.

trial balance (p. 115) A two-column schedule listing the names and the debit or credit balances of all accounts in the ledger.

DEMONSTRATION PROBLEM

Epler Consulting Services, Inc., opened for business on January 25, 2002. The company maintains the following ledger accounts:

Cash	Capital Stock
Accounts Receivable	Retained Earnings
Office Supplies	Consulting Revenue
Office Equipment	Rent Expense
Accounts Payable	Utilities Expense

The company engaged in the following business activity in January:

Jan. 20 Issued 5,000 shares of capital stock for $50,000.

Jan. 20 Paid $400 office rent for the remainder of January.

Jan. 21 Purchased office supplies for $200. The supplies will last for several months, and payment is not due until February 15.

Jan. 22 Purchased office equipment for $15,000 cash.

Jan. 26 Performed consulting services and billed clients $2,000. The entire amount will not be collected until February.

Jan. 31 Recorded $100 utilities expense. Payment is not due until February 20.

Instructions

a. Record each of the above transactions in general journal form.
b. Post each entry to the appropriate ledger accounts.
c. Prepare a trial balance dated January 31, 2002.
d. Explain why the Retained Earnings account has a zero balance in the trial balance.

Solution to the Demonstration Problem

a.

EPLER CONSULTING SERVICES, INC.
General Journal

Date	Account Titles and Explanation	Debit	Credit
2002			
Jan. 20	Cash	50,000	
	Capital Stock		50,000
	To record the issue of 5,000 shares of capital stock at $10 per share.		
20	Rent Expense	400	
	Cash		400
	To record payment of January rent expense.		
21	Office Supplies	200	
	Accounts Payable		200
	To record purchase of office supplies on account.		
22	Office Equipment	15,000	
	Cash		15,000
	To record the purchase of office equipment.		
26	Accounts Receivable	2,000	
	Consulting Revenue		2,000
	Billed clients for consulting services rendered.		
31	Utilities Expense	100	
	Accounts Payable		100
	To record January utilities expense due in February.		

b.

EPLER CONSULTING SERVICES, INC.
The Ledger
January 20–31, 2002

Asset Accounts			Liability and Owners' Equity Accounts	
Cash			**Accounts Payable**	
1/20 50,000	1/20 400			1/21 200
	1/22 15,000			1/31 100
Bal. $34,600				Bal. $300
Accounts Receivable			**Capital Stock**	
1/26 2,000				1/20 50,000
Bal. $2,000				Bal. $50,000
Office Supplies			**Retained Earnings**	
1/21 200				
Bal. $200				Bal. $0
Office Equipment			**Consulting Revenue**	
1/22 15,000				1/26 2,000
Bal. $15,000				Bal. $2,000
			Rent Expense	
			1/20 400	
			Bal. $400	
			Utilities Expense	
			1/31 100	
			Bal. $100	

c.

EPLER CONSULTING SERVICES, INC.
Trial Balance
January 31, 2002

Cash	$34,600	
Accounts receivable	2,000	
Office supplies	200	
Office equipment	15,000	
Accounts payable		$ 300
Capital stock		50,000
Retained earnings		0
Consulting revenue		2,000
Rent expense	400	
Utilities expense	100	
	$52,300	$52,300

d. Epler's Retained Earnings account balance is zero because the company has been in business for only one week and has not yet updated the Retained Earnings account for *any* revenue or expense activities. The periodic adjustment needed to update the Retained Earnings account is discussed in Chapter 5.

SELF-TEST QUESTIONS

Answers to these questions appear on page 133.

1. According to the rules of debit and credit for balance sheet accounts:
   a. Increases in asset, liability, and owners' equity accounts are recorded by debits.
   b. Decreases in asset and liability accounts are recorded by credits.
   c. Increases in asset and owners' equity accounts are recorded by debits.
   d. Decreases in liability and owners' equity accounts are recorded by debits.
2. Sunset Tours has a $3,500 account receivable from the Del Mar Rotary. On January 20, the Rotary makes a partial payment of $2,100 to Sunset Tours. The journal entry made on January 20 by Sunset Tours to record this transaction includes:
   a. A debit to the Cash Received account of $2,100.
   b. A credit to the Accounts Receivable account of $2,100.
   c. A debit to the Cash account of $1,400.
   d. A debit to the Accounts Receivable account of $1,400.
3. Indicate all of the following statements that correctly describe net income. Net income:
   a. Is equal to revenue minus expenses.
   b. Is equal to revenue minus the sum of expenses and dividends.
   c. Increases owners' equity.
   d. Is reported by a company for a specific period of time.
4. Which of the following is provided by a trial balance in which total debits equal total credits?
   a. Proof that no transaction was completely omitted from the ledger during the posting process.
   b. Proof that the correct debit or credit balance has been computed for each account.
   c. Proof that the ledger is in balance.
   d. Proof that transactions have been correctly analyzed and recorded in the proper accounts.
5. Which of the following explains the debit and credit rules relating to the recording of revenue and expenses?

a. Expenses appear on the left side of the balance sheet and are recorded by debits; revenue appears on the right side of the balance sheet and is recorded by credits.
   b. Expenses appear on the left side of the income statement and are recorded by debits; revenue appears on the right side of the income statement and is recorded by credits.
   c. The effects of revenue and expenses on owners' equity.
   d. The realization principle and the matching principle.
6. Which of the following is *not* considered an analytical aspect of the accounting profession?
   a. Evaluating an organization's operational efficiency.
   b. Forecasting the probable results of future operations.
   c. Designing systems that provide information to decision makers.
   d. Journalizing and posting business transactions.
7. Indicate all correct answers. In the accounting cycle
   a. Transactions are posted before they are journalized.
   b. A trial balance is prepared after journal entries have been posted.
   c. The Retained Earnings account is not shown as an up-to-date figure in the trial balance.
   d. Journal entries are posted to appropriate ledger accounts.
8. Indicate all correct answers. Dividends
   a. Decrease owners' equity.
   b. Decrease net income.
   c. Are recorded by debiting the Dividend account.
   d. Are a business expense.

ASSIGNMENT MATERIAL

DISCUSSION QUESTIONS

1. Baker Construction is a small corporation owned and managed by Tom Baker. The corporation has 21 employees, few creditors, and no investor other than Tom Baker. Thus, like many small businesses, it has no obligation to issue financial statements to creditors or investors. Under these circumstances, is there any reason for this corporation to maintain accounting records?
2. In its simplest form, an account has only three elements or basic parts. What are these three elements?
3. At the beginning of the year, the Office Equipment account of Gulf Coast Airlines had a debit balance of *$126,900*. During the year, debit entries of *$23,400* and credit entries of *$38,200* were posted to the account. What was the balance of this account at the end of the year? (Indicate debit or credit balance.)
4. What relationship exists between the position of an account on the balance sheet and the rules for recording increases in that account?
5. State briefly the rules of debit and credit as applied to asset accounts and as applied to liability and owners' equity accounts.
6. Does the term *debit* mean increase and the term *credit* mean decrease? Explain.
7. What requirement is imposed by the double-entry system in the recording of any business transaction?
8. Explain precisely what is meant by each of the phrases listed below. Whenever appropriate, indicate whether the left or right side of an account is affected and whether an increase or decrease is indicated.
   a. A debit of $200 to the Cash account.
   b. A debit of $600 to Accounts Payable.
   c. A credit of $50 to Accounts Receivable.
   d. A debit to the Land account.
   e. Credit balance.
   f. Credit side of an account.

9. For each of the following transactions, indicate whether the account in parentheses should be debited or credited, and *give the reason* for your answer.
   a. Purchased land for cash. (Cash)
   b. Sold an old, unneeded computer on 30-day credit. (Office Equipment)
   c. Obtained a loan of $30,000 from a bank. (Cash)
   d. Purchased a copying machine on credit, promising to make payment in full within 30 days. (Accounts Payable)
   e. Williams Word Processing, Inc., issued 10,000 shares of capital stock. (Capital Stock)
10. Explain the effect of operating profitably on the balance sheet of a business entity.
11. Does net income represent a supply of cash that could be distributed to stockholders in the form of dividends? Explain.
12. What is the meaning of the term *revenue?* Does the receipt of cash by a business indicate that revenue has been earned? Explain.
13. What is the meaning of the term *expenses?* Does the payment of cash by a business indicate that an expense has been incurred? Explain.
14. A service enterprise performs services in the amount of $500 for a customer in May and receives payment in June. In which month is the $500 of revenue recognized? What is the journal entry to be made in May and the entry to be made in June?
15. When do accountants consider revenue to be realized? What basic question about recording revenue in accounting records is answered by the *realization principle?*
16. Late in March, Classic Auto Painters purchased paint on account, with payment due in 60 days. The company used the paint to paint customers' cars during the first three weeks of April. Late in May, the company paid the paint store from which the paint had been purchased. In which month should Classic Auto Painters recognize the cost of this paint as expense? What generally accepted accounting principle determines the answer to this question?
17. In what accounting period does the *matching principle* indicate that an expense should be recognized?
18. Explain the rules of debit and credit with respect to transactions recorded in revenue and expense accounts.
19. What are some of the limitations of a trial balance?
20. How do dividends affect owners' equity? Are they treated as a business expense? Explain.
21. How does the accrual basis of accounting differ from the cash basis of accounting? Which gives a more accurate picture of the profitability of a business? Explain.

EXERCISES

EXERCISE 3.1

Accounting Terminology

LO 1–10

Listed below are eight technical accounting terms introduced in this chapter:

Realization principle	Credit
Time period principle	Accounting period
Matching principle	Expenses
Net income	Accounting cycle

Each of the following statements may (or may not) describe one of these technical terms. For each statement, indicate the term described, or answer "None" if the statement does not correctly describe any of the terms.

a. The span of time covered by an income statement.
b. The sequence of accounting procedures used to record, classify, and summarize accounting information.
c. The traditional accounting practice of resolving uncertainty by choosing the solution that leads to the lowest amount of income being recognized.
d. An increase in owners' equity resulting from profitable operations.
e. The generally accepted accounting principle that determines when revenue should be recorded in the accounting records.

Exercises

f. The type of entry used to decrease an asset or increase a liability or owners' equity account.
g. The generally accepted accounting principle of offsetting revenue earned during an accounting period with the expenses incurred in generating that revenue.
h. The costs of the goods and services used up in the process of generating revenue.

EXERCISE 3.2

The Accounting Cycle

LO 1, 2, 5, 9, 10

Listed below in *random order* are the eight steps comprising a complete accounting cycle:
- Prepare a trial balance. 3
- Journalize and post the closing entries. 7
- Prepare financial statements. 6
- Post transaction data to the ledger. 2
- Prepare an adjusted trial balance. 5
- Make end-of-period adjustments. 4
- Journalize transactions. 1
- Prepare an after-closing trial balance. 8

a. List these steps in the sequence in which they would normally be performed. (A detailed understanding of these eight steps is not required until Chapters 4 and 5.)
b. Describe ways in which the information produced through the accounting cycle is used by a company's management and employees.

EXERCISE 3.3

The Matching Principle: You as a Driver

LO 6, 7

The purpose of this exercise is to demonstrate the *matching principle* in a familiar setting. Assume that you own a car that you drive about 15,000 miles each year.

a. List the various costs to you associated with owning and operating this car. Make an estimate of the total annual cost of owning and operating the car, as well as the average cost-per-mile that you drive.
b. Assume also that you have a part-time job. You usually do not use your car in this job, but today your employer asks you to drive 100 miles (round trip) to deliver some important documents. Your employer offers to "reimburse you for your driving expenses."

You already have a full tank of gas, so you are able to drive the whole 100 miles without stopping and you don't actually spend any money during the trip. Does this mean that you have incurred no "expenses" for which you should be reimbursed? Explain.

EXERCISE 3.4

Recording Transactions in a Journal

LO 3, 4, 5

Record the following selected transactions in general journal form for Sun Orthopedic Clinic, Inc. Include a brief explanation of the transaction as part of each journal entry.

Oct. 1 The clinic issued 4,000 additional shares of capital stock to Doctor Soges at $50 per share.
Oct. 4 The clinic purchased diagnostic equipment. The equipment cost $75,000, of which $25,000 was paid in cash; a note payable was issued for the balance.
Oct. 12 Issued a check for $9,000 in full payment of an account payable to Zeller Laboratories.
Oct. 19 Purchased surgical supplies for $2,600. Payment is not due until November 28.
Oct. 25 Collected a $24,000 account receivable from Health One Insurance Company.
Oct. 30 Declared and paid a $300,000 cash dividend to stockholders.

EXERCISE 3.5

Relationship between Journal and Ledger Accounts

LO 2, 3, 4, 5

Transactions are *first* journalized and *then* posted to ledger accounts. In this exercise, however, your understanding of the relationship between the journal and the ledger is tested by asking you to study some ledger accounts and determine the journal entries that probably were made to produce these ledger entries. The following accounts show the first six transactions of Avenson Insurance Company. Prepare a journal entry (including a written explanation) for each transaction.

	Cash				Vehicles		
Nov. 1	120,000	Nov. 8	33,600	Nov. 30	9,400		
		Nov. 25	12,000				
		Nov. 30	1,400				

	Land			Notes Payable	
Nov. 8	70,000	Nov. 25	12,000	Nov. 8	95,000
				Nov. 30	8,000

	Building			Accounts Payable	
Nov. 8	58,600	Nov. 21	480	Nov. 15	3,200

	Office Equipment			Capital Stock	
Nov. 15	3,200	Nov. 21	480		Nov. 1	120,000

EXERCISE 3.6

Preparing a Trial Balance

LO 9

Using the information in the ledger accounts presented in Exercise 3.5, prepare a trial balance for Avenson Insurance Company dated November 30.

EXERCISE 3.7

Relationship between Net Income and Equity

LO 6, 8

The following information came from a recent balance sheet of **Apple Computer, Inc.**:

	End of Year	Beginning of Year
Assets	$6.8 billion	$5.1 billion
Liabilities	$2.7 billion	?
Owner's Equity	?	$3.1 billion

a. Determine the amount of total liabilities reported in **Apple Computer**'s balance sheet at the beginning of the year.

b. Determine the amount of total owners' equity reported in **Apple Computer**'s balance sheet at the end of the year.

c. Capital stock reported in **Apple Computer**'s year-end balance sheet was $220 million more than the amount reported in the company's beginning balance sheet. If the company did not declare any dividends, determine its net income for the year.

EXERCISE 3.8

Effects of Transactions on the Accounting Equation

LO 2, 3, 4, 5, 6

Satka Fishing Expeditions, Inc., recorded the following transactions in July:

1. Provided an ocean fishing expedition for a credit customer; payment is due August 10.
2. Paid Marine Service Center for repairs to boats performed in June. (In June, Satka Fishing Expeditions, Inc., had received and properly recorded the invoice for these repairs.)
3. Collected the full amount due from a credit customer for a fishing expedition provided in June.
4. Received a bill from Baldy's Bait Shop for bait purchased and used in July. Payment is due August 3.
5. Purchased a new fishing boat on July 28, paying part cash and issuing a note payable for the balance. The new boat is first scheduled for use on August 5.
6. Declared and paid a cash dividend on July 31.

Indicate the effects that each of these transactions will have upon the following six *total amounts* in the company's financial statements for the month of July. Organize your answer in tabular form, using the column headings shown, and use the code letters **I** for increase, **D** for decrease, and **NE** for no effect. The answer to transaction **1** is provided as an example.

Transaction	Income Statement			Balance Sheet		
	Revenue −	Expenses =	Net Income	Assets =	Liabilities +	Owners' Equity
(1)	I	NE	I	I	NE	I

EXERCISE 3.9
Effects of Transactions on the Accounting Equation
LO 2, 3, 4, 5, 6

A number of transactions of Claypool Construction are described below in terms of accounts debited and credited:

1. Debit Wages Expense; credit Wages Payable.
2. Debit Accounts Receivable; credit Construction Revenue.
3. Debit Dividends; credit Cash.
4. Debit Office Supplies; credit Accounts Payable.
5. Debit Repairs Expense; credit Cash.
6. Debit Cash; credit Accounts Receivable.
7. Debit Tools and Equipment; credit Cash and Notes Payable.
8. Debit accounts Payable; credit Cash.

a. Indicate the effects of each transaction upon the elements of the income statement and the balance sheet. Use the code letters **I** for increase, **D** for decrease, and **NE** for no effect. Organize your answer in tabular form using the column headings shown below. The answer for transaction **1** is provided as an example.

Transaction	Income Statement			Balance Sheet		
	Revenue −	Expenses =	Net Income	Assets =	Liabilities +	Owners' Equity
(1)	NE	I	D	NE	I	D

b. Write a one-sentence description of each transaction.

EXERCISE 3.10
When Is Revenue Realized?
LO 6, 7

The following transactions were carried out during the month of May by M. Palmer and Company, a firm of design architects. For each of the five transactions, you are to state whether the transaction represented revenue to the firm during the month of May. Give reasons for your decision in each case.

a. M. Palmer and Company received $25,000 cash by issuing additional shares of capital stock.
b. Collected cash of $2,400 from an account receivable. The receivable originated in April from services rendered to a client.
c. Borrowed $12,800 from Century Bank to be repaid in three months.
d. Earned $83 interest on a company bank account during the month of May. No withdrawals were made from this account in May.
e. Completed plans for guest house, pool, and spa for a client. The $5,700 fee for this project was billed to the client in May, but will not be collected until June 25.

EXERCISE 3.11
When Are Expenses Incurred?
LO 6, 7

During March, the activities of Evergreen Landscaping included the following transactions and events, among others. Which of these items represented expenses in March? Explain.

a. Purchased a copying machine for $2,750 cash.
b. Paid $192 for gasoline purchases for a delivery truck during March.
c. Paid $2,280 salary to an employee for time worked during March.
d. Paid an attorney $560 for legal services rendered in January.
e. Declared and paid an $1,800 dividend to shareholders.

EXERCISE 3.12
Preparing Journal Entries for Revenue, Expenses, and Dividends
LO 4, 6, 7, 8

Shown below are selected transactions of the architectural firm of Baxter, Claxter, and Stone, Inc.

April 5 Prepared building plans for Spangler Construction Company. Sent Spangler an invoice for $900 requesting payment within 30 days. (The appropriate revenue account is entitled Drafting Fees Earned.)

May 17 Declared a cash dividend of $5,000. The dividend will not be paid until June 25.

May 29   Received a $2,000 bill from Bob Needham, CPA, for accounting services performed during May. Payment is due by June 10. (The appropriate expense account is entitled Professional Expenses.)

June 4   Received full payment from Spangler Construction Company for the invoice sent on April 5.

June 10   Paid Bob Needham, CPA, for the bill received on May 29.

June 25   Paid the cash dividend declared on May 17.

a. Prepare journal entries to record the transactions in the firm's accounting records.

b. Identify any of the above transactions that *will not* result in a change in the company's net income.

EXERCISE 3.13

Annual Report; Appendix A

LO 1, 2, 3, 7, 10

Throughout this text we have many assignments based on the annual report of **Tootsie Roll Industries, Inc.**, in Appendix A. Refer to this annual report to respond to the following items:

a. Does the company's fiscal year end on December 31? How can you tell?

b. State the company's balance sheet in terms of A = L + E.

d. Did the company post more debits to the Cash account during the year than credits? How can you tell?

PROBLEMS

PROBLEM 3.1

Journalizing Transactions

LO 3, 4, 5

Glenn Grimes is the founder and president of Heartland Construction, a real estate development venture. The business transactions during February while the company was being organized are listed below.

Feb. 1   Grimes and several others invested $500,000 cash in the business in exchange for 25,000 shares of capital stock.

Feb. 10   The company purchased office facilities for $300,000, of which $100,000 was applicable to the land, and $200,000 to the building. A cash payment of $60,000 was made and a note payable was issued for the balance of the purchase price.

Feb. 16   Computer equipment was purchased from PCWorld for $12,000 cash.

Feb. 18   Office furnishings were purchased from Hi-Way Furnishings at a cost of $9,000. A $1,000 cash payment was made at the time of purchase, and an agreement was made to pay the remaining balance in two equal installments due March 1 and April 1. Hi-Way Furnishings did not require that Heartland sign a promissory note.

Feb. 22   Office supplies were purchased from Office World for $300 cash.

Feb. 23   Heartland discovered that it paid too much for a computer printer purchased on February 16. The unit should have cost only $359, but Heartland was charged $395. PCWorld promised to refund the difference within seven days.

Feb. 27   Mailed Hi-Way Furnishings the first installment due on the account payable for office furnishings purchased on February 18.

Feb. 28   Received $36 from PCWorld in full settlement of the account receivable created on February 23.

Instructions

a. Prepare journal entries to record the above transactions. Select the appropriate account titles from the following chart of accounts:

Cash	Land
Accounts Receivable	Office Building
Office Supplies	Notes Payable
Office Furnishings	Accounts Payable
Computer Systems	Capital Stock

b. Indicate the effects of each transaction on the company's assets, liabilities, and owners' equity for the month of February. Organize your analysis in tabular form as shown for the February 1 transaction:

Transaction	Assets	=	Liabilities	+	Owners' Equity
Feb. 1	+$500,000 (Cash)		$0		+$500,000 (Capital Stock)

PROBLEM 3.2

Analyzing and Journalizing Transactions

LO 3, 4, 5, 6, 7, 8

Environmental Services, Inc., performs various tests on wells and septic systems. A few of the company's business transactions occurring during August are described below:

1. On August 1, the company billed customers $2,500 on account for services rendered. Customers are required to make full payment within 30 days.
2. On August 3, purchased testing supplies costing $3,800, paying $800 cash and charging the remainder on the company's 30-day account at Penn Chemicals. The testing supplies are expected to last several months.
3. On August 5, returned to Penn Chemicals $100 of testing supplies that were not needed. The return of these supplies reduced by $100 the amount owed to Penn Chemicals.
4. On August 17, the company issued an additional 2,500 shares of capital stock at $8 per share. The cash raised will be used to purchase new testing equipment in September.
5. On August 22, the company received $600 cash from customers it had billed on August 1.
6. On August 29, the company paid its outstanding account payable to Penn Chemicals.
7. On August 30, a cash dividend totaling $6,800 was declared and paid to the company's stockholders.

Instructions

a. Prepare an analysis of each of the above transactions. Transaction 1 serves as an example of the form of analysis to be used.
   1. (a) The asset Accounts Receivable was increased. Increases in assets are recorded by debits. Debit Accounts Receivable, $2,500.
      (b) Revenue has been earned. Revenue increases owners' equity. Increases in owners' equity are recorded by credits. Credit Testing Service Revenue, $2,500.
b. Prepare journal entries, including explanations, for the above transactions.
c. How does the *realization principle* influence the manner in which the August 1 billing to customers is recorded in the accounting records?
d. How does the *matching principle* influence the manner in which the August 3 purchase of testing supplies is recorded in the accounting records?

PROBLEM 3.3

Analyzing and Journalizing Transactions

LO 3, 4, 5, 6, 7, 8

Weida Surveying, Inc., provides land surveying services. During September, its transactions included the following:

Sept. 1 Paid rent for the month of September, $4,400.
Sept. 3 Billed Fine Line Homes $5,620 for surveying services. The entire amount is due on or before September 28. (Weida uses an account entitled Surveying Revenue when billing clients.)
Sept. 9 Provided surveying services to Sunset Ridge Developments for $2,830. The entire amount was collected on this date.
Sept. 14 Placed a newspaper advertisement in the *Daily Item* to be published in the September 20 issue. The cost of the advertisement was $165. Payment is due in 30 days.
Sept. 25 Received a check for $5,620 from Fine Line Homes for the amount billed on September 3.
Sept. 26 Provided surveying services to Thompson Excavating Company for $1,890. Weida collected $400 cash, with the balance due in 30 days.
Sept. 29 Sent a check to the *Daily Item* in full payment of the liability incurred on September 14.
Sept. 30 Declared and paid a $7,600 cash dividend to the company's stockholders.

Instructions

a. Analyze the effects that each of these transactions will have on the following six components of the company's financial statements for the month of September. Organize your answer in tabular form, using the column headings shown. Use **I** for increase, **D** for decrease, and **NE** for no effect. The September 1 transaction is provided for you:

	Income Statement	Balance Sheet
Transaction	Revenue − Expenses = Net Income	Assets = Liabilities + Owners' Equity
Sept. 1	NE I D	D NE D

b. Prepare a journal entry (including explanation) for each of the above transactions.

c. Three of September's transactions involve cash payments, yet only one of these transactions is recorded as an expense. Describe three situations in which a cash payment would *not* involve recognition of an expense.

PROBLEM 3.4
The Accounting Cycle: Journalizing, Posting, and Preparing a Trial Balance

LO 1–10

In June 2002, Wendy Winger organized a corporation to provide aerial photography services. The company, called Aerial Views, began operations immediately. Transactions during the month of June were as follows:

June 1 The corporation issued 60,000 shares of capital stock to Wendy Winger in exchange for $60,000 cash.

June 2 Purchased a plane from Utility Aircraft for $220,000. Made a $40,000 cash down payment and issued a note payable for the remaining balance.

June 4 Paid Woodrow Airport $2,500 to rent office and hangar space for the month.

June 15 Billed customers $8,320 for aerial photographs taken during the first half of June.

June 15 Paid $5,880 in salaries earned by employees during the first half of June.

June 18 Paid Hannigan's Hangar $1,890 for maintenance and repair services on the company plane.

June 25 Collected $4,910 of the amounts billed to customers on June 15.

June 30 Billed customers $16,450 for aerial photographs taken during the second half of the month.

June 30 Paid $6,000 in salaries earned by employees during the second half of the month.

June 30 Received a $2,510 bill from Peatree Petroleum for aircraft fuel purchased in June. The entire amount is due July 10.

June 30 Declared a $2,000 dividend payable on July 15.

The account titles used by Aerial Views are

Cash	Retained Earnings
Accounts Receivable	Dividends
Aircraft	Aerial Photography Revenue
Notes Payable	Maintenance Expense
Accounts Payable	Fuel Expense
Dividends Payable	Salaries Expense
Capital Stock	Rent Expense

Instructions

a. Analyze the effects that each of these transactions will have on the following six components of the company's financial statements for the month of June. Organize your answer in tabular form, using the column headings shown on the facing page. Use **I** for increase, **D** for decrease, and **NE** for no effect. The June 1 transaction is provided for you:

	Income Statement	Balance Sheet
Transaction	Revenue − Expenses = Net Income	Assets = Liabilities + Owners' Equity
June 1	NE NE NE	I NE I

b. Prepare journal entries (including explanations) for each transaction.

c. Post each transaction to the appropriate ledger accounts (use a running balance format as illustrated in Exhibit 3–3).

d. Prepare a trial balance dated June 30, 2002.

Cases and Unstructured Problems

e. Using figures from the trial balance prepared in part **d,** compute total assets, total liabilities, and owners' equity. Are these the figures that the company will report in its June 30 balance sheet? Explain your answer briefly.

PROBLEM 3.5

The Accounting Cycle: Journalizing, Posting, and Preparing a Trial Balance

LO 1–10

Dr. Schekter, DVM, opened a veterinary clinic on May 1. The business transactions for May are shown below:

May 1 Dr. Schekter invested $400,000 cash in the business in exchange for 5,000 shares of capital stock.

May 4 Land and a building were purchased for $250,000. Of this amount, $70,000 applied to the land, and $180,000 to the building. A cash payment of $100,000 was made at the time of the purchase, and a note payable was issued for the remaining balance.

May 9 Medical instruments were purchased for $130,000 cash.

May 16 Office fixtures and equipment were purchased for $50,000. Dr. Schekter paid $20,000 at the time of purchase and agreed to pay the entire remaining balance in 15 days.

May 21 Office supplies expected to last several months were purchased for $5,000 cash.

May 24 Dr. Schekter billed clients $2,200 for services rendered. Of this amount, $1,900 was received in cash, and $300 was billed on account (due in 30 days).

May 27 A $400 invoice was received for several radio advertisements aired in May. The entire amount is due on June 5.

May 28 Received a $100 payment on the $300 account receivable recorded May 24.

May 31 Paid employees $2,800 for salaries earned in May.

A partial list of account titles used by Dr. Schekter includes:

Cash	Notes Payable
Accounts Receivable	Accounts Payable
Office Supplies	Capital Stock
Medical Instruments	Veterinary Service Revenue
Office Fixtures and Equipment	Advertising Expense
Land	Salary Expense
Building	

Instructions

a. Analyze the effects that each of these transactions will have on the following six components of the company's financial statements for the month of May. Organize your answer in tabular form, using the column headings shown below. Use **I** for increase, **D** for decrease, and **NE** for no effect. The May 1 transaction is provided for you:

	Income Statement			Balance Sheet		
Transaction	Revenue	− Expenses	= Net Income	Assets	= Liabilities	+ Owners' Equity
May 1	NE	NE	NE	I	NE	I

b. Prepare journal entries (including explanations) for each transaction.
c. Post each transaction to the appropriate ledger accounts (use T account format as illustrated on page 114).
d. Prepare a trial balance dated May 31, 2002.
e. Using figures from the trial balance prepared in part **d,** compute total assets, total liabilities, and owners' equity. Did May appear to be a profitable month?

CASES AND UNSTRUCTURED PROBLEMS

CASE 3.1

Revenue Recognition

LO 7, 10

The realization principle determines when a business should recognize revenue. Listed next are three common business situations involving revenue. After each situation, we give two alternatives as to the accounting period (or periods) in which the business might recognize this revenue. Select the appropriate alternative by applying the realization principle, and explain your reasoning.

a. Airline ticket revenue: Most airlines sell tickets well before the scheduled date of the flight. (Period ticket sold; period of flight)
b. Sales on account: In June 2002, a San Diego–based furniture store had a big sale, featuring "No payments until 2003." (Period furniture sold; periods that payments are received from customers)
c. Magazine subscriptions revenue: Most magazine publishers sell subscriptions for future delivery of the magazine. (Period subscription sold; periods that magazines are mailed to customers)

CASE 3.2

Measuring Income Fairly

LO 6, 7, 10

Kim Morris purchased Print Shop, Inc., a printing business, from Chris Stanley. Morris made a cash down payment and agreed to make annual payments equal to 40% of the company's net income in each of the next three years. (Such "earn-outs" are a common means of financing the purchase of a small business.) Stanley was disappointed, however, when Morris reported a first year's net income far below Stanley's expectations.

The agreement between Morris and Stanley did not state precisely how "net income" was to be measured. Neither Morris nor Stanley was familiar with accounting concepts. Their agreement stated only that the net income of the corporation should be measured in a "fair and reasonable manner."

In measuring net income, Morris applied the following policies:

1. Revenue was recognized when cash was received from customers. Most customers paid in cash, but a few were allowed 30-day credit terms.
2. Expenditures for ink and paper, which are purchased weekly, were charged directly to Supplies Expense, as were the Morris family's weekly grocery and dry cleaning bills.
3. Morris set her annual salary at $60,000, which Stanley had agreed was reasonable. She also paid salaries of $30,000 per year to her husband and to each of her two teenage children. These family members did not work in the business on a regular basis, but they did help out when things got busy.
4. Income taxes expense included the amount paid by the corporation (which was computed correctly), as well as the personal income taxes paid by various members of the Morris family on the salaries they earned working for the business.
5. The business had state-of-the-art printing equipment valued at $150,000 at the time Morris purchased it. The first-year income statement included a $150,000 equipment expense related to these assets.

Instructions

a. Discuss the fairness and reasonableness of these income-measurement policies. (Remember, these policies do *not* have to conform to generally accepted accounting principles. But they should be *fair* and *reasonable*.)
b. Do you think that the net *cash flow* generated by this business (cash receipts less cash outlays) is higher or lower than the net income as measured by Morris? Explain.

BUSINESS WEEK ASSIGNMENT

CASE 3.3

Critical Path and Accounting Principles

LO 7

The August 6, 2001, *Business Week* article "Critical Errors at Critical Path" by Ben Elgin details recent problems experienced by **Critical Path Inc.**, a company that managed e-mail for corporations. On February 2, 2001, **Critical Path** disclosed that its fourth-quarter earnings report may have contained accounting irregularities. In its first quarter ended March 31 2001, **Critical Path** was facing investigation by the Securities and Exchange Commission and more than two dozen lawsuits, claiming that the company artificially inflated its stock with unrealistic revenue and profit projections.

What happened? According to several current and former executives, the company backdated sales contracts, pushing deals forward by several days so they would count in an earlier quarter. It also relied on so-called side-letter deals, which made it appear as if **Critical Path**'s services were being ordered by clients. In reality, **Critical Path**'s management knew these side-letters would allow customers to renege on purchase agreements without penalties.

Instructions

Write a brief paragraph explaining whether you believe **Critical Path Inc.** followed the realization and matching principles. Include examples from the *Business Week* story above and provide a clear explanation about why the examples support your beliefs.

INTERNET ASSIGNMENT

INTERNET 3.1

Revenue from Various Sources

LO 6

Visit the EDGAR database of the Security and Exchange Commission at the following Internet location:

www.sec.gov/cgi-bin/srch-edgar

Enter **PC Connection** in the search box and access the company's most recent 10-K report. What percent of the company's total revenue was generated by desktop computers? What percent of the company's total revenue is generated by the sale of Macintosh systems manufactured by **Apple Computer**? Have sales of Macintosh systems as a percentage of total revenue increased or decreased during the past three years? Approximately how many catalogs does the company mail each year to potential customers?

Internet sites are time and date sensitive. It is the purpose of these exercises to have you explore the Internet. You may need to use the Yahoo! search engine **http://www.yahoo.com** *(or other favorite search engines) to find a company's current Web address.*

OUR COMMENTS ON THE "YOUR TURN" CASES

You as a Student (p. 92) The concept of double-entry accounting *does* apply to your personal financial position. The financial position of an individual may be described by the equation:

Assets = Liabilities + Net Worth

Any change in the amount of any asset or liability causes an offsetting change *elsewhere* in the equation. Thus two or more accounts within the accounting equation must change—this is what is meant by double-entry.

For example, your spending cash results in the acquisition of another asset, in the reduction of a liability, or in the reduction of your personal net worth (the equivalent of owners' equity in a business organization). A cash receipt implies the reduction of another asset, an increase in liabilities, or an increase in net worth.

Although individuals usually do not use debits and credits to record changes in their financial positions, the concept of double-entry—that is, corresponding changes in the accounting equation—still applies.

You as a Business Owner (p. 105) Indeed it does. If the business is *unincorporated,* its assets belong to you. Thus, you may withdraw these assets from the business at any time and use them for any purpose. But if the business is a corporation, these assets belong to *the corporate entity.* Even though you are the sole owner of the company, you may *not* withdraw assets from the business without *proper authorization.* Thus, your personal use of corporate assets must be viewed as compensation to you (i.e., salary), a loan, or a dividend.

Note: For income tax purposes, treating this expenditure as a loan probably is the best alternative. If you treat it as either salary or a dividend, you are receiving taxable income. Tax planning often plays a major role in transactions between a corporation and its owners.

You as Overnight Auto Service's Accountant (p. 110) You should tell Fred that the information he requests is confidential and you cannot provide it to him. The Institute of Management Accountants (IMA) has established a code of ethics that includes a requirement of confidentiality. Confidentiality means that accounting personnel should refrain from disclosing confidential information. The request from Fred Jonas would require you to violate the confidentiality requirement. For more information on the IMA's code of ethics, visit their website at:
www.imanet.org/Content/About_IMA/EthicsCenter/Code_of_Ethics/Ethical_Standards.htm

ANSWERS TO SELF-TEST QUESTIONS

1. d 2. b 3. a, c, and d 4. c 5. c 6. d 7. b, c, and d
8. a and c

CHAPTER 4

THE ACCOUNTING CYCLE:

Accruals and Deferrals

Learning Objectives

After studying this chapter, you should be able to:

1. Explain the purpose of adjusting entries.
2. Describe and prepare the four basic types of adjusting entries.
3. Prepare adjusting entries to convert assets to expenses.
4. Prepare adjusting entries to convert liabilities to revenue.
5. Prepare adjusting entries to accrue unpaid expenses.
6. Prepare adjusting entries to accrue uncollected revenue.
7. Explain how the principles of *realization* and *matching* relate to adjusting entries.
8. Explain the concept of *materiality*.
9. Prepare an adjusted trial balance and describe its purpose.

Reuters

Carnival Corporation

When is revenue actually *earned* by a company? In many cases, revenue is earned when cash is received at the point of sale. For instance, when a taxicab driver takes someone to the airport, revenue is earned when the passenger is dropped off at the appropriate terminal and the fare is collected.

Suppose the same passenger boards a **Carnival** cruise ship to the Bahamas using a ticket that was purchased six months in advance. At what point should the cruise line recognize that ticket revenue has been earned? A recent **Carnival Corporation** balance sheet provides the answer to this question.

In its balance sheet, **Carnival Corporation** reports a $771 million liability account called Customer Deposits. As passengers purchase tickets in advance, **Carnival Corporation** credits the Customer Deposits account for an amount equal to the cash it receives. It is not until passengers actually *use* their tickets that the company reduces this liability account and records Passenger Revenue in its income statement.

• • •

For most companies, revenue is *not* always earned as cash is received, nor is an expense necessarily incurred as cash is disbursed. Timing differences between cash flows and the recognition of revenue and expenses are referred to as *accruals* and *deferrals*. In this chapter we examine how accounting information must be adjusted for accruals and deferrals prior to the preparation of financial statements.

The first three steps of the accounting cycle were discussed in Chapter 3. They included (1) recording transactions, (2) posting transactions, and (3) preparing a trial balance. In this chapter, we focus solely upon the fourth step of the accounting cycle: Performing the end-of-period adjustments required to measure business income. The remaining steps of the cycle are covered in Chapter 5.

ADJUSTING ENTRIES

There is more to the measurement of business income than merely recording simple revenue and expense transactions that affect only a single accounting period. Certain transactions affect the revenue or expenses of *two or more* accounting periods. The purpose of adjusting entries is to assign to each accounting period appropriate amounts of revenue and expense. For example, Overnight Auto Service purchased shop supplies that will be used for several months. Thus, an adjusting entry is required to record the expense associated with the shop supplies that Overnight *uses* each month.

The Need for Adjusting Entries

For purposes of measuring income and preparing financial statements, the life of a business is divided into a series of *accounting periods*. This practice enables decision makers to compare the financial statements of successive periods and to identify significant trends.

But measuring net income for a relatively short accounting period—such as a month or even a year—poses a problem because, as mentioned above, some business activities affect the revenue and expenses of *multiple accounting periods*. Therefore, **adjusting entries** are needed at the end of each accounting period to make certain that appropriate amounts of revenue and expense are reported in the company's income statement.

For example, magazine publishers often sell two- or three-year subscriptions to their publications. At the end of each accounting period, these publishers make adjusting entries recognizing the portion of their advance receipts that have been earned during the current period. Most companies also purchase insurance policies that benefit more than one period. Therefore, an adjusting entry is needed to make certain that an appropriate portion of each policy's total cost is reported in the income statement as insurance expense for the period. In short, adjusting entries are needed whenever transactions affect the revenue or expenses of more than one accounting period. These entries assign revenues to the period in which they are *earned,* and expenses to the periods in which related goods or services are *used.*

In theory, a business could make adjusting entries on a daily basis. But as a practical matter, these entries are made *only at the end of each accounting period.* For most companies, adjusting entries are made on a monthly basis.

Types of Adjusting Entries

The number of adjustments needed at the end of each accounting period depends entirely upon the nature of the company's business activities. However, most adjusting entries fall into one of four general categories:[1]

1. *Converting assets to expenses.* A cash expenditure (or cost) that will benefit more than one accounting period usually is recorded by debiting an asset account (for

---

[1] A fifth category of adjusting entries consists of adjustments related to the valuation of certain assets, such as marketable securities and accounts receivable. These valuation adjustments are explained and illustrated in Chapter 7.

example, Supplies, Unexpired Insurance, and so on) and by crediting Cash. The asset account created actually represents the *deferral* (or the postponement) of an expense. In each future period that benefits from the use of this asset, an adjusting entry is made to allocate a portion of the asset's cost from the balance sheet to the income statement as an expense. This adjusting entry is recorded by debiting the appropriate expense account (for example, Supplies Expense or Insurance Expense) and crediting the related asset account (for example, Supplies or Unexpired Insurance).

2. *Converting liabilities to revenue.* A business may collect cash in advance for services to be rendered in future accounting periods. Transactions of this nature are usually recorded by debiting Cash and by crediting a liability account (typically called Unearned Revenue). Here, the liability account created represents the *deferral* (or the postponement) of a revenue. In the period that services are actually rendered (or that goods are sold), an adjusting entry is made to allocate a portion of the liability from the balance sheet to the income statement to recognize the revenue earned during the period. The adjusting entry is recorded by debiting the liability (Unearned Revenue) and by crediting *Revenue Earned* (or a similar account) for the value of the services.

3. *Accruing unpaid expenses.* An expense may be incurred in the current accounting period even though no cash payment will occur until a future period. These *accrued* expenses are recorded by an adjusting entry made at the end of each accounting period. The adjusting entry is recorded by debiting the appropriate expense account (for example, Interest Expense or Salary Expense) and by crediting the related liability (for example, Interest Payable or Salaries Payable).

4. *Accruing uncollected revenue.* Revenue may be earned (or *accrued*) during the current period, even though the collection of cash will not occur until a future period. Unrecorded earned revenue, for which no cash has been received, requires an adjusting entry at the end of the accounting period. The adjusting entry is recorded by debiting the appropriate asset (for example, Accounts Receivable or Interest Receivable) and by crediting the appropriate revenue account (for example, Service Revenue Earned or Interest Earned).

Each of these adjusting entry categories is illustrated in Exhibit 4–1.

CASH EFFECTS

In an accrual accounting system, there are often "timing differences" between cash flows and the recognition of expenses or revenue. A company can pay cash in advance of incurring certain expenses, and it can receive cash before earning certain revenue. Likewise, it can incur certain expenses before it pays any cash, and it can earn certain revenue before it receives any cash. These timing differences, and the related adjusting entries that result from them, are summarized below:

- Adjusting entries to convert assets to expenses result from cash being paid prior to an expense being incurred.
- Adjusting entries to convert liabilities to revenue result from cash being received prior to revenue being earned.
- Adjusting entries to accrue unpaid expenses result from expenses being incurred before cash is paid.
- Adjusting entries to accrue uncollected revenue result from revenue being earned before cash is received.

Characteristics of Adjusting Entries

Keep in mind two important characteristics of all adjusting entries: First, every adjusting entry *involves the recognition of either revenue or expenses.* Revenue and expenses

Exhibit 4–1   **ADJUSTING ENTRIES LINK ACCOUNTING**

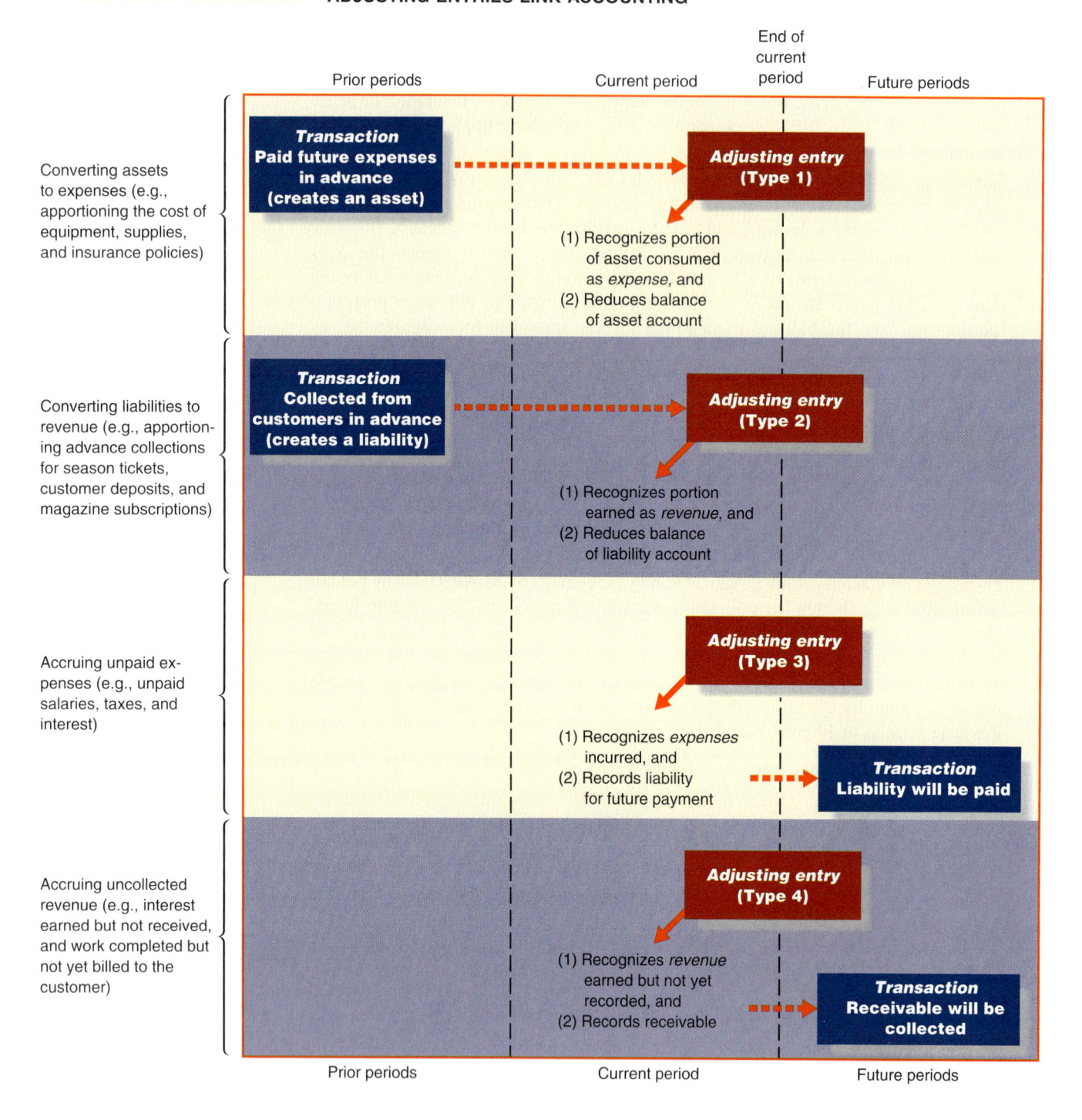

	Prior periods	Current period	End of current period	Future periods

Converting assets to expenses (e.g., apportioning the cost of equipment, supplies, and insurance policies)

- Transaction: Paid future expenses in advance (creates an asset) → Adjusting entry (Type 1)
  - (1) Recognizes portion of asset consumed as *expense*, and
  - (2) Reduces balance of asset account

Converting liabilities to revenue (e.g., apportioning advance collections for season tickets, customer deposits, and magazine subscriptions)

- Transaction: Collected from customers in advance (creates a liability) → Adjusting entry (Type 2)
  - (1) Recognizes portion earned as *revenue*, and
  - (2) Reduces balance of liability account

Accruing unpaid expenses (e.g., unpaid salaries, taxes, and interest)

- Adjusting entry (Type 3)
  - (1) Recognizes *expenses* incurred, and
  - (2) Records liability for future payment → Transaction: Liability will be paid

Accruing uncollected revenue (e.g., interest earned but not received, and work completed but not yet billed to the customer)

- Adjusting entry (Type 4)
  - (1) Recognizes *revenue* earned but not yet recorded, and
  - (2) Records receivable → Transaction: Receivable will be collected

represent changes in owners' equity. However, owners' equity cannot change by itself; *there also must be a corresponding change in either assets or liabilities.* Thus every adjusting entry affects both an income statement account (revenue or expense) and a balance sheet account (asset or liability). Rarely do adjusting entries include an entry to Cash.

Second, adjusting entries are based on the concepts of accrual accounting, *not upon monthly bills or month-end transactions.* No one sends Overnight Auto Service a bill saying, "Shop Supply Expense for the month is $500." Yet, Overnight must be aware of the need to record the estimated cost of shop supplies consumed if it is to measure income properly for the period. Making adjusting entries requires a greater understanding of

Adjusting Entries

accrual accounting concepts than does the recording of routine business transactions. In many businesses, the adjusting process is performed by the controller or by a professional accountant, rather than by the regular accounting staff.

Year-End at Overnight Auto Service

To illustrate the various types of adjusting entries, we will again use our example involving Overnight Auto Service. Chapter 3 concluded with Overnight's trial balance dated February 28, 2002 (the end of the company's second month of operations). We will now skip ahead to *December 31, 2002*—the end of Overnight's first *year* of operations. This will enable us to illustrate the preparation of *annual* financial statements, rather than statements that cover only a single month.

Most companies make adjusting entries every *month*. We will assume that Overnight has been following this approach throughout 2002. The company's *unadjusted* trial balance dated December 31, 2002, appears in Exhibit 4–2. It is referred to as an unadjusted trial balance because Overnight last made adjusting entries on *November 30;* therefore, it is still necessary to make adjusting entries for the month of December.

OVERNIGHT AUTO SERVICE
Trial Balance
December 31, 2002

Cash	$ 18,592	
Accounts receivable	6,500	
Shop supplies	1,800	
Unexpired insurance	4,500	
Land	52,000	
Building	36,000	
Accumulated depreciation: building		$ 1,500
Tools and equipment	12,000	
Accumulated depreciation: tools and equipment		2,000
Notes payable		4,000
Accounts payable		2,690
Income taxes payable		1,560
Unearned rent revenue		9,000
Capital stock		80,000
Retained earnings		0
Dividends	14,000	
Repair service revenue		171,250
Advertising expense	3,900	
Wages expense	56,800	
Supplies expense	6,900	
Depreciation expense: building	1,500	
Depreciation expense: tools and equipment	2,000	
Utilities expense	19,400	
Insurance expense	13,500	
Income taxes expense	22,608	
	$272,000	$272,000

Exhibit 4–2

UNADJUSTED TRIAL BALANCE

In the next few pages we illustrate several transactions, as well as the related adjusting entries. Both are shown in the format of general journal entries. To help distinguish between transactions and adjusting entries, transactions are printed in *blue*, and adjusting entries in *red*.

LO 3
Prepare adjusting entries to convert assets to expenses.

Converting Assets to Expenses

When a business makes an expenditure that will benefit more than one accounting period, the amount usually is debited to an asset account. At the end of each period benefiting from this expenditure, an adjusting entry is made to transfer an appropriate portion of the cost from the asset account to an expense account. This adjusting entry reflects the fact that part of the asset has been used up—or become an expense—during the current accounting period.

An adjusting entry to convert an asset to an expense consists of a debit to an expense account and a credit to an asset account (or contra-asset account). Examples of these adjustments include the entries to apportion the costs of **prepaid expenses** and entries to record depreciation expense.

Prepaid Expenses Payments in advance often are made for such items as insurance, rent, and office supplies. If the advance payment (or prepayment) will benefit more than just the current accounting period, the cost *represents an asset* rather than an expense. The cost of this asset will be allocated to expense in the accounting periods in which the services or the supplies are used. In summary, *prepaid expenses are assets;* they become expenses only as the goods or services are used up.

MANAGEMENT STRATEGY AND FINANCIAL REPORTING

Cindy Charles/PhotoEdit

Deciding when and under what circumstances to prepay expenses may involve some strategic thinking. Some expenses, such as insurance and rent, must be paid in advance. Other items, such as maintaining an inventory of supplies, require strategic decisions about the timing and the amount of cash prepayment necessary. In making these decisions, managers consider the carrying costs associated with maintaining a supplies inventory (e.g., storage and inventory monitoring costs), as well as lost opportunities to use the cash invested in supplies for other purposes. Managers must weigh these issues against the inconvenience of not having supplies on hand as needed.

In the case of Overnight Auto, management has decided that the costs and inconvenience of not having the appropriate supplies on hand outweigh the costs associated with maintaining an inventory of supplies.

Shop Supplies To illustrate, consider Overnight's accounting policies for shop supplies. As supplies are purchased, their cost is debited to the asset account Shop Supplies. It is not practical to make journal entries every few minutes as supplies are used. Instead, an estimate is made of the supplies remaining on hand at the end of each month; the supplies that are "missing" are assumed to have been used.

Prior to making adjusting entries at December 31, the balance in Overnight's Shop Supplies account is $1,800. The balance of this asset account represents shop supplies on hand on November 30. The Supplies Expense account shows a balance of $6,900, which represents the cost of supplies used through November 30. Assume that approximately $1,200 of shop supplies remain on hand at December 31. This suggests that supplies costing about $600 have been *used in December;* thus, the following *adjusting entry* is made:

Dec. 31	Supplies Expense	600	
	Shop Supplies		600
	Estimate of shop supplies used in December.		

My Notes
Transferring the cost of supplies used from the asset account to expense

This adjusting entry serves two purposes: (1) it charges to expense the cost of supplies used in December, and (2) it reduces the balance of the Shop Supplies account to $1,200—the amount of supplies estimated to be on hand at December 31.

Insurance Policies Insurance policies also are a prepaid expense. These policies provide a service, insurance protection, over a specific period of time. As the time passes, the insurance policy *expires*—that is, it is used up in business operations.

To illustrate, assume that on March 1, Overnight purchased for $18,000 a one-year insurance policy providing comprehensive liability insurance and insurance against fire and damage to customers' vehicles while in Overnight's facilities. This expenditure (a *transaction*) was debited to an asset account, as follows:

Mar. 1	Unexpired Insurance	18,000	
	Cash		18,000
	Purchased an insurance policy providing coverage for the next 12 months.		

My Notes
Purchase 12 months of insurance coverage

This $18,000 expenditure provides insurance coverage for a period of one full year. Therefore, 1/12 of this cost, or $1,500, is recognized as insurance expense every month. The $13,500 insurance expense reported in Overnight's trial balance represents the portion of the insurance policy that has expired between March 1 and November 30 ($1,500/mo. × 9 months). The $4,500 amount of unexpired insurance shown in the trial balance is the remaining cost of the 12-month policy still in effect as of November 30 ($1,500/mo. × 3 months). By December 31, another full month of the policy has expired. Thus, the insurance expense for December is recorded by the following *adjusting entry* at month-end:

Dec. 31	Insurance Expense	1,500	
	Unexpired Insurance		1,500
	Insurance expense for December.		

My Notes
Cost of insurance coverage expiring in December

Notice the similarities between the *effects* of this adjusting entry and the one that we made previously for shop supplies. In both cases, the entries transfer to expense that portion of an asset used up during the period. This flow of costs from the balance sheet to the income statement is illustrated in Exhibit 4–3.

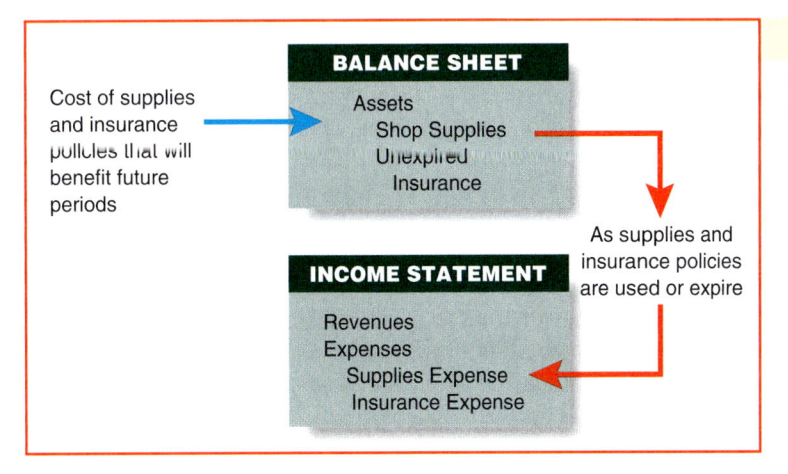

Exhibit 4–3

AN EXPIRED ASSET BECOMES AN EXPENSE

Cost of supplies and insurance policies that will benefit future periods → **BALANCE SHEET** — Assets: Shop Supplies, Unexpired Insurance

As supplies and insurance policies are used or expire →

INCOME STATEMENT — Revenues, Expenses: Supplies Expense, Insurance Expense

YOUR TURN

You as a Car Owner

Car owners typically pay insurance premiums six months in advance. Assume that you recently paid your six-month premium of $600 on February 1 (for coverage through July 31). On March 31, you decide to switch insurance companies. You call your existing agent and ask that your policy be canceled. Are you entitled to a refund? If so, why, and how much will it be?

*Our comments appear on page 173.

Recording Prepayments Directly in the Expense Accounts In our illustration, payments for shop supplies and for insurance covering more than one period were debited to asset accounts. However, some companies follow an alternative policy of debiting such prepayments directly to an expense account, such as Supplies Expense. At the end of the period, the adjusting entry then would be to debit Shop Supplies and credit Supplies Expense for the cost of supplies that had *not* been used.

This alternative method leads to the *same results* as does the procedure used by Overnight. Under either approach, the cost of supplies used during the current period is treated as an *expense,* and the cost of supplies still on hand is carried forward in the balance sheet as an *asset*.

In this text, we will follow Overnight's practice of recording prepayments in asset accounts and then making adjustments to transfer these costs to expense accounts as the assets expire. This approach correctly describes the *conceptual flow of costs* through the elements of financial statements. That is, a prepayment *is* an asset that later becomes an expense. The alternative approach is used widely in practice only because it is an efficient "shortcut," which standardizes the recording of transactions and may reduce the number of adjusting entries needed at the end of the period. Remember, our goal in this course is to develop your ability to understand and use accounting information, not to train you in alternative bookkeeping procedures.

The idea of shop supplies and insurance policies being used up over several months is easy to understand. But the same concept also applies to assets such as buildings and equipment. These assets are converted to expenses through the process of *depreciation*.

The Concept of Depreciation

Depreciable assets are *physical objects* that retain their size and shape but that eventually wear out or become obsolete. They are not physically consumed, as are assets such as supplies, but nonetheless their economic usefulness diminishes over time. Examples of depreciable assets include buildings and all types of equipment, fixtures, furnishings—and even railroad tracks. Land, however, is *not* viewed as a depreciable asset, as it has an *unlimited* useful life.

Each period, a portion of a depreciable asset's usefulness *expires*. Therefore, a corresponding portion of its cost is recognized as *depreciation expense.*

What Is Depreciation? In accounting, the term **depreciation** means the *systematic allocation of the cost of a depreciable asset to expense* over the asset's useful life. This process is illustrated in Exhibit 4–4. Notice the similarities between Exhibit 4–4 and Exhibit 4–3.

Depreciation *is not* an attempt to record changes in the asset's market value. In the short run, the market value of some depreciable assets may even increase, but the process of depreciation continues anyway. The rationale for depreciation lies in the *matching principle.* Our goal is to offset a reasonable portion of the asset's cost against revenue in each period of the asset's **useful life**.

Depreciation expense occurs continuously over the life of the asset, but there are no daily "depreciation transactions." In effect, depreciation expense is paid in advance when

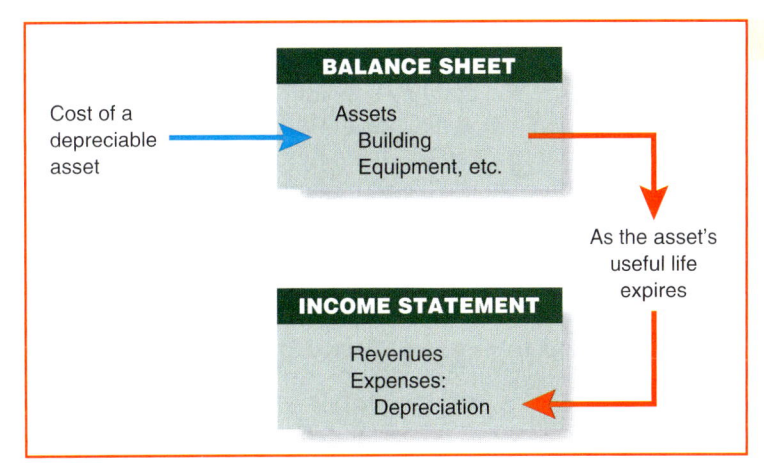

Exhibit 4–4

THE DEPRECIATION PROCESS

```
                    BALANCE SHEET
Cost of a           Assets
depreciable   →       Building
asset                 Equipment, etc.
                                          As the asset's
                                          useful life
                                          expires
                    INCOME STATEMENT
                      Revenues
                      Expenses:
                        Depreciation
```

the asset is originally purchased. Therefore, *adjusting entries* are needed at the end of each accounting period to transfer an appropriate amount of the asset's cost to depreciation expense.

Depreciation Is Only an Estimate The appropriate amount of depreciation expense is *only an estimate.* After all, we cannot look at a building or a piece of equipment and determine precisely how much of its economic usefulness has expired during the current period.

The most widely used means of estimating periodic depreciation expense is the **straight-line method of depreciation**. Under the straight-line approach, an *equal portion* of the asset's cost is allocated to depreciation expense in every period of the asset's estimated useful life. The formula for computing depreciation expense by the straight-line method is:[2]

$$\text{Depreciation expense (per period)} = \frac{\text{Cost of the asset}}{\text{Estimated useful life}}$$

The use of an *estimated useful life* is the major reason that depreciation expense is *only an estimate.* In most cases, management does not know in advance exactly how long the asset will remain in use.

CASE IN POINT

How long does a building last? For purposes of computing depreciation expense, most companies estimate about 30 or 40 years. But the Empire State Building was built in 1931, and it's not likely to be torn down anytime soon. And how about Windsor Castle? While these are not typical examples, they illustrate the difficulty in estimating in avance just how long depreciable assets may remain in use.

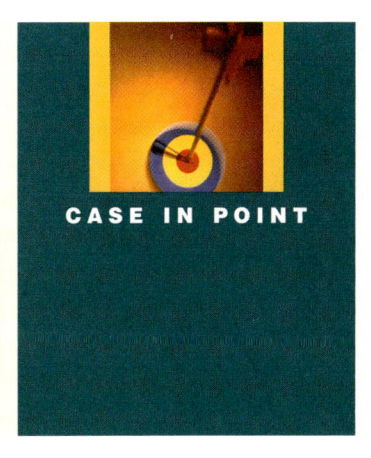

Reuters

---

[2] At this point in our discussion, we are ignoring any possible *residual value* that might be recovered upon disposal of the asset. Residual values are discussed in Chapter 9. We will assume that Overnight Auto Service depreciates its assets using the straight-line method computed without any residual values.

Depreciation of Overnight's Building Overnight purchased its building for $36,000 on January 22. Because the building was old, its estimated remaining useful life is only 20 years. Therefore, the building's monthly depreciation expense is $150 ($36,000 cost ÷ 240 months). We will assume that Overnight did *not* record any depreciation expense in January because it operated for only a small part of the month. Thus, the building's $1,500 depreciation expense reported in Overnight's trial balance illustrated in Exhibit 4–2 on page 139 represents 10 *full months* of depreciation recorded in 2002, from February 1 through November 30 ($150/mo. × 10 months). An additional $150 of depreciation expense is still needed on the building for December (bringing the total to be reported in the income statement for the year to $1,650).

The adjusting entry to record depreciation expense on Overnight's building for the month of December is:

> **My Notes**
> The adjusting entry for monthly depreciation on the building

Dec. 31	Depreciation Expense: Building	150	
	Accumulated Depreciation: Building		150
	Monthly depreciation on building ($36,000 ÷ 240 mo.).		

The *Depreciation Expense: Building* account will appear in Overnight's income statement along with other expenses for the year ended December 31, 2002. The balance in the **Accumulated Depreciation:** Building account will be reported in the December 31 balance sheet as a *deduction* from the Building Account, as shown below.

> **My Notes**
> How accumulated depreciation appears in the balance sheet

Building	$36,000
Less: Accumulated Depreciation: Building	(1,650)
Book Value	$34,350

Accumulated Depreciation: Building is an example of a **contra-asset account** because (1) it has a credit balance, and (2) it is offset against an asset account (Building) to produce the book value for the asset. Accountants often use the term **book value** (or *carrying value*) to describe the net valuation of an asset in a company's accounting records. For depreciable assets, such as buildings and equipment, book value is equal to the cost of the asset, less the related amount of accumulated depreciation. The end result of crediting the Accumulated Depreciation: Building account is much the same as if the credit had been made directly to the Building account; that is, the book value reported in the balance sheet for the building is reduced from $36,000 to $34,350.

Book value is of significance primarily for accounting purposes. It represents costs that will be offset against the revenue of future periods. It also gives users of financial statements an indication of the age of a company's depreciable assets (older assets tend to have larger amounts of accumulated depreciation associated with them than newer assets). It is important to realize that the computation of book value is based upon an asset's *historical* cost. Thus, book value is *not* intended to represent an asset's current *market value*.

Depreciation of Tools and Equipment Overnight depreciates its tools and equipment over a period of five years (60 months) using the straight-line method. The December 31 trial balance shows that the company owns tools and equipment that cost $12,000. Therefore, the adjusting entry to record December's depreciation expense is:

> **My Notes**
> Monthly depreciation on tools and equipment

Dec. 31	Depreciation Expense: Tools and Equipment	200	
	Accumulated Depreciation: Tools and Equipment		200
	Monthly depreciation on tools and equipment ($12,000 ÷ 60 months = $200 mo.)		

Again, we assume that Overnight did *not* record depreciation expense for tools and equipment in January because it operated for only a small part of the month. Thus, the related $2,000 depreciation expense reported in Overnight's trial balance in Exhibit 4–2 represents 10 *full months* of depreciation, from February 1 through November 30 ($200/mo. × 10 months). The tools and equipment still require an additional $200 of depreciation for December (bringing the total to be reported in the income statement for the year to $2,200).

What is the book value of Overnight's tools and equipment at December 31, 2002? If you said *$9,800,* you're right.[3]

CASH EFFECTS

Depreciation is a "noncash" expense. We have made the point that net income does *not* represent an inflow of cash or any other asset. Rather, it is a *computation* of the overall effect of certain business transactions on owners' equity. The computation and recognition of depreciation expense illustrate this point.

As depreciable assets "expire," owners' equity declines; but there is no corresponding cash outlay in the current period. For this reason, depreciation is called a noncash expense. Often it represents the largest difference between net income and the cash flows resulting from business operations.

Converting Liabilities to Revenue

LO 4
Prepare adjusting entries to convert liabilities to revenue.

In some instances, customers may *pay in advance* for services to be rendered in later accounting periods. For example, a football team collects much of its revenue in advance through the sale of season tickets. Health clubs collect in advance by selling long-term membership contracts. Airlines sell many of their tickets well in advance of scheduled flights.

For accounting purposes, amounts collected in advance *do not represent revenue,* because these amounts have *not yet been earned.* Amounts collected from customers in advance are recorded by debiting the Cash account and crediting an *unearned revenue* account. Unearned revenue also may be called *deferred revenue.*

When a company collects money in advance from its customers, it has an *obligation* to render services in the future. Therefore, the balance of an unearned revenue account is considered to be a liability; *it appears in the liability section of the balance sheet, not in the income statement.* Unearned revenue differs from other liabilities because it usually will be settled by rendering services, rather than by making payment in cash. In short, it will be *worked off* rather than *paid off.* Of course, if the business is unable to render the service, it must discharge this liability by refunding money to its customers.

CASE IN POINT

The largest liability in the balance sheet of **UAL Corporation (United Airlines)** is Advance Ticket Sales. This account, with a balance of more than $1.8 billion, represents unearned revenue resulting from the sale of tickets for future flights. Most of this unearned revenue will be earned as the future flights occur. Some customers, however, will change their plans and will return their tickets to **United Airlines** for a cash refund.

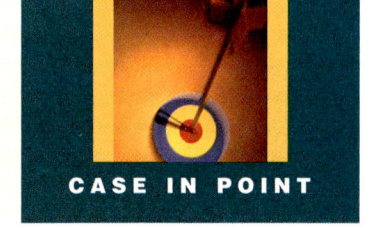

When the company renders the services for which customers have paid in advance, it is working off its liability to these customers and is earning the revenue. At the end of the accounting period, an adjusting entry is made to transfer an appropriate amount from the unearned revenue account to a revenue account. This adjusting entry consists of a debit to a liability account (unearned revenue) and a credit to a revenue account.

---

[3] Cost, $12,000, less accumulated depreciation, which amounts to $2,200 after the December 31 adjusting entry.

To illustrate these concepts, assume that on December 1, Harbor Cab Co. agreed to rent space in Overnight's building to provide indoor storage for some of its cabs. The agreed-upon rent is $3,000 per month, and Harbor Cab paid for the first three months in advance. The journal entry to record this *transaction* on December 1 was:

Dec. 1	Cash	9,000	
	Unearned Rent Revenue		9,000
	Collected in advance from Harbor Cab for rental of storage space for three months.		

My Notes
An "advance"—it's not revenue; it's a liability

Remember that Unearned Rent Revenue is a *liability* account, *not a revenue account*. Overnight will earn rental revenue *gradually* over a three-month period as it provides storage facilities for Harbor Cab. At the end of each of these three months, Overnight will make an *adjusting entry*, transferring $3,000 from the Unearned Rent Revenue account to an earned revenue account, Rent Revenue Earned, which will appear in Overnight's income statement. The first in this series of monthly transfers will be made at December 31 with the following adjusting entry:

My Notes
An adjusting entry showing that some unearned revenue has now been earned

Dec. 31	Unearned Rent Revenue	3,000	
	Rent Revenue Earned		3,000
	Portion of rent received in advance from Harbor Cab that was earned in December ($9,000 ÷ 3 mo.).		

After this adjusting entry has been posted, the Unearned Rent Revenue account will have a $6,000 credit balance. This balance represents Overnight's obligation to render $6,000 worth of service over the next two months and will appear in the liability section of the company's balance sheet. The Rent Revenue Earned account will appear in Overnight's income statement.

The transfer of unearned revenue to earned revenue is illustrated in Exhibit 4–5.

Exhibit 4–5

UNEARNED REVENUE BECOMES EARNED REVENUE

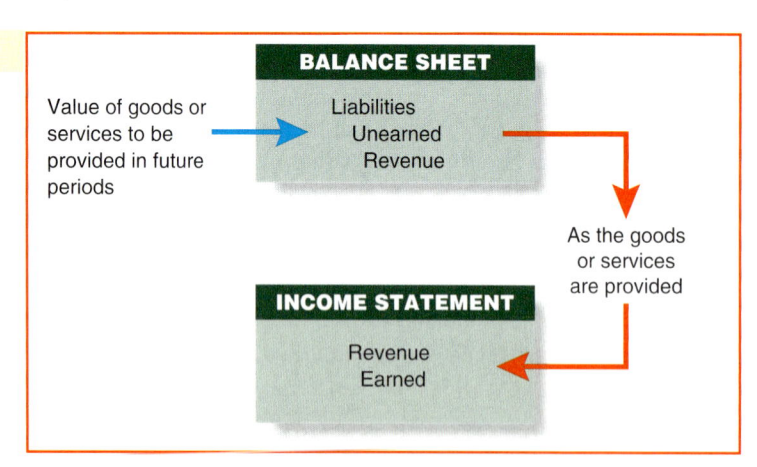

Value of goods or services to be provided in future periods → **BALANCE SHEET** Liabilities Unearned Revenue

As the goods or services are provided →

INCOME STATEMENT Revenue Earned

Recording Advance Collections Directly in the Revenue Accounts We have stressed that amounts collected from customers in advance represent liabilities, not revenue. However, some companies follow an accounting policy of crediting these advance collections directly to revenue accounts. The adjusting entry then should consist of a debit to the revenue account and a credit to the unearned revenue account for the portion of the advance payments *not yet earned*. This alternative accounting practice leads to the same results as does the method used in our illustration.

In this text, we will follow the originally described practice of crediting advance payments from customers to an unearned revenue account.

Accruing Unpaid Expenses

This type of adjusting entry recognizes expenses that will be paid in *future* transactions; therefore, no cost has yet been recorded in the accounting records. Salaries of employees and interest on borrowed money are common examples of expenses that accumulate from day to day but that usually are not recorded until they are paid. These expenses are said to **accrue** over time, that is, to grow or to accumulate. At the end of the accounting period, an adjusting entry should be made to record any expenses that have accrued but that have not yet been recorded. Since these expenses will be paid at a future date, the adjusting entry consists of a debit to an expense account and a credit to a liability account. We shall now use the example of Overnight Auto Service to illustrate this type of adjusting entry.

LO 5
Prepare adjusting entries to accrue unpaid expenses.

Accrual of Wages (or Salaries) Expense Overnight, like many businesses, pays its employees every other Friday. This month, however, ends on a Tuesday—three days before the next scheduled payday. Thus Overnight's employees have worked for more than a week in December *for which they have not yet been paid.*

Time cards indicate that since the last payroll date, Overnight's employees have worked a total of 130 hours. Including payroll taxes, Overnight's wage expense averages about $15 per hour. Therefore, at December 31, the company owes its employees approximately *$1,950* for work performed in December.[4] The following adjusting entry should be made to record this amount both as wages expense of the current period and as a liability:

Dec. 31	Wages Expense	1,950	
	Wages Payable		1,950
	To accrue wages owed to employees but unpaid as of month-end.		

My Notes
Wages owed as of month-end

This adjusting entry increases Overnight's wages expense for 2002 and also creates a liability—wages payable—that will appear in the December 31 balance sheet.

On Friday, January 3, Overnight will pay its regular biweekly payroll. Let us assume that this payroll amounts to $2,397. In this case, the entry to record payment is as follows:[5]

2003			
Jan. 3	Wages Expense (for January)	447	
	Wages Payable (accrued in December)	1,950	
	Cash		2,397
	Biweekly payroll, $1,950 of which had been accrued at December 31.		

My Notes
Payment of wages earned in two accounting periods

Accrual of Interest Expense On January 22, 2002, Overnight purchased its building, an old bus garage, from Metropolitan Transit District for $36,000. Overnight paid $6,000 cash, and issued a $30,000, 90-day note payable for the balance owed. Overnight paid the $30,000 obligation in April. There was no interest expense associated with this note payable because it was *non-interest-bearing.*

---

[4] In preparing a formal payroll, wages and payroll taxes must be computed "down to the last cent." But this is not a payroll; it is an amount to be used in the company's financial statements. Therefore, a reasonable estimate will suffice. The accounting principle of *materiality* is discussed later in this chapter.

[5] In this illustration, we do not address the details associated with payroll taxes and amounts withheld. These topics are discussed in Chapter 10.

On November 30, 2002, Overnight borrowed $4,000 from American National Bank by issuing an *interest-bearing* note payable. This loan is to be repaid in three months (on February 28, 2003), along with interest computed at an annual rate of 9%. The entry made on November 30 to record this borrowing transaction is:

Nov. 30	Cash 4,000	
	Notes Payable	4,000
	Borrowed cash from American National Bank, issuing	
	a 9%, $4,000 note payable, due in three months.	

On February 28, Overnight must pay the bank $4,090. This represents the $4,000 amount borrowed, *plus $90 interest* ($4,000 × .09 × 3/12). The $90 interest charge covers a period of *three months*. Although no payment will be made until February 28, 2003, interest expense is *incurred* (or accrued) at a rate of $30 per month, as shown in Exhibit 4–6.

Exhibit 4–6
ACCRUAL OF INTEREST

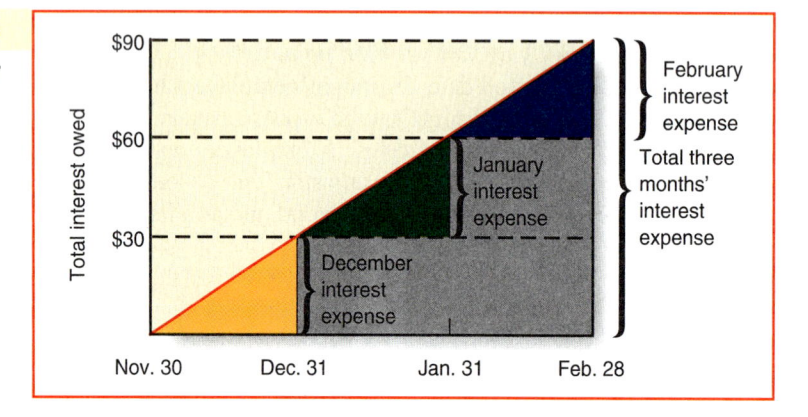

The following adjusting entry is made at December 31 to charge December operations with one month's interest expense and to record the amount of interest owed to the bank at month-end:

My Notes

Adjusting entry for interest expense accrued in December

Dec. 31	Interest Expense 30	
	Interest Payable	30
	Interest expense accrued during December	
	on note payable ($4,000 × .09 × 1/12).	

The $30 interest expense that accrued in December will appear in Overnight's 2002 income statement. Both the $30 interest payable and the $4,000 note payable to American National Bank will appear as *liabilities* in the December 31, 2002, balance sheet.

Overnight will make a second adjusting entry recognizing another $30 in interest expense on January 31 of the coming year. The entry on February 28 to record the repayment of this loan, including $90 in interest charges, is:

My Notes

Payment of interest expense accrued over three months

2003		
Feb. 28	Notes Payable 4,000	
	Interest Payable (from December and January) 60	
	Interest Expense (February only) 30	
	Cash	4,090
	Repaid $4,000 note payable to American National	
	Bank, including $90 in interest charges.	

Adjusting Entries

Accruing Uncollected Revenue

A business may earn revenue during the current accounting period but not bill the customer until a future accounting period. This situation is likely to occur if additional services are being performed for the same customer, in which case the bill might not be prepared until all services are completed. Any revenue that has been *earned but not recorded* during the current accounting period should be recorded at the end of the period by means of an adjusting entry. This adjusting entry consists of a debit to an account receivable and a credit to the appropriate revenue account. The term *accrued revenue* often is used to describe revenue that has been earned during the period but that has not been recorded prior to the closing date.

To illustrate this type of adjusting entry, assume that in December, Overnight entered into an agreement to perform routine maintenance on several vans owned by Airport Shuttle Service. Overnight agreed to maintain these vans for a flat fee of $1,500 per month, payable on the fifteenth of each month.

No entry was made to record the signing of this agreement, because no services had yet been rendered. Overnight began rendering services on *December 15,* but the first monthly payment will not be received until January 15. Therefore, Overnight should make the following adjusting entry at December 31 to record the revenue *earned* from Airport Shuttle during the month:

LO 6
Prepare adjusting entries to accrue uncollected revenue.

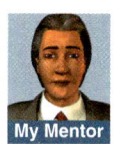

Dec. 31	Accounts Receivable	750	
	Repair Service Revenue		750
	To recognize revenue from services rendered on Airport Shuttle maintenance contract during December. Account is settled on the fifteenth of each month.		

My Notes
Adjusting entry recognizing revenue earned but not yet billed or collected

You as Overnight Auto's Service Department Manager

As part of your employment agreement with Overnight Auto, you earn a 5% bonus based on Overnight's profits each year. You were discussing this arrangement with friends after bowling at Jill's Lounge, when one of them asked if your bonus would not be higher if the entire month's revenue from Airport Shuttle Service ($1,500) were recognized in December rather than only 1/2 of the revenue ($750) as illustrated above. How would you respond?

*Our answer is on page 173.

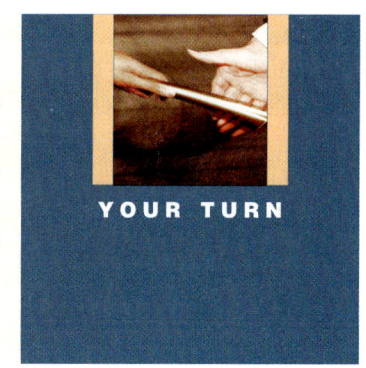

YOUR TURN

The collection of the first monthly fee from Airport Shuttle will occur in the next accounting period (January 15, to be exact). Of this $1,500 cash receipt, half represents collection of the receivable recorded on December 31; the other half represents revenue earned in January. Thus the entry to record the receipt of $1,500 from Airport Shuttle on January 15 will be:

2003			
Jan. 15	Cash	1,500	
	Accounts Receivable		750
	Repair Service Revenue		750
	Collected from Airport Shuttle for van maintenance, Dec. 15 through Jan. 15.		

My Notes
Entry to record collection of accrued revenue

The net result of the December 31 adjusting entry has been to divide the revenue from maintenance of Airport Shuttle's vans between December and January in proportion to the services rendered during each month.

Accruing Income Taxes Expense: The Final Adjusting Entry

As a corporation earns taxable income, it incurs income taxes expense, and also a liability to governmental tax authorities. This liability is paid in four installments called *estimated quarterly payments.* The first three payments normally are made on April 15, June 15, and September 15. The final installment actually is due on *December 15;* but for purposes of our illustration and assignment materials, we will assume the final payment is not due until *January 15* of the following year.[6]

In its unadjusted trial balance (Exhibit 4–2 on page 139), Overnight shows income taxes expense of $22,608. This is the income taxes expense recognized from January 20, 2002 (the date Overnight opened for business) through November 30, 2002. Income taxes accrued through September 30 have already been paid. Thus, the $1,560 liability for income taxes payable represents only the income taxes accrued in *October* and *November.*

The amount of income taxes expense accrued for any given month is only an *estimate.* The actual amount of income taxes cannot be determined until the company prepares its annual income tax return. In our illustrations and assignment materials, we estimate income taxes expense at *40% of taxable income.* We also assume that taxable income is equal to *income before income taxes,* a subtotal often shown in an income statement. This subtotal is total revenue less all expenses *other than* income taxes.

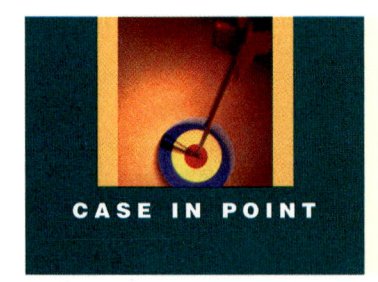

CASE IN POINT

Corporate income tax rates vary around the world. A recent survey shows that rates range from 15% in Chile to 43% in Pakistan.* In addition to corporate income taxes, some countries also (1) withhold taxes on dividends, interest, and royalties, (2) charge value-added taxes at specified production and distribution points, and (3) impose border taxes such as customs and import duties.

*KPMG Corporate Tax Rate Survey (January 2000).

In 2002, Overnight earned income before income taxes of $66,570 (see the income statement in Exhibit 5–2, page 178, in Chapter 5). Therefore, income taxes expense *for the entire year* is estimated at $26,628 ($66,570 × 40%). Given that income taxes expense recognized through November 30 amounts to $22,608 (see the unadjusted trial balance in Exhibit 4–2), an additional $4,020 in income taxes expense must have accrued during *December* ($26,628 − $22,608). The adjusting entry to record this expense is:

My Notes

Adjusting entry to record income taxes for December

Dec. 31	Income Taxes Expense	4,020	
	Income Taxes Payable		4,020
	Estimated income taxes applicable to taxable income earned during December.		

This entry increases the balance in the Income Taxes Expense account to the $26,628 amount required for the year ended December 31, 2002. It also increases the liability for

---

[6] This assumption enables us to accrue income taxes in December in the same manner as in other months. Otherwise, income taxes for this month would be recorded as a mid-month transaction, rather than in an end-of-month adjusting entry. The adjusting entry for income taxes is an example of an accrued, but unpaid, expense.

income taxes payable to $5,580 ($1,560 + $4,020). The entry to record the payment of this liability on January 15, 2003, will be:

2003			
Jan. 15	Income Taxes Payable	5,580	
	Cash		5,580
	Paid final installment on 2002 income tax liability.		

The above transaction is simply the payment of an outstanding liability; therefore, it is *not* considered an adjusting entry.

Income Taxes in Unprofitable Periods What happens to income taxes expense when *losses* are incurred? In these situations, the company recognizes a "negative amount" of income taxes expense. The adjusting entry to record income taxes at the end of an *unprofitable* accounting period consists of a *debit* to Income Taxes Payable and a *credit* to Income Taxes Expense.

"Negative" income taxes expense means that the company may be able to recover from the government some of the income taxes recognized as expense in prior periods.[7] If the Income Taxes Payable account has a *debit* balance at year-end, it is reclassified as an *asset*, called "Income Tax Refund Receivable." A credit balance in the Income Taxes Expense account is offset against the amount of the before-tax loss, as shown in Exhibit 4–7.

My Notes

Income tax benefit can reduce a pretax loss

Partial Income Statement — for an *Unprofitable* Period	
Income (loss) before income taxes	$(20,000)
Income tax benefit (recovery of previously recorded taxes)	8,000
Net loss	$(12,000)

Exhibit 4–7

PARTIAL INCOME STATEMENT

We have already seen that income taxes *expense* reduces the amount of before-tax *profits*. Notice now that income tax *benefits*—in the form of tax refunds—can reduce the amount of a pretax *loss*. Thus, income taxes reduce the size of *both* profits and losses. The detailed reporting of profits and losses in the income statement is illustrated in Chapter 5.

ADJUSTING ENTRIES AND ACCOUNTING PRINCIPLES

Adjusting entries are *tools* by which accountants apply the **realization** and **matching** principles. Through these entries, revenues are recognized as they are *earned,* and expenses are recognized as resources are *used* or consumed in producing the related revenue.

In most cases, the realization principle indicates that revenue should be recognized *at the time goods are sold or services are rendered.* At this point the business has essentially completed the earning process and the sales value of the goods or services can be measured objectively. At any time prior to sale, the ultimate sales value of the goods or services sold can only be estimated. After the sale, the only step that remains is to collect from the customer, and this is usually a relatively certain event.

The matching principle underlies such accounting practices as depreciating plant assets, measuring the cost of goods sold, and amortizing the cost of unexpired insurance

---

[7] Tax refunds may be limited to tax payments in recent years. In this introductory discussion, we assume the company has paid sufficient taxes in prior years to permit a full recovery of any "negative tax expense" relating to the loss in the current period.

LO 7

Explain how the principles of *realization* and *matching* relate to adjusting entries.

policies. All end-of-the-period adjusting entries involving recognition of expense are applications of the matching principle.

Costs are matched with revenue in one of two ways:

1. *Direct association of costs with specific revenue transactions.* The ideal method of matching revenue with expenses is to determine the amount of expense associated with the specific revenue transactions occurring during the period. However, this approach works only for those costs and expenses that can be directly associated with specific revenue transactions. Commissions paid to salespeople are an example of costs that can be *directly associated* with the revenue of a specific accounting period.

2. *Systematic allocation of costs over the useful life of the expenditure.* Many expenditures contribute to the earning of revenue for a number of accounting periods but cannot be directly associated with specific revenue transactions. Examples include the costs of insurance policies, depreciable assets, and intangible assets such as patents. In these cases, accountants attempt to match revenue and expenses by *systematically allocating the cost to expense* over its useful life. Straight-line depreciation is an example of a systematic technique used to match revenue with the related costs and expenses.

YOUR TURN

You as Overnight Auto's Service Department Manager

You just found out that Betty, one of the best mechanics that you supervise for Overnight Auto, has taken home small items from the company's supplies, such as a screwdriver and a couple of cans of oil. When you talk to Betty, she suggests that these items are immaterial to Overnight Auto because they are not recorded in the inventory and they are expensed when they are purchased. How should you respond to Betty?

*Our answer is on page 173.

The Concept of Materiality

LO 8
Explain the concept of materiality.

Another generally accepted accounting principle also plays a major role in the making of adjusting entries—the concept of **materiality**. The term *materiality* refers to the *relative importance* of an item or an event. An item is considered material if knowledge of the item might reasonably *influence the decisions* of users of financial statements. Accountants must be sure that all material items are properly reported in financial statements.

However, the financial reporting process should be *cost-effective*—that is, the value of the information should exceed the cost of its preparation. By definition, the accounting treatment accorded to **immaterial** items is of *little or no consequence to decision makers*. Therefore, accountants do not waste time accounting for immaterial items; these items may be handled in the *easiest and most convenient manner.*

In summary, the concept of materiality allows accountants to use estimated amounts and even to ignore other accounting principles if the results of these actions do not have an important impact on the financial statements. Materiality is one of the most important generally accepted accounting principles; you will encounter applications of this concept throughout the study of accounting.

Materiality and Adjusting Entries The concept of materiality enables accountants to shorten and simplify the process of making adjusting entries in several ways. For example:

1. Businesses purchase many assets that have a very low cost or that will be consumed quickly in business operations. Examples include wastebaskets, lightbulbs, and janitorial supplies. The materiality concept permits charging such purchases *directly to*

expense accounts, rather than to asset accounts. This treatment conveniently eliminates the need for an adjusting entry at the end of the period to transfer a portion of these costs from an asset account to expense. This accounting shortcut is acceptable as long as the cost of the *unused* items on hand at the end of the period is immaterial.

2. Some expenses, such as telephone bills and utility bills, may be charged to expenses as the bills are *paid,* rather than as the services are used. Technically this treatment violates the *matching principle.* However, accounting for utility bills on a cash basis is very convenient, as the monthly cost of utility service is not even known until the utility bill is received. Under this cash basis approach, one month's utility bill is charged to an expense each month. Although the bill charged to expense is actually the *prior* month's bill, the resulting "error" in the financial statements is not likely to be material.

3. Adjusting entries to accrue unrecorded expenses or unrecorded revenue may be ignored if the dollar amounts are immaterial.

4. If the amount of error is not likely to be material, adjusting entries may be based on *estimates.* For example, earlier we illustrated an adjusting entry allocating part of the $1,800 balance in the Supplies account to an expense. The amount of supplies used during the period ($600) was based on an *estimate* of the supplies still on hand ($1,200). This $1,200 estimate is an educated guess; no one actually counts all of the shop supplies on hand and looks up their cost. The adjusting entry recording accrued wages payable also was based on an estimate, not a detailed calculation.

Materiality Is a Matter of Professional Judgment Whether a specific item or event is material is a matter of *professional judgment.* In making these judgments, accountants consider several factors.

First, what constitutes a material amount varies with the size of the organization. For example, a $1,000 expenditure may be material in relation to the financial statements of a small business but not to the statements of a large corporation such as **General Electric**.[8] There are no official rules as to what constitutes a material amount, but most accountants would consider amounts of less than 2% or 3% of net income to be immaterial, unless there were other factors to consider. One such other factor is the *cumulative effect* of numerous immaterial events. Each of a dozen items may be immaterial when considered by itself. When viewed together, however, the combined effect of all 12 items may be material.

Finally, materiality depends on the *nature* of the item, as well as its dollar amount. Assume, for example, that several managers systematically have been stealing money from the company that they manage. Stockholders probably would consider this fact important even if the dollar amounts were small in relation to the company's total resources.

Note to students: In the assignment material accompanying this textbook, you are to consider all dollar amounts to be material, unless the problem specifically raises the question of materiality.

Effects of the Adjusting Entries

We now have discussed nine separate adjusting entries that Overnight will make at December 31. These adjustments appear in the format of general journal entries in Exhibit 4–8. (Overnight also recorded many transactions throughout the month of

---

[8] This point is emphasized by the fact that General Electric rounds the dollar amounts shown in its financial statements to the nearest $1 million. This rounding of financial statement amounts is, in itself, an application of the materiality concept.

December. The company's December transactions are not illustrated here but were accounted for in the manner described in Chapter 3.)

Exhibit 4–8
ADJUSTING ENTRIES

My Notes
Adjusting entries are recorded only at the end of the period

OVERNIGHT AUTO SERVICE
General Journal
December 31, 2002

Date	Account Titles and Explanation	Debit	Credit
2002			
Dec. 31	Supplies Expense	600	
	Shop Supplies		600
	Shop supplies used during December.		
31	Insurance Expense	1,500	
	Unexpired Insurance		1,500
	Insurance expense for December.		
31	Depreciation Expense: Building	150	
	Accumulated Depreciation: Building		150
	Monthly depreciation on building ($36,000 ÷ 240 mo.).		
31	Depreciation Expense: Tools and Equipment	200	
	Accumulated Depreciation: Tools and Equipment		200
	Monthly depreciation on tools and equipment ($12,000 ÷ 60 mo.)		
31	Unearned Rent Revenue	3,000	
	Rent Revenue Earned		3,000
	Portion of rent received in advance from Harbor Cab that was earned in December ($9,000 ÷ 3 mo.).		
31	Wages Expense	1,950	
	Wages Payable		1,950
	To accrue wages owed to employees but unpaid as of month-end.		
31	Interest Expense	30	
	Interest Payable		30
	Interest expense accrued during December on note payable ($4,000 × .09 × 1/12).		
31	Accounts Receivable	750	
	Repair Service Revenue		750
	To recognize revenue from services rendered on Airport Shuttle maintenance contract during December.		
31	Income Taxes Expense	4,020	
	Income Taxes Payable		4,020
	Estimated income taxes applicable to taxable income earned in December.		

After these adjustments are posted to the ledger, Overnight's ledger accounts will be up-to-date (except for the balance in the Retained Earnings account).[9] The

---
[9] The balance in the Retained Earnings account will be brought up-to-date during the closing process, discussed in Chapter 5.

Concluding Remarks

company's *adjusted trial balance* at December 31, 2002, appears in Exhibit 4–9. (For emphasis, those accounts affected by the month-end adjusting entries are shown in red.)

Overnight's financial statements are prepared directly from the adjusted trial balance. Note the order of the accounts: all balance sheet accounts are followed by the statement of retained earnings accounts and then the income statement accounts. In Chapter 5, we illustrate exactly how these three financial statements are prepared.

Exhibit 4–9

ADJUSTED TRIAL BALANCE

LO 9 Prepare an adjusted trial balance and describe its purpose.

OVERNIGHT AUTO SERVICE
Adjusted Trial Balance
December 31, 2002

Account	Debit	Credit
Cash	$ 18,592	
Accounts receivable	7,250	
Shop supplies	1,200	
Unexpired insurance	3,000	
Land	52,000	
Building	36,000	
Accumulated depreciation: building		$ 1,650
Tools and equipment	12,000	
Accumulated depreciation: tools and equipment		2,200
Notes payable		4,000
Accounts payable		2,690
Wages payable		1,950
Income taxes payable		5,580
Interest payable		30
Unearned rent revenue		6,000
Capital stock		80,000
Retained earnings (*Note:* still must be updated for transactions recorded in the accounts listed below. Closing entries serve this purpose.)		0
Dividends	14,000	
Repair service revenue		172,000
Rent revenue earned		3,000
Advertising expense	3,900	
Wages expense	58,750	
Supplies expense	7,500	
Depreciation expense: building	1,650	
Depreciation expense: tools and equipment	2,200	
Utilities expense	19,400	
Insurance expense	15,000	
Interest expense	30	
Income taxes expense	26,628	
	$279,100	$279,100

Balance sheet accounts (Cash through Capital stock)

Statement of retained earnings accounts (Retained earnings, Dividends)

Income statement accounts (Repair service revenue through Income taxes expense)

CONCLUDING REMARKS

Throughout this chapter, we illustrated end-of-period adjusting entries arising from *timing differences* between cash flows and revenue or expense recognition. In short, the adjusting process helps to ensure that appropriate amounts of revenue and expense are measured and reported in a company's income statement.

In Chapter 5, we continue with our illustration of Overnight Auto Service and demonstrate how adjusting entries are reflected throughout a company's financial statements.

Later chapters explain why accurate income measurement is of critical importance to investors and creditors in estimating the timing and amounts of a company's future cash flows. We also illustrate how understanding certain timing differences enables managers to budget and to plan for future operations.

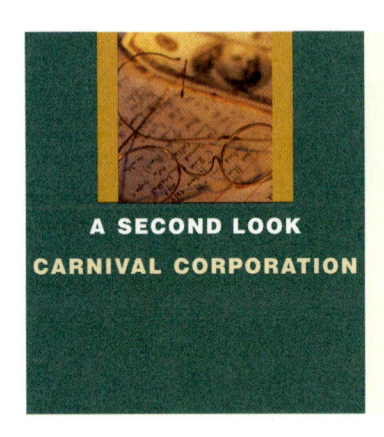

**A SECOND LOOK
CARNIVAL CORPORATION**

We have seen why Customer Deposits are reported in **Carnival Corporation**'s balance sheet as a liability account. This account represents revenue that must be *deferred* (remain unearned) until future cruise services are provided to passengers who have purchased tickets in advance. At the end of each accounting period, **Carnival Corporation** makes an adjusting entry to account for the portion of any unearned revenue that has been *earned* at the balance sheet date. It does so in much the same way as Overnight Auto Service adjusted its Unearned Revenue account. Other accounts similar to those used by Overnight Auto Service can be identified in **Carnival Corporation**'s balance sheet as candidates for adjusting entries. Examples include Prepaid Expenses, Accumulated Depreciation, and Accrued Liabilities.

END-OF-CHAPTER REVIEW

SUMMARY OF LEARNING OBJECTIVES

LO 1
Explain the purpose of adjusting entries.
The purpose of adjusting entries is to allocate revenue and expenses among accounting periods in accordance with the realization and matching principles. These end-of-period entries are necessary because revenue may be earned and expenses may be incurred in periods other than the period in which related cash flows are recorded.

LO 2
Describe and prepare the four basic types of adjusting entries.
The four basic types of adjusting entries are made to (1) convert assets to expenses, (2) convert liabilities to revenue, (3) accrue unpaid expenses, and (4) accrue uncollected revenue. Often a transaction affects the revenue or expenses of *two or more* accounting periods. The related cash inflow or outflow does not always coincide with the period in which these revenue or expense items are recorded. Thus, the need for adjusting entries results from *timing differences* between the receipt or disbursement of cash and the recording of revenue or expenses.

LO 3
Prepare adjusting entries to convert assets to expenses.
When an expenditure is made that will benefit more than one accounting period, an asset account is debited and cash is credited. The asset account is used to *defer* (or postpone) expense recognition until a later date. At the end of each period benefiting from this expenditure, an adjusting entry is made to transfer an appropriate amount from the asset account to an *expense* account. This adjustment reflects the fact that part of the asset's cost has been *matched* against revenue in the measurement of income for the current period.

LO 4
Prepare adjusting entries to convert liabilities to revenue.
Customers sometimes pay in advance for services to be rendered in later accounting periods. For accounting purposes, the cash received does *not* represent revenue until it has been *earned*. Thus, the recognition of revenue must be *deferred* until it is earned. Advance collections from customers are recorded by debiting Cash and by crediting a *liability* account for *unearned* revenue. This liability is sometimes called Customer Deposits, Advance Sales, or Deferred Revenue. As unearned revenue becomes earned, an adjusting entry is made at the end of each period to transfer an appropriate amount from the liability account to a *revenue* account. This adjustment reflects the fact that all or part of the company's obligation to its customers has been fulfilled and that revenue has been realized.

LO 5
Prepare adjusting entries to accrue unpaid expenses.
Some expenses accumulate (or *accrue*) in the current period but are not *paid* until a future period. These accrued expenses are recorded as part of the adjusting process at the end of each period by debiting the appropriate expense (e.g., Salary Expense, Interest Expense, or Income Taxes Expense), and by crediting a liability account (e.g., Salaries Payable, Interest Payable, or Income Taxes Payable). In future periods, as cash is disbursed in settlement of these liabilities, the appropriate liability account is debited and Cash is credited. *Note:* Recording the accrued expense in the current period is the adjusting entry. Recording the disbursement of cash in a future period is *not* considered an adjusting entry.

LO 6
Prepare adjusting entries to accrue uncollected revenue.
Some revenues are earned (or *accrued*) in the current period but are not *collected* until a future period. These revenues are normally recorded as part of the adjusting process at the end of each period by debiting an asset account called Accounts Receivable, and by crediting the appropriate revenue account. In future periods, as cash is collected in settlement of outstanding receivables, Cash is debited and Accounts Receivable is credited. *Note:* Recording the accrued revenue in the current period is the adjusting entry. Recording the receipt of cash in a future period is *not* considered an adjusting entry.

LO 7
Explain how the principles of *realization* and *matching* relate to adjusting entries.
Adjusting entries are the *tools* by which accountants apply the realization and matching principles. Through these entries, revenues are recognized as they are *earned,* and expenses are recognized as resources are *used* or consumed in producing the related revenue.

LO 8
Explain the concept of *materiality*.
The concept of materiality allows accountants to use estimated amounts and to ignore certain accounting principles if these actions will not have a material effect on the financial statements. A material effect is one that might reasonably be expected to influence the decisions made by the users of financial statements. Thus, accountants may account for immaterial items and events in the easiest and most convenient manner.

LO 9
Prepare an adjusted trial balance and describe its purpose.
The adjusted trial balance reports all of the balances in the general ledger *after* the end-of-period adjusting entries have been

made and posted. Generally, all of a company's balance sheet accounts are listed, followed by the statement of retained earnings accounts, and finally, the income statement accounts. The amounts shown in the adjusted trial balance are carried forward directly to the financial statements. The adjusted trial balance is *not* considered one of the four general purpose financial statements introduced in Chapter 2. Rather, it is simply a *schedule* (or tool) used in preparing the financial statements.

KEY TERMS INTRODUCED OR EMPHASIZED IN CHAPTER 4

accrue (p. 147)   To grow or accumulate over time; for example, interest expense.

Accumulated Depreciation (p. 144)   A contra-asset account shown as a deduction from the related asset account in the balance sheet. Depreciation taken throughout the useful life of an asset is accumulated in this account.

adjusted trial balance (p. 155)   A schedule indicating the balances in ledger accounts *after* end-of-period adjusting entries have been posted. The amounts shown in the adjusted trial balance are carried directly into financial statements.

adjusting entries (p. 136)   Entries made at the end of the accounting period for the purpose of recognizing revenue and expenses that are not properly measured as a result of journalizing transactions as they occur.

book value (p. 144)   The net amount at which an asset appears in financial statements. For depreciable assets, book value represents cost minus accumulated depreciation. Also called *carrying value*.

contra-asset account (p. 144)   An account with a credit balance that is offset against or deducted from an asset account to produce the proper balance sheet amount for the asset.

depreciable assets (p. 142)   Physical objects with a limited life. The cost of these assets is gradually recognized as depreciation expense.

depreciation (p. 142)   The systematic allocation of the cost of an asset to expense during the periods of its useful life.

immaterial (p. 152)   Something of little or no consequence. Immaterial items may be accounted for in the most convenient manner, without regard to other theoretical concepts.

matching (principle) (p. 151)   The accounting principle of offsetting revenue with the expenses incurred in producing that revenue. Requires recognition of expenses in the periods that the goods and services are used in the effort to produce revenue.

materiality (p. 152)   The relative importance of an item or amount. Items significant enough to influence decisions are said to be *material*. Items lacking this importance are considered *immaterial*. The accounting treatment accorded to immaterial items may be guided by convenience rather than by theoretical principles.

prepaid expenses (p. 140)   Assets representing advance payment of the expenses of future accounting periods. As time passes, adjusting entries are made to transfer the related costs from the asset account to an expense account.

realization (principle) (p. 151)   The accounting principle that governs the timing of revenue recognition. Basically, the principle indicates that revenue should be recognized in the period in which it is earned.

straight-line method of depreciation (p. 143)   The widely used approach of recognizing an equal amount of depreciation expense in each period of a depreciable asset's useful life.

unearned revenue (p. 145)   An obligation to deliver goods or render services in the future, stemming from the receipt of advance payment.

useful life (p. 142)   The period of time that a depreciable asset is expected to be useful to the business. This is the period over which the cost of the asset is allocated to depreciation expense.

DEMONSTRATION PROBLEM

Internet Consulting Service, Inc., adjusts its accounts every month. The following is the company's year-end *unadjusted* trial balance dated December 31, 2002. (Bear in mind that adjusting entries already have been made for the first 11 months of 2002, but have *not* for December.)

Demonstration Problem

INTERNET CONSULTING SERVICE, INC.
Unadjusted Trial Balance
December 31, 2002

Cash	$ 49,100	
Consulting fees receivable	23,400	
Prepaid office rent	6,300	
Prepaid dues and subscriptions	300	
Supplies	600	
Equipment	36,000	
Accumulated depreciation: equipment		$ 10,200
Notes payable		5,000
Income taxes payable		12,000
Unearned consulting fees		5,950
Capital stock		30,000
Retained earnings		32,700
Dividends	60,000	
Consulting fees earned		257,180
Salaries expense	88,820	
Telephone expense	2,550	
Rent expense	22,000	
Income taxes expense	51,000	
Dues and subscriptions expense	560	
Supplies expense	1,600	
Depreciation expense: equipment	6,600	
Miscellaneous expenses	4,200	
	$353,030	$353,030

Other Data

a. On December 1, the company signed a new rental agreement and paid three months' rent in advance at a rate of $2,100 per month. This advance payment was debited to the Prepaid Office Rent account.

b. Dues and subscriptions expiring during December amounted to $50.

c. An estimate of supplies on hand was made at December 31; the estimated cost of the unused supplies was $450.

d. The useful life of the equipment has been estimated at five years (60 months) from date of acquisition.

e. Accrued interest on notes payable amounted to $100 at year-end. (Set up accounts for Interest Expense and for Interest Payable.)

f. Consulting services valued at $2,850 were rendered during December to clients who had made payment in advance.

g. It is the custom of the firm to bill clients only when consulting work is completed or, in the case of prolonged engagements, at monthly intervals. At December 31, consulting services valued at $11,000 had been rendered to clients but not yet billed. No advance payments had been received from these clients.

h. Salaries earned by employees but not paid as of December 31 amount to $1,700.

i. Income taxes expense for the year is estimated at $56,000. Of this amount, $51,000 has been recognized as expense in prior months, and $39,000 has been paid to tax authorities. The company plans to pay the $17,000 remainder of its income tax liability on January 15.

Instructions

a. Prepare the necessary adjusting journal entries on December 31, 2002.

b. Determine the amounts to be reported in the company's year-end adjusted trial balance for each of the following accounts:

    Consulting Fees Earned   Dues and Subscriptions Expense

    Salaries Expense   Depreciation Expense: Equipment

    Telephone Expense   Miscellaneous Expenses

    Rent Expense   Interest Expense

    Supplies Expense   Income Taxes Expense

c. Determine the company's net income for the year ended December 31, 2002. (*Hint:* Use the amounts determined in part **b** above.)

Solution to the Demonstration Problem

a.

INTERNET CONSULTING SERVICE, INC.
General Journal
December 31, 2002

Date	Account Titles and Explanation	Debit	Credit
Dec. 31 2002			
a.	Rent Expense	2,100	
	Prepaid Office Rent		2,100
	Rent expense for December.		
b.	Dues and Subscriptions Expense	50	
	Prepaid Dues and Subscriptions		50
	Dues and subscriptions expense for December.		
c.	Supplies Expense	150	
	Supplies		150
	Supplies used during December.		
d.	Depreciation Expense: Equipment	600	
	Accumulated Depreciation: Equipment		600
	Depreciation expense for December ($36,000 ÷ 60 mos.).		
e.	Interest Expense	100	
	Interest Payable		100
	Interest accrued on notes payable in December.		
f.	Unearned Consulting Fees	2,850	
	Consulting Fees Earned		2,850
	Consulting services performed for clients who paid in advance.		
g.	Consulting Fees Receivable	11,000	
	Consulting Fees Earned		11,000
	Consulting services performed in December for which billings have not been made nor payments received.		
h.	Salaries Expense	1,700	
	Salaries Payable		1,700
	Salaries accrued in December but not yet paid.		
i.	Income Taxes Expense	5,000	
	Income Taxes Payable		5,000
	Estimated income taxes accrued on income in December.		

b.

INTERNET CONSULTING SERVICE, INC.
Adjusted Trial Balance
December 31, 2002

	Unadjusted Trial Balance Amount	+	Adjustment	=	Adjusted Trial Balance Amount
Consulting Fees Earned	$257,180		(f) $ 2,850		
			(g) $11,000		$271,030
Salaries Expense	$ 88,820		(h) $ 1,700		$ 90,520
Telephone Expense	$ 2,550		None		$ 2,550
Rent Expense	$ 22,000		(a) $ 2,100		$ 24,100
Supplies Expense	$ 1,600		(c) $ 150		$ 1,750
Dues and Subscriptions Expense	$ 560		(b) $ 50		$ 610
Depreciation Expense: Equipment	$ 6,600		(d) $ 600		$ 7,200
Miscellaneous Expenses	$ 4,200		None		$ 4,200
Interest Expense	None		(e) $ 100		$ 100
Income Taxes Expense	$ 51,000		(i) $ 5,000		$ 56,000

c. Using the figures computed in part **b**, net income for the year is computed as follows:

Consulting Fees Earned		$271,030
Salaries Expense	$90,520	
Telephone Expense	2,550	
Rent Expense	24,100	
Supplies Expense	1,750	
Dues and Subscriptions Expense	610	
Depreciation Expense: Equipment	7,200	
Miscellaneous	4,200	
Interest Expense	100	
Income Taxes Expense	56,000	(187,030)
Net Income		$ 84,000

SELF-TEST QUESTIONS

The answers to these questions appear on page 173.

1. The purpose of adjusting entries is to:
   a. Adjust the Retained Earnings account for the revenue, expense, and dividends recorded during the accounting period.
   b. Adjust daily the balances in asset, liability, revenue, and expense accounts for the effects of business transactions.
   c. Apply the realization principle and the matching principle to transactions affecting two or more accounting periods.
   d. Prepare revenue and expense accounts for recording the transactions of the next accounting period.

2. Before month-end adjustments are made, the January 31 trial balance of Rover Excursions contains revenue of $27,900 and expenses of $17,340. Adjustments are necessary for the following items:

   Portion of prepaid rent applicable to January, $2,700
   Depreciation for January, $1,440
   Portion of fees collected in advance earned in January, $3,300
   Fees earned in January, not yet billed to customers, $1,950

   Net income for January is:
   a. $10,560   **b.** $17,070   **c.** $7,770   **d.** Some other amount

3. The CPA firm auditing Mason Street Recording Studios found that total stockholders' equity was understated and liabilities were overstated. Which of the following errors could have been the cause?
   a. Making the adjustment entry for depreciation expense twice.
   b. Failure to record interest accrued on a note payable.
   c. Failure to make the adjusting entry to record revenue that had been earned but not yet billed to clients.
   d. Failure to record the earned portion of fees received in advance.

4. Assume Fisher Corporation usually earns taxable income, but sustains a *loss* in the current period. The entry to record income taxes expense in the current period will most likely: (Indicate all correct answers.)
   a. Increase the amount of that loss.
   b. Include a credit to the Income Taxes Expense account.
   c. Be an adjusting entry, rather than an entry to record a transaction completed during the period.
   d. Include a credit to Income Taxes Payable.

5. The concept of *materiality:* (Indicate all correct answers.)
   a. Requires that financial statements be accurate to the nearest dollar, but need not show cents.
   b. Is based upon what users of financial statements are thought to consider important.
   c. Permits accountants to ignore generally accepted accounting principles in certain situations.
   d. Permits accountants to use the easiest and most convenient means of accounting for events that are *immaterial*.

ASSIGNMENT MATERIAL
DISCUSSION QUESTIONS

1. What is the purpose of making adjusting entries? Your answer should relate adjusting entries to the goals of accrual accounting.
2. Do all transactions involving revenue or expenses require adjusting entries at the end of the accounting period? If not, what is the distinguishing characteristic of those transactions that do require adjusting entries?
3. Do adjusting entries affect income statement accounts, balance sheet accounts, or both? Explain.
4. Why does the recording of adjusting entries require a better understanding of the concepts of accrual accounting than does the recording of routine revenue and expense transactions occurring throughout the period?
5. Why does the purchase of a one-year insurance policy four months ago give rise to insurance expense in the current month?
6. If services have been rendered to customers during the current accounting period but no revenue has been recorded and no bill has been sent to the customers, why is an adjusting entry needed? What types of accounts should be debited and credited by this entry?
7. What is meant by the term *unearned revenue*? Where should an unearned revenue account appear in the financial statements? As the work is done, what happens to the balance of an unearned revenue account?

8. The weekly payroll for employees of Ryan Company, who work a five-day week, amounts to $20,000. All employees are paid up-to-date at the close of business each Friday. If December 31 falls on Thursday, what year-end adjusting entry is needed?

9. At year-end the adjusting entry to reduce the Unexpired Insurance account by the amount of insurance premium applicable to the current period was accidentally omitted. Which items in the income statement will be in error? Will these items be overstated or understated? Which items in the balance sheet will be in error? Will they be overstated or understated?

10. Briefly explain the concept of *materiality*. If an item is not material, how is the item treated for financial reporting purposes?

11. Assets are defined as economic resources owned by a business and expected to benefit future business operations. By this definition, the gasoline in the tank of a business automobile, unused printer cartridges, and even ballpoint pens are actually assets. Why, then, are purchases of such items routinely charged directly to expense?

EXERCISES

EXERCISE 4.1
Accounting Terminology
LO 1–9

Listed below are nine technical accounting terms used in this chapter:

Unrecorded revenue	Adjusting entries	Accrued expenses
Book value	Matching principle	Accumulated depreciation
Unearned revenue	Materiality	Prepaid expenses

Each of the following statements may (or may not) describe one of these technical terms. For each statement, indicate the accounting term described, or answer "None" if the statement does not correctly describe any of the terms.

a. The net amount at which an asset is carried in the accounting records as distinguished from its market value.

b. An accounting concept that may justify departure from other accounting principles for purposes of convenience and economy.

c. The offsetting of revenue with expenses incurred in generating that revenue.

d. Revenue earned during the current accounting period but not yet recorded or billed, which requires an adjusting entry at the end of the period.

e. Entries made at the end of the period to achieve the goals of accrual accounting by recording revenue when it is earned and by recording expenses when the related goods and services are used.

f. A type of account credited when customers pay in advance for services to be rendered in the future.

g. A balance sheet category used for reporting advance payments of such items as insurance, rent, and office supplies.

h. An expense representing the systematic allocation of an asset's cost over its useful life.

EXERCISE 4.2
Effects of Adjusting Entries
LO 1–6, 9

Security Service Company adjusts its accounts at the end of the month. On November 30, adjusting entries are prepared to record:

a. Depreciation expense for November.
b. Interest expense that has accrued during November.
c. Revenue earned during November that has not yet been billed to customers.
d. Salaries, payable to company employees, that have accrued since the last payday in November.
e. The portion of the company's prepaid insurance that has expired during November.
f. Earning a portion of the amount collected in advance from a customer, Harbor Restaurant.

Indicate the effect of each of these adjusting entries on the major elements of the company's income statement and balance sheet—that is, on revenue, expenses, net income, assets, liabilities, and owners' equity. Organize your answer in tabular form, using the column headings shown and the symbols **I** for increase, **D** for decrease, and **NE** for no effect. The answer for adjusting entry **a** is provided as an example.

	Income Statement	Balance Sheet
Adjusting Entry	Revenue − Expenses = Net Income	Assets = Liabilities + Owners' Equity
a	NE I D	D NE D

EXERCISE 4.3
Preparing Adjusting Entries to Convert an Asset to an Expense and to Convert a Liability to Revenue

LO 1–7

The Golden Goals, a professional soccer team, prepare financial statements on a monthly basis. The soccer season begins in May, but in April the team engaged in the following transactions:

1. Paid $1,200,000 to the municipal stadium as advance rent for use of the facilities for the five-month period from May 1 through September 30. This payment was initially recorded as Prepaid Rent.
2. Collected $4,500,000 cash from the sale of season tickets for the team's home games. The entire amount was initially recorded as Unearned Ticket Revenue. During the month of May, the Golden Goals played several home games at which $148,800 of the season tickets sold in April were used by fans.

Prepare the two adjusting entries required on May 31.

EXERCISE 4.4
Preparing Adjusting Entries to Convert an Asset to an Expense and to Convert a Liability to Revenue

LO 1–7

Carnival Corporation is the world's largest cruise line company. Its printing costs for brochures are initially recorded as Prepaid Advertising and are later charged to Advertising Expense when they are mailed. Passenger deposits for upcoming cruises are considered unearned revenue and are recorded as Customer Deposits as cash is received. Deposited amounts are later converted to Cruise Revenue as voyages are completed.

a. Where in its financial statements does **Carnival Corporation** report Prepaid Advertising? Where in its financial statements does it report Customer Deposits?
b. In its most recent annual report, **Carnival Corporation** reported Prepaid Advertising of $23 million. Prepare the adjusting entry necessary in the following year when brochures costing $18 million are mailed.
c. In its most recent annual report, **Carnival Corporation** reported Customer Deposits of $771 million. Prepare the adjusting entry necessary in the following year as $90 million of this amount is earned.
d. Consider the entire adjusting process at **Carnival Corporation**. Which adjusting entry do you think results in the most significant expense reported in the company's income statement?

EXERCISE 4.5
Preparing Adjusting Entries to Accrue Revenue and Expenses for Which No Cash Has Been Received

LO 1–7

The geological consulting firm of Gilbert, Marsh, & Kester prepares adjusting entries on a monthly basis. Among the items requiring adjustment on December 31, 2002, are the following:

1. The company has outstanding a $50,000, 9%, 2-year note payable issued on July 1, 2001. Payment of the $50,000 note, *plus* all accrued interest for the 2-year loan period, is due in full on June 30, 2003.
2. The firm is providing consulting services to the Texas Oil Company at an agreed-upon rate of $1,000 per day. At December 31, 10 days of unbilled consulting services have been provided.

a. Prepare the two adjusting entries required on December 31 to record the accrued interest expense and the accrued consulting revenue earned.
b. Assume that the $50,000 note payable plus all accrued interest are paid in full on June 30, 2003. What portion of the total interest expense associated with this note will be reported in the firm's *2003* income statement?
c. Assume that on January 30, 2003, Gilbert, Marsh, & Kester receive $25,000 from the Texas Oil Company in full payment of the consulting services provided in December and January. What portion of this amount constitutes revenue earned in *January?*

EXERCISE 4.6
Deferred Revenue

LO 1, 2, 4

When **American Airlines** sells tickets for future flights, it debits Cash and credits an account entitled Air Traffic Liability (as opposed to crediting Passenger Revenue Earned). This account, reported recently at $2.7 billion, is among the largest liabilities appearing in the company's balance sheet.

a. Explain why this liability is often referred to as a deferred revenue account.
b. What activity normally *reduces* this liability? Can you think of any *other* transaction that would also reduce this account?

c. Assume that in a recent flight, passengers of the airline used tickets that they had purchased in advance for $200,000. Record the entry **American Airlines** would make upon completion of this flight.

EXERCISE 4.7

Preparing Various Adjusting Entries

LO 1–6, 9

Sweeney & Associates, a large marketing firm, adjusts its accounts at the end of each month. The following information is available:

1. A bank loan had been obtained on December 1. Accrued interest on the loan at December 31 amounts to $1,200. No interest expense has yet been recorded.
2. Depreciation of the firm's office building is based on an estimated life of 25 years. The building was purchased in 1998 for $330,000.
3. Accrued, but unbilled, revenue during December amounts to $64,000.
4. On March 1, the firm paid $1,800 to renew a 12-month insurance policy. The entire amount was recorded as Prepaid Insurance.
5. The firm received $14,000 from the King Biscuit Company in advance of developing a six-month marketing campaign. The entire amount was initially recorded as Unearned Revenue. At December 31, $3,500 had actually been *earned* by the firm.
6. The company's policy is to pay its employees every Friday. Since December 31 fell on a Wednesday, there was an accrued liability for salaries amounting to $2,400.

a. Record the necessary adjusting journal entries on December 31, 2002.
b. By how much did Sweeney & Associates' net income increase or decrease as a result of the adjusting entries performed in part **a**? (Ignore income taxes.)

EXERCISE 4.8

Notes Payable and Interest

LO 1, 2, 5

Ventura Company adjusts its accounts *monthly* and closes its accounts on December 31. On October 31, 2002, Ventura Company signed a note payable and borrowed $120,000 from a bank for a period of six months at an annual interest rate of 9%.

a. How much is the total interest expense over the life of the note? How much is the monthly interest expense? (Assume equal amounts of interest expense each month.)
b. In the company's annual balance sheet at December 31, 2002, what is the amount of the liability to the bank?
c. Prepare the journal entry to record issuance of the note payable on October 31, 2002.
d. Prepare the adjusting entry to accrue interest on the note at December 31, 2002.
e. Assume the company prepared a balance sheet at March 31, 2003. State the amount of the liability to the bank at this date.

EXERCISE 4.9

Relationship of Adjusting Entries to Business Transactions

LO 1–7, 9

Among the ledger accounts used by Glenwood Speedway are the following: Prepaid Rent, Rent Expense, Unearned Admissions Revenue, Admissions Revenue, Prepaid Printing, Printing Expense, Concessions Receivable, and Concessions Revenue. For each of the following items, provide the journal entry (if one is needed) to record the initial transaction and provide the adjusting entry, if any, required on May 31, the end of the fiscal year.

a. On May 1, borrowed $300,000 cash from National Bank by issuing a 12% note payable due in three months.
b. On May 1, paid rent for six months beginning May 1 at $30,000 per month.
c. On May 2, sold season tickets for a total of $910,000 cash. The season includes 70 racing days: 20 in May, 25 in June, and 25 in July.
d. On May 4, an agreement was reached with Snack-Bars, Inc., allowing that company to sell refreshments at the track in return for 10% of the gross receipts from refreshment sales.
e. On May 6, schedules for the 20 racing days in May and the first 10 racing days in June were printed and paid for at a cost of $12,000.
f. On May 31, Snack-Bars, Inc., reported that the gross receipts from refreshment sales in May had been $165,000 and that the 10% owed to Glenwood Speedway would be remitted on June 10.

Something to Consider Assume that the May 1 payment of $180,000 rent was properly recorded as Prepaid Rent, but that the May 31 adjusting entry for this item was inadvertently omitted. What is the effect of this omission on Glenwood's financial statements at May 31? (Specifically consider the financial statement elements revenue, expense, net income, assets, liabilities, and owners' equity at May 31; indicate whether each would be overstated, understated, or not affected by the omission.)

EXERCISE 4.10
Concept of Materiality
LO 8

The concept of materiality is a generally accepted accounting principle.
a. Briefly explain the concept of materiality.
b. Is $2,500 a "material" dollar amount? Explain.
c. Describe two ways in which the concept of materiality may save accountants' time and effort in making adjusting entries.

EXERCISE 4.11
Accounting Principles
LO 1–8

For each of the situations described below, indicate the generally accepted accounting principle that is being *violated*. Choose from the following principles:

Matching   Materiality
Cost   Realization
Objectivity

If you do not believe that the practice violates any of these principles, answer "None" and explain.

a. The bookkeeper of a large metropolitan auto dealership depreciates the $7.20 cost of metal wastebaskets over a period of 10 years.
b. A small commuter airline recognizes no depreciation expense on its aircraft because the planes are maintained in "as good as new" condition.
c. Palm Beach Hotel recognizes room rental revenue on the date that a reservation is received. For the winter season, many guests make reservations as much as a year in advance.

EXERCISE 4.12
Examining an Annual Report
LO 1, 2

The annual report of **Tootsie Roll Industries, Inc.**, appears in Appendix A at the end of this textbook. Examine the company's consolidated balance sheet and identify specific accounts that may have required adjusting entries at the end of the year.

PROBLEMS

PROBLEM 4.1
Preparing Adjusting Entries
LO 1–7

Florida Palms Country Club adjusts its accounts *monthly* and closes its accounts annually. Club members pay their annual dues in advance by January 4. The entire amount is initially credited to Unearned Membership Dues. At the end of each month, an appropriate portion of this amount is credited to Membership Dues Earned. Guests of the club normally pay green fees before being allowed on the course. The amounts collected are credited to Green Fee Revenue at the time of receipt. Certain guests, however, are billed for green fees at the end of the month. The following information is available as a source for preparing adjusting entries at December 31:

1. Salaries earned by golf course employees that have not yet been recorded or paid amount to $9,600.
2. The Tampa University golf team used Florida Palms for a tournament played on December 30 of the current year. At December 31, the $1,800 owed by the team for green fees had not yet been recorded or billed.
3. Membership dues earned in December, for collections received in January, amount to $106,000.
4. Depreciation of the country club's golf carts is based on an estimated life of 15 years. The carts had originally been purchased for $180,000. The straight-line method is used.
   (*Note:* The clubhouse building was constructed in 1925 and is fully depreciated.)
5. A 12-month bank loan in the amount of $45,000 had been obtained by the country club on November 1. Interest is computed at an annual rate of 8%. The entire $45,000, plus all of the interest accrued over the 12-month life of the loan, is due in full on October 31 of the upcoming year. The necessary adjusting entry was made on November 30 to record the first month of accrued interest expense. However, no adjustment has been made to record interest expense accrued in December.
6. A one-year property insurance policy had been purchased on March 1. The entire premium of $7,800 was initially recorded as Unexpired Insurance.
7. In December, Florida Palms Country Club entered into an agreement to host the annual tournament of the Florida Seniors Golf Association. The country club expects to generate green fees of $4,500 from this event.

Problems

8. Unrecorded Income Taxes Expense accrued in December amounts to $19,000. This amount will not be paid until January 15.

Instructions

a. For each of the above numbered paragraphs, prepare the necessary adjusting entry (including an explanation). If no adjusting entry is required, explain why.

b. Four types of adjusting entries are described at the beginning of the chapter. Using these descriptions, identify the type of each adjusting entry prepared in part **a** above.

c. Although Florida Palms' clubhouse building is fully depreciated, it is in excellent physical condition. Explain how this can be.

PROBLEM 4.2
Preparing and Analyzing the Effects of Adjusting Entries
LO 1–6, 9

Enchanted Forest, a large campground in South Carolina, adjusts its accounts *monthly* and closes its accounts annually on December 31. Most guests of the campground pay at the time they check out, and the amounts collected are credited to Camper Revenue. The following information is available as a source for preparing the adjusting entries at December 31:

1. Enchanted Forest invests some of its excess cash in certificates of deposit (CDs) with its local bank. Accrued interest revenue on its CDs at December 31 is $400. None of the interest has yet been received. (Debit Interest Receivable.)

2. A six-month bank loan in the amount of $12,000 had been obtained on September 1. Interest is to be computed at an annual rate of 8.5% and is payable when the loan becomes due.

3. Depreciation on buildings owned by the campground is based on a 25-year life. The original cost of the buildings was $600,000. The Accumulated Depreciation: Buildings account has a credit balance of $310,000 at December 31, prior to the adjusting entry process. The straight-line method of depreciation is used.

4. Management signed an agreement to let Boy Scout Troop 538 of Lewisburg, Pennsylvania, use the campground in June of next year. The agreement specifies that the Boy Scouts will pay a daily rate of $15 per campsite, with a clause providing a minimum total charge of $1,475.

5. Salaries earned by campground employees that have not yet been paid amount to $1,250.

6. As of December 31, Enchanted Forest has earned $2,400 of revenue from current campers who will not be billed until they check out. (Debit Camper Revenue Receivable.)

7. Several lakefront campsites are currently being leased on a long-term basis by a group of senior citizens. Six months' rent of $5,400 was collected in advance and credited to Unearned Camper Revenue on October 1 of the current year.

8. A bus to carry campers to and from town and the airport had been rented the first week of December at a daily rate of $40. At December 31, no rental payment has been made, although the campground has had use of the bus for 25 days.

9. Unrecorded Income Taxes Expense accrued in December amounts to $8,400. This amount will not be paid until January 15.

Instructions

a. For each of the above numbered paragraphs, prepare the necessary adjusting entry (including an explanation). If no adjusting entry is required, explain why.

b. Four types of adjusting entries are described at the beginning of the chapter. Using these descriptions, identify the type of each adjusting entry prepared in part **a** above.

c. Indicate the effects that each of the adjustments in part **a** will have on the following six *total amounts* in the campground's financial statements for the month of *December*. Organize your answer in tabular form, using the column headings shown below. Use the letters **I** for increase, **D** for decrease, and **NE** for no effect. Adjusting entry **1** is provided as an example.

	Income Statement			Balance Sheet		
Adjusting	Revenue	− Expenses	= Net Income	Assets	= Liabilities	+ Owners' Equity
1	I	NE	I	I	NE	I

d. What is the amount of interest expense recognized for the *entire current year* on the $12,000 bank loan obtained September 1?

e. Compute the *book value* of the campground's buildings to be reported in the current year's December 31 balance sheet. (Refer to paragraph **3**.)

PROBLEM 4.3
Analysis of Adjusted Data
LO 1–7, 9

Gunflint Adventures operates an airplane service that takes fishing parties to a remote lake resort in northern Manitoba, Canada. Individuals *must* purchase their tickets at least one month in advance during the busy summer season. The company adjusts its accounts only once each month. Selected balances appearing in the company's June 30 *adjusted* trial balance appear as follows:

	Debit	Credit
Prepaid Airport Rent	$ 7,200	
Unexpired Insurance	3,500	
Airplane	240,000	
Accumulated Depreciation: Airplane		$36,000
Unearned Passenger Revenue		90,000

Other Information

1. The airplane is being depreciated over a 20-year life with no residual value.
2. Unearned passenger revenue represents advance ticket sales for bookings in July and August at $300 per ticket.
3. Six months' of airport rent had been prepaid on May 1.
4. The unexpired insurance is what remains of a 12-month policy purchased on February 1.
5. Passenger revenue earned in June totaled $75,000.

Instructions

a. Determine the following:
   1. The age of the airplane in months.
   2. The monthly airport rent expense.
   3. The amount paid for the 12-month insurance policy on February 1.
b. Prepare the adjusting entries made on June 30 involving the following accounts:
   1. Depreciation Expense: Airplane
   2. Airport Rent Expense
   3. Insurance Expense
   4. Passenger Revenue Earned

PROBLEM 4.4
Preparing Adjusting Entries from a Trial Balance
LO 1–7, 9

The Campus Theater adjusts its accounts every *month*. Below is the company's *unadjusted* trial balance dated August 31, 2002. Additional information is provided for use in preparing the company's adjusting entries for the month of August. (Bear in mind that adjusting entries *have* already been made for the first seven months of 2002, but *not* for August.)

CAMPUS THEATER
Unadjusted Trial Balance
August 31, 2002

Account	Debit	Credit
Cash	$ 20,000	
Prepaid film rental	31,200	
Land	120,000	
Building	168,000	
Accumulated depreciation: building		$ 14,000
Fixtures and equipment	36,000	
Accumulated depreciation: fixtures and equipment		12,000
Notes payable		180,000
Accounts payable		4,400
Unearned admissions revenue (YMCA)		1,000
Income taxes payable		4,740
Capital stock		40,000
Retained earnings		46,610
Dividends	15,000	
Admissions revenue		305,200
Concessions revenue		14,350
Salaries expense	68,500	
Film rental expense	94,500	
Utilities expense	9,500	
Depreciation expense: building	4,900	
Depreciation expense: fixtures and equipment	4,200	
Interest expense	10,500	
Income taxes expense	40,000	
	$622,300	$622,300

Other Data

1. Film rental expense for the month is $15,200. However, the film rental expense for several months has been paid in advance.
2. The building is being depreciated over a period of 20 years (240 months).
3. The fixtures and equipment are being depreciated over a period of 5 years (60 months).
4. On the first of each month, the theater pays the interest that accrued in the prior month on its note payable. At August 31, accrued interest payable on this note amounts to $1,500.
5. The theater allows the local YMCA to bring children attending summer camp to the movies on any weekday afternoon for a fixed fee of $500 per month. On June 28, the YMCA made a $1,500 advance payment covering the months of July, August, and September.
6. The theater receives a percentage of the revenue earned by Tastie Corporation, the concessionaire operating the snack bar. For snack bar sales in August, Tastie owes Campus Theater $2,250, payable on September 10. No entry has yet been made to record this revenue. (Credit Concessions Revenue.)
7. Salaries earned by employees, but not recorded or paid as of August 31, amount to $1,700. No entry has yet been made to record this liability and expense.
8. Income taxes expense for August is estimated at $4,200. This amount will be paid in the September 15 installment payment.
9. Utilities expense is recorded as monthly bills are received. No adjusting entries for utilities expense are made at month-end.

Instructions

a. For each of the numbered paragraphs, prepare the necessary adjusting entry (including an explanation).

b. Refer to the balances shown in the *unadjusted* trial balance at August 31. How many *months* of expense are included in each of the following account balances? (Remember, Campus Theater adjusts its accounts *monthly*. Thus, the accounts shown were last adjusted on 7/31/02.)

  1. Utilities Expense
  2. Depreciation Expense
  3. Accumulated Depreciation: Building

c. Assume the theater has been operating profitably all year. Although the August 31 trial balance shows substantial income taxes *expense,* income taxes *payable* is a much smaller amount. This relationship is quite normal throughout much of the year. Explain.

PROBLEM 4.5
Preparing Adjusting Entries from a Trial Balance
LO 1–7, 9

Ken Hensley Enterprises, Inc., is a small recording studio in St. Louis. Rock bands use the studio to mix high-quality demo recordings distributed to talent agents. New clients are required to pay in advance for studio services. Bands with established credit are billed for studio services at the end of each month. Adjusting entries are performed on a *monthly* basis. An *unadjusted* trial balance dated December 31, 2002, follows. (Bear in mind that adjusting entries already have been made for the first eleven months of 2002, but *not* for December.)

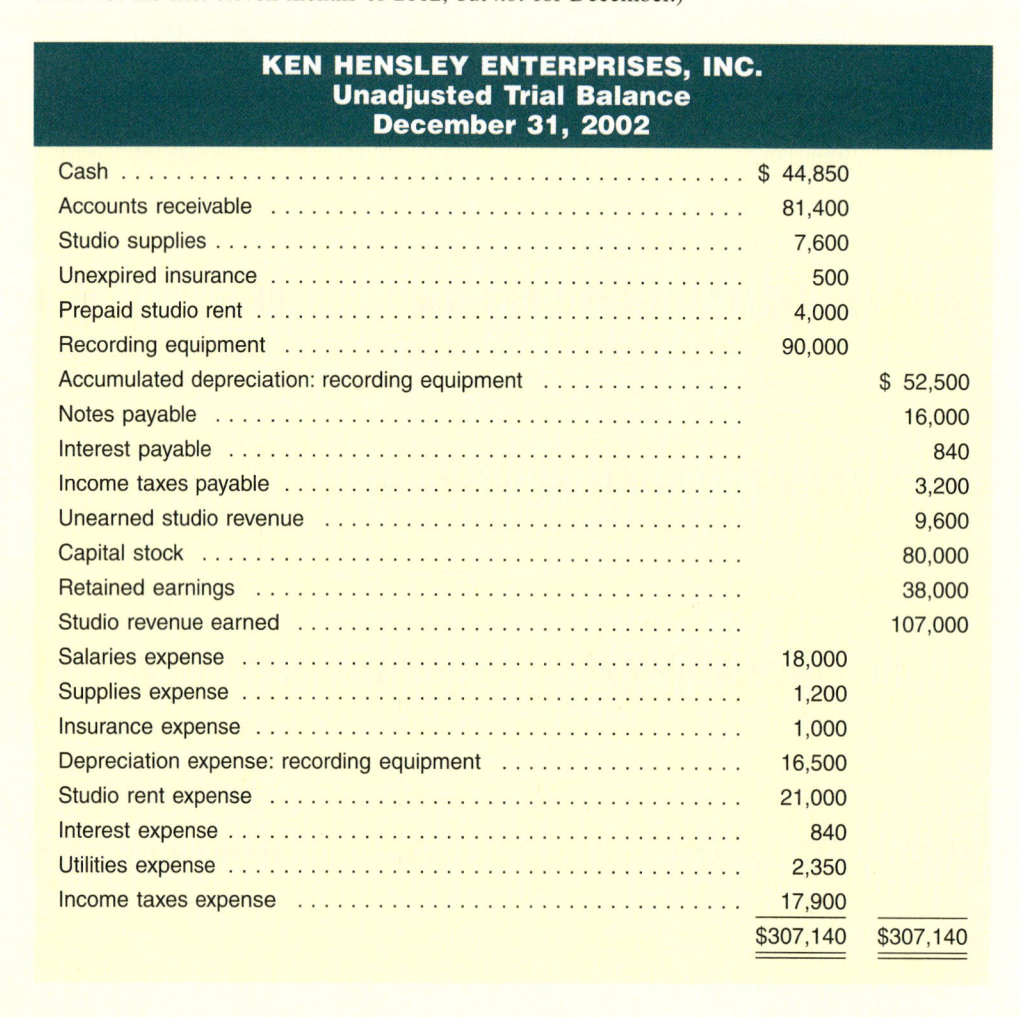

KEN HENSLEY ENTERPRISES, INC.
Unadjusted Trial Balance
December 31, 2002

Cash	$ 44,850	
Accounts receivable	81,400	
Studio supplies	7,600	
Unexpired insurance	500	
Prepaid studio rent	4,000	
Recording equipment	90,000	
Accumulated depreciation: recording equipment		$ 52,500
Notes payable		16,000
Interest payable		840
Income taxes payable		3,200
Unearned studio revenue		9,600
Capital stock		80,000
Retained earnings		38,000
Studio revenue earned		107,000
Salaries expense	18,000	
Supplies expense	1,200	
Insurance expense	1,000	
Depreciation expense: recording equipment	16,500	
Studio rent expense	21,000	
Interest expense	840	
Utilities expense	2,350	
Income taxes expense	17,900	
	$307,140	$307,140

Other Data

1. Records show that $4,400 in studio revenue had not yet been billed or recorded as of December 31.
2. Studio supplies on hand at December 31 amount to $6,900.
3. On August 1, 2002, the studio purchased a six-month insurance policy for $1,500. The entire premium was initially debited to Unexpired Insurance.
4. The studio is located in a rented building. On November 1, 2002, the studio paid $6,000 rent in advance for November, December, and January. The entire amount was debited to Prepaid Studio Rent.

5. The useful life of the studio's recording equipment is estimated to be five years (or 60 months). The straight-line method of depreciation is used.
6. On May 1, 2002, the studio borrowed $16,000 by signing a 12-month, 9% note payable to First Federal Bank of St. Louis. The entire $16,000 plus 12 months' interest is due in full on April 30, 2003.
7. Records show that $3,600 of cash receipts originally recorded as Unearned Studio Revenue had been earned as of December 31.
8. Salaries earned by recording technicians that remain unpaid at December 31 amount to $540.
9. The studio's accountant estimates that income taxes expense for the *entire year* ended December 31, 2002, is $19,600. (Note that $17,900 of this amount has already been recorded.)

Instructions

a. For each of the above numbered paragraphs, prepare the necessary adjusting entry (including an explanation). If no adjusting entry is required, explain why.
b. Using figures from the company's unadjusted trial balance in conjunction with the adjusting entries made in part **a**, compute net income for the year ended December 31, 2002.
c. Was the studio's monthly rent for the last 2 months of 2002 more or less than during the first 10 months of the year? Explain your answer.

PROBLEM 4.6

Understanding the Effects of Various Errors

LO 1–7, 9

Koyne Corporation recently hired Jane McDonald as its new bookkeeper. McDonald was not very experienced and made six recording errors during the last accounting period. The nature of each error is described in the following table.

Instructions

Indicate the effect of the following errors on each of the financial statement elements described in the column headings in the table. Use the following symbols: **O** = overstated, **U** = understated, and **NE** = no effect.

	Error	Total Revenue	Total Expenses	Net Income	Total Assets	Total Liabilities	Owners' Equity
a.	Recorded a dividend as an expense reported in the income statement.						
b.	Recorded the payment of an account payable as a debit to accounts payable and a credit to an expense account.						
c.	Failed to record depreciation expense.						
d.	Recorded the sale of capital stock as a debit to cash and a credit to retained earnings.						
e.	Recorded the receipt of a customer deposit as a debit to cash and a credit to fees earned.						
f.	Failed to record expired portion of an insurance policy.						
g.	Failed to record accrued interest earned on an outstanding note receivable.						

CASES AND UNSTRUCTURED PROBLEMS

CASE 4.1

Should This Be Adjusted?

LO 1–7

Property Management Professionals provides building management services to owners of office buildings and shopping centers. The company closes its accounts at the *end of the calendar year*. The manner in which the company has recorded several transactions occurring during 2002 is described as follows:

a. On September 1, received advance payment from a shopping center for property management services to be performed over the three-month period beginning September 1. The entire amount received was credited directly to a *revenue* account.

b. On December 1, received advance payment from the same customer described in part a for services to be rendered over the three-month period beginning December 1. This time, the entire amount received was credited to an *unearned* revenue account.

c. Rendered management services for many customers in December. Normal procedure is to record revenue on the date the customer is billed, which is early in the month after the services have been rendered.

d. On December 15, made full payment for a one-year insurance policy that goes into effect on January 2, 2003. The cost of the policy was debited to Unexpired Insurance.

e. Numerous purchases of equipment were debited to asset accounts, rather than to expense accounts.

f. Payroll expense is recorded when employees are paid. Payday for the last two weeks of December falls on January 2, 2003.

Instructions

For each item above, explain whether an adjusting entry is needed at *December 31, 2002,* and state the reasons for your answer. If you recommend an adjusting entry, explain the effects this entry would have on assets, liabilities, owners' equity, revenue, and expense in the 2002 financial statements.

CASE 4.2

The Concept of Materiality

LO 8

The concept of materiality is one of the most basic generally accepted accounting principles.

a. Answer the following questions:
  1. Why is the materiality of a transaction or an event a matter of professional judgment?
  2. What criteria should accountants consider in determining whether a transaction or an event is material?
  3. Does the concept of materiality mean that financial statements are not precise, down to the last dollar? Does this concept make financial statements less useful to most users?

b. **Avis Rent-a-Car** purchases a large number of cars each year for its rental fleet. The cost of any individual automobile is immaterial to **Avis**, which is a very large corporation. Would it be acceptable for **Avis** to charge the purchase of automobiles for its rental fleet directly to expense, rather than to an asset account? Explain.

BUSINESS WEEK ASSIGNMENT

CASE 4.3

Deferred Expenses at Pre-Paid Legal Services

LO 3, 5, 7

Pre-Paid Legal Services Inc. is a company that sells memberships allowing persons to access legal services when they need legal help. **Pre-Paid** associates recruit new members throughout the country and are compensated by commissions. The company records the payment of commissions by debiting an asset account (Prepaid Commissions) and by crediting Cash. As members access legal services, the company debits Commissions Expense and credits Prepaid Commissions.

On June 28, 2001, **Pre-Paid Legal Services Inc.** was asked by the Securities and Exchange Commission (SEC) to correct its books. In short, the SEC wanted the company to record Commissions Expense when the commissions were *paid,* not when members' services were *used.* A story in the July 23, 2001, *Business Week* article by David Henry, "For Accountants, a Major Credibility GAAP," explains that the correction could erase half the earnings **Pre-Paid** reported in the previous two years, and three-fourths of its net worth.

SEC auditors were concerned that by deferring commission expenses, **Pre-Paid** had inflated both its earnings and its assets. **Pre-Paid** says it complies with generally accepted accounting principles (GAAP) and logically aligns the expense with future revenue.

Instructions

Choose one of the following positions and be prepared to defend it in a class discussion:

a. **Pre-Paid**'s practice of treating commission payments as prepaid expenses is appropriate.

b. **Pre-Paid**'s practice of treating commission payments as prepaid expenses is inappropriate.

INTERNET ASSIGNMENT

INTERNET 4.1

Identifying Accounts Requiring Adjusting Entries

LO 1–6

Visit **Hershey's** home page at:

www.hersheys.com

From **Hershey's** home page, access its most recent annual report (see the Investor Relations link). Examine the company's balance sheet and identify the accounts most likely to have been involved in the end-of-year adjusting entry process.

Internet sites are time and date sensitive. It is the purpose of these exercises to have you explore the Internet. You may need to use the Yahoo! search engine **http://www.yahoo.com** *(or another favorite search engine) to find a company's current Web address.*

OUR COMMENTS ON THE "YOUR TURN" CASES

You as a Car Owner (p. 142) Yes, in most cases you will receive a full refund equal to the unexpired portion of your policy. You are entitled to a refund because you will not consume four full months of coverage that remain on your policy at the time of cancellation. Thus you should receive a check for $400 (or $100 per month for April, May, June, and July).

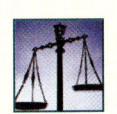

You as Overnight Auto's Service Department Manager (p. 149) It is true that by accruing an entire month's revenue from Airport Shuttle Services, Overnight's reported income for December would have increased by $750 (the difference between recognizing the entire month's revenue of $1,500 and the $750 already recorded). However, to record revenue for services not yet performed is in conflict with generally accepted accounting principles (GAAP). Furthermore, the practice of overstating revenue to increase one's bonus is also unethical.

The timing of revenue recognition is a complex issue faced by business managers, auditors, tax authorities, and the financial reporting enforcement arm of the SEC. For instance, **McKesson HBOC** had reported more than $44 million in revenues that had not, in fact, been realized. As this information became public, **McKesson**'s shareholders filed lawsuits and the company's stock price dropped by nearly 50%.

You as Overnight Auto's Service Department Manager (p. 152) It is true that Overnight Auto might consider the items Betty took home as immaterial for the preparation of their financial records. Thus, Overnight Auto might choose to account for screwdrivers and cans of oil in the easiest and most convenient manner by expensing the costs as they are incurred.

However, the materiality issue is unrelated to the ethical issue of stealing from the company. Betty should either be fired or asked to return and/or replace the missing items. Another option would be to put Betty on probation and monitor supplies for missing items. As the manager of the department you might wish to implement sign-out procedures for supplies that would allow you to monitor the use and location of equipment used in servicing vehicles.

ANSWERS TO SELF-TEST QUESTIONS

1. c.
2. d $11,670 ($27,900 − $17,340 − $2,700 − $1,440 + $3,300 + $1,950)
3. d
4. b, c
5. b, c, d

CHAPTER 5

THE ACCOUNTING CYCLE:

Reporting Financial Results

Learning Objectives

After studying this chapter, you should be able to:

1. Prepare an income statement, a statement of retained earnings, and a balance sheet.

2. Explain how the income statement and the statement of retained earnings relate to the balance sheet.

3. Explain the concept of *adequate disclosure.*

4. Explain the purposes of *closing entries;* prepare these entries.

5. Prepare an after-closing trial balance.

6. Use financial statement information to evaluate profitability and liquidity.

7. Explain how *interim* financial statements are prepared in a business that closes its accounts only at year-end.

8. Prepare a worksheet and explain its uses.*

---

*Supplemental Topic, "The Worksheet."

Spencer Grant/PhotoEdit

Circuit City

Circuit City is a national retailer of televisions, video equipment, stereo systems, personal computers, cellular phones, and an array of other consumer electronic devices. Throughout its history, the company has also offered a wide selection of major household appliances such as washers, dryers, refrigerators, and freezers. Recently, however, **Circuit City** made a strategic decision to exit the major appliance market in order to expand its selection of consumer electronics and home office products. The decision was based on slumping sales forecasts and the threat of increased competition.

To discontinue its appliance business, **Circuit City** was forced to terminate hundreds of employees and close numerous sales and distribution centers. Company management anticipates this major shift in strategic direction will improve **Circuit City**'s future profitability and solvency.

• • •

176 Chapter 5 The Accounting Cycle

In this chapter, we examine how companies prepare general purpose financial statements used by investors, creditors, and managers. In addition, we discuss how certain events, such as **Circuit City**'s decision to discontinue selling major appliances, are disclosed in the notes that accompany financial statements. We also illustrate several methods of evaluating liquidity and profitability using financial statement information.

In Chapter 3, we introduced the first of the eight steps in the accounting cycle by illustrating how Overnight Auto Service (1) captured (journalized) economic events, (2) posted these transactions to its general ledger, and (3) prepared an *unadjusted* trial balance from its general ledger account balances. We continued our illustration of the accounting cycle in Chapter 4 by (4) performing the adjusting entries made by Overnight and (5) presenting the company's *adjusted* trial balance at year-end.

In this chapter, we complete the accounting cycle by (6) preparing Overnight's financial statements, (7) performing year-end closing entries, and (8) presenting the company's *after-closing* trial balance.

PREPARING FINANCIAL STATEMENTS

LO 1
Prepare an income statement, a statement of retained earnings, and a balance sheet.

Publicly owned companies—those with shares listed on a stock exchange—have obligations to release annual and quarterly information to their stockholders and to the public. These companies don't simply prepare financial statements—they publish *annual reports*.

An annual report *includes* comparative financial statements for several years and a wealth of other information about the company's financial position, business operations, and future prospects. (For illustrative purposes, the 2000 annual report of **Tootsie Roll Industries, Inc.,** appears in Appendix A.) Before an annual report is issued, the financial statements must be *audited* by a firm of certified public accountants (CPAs). Publicly owned companies must file their audited financial statements and detailed supporting schedules with the Securities and Exchange Commission (SEC).

The activities surrounding the preparation of an annual report become very intense as the new year approaches. Once the fiscal year has ended, it often takes several *months* before the annual report is available for distribution. Thus, many accountants refer to the months of December through March as the "busy season."[1] We cannot adequately discuss all of the activities associated with the preparation of an annual report in a single chapter. Thus, here we focus on the *preparation of financial statements*.

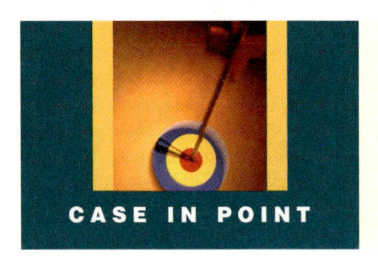

CASE IN POINT

The timeliness of annual reports varies significantly from country to country. To illustrate, consider the amount of time that elapses between the year-end date and the date of the auditor's report. In Brazil, Mexico, and the United States the average time is between 31 and 60 days. However, in Austria, France, Hong Kong, and Germany, the average time is between 91 and 120 days.

The adjusted trial balance prepared in Chapter 4 is reprinted in Exhibit 5–1. The income statement, statement of retained earnings, and balance sheet can be prepared *directly from the amounts shown in this adjusted trial balance*. For illustrative purposes, we have made marginal notes indicating which accounts appear in which financial statements. Overnight's financial statements for the year ended December 31, 2002, are illustrated in Exhibit 5–2.

---

[1] Some companies elect to end their fiscal year during a seasonal low point in business activity. However, most companies *do* end their fiscal year on December 31.

Exhibit 5–1
ADJUSTED TRIAL BALANCE

OVERNIGHT AUTO SERVICE
Adjusted Trial Balance
December 31, 2002

Cash	$ 18,592	
Accounts receivable	7,250	
Shop supplies	1,200	
Unexpired insurance	3,000	
Land	52,000	
Building	36,000	
Accumulated depreciation: building		$ 1,650
Tools and equipment	12,000	
Accumulated depreciation: tools and equipment		2,200
Notes payable		4,000
Accounts payable		2,690
Wages payable		1,950
Income taxes payable		5,580
Interest payable		30
Unearned rent revenue		6,000
Capital stock		80,000
Retained earnings (*Note:* still must be updated for transactions recorded in the accounts listed below. Closing entries serve this purpose.)		0
Dividends	14,000	
Repair service revenue		172,000
Rent revenue earned		3,000
Advertising expense	3,900	
Wages expense	58,750	
Supplies expense	7,500	
Depreciation expense: building	1,650	
Depreciation expense: tools and equipment	2,200	
Utilities expense	19,400	
Insurance expense	15,000	
Interest expense	30	
Income taxes expense	26,628	
	$279,100	$279,100

Balance sheet accounts (Cash through Capital stock)
Statement of retained earnings accounts (Retained earnings and Dividends)
Income statement accounts (Repair service revenue through Income taxes expense)

The income statement is prepared first because it determines the amount of net income to be reported in the statement of retained earnings. The statement of retained earnings is prepared second because it determines the amount of retained earnings to be reported in the balance sheet. Note that we have not included Overnight's statement of cash flows with the other three reports. An in-depth discussion of the statement of cash flows is the primary focus of Chapter 13.

The Income Statement

Alternative titles for the income statement include *earnings statement, statement of operations,* and *profit and loss statement.* However, *income statement* is the most popular term for this important financial statement. The income statement is used to summarize the *operating* results of a business by matching the revenue earned during a given period of time with the expenses incurred in generating that revenue.

The revenue and expenses shown in Overnight's income statement are taken directly from the company's adjusted trial balance. Overnight's 2002 income statement shows

LO 2
Explain how the income statement and the statement of retained earnings relate to the balance sheet.

Exhibit 5–2

OVERNIGHT AUTO SERVICE'S FINANCIAL STATEMENTS

OVERNIGHT AUTO SERVICE
Income Statement
For the Year Ended December 31, 2002

Revenue:

Repair service revenue		$172,000
Rent revenue earned		3,000
Total revenue		$175,000

Expenses:

Advertising	$ 3,900	
Wages expense	58,750	
Supplies expense	7,500	
Depreciation: building	1,650	
Depreciation: tools and equipment	2,200	
Utilities expense	19,400	
Insurance	15,000	
Interest	30	108,430
Income before income taxes		$ 66,570
Income taxes		26,628
Net income		$ 39,942

My Notes

Amounts are taken directly from the adjusted trial balance

My Notes

Net income also appears in the statement of retained earnings

OVERNIGHT AUTO SERVICE
Statement of Retained Earnings
For the Year Ended December 31, 2002

Retained earnings, Jan. 20, 2002	$ 0
Add: Net income	39,942
Subtotal	$39,942
Less: Dividends	14,000
Retained earnings, Dec. 31, 2002	$25,942

My Notes

The ending balance in the Retained Earnings account also appears in the balance sheet

OVERNIGHT AUTO SERVICE
Balance Sheet
December 31, 2002

Assets

Cash		$ 18,592
Accounts receivable		7,250
Shop supplies		1,200
Unexpired insurance		3,000
Land		52,000
Building	$36,000	
Less: Accumulated depreciation	1,650	34,350
Tools and equipment	$12,000	
Less: Accumulated depreciation	2,200	9,800
Total assets		$126,192

Liabilities & Stockholders' Equity

Liabilities:

Notes payable	$ 4,000
Accounts payable	2,690
Wages payable	1,950
Income taxes payable	5,580
Interest payable	30
Unearned rent revenue	6,000
Total liabilities	$ 20,250

Stockholders' equity:

Capital stock	80,000
Retained earnings	25,942
Total stockholders' equity	$105,942
Total liabilities and stockholders' equity	$126,192

that revenue exceeded expenses for the year, thus producing a net income of $39,942. Bear in mind, however, that this measurement of net income is not absolutely accurate or precise due to the *assumptions and estimates* in the accounting process.

An income statement has certain limitations. For instance, the amounts shown for depreciation expense are based upon estimates of the useful lives of the company's building and equipment. Also, the income statement includes only those events that have been evidenced by actual business transactions. Perhaps during the year Overnight's advertising has caught the attention of many potential customers. A good "customer base" is certainly an important step toward profitable operations; however, the development of a customer base is not reflected in the income statement because its value cannot be measured *objectively* until actual transactions take place. Despite these limitations, the income statement is of vital importance to the users of a company's financial statements.

The Statement of Retained Earnings

Retained Earnings is that portion of stockholders' (owners') equity created by earning net income and retaining the related resources in the business. The resources retained from being profitable may include, but are certainly not limited to, *cash*. The statement of retained earnings summarizes the increases and decreases in retained earnings resulting from business operations during the period. Increases in retained earnings result from earning net income; decreases result from net losses and from the declaration of dividends.

The format of this financial statement is based upon the following relationships:

Retained Earnings at the beginning of the period + **Net Income** − **Dividends** = **Retained Earnings at the end of the period**

> **My Notes**
> Statement of retained earnings

The amount of retained earnings at the *beginning* of the period is shown at the top of the statement. Next, the net income for the period is added (or net loss subtracted), and any dividends declared during the period are deducted. This short computation determines the amount of retained earnings at the *end* of the accounting period. The ending retained earnings ($25,942 in our example) appears at the bottom of the statement and also in the company's year-end balance sheet.

Our illustration of the statement of retained earnings for Overnight is unusual in that the beginning balance of retained earnings at the date of the company's formation (January 20, 2002) was *$0*. This occurred only because 2002 was the *first year* of Overnight's business operations. The ending retained earnings ($25,942) becomes the beginning retained earnings for the following year.

A Word about Dividends In Chapter 3, the declaration and payment of a cash dividend were treated as a single event recorded by one journal entry. A small corporation with only a few stockholders may choose to declare and pay a dividend on the same day. In large corporations, an interval of a month or more will separate the date of declaration from the later date of payment. A liability account, Dividends Payable, comes into existence when the dividend is declared, and is discharged when the dividend is paid. Because Overnight reports no dividends payable in its adjusted trial balance, we may assume that it declared and had paid the entire $14,000 at December 31, 2002.[2]

Finally, it is important to realize that dividends paid to stockholders are *not* reported in the income statement as an expense. In short, dividends represent a decision by a corporation to distribute a portion of its income to stockholders. Thus, the amount of the dividend is not included in the computation of income.

---

[2] Details related to the declaration and payment of dividends are discussed in Chapter 12.

The Balance Sheet

The balance sheet lists the amounts of the company's assets, liabilities, and owners' equity at the *end* of the accounting period. The balances of Overnight's asset and liability accounts are taken directly from the adjusted trial balance in Exhibit 5–1. The amount of retained earnings at the end of the period, $25,942, was determined in the *statement of retained earnings.*

Balance sheets can be presented with asset accounts appearing on the left and liabilities and owners' equity accounts appearing on the right. They may also be presented in *report form,* with liabilities and owners' equity listed *below* (rather than to the right of) the asset section. It is also common for corporations to refer to owners' equity as *stockholders'* equity.

Separate Balance Sheet Subtotals Many companies group together as separate balance sheet subtotals those assets and liabilities that are considered *current.* To be classified as a **current asset**, an asset must already be cash or must be capable of *being converted into cash* within a relatively short period of time. For most companies, this period of time is usually one year or less. Those assets that get used up quickly (e.g., insurance policies and office supplies) are also classified as current assets. Of Overnight's $126,192 in total assets shown in Exhibit 5–2, the current assets include Cash, Accounts Receivable, Shop Supplies, and Unexpired Insurance. Thus, $30,042 of Overnight's total assets is considered *current.*

A **current liability** is an existing debt or obligation that a company expects to satisfy relatively soon using its current assets. Once again, this period of time is typically one year or less. While not a *debt,* often unearned revenue is considered a current liability also. *All* of Overnight's $20,250 in total liabilities shown in Exhibit 5–2 are considered current liabilities.

Computing separate subtotals for current assets and current liabilities is very useful when evaluating a company's ability to pay its debts as they come due (see this chapter's Financial Analysis discussion). The annual report of **Tootsie Roll Industries, Inc.**, in Appendix A at the end of this textbook, illustrates how subtotals for current assets and current liabilities are presented in the balance sheet. Coverage of several other balance sheet subtotals appears in Chapter 14.

RELATIONSHIPS AMONG THE FINANCIAL STATEMENTS

A set of financial statements becomes easier to understand if we recognize that the income statement, statement of retained earnings, and balance sheet all are *related to one another.* These relationships are emphasized by the arrows in the right-hand margin of Exhibit 5–2.

The balance sheet prepared at the end of the preceding period and the one prepared at the end of the current period both include the amount of retained earnings at the respective balance sheet dates. The statement of retained earnings summarizes the factors (net income and dividends) that have caused the amount of retained earnings to change between these two balance sheet dates. The income statement explains in greater detail the change in retained earnings resulting from profitable (or unprofitable) operation of the business. Thus, the income statement and the retained earnings statement provide informative links between successive balance sheets.

Drafting the Notes That Accompany Financial Statements

To the users of financial statements, **adequate disclosure** is perhaps the most important accounting principle. This principle simply means that financial statements should be accompanied by any information necessary for the statements to be *interpreted properly.*

LO 3
Explain the concept of *adequate disclosure.*

Most disclosures appear within the several pages of notes that accompany the financial statements. Drafting these notes can be one of the most challenging tasks confronting accountants at the end of the period. The content of these notes often cannot be drawn directly from the accounting records. Rather, drafting these notes requires an *in-depth understanding* of the company and its operations, of accounting principles, and of how decision makers interpret and use accounting information.

Two items always disclosed in the notes to financial statements are the accounting methods in use and the due dates of major liabilities. Thus Overnight's 2002 financial statements should include the following notes:

Note 1: Depreciation policies
Depreciation expense in the financial statements is computed by the straight-line method. Estimated useful lives are 20 years for the building and 5 years for tools and equipment.

Note 2: Maturity dates of liabilities
The Company's notes payable consist of a single obligation that matures on February 28 of the coming year. The maturity value of this note, including interest charges, will amount to $4,090.

CASH EFFECTS

Note 2 above, maturity dates of liabilities, should be of particular importance to American National Bank. Specifically, bankers will want to know if Overnight will have enough cash to pay this $4,090 liability in just two months. The company's balance sheet reports cash of $18,592. However, it also reports additional liabilities coming due, other than the note payable, in excess of $10,000. Furthermore, the company has an $18,000 insurance policy to renew on March 1. Even though Overnight's income statement reports net income of $39,942, the company's balance sheet doesn't report enough liquid assets to satisfy all of its upcoming obligations.

What Types of Information Must Be Disclosed?

There is no comprehensive list of all information that should be disclosed in financial statements. The adequacy of disclosure is based on a combination of official rules, tradition, and accountants' professional judgment.

As a general rule, a company should disclose any facts that an intelligent person would consider necessary for the statements to be *interpreted properly*. In addition to accounting methods in use and the due dates of major liabilities, businesses may need to disclose such matters as the following:

- Lawsuits pending against the business
- Scheduled plant closings
- Governmental investigations into the safety of the company's products or the legality of its pricing policies
- Significant events occurring *after* the balance sheet date but before the financial statements are actually issued
- Specific customers that account for a large portion of the company's business
- Unusual transactions or conflicts of interest between the company and its key officers

Let us stress again that *there is no comprehensive list of items that must be disclosed.* Throughout this course, we will identify and discuss many items that may require disclosure in financial statements.

In some cases, companies must even disclose information that could have a *damaging effect* on the business. For example, a manufacturer may need to disclose that it is being sued by customers who have been injured by its products. The fact that a disclosure might prove embarrassing—or even damaging to the business—is *not* a valid reason for not disclosing the information. The concept of adequate disclosure demands a *good faith effort* by management to keep the users of financial statements informed about the company's operations.

Companies are *not* required to disclose information that is immaterial or that does not have a direct *financial* impact on the business. For example, a company is not required by generally accepted accounting principles to disclose the resignation, firing, or death of a key executive. Of course, companies often *do* disclose such nonfinancial events on a voluntary basis.

Disclosures that accompany financial statements should be limited to *facts* and *reasonable estimates*. They should not include *optimistic speculation* that cannot be substantiated.

For a look at the types of disclosure made by publicly owned corporations, see the **Tootsie Roll Industries, Inc.**, annual report, which appears in Appendix A.

YOUR TURN

You as Overnight Auto's Independent Auditor

Assume that Overnight Auto Service is being sued by a former employee injured while on the job. The person claims that Overnight had been negligent in providing a safe work environment. If the plaintiff prevails, Overnight may have to pay damages well in excess of what is covered by its insurance policies. As Overnight's independent auditor, you have asked that the company disclose information about this lawsuit in the notes that accompany the financial statements. Overnight's management disagrees with your suggestion because in its opinion, the likelihood of the plaintiff prevailing is extremely remote. How should you respond?

John Neubauer/PhotoEdit

*Our answer is on page 216.

CLOSING THE TEMPORARY EQUITY ACCOUNTS

LO 4
Explain the purpose of *closing entries;* prepare these entries.

As previously stated, revenue increases retained earnings, and expenses and dividends decrease retained earnings. If the only financial statement that we needed was a balance sheet, these changes in retained earnings could be recorded directly in the Retained Earnings account. However, owners, managers, investors, and others need to know amounts of specific revenues and expenses, and the amount of net income earned in the period. Therefore, we maintain *separate ledger accounts* to measure each type of revenue and expense, and the dividends distributed.

These revenue, expense, and dividends accounts are called *temporary,* or *nominal,* accounts, because they accumulate the transactions of *only one accounting period.* At the end of this accounting period, the changes in retained earnings accumulated in these temporary accounts are transferred into the Retained Earnings account. This process serves two purposes. First, it *updates the balance of the Retained Earnings account* for changes in retained earnings occurring during the accounting period. Second, it *returns the balances of the temporary accounts to zero,* so that they are ready for measuring the revenue, expenses, and dividends of the next accounting period.

The Retained Earnings account and other balance sheet accounts are called *permanent,* or *real,* accounts, because their balances continue to exist beyond the current accounting period. The process of transferring the balances of the temporary accounts into the Retained Earnings account is called *closing* the accounts. The journal entries made for the purpose of closing the temporary accounts are called **closing entries**.

Revenue and expense accounts are closed at the end of each accounting period by *transferring their balances* to a summary account called **Income Summary**. When the credit balances of the revenue accounts and the debit balances of the expense accounts have been transferred into one summary account, the balance of the Income Summary account will be the *net income* or *net loss* for the period. If revenues (credit balances) exceed expenses (debit balances), the Income Summary account will have a credit balance representing net income. Conversely, if expenses exceed revenues, the Income Summary account will have a debit balance representing net loss. This is consistent with the rule that increases in owners' equity are recorded by credits and decreases are recorded by debits.

While adjusting entries are usually made on a monthly basis, it is common practice to close accounts only *once each year.* Thus, we will demonstrate the closing of the temporary accounts of Overnight Auto Service at December 31, 2002, the end of its first year of operations.

On the following pages, Overnight's temporary accounts are illustrated in T account form. We have eliminated the detail of every transaction posted to each account throughout the year. Therefore, each account shows only its December 31, 2002, balance as reported in the adjusted trial balance in Exhibit 5–1.

Closing Entries for Revenue Accounts

Revenue accounts have credit balances. Therefore, closing a revenue account means transferring its credit balance to the Income Summary account. This transfer is accomplished by a journal entry debiting the revenue account in an amount equal to its credit balance, with an offsetting credit to the Income Summary account. The debit portion of this closing entry returns the balance of the revenue account to zero; the credit portion transfers the former balance of the revenue account into the Income Summary account.

Overnight uses two revenue accounts: (1) Repair Service Revenue, which had a credit balance of $172,000 at December 31, 2002, and (2) Rent Revenue Earned, which had a credit balance of $3,000 at December 31, 2002. Two separate journal entries could be made to close these accounts, but the use of one *compound journal entry* is an easier, time-saving method of closing more than one account. A compound journal entry is an entry that includes debits or credits to more than one account. The compound closing entry for Overnight's revenue accounts is displayed in Exhibit 5–3.

OVERNIGHT AUTO SERVICE
General Journal
December 31, 2002

Date	Account Titles and Explanation	Debit	Credit
2002			
Dec. 31	Repair Service Revenue	172,000	
	Rent Revenue Earned	3,000	
	Income Summary		175,000
	To close the Repair Service Revenue and Rent Revenue Earned accounts.		

Exhibit 5–3

CLOSING OF REVENUE ACCOUNTS

After this closing entry has been posted, the two revenue accounts each have *zero* balances, whereas Income Summary has a credit balance of $175,000, as illustrated in Exhibit 5–4.

184 Chapter 5 The Accounting Cycle

Exhibit 5–4

TRANSFERRING REVENUE ACCOUNT BALANCES TO THE INCOME SUMMARY

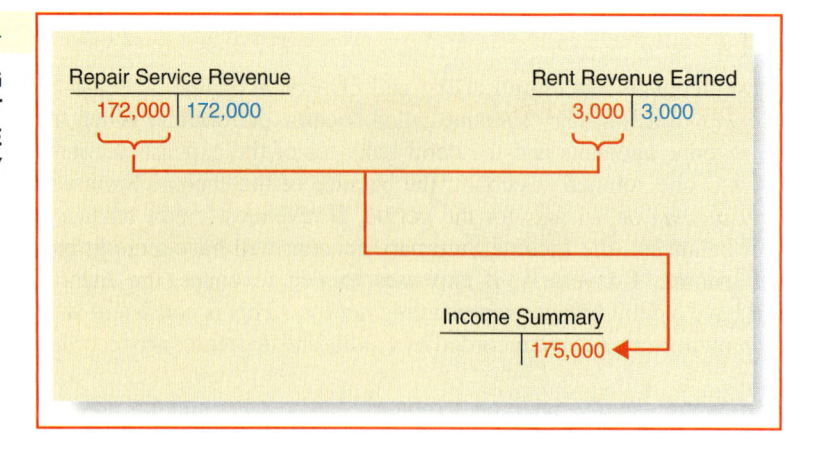

Repair Service Revenue			Rent Revenue Earned	
172,000	172,000		3,000	3,000

Income Summary
| | 175,000 |

Closing Entries for Expense Accounts

Expense accounts have debit balances. Closing an expense account means transferring its debit balance to the Income Summary account. The journal entry to close an expense, therefore, consists of a credit to the expense account in an amount equal to its debit balance, with an offsetting debit to the Income Summary account.

There are nine expense accounts in Overnight's ledger (see the adjusted trial balance in Exhibit 5–1). Again, a compound journal entry is used to close each of these accounts. The required closing entry is displayed in Exhibit 5–5.

Exhibit 5–5

CLOSING OF EXPENSE ACCOUNTS

OVERNIGHT AUTO SERVICE
General Journal
December 31, 2002

Date	Account Titles and Explanation	Debit	Credit
2002			
Dec. 31	Income Summary	135,058	
	Advertising Expense		3,900
	Wages Expense		58,750
	Supplies Expense		7,500
	Depreciation Expense: Building		1,650
	Depreciation Expense: Tools and Equipment		2,200
	Utilities Expense		19,400
	Insurance Expense		15,000
	Interest Expense		30
	Income Taxes Expense		26,628
	To close the expense accounts.		

After this closing entry has been posted, the Income Summary account has a credit balance of *$39,942* ($175,000 credit posted − $135,058 debit posted), and the nine expense accounts each have zero balances as shown in Exhibit 5–6. This $39,942 credit balance equals the net income reported in Overnight's income statement. Had the company's income statement reported a *net loss* for the year, the Income Summary account would have a *debit balance* equal to the amount of the loss reported.

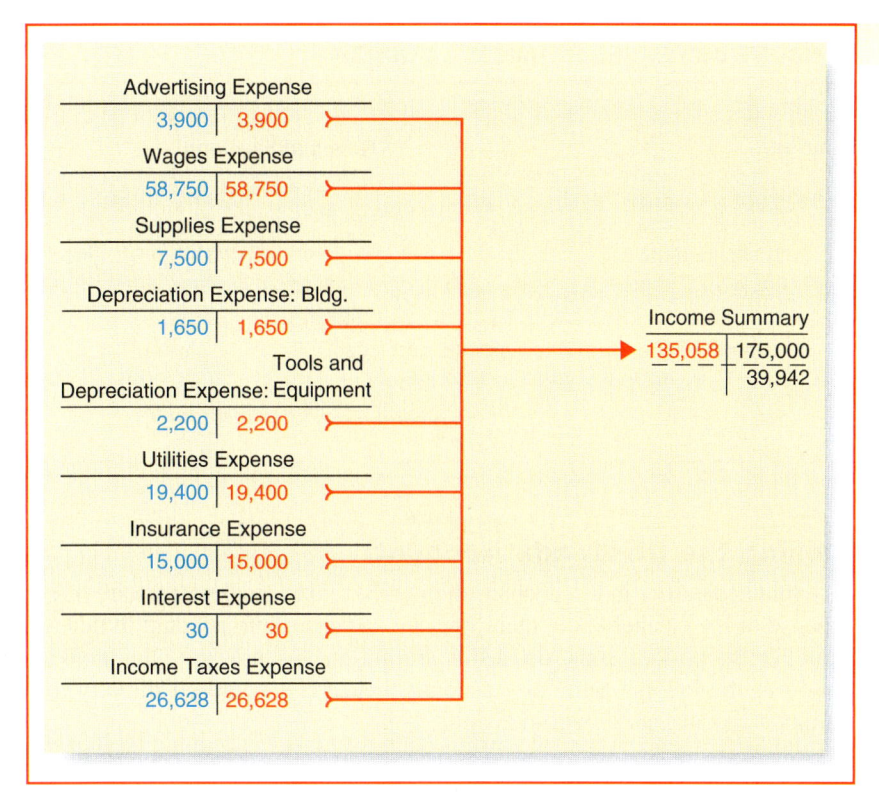

Exhibit 5–6

TRANSFERRING EXPENSE ACCOUNT BALANCES TO THE INCOME SUMMARY

```
        Advertising Expense
         3,900 │ 3,900
         Wages Expense
        58,750 │ 58,750
         Supplies Expense
         7,500 │ 7,500
     Depreciation Expense: Bldg.                Income Summary
         1,650 │ 1,650                         135,058 │ 175,000
               Tools and                                │  39,942
     Depreciation Expense: Equipment
         2,200 │ 2,200
         Utilities Expense
        19,400 │ 19,400
         Insurance Expense
        15,000 │ 15,000
         Interest Expense
            30 │    30
        Income Taxes Expense
        26,628 │ 26,628
```

Closing the Income Summary Account

The nine expense accounts have now been closed, and the total amount of $135,058 formerly contained in these accounts appears in the debit column of the Income Summary account. The revenue of $175,000 earned during 2002 appears in the credit column of the Income Summary account. Since the credit entry representing revenue of $175,000 is larger than the debit entry representing total expenses of $135,058, the Income Summary has a credit balance of $39,942.

The net income of $39,942 earned during the year causes an increase in Overnight's owners' equity. Thus, the $39,942 credit balance of the Income Summary account is transferred to the Retained Earnings account by the closing entry in Exhibit 5–7.

OVERNIGHT AUTO SERVICE
General Journal
December 31, 2002

Date	Account Titles and Explanation	Debit	Credit
2002			
Dec. 31	Income Summary	39,942	
	Retained Earnings		39,942
	Transferring net income earned in 2002 to the Retained Earnings account.		

Exhibit 5–7

CLOSING THE INCOME SUMMARY ACCOUNT

After this closing entry has been posted, the Income Summary account has a zero balance, and the net income for the year ended December 31, 2002, appears as an increase (or credit entry) in the Retained Earnings account as shown in Exhibit 5–8.

Exhibit 5-8

INCOME INCREASES RETAINED EARNINGS

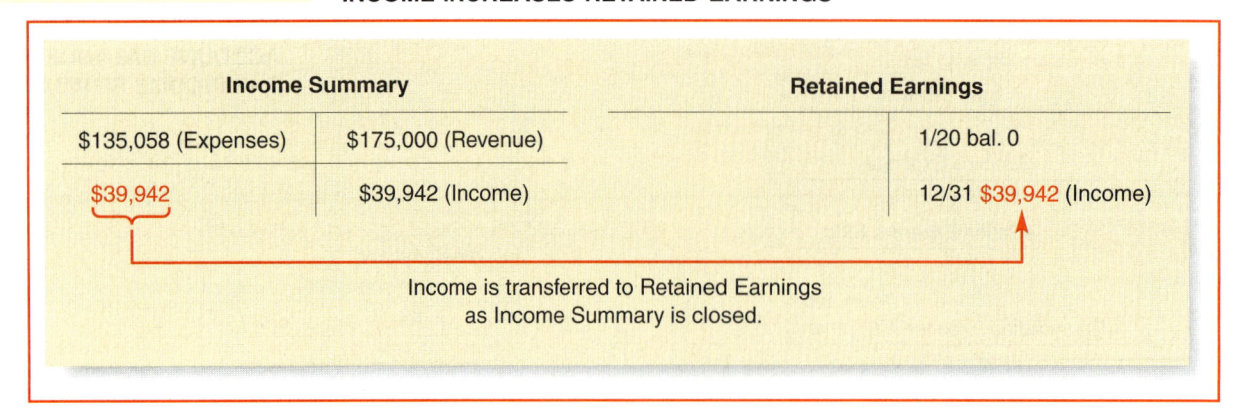

Income Summary		Retained Earnings
$135,058 (Expenses)	$175,000 (Revenue)	1/20 bal. 0
$39,942	$39,942 (Income)	12/31 $39,942 (Income)

Income is transferred to Retained Earnings as Income Summary is closed.

Closing the Dividends Account

As explained earlier in the chapter, dividends paid to stockholders are *not* considered an expense of the business and, therefore, are *not* taken into account in determining net income for the period. Since dividends are not an expense, the Dividends account is *not* closed to the Income Summary account. Instead, it is closed directly to the Retained Earnings account, as shown in Exhibit 5–9.

Exhibit 5-9

CLOSING THE DIVIDENDS ACCOUNT

OVERNIGHT AUTO SERVICE
General Journal
December 31, 2002

Date	Account Titles and Explanation	Debit	Credit
2002			
Dec. 31	Retained Earnings	14,000	
	Dividends		14,000
	To transfer dividends declared in 2002 to the Retained Earnings account.		

After this closing entry has been posted, the Dividends account will have a zero balance, and the Retained Earnings account will have an ending credit balance of $25,942, as shown in Exhibit 5–10.

Exhibit 5-10

DIVIDENDS DECREASE RETAINED EARNINGS

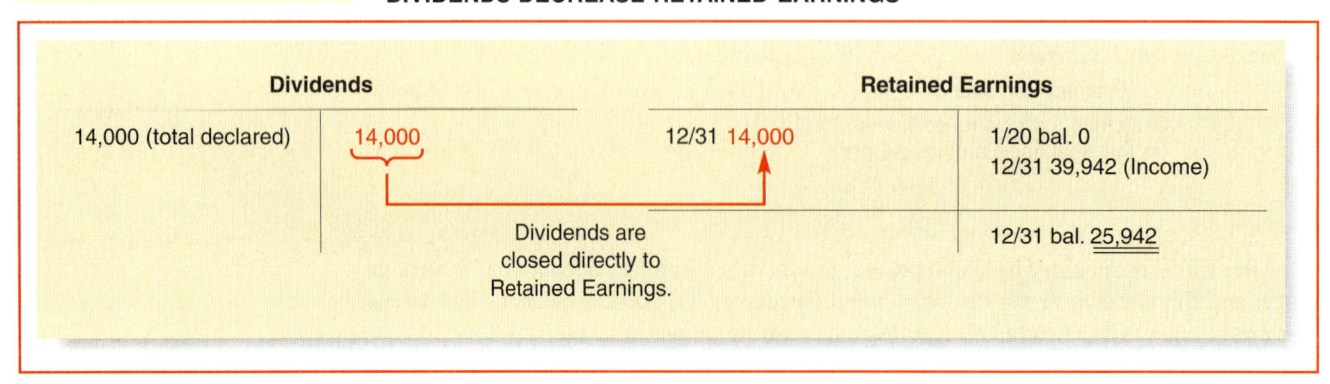

Dividends		Retained Earnings
14,000 (total declared)	14,000	12/31 14,000	1/20 bal. 0
			12/31 39,942 (Income)
	Dividends are closed directly to Retained Earnings.		12/31 bal. 25,942

You as a Software Developer

Assume that you are the developer of business software applications. How might you design an accounting software package that would enable a business to perform its year-end closing process *without* having to make all of the general journal entries illustrated in Exhibits 5–3, 5–5, 5–7, and 5–9.

*Our answer is on page 216.

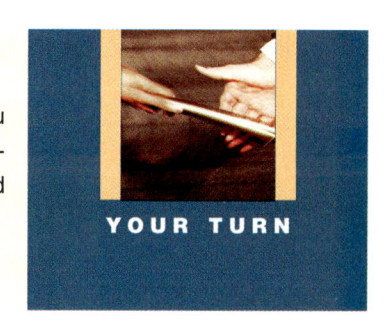

SUMMARY OF THE CLOSING PROCESS

Let us now summarize the process of closing the accounts.

1. Close the various *revenue* accounts by transferring their balances into the Income Summary account.
2. Close the various *expense* accounts by transferring their balances into the Income Summary account.
3. Close the *Income Summary* account by transferring its balance into the Retained Earnings account.
4. Close the *Dividends* account by transferring its balance into the Retained Earnings account.

The entire closing process is illustrated in Exhibit 5–11 using T accounts.

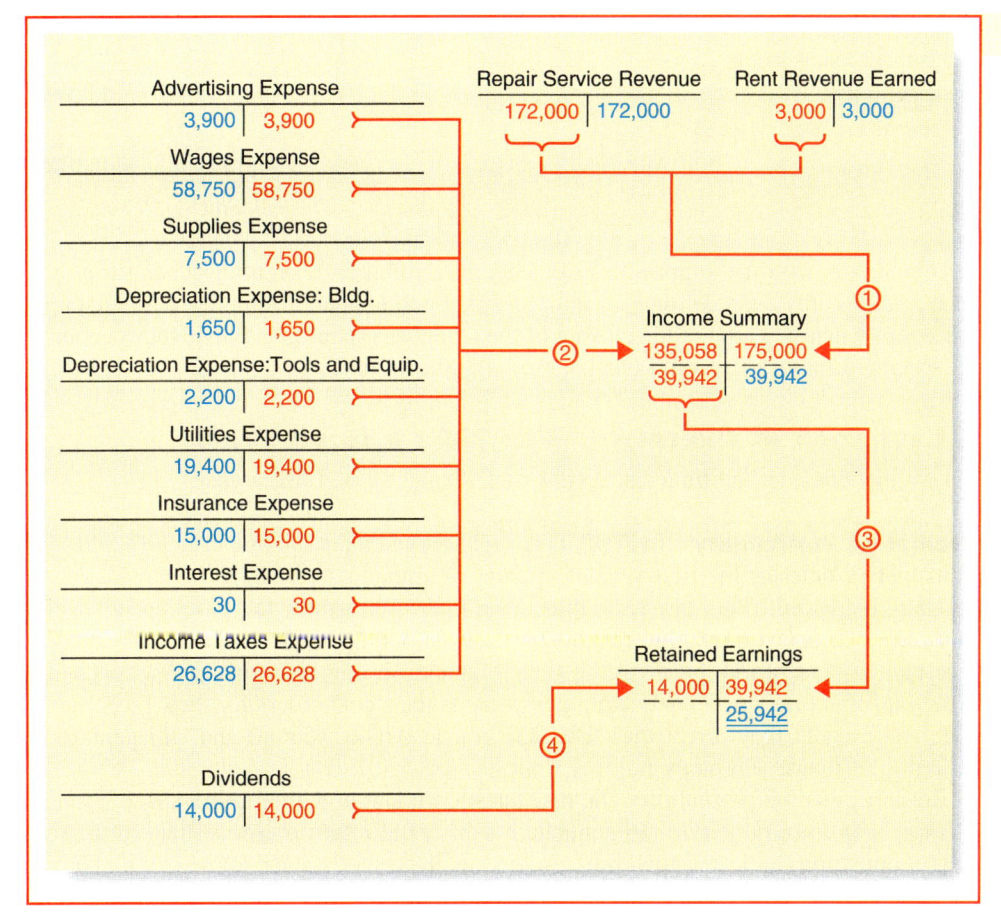

Exhibit 5–11

FLOWCHART OF THE CLOSING PROCESS

Advertising Expense	
3,900	3,900

Wages Expense	
58,750	58,750

Supplies Expense	
7,500	7,500

Depreciation Expense: Bldg.	
1,650	1,650

Depreciation Expense: Tools and Equip.	
2,200	2,200

Utilities Expense	
19,400	19,400

Insurance Expense	
15,000	15,000

Interest Expense	
30	30

Income Taxes Expense	
26,628	26,628

Dividends	
14,000	14,000

Repair Service Revenue	
172,000	172,000

Rent Revenue Earned	
3,000	3,000

Income Summary	
135,058	175,000
39,942	39,942

Retained Earnings	
14,000	39,942
	25,942

AFTER-CLOSING TRIAL BALANCE

LO 5
Prepare an after-closing trial balance.

After the revenue and expense accounts have been closed, it is desirable to prepare an **after-closing trial balance** that consists solely of balance sheet accounts. There is always the possibility that an error in posting the closing entries may have upset the equality of debits and credits in the ledger. The after-closing trial balance, or *post-closing trial balance* as it is often called, is prepared from the ledger. It gives assurance that the accounts are in balance and ready for recording transactions in the new accounting period. The after-closing trial balance of Overnight Auto Service is shown in Exhibit 5–12.

Exhibit 5–12

TEMPORARY EQUITY ACCOUNTS CLOSED INTO RETAINED EARNINGS

OVERNIGHT AUTO SERVICE
After-Closing Trial Balance
December 31, 2002

Cash	$ 18,592	
Accounts receivable	7,250	
Shop supplies	1,200	
Unexpired insurance	3,000	
Land	52,000	
Building	36,000	
Accumulated depreciation: building		$ 1,650
Tools and equipment	12,000	
Accumulated depreciation: tools and equipment		2,200
Notes payable		4,000
Accounts payable		2,690
Wages payable		1,950
Income taxes payable		5,580
Interest payable		30
Unearned rent revenue		6,000
Capital stock		80,000
Retained earnings, Dec. 31		25,942
	$130,042	$130,042

In comparison with the adjusted trial balance in Exhibit 5–1, an after-closing trial balance contains only *balance sheet* accounts. Also, the Retained Earnings account no longer has a zero balance. Through the closing of the revenue, expense, and dividends accounts, the Retained Earnings account has been brought up-to-date.

A Last Look at Overnight: Was 2002 a Good Year?

Let us now consider the financial results of Overnight's first fiscal year.

LO 6
Use financial statement information to evaluate profitability and liquidity.

Evaluating Profitability In 2002, Overnight earned a net income of nearly *$40,000.* Thus, net income for the first year of operations amounts to 50% of the stockholders' $80,000 investment. This is a very impressive rate of return for the first year of operations. Of course, Overnight's stockholders (members of the McBryan family) have taken a certain amount of risk by investing their financial resources in this business. Does a 50% *return on investment* adequately compensate the stockholders for their risk? Stated differently, could they invest their $80,000 in a less risky venture and still generate a 50% rate of return? Probably not.

But in evaluating profitability, the real question is not how the business *did,* but how it *is likely to do in the future.* To generate a substantial return on investment in the first year of operations indicates good profit potential. Overnight's rental contract with Harbor Cab Company is also promising. In 2002, only $3,000 in revenue was earned by renting storage space to the company for its cabs (December's rent). In 2003, Overnight will earn 12 full months of rent revenue from Harbor Cab ($33,000 more than it earned in 2002). In addition, if Harbor Cab stores its cabs in Overnight's garage, Overnight becomes the likely candidate to perform any necessary maintenance and repairs.

One of the primary uses of accounting information is to direct management's attention to problems and opportunities. The Harbor Cab Co. rental agreement presents a strategic business opportunity to Overnight Auto—to obtain the right to service cabs stored in Overnight's facility.

Overnight's management should also direct its attention to the expense section of the income statement. The expense amounts for insurance and utilities may be excessive and offer a potential for significant cost savings. Before renewing its insurance policies, Overnight should obtain competitive quotes from several insurance companies. Perhaps comparable insurance is available for substantially less than $18,000 per year. To reduce utility expense management should consider:

- Is the lighting system efficient?
- Is the heating system efficient and is the building adequately insulated?
- Are employees using company phones for personal calls?

At first glance these items may seem small and unimportant. But if Overnight could save just 10% on its insurance and utility bills, it would have increased net income in 2002 by more than $300 per month.

MANAGEMENT STRATEGY AND FINANCIAL REPORTING

Evaluating Liquidity   *Liquidity* refers to a company's ability to meet its cash obligations as they become due. Liquidity, at least in the short term, may be independent of profitability. And in the short term, Overnight appears to have *potential* cash flow problems. In the very near future, Overnight must make cash expenditures for the following items:

Note and interest payable	$ 4,090
Accounts payable	2,690
Wages payable	1,950
Income taxes payable	5,580
Insurance policy renewal	18,000
Total expenditures coming due	$32,310

My Notes

Items requiring cash payment in near future

These outlays exceed the company's liquid assets (cash and accounts receivable) reported in its December 31, 2002, balance sheet.

The liquid assets reported in Overnight's balance sheet represent cash and accounts receivable at a *point in time* (December 31, 2002). Thus, while these liquid assets are currently insufficient to cover the cash expenditures coming due, this may not be the case for long. Based on its past performance, Overnight is likely to generate revenue in excess of $40,000 during the next several months. If a substantial amount of this revenue is received in cash, and expenses are kept under control, the company may actually become more liquid than it appears to be now.

CASH EFFECTS

FINANCIAL ANALYSIS

Other commonly used measures of Overnight's *profitability* include:

Measure	Computation	Overnight's Performance
Net Income Percentage	$\dfrac{\text{Net Income}}{\text{Total Revenue}}$	$\dfrac{\$39{,}942}{\$175{,}000} = 22.8\%$

Significance: An indicator of management's ability to control costs.

Return on Equity	$\dfrac{\text{Net Income}}{\text{Average Stockholders' Equity}}$	$\dfrac{\$39{,}942}{\$92{,}971} = 43.0\%$

Significance: A measure of income generated per average dollar of stockholders' equity.

*Average stockholders' equity of $92,971 is simply the average of Overnight's beginning stockholders' equity of $80,000, and its ending stockholders' equity of $105,942.

Other commonly used measures of Overnight's *liquidity* include:

Measure	Computation	Overnight's Performance
Working Capital	Current Assets − Current Liabilities	$30,042 − $20,250 = $9,792

Significance: A measure of short-term debt paying ability expressed in dollars.

Current Ratio	$\dfrac{\text{Current Assets}}{\text{Current Liabilities}}$	$\dfrac{\$30{,}042}{\$20{,}250} = 1.48:1$

Significance: A measure of short-term debt paying ability expressed as a ratio.

*Current assets are those assets expected to leave the balance sheet in the near future, several of which are very liquid. For Overnight, current assets include Cash, Accounts Receivable, Shop Supplies, and Unexpired Insurance. Current liabilities are those liabilities expected to leave the balance sheet in the near future, most of which must be settled in cash. All of Overnight's liabilities are considered current liabilities.

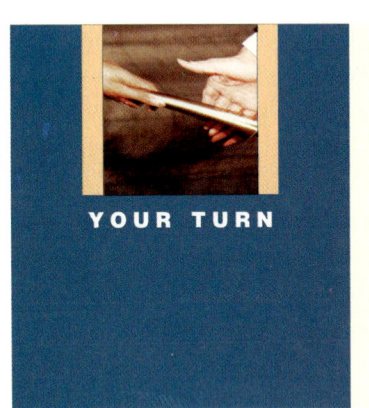

YOUR TURN — You as a Potential Owner of Overnight Auto Service

Assume you have the opportunity to purchase some shares in Overnight Auto from a member of the McBryan family. The family member suggests that Overnight's profitability is really stronger than the closing numbers indicate because advertising expense should have been capitalized (recorded as an asset account—Prepaid Advertising). The family member argues that the $3,900 advertising cost will generate future revenues and that the matching principle makes recording the advertising expenditure as an asset appropriate. How would you respond?

*Our answer is on page 216.

Preparing Financial Statements Covering Different Periods of Time

LO 7 Explain how interim financial statements are prepared in a business that closes its accounts only at year-end.

Many businesses prepare financial statements every quarter, as well as at year-end. In addition, they may prepare financial statements covering other time periods, such as one month or the year-to-date.

When a business closes its accounts only at year-end, the revenue, expense, and dividends accounts have balances representing the activities of the *year-to-date.* Thus, at *June 30,* these account balances represent the activities recorded over the past six months. Year-to-date financial statements can be prepared directly from an adjusted trial balance.

But how might this business prepare **interim financial statements** covering only the month of June? Or the quarter (three months) ended June 30?

The answer is by doing a little *subtraction.* As an example, assume that the adjusted balance in Overnight's Repair Service Revenue account at the ends of the following months was as shown:

March 31 (end of the first quarter)	$38,000
May 31	67,000
June 30	80,000

My Notes

Revenue amounts are for the year-to-date

At each date, the account balance represents the revenue earned since January 1. Thus the March 31 balance represents three months' revenue; the May 31 balance, five months' revenue; and the June 30 balance, the revenue earned over a period of six months.

To prepare an income statement for the *six months* ended June 30, we simply use the June 30 balance in the revenue account—*$80,000.* But to prepare an income statement for the *month* ended June 30, we would have to subtract from the June 30 balance of this account its balance as of May 31. The remainder, *$13,000,* represents the amount of revenue recorded in the account during June ($80,000 − $67,000 = $13,000).

To prepare an income statement for the *quarter* ended June 30, we would subtract from the June 30 balance in this revenue account its balance as of March 31. Thus the revenue earned during the second quarter (April 1 through June 30) amounts to *$42,000* ($80,000 − $38,000 = $42,000).

This process of subtracting prior balances from the current balance is repeated for each revenue and expense account, as well as for the dividends account.

This sounds like a bigger job than it really is. There are only about 10 or 15 accounts involved, and in a computerized system, the entire process is done automatically. Even in a manual system, a person using a calculator can complete this process in a few minutes.

Computations like these are not required for the balance sheet accounts. A balance sheet always is based on the account balances *at the balance sheet date.* Therefore, a June 30 balance sheet looks exactly the same *regardless* of the time period covered by the other financial statements.

CONCLUDING REMARKS

We have now completed the *entire accounting cycle*—from the initial recording of transactions in Chapter 3, through an after-closing trial balance in this chapter. The steps comprising this cycle are listed below and illustrated in a flow chart diagram in Exhibit 5–13.

1. *Journalize (record) transactions.* Enter all transactions in the journal, thus creating a chronological record of events.
2. *Post to ledger accounts.* Post debits and credits from the journal to the proper ledger accounts, thus creating a record classified by accounts.
3. *Prepare a trial balance.* Prove the equality of debits and credits in the ledger.
4. *Make end-of-period adjustments.* Make adjusting entries in the general journal and post to ledger accounts.
5. *Prepare an adjusted trial balance.* Prove again the equality of debits and credits in the ledger. (*Note:* These are the amounts used in the preparation of financial statements.)
6. *Prepare financial statements and appropriate disclosures.* An income statement shows the results of operation for the period. A statement of retained earnings shows changes in retained earnings during the period. A balance sheet shows the financial position of the business at the end of the period. Financial statements should be accompanied by *notes* disclosing facts necessary for the proper interpretation of those statements.

Exhibit 5-13 THE ACCOUNTING CYCLE

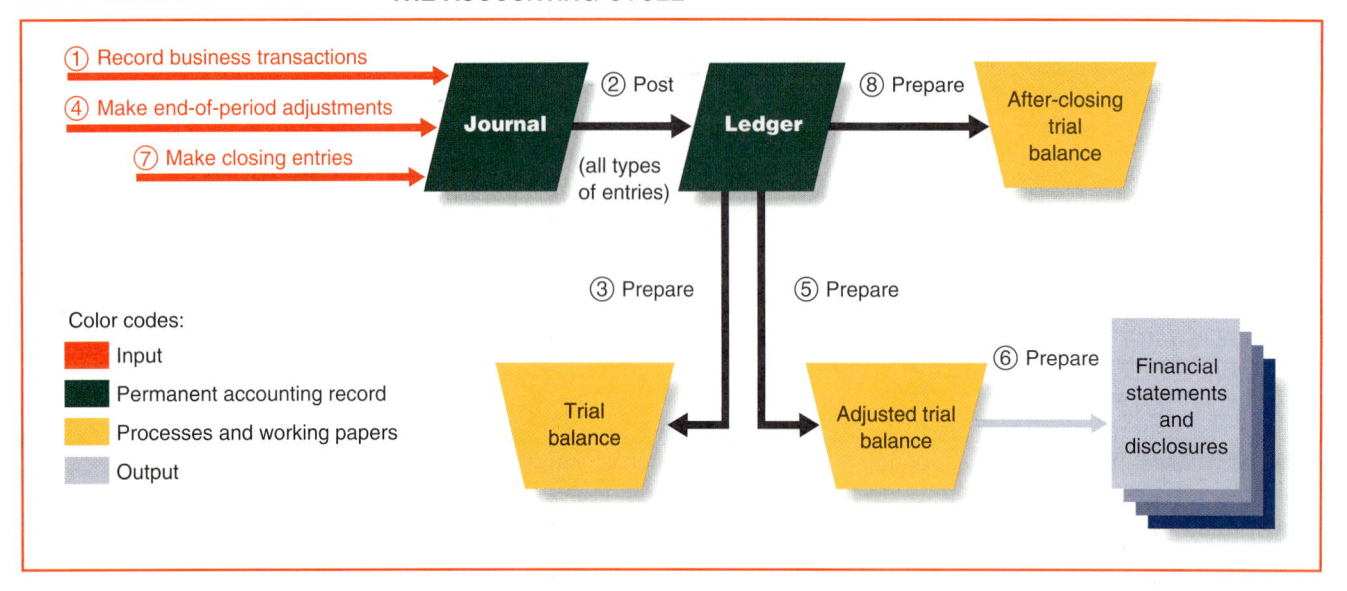

① Record business transactions
④ Make end-of-period adjustments
⑦ Make closing entries

Journal (all types of entries) → ② Post → Ledger
Ledger → ⑧ Prepare → After-closing trial balance
Ledger → ③ Prepare → Trial balance
Ledger → ⑤ Prepare → Adjusted trial balance
Adjusted trial balance → ⑥ Prepare → Financial statements and disclosures

Color codes:
- Input
- Permanent accounting record
- Processes and working papers
- Output

---

7. *Journalize and post the closing entries.* The closing entries "zero" the revenue, expense, and dividends accounts, making them ready for recording the events of the next accounting period. These entries also bring the balance in the Retained Earnings account up-to-date.

8. *Prepare an after-closing trial balance.* This step ensures that the ledger remains in balance after posting of the closing entries.

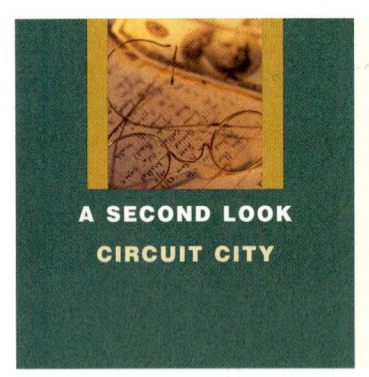

A SECOND LOOK — CIRCUIT CITY

The decision to discontinue its appliance business was a major event in the life of **Circuit City**. Management made numerous disclosures pertaining to this decision in the notes to the company's financial statements. These disclosures revealed the number of employees terminated and specified how many distribution and service centers had been closed as a direct result of exiting the appliance business.

In addition to footnote disclosures, the actual financial ramifications of **Circuit City**'s decision were reported in the company's income statement as *exit costs* totaling nearly $30 million. In Chapter 12, we will examine ways in which companies report these and other significant nonrecurring events as components of net income.

SUPPLEMENTAL TOPIC

THE WORKSHEET

LO 8 Prepare a worksheet and explain its uses.

A **worksheet** illustrates in one place the relationships among the unadjusted trial balance, proposed adjusting entries, and the financial statements. A worksheet is prepared at the end of the period, but *before* the adjusting entries are formally recorded in the accounting records. It is not a formal step in the accounting cycle. Rather, it is a tool used by accountants to work out the details of the proposed end-of-period adjustments. It also provides them with a preview of how the financial statements will look.

You can see a worksheet for Overnight Auto Service at December 31, 2002, in Exhibit 5–14.

Exhibit 5–14

WORKSHEET

OVERNIGHT AUTO SERVICE
Worksheet
For the Year Ended December 31, 2002

	Trial Balance Dr	Trial Balance Cr	Adjustments* Dr	Adjustments* Cr	Adjusted Trial Balance Dr	Adjusted Trial Balance Cr	Income Statement Dr	Income Statement Cr	Balance Sheet Dr	Balance Sheet Cr
Balance sheet accounts:										
Cash	18,592				18,592				18,592	
Accounts Receivable	6,500		(h) 750		7,250				7,250	
Shop Supplies	1,800			(a) 600	1,200				1,200	
Unexpired Insurance	4,500			(b) 1,500	3,000				3,000	
Land	52,000				52,000				52,000	
Building	36,000				36,000				36,000	
Accumulated Depreciation: Building		1,500		(c) 150		1,650				1,650
Tools and Equipment	12,000				12,000				12,000	
Accumulated Depreciation: Tools and Equipment		2,000		(d) 200		2,200				2,200
Notes Payable		4,000				4,000				4,000
Accounts Payable		2,690				2,690				2,690
Income Taxes Payable		1,560		(i) 4,020		5,580				5,580
Unearned Rent Revenue		9,000	(e) 3,000			6,000				6,000
Capital Stock		80,000				80,000				80,000
Retained Earnings		0				0				0
Dividends	14,000				14,000				14,000	
Wages Payable				(f) 1,950		1,950				1,950
Interest Payable				(g) 30		30				30
Income statement accounts:										
Repair Service Revenue		171,250		(h) 750		172,000		172,000		
Advertising Expense	3,900				3,900		3,900			
Wages Expense	56,800		(f) 1,950		58,750		58,750			
Supplies Expense	6,900		(a) 600		7,500		7,500			
Depreciation Expense: Building	1,500		(c) 150		1,650		1,650			
Depreciation Expense: Tools and Equipment	2,000		(d) 200		2,200		2,200			
Utilities Expense	19,400				19,400		19,400			
Insurance Expense	13,500		(b) 1,500		15,000		15,000			
Income Taxes Expense	22,608		(i) 4,020		26,628		26,628			
Rent Revenue Earned				(e) 3,000		3,000		3,000		
Interest Expense			(g) 30		30		30			
	272,000	272,000	12,200	12,200	279,100	279,100	135,058	175,000	144,042	104,100
Net income							39,942			39,942
Totals							175,000	175,000	144,042	144,042

*Adjustments:
(a) Shop supplies used in December.
(b) Portion of insurance cost expiring in December.
(c) Depreciation on building for December.
(d) Depreciation of tools and equipment for December.
(e) Earned one-third of rent revenue collected in advance from Harbor Cab.
(f) Unpaid wages owed to employees at December 31.
(g) Interest payable accrued during December.
(h) Repair service revenue earned in December but not yet billed.
(i) Income taxes expense for December.

Isn't This Really a Spreadsheet?

Yes. The term *worksheet* is a holdover from the days when these schedules were prepared manually on large sheets of columnar paper. Today, most worksheets are prepared on a computer using spreadsheet software, such as *Excel*™, or with **general ledger software** such as *Peachtree*™ or *Dac-Easy*™.

Since the worksheet is simply a tool used by accountants, it often isn't printed out in hard copy—it may exist only on a computer screen. But the concept remains the same; the worksheet displays *in one place* the unadjusted account balances, proposed adjusting entries, and financial statements as they will appear if the proposed adjustments are made.

How Is a Worksheet Used?

A worksheet serves several purposes. It allows accountants to *see the effects* of adjusting entries without actually entering these adjustments in the accounting records. This makes it relatively easy for them to correct errors or make changes in estimated amounts. It also enables accountants and management to preview the financial statements before the final drafts are developed. Once the worksheet is complete, it serves as the source for recording adjusting and closing entries in the accounting records and for preparing financial statements.

Another important use of the worksheet is in the preparation of *interim financial statements*. Interim statements are financial statements developed at various points *during* the fiscal year. Most companies close their accounts only once each year. Yet they often need to develop quarterly or monthly financial statements. Through the use of a worksheet, they can develop these interim statements *without* having to formally adjust and close their accounts.

The Mechanics: How It's Done

Whether done manually or on a computer, the preparation of a worksheet involves five basic steps. We begin by describing these steps as if the worksheet were being prepared manually. Afterward, we explain how virtually all of the mechanical steps can be performed automatically by a computer.

1. *Enter the ledger account balances in the Trial Balance columns.* The worksheet begins with an unadjusted trial balance—that is, a listing of the ledger account balances at the end of the period *prior* to making any adjusting entries. In our illustration, the unadjusted trial balance appears in *blue*.

    Notice our inclusion of the captions "Balance sheet accounts" and "Income statement accounts." These captions are optional, but they help clarify the relationships between the ledger accounts and the financial statements. (*Hint:* A few lines should be left blank immediately below the last balance sheet account. It is often necessary to add a few more accounts during the adjusting process. Additional income statement accounts may also be necessary.)

2. *Enter the adjustments in the Adjustments columns.* The next step is the most important: Enter the appropriate end-of-period adjustments in the Adjustments columns. In our illustration, these adjustments appear in *red*.

    Notice that each adjustment includes both debit and credit entries, which are linked together by the small key letters appearing to the left of the dollar amount. Thus, adjusting entry *a* consists of a $600 debit to Supplies Expense and a $600 credit to Shop Supplies. Because the individual adjusting entries include equal debit and credit amounts, the totals of the debit and credit Adjustment columns should be equal.

    Sometimes the adjustments require adding accounts to the original trial balance. (The four ledger account titles printed in *red* were added during the adjusting process.)

3. *Prepare an adjusted trial balance.* Next, an adjusted trial balance is prepared. The balances in the original trial balance (*blue*) are adjusted for the debit or credit amounts in the Adjustments columns (*red*). This process of horizontal addition or subtraction is called *cross-footing.* The adjusted trial balance is totaled to determine that the accounts remain in balance.

   At this point, the worksheet is almost complete. We have emphasized that financial statements are prepared *directly from the adjusted trial balance.* Thus we have only to arrange these accounts into the format of financial statements. For this reason, we show the adjusted trial balance amounts in *blue*—both in the Adjusted Trial Balance columns and when these amounts are *extended* (carried forward) into the financial statement columns.

4. *Extend the adjusted trial balance amounts into the appropriate financial statement columns.* The balance sheet accounts—assets, liabilities, and owners' equity—are extended into the Balance Sheet columns; income statement amounts, into the Income Statement columns. (The "Balance Sheet" and "Income Statement" captions in the original trial balance should simplify this procedure. Notice each amount is extended to only one column. Also, the account retains the same debit or credit balance as shown in the adjusted trial balance.)

5. *Total the financial statement columns; determine and record net income or net loss.* The final step in preparing the worksheet consists of totaling the Income Statement and Balance Sheet columns and then bringing each set of columns into balance. These tasks are performed on the bottom three lines of the worksheet. In our illustration, the amounts involved in this final step are shown in *black.*

When the Income Statement and Balance Sheet columns are first totaled, the debit and credit columns will not agree. But each set of columns should be out-of-balance by the *same amount*—and that amount should be the amount of net income or net loss for the period.

Let us briefly explain *why* both sets of columns initially are out-of-balance by this amount. First consider the Income Statement columns. The Credit column contains the revenue accounts, and the Debit column, the expense accounts. The difference, therefore, represents the net income (net loss) for the period.

Now consider the Balance Sheet columns. All of the balance sheet amounts are shown at up-to-date amounts *except* for the Retained Earnings account, which still contains the balance from the *beginning* of the period. To bring the Retained Earnings account up-to-date, we must add net income and subtract any dividends. The dividends already appear in the Balance Sheet Debit column. So what's the only thing missing? The net income (or net loss) for the period.

To bring both sets of columns into balance, we enter the net income (or net loss) on the next line. The same amount will appear in both the Income Statement columns and the Balance Sheet columns. But in one set of columns it appears as a debit, and in the other, it appears as a credit.[1] After this amount is entered, each set of columns should balance.

Computers Do the Pencil-Pushing When a worksheet is prepared by computer, accountants perform only *one* of the steps listed above—*entering the adjustments.* The computer automatically lists the ledger accounts in the form of a trial balance. After the accountant has entered the adjustments, it automatically computes the adjusted account balances and completes the worksheet. (Once the adjusted balances are determined, completing the worksheet involves nothing more than putting these amounts in the appropriate column and determining the column totals.)

---

[1] To bring the Income Statement columns into balance, net *income* is entered in the *Debit column.* This is because the Credit column (revenue) exceeds the Debit column (expenses). But in the balance sheet, net income is an element of owners' equity, which is represented by a credit. In event of a net *loss,* this situation reverses.

What-If: A Special Application of Worksheet Software

We have discussed a relatively simple application of the worksheet concept—illustrating the effects of proposed *adjusting entries* on account balances. But the same concept can be applied to proposed *future transactions.* The effects of the proposed transactions simply are entered in the "Adjustments" columns. Thus, without disrupting the accounting records, accountants can prepare schedules showing how the company's financial statements might be affected by such events as a merger with another company, a 15% increase in sales volume, or the closure of a plant.

There is a tendency to view worksheets as mechanical and old-fashioned. This is not at all the case. Today, the mechanical aspects are handled entirely by computer. The real purpose of a worksheet is to show quickly and efficiently how specific events or transactions will affect the financial statements. This isn't bookkeeping—it's *planning*.

END-OF-CHAPTER REVIEW

SUMMARY OF LEARNING OBJECTIVES

LO 1

Prepare an income statement, a statement of retained earnings, and a balance sheet.
The financial statements are prepared directly from the adjusted trial balance. The income statement is prepared by reporting all revenue earned during the period, less all expenses incurred in generating the related revenue. The statement of retained earnings reconciles the *beginning* Retained Earnings account balance with its *ending* balance. The retained earnings statement reports any increase to Retained Earnings resulting from net income earned for the period, as well as any decreases to Retained Earnings resulting from dividends declared or a net loss incurred for the period. The balance sheet reveals the company's financial position by reporting its economic resources (assets), and the claims against those resources (liabilities and owners' equity).

LO 2

Explain how the income statement and the statement of retained earnings relate to the balance sheet.
An income statement shows the revenue and expenses of a business for a specified accounting period. In the statement of retained earnings, the net income figure from the income statement is added to the beginning Retained Earnings balance, while dividends declared during the period are subtracted, in arriving at the ending Retained Earnings balance. The ending Retained Earnings balance is then reported in the balance sheet as a component of owners' equity.

LO 3

Explain the concept of *adequate disclosure*.
Adequate disclosure is a generally accepted accounting principle, meaning that financial statements should include any information that an informed user needs to interpret the statements properly. The appropriate disclosures usually are contained in several pages of notes that accompany the statements.

LO 4

Explain the purposes of *closing entries*; prepare these entries.
Closing entries serve two basic purposes. The first is to return the balances of the temporary owners' equity accounts (revenue, expenses, and dividend accounts) to zero so that these accounts may be used to measure the activities of the next reporting period. The second purpose of closing entries is to update the balance of the Retained Earnings account. Four closing entries generally are needed: (1) close the revenue accounts to the Income Summary account, (2) close the expense accounts to the Income Summary account, (3) close the balance of the Income Summary account to the Retained Earnings account, and (4) close the Dividends account to the Retained Earnings account.

LO 5

Prepare an after-closing trial balance.
After the revenue and expense accounts have been closed, it is desirable to prepare an after-closing trial balance consisting solely of balance sheet accounts. The after-closing trial balance, or post-closing trial balance, gives assurance that the accounts of the general ledger are in balance and ready for recording transactions for the new accounting period.

LO 6

Use financial statement information to evaluate profitability and liquidity.
Profitability is an increase in stockholders' equity resulting from revenue exceeding expenses, whereas liquidity refers to a company's ability to meet its cash obligations as they come due. Liquidity, at least in the short term, may be *independent* of profitability. Financial statements are useful tools for evaluating both profitability and liquidity. Used separately, or in combination, the income statement and balance sheet help interested parties to measure a company's current financial performance, and to forecast its profit and cash flow potential. In the Financial Analysis feature, we illustrated several measures of profitability and liquidity computed using financial statement information. Throughout the remainder of this text we introduce and discuss many additional measures.

LO 7

Explain how *interim* financial statements are prepared in a business that closes its accounts only at year-end.
When a business closes its accounts only at year-end, the revenue, expense, and dividend accounts have balances representing the activities of the year-to-date. To prepare an income statement for any period shorter than the year-to-date, we subtract from the current balance in the revenue or expense account the balance in the account as of the beginning of the desired period. This process of subtracting prior balances from the current balance is repeated for each revenue and expense account and for the dividend account. No computations of this type are required for the balance sheet accounts, as a balance sheet is based on the account balances at the balance sheet date.

*LO 8

Prepare a worksheet and explain its uses.
A worksheet is a "testing ground" on which the ledger accounts are adjusted, balanced, and arranged in the format of financial statements. A worksheet consists of a trial balance, the end-of-period adjusting entries, an adjusted trial balance, and columns showing the ledger accounts arranged as an income statement and as a balance sheet. The completed worksheet is used as the basis for preparing financial statements and for recording adjusting and closing entries in the formal accounting records.

Supplemental Topic, "The Worksheet."

KEY TERMS INTRODUCED OR EMPHASIZED IN CHAPTER 5

adequate disclosure (p. 180)   The generally accepted accounting principle of providing with financial statements any information that users need to interpret those statements properly.

after-closing trial balance (p. 188)   A trial balance prepared after all closing entries have been made. Consists only of accounts for assets, liabilities, and owners' equity.

closing entries (p. 183)   Journal entries made at the end of the period for the purpose of closing temporary accounts (revenue, expense, and dividend accounts) and transferring balances to the Retained Earnings account.

current assets (p. 180)   Cash and other assets that can be converted into cash or used up within a relatively short period of time without interfering with normal business operations.

current liabilities (p. 180)   Existing obligations that are expected to be satisfied with a company's current assets within a relatively short period of time.

general ledger software (p. 194)   Computer software used for recording transactions, maintaining journals and ledgers, and preparing financial statements. Also includes spreadsheet capabilities for showing the effects of proposed adjusting entries or transactions on the financial statements without actually recording these entries in the accounting records.

Income Summary (p. 183)   The summary account in the ledger to which revenue and expense accounts are closed at the end of the period. The balance (credit balance for a net income, debit balance for a net loss) is transferred to the Retained Earnings account.

interim financial statements (p. 191)   Financial statements prepared for periods of less than one year (includes monthly and quarterly statements).

notes (accompanying financial statements) (p. 181)   Supplemental disclosures that accompany financial statements. These notes provide users with various types of information considered necessary for the proper interpretation of the statements.

worksheet (p. 192)   A multicolumn schedule showing the relationships among the current account balances (a trial balance), proposed or actual adjusting entries or transactions, and the financial statements that would result if these adjusting entries or transactions were recorded. Used both at the end of the accounting period as an aid to preparing financial statements and for planning purposes.

DEMONSTRATION PROBLEM

Jan's Dance Studio, Inc., performs adjusting entries every month, but closes its accounts only at year-end. The studio's year-end *adjusted trial balance* dated December 31, 2002, appears below. (Bear in mind, the balance shown for Retained Earnings was last updated on December 31, *2001*).

JAN'S DANCE STUDIO, INC.
Adjusted Trial Balance
December 31, 2002

Cash	$171,100	
Accounts receivable	9,400	
Prepaid studio rent	3,000	
Unexpired insurance	7,200	
Supplies	500	
Equipment	18,000	
Accumulated depreciation: equipment		$ 7,200
Notes payable		10,000
Accounts payable		3,200
Salaries payable		4,000
Income taxes payable		6,000
Unearned studio revenue		8,800
Capital stock		100,000
Retained earnings		40,000
Dividends	6,000	
Studio revenue earned		165,000
Salary expense	85,000	
Supply expense	3,900	
Rent expense	12,000	
Insurance expense	1,900	
Advertising expense	500	
Depreciation expense: equipment	1,800	
Interest expense	900	
Income taxes expense	23,000	
	$344,200	$344,200

Instructions

a. Prepare an income statement and statement of retained earnings for the year ended December 31, 2002. Also prepare the studio's balance sheet dated December 31, 2002.
b. Prepare the necessary closing entries at December 31, 2002.
c. Prepare an after-closing trial balance dated December 31, 2002.

Solution to the Demonstration Problem

a.

JAN'S DANCE STUDIO, INC.
Income Statement
For the Year Ended December 31, 2002

Revenue:		
Studio revenue earned		$165,000
Expenses:		
Salary expense	$85,000	
Supply expense	3,900	
Rent expense	12,000	
Insurance expense	1,900	
Advertising expense	500	
Depreciation expense: equipment	1,800	
Interest expense	900	106,000
Income before income taxes		$ 59,000
Income taxes expense		23,000
Net income		$ 36,000

JAN'S DANCE STUDIO, INC.
Statement of Retained Earnings
For the Year Ended December 31, 2002

Retained earnings, January 1, 2002	$40,000
Add: Net income earned in 2002	36,000
Subtotal	$76,000
Less: Dividends declared in 2002	6,000
Retained earnings, December 31, 2002	$70,000

JAN'S DANCE STUDIO, INC.
Balance Sheet
December 31, 2002

Assets

Cash		$171,100
Accounts receivable		9,400
Prepaid studio rent		3,000
Unexpired insurance		7,200
Supplies		500
Equipment	$18,000	
Less: Accumulated depreciation: equipment	7,200	10,800
Total assets		$202,000

Liabilities & Stockholders' Equity

Liabilities:

Notes payable	$ 10,000
Accounts payable	3,200
Salaries payable	4,000
Income taxes payable	6,000
Unearned studio revenue	8,800
Total liabilities	$ 32,000

Stockholders' equity:

Capital stock	$100,000
Retained earnings	70,000
Total stockholders' equity	$170,000
Total liabilities and stockholders' equity	$202,000

b.

JAN'S DANCE STUDIO, INC.
General Journal
December 31, 2002

Date	Account Titles and Explanation	Debit	Credit
Dec. 31 2002			
1.	Studio Revenue Earned	165,000	
	Income Summary		165,000
	To close Studio Revenue Earned.		
2.	Income Summary	129,000	
	Salary Expense		85,000
	Supply Expense		3,900
	Rent Expense		12,000
	Insurance Expense		1,900
	Advertising Expense		500
	Depreciation Expense: Equipment		1,800
	Interest Expense		900
	Income Taxes Expense		23,000
	To close all expense accounts.		
3.	Income Summary	36,000	
	Retained Earnings		36,000
	To transfer net income earned in 2002 to the Retained Earnings account ($165,000 − $129,000 = $36,000).		
4.	Retained Earnings	6,000	
	Dividends		6,000
	To transfer dividends declared in 2002 to the Retained Earnings account.		

c.

JAN'S DANCE STUDIO, INC.
After-Closing Trial Balance
December 31, 2002

Cash	$171,100	
Accounts receivable	9,400	
Prepaid studio rent	3,000	
Unexpired insurance	7,200	
Supplies	500	
Equipment	18,000	
Accumulated depreciation: equipment		$ 7,200
Notes payable		10,000
Accounts payable		3,200
Salaries payable		4,000
Income taxes payable		6,000
Unearned studio revenue		8,800
Capital stock		100,000
Retained earnings, December 31		70,000
	$209,200	$209,200

SELF-TEST QUESTIONS

The answers to these questions appear on page 216.

1. For a publicly owned company, indicate which of the following accounting activities are likely to occur at or shortly after year-end. (More than one answer may be correct.)
    a. Preparing of income tax returns.
    b. Adjusting and closing the accounts.
    c. Drafting disclosures that accompany the financial statements.
    d. An audit of the financial statements by a firm of CPAs.

2. Which of the following financial statements is generally prepared first?
    a. Income statement.
    b. Balance sheet.
    c. Statement of retained earnings.
    d. Statement of cash flows.

3. Which of the following accounts would *never* be reported in the income statement as an expense?
    a. Depreciation expense.
    b. Income taxes expense.
    c. Interest expense.
    d. Dividends expense.

4. Which of the following accounts would *never* appear in the after-closing trial balance? (More than one answer may be correct.)
    a. Unearned revenue.
    b. Dividends.
    c. Accumulated depreciation.
    d. Income taxes expense.

5. Which of the following journal entries is required to close the Income Summary account of a profitable company?
    a. Debit Income Summary, credit Retained Earnings.
    b. Credit Income Summary, debit Retained Earnings.

c. Debit Income Summary, credit Capital Stock.
   d. Credit Income Summary, debit Capital Stock.

6. Indicate those items for which generally accepted accounting principles *require* disclosure in notes accompanying the financial statements. (More than one answer may be correct.)
   a. A large lawsuit was filed against the company two days *after* the balance sheet date.
   b. The depreciation method in use, given that several different methods are acceptable under generally accepted accounting principles.
   c. Whether small but long-lived items—such as electric pencil sharpeners and handheld calculators—are charged to asset accounts or to expense accounts.
   d. As of year-end, the chief executive officer had been hospitalized because of chest pains.

7. Ski West adjusts its accounts at the end of each month, but closes them only at the end of the calendar year (December 31). The ending balances in the Equipment Rental Revenue account and the Cash account in February and March appear below.

	Feb. 28	Mar. 31
Cash	$14,200	$26,500
Equipment rental revenue	12,100	18,400

Ski West prepares financial statements showing separately the operating results of each month. In the financial statements prepared for the *month* ended March 31, Equipment Rental Revenue and Cash should appear as follows:
   a. Equipment Rental Revenue, $18,400; Cash, $26,500
   b. Equipment Rental Revenue, $18,400; Cash, $12,300
   c. Equipment Rental Revenue, $6,300; Cash, $26,500
   d. Equipment Rental Revenue, $6,300; Cash, $12,300

8. Which of the following accounts is *not* closed to the Income Summary account at the end of the accounting period? (More than one answer may be correct.)
   a. Rent Expense.
   b. Accumulated Depreciation.
   c. Unearned Revenue.
   d. Supplies Expense.

ASSIGNMENT MATERIAL
DISCUSSION QUESTIONS

1. Explain briefly the items generally included in a company's annual report. (You may use the annual report appearing in Appendix A to support your answer.)
2. Discuss several limitations of the income statement.
3. Some people think that a company's retained earnings represent *cash* reserved for the payment of dividends. Are they correct? Explain.
4. Are dividends paid to stockholders ever reported in the income statement as an expense? Explain.
5. Discuss the relationship among the income statement, the statement of retained earnings, and the balance sheet.
6. Identify several items that may require disclosure in the notes that accompany financial statements.
7. What type of accounts are referred to as *temporary* or *nominal* accounts? What is meant by these terms?
8. What type of accounts are referred to as *permanent* or *real* accounts? What is meant by these terms?
9. Explain *why* the Dividends account is closed directly to the Retained Earnings account.
10. Which accounts appear in a company's after-closing trial balance? How do these accounts differ from those reported in an adjusted trial balance?
11. Can a company be both profitable *and* insolvent? Explain.

12. What are interim financial statements? Do accounts that appear in a company's interim balance sheet require any special computations to be reported correctly? Explain.
13. Explain the accounting principle of *adequate disclosure.*
14. Briefly describe the content of the *notes* that accompany financial statements.
15. How does depreciation expense differ from other operating expenses?
16. Explain the need for closing entries and describe the process by which temporary owners' equity accounts are closed at year-end.
*17. Explain several purposes that may be served by preparing a worksheet (or using computer software that achieves the goals of a worksheet).

EXERCISES

EXERCISE 5.1
Accounting Terminology
LO 1–7

Listed below are nine technical terms used in this chapter:

Liquidity	Nominal accounts	Real accounts
Adequate disclosure	After-closing trial balance	Closing entries
Income summary	Interim financial statements	Dividends

Each of the following statements may (or may not) describe one of these technical terms. For each statement, indicate the accounting term described, or answer "None" if the statement does not describe any of the items.

a. The accounting principle intended to assist users in *interpreting* financial statements.
b. A term used to describe a company's ability to pay its obligations as they come due.
c. A term used in reference to accounts that are closed at year-end.
d. A term used in reference to accounts that are not closed at year-end.
e. A document prepared to assist management in detecting whether any errors occurred in posting the closing entries.
f. A policy decision by a corporation to distribute a portion of its income to stockholders.
g. The process by which the Retained Earnings account is updated at year-end.
h. Entries made during the accounting period to correct errors in the original recording of complex transactions.

EXERCISE 5.2
Financial Statement Preparation
LO 1, 2, 6

Tutors for Rent, Inc., performs adjusting entries every month, but closes its accounts *only at year-end.* The company's year-end *adjusted trial balance* dated December 31, 2002, was:

---
*Supplemental Topic, "The Worksheet."

TUTORS FOR RENT, INC.
Adjusted Trial Balance
December 31, 2002

Cash	$ 91,100	
Accounts receivable	4,500	
Supplies	300	
Equipment	12,000	
Accumulated depreciation: equipment		$ 5,000
Accounts payable		1,500
Income taxes payable		3,500
Capital stock		25,000
Retained earnings		45,000
Dividends	2,000	
Tutoring revenue earned		96,000
Salary expense	52,000	
Supply expense	1,200	
Advertising expense	300	
Depreciation expense: equipment	1,000	
Income taxes expense	11,600	
	$176,000	$176,000

a. Prepare an income statement and statement of retained earnings for the year ended December 31, 2002. Also prepare the company's balance sheet dated December 31, 2002.
b. Does the company appear to be liquid? Defend your answer.
c. Has the company been profitable in the past? Explain.

EXERCISE 5.3
Financial Statement Preparation
LO 1, 2, 6

Wilderness Guide Services, Inc., performs adjusting entries every month, but closes its accounts *only at year-end*. The company's year-end *adjusted trial balance* dated December 31, 2002, follows:

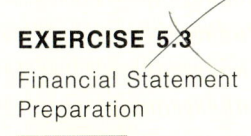

WILDERNESS GUIDE SERVICES, INC.
Adjusted Trial Balance
December 31, 2002

Cash	$ 12,200	
Accounts receivable	31,000	
Camping supplies	7,900	
Unexpired insurance policies	2,400	
Equipment	70,000	
Accumulated depreciation: equipment		$ 60,000
Notes payable (due 4/1/03)		18,000
Accounts payable		9,500
Capital stock		25,000
Retained earnings		15,000
Dividends	1,000	
Guide revenue earned		102,000
Salary expense	87,500	
Camping supply expense	1,200	
Insurance expense	9,600	
Depreciation expense: equipment	5,000	
Interest expense	1,700	
	$229,500	$229,500

a. Prepare an income statement and statement of retained earnings for the year ended December 31, 2002. Also prepare the company's balance sheet dated December 31, 2002. (*Hint:* Unprofitable companies have no income taxes expense.)
b. Does the company appear to be liquid? Defend your answer.
c. Has the company been profitable in the past? Explain.

EXERCISE 5.4
Preparing Closing Entries and an After-Closing Trial Balance
LO 2, 4, 5

Refer to the adjusted trial balance of Tutors for Rent, Inc., illustrated in Exercise 5.2 to respond to the following items:
a. Prepare all necessary closing entries at December 31, 2002.
b. Prepare an after-closing trial balance dated December 31, 2002.
c. Compare the Retained Earnings balance reported in the after-closing trial balance prepared in part **b** to the balance reported in the adjusted trial balance. Explain *why* the two balances are different. (Include in your explanation why the balance reported in the after-closing trial balance has increased or decreased subsequent to the closing process.)

EXERCISE 5.5
Preparing Closing Entries and an After-Closing Trial Balance
LO 2, 4, 5

Refer to the adjusted trial balance of Wilderness Guide Services, Inc., illustrated in Exercise 5.3 to respond to the following items:
a. Prepare all necessary closing entries at December 31, 2002.
b. Prepare an after-closing trial balance dated December 31, 2002.
c. Compare the Retained Earnings balance reported in the after-closing trial balance prepared in part **b** to the balance reported in the adjusted trial balance. Explain *why* the two balances are different. (Include in your explanation why the balance reported in the after-closing trial balance has increased or decreased subsequent to the closing process.)

EXERCISE 5.6
Preparing Closing Entries
LO 2, 4

Gerdes Psychological Services, Inc., closes its temporary owners' equity accounts once each year on December 31. The company recently issued the following income statement as part of its annual report:

GERDES PSYCHOLOGICAL SERVICES, INC.
Income Statement
For the Year Ended December 31, 2002

Revenue:		
Counseling revenue		$225,000
Expenses:		
Advertising expense	$ 1,800	
Salaries expense	94,000	
Office supplies expense	1,200	
Utilities expense	850	
Malpractice insurance expense	6,000	
Office rent expense	24,000	
Continuing education expense	2,650	
Depreciation expense: fixtures	4,500	
Miscellaneous expense	6,000	
Income taxes expense	29,400	170,400
Net income		$ 54,600

The firm's statement of retained earnings indicates that a $6,000 cash dividend was declared and paid during 2002.
a. Prepare the necessary closing entries on December 31, 2002.
b. If the firm's Retained Earnings account had a $92,000 balance on January 1, 2002, at what amount should Retained Earnings be reported in the firm's balance sheet dated December 31, 2002?

EXERCISE 5.7
Distinction between the Adjusting and the Closing Process
LO 2, 4

When Torretti Company began business on August 1, it purchased a one-year fire insurance policy and debited the entire cost of $7,200 to Unexpired Insurance. Torretti *adjusts* its accounts at the end of each month and *closes* its books at the end of the year.

a. Give the *adjusting entry* required at December 31 with respect to this insurance policy.

b. Give the *closing entry* required at December 31 with respect to insurance expense. Assume that this policy is the only insurance policy Torretti had during the year.

c. Compare the dollar amount appearing in the December 31 adjusting entry (part **a**) with that in the closing entry (part **b**). Are the dollar amounts the same? Why or why not? Explain.

EXERCISE 5.8
Interim Results
LO 1, 2, 7

Ski Powder Resort ends its fiscal year on April 30. The business adjusts its accounts monthly, but *closes them only at year-end* (April 30). The resort's busy season is from December 1 through March 31.

Adrian Pride, the resort's chief financial officer, keeps a close watch on Lift Ticket Revenue and Cash. The balances of these accounts at the ends of each of the last five months are as follows:

	Lift Ticket Revenue	Cash
November 30	$ 30,000	$ 9,000
December 31	200,000	59,000
January 31	640,000	94,000
February 28	850,000	116,000
March 31	990,000	138,000

Mr. Pride prepares income statements and balance sheets for the resort. Indicate what amounts will be shown in these statements for (1) Lift Ticket Revenue and (2) Cash, assuming they are prepared for:

a. The *month* ended February 28.

b. The entire "busy season to date"—that is, December 1 through March 31.

c. In terms of Lift Ticket Revenue and increases in Cash, which has been the resort's best month? (Indicate the dollar amounts.)

EXERCISE 5.9
Understanding the Effects of Errors on the Financial Statements
LO 2, 3

Indicate the effect of the following errors on each of the financial statement elements described in the column headings in the table below. Use the following symbols: **O** = overstated, **U** = understated, and **NE** = no effect.

	Error	Net Income	Total Assets	Total Liabilities	Retained Earnings
a.	Recorded a dividend as an *expense* in the income statement				
b.	Recorded unearned revenue as *earned* revenue in the income statement.				
c.	Failed to record accrued wages payable at the end of the accounting period.				
d.	Recorded a declared but unpaid dividend by debiting Dividends and crediting Cash.				
e.	Failed to disclose a pending lawsuit in the notes accompanying the financial statements.				

EXERCISE 5.10
Examining an Annual Report
LO 3, 6

The annual report of **Tootsie Roll Industries, Inc.,** appears in Appendix A at the end of this textbook.

a. Review the notes accompanying the company's consolidated financial statements. Identify the major topic headings.
b. Does the company use straight-line depreciation? How can you tell?
c. What portion of the company's total revenue came from a single major customer in each of the three years reported?
d. Using information from the consolidated financial statements, evaluate briefly the company's profitability and liquidity.

PROBLEMS

PROBLEM 5.1
Correcting Classification Errors
LO 1, 2, 4, 6

Party Wagon, Inc., provides musical entertainment at weddings, dances, and various other functions. The company performs adjusting entries *monthly,* but prepares closing entries *annually* on December 31. The company recently hired Jack Armstrong as its new accountant. Jack's first assignment was to prepare an income statement, a statement of retained earnings, and a balance sheet using an *adjusted* trial balance given to him by his predecessor, dated December 31, 2002.

From the adjusted trial balance, Jack prepared the following set of financial statements:

PARTY WAGON, INC.
Income Statement
For the Year Ended December 31, 2002

Revenue:		
Party revenue earned		$130,000
Unearned party revenue		1,800
Accounts receivable		9,000
Total revenue		$140,800
Expenses:		
Insurance expense	$ 1,800	
Office rent expense	12,000	
Supplies expense	1,200	
Dividends	1,000	
Salary expense	75,000	
Accumulated depreciation: Van	16,000	
Accumulated depreciation: Equipment and music	14,000	
Repair and maintenance expense	2,000	
Travel expense	6,000	
Miscellaneous expense	3,600	
Interest expense	4,400	137,000
Income before income taxes		$ 3,800
Income taxes payable		400
Net income		$ 3,400

PARTY WAGON, INC.
Statement of Retained Earnings
For the Year Ended December 31, 2002

Retained earnings (per adjusted trial balance)	$15,000
Add: Income	3,400
Less: Income taxes expense	2,000
Retained earnings (12/31/02)	$16,400

PARTY WAGON, INC.
Balance Sheet
December 31, 2002

Assets

Cash		$15,000
Supplies		500
Van	$40,000	
Less: Depreciation expense: Van	8,000	32,000
Equipment and music	$35,000	
Less: Depreciation expense: Music and equipment	7,000	28,000
Total assets		$75,500

Liabilities & Stockholders' Equity

Liabilities:

Accounts payable	$ 7,000
Notes payable	39,000
Salaries payable	1,600
Prepaid rent	2,000
Unexpired insurance	4,500
Total liabilities	$54,100

Stockholders' Equity:

Capital stock	5,000
Retained earnings	16,400
Total stockholders' equity	$21,400
Total liabilities and stockholders' equity	$75,500

Instructions

a. Prepare a corrected set of financial statements dated December 31, 2002. (You may assume that all of the figures in the company's adjusted trial balance were reported correctly except for Interest Payable of $200, which was mistakenly omitted in the financial statements prepared by Jack.)

b. Prepare the necessary year-end closing entries.

c. Using the financial statements prepared in part a, briefly evaluate the company's profitability and liquidity.

PROBLEM 5.2
Preparing Financial Statements and Closing Entries of a Profitable Company

LO 1, 2, 4, 5, 6

Lawn Pride, Inc., provides lawn mowing services to both commercial and residential customers. The company performs adjusting entries on a *monthly* basis, whereas closing entries are prepared *annually* at December 31. An *adjusted* trial balance dated December 31, 2002, follows.

LAWN PRIDE, INC.
Adjusted Trial Balance
December 31, 2002

	Debits	Credits
Cash	$ 58,525	
Accounts receivable	4,800	
Unexpired insurance	8,000	
Prepaid rent	3,000	
Supplies	1,075	
Trucks	150,000	
Accumulated depreciation: Trucks		$120,000
Mowing equipment	20,000	
Accumulated depreciation: Mowing equipment		12,000
Accounts payable		1,500
Notes payable		50,000
Salaries payable		900
Interest payable		150
Income taxes payable		1,050
Unearned mowing revenue		900
Capital stock		20,000
Retained earnings		30,000
Dividends	5,000	
Mowing revenue earned		170,000
Insurance expense	2,400	
Office rent expense	36,000	
Supplies expense	5,200	
Salary expense	60,000	
Depreciation expense: Trucks	30,000	
Depreciation expense: Mowing equipment	4,000	
Repair and maintenance expense	3,000	
Fuel expense	1,500	
Miscellaneous expense	5,000	
Interest expense	3,000	
Income taxes expense	6,000	
	$406,500	$406,500

Instructions

a. Prepare an income statement and statement of retained earnings for the year ended December 31, 2002. Also prepare the company's balance sheet dated December 31, 2002.
b. Prepare the necessary year-end closing entries.
c. Prepare an after-closing trial balance.
d. Using the financial statements prepared in part **a**, briefly evaluate the company's profitability and liquidity.

PROBLEM 5.3
Preparing Financial Statements and Closing Entries of an Unprofitable Company

LO 1–4, 6

Mystic Masters, Inc., provides fortune-telling services over the Internet. In recent years the company has experienced severe financial difficulty. Its accountant prepares adjusting entries on a *monthly* basis, and closing entries on an *annual* basis, at December 31. An *adjusted* trial balance dated December 31, 2002, follows.

MYSTIC MASTERS, INC.
Adjusted Trial Balance
December 31, 2002

	Debits	Credits
Cash	$ 960	
Accounts receivable	300	
Unexpired insurance	2,000	
Prepaid rent	1,500	
Supplies	200	
Furniture and fixtures	8,400	
Accumulated depreciation: Furniture and fixtures		$ 5,200
Accounts payable		6,540
Notes payable		24,000
Salaries payable		1,700
Interest payable		360
Unearned client revenue		200
Capital stock		4,000
Retained earnings		2,600
Client revenue earned		52,000
Insurance expense	6,000	
Office rent expense	9,000	
Supplies expense	440	
Salary expense	48,000	
Depreciation expense: Furniture and fixtures	1,400	
Office and telephone expense	3,000	
Internet service expense	4,900	
Legal expense	1,500	
Interest expense	4,000	
Miscellaneous expense	5,000	
	$96,600	$96,600

Instructions

a. Prepare an income statement and statement of retained earnings for the year ended December 31, 2002. Also prepare the company's balance sheet dated December 31, 2002. (*Hint*: The company incurred no income taxes expense in 2002.)
b. Prepare the necessary year-end closing entries.
c. Prepare an after-closing trial balance.
d. Using the financial statements prepared in part **a**, briefly evaluate the company's performance.
e. Identify information that the company is apt to disclose in the notes that accompany the financial statements prepared in part **a**.

PROBLEM 5.4
Interim Financial Statements

LO 1, 2, 7

Guardian Insurance Agency adjusts its accounts monthly but closes them only at the end of the calendar year. Below are the adjusted balances of the revenue and expense accounts at September 30 of the current year and at the ends of two earlier months:

	Sept. 30	Aug. 31	June 30
Commissions Earned	$144,000	$128,000	$90,000
Advertising Expense	28,000	23,000	15,000
Salaries Expense	36,000	32,000	24,000
Rent Expense	22,500	20,000	15,000
Depreciation Expense	2,700	2,400	1,800

Instructions

a. Prepare a three-column income statement, showing net income for three separate time periods, all of which end on September 30. Use the format illustrated below. Show supporting computations for the amounts of revenue reported in the first two columns.

GUARDIAN INSURANCE AGENCY
Income Statement
For the Following Time Periods in 2002

	Month Ended Sept. 30	Quarter Ended Sept. 30	9 Months Ended Sept. 30
Revenue:			
Commissions Earned	$	$	$
Expenses:			

b. Briefly explain how you determined the dollar amounts for each of the three time periods. Would you apply the same process to the balances in Guardian's balance sheet accounts? Explain.

c. Assume that Guardian adjusts *and closes* its accounts at the end of *each month*. Briefly explain how you then would determine the revenue and expenses that would appear in each of the three columns of the income statement prepared in part **a**.

PROBLEM 5.5
Short Comprehensive Problem Including Both Adjusting and Closing Entries

LO 1–4, 6

Brushstroke Art Studio, Inc., provides quality instruction to aspiring artists. The business adjusts its accounts *monthly,* but performs closing entries *annually* on December 31. This is the studio's *unadjusted* trial balance dated December 31, 2002.

BRUSHSTROKE ART STUDIO, INC.
Unadjusted Trial Balance
December 31, 2002

	Debits	Credits
Cash	$ 22,380	
Client fees receivable	71,250	
Supplies	6,000	
Prepaid studio rent	2,500	
Studio equipment	96,000	
Accumulated depreciation: Studio equipment		$ 52,000
Accounts payable		6,420
Note payable		24,000
Interest payable		480
Unearned client fees		8,000
Income taxes payable		5,000
Capital stock		50,000
Retained earnings		20,000
Client fees earned		82,310
Supply expense	4,000	
Salary expense	17,250	
Interest expense	480	
Studio rent expense	11,250	
Utilities expense	3,300	
Depreciation expense: Studio equipment	8,800	
Income taxes expense	5,000	
	$248,210	$248,210

Other Data

1. Supplies on hand at December 31, 2002, total $1,000.
2. The studio pays rent quarterly (every 3 months). The last payment was made November 1, 2002. The next payment will be made early in February 2003.
3. Studio equipment is being depreciated over 120 months (10 years).
4. On October 1, 2002, the studio borrowed $24,000 by signing a 12-month, 12%, note payable. The entire amount, plus interest, is due on September 30, 2003.
5. At December 31, 2002, $3,000 of previously unearned client fees had been *earned.*
6. Accrued, but *unrecorded* and uncollected client fees earned total $690 at December 31, 2002.
7. Accrued, but *unrecorded* and unpaid salary expense totals $750 at December 31, 2002.
8. Accrued income taxes payable for the *entire year* ending December 31, 2002, *total* $7,000. The full amount is due early in 2003.

Instructions

a. Prepare the necessary adjusting journal entries on December 31, 2002. Prepare also an *adjusted trial balance* dated December 31, 2002.
b. From the adjusted trial balance prepared in part **a**, prepare an income statement and statement of retained earnings for the year ended December 31, 2002. Also prepare the company's balance sheet dated December 31, 2002.
c. Prepare the necessary year-end closing entries.
d. Prepare an after-closing trial balance.
e. Has the studio's monthly office rent remained the same throughout the year? If not, has it gone up or down? Explain.

*PROBLEM 5.6

Short Comprehensive Problem Including Adjusting Entries, Closing Entries, and Worksheet Preparation

LO 8

Refer to the Demonstration Problem illustrated in the previous chapter. Prepare a 10-column worksheet for Internet Consulting Service, Inc., dated December 31, 2002. At the bottom of your worksheet, prepare a brief explanation keyed to each adjusting entry.

*PROBLEM 5.7

Short Comprehensive Problem Including Adjusting Entries, Closing Entries, and Worksheet Preparation

LO 8

Refer to Problem 4.4 in the previous chapter. Prepare a 10-column worksheet for Campus Theater dated August 31, 2002. At the bottom of your worksheet, prepare a brief explanation keyed to each adjusting entry.

PROBLEM 5.8

Evaluating Profitability and Liquidity

LO 6

A recent annual report issued by **Circuit City** revealed the following data:

	End of Year	Beginning of Year
Current assets	$2.85 billion	$2.94 billion
Current liabilities	$1.29 billion	$1.41 billion
Stockholders' equity	$2.36 billion	$2.14 billion

The company's income statement reported total annual revenue of $12.96 billion, and net income for the year of $161 million.

Instructions

a. Evaluate **Circuit City**'s profitability by computing its net income percentage and its return on equity for the year.
b. Evaluate **Circuit City**'s liquidity by computing its working capital and its current ratio at the beginning of the year and at the end of the year.
c. Does **Circuit City** appear to be both profitable and liquid? Explain.

CASES AND UNSTRUCTURED PROBLEMS

CASE 5.1

Working for the Competition

LO 1

This problem focuses on the following question: *Is it ethical for a CPA (or CPA firm) to provide similar services to companies that compete directly with one another?* These services may include assistance in the preparation of financial statements, income tax services, consulting engagements, and audit work.

Instructions

a. *Before* doing any research, discuss this question as a group. Identify potential arguments on *each side* of the issue.
b. Arrange an interview with a practicing (or retired) public accountant. Learn the accounting profession's position on this issue, and discuss the various arguments developed in part **a**.
c. Develop your group's position on this issue and be prepared to explain it in class. Explain why you have chosen to overlook the conflicting arguments developed in part **a**. (If your group is not in agreement, dissenting members may draft a dissenting opinion.)

---

*Supplemental Topic, "The Worksheet."

CASE 5.2

Adequate Disclosure

LO 3

Listed below are five items that may—or may not—require disclosure in the notes that accompany financial statements.

a. Mandella Construction Co. uses the percentage-of-completion method to recognize revenue on long-term construction contracts. This is one of two acceptable methods of accounting for such projects. Over the life of the project, both methods produce the same overall results; but the annual results may differ substantially.

b. One of the most popular artists at Spectacular Comics is leaving the company and going to work for a competitor.

c. Shortly after the balance sheet date, but before the financial statements are issued, one of Coast Foods' two processing plants was damaged by a tornado. The plant will be out of service for at least three months.

d. The management of Soft Systems believes that the company has developed systems software that will make Windows® virtually obsolete. If they are correct, the company's profits could increase by 10-fold or more.

e. College Property Management (CPM) withheld a $500 security deposit from students who, in violation of their lease, kept a dog in their apartment. The students have sued CPM for this amount in small claims court.

Instructions

For each case, explain what, if any, disclosure is required under generally accepted accounting principles. Explain your reasoning.

BUSINESS WEEK ASSIGNMENT

CASE 5.3

Yahoo, Inc., and Proforma Financial Information

LO 2, 3, 6

Dave Henry reports in a May 14, 2001, *Business Week* article, "The Numbers Game," that companies are using every trick in the book to boost earnings and fool investors. He reports that some companies believe Generally Accepted Accounting Principles (GAAP) do not give investors the full picture. For example, small biotech start-ups must apply GAAP the same way as a fast-food empire or a giant automaker with billions invested in plants.

In an attempt to persuade investors about the shortfalls of GAAP, some companies issue pro forma statements that do not adhere to GAAP. They include these statements in their annual reports in addition to the GAAP statements. Recently, **Yahoo!, Inc.** presented pro forma results 35% better than GAAP figures by excluding a variety of expenses associated with buying Internet companies. (**Yahoo!, Inc.** recorded certain costs as assets instead of expenses.)

Instructions

a. Be prepared to explain how **Yahoo!, Inc.**'s income statement, balance sheet, and statement of retained earnings would be affected by excluding certain costs from its pro forma statements. Think about the articulation of these statements.

b. Some financial analysts and Securities and Exchange Commission accountants believe pro forma statements are designed to mislead investors. However, some CEOs and CFOs say they are simply providing investors and creditors with adequate disclosure, an important accounting principle. Do you support including pro forma statements with a company's annual report? Defend your answer.

INTERNET ASSIGNMENT

INTERNET 5.1

Annual Report Disclosures

LO 3

Visit the home page of the **Ford Motor Company** at:

www.ford.com

From Ford's home page, access the company's most recent annual report. Locate the notes to the financial statements and identify the kinds of information disclosed in these footnotes.

Internet sites are time and date sensitive. It is the purpose of these exercises to have you explore the Internet. You may need to use the Yahoo! search engine **http://www.yahoo.com** *(or other favorite search engine) to find a company's current Web address.*

OUR COMMENTS ON THE "YOUR TURN" CASES

You as an Independent Auditor (p. 182) Pending lawsuits are usually disclosed in the notes to the financial statements only if there is *reasonable certainty* that the defendant will incur a significant loss. Thus, Overnight need *not* disclose its pending lawsuit if the risk of it sustaining a material loss is *remote*. This is certainly an issue requiring the *professional judgments* of the company's management, accountants, legal counsel, and its auditors. Coverage of financial uncertainties such as pending lawsuits is addressed in Chapter 10 of this textbook.

You as a Business Software Developer (p. 187) Most accounting software packages streamline the steps of the closing process illustrated in this chapter. Before using the software for the first time, the business designates which account numbers in its chart of accounts correspond to *revenues, expenses, and dividends,* and which account numbers correspond to balance sheet items. At the end of the accounting period, a menu item is selected to initiate the closing process. The software then identifies the *temporary accounts* and closes them *automatically* by following the logic presented in the flowchart in Exhibit 5–11.

You as a Potential Owner of Overnight Auto Service (p. 190) The matching principle does not apply because the future revenues are uncertain. The realization principle suggests that revenue should be recognized at the time goods are sold or services are rendered. Because of the uncertainty of future revenues, and because they cannot be clearly traced to current advertising costs, capitalizing these costs would not be appropriate.

It is not unusual for managers and owners to try making financial statements appear more profitable to attract potential investors. Recently, some companies have been using pro forma reporting, including a second set of figures published in their annual reports. These figures do not necessarily comply with generally accepted accounting principles (GAAP). Some financial analysts and members of the Securities and Exchange Commission have suggested that pro forma statements are used to mislead investors. Their concerns reveal ethical issues associated with pro forma reports.

ANSWERS TO SELF-TEST QUESTIONS

1. a, b, c, d   **2.** a.   **3.** d   **4.** b, d   **5.** a   **6.** a, b   **7.** c   **8.** b, c

COMPREHENSIVE PROBLEM 1

West Branch Rent All

A COMPREHENSIVE ACCOUNTING CYCLE PROBLEM

On September 1, 2002, John and Patty Driver formed a corporation called West Branch Rent All to rent equipment. The new corporation was able to begin operations immediately by purchasing the assets and taking over the location of Rent-It, an equipment rental company that was going out of business. West Branch Rent All uses the following accounts:

Cash	Income Taxes Payable
Accounts Receivable	Capital Stock
Prepaid Rent	Retained Earnings
Unexpired Insurance	Dividends
Office Supplies	Income Summary
Rental Equipment	Rental Fees Earned
Accumulated Depreciation:	Salaries Expense
Rental Equipment	Maintenance Expense
Notes Payable	Utilities Expense
Accounts Payable	Rent Expense
Interest Payable	Office Supplies Expense
Salaries Payable	Depreciation Expense
Dividends Payable	Interest Expense
Unearned Rental Fees	Income Taxes Expense

The corporation closes its accounts and prepares financial statements at the end of each month. During September, the corporation entered into the following transactions:

Sept. 1 Issued to John and Patty Driver 20,000 shares of capital stock in exchange for a total of $100,000 cash.

Sept. 1 Purchased for $180,000 all of the equipment formerly owned by Rent-It. Paid $70,000 cash and issued a one-year note payable for $110,000.

Sept. 1 Paid $9,000 to Shapiro Realty as three months' advance rent on the rental yard and office formerly occupied by Rent-It.

Sept. 4 Purchased office supplies on account from Modern Office Co., $2,000. Payment due in 30 days. (These supplies are expected to last for several months; debit the Office Supplies asset account.)

Sept. 8 Received $20,000 cash as advance payment on equipment rental from McNamer Construction Company. (Credit Unearned Rental Fees.)

Sept. 12 Paid salaries for the first two weeks in September, $4,100.

Sept. 15 Excluding the McNamer advance, equipment rental fees earned during the first 15 days of September amounted to $9,000 of which $8,000 was received in cash.

Sept. 17 Purchased on account from Earth Movers, Inc., $500 in parts needed to repair a rental tractor. (Debit an expense account.) Payment is due in 10 days.

Sept. 23 Collected $300 of the accounts receivable recorded on September 15.

Sept. 25 Rented a backhoe to Mission Landscaping at a price of $100 per day, to be paid when the backhoe is returned. Mission Landscaping expects to keep the backhoe for about two or three weeks.

Sept. 26 Paid biweekly salaries, $4,100.

Sept. 27 Paid the account payable to Earth Movers, Inc., $500.

Sept. 28 Declared a dividend of 20 cents per share, payable on October 15.

Sept. 29 West Branch Rent All was named, along with Mission Landscaping and Collier Construction, as a co-defendant in a $25,000 lawsuit filed on behalf of Kevin Davenport. Mission Landscaping had left the rented backhoe in a fenced construction site owned by Collier Construction. After working hours on September 26, Davenport had climbed the fence to play on parked construction equipment. While playing on the backhoe, he fell and broke his arm. The extent of the company's legal and financial responsibility for this accident, if any, cannot be determined at this time. (*Note*: This event does not require a journal entry at this time, but may require disclosure in notes accompanying the statements.)

Sept. 29 Purchased a 12-month public-liability insurance policy for $2,700. This policy protects the company against liability for injuries and property damage caused by its equipment. However, the policy goes into effect on October 1, and affords no coverage for the injuries sustained by Kevin Davenport on September 26.

Sept. 30 Received a bill from Universal Utilities for the month of September, $600. Payment is due in 30 days.

Sept. 30 Equipment rental fees earned during the second half of September and received in cash amounted to $10,000.

Data for Adjusting Entries

a. The advance payment of rent on September 1 covered a period of three months.

b. Interest accrued on the note payable to Rent-It amounted to $800 at September 30.

c. The rental equipment is being depreciated by the straight-line method over a period of 10 years.

d. Office supplies on hand at September 30 are estimated at $1,100.

e. During September, the company earned $12,000 of the rental fees paid in advance by McNamer Construction Co. on September 8.

f. As of September 30, West Branch Rent All has earned five days' rent on the backhoe rented to Mission Landscaping on September 25.

g. Salaries earned by employees since the last payroll date (September 26) amounted to $1,000 at month-end.

h. It is estimated that West Branch Rent All is subject to a combined federal and state income tax rate of 40% of income before income taxes (total revenue minus all expenses *other than* income taxes). These taxes will be payable on December 15.

Instructions

a. Journalize the above transactions.

b. Post to ledger accounts.

c. Prepare a 10-column worksheet for the month ended September 30, 2002.

d. Prepare an income statement and a statement of retained earnings for the month of September, and a balance sheet (in report form) as of September 30.

e. Prepare required disclosures to accompany the September 30 financial statements of West Branch Rent All. Your solution should include a separate note addressing each of the following areas: (1) depreciation policy, (2) maturity dates of major liabilities, and (3) potential liability due to pending litigation.

f. Prepare adjusting and closing entries and post to ledger accounts.

g. Prepare an after-closing trial balance as of September 30.

h. During September, this company's cash balance has fallen from $100,000 to less than $48,000. Does it appear headed for insolvency in the near future? Explain your reasoning.

i. Would it be ethical for Patty Driver to maintain the accounting records for this company, or must they be maintained by someone who is *independent* of the organization?

CHAPTER 6: MERCHANDISING ACTIVITIES

Learning Objectives

After studying this chapter, you should be able to:

1. Describe the *operating cycle* of a merchandising company.
2. Define *subsidiary ledgers* and explain their usefulness.
3. Account for purchases and sales of merchandise in a *perpetual* inventory system.
4. Explain how a *periodic* inventory system operates.
5. Discuss the factors to be considered in selecting an inventory system.
6. Define *special journals* and explain their usefulness.
7. Account for additional merchandising transactions related to purchases and sales.
8. Measure the performance of a merchandising business.

Felicia Martinez/PhotoEdit

Rite Aid Corporation

Rite Aid Corporation is the second largest retail pharmacy chain in the United States based on store count, and the third largest based on sales. The company operates nearly 3,500 pharmacies in 30 states. Its stores average 12,663 square feet.

Rite Aid fills over 200 million prescriptions each year and generates revenue in excess of $14 billion. Nearly 40% of its revenue comes from the sale of nonprescription medications, health and beauty aids, convenience foods, greeting cards, and other household products. The company's sophisticated information system tracks detailed sales and inventory data from each of its stores. The information is consolidated and reported in the financial statements as part of the company's annual report.

Rite Aid's financial statements are very similar in format to those illustrated in previous chapters. They differ, however, because **Rite Aid** not only provides the services of registered pharmacists but also sells *merchandise* to its customers. Companies that sell merchandise must report information about inventory costs in their financial statements.

• • •

In this chapter we examine accounting issues related to merchandising businesses, such as retail pharmacies and grocery stores. In addition to discussing the unique features of a merchandising company's financial statements, we illustrate ways to use financial information to evaluate the performance of these companies.

Rite Aid Corporation's retail pharmacies are good examples of merchandising outlets. Managing **inventory** (goods that are purchased for the purpose of resale to customers) is of utmost importance to merchandising businesses. For a large chain like **Rite Aid** to be successful, its stores must acquire thousands of inventory items and sell them quickly at competitive prices.

In most merchandising companies, inventory is a relatively liquid asset—that is, it usually is sold within a few days or weeks. For this reason, inventory appears near the top of the balance sheet, immediately below accounts receivable.

MERCHANDISING COMPANIES

The Operating Cycle of a Merchandising Company

LO 1
Describe the *operating cycle* of a merchandising company.

The series of transactions through which a business generates its revenue and its cash receipts from customers is called the **operating cycle**. The operating cycle of a merchandising company consists of the following basic transactions: (1) purchases of merchandise; (2) sales of the merchandise, often on account; and (3) collection of the accounts receivable from customers. As the word *cycle* suggests, this sequence of transactions repeats continuously. Some of the cash collected from the customers is used to purchase more merchandise, and the cycle begins anew. This continuous sequence of merchandising transactions is illustrated in Exhibit 6–1.

Exhibit 6–1

THE OPERATING CYCLE

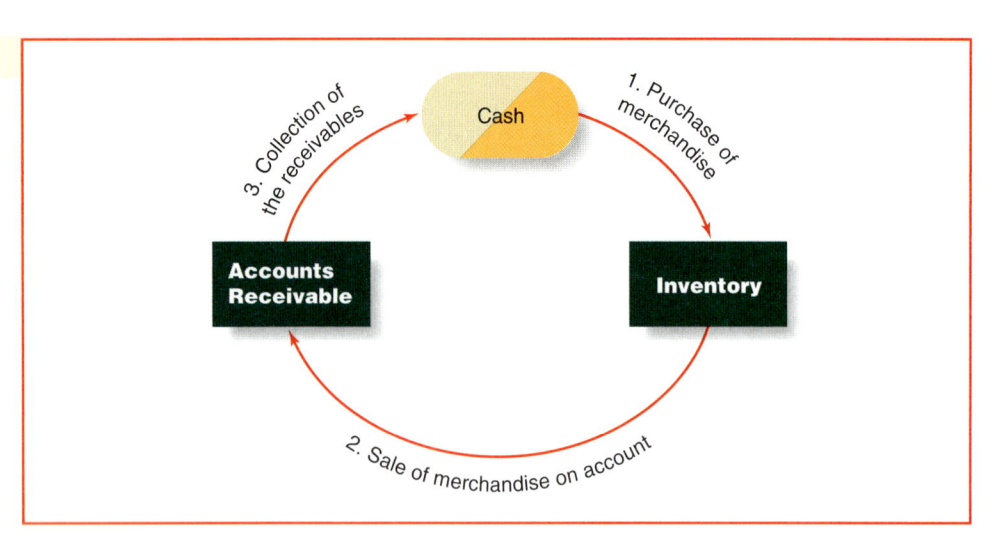

Comparing Merchandising Activities with Manufacturing Activities   Most merchandising companies purchase their inventories from other business organizations in a *ready-to-sell* condition. Companies that manufacture their inventories, such as **General Motors**, **IBM**, and **Boeing Aircraft**, are called *manufacturers,* rather than merchandisers. The operating cycle of a manufacturing company is longer and more complex than that of a merchandising company, because the first transaction—purchasing merchandise—is replaced by the many activities involved in manufacturing the merchandise.

Our examples and illustrations in this chapter are limited to companies that purchase their inventory in a ready-to-sell condition. The basic concepts, however, also apply to manufacturers.

Retailers and Wholesalers   Merchandising companies include both retailers and wholesalers. A *retailer* is a business that sells merchandise directly to the public. Retailers may be large or small; they vary in size from giant department store chains, such as **Rite**

Merchandising Companies

Aid Corporation, **CVS**, **Sears**, **Roebuck & Co.**, and **Wal-Mart**, to small neighborhood businesses, such as gas stations and convenience stores. In fact, more businesses engage in retail sales than in any other type of business activity.

The other major type of merchandising company is the *wholesaler*. Wholesalers buy large quantities of merchandise from several different manufacturers and then resell this merchandise to many different retailers. As wholesalers do not sell directly to the public, even the largest wholesalers are not well known to most consumers. Nonetheless, wholesaling is a major type of merchandising activity.

> The Internet has allowed wholesalers to become more visible to the global business community. A case in point is **KG Instruments® International**, a business that specializes in the development and distribution of fine stringed instruments and their accessories. The trading office and showroom are located at Campsie, New South Wales, Australia. The company welcomes business from importers, wholesalers, and dealers.
>
> **CASE IN POINT**

The concepts discussed in the remainder of this chapter apply equally to retailers and to wholesalers.

Income Statement of a Merchandising Company

Selling merchandise introduces a new and major cost of doing business: the *cost* to the merchandising company of the goods that it resells to its customers. This cost is termed the **cost of goods sold**. In essence, the cost of goods sold is an *expense;* however, this item is of such importance to a merchandising company that it is shown separately from other expenses in the income statement.

A highly condensed income statement for a merchandising business appears in Exhibit 6–2. In comparison with the income statement of a service-type business, the new features of this statement are the inclusion of *cost of goods sold* and a subtotal called *gross profit*.

COMPUTER CITY Condensed Income Statement For the Year Ended December 31, 2002	
Revenue from sales	$900,000
Less: Cost of goods sold	540,000
Gross profit	$360,000
Less: Expenses	270,000
Net income	$ 90,000

Exhibit 6–2

CONDENSED INCOME STATEMENT

Revenue from sales represents the *sales price* of merchandise sold to customers during the period. The cost of goods sold, on the other hand, represents the *cost* incurred by the merchandising company for purchasing these goods from the company's suppliers. The difference between revenue from sales and the cost of goods sold is called **gross profit** (or gross margin).

Gross profit is a useful means of measuring the profitability of sales transactions, but it does *not* represent the overall profitability of the business. A merchandising company has many expenses other than the cost of goods sold. Examples include salaries, rent, advertising, and depreciation. The company earns a net income only if its gross profit exceeds the sum of its other expenses.

What Accounting Information Does a Merchandising Company Need?

Before we illustrate how a merchandising company accounts for the transactions in its operating cycle, let us consider the basic types of information that the company's accounting system should develop. The company needs accounting information that will (1) meet its financial reporting requirements, (2) serve the needs of company personnel in conducting daily business operations, and (3) meet any special reporting requirements, such as information required by income tax authorities.

To meet its financial reporting requirements, a merchandising company must measure and record its revenue from sales transactions, as well as the cost of goods sold. (Other types of revenue and expenses must also be recorded, but this is done in the same manner as in a service-type business.) In addition, the accounting system must provide a complete record of the company's assets and liabilities.

The information appearing in financial statements is very condensed. For example, the amount shown as accounts receivable in a balance sheet represents the *total* accounts receivable at the balance sheet date. Managers and other employees need much more detailed accounting information than that provided in financial statements. In billing customers, for example, managers need to know the amount receivable from each credit customer. In addition, the accounting system must provide the dates and amounts of all charges and payments affecting each customer's account.

In most respects, the information needed for income tax purposes parallels that used in the financial statements. Differences between income tax rules and financial reporting requirements will be discussed in later chapters.

Let us now see how the accounting system of a merchandising company meets the company's needs for financial information.

General Ledger Accounts

Up to now, we have been posting transactions only in *general ledger* accounts. These general ledger accounts are used to prepare financial statements and other accounting reports that *summarize* the financial position of a business and the results of its operations.

Although general ledger accounts provide a useful *overview* of a company's financial activities, they do not provide much of the *detailed information* needed by managers and other company employees in daily business operations. This detailed information is found in accounting records called *subsidiary ledgers*.

Subsidiary Ledger Accounts

LO 2
Define *subsidiary ledgers* and explain their usefulness.

A **subsidiary ledger** contains a separate account for each of the *items* included in the balance of a general ledger account. For example, an *accounts receivable subsidiary ledger* contains a separate account for *each credit customer*. If the company has 500 credit customers, there are 500 accounts in the accounts receivable subsidiary ledger. The balances of these 500 subsidiary ledger accounts add up to the balance in the general ledger account.

An accounts receivable subsidiary ledger provides the information used in billing credit customers and in reviewing their creditworthiness. The account includes information on the dates and amounts of past charges and payments, the current balance owed, and the customer's billing address. In fact, each account provides a *complete history* of the credit transactions between the company and the individual customer.

CASE IN POINT

When you call the phone company, electric company, or other businesses to inquire about your bill, they always ask you for your account number. This is the number assigned to your account in their accounts receivable subsidiary ledger. The company representative then views your account on a computer screen and is able to discuss the details of your past transactions.

Most businesses maintain a number of different subsidiary ledgers, each providing detailed information about a different general ledger account. A general ledger account that summarizes the content of a subsidiary ledger is called a **controlling account** (or control account).

For convenience, the word *subsidiary* can be omitted in describing a specific subsidiary ledger. Thus the accounts receivable subsidiary ledger might simply be called the *accounts receivable ledger* (or *customer ledger*).

Subsidiary Ledgers Needed for Merchandising Transactions In addition to a subsidiary ledger for accounts receivable, every merchandising company also maintains an *accounts payable subsidiary ledger,* showing the amount owed to each creditor. Many merchandising companies also maintain an *inventory subsidiary ledger,* with a separate account for each type of merchandise that the company sells. Thus the inventory ledger of a large department store contains thousands of accounts. Each of these accounts shows, for *one type of product,* the quantities, unit costs, and total costs of all units purchased, sold, and currently in inventory.

In Exhibit 6–3 we show the relationship between several subsidiary ledgers and the related controlling accounts in the general ledger.

Exhibit 6–3

THE GENERAL LEDGER AND SUBSIDIARY LEDGERS

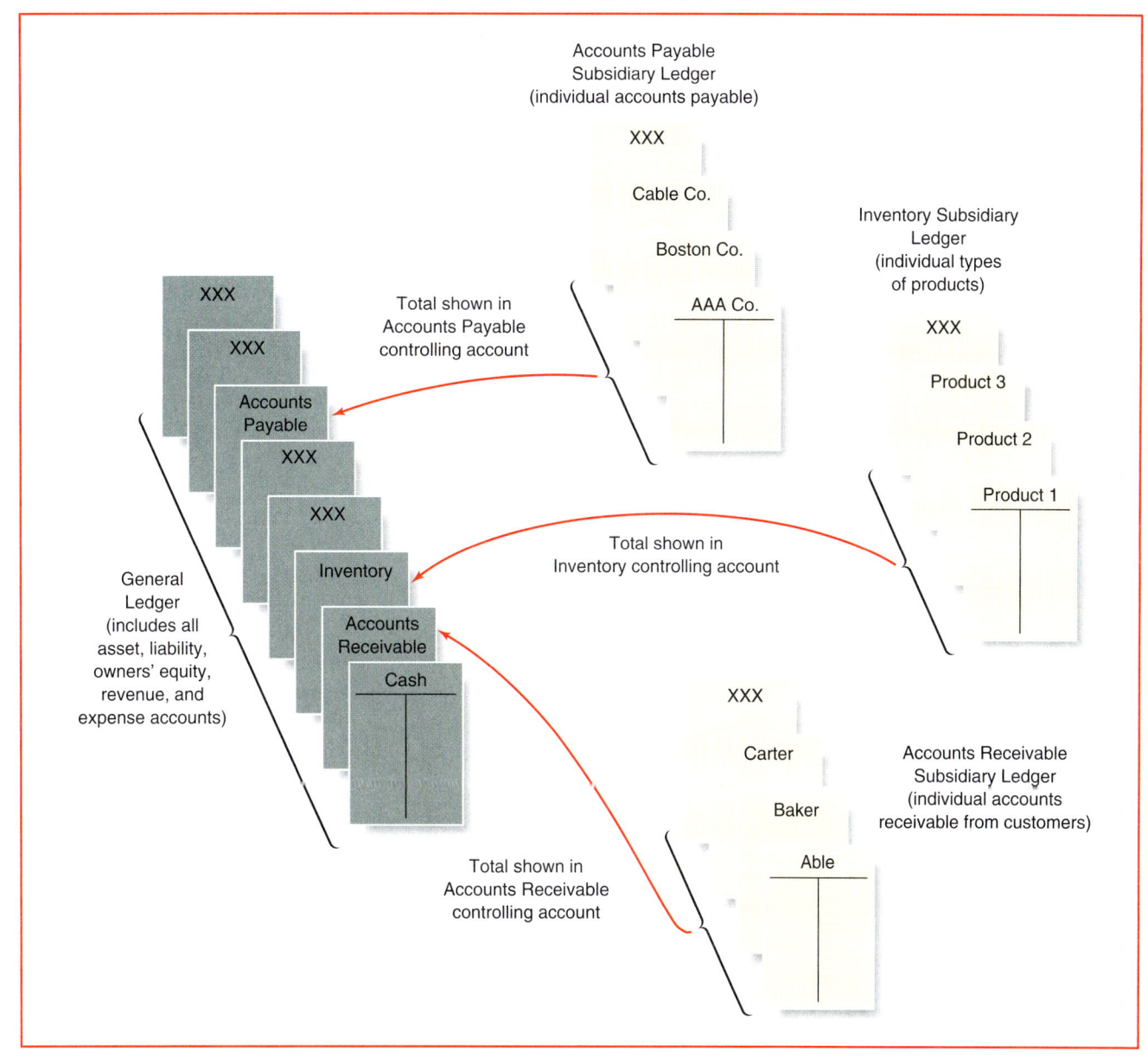

Other Types of Subsidiary Ledgers In this chapter we discuss the subsidiary ledgers for inventory, accounts payable, and accounts receivable. However, subsidiary ledgers also are maintained for many other general ledger accounts. In Exhibit 6–4 we list some of the general ledger accounts usually supported by a subsidiary ledger.

Exhibit 6–4

GENERAL LEDGER AND SUBSIDIARY LEDGER RELATIONSHIPS

Controlling Account in the General Ledger	Unit of Organization within the Subsidiary Ledger
Cash	Each bank account
Notes Receivable	Each note receivable
Accounts Receivable	Each credit customer
Inventory	Each type of product offered for sale
Plant Assets	Each asset (or group of similar assets)
Notes Payable	Each note payable
Accounts Payable	Each creditor
Capital Stock (only in a business organized as a corporation)	Each stockholder (this ledger shows each stockholder's name, address, and the number of shares owned)
Sales (or any revenue account)	Each department, branch location, or product line
Cost of Goods Sold	Same organization as the sales ledger
Many expense accounts	Each department incurring these types of expense
Payroll Expenses (including payroll taxes)	Each employee

Subsidiary ledgers are intended to meet the information needs of the company's *managers and employees*. These accounting records are *not* used in the preparation of financial statements, nor are they usually made available to persons outside of the business organization.

Subsidiary Ledgers in Computer-Based Systems At first, it may seem that maintaining subsidiary ledgers with hundreds or thousands of separate accounts would involve a great deal of work. However, business organizations big enough to require large subsidiary ledgers use computer-based accounting systems. In a computer-based accounting system, subsidiary ledger accounts and general ledger control accounts are posted *automatically* as transactions are recorded. In addition, the computer automatically reconciles the subsidiary ledgers with the controlling accounts. Thus no significant effort is required of accounting personnel to maintain subsidiary ledgers in a computer-based system.

YOUR TURN

You as a Credit Manager

Assume you are the credit manager for Wilson, Inc., a small manufacturer of toys. You have just received a request from Dave's Toy Store asking that the store's credit limit be increased from $30,000 to $50,000. Dave has been a customer of Wilson for the past five years.

Describe the information that you can obtain from the accounts receivable ledger that will assist you in making the decision about whether to increase Dave's credit limit. What *other information* would assist you in making this decision?

*Our comments appear on page 260.

Two Approaches Used in Accounting for Merchandising Transactions

Either of two approaches may be used in accounting for merchandising transactions: (1) a *perpetual inventory system* or (2) a *periodic inventory system*. In the past, both systems were in widespread use. Today, however, most large businesses (and many smaller ones) use computers to assist in maintaining perpetual systems. Periodic systems are used primarily in small businesses with manual accounting systems.

PERPETUAL INVENTORY SYSTEMS

In a **perpetual inventory system**, merchandising transactions are recorded immediately *as they occur*. The system draws its name from the fact that the accounting records are kept perpetually up-to-date. Purchases of merchandise are recorded by debiting an asset account entitled Inventory. When merchandise is sold, two entries are necessary: one to recognize the *revenue earned* and the second to recognize the related *cost of goods sold*.[1] This second entry also reduces the balance of the Inventory account to reflect the sale of some of the company's inventory.

LO 3
Account for purchases and sales of merchandise in a *perpetual* inventory system.

A perpetual inventory system uses an *inventory subsidiary ledger*. This ledger provides company personnel with up-to-date information about each type of product that the company buys and sells, including the per-unit cost and the number of units purchased, sold, and currently on hand.

To illustrate the perpetual inventory system, we follow specific items of merchandise through the operating cycle of Computer City, a retail store. The transactions comprising this illustration are as follows:

Sept. 1 Purchased 10 Regent 21-inch computer monitors on account from Okawa Wholesale Co. The monitors cost $600 each, for a total of $6,000; payment is due in 30 days.

Sept. 7 Sold two monitors on account to RJ Travel Agency at a retail sales price of $1,000 each, for a total of $2,000. Payment is due in 30 days.

Oct. 1 Paid the $6,000 account payable to Okawa Wholesale Co.

Oct. 7 Collected the $2,000 account receivable from RJ Travel Agency.

In addition to a general ledger, Computer City maintains separate subsidiary ledgers for accounts receivable, inventory, and accounts payable.

Purchases of Merchandise Purchases of inventory are recorded at cost. Thus Computer City records its purchase of the 10 computer monitors on September 1 as follows:

Inventory	6,000	
Accounts Payable (Okawa Wholesale Co.)		6,000
Purchased 10 Regent 21-inch computer monitors for $600 each; payment due in 30 days.		

My Notes

Purchase of merchandise: the start of the cycle

The data contained in this entry are posted to the general ledger *and to the subsidiary ledgers*. First, the entry is posted to the Inventory and Accounts Payable controlling accounts in the general ledger. The debit to Inventory also is posted to the Regent 21-inch Monitors account in the inventory subsidiary ledger.[2] The quantity of monitors purchased

---

[1] In some perpetual systems, only the number of *units* sold is recorded at the time of sale, and the dollar costs are entered at a later date—perhaps monthly. Such variations in perpetual systems are discussed in Chapter 8.

[2] In journal entries, it is common practice to indicate specific suppliers and customers using a parenthetical note following the account title Accounts Payable or Accounts Receivable. Similar notations usually are *not* used with the Inventory account, because *many different types of products* may be purchased or sold in a single transaction. The detailed product information used in posting to the inventory ledger is found in the *invoice* (bill) that the seller sends to the buyer.

(10) and the per-unit cost ($600) also are recorded in this subsidiary ledger account. (As shown in Exhibit 6–5.) The credit to Accounts Payable also is posted to the account for Okawa Wholesale Co. in Computer City's accounts payable subsidiary ledger.

Sales of Merchandise The revenue earned in a sales transaction is equal to the *sales price* of the merchandise and is credited to a revenue account entitled Sales. Except in rare circumstances, sales revenue is considered realized when the merchandise is *delivered to the customer*, even if the sale is made on account. Therefore, Computer City will recognize the revenue from the sale to RJ Travel Agency on September 7, as follows:

> **My Notes**
> Entries to record a sale . . .

```
Accounts Receivable (RJ Travel Agency) . . . . . . . . . . . . . . . . . . . . . . . .   2,000
    Sales . . . . . . . . . . . . . . . . . . . . . . . . . . . . . . . . . . . . . . . . . . . . . . . . . . . .         2,000
Sold two Regent 21-inch monitors for $1,000 each;
    payment due in 30 days.
```

The *matching principle* requires that revenue be matched (offset) with all of the costs and expenses incurred in producing that revenue. Therefore, a *second journal entry* is required at the date of sale to record the cost of goods sold.

> **My Notes**
> and the related cost of goods sold

```
Cost of Goods Sold . . . . . . . . . . . . . . . . . . . . . . . . . . . . . . . . . . . . . . . . . .   1,200
    Inventory . . . . . . . . . . . . . . . . . . . . . . . . . . . . . . . . . . . . . . . . . . . . . . .         1,200
To transfer the cost of two Regent 21-inch monitors ($600 each)
    from Inventory to the Cost of Goods Sold account.
```

Notice that this second entry is based on the *cost* of the merchandise to Computer City, not on its retail sales price. The per-unit cost of the Regent monitors ($600) was determined from the inventory subsidiary ledger (see Exhibit 6–5).

Both of the journal entries relating to this sales transaction are posted to Computer City's general ledger. In addition, the $2,000 debit to Accounts Receivable (first entry) is posted to the account for RJ Travel Agency in the accounts receivable ledger. The credit to Inventory (second entry) also is posted to the Regent 21-inch Monitors account in the inventory subsidiary ledger.

Payment of Accounts Payable to Suppliers The payment to Okawa Wholesale Co. on October 1 is recorded as follows:

> **My Notes**
> Payment of an account payable

```
Accounts Payable (Okawa Wholesale Co.) . . . . . . . . . . . . . . . . . . . . . . .   6,000
    Cash . . . . . . . . . . . . . . . . . . . . . . . . . . . . . . . . . . . . . . . . . . . . . . . . . .         6,000
Paid account payable.
```

Both portions of this entry are posted to the general ledger. In addition, payment of the account payable is entered in the Okawa Wholesale Co. account in the Computer City's accounts payable subsidiary ledger.

Collection of Accounts Receivable from Customers On October 7, collection of the account receivable from RJ Travel Agency is recorded as follows:

> **My Notes**
> Collection of an account receivable

```
Cash . . . . . . . . . . . . . . . . . . . . . . . . . . . . . . . . . . . . . . . . . . . . . . . . . . . . . .   2,000
    Accounts Receivable (RJ Travel Agency) . . . . . . . . . . . . . . . . . . . . .         2,000
Collected an account receivable from a credit customer.
```

Both portions of this entry are posted to the general ledger; the credit to Accounts Receivable also is posted to the RJ Travel Agency account in the accounts receivable ledger.

Collection of the cash from RJ Travel Agency completes Computer City's operating cycle with respect to these two units of merchandise.

The Inventory Subsidiary Ledger An inventory subsidiary ledger includes a separate account for each type of product in the company's inventory. Computer City's subsidiary inventory record for Regent monitors is illustrated in Exhibit 6–5.

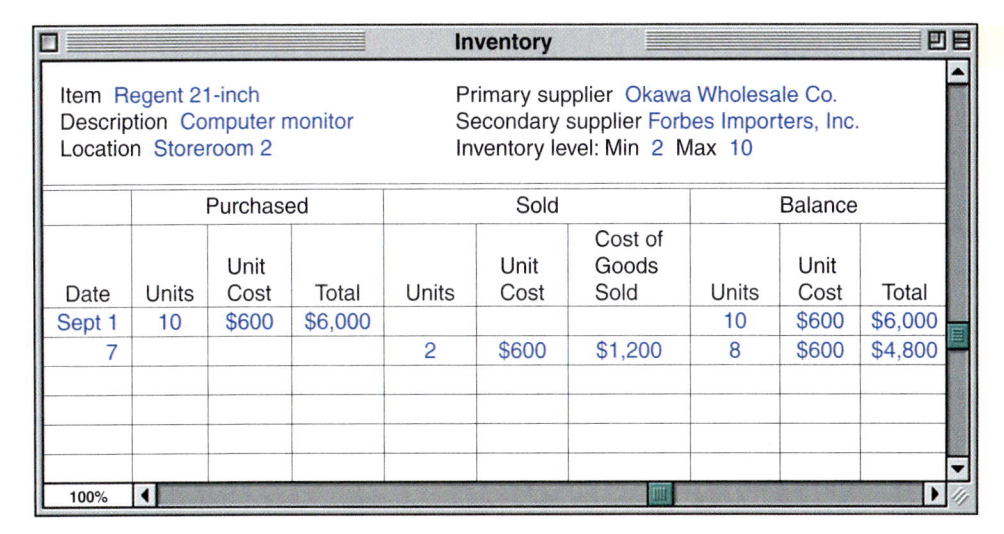

Exhibit 6–5

INVENTORY SUBSIDIARY LEDGER

Inventory

Item: Regent 21-inch
Description: Computer monitor
Location: Storeroom 2

Primary supplier: Okawa Wholesale Co.
Secondary supplier: Forbes Importers, Inc.
Inventory level: Min 2 Max 10

	Purchased			Sold			Balance		
Date	Units	Unit Cost	Total	Units	Unit Cost	Cost of Goods Sold	Units	Unit Cost	Total
Sept 1	10	$600	$6,000				10	$600	$6,000
7				2	$600	$1,200	8	$600	$4,800

When Regent 21-inch monitors are purchased, the quantity, unit cost, and total cost are entered in this subsidiary ledger account. When any of these monitors are sold, the number of units, unit cost, and total cost of the units sold also are recorded in this subsidiary ledger account. After each purchase or sales transaction, the Balance columns are updated to show the quantity, unit cost, and total cost of the monitors still on hand.[3]

An inventory ledger provides useful information to a variety of company personnel. A few examples of the company personnel who utilize this information on a daily basis are the following:

- *Sales managers* use the inventory ledger to see at a glance which products are selling quickly and which are not.
- *Accounting personnel* use these records to determine the unit costs of merchandise sold.
- *Sales personnel* use this subsidiary ledger to determine the quantities of specific products currently on hand and the physical location of this merchandise.
- *Employees responsible for ordering merchandise* refer to the inventory ledger to determine when specific products should be reordered, the quantities to order, and the names of major suppliers.

Taking a Physical Inventory

The basic characteristic of the perpetual inventory system is that the Inventory account is *continuously updated* for all purchases and sales of merchandise. When a *physical inventory* is taken, management uses the inventory ledger to determine on a product-by-product basis whether inventory on hand corresponds to the amount indicated in the

---

[3] In our illustration, all of the Regent monitors were purchased on the same date and have the same unit cost. Often a company's inventory of a given product includes units acquired at several *different* per-unit costs. This situation is addressed in Chapter 8.

inventory subsidiary ledger. Over time normal inventory shrinkage may cause some discrepancies between the quantities of merchandise shown in the inventory records and the quantities actually on hand. **Inventory shrinkage** refers to unrecorded decreases in inventory resulting from such factors as breakage, spoilage, employee theft, and shoplifting.

In order to ensure the accuracy of their perpetual inventory records, most large corporations are required to take a *complete physical count* of the merchandise on hand at least once a year. This procedure is called **taking a physical inventory**, and it usually is performed near year-end.

Once the quantity of merchandise on hand has been determined by a physical count, the per-unit costs in the inventory ledger accounts are used to determine the total cost of the inventory. The Inventory controlling account and the accounts in the inventory subsidiary ledger then are *adjusted* to the quantities and dollar amounts indicated by the physical inventory.

To illustrate, assume that at year-end the Inventory controlling account and inventory subsidiary ledger of Computer City both show an inventory with a cost of $72,200. A physical count, however, reveals that some of the merchandise listed in the accounting records is missing; the items actually on hand have a total cost of $70,000. Computer City would make the following adjusting entry to correct its Inventory controlling account:

My Notes

Adjusting for inventory shrinkage

Cost of Goods Sold	2,200	
Inventory		2,200
To adjust the perpetual inventory records to reflect the results of the year-end physical count.		

Computer City also will adjust the appropriate accounts in its inventory subsidiary ledger to reflect the quantities indicated by the physical count.

Reasonable amounts of inventory shrinkage are viewed as a normal cost of doing business and simply are debited to the Cost of Goods Sold account, as illustrated above.[4]

Closing Entries in a Perpetual Inventory System

As explained and illustrated in the previous chapters, revenue and expense accounts are *closed* at the end of each accounting period. A merchandising business with a perpetual inventory system makes closing entries that parallel those of a service-type business. The Sales account is a revenue account and is closed into the Income Summary account along with other revenue accounts. The Cost of Goods Sold account is closed into the Income Summary account in the same manner as the other expense accounts.

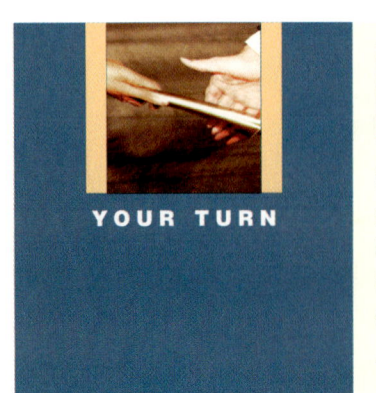

YOUR TURN

You as the Inventory Manager for Computer City

Assume you are the inventory manager for the largest store owned by Computer City. You are very busy one day when Fran Mally, an auditor from the accounting firm employed by Computer City, arrives and asks for assistance in determining the store's physical inventory on hand. You are overwhelmed with work and tell Fran that you do not have the time or the personnel needed to assist her in this task. You are also annoyed because you were not told that she was coming today to complete the physical inventory count. What should you do?

*Our answer is on page 260.

---

[4] If a large inventory shortage is caused by an event such as a fire or theft, the cost of the missing or damaged merchandise may be debited to a special loss account, such as Fire Loss. In the income statement, a loss is deducted from revenue in the same manner as an expense.

PERIODIC INVENTORY SYSTEMS

A **periodic inventory system** is an *alternative* to a perpetual inventory system. In a periodic inventory system, no effort is made to keep up-to-date records of either the inventory or the cost of goods sold. Instead, these amounts are determined only periodically—usually at the end of each year.

Operation of a Periodic Inventory System

A traditional periodic inventory system operates as follows. When merchandise is purchased, its cost is debited to an account entitled *Purchases,* rather than to the Inventory account. When merchandise is sold, an entry is made to recognize the sales revenue, but *no entry* is made to record the cost of goods sold or to reduce the balance of the Inventory account. As the inventory records are not updated as transactions occur, there is no inventory subsidiary ledger.

The foundation of the periodic inventory system is the taking of a *complete physical inventory* at year-end. This physical count determines the amount of inventory appearing in the balance sheet. The cost of goods sold for the entire year then is determined by a short computation.

LO 4 Explain how a *periodic* inventory system operates.

Data for an Illustration To illustrate, assume that one of Computer City's suppliers, Wagner Office Products, has a periodic inventory system. At December 31, 2002, the following information is available:

1. The inventory on hand at the end of *2001* cost $14,000.
2. During *2002,* purchases of merchandise for resale to customers totaled $130,000.
3. Inventory on hand at the end of *2002* cost $12,000.

The inventories at the end of 2001 and at the end of 2002 were determined by taking a complete physical inventory at (or very near) each year-end. (Because the Inventory account was not updated as transactions occurred during 2002, it still shows a balance of $14,000—the inventory on hand at the *beginning* of the year.)

The $130,000 cost of merchandise purchased during 2002 was recorded in the Purchases account.

Recording Purchases of Merchandise Wagner Office Products made many purchases of merchandise during 2002. The entry to record the first of these purchases is as follows:

Jan. 6	Purchases 2,000	
	Accounts Payable (Ink Jet Solutions)	2,000
	Purchased inventory on account; payment due in 30 days.	

This entry was posted to the Purchases and Accounts Payable accounts in the general ledger. The credit portion also was posted to the account for Ink Jet Solutions in Wagner's accounts payable subsidiary ledger. The debit to Purchases was *not* "double-posted," as there is *no inventory subsidiary ledger* in a periodic system.

Computing the Cost of Goods Sold The year-end inventory is determined by taking a complete physical count of the merchandise on hand. Once the ending inventory is known, the cost of goods sold for the entire year can be determined by a short computation. The following computation uses the three information items for Wagner Office Products just presented:

My Notes

Computation of the cost of goods sold

Inventory (beginning of the year) (1)	$ 14,000
Add: Purchases (2)	130,000
Cost of goods available for sale	$144,000
Less: Inventory (end of the year) (3)	12,000
Cost of goods sold	$132,000

Recording Inventory and the Cost of Goods Sold Wagner has now determined its inventory at the end of 2002 and its cost of goods sold for the year. But neither of these amounts has yet been recorded in the company's accounting records.

In a periodic system, the ending inventory and the cost of goods sold are recorded during the company's year-end *closing procedures*. (The term *closing procedures* refers to the end-of-period adjusting and closing entries.)

Closing Process in a Periodic Inventory System

There are several different ways of recording the ending inventory and cost of goods sold in a periodic system, but they all produce the same results. One approach is to *create* a Cost of Goods Sold account with the proper balance as part of the closing process. Once this account has been created, the company can complete its closing procedures in the same manner as if a perpetual inventory system had been in use.

Creating a Cost of Goods Sold Account A Cost of Goods Sold account is created with two special closing entries. The first entry creates the new account by bringing together the costs contributing toward the cost of goods sold. The second entry adjusts the Cost of Goods Sold account to its proper balance and records the ending inventory in the Inventory account.

The costs contributing to the cost of goods sold include (1) beginning inventory and (2) purchases made during the year. These costs are brought together by closing both the Inventory account (which contains its beginning-of-the-year balance) and the Purchases account into a new account entitled Cost of Goods Sold. This year-end closing entry is:

My Notes

Creating a Cost of Goods Sold account . . .

Dec. 31	Cost of Goods Sold	144,000	
	Inventory (beginning balance)		14,000
	Purchases		130,000
	To close the accounts contributing to the cost of goods sold for the year.		

Wagner's Cost of Goods Sold account now includes the cost of all goods *available for sale* during the year. Of course, not all of these goods were sold; the physical inventory taken at the end of 2002 shows that merchandise costing $12,000 is still on hand. Therefore, a second closing entry is made transferring the cost of merchandise still on hand *out* of the Cost of Goods Sold account and *into* the Inventory account. For Wagner, this second closing entry is:

My Notes

. . . and adjusting its balance

Dec. 31	Inventory (year-end balance)	12,000	
	Cost of Goods Sold		12,000
	To reduce the balance of the Cost of Goods Sold account by the cost of merchandise still on hand at year-end.		

With these two entries, Wagner has created a Cost of Goods Sold account with a balance of $132,000 ($144,000 − $12,000) and has brought its Inventory account up-to-date.

Completing the Closing Process Wagner may now complete its closing process in the same manner as a company using a perpetual inventory system. The company will make the usual four closing entries, closing the (1) revenue accounts, (2) expense accounts (including Cost of Goods Sold), (3) Income Summary account, and (4) Dividends account.

Comparison of Perpetual and Periodic Inventory Systems

Exhibit 6–6 provides a comparison of the way in which various events are recorded in perpetual and periodic systems. Perpetual systems are used when management needs information throughout the year about inventory levels and gross profit. Periodic systems are used when the primary goals are to develop annual data and to minimize record-keeping requirements. A single business may use *different inventory systems* to account for *different types of merchandise*.

Exhibit 6–6

SUMMARY OF THE JOURNAL ENTRIES MADE IN PERPETUAL AND PERIODIC INVENTORY SYSTEMS

Event	Perpetual System	Periodic System

Acquiring merchandise inventory	Inventory ... xxx
	    Accounts Payable (or Cash) ... xxx
	To record the purchase of merchandise inventory.
		Purchases ... xxx
		    Accounts Payable (or Cash) .. xxx
		To record the purchase of merchandise inventory.

Sale of merchandise inventory	Accounts Receivable (or Cash) ... xxx
	    Sales ... xxx
	To record the sale of merchandise inventory.
	Cost of Goods Sold ... xxx
	    Inventory ... xxx
	To update Cost of Goods Sold and Inventory accounts.
		Accounts Receivable (or Cash) ... xxx
		    Sales ... xxx
		To record the sale of merchandise inventory.
		No entry at the time of sale is made in a periodic system to update the Cost of Goods Sold and Inventory accounts.

Settlement of Accounts Payable to suppliers	Accounts Payable ... xxx
	    Cash ... xxx
	To record payment for merchandise inventory purchased on account.
		Accounts Payable ... xxx
		    Cash ... xxx
		To record payment for merchandise inventory purchased on account.

Collections from credit customers	Cash ... xxx
	    Accounts Receivable ... xxx
	To record cash collections from credit customers.
		Cash ... xxx
		    Accounts Receivable ... xxx
		To record cash collections from credit customers.

Creating year-end balances for Cost of Goods Sold and Inventory accounts	No entry necessary. Cost of Goods Sold and Inventory accounts should both reflect year-end balances in a perpetual system. If a year-end physical count reveals less inventory on hand than reported in the Inventory account, the following entry is needed to record inventory shrinkage:
	Cost of Goods Sold ... xxx
	    Inventory (shrinkage amount) ... xxx
	To reduce year-end inventory balance for shrinkage.
		Cost of Goods Sold ... xxx
		    Inventory (beginning bal.) ... xxx
		    Purchases ... xxx
		To close the Purchases and Inventory balances to the Cost of Goods Sold account.
		Inventory (ending balance) ... xxx
		    Cost of Goods Sold ... xxx
		To create the year-end balance in the Inventory account.

Note: In a periodic inventory system, the Cost of Goods Sold account is both debited and credited to create its year-end balance.

Who Uses Perpetual Systems? When management or employees *need up-to-date information about inventory levels,* there is no substitute for a perpetual inventory system. Almost all manufacturing companies use perpetual systems. These businesses need current information to coordinate their inventories of raw materials with their production schedules. Most large merchandising companies—and many small ones—also use perpetual systems.

In the days when all accounting records were maintained by hand, businesses that sold many types of low-cost products had no choice but to use periodic inventory systems. A **Wal-Mart** store, for example, may sell several thousand items *per hour*. Imagine the difficulty of keeping a perpetual inventory system up-to-date if the records were maintained by hand. But with today's *point-of-sale terminals* and *bar-coded merchandise,* many high-volume retailers now use perpetual inventory systems. In fact, **Wal-Mart** has been a leader among retailers in developing perpetual inventory systems.

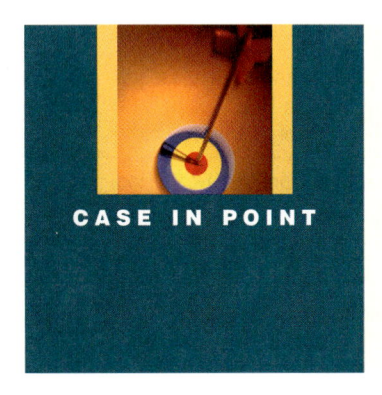

AP Wide World Photo

CASE IN POINT

Wal-Mart, referred to as the company Sam Walton built, is the world's largest retailer. By diversifying from its original discount stores to include **Sam's Clubs** and Super Stores, **Wal-Mart** has fueled its retail engine. International expansion includes 174 stores in Canada, 429 in Mexico, 241 in the United Kingdom, 94 German stores, 20 stores in Brazil, 11 Chinese stores, 11 stores in Argentina, and 6 South Korean stores. According to a recent annual report, 17 percent of total sales came from international locations, and international sales grew at 41 percent. **Wal-Mart** employs nearly 1,000,000 associates in the United States, and nearly 300,000 internationally.

Perpetual inventory systems are not limited to businesses with point-of-sale terminals. Many small businesses with manual accounting systems also use perpetual inventory systems. However, these businesses may update their inventory records on a weekly or a monthly basis, rather than at the time of each sales transaction.

Whether accounting records are maintained manually or by computer, most businesses use perpetual inventory systems in accounting for products with a *high per-unit cost*. Examples include automobiles, heavy machinery, electronic equipment, home appliances, and jewelry. Management has a greater interest in keeping track of inventory when the merchandise is expensive. Also, sales volume usually is low enough that a perpetual system can be used, even if accounting records are maintained by hand.

Who Uses Periodic Systems? Periodic systems are used when the need for current information about inventories and sales *does not justify the cost* of maintaining a perpetual system. In a small retail store, for example, the owner may be so familiar with the inventory that formal perpetual inventory records are unnecessary. Most businesses—large and small—use periodic systems for inventories that are *immaterial* in dollar amount, or when management has little interest in the quantities on hand. As stated previously, businesses that sell many low-cost items and have manual accounting systems sometimes have no choice but to use the periodic method.

CASE IN POINT

Foodtown is a small grocery store in Lewisburg, Pennsylvania. Sales are recorded on a single cash register at the checkout stand. The daily register tapes show only the sales prices of the items sold. Even if **Foodtown**'s owner was willing to spend all night updating his inventory records, he has no place to start. His accounting system does not indicate the types or costs of products sold during the day.

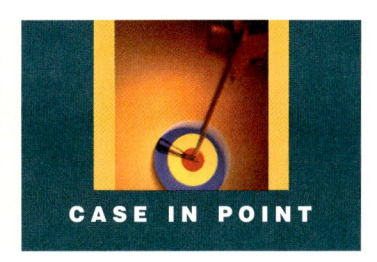

Selecting an Inventory System

Accountants—and business managers—often must select an inventory system appropriate for a particular situation. Some of the factors usually considered in these decisions are listed in Exhibit 6–7.

LO 5 Discuss the factors to be considered in selecting an inventory system.

Exhibit 6–7

FACTORS INFLUENCING CHOICE OF INVENTORY SYSTEM

Factors Suggesting a Perpetual Inventory System	Factors Suggesting a Periodic Inventory System
Large company with professional management.	Small company, run by owner.
Management and employees wanting information about items in inventory and the quantities of specific products that are selling.	Accounting records of inventories and specific product sales not needed in daily operations; such information developed primarily for use in annual income tax returns.
Items in inventory with a high per-unit cost.	Inventory with many different kinds of low-cost items.
Low volume of sales transactions or a computerized accounting system (for example, point-of-sale terminals).	High volume of sales transactions and a manual accounting system.
	Lack of full-time accounting personnel.
Merchandise stored at multiple locations or in warehouses separate from the sales sites.	All merchandise stored at the sales site (for example, in the store).

The Trend in Today's Business World Advances in technology are quickly extending the use of perpetual inventory systems to more businesses and more types of inventory. This trend is certain to continue. Throughout this textbook, you may assume that a *perpetual inventory system* is in use unless we specifically state otherwise.

You as a Buyer for a Retail Business

Assume you are in charge of purchasing merchandise for **Ace Hardware Stores**. You are currently making a decision about the purchase of barbecue grills for sale during the upcoming summer season. You must decide how many of each brand and type of grill to order. Describe the types of accounting information that would be useful in making this decision and where this information might be found.

Spencer Grant/PhotoEdit

YOUR TURN

*Our comments appear on page 260.

MODIFYING AN ACCOUNTING SYSTEM

LO 6
Define *special journals* and explain their usefulness.

Throughout this textbook we illustrate the effects of many transactions using the format of a two-column *general journal*. This format is ideal for textbook illustrations, as it allows us to concisely show the effects of *any type* of business transactions.

But while general journal entries are useful for our purposes, they are not the most efficient way for a business to record routine transactions. A supermarket, for example, may sell 10,000 to 15,000 items *per hour*. Clearly, it would not be practical to make a general journal entry to record each of these sales transactions. Therefore, most businesses use *special journals,* rather than a general journal, to record *routine transactions that occur frequently*.

Special Journals Provide Speed and Efficiency

A **special journal** is an accounting record or device designed to record *a specific type of routine transaction quickly and efficiently.*

Some special journals are maintained by hand. An example is the *check register* in your personal checkbook. If properly maintained, this special journal provides an efficient record of all cash disbursements made by check.

But many special journals are highly automated. Consider the **point-of-sale (POS) terminals** that you see in supermarkets and large retail stores. These devices record sales transactions and the related cost of goods sold as quickly as the bar-coded merchandise can be passed over the scanner.

Relative to the general journal, the special journals offer the following advantages:

- Transactions are recorded faster and more efficiently.
- Many special journals may be in operation at one time, further increasing the company's ability to handle a large volume of transactions.
- Automation may reduce the risk of errors.
- Employees maintaining special journals generally do not need expertise in accounting.
- The recording of transactions may be an automatic side effect of other basic business activities, such as collecting cash from customers.

Most businesses use separate special journals to record repetitive transactions such as sales of merchandise, cash receipts, cash payments, purchases of merchandise on account, and payrolls. There are no rules for the design or content of special journals. Rather, they are tailored to suit the needs, activities, and resources of the particular business organization.

Let us stress that the *accounting principles* used in special journals are the *same* as those used for transactions recorded in a general journal. The differences lie in the *recording techniques,* not in the information that is recorded.

Remember also that special journals are *highly specialized* in terms of the transactions they can record. Thus every business still needs a general journal to record transactions that do not fit into any of its special journals, including, for example, adjusting entries, closing entries, and unusual events such as a loss sustained from a fire.

TRANSACTIONS RELATING TO PURCHASES

LO 7
Account for additional merchandising transactions related to purchases and sales.

In addition to the basic transactions illustrated and explained in this chapter, merchandising companies must account for a variety of additional transactions relating to purchases of merchandise. Examples include discounts offered for prompt payment, merchandise returns, and transportation costs. In our discussion of these transactions, we continue to assume the use of a *perpetual* inventory system.

Credit Terms and Cash Discounts

Manufacturers and wholesalers normally sell their products to merchandisers *on account*. The credit terms are stated in the seller's bill, or *invoice*. One common example of credit terms is "net 30 days," or "n/30," meaning full payment is due in 30 days. Another common form of credit terms is "10 eom," meaning payment is due 10 days after the end of the month in which the purchase occurred.

Manufacturers and wholesalers usually allow their customers 30 or 60 days in which to pay for credit purchases. Frequently, however, sellers offer their customers a small discount to encourage earlier payment.

Perhaps the most common credit terms offered by manufacturers and wholesalers are *2/10, n/30*. This expression is read "2, 10, net 30," and means that full payment is due in 30 days, but that the buyer may take a *2% discount* if payment is made within 10 days. The period during which the discount is available is termed the *discount period*. Because the discount provides an incentive for the customer to make an early cash payment, it is called a *cash discount*. Buyers, however, often refer to these discounts as *purchase discounts,* while sellers frequently call them *sales discounts*.

Most well-managed companies have a policy of taking advantage of all cash discounts available on purchases of merchandise.[5] These companies initially record purchases of merchandise at the *net cost*—that is, the invoice price *minus* any available discount. After all, this is the amount that the company expects to pay.

To illustrate, assume that on November 3 Computer City purchases 100 spreadsheet programs from PC Products. The cost of these programs is $100 each, for a total of $10,000. However, PC Products offers credit terms of 2/10, n/30. If Computer City pays for this purchase within the discount period, it will have to pay only *$9,800,* or 98% of the full invoice price. Therefore, Computer City will record this purchase as follows:

Inventory	9,800	
Accounts Payable (PC Products)		9,800
To record purchase of 100 spreadsheet programs at net cost ($100 × 98% × 100 units).		

My Notes

Purchase recorded at net cost

If the invoice is paid within the discount period, Computer City simply records payment of a $9,800 account payable.

Through oversight or carelessness, Computer City might fail to make payment within the discount period. In this event, Computer City must pay PC Products the entire invoice price of *$10,000,* rather than the recorded liability of $9,800. The journal entry to record payment *after the discount period*—on, say, December 3—is:

Accounts Payable (PC Products)	9,800	
Purchase Discounts Lost	200	
Cash		10,000
To record payment of invoice after expiration of discount period.		

My Notes

Recording the loss of a cash discount

Notice that the $200 paid above the $9,800 recorded amount is debited to an account entitled Purchase Discounts Lost. Purchase Discounts Lost is an *expense account*. The only benefit to Computer City from this $200 expenditure was a *20-day delay* in paying an account payable. Thus the lost purchase discount is basically a *finance charge,* similar to interest expense. In an income statement, finance charges usually are classified as nonoperating expenses.

The fact that purchase discounts *not taken* are recorded in a separate expense account is the primary reason why a company should record purchases of merchandise at *net*

---

[5] The terms 2/10, n/30 offer the buyer a 2% discount for paying 20 days prior to when the full amount is due. Saving 2% over only 20 days is equivalent to earning an annual rate of return of more than 36% (2% × 365/20 = 36.5%). Thus, taking cash discounts represents an excellent investment opportunity. Most companies take advantage of all cash discounts, even if they must borrow the necessary cash from a bank to make payment within the discount period.

cost. The use of a Purchase Discounts Lost account immediately brings to management's attention any failure to take advantage of the cash discounts offered by suppliers.

Recording Purchases at Gross Invoice Price As an alternative to recording purchases at net cost, some companies record merchandise purchases at the gross (total) invoice price. If payment is made within the discount period, these companies must record the amount of the purchase discount *taken*.

To illustrate, assume that Computer City followed a policy of recording purchases at gross invoice price. The entry on November 3 to record the purchase from PC Products would have been:

My Notes

Purchases recorded at gross price

Inventory	10,000	
Accounts Payable (PC Products)		10,000
To record purchase of 100 spreadsheet programs at gross invoice price ($100 × 100 units).		

If payment is made within the discount period, Computer City will discharge this $10,000 account payable by paying only $9,800. The entry will be:

My Notes

Buyer records discounts taken

Accounts Payable (PC Products)	10,000	
Cash		9,800
Purchase Discounts Taken		200
Paid a $10,000 invoice within the discount period; taking a 2% purchase discount.		

Purchase Discounts Taken is treated as a reduction in the cost of goods sold.

Both the net cost and gross price methods are widely used and produce substantially the same results in financial statements.[6]

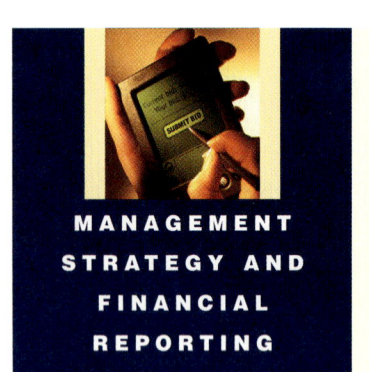

MANAGEMENT STRATEGY AND FINANCIAL REPORTING

A shortcoming of the gross price method as compared to the net cost method for valuing inventory is that it does not direct management's attention to discounts lost. Instead these discounts are buried in the costs assigned to inventory. Management can use financial reporting policies to motivate the purchasing staff to take advantage of purchase discounts when possible. By recording inventory with the net cost method, management can highlight the success of their purchasing efforts to obtain the lowest possible costs for purchased inventory. Because of the advantage of the net cost method, it is the approach recommended by the authors of this textbook.

Returns of Unsatisfactory Merchandise

On occasion, a buyer may find the purchased merchandise unsatisfactory and want to return it to the seller for a refund. Most sellers permit such returns.

To illustrate, assume that on November 9 Computer City returns to PC Products five of the spreadsheet programs purchased on November 3, because these programs were not properly labeled. As Computer City has not yet paid for this merchandise, the return will reduce the amount that Computer City owes PC Products. The gross invoice price of the returned merchandise was $500 ($100 per program). Assume that Computer City

---

[6] The net cost method values the ending inventory at net cost, whereas the gross cost method shows this inventory at gross invoice price. This difference, however, is usually *immaterial*.

records purchases at *net cost*. Therefore, these spreadsheet programs are carried in Computer City's inventory subsidiary ledger at a per-unit cost of *$98,* or $490 for the five programs being returned. The entry to record this purchase return is:

Accounts Payable (PC Products)	490	
Inventory		490
Returned five mislabeled spreadsheet programs to supplier. Net cost of the returned items, $490 ($100 × 98% × 5 units).		

My Notes

Return is based on recorded acquisition cost

The reduction in inventory must also be recorded in the subsidiary ledger accounts.

Transportation Costs on Purchases

The purchaser sometimes may pay the costs of having the purchased merchandise delivered to its premises. Transportation costs relating to the *acquisition* of inventory, or any other asset, are *not expenses* of the current period; rather, these charges are *part of the cost of the asset* being acquired.[7] If the purchaser is able to associate transportation costs with specific products, these costs should be debited directly to the Inventory account as part of the cost of the merchandise.

Often, many different products arrive in a single shipment. In such cases, it may be impractical for the purchaser to determine the amount of the total transportation cost applicable to each product. For this reason, many companies follow the convenient policy of debiting all transportation costs on inbound shipments of merchandise to an account entitled *Transportation-in*. The dollar amount of transportation-in usually is too small to show separately in the financial statements. Therefore, it is often simply added to the amount reported in the income statement as cost of goods sold.

This treatment of transportation costs is not entirely consistent with the *matching principle*. Some of the transportation costs apply to merchandise still in inventory rather than to goods sold during the current period. We have mentioned, however, that transportation costs are relatively small in dollar amount. The accounting principle of *materiality,* therefore, usually justifies accounting for these costs in the most convenient manner.

TRANSACTIONS RELATING TO SALES

Credit terms and merchandise returns also affect the amount of sales revenue earned by the seller. To the extent that credit customers take advantage of cash discounts or return merchandise for a refund, the seller's revenue is reduced. Thus revenue shown in the income statement of a merchandising concern is often called *net sales*.

The term **net sales** means total sales revenue *minus* sales returns and allowances and *minus* sales discounts. The partial income statement in Exhibit 6–8 illustrates this relationship.

COMPUTER CITY
Partial Income Statement
For the Year Ended December 31, 2002

Revenue:		
Sales		$912,000
Less: Sales returns and allowances	$8,000	
Sales discounts	4,000	12,000
Net sales		$900,000

Exhibit 6–8

PARTIAL INCOME STATEMENT

---

[7] The cost of an asset includes all reasonable and necessary costs of getting the asset to an appropriate location and putting it into usable condition.

The details of this computation seldom are shown in an actual income statement. The normal practice is to begin the income statement with the amount of net sales.

Sales Returns and Allowances

Most merchandising companies allow customers to obtain a refund by returning any merchandise considered to be unsatisfactory. If the merchandise has only minor defects, customers sometimes agree to keep the merchandise if an *allowance* (reduction) is made in the sales price.

Under the perpetual inventory system, two entries are needed to record the sale of merchandise: one to recognize the revenue earned and the other to transfer the cost of the merchandise from the Inventory account to Cost of Goods Sold. If some of the merchandise is returned, both of these entries are partially reversed.

First, let us consider the effects on revenue of granting either a refund or an allowance. Both refunds and allowances have the effect of nullifying previously recorded sales and reducing the amount of revenue earned by the business. This journal entry reduces sales revenue as the result of a sales return (or allowance):

My Notes

A sales return reverses recorded revenue . . .

Sales Returns and Allowances	200	
Accounts Receivable (or Cash)		200
Customer returned merchandise purchased on account for $200. Allowed customer full credit for returned merchandise.		

Sales Returns and Allowances is a **contra-revenue account**—that is, it is deducted from gross sales revenue as a step in determining net sales.

Why use a separate Sales Returns and Allowances account rather than merely debiting the Sales account? The answer is that using a separate contra-revenue account enables management to see both the total amount of sales *and* the amount of sales returns. The relationship between these amounts gives management an indication of *customer satisfaction* with the merchandise.

If merchandise is returned by the customer, a second entry is made to remove the cost of this merchandise from the Cost of Goods Sold account and restore it to the inventory records. This entry is:

My Notes

and the recorded cost of goods sold

Inventory	160	
Cost of Goods Sold		160
To restore in the Inventory account the cost of merchandise returned by a customer.		

Notice that this entry is based on the *cost* of the returned merchandise to the seller, *not on its sales price*. (This entry is not necessary when a sales *allowance* is granted to a customer who keeps the merchandise.)

Special accounts are maintained in the inventory subsidiary ledger for returned merchandise. Often this merchandise will be returned to the supplier or sold to a damaged-goods liquidator rather than being offered again for sale to the company's regular customers.[8]

Sales Discounts

We have explained that sellers frequently offer cash discounts, such as 2/10, n/30, to encourage customers to make early payments for purchases on account.

---

[8] An inventory of returned merchandise should not be valued in the accounting records at a cost that exceeds its *net realizable value*. The possible need to write down the carrying value of inventory is discussed in Chapter 8.

Sellers and buyers account for cash discounts quite differently. To the seller, the cost associated with cash discounts is not the discounts *lost* when payments are delayed, but rather the discounts *taken* by customers who do pay within the discount period. Therefore, sellers design their accounting systems to measure the sales discounts *taken* by their customers. To achieve this goal, the seller records the sale and the related account receivable at the *gross* (full) invoice price.

To illustrate, assume that Computer City sells merchandise to the Highlander Pub for $1,000, offering terms of 2/10, n/30. The sales revenue is recorded at the full invoice price, as follows:

Accounts Receivable (Highlander Pub)	1,000	
Sales		1,000
Sold merchandise on account. Invoice price, $1,000; terms, 2/10, n/30.		

My Notes

Sales are recorded at the gross sales price

If the Highlander Pub makes payment after the discount period has expired, Computer City records the receipt of $1,000 cash in full payment of this account receivable. If it pays *within* the discount period, however, the pub will pay only *$980* to settle its account. In this case, Computer City will record the receipt of the pub's payment as follows:

Cash	980	
Sales Discounts	20	
Accounts Receivable (Highlander Pub)		1,000
Collected a $1,000 account receivable from a customer who took a 2% discount for early payment.		

My Notes

Seller records discounts taken by customers

Sales Discounts is another contra-revenue account. In computing net sales, sales discounts are deducted from gross sales along with any sales returns and allowances. (If the customer has returned part of the merchandise, a discount may be taken only on the gross amount owed *after* the return.)

Contra-revenue accounts have much in common with expense accounts; both are deducted from gross revenue in determining net income, and both have debit balances. Thus contra-revenue accounts (Sales Returns and Allowances and Sales Discounts) are closed to the Income Summary account *in the same manner as expense accounts*.

Delivery Expenses

If the seller incurs any costs in delivering merchandise to the customer, these costs are debited to an expense account entitled Delivery Expense. In an income statement, delivery expense is classified as a regular operating expense, not as part of the cost of goods sold.

Accounting for Sales Taxes

Sales taxes are levied by many states and cities on retail sales.[9] Sales taxes actually are imposed on the consumer, not on the seller. However, the seller must collect the tax, file tax returns at times specified by law, and remit to governmental agencies the taxes collected.

For cash sales, sales tax is collected from the customer at the time of the sales transaction. For credit sales, the sales tax is included in the amount charged to the customer's account. The liability to the governmental unit for sales taxes may be recorded at the time the sale is made, as shown in the following journal entry:

---

[9] Sales taxes are applicable only when merchandise is sold to the *final consumer;* thus no sales taxes are normally levied when manufacturers or wholesalers sell merchandise to retailers.

My Notes

Sales tax recorded at time of sale

```
Cash (or Accounts Receivable) .................................. 1,070
    Sales Tax Payable .........................................        70
    Sales .....................................................     1,000
To record sales of $1,000, subject to 7% sales tax.
```

This approach requires a separate credit entry to the Sales Tax Payable account for each sale. At first glance, this may seem to require an excessive amount of bookkeeping. However, today's point-of-sale terminals automatically record the sales tax liability at the time of each sale.

EVALUATING THE PERFORMANCE OF A MERCHANDISING COMPANY

LO 8 Measure the performance of a merchandising business.

In evaluating the performance of a merchandising business, managers and investors look at more than just net income. Two key measures of past performance and future prospects are trends in the company's *net sales* and *gross profit*.

Net Sales

Most investors and business managers consider the *trend* in net sales to be a key indicator of both past performance and future prospects. Increasing sales suggest the probability of larger profits in future periods. Declining sales, on the other hand, may provide advance warning of financial difficulties.

FINANCIAL ANALYSIS

As a measure of performance, the trend in net sales has some limitations, especially when the company is adding new stores. For these companies, an increase in overall net sales in comparison to the prior year may have resulted solely from sales at the new stores. Sales at existing stores may even be declining. Business managers and investors often focus on measures that adjust for changes in the number of stores from period to period, and on measures of space utilization. These measures include:

1. **Comparable store sales.** Net sales at established stores, excluding new stores opened during the period. Indicates whether customer demand is rising or falling at established locations. (Also called *same-store sales.*)
2. **Sales per square foot of selling space.** A measure of how effectively the company is using its physical facilities (such as floor space or, in supermarkets, shelf space).

Gross Profit Margins

Increasing net sales is *not enough* to ensure increasing profitability. Some products are more profitable than others. In evaluating the profitability of sales transactions, managers and investors keep a close eye on the company's **gross profit margin** (also called *gross profit rate*).

Gross profit margin is the dollar amount of gross profit, expressed as a *percentage* of net sales revenue. Gross profit margins can be computed for the business as a whole, for specific sales departments, and for individual products.

To illustrate the computation of gross profit margin, assume that Computer City has two separate sales departments. One of these departments sells computer hardware, and the other sells software. The sales, cost of goods sold, and gross profit of these departments in 2002 are as follows:

	Hardware Department	Software Department	The Entire Company
Net sales	$400,000	$500,000	$900,000
Cost of goods sold	300,000	240,000	540,000
Gross profit	$100,000	$260,000	$360,000

Assume that two products sold in the Software Department: Report Writer (a word processing program) and Dragon Slayer (a computer game). *Per-unit* information about these products follows:

	Report Writer	Dragon Slayer
Sales price	$100	$50
Cost of goods sold	65	20
Gross profit	$ 35	$30

The Overall Gross Profit Margin The average gross profit margin (gross profit rate) earned by Computer City in 2002 is 40% (gross profit, $360,000, divided by net sales, $900,000 = 40%). But each sales department may have a gross profit margin that differs from that of the business viewed as a whole.

Departmental Gross Profit Margins Departmental profit margins are computed using *departmental* gross profit and net sales information, as follows:

Hardware Department ($100,000 ÷ $400,000)	25%
Software Department ($260,000 ÷ $500,000)	52%

Gross Profit Margins for Individual Products Finally, profit margins can be computed for specific products using *per-unit* amounts:

Report Writer ($35 ÷ $100)	35%
Dragon Slayer ($30 ÷ $50)	60%

Notice that Dragon Slayer has a higher profit margin, even though Report Writer is the more expensive product. This higher profit margin means that *at a given dollar of sales volume* (say, $10,000 in sales) Dragon Slayer is the more profitable product.

Using Information about Gross Profit Margins Investors usually compute companies' overall gross profit rates from one period to the next. High—or increasing—margins generally indicate popular products and successful marketing strategies. A substandard or declining profit margin, on the other hand, often indicates weak customer demand or intense price competition.[10]

---

[10] We discuss the interpretation of gross profit in greater depth in Chapter 14.

CASH EFFECTS Increasing gross margins do not always result in increased cash flows from operations. In fact, a company with increasing gross margins may actually have *negative* operating cash flows if it is experiencing (1) difficulty in collecting outstanding accounts receivable, (2) a buildup of unsold inventory, or (3) rapidly increasing selling and administrative expenses.

Management uses information about departments and products for many purposes. These include setting prices, deciding which products to carry and to advertise, and evaluating the performance of departmental managers. By concentrating sales efforts on the products and departments with the *highest margins,* management usually can increase the company's overall gross profit rate.

CONCLUDING REMARKS

The Overnight Auto Service illustration presented in Chapter 2 through Chapter 5 addressed measurement and reporting issues pertaining to a service-type business. Throughout this chapter, we have had an opportunity to see how merchandising companies measure and report the results for their operations. Many of the illustrations and assignments throughout the remainder of this textbook are based upon merchandising enterprises.

In Chapter 7, we examine accounts receivable and other liquid assets common to merchandisers. In Chapter 8, we focus upon issues related to merchandise inventories. Measurement and reporting issues that pertain primarily to manufacturing companies are generally covered in a subsequent course.

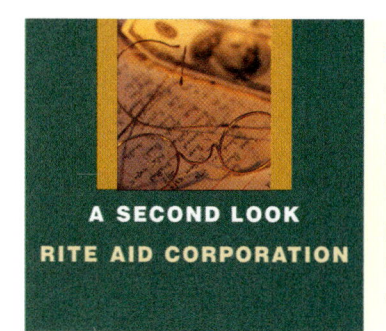

A SECOND LOOK — RITE AID CORPORATION

Rite Aid Corporation, with its 3,700 retail pharmacies, is an excellent example of a merchandising company. Throughout this chapter, we have discussed issues related to how these businesses manage and track inventory sales. Retail enterprises understand the importance of selling inventory quickly and collecting outstanding receivables on a timely basis. In Exercise 6.11, we examine how well **Rite Aid** performed relative to its competitors using performance measures discussed in the chapter. We also illustrate the cyclical nature of inventory and receivables management in terms of a company's operating cycle.

END-OF-CHAPTER REVIEW

SUMMARY OF LEARNING OBJECTIVES

LO 1
Describe the *operating cycle* of a merchandising company.
The operating cycle is the repeating sequence of transactions by which a company generates revenue and cash receipts from customers. In a merchandising company, the operating cycle consists of the following transactions: (1) purchases of merchandise, (2) sale of the merchandise—often on account, and (3) collection of accounts receivable from customers.

LO 2
Define *subsidiary ledgers* and explain their usefulness.
Subsidiary ledgers provide a detailed record of the individual items comprising the balance of a general ledger controlling account. With respect to merchandising transactions, subsidiary ledgers are needed to keep track of the amounts receivable from individual customers, the amounts owed to specific suppliers, and the quantities of specific products in inventory.

LO 3
Account for purchases and sales of merchandise in a *perpetual* inventory system.
In a perpetual inventory system, purchases of merchandise are recorded by debiting the asset Inventory account. Two entries are required to record each sale: one to recognize sales revenue and the second to record the cost of goods sold. This second entry consists of a debit to Cost of Goods Sold and a credit to Inventory.

LO 4
Explain how a *periodic* inventory system operates.
In a periodic system, up-to-date records are *not* maintained for inventory or the cost of goods sold. Thus less record keeping is required than in a perpetual system.

The beginning and ending inventories are determined by taking a complete physical count at each year-end. Purchases are recorded in a Purchases account, and no entries are made to record the cost of individual sales transactions. Instead, the cost of goods sold is determined at year-end by a computation such as the following (dollar amounts are provided only for purposes of example):

Beginning inventory	$ 30,000
Add: Purchases	180,000
Cost of goods available for sale	$210,000
Less: Ending inventory	40,000
Cost of goods sold	$170,000

The amounts of inventory and the cost of goods sold are recorded in the accounting records during the year-end closing procedures.

LO 5
Discuss the factors to be considered in selecting an inventory system.
In general terms, a perpetual system should be used when (1) management and employees need timely information about inventory levels and product sales, and (2) the company has the resources to develop this information at a reasonable cost. A periodic system should be used when the usefulness of current information about inventories does not justify the cost of maintaining a perpetual system.

Perpetual systems are most widely used in large companies with computerized accounting systems and in businesses that sell high-cost merchandise. Periodic systems are most often used in small businesses with manual accounting systems and that sell many types of low-cost merchandise.

LO 6
Define *special journals* and explain their usefulness.
Special journals are accounting records or devices designed to record a specific type of transaction in a highly efficient manner. Because a special journal is used only to record a specific type of transaction, the journal may be located at the transaction site and maintained by employees other than accounting personnel. Thus special journals reduce the time, effort, and cost of recording routine business transactions.

LO 7
Account for additional merchandising transactions related to purchases and sales.
Buyers should record purchases at the net cost and record any cash discounts lost in an expense account. Sellers record sales at the gross sales price and record in a contra-revenue account all cash discounts taken by customers.

The buyer records a purchase return by crediting the Inventory account for the net cost of the returned merchandise. In recording a sales return, the seller makes two entries: one to record Sales Returns and Allowances (a contra-revenue account) for the amount of the refund and the other to transfer the cost of the returned merchandise from the Cost of Goods Sold account back into the Inventory account.

Buyers record transportation charges on purchased merchandise either as part of the cost of the merchandise or directly as part of the cost of goods sold. Sellers view the cost of delivering merchandise to customers as an operating expense.

Sales taxes are collected by retailers from their customers and paid to state and city governments. Thus collecting sales taxes increases the retailer's assets and liabilities. Paying the sales tax to the government is payment of the liability, not an expense.

LO 8
Measure the performance of a merchandising business.
There are numerous measures used to evaluate the performance of merchandising businesses. In this chapter, we introduced three

of these measures: (1) comparable store sales, which helps determine whether customer demand is rising or falling at established locations, (2) sales per square foot of selling space, which is a measure of how effectively a merchandising business is using its facilities to generate revenue, and (3) gross profit percentages, which help users of financial statements gain insight about a company's pricing policies and the demand for its products.

KEY TERMS INTRODUCED OR EMPHASIZED IN CHAPTER 6

comparable store sales (p. 242) A comparison of sales figures at established stores with existing "track records." (Also called *same-store sales*.)

contra-revenue account (p. 240) A debit balance account that is offset against revenue in the income statement. Examples include Sales Discounts and Sales Returns and Allowances.

controlling account (p. 225) A general ledger account that summarizes the content of a specific subsidiary ledger.

cost of goods sold (p. 223) The cost to a merchandising company of the goods it has sold to its customers during the period.

gross profit (p. 223) Net sales revenue minus the cost of goods sold.

gross profit margin (p. 242) Gross profit expressed as a percentage of net sales. Also called *gross profit rate*.

inventory (p. 222) Merchandise intended for resale to customers.

inventory shrinkage (p. 230) The loss of merchandise through such causes as shoplifting, breakage, and spoilage.

net sales (p. 239) Gross sales revenue less sales returns and allowances and sales discounts. The most widely used measure of dollar sales volume; usually the first figure shown in an income statement.

operating cycle (p. 222) The repeating sequence of transactions by which a business generates its revenue and cash receipts from customers.

periodic inventory system (p. 231) An alternative to the perpetual inventory system. It eliminates the need for recording the cost of goods sold as sales occur. However, the amounts of inventory and the cost of goods sold are not known until a complete physical inventory is taken at year-end.

perpetual inventory system (p. 227) A system of accounting for merchandising transactions in which the Inventory and Cost of Goods Sold accounts are kept perpetually up-to-date.

point-of-sale (POS) terminals (p. 236) Electronic cash registers used for computer-based processing of sales transactions. The POS terminal identifies each item of merchandise from its bar code and then automatically records the sale and updates the computer-based inventory records. These terminals permit the use of perpetual inventory systems in many businesses that sell a high volume of low-cost merchandise.

sales per square foot of selling space (p. 242) A measure of efficient use of available space.

special journal (p. 236) An accounting record or device designed for recording large numbers of a particular type of transaction quickly and efficiently. A business may use many different kinds of special journals.

subsidiary ledger (p. 224) A ledger containing separate accounts for each of the items making up the balance of a controlling account in the general ledger. The total of the account balances in a subsidiary ledger are equal to the balance in the general ledger controlling account.

taking a physical inventory (p. 230) The procedure of counting all merchandise on hand and determining its cost.

DEMONSTRATION PROBLEM

STAR-TRACK sells satellite tracking systems for receiving television broadcasts from communications satellites in space. At December 31, 2001, the company's inventory amounted to $44,000. During the first week in January 2002, STAR-TRACK made only one purchase and one sale. These transactions were as follows:

Jan. 3 Sold a tracking system to Mystery Mountain Resort for $20,000 cash. The system consisted of seven different devices, which had a total cost to STAR-TRACK of $11,200.

Jan. 7 Purchased two Model 400 and four Model 800 satellite dishes from Yamaha Corp. The total cost of this purchase amounted to $10,000; terms 2/10, n/30.

STAR-TRACK records purchases of merchandise at net cost. The company has full-time accounting personnel and uses a manual accounting system.

Instructions

a. Briefly describe the operating cycle of a merchandising company.

b. Prepare journal entries to record these transactions, assuming that STAR-TRACK uses a perpetual inventory system.

c. Explain what information in part **b** should be posted to subsidiary ledger accounts.

Demonstration Problem

d. Compute the balance in the Inventory controlling account at January 7.
e. Prepare journal entries to record the two transactions, assuming that STAR-TRACK uses a *periodic* inventory system.
f. Compute the cost of goods sold for the first week of January, assuming use of the periodic system. As the amount of ending inventory, use your answer to part **d**.
g. Which type of inventory system do you think STAR-TRACK should use? Explain your reasoning.
h. Determine the gross profit margin on the January 3 sales transaction.

Solution to the Demonstration Problem

a. The operating cycle of a merchandising company consists of purchasing merchandise, selling that merchandise to customers (often on account), and collecting the sales proceeds from these customers. In the process, the business converts cash into inventory, the inventory into accounts receivable, and the accounts receivable into cash.

b. Journal entries assuming use of a *perpetual* inventory system:

GENERAL JOURNAL			
Date	Account Titles and Explanation	Debit	Credit
2002			
Jan. 3	Cash	20,000	
	Sales		20,000
	Sold tracking system to Mystery Mountain Resort.		
3	Cost of Goods Sold	11,200	
	Inventory		11,200
	To record cost of merchandise sold.		
7	Inventory	9,800	
	Accounts Payable (Yamaha Corp.)		9,800
	Purchased merchandise. Terms, 2/10, n/30; net cost, $9,800 ($10,000, less 2%).		

c. The debits and credits to the Inventory account should be posted to the appropriate accounts in the inventory subsidiary ledger. The information posted would be the costs and quantities of the types of merchandise purchased or sold. The account payable to Yamaha also should be posted to the Yamaha account in STAR-TRACK's accounts payable ledger. No postings are required to the accounts receivable ledger, as this was a cash sale. If STAR-TRACK maintains more than one bank account, however, the debit to cash should be posted to the proper account in the cash subsidiary ledger.

d. $42,600 ($44,000 beginning balance, less $11,200, plus $9,800).

e. Journal entries assuming use of a *periodic* inventory system:

GENERAL JOURNAL			
Date	Account Titles and Explanation	Debit	Credit
2002			
Jan. 3	Cash	20,000	
	Sales		20,000
	Sold tracking system to Mystery Mountain Resort.		
7	Purchases	9,800	
	Accounts Payable (Yamaha Corp.)		9,800
	Purchased merchandise. Terms, 2/10, n/30; net cost, $9,800 ($10,000, less 2%).		

f. Computation of the cost of goods sold:

Inventory, January 1	$44,000
Add: Purchases	9,800
Cost of goods available for sale	$53,800
Less: Inventory, January 7 (per part **d**)	42,600
Cost of goods sold	$11,200

g. STAR-TRACK should use a *perpetual* inventory system. The items in its inventory have a high per-unit cost. Therefore, management will want to know the costs of the individual products included in specific sales transactions and will want to keep track of the items in stock. Although the company has a manual accounting system, its volume of sales transactions is low enough that maintaining a perpetual inventory record will not be difficult.

h. Gross profit = Sales revenue − Cost of goods sold
= $20,000 − $11,200
= $8,800
Gross profit margin = Gross profit ÷ Sales revenue
= $8,800 ÷ $20,000
= 44%

SELF-TEST QUESTIONS

Answers to these questions appear on page 260.

1. Mark and Amanda Carter own an appliance store and a restaurant. The appliance store sells merchandise on a 12-month installment plan; the restaurant sells only for cash. Which of the following statements are true? (More than one answer may be correct.)
   a. The appliance store has a longer operating cycle than the restaurant.
   b. The appliance store probably uses a perpetual inventory system, whereas the restaurant probably uses a periodic system.
   c. Both businesses require subsidiary ledgers for accounts receivable and inventory.
   d. Both businesses probably have subsidiary ledgers for accounts payable.

2. Which of the following types of information are found in subsidiary ledgers, but *not* in the general ledger? (More than one answer may be correct.)
   a. Total cost of goods sold for the period.
   b. The quantity of a particular product sold during the period.
   c. The dollar amount owed to a particular creditor.
   d. The portion of total current assets that consists of cash.

3. Marietta Corporation uses a *perpetual* inventory system. The company sells merchandise costing $3,000 at a sales price of $4,300. In recording this transaction, Marietta will make all of the following entries *except:*
   a. Credit Sales, $4,300.
   b. Credit Inventory, $4,300.
   c. Debit Cost of Goods Sold, $3,000.
   d. Credit one or more accounts in the inventory subsidiary ledger for amounts totaling $3,000.

4. Fashion House uses a *perpetual* inventory system. At the beginning of the year, inventory amounted to $50,000. During the year, the company purchased merchandise for $230,000, and sold merchandise costing $245,000. A physical inventory taken at year-end indicated shrinkage losses of $4,000. *Prior* to recording these shrinkage losses, the year-end balance in the company's Inventory account was:
   a. $31,000.   b. $35,000.   c. $50,000.   d. Some other amount.

5. Best Hardware uses a *periodic* inventory system. Its inventory was $38,000 at the beginning of the year and $40,000 at the end. During the year, Best made purchases of merchandise totaling $107,000. Identify all of the correct answers:

a. To use this system, Best must take a complete physical inventory twice each year.
b. Prior to making adjusting and closing entries at year-end, the balance in Best's Inventory account is $38,000.
c. The cost of goods sold for the year is $109,000.
d. As sales transactions occur, Best makes no entries to update its inventory records or record the cost of goods sold.

6. The two basic approaches to accounting for inventory and the cost of goods sold are the *perpetual* inventory system and the *periodic* inventory system. Indicate which of the following statements are correct. (More than one answer may be correct.)
    a. Most large merchandising companies and manufacturing businesses use periodic inventory systems.
    b. As a practical matter, a grocery store or a large department store could not maintain a perpetual inventory system without the use of point-of-sale terminals.
    c. In a periodic inventory system, the cost of goods sold is not determined until a complete physical inventory is taken.
    d. In a perpetual inventory system, the Cost of Goods Sold account is debited promptly for the cost of merchandise sold.

7. Big Brother, a retail store, purchased 100 television sets from Krueger Electronics on account at a cost of $200 each. Krueger offers credit terms of 2/10, n/30. Big Brother uses a perpetual inventory system and records purchases at *net cost*. Big Brother determines that 10 of these television sets are defective and returns them to Krueger for full credit. In recording this return, Big Brother will:
    a. Debit Sales Returns and Allowances.
    b. Debit Accounts Payable, $1,960.
    c. Debit Cost of Goods Sold, $1,960.
    d. Credit Inventory, $2,000.

8. Two of the lawn mowers sold by Garden Products Co. are the LawnMaster and the Mark 5. LawnMasters sell for $250 apiece, which results in a 35% gross profit margin. Each Mark 5 costs Garden Products $300 and sells for $400. Indicate all correct answers.
    a. The dollar amount of gross profit is greater on the sale of a Mark 5 than a LawnMaster.
    b. The gross profit margin is higher on Mark 5s than on LawnMasters.
    c. Garden profits more by selling one Mark 5 than by selling one LawnMaster.
    d. Garden profits more by selling $2,000 worth of Mark 5s than $2,000 worth of LawnMasters.

ASSIGNMENT MATERIAL
DISCUSSION QUESTIONS

1. Describe the operating cycle of a merchandising company.
2. Compare and contrast the merchandising activities of a wholesaler and a retailer.
3. The income statement of a merchandising company includes a major type of cost that does not appear in the income statement of a service-type business. Identify this cost and explain what it represents.
4. During the current year, Green Bay Company earned a gross profit of $350,000, whereas New England Company earned a gross profit of only $280,000. Both companies had net sales of $900,000. Does this mean that Green Bay is more profitable than New England? Explain.
5. Thornhill Company's income statement shows gross profit of $432,000, cost of goods sold of $638,000, and other expenses totaling $390,000. Compute the amounts of (a) revenue from sales (net sales) and (b) net income.
6. Explain the need for subsidiary ledgers in accounting for merchandising activities.
7. All Night Auto Parts, Inc., maintains subsidiary ledgers for accounts receivable, inventory, and accounts payable. Explain in detail what information from the following journal entry should be posted and to which subsidiary and general ledger accounts:

> Inventory 420
>   Accounts Payable (Boss Automotive) 420
> Purchased 12 Boss LoadMaster II shock absorbers. Cost,
> $35 per unit.

8. What is meant by the phrase "reconciling a subsidiary ledger"? In general terms, what is the purpose of this procedure?

9. Define the term *inventory shrinkage*. How is the amount of inventory shrinkage determined in a business using a perpetual inventory system, and how is this shrinkage recorded in the accounting records?

10. Briefly contrast the accounting procedures in *perpetual* and *periodic* inventory systems.

11. Miracle Home Cleanser uses a *periodic* inventory system. During the current year the company purchased merchandise with a cost of $55,000. State the cost of goods sold for the year under each of the following alternative assumptions:

    a. No beginning inventory; ending inventory $3,500.
    b. Beginning inventory $10,000; no ending inventory.
    c. Beginning inventory $2,000; ending inventory $7,200.
    d. Beginning inventory $8,000; ending inventory $1,400.

12. Evaluate the following statement: "Without electronic point-of-sale terminals, it simply would not be possible to use perpetual inventory systems in businesses that sell large quantities of many different products."

13. Explain the distinguishing characteristics of (a) a general journal and (b) a special journal.

14. How does a balance arise in the Purchase Discounts Lost account? Why does management pay careful attention to the balance (if any) in this account?

15. European Imports pays substantial freight charges to obtain inbound shipments of purchased merchandise. Should these freight charges be debited to the company's Delivery Expense account? Explain.

16. Outback Sporting Goods purchases merchandise on terms of 4/10, n/60. The company has a line of credit that enables it to borrow money as needed from Northern Bank at an annual interest rate of 13%. Should Outback pay its suppliers within the 10-day discount period if it must draw on its line of credit (borrow from Northern Bank) to make these early payments? Explain.

17. TireCo is a retail store in a state that imposes a 6% sales tax. Would you expect to find sales tax expense and sales tax payable in TireCo's financial statements? Explain.

18. A seller generally records sales at the full invoice price, but the buyer often records purchases at *net cost*. Explain the logic of the buyer and seller recording the transaction at different amounts.

19. Western Stores, a chain of hardware stores, had an increase in net sales of 8% for this year in relation to the prior year. Does this mean that the company's marketing strategies, such as advertising, pricing, and product mix, are succeeding?

20. Define the term *gross profit margin*. Explain several ways in which management might improve a company's overall profit margin.

EXERCISES

EXERCISE 6.1

You as a Student

LO 1, 7

As a fund-raiser, the pep band at Melrose University sells T-shirts fans can wear when attending the school's 12 home basketball games. As the band's business manager, you must choose among several options for ordering and selling the T-shirts.

1. Place a single order in October large enough to last the entire season. The band must pay for the shirts in full when the order is placed. A 5% quantity discount applies to this option.

2. Place a series of small orders, as needed, throughout the season. Again, payment in full is due when the order is submitted. No discount applies to this option.

3. Have band members sell shirts directly to members of the student body. Cash is collected immediately as sales are made.

Exercises

4. Sell all of the T-shirts through the university bookstore. The bookstore would receive a 6% commission on total sales and would remit to the band its share of the proceeds in a lump-sum payment at the end of the season.

a. Describe which combination of options would give the pep band the shortest operating cycle.
b. Describe which combination of options would give the pep band the longest operating cycle.
c. Discuss briefly the advantages and disadvantages of each option.

EXERCISE 6.2
Effects of Basic Merchandising Transactions
LO 1

Shown below are selected transactions of Konshock's, a retail store that uses a perpetual inventory system.

a. Purchased merchandise on account.
b. Recognized the revenue from a sale of merchandise on account. (Ignore the related cost of goods sold.)
c. Recognized the cost of goods sold relating to the sale in transaction **b**.
d. Collected in cash the account receivable from the customer in transaction **b**.
e. Following the taking of a physical inventory at year-end, made an adjusting entry to record a normal amount of inventory shrinkage.

Indicate the effects of each of these transactions on the elements of the company's financial statements shown below. Organize your answer in tabular form, using the column headings shown below. (Notice that the cost of goods sold is shown separately from all other expenses.) Use the code letters **I** for increase, **D** for decrease, and **NE** for no effect.

	Income Statement				Balance Sheet		
Transaction	Net Sales −	Cost of Goods Sold −	All Other Expenses =	Net Income	Assets =	Liabilities +	Owners' Equity
a	___	___	___	___	___	___	___

EXERCISE 6.3
Subsidiary Ledgers
LO 2, 7

Listed below are eight typical merchandising transactions of Cramer Fabrics, a retail fabric outlet:

a. Purchased merchandise from New York Importers on account.
b. Paid an account payable to a supplier.
c. Sold merchandise for cash.
d. Sold merchandise on account.
e. Collected an account receivable from a customer.
f. Returned merchandise to a supplier, receiving credit against the amount owed.
g. Gave a cash refund to a customer who returned merchandise.
h. Reduced the account receivable from a credit customer who returned merchandise.

Among the accounting records of Cramer Fabrics are subsidiary ledgers for inventory, accounts receivable, and accounts payable. For each of the eight transactions, you are to indicate any subsidiary ledger (or ledgers) to which the transaction would be posted. Use the following codes:

Inv = Inventory subsidiary ledger
AR = Accounts receivable subsidiary ledger
AP = Accounts payable subsidiary ledger

Also indicate whether each posting causes the balance in the subsidiary ledger account to *increase* or *decrease*. Organize your answer in tabular form as illustrated below. The answer for transaction **a** is provided as an example.

Transaction	Subsidiary Ledger	Effect on Subsidiary Account Balance
a	Inv	Increase
	AP	Increase

EXERCISE 6.4
Perpetual Inventory Systems
LO 3, 8

Ranns Supply uses a perpetual inventory system. On January 1, its inventory account had a beginning balance of $6,450,000. Ranns engaged in the following transactions during the year:
1. Purchased merchandise inventory for $9,500,000.
2. Generated net sales of $26,000,000.
3. Recorded inventory shrinkage of $10,000 after taking a physical inventory at year-end.
4. Reported gross profit for the year of $15,000,000 in its income statement.

a. At what amount was Cost of Goods Sold reported in the company's year-end income statement?
b. At what amount was Merchandise Inventory reported in the company's year-end balance sheet?
c. Immediately prior to recording inventory shrinkage at the end of the year, what was the balance of the Cost of Goods Sold account? What was the balance of the Merchandise Inventory account?

EXERCISE 6.5
Evaluating Performance
LO 7, 8

These selected statistics are from recent annual reports of two well-known retailers (the **Kmart** figures were generated just prior to its filing for bankruptcy):

	Wal-Mart	Kmart
Percentage increase (decrease) in net sales	16%	3%
Percentage increase (decrease) in gross profit rate	0	(9)
Percentage increase (decrease) in comparable store net sales	5	1

a. Explain the significance of each of these three measures.
b. Evaluate briefly the performance of each company based upon these three measures.

EXERCISE 6.6
Taking a Physical Inventory
LO 3

Frisbee Hardware uses a perpetual inventory system. At year-end, the Inventory account has a balance of $250,000, but a physical count shows that the merchandise on hand has a cost of only $246,000.

a. Explain the probable reason(s) for this discrepancy.
b. Prepare the journal entry required in this situation.
c. Indicate all the accounting records to which your journal entry in part **b** should be posted.

EXERCISE 6.7
Periodic Inventory Systems
LO 4

Boston Bait Shop uses a periodic inventory system. At December 31, Year 1, the accounting records include the following information:

Inventory (as of December 31, Year 1)	$ 2,800
Net sales	79,600
Purchases	30,200

A complete physical inventory taken at December 31, Year 2, indicates merchandise costing $3,000 remains in stock.

a. How were the amounts of beginning and ending inventory determined?
b. Compute the amount of the cost of goods sold in Year 2.
c. Prepare two closing entries at December 31, Year 2: the first to create a Cost of Goods Sold account with the appropriate balance and the second to bring the Inventory account up-to-date.
d. Prepare a partial income statement showing the shop's gross profit for the year.
e. Describe why a company such as Boston Bait Shop would use a periodic inventory system rather than a perpetual inventory system.

EXERCISE 6.8
Relationships within Periodic Inventory Systems
LO 4

This exercise stresses the relationships between the information recorded in a periodic inventory system and the basic elements of an income statement. Each of the five lines represents a separate set of information. You are to fill in the missing amounts. A net loss in the right-hand column is to be indicated by placing brackets around the amount, as for example, in line **e** <15,000>.

Exercises

	Net Sales	Beginning Inventory	Net Purchases	Ending Inventory	Cost of Goods Sold	Gross Profit	Expenses	Net Income or (Loss)
a.	240,000	76,000	104,000	35,200	?	95,200	72,000	?
b.	480,000	72,000	272,000	?	264,000	?	?	20,000
c.	630,000	207,000	?	166,500	441,000	189,000	148,500	?
d.	810,000	?	450,000	135,000	?	234,000	270,000	?
e.	?	156,000	?	153,000	396,000	135,000	?	<15,000>

EXERCISE 6.9

Selecting an Inventory System

LO 5, 8

Year after year three huge supermarket chains—**Albertsons, Inc.**; **Safeway, Inc.**; and **Kroger Company**—consistently reported gross profit rates between 27% and 29%. Each uses a sophisticated perpetual inventory system to account for billions of dollars in inventory transactions.

a. Discuss reasons why these firms consistently report such similar and stable gross profit rates.
b. What technologies make it possible for these retailing giants to use perpetual inventory systems?

EXERCISE 6.10

Cash Discounts

LO 7

Golf World sold merchandise to Mulligans for $10,000, offering terms of 1/15, n/30. Mulligans paid for the merchandise within the discount period. Both companies use perpetual inventory systems.

a. Prepare journal entries in the accounting records of Golf World to account for this sale and the subsequent collection. Assume the original cost of the merchandise to Golf World had been $6,500.
b. Prepare journal entries in the accounting records of Mulligans to account for the purchase and subsequent payment. Mulligans records purchases of merchandise at *net cost*.
c. Assume that because of a change in personnel, Mulligans failed to pay for this merchandise within the discount period. Prepare the journal entry in the accounting records of Mulligans to record payment *after* the discount period.

EXERCISE 6.11

Evaluating Performance

LO 8

This selected information is from recent annual reports of the three largest retail pharmaceutical companies in the United States. (Dollar amounts are stated in billions.)

	Rite Aid Corporation	CVS Corporation	Walgreen Company
Net sales	$14.5	$?	$21.2
Cost of goods sold	11.2	14.7	?
Gross profit	?	5.4	?
Gross profit margin (or rate)	?%	?%	27%
Total square feet of selling space	46.2 million	30.8 million	33.7 million
Sales per square foot of selling space	?	?	?

a. Fill in the missing amounts and percentages. (Round dollar amounts to the nearest billion, and percentages to the nearest whole percent.)
b. A significant portion of any retail pharmacy's revenue is from third-party sales. A third-party sale occurs when an insurance company is responsible for paying for a customer's prescription medicine. Insurance companies rarely reimburse retail pharmacies the full price for medications purchased by customers covered under prescription drug plans.

   One of the three retail pharmacy chains listed above reported recently that its percentage of total prescription drug revenue from third-party sales had risen from 85% to over 90%, making its percentage of total prescription revenue from third-party sales one of the highest in the industry. Identify this retailer based on the information provided and from the figures computed in part **a**. Defend your answer.

EXERCISE 6.12

Comparison of Inventory Systems

LO 3, 4, 5

Sky Probe sells state-of-the-art telescopes to individuals and organizations interested in studying the solar system. At December 31 last year, the company's inventory amounted to $250,000. During the first week of January this year, the company made only one purchase and one sale. These transactions were as follows:

Jan. 2 Sold one telescope costing $90,000 to Central State University for cash, $117,000.

Jan. 5 Purchased merchandise on account from Lunar Optics, $50,000. Terms, net 30 days.

a. Prepare journal entries to record these transactions assuming that Sky Probe uses the perpetual inventory system. Use separate entries to record the sales revenue and the cost of goods sold for the sale on January 2.

b. Compute the balance of the Inventory account on January 7.

c. Prepare journal entries to record the two transactions, assuming that Sky Probe uses the periodic inventory system.

d. Compute the cost of goods sold for the first week of January assuming use of a periodic inventory system. Use your answer to part **b** as the ending inventory.

e. Which inventory system do you believe that a company such as Sky Probe would probably use? Explain your reasoning.

EXERCISE 6.13
The Periodic Inventory System
LO 4, 5

Mountain Mabel's is a small general store located just outside of Yellowstone National Park. The store uses a periodic inventory system. Every January 1, Mabel and her husband close the store and take a complete physical inventory while watching the Rose Parade on television. Last year, the inventory amounted to $6,240; this year it totaled $4,560. During the current year, the business recorded sales of $150,000 and purchases of $74,400.

a. Compute the cost of goods sold for the current year.

b. Explain why a small business such as this might use the periodic inventory system.

c. Explain some of the *disadvantages* of the periodic system to a larger business, such as a **Sears** store.

EXERCISE 6.14
Using an Annual Report
LO 8

The annual report of **Tootsie Roll Industries, Inc.**, appears in Appendix A at the end of this textbook. Use this report to complete the following requirements:

a. Calculate the gross profit percentage of **Tootsie Roll Industries** for each of the years shown in the company's income statements.

b. Evaluate the company's trend in sales and gross profit to date.

c. Does management seem optimistic about future trends in sales and gross profit? Explain.

PROBLEMS

PROBLEM 6.1
Evaluating Profitability
LO 1, 3, 8

Claypool Hardware is the only hardware store in a remote area of northern Minnesota. Some of Claypool's transactions during the current year are as follows:

Nov. 5 Sold lumber on account to Bemidji Construction, $13,390. The inventory subsidiary ledger shows the cost of this merchandise was $9,105.

Nov. 9 Purchased tools on account from Owatonna Tool Company, $3,800.

Dec. 5 Collected in cash the $13,390 account receivable from Bemidji Construction.

Dec. 9 Paid the $3,800 owed to Owatonna Tool Company.

Dec. 31 Claypool's personnel counted the inventory on hand and determined its cost to be $182,080. The accounting records, however, indicate inventory of $183,790 and a cost of goods sold of $695,222. The physical count of the inventory was observed by the company's auditors and is considered correct.

Instructions

a. Prepare journal entries to record these transactions and events in the accounting records of Claypool Hardware. (The company uses a perpetual inventory system.)

b. Prepare a partial income statement showing the company's gross profit for the year. (Net sales for the year amount to $1,024,900.)

c. Claypool purchases merchandise inventory at the same wholesale prices as other hardware stores. Due to its remote location, however, the company must pay between $18,000 and $20,000 per year in extra transportation charges to receive delivery of merchandise. (These additional charges are included in the amount shown as cost of goods sold.)

Assume that an index of key business ratios in your library shows hardware stores of Claypool's approximate size (in total assets) average net sales of $1 million per year and a gross profit margin of 25%.

Is Claypool able to pass its extra transportation costs on to its customers? Does the business appear to suffer or benefit financially from its remote location? Explain your reasoning and support your conclusions with specific accounting data comparing the operations of Claypool Hardware with the industry averages.

PROBLEM 6.2

Perpetual Inventory System and an Inventory Subsidiary Ledger

LO 1, 2, 3

Office Solutions sells fax machines, copiers, and other types of office equipment. On May 10, the company purchased for the first time a new plain-paper fax machine manufactured by Mitsui Corporation. Transactions relating to this product during May and June were as follows:

May 10 Purchased five P-500 fax machines on account from Mitsui Corporation, at a cost of $300 each. Payment due in 30 days.

May 23 Sold four P-500 fax machines on account to Foster & Cole, stockbrokers; sales price, $500 per machine. Payment due in 30 days.

May 24 Purchased an additional seven P-500 fax machines on account from Mitsui. Cost, $300 per machine; payment due in 30 days.

June 9 Paid $1,500 cash to Mitsui Corporation for the fax machines purchased on May 10.

June 19 Sold two P-500 fax machines to Tri-State Realty for cash. Sales price, $525 per machine.

June 22 Collected $2,000 from Foster & Cole in full settlement of the credit sale on May 23.

Instructions

a. Prepare journal entries to record these transactions in the accounting records of Office Solutions. (The company uses a perpetual inventory system.)

b. Post the appropriate information from these journal entries to an inventory subsidiary ledger account like the one illustrated on page 229.)

c. How many Mitsui P-500 fax machines were in inventory on May 31? From what accounting record did you obtain the answer to this question?

d. Describe the types of information contained in any inventory subsidiary ledger account and explain how this information may be useful to various company personnel in conducting daily business operations.

PROBLEM 6.3

Trend Analysis

LO 8

Shown below is information from the financial reports of Knauss Supermarkets for the past few years.

	2002	2001	2000
Net sales (in millions)	$5,495	$5,184	$4,800
Number of stores	448	445	430
Square feet of selling space (in millions)	11.9	11.1	10.0
Average net sales of comparable stores (in millions)	$ 10.8	$ 11.0	$ 11.4

Instructions

a. Calculate the following statistics for Knauss Supermarkets:

1. The percentage change in net sales from 2000 to 2001 and 2001 to 2002. *Hint*: The percentage change is computed by dividing the dollar amount of the change between years by the amount of the base year. For example, the percentage change in net sales from 2000 to 2001 is computed by dividing the difference between 2001 and 2000 net sales by the amount of 2000 net sales, or ($5,184 − $4,800) ÷ $4,800 = 8% increase.

2. The percentage change in net sales per square foot of selling space from 2000 to 2001 and 2001 to 2002.

3. The percentage change in comparable store sales from 2000 to 2001 and 2001 to 2002.

b. Evaluate the sales performance of Knauss Supermarkets.

PROBLEM 6.4
Comparison of Net Cost and Gross Price Methods

LO 3, 7

Lamprino Appliance uses a perpetual inventory system. The following are three recent merchandising transactions:

June 10 Purchased 10 televisions from Mitsu Industries on account. Invoice price, $300 per unit, for a total of $3,000. The terms of purchase were 2/10, n/30.

June 15 Sold one of these televisions for $450 cash.

June 20 Paid the account payable to Mitsu Industries within the discount period.

Instructions

a. Prepare journal entries to record these transactions assuming that Lamprino records purchases of merchandise at:
   1. Net cost
   2. Gross invoice price

b. Assume that Lamprino did *not* pay Mitsu Industries within the discount period but instead paid the full invoice price on July 10. Prepare journal entries to record this payment assuming that the original liability had been recorded at:
   1. Net cost
   2. Gross invoice price

c. Assume that you are evaluating the efficiency of Lamprino's bill-paying procedures. Which accounting method—net cost or gross invoice price—provides you with the most *useful* information? Explain.

PROBLEM 6.5
Merchandising Transactions

LO 3, 7

The following is a series of related transactions between Siogo Shoes, a shoe wholesaler, and Sole Mates, a chain of retail shoe stores:

Feb. 9 Siogo Shoes sold Sole Mates 100 pairs of hiking boots on account, terms 1/10, n/30. The cost of these boots to Siogo Shoes was $60 per pair, and the sales price was $100 per pair.

Feb. 12 United Express charged $80 for delivering this merchandise to Sole Mates. These charges were split evenly between the buyer and seller, and were paid immediately in cash.

Feb. 13 Sole Mates returned 10 pairs of boots to Siogo Shoes because they were the wrong size. Siogo Shoes allowed Sole Mates full credit for this return.

Feb. 19 Sole Mates paid the remaining balance due to Siogo Shoes within the discount period.

Both companies use a perpetual inventory system.

Instructions

a. Record this series of transactions in the general journal of Siogo Shoes. (The company records sales at gross sales price.)

b. Record this series of transactions in the general journal of Sole Mates. (The company records purchases of merchandise at *net cost* and uses a Transportation-in account to record transportation charges on inbound shipments.)

c. Sole Mates does not always have enough cash on hand to pay for purchases within the discount period. However, it has a line of credit with its bank, which enables Sole Mates to easily borrow money for short periods of time at an annual interest rate of 11%. (The bank charges interest only for the number of days until Sole Mates repays the loan.) As a matter of general policy, should Sole Mates take advantage of 1/10, n/30 cash discounts even if it must borrow the money to do so at an annual rate of 11%? Explain fully—and illustrate any supporting computations.

PROBLEM 6.6
A Comprehensive Problem

LO 1-8

CPI sells computer peripherals. At December 31, 2001, CPI's inventory amounted to $500,000. During the first week in January 2002, the company made only one purchase and one sale. These transactions were as follows:

Jan. 2 Purchased 20 modems and 80 printers from Sharp. The total cost of these machines was $25,000, terms 3/10, n/60.

Jan. 6 Sold 30 different types of products on account to Pace Corporation. The total sales price was $10,000, terms 5/10, n/90. The total cost of these 30 units to CPI was $6,100 (net of the purchase discount).

CPI has a full-time accountant and a computer-based accounting system. It records sales at the gross sales price and purchases at net cost and maintains subsidiary ledgers for accounts receivable, inventory, and accounts payable.

Instructions

a. Briefly describe the operating cycle of a merchandising company. Identify the assets and liabilities directly affected by this cycle.
b. Prepare journal entries to record these transactions, assuming that CPI uses a *perpetual* inventory system.
c. Explain the information in part **b** that should be posted to subsidiary ledger accounts.
d. Compute the balance in the Inventory controlling account at the close of business on January 6.
e. Prepare journal entries to record the two transactions, assuming that CPI uses a *periodic* inventory system.
f. Compute the cost of goods sold for the first week of January assuming use of the periodic system. (Use your answer to part **d** as the ending inventory.)
g. Which type of inventory system do you think CPI most likely would use? Explain your reasoning.
h. Compute the gross profit margin on the January 6 sales transaction.

CASES AND UNSTRUCTURED PROBLEMS

CASE 6.1

Selecting an Inventory System

LO 5

In each of the following situations, indicate whether you would expect the business to use a periodic inventory system or a perpetual inventory system. Explain the reasons for your answer.

a. The Frontier Shop is a small retail store that sells boots and Western clothing. The store is operated by the owner, who works full-time in the business, and by one part-time salesclerk. Sales transactions are recorded on an antique cash register. The business uses a manual accounting system, which is maintained by ACE Bookkeeping Service. At the end of each month, an employee of ACE visits The Frontier Shop to update its accounting records, prepare sales tax returns, and perform other necessary accounting services.
b. Allister's Corner is an art gallery in the Soho district of New York. All accounting records are maintained manually by the owner, who works in the store on a full-time basis. The store sells three or four paintings each week, at sales prices ranging from about $5,000 to $50,000 per painting.
c. A publicly owned corporation publishes about 200 titles of college-level textbooks. The books are sold to college bookstores throughout the country. Books are distributed to these bookstores from four central warehouses, located in California, Texas, Ohio, and Virginia.
d. Toys-4-You operates a national chain of 86 retail toy stores. The company has a state-of-the-art computerized accounting system. All sales transactions are recorded on electronic point-of-sale terminals. These terminals are tied into a central computer system that provides the national headquarters with information about the profitability of each store on a weekly basis.
e. Mr. Jingles is an independently owned and operated ice cream truck.
f. TransComm is a small company that sells very large quantities of a single product. The product is a low-cost, 3.5-inch, double-sided, double-density floppy computer disc, manufactured by a large Japanese company. Sales are made only in large quantities, primarily to chains of computer stores and large discount stores. This year, the average sales transaction amounted to $14,206 of merchandise. All accounting records are maintained by a full-time employee using commercial accounting software and a personal computer.

CASE 6.2

A Cost-Benefit Analysis

LO 4, 8

Village Hardware is a retail store selling hardware, small appliances, and sporting goods. The business follows a policy of selling all merchandise at exactly twice the amount of its cost to the store and uses a *periodic* inventory system.

At year-end, the following information is taken from the accounting records:

Net sales	$580,000
Inventory, January 1	58,000
Purchases	$297,250

A physical count indicates merchandise costing $49,300 is on hand at December 31.

Instructions

a. Prepare a partial income statement showing computation of the gross profit for the year.

b. On seeing your income statement, the owner of the store makes the following comment: "Inventory shrinkage losses are really costing me. If it weren't for shrinkage losses, the store's gross profit would be 50% of net sales. I'm going to hire a security guard and put an end to shoplifting once and for all."

   Determine the amount of loss from inventory shrinkage stated (1) at cost and (2) at retail sales value. (*Hint*: Without any shrinkage losses, the cost of goods sold and the amount of gross profit would each amount to 50% of net sales.)

c. Assume that Village Hardware could virtually eliminate shoplifting by hiring a security guard at a cost of $1,800 per month. Would this strategy be profitable? Explain your reasoning.

CASE 6.3
Out of Balance

LO 2

Marcus Dean works in the accounts payable department of Artistic Furniture, a large retail furniture store. At month-end, Dean's supervisor assigned him the task of reconciling the accounts payable subsidiary ledger with the controlling account.

Dean found that the balance of the controlling account was $4,500 higher than the sum of the subsidiary ledger accounts. He traced this error to a transaction occurring early in the month. Artistic had purchased $9,400 in merchandise on account from Appalachian Woods, a regular supplier. The transaction had been recorded correctly in Artistic's journal and posted correctly to the Inventory and Accounts Payable accounts in the general ledger. The $9,400 credit to Accounts Payable, however, had erroneously been posted as *$4,900* to the Appalachian Woods account in Artistic's accounts payable subsidiary ledger.

Artistic uses its subsidiary ledger as the basis for making payment to its suppliers. In the middle of the month, Artistic had sent a check to Appalachian in the amount of $4,900. This $4,900 payment was recorded and posted correctly to both the general and subsidiary ledger accounts. Thus, at the end of the month, the subsidiary ledger account for Appalachian Woods had a zero balance.

Dean learned that Appalachian had failed to detect Artistic's error. The month-end statement from Appalachian simply said, "Account paid in full." Therefore, Dean proposed the following "correcting entry" to bring Artistic's controlling account into balance with the subsidiary ledger and the supplier's month-end statement:

Accounts Payable	4,500	
Miscellaneous Revenue		4,500
To reduce Accounts Payable controlling account for unpaid amount that was not rebilled by the supplier.		

This entry is to be posted to the general ledger accounts, but not to the accounts payable subsidiary ledger.

Instructions

a. Will the proposed correcting entry bring the Accounts Payable controlling account into agreement with the accounts in the subsidiary ledger?

b. Identify and discuss any ethical considerations that you see in this situation, and suggest an appropriate course of action.

CASE 6.4
Group Assignment with Business Community Involvement

LO 3, 4, 5, 6

Identify one local business that uses a perpetual inventory system and another that uses a periodic system. Interview an individual in each organization who is familiar with the inventory system and the recording of sales transactions.

Instructions

Separately for each business organization:

a. Describe the procedures used in accounting for sales transactions, keeping track of inventory levels, and determining the cost of goods sold.

b. Explain the reasons offered by the person interviewed as to *why* the business uses this type of system.
c. Indicate whether your group considers the system in use appropriate under the circumstances. If not, recommend specific changes. *Explain your reasoning.*

BUSINESS WEEK ASSIGNMENT

CASE 6.5

Retail Chain Performance Measures

LO 1, 8

Despite the worst slowdown in the retail sector since the early 1990s, a raft of teen retailers are branching out into ever smaller slices of the highly segmented youth market. In a July 30, 2001, *Business Week* story titled, "Just How Deep Are Those Teen Pockets?" Robert Berner reported that several major retail chains, including **Abercrombie & Fitch** and **Limited Too**, are creating new stores aimed at teenage and younger buyers. Berner reported that because teenagers are the fastest growing population segment, openings of specialty stores aimed at youths are growing at a 17% clip—more than double the rate of the specialty-apparel sector overall. However, it is unclear if this new strategy will prove successful because most retailers—including many aimed at youths—reported lower year-over-year same-store sales for June, the seventh straight soft month for specialty stores.

Instructions

Explain what is meant by the article's references to *same-store sales*. Identify other measures management could use to assess the performance of each individual store in retail chains like **Limited Too**. Describe how the operating cycle of a clothing chain store such as **Abercrombie & Fitch** would differ from the cycle of a manufacturer of furniture.

INTERNET ASSIGNMENT

INTERNET 6.1

Exploring the Annual Report of **Gap, Inc.**

LO 8

You can find a large amount of information on the Internet to evaluate the performance of companies. Many firms provide links to this information on their home pages.

Access the home page of **Gap, Inc.**, at the following Internet location:

www.gapinc.com

Instructions

a. What links to financial information are available on the company's home page?
b. Download the company's most recent annual report and use it to answer the following questions:
   1. By what percentage amounts did net sales increase or decrease in each of the three years reported?
   2. What was the company's gross profit rate for each of the three years reported?
   3. What were the company's sales per square foot of selling space for each of the three years reported?
   4. For the most recent year reported, how many new stores were opened? How many existing stores, if any, were closed?
   5. By what percentage amounts did comparable store sales increase or decrease in each of the three years reported?
   6. What dollar amount of inventory does the company report in its most recent balance sheet?

Internet sites are time and date sensitive. It is the purpose of these exercises to have you explore the Internet. You may need to use the Yahoo! search engine **http://www.yahoo.com** *(or other favorite search engine) to find a company's current Web address.*

OUR COMMENTS ON THE "YOUR TURN" CASES

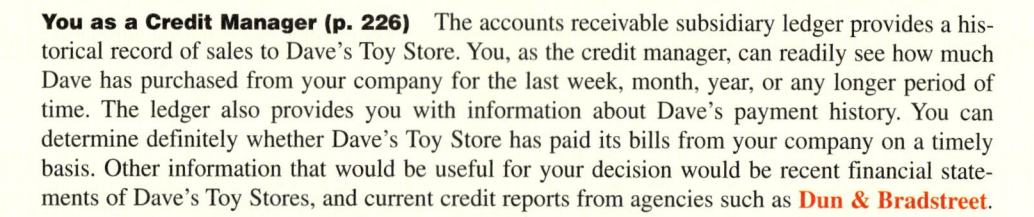

You as a Credit Manager (p. 226) The accounts receivable subsidiary ledger provides a historical record of sales to Dave's Toy Store. You, as the credit manager, can readily see how much Dave has purchased from your company for the last week, month, year, or any longer period of time. The ledger also provides you with information about Dave's payment history. You can determine definitely whether Dave's Toy Store has paid its bills from your company on a timely basis. Other information that would be useful for your decision would be recent financial statements of Dave's Toy Stores, and current credit reports from agencies such as **Dun & Bradstreet**.

You as the Inventory Manager for Computer City (p. 230) An issue of key importance in auditing inventory is that *the auditor be present* when the physical inventory count is made and that no advance notice of the physical inventory be provided to management. A major fraud discovered at **McKesson & Robbins Company** in 1938 motivated the accounting profession to change audit procedures to include the physical observation of inventory. Prior to that time, auditors avoided responsibility for determining either the physical existence or the accuracy of the count of inventory. In 1937 **McKesson & Robbins** reported assets of $87 million of which approximately $10 million of inventory was subsequently determined to be nonexistent.

You should support the auditor's access to the physical inventory. It is Computer City's responsibility to allow access to the physical inventory or the auditor may not issue a clean audit opinion.

You as a Buyer for a Retail Business (p. 235) If **Ace Hardware** maintains perpetual inventory records, these records would provide a host of information that would be useful to your purchasing decision. From the perpetual inventory records, you can determine the number, brand, and type of grills currently on hand and the number of each sold in prior summer seasons. This information will be very useful in estimating the merchandise needs for the current season.

If **Ace Hardware** does not have perpetual inventory records, you would be forced to make your decision without this information about inventory on hand and prior sales, or to spend a significant amount of time developing the information.

ANSWERS TO SELF-TEST QUESTIONS

1. a, b, d   2. b, c   3. b   4. b   5. b, d   6. b, c, d   7. b   8. a, c

CHAPTER 7
FINANCIAL ASSETS

Learning Objectives

After studying this chapter, you should be able to:

1. Define financial assets and explain their valuation in the balance sheet.
2. Describe the objectives of cash management.
3. Explain means of achieving internal control over cash transactions.
4. Prepare a bank reconciliation and explain its purpose.
5. Account for uncollectible receivables using the allowance and direct write-off methods.
6. Evaluate the liquidity of various financial assets.
7. Explain how transactions discussed in this chapter affect net income and cash flows.
*8. Account for transactions involving marketable securities.
†9. Explain, compute, and account for the accrual of interest revenue.

---

*Supplemental Topic A, "Accounting for Marketable Securities."
†Supplemental Topic B, "Notes Receivable and Interest Revenue."

© AFP/Corbis

Microsoft Corporation

Microsoft Corporation is a multibillion-dollar company that develops, manufactures, licenses, and supports a wide range of software products. The company operates facilities in Ireland, Singapore, and the Greater Seattle area.

You might think that **Microsoft** would have most of its resources tied up in plant assets. In fact, the company's balance sheet recently reported property and equipment in excess of $2.3 billion. The same balance sheet, however, shows total assets in excess of $59 billion. Thus, property and equipment comprise less than 4% of **Microsoft**'s total assets.

Financial assets of $35.3 billion account for 60% of **Microsoft**'s total assets. Financial assets are a company's most liquid resources. They include cash, cash equivalents, certain investments in marketable securities, and accounts receivable.

• • •

Financial assets are a company's most liquid (or cash-like) resources. The ability of a company to service its debt, purchase inventory, pay taxes, and cover payroll obligations hinges on the availability of these highly liquid assets. In this chapter, we will examine how companies determine and report the *current values* of financial assets, and how effective companies quickly convert certain financial assets into cash.

How Much Cash Should a Business Have?

Most businesspeople would say, "As little as necessary."

In a well-managed company, daily cash receipts are deposited promptly in the bank. Often, a principal source of these daily receipts is the collection of accounts receivable. If the daily receipts exceed routine cash outlays, the company can meet its obligations while maintaining relatively low balances in its bank accounts.

Cash that will not be needed in the immediate future often is invested in highly liquid, short-term securities. These investments are more productive than cash because they earn revenue in the forms of interest and dividends. If the business should need more cash than it has in its bank accounts, it can easily convert some of its investments back into cash.

LO 1
Define financial assets and explain their valuation in the balance sheet.

The term **financial assets** describes not just cash but also those assets easily and directly *convertible into known amounts of cash*. These assets include cash, short-term investments (also called **marketable securities**), and receivables. We address these three types of financial assets in a single chapter because they are so closely related. All of these assets represent *forms of money;* financial resources flow quickly among these asset categories.

In summary, businesses "store" money in three basic forms: cash, short-term investments, and receivables. The flow of cash among these types of financial assets is illustrated in Exhibit 7–1.

Exhibit 7–1

MONEY FLOWS AMONG THE FINANCIAL ASSETS

Accounts receivable → Collections from customers → Cash (and cash equivalents) → Cash payments

"Excess" cash is invested temporarily ↓ ↑ Investments are sold as cash is needed

Marketable securities

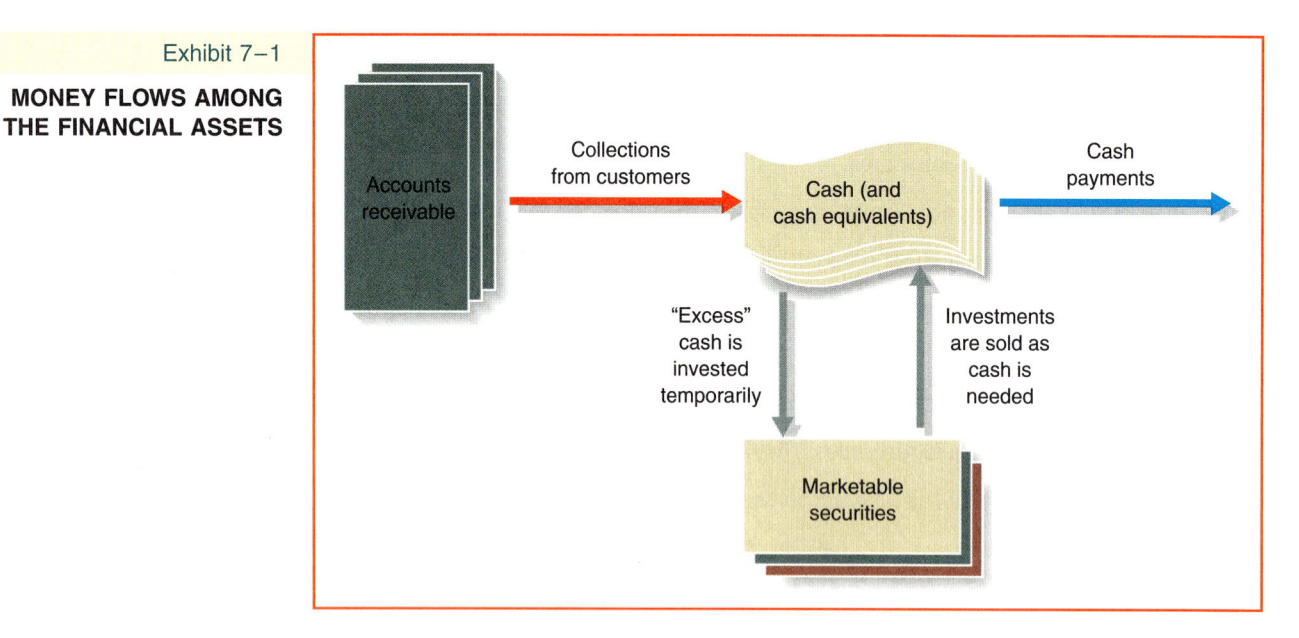

The Valuation of Financial Assets

In the balance sheet, financial assets are shown at their *current values,* meaning the amounts of cash that these assets represent. Interestingly, current value is measured differently for each type of financial asset.

The current value of cash is simply its face amount. But the current value of marketable securities may change daily, based on fluctuations in stock prices, interest rates, and other factors. Therefore, most short-term investments appear in the balance sheet at their current *market values.* (Notice that the valuation of these investments represents an exception to the cost principle.)

Accounts receivable, like cash, have stated face amounts. But large companies usually do not expect to collect every dollar of their accounts receivable. Some customers simply will be unable to make full payment. Therefore, receivables appear in the balance sheet at the estimated *collectible* amount—called **net realizable value**.

The three methods of measuring the current value of financial assets are summarized in Exhibit 7–2.

Type of Financial Asset	Basis for Valuation in the Balance Sheet
Cash (and cash equivalents)	Face amount
Short-term investments (marketable securities)	Current market value
Receivables	Net realizable value

Exhibit 7–2

METHODS OF MEASURING THE CURRENT VALUE OF FINANCIAL ASSETS

CASH

Accountants define *cash* as money on deposit in banks and any items that banks will accept for deposit. These items include not only coins and paper money, but also checks, money orders, and travelers' checks. Banks also accept drafts signed by customers using bank credit cards, such as **Visa** and **MasterCard**. Thus sales to customers using bank cards are considered *cash sales,* not credit sales, to the enterprise that makes the sale.

Most companies maintain several bank accounts as well as keep a small amount of cash on hand. Therefore, the Cash account in the general ledger is often a *controlling account*. A cash subsidiary ledger includes separate accounts corresponding to each bank account and each supply of cash on hand within the organization.

Reporting Cash in the Balance Sheet

Cash is listed first in the balance sheet because it is the most liquid of all assets. For purposes of balance sheet presentation, the balance in the Cash controlling account is combined with that of the controlling account for **cash equivalents**.

Cash Equivalents   Some short-term investments are so liquid that they are termed *cash equivalents*. Examples include money market funds, U.S. Treasury bills, and high-grade commercial paper (very short-term notes payable that are issued by large, creditworthy corporations). These assets are considered so similar to cash that they are combined with the amount of cash in the balance sheet. Therefore, the first asset listed in the balance sheet often is called Cash and Cash Equivalents.

To qualify as a cash equivalent, an investment must be very safe, have a very stable market value, and mature within 90 days of the date of acquisition. Investments in even the highest quality stocks and bonds of large corporations are *not* viewed as meeting these criteria. Short-term investments that do not qualify as cash equivalents are listed in the balance sheet as Marketable Securities.

Restricted Cash   Some bank accounts are restricted as to their use, so they are not available to meet the normal operating needs of the company. For example, a bank account may contain cash specifically earmarked for the repayment of a noncurrent liability, such as a bond payable. Restricted cash should be presented in the balance sheet as part of the section entitled "Investments and Funds."

As a condition for granting a loan, banks often require the borrower to maintain a **compensating balance** (minimum average balance) on deposit in a non-interest-bearing checking account. This agreement does not actually prevent the borrower from using the cash, but it does mean the company must quickly replenish this bank account. Compensating balances are included in the amount of cash listed in the balance sheet, but these balances should be disclosed in the notes accompanying the financial statements.

Lines of Credit Many businesses arrange **lines of credit** with their banks. A line of credit means that the bank has agreed *in advance* to lend the company any amount of money up to a specified limit. The company can borrow this money at any time simply by drawing checks on a special bank account. A liability to the bank arises as soon as any money is borrowed—that is, as soon as a portion of the credit line is used.

The *unused* portion of a line of credit is neither an asset nor a liability; it represents only the *ability* to borrow money quickly and easily. Although an unused line of credit does not appear as an asset or a liability in the balance sheet, it increases the company's liquidity. Thus unused lines of credit usually are *disclosed* in notes accompanying the financial statements.

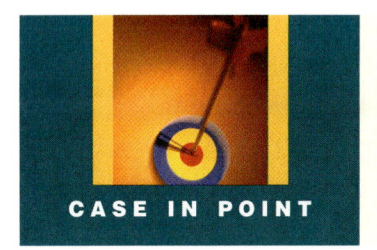

CASE IN POINT

A recent annual report of **Central Hudson Gas & Electric Corporation** included the following footnote related to its confirmed lines of credit:

Central Hudson maintains confirmed lines of credit totaling $1.5 million with regional banks. These agreements give the company competitive options to minimize its cost of short-term borrowing.

The Statement of Cash Flows

A balance sheet shows the cash owned at the end of the accounting period. As we learned in Chapter 2, cash *transactions* of the accounting period are summarized in the statement of cash flows.

In both the balance sheet and the statement of cash flows, the term *cash* includes cash equivalents. Transfers of money between bank accounts and cash equivalents do *not* appear in a statement of cash flows, because these transactions do not change the amount of cash owned. However, any *interest* received from owning cash equivalents is included in the statement of cash flows as cash receipts from operating activities.

Cash Management

LO 2
Describe the objectives of cash management.

The term **cash management** refers to planning, controlling, and accounting for cash transactions and cash balances. Because cash moves so readily between bank accounts and other financial assets, cash management really means the management of *all financial resources*. Efficient management of these resources is essential to the success—even to the survival—of every business organization. The basic objectives of cash management are as follows:

- *Provide accurate accounting for cash receipts, cash disbursements, and cash balances.* Many business transactions involve the receipt or disbursement of cash. Also, cash transactions affect every classification within the financial statements—assets, liabilities, owners' equity, revenue, and expenses. If financial statements are to be reliable, it is *absolutely essential* that cash transactions be recorded correctly.
- *Prevent or minimize losses from theft or fraud.* Cash is more susceptible to theft than any other asset and, therefore, requires physical protection.
- *Anticipate the need for borrowing and assure the availability of adequate amounts of cash for conducting business operations.* Every business organization must have sufficient cash to meet its financial obligations as they come due. Otherwise, its creditors may force the business into bankruptcy.
- *Prevent unnecessarily large amounts of cash from sitting idle in bank accounts that produce no revenue.* Well-managed companies frequently review their bank balances for the purpose of transferring any excess cash into cash equivalents or other investments that generate revenue.

Using Excess Cash Balances Efficiently Cash equivalents are safe, liquid investments, but they generate only a modest rate of return. These investments are useful for investing *temporary* surpluses of cash, which soon will be needed for other purposes. If a business has large amounts of cash that can be invested on a long-term basis, however, it should expect to earn a higher rate of return than is available from cash equivalents. Cash that is available for long-term investment may be used to finance growth and expansion of the business, or to repay debt. If the cash is not needed for business purposes, it may be distributed to the company's stockholders.

You as a Financial Advisor

Assume that you were hired by Whitlock Corporation to help manage its financial assets. The company historically has kept an average cash balance of $5 million in a corporate checking account. Whitlock's chief financial officer is very conservative and risk averse. On numerous occasions he has openly refused to "play the stock market" with company funds.

As a financial advisor, propose several low-risk investment alternatives for the company's $5 million cash surplus.

*Our comments appear on page 316.

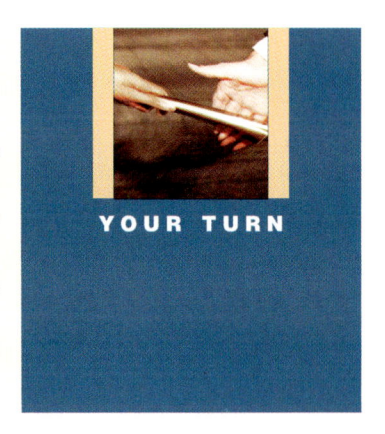

Internal Control over Cash

Internal control over cash is sometimes regarded merely as a means of preventing fraud and theft. A good system of internal control, however, will also aid in achieving the other objectives of efficient cash management, including accurate accounting for cash transactions, anticipating the need for borrowing, and the maintenance of adequate but not excessive cash balances.

The major steps in achieving internal control over cash transactions and cash balances include the following:

- Separate the function of handling cash from the maintenance of accounting records. Employees who handle cash *should not have access to the accounting records*, and accounting personnel should not have access to cash.
- For each department within the organization, prepare a *cash budget* (or forecast) of planned cash receipts, cash payments, and cash balances, scheduled month-by-month for the coming year.
- Prepare a *control listing* of cash receipts at the time and place the money is received. For cash sales, this listing may be a cash register tape, created by ringing up each sale on a cash register. For checks received through the mail, a control listing of incoming checks should be prepared by the employee assigned to open the mail.
- Require that all cash receipts be *deposited daily* in the bank.
- Make all payments *by check*. The only exception should be for small payments to be made in cash from a *petty cash fund*. (Petty cash funds are discussed later in this chapter.)
- Require that the validity and amount of every expenditure be verified *before* a check is issued in payment. Separate the function of approving expenditures from the function of signing checks.
- Promptly reconcile bank statements with the accounting records.

A company may supplement its system of internal control by obtaining a fidelity bond from an insurance company. Under a fidelity bond, the insurance company agrees to reimburse an employer for *proven* losses resulting from fraud or embezzlement by bonded employees.

Cash Over and Short In handling over-the-counter cash receipts, a few errors in making change inevitably will occur. These errors may cause a cash shortage or overage at the end of the day when the cash is counted and compared with the reading on the cash register.

For example, assume that total cash sales recorded on the point-of-sale terminals during the day amount to $4,500.00. However, the cash receipts in the register drawers total only $4,487.30. The following entry would be made to adjust the accounting records for this $12.70 shortage in the cash receipts:

Cash Over and Short	12.70	
Cash		12.70
To record a $12.70 shortage in cash receipts for the day ($4,500.00 − $4,487.30).		

The account entitled Cash Over and Short is debited with shortages and credited with overages. If the account has a debit balance, it appears in the income statement as a miscellaneous expense; if it has a credit balance, it is shown as a miscellaneous revenue.

Cash Disbursements

To achieve adequate internal control over cash disbursements, all payments—except those from petty cash—should be *made by check*. The use of checks automatically provides a written record of each cash payment. In addition, adequate internal control requires that every transaction requiring a cash payment be *verified, approved,* and *recorded* before a check is issued. Responsibility for approving cash disbursements should be *clearly separated* from the responsibility for signing checks.

The Voucher System One widely used method of establishing internal control over cash disbursements is a voucher system. In a typical voucher system, the accounting department is responsible for approving cash payments and for recording the transactions. In approving an expenditure, the accounting department will examine such supporting documents as the supplier's invoice, the purchase order, and the receiving report. Once payment has been approved, the accounting department signs a voucher authorizing payment and records the transaction in the accounting records. (Other names for a "voucher" include *invoice approval form* and *check authorization.*)

The voucher and supporting documents then are sent to the treasurer or other official in the finance department. This official reviews the voucher and supporting documents before issuing a check. When the check is signed, the voucher and supporting documents are perforated or stamped "PAID" to eliminate any possibility of their being presented later in support of another check.

Notice that neither the personnel in the accounting department nor the personnel in the finance department are in a position to make unapproved cash disbursements. Accounting personnel who approve and record disbursements are not authorized to sign checks. Finance department personnel, who issue and sign checks, are not authorized to issue a check unless they have first received an authorization voucher from the accounting department.

Bank Statements

Each month the bank provides the depositor with a statement of the depositor's account, accompanied by the checks paid and charged to the account during the month.[1] As illustrated in Exhibit 7–3, a bank statement shows the account balance at the beginning of the month, the deposits, the checks paid, any other additions and subtractions

---

[1] Large businesses may receive bank statements on a weekly basis.

during the month, and the new balance at the end of the month. (To keep the illustration short, we have shown a limited number of deposits rather than one for each business day in the month.)

Exhibit 7–3

A BANK STATEMENT

Western National Bank
100 Olympic Boulevard
Los Angeles, CA

Customer Account No. 501390
Parkview Company
109 Parkview Road
Los Angeles, CA

Bank Statement for the Month Ended July 31, 2002

Date			Amount
June 30	Previous statement balance		$ 5,029.30
	Deposits and Other Increases (Credits)		
July 1		300.00	
July 2		1,250.00	
July 8		993.60	
July 12		1,023.77	
July 18		1,300.00	
July 22		500.00 CM	
July 24		1,083.25	
July 30		711.55	
July 31		24.74 INT	
	Total deposits and other increases (credits)		7,186.91
	Checks Written and Other Decreases (Debits)		
July 2	Ck. 882	1,100.00	
July 3	Ck. 883	415.20	
July 3	Ck. 884	10.00	
July 10	Ck. 885	96.00	
July 10	Ck. 886	400.00	
July 12	Ck. 887	1,376.57	
July 15	Ck. 889	425.00	
July 18	Ck. 892	2,095.75	
July 22	Ck. 893	85.00	
July 22		5.00 DM	
July 24	Ck. 894	1,145.27	
July 30		50.25 NSF	
July 31		12.00 SC	
	Total checks written and other decreases (debits)		(7,216.04)
July 31	Balance this statement		$5,000.17

Explanation of Symbols	
CM	Credit Memoranda
DM	Debit Memoranda
INT	Interest Earned on Average Balance
NSF	Not Sufficient Funds
SC	Service Charge

Reconciling the Bank Statement

A **bank reconciliation** is a schedule *explaining any differences* between the balance shown in the bank statement and the balance shown in the depositor's accounting records. Remember that both the bank and the depositor are maintaining independent records of the deposits, the checks, and the current balance of the bank account. Each month, the depositor should prepare a bank reconciliation to verify that these independent sets of records are in agreement. This reconciliation may disclose internal control failures, such as unauthorized cash disbursements or failures to deposit cash receipts, as well as errors in either the bank statement or the depositor's accounting records. In addition, the

LO 4
Prepare a bank reconciliation and explain its purpose.

reconciliation identifies certain transactions that must be recorded in the depositor's accounting records and helps to determine the actual amount of cash on deposit.

For strong internal control, the employee who reconciles the bank statement should not have any other responsibilities for physically handling cash.

Normal Differences between Bank Records and Accounting Records The balance shown in a monthly bank statement seldom equals the balance appearing in the depositor's accounting records. Certain transactions recorded by the depositor may not have been recorded by the bank. The most common examples are:

- *Outstanding checks.* Checks issued and recorded by the company but not yet presented to the bank for payment.
- *Deposits in transit.* Cash receipts recorded by the depositor that reached the bank too late to be included in the bank statement for the current month.

In addition, certain transactions appearing in the bank statement may not have been recorded by the depositor. For example:

- *Service charges.* Banks often charge a fee for handling small accounts. The amount of this charge usually depends on both the average balance of the account and the number of checks paid during the month.
- *Charges for depositing NSF checks.* NSF stands for "Not Sufficient Funds." When checks from customers are deposited, the bank generally gives the depositor immediate credit. On occasion, one of these checks may prove to be uncollectible, because the customer who wrote the check did not have sufficient funds in his or her account. In such cases, the bank will reduce the depositor's account by the amount of this uncollectible item and return the check to the depositor marked "NSF." The depositor should view an NSF check as an account receivable from the customer, not as cash.
- *Credits for interest earned.* The checking accounts of *unincorporated* businesses often earn interest. At month-end, this interest is credited to the depositor's account and reported in the bank statement. (Current law prohibits interest on corporate checking accounts.)
- *Miscellaneous bank charges and credits.* Banks charge for services—such as printing checks, handling collections of notes receivable, and processing NSF checks. The bank *deducts* these charges from the depositor's account and notifies the depositor by including a debit memorandum in the monthly bank statement. If the bank collects a note receivable on behalf of the depositor, it credits the depositor's account and issues a credit memorandum.[2]

In a bank reconciliation, the balances shown in the bank statement and in the accounting records both are *adjusted for any unrecorded transactions.* Additional adjustment may be required to correct any errors discovered in the bank statement or in the accounting records.

Steps in Preparing a Bank Reconciliation The specific steps in preparing a bank reconciliation are as follows:

1. Compare deposits listed in the bank statement with the deposits shown in the accounting records. Any deposits not yet recorded by the bank are deposits in transit and should be added to the balance shown in the bank statement.
2. Arrange paid checks in sequence by serial numbers and compare each check with the corresponding entry in the accounting records. Any checks issued but not yet paid by the bank should be listed as outstanding checks to be deducted from the balance reported in the bank statement.

---

[2] Banks view each depositor's account as a *liability*. Debit memoranda are issued for transactions that reduce this liability, such as bank service charges. Credit memoranda are issued to recognize an increase in this liability, as results, for example, from interest earned by the depositor.

3. Add to the balance per the depositor's accounting records any credit memoranda issued by the bank that have not been recorded by the depositor.
4. Deduct from the balance per the depositor's records any debit memoranda issued by the bank that have not been recorded by the depositor.
5. Make appropriate adjustments to correct any errors in either the bank statement or the depositor's accounting records.
6. Determine that the adjusted balance of the bank statement is equal to the adjusted balance in the depositor's records.
7. Prepare journal entries to record any items in the bank reconciliation listed as adjustments to the balance per the depositor's records.

Illustration of a Bank Reconciliation The July bank statement sent by the bank to Parkview Company was illustrated in Exhibit 7–3. This statement shows a balance of cash on deposit at July 31 of *$5,000.17*. Assume that on July 31, Parkview's ledger shows a bank balance of *$4,262.83*. The employee preparing the bank reconciliation has identified the following reconciling items:

1. A deposit of $410.90 made after banking hours on July 31 does not appear in the bank statement.
2. Four checks issued in July have not yet cleared the bank. These checks are:

Check No.	Date	Amount
881	July 1	$100.00
888	July 14	10.25
890	July 16	402.50
891	July 17	205.00

3. Two credit memoranda were included in the bank statement:

Date	Amount	Explanation
July 22	$500.00	Proceeds from collection of a non-interest-bearing note receivable from J. David. The bank's collection department collected this note for Parkview Company.
July 31	24.74	Interest earned on average account balance during July.

4. Three debit memoranda accompanied the bank statement:

Date	Amount	Explanation
July 22	$ 5.00	Fee charged by bank for handling collection of note receivable.
July 30	50.25	Check from customer J. B. Ball deposited by Parkview Company charged back as NSF.
July 31	12.00	Service charge by bank for the month of July.

5. Check no. 875 was issued to the telephone company in the amount of $85 but was erroneously recorded in the cash payments journal as $58. The check, in payment of telephone expense, was paid by the bank and correctly listed at $85 in the bank statement. In Parkview's ledger, the Cash account is *overstated* by $27 because of this error ($85 − $58 = $27).

272   Chapter 7 Financial Assets

The July 31 bank reconciliation for Parkview Company is shown in Exhibit 7–4. (The numbered arrows coincide both with the steps in preparing a bank reconciliation and with the reconciling items just listed.)

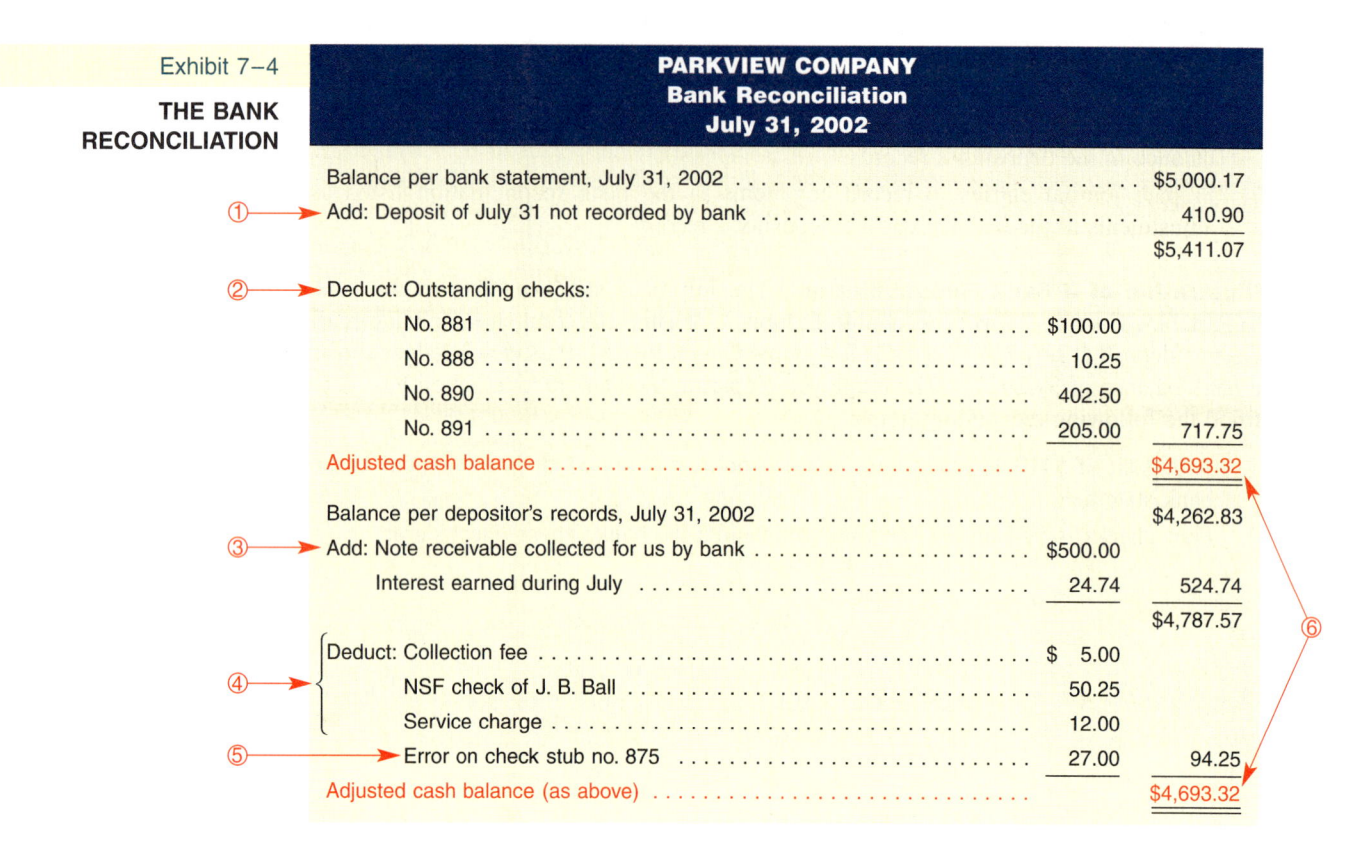

Exhibit 7–4

THE BANK RECONCILIATION

PARKVIEW COMPANY
Bank Reconciliation
July 31, 2002

Balance per bank statement, July 31, 2002			$5,000.17
① Add: Deposit of July 31 not recorded by bank			410.90
			$5,411.07
② Deduct: Outstanding checks:			
No. 881		$100.00	
No. 888		10.25	
No. 890		402.50	
No. 891		205.00	717.75
Adjusted cash balance			$4,693.32
Balance per depositor's records, July 31, 2002			$4,262.83
③ Add: Note receivable collected for us by bank		$500.00	
Interest earned during July		24.74	524.74
			$4,787.57
④ Deduct: Collection fee		$ 5.00	
NSF check of J. B. Ball		50.25	
Service charge		12.00	
⑤ Error on check stub no. 875		27.00	94.25
Adjusted cash balance (as above)			$4,693.32

⑥

Updating the Accounting Records The last step in reconciling a bank statement is to update the depositor's accounting records for any unrecorded cash transactions brought to light. In the bank reconciliation, every adjustment to the *balance per depositor's records* is a cash receipt or a cash payment that has not been recorded in the depositor's accounts. Therefore, *each of these items should be recorded.*

In this illustration and in our assignment material, we follow a policy of making one journal entry to record the unrecorded cash receipts and another to record the unrecorded cash reductions. (Acceptable alternatives would be to make separate journal entries for each item or to make one compound entry for all items.) Based on our recording policy, the entries to update the accounting records of Parkview Company are:

My Notes

Per bank credit memoranda . . .

per bank debit memoranda (and correction of an error)

Cash	524.74	
Notes Receivable		500.00
Interest Revenue		24.74
To record collection of note receivable from J. David collected by bank and interest earned on bank account in July.		
Bank Service Charges	17.00	
Accounts Receivable (J. B. Ball)	50.25	
Telephone Expense	27.00	
Cash		94.25
To record bank charges (service charge, $12; collection fee, $5); to reclassify NSF check from customer J. B. Ball as an account receivable; and to correct understatement of cash payment for telephone expense.		

Petty Cash Funds

We have emphasized the importance of making all significant cash disbursements by check. However, every business finds it convenient to have a small amount of cash on hand with which to make some minor expenditures. Examples of these expenditures include such things as small purchases of office supplies, taxi fares, and doughnuts for an office meeting.

To create a petty cash fund, a check is drawn payable to "Petty Cash" for a round amount, such as $200, which will cover these small expenditures for a period of two or three weeks. This check is cashed and the money is kept on hand in a petty cash box. One employee is designated as the *custodian* of the fund.

The custodian makes all payments from this fund and obtains a receipt or prepares a "petty cash voucher" explaining the nature and amount of each expenditure. At the end of the period (or when the fund runs low), a check is drawn payable to Petty Cash reimbursing the fund for the expenditures made during the period. The issuance of this check is recorded by debiting the appropriate expense accounts and crediting Cash. As a practical matter, because of the small amount of petty cash expenditures, the entire debit portion of this entry often is charged to the Miscellaneous Expense account.

The Cash Budget as a Control Device

Many businesses prepare detailed *cash budgets* that include forecasts of the monthly cash receipts and expenditures of each department within the organization. Management (or the internal auditors) will investigate any cash flows that differ significantly from the budgeted amounts. Thus each department manager is held accountable for the monthly cash transactions occurring within his or her department.

SHORT-TERM INVESTMENTS

Companies with large amounts of liquid resources often hold most of these resources in the form of marketable securities rather than cash.

CASE IN POINT

It is common for enterprises to invest a portion of their excess cash in marketable securities in anticipation of earning higher returns than they would by keeping these funds in the form of cash and cash equivalents. The following sample taken from recently issued balance sheets illustrates the willingness of companies to invest millions, even billions, of dollars in marketable securities:

	Amount Invested
Papa John's Pizza International	$ 5.7 million
Alcoa, Incorporated	12.0 million
Dell Computer Corporation	405.0 million
J.C. Penney Company	935.0 million
General Motors Corporation	1.1 billion
American Airlines, Inc.	2.3 billion
Pfizer, Inc.	7.7 billion
Microsoft Corporation	27.7 billion

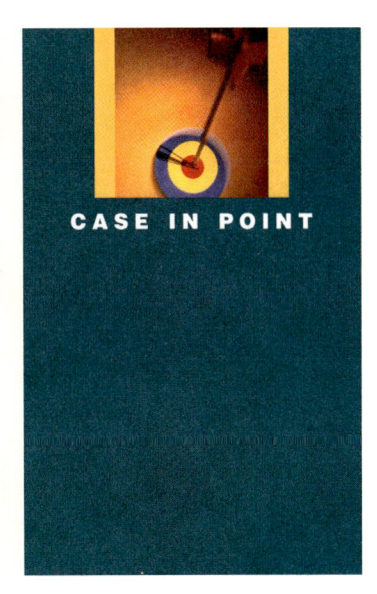

Marketable securities consist primarily of investments in bonds and in the capital stocks of publicly owned corporations. These marketable securities are traded (bought and sold) daily on organized securities exchanges, such as the **New York Stock Exchange**, the **Tokyo Stock Exchange**, and **Mexico's Bolsa**. A basic characteristic of all marketable securities is that they are *readily marketable*—meaning that they can be purchased or sold quickly and easily *at quoted market prices.*

Investments in marketable securities earn a return for the investor in the form of interest, dividends, and—if all goes well—an increase in market value. Meanwhile, these investments are *almost as liquid as cash itself.* They can be sold immediately over the telephone, simply by placing a "sell order" with a brokerage firm such as **Merrill Lynch** or **Salomon Smith Barney**, or on the Internet, by using an online brokerage firm such as **CSFB Direct**.

Because of their liquidity, investments in marketable securities usually are listed immediately after cash in the balance sheet.

Mark-to-Market: A Principle of Asset Valuation

Accounting principles are not carved in stone. Rather, they evolve and change as the accounting profession seeks to increase the usefulness of accounting information. A 1993 change in the way companies account for short-term investments provides an excellent case in point.

Short-term investments once appeared in the balance sheet at the lower of their cost or current market value. This valuation method reflected the *cost principle,* tempered by *conservatism.* But in 1993, the FASB changed the rules. Most short-term investments in marketable securities now appear in the balance sheet at their *current market value* as of the balance sheet date.[3]

Marketable securities are classified as one of three types: (1) available-for-sale securities, (2) trading securities, or (3) held-to-maturity securities. These classifications are based, in large part, on management's *intent* regarding the length of time the securities will be held. Most corporations classify their marketable securities as *available for sale.* In view of this fact, the remainder of our discussion focuses exclusively on this particular classification.

To achieve the objective of presenting marketable securities classified as available for sale at current market value, the balance sheet valuation of these investments is *adjusted to market value* at the balance sheet date. Hence, this valuation principle often is called **mark-to-market**. When the value of marketable securities is adjusted to current market value, an offsetting entry is made to an account entitled **Unrealized Holding Gain (or Loss) on Investments**. This account appears as a special stockholders' equity account in the balance sheet.

The following table summarizes the intent and the corresponding treatment of unrealized holding gains and losses of available-for-sale investments.

Classification	Management's Intent	Treatment of Unrealized Holding Gains and Losses
Available-for-sale securities	Held for short-term resale (often 6 to 18 months)	Reported in stockholders' equity section of the balance sheet

To illustrate, assume that Foster Corporation classifies all of its short-term investments as available for sale. The company currently owns marketable securities that had cost *$200,000,* but now have a market value of *$230,000.* Exhibit 7–5 illustrates Foster's condensed balance sheet.

---

[3] FASB, *Statement of Financial Accounting Standards No. 115,* "Accounting for Certain Investments in Debt and Equity Securities" (Norwalk, Conn., 1993).

Exhibit 7–5

PRESENTATION OF MARKETABLE SECURITIES IN THE BALANCE SHEET

FOSTER CORPORATION
Balance Sheet
December 31, 2002

Assets		Liabilities & Stockholders' Equity	
Current assets:		**Liabilities:**	
Cash	$ 50,000	(Detail not shown)	$350,000
Marketable securities (cost, $200,000; market value, $230,000)	230,000	**Stockholders' equity:**	
		Capital stock	100,000
		Retained earnings	420,000
Accounts receivable	300,000	Unrealized holding gain on investments	30,000
Total current assets	$580,000		
Other assets:		Total Stockholders' Equity	$550,000
(Detail not shown)	320,000		
Total	$900,000	Total	$900,000

Although the $200,000 cost of the marketable securities is *disclosed* in the balance sheet, the basis for the amount in the money columns is *$230,000*—the securities' *current market value.*

The difference between cost and current market value also appears as an *element of stockholders' equity,* labeled Unrealized Holding Gain (or Loss) on Investments. When the market value of the investments is *above* cost, as in the case just presented, this special equity account represents a holding *gain*. But if the market value is below cost, the equity account represents a holding *loss* and is shown as a *reduction* in total stockholders' equity.

Unrealized holding gains and losses are *not* subject to income taxes. Income taxes are levied on gains and losses only when the investments are sold. Nonetheless, unrealized gains and losses are shown in the balance sheet net of the expected *future* income tax effects. These expected future tax effects are included in the company's tax liability rather than in the amount shown as unrealized holding gain or loss. Such "deferred tax adjustments" are beyond the scope of our introductory discussion and are addressed in later accounting courses. In the discussions and assignment materials of this chapter, holding gains and losses simply represent the difference between the cost and the current market value of the securities owned.

Accounting for marketable securities, including the mark-to-market adjustments, is discussed further in *Supplemental Topic A* at the end of this chapter.

Our Assessment of Mark-to-Market The authors of this text commend the FASB on this change in accounting principles. Reporting short-term investments at market value substantially enhances the usefulness of the balance sheet in evaluating the liquidity of a business.

Mark-to-market is not always used internationally for valuing short-term investments. Germany and Japan continue to use the lower of cost or market valuation techniques because their accounting standards setters (Ministry of Finance for Japan and the German government) believe the techniques are more conservative.

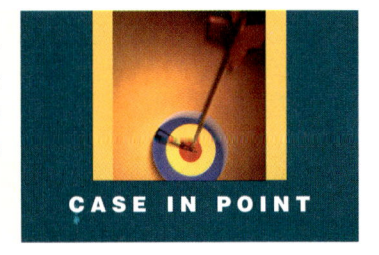

CASE IN POINT

ACCOUNTS RECEIVABLE

One of the key factors underlying the growth of the American economy is the trend toward selling goods and services on credit. Accounts receivable comprise the largest financial asset of many merchandising companies.

Accounts receivable are relatively liquid assets, usually converting into cash within a period of 30 to 60 days. Therefore, accounts receivable from customers usually appear in the balance sheet immediately after cash and short-term investments in marketable securities.

In Chapter 5, we explained that assets capable of being converted quickly into cash are classified in the balance sheet as current assets. The period used to define current assets is typically one year or the company's operating cycle, whichever is longer. The operating cycle was defined in Chapter 6 as the normal period of time required to convert cash into inventory, inventory into accounts receivable, and accounts receivable back into cash. Some companies sell merchandise on long-term installment plans that require accounts receivable be outstanding for 12, 24, or even 48 months before being collected. These receivables are part of the company's normal operating cycle. Therefore, *all* accounts receivable arising from normal sales activity are generally classified as current assets, even if the credit terms extend beyond one year.[4]

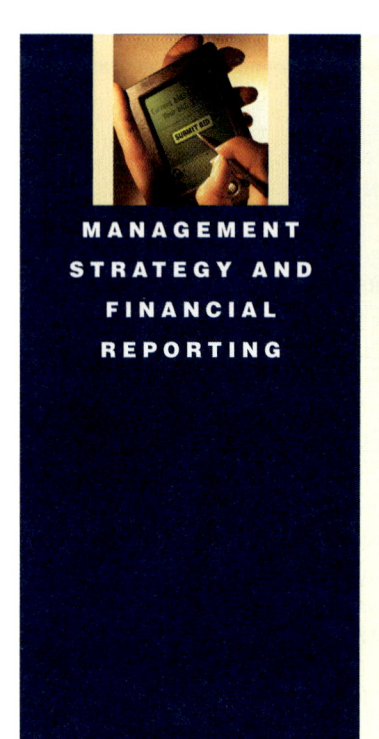

MANAGEMENT STRATEGY AND FINANCIAL REPORTING

Courtesy Dell

In a statement of cash flows, the cash receipts from collecting receivables are included in the subtotal, net cash flow from operating activities. Collections of accounts receivable often represent a company's largest and most consistent source of cash receipts. Thus monitoring the collection of receivables is an important part of efficient cash management.

Dell Computer Corp. learned that managing to squeeze time out of every step in its operating cycle between taking an order and collecting the cash can pay off. **Dell** converts the average sale to cash in less than 24 hours through the use of Internet ordering, credit cards, and electronic payment. By contrast, competitors, such as **Apple Computer** and **Gateway** take 45 days and 16 days, respectively.

A company's ability to generate the cash needed for routine business operations often depends on the amount, collectibility, and maturity dates of its receivables. Users of financial reports can judge a company's ability to collect receivables by looking at the cash flow statement and by analyzing accounts receivable performance measures presented in Exhibit 7–9 (on page 286).

Uncollectible Accounts

LO 5
Account for uncollectible receivables using the allowance and direct write-off methods.

We have stated that accounts receivable are shown in the balance sheet at the estimated collectible amount—called *net realizable value*. No business wants to sell merchandise on account to customers who will be unable to pay. Many companies maintain their own credit departments that investigate the creditworthiness of each prospective customer. Nonetheless, if a company makes credit sales to hundreds—perhaps thousands—of customers, some accounts inevitably will turn out to be uncollectible.

A limited amount of uncollectible accounts is not only expected—it is evidence of a sound credit policy. If the credit department is overly cautious, the business may lose many sales opportunities by rejecting customers who should have been considered acceptable credit risks.

Reflecting Uncollectible Accounts in the Financial Statements An account receivable that has been determined to be uncollectible is no longer an asset. The loss of this asset represents an *expense*, termed Uncollectible Accounts Expense.

---
[4] We discuss the classification of certain assets as current assets in greater depth in Chapter 14.

In measuring business income, one of the most fundamental principles of accounting is that revenue should be *matched* with (offset by) the expenses incurred in generating that revenue. Uncollectible accounts expense is *caused by selling goods* on credit to customers who fail to pay their bills. Therefore, this expense is incurred in the time period in which the *related sales* are made, even though specific accounts receivable may not be determined to be uncollectible until a later accounting period. Thus an account receivable that originates from a credit sale in January and is determined to be uncollectible in August represents an expense in *January*. Accurately estimating the amount of uncollectible receivables requires significant judgment on the part of accountants.

To illustrate, assume that World Famous Toy Co. begins business on January 1, 2002, and makes most of its sales on account. At January 31, accounts receivable amount to $250,000. On this date, the credit manager reviews the accounts receivable and estimates that approximately $10,000 of these accounts will prove to be uncollectible. The following adjusting entry should be made at January 31:

Uncollectible Accounts Expense	10,000	
Allowance for Doubtful Accounts		10,000
To record the portion of total accounts receivable estimated to be uncollectible.		

My Notes

Provision for uncollectible accounts

The Uncollectible Accounts Expense account created by the debit part of this entry is closed into the Income Summary account in the same manner as any other expense account. The Allowance for Doubtful Accounts that was credited in the above journal entry appears in the balance sheet as a deduction from the face amount of the accounts receivable. It reduces the accounts receivable to their *net realizable value* in the balance sheet, as shown in Exhibit 7–6.

WORLD FAMOUS TOY CO.
Partial Balance Sheet
January 31, 2002

Current assets:		
Cash and cash equivalents		$ 75,000
Marketable securities		25,000
Accounts receivable	$250,000	
Less: Allowance for doubtful accounts	10,000	240,000
Inventory		300,000
Total current assets		$640,000

Exhibit 7–6

REPORTING ACCOUNTS RECEIVABLE AT ESTIMATED NET REALIZABLE VALUE

The Allowance for Doubtful Accounts

There is no way of telling in advance *which* accounts receivable will prove to be uncollectible. It is therefore not possible to credit the accounts of specific customers for our estimate of probable uncollectible accounts. Neither should we credit the Accounts Receivable controlling account in the general ledger. If the Accounts Receivable controlling account were to be credited with the estimated amount of doubtful accounts, this controlling account would no longer be in balance with the total of the numerous customers' accounts in the subsidiary ledger. A practical alternative, therefore, is to credit a separate account called **Allowance for Doubtful Accounts** with the amount estimated to be uncollectible.

The Allowance for Doubtful Accounts often is described as a *contra-asset* account or a *valuation* account. Both of these terms indicate that the Allowance for Doubtful Accounts has a credit balance, which is offset against the asset Accounts Receivable to produce a more useful and reliable measure of a company's liquidity.

Estimating the Amount of Uncollectible Accounts Before financial statements are prepared at the end of the accounting period, an estimate of the expected amount of uncollectible accounts receivable should be made. This estimate is based on past experience and modified in accordance with current business conditions. Losses from uncollectible receivables tend to be greater during periods of recession than in periods of growth and prosperity. Because the allowance for doubtful accounts is an estimate and not a precise calculation, *professional judgment* plays a considerable part in determining the size of this valuation account.

Monthly Adjustments of the Allowance Account In the adjusting entry made by World Famous Toy Co. at January 31, the amount of the adjustment ($10,000) was equal to the estimated amount of uncollectible accounts. This is true only because January was the first month of operations and this was the company's first estimate of its uncollectible accounts. In future months, the amount of the adjusting entry will depend on two factors: (1) the *estimate* of uncollectible accounts and (2) the *current balance* in the Allowance for Doubtful Accounts. Before we illustrate the adjusting entry for a future month, let us see why the balance in the allowance account may change during the accounting period.

Writing Off an Uncollectible Account Receivable

Whenever an account receivable from a specific customer is determined to be uncollectible, it no longer qualifies as an asset and should be written off. To *write off* an account receivable is to reduce the balance of the customer's account to zero. The journal entry to accomplish this consists of a credit to the Accounts Receivable controlling account in the general ledger (and to the customer's account in the subsidiary ledger) and an offsetting debit to the Allowance for Doubtful Accounts.

To illustrate, assume that early in February, World Famous Toy Co. learns that Discount Stores has gone out of business and that the $4,000 account receivable from this customer is now worthless. The entry to write off this uncollectible account receivable is:

My Notes

Writing off a receivable "against the allowance"

Allowance for Doubtful Accounts	4,000	
Accounts Receivable (Discount Stores)		4,000
To write off the receivable from Discount Stores as uncollectible.		

The important thing to note in this entry is that the debit is made to the Allowance for Doubtful Accounts and *not* to the Uncollectible Accounts Expense account. The estimated expense of credit losses is charged to the Uncollectible Accounts Expense account at the end of each accounting period. When a specific account receivable is later determined to be worthless and is written off, this action does not represent an additional expense but merely confirms our previous estimate of the expense. If the Uncollectible Accounts Expense account were first charged with *estimated* credit losses and then later charged with *proven* credit losses, we would be double-counting the actual uncollectible accounts expense.

Notice also that the entry to write off an uncollectible account receivable reduces both the asset account and the contra-asset account by the same amount. Thus writing off an uncollectible account *does not change* the net realizable value of accounts receivable in the balance sheet. The net realizable value of World Famous Toy Co.'s accounts receivable before and after the write-off of the account receivable from Discount Stores is:

My Notes

What happens to net realizable value?

Before the Write-off		After the Write-off	
Accounts Receivable	$250,000	Accounts Receivable	$246,000
Less: Allowance for Doubtful Accounts	10,000	Less: Allowance for Doubtful Accounts	6,000
Net Realizable Value	$240,000	Net Realizable Value	$240,000

Let us repeat the point that underlies the allowance approach. Credit losses are recognized as an expense in the period in which the *sale occurs,* not the period in which the account is determined to be uncollectible. The reasoning for this position is based on the *matching principle.*

Write-offs Seldom Agree with Previous Estimates The total amount of accounts receivable actually written off will seldom, if ever, be exactly equal to the estimated amount previously credited to the Allowance for Doubtful Accounts.

If the amounts written off as uncollectible turn out to be less than the estimated amount, the Allowance for Doubtful Accounts will continue to show a credit balance. If the amounts written off as uncollectible are greater than the estimated amount, the Allowance for Doubtful Accounts will acquire a *temporary debit balance,* which will be eliminated by the adjustment at the end of the period.

Recovery of an Account Receivable Previously Written Off

Occasionally a receivable that has been written off as worthless will later be collected in full or in part. Such collections are often referred to as *recoveries* of bad debts. Collection of an account receivable previously written off is evidence that the write-off was an error; the receivable should therefore be reinstated as an asset.

Let us assume, for example, that a past-due account receivable in the amount of $200 from J. B. Barker was written off on February 16 by the following entry:

Allowance for Doubtful Accounts	200	
Accounts Receivable (J. B. Barker)		200
To write off the receivable from J. B. Barker as uncollectible.		

My Notes
Barker account considered uncollectible

On February 27, the customer, J. B. Barker, pays the account in full. The entry to restore Barker's account will be:

Accounts Receivable (J. B. Barker)	200	
Allowance for Doubtful Accounts		200
To reinstate as an asset an account receivable previously written off.		

My Notes
Barker account reinstated

Notice that this entry is *exactly the opposite* of the entry made when the account was written off as uncollectible. A separate entry will be made in the cash receipts journal to record the collection from Barker:

Cash	200	
Accounts Receivable (J. B. Barker)		200
To record the collection of receivable from J. B. Barker.		

Monthly Estimates of Credit Losses

At the end of each month, management should again estimate the probable amount of uncollectible accounts and adjust the Allowance for Doubtful Accounts to this new estimate.

To illustrate, assume that at the end of February the credit manager of World Famous Toy Co. analyzes the accounts receivable and estimates that approximately *$11,000* of these accounts will prove uncollectible. Currently, the Allowance for Doubtful Accounts has a credit balance of only *$6,000,* determined as follows:

My Notes

Current balance in the allowance account

Balance at January 31 (credit)		$10,000
Less: Write-offs of accounts considered worthless:		
Discount Stores	$4,000	
J. B. Barker	200	4,200
Subtotal		$ 5,800
Add: Recoveries of accounts previously written off: J. B. Barker		200
Balance at end of February (prior to adjusting entry)		$ 6,000

To increase the balance in the allowance account to $11,000 at February 28, the month-end adjusting entry must add $5,000 to the allowance. The entry will be:

My Notes

Increasing the allowance for doubtful accounts

Uncollectible Accounts Expense	5,000	
Allowance for Doubtful Accounts		5,000
To increase the Allowance for Doubtful Accounts to $11,000, computed as follows:		
Required allowance at Feb. 28	$11,000	
Credit balance prior to adjustment	6,000	
Required adjustment	$ 5,000	

Estimating Credit Losses—The Balance Sheet Approach The most widely used method of estimating the probable amount of uncollectible accounts is based on *aging the accounts receivable*. This method is sometimes called the *balance sheet* approach because the method emphasizes the proper balance sheet valuation of accounts receivable.

"Aging" accounts receivable means classifying each receivable according to its age. An aging schedule for the accounts receivable of Valley Ranch Supply is illustrated in Exhibit 7–7.

Exhibit 7–7

ACCOUNTS RECEIVABLE AGING SCHEDULE

VALLEY RANCH SUPPLY
Analysis of Accounts Receivable by Age
December 31, 2002

	Total	Not Yet Due	1–30 Days Past Due	31–60 Days Past Due	61–90 Days Past Due	Over 90 Days Past Due
Animal Care Center	$ 9,000	$ 9,000				
Butterfield, John D.	2,400			$ 2,400		
Citrus Groves, Inc.	4,000	3,000	$ 1,000			
Dairy Fresh Farms	1,600				$ 600	$1,000
Eastlake Stables	13,000	7,000	6,000			
(Other customers)	70,000	32,000	22,000	9,600	2,400	4,000
Totals	$100,000	$51,000	$29,000	$12,000	$3,000	$5,000

An aging schedule is useful to management in reviewing the status of individual accounts receivable and in evaluating the overall effectiveness of credit and collection policies. In addition, the schedule is used as the basis for estimating the amount of uncollectible accounts.

The longer an account is past due, the greater the likelihood that it will not be collected in full. Based on past experience, the credit manager estimates the percentage of credit losses likely to occur in each age group of accounts receivable. This percentage, when applied to the total dollar amount in the age group, gives the estimated uncollectible portion for that group. By adding together the estimated uncollectible portions for all age groups, the *required balance* in the Allowance for Doubtful Accounts is determined. Exhibit 7–8 provides a schedule listing the group totals from the aging schedule and shows how the estimated total amount of uncollectible accounts is computed.

VALLEY RANCH SUPPLY
Estimated Uncollectible Accounts Receivable
December 31, 2002

	Age Group Total		Percentage Considered Uncollectible*		Estimated Uncollectible Accounts
Not yet due	$ 51,000	×	1%	=	$ 510
1–30 days past due	29,000	×	3%	=	870
31–60 days past due	12,000	×	10%	=	1,200
61–90 days past due	3,000	×	20%	=	600
Over 90 days past due	5,000	×	50%	=	2,500
Totals	$100,000				$5,680

Exhibit 7–8

ESTIMATED DOLLAR AMOUNT OF UNCOLLECTIBLE ACCOUNTS

*These percentages are estimated each month by the credit manager, based on recent experience and current economic conditions.

At December 31, Valley Ranch Supply has total accounts receivable of $100,000, of which $5,680 are estimated to be uncollectible. Thus an adjusting entry is needed to increase the Allowance for Doubtful Accounts from its present level to $5,680. If the allowance account currently has a credit balance of, say, $4,000, the month-end adjusting entry should be in the amount of *$1,680.*[5]

An Alternative Approach to Estimating Credit Losses The procedures just discussed describe the *balance sheet* approach to estimating and recording credit losses. This approach is based on an aging schedule, and the Allowance for Doubtful Accounts is *adjusted to a required balance.* An alternative method, called the *income statement* approach, focuses on estimating the uncollectible accounts *expense* for the period. Based on past experience, the uncollectible accounts expense is estimated at some percentage of net credit sales. The adjusting entry is made in the *full amount of the estimated expense,* without regard for the current balance in the Allowance for Doubtful Accounts.

---

[5] If accounts receivable written off during the period *exceed* the Allowance for Doubtful Accounts at the last adjustment date, the allowance account temporarily acquires a *debit balance.* This situation seldom occurs if the allowance is adjusted each month but often occurs if adjusting entries are made only at year-end.

If Valley Ranch Supply makes only an annual adjustment for uncollectible accounts, the allowance account might have a debit balance of, say, $10,000. In this case, the year-end adjusting entry should be for *$15,680* in order to bring the allowance to the required credit balance of $5,680.

Regardless of how often adjusting entries are made, the balance in the allowance account of Valley Ranch Supply should be *$5,680 at year-end.* Uncollectible accounts expense will be the same for the year, regardless of whether adjusting entries are made annually or monthly. The only difference is in whether this expense is recognized in one annual adjusting entry or in 12 monthly adjusting entries, each for a smaller amount.

To illustrate, assume that a company's past experience indicates that about 2% of its credit sales will prove to be uncollectible. If credit sales for September amount to $150,000, the month-end adjusting entry to record uncollectible accounts expense is:

> **My Notes**
>
> The income statement approach

Uncollectible Accounts Expense	3,000	
Allowance for Doubtful Accounts		3,000
To record uncollectible accounts expense, estimated at 2% of credit sales ($150,000 × 2% = $3,000).		

This approach is fast and simple—no aging schedule is required and no consideration is given to the existing balance in the Allowance for Doubtful Accounts. The aging of accounts receivable, however, provides a more reliable estimate of uncollectible accounts because of the consideration given to the age and collectibility of specific accounts receivable at the balance sheet date.

In past years, many small companies used the income statement approach in preparing monthly financial statements but used the balance sheet method in annual financial statements. Today, however, most businesses have computer software that quickly and easily prepares monthly aging schedules of accounts receivable. Thus most businesses today use the *balance sheet approach* in their monthly as well as annual financial statements.

Conservatism in the Valuation of Accounts Receivable We previously have made reference to the accounting concept of **conservatism**. In accounting, conservatism means resolving uncertainty in a manner that minimizes the risk of overstating the company's current financial position. With respect to the valuation of accounts receivable, conservatism suggests that the allowance for doubtful accounts should be *at least adequate*. That is, it is better to err on the side of the allowance being a little too large, rather than a little too small.

Notice that conservatism in the valuation of assets also leads to a conservative measurement of net income in the current period. The larger the valuation allowance, the larger the current charge to uncollectible accounts expense.

Direct Write-off Method

Some companies do not use any valuation allowance for accounts receivable. Instead of making end-of-period adjusting entries to record uncollectible accounts expense on the basis of estimates, these companies recognize no uncollectible accounts expense until specific receivables are determined to be worthless. This method makes no attempt to match revenue with the expense of uncollectible accounts.

When a particular customer's account is determined to be uncollectible, it is written off directly to Uncollectible Accounts Expense, as follows:

Uncollectible Accounts Expense	250	
Accounts Receivable (Bell Products)		250
To write off the receivable from Bell Products as uncollectible.		

When the **direct write-off method** is used, the accounts receivable will be listed in the balance sheet at their gross amount, and *no valuation allowance* will be used. The receivables, therefore, are not stated at estimated net realizable value.

The allowance method is preferable to the direct write-off method because the allowance method does a better job of matching revenues and expenses. In some situations, however, use of the direct write-off method is acceptable. If a company makes most of its sales for cash, the amount of its accounts receivable will be small in relation to other assets. The expense from uncollectible accounts should also be small. Consequently, the direct write-off method is acceptable because its use does not have a *material* effect on the reported net income. Another situation in which the direct write-off method works satisfactorily is in a company that sells all or most of its output to a few large companies that are financially strong. In this setting there may be no basis for making advance estimates of any credit losses.

Income Tax Regulations and Financial Reporting

In previous chapters we made the point that companies often use different accounting methods in preparing their income tax returns and their financial statements. The accounting treatments accorded to uncollectible accounts receivable provide an excellent example of this concept.

Current income tax regulations *require* taxpayers to use the direct write-off method in determining the uncollectible accounts expense used in computing *taxable income*. From the standpoint of accounting theory, the allowance method is better because it enables expenses to be *matched* with the related revenue and thus provides a more logical measurement of net income. Therefore, most companies use the allowance method in their financial statements.[6]

Internal Controls for Receivables

One of the most important principles of internal control is that employees who have custody of cash or other negotiable assets must not maintain accounting records. In a small business, one employee often is responsible for handling cash receipts, maintaining accounts receivable records, issuing credit memoranda, and writing off uncollectible accounts. Such a combination of duties is an invitation to fraud. The employee in this situation is able to remove the cash collected from a customer without making any record of the collection. The next step is to dispose of the balance in the customer's account. This can be done by issuing a credit memo indicating that the customer has returned merchandise, or by writing off the customer's account as uncollectible. Thus the employee has the cash, the customer's account shows a zero balance due, and the books are in balance.

In summary, employees who maintain the accounts receivable subsidiary ledger should *not have access* to cash receipts. The employees who maintain accounts receivable or handle cash receipts should *not* have authority to issue credit memoranda or to authorize the write-off of receivables as uncollectible. These are classic examples of incompatible duties.

Management of Accounts Receivable

Management has two conflicting objectives with respect to the accounts receivable. On the one hand, management wants to generate as much sales revenue as possible. Offering customers lengthy credit terms, with little or no interest, has proven to be an effective means of generating sales revenue.

Every business, however, would rather sell for cash than on account. Unless receivables earn interest, which usually is not the case, they are nonproductive assets that produce no revenue as they await collection. Therefore, another objective of cash management is to minimize the amount of money tied up in the form of accounts receivable.

---

[6] An annual survey of accounting practices of 600 publicly owned corporations consistently shows more than 500 of these companies using the allowance method in their financial statements. All of these companies, however, use the direct write-off method in their income tax returns.

Several tools are available to a management that must offer credit terms to its customers yet wants to minimize the company's investment in accounts receivable. We have already discussed offering credit customers cash discounts (such as 2/10, n/30) to encourage early payment. Other tools include *factoring* accounts receivable and selling to customers who use national credit cards.

Factoring Accounts Receivable

The term **factoring** describes transactions in which a business either sells its accounts receivable to a financial institution (often called a *factor*) or borrows money by pledging its accounts receivable as collateral (security) for a loan. In either case, the business obtains cash immediately instead of having to wait until the receivables can be collected.

Factoring accounts receivable is a practice limited primarily to small business organizations that do not have well-established credit. Large and liquid organizations usually are able to borrow money using unsecured lines of credit, so they need not factor their accounts receivable.

YOUR TURN

You as a Used Car Purchaser

Assume you purchased a car from John's Used Cars for $500 down and 24 payments of $150 per month. After making three months of payments to John's Used Cars, you are notified that John's plans to factor your account receivable to the Barb Smith Collection Agency. You are concerned about owing money to this particular collection agency because you have heard it uses very aggressive tactics to collect overdue payments. You call the car lot and speak directly with John. You question the legality and ethics of factoring accounts receivable. You state that you entered into a contract to him and not a collection agency. You state that you did not give permission to sell your receivable and that selling the receivable to another organization eliminates your obligation to pay it. John says factoring accounts receivable is legal and suggests that you consult the Uniform Commercial Code. What would you do?

David Young-Wolff/PhotoEdit

*Our comments appear on page 317.

Credit Card Sales

Many retailing businesses minimize their investment in receivables by encouraging customers to use credit cards such as **American Express**, **Visa**, and **MasterCard**. A customer who makes a purchase using one of these cards signs a multiple-copy form, which includes a *credit card draft*. A credit card draft is similar to a check that is drawn on the funds of the credit card company rather than on the personal bank account of the customer. The credit card company promptly pays a discounted amount of cash to the merchant to redeem these drafts. At the end of each month, the credit card company bills the credit card holder for all the drafts it has redeemed during the month. If the credit card holder fails to pay the amount owed, the credit card company sustains the loss.

By making sales through credit card companies, merchants receive cash more quickly from credit sales and avoid uncollectible accounts expense. Also, the merchant avoids the expenses of investigating customers' credit, maintaining an accounts receivable subsidiary ledger, and making collections from customers.

Bank Credit Cards   Some widely used credit cards (such as **Visa** and **MasterCard**) are issued by banks. When the credit card company is a bank, the retailing business may deposit the signed credit card drafts directly in its bank account. Because banks accept these credit card drafts for immediate deposit, sales to customers using bank credit cards are recorded as *cash sales*.

In exchange for handling the credit card drafts, the bank makes a monthly service charge that usually runs between 1¼% and 3½% of the amount of the drafts. This monthly service charge is deducted from the merchant's bank account and appears with other bank service charges in the merchant's monthly bank statement.

Other Credit Cards   When customers use nonbank credit cards (such as **American Express** and **Carte Blanche**), the retailing business cannot deposit the credit card drafts directly in its bank account. Instead of debiting Cash, the merchant records an account receivable from the credit card company. Periodically, the credit card drafts are mailed (or transmitted electronically) to the credit card company, which then sends a check to the merchant. Credit card companies, however, do not redeem the drafts at the full sales price. The agreement between the credit card company and the merchant usually allows the credit card company to take a discount of between 3½% and 5% when redeeming the drafts.

To illustrate, assume that Bradshaw Camera Shop sells a camera for $1,200 to a customer who uses a Quick Charge credit card. The entry would be:

Accounts Receivable (Quick Charge Co.)	1,200	
Sales		1,200
To record sale to customer using Quick Charge credit card.		

My Notes

This receivable is from the credit card company

At the end of the week, Bradshaw Camera Shop mails the $1,200 credit card draft to Quick Charge Company, which redeems the draft after deducting a 5% discount. When payment is received by Bradshaw, the entry is:

Cash	1,140	
Credit Card Discount Expense	60	
Accounts Receivable (Quick Charge Co.)		1,200
To record collection of account receivable from Quick Charge Co., less 5% discount.		

The expense account, Credit Card Discount Expense, is included among the selling expenses in the income statement of Bradshaw Camera Shop.

FINANCIAL ANALYSIS

Collecting accounts receivable *on time* is important; it spells the success or failure of a company's credit and collection policies. A past-due receivable is a candidate for write-off as a credit loss. To help us judge how good a job a company is doing in granting credit and collecting its receivables, we compute the ratio of net sales to average

LO 6
Evaluate the liquidity of various financial assets.

receivables. This **accounts receivable turnover rate** tells us how many times the company's average investment in receivables was converted into cash during the year. The ratio is computed by dividing annual net sales by average accounts receivable.[7] The higher the turnover rate, the more liquid the company's receivables. Dividing 365 days by the turnover rate provides an estimate of the average number of *days* an account receivable remains outstanding before it is collected. High turnover rates result in shorter collection periods than low turnover rates.

In some companies, such as restaurants, hotels, and public utilities, turnover rates are relatively high. For other enterprises, such as large manufacturing firms, turnover rates are relatively low, making the average time it takes to collect an outstanding receivable much longer.

To illustrate, Exhibit 7–9 contains information taken from recent financial statements issued by **Minnesota Power, Inc.**, and **3M (Minnesota Mining and Manufacturing Company)**.

Exhibit 7–9

ACCOUNTS RECEIVABLE COLLECTION PERFORMANCE

		Minnesota Power, Inc.	3M
a.	Net sales	$1.1 billion	$16.7 billion
	Accounts receivable (beginning of year)	$111 million	$2.9 billion
	Accounts receivable (end of year)	113 million	2.7 billion
		$224 million	$5.6 billion
		÷ 2	÷ 2
b.	Average accounts receivable	$112 million	$2.8 billion
c.	Accounts receivable turnover rate (a ÷ b)	9.8 times	6.0 times
	Average days outstanding (365 days ÷ c)	37 days	61 days

As shown in Exhibit 7–9, **Minnesota Power**'s accounts receivable turnover rate is *9.8 times* ($1.1 billion net sales ÷ $112 million average accounts receivable), compared to **3M**'s turnover rate of only *6 times* ($16.7 billion net sales ÷ $2.8 billion average accounts receivable). Thus, **Minnesota Power**'s accounts receivable remain outstanding an average of *37 days* before being collected (365 days ÷ 9.8 turnover rate), whereas **3M**'s accounts receivable remain outstanding an average of *61 days* prior to collection (365 days ÷ 6.0 turnover rate).

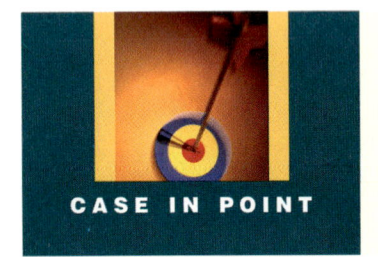

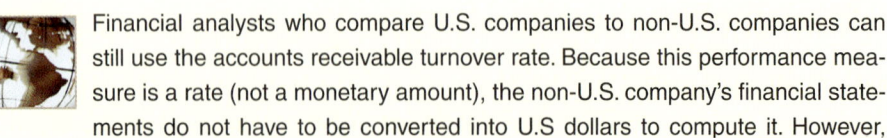

CASE IN POINT

Financial analysts who compare U.S. companies to non-U.S. companies can still use the accounts receivable turnover rate. Because this performance measure is a rate (not a monetary amount), the non-U.S. company's financial statements do not have to be converted into U.S dollars to compute it. However, when using rates to compare U.S. and non-U.S. companies, financial analysts must take into account any differences in acceptable business practices between the two countries.

---

[7] From a conceptual point of view, net *credit* sales should be used in computing the accounts receivable turnover rate. It is common practice, however, to use the net sales figure, as the portion of net sales made on account usually is not disclosed in financial statements.

Management closely monitors these performance measures in evaluating the company's policies for extending credit to customers and the effectiveness of its collection procedures. Short-term creditors, such as factors, banks, and merchandise suppliers, also use these ratios to evaluate a company's ability to generate the cash necessary to pay its short-term liabilities.

In the annual audit of a company by a CPA firm, the independent auditors will verify receivables by communicating directly with the people who owe the money. This *confirmation* process is designed to provide evidence that the customers and other debtors actually exist and that they acknowledge their indebtedness. The CPA firm also may verify the credit rating of major debtors.

YOUR TURN

You as a Credit Manager

Assume that you were hired by Regis Department Stores in 1999 to develop and implement a new credit policy. At the time of your hire, the average collection period for an outstanding receivable was in excess of 90 days (far greater than the industry average). Thus the primary purpose of the new policy was to better screen credit applicants in an attempt to improve the quality of the company's accounts receivable.

Shown below are sales and accounts receivable data for the past four years (in thousands):

	2002	2001	2000	1999
Sales	$17,000	$14,580	$9,600	$9,000
Average Accounts Receivable	$ 1,700	$ 1,620	$1,600	$1,800

Based on the above data, was the credit policy you developed successful? Explain.

*Our comments appear on page 317.

Concentrations of Credit Risk

Assume that a business operates a single retail store in a town in which the major employer is a steel mill. What would happen to the collectibility of the store's accounts receivable if the steel mill were to close, leaving most of the store's customers unemployed? This situation illustrates what accountants call a *concentration of credit risk*, because many of the store's credit customers can be affected *in a similar manner* by certain changes in economic conditions. Concentrations of credit risk occur if a significant portion of a company's receivables are due from a few major customers or from customers operating in the same industry or geographic region.

The FASB requires companies to disclose all significant concentrations of credit risk in the notes accompanying their financial statements. The basic purpose of these disclosures is to assist users of the financial statements in evaluating the extent of the company's vulnerability to credit losses stemming from changes in specific economic conditions.

Notes Receivable and Interest Charges

Accounts receivable usually do not bear interest. When interest will be charged, creditors usually require the debtor to sign a formal promissory note. Accounting for notes receivable and interest charges is discussed in *Supplemental Topic B* at the end of this chapter.

LO 7
Explain how transactions discussed in this chapter affect net income and cash flows.

CASH EFFECTS

In Exhibit 7–2, we summarized the valuation of financial assets in the balance sheet. The following table summarizes the reporting of transactions involving these assets in the *income statement* and any cash effects to be presented in the *statement of cash flows*. Note that most of these transactions have no cash flow effects.

Transactions	Presentation in the: Income Statement	Statement of Cash Flows
Cash sales	Included in net sales	Cash receipts from operating activities
Investments in cash equivalents	No effect	Omitted—does not change cash total
Conversion of cash equivalents back into cash	No effect	Omitted—does not change cash total
Interest received from cash equivalents	*Nonoperating revenue	Cash receipts from operating activities
Investments in marketable securities	No effect	Cash used in investing activities
Conversion of marketable securities into cash	Nonoperating item (only the amount of gain or loss)	Cash receipts from investing activities (total proceeds)
*Interest and dividends from investments	*Nonoperating revenue (recognized *as received*)	Cash receipts from operating activities
*Year-end mark-to-market adjustment of available-for-sale marketable securities	No effect	Omitted—not a cash transaction
Sales on account	Included in net sales	Omitted—not a cash transaction
Collections of accounts receivable	No effect	Cash receipts from operating activities
Addition to an allowance for doubtful accounts	Operating expense	Omitted—not a cash transaction
Write-off of an uncollectible account against the allowance	No effect	Omitted—not a cash transaction
Write-off of an account using the direct write-off method	Operating expense	Omitted—not a cash transaction
†Interest revenue on notes receivable	Nonoperating revenue (recognized *as earned*)	Cash receipts from operating activities (recognized *as received*)

*Topic is covered in *Supplemental Topic A*.
†Topic is covered in *Supplemental Topic B*.

CONCLUDING REMARKS

This is the first of three chapters in which we explore the issues involved in accounting for assets. The central theme in these chapters is the valuation of assets.

The valuation of assets affects not only the balance sheet but also the measurement of net income. With respect to cash, there is little question as to the appropriate valuation. The valuation of notes receivable however, requires professional judgment and can be a measurement of critical importance.

In the next two chapters, we explore the valuation of inventories and of plant assets. For each of these assets, you will see that several *alternative* valuation methods are acceptable. These different methods, however, may produce *significantly different results*. An understanding of these alternative accounting methods is essential to the proper use and interpretation of financial statements and in the preparation of income tax returns.

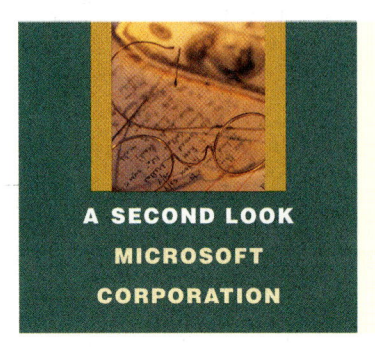

A SECOND LOOK — MICROSOFT CORPORATION

Would any company want billions of dollars sitting idle in their corporate checking account earning no interest or dividends whatsoever? Certainly not Microsoft. In its recent financial statements, Microsoft reported cash, cash equivalents, and marketable securities totaling $31.7 billion. Of this amount, only about 1% was held as cash. The remaining $31.4 billion was invested in cash equivalents and marketable securities. If we assume that Microsoft is able to generate a return on these investments of, say, 7%, that's nearly $2.2 billion in interests, dividends, and capital appreciation per year.

Supplemental Topic A

SUPPLEMENTAL TOPIC A

ACCOUNTING FOR MARKETABLE SECURITIES

There are four basic accountable events relating to investments in marketable securities: (1) purchase of the investments, (2) receipt of dividend revenue and interest revenue, (3) sales of securities owned, and (4) end-of-period mark-to-market adjustment.

LO 8
Account for transactions involving marketable securities.

Purchases of Marketable Securities

Investments in marketable securities originally are recorded at cost, which includes any brokerage commissions.[1] To illustrate, assume that MedCo purchases as a short-term investment 4,000 shares of the capital stock of **Coca-Cola** Company. The purchase price is *$50 per share*, plus a brokerage commission of *$800*. The entry to record the purchase of these shares is:

Marketable Securities (**Coca-Cola** capital stock)	200,800	
Cash		200,800
Purchased 4,000 shares of **Coca-Cola** capital stock. Total cost, $200,800 ($50 × 4,000 shares + $800); cost per share, $50.20 ($200,800 ÷ 4,000 shares).		

Marketable Securities is a controlling account, representing the balance sheet value of *all* of MedCo's short-term investments. MedCo—like most investors—also maintains a *marketable securities subsidiary ledger*, with a separate account for each security owned. (Notice the computation in the explanation of our journal entry of the $50.20 *cost per share*. This amount will be used in computing any gains or losses when MedCo sells some of these investment shares.)

Recognition of Investment Revenue

Most investors recognize interest and dividend revenue *as it is received*. Thus the entries involve a debit to Cash and a credit to either Interest Revenue or Dividend Revenue.

To illustrate, assume that MedCo receives an $0.80 per share dividend on its 4,000 shares of **Coca-Cola**. The entry to record this cash receipt is:

Cash	3,200	
Dividend Revenue		3,200
Received a quarterly cash dividend of 80 cents per share on 4,000 shares of **Coca-Cola** capital stock.		

The policy of recognizing revenue as it is received eliminates the need for adjusting entries to accrue any investment revenue receivable at year-end.[2]

---

[1] In purchasing some types of interest-bearing securities, the investors also must purchase any accrued interest. The amount of accrued interest should be debited to a separate account, entitled Accrued Interest Receivable. Accounting for accrued interest is explained in *Supplemental Topic B*, beginning on page 292.

[2] Dividend revenue does not accrue from day to day, but interest revenue does. There is nothing wrong with accruing interest revenue receivable at the end of each accounting period, but this usually is unnecessary. Accountants seldom make adjusting entries for immaterial amounts. In most cases, recognizing interest revenue as it is *received* produces essentially the same annual results as recording this revenue as it accrues. Thus the convenient practice of recognizing interest revenue as it is received often is justified by the principle of *materiality*.

Sales of Investments

When an investment is sold, a gain or a loss often results. A sales price in excess of cost produces a **gain**, whereas a sales price below cost results in a **loss**.

Sale at a Price Resulting in a Gain To illustrate, assume that MedCo sells 1,000 shares of its **Coca-Cola** stock for $55 per share, less a brokerage commission of $200. The entry would be:

Cash	54,800	
Marketable Securities (**Coca-Cola** capital stock)		50,200
Gain on Sale of Investments		4,600
Sold 1,000 shares of **Coca-Cola** capital stock at a gain:		
Sales price ($55 × 1,000 shares − $200) $54,800		
Cost ($50.20 per share × 1,000 shares) 50,200		
Gain on sale . . . . $ 4,600		

This transaction results in a gain because MedCo sold the shares at a price above cost. The gain—representing the profit on the sale—increases MedCo's net income for the period. At the end of the period, the credit balances in any gain accounts are closed into the Income Summary account, along with the credit balances of the revenue accounts.

Sale at a Price Resulting in a Loss Assume that several months later, MedCo sells another 1,000 shares of its **Coca-Cola** stock, this time at a price *below* cost. The sales price is $48 per share, again less a brokerage commission of $200. The entry would be:

Cash	47,800	
Loss on Sale of Investments	2,400	
Marketable Securities (**Coca-Cola** capital stock)		50,200
Sold 1,000 shares of **Coca-Cola** capital stock at a loss:		
Sales price ($48 × 1,000 shares − $200) $47,800		
Cost ($50.20 per share × 1,000 shares) 50,200		
Loss on sale . . . . $ (2,400)		

This loss decreases MedCo's net income for the period. At the end of the period, the debit balances in any loss accounts are closed into the Income Summary account, along with the debit balances of expense accounts.

Adjusting Marketable Securities to Market Value

At the end of each accounting period, the balance in the Marketable Securities account is adjusted to its *current market value*. Hence, this adjustment is described by the phrase "mark-to-market." Mark-to-market is an interesting concept because it represents a *departure from the cost principle*. At present, marketable securities are the only assets likely to appear in the balance sheet at an amount *above cost*.

The mark-to-market adjustment is easy to make and involves only two accounts: (1) the Marketable Securities controlling account and (2) a special owners' equity account, entitled Unrealized Holding Gain (or Loss) on Investments. The adjustment to the Marketable Securities account may be either a debit or a credit—whichever is necessary to adjust the account's balance to current market value.[3] (The market values of securities owned can be determined easily from the newspaper—remember, marketable securities trade daily at *quoted market prices.*)

When we change the valuation of an asset, there is a corresponding change in either total liabilities or total owners' equity. In the case of the mark-to-market adjustment, the corresponding change is recorded in the owners' equity account, Unrealized Holding Gain (or Loss) on Investments.

The Mark-to-Market Adjustment: An Illustration Assume that prior to making any adjusting entry, MedCo's Marketable Securities account has a balance of *$250,000* at year-end. If the current market value of the securities owned is, say, *$265,000,* MedCo will make the following adjustment at year-end:

Marketable Securities	15,000	
Unrealized Holding Gain (or Loss) on Investments		15,000
To adjust the balance sheet valuation of marketable securities to their current market value of $265,000.		

But if the market value of the securities were only *$240,000—$10,000 less* than the balance in the Marketable Securities account—the adjusting entry would be:

Unrealized Holding Gain (or Loss) on Investments	10,000	
Marketable Securities		10,000
To adjust the balance sheet valuation of marketable securities owned to a market value of $240,000.		

Notice that the Unrealized Holding Gain (or Loss) account may have either a debit or credit balance. A debit balance represents an unrealized holding *loss,* meaning that the current market value of the securities owned is *below* the investor's cost. A credit balance represents an unrealized holding *gain,* indicating that market value of the securities *exceeds* the investor's cost.

Mark-to-Market Affects Only the Balance Sheet In Chapter 4 we made the point that adjusting entries usually affect both the balance sheet and the income statement. The mark-to-market adjustment of marketable securities is an exception to this rule—it affects *only the balance sheet.*[4]

The gains and losses recorded in the mark-to-market adjusting entries are *unrealized*—that is, they have not been finalized through sales of the securities. These unrealized gains and losses are *not* included in the investor's income statement. Rather, the Unrealized Holding Gain (or Loss) account appears in the *stockholders' equity section of the balance sheet.*

---

[3] The adjustment to the Marketable Securities account does *not* change the carrying value of individual securities. This adjustment is based on the total value of *all* securities owned. Thus mark-to-market adjustments *do not affect* the amounts of realized gains or losses recognized when specific securities are sold. Realized gains and losses are determined by comparing the *cost* of the securities sold with the proceeds from the sale.

[4] This exception applies only to those short-term investments classified as available for sale. It does not apply to short-term investments classified as trading securities. Held-to-maturity securities and trading securities are addressed in more advanced accounting courses.

Because the Unrealized Holding Gain (or Loss) account does not enter into the determination of net income, it is not closed at the end of the accounting period. Instead, its balance is adjusted from one period to the next. At any balance sheet date, the Unrealized Holding Gain (or Loss) account represents the *difference between* the cost of the marketable securities owned and their current market value.

Reporting Investment Transactions in the Financial Statements

In a multiple-step income statement, interest revenue, dividend revenue, and gains and losses from sales of investments usually appear as *nonoperating items,* after the determination of income from operations.

In a statement of *cash flows,* receipts of dividends and interest are classified as *operating activities.* Purchases and sales of marketable securities classified as available for sale are presented as *investing activities,* regardless of whether sales transactions result in a gain or a loss. (In the statement of cash flows, the *total sales proceeds* are listed as cash receipts from investing activities, regardless of whether the investment is sold at a gain or at a loss.)

Mark-to-Market and Income Taxes In income tax returns, the gains and losses on sales of investments are called *capital gains* and *capital losses.* Capital gains and losses are included in income tax returns only when the securities are *sold.* Thus mark-to-market adjustments *do not* enter into the computation of taxable income.

SUPPLEMENTAL TOPIC B

NOTES RECEIVABLE AND INTEREST REVENUE

A promissory note is an unconditional promise in writing to pay on demand or at a future date a definite sum of money.

The person who signs the note and thereby promises to pay is called the *maker* of the note. The person to whom payment is to be made is called the *payee* of the note. In Exhibit 7–10, Pacific Rim Corp. is the maker of the note and First National Bank is the payee.

Exhibit 7–10
SIMPLIFIED FORM OF PROMISSORY NOTE

$100,000   Los Angeles, California   July 10, 2002

One year   AFTER DATE   Pacific Rim Corp.   PROMISES TO PAY

TO THE ORDER OF   First National Bank

---One hundred thousand and no/100---   DOLLARS

PLUS INTEREST COMPUTED AT THE RATE OF   12% per annum

SIGNED   G. L. Smith

TITLE   Treasurer

From the viewpoint of the maker, Pacific Rim, the illustrated note is a liability and is recorded by crediting the Notes Payable account. However, from the viewpoint of the payee, First National Bank, this same note is an asset and is recorded by debiting the Notes Receivable account. The maker of a note expects to pay cash at the *maturity date* (or due date); the payee expects to receive cash at that date.

Nature of Interest

Interest is a charge made for the use of money. A borrower incurs interest expense. A lender earns interest revenue. When you encounter notes payable in a company's financial statements, you know that the company is borrowing and you should expect to find interest expense. When you encounter notes receivable, you should expect interest revenue.

LO 9
Explain, compute, and account for the accrual of interest revenue.

Computing Interest   A formula used in computing interest is as follows:

$$\text{Interest} = \text{Principal} \times \text{Rate of Interest} \times \text{Time}$$

(This formula is often expressed as $I = P \times R \times T$.)

Interest rates usually are stated on an *annual basis*. For example, the total interest charge on a $100,000, one-year, 12% note receivable is computed as follows:

$$P \times R \times T = \$100,000 \times .12 \times 1 = \$12,000$$

If the term of the note were only *four months* instead of one year, the total interest revenue earned in the life of the note would be $4,000, computed as follows:

$$P \times R \times T = \$100,000 \times .12 \times {}^{4}/_{12} = \$4,000$$

In making interest computations, it is convenient to assume that each month has *30* days. Thus a year has *360* days and each month represents $^{1}/_{12}$ of the year. As these assumptions greatly simplify the computation of interest and assist students in focusing on the underlying concepts, we will use them in our illustrations and assignment material.[1]

If the term of a note is expressed in days, the exact number of days in each month must be considered in determining the maturity date of the note. The day on which a note is dated is not counted, but the date on which it matures is. Thus a two-day note dated today matures the day *after* tomorrow.

To illustrate these concepts, assume that a 60-day, 12% note for $100,000 is drawn on June 10. The *total* interest charge on this note will be $2,000, computed as follows:

$$P \times R \times T = \$100,000 \times .12 \times {}^{60}/_{360} = \$2,000$$

The $102,000 **maturity value** of the note ($100,000 principal, plus $2,000 interest) will be payable on *August 9*. The **maturity date** is determined as follows:

Days remaining in June (30 − 10)	20
Days in July	31
Subtotal	51
Days in August needed to complete the term of the note (including maturity date)	9
Specified term of note (in days)	60

Accounting for Notes Receivable

In most fields of business, notes receivable are seldom encountered; in some fields they occur frequently and may constitute an important part of total assets. In banks and financial institutions, for example, notes receivable often represent the company's largest asset category and generate most of the company's revenue. Some retailers that sell on installment plans, such as **Sears, Roebuck & Co.**, also own large amounts of notes receivable from customers.

---

[1] Prior to the widespread use of computers, these assumptions were widely used in the business community. Today, however, most financial institutions compute interest using a 365-day year and the actual number of days in each month. The differences between these assumptions usually are *not material* in dollar amount.

All notes receivable are usually posted to a single account in the general ledger. A subsidiary ledger is not essential because the notes themselves, when filed by due dates, are the equivalent of a subsidiary ledger and provide any necessary information as to maturity, interest rates, collateral pledged, and other details. The amount debited to Notes Receivable is always the *face amount* of the note, regardless of whether the note bears interest. When an interest-bearing note is collected, the amount of cash received may be larger than the face amount of the note. The interest collected is credited to an Interest Revenue account, and only the face amount of the note is credited to the Notes Receivable account.

Illustrative Entries Assume that on December 1 a 90-day, 12% note receivable is acquired from a customer, Marvin White, in settlement of an existing account receivable of $30,000. The entry for acquisition of the note is as follows:

> **My Notes**
> Note received to replace account receivable

Notes Receivable	30,000	
Accounts Receivable (Marvin White)		30,000
Accepted 90-day, 12% note in settlement of account receivable.		

At December 31, the end of the company's fiscal year, the interest earned to date on notes receivable should be accrued by an adjusting entry as follows:

> **My Notes**
> Adjusting entry for interest revenue earned in December

Interest Receivable	300	
Interest Revenue		300
To accrue interest for the month of December on Marvin White note ($30,000 × 12% × 1/12 = $300).		

To simplify this illustration, we will assume our company makes adjusting entries *only at year-end*. Therefore, no entries are made to recognize the interest revenue accruing during January and February.

On March 1 (90 days after the date of the note) the note matures. The entry to record collection of the note will be:

> **My Notes**
> Collection of principal and interest

Cash	30,900	
Notes Receivable		30,000
Interest Receivable		300
Interest Revenue		600
Collected 90-day, 12% note from Marvin White ($30,000 × 12% × 3/12 = $900 interest, of which $600 was earned in current year).		

The preceding three entries show that interest is being earned throughout the term of the note and that the interest should be apportioned between years on a time basis. The revenue of each year will then include the interest actually earned in that year.

If the Maker of a Note Defaults A note receivable that cannot be collected at maturity is said to have been **defaulted** by the maker. Immediately after the default of a note, an entry should be made by the holder to transfer the amount due from the Notes Receivable account to an account receivable from the debtor.

To illustrate, assume that on March 1, our customer, Marvin White, had defaulted on the note used in the preceding example. In this case, the entry on March 1 would have been:

Accounts Receivable (Marvin White) 30,900		
Notes Receivable	30,000	
Interest Receivable	300	
Interest Revenue	600	
To record default by Marvin White on 90-day, 12% note.		

Notice that the interest earned on the note is recorded through the maturity date and is included in the account receivable from the maker. The interest receivable on a defaulted note is just as valid a claim against the maker as is the principal amount of the note.

If the account receivable from White cannot be collected, it ultimately will be written off against the Allowance for Doubtful Accounts. Therefore, the balance in the Allowance for Doubtful Accounts should provide for estimated uncollectible *notes* receivable as well as uncollectible *accounts* receivable.

CASE IN POINT

For many companies, the provision for doubtful accounts is small and does not have a material effect on net income for the period. Notes receivable, however, are the largest and most important asset for nearly every bank. Interest on these notes is a bank's largest and most important type of revenue. Thus the collectibility of notes owned by a bank is a key factor in determining the success or failure of that bank.

Citicorp, the nation's largest bank, recently added a staggering $3 billion to its allowance for doubtful loans to developing countries. The related expense caused **Citicorp** to report one of the largest net losses for a single quarter (three-month period) in the history of American business. **Citicorp** is not alone in having problems with uncollectible loans. In recent years, uncollectible loans have been the largest expense in the income statements of many American banks and savings and loan associations.

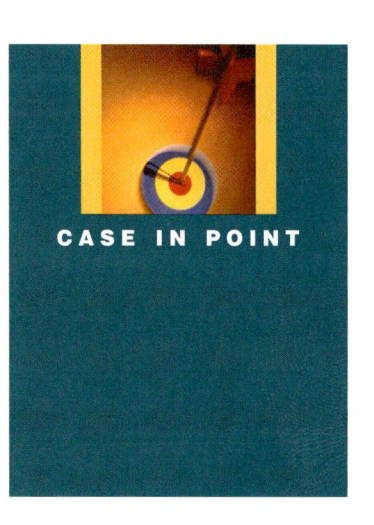

Discounting Notes Receivable In past years some companies sold their notes receivable to banks in order to obtain cash prior to the maturity dates of these notes. As the banks purchased these notes at a "discount" from their maturity values, this practice became known as *discounting* notes receivable.

Discounting notes receivable is not a widespread practice today because most banks no longer purchase notes receivable from their customers. Interestingly, the practice of discounting notes receivable is most widespread among banks themselves. Many banks sell large packages of their notes receivable (loans) to agencies of the federal government or to other financial institutions. From a conceptual point of view, discounting notes receivable is essentially the same as selling accounts receivable to a factor.

The Decision of Whether to Accrue Interest

The concept of interest accruing from day to day applies not only to notes receivable but to all interest-bearing investments (such as cash equivalents and bonds) and to interest-bearing debt. But in our discussions of cash equivalents and marketable securities, we stated that investors generally recognize interest revenue as it is received. In accounting for notes receivable, why did we accrue the interest earned, instead of recognizing revenue as cash was received?

The answer lies in the concept of *materiality*. Interest does, in fact, accrue from day to day. But the interest revenue earned from cash equivalents and investments in marketable securities usually represents only a small part of the investor's total revenue. In short, it usually is *not material* in relation to other financial statement amounts. Thus the principle of materiality often justifies investors' accounting for this revenue in the most convenient manner.

Most notes receivable, however, are owned by *financial institutions.* For these businesses, interest revenue *is* material. In fact, it generally is the company's primary source of revenue. In these circumstances, greater care must be taken to assign interest revenue to the period in which it actually is *earned.*

END-OF-CHAPTER REVIEW

SUMMARY OF LEARNING OBJECTIVES

LO 1
Define financial assets and explain their valuation in the balance sheet.
Financial assets are cash and other assets that convert directly into *known amounts* of cash. The three basic categories are cash, marketable securities, and receivables. In the balance sheet, financial assets are listed at their *current value*. For cash, this means the face amount; for marketable securities, current market value; and for receivables, net realizable value.

LO 2
Describe the objectives of cash management.
The objectives of cash management are accurate accounting for cash transactions, the prevention of losses through theft or fraud, and maintaining adequate—but not excessive—cash balances.

LO 3
Explain means of achieving internal control over cash transactions.
The major steps in achieving internal control over cash transactions are as follows: (1) separate cash handling from the accounting function, (2) prepare departmental cash budgets, (3) prepare a control listing of all cash received through the mail and from over-the-counter cash sales, (4) deposit all cash receipts in the bank daily, (5) make all payments by check, (6) verify every expenditure before issuing a check in payment, and (7) promptly reconcile bank statements.

LO 4
Prepare a bank reconciliation and explain its purpose.
The cash balance shown in the month-end bank statement usually will differ from the amount of cash shown in the depositor's ledger. The difference is caused by items that have been recorded by either the depositor or the bank, but not recorded by both. Examples are outstanding checks and deposits in transit. The bank reconciliation adjusts the cash balance per the books and the cash balance per the bank statement for any unrecorded items and thus produces the correct amount of cash to be included in the balance sheet at the end of the month.

The purpose of a bank reconciliation is to achieve the control inherent in the maintenance of two independent records of cash transactions: one record maintained by the depositor and the other by the bank. When these two records are reconciled (brought into agreement), we gain assurance of a correct accounting for cash transactions.

LO 5
Account for uncollectible receivables using the allowance and direct write-off methods.
Under the allowance method, the portion of each period's credit sales expected to prove uncollectible is *estimated*. This estimated amount is recorded by a debit to Uncollectible Accounts Expense and a credit to the contra-asset account Allowance for Doubtful Accounts. When specific accounts are determined to be uncollectible, they are written off by debiting Allowance for Doubtful Accounts and crediting Accounts Receivable.

Under the direct write-off method, uncollectible accounts are charged to expense in the period that they are determined to be worthless.

The allowance method is theoretically preferable because it is based on the matching principle. However, only the direct write-off method may be used in income tax returns.

LO 6
Evaluate the liquidity of various financial assets.
The most liquid financial asset is cash, followed by cash equivalents, marketable securities, and receivables. The liquidity of receivables varies depending on their collectibility and maturity dates.

The allowance for doubtful accounts should provide for those receivables that may prove to be uncollectible. However, users of financial statements may also want to evaluate the concentrations-of-credit-risk disclosure and, perhaps, the credit ratings of major debtors. The accounts receivable turnover rate provides insight as to how quickly receivables are collected.

LO 7
Explain how transactions discussed in this chapter affect net income and cash flows.
These effects are summarized in the table on page 288.

*LO 8
Account for transactions involving marketable securities.
When securities are purchased, they are recorded at cost. Interest and dividends generally are recognized as revenue when they are received. When securities are sold, the cost is compared to the sales price, and the difference is recorded as a gain or a loss. At the end of each accounting period, the balance of the controlling account is adjusted to reflect the *current market value* of the securities owned.

†LO 9
Explain, compute, and account for the accrual of interest revenue.
Interest is a contractual amount that accumulates (accrues) day by day. The amount of interest accruing over a time period may be computed by the formula *Principal × Rate × Time*.

Whether interest revenue is recognized as it *accrues* or as it *is received* depends on the *materiality* of the amounts involved.

---

*Supplemental Topic A, "Accounting for Marketable Securities."

†Supplemental Topic B, "Notes Receivable and Interest Revenue."

KEY TERMS INTRODUCED OR EMPHASIZED IN CHAPTER 7

accounts receivable turnover rate (p. 286)   A ratio used to measure the liquidity of accounts receivable and the reasonableness of the accounts receivable balance. Computed by dividing net sales by average receivables.

aging the accounts receivable (p. 280)   The process of classifying accounts receivable by age groups such as current, 1–30 days past due, 31–60 days past due, etc. A step in estimating the uncollectible portion of the accounts receivable.

Allowance for Doubtful Accounts (p. 277)   A valuation account or contra-account relating to accounts receivable and showing the portion of the receivables estimated to be uncollectible.

bank reconciliation (p. 269)   An analysis that explains the difference between the balance of cash shown in the bank statement and the balance of cash shown in the depositor's records.

cash equivalents (p. 265)   Very short-term investments that are so liquid that they are considered equivalent to cash. Examples include money market funds, U.S. Treasury bills, certificates of deposit, and commercial paper. These investments must mature within 90 days of acquisition.

cash management (p. 266)   Planning, controlling, and accounting for cash transactions and cash balances.

compensating balance (p. 265)   A minimum average balance that a bank may require a borrower to leave on deposit in a non-interest-bearing account.

conservatism (p. 282)   A traditional practice of resolving uncertainties by choosing an asset valuation at the lower end of the range of reasonableness. Also refers to the policy of postponing recognition of revenue to a later date when a range of reasonable choice exists. Designed to avoid overstatement of financial strength and earnings.

default (p. 294)   Failure to pay interest or principal of a promissory note at the due date.

direct write-off method (p. 282)   A method of accounting for uncollectible receivables in which no expense is recognized until individual accounts are determined to be worthless. At that point the account receivable is written off, with an offsetting debit to uncollectible accounts expense. Fails to match revenue and related expenses.

factoring (p. 284)   Transactions in which a business either sells its accounts receivable to a financial institution (often called a *factor*) or borrows money by pledging its accounts receivable as collateral.

financial assets (p. 264)   Cash and assets convertible directly into known amounts of cash (such as marketable securities and receivables).

gain (p. 290)   An increase in owners' equity resulting from a transaction other than earning revenue or investment by the owners. The most common example is the sale of an asset at a price above book value.

line of credit (p. 266)   A prearranged borrowing agreement in which a bank stands ready to advance the borrower without delay any amount up to a specified credit limit. Once used, a line of credit becomes a liability. The unused portion of the line represents the ability to borrow cash without delay.

loss (p. 290)   A decrease in owners' equity resulting from any transaction other than an expense or a distribution to the owners. The most common example is sale of an asset at a price below book value.

marketable securities (p. 264)   Highly liquid investments, primarily in stocks and bonds, that can be sold at quoted market prices in organized securities exchanges.

mark-to-market (p. 274)   The balance sheet valuation standard applied to investments in marketable securities. Involves adjusting the controlling account for securities owned to its total market value at each balance sheet date. (Represents an exception to the cost principle.)

maturity date (p. 293)   The date on which a note becomes due and payable.

maturity value (p. 293)   The value of a note at its maturity date, consisting of principal plus interest.

net realizable value (p. 265)   The balance sheet valuation standard applied to receivables. Equal to the gross amount of accounts and notes receivable, less an estimate of the portion that may prove to be uncollectible.

NSF check (p. 270)   A customer's check that was deposited but returned because of a lack of funds (Not Sufficient Funds) in the account on which the check was drawn.

Unrealized Holding Gain (or Loss) on Investments (p. 274)   A special owners' equity account representing the difference between the cost of investments owned and their market value at the balance sheet date. In short, gains or losses on these investments that have not been "realized" through sale of the securities.

voucher (p. 268)   A written authorization used to approve a transaction for recording and payment.

voucher system (p. 268)   An accounting system designed to provide strong internal control over cash disbursements. Requires that every transaction that will result in a cash payment be verified, approved, and recorded before a check is prepared.

DEMONSTRATION PROBLEM

Shown below are selected transactions of Gulf Corp. during the month of December.

Dec. 5 Sold 2,000 shares of **General Motors** capital stock at $53 per share, less a brokerage commission of $200. These marketable securities had been acquired nine months earlier at a total cost of $112,000.

Dec. 8 An account receivable from S. Willis in the amount of $700 is determined to be uncollectible and is written off against the Allowance for Doubtful Accounts.

Dec. 15 Unexpectedly received $200 from F. Hill in full payment of her account. The $200 account receivable from Hill previously had been written off as uncollectible.

Dec. 20 Sold 1,000 shares of **Merck & Company** capital stock at a price of $60 per share, less a brokerage commission of $150. These investment shares had been acquired at a total cost of $52,000.

Dec. 31 Replenished the petty cash fund. Petty cash vouchers indicated office supplies expense, $44; miscellaneous expense, $32.

Dec. 31 The month-end bank reconciliation includes the following items: outstanding checks, $12,320; deposit in transit, $3,150; check from customer T. Jones returned "NSF," $358; bank service charges, $10; bank collected $20,000 in maturing U.S. Treasury bills (a cash equivalent) on the company's behalf. (These Treasury bills had cost $19,670, so the amount collected includes $330 interest revenue.)

Data for Adjusting Entries

1. An aging of accounts receivable indicates probable uncollectible accounts totaling $9,000. Prior to the month-end adjustment, the Allowance for Doubtful Accounts had a credit balance of $5,210.

2. Prior to any year-end adjustment, the balance in the Marketable Securities account was $213,800. At year-end, marketable securities owned had a cost of $198,000 and a market value of $210,000.

Instructions

a. Prepare entries in general journal entry form for the December transactions. In adjusting the accounting records from the bank reconciliation, make one entry to record any increases in the Cash account and a separate entry to record any decreases.

b. Prepare the month-end adjustments indicated by the two numbered paragraphs.

c. What is the adjusted balance in the Unrealized Gain (or Loss) on Investments account at December 31? Where in the financial statements does this account appear?

Solution to the Demonstration Problem

a.   **General Journal**

Dec.	5	Cash	105,800	
		Loss on Sale of Investments	6,200	
		Marketable Securities		112,000
		Sold 2,000 shares of **General Motors** capital stock at a price below cost.		
	8	Allowance for Doubtful Accounts	700	
		Accounts Receivable (S. Willis)		700
		To write off receivable from S. Willis as uncollectible.		
	15	Accounts Receivable (F. Hill)	200	
		Allowance for Doubtful Accounts		200
		To reinstate account receivable previously written off as uncollectible.		
	15	Cash	200	
		Accounts Receivable (F. Hill)		200
		To record collection of account receivable.		
	20	Cash	59,850	
		Marketable Securities		52,000
		Gain on Sale of Investments		7,850
		Sold 1,000 shares of **Merck & Company** at a price above cost.		
	31	Office Supplies Expense	44	
		Miscellaneous Expense	32	
		Cash		76
		To replenish petty cash fund.		
	31	Cash	20,000	
		Cash Equivalents		19,670
		Interest Revenue		330
		To record collection of maturing T-bills by bank.		
	31	Accounts Receivable (T. Jones)	358	
		Bank Service Charges	10	
		Cash		368
		To record bank service charge and to reclassify NSF check from T. Jones as an account receivable.		

b.   **Adjusting Entries**

Dec.	31	Uncollectible Accounts Expense	3,790	
		Allowance for Doubtful Accounts		3,790
		To increase Allowance for Doubtful Accounts to $9,000 ($9,000 − $5,210 = $3,790).		
	31	Unrealized Gain (or Loss) on Investments	3,800	
		Marketable Securities		3,800
		To reduce the balance in the Marketable Securities account to a market value of $210,000.		

c. The Unrealized Gain (or Loss) on Investments account has a *$12,000 credit balance*, representing the unrealized gain on securities owned as of December 31. (The unrealized gain is equal to the $210,000 market value of these securities, less their $198,000 cost.) The account appears in the stockholders' equity section of Gulf Corp.'s balance sheet.

SELF-TEST QUESTIONS

Answers to these questions appear on page 317.

1. In general terms, financial assets appear in the balance sheet at:
   a. Face value.
   b. Current value.
   c. Cost.
   d. Estimated future sales value.

2. Which of the following practices contributes to efficient cash management?
   a. Never borrow money—maintain a cash balance sufficient to make all necessary payments.
   b. Record all cash receipts and cash payments at the end of the month when reconciling the bank statements.
   c. Prepare monthly forecasts of planned cash receipts, payments, and anticipated cash balances up to a year in advance.
   d. Pay each bill as soon as the invoice arrives.

3. Each of the following measures strengthens internal control over cash receipts *except:*
   a. The use of a voucher system.
   b. Preparation of a daily listing of all checks received through the mail.
   c. The deposit of cash receipts in the bank on a daily basis.
   d. The use of cash registers.

Use the following data for questions 4 and 5

Quinn Company's bank statement at January 31 shows a balance of $13,360, while the ledger account for Cash in Quinn's ledger shows a balance of $12,890 at the same date. The only reconciling items are the following:

- Deposit in transit, $890.
- Bank service charge, $24.
- NSF check from customer Greg Denton in the amount of $426.
- Error in recording check No. 389 for rent: check was written in the amount of $1,320, but was recorded improperly in the accounting records as $1,230.
- Outstanding checks, $?????

4. What is the total amount of outstanding checks at January 31?
   a. $1,048.   b. $868.   c. $1,900.   d. $1,720.

5. Assuming a single journal entry is made to adjust Quinn Company's accounting records at January 31, the journal entry includes:
   a. A debit to Rent Expense for $90.
   b. A credit to Accounts Receivable, G. Denton, for $426.
   c. A credit to Cash for $450.
   d. A credit to Cash for $1,720.

6. Which of the following best describes the application of generally accepted accounting principles to the valuation of accounts receivable?
   a. Realization principle—Accounts receivable are shown at their net realizable value in the balance sheet.
   b. Matching principle—The loss due to an uncollectible account is recognized in the period in which the sale is made, not in the period in which the account receivable is determined to be worthless.
   c. Cost principle—Accounts receivable are shown at the initial cost of the merchandise to customers, less the cost the seller must pay to cover uncollectible accounts.
   d. Principle of conservatism—Accountants favor using the lowest reasonable estimate for the amount of uncollectible accounts.

7. On January 1, Dillon Company had a $3,100 credit balance in the Allowance for Doubtful Accounts. During the year, sales totaled $780,000 and $6,900 of accounts receivable were written off as uncollectible. A December 31 aging of accounts receivable indicated the amount probably uncollectible to be $5,300. (No recoveries of accounts previously written off were made during the year.) Dillon's financial statements for the current year should include:
   a. Uncollectible accounts expense of $9,100.
   b. Uncollectible accounts expense of $5,300.
   c. Allowance for Doubtful Accounts with a credit balance of $1,500.
   d. Allowance for Doubtful Accounts with a credit balance of $8,400.

8. Under the *direct write-off* method of accounting for uncollectible accounts:
   a. The current year uncollectible accounts expense is less than the expense would be under the allowance approach.
   b. The relationship between the current period net sales and current period uncollectible accounts expense illustrates the matching principle.
   c. The Allowance for Doubtful Accounts is debited when specific accounts receivable are determined to be worthless.
   d. Accounts receivable are not stated in the balance sheet at net realizable value, but at the balance of the Accounts Receivable controlling account.

9. Which of the following actions is *least* likely to increase a company's accounts receivable turnover?
   a. Encouraging customers to use bank credit cards, such as **Visa** and **MasterCard**, rather than other national credit cards, such as **American Express** and **Diners' Club**.
   b. Offer customers larger cash discounts for making early payments.
   c. Reduce the interest rate charged to credit customers.
   d. Sell accounts receivable to a factor.

*10. Puget Sound Co. sold marketable securities costing $80,000 for $92,000 cash. In the company's income statement and statement of cash flows, respectively, this will appear as:
   a. A $12,000 gain and a $92,000 cash receipt.
   b. A $92,000 gain and an $8,000 cash receipt.
   c. A $12,000 gain and an $80,000 cash receipt.
   d. A $92,000 sale and a $92,000 cash receipt.

†11. On October 1, *2001,* Coast Financial loaned Barr Corporation $300,000, receiving in exchange a nine-month, 12% note receivable. Coast ends its fiscal year on December 31 and makes adjusting entries to accrue interest earned on all notes receivable. The interest earned on the note receivable from Barr Corporation during *2002* will amount to:
   a. $9,000.   b. $18,000.   c. $27,000.   d. $36,000.

ASSIGNMENT MATERIAL
DISCUSSION QUESTIONS

1. Briefly describe the flow of cash among receivables, cash, and marketable securities.
2. Different categories of financial assets are valued differently in the balance sheet. These different valuation methods have one common goal. Explain.
3. What are *cash equivalents?* Provide two examples. Why are these items often combined with cash for the purpose of balance sheet presentation?
4. What are lines of credit? From the viewpoint of a short-term creditor, why do lines of credit increase a company's liquidity? How are the unused portions of these lines presented in financial statements?

---

*Supplemental Topic A, "Accounting for Marketable Securities."

†Supplemental Topic B, "Notes Receivable and Interest Revenue."

Discussion Questions

5. Does the expression "efficient management of cash" mean anything more than procedures to prevent losses from fraud or theft? Explain.
6. Why are cash balances in *excess* of those needed to finance business operations viewed as relatively nonproductive assets? Suggest several ways in which these excess cash balances may be utilized effectively.
7. List several principles to be observed by a business in establishing strong internal control over cash receipts.
8. What is the basic control feature in a *voucher system?*
9. List two items often encountered in reconciling a bank statement that may cause cash per the bank statement to be *larger* than the balance of cash shown in the depositor's accounting records.
10. Describe the nature and usefulness of a *cash budget.*
11. Why are investments in marketable securities shown separately from cash equivalents in the balance sheet?
12. Why must an investor who owns numerous marketable securities maintain a marketable securities subsidiary ledger?
13. Explain the valuation procedure termed *mark-to-market* for short-term investments classified as available-for-sale securities.
14. What does the account Unrealized Holding Gain (or Loss) on Investment represent? How is this account presented in the financial statements for short-term investments classified as available-for-sale securities?
15. Explain the relationship between the *matching principle* and the need to estimate uncollectible accounts receivable.
16. In making the annual adjusting entry for uncollectible accounts, a company may utilize a *balance sheet approach* to make the estimate, or it may use an *income statement approach.* Explain these two alternative approaches.
17. What is the direct write-off method of handling credit losses as opposed to the allowance method? What is its principal shortcoming?
18. Must companies use the same method of accounting for uncollectible accounts receivable in their financial statements and in their income tax returns? Explain.
19. What are the advantages to a retailer of making credit sales only to customers who use nationally recognized credit cards?
20. Alta Mine Company, a restaurant that had always made cash sales only, adopted a new policy of honoring several nationally known credit cards. Sales did not increase, but many of Alta Mine's regular customers began charging dinner bills on the credit cards. Has the new policy been beneficial to Alta Mine Company? Explain.
21. How is the accounts receivable turnover rate computed? Why is this rate significant to short-term creditors?
22. How does an annual audit by a CPA firm provide assurance that a company's accounts receivable and notes receivable are fairly presented in the company's financial statements?
23. Explain how each of the following is presented in (1) a multiple-step income statement and (2) a statement of cash flows.
    a. Sale of marketable securities at a loss.
    b. Adjusting entry to create (or increase) the allowance for doubtful accounts.
    c. Entry to write off an uncollectible account against the allowance.
    d. Adjusting entry to increase the balance in the Marketable Securities account to a higher market value (assume these investments are classified as available-for-sale securities).
*24. The market values of some marketable securities may change from day to day. How do these changes in market value affect the investor's *taxable income?*
†25. Determine the maturity date and maturity value of each of the following notes. (Assume a 360-day year in computing interest and maturity values, but count actual days to the maturity dates.)
    a. A $10,000, 9%, one-year note dated July 1, 2001.
    b. A $20,000, 8%, 90-day note dated March 11.

---

*Supplemental Topic A, "Accounting for Marketable Securities."
†Supplemental Topic B, "Notes Receivable and Interest Revenue."

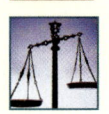

EXERCISES

EXERCISE 7.1
You as a Student
LO 4

Assume that the following information relates to your most recent bank statement dated September 30:

Balance per bank statement at September 30	$3,400

Checks written that had not cleared the bank as of September 30:

#203	University tuition	$1,500
#205	University bookstore	350
#208	Rocco's pizza	25
#210	Stereo purchase	425
#211	October apartment rent	500

Interest amounting to $4 was credited to your account by the bank in September. The bank's service charge for the month was $5. In addition to your bank statement, you received a letter from your parents informing you that they had made a $2,400 electronic funds transfer directly into your account on October 2. After reading your parents' letter, you looked in your checkbook and discovered its balance was $601. Adding your parents' deposit brought that total to $3,001.

Prepare a bank reconciliation to determine your correct checking account balance. Explain why neither your bank statement nor your checkbook shows this amount.

EXERCISE 7.2
Financial Assets
LO 1, 2

The following financial assets appeared in a recent balance sheet of **Apple Computer, Inc.** (dollar amounts are stated in millions):

Cash and cash equivalents	$1,191
Marketable securities (short-term investments)	2,836
Accounts receivable (net of allowance for doubtful accounts of $64)	953

a. Define *financial assets*.
b. A different approach is used in determining the balance sheet value for each category of **Apple Computer**'s financial assets, although each approach serves a common goal. Explain.
c. Why do companies like **Apple Computer** hold so much of their financial assets in the form of marketable securities and receivables?
d. What types of investments might **Apple Computer** own that are considered cash equivalents?
e. Explain what is meant by the balance sheet presentation of **Apple Computer**'s Accounts Receivable as shown above.

EXERCISE 7.3
Grandmother's Secret
LO 2, 3

The former bookkeeper of **White Electric Supply** is serving time in prison for embezzling nearly $416,000 in less than five years. She describes herself as "an ordinary mother of three kids and a proud grandmother of four." Like so many other "ordinary" employees, she started out by taking only small amounts. By the time she was caught, she was stealing lump sums of $5,000 and $10,000.

Her method was crude and simple. She would write a check for the correct amount payable to a supplier for, say, $15,000. However, she would record in the company's check register an amount significantly greater, say, $20,000. She would then write a check payable to herself for the $5,000 difference. In the check register, next to the number of each check she had deposited in her personal bank account, she would write the word "void," making it appear as though the check had been destroyed. This process went undetected for nearly five years.

a. What controls must have been lacking at **White Electric Supply** to enable the bookkeeper to steal nearly $416,000 before being caught?

b. What the bookkeeper did was definitely unethical. But *what if* one of her grandchildren had been ill and needed an expensive operation? If this had been the case, would it have been ethical for her to take company funds to pay for the operation if she intended to pay the company back in full? Defend your answer.

EXERCISE 7.4
Embezzlement Issues
LO 2, 3

D. J. Fletcher, a trusted employee of Bluestem Products, found himself in personal financial difficulties and decided to "borrow" $3,000 from the company and to conceal his theft.

As a first step, Fletcher removed $3,000 in currency from the cash register. This amount represented the bulk of the cash received in over-the-counter sales during the three business days since the last bank deposit. Fletcher then removed a $3,000 check from the day's incoming mail; this check had been mailed in by a customer, Michael Adams, in full payment of his account. Fletcher made no journal entry to record the $3,000 collection from Adams, but deposited the check in Bluestem Products' bank account in place of the $3,000 over-the-counter cash receipts he had stolen.

In order to keep Adams from protesting when his month-end statement reached him, Fletcher made a journal entry debiting Sales Returns and Allowances and crediting Accounts Receivable—Michael Adams. Fletcher posted this entry to the two general ledger accounts affected and to Adams's account in the subsidiary ledger for accounts receivable.

a. Did these actions by Fletcher cause the general ledger to be out of balance or the subsidiary ledger to disagree with the controlling account? Explain.

b. Assume that Bluestem Products prepares financial statements at the end of the month without discovering the theft. Would any items in the balance sheet or the income statement be in error? Explain.

c. Several weaknesses in internal control apparently exist in Bluestem Products. Indicate three specific changes needed to strengthen internal control over cash receipts.

EXERCISE 7.5
Bank Reconciliation
LO 4

Shown below is the information needed to prepare a bank reconciliation for Warren Electric at December 31:

1. At December 31, cash per the bank statement was $15,200; cash per the company's records was $17,500.
2. Two debit memoranda accompanied the bank statement: service charges for December of $25, and a $775 check drawn by Jane Jones marked "NSF."
3. Cash receipts of $10,000 on December 31 were not deposited until January 4.
4. The following checks had been issued in December but were not included among the paid checks returned by the bank: no. 620 for $1,000, no. 630 for $3,000, and no. 641 for $4,500.

a. Prepare a bank reconciliation at December 31.

b. Prepare the necessary journal entry or entries to update the accounting records.

c. Assume that the company normally is *not* required to pay a bank service charge if it maintains a minimum average daily balance of $1,000 throughout the month. If the company's average daily balance for December had been $8,000, why did it have to pay a $25 service charge?

EXERCISE 7.6
Cash and Cash Equivalents
LO 1, 2

The following footnote appeared in a recent financial statement of **Westinghouse Electric**:

> The Corporation considers all investment securities with a maturity of three months or less when acquired to be cash equivalents. All cash and temporary investments are placed with high-credit-quality financial institutions, and the amount of credit exposure to any one financial institution is limited. At December 31, cash and cash equivalents include restricted funds of $42 million.

a. Are the company's cash equivalents debt or equity securities? How do you know?

b. Explain what is meant by the statement that "the credit exposure to any one financial institution is limited."

c. Explain what is meant by the term *restricted funds* used in the footnote.

EXERCISE 7.7
Evaluating Cash Equivalents

LO 1, 2

Tyson Furniture has $100,000 in excess cash that it wants to invest in one or more cash equivalents. The treasurer has researched two money market accounts and two certificates of deposit (CDs) offered by four major banks. This is the information she gathered:

Investment Institution	Investment Type	Minimum Investment	Interest Rate	Penalty for Early Withdrawal?	Financial Risk
Nexity Bank	Money market account	$ 1,000	3.14%	No	Very low
MBNA America Bank	Money market account	50,000	3.15	No	Very low
IndyMac Bank	90-day CD	5,000	3.20	Yes	Very low
Next Bank	90-day CD	100,000	3.30	Yes	Very low

The two 90-day certificates of deposit are FDIC insured for up to $100,000. The money market accounts are not FDIC insured.

Suggest how Tyson Furniture might allocate its $100,000 cash among these four opportunities. Discuss the trade-offs that management must consider.

EXERCISE 7.8
The Nature of Marketable Securities

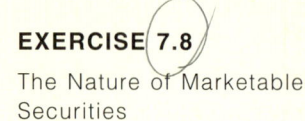

LO 1, 8

Many companies hold a significant portion of their financial assets in the form of marketable securities. For example, **Microsoft Corporation** recently reported investments in marketable securities totaling $27.7 billion, an amount equal to 79% of its total financial assets. In contrast, only 3% of its financial assets were in the form of accounts receivable.

a. Define *marketable securities* (also referred to as short-term investments). What characteristics of these securities justify classifying them as financial assets?

b. What is the basic advantage of **Microsoft Corporation** keeping financial assets in the form of marketable securities instead of cash? Is there any disadvantage?

c. Explain how **Microsoft Corporation** values these investments in its balance sheet.

d. Discuss whether the valuation of marketable securities represents a departure from (1) the cost principle and (2) the objectivity principle.

e. Explain how *mark-to-market* benefits the *users* of **Microsoft Corporation**'s financial statements.

EXERCISE 7.9
Reporting Uncollectable Accounts

LO 1, 5

The credit manager of Montour Fuel has gathered the following information about the company's accounts receivable and credit losses during the current year:

Net credit sales for the year		$8,000,000
Accounts receivable at year-end		1,750,000
Uncollectible accounts receivable:		
Actually written off during the year	$96,000	
Estimated portion of year-end receivables expected to prove uncollectible (per aging schedule)	84,000	180,000

Prepare one journal entry summarizing the recognition of uncollectible accounts expense for the entire year under each of the following independent assumptions:

a. Uncollectible accounts expense is estimated at an amount equal to 2.5% of net credit sales.

b. Uncollectible accounts expense is recognized by adjusting the balance in the Allowance for Doubtful Accounts to the amount indicated in the year-end aging schedule. The balance in the allowance account at the *beginning* of the current year was $25,000. (Consider the effect of the write-offs during the year on the balance in the Allowance for Doubtful Accounts.)

c. The company uses the direct write-off method of accounting for uncollectible accounts.

d. Which of the three methods gives investors and creditors the most accurate assessment of a company's liquidity? Defend your answer.

Exercises

EXERCISE 7.10

Industry Characteristics and Collection Performance

LO 6

The following information was taken from recent annual reports of **Huffy Corporation**, a manufacturer of bicycles sold primarily by large retail chains, and **Pennsylvania Power Company**, a public utility (dollar amounts are stated in thousands):

	Huffy	PPC
Net sales	$488,181	$7,028,961
Average accounts receivable	68,304	291,601

a. Compute for each company the accounts receivable turnover rate for the year.
b. Compute for each company the average number of days required to collect outstanding receivables (round answers to nearest whole day).
c. Explain why the figures computed for **Huffy Corporation** in parts **a** and **b** are so different from those computed for **Pennsylvania Power Company**.

EXERCISE 7.11

Analyzing the Effects of Transactions

LO 1, 7

Six events pertaining to financial assets are described as follows:

a. Invested idle cash in marketable securities and classified them as available for sale.
b. Collected an account receivable.
c. Sold marketable securities at a loss (proceeds from the sale were equal to the market value reflected in the last balance sheet).
d. Determined a particular account receivable to be uncollectible and wrote it off against the allowance for doubtful accounts.
e. Received interest earned on an investment in marketable securities (company policy is to recognize interest as revenue *when received*).
f. Made a mark-to-market adjustment increasing the balance in the Marketable Securities account to reflect a rise in the market value of securities owned.

Indicate the effects of each transaction or adjusting entry upon the financial measurements in the four column headings listed below. Use the code letters **I** for increase, **D** for decrease, and **NE** for no effect.

Transaction	Total Assets	Net Income	Net Cash Flow from Operating Activities	Net Cash Flow (from any source)
a				

EXERCISE 7.12

Industry Characteristics and Allowances for Doubtful Accounts

LO 5

The following percentages were computed using figures from recent annual reports of **Albertsons Inc.**, a large grocery store chain, and **Sprint Corporation**, a provider of telecommunication services:

	Albertsons	Sprint
Allowance for doubtful accounts as a percentage of net sales	0.09%	1.5%
Accounts receivable as a percentage of net sales	1.4	14.2

Explain why **Sprint**'s percentages are so much larger than **Albertson**'s percentages.

EXERCISE 7.13
Reporting Financial Assets
LO 1

Explain how each of the following items is reported in a complete set of financial statements, including the accompanying notes. (In one or more cases, the item may not appear in the financial statements.) The answer to the first item is provided as an example.

a. Cash equivalents.
b. Cash in a special fund being accumulated as legally required for the purpose of retiring a specific long-term liability.
c. Compensating balances.
d. The amount by which the current market value of securities classified as available for sale exceeds their cost.
e. The allowance for doubtful accounts receivable.
f. The accounts receivable turnover rate.
g. Realized gains and losses on investments sold during the period.
h. Proceeds from converting cash equivalents into cash.
i. Proceeds from converting investments in marketable securities into cash.

Example: a. Cash equivalents normally are *not* shown separately in financial statements. Rather, they are combined with other types of cash and reported under the caption "Cash and Cash Equivalents." A note to the statements often shows the breakdown of this asset category.

EXERCISE 7.14
Analyzing Accounts Receivable
LO 1, 5, 6

Following are the average accounts receivable and net sales reported recently by two large beverage companies (dollar amounts are stated in millions):

	Average Accounts Receivable	Net Sales
Adolph Coors Company	$114	$ 2,842
Anheuser-Busch Companies, Inc.	615	12,262

a. Compute the accounts receivable turnover rate for each company (round your results to the nearest whole number).
b. Compute the average number of days that it takes for each company to collect its accounts receivable (round your results to the nearest whole day).
c. Based upon your computations in **a** and **b**, which company's accounts receivable appear to be most liquid? Defend your answer.

*EXERCISE 7.15
Mark-to-Market
LO 1, 7, 8

Weis Markets accumulates large amounts of excess cash throughout the year. It typically invests these funds in marketable securities until they are needed. The company's most recent financial statements revealed a nearly $14 million unrealized gain on short-term investments. Footnotes to the financial statements disclosed that **Weis** classifies its short-term investments as available-for-sale securities.

a. Explain the meaning of the company's unrealized gain on short-term investments.
b. How does the unrealized gain impact the company's financial statements?
c. Is the unrealized gain included in the computation of the company's taxable income? Explain.
d. Evaluate the mark-to-market concept from the perspective of the company's creditors.

*EXERCISE 7.16
Accounting for Marketable Securities
LO 1, 7, 8

McGoun Industries pays income taxes on capital gains at a rate of 30%. At December 31, *2001*, the company owns marketable securities that cost $90,000, but have a current market value of $260,000.

a. How will users of McGoun's financial statements be made aware of this substantial increase in the market value of the company's investments?
b. As of December 31, 2001, what income taxes has McGoun paid on the increase in value of these investments? Explain.
c. Prepare a journal entry at January 4, 2002, to record the cash sale of these investments at $260,000.
d. What effect will the sale recorded in part **c** have on McGoun's tax obligation for 2002?

---
*Supplemental Topic A, "Accounting for Marketable Securities."

†EXERCISE 7.17

Notes and Interest

LO 9

On September 1, Health Wise International acquired a 12%, nine-month note receivable from Herbal Innovations, a credit customer, in settlement of a $22,000 account receivable. Prepare journal entries to record the following:

a. The receipt of the note on September 1 in settlement of the account receivable.
b. The adjustment to record accrued interest revenue on December 31.
c. The collection of the principal and interest on May 31.

EXERCISE 7.18

Using the Annual Report of **Tootsie Roll Industries, Inc.**

LO 1, 6

The annual report of **Tootsie Roll Industries, Inc.**, appears in Appendix A at the end of this textbook. Use this report to answer the following questions:

a. What is the total dollar value of the company's financial assets for the most current year reported?
b. Does the company report any investments in marketable securities? If so, how does it report unrealized gains and losses?
c. What is the company's allowance for uncollectible accounts for the most current year reported?
d. On average, for how many days do the company's accounts receivable remain outstanding before collection?

PROBLEMS

PROBLEM 7.1

Bank Reconciliation

LO 1, 4

The cash transactions and cash balances of Banner, Inc., for July were as follows:

1. The ledger account for Cash showed a balance at July 31 of $125,568.
2. The July bank statement showed a closing balance of $114,828.
3. The cash received on July 31 amounted to $16,000. It was left at the bank in the night depository chute after banking hours on July 31 and therefore was not recorded by the bank on the July statement.
4. Also included with the July bank statement was a debit memorandum from the bank for $50 representing service charges for July.
5. A credit memorandum enclosed with the July bank statement indicated that a non-interest-bearing note receivable for $4,000 from Rene Manes, left with the bank for collection, had been collected and the proceeds credited to the account of Banner, Inc.
6. Comparison of the paid checks returned by the bank with the entries in the accounting records revealed that check no. 821 for $519, issued July 15 in payment for office equipment, had been erroneously entered in Banner's records as $915.
7. Examination of the paid checks also revealed that three checks, all issued in July, had not yet been paid by the bank: no. 811 for $314; no. 814 for $625; no. 823 for $175.
8. Included with the July bank statement was a $200 check drawn by Howard Williams, a customer of Banner, Inc. This check was marked "NSF." It had been included in the deposit of July 27 but had been charged back against the company's account on July 31.

Instructions

a. Prepare a bank reconciliation for Banner, Inc., at July 31.
b. Prepare journal entries (in general journal form) to adjust the accounts at July 31. Assume that the accounts have not been closed.
c. State the amount of cash that should be included in the balance sheet at July 31.
d. Explain why the balance per the company's bank statement is often larger than the balance shown in its accounting records.

---

†*Supplemental Topic B*, "Notes Receivable and Interest Revenue."

PROBLEM 7.2
Protecting Cash

LO 2, 3, 4

Osage Farm Supply had poor internal control over its cash transactions. Facts about the company's cash position at November 30 are described below.

The accounting records showed a cash balance of $35,400, which included a deposit in transit of $1,245. The balance indicated in the bank statement was $20,600. Included in the bank statement were the following debit and credit memoranda:

Debit Memoranda:	
Check from customer G. Davis, deposited by Osage Farm Supply, but charged back as NSF	$ 130
Bank service charges for November	15
Credit Memorandum:	
Proceeds from collection of a note receivable from Regal Farms, which Osage Farm Supply had left with the bank's collection department	$6,255

Outstanding checks as of November 30 were as follows:

Check No.	Amount
8231	$ 400
8263	524
8288	176
8294	5,000

Bev Escola, the company's cashier, has been taking portions of the company's cash receipts for several months. Each month, Escola prepares the company's bank reconciliation in a manner that conceals her thefts. Her bank reconciliation for November was as follows:

Balance per bank statement, Nov. 30			$20,600
Add: Deposits in transit		$2,145	
Collection of note from Regal Farms		6,255	8,400
Subtotal			$30,000
Less: Outstanding checks:			
No. 8231		$400	
8263		524	
8288		176	1,000
Adjusted cash balance per bank statement			$29,000
Balance per accounting records, Nov. 30			$35,400
Add: Credit memorandum from bank			6,255
Subtotal			$29,145
Less: Debit memoranda from bank:			
NSF check of G. Davis		$ 15	
Bank service charges		130	145
Adjusted cash balance per accounting records			$29,000

Instructions

a. Determine the amount of the cash shortage that has been concealed by Escola in her bank reconciliation. (As a format, we suggest that you prepare the bank reconciliation correctly.

the amount of the shortage then will be the difference between the adjusted balances per the bank statement and per the accounting records. You can then list this unrecorded cash shortage as the final adjustment necessary to complete your reconciliation.)

b. Carefully review Escola's bank reconciliation and explain in detail how she concealed the amount of the shortage. Include a listing of the dollar amounts that were concealed in various ways. This listing should total the amount of the shortage determined in part **a**.

c. Suggest some specific internal control measures that appear to be necessary for Osage Farm Supply.

PROBLEM 7.3
Aging Accounts Receivable; Write-offs
LO 1, 5

Super Star, a Hollywood Publicity firm, uses the balance sheet approach to estimate uncollectible accounts expense. At year-end an aging of the accounts receivable produced the following classification:

Not yet due	$500,000
1–30 days past due	210,000
31–60 days past due	80,000
61–90 days past due	15,000
Over 90 days past due	30,000
Total	$835,000

On the basis of past experience, the company estimated the percentages probably uncollectible for the above five age groups to be as follows: Group 1, 1%; Group 2, 3%; Group 3, 10%; Group 4, 20%; and Group 5, 50%.

The Allowance for Doubtful Accounts before adjustment at December 31 showed a credit balance of $11,800.

Instructions

a. Compute the estimated amount of uncollectible accounts based on the above classification by age groups.

b. Prepare the adjusting entry needed to bring the Allowance for Doubtful Accounts to the proper amount.

c. Assume that on January 10 of the following year, Super Star learned that an account receivable that had originated on September 1 in the amount of $8,250 was worthless because of the bankruptcy of the client, April Showers. Prepare the journal entry required on January 10 to write off this account.

d. The firm is considering the adoption of a policy whereby clients whose outstanding accounts become more than 60 days past due will be required to sign an interest-bearing note for the full amount of their outstanding balance. What advantages would such a policy offer?

PROBLEM 7.4
Accounting for Uncollectible Accounts
LO 1, 5

Wilcox Mills is a manufacturer that makes all sales on 30-day credit terms. Annual sales are approximately $30 million. At the end of 2001, accounts receivable were presented in the company's balance sheet as follows:

Accounts Receivable from Clients	$3,100,000
Less: Allowance for Doubtful Accounts	80,000

During 2002, $165,000 of specific accounts receivable were written off as uncollectible. Of these accounts written off, receivables totaling $15,000 were subsequently collected. At the end of 2002, an aging of accounts receivable indicated a need for an $90,000 allowance to cover possible failure to collect the accounts currently outstanding.

Wilcox Mills makes adjusting entries in its accounting records *only at year-end*. Monthly and quarterly financial statements are prepared from worksheets, without any adjusting or closing entries actually being entered in the accounting records. (In short, you may assume the company adjusts its accounts only at year-end.)

Instructions

a. Prepare the following general journal entries:
   1. One entry to summarize all accounts written off against the allowance for doubtful accounts during 2002.
   2. Entries to record the $15,000 in accounts receivable that were subsequently collected.
   3. The adjusting entry required at December 31, 2002, to increase the allowance for doubtful accounts to $90,000.

b. Notice that the allowance for doubtful accounts was only $80,000 at the end of 2001, but uncollectible accounts during 2002 totaled $150,000 ($165,000 less the $15,000 reinstated). Do these relationships appear reasonable, or was the allowance for doubtful accounts greatly understated at the end of 2001? Explain.

*PROBLEM 7.5
Accounting for Marketable Securities
LO 1, 8

At December 31, *2001,* Weston Manufacturing Co. owned the following investments in capital stock of publicly traded companies (classified as available-for-sale securities):

	Cost	Current Market Value
Footlocker, Inc. (5,000 shares: cost, $17 per share; market value, $20)	$ 85,000	$100,000
Gap, Inc. (4,000 shares: cost, $17 per share; market value, $15)	68,000	60,000
	$153,000	$160,000

In *2002,* Weston engaged in the following two transactions:

April 10 Sold 1,000 shares of its investment in **Footlocker, Inc.**, at a price of $21 per share, less a brokerage commission of $50.

August 7 Sold 2,000 shares of its investment in **Gap, Inc.**, at a price of $14 per share, less a brokerage commission of $60.

At December 31, 2002, the market values of these stocks were **Footlocker, Inc.**, $18 per share and **Gap, Inc.**, $16 per share.

Instructions

a. Illustrate the presentation of marketable securities and the unrealized holding gain or loss in Weston's balance sheet at December 31, *2001*. Include a caption indicating the section of the balance sheet in which each of these accounts appears.
b. Prepare journal entries to record the transactions on April 10 and August 7.
c. Prior to making a mark-to-market adjustment at the end of 2002, determine the unadjusted balance in the Marketable Securities controlling account and the Unrealized Holding Gain (or Loss) on Investments. (Assume that no unrealized gains or losses have been recognized since last year.)
d. Prepare a schedule showing the cost and market values of securities owned at the end of 2002. (Use the same format as the schedule illustrated above.)
e. Prepare the "mark-to-market" adjusting entry required at December 31, 2002.
f. Illustrate the presentation of the marketable securities and unrealized holding gain (or loss) in the balance sheet at December 31, *2002*. (Follow the same format as in part **a**.)
g. Illustrate the presentation of the net *realized* gains (or losses) in the 2002 income statement. Assume a multiple-step income statement and show the caption identifying the section in which this amount would appear.
h. Explain how both the realized and unrealized gains and losses will affect the company's 2002 income tax return.

Supplemental Topic A, "Accounting for Marketable Securities."

†PROBLEM 7.6
Notes Receivable
LO 9

Eastern Supply sells a variety of merchandise to retail stores on open account, but it insists that any customer who fails to pay an invoice when due must replace it with an interest-bearing note. The company adjusts and closes its accounts at December 31. Among the transactions relating to notes receivable were the following:

Sept. 1 Received from a customer (Party Plus) a nine-month, 10% note for $75,000 in settlement of an account receivable due today.

June 1 Collected in full the nine-month, 10% note receivable from Party Plus, including interest.

Instructions

a. Prepare journal entries (in general journal form) to record: (1) the receipt of the note on September 1; (2) the adjustment for interest on December 31; and (3) collection of principal and interest on June 1. (To better illustrate the allocation of interest revenue between accounting periods, we will assume Eastern Supply makes adjusting entries *only at year-end*.)

b. Assume that instead of paying the note on June 1, the customer (Party Plus) had defaulted. Give the journal entry by Eastern Supply to record the default. Assume that Party Plus has sufficient resources that the note eventually will be collected.

c. Explain why the company insists that any customer who fails to pay an invoice when due must replace it with an interest-bearing note.

CASES AND UNSTRUCTURED PROBLEMS

CASE 7.1
Cash Management
LO 2

Most banks offer a variety of cash management options to individuals and small businesses. These include, for example, T-bills, money market funds, daily "sweeps" of checking accounts, and CDs.

Instructions

a. Arrange an interview with a representative of a local bank. Inquire as to the options the bank provides for temporarily investing cash balances not needed in the near future. Gain an understanding of the various cash management options available to individuals and to small businesses, including the expected yields.

b. Briefly explain each of the options discussed in this interview, along with the expected yields (if determinable). Identify the option you consider best suited to:

1. An individual whose checking account often has as much as $10,000 that will not be needed within the next 30 days.
2. A small business that has about $400,000 in liquid resources that will not be needed for the next nine months.

Explain the reasons for your choices and be prepared to explain these reasons in class.

CASE 7.2
"Improving" the Balance Sheet
LO 1, 2, 4, 5, 6, 8

Affections manufactures candy and sells only to retailers. It is not a publicly owned company and its financial statements are not audited. But the company frequently must borrow money. Its creditors insist that the company provide them with unaudited financial statements at the end of each quarter.

In October, management met to discuss the fiscal year ending next December 31. Due to a sluggish economy, Affections was having difficulty collecting its accounts receivable, and its cash position was unusually low. Management knew that if the December 31 balance sheet did not look good, the company would have difficulty borrowing the money it would need to boost production for Valentine's Day.

Thus the purpose of the meeting was to explore ways in which Affections might improve its December 31 balance sheet. Some of the ideas discussed are as follows:

1. Offer customers purchasing Christmas candy a 10% discount if they make payment within 30 days.
2. Allow a 30-day grace period on all accounts receivable overdue at the end of the year. As these accounts will no longer be overdue, the company will not need an allowance for overdue accounts.

†*Supplemental Topic B,* "Notes Receivable and Interest Revenue."

3. For purposes of balance sheet presentation, combine all forms of cash, including cash equivalents, compensating balances, and unused lines of credit.
4. Require officers who have borrowed money from the company to repay the amounts owed at December 31. This would convert into cash the "notes receivable from officers," which now appear in the balance sheet as noncurrent assets. The loans could be renewed immediately after year-end.
5. Present investments in marketable securities at their market value, rather than at cost.
6. Treat inventory as a financial asset and show it at current sales value. As Affections is not a publicly owned company, it is not legally required to prepare its financial statements in conformity with generally accepted accounting principles.
7. On December 31, draw a large check against one of the company's bank accounts and deposit it in another of the company's accounts in a different bank. The check won't clear the first bank until after year-end. This will substantially increase the amount of cash in bank accounts at year-end.

Instructions

a. Separately evaluate each of these proposals. Consider ethical issues as well as accounting issues.
b. Do you consider it ethical for management to hold this meeting in the first place? That is, should management plan in advance how to improve financial statements that will be distributed to creditors and investors?

CASE 7.3

Accounting Principles

LO 1, 5, 9

In each of the situations described below, indicate the accounting principles or concepts, if any, that have been violated and explain briefly the nature of the violation. If you believe the practice is *in accord* with generally accepted accounting principles, state this as your position and defend it.

a. A small business in which credit sales fluctuate greatly from year to year uses the direct write-off method both for income tax purposes and in its financial statements.
b. A manufacturing company charges all of its petty cash expenditures to Miscellaneous Expense, rather than to the various expense accounts that reflect the nature of each expenditure.
c. Computer Systems often sells merchandise in exchange for interest-bearing notes receivable, maturing in 6, 12, or 24 months. The company records these sales transactions by debiting Notes Receivable for the maturity value of the notes, crediting Sales for the sales price of the merchandise, and crediting Interest Revenue for the balance of the maturity value of the note. The cost of goods sold also is recorded.
d. A company has $400,000 in unrestricted cash, $1 million in a bank account specifically earmarked for the construction of a new factory, and $2 million in cash equivalents. In the balance sheet, these amounts are combined and shown as "Cash and cash equivalents . . . $3.4 million."

CASE 7.4

If Things Get Any Better, We'll Be Broke

LO 6, 7

Rock, Inc., sells stereo equipment. Traditionally, the company's sales have been in the following categories: cash sales, 25%; customers using national credit cards, 35%; sales on account (due in 30 days), 40%. With these policies, the company earned a modest profit, and monthly cash receipts exceeded monthly cash payments by a comfortable margin. Uncollectible accounts expense was approximately 1% of net sales. (The company uses the direct write-off method in accounting for uncollectible accounts receivable.)

Two months ago, the company initiated a new credit policy, which it calls "Double Zero." Customers may purchase merchandise on account, with no down payment and no interest charges. The accounts are collected in 12 monthly installments of equal amounts.

The plan has proven quite popular with customers, and monthly sales have increased dramatically. Despite the increase in sales, however, Rock is experiencing cash flow problems— it hasn't been generating enough cash to pay its suppliers, most of which require payment within 30 days.

The company's bookkeeper has prepared the following analysis of monthly operating results:

Sales	Before Double Zero	Last Month
Cash	$12,500	$ 5,000
National credit card	17,500	10,000
30-day accounts	20,000	–0–
Double Zero accounts	–0–	75,000
Total monthly sales	$50,000	$ 90,000
Cost of goods sold and expenses	40,000	65,000
Net income	$10,000	$ 25,000
Cash receipts		
Cash sales	$12,500	$ 5,000
National credit card companies	17,500	10,000
30-day accounts	19,500	–0–
Double Zero accounts	–0–	11,250
Total monthly cash receipts	$49,500	$ 26,250
Accounts written off as uncollectible	$ 500	$ –0–
Accounts receivable at month-end	$20,000	$135,000

The bookkeeper offered the following assessment: "Double Zero is killing us. Since we started that plan, our accounts receivable have increased nearly sevenfold, and they're still growing. We can't afford to carry such a large nonproductive asset on our books. Our cash receipts are down to nearly half of what they used to be. If we don't go back to more cash sales and receivables that can be collected more quickly, we'll become insolvent."

In reply Maxwell "Rock" Swartz, founder and chief executive officer, shouted out: "Why do you say that our accounts receivable are nonproductive? They're the most productive asset we have! Since we started Double Zero, our sales have nearly doubled, our profits have more than doubled, and our bad debt expense has dropped to nothing!"

Instructions

a. Is it logical that the Double Zero plan is causing sales and profits to increase while also causing a decline in cash receipts? Explain.

b. Why has the uncollectible accounts expense dropped to zero? What would you expect to happen to the company's uncollectible accounts expense in the future—say, next year? Why?

c. Do you think that the reduction in monthly cash receipts is permanent or temporary? Explain.

d. In what sense are the company's accounts receivable a "nonproductive" asset?

e. Suggest several ways that Rock may be able to generate the cash it needs to pay its bills without terminating the Double Zero plan.

f. Would you recommend that the company continue offering Double Zero financing, or should it return to the use of 30-day accounts? Explain the reasons for your answer, and identify any unresolved factors that might cause you to change this opinion in the future.

BUSINESS WEEK ASSIGNMENT

CASE 7.5

Cash Management

LO 6, 7

Effective cash management is critical to the survival of any business. In her January 22, 2001, *Business Week* article, "The Ins and Outs of Cash Flow," Anne Tergesen wrote:

> Accounting experts pay a lot of attention to accounts receivable. . . . When receivables rise at a faster pace than sales, the company may be having trouble collecting what it is owed.

Instructions

a. Discuss how the management of accounts receivable is related to the management of cash.

b. What performance measures described in this chapter provide information about the management of cash and the management of accounts receivable? Which users of financial information might be interested in these measures?

INTERNET ASSIGNMENT

INTERNET 7.1

Returns on Idle Cash from Various Cash Equivalents

LO 1, 2, 6

Prudent cash management is an important function in any business. Large amounts of cash sitting idle in non-interest-bearing checking accounts can cost a company thousands—even millions—of dollars annually in forgone revenue. Thus, many businesses invest large amounts of idle cash in Treasury bills, certificates of deposit (CDs), and money market accounts.

Visit the **Bloomberg** homepage at the following address:

www.bloomberg.com

Search the **Bloomberg** site for information on Treasury bills, CDs, and money market accounts. The site's main page has a direct link to Treasury bills. CDs and money market account information can be found through a link to banking and loans. Look for a pull-down menu to select interest-bearing products.

Instructions

a. Prepare a table showing the current interest rates on Treasury bills, various CDs, and money market accounts.

b. If you were in charge of investing $1 million among the cash equivalents identified in part **a**, how would you make your allocation? Defend your answer.

Internet sites are time and date sensitive. It is the purpose of these exercises to have you explore the Internet. You may need to use the Yahoo! search engine **http://www.yahoo.com** *(or another favorite search engine) to find a company's current Web address.*

OUR COMMENTS ON THE "YOUR TURN" CASES

You as a Financial Advisor (p. 267) Alternative uses for the company's cash surplus may include investments in (1) certificates of deposit—CDs—with staggered maturity dates, (2) short-term notes issued by the U.S. Treasury Department, or (3) money market accounts. If these alternatives are deemed unacceptable, management may wish to distribute a cash dividend to the company's shareholders. As a financial advisor, you should alert management to the fact that the $5 million checking account balance may not be entirely safe. Should the bank run into financial problems, the FDIC would insure only a fraction of the $5 million total.

You as a Used Car Purchaser (p. 284) Whether you read the Uniform Commercial Code or consult a lawyer, you will find that factoring accounts receivable is neither illegal nor unethical. Your contract to make the monthly payments most likely includes a clause to pay whoever owns the receivable. Article 9 of the Uniform Commercial Code provides the legal requirements for the sale of accounts receivables to a third party.* The ethics of the situation may depend on what customers were promised when they made purchases on account. At a minimum, a letter should be sent to all customers explaining that the receivables have been sold and will now be collected by a collection agency. Many customers do not like their accounts receivable to be sold to a third party. Thus, using factoring as a short-term solution to a cash flow problem may cause long-term problems with lost customers and ultimately lost revenues.

You as a Credit Manager (p. 287) Shown below are accounts receivable turnover rates and average-days-outstanding figures for the past four years.

Note: Days outstanding were computed by dividing 365 days by the turnover rate.

	2002	2001	2000	1999
Sales	$17,000	$14,580	$9,600	$9,000
Divided by Average accounts receivable	1,700	1,620	1,600	1,800
Turnover rate	10 times	9 times	6 times	5 times
Days outstanding	37 days	41 days	61 days	73 days

Based on these data, it appears that the new credit policy was successful in two ways. First, over the four-year period, it resulted in the doubling of the company's accounts receivable turnover rate (and thereby reduced its average collection period from 73 days to 37 days). Furthermore, the new policy successfully improved the quality of accounts receivable without adversely affecting sales growth.

ANSWERS TO SELF-TEST QUESTIONS

1. b 2. c 3. a 4. c 5. a 6. b 7. a 8. d 9. c
10. a 11. b ($300,000 × 12% × 6/12)

---

*See **www.law.cornell.edu/ucc/ucc.table.html** for more details about the Uniform Commercial Code.

CHAPTER 8
INVENTORIES AND THE COST OF GOODS SOLD

Learning Objectives

After studying this chapter, you should be able to:

1. In a perpetual inventory system, determine the cost of goods sold using (a) specific identification, (b) average cost, (c) FIFO, and (d) LIFO. Discuss the advantages and shortcomings of each method.

2. Explain the need for taking a physical inventory.

3. Record shrinkage losses and other year-end adjustments to inventory.

4. In a periodic inventory system, determine the ending inventory and the cost of goods sold using (a) specific identification, (b) average cost, (c) FIFO, and (d) LIFO.

5. Explain the effects on the income statement of errors in inventory valuation.

6. Estimate the cost of goods sold and ending inventory by the gross profit method and by the retail method.

7. Compute the inventory turnover rate and explain its uses.

*8. Define a "LIFO reserve" and explain its implications to users of financial statements.

---

*Supplemental Topic, "LIFO Reserves."

© Wolfgang Kaehler/CORBIS

Safeway, Inc.

Having the right merchandise available at the right time and in the right place is critically important to all companies that sell products to their customers. These businesses include chain stores such as grocery stores, drugstores, and department stores.

Consider **Safeway, Inc.**,—a giant grocery chain with nearly 1,700 stores nationwide. When customers shop at **Safeway**, they expect to find the items they want in stock and ready to purchase. If not, they most likely will find another place to shop. To meet the needs of every customer, each **Safeway** store must stock more than 10,000 products. To control such a diverse selection of inventory is a major challenge in the highly competitive environment of food retailing.

• • •

Accounting for merchandise inventory presents one of the greatest challenges for merchandising companies. These companies must maintain not only a record of inventory items for sale but also the prices at which these items are purchased and sold, both of which change over time. This adds a significant complication to accounting for inventory and the expense included in the income statement when inventory is sold to customers. You learn how to account for inventory and its cost in this chapter.

Inventory Defined

In a merchandising company, inventory consists of all goods owned and held for sale to customers. Inventory is expected to be converted into cash within the company's *operating cycle*.[1] In the balance sheet, inventory is listed immediately after accounts receivable, because it is just one step farther removed from conversion into cash than customer receivables.

THE FLOW OF INVENTORY COSTS

Inventory is a nonfinancial asset and usually is shown in the balance sheet at its cost.[2] As items are sold from inventory, their costs are removed from the balance sheet and transferred to the cost of goods sold, which is offset against sales revenue in the income statement. This flow of costs is illustrated in Exhibit 8–1.

Exhibit 8–1

THE FLOW OF COSTS THROUGH FINANCIAL STATEMENTS

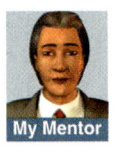

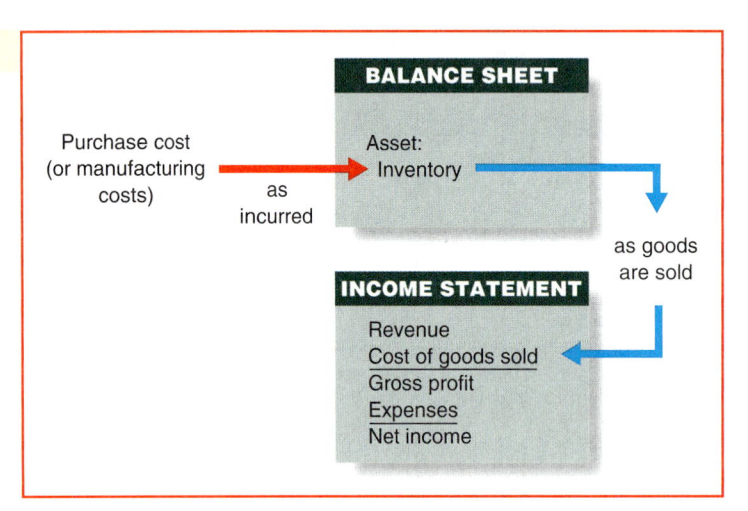

In a perpetual inventory system, entries in the accounting records parallel this flow of costs. When merchandise is purchased, its cost (net of allowable cash discounts) is added to the asset account Inventory. As the merchandise is sold, its cost is removed from the Inventory account and transferred to the Cost of Goods Sold account.

The valuation of inventory and of the cost of goods sold is of critical importance to managers and to external users of financial statements. In many cases, inventory is a company's largest asset, and the cost of goods sold is its largest expense. These two accounts have a significant effect on the financial statement subtotals and ratios used in evaluating the liquidity and profitability of the business.

---

[1] As explained in Chapter 6, the *operating cycle* of a merchandising business is the period of time required to convert cash into inventory, inventory into accounts receivable, and accounts receivable into cash. Assets expected to be converted into cash within one year or the operating cycle, whichever is longer, are regarded as current assets.

[2] Some companies deal in inventories that can be sold in a worldwide market at quoted market prices. Examples include mutual funds, stock brokerages, and companies that deal in commodities such as agricultural crops or precious metals. Often these companies value their inventories at market price rather than at cost. Our discussions in this chapter are directed to the far more common situation in which inventories are valued at cost.

The Flow of Inventory Costs

Several different methods of pricing inventory and of measuring the cost of goods sold are acceptable under generally accepted accounting principles. These different methods may produce significantly different results, both in a company's financial statements and in its income tax returns. Therefore, managers and investors should understand the effects of the different inventory valuation methods.

Which Unit Did We Sell?

Purchases of merchandise are recorded in the same manner under all of the inventory valuation methods. The differences in these methods lie in determining *which costs* should be removed from the Inventory account when merchandise is sold.

We illustrated the basic entries relating to purchases and sales of merchandise in Chapter 6. In that introductory discussion, however, we made a simplifying assumption: All of the units in inventory had been acquired at the same unit cost. In practice, a company often has in its inventory identical units of a given product that were acquired at *different costs*. Acquisition costs may vary because the units were purchased at different dates, from different suppliers, or in different quantities.

When identical units of inventory have different unit costs, a question arises as to *which of these costs* should be used in measuring the cost of goods sold.

Data for an Illustration

To illustrate the alternative methods of measuring the cost of goods sold, assume that Mead Electric Company sells electrical equipment and supplies. Included in the company's inventory are five Elco AC-40 generators. These generators are identical; however, two were purchased on January 5 at a per-unit cost of *$1,000*, and the other three were purchased a month later, shortly after Elco had announced a price increase, at a per-unit cost of *$1,200*. These purchases are reflected in Mead's inventory subsidiary ledger in Exhibit 8–2.

Exhibit 8–2

INVENTORY SUBSIDIARY LEDGER

Item Elco AC-40				Primary supplier Elco Manufacturing					
Description Portable generator				Secondary supplier Vegas Wholesale Co.					
Location Daily St. warehouse				Inventory level: Min: 2 Max: 5					

	Purchased			Sold			Balance		
Date	Units	Unit Cost	Total	Units	Unit Cost	Cost of Goods Sold	Units	Unit Cost	Total
Jan. 5	2	$1,000	$2,000				2	$1,000	$2,000
Feb. 5	3	1,200	3,600				{2	1,000}	
							{3	1,200}	5,600

Notice that on February 5, the Balance columns contain two "layers" of unit cost information, representing the units purchased at the two different unit costs. A new **cost layer** is created whenever units are acquired at a different per-unit cost. (As all units comprising a cost layer are sold, the layer is eliminated from the inventory. Therefore, a business is unlikely to have more than three or four cost layers in its inventory at any given time.)

Now assume that on March 1, Mead sells one of these Elco generators to Boulder Construction Company for $1,800 cash. What cost should be removed from the Inventory account and recognized as the cost of goods sold—$1,000 or $1,200?

In answering such questions, accountants may use an approach called **specific identification**, or they may adopt a cost **flow assumption**. Either of these approaches is

LO 1
In a perpetual inventory system, determine the cost of goods sold using (a) specific identification, (b) average cost, (c) FIFO, and (d) LIFO. Discuss the advantages and shortcomings of each method.

acceptable. Once an approach has been selected, however, it should be *applied consistently* in accounting for all sales of this particular type of merchandise.

Specific Identification

The specific identification method can be used only when the actual costs of individual units of merchandise can be determined from the accounting records. For example, each of the generators in Mead's inventory may have an identification number, and these numbers may appear on the purchase invoices. With this identification number, Mead's accounting department can determine whether the generator sold to Boulder Construction cost $1,000 or $1,200. The *actual cost* of this particular unit then is used in recording the cost of goods sold.

Cost Flow Assumptions

If the items in inventory are *homogeneous* in nature (identical, except for insignificant differences), it is *not necessary* for the seller to use the specific identification method. Rather, the seller may follow the more convenient practice of using a *cost flow assumption*. Using a cost flow assumption, often referred to as simply a flow assumption, is particularly common where the company has a large number of virtually identical inventory items.

When a flow assumption is in use, the seller simply makes an *assumption* as to the sequence in which units are withdrawn from inventory. For example, the seller might assume that the oldest merchandise always is sold first or that the most recently purchased items are the first to be sold.

Three flow assumptions are in widespread use:

1. *Average cost.* This assumption values all merchandise—units sold and units remaining in inventory—at the *average* per-unit cost. (In effect, the average-cost method assumes that units are withdrawn from the inventory in random order.)
2. *First-in, first-out (FIFO).* As the name implies, FIFO involves the assumption that goods sold are the *first* units that were purchased—that is, the *oldest* goods on hand. Thus the remaining inventory is comprised of the most recent purchases.
3. *Last-in, first-out (LIFO).* Under LIFO, the units sold are assumed to be those *most recently* acquired. The remaining inventory, therefore, is assumed to consist of the earliest purchases.

The cost flow assumption selected by a company *need not* correspond to the actual physical movement of the company's merchandise. When the units of merchandise are identical (or nearly identical), it *does not matter* which units are delivered to the customer in a particular sales transaction. Therefore, in measuring the income of a business that sells units of identical merchandise, accountants consider the flow of *costs* to be more important than the physical flow of the merchandise.

The use of a flow assumption *eliminates the need for separately identifying each unit sold and looking up its actual cost.* Experience has shown that these flow assumptions provide useful and reliable measurements of the cost of goods sold, as long as they are applied consistently to all sales of the particular type of merchandise.

Average-Cost Method

When the **average-cost method** is in use, the *average cost* of all units in inventory is computed after every purchase. This average cost is computed by dividing the total cost of goods available for sale by the number of units in inventory. Because the average cost may change following each purchase, this method also is called the *moving average method.*

As of January 5, Mead had only two Elco generators in its inventory, each acquired at a purchase cost of $1,000. Therefore, the average cost is $1,000 per unit. After the purchase on February 5, Mead had five Elco generators in inventory, acquired at a total

The Flow of Inventory Costs

cost of $5,600 (2 units @ $1,000, plus 3 units @ $1,200 = $5,600). Therefore, the *average* per-unit cost now is *$1,120* ($5,600 ÷ 5 units = $1,120).

On March 1, two entries are made to record the sale of one of these generators to Boulder Construction Company. The first recognizes the revenue from this sale, and the second recognizes the cost of the goods sold. These entries follow, with the cost of goods sold measured by the average-cost method:

```
Cash ............................................. 1,800
    Sales ............................................ 1,800
To record the sale of one Elco AC-40 generator.

Cost of Goods Sold ................................. 1,120
    Inventory ........................................ 1,120
To record the cost of one Elco AC-40 generator sold to Boulder
    Construction Co. Cost determined by the average-cost method.
```

(The entry to recognize the $1,800 in sales revenue is the same, regardless of the inventory method in use. Therefore, we will not repeat this entry in our illustrations of the other cost flow assumptions.)

When the average-cost method is in use, the inventory subsidiary ledger is modified slightly from the format in Exhibit 8–2. Following the sale on March 1, Mead's subsidiary ledger card for Elco generators would be modified to show the average unit cost as in Exhibit 8–3.

| | Purchased ||| Sold ||| Balance |||
Date	Units	Unit Cost	Total	Units	Unit Cost	Cost of Goods Sold	Units	Unit Cost	Total
Jan. 5	2	$1,000	$2,000				2	$1,000*	$2,000
Feb. 5	3	1,200	3,600				5	$1,120**	5,600
Mar. 1				1	$1,120	$1,120	4	$1,120	4,480

Exhibit 8–3

INVENTORY SUBSIDIARY LEDGER—AVERAGE-COST BASIS

*$2,000 total cost ÷ 2 units = $1,000.
**$5,600 total cost ÷ 5 units = $1,120.

Notice that the Unit Cost column for purchases still shows actual unit costs—$1,000 and $1,200. The Unit Cost columns relating to sales and to the remaining inventory, however, show the *average unit cost* ($5,600 total ÷ 5 units = $1,120). As all units are valued at this same average cost, the inventory has only one cost layer.

Under the average-cost assumption, all items in inventory are assigned the *same* per-unit cost (the average cost). Hence, it does not matter which units are sold; the cost of goods sold always is based on the current average unit cost. When one generator is sold on March 1, the cost of goods sold is $1,120; if three generators had been sold on this date, the cost of goods sold would have been $3,360 (3 units × $1,120 per unit).

First-In, First-Out Method

The **first-in, first-out method**, often called *FIFO*, is based on the assumption that the *first merchandise purchased is the first merchandise sold*. Thus the accountant for Mead Electric would assume that the generator sold on March 1 was one of those purchased on *January 5*. The entry to record the cost of goods sold would be:

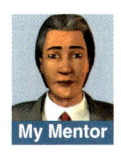

Cost of Goods Sold	1,000	
Inventory		1,000

To record the cost of one Elco AC-40 generator sold to Boulder Construction Co. Cost determined by the FIFO flow assumption.

Following this sale, Mead's inventory ledger would appear as shown in Exhibit 8–4.

Exhibit 8–4
INVENTORY SUBSIDIARY LEDGER—FIFO BASIS

	Purchased			Sold			Balance		
Date	Units	Unit Cost	Total	Units	Unit Cost	Cost of Goods Sold	Units	Unit Cost	Total
Jan. 5	2	$1,000	$2,000				2	$1,000	$2,000
Feb. 5	3	1,200	3,600				{ 2 { 3	1,000 1,200	5,600
Mar. 1				1	$1,000	$1,000	{ 1 { 3	1,000 1,200	4,600

Notice that FIFO uses actual purchase costs, rather than an average cost. Thus, if merchandise has been purchased at several different costs, the inventory will include several different cost layers. The cost of goods sold for a given sales transaction also may involve several different cost layers. To illustrate, assume that Mead had sold *four* generators to Boulder Construction, instead of only one. Under the FIFO flow assumption, Mead would assume that it first sold the two generators purchased on January 5 and then two of those purchased on February 5. Thus the total cost of goods sold ($4,400) would include items at *two different unit costs,* as shown here:

2 generators from Jan. 5 purchase @ $1,000	$2,000
2 generators from Feb. 5 purchase @ $1,200	$2,400
Total cost of goods sold (4 units)	$4,400

As the cost of goods sold always is recorded at the oldest available purchase costs, the units remaining in inventory are valued at the more recent acquisition costs.

Last-In, First-Out Method

The **last-in, first-out method**, commonly known as *LIFO,* is among the most widely used methods of determining the cost of goods sold and valuing inventory. As the name suggests, the *most recently* purchased merchandise (the last in) is assumed to be sold first. If Mead were using the LIFO method, it would assume that the generator sold on March 1 was one of those acquired on *February 5,* the most recent purchase date. Thus, the cost transferred from inventory to the cost of goods sold would be *$1,200.*

The journal entry to record the cost of goods sold appears below. The inventory subsidiary ledger record after this entry has been posted is in Exhibit 8–5.

Cost of Goods Sold	1,200	
Inventory		1,200

To record the cost of one Elco AC-40 generator sold to Boulder Construction Co. Cost determined by the LIFO flow assumption.

The Flow of Inventory Costs

Exhibit 8–5

INVENTORY SUBSIDIARY LEDGER—LIFO BASIS

	Purchased			Sold			Balance		
Date	Units	Unit Cost	Total	Units	Unit Cost	Cost of Goods Sold	Units	Unit Cost	Total
Jan. 5	2	$1,000	$2,000				2	$1,000	$2,000
Feb. 5	3	1,200	3,600				{ 2	1,000	
							3	1,200 }	5,600
Mar. 1				1	$1,200	$1,200	{ 2	1,000	
							2	1,200 }	4,400

Like FIFO, the LIFO method uses actual purchase costs, rather than an average cost. Thus the inventory may have several different cost layers. If a sale includes more units than are included in the most recent cost layer, some of the goods sold are assumed to come from the next most recent layer. For example, if Mead had sold four generators (instead of one) on March 1, the cost of goods sold determined under the LIFO assumption would be $4,600:

3 generators from Feb. 5 purchase @ $1,200	$3,600
1 generator from Jan. 5 purchase @ $1,000	$1,000
Total cost of goods sold (4 units)	$4,600

As LIFO transfers the most recent purchase costs to the cost of goods sold, the goods remaining in inventory are valued at the oldest acquisition costs.

Evaluation of the Methods

All three of the cost flow assumptions just described are acceptable for use in financial statements and in income tax returns. As we have explained, it is not necessary that the physical flow of merchandise correspond to the cost flow assumption. Different flow assumptions may be used for different types of inventory or for inventories in different geographical locations.

The only requirement for using a flow assumption is that the units to which the assumption is applied should be *homogeneous* in nature—that is, virtually identical to one another. If each unit is unique, such as the sale of portraits by an art studio, only the specific identification method can properly match sales revenue with the cost of goods sold.

Each inventory valuation method has certain advantages and shortcomings. In the final analysis, the selection of inventory valuation methods is a managerial decision. However, the method (or methods) used in financial statements always should be disclosed in notes accompanying the statements.

Specific Identification The specific identification method is best suited to inventories of high-priced, low-volume items. This is the only method that exactly parallels the physical flow of the merchandise. If each item in the inventory is unique, as in the case of valuable paintings, custom jewelry, and most real estate, specific identification is clearly the logical choice.

The specific identification method has an intuitive appeal, because it assigns actual purchase costs to the specific units of merchandise sold or in inventory. However, when the units in inventory are identical (or nearly identical), the specific identification method may produce *misleading results* by implying differences in value that—under current market conditions—do not exist.

As an example, assume that a coal dealer has purchased 100 tons of coal at a cost of $60 per ton. A short time later, the company purchases another 100 tons of the *same grade* of coal—but this time, the cost is $80 per ton. The two purchases are in separate piles; thus it would be possible for the company to use the specific identification method in accounting for sales.

Assume now that the company has an opportunity to sell 10 tons of coal at a retail price of $120 per ton. Does it really matter from which pile this coal is removed? The answer is *no;* the coal is a homogeneous product. Under current market conditions, the coal in each pile is equally valuable. To imply that it is more profitable to sell coal from one pile rather than the other is an argument of questionable logic.

Let us try to make this point in a more personal way: Would you be willing to shovel the more recently purchased coal out of the way so that the customer can get its truck back to the lower-cost coal pile?

Average Cost Identical items will have the same accounting values only under the average-cost method. Assume, for example, that a hardware store sells a given size nail for 65 cents per pound. The hardware store buys the nails in 100-pound quantities at different times at prices ranging from 40 to 50 cents per pound. Several hundred pounds of nails are always on hand, stored in a large bin. The average-cost method properly recognizes that when a customer buys a pound of nails it is not necessary to know exactly which nails the customer selected from the bin in order to measure the cost of goods sold. Therefore, the average-cost method avoids the shortcomings of the specific identification method. It is not necessary to keep track of the specific items sold and of those still in inventory. Also, it is not possible to manipulate income merely by selecting the specific items to be delivered to customers.

A shortcoming of the average-cost method is that changes in current replacement costs of inventory are concealed because these costs are averaged with older costs. Thus neither the valuation of ending inventory nor the cost of goods sold will quickly reflect changes in the current replacement cost of merchandise.

First-In, First-Out The distinguishing characteristic of the FIFO method is that the oldest purchase costs are transferred to the cost of goods sold, while the most recent costs remain in inventory.

Over the past 50 years, we have lived in an inflationary economy, which means that most prices tend to rise over time. When purchase costs are rising, the FIFO method assigns *lower* (older) costs to the cost of goods sold and the higher (more recent) costs to the goods remaining in inventory.

By assigning lower costs to the cost of goods sold, FIFO usually causes a business to report somewhat *higher profits* than would be reported under the other inventory valuation methods. Some companies favor the FIFO method for financial reporting purposes, because their goal is to report the highest net income possible. For income tax purposes, however, reporting more income than necessary results in paying more income taxes than necessary.

Some accountants and decision makers believe that FIFO tends to *overstate* a company's profitability. Revenue is based on current market conditions. By offsetting this revenue with a cost of goods sold based on older (and lower) prices, gross profits may be overstated consistently.

A conceptual advantage of the FIFO method is that in the balance sheet inventory is valued at recent purchase costs. Therefore, this asset appears in the balance sheet at an amount closely approximating its current replacement cost.

Last-In, First-Out The LIFO method is one of the most interesting and controversial flow assumptions. The basic assumption in the LIFO method is that the most recently purchased units are sold first and that the older units remain in inventory. This assumption is *not* in accord with the physical flow of merchandise in most businesses. Yet there are strong logical arguments in support of the LIFO method, in addition to income tax considerations.

For the purpose of measuring income, most accountants consider the *flow of costs* more important than the physical flow of merchandise. Supporters of the LIFO method contend that the measurement of income should be based on *current market conditions.* Therefore, current sales revenue should be offset by the *current* cost of the merchandise sold. By the LIFO method, the costs assigned to the cost of goods sold are relatively current because they reflect the most recent purchases. By the FIFO method, on the other hand, the cost of goods sold is based on older costs.

Income tax considerations, however, provide the principal reason for the popularity of the LIFO method. Remember that the LIFO method assigns the most recent inventory purchase costs to the cost of goods sold. In the common situation of rising prices, these most recent costs are also the highest costs. By reporting a higher cost of goods sold than results from other inventory valuation methods, the LIFO method usually results in *lower taxable income.* In short, if inventory costs are rising, a company can reduce the amount of its income tax obligation by using the LIFO method in its income tax return.

It may seem reasonable that a company would use the LIFO method in its tax return to reduce taxable income and use the FIFO method in its financial statements to increase the amount of net income reported to investors and creditors. However, income tax regulations allow a corporation to use LIFO in its income tax return *only* if the company also uses LIFO in its financial statements. Thus income tax considerations often provide the overriding reason for selecting the LIFO method.

There is one significant shortcoming to the LIFO method. The valuation of the asset inventory is based on the company's oldest inventory acquisition costs. After the company has been in business for many years, these oldest costs may greatly understate the current replacement cost of the inventory. Thus, when an inventory is valued by the LIFO method, the company also should disclose the current replacement cost of the inventory in a note to the financial statements.

During periods of rising inventory replacement costs, the LIFO method results in the lowest valuation of inventory and measurement of net income. Therefore, LIFO is regarded as the most *conservative* of the inventory pricing methods. FIFO, on the other hand, is the least conservative method.[3]

Do Inventory Methods Really Affect Performance?

Except for their effects on income taxes, the answer to this question is *no.*

During a period of rising prices, a company might *report* higher profits by using FIFO instead of LIFO. But the company would not really *be* any more profitable. An inventory valuation method affects only the *allocation of costs* between the Inventory account and the Cost of Goods Sold account. It has *no effect* on the total costs actually *incurred* in purchasing or manufacturing inventory. Except for income taxes, differences in the profitability reported under different inventory methods exist "only on paper."

The inventory method in use *does* affect the amount of income taxes owed. To the extent that an inventory method reduces these taxes, it *does* increase profitability. In Exhibit 8–6 we summarize characteristics of the basic inventory valuation methods.

CASH EFFECTS

The cash payments relating to inventory occur when suppliers are *paid.* In a statement of cash flows, these outlays are included among the cash payments for operating activities. For merchandising and manufacturing businesses, these payments often represent the largest use of cash. It is important to note that inventory valuation methods have *no effect* on the cash paid to purchase or manufacture inventory. They do, however, affect cash payments for income taxes.

---

[3] During a prolonged period of *declining* inventory replacement costs, this situation reverses: FIFO becomes the most conservative method, and LIFO the least conservative.

Exhibit 8–6 SUMMARY OF INVENTORY VALUATION METHODS

	Costs Allocated to:		
Valuation Method	**Cost of Goods Sold**	**Inventory**	**Comments**
Specific identification	Actual costs of the units sold	Actual cost of units remaining	• Parallels physical flow • Logical method when units are unique • May be misleading when the units are identical
Flow assumptions (acceptable only for an inventory of *homogeneous units*):			
Average cost	Number of units sold times the *average unit cost*	Number of units on hand times the *average unit cost*	• Assigns all units the same *average unit cost* • Current costs are averaged in with older costs
First-in, first-out (FIFO)	Costs of *earliest purchases* on hand at the time of the sale (first-in, first-out)	Cost of *most recently* purchased units	• Cost of goods sold is based on older costs • Inventory valued at most recent costs • May overstate income during periods of rising prices; may increase income taxes due
Last-in, first-out (LIFO)	Cost of *most recently purchased* units (last-in, first-out)	Costs of *earliest* purchases (assumed *still* to be in inventory)	• Cost of goods sold shown at most recent prices • Inventory shown at old (and perhaps out-of-date) costs • Most conservative method during periods of rising prices; often results in lower income taxes

The Principle of Consistency

The principle of **consistency** is one of the basic concepts underlying reliable financial statements. This principle means that once a company has adopted a particular accounting method, it should *follow that method consistently,* rather than switch methods from one year to the next. Thus, once a company has adopted a particular inventory flow assumption (or the specific identification method), it should continue to apply that assumption to all sales of that type of merchandise.

The principle of consistency does *not* prohibit a company from *ever* changing its accounting methods. If a change is made, however, the reasons for the change must be explained, and the effects of the change on the company's net income must be fully disclosed.[4]

Just-in-Time (JIT) Inventory Systems

In recent years, much attention has been paid to the **just-in-time (JIT) inventory system** in manufacturing operations. The phrase "just-in-time" usually means that purchases of raw materials and component parts arrive just in time for use in the manufacturing process—often within a few hours of the time they are scheduled for use. A second

---

[4] Disclosure of the effects of such "accounting changes" is discussed in Chapter 11. A change in the method of pricing inventory for tax purposes requires the approval of the Internal Revenue Service.

application of the just-in-time concept is completing the manufacturing process just in time to ship the finished goods to customers.

> A major advantage of a just-in-time system is reducing the amount of money tied up in inventories of raw materials and finished goods. **Boeing Co.** uses lean manufacturing and just-in-time inventory management. At **Boeing**'s vast assembly plant for 737s in Renton, Washington, just-in-time procedures are cutting waste, shrinking factory space, and eliminating unnecessary inventory. **Boeing** found it needed to make some changes, however, after an attempt to double production led to a disastrous $1.6 billion loss in its 1997 financial statements.
>
> **Boeing**'s 1997 problems illustrate one disadvantage of a just-in-time system: Parts supply problems forced the company to shut down its 747 and 737 assembly lines. To be effective, just-in-time systems cannot tolerate delays in the arrival of essential materials because manufacturing operations come to a halt. Therefore, just-in-time scheduling of incoming materials is feasible only when the suppliers and the transportation systems are highly reliable.
>
> After solving the parts supply problems, **Boeing** is reaping the benefits of lean manufacturing and just-in-time inventory management techniques. For example, mechanics used to take 42 hours to install 204 parts that make up a mixer bay assembly, which circulates cabin air. Now, because parts come preassembled from suppliers in a just-in-time system, the job is completed in just 16 hours, cutting time by 62%.

MANAGEMENT STRATEGY AND FINANCIAL REPORTING

Although a just-in-time system reduces the size of a company's inventories, it does not eliminate them entirely. A recent annual report of **Dell Computer Corporation**, for example, shows inventories in excess of *$273 million* (**Dell** reports its inventories by the FIFO method).

> **Dell Computer Corporation** generates millions in revenue each day by selling computers on the Internet. The company has long been a model of just-in-time manufacturing. **Dell** doesn't start ordering components or assembling computers until an order has been booked. Most of its suppliers keep components warehoused just minutes from **Dell**'s factories. The JIT philosophy applies to suppliers, assemblers, and distributors. A customer order placed Monday morning can be on a delivery truck by Tuesday evening.

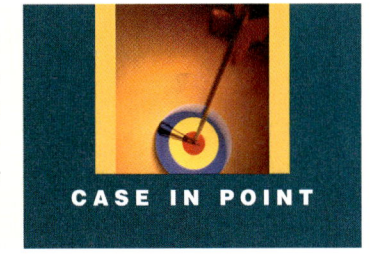

CASE IN POINT

The concept of minimizing inventories applies more to manufacturing operations than to retailers. Ideally, manufacturers have buyers "lined up" for their merchandise even before the goods are produced. Many retailers, in contrast, want to offer their customers a large selection of in-stock merchandise—which means a big inventory.

The just-in-time concept actually involves much more than minimizing the size of inventories. It has been described as the philosophy of constantly working to increase efficiency throughout the organization. One basic goal of an accounting system is to provide management with useful information about the efficiency—or inefficiency—of operations.

TAKING A PHYSICAL INVENTORY

In Chapter 6 we explained the need for businesses to make a complete physical count of the merchandise on hand at least once a year. The primary reason for this procedure of "taking inventory" is to adjust the perpetual inventory records for unrecorded **shrinkage losses**, such as theft, spoilage, or breakage.

LO 2
Explain the need for taking a physical inventory.

The **physical inventory** usually is taken at (or near) the end of the company's fiscal year.[5] Often a business selects a fiscal year ending in a season of low activity. For example, many large retailers use a fiscal year that starts February 1 and ends January 31.

Recording Shrinkage Losses

In most cases, the year-end physical count of the inventory reveals some shortages or damaged merchandise. The costs of missing or damaged units are removed from the inventory records using the same flow assumption as is used in recording the costs of goods sold.

To illustrate, assume that a company's inventory subsidiary ledger shows the following 158 units of a particular product in inventory at year-end:

8 units purchased Nov. 2 @ $100	$ 800
150 units purchased Dec. 10 @ $115	17,250
Total (158 units)	$18,050

A year-end physical count, however, discloses that only *148* of these units actually are on hand. Based on this physical count, the company should adjust its inventory records to reflect the loss of 10 units.

The inventory flow assumption in use affects the measurement of shrinkage losses in the same way it affects the cost of goods sold. If the company uses *FIFO,* for example, the missing units will be valued at the oldest purchase costs shown in the inventory records. Thus 8 of the missing units will be assumed to have cost $100 per unit and the other 2, $115 per unit. Under FIFO, the shrinkage loss amounts to *$1,030* (8 units @ $100 + 2 units @ $115). But if this company uses *LIFO,* the missing units all will be assumed to have come from the most recent purchase (on December 10). Therefore, the shrinkage loss amounts to *$1,150* (10 units @ $115).

If shrinkage losses are small, the costs removed from inventory may be charged (debited) directly to the Cost of Goods Sold account. If these losses are *material* in amount, the offsetting debit should be entered in a special loss account, such as Inventory Shrinkage Losses. In the income statement, a loss account is deducted from revenue in the same manner as an expense account.

LCM and Other Write-Downs of Inventory

In addition to shrinkage losses, the value of inventory may decline because the merchandise has become obsolete or is unsalable for other reasons. If inventory has become obsolete or is otherwise unsalable, its carrying value in the accounting records should be *written down* to zero (or to its "scrap value," if any). A **write-down** of inventory reduces both the carrying amount of the inventory in the balance sheet and the net income of the current period. The reduction in income is handled in the same manner as a shrinkage loss. If the write-down is relatively small, the loss is debited directly to the Cost of Goods Sold account. If the write-down is *material in amount,* however, it is charged to a special loss account, perhaps entitled Loss from Write-Down of Inventory.

---

[5] The reason for taking a physical inventory near year-end is to ensure that any shrinkage losses are reflected in the annual financial statements. The stronger the company's system of internal control over inventories, the farther away this procedure may be moved from the balance sheet date. Obviously, no one wants to spend New Year's Eve counting inventory.

> **CASE IN POINT**
>
> Determining the materiality of an inventory write-down is a matter of professional judgment. For example, Guess, Inc., a leading clothing retailer for young women, generally charges the entire cost of obsolete inventory directly to the Cost of Goods Sold account, thereby reducing its gross profit. In a recent income statement, Guess, Inc., reported a gross profit rate of 37% of sales. This figure, however, included a $6 million inventory write-down. Had it been charged to a separate account for inventory losses, the gross profit rate would have been nearly 40% of sales. Given the magnitude of this write-down, some might argue that it should have been treated separately.
>
> © Felicia Martinez/PhotoEdit

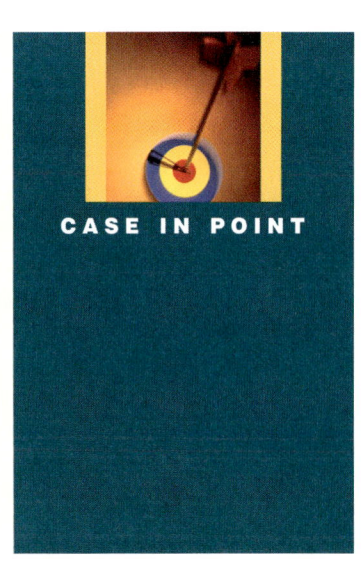

The Lower-of-Cost-or-Market (LCM) Rule An asset is an economic resource. It may be argued that no economic resource is worth more than it would cost to *replace* that resource in the open market. For this reason, accountants traditionally have valued inventory in the balance sheet at the lower of its (1) cost or (2) market value. In this context, "market value" means *current replacement cost*. Thus the inventory is valued at the lower of its historical cost or its current replacement cost.

The lower-of-cost-or-market rule may be applied in conjunction with any flow assumption as well as with the specific identification method. If the current replacement cost of the ending inventory is substantially *below* the cost shown in the accounting records, the inventory is written down to this replacement cost. The offsetting debit is charged to either the Cost of Goods Sold account or the Loss from Write-Down of Inventory account, depending on the materiality of the dollar amount.

In their financial statements, most companies state that inventory is valued at the lower-of-cost-or-market. In our inflationary economy, however, the lower of these two amounts usually is cost, especially for companies using LIFO.[6]

The Year-End Cutoff of Transactions

Making a proper *cutoff* of transactions is an essential step in the preparation of reliable financial statements. A proper cutoff simply means that the transactions occurring near year-end are *recorded in the right accounting period*.

One aspect of a proper cutoff is determining that all purchases of merchandise through the end of the period are recorded in the inventory records and included in the physical count of merchandise on hand at year-end. Of equal importance is determining that the cost of all merchandise sold through the end of the period has been removed from the inventory accounts and charged to the Cost of Goods Sold. This merchandise should *not* be included in the year-end physical count.

If some sales transactions have not been recorded as of year-end, the quantities of merchandise shown in the inventory records will exceed the quantities actually on hand. When the results of the physical count are compared with the inventory records, these unrecorded sales easily could be mistaken for inventory shortages.

---

[6] A notable exception is the petroleum industry, in which the replacement cost of inventory can fluctuate very quickly and in either direction. Large oil companies occasionally report LCM adjustments of several hundred million dollars in a single year.

Making a proper cutoff may be difficult if sales transactions are occurring while the merchandise is being counted. For this reason, many businesses count their physical inventory during nonbusiness hours, even if they must shut down their sales operations for a day.

Matching Revenue and the Cost of Goods Sold Accountants must determine that both the sales revenue and the cost of goods sold relating to sales transactions occurring near year-end are recorded in the *same* accounting period. Otherwise, the revenues and expenses from these transactions will not be properly matched in the company's income statements.

Goods in Transit A sale should be recorded *when title to the merchandise passes to the buyer.* In making a year-end cutoff of transactions, questions may arise when goods are in transit between the seller and the buyer as to which company owns the merchandise. The answer to such questions lies in the terms of shipment. If these terms are **F.O.B. (free on board) shipping point**, title passes at the point of shipment and the goods are the property of the buyer while in transit. If the terms of the shipment are **F.O.B. destination**, title does not pass until the shipment reaches its destination and the goods belong to the seller while in transit.

Many companies ignore these distinctions, because goods in transit usually arrive within a day or two. In such cases, the amount of merchandise in transit usually is *not material* in dollar amount, and the company may follow the *most convenient* accounting procedures. It usually is most convenient to record all purchases when the inbound shipments arrive and all sales when the merchandise is shipped to the customer.

In some industries, however, goods in transit may be very material. Oil companies, for example, often have millions of dollars of inventory in transit in pipelines and supertankers. In these situations, the company must consider the terms of each shipment in recording its purchases and sales.

YOUR TURN

You as a Sales Manager

As sales manager for Tempto Co., a producer of the fine home furnishings, you have responsibility for the northeast region of the country. Assume you have just returned from the company's annual sales managers' conference in New Orleans. At the conference, while strolling with some of the regional managers in the French Quarter, you became aware that several managers report sales that are scheduled for shipment in early January as if they were shipped in late December. What should you do?

*Our comments appear on page 361.

Periodic Inventory Systems

In our preceding discussions, we have emphasized the perpetual inventory system—that is, inventory records that are kept continuously up-to-date. Virtually all large business organizations use perpetual inventory systems.

Some small businesses, however, use *periodic* inventory systems. In a periodic inventory system, the cost of merchandise purchased during the year is debited to a *Purchases* account, rather than to the Inventory account. When merchandise is sold to a customer, an entry is made recognizing the sales revenue, but no entry is made to reduce the inventory account or to recognize the cost of goods sold.

The inventory on hand and the cost of goods sold for the year are not determined until year-end. At the end of the year, all goods on hand are counted and priced at cost. The cost assigned to this ending inventory is then used to compute the cost of goods sold. (The dollar amounts are assumed for the purpose of completing this illustration.)

LO 4
In a periodic inventory system, determine the ending inventory and the cost of goods sold using (a) specific identification, (b) average cost, (c) FIFO, and (d) LIFO.

Inventory at the beginning of the year		$10,000
Add: Purchases during the year		80,000
Cost of goods available for sale during the year		$90,000
Less: Inventory at the end of the year		7,000
Cost of goods sold		$83,000

The only item in this computation that is kept continuously up-to-date in the accounting records is the Purchases account. The amounts of inventory at the beginning and end of the year are determined by annual physical observation.

Determining the cost of the year-end inventory involves two distinct steps: counting the merchandise and pricing the inventory—that is, determining the cost of the units on hand. Together, these procedures determine the proper valuation of inventory and the cost of goods sold.

Applying Flow Assumptions in a Periodic System In our discussion of perpetual inventory systems, we have emphasized the costs that are transferred from inventory *to the cost of goods sold*. In a periodic system, the emphasis shifts to determining the costs that should be assigned *to inventory* at the end of the period.

To illustrate, assume that The Kitchen Counter, a retail store, uses a periodic inventory system. The year-end physical inventory indicates that 12 units of a particular model food processor are on hand. Purchases of these food processors during the year are listed in Exhibit 8–7.

	Number of Units	Cost per Unit	Total Cost
Beginning inventory	10	$ 80	$ 800
First purchase (Mar. 1)	5	90	450
Second purchase (July 1)	5	100	500
Third purchase (Oct. 1)	5	120	600
Fourth purchase (Dec. 1)	5	130	650
Available for sale	30		$3,000
Units in ending inventory	12		
Units sold	18		

Exhibit 8–7

SUMMARY OF INVENTORY PURCHASES

In Exhibit 8–7, note that of the 30 food processors available for sale in the course of the year, 12 are still on hand. Thus 18 of these food processors apparently were sold.[7] We will now use these data to determine the cost of the year-end inventory and the cost of goods sold using the specific identification method and the average-cost, FIFO, and LIFO flow assumptions.

Specific Identification If specific identification is used, the company must identify the 12 food processors on hand at year-end and determine their actual costs from purchase invoices. Assume that these 12 units have an actual total cost of $1,240. The cost of goods sold then is determined by subtracting this ending inventory from the cost of goods available for sale as shown below:

Cost of goods available for sale	$3,000
Less: Ending inventory (specific identification)	1,240
Cost of goods sold	$1,760

---

[7] The periodic inventory method does not distinguish between merchandise sold and shrinkage losses. Shrinkage losses are included automatically in the cost of goods sold.

Average Cost The average cost is determined by dividing the total cost of goods available for sale during the year by the total number of units available for sale. Thus the average per-unit cost is *$100* ($3,000 ÷ 30 units). Under the average-cost method, the ending inventory would be priced at $1,200 (12 units × $100 per unit), and the cost of goods sold would be *$1,800* ($3,000 cost of goods available for sale, less $1,200 in costs assigned to the ending inventory).

FIFO Under the FIFO flow assumption, the oldest units are assumed to be the first sold. The ending inventory, therefore, is assumed to consist of the *most recently* acquired goods. (Remember, we are now talking about the goods *remaining in inventory,* not the goods sold.) Thus the inventory of 12 food processors would be valued at the following costs:

5 units from the Dec. 1 purchase @ $130	$ 650
5 units from the Oct. 1 purchase @ $120	600
2 units from the July 1 purchase @ $100	200
Ending inventory, 12 units at FIFO cost	$1,450

The cost of goods sold would be *$1,550* ($3,000 − $1,450).

Notice that the FIFO method results in an inventory valued at relatively recent purchase costs. The cost of goods sold, however, is based on the older acquisition costs.

LIFO Under LIFO, the last units purchased are considered to be the first goods sold. Therefore, the ending inventory is assumed to contain the *earliest* purchases. The 12 food processors in inventory would be valued as:

10 units from the beginning inventory @ $80	$800
2 units from the Mar. 1 purchase @ $90	180
Ending inventory, 12 units at LIFO cost	$980

The cost of goods sold under the LIFO method is *$2,020* ($3,000 − $980).

Notice that the cost of goods sold under LIFO is *higher* than that determined by the FIFO method ($2,020 under LIFO, as compared with $1,550 under FIFO). LIFO always results in a higher cost of goods sold when purchase costs are rising. Thus LIFO tends to minimize reported net income and income taxes during periods of rising prices in both perpetual and periodic systems.

Notice also that the LIFO method may result in an ending inventory that is priced *well below* its current replacement cost. In this illustration, ending inventory is determined at $80 and $90 per unit, but the most recent purchase price is $130 per unit.

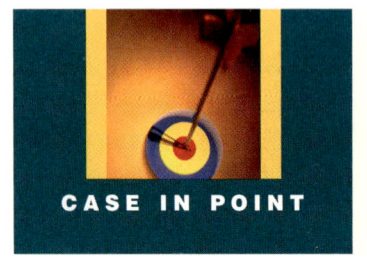

CASE IN POINT

Although FIFO techniques are allowed for financial reporting in nearly all countries, LIFO is more controversial. The International Accounting Standards Committee's conceptual framework does not embrace LIFO because it leads to outdated numbers in the balance sheet. Australia, New Zealand, and Sweden are countries that do not permit the use of LIFO inventory valuation techniques for financial reporting purposes.

Receiving the Maximum Tax Benefit from the LIFO Method Many companies that use LIFO in a perpetual inventory system *restate* their year-end inventory at the costs indicated by the *periodic* LIFO costing procedures illustrated above. This restatement is accomplished by either debiting or crediting the Inventory account and making an offsetting entry to the Cost of Goods Sold account.

Often, restating ending inventory using periodic costing procedures results in older (and lower) unit costs than those shown in the periodic inventory records. By assigning less cost to the ending inventory, it follows that more of these costs will be assigned to the cost of goods sold. A higher cost of goods sold, in turn, means less taxable income.

Let us briefly explain why applying LIFO at year-end may result in a lower valuation of inventory than does applying LIFO on a perpetual basis. Consider the last purchase in our example. This purchase of five food processors was made on December 1, at the relatively high unit cost of $130. Assuming that no additional units were sold in December, they would be included in the year-end inventory in perpetual inventory records, even if these records were maintained on a LIFO basis. When the ending inventory is priced using "periodic LIFO," however, a last-minute purchase is *not* included in inventory, but rather is transferred to the income statement as part of cost of goods sold.

Both the LIFO and average-cost methods produce different valuations of inventory under perpetual and periodic costing procedures. Only companies using LIFO, however, usually adjust their perpetual records to indicate the unit costs determined by periodic costing procedures. When FIFO is in use, the perpetual and periodic costing procedures result in exactly the same valuation of inventory.

> In Brazil, the government, corporation, law, and tax regulation have a strong influence on accounting and financial reporting practices. Because Brazilian stock markets are very small, reporting is oriented toward creditors (the major source of capital) and tax authorities. The tax authorities in Brazil do not allow LIFO inventory valuation techniques. As a result, Brazilian companies almost exclusively use FIFO and average cost methods for financial reporting purposes.

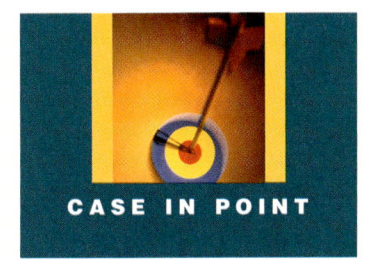

CASE IN POINT

Pricing the Year-End Inventory by Computer If purchase records are maintained by computer, as is now the case for most companies, the value of the ending inventory can be computed automatically using any of the flow assumptions that have been discussed. Only the number of units must be entered at year-end. A computer also can apply the specific identification method, but the system requires an identification number for each unit in the ending inventory. This is one reason why the specific identification method usually is not used for inventories consisting of a large number of low-cost items.

Importance of an Accurate Valuation of Inventory

The most important liquid assets in the balance sheets of most companies are cash, accounts receivable, and inventory. Of these assets, inventory often is the largest. It also is the only one of these assets for which alternative valuation methods are considered acceptable.

Because of the relatively large size of inventory, and many different products may be stored in different locations, an error in inventory valuation may not be readily apparent. Even a small error in the valuation of inventory may have a material effect on net income. Therefore, care must be taken in counting and pricing the inventory at year-end.

An error in the valuation of inventory will affect several balance sheet measurements, including assets and total owners' equity. It also will affect key figures in the *income statement,* including the cost of goods sold, gross profit, and net income. And remember that the ending inventory of one year is the beginning inventory of the next. Thus an error in inventory valuation will *carry over* into the financial statements of the following year.

Effects of an Error in Valuing Ending Inventory To illustrate, assume that some items of merchandise in a company's inventory are overlooked during the year-end physical count. As a result of this error, the ending inventory will be *understated*. The costs of the uncounted merchandise erroneously will be transferred out of the Inventory account and included in the cost of goods sold. This overstatement of the cost of goods sold, in turn, results in an understatement of gross profit and net income.[8]

Inventory Errors Affect Two Years An error in the valuation of ending inventory affects not only the financial statements of the current year but also the income statement for the *following* year.

Assume that the ending inventory in 2001 is *understated* by $10,000. As we have described above, the cost of goods sold in 2001 is also overstated by this amount, and both gross profit and net income are *understated*.

The ending inventory in 2001, however, becomes the *beginning inventory* in 2002. An understatement of the beginning inventory results in an understatement of the cost of goods sold and, therefore, an *overstatement* of gross profit and net income in 2002.

Notice that the original error has exactly the *opposite effects* on the net incomes of the two successive years. Net income was *understated* by the amount of the error in 2001 and *overstated* by the same amount in 2002. For this reason, inventory errors are said to be "counterbalancing" or "self-correcting" over a two-year period.

The fact that offsetting errors occur in the financial statements of two successive years does not lessen the consequences of errors in inventory valuation. Rather, it *exaggerates* the misleading effects of the error on *trends* in the company's performance from one year to the next.

LO 5
Explain the effects on the income statement of errors in inventory valuation.

CASE IN POINT

Some small businesses purposely have understated ending inventory in their income tax returns as an easy—though fraudulent—means of understating taxable income. In the following year, however, the effect of this error will reverse, and taxable income will be overstated. To avoid paying income taxes on this overstated income, the business may again understate its ending inventory, this time by an even greater amount. If this type of fraud continues for very long, the inventory becomes so understated that the situation becomes obvious.

When the Internal Revenue Service audits the income tax return of a small business, the IRS agents invariably try to determine whether inventory has been understated. If such an understatement exists, they will try to determine the taxpayer's intent. If the understatement has been allowed to reverse itself in the following year, the auditors probably will view the incident as an honest mistake. If they find a consistent pattern of understated inventories, however, they may prosecute the taxpayer for income tax evasion—a criminal offense.

Effects of Errors in Inventory Valuation: A Summary In Exhibit 8–8 we summarize the effects of an error in the valuation of ending inventory over two successive years. In this table we indicate the effects of the error on various financial statement measurements using the code letters **U** (understated), **O** (overstated), and **NE** (no effect). The effects of errors in the valuation of inventory are the same regardless of whether the company uses a perpetual or a periodic inventory system. The NE for owners' equity at year-end in the Following Year column results from the offsetting of the first-year error in the second year.

---

[8] If income tax effects are ignored, the amount of the error is exactly the same in inventory, gross profit, and net income. If tax effects are considered, the amount of the error may be lessened in the net income figure.

Exhibit 8–8

EFFECTS OF INVENTORY ERRORS

Original Error: Ending Inventory Understated	Year of the Error	Following Year
Beginning inventory	NE	U
Cost of goods available for sale	NE	U
Ending inventory	U	NE
Cost of goods sold	O	U
Gross profit	U	O
Net income	U	O
Owners' equity at year-end	U	NE

Original Error: Ending Inventory Overstated	Year of the Error	Following Year
Beginning inventory	NE	O
Cost of goods available for sale	NE	O
Ending inventory	O	NE
Cost of goods sold	U	O
Gross profit	O	U
Net income	O	U
Owners' equity at year-end	O	NE

Techniques for Estimating the Cost of Goods Sold and the Ending Inventory

Taking a physical inventory every month would be very expensive and time-consuming. Therefore, if a business using a periodic inventory system prepares monthly or quarterly financial statements, it usually *estimates* the amounts of its inventory and cost of goods sold. One approach to making these estimates is called the gross profit method; another—used primarily by retail stores—is the retail method.

The Gross Profit Method

The **gross profit method** is a quick and simple technique for estimating the cost of goods sold and the amount of inventory on hand. In using this method, it is assumed that the rate of gross profit earned in the preceding year (or several years) will remain the same for the current year. When we know the rate of gross profit, we can divide the dollar amount of net sales into two elements: (1) the gross profit and (2) the cost of goods sold. We view net sales as 100%. If the gross profit rate, for example, is 40% of net sales, the cost of goods sold must be 60%. In other words, the cost of goods sold percentage (or **cost ratio**) is determined by deducting the gross profit rate from 100%.

LO 6
Estimate the cost of goods sold and the ending inventory by the gross profit method and by the retail method.

When the gross profit rate is known, the ending inventory can be estimated by the following procedures:

1. Determine the *cost of goods available for sale* from the general ledger records of beginning inventory and net purchases.
2. Estimate the *cost of goods sold* by multiplying the net sales by the cost ratio.
3. Deduct the estimated *cost of goods sold* from the *cost of goods available for sale* to find the estimated ending inventory.

To illustrate, assume that Metro Hardware has a beginning inventory of $50,000 on January 1. During the month of January, net purchases amount to $20,000 and net sales total $30,000. Assume that the company's normal gross profit rate is 40% of net sales; it follows that the cost ratio is 60%. Using these facts, the inventory on January 31 may be estimated as:

My Notes

Step 1 . . .

Step 2 . . .
Step 3 . . .

Goods available for sale:		
Beginning inventory, Jan. 1		$50,000
Purchases		20,000
Cost of goods available for sale		$70,000
Deduct: Estimated cost of goods sold:		
Net sales	$30,000	
Cost ratio (100% − 40%)	60%	
Estimated cost of goods sold ($30,000 × 60%)		18,000
Estimated ending inventory, Jan. 31		$52,000

The gross profit method of estimating inventory has several uses apart from the preparation of monthly financial statements. For example, if an inventory is destroyed by fire, the company must estimate the amount of the inventory on hand at the date of the fire to file an insurance claim. The most convenient way to determine this inventory amount may be the gross profit method.

The gross profit method is also used at year-end after the taking of a physical inventory to confirm the overall reasonableness of the amount determined by the counting and pricing process. The gross profit method is not, however, a satisfactory substitute for periodically taking an actual physical inventory.

The Retail Method

The **retail method** of estimating inventory and the cost of goods sold is similar to the gross profit method. The basic difference is that the retail method requires that management determine the value of ending inventory at *retail* prices. The retail value of ending inventory is then converted to its approximate cost using a cost ratio.

To determine the cost ratio, a business must keep track of goods available for sale at both cost and at retail prices. To illustrate, assume that Ski Valley had merchandise available for sale costing $450,000 for the year, and that management had offered this merchandise for sale to customers at *retail* prices totaling $1,000,000. Thus Ski Valley's cost ratio for the year was 45% ($450,000 ÷ $1,000,000). Ski Valley will use this ratio to convert the retail value of its ending merchandise inventory to its estimated *cost*.

Assume that Ski Valley's employees determined that inventory on hand at the end of the year had a total *retail* value of $300,000. This amount is converted easily to *cost* using the 45% cost ratio as follows:

a	Goods available for sale at *cost*	$ 450,000
b	Goods available for sale at *retail*	1,000,000
c	Cost ratio [a ÷ b]	45%
d	Physical count of ending inventory priced at *retail*	300,000
e	Estimated ending inventory at cost [c × d]	$ 135,000

This application of the retail method approximates a valuation of ending inventory at its average cost. A widely used variation of this method enables management to estimate a LIFO valuation of ending inventory.

"Textbook" Inventory Systems Can Be Modified . . . and They Often Are

In this chapter we have described the basic characteristics of the most common inventory systems. In practice, businesses often modify these systems to suit their particular needs. Some businesses also use *different inventory systems for different purposes*.

Financial Analysis

We described one modification in Chapter 6—a company that maintains very little inventory may simply charge (debit) all purchases directly to the cost of goods sold. Another common modification is to maintain perpetual inventory records showing only the *quantities* of merchandise bought and sold, with no dollar amounts. Such systems require less record keeping than a full-blown perpetual system, and they still provide management with useful information about sales and inventories. To generate the dollar amounts needed in financial statements and tax returns, these companies might use the gross profit method, the retail method, or a periodic inventory system.

CASE IN POINT

Apple Computer maintains a perpetual inventory system. The daily entries reflect only the *quantities* of units produced and sold—not the dollar costs. Dollar amounts are computed and recorded in the inventory records at the end of the month. In transferring costs from inventory accounts to the cost of goods sold, **Apple** uses a FIFO flow assumption. But the inventory cost layers don't represent units purchased at different prices—they represent units manufactured in different months.

Sears and **Wal-Mart** maintain perpetual inventory records showing both quantities and dollar amounts. But the dollar amounts are recorded at *retail prices*. When cost data are needed, these companies apply cost ratios to the retail amounts.

Fleming Cos. is the world's largest food wholesaler. To assist management in monitoring sales, profit margins, and inventory, **Fleming** maintains a perpetual inventory system. In its interim financial statements, however, it uses the *gross profit method*. Why? Some of **Fleming**'s inventories are subject to significant spoilage losses. The gross profit method automatically provides for normal amounts of shrinkage. Adjusting the perpetual records to reflect these losses would require a complete physical inventory.

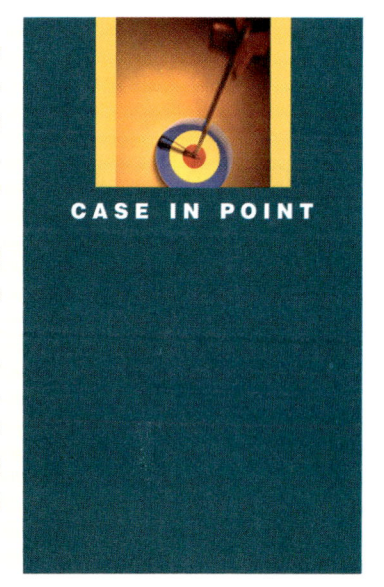

Businesses such as restaurants often update their inventory records by physically counting products on a daily or weekly basis. In effect, they use frequent periodic counts as the basis for maintaining a perpetual inventory system.

In summary, real-world inventory systems often differ from the illustrations in a textbook. But the underlying principles remain much the same.

FINANCIAL ANALYSIS

Inventory often is the largest of a company's current assets. But how liquid is this asset? How quickly will it be converted into cash? As a step toward answering these questions, short-term creditors often compute the **inventory turnover rate**.

LO 7
Compute the inventory turnover rate and explain its uses.

Inventory Turnover Rate

The inventory turnover rate is equal to the cost of goods sold divided by the average amount of inventory (beginning inventory plus ending inventory, divided by 2). This ratio indicates how many *times* in the course of a year the company is able to sell the amount of its average inventory. The higher this rate, the more quickly the company sells its inventory.

To illustrate, a recent annual report of **J.C. Penney** shows a cost of goods sold of $23 billion and average inventory of $5.6 billion. The inventory turnover rate for **Penney**'s, therefore, is *4.1* ($23 billion ÷ $5.6 billion). We may compute the number of *days* required for the company to sell its inventory by dividing 365 days by the turnover rate. Thus **J.C. Penney** requires *89 days* to turn over (sell) the amount of its average inventory (365 days ÷ 4.1). The computation of **J.C. Penney**'s inventory turnover rate and the average number of days required to sell its inventory is summarized as follows:

Unicorn Stock Photos

Inventory Turnover Rate

$$\frac{\text{Cost of Goods Sold}}{\text{Average Inventory*}} = \frac{\$23 \text{ billion}}{\$5.6 \text{ billion}} = \underline{\underline{4.1 \text{ times}}}$$

Average Number of Days to Sell Inventory

$$\frac{\text{Days in the Year}}{\text{Inventory Turnover}} = \frac{365 \text{ days}}{4.1 \text{ times}} = \underline{\underline{89 \text{ days}}}$$

*Average Inventory = (Beginning Inventory + Ending Inventory) ÷ 2

Users of financial statements find the inventory turnover rate useful in evaluating the liquidity of the company's inventory. In addition, managers and independent auditors use this computation to help identify inventory that is not selling well and that may have become obsolete. A declining turnover rate indicates that merchandise is not selling as quickly as it used to. Comparing a company's inventory turnover with that of competitors is particularly useful in evaluating how effective a company is at managing its inventory, often one of its largest assets.

CASH EFFECTS

Most businesses sell merchandise on account. Therefore, the sale of inventory often does not provide an immediate source of cash. To determine how quickly inventory is converted into cash, the number of days required to *sell the inventory* must be combined with the number of days required to *collect the accounts receivable*.

The number of days required to collect accounts receivable depends on a company's *accounts receivable turnover rate*. This figure is computed by dividing net sales by the average accounts receivable. The number of days required to collect these receivables then is determined by dividing 365 days by the turnover rate. Data for the **J.C. Penney** annual report indicate that the company needed *11 days* (on average) for receivables to convert to cash.

Length of the Operating Cycle The *operating cycle* of a merchandising company is the average time period between the purchase of merchandise and the conversion of this merchandise back into cash. In other words, the merchandise acquired as inventory gradually is converted into accounts receivable by sale of the goods on account, and these receivables are converted into cash through the process of collection.

The operating cycle of **J.C. Penney** was approximately *100 days,* computed by adding the average *89 days* required to sell its inventory and the *11 days* required to collect cash from customers. From the viewpoint of short-term creditors, the shorter the operating cycle, the higher the quality of the company's liquid assets because they will be converted into cash more quickly.

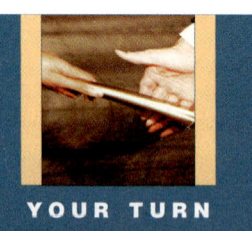

YOUR TURN

You as a Banker

Assume that you are a commercial loan officer at a large bank. One of your clients recently submitted an application for a $300,000 five-year loan. You have worked with this business on numerous occasions and have periodically been forced to deal with late and missed payments attributed to cash flow problems. Thus you are surprised to see in the business plan accompanying the application that management expects to reduce the company's operating cycle from 190 days to 90 days. A note to the business plan indicates that the reduction in the operating cycle will result from (1) a tighter credit policy and (2) the implementation of a just-in-time inventory system.

As a banker, are you comfortable that these changes are related to the company's operating cycle?

*Our comments appear on page 361.

Accounting Methods Can Affect Financial Ratios

The accounting methods selected by a company may affect the ratios and financial statement subtotals used in evaluating the company's financial position and the results of its operations. To illustrate, let us consider the effects of inventory valuation methods on inventory turnover rates.

Assume that during a period of rising prices Alpha Company uses LIFO, whereas Beta Company uses FIFO. In all other respects, the two companies *are identical;* they have the same size inventories, and they purchase and sell the same quantities of merchandise at the same prices and on the same dates. Thus each company *physically* turns over its inventory at *exactly the same rate.*

Because Alpha uses the LIFO method, however, its inventory is valued at older (and lower) costs than is the inventory of Beta Company. Also, Alpha's cost of goods sold includes more recent (and higher) costs than does Beta's. When these amounts are used in computing the inventory turnover rate (cost of goods sold divided by average inventory), Alpha's rate *appears* to be higher than Beta's.

We already have stated that the physical inventories of these two companies are turning over at exactly the same rate. Therefore, the differences in the turnover rates computed from the companies' financial statements are caused *solely by the different accounting methods used in the valuation of the companies' inventories.*

Inventory turnover is not the only ratio that will be affected. Alpha will report less gross profit and lower net income than Beta.

Users of financial statements must understand the effects of using different accounting methods. Also, a financial analyst should be able to restate on a *comparable basis* the financial statements of companies that use different accounting methods. Notes accompanying the financial statements sometimes provide the information necessary for comparing the operating results of companies using LIFO with those of companies using the FIFO method.

ISCO., Inc., Manufactures various lines of measuring instruments. The company uses LIFO to account for inventories. A recent note accompanying its financial statements reads, in part:

> The company uses LIFO to account for inventories. Had inventories been valued on the FIFO basis, they would have been approximately $1,967,000 higher than under LIFO.

This information enables users of the company's financial statements to estimate the amount by which cost of goods sold and income would have differed had FIFO been used.

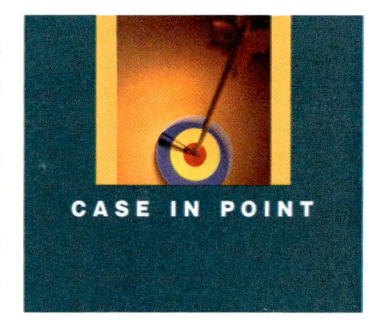

CASE IN POINT

CONCLUDING REMARKS

Throughout this chapter we have learned about different inventory valuation methods. Each method is based upon a particular assumption about cost flows, and does not necessarily parallel the physical movement of merchandise. Moreover, the choice of valuation by management can have significant effects on a company's income statement, balance sheet, and tax returns.

In the following chapter, we will see that a similar situation exists with respect to alternative methods used to account for plant and equipment.

Having the right inventory available to meet the needs of customers is of critical importance to retail enterprises such as **Safeway**. In a recent balance sheet, **Safeway** reported inventory of nearly $2.5 billion, or 78% of its total current assets (i.e., cash, receivables, inventories, and prepaid items). **Safeway** inventory turnover is remarkably fast, averaging 12 to 13 times during the past several years. This means that **Safeway** turns over its entire $2.5 billion inventory nearly once every 30 days. Of course, to effectively evaluate its performance, one needs comparative information about **Safeway**'s major competitors.

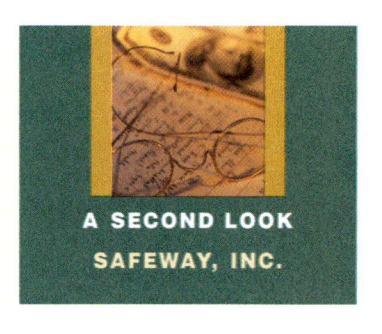

A SECOND LOOK — SAFEWAY, INC.

SUPPLEMENTAL TOPIC

LIFO RESERVES

LO 8
Define a "LIFO reserve" and explain its implications to users of financial statements.

We have stated that a significant shortcoming in the LIFO method is that the asset inventory is valued at the company's oldest inventory acquisition costs. After a period of years, these outdated costs may significantly understate the current replacement cost of the inventory. The difference between the LIFO cost of an inventory and its current replacement cost often is called a **LIFO reserve**.[1]

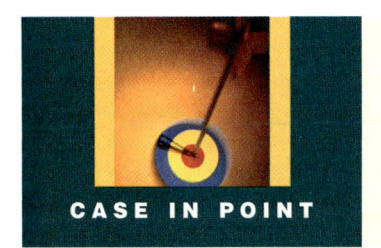

CASE IN POINT

In a recent balance sheet, **Ford Motor Company** reported inventories of approximately $5.7 billion valued by the LIFO method. A note accompanying the balance sheet, however, explained that the current replacement cost of these inventories exceeded $6.9 billion. Therefore, **Ford** had a LIFO reserve of more than $1.2 billion.

The Significance of a LIFO Reserve

Users of financial statements should understand the implications of a large LIFO reserve.

Comparing LIFO and FIFO Inventories A LIFO reserve indicates that the company's inventory is *undervalued* in terms of its current replacement cost and the valuation that would have resulted from use of the FIFO method. Thus the inventories of companies using LIFO are not directly comparable to those of companies using FIFO. Fortunately, this problem is solved in the notes to the financial statements: Companies using LIFO disclose the current replacement cost (or FIFO cost) of their inventories.

Liquidation of a LIFO Reserve The existence of a LIFO reserve may cause a company's profits to rise dramatically if inventory falls to an abnormally low level at year-end. As the company reduces its inventories, the costs transferred to the cost of goods sold come from older—and lower—cost layers. The inclusion of these old and low costs in the cost of goods sold can cause the company's gross profit rate to soar. This situation is often referred to as a **liquidation of a LIFO reserve**.

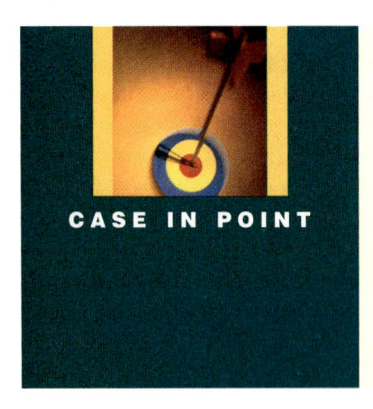

CASE IN POINT

Oshkosh B' Gosh, Inc., (a publicly owned maker of children's clothing) uses LIFO. A note accompanying a recent annual report makes reference to the company's increase in gross profit resulting from the liquidation of a LIFO reserve. The note reads in part:

> As a result of a substantial reduction of the company's inventory levels, the gross profit margin was favorably impacted by approximately $2.2 million related to the liquidation of certain LIFO layers.

The note goes on to explain that the favorable impact on gross profit resulted from the LIFO valuations used to compute cost of goods sold being significantly lower than the current replacement cost of the inventory sold.

Many factors may cause the liquidation of a LIFO reserve. For example, the company may be unable to make the purchases necessary to replenish its inventory because of

---

[1] The phrase "LIFO reserve" is used by accountants, investors, and business managers in conversation and many types of financial literature. The FASB, however, discourages use of the word "reserve" in formal financial statements, as this word has several different meanings. Therefore, in financial statements a LIFO reserve is more appropriately described as "the difference between the LIFO cost and current (replacement) cost of inventory."

shortages or strikes. Often a company discontinues a particular product line and sells its entire inventory of this merchandise. Also, management deliberately may delay making normal year-end purchases to liquidate a portion of the company's LIFO reserve.

Users of financial statements should recognize that the abnormal profits that result from the liquidation of a LIFO reserve *do not* represent an improvement in financial performance. Rather, these profits are a one-time occurrence, resulting from old and relatively low unit costs temporarily being used in measuring the cost of goods sold. Users of financial statements easily can determine whether a company's reported earnings are affected by the liquidation of a LIFO reserve. This liquidation occurs whenever a company using LIFO ends its fiscal year with its inventory at a substantially lower level than at the beginning of the year. If material in dollar amount, the financial impact of this liquidation should be disclosed in notes accompanying the financial statements.

CASH EFFECTS

The inclusion of outdated figures in the cost of goods sold resulting from the liquidation of the LIFO reserve can cause taxable income to soar. Unfortunately, when taxable income soars, cash expenditures made for income taxes soar as well. When this happens, the amount of cash available (after taxes) may fall short of what is needed to replenish depleted levels of inventory.

Assessing the Income Tax Benefits of Using LIFO   A LIFO reserve represents the amount by which a company has reduced its taxable income over the years through use of the LIFO method. Referring to a previous Case in Point, **Ford Motor Company** has reduced its taxable income (over a long span of years) by more than $1.2 billion. If we assume that **Ford** pays income taxes at a rate of 33%, using LIFO has saved the company about $400 million in income taxes.

You as a Business Owner

Assume that you have been using the LIFO inventory method in your building supply business for the past 10 years. Each year, your accountant brings to your attention the significant tax savings that have resulted from your decision to use LIFO instead of FIFO.

During December, a major supplier was unable to make deliveries due to a strike by the truck drivers' union. As a consequence, inventory levels at year-end were nearly depleted. You have just received a call from your accountant informing you that taxable income for the year ended December 31 was unexpectedly high, and that the estimated tax payments made throughout the year fell far short of the company's actual tax liability.

The news from your accountant made you angry and confused, as you were certain that LIFO always results in the lowest possible taxable income during periods of rising prices. While the past year was inflationary, income taxes were much higher than expected. What happened?

*Our comments appear on page 361.

END-OF-CHAPTER REVIEW

SUMMARY OF LEARNING OBJECTIVES

LO 1
In a perpetual inventory system, determine the cost of goods sold using (a) specific identification, (b) average cost, (c) FIFO, and (d) LIFO. Discuss the advantages and shortcomings of each method.

By the *specific identification method,* the actual costs of the specific units sold are transferred from inventory to the cost of goods sold. (Debit Cost of Goods Sold; credit Inventory.) This method achieves the proper matching of sales revenue and cost of goods sold when the individual units in the inventory are unique. However, the method becomes cumbersome and may produce misleading results if the inventory consists of homogeneous items.

The remaining three methods are flow assumptions, which should be applied only to an inventory of homogeneous items.

By the *average-cost method,* the average cost of all units in the inventory is computed and used in recording the cost of goods sold. This is the only method in which all units are assigned the same (average) per-unit cost.

FIFO (first-in, first-out) is the assumption that the first units purchased are the first units sold. Thus inventory is assumed to consist of the most recently purchased units. FIFO assigns current costs to inventory but older (and often lower) costs to the cost of goods sold.

LIFO (last-in, first-out) is the assumption that the most recently acquired goods are sold first. This method matches sales revenue with relatively current costs. In a period of inflation, LIFO usually results in lower reported profits and lower income taxes than the other methods. However, the oldest purchase costs are assigned to inventory, which may result in inventory becoming grossly understated in terms of current replacement costs.

LO 2
Explain the need for taking a physical inventory.

In a perpetual inventory system, a physical inventory is taken to adjust the inventory records for shrinkage losses. In a periodic inventory system, the physical inventory is the basis for determining the cost of the ending inventory and for computing cost of goods sold.

LO 3
Record shrinkage losses and other year-end adjustments to inventory.

Shrinkage losses are recorded by removing from the Inventory account the cost of the missing or damaged units. The offsetting debit may be to Cost of Goods Sold, if the shrinkage is normal in amount, or to a special loss account. If inventory is found to be obsolete and unlikely to be sold, it is written down to zero (or its scrap value, if any). If inventory is valued at the lower-of-cost-or-market, it is written down to its current replacement cost, if at year-end this amount is substantially below the cost shown in the inventory records.

LO 4
In a periodic inventory system, determine the ending inventory and the cost of goods sold using (a) specific identification, (b) average cost, (c) FIFO, and (d) LIFO.

The cost of goods sold is determined by combining the beginning inventory with the purchases during the period and subtracting the cost of the ending inventory. Thus the cost assigned to ending inventory also determines the cost of goods sold.

By the specific identification method, the ending inventory is determined by the specific costs associated with the units on hand. By the average-cost method, the ending inventory is determined by multiplying the number of units on hand by the average cost of the units available for sale during the year. By FIFO, the units in inventory are priced using the unit costs from the most recent cost layers. By the LIFO method, inventory is priced using the unit costs in the oldest cost layers.

LO 5
Explain the effects on the income statement of errors in inventory valuation.

In the current year, an error in the costs assigned to ending inventory will cause an opposite error in the cost of goods sold and, therefore, a repetition of the original error in the amount of gross profit. For example, understating ending inventory results in an overstatement of the cost of goods sold and an understatement of gross profit.

The error has exactly the opposite effects on the cost of goods sold and the gross profit of the following year, because the error is now in the cost assigned to *beginning* inventory.

LO 6
Estimate the cost of goods sold and ending inventory by the gross profit method and by the retail method.

Both the gross profit and retail methods use a cost ratio to estimate the cost of goods sold and ending inventory. The cost of goods sold is estimated by multiplying net sales by this cost ratio; ending inventory then is estimated by subtracting this cost of goods sold from the cost of goods available for sale.

In the gross profit method, the cost ratio is 100% minus the company's historical gross profit rate. In the retail method, the cost ratio is the percentage of cost to the retail prices of merchandise available for sale.

LO 7
Compute the inventory turnover rate and explain its uses.

The inventory turnover rate is equal to the cost of goods sold divided by the average inventory. Users of financial statements find the inventory turnover rate useful in evaluating the liquidity of the company's inventory. In addition, managers and independent auditors use this computation to help identify inventory that is not selling well and that may have become obsolete.

End of Chapter Review

*LO 8
Define a "LIFO reserve" and explain its implications to users of financial statements.

A LIFO reserve is the amount by which the current replacement cost of inventory exceeds the LIFO cost shown in the accounting records.

If a company has a large LIFO reserve, neither its inventory nor its cost of goods sold are comparable to those of a company using FIFO. Also, a LIFO reserve may cause earnings to increase dramatically if inventory falls below normal levels. Notes accompanying the financial statements provide the statement users with information useful in evaluating the implications of a LIFO reserve.

KEY TERMS INTRODUCED OR EMPHASIZED IN CHAPTER 8

average-cost method (p. 322)   A method of valuing all units in inventory at the same average per-unit cost, which is recomputed after every purchase.

consistency (in inventory valuation) (p. 328)   An accounting principle that calls for the use of the same method of inventory pricing from year to year, with full disclosure of the effects of any change in method. Intended to make financial statements comparable.

cost layer (p. 321)   Units of merchandise acquired at the same unit cost. An inventory comprised of several cost layers is characteristic of all inventory valuation methods except *average cost*.

cost ratio (p. 337)   The cost of merchandise expressed as a percentage of its retail selling price. Used in inventory estimating techniques, such as the gross profit method and the retail method.

first-in, first-out (FIFO) method (p. 323)   A method of computing the cost of inventory and the cost of goods sold based on the assumption that the first merchandise acquired is the first merchandise sold and that the ending inventory consists of the most recently acquired goods.

flow assumption (p. 321)   Assumption as to the sequence in which units are removed from inventory for the purpose of sale. Is not required to parallel the physical movement of merchandise if the units are homogeneous.

F.O.B. destination (p. 332)   A term meaning the seller bears the cost of shipping goods to the buyer's location. Title to the goods remains with the seller while the goods are in transit.

F.O.B. shipping point (p. 332)   The buyer of goods bears the cost of transportation from the seller's location to the buyer's location. Title to the goods passes at the point of shipment, and the goods are the property of the buyer while in transit.

gross profit method (p. 337)   A method of estimating the cost of the ending inventory based on the assumption that the rate of gross profit remains approximately the same from year to year.

inventory turnover rate (p. 339)   The cost of goods sold divided by the average amount of inventory. Indicates how many times the average inventory is sold during the course of the year.

just-in-time (JIT) inventory system (p. 328)   A technique designed to minimize a company's investment in inventory. In a manufacturing company, this means receiving purchases of raw materials just in time for use in the manufacturing process and completing the manufacture of finished goods just in time to fill sales orders. Just-in-time also may be described as the philosophy of constantly striving to become more efficient by purchasing and storing less inventory.

last-in, first-out (LIFO) method (p. 324)   A method of computing the cost of goods sold by use of the prices paid for the most recently acquired units. Ending inventory is valued on the basis of prices paid for the units first acquired.

LIFO reserve (p. 342)   The difference between the current replacement cost of a company's inventory and the LIFO cost shown in the accounting records. The fact that a LIFO reserve can become very large is the principal shortcoming of the LIFO method.

liquidation of a LIFO reserve (p. 342)   Selling merchandise from a LIFO inventory to the point at which old and relatively low costs are transferred from inventory into the cost of goods sold. Tends to inflate reported profits.

lower-of-cost-or-market (LCM) (p. 331)   A method of inventory pricing in which goods are valued at original cost or replacement cost (market), whichever is lower.

physical inventory (p. 330)   A systematic count of all goods on hand, followed by the application of unit prices to the quantities counted and development of a dollar valuation of the ending inventory.

retail method (p. 338)   A method of estimating the cost of goods sold and ending inventory. Similar to the gross profit method, except that the cost ratio is based on current cost-to-retail price relationships rather than on those of the prior year.

shrinkage losses (p. 329)   Losses of inventory resulting from theft, spoilage, or breakage.

specific identification (p. 321)   Recording as the cost of goods sold the actual costs of the specific units sold. Necessary if each unit in inventory is unique, but not if the inventory consists of homogeneous products.

write-down (of an asset) (p. 330)   A reduction in the carrying amount of an asset because it has become obsolete or its usefulness has otherwise been impaired. Involves a credit to the appropriate asset account, with an offsetting debit to a loss account.

---
*Supplemental Topic, "LIFO Reserves."

DEMONSTRATION PROBLEM

The Audiophile sells high-performance stereo equipment. Massachusetts Acoustic recently introduced the Carnegie-440, a state-of-the-art speaker system. During the current year, The Audiophile purchased nine of these speaker systems at the following dates and acquisition costs:

Date	Units Purchased	Unit Cost	Total Cost
Oct. 1	2	$3,000	$ 6,000
Nov. 17	3	3,200	9,600
Dec. 1	4	3,250	13,000
Available for sale during the year	9		$28,600

On *November 21,* The Audiophile sold four of these speaker systems to the Boston Symphony. The other five Carnegie-440s remained in inventory at December 31.

Instructions

Assume that The Audiophile uses a *perpetual inventory system.* Compute (1) the cost of goods sold relating to the sale of Carnegie-440 speakers to the Boston Symphony and (2) the ending inventory of these speakers at December 31, using each of the following flow assumptions:

a. Average cost
b. First-in, first-out (FIFO)
c. Last-in, first-out (LIFO)

Show the number of units and the unit costs of the cost layers comprising the cost of goods sold and the ending inventory.

Solution to the Demonstration Problem

a. 1. Cost of goods sold (at average cost):
   Average unit cost at Nov. 21 [($6,000 + $9,600) ÷ 5 units] ...... $ 3,120
   Cost of goods sold (4 units × $3,120 per unit) $12,480
   2. Inventory at Dec. 31 (at average cost):
   Units remaining after sale of Nov. 21 (1 unit @ $3,120) .... $ 3,120
   Units purchased on Dec. 1 (4 units @ $3,250) 13,000
   Total cost of 5 units in inventory $16,120
   Average unit cost at Dec. 31 ($16,120 ÷ 5 units) .... $ 3,224
   Inventory at Dec. 31 (5 units × $3,224 per unit) $16,120

b. 1. Cost of goods sold (FIFO basis):
   (2 units @ $3,000 + 2 units @ $3,200) $12,400
   2. Inventory at Dec. 31 (4 units @ $3,250 + 1 unit @ $3,200) $16,200

c. 1. Cost of goods sold (LIFO basis):
   (3 units @ $3,200 + 1 unit @ $3,000) $12,600
   2. Inventory at Dec. 31 (4 units @ $3,250 + 1 unit @ $3,000) $16,000

SELF-TEST QUESTIONS

Answers to these questions appear on page 362.

1. The primary purpose for using an inventory flow *assumption* is to:
   a. Parallel the physical flow of units of merchandise.
   b. Offset against revenue an appropriate cost of goods sold.

c. Minimize income taxes.
d. Maximize the reported amount of net income.

2. Ace Auto Supply uses a perpetual inventory record. On March 10, the company sells two Shelby four-barrel carburetors. Immediately prior to this sale, the perpetual inventory records indicate three of these carburetors on hand, as follows:

Date	Quantity Purchased	Unit Cost	Units on Hand	Total Cost
Feb. 4	1	$220	1	$220
Mar. 2	2	235	3	690

With respect to the sale on March 10: (More than one of the following answers may be correct.)
a. If the average-cost method is used, the cost of goods sold is $460.
b. If these carburetors have identification numbers, Ace must use the specific identification method to determine the cost of goods sold.
c. If the company uses LIFO, the cost of goods sold will be $15 higher than if it were using FIFO.
d. If the company uses LIFO, the carburetor *remaining* in inventory after the sales will be assumed to have cost $220.

3. T-Shirt City uses a *periodic* inventory system. During the first year of operations, the company made four purchases of a particular product. Each purchase was for 500 units and the prices paid were $9 per unit in the first purchase, $10 per unit in the second purchase, $12 per unit in the third purchase, and $13 per unit in the fourth purchase. At year-end, 650 of these units remained unsold. Compute the cost of goods sold under the FIFO method and LIFO method, respectively.
a. $13,700 (FIFO) and $16,000 (LIFO).
b. $8,300 (FIFO) and $6,000 (LIFO).
c. $16,000 (FIFO) and $13,700 (LIFO).
d. $6,000 (FIFO) and $8,300 (LIFO).

4. Trent Department Store uses a perpetual inventory system but adjusts its inventory records at year-end to reflect the results of a complete physical inventory. In the physical inventory taken at the ends of 2001 and 2002, Trent's employees failed to count the merchandise in the store's window displays. The cost of this merchandise amounted to $13,000 at the end of 2001 and $19,000 at the end of 2002. As a result of these errors, the cost of goods sold for 2002 will be:
a. Understated by $19,000.
b. Overstated by $6,000.
c. Understated by $6,000.
d. None of the above.

5. In July 2002, the accountant for LBJ Imports is in the process of preparing financial statements for the quarter ended June 30, 2002. The physical inventory, however, was last taken on June 5 and the accountant must establish the approximate cost at June 30 from the following data:

Physical inventory, June 5, 2002	$900,000
Transactions for the period June 5–June 30:	
Sales	700,000
Purchases	400,000

The gross profit on sales has consistently averaged 40% of sales. Using the gross profit method, compute the approximate inventory cost at June 30, 2002.
a. $420,000.   b. $880,000.   c. $480,000.   d. $1,360,000.

6. Allied Products maintains a large inventory. The company has used the LIFO inventory method for many years, during which the purchase costs of its products have risen substantially. (More than one of the following answers may be correct.)
   a. Allied would have reported a *higher* net income in past years if it had been using the average-cost method.
   b. Allied's financial statements imply a *lower* inventory turnover rate than they would if the company were using FIFO.
   c. If Allied were to let its inventory fall far below normal levels, the company's gross profit rate would *decline*.
   d. Allied would have paid more income taxes in past years if it had been using the FIFO method.

ASSIGNMENT MATERIAL

DISCUSSION QUESTIONS

1. Is the cost of merchandise acquired during the period classified as an asset or an expense? Explain.
2. Briefly describe the advantages of using a cost flow assumption, rather than the specific identification method, to value an inventory.
3. Under what circumstances do generally accepted accounting principles permit the use of an inventory cost flow assumption? Must a flow assumption closely parallel the physical movement of the company's merchandise?
4. Assume that a company has in its inventory units of a particular product that were purchased at several different per-unit costs. When some of these units are sold, explain how the cost of goods sold is measured under each of the following cost flow assumptions in a perpetual inventory system:
   a. Average cost
   b. FIFO
   c. LIFO
5. A large art gallery has in inventory more than 100 paintings. No two are alike. The least expensive is priced at more than $1,000 and the higher-priced items carry prices of $100,000 or more. Which of the four methods of inventory valuation discussed in this chapter would you consider to be most appropriate for this business? Give reasons for your answer.
6. During a period of steadily increasing purchase costs, which inventory flow assumption results in the highest reported profits? The lowest taxable income? The valuation of inventory that is closest to current replacement cost? Briefly explain your answers.
7. Assume that during the first year of Hatton Corporation's operation, there were numerous purchases of identical items of merchandise. However, there was no change during the year in the prices paid for this merchandise. Under these special circumstances, how would the financial statements be affected by the choice between the FIFO and LIFO methods of inventory valuation?
8. Apex Corporation operates in two locations: New York and Oregon. The LIFO method is used in accounting for inventories at the New York facility and the specific identification method for inventories at the Oregon location. Does this concurrent use of two inventory methods indicate that Apex is violating the accounting principle of consistency? Explain.
9. What are the characteristics of a *just-in-time* inventory system? Briefly explain some advantages and risks of this type of system.
10. Why do companies that use perpetual inventory systems also take an annual *physical inventory?* When is this physical inventory usually taken? Why?
11. Under what circumstances might a company write down its inventory to carrying value below cost?
12. What is meant by the year-end *cutoff* of transactions? If merchandise in transit at year-end is material in dollar amount, what determines whether these goods should be included in the inventory of the buyer or the seller? Explain.

Discussion Questions

13. Briefly explain the operation of a *periodic* inventory system. Include an explanation of how the cost of goods sold is determined.

14. Assume that a *periodic* inventory system is in use. Explain which per-unit acquisition costs are assigned to the year-end inventory under each of the following inventory costing procedures:
   a. The average-cost method
   b. FIFO
   c. LIFO

15. Why do companies using LIFO in a perpetual inventory system often restate their ending inventory at the per-unit costs that result from applying *periodic* LIFO costing procedures?

16. Explain why errors in the valuation of inventory at the end of the year are sometimes called "counterbalancing" or "self-correcting."

17. Briefly explain the *gross profit method* of estimating inventories. In what types of situations is this technique likely to be useful?

18. Estimate the ending inventory by the gross profit method, given the following data: beginning inventory, $40,000; net purchases, $100,000; net sales, $112,000; average gross profit rate, 25% of net sales.

19. A store using the *retail inventory method* takes its physical inventory by applying current retail prices as marked on the merchandise to the quantities counted. Does this procedure mean that the inventory will appear in the financial statements at retail selling price? Explain.

20. How is the *inventory turnover rate* computed? Why is this measurement of interest to short-term creditors?

21. Baxter Corporation has been using FIFO during a period of rising costs. Explain whether you would expect each of the following measurements to be higher or lower if the company had been using LIFO.
   a. Net income
   b. Inventory turnover rate
   c. Income taxes expense

22. In anticipation of *declining* inventory replacement costs, the management of Computer Products Co. elects to use the *FIFO* inventory method rather than LIFO. Explain how this decision should affect the company's future:
   a. Rate of gross profit.
   b. Net cash flow from operating activities.

23. Notes to the financial statements of two well-known clothing manufacturers follow:

   J. P. Stevens & Co., Inc.

   Inventories: The inventories are stated at the lower of cost, determined principally by the LIFO method, or market.

   Bobbie Brooks, Incorporated

   Inventories: Inventories are stated at the lower of cost (first-in, first-out method) or market value assuming a period of rising prices.

   a. Which company is using the more conservative method of pricing its inventories? Explain.
   b. Based on the inventory methods in use in their financial statements, which company is in the better position to minimize the amount of income taxes that it must pay? Explain.
   c. Could either company increase its cash collections from customers or reduce its cash payments to suppliers of merchandise by switching from FIFO to LIFO, or from LIFO to FIFO? Explain.

*24. What is a *LIFO reserve?* What is likely to happen to the gross profit rate of a company with a large LIFO reserve if it sells most of its inventory?

---

*Supplemental Topic, "LIFO Reserves."

EXERCISES

EXERCISE 8.1
Accounting Terminology
LO 1–8

Listed below are nine technical accounting terms introduced in this chapter.

Retail method	FIFO method	Average-cost method
Gross profit method	LIFO method	Lower-of-cost-or-market
Flow assumption	*LIFO reserve	Specific identification

Each of the following statements may (or may not) describe one of these technical terms. For each statement, indicate the term described, or answer "None" if the statement does not correctly describe any of the terms.

a. A pattern of transferring unit costs from the Inventory account to the cost of goods sold that may (or may not) parallel the physical flow of merchandise.

b. The excess of the current replacement cost of any inventory of merchandise over the cost of the inventory determined by the LIFO assumption.

c. The only flow assumption in which all units of merchandise are assigned the same per-unit cost.

d. The method used to record the cost of goods sold when each unit in the inventory is unique.

e. The most conservative of the flow assumptions during a period of sustained inflation.

f. The flow assumption that provides the most current valuation of inventory in the balance sheet.

g. A technique for estimating the cost of goods sold and the ending inventory that is based on the relationship between cost and sales price during the *current* accounting period.

EXERCISE 8.2
Cost Flow Assumptions
LO 1

On May 10, Hudson Computing sold 90 Millennium laptop computers to Apex Publishers. At the date of this sale, Hudson's perpetual inventory records included the following cost layers for the Millennium laptops:

Purchase Date	Quantity	Unit Cost	Total Cost
Apr. 9	70	$1,500	$105,000
May 1	30	$1,600	48,000
Total on hand	100		$153,000

Prepare journal entries to record the cost of the 90 Millennium laptops sold on May 10, assuming that Hudson Computing uses the:

a. Specific identification method (62 of the units sold were purchased on April 9, and the remaining units were purchased on May 1).

b. Average-cost method.

c. FIFO method.

d. LIFO method.

e. Discuss briefly the financial reporting differences that may arise from choosing the FIFO method over the LIFO method.

EXERCISE 8.3
Physical Flow versus Cost Flow
LO 1

The Warm-Up Shop sells heating oil, coal, and kerosene fuel to residential customers. Heating oil is kept in large storage tanks that supply the company's fleet of delivery trucks. Coal is kept in huge bins that are loaded and emptied from the top by giant scooping machines. Kerosene is sold "off the shelf" in five-gallon containers at the company's retail outlet. Separate inventory records are maintained for each fuel type.

a. Which of the cost flow assumptions (average-cost, FIFO, or LIFO) best describes the *physical flow* of:

1. The heating oil inventory? Explain.
2. The coal inventory? Explain.
3. The kerosene inventory? Explain.

Supplemental Topic, "LIFO Reserves."

Exercises

EXERCISE 8.4
Effects of Different Flow Assumptions
LO 1

b. Which of these cost flow assumptions is likely to result in the *lowest* income tax liability for the company? Explain.
c. Explain why management keeps separate inventory records for its heating oil, coal, and kerosene inventories.

La-Z-Boy, Inc., is a giant provider of home furnishings. The company uses the FIFO inventory method. The following information was taken from the company's recent financial statements (dollar amounts are in thousands):

Cost of goods sold	$1,753,000
Income before taxes	112,044
Income taxes expense (and payments)	44,818
Net income	67,226
Net cash provided by operating activities	116,009

The financial statements also revealed that had **La-Z-Boy** been using *LIFO*, its cost of goods sold would have been $1,763,384. The company's income taxes and payments amount to approximately 40% of income before taxes.

a. Explain how LIFO can result in higher cost of goods sold. Would you expect LIFO to result in a greater or lesser valuation of the company's ending inventories? Defend your answer.
b. Assuming that **La-Z-Boy** had been using *LIFO*, compute the following amounts for the current year. Show your supporting computations, with dollar amounts in thousands.
   1. Income before taxes
   2. Income taxes expense (which are assumed equal to income taxes actually paid)
   3. Net income
   4. Net cash provided by operating activities

EXERCISE 8.5
Transfer of Title
LO 2

Jensen Tire had two large shipments in transit at December 31. One was a $125,000 inbound shipment of merchandise (shipped December 28, F.O.B. shipping point), which arrived at Jensen's receiving dock on January 2. The other shipment was a $95,000 outbound shipment of merchandise to a customer, which was shipped and billed by Jensen on December 30 (terms F.O.B. shipping point) and reached the customer on January 3.

In taking a physical inventory on December 31, Jensen counted all goods on hand and priced the inventory on the basis of average cost. The total amount was $600,000. No goods in transit were included in this figure.

What amount should appear as inventory on the company's balance sheet at December 31? Explain. If you indicate an amount other than $600,000, state which asset or liability other than inventory also would be changed in amount.

EXERCISE 8.6
Inventory Write-Downs
LO 3

Late in the year, Software City began carrying WordCrafter, a new word processing software program. At December 31, Software City's perpetual inventory records included the following cost layers in its inventory of WordCrafter programs:

Purchase Date	Quantity	Unit Cost	Total Cost
Nov. 14	8	$400	$3,200
Dec. 12	20	310	6,200
Total available for sale at Dec. 31	28		$9,400

a. At December 31, Software City takes a physical inventory and finds that all 28 units of WordCrafter are on hand. However, the current replacement cost (wholesale price) of this product is only $250 per unit. Prepare the entries to record:

1. This write-down of the inventory to the lower-of-cost-or-market at December 31.
2. The cash sale of 15 WordCrafter programs on January 9, at a retail price of $350 each. Assume that Software City uses the FIFO flow assumption. (Company policy is to charge LCM adjustments of less than $2,000 to Cost of Goods Sold and larger amounts to a separate loss account.)

b. Now assume that the current replacement cost of the WordCrafter programs is $405 each. A physical inventory finds only 25 of these programs on hand at December 31. (For this part, return to the original information and ignore what you did in part **a**.)

1. Prepare the journal entry to record the shrinkage loss assuming that Software City uses the FIFO flow assumption.
2. Prepare the journal entry to record the shrinkage loss assuming that Software City uses the LIFO flow assumption.
3. Which cost flow assumption (FIFO or LIFO) results in the lowest net income for the period? Would using this assumption really mean that the company's operations are less efficient? Explain.

EXERCISE 8.7
Costing Inventory in a Periodic System
LO 4

Pemberton Products uses a *periodic* inventory system. The company's records show the beginning inventory of PH4 oil filters on January 1, and the purchases of this item during the current year to be as follows:

Jan. 1	Beginning inventory		9 units @ $3.00	$ 27.00
Feb. 23	Purchase		12 units @ $3.50	42.00
Apr. 20	Purchase		30 units @ $3.80	114.00
May 4	Purchase		40 units @ $4.00	160.00
Nov. 30	Purchase		19 units @ $5.00	95.00
	Totals		110 units	$438.00

A physical count indicates 20 units in inventory at year-end.

Determine the cost of the ending inventory, based on each of the following methods of inventory valuation. (Remember to use *periodic* inventory costing procedures.)

a. Average cost
b. FIFO
c. LIFO
d. Which of the above methods (if any) results in the same ending inventory valuation under *both* periodic and perpetual costing procedures? Explain.

EXERCISE 8.8
Effects of Errors in Inventory Valuation
LO 5

Boswell Electric prepared the following condensed income statements for two successive years:

	2002	2001
Sales	$2,000,000	$1,500,000
Cost of goods sold	1,250,000	900,000
Gross profit on sales	$ 750,000	$ 600,000
Operating expenses	400,000	350,000
Net income	$ 350,000	$ 250,000

At the end of 2001 (right-hand column above), the inventory was understated by $40,000, but the error was not discovered until after the accounts had been closed and financial statements prepared at the end of 2002. The balance sheets for the two years showed owner's equity of $500,000 at the end of 2001 and $580,000 at the end of 2002. (Boswell is organized as a sole proprietorship and does not incur income taxes expense.)

a. Compute the corrected net income figures for 2001 and 2002.
b. Compute the gross profit amounts and the gross profit percentages for each year based on corrected data.

c. What correction, if any, should be made in the amounts of the company's owner's equity at the end of 2001 and at the end of 2002?

EXERCISE 8.9

Estimating Inventory by the Gross Profit Method

LO 6

When Laura Rapp arrived at her store on the morning of January 29, she found empty shelves and display racks; thieves had broken in during the night and stolen the entire inventory. Rapp's accounting records showed that she had inventory costing $50,000 on January 1. From January 1 to January 29, she had made net sales of $70,000, and net purchases of $80,000. The gross profit during the past several years had consistently averaged 45% of net sales. Rapp wishes to file an insurance claim for the theft loss.

a. Using the gross profit method, estimate the cost of Rapp's inventory at the time of the theft.
b. Does Rapp use the periodic inventory method or does she account for inventory using the perpetual method? Defend your answer.

EXERCISE 8.10

Estimating Inventory by the Retail Method

LO 6

Phillips Supply uses a periodic inventory system but needs to determine the approximate amount of inventory at the end of each month without taking a physical inventory. Phillips has provided the following inventory data:

	Cost Price	Retail Selling Price
Inventory of merchandise, June 30	$300,000	$500,000
Purchases during July	222,000	400,000
Goods available for sale during July	$522,000	$900,000
Net sales during July		$600,000

a. Estimate the cost of goods sold and the cost of the July 31 ending inventory using the retail method of evaluation.
b. Was the cost of Phillips inventory, as a percentage of retail selling prices, higher or lower in July than it was in June? Explain.

EXERCISE 8.11

Evaluating Cost Flow Assumptions

LO 1, 7

A note to a recent annual report issued by the **Quaker Oats Company** includes the following information:

> Inventories are valued using various cost methods. The percentage of year-end inventories valued using each of these methods is:
> Average costs 53%
> LIFO 45%
> FIFO 2%
> If the LIFO method of valuation had *not* been used, total inventories would have been $2.4 million *lower* than reported.

a. Does the company's use of three different inventory methods violate the accounting principle of consistency? Defend your answer.
b. Had the LIFO assumption *not* been used, would the company's gross profit reported in its income statement have been higher or lower? Explain.
c. Based on the information from the company's annual report, do its inventory replacement costs appear to be rising or falling? Explain.

EXERCISE 8.12

FIFO versus LIFO: A Challenging Analysis

LO 1, 7

Ford Motor Company uses LIFO to account for all of its domestic inventories. A note to the company's recent financial statements reads in part:

> If the FIFO method had been used instead of the LIFO method, inventories would have been higher by $1.1 billion.

a. Indicate whether each of the following financial measurements would have been *higher, lower,* or *unaffected* had **Ford Motor Company** used FIFO instead of LIFO. Explain the reasoning behind your answers.

1. Gross profit rate
2. Reported net income
3. Current ratio (**Ford**'s current ratio is greater than 1 to 1)
4. Inventory turnover rate
5. Accounts receivable turnover rate
6. Cash payments made to suppliers
7. Net cash flow from operations (**Ford**'s operating cash flows are positive)

b. Provide *your own* assessment of whether using LIFO has made **Ford Motor Company** more or less (1) liquid and (2) well-off. Defend your answers.

EXERCISE 8.13
Inventory Turnover Rate
LO 7

A recent annual report of **Gateway, Inc.**, reveals the following information (dollar amounts are stated in millions):

Cost of goods sold	$7,542
Inventory (beginning of year)	193
Inventory (end of year)	315
Average time required to collect accounts receivable	22 days

a. Compute **Gateway**'s inventory turnover rate for the year (round to nearest tenth).
b. Compute the number of days required by **Gateway** to sell its average inventory (round to the nearest day).
c. What is the length of **Gateway**'s *operating cycle?*
d. **Gateway**'s inventory turnover rate is much higher than the inventory turnover of a retail computer business such as **Comp USA**. Explain why.

*EXERCISE 8.14
Cost Flows, Cash Flows, and LIFO Reserves
LO 8

A recent balance sheet of **Safeway, Inc.**, contains the following information about inventories:

Inventories	
At replacement cost	$2,588 million
Less: LIFO reserve	80 million
Inventory at LIFO cost	$2,508 million

Safeway's income statement reveals that the company's income taxes equal approximately 35% of income before taxes.

a. Assume that if **Safeway** had used *FIFO*, inventory would appear at the amount shown as replacement cost. Over the life of the company, determine the *cumulative amounts* by which the use of LIFO has *reduced* the following financial statement amounts. (Include a brief explanation for each answer.)
  1. Taxable income
  2. Income taxes expense
  3. Net income
b. How would **Safeway**'s cash flows from operating activities have differed had the company used FIFO instead of LIFO? Defend your answer.
c. Assume that in the coming year, **Safeway** liquidates some of its LIFO reserve. What effect would you expect this action to have on the company's *gross profit rate?* Explain.

Supplemental Topic, "LIFO Reserves."

Problems

EXERCISE 8.15
Using an Annual Report
LO 7

The annual report of **Tootsie Roll Industries, Inc.** appears in Appendix A at the end of this textbook. Using figures from the income statement and balance sheet, answer the following questions:

a. What was the company's inventory turnover rate for the most recent year reported?
b. Using your answer from part **a**, what was the average number of days that merchandise remained in inventory before it was sold?
c. Is the company's operating cycle influenced significantly by its accounts receivable turnover rate? Explain.

PROBLEMS

PROBLEM 8.1
Four Methods of Inventory Valuation
LO 1

On January 15, 2002, BassTrack sold 1,000 Ace-5 fishing reels to Angler's Warehouse. Immediately prior to this sale, BassTrack's perpetual inventory records for Ace-5 reels included the following cost layers:

Purchase Date	Quantity	Unit Cost	Total Cost
Dec. 12, 2001	600	$29	$17,400
Jan. 9, 2002	900	32	28,800
Total on hand	1,500		$46,200

Instructions

Note: We present this problem in the normal sequence of the accounting cycle—that is, journal entries before ledger entries. However, you may find it helpful to work part **b** first.

a. Prepare a separate journal entry to record the cost of goods sold relating to the January 15 sale of 1,000 Ace-5 reels, assuming that BassTrack uses:
  1. Specific identification (500 of the units sold were purchased on December 12, and the remaining 500 were purchased on January 9)
  2. Average cost
  3. FIFO
  4. LIFO
b. Complete a subsidiary ledger record for Ace-5 reels using each of the four inventory valuation methods listed above. Your inventory records should show both purchases of this product, the sale on January 15, and the balance on hand at December 12, January 9, and January 15. Use the formats for inventory subsidiary records illustrated on pages 323–325 of this chapter.
c. Refer to the cost of goods sold figures computed in part **a**. For financial reporting purposes, can the company use the valuation method that resulted in the *lowest* cost of goods sold if, for tax purposes, it used the method that resulted in the *highest* cost of goods sold? Explain.

Problems 8.2 and 8.3 are based on the following data

Speed World Cycles sells high-performance motorcycles and Motocross racers. One of Speed World's most popular models is the Kazomma 900 dirt bike. During the current year, Speed World purchased eight of these cycles at the following costs:

Purchase Date	Units Purchased	Unit Cost	Total Cost
July 1	2	$4,950	$ 9,900
July 22	3	5,000	15,000
Aug. 3	3	5,100	15,300
	8		$40,200

PROBLEM 8.2
Alternative Cost Flow Assumptions in a Perpetual System
LO 1

On *July 28*, Speed World sold four Kazomma 900 dirt bikes to the Vince Wilson racing team. The remaining four bikes remained in inventory at September 30, the end of Speed World's fiscal year.

Assume that Speed World uses a *perpetual inventory system*. (See the data given following Problem 8.1.)

Instructions

a. Compute (a) the cost of goods sold relating to the sale on July 28 and (b) the ending inventory of Kazomma 900 dirt bikes at September 30, using the following cost flow assumptions:
   1. Average cost
   2. FIFO
   3. LIFO

   Show the number of units and the unit costs of each layer comprising the cost of goods sold and ending inventory.

b. Using the cost figures computed in part **a**, answer the following questions:
   1. Which of the three cost flow assumptions will result in Speed World Cycles reporting the *highest net income* for the current year? Would this always be the case? Explain.
   2. Which of the three cost flow assumptions will *minimize the income taxes owed* by Speed World Cycles for the year. Would you expect this usually to be the case? Explain.
   3. May Speed World Cycles use the cost flow assumption that results in the highest net income for the current year in its financial statements, but use the cost flow assumption that minimizes taxable income for the current year in its income tax return? Explain.

PROBLEM 8.3
Alternative Cost Flow Assumptions in a Periodic System
LO 4

Assume that Speed World uses a *periodic inventory system*. (See the data given following Problem 8.1.)

Instructions

a. Compute (a) the cost of goods sold relating to the sale on July 28 and (b) the ending inventory of Kazomma 900 dirt bikes at September 30, using the following cost flow assumptions:
   1. Average cost
   2. FIFO
   3. LIFO

   Show the number of units and unit costs in each cost layer of the *ending inventory*. You may determine the cost of goods sold by deducting ending inventory from the cost of goods available for sale.

b. If Speed World Cycles uses the LIFO cost flow assumption for financial reporting purposes, can it use the FIFO method for income tax purposes? Explain.

PROBLEM 8.4
Year-End Adjustments; Shrinkage Losses and LCM
LO 1, 2, 3

Mario's Nursery uses a perpetual inventory system. At December 31, the perpetual inventory records indicate the following quantities of a particular blue spruce tree:

	Quantity	Unit Cost	Total Cost
First purchase (oldest)	130	$25.00	$ 3,250
Second purchase	120	28.50	3,420
Third purchase	100	39.00	3,900
Total	350		$10,570

A year-end physical inventory, however, shows only 310 of these trees on hand.

In its financial statements, Mario's values its inventories at the lower-of-cost-or-market. At year-end, the per-unit replacement cost of this tree is $40. (Use $3,500 as the "level of materiality" in deciding whether to debit losses to Cost of Goods Sold or to a separate loss account.)

Problems

Instructions

Prepare the journal entries required to adjust the inventory records at year-end, assuming that:

a. Mario's uses:
   1. Average cost
   2. Last-in, first-out

b. Mario's uses the first-in, first-out method. However, the replacement cost of the trees at year-end is $20 apiece, rather than the $40 stated originally. [Make separate journal entries to record (1) the shrinkage losses and (2) the restatement of the inventory at a market value lower than cost. Record the shrinkage losses first.]

c. Assume that the company had been experiencing monthly inventory shrinkage of 30 to 60 trees for several months. In response, management placed several hidden security cameras throughout the premises. Within days, an employee was caught on film loading potted trees into his pickup truck. The employee's attorney asked that the case be dropped because the company had "unethically used a hidden camera to entrap his client." Do you agree with the attorney? Defend your answer.

PROBLEM 8.5
Periodic Inventory Costing Procedures

LO 4

Mach IV Audio uses a periodic inventory system. One of the store's most popular products is a minidisc car stereo system. The inventory quantities, purchases, and sales of this product for the most recent year are as follows:

	Number of Units	Cost per Unit	Total Cost
Inventory, Jan. 1	10	$299	$ 2,990
First purchase (May 12)	15	306	4,590
Second purchase (July 9)	20	308	6,160
Third purchase (Oct. 4)	8	315	2,520
Fourth purchase (Dec. 18)	19	320	6,080
Goods available for sale	72		$22,340
Units sold during the year	51		
Inventory, Dec. 31	21		

Instructions

a. Using *periodic* costing procedures, compute the cost of the December 31 inventory and the cost of goods sold for the minidisc systems during the year under each of the following cost flow assumptions:
   1. First-in, first-out
   2. Last-in, first-out
   3. Average cost (round to nearest dollar, except unit cost)

b. Which of the three inventory pricing methods provides the most realistic balance sheet valuation of inventory in light of the current replacement cost of the minidisc units? Does this same method also produce the most realistic measure of income in light of the costs being incurred by Mach IV Audio to replace the minidisc systems when they are sold? Explain.

PROBLEM 8.6
Effects of Inventory Errors on Earnings

LO 5

The owners of Hexagon Health Foods are offering the business for sale. The partial income statements of the business for the three years of its existence are summarized below.

	2002	2001	2000
Net sales	$875,000	$840,000	$820,000
Cost of goods sold	481,250	487,200	480,000
Gross profit on sales	$393,750	$352,800	$340,000
Gross profit percentage	45%	42%	41%

In negotiations with prospective buyers of the business, the owners of Hexagon are calling attention to the rising trends of the gross profit and of the gross profit percentage as very favorable elements.

Assume that you are retained by a prospective purchaser of the business to make an investigation of the fairness and reliability of the enterprise's accounting records and financial statements. You find everything in order except for the following: (1) An arithmetic error in the computation of inventory at the end of 2000 had caused a $40,000 understatement in that inventory, and (2) a duplication of figures in the computation of inventory at the end of 2002 had caused an overstatement of $81,750 in that inventory. The company uses the periodic inventory system and these errors had not been brought to light prior to your investigation.

Instructions
a. Prepare a revised three-year partial income statement summary.
b. Comment on the trend of gross profit and gross profit percentage before and after the revision.

PROBLEM 8.7
Retail Method
LO 2, 3, 6

Between The Ears is a popular Internet music store (*www.BTE.com*). During the current year, the company's cost of goods available for sale amounted to $462,000. The retail sales value of this merchandise amounted to $840,000. Sales for the year were $744,000.

Instructions
a. Using the retail method, estimate (1) the cost of goods sold during the year and (2) the inventory at the end of the year.
b. At year-end, BTE.com takes a physical inventory. The general manager walks through the warehouse counting each type of product and reading its retail price into a tape recorder. From the recorded information, another employee prepares a schedule listing the entire ending inventory at retail sales prices. The schedule prepared for the current year reports ending inventory at $84,480 at retail sales prices.
   1. Use the cost ratio computed in part **a** to reduce the inventory counted by the general manager from its retail value to an estimate of its costs.
   2. Determine the estimated shrinkage losses (measured at cost) incurred by BTE.com during the year.
   3. Compute BTE.com's gross profit for the year. (Include inventory shrinkage losses in the cost of goods sold.)
c. What controls might BTE.com implement to reduce inventory shrinkage?

PROBLEM 8.8
FIFO versus LIFO Comparisons
LO 1, 7

Wal-Mart uses LIFO to account for its inventories. Recent financial statements were used to compile the following information (dollar figures are in billions):

Average inventory (throughout the year)	$ 20.618
Current assets (at year-end)	26.555
Current liabilities (at year-end)	28.949
Net sales	191.329
Cost of goods sold	150.255
Gross profit	41.074
Average time required to collect outstanding receivables	3 days

Had **Wal-Mart** used the *FIFO* inventory method, the following differences would have occurred:
1. Average inventory would have been $20.908 billion ($290 million *higher* than the LIFO amount).
2. Ending inventory would have been $21.644 billion ($202 million *higher* than the LIFO amount).
3. The cost of goods sold would have been $150.053 billion ($202 million *lower* than the LIFO amount).

Instructions

a. Using the information provided, compute the following measures based upon the *LIFO* method:
   1. Inventory turnover rate
   2. Current ratio (see Chapter 5 for a discussion of this ratio)
   3. Gross profit rate (see Chapter 6 for a discussion of this statistic)
b. *Recompute* your results from part **a** using the *FIFO* method.
c. Notice that the cost of goods sold is *lower* under FIFO than LIFO. What circumstances must the company have encountered to cause this situation? (Were replacement costs, on average, rising or falling?)
d. Explain why the average number of days required by **Wal-Mart** to collect its accounts receivable is so low. (See Chapter 7 for a discussion of the accounts receivable turnover rate.)

CASES AND UNSTRUCTURED PROBLEMS

CASE 8.1

It's Not Right, but at Least It's Consistent

LO 5

Our Little Secret is a small manufacturer of swimsuits and other beach apparel. The company is closely held and has no external reporting obligations, other than payroll reports and income tax returns. The company's accounting system is grossly inadequate. Accounting records are maintained by clerical employees with little knowledge of accounting and with many other job responsibilities. Management has decided that the company must hire a competent controller, who can establish and oversee an adequate accounting system.

Amy Lee, CPA, has applied for this position. During a recent interview, Dean Frost, the company's director of personnel, said, "Amy, the job is yours. But you should know that we have a big inventory problem here.

"For some time now, it appears that we have been understating our ending inventory in income tax returns. No one knows when this all got started, or who was responsible. We never even counted our inventory until a few months ago. But the problem is pretty big. In our latest tax return—that's for 2002—we listed inventory at only about half its actual cost. That's an understatement of, maybe, $400,000.

"We don't know what to do. We sure don't want a big scandal—tax evasion, and all that. Maybe the best thing is continue understating inventory by the same amount as we did in 2002. That way, taxable income will be correctly stated in future years. Anyway, this is just something I thought you should know about."

Instructions

a. Briefly identify the ethical issues raised for Lee by Frost's disclosure.
b. From Lee's perspective, evaluate the possible solution proposed by Frost.
c. Identify and discuss the alternative ethical courses of action that are open to Lee.

CASE 8.2

Dealing with the Bank

LO 3

Avery Frozen Foods owes the bank $50,000 on a line of credit. Terms of the agreement specify that Avery must maintain a minimum current ratio of 1.2 to 1, or the entire outstanding balance becomes immediately due in full. To date, the company has complied with the minimum requirement. However, management has just learned that a failed warehouse freezer has ruined thousands of dollars of frozen foods inventory. If the company records this loss, its current ratio will drop to approximately 0.8 to 1.

Whether any or all of this loss may be covered by insurance currently is in dispute and will not be known for at least 90 days—perhaps much longer. There are several reasons why the insurance company may have no liability.

In trying to decide how to deal with the bank, management is considering the following options: (1) postpone recording the inventory loss until the dispute with the insurance company is resolved, (2) increase the current ratio to 1.2 to 1 by making a large purchase of inventory on account, (3) explain to the bank what has happened, and request that it be flexible until things get back to normal.

Instructions

a. Given that the company hopes for at least partial reimbursement from the insurance company, is it really unethical for management to postpone recording the inventory loss in the financial statements it submits to the bank?

b. Is it possible to increase the company's current ratio from 0.8 to 1 to 1.2 to 1 by purchasing more inventory on account? Explain.

c. What approach do you think the company should follow in dealing with the bank?

*CASE 8.3

LIFO Liquidation

LO 8

Jackson Specialties has been in business for 52 years. The company maintains a perpetual inventory system, uses a LIFO flow assumption, and ends its fiscal year at December 31. At year-end, the cost of goods sold and inventory are adjusted to reflect periodic LIFO costing procedures.

A railroad strike has delayed the arrival of purchases ordered during the past several months of 2002, and Jackson Specialties has not been able to replenish its inventories as merchandise is sold. At December 22, one product appears in the company's perpetual inventory records at the following unit costs:

Purchase Date	Quantity	Unit Cost	Total Cost
Nov. 14, 1954	3,000	$6	$18,000
Apr. 12, 1955	2,000	8	16,000
Available for sale at Dec. 22, 2002	5,000		$34,000

Jackson Specialties has another 8,000 units of this product on order at the current wholesale cost of $30 per unit. Because of the railroad strike, however, these units have not yet arrived (the terms of purchase are F.O.B. destination). Jackson Specialties also has an order from a customer who wants to purchase 4,000 units of this product at the retail sales price of $47 per unit. Jackson Specialties intends to make this sale on December 30, regardless of whether the 8,000 units on order arrive by this date. (The 4,000-unit sale will be shipped by truck, F.O.B. shipping point.)

Instructions

a. Are the units in inventory really almost 50 years old? Explain.

b. Prepare a schedule showing the sales revenue, cost of goods sold, and gross profit that will result from this sale on December 30, assuming that the 8,000 units currently on order (1) arrive before year-end and (2) do not arrive until some time in the following year. (In each computation, show the number of units comprising the cost of goods sold and their related per-unit costs.)

c. Comment on these results.

d. Might management be wise to delay this sale by a few days? Explain.

BUSINESS WEEK ASSIGNMENT

CASE 8.4

Errors in Inventory Valuation

LO 5

Nanette Byrnes and David Henry discuss the importance of careful valuation of assets including inventories in "Confused about Earnings?" in the November 26, 2001, issue of *Business Week*. They suggest that in 2001 Corporate America will charge off a record $125 billion, much of it for assets, investment, and inventory that aren't worth as much as management thought. For example on November 8, **Enron Corp.**, a Texas energy company, acknowledged that results over the previous three years were actually overstated by more than a half-billion dollars. **Enron**'s stock price dropped dramatically after these revelations.

Like **Enron**, most of the companies cited in stories about inventory errors appearing in business publications have overstated their inventory values.

**Supplemental Topic A*, "LIFO Reserves."

Instructions

Refer to Exhibit 8–8 explaining the effects of errors on inventory valuation. Explain why errors that significantly overstate inventory values are likely to be featured topics in business publications when those errors become public information.

INTERNET ASSIGNMENT

INTERNET 8.1

Inventory Turnover

LO 7

A company's inventory turnover rate is one measure of its potential to convert inventory into cash. But what is considered a good inventory turnover rate? The answer to that question depends on a variety of industry and company characteristics.

Access the EDGAR database at the following Internet address:

www.sec.gov

Locate the most recent 10K reports of **Safeway, Inc.** and **Staples, Inc.** Compute the inventory turnover rates of each company. Does the higher turnover rate computed for **Safeway** mean that the company manages its inventory more effectively than **Staples**? Explain.

Internet sites are time and date sensitive. It is the purpose of these exercises to have you explore the Internet. You may need to use the Yahoo! search engine **http://www.yahoo.com** *(or another favorite search engine) to find a company's current Web address.*

OUR COMMENTS ON THE "YOUR TURN" CASES

You as a Sales Manager (p. 332) The revelation from the other sales managers presents an ethical dilemma. It is inappropriate to mark shipments as having been shipped when in fact they will be shipped in January. Now that you know this information, you must inform upper management of the problem.

The first step is to consider whether Tempto Co. has a code of conduct or other personnel related codes that provide guidance about how potential ethical dilemmas can be resolved. If your company has no policies or the dilemma is not addressed by company policies, then consider that The International Federation of Accountants provides guidance about how to resolve ethical issues in Section 2 of its Code of Ethics for Professional Accountants.* It recommends: (1) review the conflict problem with the immediate superior. If it appears the superior is involved in the conflict problem, raise the issue with the next higher level of management. (2) Seek counseling and advice on a confidential basis with an independent advisor or the applicable professional accountancy body. (3) If the ethical issue still exists after fully exhausting all levels of internal review, as a last resort on significant matters (e.g., fraud) resign and submit an information memo to the appropriate representative of the organization.

You as a Banker (p. 340) Over time, a tighter credit policy is likely to improve the quality of the company's credit accounts and should decrease the average time that its accounts receivable remain outstanding. Tighter credit policies may, however, reduce the company's overall level of sales. The adoption of a just-in-time inventory system will increase inventory turnover and will have the potential to greatly reduce the length of time that cash remains tied up in inventory. In short, if the changes suggested by management are successful, they should result in a reduced operating cycle. Whether they will reduce the cycle by 100 days remains to be seen, however. It is the banker's professional responsibility to view these projections with cautious optimism.

You as a Business Owner (p. 343) The LIFO method normally does result in a lower taxable income during periods of rising prices, as long as the old, low-cost inventory layers are not depleted. In our example, the truck drivers' strike forced the business to sell almost all of its

---

*For more information visit **www.ifac.org**.

inventory—including the old, low-cost layers. When these items were sold, their relatively low and outdated acquisition costs were matched against the revenues of the current period. As a consequence, the unusually high gross profit on these sales drove taxable income up unexpectedly. This risk associated with the LIFO method is sometimes referred to as the *liquidation of the LIFO reserve.*

ANSWERS TO SELF-TEST QUESTIONS

1. b **2.** a, c, d **3.** a **4.** b **5.** b **6.** a, d

COMPREHENSIVE PROBLEM 2

Guitar Universe, Inc.

Guitar Universe, Inc., is a popular source of musical instruments for professional and amateur musicians. The company's accountants make necessary adjusting entries *monthly,* and make all closing entries *annually.* Guitar Universe is growing rapidly and prides itself on having no long-term liabilities.

The company has provided the following *trial balance* dated *December 31, 2002:*

GUITAR UNIVERSE, INC.
Trial Balance
December 31, 2002

Cash	$ 45,000	
Marketable securities	25,000	
Accounts receivable	125,000	
Allowance for doubtful accounts		$ 5,000
Merchandise inventory	250,000	
Office supplies	1,200	
Prepaid insurance	6,600	
Building and fixtures	1,791,000	
Accumulated depreciation		800,000
Land	64,800	
Accounts payable		70,000
Unearned customer deposits		8,000
Income taxes payable		75,000
Capital stock		1,000,000
Retained earnings		240,200
Unrealized holding gain on investments		6,000
Sales		1,600,000
Cost of goods sold	958,000	
Bank service charges	200	
Uncollectible accounts expense	9,000	
Salary and wages expense	395,000	
Office supply expense	400	
Insurance expense	6,400	
Utilities expense	3,600	
Depreciation expense	48,000	
Income taxes expense	75,000	
	$3,804,200	$3,804,200

Other information pertaining to Guitar Universe's trial balance is shown below:

1. The company's most recent bank statement reports a balance of $46,975. Included with the bank statement was a $2,500 check from Iggy Bates, a professional musician, charged back to Guitar Universe as NSF. The bank's monthly service charge was $25. Three checks written by Guitar Universe to suppliers of merchandise inventory had not yet cleared the bank for payment as of the statement date. These checks included: No. 507, $4,000; No. 511, $9,000; and No. 521, $8,000. Deposits made by Guitar Universe of $16,500 had reached the bank too late for inclusion in the current statement. The company prepares a bank reconciliation at the end of each month.

2. Guitar Universe has a portfolio of marketable securities. The initial investment in the portfolio was $19,000. As of December 31, the market value of these securities was $27,500. Management classifies all short-term investments as "available for sale."

3. During December, $6,400 of accounts receivable were written off as uncollectible. A recent aging of the company's accounts receivable helped management to conclude that an allowance for doubtful accounts of $8,500 was needed at December 31, 2002.

4. The company uses a perpetual inventory system. A year-end physical count revealed that several guitars reported in the inventory records were missing. The cost of the missing units amounted to $1,350. This amount is not considered significant relative to the total cost of inventory on hand.

5. At December 31, approximately $900 in office supplies remained on hand.

6. The company pays for its insurance policies 12 months in advance. Its most recent payment was made on November 1, 2002. The cost of this policy was slightly higher than the cost of coverage for the previous 12 months.

7. Depreciation expense related to the company's building and fixtures is $5,000 for the month ending December 31, 2002.

8. Although Guitar Universe carries an extensive inventory, it is not uncommon for musicians to order custom guitars made to their exact specifications. Manufacturers do not allow any sales returns of custom-made guitars. Thus, all customers must pay in advance for these special orders. The entire sales amount is collected at the time a custom order is placed, and is credited to an account entitled, "Unearned Customer Deposits." As of December 31, $4,800 of these deposits remained unearned. Assume that the cost of goods sold and the reduction in inventory associated with all custom orders is recorded when the custom merchandise is delivered to customers. Thus, the adjusting entry requires only a decrease to unearned customer deposits and an increase to sales.

9. Accrued income taxes payable for the *entire year ending* December 31, 2002, total $81,000. No income tax payments are due until early in 2003.

Instructions

a. Prepare a bank reconciliation and make the necessary journal entry to update the accounting records of Guitar Universe as of December 31, 2002.

b. Prepare the necessary adjusting entry to update the company's marketable securities portfolio to its mark-to-market value.

c. Prepare the adjusting entry at December 31, 2002, to report the company's accounts receivable at their net realizable value.

d. Prepare the entry to account for the guitars missing from the company's inventory at the end of the year.

e. Prepare the adjusting entry to account for the office supplies used during December.

f. Prepare the adjusting entry to account for the expiration of the company's insurance policies during December.

g. Prepare the adjusting entry to account for the depreciation of the company's building and fixtures during December.

h. Prepare the adjusting entry to report the portion of unearned customer deposits that were earned during December.

i. Prepare the adjusting entry to account for income taxes expense that accrued during December.

j. Based upon the adjustments made to the accounting records in parts **a** through **i** above, prepare the company's adjusted trial balance at December 31, 2002.

k. Using the adjusted trial balance prepared in part **j** above, prepare an *annual* income statement, statement of retained earnings, and a balance sheet dated December 31, 2002.

Comprehensive Problem 2

l. Using the financial statements prepared in part **k** above, approximately how many days does an account receivable remain outstanding before it is collected? You may assume that the company's ending accounts receivable balance on December 31 is a close approximation of its average accounts receivable balance throughout the year.

m. Using the financial statements prepared in part **k**, approximately how many days does an item of merchandise remain in stock before it is sold? You may assume that the company's ending merchandise inventory balance on December 31 is a close approximation of its average merchandise inventory balance throughout the year.

n. Using the financial statements prepared in part **k**, approximately how many days does it take to convert the company's inventory into cash? Stated differently, what is the length of the company's operating cycle?

o. Comment briefly upon the company's financial condition from the perspective of a short-term creditor.

CHAPTER 9
PLANT AND INTANGIBLE ASSETS

Learning Objectives

After studying this chapter, you should be able to:

1. Determine the cost of plant assets.
2. Distinguish between capital expenditures and revenue expenditures.
3. Compute depreciation by the straight-line and declining-balance methods.
4. Account for disposals of plant assets.
5. Explain the nature of intangible assets, including goodwill.
6. Account for the depletion of natural resources.
7. Explain the cash effects of transactions involving plant assets.
*8. Account for depreciation using methods other than straight-line or declining-balance.

---

*Supplemental Topic, "Other Depreciation Methods."

© AFP/CORBIS

Federal Express Corporation

What kind of plant and intangible assets would you expect **Federal Express Corporation** to have? Probably the first thing that comes to mind is aircraft because so much of the company's success depends on overnight air transportation throughout the world. Flight equipment is, in fact, an important plant asset for **Federal Express**—totaling almost $5 billion in the company's 2000 balance sheet! Flight equipment is not the company's only important plant asset, however. Package handling equipment, ground support equipment, and vehicles make up over $4 billion in the same balance sheet; the company also has a significant investment in computer and electronic equipment. In total, all of **Federal Express**'s plant and equipment assets make up almost $15 billion before accumulated depreciation and more than $7 billion after accumulated depreciation. This latter amount represents about 61% of the company's total assets of approximately $11.5 billion in 2000.

Plant assets are important for a company such as **Federal Express** to be successful in its daily operations. The exact types and amount of plant assets used by a particular company depend on the nature of the company and its operations. Virtually all companies need some type of plant assets to operate efficiently and be successful. In addition, some companies require certain intangible assets to do business. Intangibles are rights and privileges that have been developed or acquired, such as trade names and patents; these may be as important to a business as its equipment, buildings, and land.

• • •

In earlier chapters, we introduced the idea of plant assets and depreciation and stressed the importance of such assets to the successful functioning of businesses. In this chapter, we explore in greater depth the accounting issues surrounding plant assets and discuss intangible assets. Together, plant and intangible assets make up a significant part of corporate balance sheets because they represent major investments of resources. In many respects, the future of business enterprises depends heavily on their investment in plant and intangible assets.

Plant Assets as a "Stream of Future Services"

Plant assets represent a bundle of future services and, thus, are similar to long-term prepaid expenses. Ownership of a delivery truck, for example, may provide about 100,000 miles of transportation. The cost of the truck is entered in an asset account, which in essence represents the *advance purchase* of these transportation services. Similarly, a building represents the advance purchase of many years of housing services. As the years go by, these services are utilized by the business, and the cost of the plant asset gradually is transferred to depreciation expense.

Major Categories of Plant Assets

Plant and equipment items are often classified into the following groups:

1. Tangible plant assets. The term *tangible* denotes physical substance, as exemplified by land, a building, or a machine. This category may be further separated into two distinct classifications:
    a. Plant property subject to depreciation. Included are plant assets of limited useful life such as buildings and office equipment.
    b. Land. The only plant asset not subject to depreciation is land, which has an unlimited term of existence and whose usefulness does not decline over time.
2. Intangible assets. The term *intangible assets* is used to describe assets that are used in the operation of the business but have no physical characteristics and are noncurrent. Examples include patents, copyrights, trademarks, franchises, and goodwill. Current assets such as accounts receivable or prepaid rent are not included in the intangible classification, even though they also are lacking in physical substance.
3. Natural resources. A site acquired for the purpose of extracting or removing some valuable resource such as oil, minerals, or timber is classified as a *natural resource,* not as land. This type of plant asset is gradually converted into *inventory* as the natural resource is extracted from the site.

Accountable Events in the Lives of Plant Assets

For all categories of plant assets, there are three basic *accountable events:* (1) acquisition, (2) allocation of the acquisition cost to expense over the asset's useful life (depreciation), and (3) sale or disposal.

ACQUISITIONS OF PLANT ASSETS

LO 1
Determine the cost of plant assets.

The cost of a plant asset includes all expenditures that are *reasonable* and *necessary* for getting the asset to the desired location and *ready for use.* Thus many incidental costs may be included in the cost assigned to a plant asset. These include, for example, sales taxes on the purchase price, delivery costs, and installation costs.

Only reasonable and necessary costs should be included. Assume, for example, that a machine is dropped and damaged while it is being unloaded. The cost of repairing this damage should be recognized as an expense of the current period, *not* added to the cost of the machine. Although it is necessary to repair the machine, it was not necessary to drop it—and that's what brought about the need for the repairs.

Companies often purchase plant assets on an installment plan or by issuing a note payable. Interest charges after the asset is ready for use are recorded as interest expense, not as part of the cost of the asset. But if a company constructs a plant asset for its own use, the interest charges *during the construction period* are viewed as part of the asset's cost.[1]

Determining Cost: An Example

The concept of including in the cost of a plant asset all of the incidental charges necessary to put the asset in use is illustrated by the following example. A factory in Mississippi orders a machine from a Colorado tool manufacturer at a list price of $10,000. Payment will be made in 48 monthly installments of $250, which include $2,000 in interest charges. Sales taxes of $600 must be paid, as well as freight charges of $1,350. Installation and other set-up costs amount to $500. The cost of this machine to be established in the Machinery account is computed as follows:

List price*	$10,000
Sales taxes	600
Transportation charges	1,350
Cost of installation and set-up	500
Total	$12,450

*The $2,000 in interest charges on the installment purchase will be recognized as interest expense over the next 48 months. (Accounting for installment notes payable is discussed in the next chapter.)

My Notes

All reasonable and necessary costs are capitalized

Some Special Considerations

Land   When land is purchased, various incidental costs are generally incurred in addition to the purchase price. These additional costs may include commissions to real estate brokers, escrow fees, legal fees for examining and insuring the title, delinquent taxes paid by the purchaser, and fees for surveying, draining, clearing, and grading the property. All these expenditures become part of the cost of the land.

Sometimes land purchased as a building site has on it an old building that is not suitable for the buyer's use. In this case, the only useful asset being acquired is the land. Therefore, the entire purchase price is charged to the Land account, along with the costs of tearing down and removing the unusable building.

Land Improvements   Improvements to real estate such as driveways, fences, parking lots, landscaping, and sprinkler systems have a limited life and are therefore subject to depreciation. For this reason, they should be recorded in a separate account entitled Land Improvements.

Buildings   Old buildings are sometimes purchased with the intention of repairing them prior to placing them in use. Repairs made under these circumstances are charged to the Buildings account. After the building has been placed in use, however, ordinary repairs are considered to be maintenance expense when incurred.

Equipment   When equipment is purchased, all of the sales taxes, delivery costs, and costs of getting the equipment in good running order are treated as part of the cost of the asset. Once the equipment has been placed in operation, maintenance costs (including interest, insurance, and property taxes) are treated as expenses of the current period.

Allocation of a Lump-Sum Purchase   Several different types of plant assets may be purchased at one time. Separate controlling accounts are maintained for each type of plant asset, such as land, buildings, and equipment.[2]

---

[1] FASB Statement No. 34, "Capitalization of Interest Costs" (Norwalk, Conn.: 1979).

[2] Each controlling account is supported by a subsidiary ledger providing information about the cost, annual depreciation, and book value of each asset (or group of similar assets).

When land and buildings (and perhaps other assets) are purchased for a lump sum, the purchase price must be *allocated* among the types of assets acquired. An appraisal may be needed for this purpose. Assume, for example, that Exercise-for-Health, Inc. purchases a complete fitness center from Golden Health Spas. Exercise-for-Health purchases the entire facility at a bargain price of $800,000. The allocation of this cost on the basis of an appraisal is illustrated as follows:

My Notes

Total cost is allocated in proportion to appraised values

	Value per Appraisal	Percentage of Total Appraised Value	Allocation of $800,000 Cost
Land	$ 250,000	25%	$200,000
Land improvements	50,000	5	40,000
Building	300,000	30	240,000
Equipment	400,000	40	320,000
Total	$1,000,000	100%	$800,000

Assuming that Exercise-for-Health purchased this facility for cash, the journal entry to record this acquisition would be:

My Notes

The journal entry allocating the total cost

Land	200,000	
Land Improvements	40,000	
Building	240,000	
Equipment	320,000	
Cash		800,000

To record purchase of fitness center from Golden Health Spas for cash.

YOUR TURN

You as the New Facility Manager for Exercise-for-Health

Assume you have been hired as manager of the new Golden Health Spas facility that was recently purchased by Exercise-for-Health. One of your responsibilities as manager is to show that the facility is profitable. In fact, your contract specifies a bonus if the profits are at least 10% above the budgeted amount each year. In a recent conversation with the appraiser, it becomes clear to you that some of the items classified as land in the appraisal were really building improvements. No one at Exercise-for-Health is aware of this misclassification. As a result, the appraised value for the building asset account should be $350,000 instead of $300,000. When budgeted profits for the Golden Health Spas facility are computed each year, a charge for depreciation on the building is deducted from the profits. What impact does the improper appraisal have on your ability to achieve the bonus? What should you do?

*Our comments appear on p. 406.

Capital Expenditures and Revenue Expenditures

LO 2

Distinguish between capital expenditures and revenue expenditures.

Expenditures for the purchase or expansion of plant assets are called **capital expenditures** and are recorded in asset accounts. Accountants often use the verb **capitalize** to mean charging an expenditure to an asset account rather than to an expense account. Expenditures for ordinary repairs, maintenance, fuel, and other items necessary to the ownership and use of plant and equipment are called **revenue expenditures** and are recorded by debiting expense accounts. The charge to an expense account is based on the assumption that the benefits from the expenditure will be used up in the current period, and therefore the cost should be deducted from the revenue of the period in determining the net income. Charging an expenditure directly to an expense account is often called "expensing" the item.

A business may purchase many small items that will benefit several accounting periods but that have a relatively low cost. Examples of such items include auto batteries, wastebaskets, and pencil sharpeners. Such items are theoretically capital expenditures, but if they are recorded as assets in the accounting records it will be necessary to compute and record the related depreciation expense in future periods. We have previously mentioned the idea that the extra work involved in developing more precise accounting information should be weighed against the benefits that result. Thus, for reasons of convenience and economy, expenditures that are *not material* in dollar amount are treated in the accounting records as expenses of the current period.

In brief, any material expenditure that will benefit several accounting periods is considered a *capital expenditure.* Any expenditure that will benefit only the current period or that is not material in amount is treated as a *revenue expenditure.*

Many companies develop formal policy statements defining capital and revenue expenditures as a guide toward consistent accounting practice from year to year. These policy statements often set a minimum dollar amount (such as $500) for expenditures that are to be capitalized.

DEPRECIATION

We first introduced the concept of depreciation in Chapter 4. Now we expand that discussion to address such topics as residual values and alternative depreciation methods.

Allocating the Cost of Plant and Equipment over the Years of Use

Tangible plant assets, with the exception of land, are of use to a company for only a limited number of years. **Depreciation**, as the term is used in accounting, is the *allocation of the cost of a tangible plant asset to expense in the periods in which services are received from the asset.* In short, the basic purpose of depreciation is to offset the revenue of an accounting period with the costs of the goods and services being consumed in the effort to generate that revenue. (See Exhibit 9–1.)

Earlier in this chapter, we described a delivery truck as a stream of transportation services to be received over the years that the truck is owned and used. The cost of the truck initially is added to an asset account, because the purchase of these transportation services will benefit several future accounting periods. As these services are received, however, the cost of the truck gradually is removed from the balance sheet and allocated to expense, through the process of depreciation.

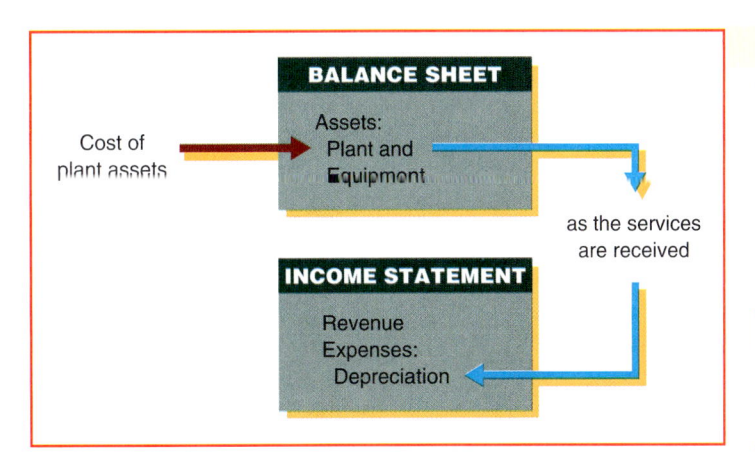

Exhibit 9–1

THE DEPRECIATION PROCESS

My Notes

Depreciation: a process of allocating the cost of an asset to expense over the asset's useful life

The journal entry to record depreciation expense consists of a debit to Depreciation Expense and a credit to Accumulated Depreciation. The credit portion of the entry removes from the balance sheet that portion of the asset's cost estimated to have been used up during the current period. The debit portion of the entry allocates this expired cost to expense.

Separate Depreciation Expense and Accumulated Depreciation accounts are maintained for different types of depreciable assets, such as factory buildings, delivery equipment, and office equipment. These separate accounts help accountants to measure separately the costs of different business activities, such as manufacturing, sales, and administration.

Depreciation Is Not a Process of Valuation Depreciation is a process of *cost allocation,* not a process of asset valuation. Accounting records do not attempt to show the current market values of plant assets. The market value of a building, for example, may increase during some accounting periods within the building's useful life. The recognition of depreciation expense continues, however, without regard to such temporary increases in market value. Accountants recognize that the building will render useful services only for a limited number of years and that the full cost of the building should be *systematically allocated to expense* during these years.

CASH EFFECTS Depreciation differs from most other expenses in that it does not depend on cash payments at or near the time the expense is recorded. For this reason, depreciation often is called a "noncash" expense. Bear in mind, however, that large cash payments usually are required at the time depreciable assets are purchased.

Book Value Plant assets are shown in the balance sheet at their book values (or *carrying values*). The book value of a plant asset is its *cost minus the related accumulated depreciation.* Accumulated depreciation is a contra-asset account, representing that portion of the asset's cost that has *already* been allocated to expense. Thus book value represents the portion of the asset's cost that remains to be allocated to expense in future periods.

Causes of Depreciation

The need to systematically allocate plant asset costs over multiple accounting periods arises from two major causes: (1) physical deterioration and (2) obsolescence.

Physical Deterioration Physical deterioration of a plant asset results from use, as well as from exposure to sun, wind, and other climatic factors. When a plant asset has been carefully maintained, it is not uncommon for the owner to claim that the asset is as "good as new." Such statements are not literally true. Although a good repair policy may greatly lengthen the useful life of a machine, every machine eventually reaches the point at which it must be discarded. In brief, the making of repairs does not eliminate the need for recognition of depreciation.

Obsolescence The term *obsolescence* means the process of becoming out of date or obsolete. An airplane, for example, may become obsolete even though it is in excellent physical condition; it becomes obsolete because better planes of superior design and performance have become available.

Depreciation

CASE IN POINT

Chrysler Corporation recently opened the Jefferson North Assembly Plant in the heart of Detroit. Did Chrysler build this plant because existing facilities had become physically deteriorated beyond use? The answer is no. While existing facilities could still be used to produce automobiles, their production methods had become obsolete.

The Jefferson North Assembly Plant employs some of the most innovative technologies in the automotive industry. As a result, Chrysler can produce vehicles of higher quality, at a lower cost, and with less pollution than ever before.

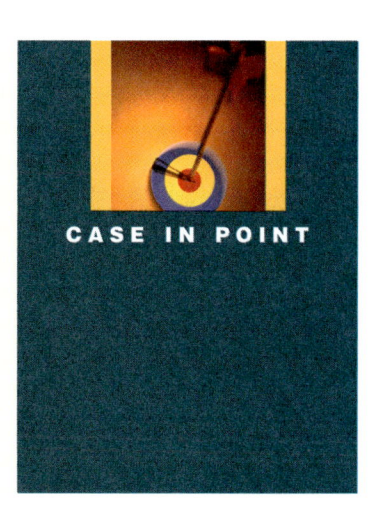

Methods of Computing Depreciation

In Chapter 4, we computed depreciation only by the **straight-line depreciation** method. Companies actually may use any of several depreciation methods. Generally accepted accounting principles require only that a depreciation method result in a *rational and systematic* allocation of cost over the asset's useful life. The straight-line method is by far the most commonly used depreciation method for financial reporting purposes.

The straight-line method allocates an *equal portion* of depreciation expense to each period of the asset's useful life. Most of the other depreciation methods are various forms of accelerated depreciation. The term **accelerated depreciation** means that larger amounts of depreciation are recognized in the early years of the asset's life, and smaller amounts are recognized in the later years. Over the entire life of the asset, however, both the straight-line method and accelerated methods recognize the same *total* amount of depreciation.

The differences between the straight-line methods and accelerated methods are illustrated in Exhibit 9–2.

LO 3
Compute depreciation by the straight-line and declining-balance methods.

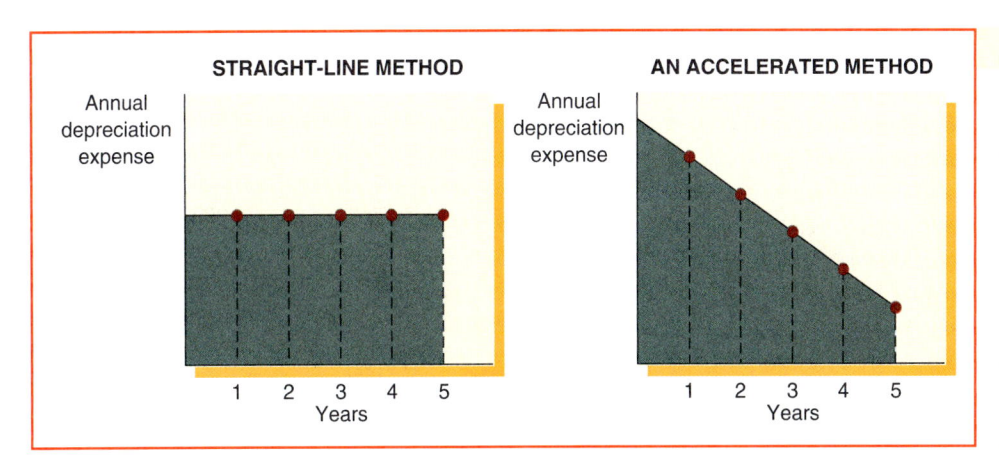

Exhibit 9–2

STRAIGHT-LINE AND ACCELERATED DEPRECIATION

My Notes

Both methods recognize the same total depreciation

There is only one straight-line method. But there are several accelerated methods, each producing slightly different results. Different depreciation methods may be used for different assets. The depreciation methods in use should be disclosed in notes accompanying the financial statements.

In this chapter, we illustrate and explain straight-line depreciation and one variation of the most widely used accelerated method, which is called *fixed-percentage-of-declining-balance,* or simply the *declining-balance* method. Other depreciation methods are discussed briefly in the *Supplemental Topic* at the end of the chapter.

Data for Our Illustrations Our illustrations of depreciation methods are based on the following data: On January 2, S&G Wholesale Grocery acquires a new delivery truck. The data and estimates needed for the computation of the annual depreciation expense are:

Cost	$17,000
Estimated residual value	$ 2,000
Estimated useful life	5 years

The Straight-Line Method

Under the straight-line method, an *equal portion* of the asset's cost is recognized as depreciation expense in each period of the asset's useful life. Annual depreciation expense is computed by deducting the estimated **residual value** (or **salvage value**) from the cost of the asset and dividing the remaining *depreciable cost* by the years of estimated useful life. Using the data in our example, the annual straight-line depreciation is computed as follows:

$$\frac{\text{Cost} - \text{Residual Value}}{\text{Years of Useful Life}} = \frac{\$17,000 - \$2,000}{5 \text{ years}} = \$3,000 \text{ per year}$$

This same depreciation computation is shown in tabular form as follows:

My Notes
Computing depreciation by the straight-line method

Cost of the depreciable asset	$17,000
Less: Estimated residual value (amount to be realized by sale of asset when it is retired from use)	2,000
Total amount to be depreciated (depreciable cost)	$15,000
Estimated useful life	5 years
Depreciation expense each year ($15,000 ÷ 5)	$ 3,000

In Exhibit 9–3, the schedule summarizes the effects of straight-line depreciation over the entire life of the asset.

Exhibit 9–3
STRAIGHT-LINE DEPRECIATION SCHEDULE

My Notes
Constant annual depreciation expense

Depreciation Schedule: Straight-Line Method

Year	Computation	Depreciation Expense	Accumulated Depreciation	Book Value
				$17,000
First	$15,000 × 1/5	$ 3,000	$ 3,000	14,000
Second	15,000 × 1/5	3,000	6,000	11,000
Third	15,000 × 1/5	3,000	9,000	8,000
Fourth	15,000 × 1/5	3,000	12,000	5,000
Fifth	15,000 × 1/5	3,000	15,000	2,000
Total		$15,000		

(We present several depreciation schedules in this chapter. In each schedule we highlight in red those features that we want to emphasize.)

Notice that the depreciation expense over the life of the truck totals *$15,000*—the cost of the truck *minus the estimated residual value.* The residual value is *not* part of the cost "used up" in business operations. Instead, the residual value is expected to be recovered in cash upon disposal of the asset.

In practice, residual values may be ignored if they are not expected to be *material* in amount. Traditionally, buildings, office equipment, furniture, fixtures, and special-purpose equipment seldom are considered to have significant residual values. Assets such as vehicles, aircraft, and construction equipment, in contrast, often do have residual values that are material in amount.

It often is convenient to state the portion of an asset's depreciable cost that will be written off during the year as a percentage, called the *depreciation rate*. When straight-line depreciation is in use, the depreciation rate is simply *1* divided by the *life* (in years) of the asset. The delivery truck in our example has an estimated life of 5 years, so the depreciation expense each year is ¹/₅, or *20%*, of the depreciable amount. Similarly, an asset with a 10-year life has a depreciation rate of ¹/₁₀, or *10%*; and an asset with an 8-year life, a depreciation rate of ¹/₈, or *12¹/₂%*.

YOUR TURN

You as a Business Owner

Assume you are the owner of a trucking company that has just invested $150,000 in a new truck. Working with your accountant, you are in the process of estimating its useful life and residual value. Your estimates will be used to compute straight-line depreciation expense for financial reporting purposes.

What factors should you take into consideration in developing these estimates? Discuss briefly how these factors will influence the amount of depreciation expense reported by your company each year.

*Our comments appear on page 406.

Depreciation for Fractional Periods When an asset is acquired in the middle of an accounting period, it is not necessary to compute depreciation expense to the nearest day or week. In fact, such a computation would give a misleading impression of great precision. Since depreciation is based on an estimated useful life of many years, the depreciation applicable to any one year is *only an approximation*.

One widely used method of computing depreciation for part of a year is to round the calculation to the nearest whole month. In our example, S&G acquired the delivery truck on January 2. Therefore, we computed a full year's depreciation for the year of acquisition. Assume, however, that the truck had been acquired later in the year on *October 1*. Thus the truck would have been in use for only 3 months (or ³/₁₂) of the first year. In this case, depreciation expense for the first year would be limited to only *$750*, or ³/₁₂ of a full year's depreciation ($3,000 × ³/₁₂ = $750).

An even more widely used approach, called the **half-year convention**, is to record six months' depreciation on all assets acquired during the year. This approach is based on the assumption that the actual purchase dates will average out to approximately midyear. The half-year convention is widely used for assets such as office equipment, automobiles, and machinery.

Assume that S&G Wholesale Grocery uses straight-line depreciation with the half-year convention. In Exhibit 9–4, we summarize depreciation on the $17,000 delivery truck with the 5-year life.

Exhibit 9–4

STRAIGHT-LINE DEPRECIATION SCHEDULE

Depreciation Schedule
Straight-Line Method with Half-Year Convention

Year	Computation	Depreciation Expense	Accumulated Depreciation	Book Value
				$17,000
First	$15,000 × ¹/₅ × ¹/₂	$ 1,500	$ 1,500	15,500
Second	15,000 × ¹/₅	3,000	4,500	12,500
Third	15,000 × ¹/₅	3,000	7,500	9,500
Fourth	15,000 × ¹/₅	3,000	10,500	6,500
Fifth	15,000 × ¹/₅	3,000	13,500	3,500
Sixth	15,000 × ¹/₅ × ¹/₂	1,500	15,000	2,000
Total		$15,000		

When the half-year convention is in use, we ignore the date on which the asset was actually purchased. We simply recognize *one-half year's depreciation* in both the first year and last year of the depreciation schedule. Notice that our depreciation schedule now includes depreciation expense in the sixth year. Taking only a partial year's depreciation in the first year always extends the depreciation program into one additional year.

The half-year convention enables us to treat similar assets acquired at different dates during the year as a single group. For example, assume that an insurance company purchases hundreds of desktop computers throughout the current year at a total cost of $600,000. The company depreciates these computers by the straight-line method, assuming a 5-year life and no residual value. Using the half-year convention, the depreciation expense on all of the computers purchased during the year may be computed as follows: $600,000 ÷ 5 years × 6/12 = $60,000. If we did not use the half-year convention, depreciation would have to be computed separately for computers purchased in different months.

The Declining-Balance Method

The most widely used accelerated depreciation method is called **fixed-percentage-of-declining-balance depreciation**. However, the method is used primarily in *income tax returns,* rather than financial statements.[3]

Under the declining-balance method, an accelerated *depreciation rate* is computed as a specified percentage of the straight-line depreciation rate. Annual depreciation expense then is computed by applying this accelerated depreciation rate to the undepreciated cost (current book value) of the asset. This computation may be summarized as follows:

$$\text{Depreciation Expense} = \text{Remaining Book Value} \times \text{Accelerated Depreciation Rate}$$

The accelerated depreciation rate *remains constant* throughout the life of the asset. Hence, the rate represents the "fixed-percentage" described in the name of this depreciation method. The book value (cost minus accumulated depreciation) *decreases every year* and represents the "declining-balance."

Thus far, we have described the accelerated depreciation rate as a "specified percentage" of the straight-line rate. Most often, this specified percentage is 200%, meaning that the accelerated rate is exactly twice the straight-line rate. As a result, the declining-balance method of depreciation often is called *double-declining-balance* (or 200% declining-balance). Tax rules, however, often specify a *lower* percentage, such as 150% of the straight-line rate. This version of the declining-balance method may be described as "150% declining-balance."[4]

Double-Declining-Balance To illustrate the double-declining-balance method, consider our example of the $17,000 delivery truck. The estimated useful life is 5 years; therefore, the straight-line depreciation rate is 20% (1 ÷ 5 years). Doubling this straight-line rate indicates an accelerated depreciation rate of 40%. Each year, we will recognize as depreciation expense 40% of the truck's current book value, as we show in Exhibit 9–5.

---

[3] In 1986, Congress adopted an accelerated method of depreciation called the *Modified Accelerated Cost Recovery System* (or MACRS). Companies may use straight-line depreciation for federal income tax purposes, but most prefer to use MACRS because of its favorable income tax consequences. MACRS is the *only* accelerated depreciation method that may be used in federal income tax returns.

[4] The higher the specified percentage of the straight-line rate, the more accelerated this depreciation becomes. Experience and tradition have established 200% of the straight-line rate as the maximum level. For federal income tax purposes, MACRS (see footnote 3 above) is based upon a 200% declining-balance for some assets, and a 150% declining-balance method for others. The 150% declining-balance slows down the rates at which taxpayers may depreciate specific types of assets in their income tax returns.

Exhibit 9–5

200% DECLINING-BALANCE DEPRECIATION SCHEDULE

Depreciation Schedule: 200% Declining-Balance Method				
Year	Computation	Depreciation Expense	Accumulated Depreciation	Book Value
				$17,000
First	$17,000 × 40%	$ 6,800	$ 6,800	10,200
Second	10,200 × 40%	4,080	10,880	6,120
Third	6,120 × 40%	2,448	13,328	3,672
Fourth	3,672 × 40%	1,469	14,797	2,203
Fifth	2,203 − $2,000	203	15,000	2,000
Total		$15,000		

Notice that the estimated residual value of the delivery truck *does not* enter into the computation of depreciation expense until the end. This is because the declining-balance method provides an *"automatic"* residual value. As long as each year's depreciation expense is equal to only a portion of the undepreciated cost of the asset, the asset *will never be entirely written off*. However, if the asset has a significant residual value, depreciation should *stop at this point*. Since our delivery truck has an estimated residual value of *$2,000*, the depreciation expense for the fifth year is *limited to $203*, rather than the $881 indicated by taking 40% of the remaining book value. By limiting the last year's depreciation expense in this manner, the book value of the truck at the end of the fifth year will be equal to its $2,000 estimated residual value.

In Exhibit 9–5 we computed a full year's depreciation in the first year because the asset was acquired on January 2. But if the half-year convention were in use, depreciation in the first year would be *reduced by half,* to $3,400. The depreciation in the second year would be ($17,000 − $3,400) × 40%, or *$5,440.*

150% Declining-Balance Now assume that we wanted to depreciate this truck using 150% of the straight-line rate. In this case, the depreciation rate will be 30%, instead of 40% (a 20% straight-line rate × 150% = 30%). This depreciation schedule is in Exhibit 9–6.

Exhibit 9–6

150% DECLINING-BALANCE DEPRECIATION SCHEDULE

Depreciation Schedule: 150% Declining-Balance Method				
Year	Computation	Depreciation Expense	Accumulated Depreciation	Book Value
				$17,000
First	$17,000 × 30%	$ 5,100	$ 5,100	11,900
Second	11,900 × 30%	3,570	8,670	8,330
Third	8,330 × 30%	2,499	11,169	5,831
Fourth	(5,831 − 2,000) ÷ 2	1,916*	13,085	3,915
Fifth	3,915 − 2,000	1,915*	15,000	2,000
Total		$15,000		

*Switched to the straight-line method for Years 4 and 5.

Notice that we switched to straight-line depreciation in the last 2 years. The undepreciated cost of the truck at the end of Year 3 was *$5,831*. To depreciate the truck to an estimated residual value of $2,000 at the end of Year 5, $3,831 in depreciation expense must be recognized over the next 2 years. At this point, *larger depreciation charges* can be recognized if we simply allocate this $3,831 by the straight-line method, rather than continuing to compute 30% of the remaining book value. (In our table, we round the allocation of this amount to the nearest dollar.)

Allocating the remaining book value over the remaining life by the straight-line method does *not* represent a change in depreciation methods. Rather, a switch to straight-line when this will result in larger depreciation is *part of the declining-balance method.* This is the way in which we arrive at the desired residual value.

Which Depreciation Methods Do Most Businesses Use?

Many businesses use the straight-line method of depreciation in their financial statements and accelerated methods in their income tax returns. The reasons for these choices are easy to understand.

Accelerated depreciation methods result in higher charges to depreciation expense early in the asset's life and, therefore, lower reported net income than straight-line depreciation. Most publicly owned companies want to appear as profitable as possible—certainly as profitable as their competitors. Therefore, the majority of publicly owned companies use straight-line depreciation in their financial statements.

For income tax purposes, it's a different story. Management usually wants to report the *lowest* possible taxable income in the company's income tax returns. Accelerated depreciation methods can substantially reduce both taxable income and tax payments for a period of years.[5]

Accounting principles and income tax laws both permit companies to use *different depreciation methods* in their financial statements and their income tax returns. Therefore, many companies use straight-line depreciation in their financial statements and accelerated methods (variations of the declining-balance method) in their income tax returns.

The Differences in Depreciation Methods: Are They "Real"? Using the straight-line depreciation method will cause a company to *report* higher profits than would be reported if an accelerated method were in use. But *is* the company better off than if it had used an accelerated method? The answer is *no!* Depreciation—no matter how it is computed—*is only an estimate.* The amount of this estimate has *no effect* on the actual financial strength of the business. Thus a business that uses an accelerated depreciation method in its financial statements is simply measuring its net income *more conservatively* than a business that uses straight-line.

CASH EFFECTS The benefits of using an accelerated method for income tax purposes are real because the amount of depreciation claimed affects the amount of taxes owed. Lower income taxes translate directly into increased cash availability.

In the preceding chapter, we made the point that if a company wants to use LIFO in its income tax return, it *must* use LIFO in its financial statements. *No similar requirement exists for depreciation methods.* A company may use an accelerated method in its income tax returns and the straight-line method in its financial statements—and most companies do.

---

[5] For a *growing* business, the use of accelerated depreciation in income tax returns may reduce taxable income *every* year. This is because a growing business may always have more assets in the early years of their recovery periods than in the later years.

You as a Business Consultant

Assume you are a consultant to a promising new service company. The company is owned privately by a pool of 100 investors. However, its goal is to "go public" after just five years of operations. The company's current investment in buildings and office equipment is expected to be adequate until its stock is traded publicly.

Management has recently given you a business plan to review. In it, you note that an accelerated method of depreciation was used in making all income projections. Using this information, you have recomputed depreciation expense under the straight-line method. A comparison of your depreciation expense figures for the next five years with those of management is shown below (based on average useful life of 20 years):

| | Annual Depreciation Expense (in 000's) ||
	Accelerated	Straight-line
Year 1	$2,000	$1,000
Year 2	1,800	1,000
Year 3	1,620	1,000
Year 4	1,450	1,000
Year 5	1,305	1,000

Explain to management why the company should consider using straight-line depreciation for financial reporting purposes instead of the accelerated method.

*Our comments appear on page 406.

Financial Statement Disclosures

A company should *disclose* in notes to its financial statements the methods used to depreciate plant assets. Readers of the statements should recognize that accelerated depreciation methods transfer the costs of plant assets to expense more quickly than the straight-line method. Thus accelerated methods result in more *conservative* (lower) balance sheet amounts of plant assets and measurements of net income.

Estimates of Useful Life and Residual Value Estimating the useful lives and residual values of plant assets is the *responsibility of management.* These estimates usually are based on the company's past experience with similar assets, but they also reflect the company's current circumstances and management's future plans. Thus the estimated lives of similar assets may vary from one company to another.

The estimated lives of plant assets affect the amount of net income reported each period. The longer the estimated useful life, the smaller the amount of cost transferred each period to depreciation expense and the larger the amount of reported net income. Bear in mind, however, that all large corporations are *audited* annually by a firm of independent public accountants. One of the responsibilities of these auditors is to determine that management's estimates of the useful lives of plant assets are reasonable under the circumstances.

Automobiles typically are depreciated over relatively short estimated lives—say, from 3 to 5 years. Most other types of equipment are depreciated over a period of from 5 to 15 years. Buildings are depreciated over much longer lives—perhaps 30 to 50 years for a new building and 15 years or more for a building acquired used.

The Principle of Consistency The *consistent* application of accounting methods is a generally accepted accounting principle. With respect to depreciation methods, this principle means that a company should *not change* from year to year the method used in computing the depreciation expense for a given plant asset. However, management *may* use different methods in computing depreciation for different assets. Also, as we have stressed repeatedly, a company may—and often *must*—use different depreciation methods in its financial statements and income tax returns.

Revision of Estimated Useful Lives What should be done if, after a few years of using a plant asset, management decides that the asset actually is going to last for a considerably longer or shorter period than was originally estimated? When this situation arises, a *revised estimate* of useful life should be made and the periodic depreciation expense decreased or increased accordingly.

The procedure for correcting the depreciation schedule is to spread the remaining undepreciated cost of the asset *over the years of remaining useful life*. This correction affects only the amount of depreciation expense that will be recorded in the current and future periods. The financial statements of past periods are *not* revised to reflect changes in the estimated useful lives of depreciable assets.

To illustrate, assume that a company acquires a $10,000 asset estimated to have a 5-year useful life and no residual value. Under the straight-line method, the annual depreciation expense is $2,000. At the end of the third year, accumulated depreciation amounts to $6,000, and the asset has an undepreciated cost (or book value) of $4,000.

At the beginning of the fourth year, it is decided that the asset will last for 5 *more* years. The revised estimate of useful life is, therefore, a total of 8 years. The depreciation expense to be recognized for the fourth year and for each of the remaining years is $800, computed as follows:

Undepreciated cost at end of third year ($10,000 − $6,000)	$4,000
Revised estimate of remaining years of useful life	5 years
Revised amount of annual depreciation expense ($4,000 ÷ 5)	$ 800

The Impairment of Plant Assets

On occasion, it may become apparent that a company cannot reasonably expect to recover the cost of certain plant assets, either through use or through sale. For example, a computer manufacturer may have paid a high price to acquire specialized production equipment. If new technology soon renders the equipment obsolete, however, it may become apparent that it is worth far less than its cost.

If the cost of an asset cannot be recovered through future use or sale, the asset should be *written down* to its net realizable value. The offsetting debit is to a loss account. These write-offs generally do *not* enter into the determination of taxable income.

CASE IN POINT

Several years ago, **Chrysler Corporation** made a strategic commitment to focus on its core automotive manufacturing business. Thus the company sold its **Thrifty Rent-A-Car** subsidiary. Realizing it could not possibly recover the cost of this subsidiary, **Chrysler** recorded a $100 million charge against income to write down **Thrifty**'s assets to their net realizable values.

DISPOSAL OF PLANT AND EQUIPMENT

LO 4
Account for disposals of plant assets.

When depreciable assets are disposed of at any date other than the end of the year, an entry should be made to record depreciation for the *fraction of the year* ending with the date of disposal. If the half-year convention is in use, six months' depreciation should be recorded on all assets disposed of during the year. In the following illustrations of the disposal of items of plant and equipment, it is assumed that any necessary entries for fractional-period depreciation already have been recorded.

As units of plant and equipment wear out or become obsolete, they must be scrapped, sold, or traded in on new equipment. Upon the disposal or retirement of a depreciable asset, the cost of the property is removed from the asset account, and the accumulated depreciation is removed from the related contra-asset account. Assume, for example, that office equipment purchased 10 years ago at a cost of $20,000 has been fully depreciated and is no longer useful. The entry to record the scrapping of the worthless equipment is as follows:

Accumulated Depreciation: Office Equipment	20,000	
Office Equipment		20,000
To remove from the accounts the cost and the accumulated depreciation on fully depreciated office equipment now being scrapped. No salvage value.		

My Notes
Scrapping a fully depreciated asset

Once an asset has been fully depreciated, no more depreciation should be recorded on it, even though the property may be in good condition and is still in use. The objective of depreciation is to spread the *cost* of an asset over the periods of its usefulness; in no case can depreciation expense be greater than the cost of the asset. When a fully depreciated asset remains in use beyond the original estimate of useful life, the asset account and the Accumulated Depreciation account should remain in the accounting records without further entries until the asset is retired.

Gains and Losses on Disposals of Plant and Equipment

Since the residual values and useful lives of plant assets are only estimates, it is not uncommon for a plant asset to be sold at a price that differs from its book value at the date of disposal. When plant assets are sold, any gain or loss on the disposal is computed by comparing the *book value with the amount received from the sale.* A sales price in excess of the book value produces a gain; a sales price below the book value produces a loss. These gains or losses, if material in amount, should be shown separately in the income statement following the computation of income from operations.

Asset dispositions occur frequently in many businesses, and the gains and losses that result often are material in amount. For instance, recent financial statements of **U.S. Steel** and **Dow Chemical** reported gains on asset dispositions of $40 million and $24 million, respectively. The income statements of **Consolidated Freightlines** and **Ford Motor Company**, on the other hand, reported losses on asset dispositions of $4 million and $235 million, respectively.

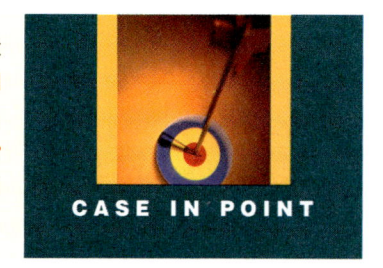

CASE IN POINT

Disposal at a Price above Book Value Assume that a machine costing $10,000 has a book value of $2,000 at the time it is sold for $3,000 cash. The journal entry to record this disposal is as follows:

Cash	3,000	
Accumulated Depreciation: Machinery	8,000	
Machinery		10,000
Gain on Disposal of Plant Assets		1,000
To record sale of machinery at a price above book value.		

My Notes
Gain on disposal of plant asset

Disposal at a Price below Book Value Now assume instead that the same machine is sold for $500. The journal entry in this case would be as follows:

Cash	500	
Accumulated Depreciation: Machinery	8,000	
Loss on Disposal of Plant Assets	1,500	
Machinery		10,000

To record sale of machinery at a price below book value.

My Notes: Loss on disposal of plant asset

The disposal of a depreciable asset at a price *equal to* book value results in neither a gain nor a loss. The entry for such a transaction consists of a debit to Cash for the amount received, a debit to Accumulated Depreciation for the balance accumulated, and a credit to the asset account for the original cost.

Trading in Used Assets for New Ones

Certain types of depreciable assets, such as automobiles and trucks, sometimes are traded in for new assets of the same kind. In most instances, a trade-in is viewed as both a *sale* of the old asset and a purchase of a new one.

To illustrate, assume that Rancho Landscape has an old pickup truck that originally cost $10,000 but that now has a book value (and tax basis) of $2,000. Rancho trades in this old truck for a new one with a fair market value of $15,000. The truck dealership grants Rancho a trade-in allowance of $3,500 for the old truck, and Rancho pays the remaining $11,500 cost of the new truck in cash. Rancho Landscape should record this transaction as follows:

Vehicles (new truck)	15,000	
Accumulated Depreciation: Trucks (old truck)	8,000	
Vehicles (old truck)		10,000
Gain on Disposal of Plant Assets		1,500
Cash		11,500

Traded in old truck for a new one costing $15,000. Received $3,500 trade-in allowance on the old truck, which had a book value of $2,000.

My Notes: Entry to record a typical trade-in

Notice that Rancho views the $3,500 trade-in allowance granted by the truck dealership as the *sales price* of the old truck. Thus Rancho recognizes a *$1,500 gain* on the disposal (trade-in) of this asset ($3,500 trade-in allowance − $2,000 book value = $1,500 gain).

For financial reporting purposes, gains and losses on routine trade-ins are recorded in the accounting records whenever the transaction also involves the payment of a significant amount of cash (or the creation of debt).[6] Income tax rules do *not* permit recognition of gains or losses on exchanges of assets that are used for similar purposes. Thus the $1,500 gain recorded in our example is not regarded as taxable income.[7]

---

[6] The FASB Emerging Issues Task Force takes the position that when 25% or more of the transaction value is comprised of cash or monetary obligations, the transaction should be viewed as *monetary*, rather than nonmonetary. Thus gains on most routine trade-ins should be *recognized in full*, rather than "deferred" as they are for income tax purposes. See *EITF Abstract Nos. 84-29, 86-29,* and *87-29*.

[7] Had the trade-in allowance been less than book value, the resulting loss would *not be deductible* in the determination of taxable income.

INTANGIBLE ASSETS

Characteristics

As the word *intangible* suggests, assets in this classification have no physical substance. Common examples are goodwill, patents, and trademarks. Intangible assets are classified in the balance sheet as a subgroup of plant assets. However, not all assets that lack physical substance are regarded as intangible assets. An account receivable, for example, has no physical attributes but is classified as a current asset and is not regarded as an intangible. In brief, *intangible assets are assets that are used in the operation of the business but that have no physical substance and are noncurrent.*

The basis of valuation for intangible assets is cost. In some companies, however, certain intangible assets such as trademarks may be of great importance but may have been acquired without incurring any significant cost. These intangible assets appear in the balance sheet at their *cost,* regardless of their value to the company. Intangible assets are listed only if significant costs are incurred in their acquisition or development. If these costs are *insignificant,* they are treated as revenue expenditures (ordinary expenses).

LO 5

Explain the nature of intangible assets, including goodwill.

Operating Expenses versus Intangible Assets

For an expenditure to qualify as an intangible asset, there must be reasonable evidence of future benefits. Many expenditures offer some prospects of yielding benefits in subsequent years, but the existence and life span of these benefits are so uncertain that most companies treat these expenditures as operating expenses. Examples are the expenditures for intensive advertising campaigns to introduce new products and the expense of training employees to work with new types of machinery or office equipment. There is little doubt that some benefits from these outlays continue beyond the current period, but because of the uncertain duration of the benefits, it is almost universal practice to treat expenditures of this nature as an expense of the current period.

Amortization

The term **amortization** describes the systematic write-off to expense of the cost of an intangible asset over its useful life. The usual accounting entry for amortization consists of a debit to Amortization Expense and a credit to the intangible asset account. There is no theoretical objection to crediting an accumulated amortization account rather than the intangible asset account, but this method is seldom encountered in practice.

Although it is difficult to estimate the useful life of an intangible such as a trademark, it is highly probable that such an asset will not contribute to future earnings on a permanent basis. The cost of the intangible asset should, therefore, be deducted from revenue during the years in which it may be expected to aid in producing revenue. The straight-line method normally is used for amortizing intangible assets.

Goodwill

The intangible asset **goodwill** is often found in corporate balance sheets. While this word has a variety of meanings in our general vocabulary, it has a specific and specialized meaning in financial reporting. Goodwill represents an amount that a company has paid to acquire certain favorable intangible attributes as part of an acquisition of another company. For example, assume a company purchases another company that has a favorable reputation for high-quality customer service. The purchasing company might be willing to pay a price to acquire this favorable attribute because of its expectations about the positive impact this customer service will have on future profitability. Even though an intangible asset such as having a favorable reputation for customer service lacks the physical qualities of land, buildings, and equipment, such service may be just as important for the future success of a company. Goodwill is a general term that encompasses a wide variety of favorable attributes expected to permit the acquiring company to operate at a greater-than-normal level of profitability. Positive attributes often included in goodwill include:

- Favorable reputation
- Positive market share
- Positive advertising image
- Reputation for high-quality and loyal employees
- Superior management
- Manufacturing and other operating efficiency

All of these attributes can be expected to contribute to positive future cash flows of the acquiring company. The **present value** of future cash flows is the amount that a knowledgeable investor would pay today for the right to receive those future cash flows. (The present value concept is discussed further in later chapters and in Appendix B.)

Goodwill is sometimes described and measured as the price paid to receive an *above-normal return* on the purchase of another company's net identifiable assets. This requires that we explain the phrase *normal return on the net identifiable assets. Net assets* refers to assets minus liabilities, or owners' equity. Goodwill is not an identifiable asset, however, and the existence of goodwill is implied by the ability of a business to earn an above-average return. The term, **net identifiable assets**, is used to mean all assets except goodwill, minus liabilities.

A *normal return* on net identifiable assets is the rate of return that investors demand in a particular industry to justify their buying a business at the fair market value of its net identifiable assets. A business has goodwill when investors will pay a *higher* price because the business earns *more* than the normal rate of return.

Assume that two similar restaurants are offered for sale and that the normal return on the fair market value of the net identifiable assets of restaurants of this type is 15% a year. The relative earning power of the two restaurants during the past five years is as follows:

My Notes

Which business is worth more?

	Mandarin Coast	Golden Dragon
Fair market value of net identifiable assets	$1,000,000	$1,000,000
Normal rate of return on net assets	15%	15%
Normal earnings, computed as 15% of net identifiable assets	150,000	150,000
Average actual net income for past five years	$ 150,000	$ 200,000
Earnings in excess of normal	$ –0–	$ 50,000

An investor presumably would be willing to pay $1,000,000 to buy Mandarin Coast, because this restaurant earns the normal 15% return that justifies the fair market value of its net identifiable assets. Although Golden Dragon has the same amount of net identifiable assets, an investor should be willing to pay *more* for Golden Dragon than for Mandarin Coast, because Golden Dragon has a record of superior earnings. The *extra amount* that a buyer pays to purchase Golden Dragon represents the value of this business's *goodwill*.

Estimating Goodwill How much will an investor pay for goodwill? Above-average earnings in past years are of significance to prospective purchasers only if they believe that these earnings *will continue* after they acquire the business. Investors' appraisals of goodwill, therefore, will vary with their estimates of the *future earning power* of the business. Very few businesses, however, are able to maintain above-average earnings for more than a few years. Consequently, the purchaser of a business will usually limit any amount paid for goodwill to not more than four or five times the amount by which annual earnings exceed normal earnings.

Estimating an amount for goodwill in the purchase of a business is a difficult and speculative process. In attempting to make such an estimate, you are essentially trying to look into the future and predict the extent to which purchasing another business will add so much value to your current business that you are willing to pay a price greater than the value of the identifiable net assets of the business you are acquiring. For example, in the previous example how much more than $1,000,000 would you be willing to pay for Golden Dragon in comparison with Mandarin Coast? History indicates that Golden Dragon is more profitable, and thus worth more, than Mandarin Coast but whether that extra profitability will continue in the future requires considerable judgment.

Several methods exist for placing a monetary value on the amount of goodwill in the purchase of a business. A widely used method that is consistent with this description of goodwill is to value the business as a whole and then subtract the current market value of the net identifiable assets to estimate the amount of goodwill. For example, assume that successful restaurants sell at about $6^1/_2$ times annual earnings.[8] This suggests that Golden Dragon is worth about $1,300,000, which is the company's $200,000 average net income times 6.5. Because the company's net identifiable assets have a fair market value of only $1,000,000, a reasonable estimate of the positive attributes of Golden Dragon, such as positive reputation or market share, is $300,000, determined as follows:

Estimated value of the business as a whole	$1,300,000
Fair market value of net identifiable assets	1,000,000
Estimated value of goodwill	$ 300,000

If a buyer of Golden Dragon pays $1,300,000 to purchase the business, $300,000 of goodwill would be recorded. On the other hand, if the buyer is able to purchase Golden Dragon for less than $1,300,000, say $1,250,000, only $250,000 of goodwill would be recorded ($1,250,000 − $1,000,000 = $250,000), even though the estimated value of goodwill is more than the amount paid.

Recording Goodwill in the Accounts Because of the difficulties in objectively estimating the value of goodwill, this asset is recorded only when it is purchased. Goodwill is purchased when one company buys another. The purchaser records the identifiable assets it has purchased at their fair market values and then establishes any additional amount paid to an asset account entitled Goodwill.

Many businesses never purchase goodwill but develop goodwill attributes like good customer relations, superior management, or other factors that result in above-average earnings. Because there is no objective way of determining the value of these qualities unless the business is sold, internally generated goodwill is *not recorded* in the accounting records. The absence of internally generated goodwill is one of the principal reasons why a balance sheet does not indicate a company's current market value.

For many years, generally accepted accounting principles required that purchased goodwill be amortized over a period not exceeding 40 years. The FASB has recently changed accounting for goodwill so that goodwill is no longer required to be amortized. The amortization of goodwill was similar to depreciation of land, equipment, and other long-lived assets in that a portion of the cost was removed from the asset account and transferred to an expense in each accounting period. As a general rule, the straight-line method was used for amortizing goodwill and is still commonly used for other intangible assets that are subject to amortization. As part of the changes that resulted in goodwill no longer being amortized, goodwill is subject to assessment for impairment in

---

[8] Investments in small businesses involve more risk and less liquidity than investments in publicly owned companies. For these reasons, the price-earnings ratios of small businesses tend to be substantially lower than those of publicly owned corporations.

value, similar to that for plant assets as explained earlier in this chapter. When the recorded amount of goodwill is no longer recoverable, an impairment loss must be recorded by reducing the asset amount and including a loss in the income statement of the same accounting period.[9]

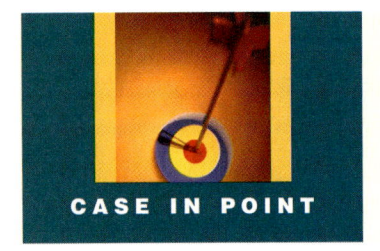

CASE IN POINT

Accounting for goodwill has significant variation around the world. For example, Denmark, Sweden, and Germany allow goodwill to be charged directly to equity with no requirement for amortization. However, Japan and South Korea severely limit the time period for amortizing goodwill to five years. Finally, China's accounting requirements make no mention of goodwill.

Patents

A patent is an exclusive right granted by the federal government for manufacture, use, and sale of a particular product. The purpose of this exclusive grant is to encourage the invention of new products and processes. When a company acquires a patent by purchase from the inventor or other holder, the purchase price should be recorded by debiting the intangible asset account Patents.

Patents are granted for 17 years, and the period of amortization should not exceed that period. However, if the patent is likely to lose its usefulness in less than 17 years, amortization should be based on the shorter estimated useful life. Assume that a patent is purchased from the inventor at a cost of $100,000 after 5 years of the legal life have expired. The remaining *legal* life is, therefore, 12 years. But if the estimated *useful* life is only 4 years, amortization should be based on this shorter period. The entry to record the annual amortization expense would be:

My Notes
Entry for amortization of patent

Amortization Expense: Patents	25,000	
Patents		25,000
To amortize cost of patent on a straight-line basis over an estimated useful life of 4 years.		

Trademarks and Trade Names

Coca-Cola's famous name, usually printed in a distinctive typeface, is a classic example of a trademark known around the world. A trademark is a name, symbol, or design that identifies a product or group of products. A permanent exclusive right to the use of a trademark, brand name, or commercial symbol may be obtained by registering it with the federal government.

The costs of developing a trademark or brand name often consist of advertising campaigns, which should be treated as expenses when incurred. If a trademark or brand name is *purchased,* however, the cost may be substantial. Such cost should be capitalized and amortized to expense over the time period the trademark or brand name is expected to be used. If the use of the trademark is discontinued or its contribution to earnings becomes doubtful, any unamortized cost should be written off immediately.

Franchises

A franchise is a right granted by a company or a governmental unit to conduct a certain type of business in a specific geographical area. An example of a franchise is the right to operate a McDonald's restaurant in a specific neighborhood. The cost of franchises

---
[9] See FASB Statement of Financial Accounting Standards No. 142, "Goodwill and Other Intangible Assets."

varies greatly and often is quite substantial. When the cost of a franchise is small, it may be charged immediately to expense or amortized over a short period such as five years. When the cost is material, amortization should be based on the life of the franchise (if limited); the amortization period, however, should not exceed the period the franchise is expected to generate revenue.

You as a Franchise Owner

As owner of a Big Barbecue franchise, each year you are required to have your financial records audited by a certified public accountant and the resulting report sent to franchise headquarters. You hired the firm Bob Jones, CPA to undertake the audit. However, Bob sent an inexperienced employee, Dan Dawts, who recently completed high school, to undertake your audit. You phoned Bob to express your reservations about Dan's competence to undertake the audit. Bob responded that he would look over his nephew Dan's work to make sure it was correct. After your conversation with Bob, you look in on Dan and he has documents and records scattered throughout the office you assigned him. Furthermore, he announces he is totally baffled about what the records mean and his assigned tasks. He asks for your help. What should you do?

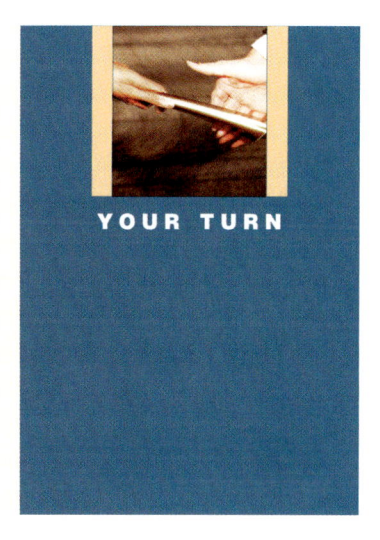

*Our comments appear on page 406.

Copyrights

A copyright is an exclusive right granted by the federal government to protect the production and sale of literary or artistic materials for the life of the creator plus 50 years. The cost of obtaining a copyright in some cases is minor and therefore is chargeable to expense when paid. Only when a copyright is *purchased* will the expenditure be *material enough* to warrant its being capitalized and spread over the useful life. The revenue from copyrights is usually limited to only a few years, and the purchase cost should, of course, be amortized over the years in which the revenue is expected.

Other Intangibles and Deferred Charges

Among the other intangibles found in the published balance sheets of large corporations are moving costs, plant rearrangement costs, formulas, processes, name lists, and film rights. Some companies group items of this type under the title of Deferred Charges, meaning expenditures that will provide benefits beyond the current year and that will be written off to expense over their useful economic lives. It is also common practice to combine these items under the heading of Other Assets, which is listed at the bottom of the balance sheet.

MANAGEMENT STRATEGY AND FINANCIAL REPORTING

Many intangible assets do not currently appear on balance sheets. Some financial analysts believe they should be included. These analysts argue that management is more likely to include these intangible assets in their strategic planning if those assets are part of their externally reported financial statements.

U.S. GAAP permits recognition of an asset if the costs are capable of specific identification and if the asset is separable from the continuing business. Thus, few internally generated intangible assets such as human resources or brand names like Coca-Cola or Sony can be reported on the audited financial statements.

The United Kingdom and Australia allow brand values to be reported on balance sheets for some companies. However, measuring the value of a brand and adjusting financial statements for year-to-year fluctuations in brand value are difficult issues to resolve. Consider that in 2000, the Yahoo! brand had an estimate value of $6.3 billion but that value dropped to $4.4 billion in 2001, a 30% drop in one year.

Research and Development (R&D) Costs

The spending of billions of dollars each year on research and development of new products is a striking characteristic of U.S. industry. The annual research and development expenditures of some companies often exceed $1 billion and account for a substantial percentage of their total costs and expenses.

In the past, some companies treated all research and development costs as expenses in the year incurred; other companies in the same industry recorded these costs as intangible assets to be amortized over future years. This diversity of practice prevented financial statements of different companies from being comparable.

The lack of uniformity in accounting for R&D ended when the Financial Accounting Standards Board ruled that all research and development expenditures should be charged to expense *when incurred*.[10] This action by the FASB had the beneficial effect of reducing the number of alternative accounting practices and helping to make financial statements of different companies more comparable.

FINANCIAL ANALYSIS

The success of many businesses depends on research and development activities (R&D). To better understand a company's commitment to funding R&D, users of financial statements often examine trends in a company's R&D expenditures as a percentage of total operating expenses:

R&D % = R&D Costs ÷ Total Operating Expenses

R&D expenditures as a percentage of total operating costs are naturally higher in some industries than in others. To illustrate this point, see the recent R&D figures of well-known companies from four industries in Exhibit 9–7.

Exhibit 9–7

COMPARATIVE R&D EXPENDITURES

	R&D Costs (in millions)	÷	Total Operating Expenses (in millions)	=	R&D%
Chemical Products					
DuPont	$1,617		$26,950		6.0%
Dow Chemical	807		17,055		4.7
Computer Hardware					
Sun Microsystems	1,263		10,205		12.4
Silicon Graphics	301		2,692		11.2
Pharmaceuticals					
Eli Lilly & Co.	1,784		6,758		26.4
Pfizer	2,279		10,950		20.8
Computer Software					
Netscape	123		396		31.1
Microsoft	3,775		12,019		31.4

NATURAL RESOURCES

Accounting for Natural Resources

LO 6 Account for the depletion of natural resources.

Mining properties, oil and gas reserves, and tracts of standing timber are leading examples of natural resources. The distinguishing characteristic of these assets is that they are

---

[10] FASB Statement No. 2, "Accounting for Research and Development Costs" (Norwalk, Conn.: 1974), par. 12.

physically removed from their natural environment and are converted into inventory. Theoretically, a coal mine might be regarded as an underground inventory of coal; however, such an inventory is certainly not a current asset. In the balance sheet, mining property and other natural resources are classified as property, plant, and equipment. Once the coal is removed from the ground, however, this coal *does* represent inventory.

We have explained that plant assets such as buildings and equipment depreciate because of physical deterioration or obsolescence. A mine or an oil reserve does not depreciate for these reasons, but it is gradually *depleted* as the natural resource is removed from the ground. Once all of the coal has been removed from a coal mine, for example, the mine is "fully depleted" and will be abandoned or sold for its residual value.

To illustrate the **depletion** of a natural resource, assume that Rainbow Minerals pays $45 million to acquire the Red Valley Mine, which is believed to contain 10 million tons of coal. The residual value of the mine after all of the coal is removed is estimated to be $5 million. The depletion that will occur over the life of the mine is the original cost minus the residual value, or $40 million. This depletion will occur at the rate of *$4 per ton* ($40 million ÷ 10 million tons) as the coal is removed from the mine. If we assume that 2 million tons are mined during the first year of operations, the entry to record the depletion of the mine would be as follows:

Inventory	8,000,000	
Accumulated Depletion: Red Valley Mine		8,000,000
To record depletion of the Red Valley Mine for the year; 2,000,000 tons mined @ $4 per ton.		

My Notes
Recording depletion

Once removed from the mine, coal becomes merchandise available for sale. Therefore, the estimated cost of this coal is debited to the Inventory account. As the coal is sold, this cost is transferred from the Inventory account to the Cost of Goods Sold account.

Accumulated Depletion is a *contra-asset account* similar to the Accumulated Depreciation account; it represents the portion of the mine that has been used up (depleted) to date. In Rainbow Mineral's balance sheet, the Red Valley Mine now appears as follows:

Property, Plant, & Equipment:		
Mining properties: Red Valley Mine	$45,000,000	
Less: Accumulated depletion	8,000,000	$37,000,000

My Notes
The mine gradually is turned into inventory

Depreciation of Buildings and Equipment Closely Related to Natural Resources Buildings and equipment installed at a mine or drilling site may be useful only at that particular location. Consequently, such assets should be depreciated over their normal useful lives or over the life of the natural resource, *whichever is shorter.* Often depreciation on such assets is computed using the units-of-output method, which is discussed in the *Supplemental Topic* at the end of this chapter.

Depreciation, Amortization, and Depletion—A Common Goal

The processes of depreciation, amortization, and depletion discussed in this chapter all have a common goal. That goal is to *allocate the acquisition cost of a long-lived asset to expense over the years in which the asset contributes to revenue.* Allocating the acquisition cost of long-lived assets over the years that benefit from the use of these assets is an important application of the *matching principle.* The determination of income requires matching revenue with the expenses incurred to produce that revenue.

PLANT TRANSACTIONS AND THE STATEMENT OF CASH FLOWS

LO 7
Explain the cash effects of transactions involving plant assets.

The cash effects of plant and equipment transactions are *very different* from the effects reported in the income statement. Cash payments for plant assets occur when those assets are *purchased*—or, more precisely, when payment is made. Cash receipts often occur when assets are sold. (These receipts are equal to the *total proceeds* received from the sale, not just the amount of any gain.) Cash flows relating to acquisitions and disposals of plant assets appear in the statement of cash flows, classified as *investing activities*.

CASH EFFECTS

Depreciation and amortization expense both *reduce net income,* but they have *no effect on cash flows.* As a result, both tend to make net income *less* than the net cash flows from operating activities. Likewise, the write-down of impaired assets is another example of a **noncash charge or expense** against income having no immediate effect on cash flows.

Noncash Investing Activities Not all purchases and sales of plant assets result in cash payments or cash receipts during the current accounting period. For example, a company may finance the purchase of plant assets by issuing notes payable, or it may sell plant assets in exchange for notes receivable. The noncash aspects of investing and financing activities are summarized in a special schedule that accompanies a statement of cash flows. This schedule will be illustrated and explained in Chapter 13.

CONCLUDING REMARKS

This chapter completes our discussion of accounting for various types of assets. To briefly review, we have seen that cash is reported in the financial statements at its face value, marketable securities at their market value, accounts receivable at their net realizable value (i.e., net amount of cash expected to be collected), inventories at the lower-of-cost-or-market, and plant assets at cost less accumulated depreciation.

Two ideas that have been consistently reflected in each of these valuation bases are the matching principle and conservatism. A major determinant of the amount at which assets are accounted for in the balance sheet is the future amount to be released as an expense into the income statement. Closely related to this is the objective of not overstating the current and future expectations of a company's financial activities by overstating assets and understating current expenses.

In the next chapter we turn our attention to the measurement and presentation of liabilities.

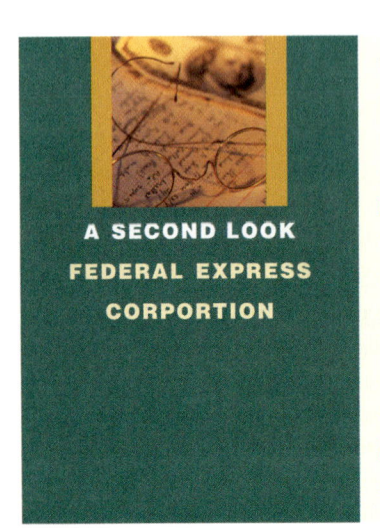

A SECOND LOOK
FEDERAL EXPRESS CORPORTION

We introduced this chapter by considering **Federal Express Corporation** and its major investment in flight equipment, ground equipment, vehicles, and other plant assets required for efficient operations. Not surprising, as **Federal Express** has grown consistently over recent years, its investment in plant assets, including equipment, has also grown. **Federal Express** also lists goodwill in its 2000 balance sheet and the balance is more than $500,000 million. This amount of goodwill resulted from the company purchasing other companies at prices in excess of the book value of the net assets acquired, as explained in this chapter.

Further evidence of the importance of plant assets to **Federal Express** is the large amount of cash paid out to acquire property and equipment, including over $1.6 billion in the year ending May 31, 2000. In short, it is reasonable to conclude that **Federal Express**'s success depends heavily on its ownership and efficient management of plant and intangible assets.

SUPPLEMENTAL TOPIC

OTHER DEPRECIATION METHODS

Most companies that prepare financial statements in conformity with generally accepted accounting principles use the straight-line method of depreciation. However, any rational and systematic method is acceptable, as long as costs are allocated to expense in a reasonable manner. Several such methods are discussed here.

LO 8
Account for depreciation using methods other than straight-line or declining-balance.

The Units-of-Output Method

Under the **units-of-output** method, depreciation is based on some measure of output *rather than* on the passage of time. When depreciation is based on units of output, more depreciation is recognized in the periods in which the assets are most heavily used.

To illustrate this method, consider S&G's delivery truck, which cost $17,000 and has an estimated salvage value of $2,000. Assume that S&G plans to retire this truck after it has been driven 100,000 miles. The depreciation rate *per mile of operation* is *15 cents*, computed as follows:

$$\frac{\text{Cost} - \text{Residual Value}}{\text{Estimated Units of Output (Miles)}} = \text{Cost per Unit of Output (Mile)}$$

$$\frac{\$17,000 - \$2,000}{100,000 \text{ miles}} = \$0.15 \text{ Depreciation per Mile}$$

At the end of each year, the amount of depreciation to be recorded is determined by multiplying the 15-cent rate by the number of miles the truck had been driven during the year. After the truck has gone 100,000 miles, it is fully depreciated, and the depreciation process is stopped.

This method provides an excellent matching of expense with revenue. However, the method should be used only when the total units of output can be estimated with reasonable accuracy. Also, this method is used only for assets such as vehicles and certain types of machinery. Assets such as buildings, computers, and furniture do not have well-defined "units of output."

In many cases, units-of-output is an *accelerated method*. Often assets are used more extensively in the earlier years of their useful lives than in the later years.

MACRS

Most businesses use a depreciation method called **MACRS** (Modified Accelerated Cost Recovery System) in their federal income tax returns. Some small businesses also use this method in their financial statements, so they do not have to compute depreciation in several different ways. MACRS is based on the declining-balance method, but should be considered for use in financial statements only if the *designated "recovery periods"* and the *assumption of no salvage value* are reasonable. For publicly traded companies, the use of MACRS in financial statements is usually not considered to be in conformity with generally accepted accounting principles.

Sum-of-the-Years' Digits

Sum-of-the-years' digits, or **SYD**, is a form of accelerated depreciation. It generally produces results that lie between the double-declining-balance and 150%-declining-balance methods.

SYD is a traditional topic that is included in many accounting textbooks. But it is the most complex of the accelerated methods—especially when partial years are involved. SYD is rarely used in today's business world. As shown in Exhibit 9–8, only 11 of the 600 corporations surveyed—less than 2%—make any use of this method. Because of its complexity, it is even less frequently used in small businesses. SYD is seldom used for income tax purposes, because tax laws usually define allowable depreciation rates in terms of the declining-balance method. For these reasons, we defer coverage of the mechanics of this method to later accounting courses.

Exhibit 9–8

COMPARATIVE USE OF DEPRECIATION METHODS

My Notes

Straight-line is clearly the method most widely used in financial statements

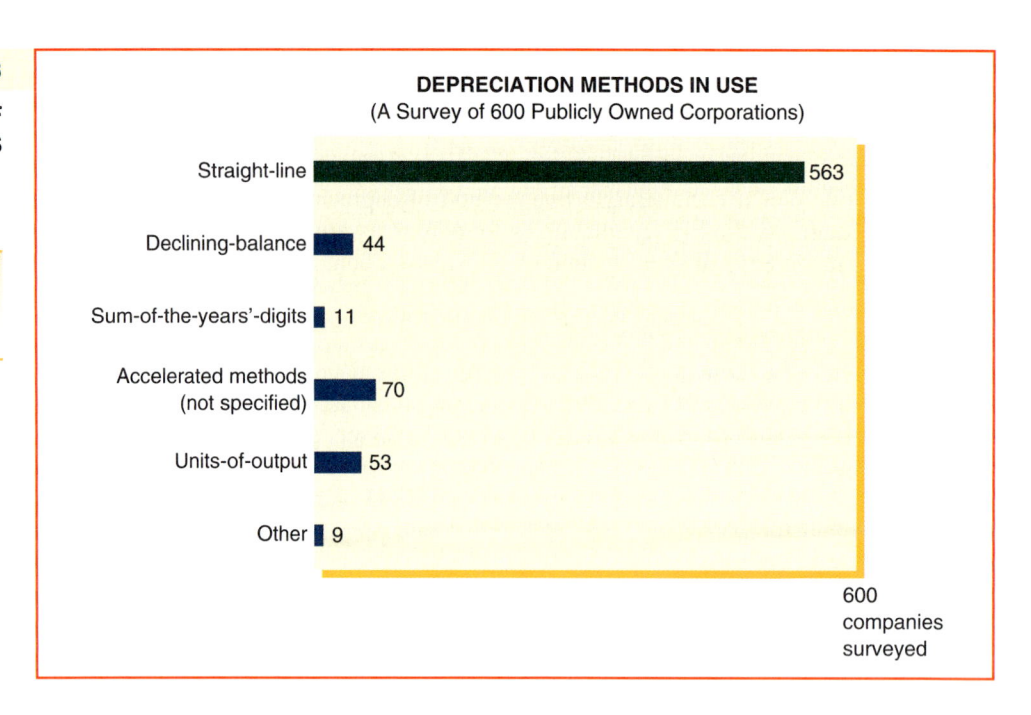

DEPRECIATION METHODS IN USE
(A Survey of 600 Publicly Owned Corporations)

- Straight-line: 563
- Declining-balance: 44
- Sum-of-the-years'-digits: 11
- Accelerated methods (not specified): 70
- Units-of-output: 53
- Other: 9

600 companies surveyed

Decelerated Depreciation Methods

Depreciation methods do exist that recognize *less* depreciation expense in the early years of an asset's useful life and *more in the later years*. Such methods may achieve a reasonable matching of depreciation expense and revenue when the plant asset is expected to become *increasingly productive* over time. Utility companies, for example, may use these methods for new power plants that will be more fully utilized as the population of the area increases.

These depreciation methods are rarely used; thus we defer coverage to later accounting courses.

Depreciation Methods in Use: A Survey

Every year, the American Institute of Certified Public Accountants conducts a survey of 600 publicly owned companies to determine the accounting methods most widely used in financial statements. The various depreciation methods in use during a recent year are summarized in Exhibit 9–8. Notice that the number of methods in use exceeds 600. This is because some companies use different depreciation methods for different types of assets.

Bear in mind this survey indicates only the depreciation methods used in financial statements. In income tax returns, most companies use accelerated depreciation methods such as MACRS.

END-OF-CHAPTER REVIEW

SUMMARY OF LEARNING OBJECTIVES

LO 1
Determine the cost of plant assets.
Plant assets are long-lived assets acquired for use in the business and not for resale to customers. The matching principle requires that we include in the plant and equipment accounts those costs that will provide services over a period of years. During these years, the use of the plant assets contributes to the earning of revenues. The cost of a plant asset includes all expenditures reasonable and necessary in acquiring the asset and placing it in a position and condition for use in the operations of the business.

LO 2
Distinguish between capital expenditures and revenue expenditures.
Capital expenditures include any material expenditure that will benefit several accounting periods. Therefore, these expenditures are charged to asset accounts (capitalized) and are recognized as expense in future periods.

Revenue expenditures are charged directly to expense accounts because either (1) there is no objective evidence of future benefits or (2) the amounts are immaterial.

LO 3
Compute depreciation by the straight-line and declining-balance methods.
Straight-line depreciation assigns an equal portion of an asset's cost to expense in each period of the asset's life. Declining-balance is an accelerated method. Each year, a fixed (and relatively high) depreciation rate is applied to the remaining book value of the asset. There are several variations of declining-balance depreciation.

LO 4
Account for disposals of plant assets.
When plant assets are disposed of, depreciation should be recorded to the date of disposal. The cost is then removed from the asset account and the total recorded depreciation is removed from the accumulated depreciation account. The sale of a plant asset at a price above or below book value results in a gain or loss to be reported in the income statement.

Because different depreciation methods are used for income tax purposes, the gain or loss reported in income tax returns may differ from that shown in the income statement. The gain or loss shown in the financial statement is recorded in the company's general ledger accounts.

LO 5
Explain the nature of intangible assets, including goodwill.
Intangible assets are assets owned by the business that have no physical substance, are noncurrent, and are used in business operations. Examples include trademarks and patents.

Among the most interesting intangible assets is goodwill. Goodwill is the present value of future earnings in excess of a normal return on net identifiable assets. It stems from such factors as a good reputation, loyal customers, and superior management. Any business that earns significantly more than a normal rate of return actually has goodwill. But goodwill is recorded in the accounts only if it is *purchased* by acquiring another business at a price higher than the fair market value of its net identifiable assets.

LO 6
Account for the depletion of natural resources.
Natural resources (or wasting assets) include mines, oil fields, and standing timber. Their cost is converted into inventory as the resource is mined, pumped, or cut. This allocation of the cost of a natural resource to inventories is called depletion. The depletion rate per unit extracted equals the cost of the resource (less residual value) divided by the estimated number of units it contains.

LO 7
Explain the cash effects of transactions involving plant assets.
Depreciation is a noncash expense; cash expenditures for the acquisition of plant assets are independent of the amount of depreciation for the period. Cash payments to acquire plant assets (and cash receipts from disposals) appear in the statement of cash flows, classified as investing activities.

Write-downs of plant assets also are noncash charges, which do not involve cash payments.

*LO 8
Account for depreciation using methods other than straight-line or declining-balance.
Most companies that prepare financial statements in conformity with generally accepted accounting principles use the straight-line method of depreciation (see survey results in Exhibit 9–8). Other accepted methods include the units-of-output method, sum-of-the-years' digits, and in rare circumstances, decelerated depreciation methods.

Supplemental Topic, "Other Depreciation Methods."

KEY TERMS INTRODUCED OR EMPHASIZED IN CHAPTER 9

accelerated depreciation (p. 373) Methods of depreciation that call for recognition of relatively large amounts of depreciation in the early years of an asset's useful life and relatively small amounts in the later years.

amortization (p. 383) The systematic write-off to expense of the cost of an intangible asset over the periods of its economic usefulness.

book value (p. 372) The cost of a plant asset minus the total recorded depreciation, as shown by the Accumulated Depreciation account. The remaining undepreciated cost is also known as *carrying value*.

capital expenditures (p. 370) Costs incurred to acquire a long-lived asset. Expenditures that will benefit several accounting periods.

capitalize (p. 370) A verb with two different meanings in accounting. The first is to debit an expenditure to an asset account, rather than directly to expense. The second is to estimate the value of an investment by dividing the annual return by the investor's required rate of return.

depletion (p. 389) Allocating the cost of a natural resource to the units removed as the resource is mined, pumped, cut, or otherwise consumed.

depreciation (p. 371) The systematic allocation of the cost of an asset to expense over the years of its estimated useful life.

fixed-percentage-of-declining-balance depreciation (p. 376) An accelerated method of depreciation in which the rate is a multiple of the straight-line rate and is applied each year to the undepreciated cost of the asset. The most commonly used rate is double the straight-line rate.

goodwill (p. 383) The present value of expected future earnings of a business in excess of the earnings normally realized in the industry. Recorded when a business entity is purchased at a price in excess of the fair value of its net identifiable assets (excluding goodwill) less liabilities.

half-year convention (p. 375) The practice of taking six months' depreciation in the year of acquisition and in the year of disposition, rather than computing depreciation for partial periods to the nearest month. This method is widely used and is acceptable for both income tax reporting and financial reports, as long as it is applied to all assets of a particular type acquired during the year. The half-year convention generally is not used for buildings.

intangible assets (p. 368) Those assets that are used in the operation of a business but that have no physical substance and are noncurrent.

MACRS (p. 391) The Modified Accelerated Cost Recovery System. The accelerated depreciation method permitted in federal income tax returns for assets acquired after December 31, 1986. Depreciation is based on prescribed recovery periods and depreciation rates.

natural resources (p. 368) Mines, oil fields, standing timber, and similar assets that are physically consumed and converted into inventory.

net identifiable assets (p. 384) Total of all assets, except goodwill, minus liabilities.

noncash charge or expense (p. 390) A charge against earnings—either an expense or a loss—that does not require a cash expenditure at or near the time of recognition. Thus, the charge reduces net income, but does not affect cash flows (except, perhaps, for income tax payments). Examples are depreciation and the write-off of asset values because an asset has become impaired.

plant assets (p. 368) Long-lived assets that are acquired for use in business operations rather than for resale to customers.

present value (p. 384) The amount that a knowledgeable investor would pay today for the right to receive future cash flows. The present value is always less than the sum of the future cash flows because the investor requires a return on the investment.

residual (salvage) value (p. 374) The portion of an asset's cost expected to be recovered through sale or trade-in of the asset at the end of its useful life.

revenue expenditures (p. 370) Expenditures that will benefit only the current accounting period.

straight-line depreciation (p. 373) A method of depreciation that allocates the cost of an asset (minus any residual value) equally to each year of its useful life.

sum-of-the-years' digits (SYD) depreciation (p. 391) A long-established but seldom-used method of accelerated depreciation. Usually produces results that lie in between 200%- and 150%-declining-balance.

tangible plant assets (p. 368) Plant assets that have physical substance but that are not natural resources. Include land, buildings, and all types of equipment.

units-of-output (p. 391) A depreciation method in which cost (minus residual value) is divided by the estimated units of lifetime output. The unit depreciation cost is multiplied by the actual units of output each year to compute the annual depreciation expense.

DEMONSTRATION PROBLEM

On April 1, 2002, Argo Industries purchased new equipment at a cost of $325,000. The useful life of this equipment was estimated at 5 years, with a residual value of $25,000.

Instructions
Compute the annual depreciation expense for each year until this equipment becomes fully depreciated under each depreciation method listed below. Because you will record depreciation for only a fraction of a year in 2002, depreciation will extend through 2007 for both methods. Show supporting computations.
a. Straight-line, with depreciation for fractional years rounded to the nearest whole month.
b. 200% declining-balance, with the half-year convention. Limit depreciation in 2007 to an amount that reduces the undepreciated cost to the estimated residual value.
c. Assume that the equipment is sold at the end of December 2004, for $182,500 cash. Record the necessary gain or loss resulting from the sale under the straight-line method.

Solution to the Demonstration Problem

Expense under Each Method of Depreciation

Year	a Straight-Line	b 200% Declining-Balance
2002	$ 45,000	$ 65,000
2003	60,000	104,000
2004	60,000	62,400
2005	60,000	37,440
2006	60,000	22,464
2007	15,000	8,696
Totals	$300,000	$300,000

c. Entry to record sale of equipment in 2004:

Cash	182,500	
Accumulated Depreciation: Equipment	165,000	
Equipment		325,000
Gain on Sale of Equipment		22,500

Supporting computations:
a. 2002: ($325,000 − $25,000) × 1/5 × 9/12 = $45,000
    2003–2006: $300,000 × 1/5 = $60,000
    2007: $300,000 × 1/5 × 3/12 = $15,000
b.

	Undepreciated Cost	Rate	Depreciation Expense
2002	$325,000	× 40% × 1/2 =	$ 65,000
2003	260,000	× 40% =	104,000
2004	156,000	× 40% =	62,400
2005	93,600	× 40% =	37,440
2006	56,160	× 40% =	22,464
2007	33,696	− $25,000 =	8,696

c. Accumulated depreciation at the end of 2004:

Depreciation expense, 2002	$ 45,000
Depreciation expense, 2003	60,000
Depreciation expense, 2004	60,000
Accumulated depreciation at the end of 2004	$165,000
Original cost of equipment in 2002	$325,000
Less: Accumulated depreciation at the end of 2004	(165,000)
Book value of equipment at time of disposal	$160,000
Cash proceeds from sale	$182,500
Less: Book value of equipment at time of disposal	(160,000)
Gain on sale of disposal	$ 22,500

SELF-TEST QUESTIONS

Answers to these questions appear on page 407.

1. In which of the following situations should the named company *not* record any depreciation expense on the asset described?
   a. Commuter Airline is required by law to maintain its aircraft in "as good as new" condition.
   b. Metro Advertising owns an office building that has been increasing in value each year since it was purchased.
   c. Computer Sales Company has in inventory a new type of computer, designed "never to become obsolete."
   d. None of the above answers is correct—in each case, the named company should record depreciation on the asset described.

2. Which of the following statements is (are) correct?
   a. Accumulated depreciation represents a cash fund being accumulated for the replacement of plant assets.
   b. The cost of a machine includes the cost of repairing damage to the machine during the installation process.
   c. A company may use different depreciation methods in its financial statements and its income tax return.
   d. The use of an accelerated depreciation method causes an asset to wear out more quickly than does use of the straight-line method.

3. On April 1, 2001, Sanders Construction paid $10,000 for equipment with an estimated useful life of 10 years and a residual value of $2,000. The company uses the double-declining-balance method of depreciation and applies the half-year convention to fractional periods. In 2002, the amount of depreciation expense to be recognized on this equipment is:
   a. $1,600   b. $1,440   c. $1,280   d. Some other amount

4. Evergreen Mfg. is a rapidly growing company that acquires more equipment every year. Evergreen uses straight-line depreciation in its financial statements and an accelerated method in its tax returns. Identify all correct statements:
   a. Using straight-line depreciation in the financial statements instead of an accelerated method increases Evergreen's reported net income.
   b. Using straight-line depreciation in the financial statements instead of an accelerated method increases Evergreen's annual net cash flow.
   c. Using an accelerated method instead of straight-line in income tax returns increases Evergreen's net cash flow.
   d. As long as Evergreen keeps growing, it will probably report more depreciation in its income tax returns *each year* than it does in its financial statements.

5. Delta Company sold a plant asset that originally cost $50,000 for $22,000 cash. If Delta correctly reports a $5,000 gain on this sale, the *accumulated depreciation* on the asset at the date of sale must have been:
   a. $33,000   b. $28,000   c. $23,000   d. Some other amount

6. In which of the following situations would Burton Industries include goodwill in its balance sheet?
   a. The fair market value of Burton's net identifiable assets amounts to $2,000,000. Normal earnings for this industry are 15% of net identifiable assets. Burton's net income for the past five years has averaged $390,000.
   b. Burton spent $800,000 during the current year for research and development for a new product that promises to generate substantial revenue for at least 10 years.
   c. Burton acquired Baxter Electronics at a price in excess of the fair market value of Baxter's net identifiable assets.
   d. A buyer wishing to purchase Burton's entire operation has offered a price in excess of the fair market value of Burton's net identifiable assets.

ASSIGNMENT MATERIAL
DISCUSSION QUESTIONS

1. **Coca-Cola**'s distinctive trademark is more valuable to the company than its bottling plants. But the company's bottling plants are listed in the balance sheet, and the famous trademark isn't. Explain.
2. Identify the basic "accountable events" in the life of a depreciable plant asset. Which of these events directly affect the net income of the current period? Which directly affect cash flows (other than income tax payments)?
3. Which of the following characteristics would prevent an item from being included in the balance sheet classification of plant and equipment? (a) Intangible, (b) limited life, (c) unlimited life, (d) held for sale in the regular course of business, (e) not capable of rendering benefits to the business in the future.
4. The following expenditures were incurred in connection with a large new machine acquired by a metals manufacturing company. Identify those that should be included in the cost of the asset. (a) Freight charges, (b) sales tax on the machine, (c) payment to a passing motorist whose car was damaged by the equipment used in unloading the machine, (d) wages of employees for time spent in installing and testing the machine before it was placed in service, (e) wages of employees assigned to lubricate and make minor adjustments to the machine one year after it was placed in service.
5. What is the distinction between a *capital expenditure* and a *revenue expenditure*?
6. If a capital expenditure is erroneously treated as a revenue expenditure, will the net income of the current year be overstated or understated? Will this error have any effect on the net income reported in future years? Explain.
7. Shoppers' Market purchased for $245,000 a site on which it planned to build a new store. The site consisted of three acres of land and included an old house and two barns. County property tax records showed the following appraised values for this property: land, $160,000; buildings, $40,000. Indicate what Shoppers' should do with this $245,000 cost in its financial statements, and explain your reasoning.
8. Which of the following statements best describes the nature of depreciation?
   a. Regular reduction of asset value to correspond to the decline in market value as the asset ages.
   b. A process of correlating the book value of an asset with its gradual decline in physical efficiency.
   c. Allocation of cost in a manner that will ensure that plant and equipment items are not carried on the balance sheet at amounts in excess of net realizable value.
   d. Allocation of the cost of a plant asset to the periods in which benefits are received.
9. Should depreciation continue to be recorded on a building when ample evidence exists that the current market value is greater than original cost and that the rising trend of market values is continuing? Explain.
10. Explain what is meant by an *accelerated* depreciation method. Are accelerated methods more widely used in financial statements or in income tax returns? Explain.
11. One accelerated depreciation method is called *fixed-percentage-of-declining-balance*. Explain what is meant by the terms "fixed-percentage" and "declining-balance." For what purpose is this method most widely used?

12. An accountant for a large corporation said the company computes depreciation on its plant assets by using several different methods. But a note to the company's financial statements says all depreciation is computed by the straight-line method. Explain.

13. Criticize the following quotation: "We shall have no difficulty in paying for new plant assets needed during the coming year because our estimated outlays for new equipment amount to only $80,000, and we have more than twice that amount in our accumulated depreciation account at present."

14. Explain two approaches to computing depreciation for a fractional period in the year in which an asset is purchased. (Neither of your approaches should require the computation of depreciation to the nearest day or week.)

15. a. Does the accounting principle of consistency require a company to use the same method of depreciation for all of its plant assets?
    b. Is it acceptable for a corporation to use different depreciation methods in its financial statements and its income tax returns?

16. After 4 years of using a machine acquired at a cost of $15,000, Miller Construction Company determined that the original estimated life of 10 years had been too short and that a total useful life of 12 years was a more reasonable estimate. Explain briefly the method that should be used to revise the depreciation program, assuming that straight-line depreciation has been used. Assume that the revision is made after recording depreciation and closing the accounts at the end of 4 years of use.

17. Define *intangible assets*. Would an account receivable arising from a sale of merchandise under terms of 2/10, n/30 qualify as an intangible asset under your definition?

18. Over what period of time should the cost of various types of intangible assets be amortized by regular charges against revenue? (Your answer should be in the form of a principle or guideline rather than a specific number of years.) What method of amortization is generally used?

19. Under what circumstances should *goodwill* be recorded in the accounts?

20. In reviewing the financial statements of Digital Products Company with a view to investing in the company's stock, you notice that net tangible assets total $1 million, that goodwill is listed at $400,000, and that average earnings for the past five years have been $50,000 a year. How would these relationships influence your thinking about the company?

21. Mineral World recognizes $20 depletion for each ton of ore mined. During the current year the company mined 600,000 tons but sold only 500,000 tons, as it was attempting to build up inventories in anticipation of a possible strike by employees. How much depletion should be deducted from revenue of the current year?

22. Explain the meaning of an *impairment* of an asset. Provide several examples. What accounting event should occur when an asset has become substantially impaired?

23. Several years ago March Metals purchased for $120,000 a well-known trademark for padlocks and other security products. After using the trademark for three years, March Metals discontinued it altogether when the company withdrew from the lock business and concentrated on the manufacture of aircraft parts. Amortization of the trademark at the rate of $3,000 a year is being continued on the basis of a 20-year life, which the owner of March Metals says is consistent with accounting standards. Do you agree? Explain.

EXERCISES

EXERCISE 9.1

You as a Student

LO 2, 3

Assume that you recently applied for a student loan to go to graduate school. As part of the application process, your bank requested a list of your assets. Aside from an extensive CD collection, your only other asset is a pickup truck. You purchased the truck six years ago for $15,000. Its current fair market value is approximately $5,000.

a. What factors caused your pickup truck to depreciate $10,000 in value?

b. Assume that the bank is willing to lend you money for graduate school. Even with the loan, however, you still need to raise an additional $5,000. Do you think that the bank will lend you $5,000 more for graduate school if you agree to use your truck as collateral? Explain.

EXERCISE 9.2
Distinguishing Capital Expenditures from Revenue Expenditures

LO 1, 2

c. Assume that the truck has been used solely in a delivery service business that you operated while in college. Would your balance sheet necessarily show $10,000 in accumulated depreciation related to the truck? Explain.

Identify the following expenditures as capital expenditures or revenue expenditures:

a. Immediately after acquiring a new delivery truck, paid $225 to have the name of the store and other advertising material painted on the vehicle.
b. Painted delivery truck at a cost of $250 after 2 years of use.
c. Purchased new battery at a cost of $40 for 2-year-old delivery truck.
d. Installed an escalator at a cost of $12,500 in a three-story building that had been used for some years without elevators or escalators.
e. Purchased a pencil sharpener at a cost of $8.50.
f. Original life of the delivery truck had been estimated at 4 years and straight-line depreciation of 25% yearly had been recognized. After 3 years' use, however, it was decided to recondition the truck thoroughly, including adding a new engine.

EXERCISE 9.3
Depreciation for Fractional Years

LO 3

On August 3, Srini Construction purchased special-purpose equipment at a cost of $1,000,000. The useful life of the equipment was estimated to be 8 years, with a residual value of $50,000.

a. Compute the depreciation expense to be recognized each calendar year for financial reporting purposes under the straight-line depreciation method (half-year convention).
b. Compute the depreciation expense to be recognized each calendar year for financial reporting purposes under the 200% declining-balance method (half-year convention).
c. Which of these two depreciation methods (straight-line or double-declining-balance) results in the highest net income for financial reporting purposes during the first two years of the equipment's use? Explain.

EXERCISE 9.4
Depreciation Methods

LO 3

On January 2, 2002, Jansing Corporation acquired a new machine with an estimated useful life of 5 years. The cost of the equipment was $40,000 with a residual value of $5,000.

a. Prepare a complete depreciation table under the three depreciation methods listed below. Use a format similar to the illustrations in Exhibits 9–4, 9–5, and 9–6. In each case, assume that a full year of depreciation was taken in 2002.
  1. Straight-line.
  2. 200% declining-balance.
  3. 150% declining-balance.
b. Comment on significant differences or similarities that you observe among the patterns of depreciation expense recognized under each of these methods.

EXERCISE 9.5
Evaluation of Disclosures in Annual Reports

LO 3

A recent annual report of **H. J. Heinz Company** includes the following note:

Depreciation: For financial reporting purposes, depreciation is provided on the straight-line method over the estimated useful lives of the assets. Accelerated depreciation methods generally are used for income tax purposes.

a. Is the company violating the accounting principle of consistency by using different depreciation methods in its financial statements than in its income tax returns? Explain.
b. *Why* do you think that the company uses accelerated depreciation methods in its income tax returns?
c. Would the use of accelerated depreciation in the financial statements be more conservative or less conservative than the current practice of using the straight-line method? Explain.

EXERCISE 9.6
Revision of Depreciation Estimates

LO 3

Swindall Industries uses straight-line depreciation on all of its depreciable assets. The company records annual depreciation expense at the end of each calendar year. On January 11, 2002, the company purchased a machine costing $90,000. The machine's useful life was estimated to be 12 years with a residual value of $18,000. Depreciation for partial years is recorded to the nearest full month.

In 2006, after almost 5 years of experience with the machine, management decided to revise its estimated life from 12 years to 20 years. No change was made in the estimated residual value. The revised estimate of the useful life was decided *prior* to recording annual depreciation expense for the year ended December 31, 2006.

a. Prepare journal entries in chronological order for the above events, beginning with the purchase of the machinery on January 11, 2002. Show separately the recording of depreciation expense in 2002 through 2006.

b. What factors may have caused the company to revise its estimate of the machine's useful life?

EXERCISE 9.7
Accounting for Trade-ins
LO 4

Wilford Bus Service traded in a used bus for a new one. The original cost of the old bus was $52,000. Accumulated depreciation at the time of the trade-in amounted to $34,000. The new bus costs $65,000 but Wilford was given a trade-in allowance of $10,000.

a. What amount of cash must Wilford pay to acquire the new bus?

b. Compute the gain or loss on the disposal for financial reporting purposes.

c. Explain how the gain or loss would be reported in the company's income statement.

EXERCISE 9.8
Estimating Goodwill
LO 5

During the past several years the annual net income of Goldtone Appliance Company has averaged $540,000. At the present time the company is being offered for sale. Its accounting records show the book value of net assets (total assets minus all liabilities) to be $2,800,000. The fair market value of Goldtone's net identifiable assets, however, is $3,000,000.

An investor negotiating to buy the company offers to pay an amount equal to the fair market value for the net identifiable assets and to assume all liabilities. In addition, the investor is willing to pay for goodwill an amount equal to the above-average earnings for five years.

On the basis of this agreement, what price should the investor offer for Goldtone Appliance? A normal return on the fair value of net assets in this industry is 15%.

EXERCISE 9.9
The Write-Down of Impaired Assets
LO 4, 7

For several years, a number of **Food Lion, Inc.**, grocery stores were unprofitable. The company closed, and continues to close, some of these locations. It is apparent that the company will not be able to recover the cost of the assets associated with the closed stores. Thus, the current value of these impaired assets must be written down (see the Case in Point on page 380).

A recent **Food Lion** income statement reports a $9.5 million charge against income pertaining to the write-down of impaired assets.

a. Explain why **Food Lion** must write down the current carrying value of its unprofitable stores.

b. Explain why the recent $9.5 million charge to write down these impaired assets is considered a noncash expense.

EXERCISE 9.10
Ethics: "Let the Buyer Beware"
LO 1, 5

Bill Gladstone has owned and operated Gladstone's Service Station for over 30 years. The business, which is currently the town's only service station, has always been extremely profitable. Gladstone recently decided that he wanted to sell the business and retire. His asking price exceeds the fair market value of its net identifiable assets by nearly $50,000. Gladstone attributes this premium to the above-normal returns that the service station has always generated.

Gladstone recently found out about two issues that could have a profound effect upon the future of the business: (1) A well-known service station franchise will be built across the street from his station in approximately 18 months, and (2) one of his underground fuel tanks *may* have developed a very slow leak.

a. How might these issues affect the $50,000 in goodwill that Gladstone included in his selling price?

b. Assume that Gladstone is *not* disclosing this information to potential buyers. Does he have an ethical obligation to do so? Defend your answer.

EXERCISE 9.11
Depletion of Natural Resources
LO 6

Salter Mining Company purchased the Northern Tier Mine for $21 million cash. The mine was estimated to contain 2.5 million tons of ore and to have a residual value of $1 million.

During the first year of mining operations at the Northern Tier Mine, 50,000 tons of ore were mined, of which 40,000 tons were sold.

a. Prepare a journal entry to record depletion during the year.

b. Show how the Northern Tier Mine, and its accumulated depletion, would appear in Salter Mining Company's balance sheet after the first year of operations.

c. Will the entire amount of depletion computed in part **a** be deducted from revenue in the determination of income for the year? Explain.

d. Indicate how the journal entry in part **a** affects the company's current ratio (its current assets divided by its current liabilities). Do you believe that the activities summarized in this entry do, in fact, make the company any more or less liquid? Explain.

EXERCISE 9.12
Researching a Real Company

LO 5, 7

Locate an annual report in your library (or some other source) that includes a large gain or loss on the disposal of fixed assets. Report to the class the amount of the gain or loss and where in the company's income statement it is reported. Describe how the gain or loss is reported in the company's statement of cash flows. Summarize any discussion in the footnotes concerning the cause of the disposal.

*EXERCISE 9.13
Units-of-Output Method

LO 8

During the current year, Airport Auto Rentals purchased 60 new automobiles at a cost of $13,000 per car. The cars will be sold to a wholesaler at an estimated $5,000 each as soon as they have been driven 50,000 miles. Airport Auto Rentals computes depreciation expense on its automobiles by the units-of-output method, based on mileage.

a. Compute the amount of depreciation to be recognized for each mile that a rental automobile is driven.

b. Assuming that the 60 rental cars are driven a total of 1,670,000 miles during the current year, compute the total amount of depreciation expense that Airport Auto Rentals should recognize on this fleet of cars for the year.

c. In this particular situation, do you believe the units-of-output depreciation method achieves a better matching of expenses with revenue than would the straight-line method? Explain.

EXERCISE 9.14
Using an Annual Report to Determine Depreciation Methods Used

LO 1, 3

The annual report of **Tootsie Roll Industries, Inc.**, appears in Appendix A at the end of this textbook. Use this annual report to answer the following questions:

a. What method of computing depreciation expense does the company use for financial reporting purposes?

b. What method of computing depreciation expense does the company use for federal income tax purposes?

c. The company's income statement reports amortization of intangible assets. What types of intangible assets would you guess require amortization?

PROBLEMS

PROBLEM 9.1
Determining the Cost of Plant Assets

LO 1, 2, 3

Prescott College recently purchased new computing equipment for its library. The following information refers to the purchase and installation of this equipment:

1. The list price of the equipment was $275,000; however, Prescott College qualified for an "education discount" of $25,000. It paid $50,000 cash for the equipment, and issued a 3-month, 9% note payable for the remaining balance. The note, plus accrued interest charges of $4,500, was paid promptly at the maturity date.

2. In addition to the amounts described in **1**, Prescott paid sales taxes of $15,000 at the date of purchase.

3. Freight charges for delivery of the equipment totaled $1,000.

4. Installation costs related to the equipment amounted to $5,000.

5. During installation, one of the computer terminals was accidentally damaged by a library employee. It cost the college $500 to repair this damage.

6. As soon as the computers were installed, the college paid $4,000 to print admissions brochures featuring the library's new, state-of-the-art computing facilities.

Instructions

a. In one sentence, make a general statement summarizing the nature of expenditures that qualify for inclusion in the cost of plant assets such as computing equipment.

b. For each of the six numbered paragraphs, indicate which items should be included by Prescott College in the total cost debited to its Computing Equipment account. Also briefly indicate the proper accounting treatment of those items that *are not* included in the cost of the equipment.

Supplemental Topic, "Other Depreciation Methods."

c. Compute the total cost debited to the college's Computing Equipment account.
d. Prepare a journal entry at the end of the current year to record depreciation on the computing equipment. Prescott College will depreciate this equipment by the straight-line method (half-year convention) over an estimated useful life of 5 years. Assume a zero residual value.

PROBLEM 9.2

Comparison of Straight-Line and Accelerated Methods

LO 3, 4

Martin & Hiller, Inc., purchased a new machine on September 1, 2002, at a cost of $108,000. The machine's estimated useful life at the time of the purchase was 5 years, and its residual value was $8,000.

Instructions

a. Prepare a complete depreciation schedule, beginning with calendar year 2002, under each of the methods listed below (assume that the half-year convention is used):
   1. Straight-line.
   2. 200% declining-balance.
   3. 150% declining-balance.
b. Which of the three methods computed in part **a** is most common for financial reporting purposes? Explain.
c. Assume that Martin & Hiller sells the machine on December 31, 2005, for $28,000 cash. Compute the resulting gain or loss from this sale under each of the depreciation methods used in part **a**. Does the gain or loss reported in the company's income statement have any direct cash effects? Explain.

PROBLEM 9.3

Issues Involving Alternative Depreciation Methods

LO 1–4

Smart Hardware purchased new shelving for its store on April 1, 2002: The shelving is expected to have a 20-year life and no residual value. The following expenditures were associated with the purchase:

Cost of the shelving	$12,000
Freight charges	520
Sales taxes	780
Installation of shelving	2,700
Cost to repair shelf damaged during installation	400

Instructions

a. Compute depreciation expense for the years 2002 through 2005 under each depreciation method listed below:
   1. Straight-line, with fractional years rounded to the nearest whole month.
   2. 200% declining-balance, using the half-year convention.
   3. 150% declining-balance, using the half-year convention.
b. Smart Hardware has two conflicting objectives. Management wants to report the highest possible earnings in its financial statements, yet it also wants to minimize its taxable income reported to the IRS. Explain how both of these objectives can be met.
c. Which of the depreciation methods applied in part **a** resulted in the lowest reported book value at the end of 2005? Is book value an estimate of an asset's fair market value? Explain.
d. Assume that Smart Hardware sold the old shelving that was being replaced. The old shelving had originally cost $9,000. Its book value at the time of the sale was $400. Record the sale of the old shelving under the following conditions:
   1. The shelving was sold for $1,200 cash.
   2. The shelving was sold for $200 cash.

PROBLEM 9.4

Disposal of Plant Assets

LO 4

During the current year, Escola Developers disposed of plant assets in the following transactions:

Feb. 10 Office equipment costing $26,000 was given to a scrap dealer at no charge. At the date of disposal, accumulated depreciation on the office equipment amounted to $25,800.

Apr. 1 Escola sold land and a building to Claypool Associates for $900,000, receiving $100,000 cash and a 5-year, 9% note receivable for the remaining balance. Escola's records showed the following amounts: Land, $50,000; Building, $550,000; Accumulated Depreciation: Building (at the date of disposal), $250,000.

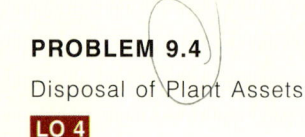

Aug. 15 Escola traded in an old truck for a new one. The old truck had cost $26,000, and its accumulated depreciation amounted to $18,000. The list price of the new truck was $39,000, but Escola received a $10,000 trade-in allowance for the old truck and paid only $29,000 in cash. Escola includes trucks in its Vehicles account.

Oct. 1 Escola traded in its old computer system as part of the purchase of a new system. The old system had cost $15,000, and its accumulated depreciation amounted to $11,000. The new computer's list price was $8,000. Escola accepted a trade-in allowance of $500 for the old computer system, paying $1,500 down in cash, and issuing a 1-year, 8% note payable for the $6,000 balance owed.

Instructions

a. Prepare journal entries to record each of the disposal transactions. Assume that depreciation expense on each asset has been recorded up to the date of disposal. Thus, you need not update the accumulated depreciation figures stated in the problem.

b. Will the gains and losses recorded in part **a** above affect the *gross profit* reported in Escola's income statement? Explain.

c. Explain how the financial reporting of gains and losses on plant assets differs from the financial reporting of *unrealized* gains and losses on marketable securities discussed in Chapter 7.

PROBLEM 9.5
Accounting for Intangible Assets under GAAP
LO 5

During the current year, White Corporation incurred the following expenditures which should be recorded either as operating expenses or as intangible assets:

a. Expenditures were made for the training of new employees. The average employee remains with the company for five years, but is trained for a new position every two years.

b. White purchased a controlling interest in a vinyl flooring company. The expenditure resulted in the recording of a significant amount of goodwill. White expects to earn above average returns on this investment indefinitely.

c. White incurred large amounts of research and development costs in developing a dirt-resistant carpet fiber. The company expects that the fiber will be patented and that sales of the resulting products will contribute to revenue for at least 20 years. The legal life of the patent, however, will be only 17 years.

d. White made an expenditure to acquire the patent on a popular carpet cleaner. The patent had a remaining legal life of 14 years, but White expects to produce and sell the product for only 6 more years.

e. White spent a large amount to sponsor the televising of the Olympic Games. White's intent was to make television viewers more aware of the company's name and its product lines.

Instructions

Explain whether each of the above expenditures should be recorded as an operating expense or an intangible asset. If you view the expenditure as an intangible asset, indicate the number of years over which the asset should be amortized, if any. Explain your reasoning.

PROBLEM 9.6
Accounting for Goodwill
LO 5

Kivi Service Stations is considering expanding its operations to include the greater Dubuque area. Rather than build new service stations in the Dubuque area, management plans to acquire existing service stations and convert them into Kivi outlets.

Kivi is evaluating two similar acquisition opportunities. Information relating to each of these service stations is presented below:

	Phil's Garage	Gas N' Go
Estimated normal rate of return on net assets	20%	20%
Fair market value of net identifiable assets	$950,000	$980,000
Actual average net income for past five years	250,000	260,000

Instructions

a. Compute an estimated fair value for any goodwill associated with Kivi purchasing Phil's Garage. Base your computation upon an assumption that successful service stations typically sell at about 9.25 times their annual earnings.

b. Compute an estimated fair value for any goodwill associated with Kivi purchasing Gas N' Go. Base your computation upon an assumption that Kivi's management expects excess earnings to continue for four years.

c. Many of Kivi's existing service stations are extremely profitable. If Kivi acquires Phil's Garage or Gas N' Go, should it also record the goodwill associated with its existing locations? Explain.

CASES AND UNSTRUCTURED PROBLEMS

CASE 9.1

Are Useful Lives "Flexible"?

LO 3

Robert Lynch is the controller of Print Technologies, a publicly owned company. The company is experiencing financial difficulties and is aggressively looking for ways to cut costs.

Suzanne Bedell, the CEO, instructs Lynch to lengthen from 5 to 10 years the useful life used in computing depreciation on certain special-purpose machinery. Bedell believes that this change represents a substantial cost savings, as it will reduce the depreciation expense on these assets by nearly one-half.

Note: The proposed change affects only the depreciation expense recognized in financial statements. Depreciation deductions in income tax returns will not be affected.

Instructions

a. Discuss the extent to which Bedell's idea will, in fact, achieve a cost savings. Consider the effects on both net income and cash flows.

b. Who is responsible for estimating the useful lives of plant assets?

c. Discuss any ethical issues that Lynch should consider with respect to Bedell's instructions.

CASE 9.2

Departures from GAAP—Are They Ethical?

LO 1

Martin Cole owns Delta Construction Co. The company maintains accounting records for the purposes of exercising control over its construction activities and meeting its reporting obligations regarding payrolls and income tax returns. As it has no other financial reporting obligations, Delta does not prepare formal financial statements.

The company owns land and several other assets with current market values well in excess of their historical costs. Cole directs the company's accountant, Maureen O'Shaughnessey, to prepare a balance sheet in which assets are shown at estimated market values. Cole says this type of balance sheet will give him a better understanding of where the business stands. He also thinks it will be useful in obtaining bank loans, as loan applications always ask for the estimated market values of real estate owned.

Instructions

a. Would the financial statements requested by Cole be in conformity with generally accepted accounting principles?

b. Is Delta Construction under any legal or ethical obligation to prepare financial statements that *do* conform to generally accepted accounting principles?

c. Discuss any ethical issues that O'Shaughnessey should consider with respect to Cole's request.

*CASE 9.3

Depreciation Policies in Annual Reports

LO 3, 8

The following is a note accompanying a recent financial statement of **International Paper Company**:

Plant, Properties, and Equipment

Plant, properties, and equipment are stated at cost less accumulated depreciation.

For financial reporting purposes, the company uses the units-of-production method of depreciating its major pulp and paper mills and certain wood products facilities, and the straight-line method for other plants and equipment.

---

*Supplemental Topic, "Other Depreciation Methods."

Annual straight-line depreciation rates for financial reporting purposes are as follows: buildings $2\frac{1}{2}$% to 8%; machinery and equipment 5% to 33%; woods equipment 10% to 16%. For tax purposes, depreciation is computed utilizing accelerated methods.

Instructions

a. Are the depreciation methods used in the company's financial statements determined by current income tax laws? If not, who is responsible for selecting these methods? Explain.

b. Does the company violate the consistency principle by using different depreciation methods for its paper mills and wood products facilities than it uses for its other plant and equipment? If not, what does the principle of consistency mean? Explain.

c. What is the estimated useful life of the machinery and equipment being depreciated with a straight-line depreciation rate of:
   1. 5%
   2. 33% (round to the nearest year)

   Who determines the useful lives over which specific assets are to be depreciated?

d. Why do you think the company uses accelerated depreciation methods for income tax purposes, rather than using the straight-line method?

BUSINESS WEEK ASSIGNMENT

CASE 9.4

Accounting for Intangibles

LO 2, 5

Neil Gross claims that the value of companies has been shifting from tangible assets—the bricks and mortar—to intangible assets, such as patents, customer lists, and brands. His article, "Valuing 'Intangibles' Is a Tough Job, but It Has to Be Done," in the August 6, 2001, issue of *Business Week,* also claims that intangibles are the keys to shareholder value in today's economy where so much value is placed on knowledge, but that accounting systems do little to acknowledge them. Gross complains that these intangibles don't appear on the balance sheet except in rare cases.

In response to concerns about the lack of information about intangibles in financial statements, the FASB has taken the issue under consideration. FASB research director Timothy S. Lucas is quoted in Gross's article as saying "there are very significant measurement and definition problems."

Instructions

Choose two other students to form a group of three (or let the instructor assign you) and prepare a one-page paper that argues in favor (or against) valuing brands (or internally generated goodwill) and classifying either as an asset on the balance sheet.

INTERNET ASSIGNMENT

INTERNET 9.1

R&D in the Pharmaceutical Industry

LO 2

The pharmaceutical industry spends billions of dollars each year on research and development. Rather than capitalize these R&D expenditures as intangible assets, companies are required to charge them to expense in the year incurred.

Perform a keyword search of Pharmaceutical Companies using the following search engine:

www.yahoo.com

Your search will result in a list of companies that research and develop pharmaceutical products. Select five of these companies and obtain their 10-K reports (using EDGAR) at the following Internet address:

www.sec.gov

Instructions

a. For each of the companies you selected, determine:
   1. Total R&D expense for the most current year.
   2. Total R&D expense as a percentage of total operating costs and expenses.
   3. Total R&D expense as a percentage of net sales.
   4. The percentage by which operating income would have increased had the entire R&D expenditure been recorded as an intangible asset instead of being charged to expense.

b. Using information from the 10-K reports, summarize briefly the kinds of drugs being researched and developed by each of these companies. To a potential investor, which company appears to be the most innovative and promising? Explain.

Internet sites are time and date sensitive. It is the purpose of these exercises to have you explore the Internet. You may need to use the Yahoo! search engine **http://www.yahoo.com** *(or another favorite search engine) to find a company's current Web address.*

OUR COMMENTS ON THE "YOUR TURN" CASES

You as the New Facility Manager for Exercise-for-Health (p. 370) Your ability to earn profits 10% over the budgeted amount will be impacted by the amount of the charge for depreciation on the building. The amount of depreciation each year will depend on the dollar amount recorded for the building asset. Thus, if you ask the bookkeeper to correct the building account, it may make it more difficult to achieve your bonus.

However, it is your ethical responsibility to inform Exercise-for-Health's management about the error in the appraisal. Management will respect your integrity. Your reputation for honesty and ethical behavior will be enhanced.

You as a Business Owner (p. 375) Several factors may influence the useful life and residual value of a truck. These factors may include (1) the miles the truck will be driven each year, (2) the amount of maintenance it receives, (3) road conditions, (4) the climate in which it is driven, and (5) new technologies that make new trucks more fuel efficient and/or powerful.

To the extent that the company can prevent excessive physical deterioration and obsolescence from occurring, estimates of the truck's useful life and residual value will increase. A prolonged life and high residual value will reduce depreciation expense reported by the company each year. If, on the other hand, the truck is expected to undergo excessive abuse or become obsolete, estimates of its useful life and residual value will decrease. This, in turn, will increase the amount of depreciation expense reported by the company each year.

You as a Business Consultant (p. 379) As shown, using the accelerated method requires higher charges to depreciation expense and, therefore, results in a lower reported net income than the straight-line method. Of course, the manner in which depreciation is computed has no *real effect* on a company's profitability or financial position. However, because this business intends to go public within five years, management may want the company to appear as profitable as generally accepted accounting principles will allow.

You as a Franchise Owner (p. 387) You should not help. You have every right to expect the audit to be completed by a competent auditor. As a licensed CPA Bob Jones is expected to discharge professional responsibilities with competence and diligence. The AICPA Code of Professional Conduct states that CPAs are expected to use due care in executing their engagements. In particular, due care requires members to plan and supervise adequately any professional activity for which they are responsible.

You could phone Bob Jones and explain that you expect him, as a CPA, to comply with the profession's code of conduct by making sure to adequately staff and supervise a professional activity for which he is responsible. If Jones continues to refuse to be cooperative, he could be reported to the state society of CPAs, which will advise you of your rights and Jones of his responsibilities. If you are not satisfied with the response you receive from Jones, you may want to consider engaging a different CPA.

ANSWERS TO SELF-TEST QUESTIONS

1. c (Depreciation is not recorded on inventory.) **2.** c **3.** d $1,800, computed 20% [$10,000 − ($10,000 × 20% × $1/2$)] **4.** a, c, d **5.** a ($22,000 selling price − $17,000 book value = $5,000 gain; $50,000 cost − $17,000 book value = $33,000 accumulated depreciation) **6.** c

CHAPTER 10
LIABILITIES

Learning Objectives

After studying this chapter, you should be able to:

1. Define *liabilities* and distinguish between current and long-term liabilities.
2. Account for notes payable and interest expense.
3. Describe the costs relating to payrolls.
4. Prepare an amortization table allocating payments between interest and principal.
5. Describe corporate bonds and explain the tax advantage of debt financing.
6. Account for bonds issued at a discount or premium.
7. Explain the concept of present value as it relates to bond prices.
8. Explain how estimated liabilities, loss contingencies, and commitments are disclosed in financial statements.
9. Evaluate the safety of creditors' claims.
*10. Describe reporting issues related to leases, postretirement benefits, and deferred taxes.

Supplemental Topic, "Special Types of Liabilities."

Courtesy DuPont

DuPont

Buying items on credit has never been easier. Each day, large retailers and credit card companies seem to encourage consumers to go deeper and deeper into debt. Add to credit card debt other long-term obligations—such as home mortgages and automobile loans—and it's no wonder that payments on total household debt consume nearly 98% of total disposable income in the United States.

Large corporations also have jumped on the bandwagon in recent years by issuing more debt than ever to finance expansion and acquisitions. The tremendous debt service costs associated with corporate borrowing can siphon away a significant portion of a company's operating cash flows.

Consider, for example, **E. I. duPont de Nemours & Co.** In a recent balance sheet, **DuPont** reports total liabilities of $27 billion in comparison to total stockholders' equity of only $13 billion. The company's disproportionate reliance on debt financing burdens the company with billions of dollars in debt service costs annually. Notes accompanying **DuPont**'s recent financial statements reveal management's intent to reduce current debt levels to improve the company's overall financial flexibility. Other major corporations are likely to do the same.

• • •

Creditors and investors evaluate carefully the liabilities appearing in financial reports. Thoroughly understanding short-term versus long-term debt is important for managers choosing how to finance their businesses. This chapter provides a basic understanding of concepts related to liabilities as well as describing how liabilities are recorded and later presented in the financial statements. In addition, the impact of debt on various financial ratios is illustrated.

The Nature of Liabilities

LO 1
Define *liabilities* and distinguish between current and long-term liabilities.

Liabilities may be defined as *debts or obligations arising from past transactions or events* that require settlement at a future date. All liabilities have certain characteristics in common; however, the specific terms of different liabilities, and the rights of the creditors, vary greatly.

Distinction between Debt and Equity Businesses have two basic sources of financing: liabilities and owners' equity. Liabilities differ from owners' equity in several respects. The feature that most clearly distinguishes the claims of creditors from owners' equity is that all liabilities eventually *mature*—that is, they come due. Owners' equity does not mature. The date on which a liability comes due is called the **maturity date**.[1]

Although all liabilities mature, their maturity dates vary. Some liabilities are so short in term that they are paid before the financial statements are prepared. Long-term liabilities, in contrast, may not mature for many years. The maturity dates of key liabilities may be a critical factor in the solvency of a business.

The providers of borrowed capital are *creditors* of the business, not owners. As creditors, they have financial claims against the business but usually do *not* have the right to control business operations. The traditional roles of owners, managers, and creditors may be modified, however, in an *indenture contract*. Creditors sometimes insist on being granted some control over business operations as a condition of making a loan, particularly if the business is in poor financial condition. Indenture contracts may impose such restrictions as limits on management salaries and on dividends, and may require the creditor's approval for additional borrowing or for large capital expenditures.

The claims of creditors have *legal priority* over the claims of owners. If a business ceases operations and liquidates, creditors must be *paid in full* before any distributions are made to the owners. The relative security of creditors' claims, however, can vary among the creditors. Sometimes the borrower pledges title to specific assets as **collateral** for a loan. If the borrower defaults on a secured loan, the creditor may foreclose on the pledged assets. Assets that have been pledged as security for loans should be identified in notes accompanying the borrower's financial statements.

Liabilities that are not secured by specific assets are termed *general credit obligations.* The priorities of general credit obligations vary with the nature of the liability and the terms of indenture contracts.

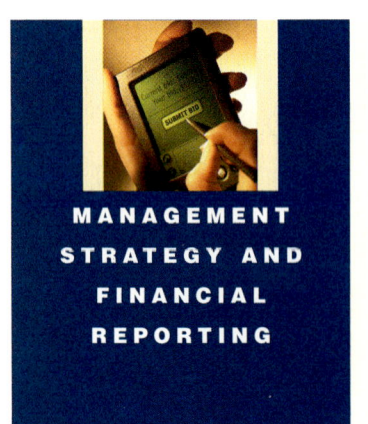

MANAGEMENT STRATEGY AND FINANCIAL REPORTING

Management strategy can be significantly affected by debt agreements linked to financial accounting numbers. Contracts for both public debt and private debt include covenants that use numbers from the published audited financial statements to restrict management's actions. Any breach of those covenants is considered a default, providing the lender with the right to take action. Covenants can include restrictions on the amount of additional borrowing, issuance of dividends, merger activity, and/or restrictions on the disposition of assets.

For example, notes accompanying recent financial statements of **Safeway, Inc.**, state:

Restrictive covenants of the bank credit agreement limit Safeway with respect to, among other things, creating liens upon its assets and disposing of material amounts of assets other than in the ordinary course of business. Safeway is also required to meet certain financial tests under the bank credit agreement.

---

[1] Some liabilities are *due on demand,* which means that the liability is payable upon the creditor's request. From a bank's point of view, customers' checking accounts are "demand liabilities." Liabilities due on demand may come due at any time and are classified as current liabilities.

Current Liabilities

Many Liabilities Bear Interest Many long-term liabilities, and some short-term ones, require the borrower to pay interest. Only interest accrued *as of the balance sheet date* appears as a liability in the borrower's balance sheet. The borrower's obligation to pay interest in *future* periods sometimes is disclosed in the notes to the financial statements, but it is not shown as an existing liability.

Estimated Liabilities Most liabilities are for a definite dollar amount, clearly stated by contract. Examples include notes payable, accounts payable, and accrued expenses, such as interest payable and salaries payable. In some cases, however, the dollar amount of a liability must be *estimated* at the balance sheet date.

Estimated liabilities have two basic characteristics: The liability is *known to exist,* and the precise dollar amount cannot be determined until a later date. For instance, the automobiles sold by most automakers are accompanied by a warranty obligating the automaker to replace defective parts for a period of several years. As each car is sold, the automaker *incurs a liability* to perform any work that may be required under the warranty. The dollar amount of this liability, however, can only be estimated.

CURRENT LIABILITIES

Current liabilities are obligations that must be paid within one year or within the operating cycle, whichever is longer. Another requirement for classification as a current liability is the expectation that the debt will be paid from current assets (or through the rendering of services). Liabilities that do not meet these conditions are classified as long-term liabilities.

The time period used in defining current liabilities parallels that used in defining current assets. The amount of *working capital* (current assets less current liabilities) and the *current ratio* (current assets divided by current liabilities) are valuable indicators of a company's ability to pay its debts in the near future.

Among the most common examples of current liabilities are accounts payable, short-term notes payable, the current portion of long-term debt, accrued liabilities (such as interest payable, income taxes payable, and payroll liabilities), and unearned revenue.

Accounts Payable

Accounts payable often are subdivided into the categories of *trade* accounts payable and *other* accounts payable. Trade accounts payable are short-term obligations to suppliers for purchases of merchandise. Other accounts payable include liabilities for any goods and services other than merchandise.

Technically, the date at which a trade account payable comes into existence depends on whether goods are purchased F.O.B. (free on board) shipping point or F.O.B. destination. Under F.O.B. shipping point, a liability arises and title to the goods transfers when the merchandise is *shipped* by the supplier. Under F.O.B. destination, a liability does not arise and title of ownership does not transfer until the goods are actually *received* by the buyer. However, unless *material* amounts of merchandise are purchased on terms F.O.B. shipping point, most companies follow the convenient practice of recording trade accounts payable when merchandise is received.

© Deborah David/PhotoEdit

Notes Payable

Notes payable are issued whenever bank loans are obtained. Other transactions that may give rise to notes payable include the purchase of real estate or costly equipment, the purchase of merchandise, and the substitution of a note for a past-due account payable.

Notes payable usually require the borrower to pay an interest charge. Normally, the interest rate is stated separately from the principal amount of the note.[2]

LO 2

Account for notes payable and interest expense.

---

[2] An alternative is to include the interest charges in the face amount of the note. This form of note is seldom used today, largely because of the disclosure requirements under "truth-in-lending" laws.

To illustrate, assume that on November 1, Porter Company borrows $10,000 from its bank for a period of six months at an annual interest rate of 12%. Six months later on May 1, Porter Company will have to pay the bank the principal amount of $10,000, plus $600 interest ($10,000 × .12 × $^6/_{12}$). As evidence of this loan, the bank will require Porter Company to issue a note payable similar to the one in Exhibit 10–1.

Exhibit 10–1

A NOTE PAYABLE

```
         Miami, Florida                                    November 1, 20__

         Six months           AFTER THIS DATE              Porter Company

    PROMISES TO PAY TO SECURITY NATIONAL BANK THE SUM OF $  $10,000

    WITH INTEREST AT THE RATE OF          12%              PER ANNUM.

                              SIGNED      John Caldwell

                              TITLE       Treasurer
```

The journal entry in Porter Company's accounting records for this November 1 borrowing is:

My Notes

The liability is recorded at the face amount of the note

Cash	10,000	
Notes Payable		10,000
Borrowed $10,000 for 6 months at 12% interest per year.		

Notice that no liability is recorded for the interest charges when the note is issued. At the date that money is borrowed, the borrower has a liability *only for the principal amount of the loan;* the liability for interest accrues day by day over the life of the loan. At December 31, two months' interest expense has accrued, and the following year-end adjusting entry is made:

My Notes

A liability for interest accrues day by day

Interest Expense	200	
Interest Payable		200
To record interest expense incurred through year-end on 12%, 6-month note dated Nov. 1 ($10,000 × 12% × $^2/_{12}$ = $200).		

For simplicity, we will assume that Porter Company makes adjusting entries *only at year-end*. Thus the entry on May 1 to record payment of the note will be:

My Notes

Payment of principal and interest

Notes Payable	10,000	
Interest Payable	200	
Interest Expense	400	
Cash		10,600
To record payment of 12%, 6-month note on maturity date and to recognize interest expense incurred since Jan. 1 ($10,000 × 12% × $^4/_{12}$ = $400).		

If Porter Company paid this note *prior* to May 1, interest charges usually would be computed only through the date of early payment.[3]

The Current Portion of Long-Term Debt

Some long-term debts, such as mortgage loans, are payable in a series of monthly or quarterly installments. In these cases, the *principal* amount due within one year (or the operating cycle) is regarded as a current liability, and the remainder of the obligation is classified as a long-term liability.

As the maturity date of a long-term liability approaches, the obligation eventually becomes due within the current period. Long-term liabilities that become payable within the coming year are *reclassified* in the balance sheet as current liabilities.[4] Changing the classification of a liability does not require a journal entry; the obligation is simply shown in a different section of the balance sheet.

Accrued Liabilities

Accrued liabilities arise from the recognition of expenses for which payment will be made in a future period. Thus accrued liabilities also are called *accrued expenses*. Examples of accrued liabilities include interest payable, income taxes payable, and a number of liabilities relating to payrolls. As accrued liabilities stem from the recording of expenses, the *matching* principle governs the timing of their recognition.

All companies incur accrued liabilities. In most cases, however, these liabilities are paid at frequent intervals. Therefore, they usually do not accumulate to large amounts. In a balance sheet, accrued liabilities frequently are included in the amount shown as accounts payable.

Payroll Liabilities

The preparation of a payroll is a specialized accounting function beyond the scope of this text. But we believe that every student should have some understanding of the various costs associated with payrolls. Employers must compute, record, and pay a number of costs in addition to the wages and salaries owed to employees. In fact, one might say that the total wages and salaries expense (or gross pay) represents only the starting point of payroll computations.

LO 3
Describe the costs relating to payrolls.

To illustrate, assume that a manufacturing company employs 50 highly skilled factory employees. If monthly wages for this workforce average $100,000, the costs incurred by this employer in a typical monthly payroll would be:

Gross pay (wages expense)	$100,000
Social Security and Medicare taxes	7,650
Federal and state unemployment taxes	6,200
Workers' compensation insurance premiums	4,000
Group health insurance premiums	10,500
Contributions to employee pension plan and other postretirement costs	5,000
Total factory payroll costs for January	$133,350

My Notes
Notice the costs in addition to employees' wages

---

[3] Computing interest charges only through the date of payment is the normal business practice. However, some notes are written in a manner requiring the borrower to pay interest for the full term of the note even if payment is made early. Borrowers should look carefully at these terms.

[4] Exceptions are made to this rule if the liability will be *refinanced* (that is, extended or renewed) on a long-term basis or if a special *sinking fund* has been accumulated for the purpose of repaying this obligation. In these cases, the debt remains classified as a long-term liability, even though it will mature within the current period.

The amounts shown in red are **payroll taxes** and insurance premiums required by law. Costs shown in green currently are not required by law but often are included in the total compensation package provided to employees.

In our example, total payroll-related costs exceed wages expense *by more than 30%*. This relationship will vary from one employer to another, but our illustration is typical of many payrolls.

Payroll Taxes and Mandated Costs All employers must pay Social Security and Medicare taxes on the wages or salary paid to each employee. These taxes currently amount to 7.65% of the employee's earnings.[5] Federal unemployment taxes apply only to the *first $7,000* earned by each employee during the year (state unemployment taxes may vary). Thus these taxes tend to drop off dramatically as the year progresses.

Workers' compensation is a state-mandated program that provides insurance to employees against job-related injury. The premiums vary greatly by state and by occupational classification. In some high-risk industries (e.g., roofers), workers' compensation premiums may exceed 50% of the employees' wages.

Other Payroll-Related Costs Many employers pay some or all of the costs of health insurance for their employees as well as make contributions to employee pension plans. Annual health insurance premiums usually cost between $1,800 and $3,600 per employee (including family members). Contributions to employees' pension plans, if any, vary greatly among employers.

Amounts Withheld from Employees' Pay Our illustration specifies only those taxes levied on the employer. Employees, too, incur taxes on their earnings. These include federal and state income taxes and the employees' shares of Social Security and Medicare taxes. Employers must withhold these amounts from the employees' pay and forward them directly to the appropriate tax authorities. (The net amount of cash actually paid to employees—that is, total wages and salaries expense less the amounts withheld—often is called the employees' *take-home pay*.)

Amounts withheld from employees' pay do *not* represent taxes on the employer. These amounts are simply portions of the original wages and salaries expense that must be sent directly to tax authorities, rather than paid to the employees. With respect to these taxes, the employer is required by law to act as the tax *collector*. In the employer's balance sheet, these withholdings represent current liabilities until they are deposited with the proper tax authorities.

Unearned Revenue

A liability for unearned revenue arises when a customer pays in advance. Upon receipt of an advance payment from a customer, the company debits Cash and credits a liability account such as Unearned Revenue or Customers' Deposits. As the services are rendered to the customer, an entry is made debiting the liability account and crediting a revenue account. Notice that the liability for unearned revenue normally is satisfied by rendering services to the creditor, rather than by making cash payments.

Unearned revenue ordinarily is classified as a current liability because activities involved in earning revenue are part of the business's normal operating cycle.

---

[5] Social Security and Medicare taxes of the *same amount* are also levied on the employees and are withheld from their paychecks. Thus total Social Security and Medicare taxes amount to more than 15% of gross wages and salaries. There is a limit on the portion of an employee's earnings subject to Social Security taxes. The current limit is approximately $85,000. There is no cap on employee wages or salaries subject to Medicare taxes.

You as a CPA for a Pawn Shop

Assume you are a sole proprietor of Balance & Income, CPAs. One of your clients is Pawn Shop, Inc., for which you undertake normal accounting duties, including preparing monthly statements, completing required tax returns, and recording monthly revenues and expenses. However, Pawn Shop cashes its own checks and pays its own bills from its own bank accounts. Mr. Swidle, the manager of Pawn Shop, asks you if you would be willing to keep a check received from a customer as a down payment for merchandise to be delivered in the future until the transaction is complete. Mr. Swidle explains that he does not want to cash the check now because he is unsure how long it will be before Pawn Shop obtains the desired merchandise. How should you respond to Mr. Swidle?

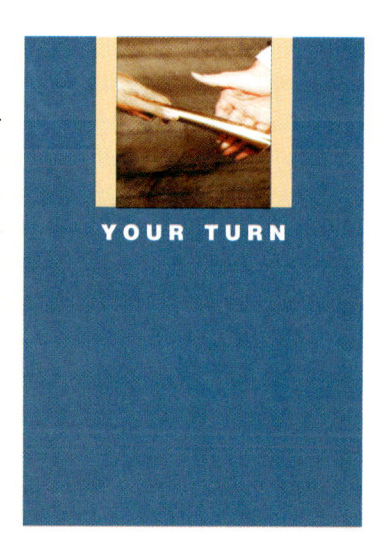

*Our comments appear on page 458.

LONG-TERM LIABILITIES

Long-term obligations usually arise from major expenditures, such as acquisitions of plant assets, the purchase of another company, or refinancing an existing long-term obligation that is about to mature. Thus transactions involving long-term liabilities are relatively few in number but often involve large dollar amounts. In contrast, current liabilities usually arise from routine operating transactions.

Many businesses regard long-term liabilities as an alternative to owners' equity as a source of permanent financing. Although long-term liabilities eventually mature, they often are *refinanced*—that is, the maturing obligation simply is replaced with a new long-term liability.

Maturing Obligations Intended to Be Refinanced

One special type of long-term liability is an obligation that will mature in the current period but that is expected to be refinanced on a long-term basis. For example, a company may have a bank loan that comes due each year but is routinely extended for the following year. Both the company and the bank may intend for this arrangement to continue on a long-term basis.

If management has both the *intent* and the *ability* to refinance soon-to-mature obligations on a long-term basis, these obligations are classified as long-term liabilities. In this situation, the accountant looks to the *economic substance* of the situation rather than to its legal form.

When the economic substance of a transaction differs from its legal form or its outward appearance, financial statements should reflect the *economic substance*. Accountants summarize this concept with the phrase *"Substance takes precedence over form."* Today's business world is characterized by transactions of ever-increasing complexity. Recognizing those situations in which the substance of a transaction differs from its form is one of the greatest challenges confronting the accounting profession.

It is typical in Japan for short-term debt to have lower interest rates than long-term debt. Thus, Japanese managers find short-term debt more attractive than long-term debt. In addition, banks are happy to renew these loans because this allows them to adjust the interest rates to changing market conditions. Thus, short-term debt in Japan works like long-term debt elsewhere. In fact, the use of short-term debt to finance long-term assets appears to be the rule, not the exception, in Japan.

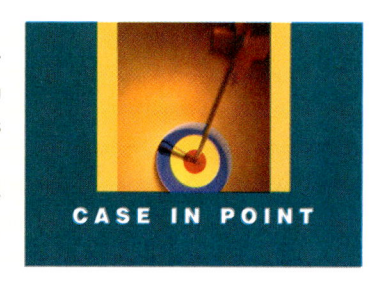

416 Chapter 10 Liabilities

Installment Notes Payable

Purchases of real estate and certain types of equipment often are financed by the issuance of long-term notes that call for a series of installment payments. These payments (often called **debt service**) may be due monthly, quarterly, semiannually, or at any other interval. If these installments continue until the debt is completely repaid, the loan is said to be "fully amortizing." Often, however, installment notes contain a due date at which the remaining unpaid balance is to be repaid in a single "balloon" payment.

Some installment notes call for installment payments equal to the periodic interest charges (an "interest only" note). Under these terms, the principal amount of the loan is payable at a specified maturity date. More often, however, the installment payments are *greater* than the amount of interest accruing during the period. Thus only a portion of each installment payment represents interest expense, and the remainder of the payment reduces the principal amount of the liability. As the amount owed is reduced by each payment, the portion of each successive payment representing interest expense will *decrease,* and the portion going toward repayment of principal will *increase.*

Allocating Installment Payments between Interest and Principal In accounting for an installment note, the accountant must determine the portion of each payment that represents interest expense and the portion that reduces the principal amount of the liability. This distinction is made in advance by preparing an **amortization table**.

To illustrate, assume that on October 15, Year 1, King's Inn purchases furnishings at a total cost of $16,398. In payment, the company issues an installment note payable for this amount, plus interest at 12% per annum (or 1% per month). This note will be paid in 18 monthly installments of $1,000 each, beginning on November 15. An amortization table for this installment note payable is shown in Exhibit 10–2 (amounts of interest expense are *rounded to the nearest dollar*).

Preparing an Amortization Table Let us explore the content of Exhibit 10–2. First, notice that the payments are made on a *monthly* basis. Therefore, the amounts of the payments (column A), interest expense (column B), and reduction in the unpaid balance (column C) are all *monthly amounts.*

The interest rate used in the table is of special importance; this rate must coincide with the period of time *between payment dates*—in this case, one month. Thus, if payments are made monthly, column B must be based on the *monthly* rate of interest. If payments were made quarterly, this column would use the quarterly rate of interest.

An amortization table begins with the original amount of the liability ($16,398) listed at the top of the Unpaid Balance column. The amounts of the monthly payments, shown in column A, are specified by the installment contract. The monthly interest expense, shown in column B, is computed for each month by applying the monthly interest rate to the unpaid balance at the *beginning of that month.* The portion of each payment that reduces the amount of the liability (column C) is simply the remainder of the payment (column A minus column B). Finally, the unpaid balance of the liability (column D) is reduced each month by the amount indicated in column C.

Rather than continuing to make monthly payments, King's Inn could settle this liability at any time by paying the amount currently shown as the unpaid balance.

Notice that the amount of interest expense listed in column B *changes every month.* In our illustration, the interest expense is *decreasing* each month, because the unpaid balance is continually decreasing.[6]

Preparing each horizontal line in an amortization table involves making the same computations, based on a new unpaid balance. Thus an amortization table of any length can

---

[6] If the monthly payments were *less* than the amount of the monthly interest expense, the unpaid balance of the note would *increase* each month. This, in turn, would cause the interest expense to increase each month. This pattern, termed *negative amortization,* occurs temporarily in some "adjustable-rate" home mortgages.

Long-Term Liabilities

Exhibit 10–2

AMORTIZATION TABLE FOR A NOTE PAYABLE

AMORTIZATION TABLE
(12% Note Payable for $16,398; Payable in 18 Monthly Installments of $1,000)

Interest Period	Payment Date	(A) Monthly Payment	(B) Interest Expense (1% of the Last Unpaid Balance)	(C) Reduction in Unpaid Balance (A) − (B)	(D) Unpaid Balance
Issue date	Oct. 15, Year 1	—	—	—	$16,398
1	Nov. 15	$1,000	$164	$836	15,562
2	Dec. 15	1,000	156	844	14,718
3	Jan. 15, Year 2	1,000	147	853	13,865
4	Feb. 15	1,000	139	861	13,004
5	Mar. 15	1,000	130	870	12,134
6	Apr. 15	1,000	121	879	11,255
7	May 15	1,000	113	887	10,368
8	June 15	1,000	104	896	9,472
9	July 15	1,000	95	905	8,567
10	Aug. 15	1,000	86	914	7,653
11	Sept. 15	1,000	77	923	6,730
12	Oct. 15	1,000	67	933	5,797
13	Nov. 15	1,000	58	942	4,855
14	Dec. 15	1,000	49	951	3,904
15	Jan. 15, Year 3	1,000	39	961	2,943
16	Feb. 15	1,000	29	971	1,972
17	Mar. 15	1,000	20	980	992
18	Apr. 15	1,000	8*	992	–0–

*In the last period, interest expense is equal to the amount of the final payment minus the remaining unpaid balance. This compensates for the cumulative effect of rounding interest amounts to the nearest dollar.

be easily and quickly prepared by computer. (Most "money management" software includes a program for preparing amortization tables.) Only three items of data need to be entered into the computer: (1) the original amount of the liability, (2) the amount of periodic payments, and (3) the interest rate (per payment period).

Examine the amortization table illustrated in Exhibit 10–2. Note that the total monthly cash payment (column A) does not change from period to period. What does change, however, is the portion of the cash payment allocated to interest expense each month (column B) versus the amount by which the outstanding loan balance is reduced (column C).

CASH EFFECTS

Using an Amortization Table Once an amortization table has been prepared, the entries to record each payment are taken directly from the amounts shown in the table. For example, the entry to record the first monthly payment (November 15, Year 1) is:

Interest Expense	164	
Installment Note Payable	836	
Cash		1,000
Made Nov. payment on installment note payable.		

My Notes

Payment is allocated between interest and principal

418 Chapter 10 Liabilities

Similarly, the entry to record the *second* payment, made on *December 15, Year 1,* is:

> **My Notes**
> Notice that interest expense is less in December

Interest Expense	156	
Installment Note Payable	844	
Cash		1,000
Made Dec. payment on installment note payable.		

At December 31, Year 1, King's Inn should make an adjusting entry to record one-half month's accrued interest on this liability. The amount of this adjusting entry is based on the unpaid balance shown in the amortization table as of the last payment (December 15). This entry is:

> **My Notes**
> Year-end adjusting entry

Interest Expense	74	
Interest Payable		74
Adjusting entry to record interest expense on installment note for the last half of Dec.: $14,718 \times 1\% \times 1/2 = $74.		

The Current Portion of Long-Term Debt Notice that as of December 31, Year 1, the unpaid balance of this note is $14,718. As of December 31, *Year 2,* however, the unpaid balance will be only $3,904. Thus the principal amount of this note will be reduced by *$10,814* during Year 2 ($14,718 − $3,904 = $10,814). In the balance sheet prepared at December 31, Year 1, the $10,814 portion of this debt that is scheduled for repayment within the *next 12 months* should be classified as a *current liability.* The remaining $3,904 should be classified as a long-term liability.

Bonds Payable

> **LO 5**
> Describe corporate bonds and explain the tax advantage of debt financing.

Financially sound corporations may arrange limited amounts of long-term financing by issuing notes payable to banks or to insurance companies. But to finance a large project, such as developing an oil field or purchasing a controlling interest in the capital stock of another company, a corporation may need more capital than any single lender can supply. When a corporation needs to raise large amounts of long-term capital—perhaps 50, 100, or 500 million dollars (or more)—it generally sells additional shares of capital stock or issues **bonds payable**.

What Are Bonds?

The issuance of bonds payable is a technique for splitting a very large loan into many transferable units, called bonds. Each bond represents a *long-term, interest-bearing note payable,* usually in the face amount (or par value) of $1,000 or some multiple of $1,000. The bonds are sold to the investing public, enabling many different investors (bondholders) to participate in the loan.

Bonds usually are very long-term notes, maturing in perhaps 30 or 40 years. The bonds are transferable, however, so individual bondholders may sell their bonds to other investors at any time. Most bonds call for semiannual interest payments to the bondholders, with interest computed at a specified *contract rate* throughout the life of the bond. Thus investors often describe bonds as "fixed income" investments.

An example of a corporate bond issue is the $8^1/_2\%$ bonds of **Pacific Bell** (a Pacific Telesis company, known as **PacBell**), due August 15, 2031. Interest on these bonds is payable semiannually on February 15 and August 15. With this bond issue, **PacBell** borrowed $225 million by issuing 225,000 bonds of $1,000 each.

PacBell did not actually print and issue 225,000 separate notes payable. Each bondholder is issued a single *bond certificate* indicating the number of bonds purchased. Each certificate is in the face amount of $25,000 and, therefore, represents ownership

Long-Term Liabilities

of 25 bonds. Investors such as mutual funds, banks, and insurance companies often buy thousands of bonds at one time.

The Issuance of Bonds Payable When bonds are issued, the corporation usually utilizes the services of an investment banking firm, called an **underwriter**. The underwriter guarantees the issuing corporation a specific price for the entire bond issue and makes a profit by selling the bonds to the investing public at a higher price. The corporation records the issuance of the bonds at the net amount received from the underwriter. The use of an underwriter assures the corporation that the entire bond issue will be sold without delay and that the entire amount of the proceeds will be available at a specific date.

Transferability of Bonds Corporate bonds, like capital stocks, are traded daily on organized securities exchanges, such as the *New York Bond Exchange*. The holders of a 25-year bond issue need not wait 25 years to convert their investments into cash. By placing a telephone call to a broker, an investor may sell bonds within a matter of minutes at the going market price. This quality of *liquidity* is one of the most attractive features of an investment in corporate bonds.

Quoted Market Prices Bond prices are quoted as a *percentage* of their face value or *maturity* value, which is usually $1,000. The maturity value is the amount the issuing company must pay to redeem the bond at the date it matures (becomes due). A $1,000 bond quoted at *102* would therefore have a market price of $1,020 (102% of $1,000). Bond prices are quoted at the nearest one-eighth of a percentage point. The following line from the financial page of a daily newspaper summarizes the previous day's trading in bonds of **Sears, Roebuck & Company**:

Bonds	Sales	High	Low	Close	Net Change
Sears R $7^7/_8$'07	245	$97^1/_2$	$95^1/_2$	97	+1

This line of condensed information indicates that 245 of Sears' $7^7/_8$%, $1,000 bonds maturing in 2007 were traded during the day. The highest price is reported as $97^1/_2$, or $975 for a bond of $1,000 face value. The lowest price was $95^1/_2$, or $955 for a $1,000 bond. The closing price (last sale of the day) was 97, or $970. This was one point above the closing price of the previous day, an increase of $10 in the price of a $1,000 bond.

Types of Bonds Bonds secured by the pledge of specific assets are called *mortgage bonds*. An unsecured bond is called a *debenture bond;* its value rests on the general credit of the corporation. A debenture bond issued by a very large and strong corporation may have a higher investment rating than a secured bond issued by a corporation in less satisfactory financial condition.

Bond interest is paid semiannually by mailing to each bondholder a check for six months' interest on the bonds he or she owns.[7] Many bonds are *callable,* which means that the corporation has the right to redeem the bonds *in advance* of the maturity date by paying a specified *call price*. To compensate bondholders for being forced to give up their investments, the call price usually is somewhat higher than the face value of the bonds.

---

[7] In recent years, corporations have issued only *registered* bonds, for which interest is paid by mailing a check to the registered owners of the bonds. In past decades, some companies issued *coupon bonds* or *bearer bonds,* which had a series of redeemable coupons attached. At each interest date, the bondholder had to "clip" the coupon and present it to a bank to collect the interest. These bonds posed a considerable hazard to investors—if the investor lost the coupon, or forgot about an interest date, he or she received no interest. In many states, issuing coupon bonds now is illegal.

Traditionally, bonds have appealed to conservative investors, interested primarily in a reliable income stream from their investments. To make a bond issue more attractive to these investors, some corporations create a bond **sinking fund**, designated for repaying the bonds at maturity. At regular intervals, the corporation deposits cash into this sinking fund. A bond sinking fund is not classified as a current asset, because it is not available for the payment of current liabilities. Such funds are shown in the balance sheet under the caption "Long-Term Investments," which appears just below the current asset section.

As an additional attraction to investors, corporations sometimes include a conversion privilege in the bond indenture. A **convertible bond** is one that may be exchanged at the option of the bondholder for a specified number of shares of capital stock. Thus the market value of a convertible bond tends to fluctuate with the market value of an equivalent number of shares of capital stock.

Junk Bonds In recent years, some corporations have issued securities that have come to be known as **junk bonds**. This term describes a bond issue that involves a substantially greater risk of default than normal. A company issuing junk bonds usually has so much long-term debt that its ability to meet interest and principal repayment obligations has become questionable. To compensate bondholders for this unusual level of risk, junk bonds promise a substantially higher rate of interest than do "investment quality" bonds.

CASE IN POINT The risk associated with junk bonds can make them a real gamble for investors in more ways than one. Donald Trump sold $1.2 billion in junk bonds, secured primarily by the Trump Taj Mahal and the Trump Plaza—the largest casino junk bond issue in history. The risk did not scare away high-rolling investors, however, who eagerly placed bets on the chance of receiving an 11.25% contract rate of interest.

Tax Advantage of Bond Financing

A principal advantage of raising money by issuing bonds instead of stock is that interest payments are *deductible* in determining income subject to corporate income taxes. Dividends paid to stockholders, however, are *not deductible* in computing taxable income.

To illustrate, assume that a corporation pays income taxes at a rate of *30%* on its taxable income. If this corporation issues $10 million of 10% bonds payable, it will incur interest expense of $1 million per year. This interest expense, however, will reduce taxable income by $1 million, thus reducing the corporation's annual income taxes by $300,000. As a result, the *after-tax* cost of borrowing the $10 million is only *$700,000:*

Interest expense ($10,000,000 × 10%)	$1,000,000
Less: Income tax savings ($1,000,000 deduction × 30%)	300,000
After-tax cost of borrowing	$ 700,000

A shortcut approach to computing the after-tax cost of borrowing is simply multiplying the interest expense by *1 minus the company's tax rate,* as follows: $1,000,000 × (1 − .30) = $700,000.

Accounting for Bonds Payable

Accounting for bonds payable closely parallels accounting for notes payable. The accountable events for a bond issue usually are (1) issuance of the bonds, (2) semiannual

Long-Term Liabilities

interest payments, (3) accrual of interest payable at the end of each accounting period, and (4) retirement of the bonds at maturity.[8]

To illustrate these events, assume that on March 1, 2002, Wells Corporation issues $1 million of 12%, 20-year bonds payable.[9] These bonds are dated March 1, 2002, and interest is computed from this date. Interest on the bonds is payable semiannually, each September 1 and March 1. If all of the bonds are sold at par value (face amount), the issuance of the bonds on March 1 will be recorded by the following entry:

Cash	1,000,000	
Bonds Payable		1,000,000
Issued 12% 20-year bonds payable at a price of 100.		

My Notes
Entry at the issuance date

Every September 1 during the term of the bond issue, Wells Corporation must pay $60,000 to the bondholders ($1,000,000 × .12 × 1/2 = $60,000). This semiannual interest payment will be recorded as shown below:

Bond Interest Expense	60,000	
Cash		60,000
Semiannual payment of bond interest.		

My Notes
Entry to record semiannual interest payments

Every December 31, Wells Corporation must make an adjusting entry to record the four months' interest that has accrued since September 1:

Bond Interest Expense	40,000	
Bond Interest Payable		40,000
To accrue bond interest payable for four months ended Dec. 31 ($1,000,000 × .12 × 4/12 = $40,000).		

My Notes
Adjusting entry at year-end

The accrued liability for bond interest payable will be paid within a few months and, therefore, is classified as a current liability.

Two months later, on March 1, a semiannual interest payment is made to bondholders. This transaction represents payment of the four months' interest accrued at December 31, and of two months' interest that has accrued since year-end. Thus the entry to record the semiannual interest payments every March 1 will be:

Bond Interest Expense	20,000	
Bond Interest Payable	40,000	
Cash		60,000
To record semiannual interest payment to bondholders, and to recognize two months' interest expense accrued since year-end ($1,000,000 × .12 × 2/12 = $20,000).		

My Notes
Interest payment following the year-end adjusting entry

---

[8] To simplify our illustrations, we assume in all of our examples and assignment material that adjusting entries for accrued bond interest payable are made *only at year-end*. In practice, these adjustments usually are made on a monthly basis.

[9] The amount of $1 million is used only for purposes of illustration. As explained earlier, actual bond issues are for many millions of dollars.

When the bonds mature 20 years later on March 1, 2022, two entries are required: one to record the regular semiannual interest payment and a second to record the retirement of the bonds. The entry to record the retirement of the bond issue is:

My Notes

Redeeming the bonds at the maturity date

Bonds Payable	1,000,000	
Cash		1,000,000
Paid face amount of bonds at maturity.		

Bonds Issued between Interest Dates The semiannual interest dates (such as January 1 and July 1, or April 1 and October 1) are printed on the bond certificates. However, bonds are often issued between the specified interest dates. The *investor* is then required to pay the interest accrued to the date of issuance *in addition* to the stated price of the bond. This practice enables the corporation to pay a full six months' interest on all bonds outstanding at the semiannual interest payment date. The accrued interest collected from investors who purchase bonds between interest payment dates is thus returned to them on the next interest payment date.

To illustrate, let us modify our illustration to assume that Wells Corporation issues $1 million of 12% bonds at a price of 100 on *May 1*—two months *after* the March interest date printed on the bonds. The amount received from the bond purchasers now will include two months' accrued interest, as follows:

[Handwritten note: NOT ON TEST]

My Notes

Bonds issued between interest dates

Cash	1,020,000	
Bonds Payable		1,000,000
Bond Interest Payable		20,000
Issued $1,000,000 face value of 12%, 20-year bonds at 100 plus accrued interest for two months ($1,000,000 × 12% × $2/12$ = $20,000).		

Four months later on the regular September 1 semiannual interest payment date, a full six months' interest ($60 per $1,000 bond) will be paid to all bondholders, *regardless of when they purchased their bonds.* The entry for the semiannual interest payment is illustrated below:

My Notes

Notice only part of the interest payment is charged to expense

Bond Interest Payable	20,000	
Bond Interest Expense	40,000	
Cash		60,000
Paid semiannual interest on $1,000,000 face value of 12% bonds.		

Now consider these interest transactions from the standpoint of the *investors.* They paid for two months' accrued interest at the time of purchasing the bonds and then received checks for six months' interest after holding the bonds for only four months. They have, therefore, been reimbursed properly for the use of their money for four months.

When bonds are subsequently sold by one investor to another, they sell at the quoted market price *plus accrued interest* since the last interest payment date. This practice enables the issuing corporation to pay all the interest for an interest period to the investor owning the bond at the interest date. Otherwise, the corporation would have to make partial payments to every investor who bought or sold the bond during the interest period.

The amount that investors will pay for bonds is the *present value* of the principal and interest payments they will receive. The concept of present value is discussed on pages 429–430. A more in-depth coverage of present value appears in Appendix B at the end of this textbook.

Long-Term Liabilities

Bonds Issued at a Discount or a Premium

Underwriters normally sell corporate bonds to investors either at par or at a price very close to par. Therefore, the underwriter usually purchases these bonds from the issuing corporation at a discount—that is, at a price below par. The discount generally is quite small—perhaps 1% or 2% of the face amount of the bonds.

When bonds are issued, the borrower records a liability equal to the *amount received.* If the bonds are issued at a small discount—which is the normal case—this liability is slightly smaller than the face value of the bond issue. At the maturity date, of course, the issuing corporation must redeem the bonds at full face value. Thus, over the term of the bond issue, the borrower's liability gradually *increases* from the original issue price to the maturity value.

LO 6
Account for bonds issued at a discount or premium.

Accounting for a Bond Discount: An Illustration

To illustrate, assume that on March 1, 2002, Wells Corporation sells $1 million of 12%, 20-year bonds payable to an underwriter at a price of *97* (meaning that the bonds were sold to the underwriter at 97% of their face value). On March 1, 2002, Wells Corporation receives $970,000 cash from the underwriter and records a *net* liability of this amount. When these bonds mature in 20 years, however, Wells will owe its bondholders the *full* $1 million face value of the bond issue. Thus, the company's liability must somehow be *increased* by $30,000 over the 20 years that the bonds are outstanding.

The gradual growth in the company's liability is illustrated in Exhibit 10–3. Notice that the liability increases at an average rate of $1,500 per year ($30,000 total increase ÷ 20-year life of the bond issue).

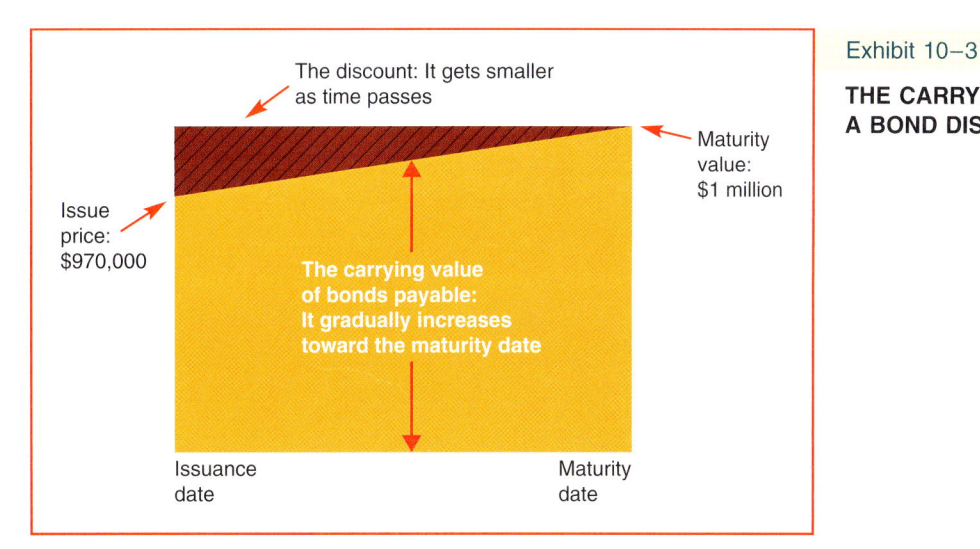

Exhibit 10–3

THE CARRYING VALUE OF A BOND DISCOUNT

Bond Discount: Part of the Cost of Borrowing When bonds are issued at a discount, the borrower must repay more than the amount originally borrowed. Thus any discount in the issuance price becomes an additional cost of the overall borrowing transaction.

In terms of cash outlays, the additional cost represented by the discount is not paid until the bonds mature. But the *matching principle* may require the borrower to recognize this cost gradually over the life of the bond issue.[10] After all, the borrower does benefit from the use of the borrowed funds throughout this entire period.

---

[10] If the amount of the discount is immaterial, it may be charged directly to expense as a matter of convenience.

When the bonds are issued, the amount of any discount is debited to an account entitled *Discount on Bonds Payable*. Thus, Wells Corporation will record the March 1 issuance as follows:

Cash	970,000	
Discount on Bonds Payable	30,000	
Bonds Payable		1,000,000
Issued 20-year bonds with $1,000,000 face value to an underwriter at a price of 97.		

Wells Corporation's liability at the date of issuance will appear in the balance sheet as follows:

Long-Term Liabilities

Bonds payable	$1,000,000
Less: Discount on bonds payable	30,000
Net carrying value of bonds payable	$ 970,000

The Discount on Bonds Payable account has a debit balance and is treated as a *contra-liability account*. As illustrated, it is shown in the balance sheet as a *reduction* in the face or par value of bonds payable. Thus, the net carrying value of the bonds payable on the date of issuance is equal to the *amount borrowed*.

Amortization of the Discount On March 1, 2002, Wells Corporation received $970,000 from the underwriter. When the bonds mature 20 years later on March 1, 2022, the company must pay its bondholders the *full* $1 million face value of the bond issue. This additional $30,000 represents *interest expense* that must be amortized over the 20-year life of the bond. At each interest payment date, an adjusting entry is made to transfer a portion of the balance in the Discount on Bonds Payable account into interest expense. Thus, over time, the discount declines and the carrying value of the bonds—the face amount less the remaining discount balance—rises toward the $1 million maturity value of the bond issue.

Each September 1, the company records the following interest expense of *$60,750:*

Semiannual interest *payment* ($1,000,000 × 12% × $\frac{1}{2}$)	$60,000
Add: Semiannual amortization of bond discount ([$30,000 discount ÷ 20 years)] × $\frac{1}{2}$)	750
Semiannual interest expense	$60,750

The entry to record interest expense on September 1 throughout the life of the bond issue is:

Bond Interest Expense	60,750	
Cash		60,000
Discount on Bonds Payable		750
To record semiannual interest expense and to recognize six months' amortization of the $30,000 discount on 20-year bonds payable.		

> **CASH EFFECTS**
>
> Notice that the amortization of the discount increases Wells Corporation's semiannual interest expense by $750. It does not, however, require any immediate cash outlay. The $30,000 interest expense represented by the *entire* amortized discount will not be paid until the bonds mature on March 1, 2022.

Every December 31, Wells Corporation must make an adjusting entry to record four months' interest expense that has accrued since September 1. The computation of this $40,500 accrual is computed as follows:

> Four months' accrued interest *payable* ($1,000,000 × 12% × 4/12) $40,000
> Add: Four months' amortization of bond discount
>   ([$30,000 discount ÷ 20 years] × 4/12) 500
> Interest accrued from September 1 through December 31 . . . . $40,500

Thus, the adjusting entry required on December 31 throughout the life of the bond issue is as follows:

> Bond Interest Expense 40,500
>   Bond Interest Payable 40,000
>   Discount on Bonds Payable 500
> To record four months' interest expense and to amortize four months'
>   of discount on 20-year bonds payable.

Two months later, on every March 1, a *full* semiannual interest payment is made to the company's bondholders, and an additional two months' amortization of the discount is recognized. The $20,250 interest expense recorded on this date is computed as:

> Two months' accrued interest *payable* ($1,000,000 × 12% × 2/12) $20,000
> Add: Two months' amortization of bond discount
>   ([$30,000 discount ÷ 20 years] × 2/12) 250
> Interest accrued from January 1 through March 1 . . . . $20,250

The semiannual interest payment recorded on March 1 throughout the life of the bond issue is:

> Bond Interest Expense 20,250
> Bond Interest Payable 40,000
>   Cash 60,000
>   Discount on Bonds Payable 250
> To record two months' interest expense, to amortize two months'
>   of discount on 20-year bonds payable, and to record semiannual
>   interest payment to bondholders.

When the bonds mature 20 years later on March 1, 2022, two entries are required: one to record the regular semiannual interest payment, and a second to record the retirement of the bonds. At this date, the original $30,000 discount will be *fully amortized* (i.e., the Discount on Bonds Payable account will have a zero balance). Thus the carrying value

426 Chapter 10 Liabilities

of the bond issue will be $1 million, and the entry required to record the retirement of the bond issue will be:

Bonds Payable	1,000,000	
Cash		1,000,000
Paid the face amount of bonds at maturity.		

It is important to realize that over the life of this bond issue, Wells Corporation recognized *total* interest expense of $2,430,000 (40 semiannual interest payments of $60,000, plus the $30,000 discount amortized).

Accounting for a Bond Premium: An Illustration

As noted previously, underwriters normally purchase bonds from the issuing corporation at a slight discount. Under some circumstances, however, an underwriter may actually pay a slight premium to the issuer—that is, a price above par.

To illustrate, assume that on March 1, 2002, Wells Corporation sells $1 million of 12%, 20-year bonds payable to an underwriter at a price of *103* (meaning that the bonds were sold to the underwriter at 103% of their face value). On March 1, 2002, Wells Corporation receives $1,030,000 cash from the underwriter and records a liability equal to this amount. When these bonds mature in 20 years, however, Wells will owe its bondholders only the $1 million *face value* of the bond issue. Thus, the company's initial liability must somehow be *reduced* by $30,000 over the 20 years that the bonds are outstanding.

The gradual decrease in the company's liability is illustrated in Exhibit 10–4. Notice that the liability decreases at an average rate of $1,500 per year ($30,000 total increase ÷ 20-year life of the bond issue).

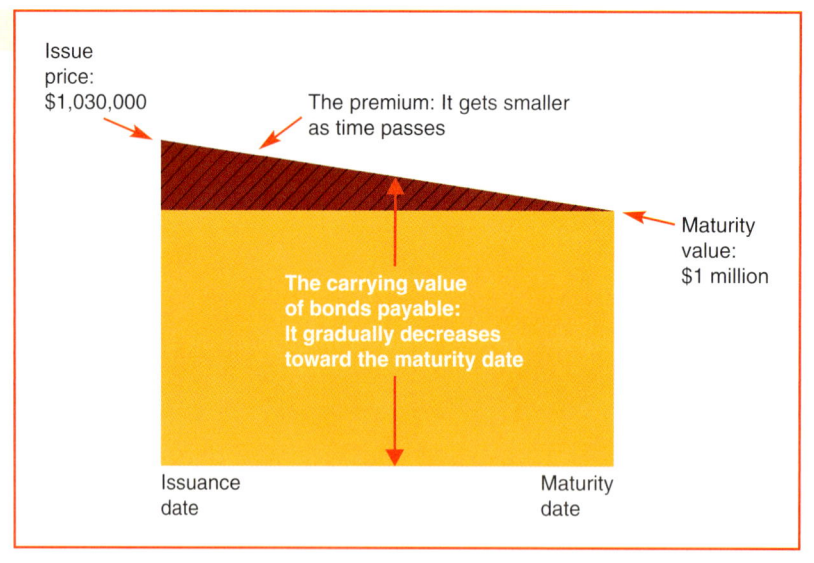

Exhibit 10–4

THE CARRYING VALUE OF A BOND PREMIUM

Issue price: $1,030,000

The premium: It gets smaller as time passes

Maturity value: $1 million

The carrying value of bonds payable: It gradually decreases toward the maturity date

Issuance date   Maturity date

Bond Premium: A Reduction in the Cost of Borrowing When bonds are issued at a premium, the borrower repays less than the amount originally received at the date of issuance. Thus, any premium actually represents a reduction in the overall cost of borrowing. Unlike bonds issued at a discount, the interest expense associated with bonds issued at a premium will be *less* than the semiannual cash payment made to bondholders.

When the bonds are issued, the amount of any premium is credited to an account entitled *Premium on Bonds Payable.* Thus, Wells Corporation will record the March 1 issuance as follows:

Long-Term Liabilities

```
Cash ............................................... 1,030,000
    Premium on Bonds Payable ...........................        30,000
    Bonds Payable ......................................     1,000,000
Issued 20-year bonds with $1,000,000 face value to
  an underwriter at a price of 103.
```

Wells Corporation's liability at the date of issuance will appear in the balance sheet as follows:

Long-Term Liabilities

Bonds Payable	$1,000,000
Add: Premium on bonds payable	30,000
Carrying value of bonds payable	$1,030,000

Note that because the Premium on Bonds Payable account has credit balance, it is shown in the balance sheet as an *increase* in the face or par value of bonds payable.

Amortization of the Premium On March 1, 2002, Wells Corporation received $1,030,000 from the underwriter. When the bonds mature 20 years later on March 1, 2022, the company must pay back its bondholders only the $1 million *face value* of the bond issue. This $30,000 reduction in the amount owed represents *interest savings* that must be amortized over the 20-year life of the bond. Thus, over time, the premium declines, and the carrying value of the bonds—the face amount plus the remaining premium balance—also declines toward the $1 million maturity value of the bond issue.

Each September 1, the company records interest expense of *$59,250*, computed as:

```
Semiannual interest payment ($1,000,000 × 12% × 1/2) ................ $60,000
Less: Semiannual amortization of bond premium
      ([$30,000 premium ÷ 20 years)] × 1/2) ......................        750
Semiannual interest expense ........................................... $59,250
```

The entry to record interest expense on September 1 throughout the life of the bond issue is:

```
Bond Interest Expense ..........................................  59,250
Premium on Bonds Payable ......................................     750
    Cash ......................................................            60,000
To record semiannual interest expense and to recognize six months'
  amortization of the $30,000 premium on 20-year bonds payable.
```

CASH EFFECTS

Notice that $60,000 semiannual interest payment is the same regardless of whether the bonds are issued at par, at a discount, or at a premium. The amortization of the premium does, however, reduce the amount of interest expense recognized by the company over the life of the bond issue.

Every December 31, Wells Corporation must make an adjusting entry to record four months' interest expense that has accrued since September 1. The $39,500 accrual is computed as follows:

Four months' accrued interest *payable* ($1,000,000 × 12% × 4/12)	$40,000
Less: Four months' amortization of bond premium ([$30,000 premium ÷ 20 years] × 4/12)	500
Interest accrued from September 1 through December 31	$39,500

Thus, the following adjusting entry is required on December 31 throughout the life of the bond issue:

Bond Interest Expense	39,500	
Premium on Bonds Payable	500	
Bond Interest Payable		40,000

To record four months' interest expense and to amortize four months' premium on 20-year bonds payable.

Two months later, on every March 1, a *full* semiannual interest payment is made to the company's bondholders, and an additional two months' amortization of the premium is recognized. The $19,750 interest expense recorded on this date is computed as:

Two months' accrued interest *payable* ($1,000,000 × 12% × 2/12)	$20,000
Less: Two months' amortization of bond premium ([$30,000 premium ÷ 20 years] × 2/12)	250
Interest accrued from January 1 through March 1	$19,750

This semiannual interest payment is recorded on March 1 throughout the life of the bond issue:

Bond Interest Expense	19,750	
Bond Interest Payable	40,000	
Premium on Bonds Payable	250	
Cash		60,000

To record two months' interest expense, to amortize two months' premium on 20-year bonds payable, and to record semiannual interest payment to bondholders.

When the bonds mature 20 years later on March 1, 2022, two entries are required: one to record the regular semiannual interest payment, and a second to record the retirement of the bonds. At this date, the original $30,000 premium will be *fully amortized* (i.e., the Premium on Bonds Payable account will have a zero balance). Thus the carrying value of the bond issue will be $1 million, and the entry required to record the retirement of the bond issue will be as follows:

Bonds Payable	1,000,000	
Cash		1,000,000

Paid the face amount of bonds at maturity.

In the previous illustration involving a bond discount, Wells Corporation recognized total interest expense of $2,430,000 over the life of the bonds. Had these same bonds been issued at a premium of 103, however, we see that the company would have incurred total interest expense of $2,370,000 (40 semiannual interest payments of $60,000, less the $30,000 premium amortized).

Bond Discount and Premium in Perspective

From a conceptual point of view, investors might pay a premium price to purchase bonds that pay an *above-market* rate of interest. If the bonds pay a *below-market* rate, investors will buy them only at a discount.

But these concepts seldom come into play when bonds are first issued. Most bonds are issued *at* the market rate of interest. Corporate bonds *almost never* are issued at a premium. Bonds often are issued at a small discount, but this discount represents only the underwriter's profit margin, not investors' response to a below-market interest rate.[11] The annual effects of amortizing bond discount or premium are diluted further because these amounts are amortized over the entire life of the bond issue—usually 20 years or more.

In summary, bond discounts and premiums *seldom have a material effect* on a company's annual interest expense or its financial position.[12] For this reason, we defer further discussion of this topic to more advanced accounting courses.

The Concept of Present Value

The concept of present value is based on the time value of money—the idea that receiving money today is preferable to receiving money at some later date. Assume, for example, that a bond will have a maturity value of $1,000 five years from today but will pay no interest in the meantime. Investors would not pay $1,000 for this bond today, because they would receive no return on their investment over the next five years. There are prices less than $1,000, however, at which investors would buy the bond. For example, if the bond could be purchased for $600, the investor could expect a return (interest) of $400 from the investment over the five-year period.

The **present value** of a future cash receipt is the amount that a knowledgeable investor will pay *today* for the right to receive that future payment. The exact amount of the present value depends on (1) the amount of the future payment, (2) the length of time until the payment will be received, and (3) the rate of return required by the investor. However, the present value will always be *less* than the future amount. This is because money received today can be invested to earn interest and grow to a larger amount in the future.

The rate of interest that will cause a given present value to grow to a given future amount is called the *discount rate* or *effective rate*. The effective interest rate required by investors at any given time is regarded as the going *market rate* of interest. (The procedures for computing the present value of a future amount are illustrated in Appendix B at the end of this textbook. The concept of present value is very useful in managing your personal financial affairs. We suggest that you read Appendix B—even if it has not been assigned.)

LO 7
Explain the concept of present value as it relates to bond prices.

The Present Value Concept and Bond Prices The price at which bonds sell is the present value to investors of the future principal and interest payments. If the bonds

---

[11] Professor Bill Schwartz of Virginia Commonwealth University conducted a study of 685 bond issues in a given year. *None* of these bonds was issued at a premium, and *over* 95% were issued either at par or at a discount of less than 2% of face value.

[12] Some companies issue *zero-coupon* bonds, which pay *no* interest but are issued at huge discounts. In these situations, amortization of the discount *is* material and may comprise much of the company's total interest expense. Zero-coupon bonds are a specialized form of financing that will be discussed in later accounting courses and courses in corporate finance.

sell at par, the market rate is equal to the *contract interest rate* (or nominal rate) printed on the bonds. The *higher* the effective interest rate that investors require, the *less* they will pay underwriters for bonds with a given contract rate of interest. For example, if investors insist on a 10% return, they will pay less than $1,000 for a 9%, $1,000 bond. Thus, if investors require an effective interest rate *greater* than the contract rate of interest, the bonds will be sold by underwriters at a *discount* (a price less than their face value). On the other hand, if market conditions support an effective interest rate of *less* than the contract rate, the bonds will sell at a *premium* (a price above their face value).

A corporation wishing to borrow money by issuing bonds must pay the going market rate of interest. Since market rates of interest fluctuate constantly, it must be expected that the contract rate of interest may vary somewhat from the market rate at the date the bonds are issued.

Bond Prices after Issuance

As stated earlier, many corporate bonds are traded daily on organized securities exchanges at quoted market prices. After bonds are issued, their market prices vary *inversely* with changes in market interest rates. As interest rates rise, investors will be willing to pay less money to own a bond that pays a given contract rate of interest. Conversely, as interest rates decline, the market prices of bonds rise.

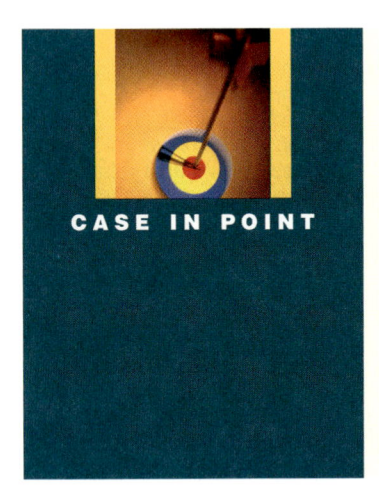

CASE IN POINT

IBM sold to underwriters $500 million of $9^{3}/_{8}$%, 25-year debenture bonds. The underwriters planned to sell the bonds to the public at a price of $99^{5}/_{8}$. Just as the bonds were offered for sale, however, a change in Federal Reserve credit policy started an upward surge in interest rates. The underwriters encountered great difficulty selling the bonds. Within one week, the market price of the bonds had fallen to $94^{1}/_{2}$. The underwriters dumped their unsold inventory at this price and sustained one of the largest underwriting losses in Wall Street history.

During the months that followed, interest rates soared to record levels. Within five months, the price of the bonds had fallen to $76^{3}/_{8}$. Thus nearly one-fourth of the market value of these bonds evaporated in less than half a year. At this time, the financial strength of **IBM** was never in question; this dramatic loss in market value was caused entirely by rising interest rates.

Changes in the current level of interest rates are not the only factors influencing the market prices of bonds. The length of time remaining until the bonds mature is another major force. As a bond nears its maturity date, its market price normally moves closer and closer to the maturity value. This trend is dependable because the bonds are redeemed at par value on the maturity date.

Volatility of Short-Term and Long-Term Bond Prices When interest rates fluctuate, the market prices of long-term bonds are affected to a far greater extent than are the market prices of bonds due to mature in the near future. To illustrate, assume that market interest rates suddenly soar from 9% to 12%. A 9% bond scheduled to mature in a few days will still have a market value of approximately $1,000—the amount to be collected in a few days from the issuing corporation. However, the market price of a 9% bond maturing in 10 years will drop significantly. Investors who must accept these below market interest payments for many years will buy the bonds only at a discounted price.

In summary, fluctuations in interest rates have a far greater effect on the market prices of long-term bonds than on the prices of short-term bonds.

Remember that after bonds have been issued, they belong to the bondholder, *not to the issuing corporation.* Therefore, changes in the market price of bonds subsequent to their issuance *do not* affect the amounts shown in the financial statements of the issuing corporation, and these changes are not recorded in the company's accounting records.

You as a Financial Advisor

Assume that you are the financial advisor for a recently retired couple. Your clients want to invest their savings in such a way as to receive a stable stream of cash flow every year throughout their retirement. They have expressed their concerns to you regarding the volatility of long-term bond prices when interest rates fluctuate.

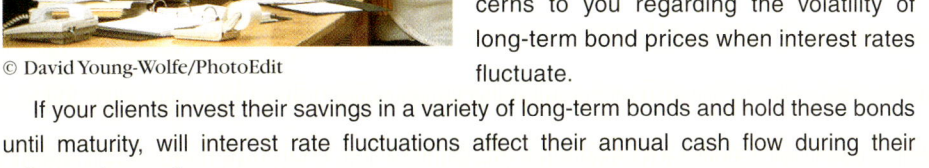

If your clients invest their savings in a variety of long-term bonds and hold these bonds until maturity, will interest rate fluctuations affect their annual cash flow during their retirement years?

*Our comments appear on page 458.

Early Retirement of Bonds Payable

Bonds are sometimes retired before the maturity date. The principal reason for retiring bonds early is to relieve the issuing corporation of the obligation to make future interest payments. If interest rates decline to the point that a corporation can borrow at an interest rate below that being paid on a particular bond issue, the corporation may benefit from retiring those bonds and issuing new bonds at a lower interest rate.

Most bond issues contain a call provision, permitting the corporation to redeem the bonds by paying a specified price, usually a few points above par. Even without a call provision, the corporation may retire its bonds before maturity by purchasing them in the open market. If the bonds can be purchased by the issuing corporation at less than their carrying value, a *gain* is realized on the retirement of the debt. If the bonds are reacquired by the issuing corporation at a price in excess of their carrying value, a *loss* must be recognized.[13]

For example, assume that Briggs Corporation has outstanding a 13%, $10 million bond issue, callable on any interest date at a price of 104. Assume also that the bonds were issued at par and will not mature for nine years. Recently, however, market interest rates have declined to less than 10%, and the market price of Briggs's bonds has increased to 106.[14]

Regardless of the market price, Briggs can call these bonds at 104. If the company exercises this call provision for 10% of the bonds ($1,000,000 face value), the entry will be:

Bonds Payable	1,000,000	
Loss on Early Retirement of Bonds	40,000	
Cash		1,040,000

To record the call of $1 million in bonds payable at a call price of 104.

Notice that Briggs *called* these bonds, rather than repurchasing them at market prices. Therefore, Briggs is able to retire these bonds at their call price of 104. (Had the market price of the bonds been *below* 104, Briggs might have been able to retire the bonds at less cost by purchasing them in the open market.)

---

[13] The FASB has ruled that the gains and losses from early retirements of debt be classified in a special section of the income statement and identified as *extraordinary items*. The presentation of extraordinary items is explained and illustrated in Chapter 12.

[14] Falling interest rates cause bond prices to rise. On the other hand, falling interest rates also provide the issuing company with an incentive to call the bonds and, perhaps, replace them with bonds bearing a lower rate of interest. For this reason, call prices often serve as an approximate "ceiling" on market prices.

ESTIMATED LIABILITIES, LOSS CONTINGENCIES, AND COMMITMENTS

Estimated Liabilities

LO 8
Explain how estimated liabilities, loss contingencies, and commitments are disclosed in financial statements.

The term *estimated liabilities* refers to *liabilities that appear in financial statements at estimated dollar amounts.* Let us consider the example of the automaker's liability to honor its new car warranties. A manufacturer's liability for warranty work is recorded by an entry debiting Warranty Expense and crediting Liability for Warranty Claims. The *matching principle* requires that the expense of performing warranty work be recognized in the period in which the products are *sold,* in order to offset this expense against the related sales revenue. As the warranty may extend several years into the future, the dollar amount of this liability (and expense) must be estimated. Because of the uncertainty regarding when warranty work will be performed, accountants traditionally have classified the liability for warranty claims as a current liability.

By definition, estimated liabilities involve some degree of uncertainty. However, (1) the liabilities are known to exist, and (2) the uncertainty as to dollar amount is *not so great* as to prevent the company from making a reasonable estimate and recording the liability.

Loss Contingencies

Loss contingencies are similar to estimated liabilities but may involve much more uncertainty. A loss contingency is a *possible loss* (or expense), stemming from *past events,* that is expected to be resolved in the future.

Central to the definition of a loss contingency is the element of *uncertainty*—uncertainty as to the amount of loss and, in some cases, uncertainty as to *whether or not any loss actually has been incurred.* A common example of a loss contingency is a lawsuit pending against a company. The lawsuit is based on past events, but until the suit is resolved, uncertainty exists as to the amount (if any) of the company's liability.

Loss contingencies differ from estimated liabilities in two ways. First, a loss contingency may involve a *greater degree of uncertainty.* Often the uncertainty extends to whether any loss or expense actually has been incurred. In contrast, the loss or expense relating to an estimated liability is *known to exist.*

Second, the concept of a loss contingency extends not only to possible liabilities, but also to possible *impairments of assets.* Assume, for example, that a bank has made large loans to a foreign country now experiencing political instability. Uncertainty exists as to the amount of loss, if any, associated with this loan. From the bank's point of view, this loan is an asset that may be impaired, not a liability.

Loss Contingencies in Financial Statements The manner in which loss contingencies are presented in financial statements depends on the *degree of uncertainty involved.*

Loss contingencies are *recorded* in the accounting records only when both of the following criteria are met: (1) It is *probable* that a loss has been incurred, and (2) the amount of loss can be *reasonably estimated.* An example of a loss contingency that usually meets these criteria and is recorded in the accounts is the obligation a company has for product warranties and defects.

When these criteria are *not* met, loss contingencies are *disclosed* in notes to the financial statements if there is a *reasonable possibility* that a material loss has been incurred. Pending lawsuits, for example, usually are disclosed in notes accompanying the financial statements, but the loss, if any, is not recorded in the accounting records until the lawsuit is settled. Companies need *not* disclose loss contingencies if the risk of a material loss having occurred is considered *remote.*

Notice the *judgmental nature* of the criteria used in accounting for loss contingencies. These criteria involve assessments as to whether the risk of material loss is "probable," "reasonably possible," or "remote." Thus the *professional judgments* of the company's management, accountants, legal counsel, and auditors are the deciding factors in accounting for loss contingencies.

When loss contingencies are disclosed in notes to the financial statements, the note should describe the nature of the contingency and, if possible, provide an estimate of the amount of possible loss. If a reasonable estimate of the amount of possible loss cannot be made, the disclosure should include the range of possible loss or a statement that an estimate cannot be made. The following note is typical of the disclosure of the loss contingency arising from pending litigation:

Note 8: Contingencies
In October of 2002, the Company was named as defendant in a $408 million patent infringement lawsuit. The Company denies all charges and is preparing its defense against them. It is not possible at this time to determine the ultimate legal or financial responsibility that may arise as a result of this litigation.

My Notes
Note disclosure of a loss contingency

Sometimes a *portion* of a loss contingency qualifies for immediate recognition, whereas the remainder only meets the criteria for disclosure. Assume, for example, that a company is required by the Superfund Act to clean up an environmental hazard over a 10-year period. The company cannot predict the total cost of the project but considers it probable that it will lose at least $1 million. The company should recognize a $1 million expected loss and record it as a liability. In addition, it should disclose in the notes to the financial statements that the actual cost ultimately may exceed the recorded amount.

DuPont accrues a liability for environmental remediation activities when it is probable that a liability has been incurred and reasonable estimates of the liability can be made. Much of this accrual relates to the Superfund Act, which mandates that the company clean up its waste sites over the next two decades.

Remediation activities tend to occur over relatively long periods of time and vary substantially in cost from site to site. The company's assessment of remediation costs is a continuous process that takes into account the relevant factors affecting each specific site. **DuPont** has accrued over $600 million related to future environmental clean-up activities. Although the company cannot estimate with precision the actual amount it will eventually incur, it apparently believes that costs of at least $600 million appear probable.

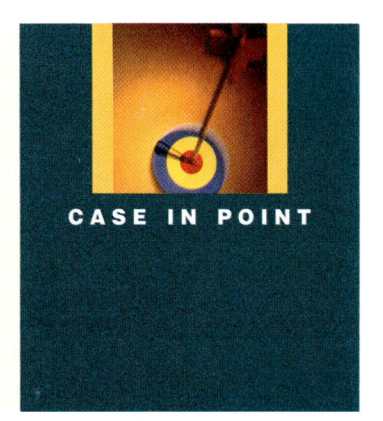

CASE IN POINT

Notice that loss contingencies relate only to possible losses from *past events*. For **DuPont**, these past events were related to the improper disposal of hazardous wastes. The risk that losses may result from *future* events is *not* a loss contingency. The risk of future losses generally is *not* disclosed in financial statements for several reasons.[15] For one, any disclosure of future losses would be sheer speculation. For another, no one can foresee all of the events that might give rise to future losses.

Commitments

Contracts for future transactions are called **commitments**. They are not liabilities, but, if material, they are disclosed in notes to the financial statements. For example, a professional baseball club may issue a three-year contract to a player at an annual salary of, say, $5 million. This is a commitment to pay for services to be rendered in the future. There is no obligation to make payment until the services are received. As liabilities stem only from *past transactions,* this commitment has not yet created a liability.

Other examples of commitments include a corporation's long-term employment contract with a key officer, a contract for construction of a new plant, and a contract to buy or sell inventory at future dates. The common quality of all these commitments is an intent to enter into transactions *in the future.* Commitments that are material in amount should be disclosed in notes to the financial statements.

---

[15] The risk of future losses *is* disclosed if this risk stems from *existing contracts*, such as a written guarantee of another company's indebtedness (called a loan guarantee, or an accommodation endorsement).

LO 9
Evaluate the safety of creditors' claims.

EVALUATING THE SAFETY OF CREDITORS' CLAIMS

Creditors, of course, want to be sure that their claims are safe—that is, that they will be paid on time. Actually, *everyone* associated with a business—management, owners, employees—should be concerned with the company's ability to pay its debts. If a business becomes *illiquid* (unable to pay its obligations), it may be forced into **bankruptcy**.[16]

Not only does management want the business to remain liquid, it wants the company to maintain a high *credit rating* with agencies such as **Dun & Bradstreet** and **Standard & Poor's**. A high credit rating helps a company borrow money more easily and at lower interest rates.

In evaluating debt-paying ability, short-term creditors and long-term creditors look at different relationships. Short-term creditors are interested in the company's *immediate* liquidity. Long-term creditors, in contrast, are interested in the company's ability to meet its interest obligations over a *period of years,* as well as its ability to repay or refinance large obligations as they come due.

In previous chapters we introduced several measures of short-term liquidity and long-term credit risk. These measures are summarized in Exhibit 10–5—along with the *interest coverage ratio,* which is discussed below.

Interest Coverage Ratio Creditors, investors, and managers all feel more comfortable when a company has enough income to cover its interest payments by a wide margin. One widely used measure of the relationship between earnings and interest expense is the **interest coverage ratio**.

The interest coverage ratio is computed by dividing *operating income* by the annual interest expense. From a creditor's point of view, the higher this ratio, the better. In past years, most companies with good credit ratings had interest coverage ratios of, perhaps, 4 to 1 or more. With the spree of junk bond financing in the 1980s, many large corporations let their interest coverage ratios decline below 2 to 1. In most cases, their credit ratings dropped accordingly.

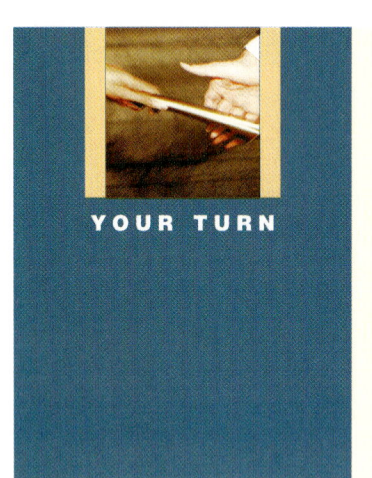

YOUR TURN

You as a Loan Officer

Assume that you are a loan officer for First Federal National Bank. A local business wishes to obtain a five-year loan in the amount of $150,000 to purchase a new piece of equipment. All of the company's liquidity ratios look promising except for its interest coverage ratio, which is 3 to 1.

The company's CEO contends that this ratio is acceptable, considering that the company's $375,000 in operating income for the year included depreciation expense of $200,000 and goodwill amortization expense of $50,000. Interest expense was, of course, $125,000 ($375,000 ÷ $125,000 = 3 times coverage).

What point was the CEO trying to make? Do you agree?

*Our comments appear on page 458.

Less Formal Means of Determining Creditworthiness Not all decisions to extend credit involve formal analysis of the borrower's financial statements. Most suppliers

---

[16] Bankruptcy is a legal status under which the company's fate is determined largely by the U.S. Bankruptcy Court. Sometimes the company is reorganized and allowed to continue its operations. In other cases, the business is closed and its assets are sold. Often managers and other employees lose their jobs. In almost all bankruptcies, the company's creditors and owners incur legal costs and sustain financial losses.

Financial Analysis

of goods or services, for example, will sell on account to almost any long-established business—unless they know the customer is in severe financial difficulty. If the customer is not a well-established business, these suppliers may investigate the customer's credit history by contacting a credit-rating agency.

In lending to small businesses organized as corporations, lenders may require key stockholders to *personally guarantee* repayment of the loan.

How Much Debt Should a Business Have?

All businesses incur some debts as a result of normal business operations. These include, for example, accounts payable and accrued liabilities. But many businesses aggressively use long-term debt, such as mortgages and bonds payable, to finance growth and expansion. Is this wise? Does it benefit the stockholders? The answer hinges on another question: *Can the borrowed funds be invested to earn a return higher than the rate of interest paid to creditors?*

Using borrowed money to finance business operations is called applying **leverage**. Extensive use of leverage—that is, a great deal of debt—sometimes benefits a business dramatically. But if things don't work out, it can "wipe out" the borrower.

If borrowed money can be invested to earn a rate of return *higher* than the interest rates paid to the lenders, net income and the return on stockholders' equity will *increase*.[17] For example, if you borrow money at an interest rate of 9% and invest it to earn 15%, you will benefit from "the spread."

But leverage is a double-edged sword—the effects may be favorable *or unfavorable*. If the rate of return earned on the borrowed money falls *below* the rate of interest being paid, the use of borrowed money *reduces* net income and the return on equity. Companies with large amounts of debt sometimes become victims of their own debt-service requirements.

The effects of leverage may be summarized as follows:

Relationship of Return on Assets to Interest Rate on Borrowed Funds	Effect on Net Income and Return on Equity
Return on Assets > Interest Rates Being Paid	Increase
Return on Assets < Interest Rates Being Paid	Decrease

Bear in mind that over time, both the return on assets and the interest rates that the company must pay may *change*.

The more leverage a company applies, the greater the effects on net income and the return on equity. Using more leverage simply means having more debt. Therefore, the *debt ratio* is a basic measure of the amount of leverage being applied.

FINANCIAL ANALYSIS

Exhibit 10–5 provides a summary of common measures used by creditors and investors to evaluate a company's *short-term and long-term debt-paying ability:*

---

[17] The rate of return earned on invested capital usually is viewed as the overall *return on assets*—that is, operating income divided by average total assets. *Return on equity* is net income expressed as a percentage of average stockholders' equity. Both of these return on investment measures are discussed in Chapter 14.

Exhibit 10–5

MEASURES OF DEBT-PAYING ABILITY

Short-Term	Long-Term
Quick ratio—Most liquid assets divided by current liabilities; a stringent measure of liquidity.	Debt ratio—Total liabilities divided by total assets. Measures percentage of capital structure financed by creditors.
Current ratio—Current assets divided by current liabilities; the most common measure of liquidity, but less stringent than the quick ratio.	Interest coverage ratio—Operating income divided by interest expense. Shows how many times the company earns its annual interest obligations.
Working capital—Current assets less current liabilities; the "uncommitted" liquid resources.	Trend in net cash flows from operating activities—Indicates trend in cash-generating ability. Determined from comparative statements of cash flow.
Turnover rates—Measures of how quickly receivables are collected or inventory is sold. (Computed separately for receivables and inventory.)	Trend in net income—Less related to debt-paying ability than cash flow, but still an excellent measure of long-term financial health.
Operating cycle—The period of time required to convert inventory into cash.	
Net cash flows from operating activities—Measures a company's ability to generate cash. (Shown in the statement of cash flows.)	
Lines of credit—Indicates ready access to additional cash should the need arise.	

CONCLUDING REMARKS

Businesses have two basic sources of financing their assets: liabilities and owners' equity. Throughout this chapter, we have studied current liabilities, long-term liabilities, and estimated liabilities common to most large businesses. We have learned that liabilities differ from owners' equity in several respects. The feature that most clearly distinguishes the claims of creditors from those of owners is that virtually all liabilities eventually mature and become due. We have also learned that the claims of creditors have legal priority over the claims of owners.

In the next two chapters, we turn our attention to owners' equity. We will examine many important topics including treasury stock transactions, cash dividends, stock dividends, stock splits, and the differences between common and preferred stockholders.

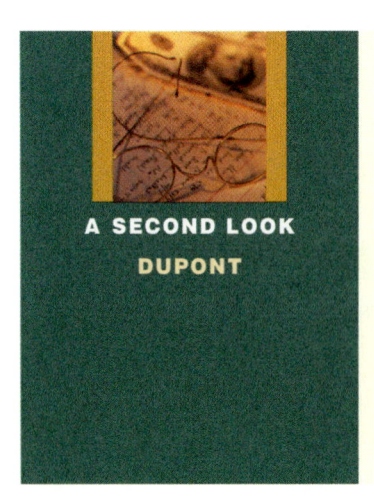

A SECOND LOOK

DUPONT

As noted at the start of this chapter, **E.I. du Pont de Nemours & Co.**'s disproportionate reliance on debt financing burdens the company with billions of dollars in debt service costs annually. The statement of cash flows enables investors and creditors to ascertain how much a company pays each year to service its debt. A statement of cash flows issued by **Dupont** reveals that the company recently made interest and principal payments exceeding $9 billion and borrowed an additional $4.9 billion through the issuance of long-term debt. These figures are staggering, given that the company's cash flows from continuing operations average less than $5 billion annually.

Principal repayment of debt obligations and the issuance of new debt instruments are reported in the statement of cash flows as *financing activities*. Other financing activities reported in **DuPont**'s statement of cash flows include treasury stock transactions and dividend payments. These activities are discussed in Chapters 11 and 12.

SUPPLEMENTAL TOPIC

SPECIAL TYPES OF LIABILITIES

The types of liabilities discussed up to this point have been those short-term and long-term obligations encountered by most organizations. Here we examine three special types of liabilities most common to very large organizations: (1) leases, (2) postretirement benefits, and (3) deferred taxes.

LO 10
Describe reporting issues related to leases, postretirement benefits, and deferred taxes.

Lease Payment Obligations

A company may purchase the assets needed in its business operations or, as an alternative, it may lease them. A *lease* is a contract in which the lessor gives the lessee the right to use an asset for a specified period of time in exchange for periodic rental payments. The **lessor** is the owner of the property; the **lessee** is a tenant or renter. Examples of assets frequently acquired by lease include automobiles, building space, computers, and equipment.

Operating Leases

When the lessor gives the lessee the right to use leased property for a limited period of time but retains the usual risks and rewards of ownership, the contract is known as an **operating lease**. An example of an operating lease is a contract leasing office space in an office building. If the building increases in value, the *lessor* can receive the benefits of this increase by either selling the building or increasing the rental rate once the lease term has expired. Likewise, if the building declines in value, it is the lessor who bears the loss.

In accounting for an operating lease, the lessor views the monthly lease payments received as rental revenue, and the lessee regards these payments as rental expense. No asset or liability (other than a short-term liability for accrued rent payable) relating to the lease appears in the lessee's balance sheet. Thus operating leases are sometimes termed **off-balance-sheet financing**.

Capital Leases

Some lease contracts are intended to provide financing to the lessee for the eventual purchase of the property or to provide the lessee with use of the property over most of its useful life. These lease contracts are called **capital leases** (or financing leases). In contrast to an operating lease, a capital lease transfers most of the risks and rewards of ownership from the lessor to the *lessee*.

From an accounting viewpoint, capital leases are regarded as *essentially equivalent to a sale* of the property by the lessor to the lessee, even though title to the leased property has not been transferred. Thus a capital lease should be recorded by the *lessor as a sale* of property and by the *lessee as a purchase.*

When equipment is acquired through a capital lease, the lessee *debits an asset account,* Leased Equipment, and *credits a liability account,* Lease Payment Obligation, for the present value of the future lease payments. Lease payments made by the lessee are allocated between Interest Expense and a reduction in the liability Lease Payment Obligation. The portion of the lease payment obligation that will be repaid within the next year is classified as a current liability, and the remainder is classified as long-term.

No rent expense is recorded by the lessee in a capital lease. The asset account Leased Equipment is usually depreciated by the lessee over the life of the equipment rather than the term of the lease. Accounting for capital leases is illustrated in Appendix B at the end of this textbook.

Distinguishing between Capital Leases and Operating Leases The FASB has taken the position that the risks and returns of ownership transfer to the lessee under any of the following circumstances:

- The lease transfers ownership of the property to the lessee at the end of the lease term.
- The lease contains a bargain purchase option.
- The lease term is equal to 75% or more of the estimated economic life of the leased property.
- The present value of the minimum lease payments amounts to 90% or more of the fair value of the lease property.

Thus, if a lease contains any of these provisions, it is viewed as a capital lease. Otherwise, it is accounted for as an operating lease.

Liabilities for Pensions and Other Postretirement Benefits

Many employers agree to pay their employees a pension; that is, monthly cash payments for life, beginning at retirement. Pensions are not an expense of the years in which cash payments are made to retired workers. Employees earn the right to receive the pension *while they are working for their employer.* Therefore, the employer's cost of future pension payments *accrues* over the years that each employee is on the payroll.

The amounts of the retirement benefits that will be paid to today's workers after they retire are not known with certainty. Among other things, these amounts depend on how long retired employees live. Therefore, the employer's obligation for future pension payments arising during the current year *can only be estimated.*

Employers do not usually pay retirement pensions directly to retired employees. Most employers meet their pension obligations by making periodic deposits in a **pension fund** (or pension plan) throughout the years of each worker's employment.

A pension fund is *not an asset* of the employer. Rather, it is an *independent entity* managed by a trustee (usually a bank or an insurance company). As the employer makes deposits in the pension fund, the trustee invests the money in securities such as stocks and bonds. Over time, the pension fund earns investment income and normally accumulates to a balance far in excess of the employer's deposits. The *pension fund*—not the employer—disburses monthly pension benefits to retired workers.

If the employer meets *all* of its estimated pension obligations by promptly depositing cash in a pension fund, the pension fund is said to be *fully funded.* If a pension plan is fully funded, *no liability* for pension payments appears in the employer's balance sheet. The employer's obligation is discharged in the *current period* through the payments made to the pension fund. The employer records each payment to this fund by debiting Pension Expense and crediting Cash.

Determining Pension Expense From a conceptual point of view, the pension expense of a given period is the *present value* of the future pension rights granted to employees as a result of their services during the period. The computation of annual pension expense is complex and involves many assumptions. The amount of this expense is computed not by accountants, but rather by an **actuary**, who considers these factors:

- Average age, retirement age, and life expectancy of employees
- Employee turnover rates
- Compensation levels and estimated rate of pay increases
- Expected rate of return to be earned on pension fund assets

For example, assume that the actuarial firm of Gibson & Holt computes a pension expense for Cramer Cable Company of $400,000 for 2002. This amount represents the present value of pension rights granted to Cramer's employees for the work they performed during the year. To fully fund this obligation, Cramer transfers $400,000 to National Trust Co., the trustee of the company's pension plan.

The following entry summarizes Cramer's fully funded pension expense for 2002:

Pension Expense	400,000	
Cash		400,000

Pension expense for the year as determined by actuarial firm of
Gibson & Holt; fully funded by payments to National Trust Co.

You as a Public Accountant for Small Businesses

Assume you are a sole proprietor of Balance & Income, CPAs. One of your clients asks you to provide help in estimating pension obligations associated with his firm. You tell the client that you do not have actuarial training; however, the client is insistent and suggests you get a book of actuarial tables and make an estimate. What should you do?

*Our comments appear on page 458.

Postretirement Benefits Other Than Pensions In addition to pension plans, many companies have promised their employees other types of *postretirement benefits*, such as continuing health insurance. In most respects, these nonpension postretirement benefits are accounted for in the same manner as are pension benefits. Most companies, however, do not fully fund their obligations for nonpension postretirement benefits. Thus recognition of the annual expense often includes a credit to an unfunded liability for part of the cost.

Continuing with our illustration of Cramer Cable Company, assume that Gibson & Holt computes for the company a $250,000 nonpension postretirement benefits expense for 2002. Unlike its pension expense, however, Cramer does *not* fully fund its nonpension obligations.

For 2002, only $140,000 of the total amount was paid in cash. The entry to summarize this expense for the year is:

Nonpension Postretirement Benefits Expense	250,000	
Cash		140,000
Unfunded Liability for Nonpension Postretirement Benefits		110,000

To record nonpension postretirement benefits expense per report of
Gibson & Holt, actuaries; expense funded to the extent of $140,000.

Any portion of the unfunded liability that the company intends to fund during the next year is classified as a *current liability;* the remainder is classified as a *long-term liability*.

Unfunded Postretirement Costs Are Noncash Expenses Postretirement costs are recognized as expenses as workers earn the right to receive these benefits. If these costs are fully funded, the company makes cash payments within the current period equal to this expense. But if these benefits are *not* funded, the cash payments are not made until after the employees retire. Thus an unfunded retirement plan involves a long lag between the recognition of expense and the related cash payments.

Unfunded retirement benefits often are called a noncash expense. That is, the expense is charged against current earnings, but there are no corresponding cash payments in the period. In the journal entry above, notice that expense exceeds the cash outlays by $110,000 ($250,000 − $140,000 = $110,000). This amount corresponds to the growth in the unfunded liability.

Unfunded Liabilities for Postretirement Costs: Can They Really Be Paid? Many of America's largest and best-known corporations have obligations for unfunded postretirement benefits that can only be described as enormous. For many companies, this liability is equal to, or *greater than,* the total amount of stockholders' equity.

CASE IN POINT

General Motors reports an unfunded liability for postretirement costs of more than *$34 billion*. That compares with total stockholders' equity of a little more than $29 billion. One might say that **GM**'s employees have a greater financial stake in the company's long-term prospects than do its stockholders.

Many users of financial statements wonder whether **General Motors** and other large corporations can really pay liabilities this large. Interesting question.

Let us suggest some things to consider in evaluating a company's ability to pay its unfunded liability for postretirement costs. First, remember that this liability represents only the *present value* of the estimated future payments. The future payments are expected to be *substantially more* than the amount shown in the balance sheet. Next, this liability may *continue to grow*, especially if the company has more employees today than in the past. On the other hand, this liability does *not* have to be paid all at once. It will be paid over a *great many years*—the life span of today's workforce.

CASH EFFECTS

In evaluating a company's ability to meet its postretirement obligations, we suggest looking to the *statement of cash flows,* rather than the balance sheet or income statement. In the statement of cash flows, payments of postretirement costs are classified as operating activities. Thus, if a company has a steadily increasing net cash flow from operating activities, it is more likely to be able to handle these costs—at least *at present.* But if the net cash flow from operating activities starts to decline, the company may have no choice but to reduce the benefits it provides to retired employees. Often these benefits are *not* contractual and can be reduced at management's discretion.

Deferred Income Taxes

We have seen in earlier chapters that differences sometimes exist between the way certain revenues or expenses are recognized in financial statements and the way these same items are reported in income tax returns. For example, most companies use the straight-line method of depreciation in their financial reports but use an accelerated method in their income tax returns. Because of such differences between accounting principles and tax rules, income appearing in the income statement today may not be subject to income taxes until future years. However, the *matching principle* requires that the income shown in an income statement be offset by all related income taxes expense, regardless of when these taxes will be paid. Thus the entry to record a corporation's income taxes expense might appear as follows:

My Notes
Payment of income taxes expense often can be deferred

Income Taxes Expense	1,000,000	
Income Taxes Payable		800,000
Deferred Income Taxes		200,000
To record corporate income taxes applicable to the income of the current year.		

Income Taxes Payable is a current liability representing the portion of the income taxes expense that must be paid when the company files its income tax return for the current year. The portion of income taxes expense that is deferred to future tax returns is credited to a liability account entitled **Deferred Income Taxes**.

Supplemental Topic

Deferred Income Taxes in Financial Statements How deferred income taxes are classified in the balance sheet depends on the classification of the assets and liabilities that *caused* the tax deferrals. Although deferred taxes often appear as liabilities, certain conditions may require that they be classified as assets. Accounting for deferred taxes involves a number of complex issues that are addressed in more advanced accounting courses.

CASE IN POINT

In some countries, financial reporting requirements are consistent with tax reporting requirements. As a result, deferred income taxes do not typically appear on the financial statements of companies in those countries. Germany, France, and Sweden are countries where tax and financial reporting requirements are consistent. A recent annual report of **Renault**, an automobile company headquartered in France and listed on the Paris Bourse (the French stock exchange), does not contain deferred income tax information.

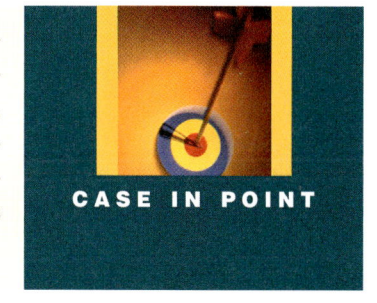

END-OF-CHAPTER REVIEW

SUMMARY OF LEARNING OBJECTIVES

LO 1
Define *liabilities* and distinguish between current and long-term liabilities.
Liabilities are debts arising from past transactions or events that require payment (or the rendering of services) at some future date. Current liabilities are those maturing within one year or the company's operating cycle (whichever is longer) and that are expected to be paid from current assets. Liabilities classified as long-term include obligations maturing more than one year in the future and shorter-term obligations that will be refinanced or paid from noncurrent assets.

LO 2
Account for notes payable and interest expense.
Initially, a liability is recorded only for the principal amount of a note—that is, the amount owed *before* including any interest charges. Interest expense accrues over time. Any accrued interest expense is recognized at the end of an accounting period by an adjusting entry that records both the expense and a short-term liability for accrued interest payable.

LO 3
Describe the costs relating to payrolls.
The basic cost of payrolls is, of course, the salaries and wages earned by employees. However, all employers also incur costs for various payroll taxes, such as the employer's share of Social Security and Medicare, workers' compensation premiums, and unemployment insurance. Many employers also incur costs for various employee benefits, such as health insurance and postretirement benefits. (These additional payroll related costs often amount to 30% to 40% of the basic wages and salaries expense.)

LO 4
Prepare an amortization table allocating payments between interest and principal.
An amortization table includes four money columns, showing (1) the amount of each payment, (2) the portion of the payment representing interest expense, (3) the portion of the payment that reduces the principal amount of the loan, and (4) the remaining unpaid balance (or principal amount). The table begins with the original amount of the loan listed in the unpaid balance column. A separate line then is completed showing the allocation of each payment between interest and principal reduction and indicating the new unpaid balance subsequent to the payment.

LO 5
Describe corporate bonds and explain the tax advantage of debt financing.
Corporate bonds are transferable long-term notes payable. Each bond usually has a face value of $1,000 (or a multiple of $1,000), calls for interest payments at a contractual rate, and has a stated maturity date. By issuing thousands of bonds to the investing public at one time, the corporation divides a very large and long-term loan into many transferable units.

The principal advantage of issuing bonds instead of capital stock is that interest payments to bondholders are deductible in determining taxable income, whereas dividend payments to stockholders are not.

LO 6
Account for bonds issued at a discount or premium.
When bonds are issued at a discount, the borrower must repay more than the amount originally borrowed. Thus any discount in the issuance price represents additional cost in the overall borrowing transaction. The matching principle requires that the borrower recognize this cost gradually over the life of the bond issue as interest expense.

If bonds are issued at a premium, the borrower will repay an amount less than the amount originally borrowed. Thus the premium serves to reduce the overall cost of the borrowing transaction. Again, the matching principle requires that this reduction in interest expense be recognized gradually over the life of the bond issue.

LO 7
Explain the concept of present value as it relates to bond prices.
The basic concept of present value is that an amount of money that will not be paid or received until some future date is equivalent to a smaller amount of money today. This is because the smaller amount available today could be invested to earn interest and thereby accumulate over time to the larger future amount. The amount today considered equivalent to the future amount is termed the present value of that future amount.

The concept of present value is used in the valuation of most long-term liabilities. It also is widely used in investment decisions. Readers who are not familiar with this concept are encouraged to read Appendix B at the end of this textbook.

LO 8
Explain how estimated liabilities, loss contingencies, and commitments are disclosed in financial statements.
Estimated liabilities, such as an automobile manufacturer's responsibility to honor new car warranties, appear in the financial statements at their estimated dollar amounts. Loss contingencies appear as liabilities *only* when it is probable that a loss has been incurred *and* the amount can be reasonably estimated. Unless both these conditions are met, loss contingencies are simply disclosed in the notes to the financial statements. Commitments are contracts for future transactions; they are *not* liabilities. However, if considered material, they are often disclosed in the notes to the financial statements.

LO 9
Evaluate the safety of creditors' claims.
Short-term creditors may evaluate the safety of their claims using such measures of liquidity as the current ratio, quick ratio, the available lines of credit, and the debtor's credit rating. Long-term creditors look more to signs of stability and long-term financial health, including the debt ratio, interest coverage ratio, and the trends in net income and net cash flow from operating activities.

*LO 10
Describe reporting issues related to leases, postretirement benefits, and deferred taxes.
Leases that are essentially equivalent to a sale of property by the lessor to the lessee are regarded as capital leases. Under a capital lease arrangement, the lessee reports in its balance sheet the present values of both an asset (e.g., leased equipment), and a liability (lease payment obligations). Lease arrangements that do not qualify as capital leases are treated as operating leases, requiring that lease payments be treated as expenses when paid.

Unfunded postretirement costs are reported in the balance sheet at their discounted present values as long-term liabilities. Unfunded postretirement benefits are often called a noncash expense. That is, the expense is charged against current earnings without a corresponding outlay of cash.

Deferred income taxes result because timing differences exist between financial accounting principles and tax rules. Thus, income appearing in the income statement today may not be subject to income taxes until future years. Likewise, income subject to income taxes today, may not appear in the company's income statement until future periods. Depending on the circumstances, deferred taxes may appear in the balance sheet as liabilities and/or assets (both current and long-term).

KEY TERMS INTRODUCED OR EMPHASIZED IN CHAPTER 10

accrued liabilities (p. 413) The liability to pay an expense that has accrued during the period. Also called *accrued expenses*.

actuary (p. 438) A statistician who performs computations involving assumptions as to human life spans. One function is computing companies' liabilities for pensions and postretirement benefits.

amortization table (p. 416) A schedule that indicates how installment payments are allocated between interest expense and repayments of principal.

bankruptcy (p. 434) A legal status in which the financial affairs of an illiquid business (or individual) are managed, in large part, by the U.S. Bankruptcy Court.

bonds payable (p. 418) Long-term debt securities that subdivide a very large and long-term corporate debt into transferable increments of $1,000 or multiples thereof.

capital lease (p. 437) A lease contract that finances the eventual purchase by the lessee of leased property. The lessor accounts for a capital lease as a sale of property; the lessee records an asset and a liability equal to the present value of the future lease payments. Also called a *financing lease*.

collateral (p. 410) Assets that have been pledged to secure specific liabilities. Creditors with secured claims can foreclose on (seize title to) these assets if the borrower defaults.

commitments (p. 433) Agreements to carry out future transactions. Not a liability because the transaction has not yet been performed, but may be disclosed in notes to the financial statements.

convertible bond (p. 420) A bond that may be exchanged (at the bondholder's option) for a specified number of shares of the company's capital stock.

debt service (p. 416) The combined cash outlays required for repayment of principal amounts borrowed and for payments of interest expense during the period.

deferred income taxes (p. 440) A liability account to pay income taxes that have been postponed to a future year's income tax return. In some cases, this account can also be an asset account representing income taxes to be saved in a future year's income tax return.

estimated liabilities (p. 411) Liabilities known to exist, but that must be recorded in the accounting records at estimated dollar amounts.

interest coverage ratio (p. 434) Operating income divided by interest expense. Indicates the number of times that the company was able to earn the amount of its interest charges.

junk bonds (p. 420) Bonds payable that involve a greater than normal risk of default and, therefore, must pay higher than normal rates of interest in order to be attractive to investors.

lessee (p. 437) The tenant, user, or renter of leased property.

lessor (p. 437) The owner of property leased to a lessee.

leverage (p. 435) The use of borrowed money to finance business operations.

loss contingencies (p. 432) Situations involving uncertainty as to whether a loss has occurred. The uncertainty will be resolved by a future event. An example of a loss contingency is the possible loss relating to a lawsuit pending against a company. Although loss contingencies are sometimes recorded in the accounts, they are more frequently disclosed only in notes to the financial statements.

maturity date (p. 410) The date on which a liability becomes due.

off-balance-sheet financing (p. 437) An arrangement in which the use of resources is financed without the obligation for

---
Supplemental Topic: "Special Types of Liabilities."

future payments appearing as a liability in the balance sheet. An operating lease is a common example of off-balance-sheet financing.

operating lease (p. 437) A lease contract which is in essence a rental agreement. The lessee has the use of the leased property, but the lessor retains the usual risks and rewards of ownership. The periodic lease payments are accounted for as rent expense by the lessee and as rental revenue by the lessor.

payroll taxes (p. 414) Taxes levied on an employer based on the amount of wages and salaries being paid to employees during the period. Include the employers' share of Social Security and Medicare taxes, unemployment taxes, and (though not called a "tax") workers' compensation premiums.

pension fund (p. 438) A fund managed by an independent trustee into which an employer company makes periodic payments. The fund is used to make pension payments to retired employees.

postretirement benefits (p. 439) Benefits that will be paid to retired workers. The present value of the future benefits earned by workers during the current period is an expense of the period. If not fully funded, this expense results in a liability for unfunded postretirement benefits. (For many companies, these liabilities have become very large.)

present value (of a future amount) (p. 429) The amount of money that an informed investor would pay today for the right to receive the future amount, based on a specific rate of return required by the investor.

principal amount (p. 411) The unpaid balance of an obligation, exclusive of any interest charges for the current period.

sinking fund (p. 420) Cash set aside by a corporation at regular intervals (usually with a trustee) for the purpose of repaying a bond issue at its maturity date.

underwriter (p. 419) An investment banking firm that handles the sale of a corporation's stocks or bonds to the public.

workers' compensation (p. 414) A state-mandated insurance program insuring workers against job-related injuries. Premiums are charged to employers as a percentage of the employees' wages and salaries. The amounts vary by state and by the employees' occupations but, in some cases, can be very substantial.

DEMONSTRATION PROBLEM

Listed below are selected items from the financial statements of G & H Pump Mfg. Co. for the year ended December 31, 2002.

Note payable to Porterville Bank	99,000
Income taxes payable	63,000
Loss contingency relating to lawsuit	200,000
Accounts payable and accrued expenses	163,230
Mortgage note payable	240,864
Bonds payable	2,200,000
Premium on bonds payable	1,406
Accrued bond interest payable	110,000
Pension expense	61,400
Unearned revenue	25,300

Other Information

1. The note payable owed to Porterville Bank is due in 30 days. G & H has arranged with this bank to renew the note for an additional two years.
2. G & H has been sued for $200,000 by someone claiming the company's pumps are excessively noisy. It is reasonably possible, but not probable, that a loss has been sustained.
3. The mortgage note is payable at $8,000 per month over the next three years. During the next 12 months, the principal amount of this note will be reduced to $169,994.
4. The bonds payable mature in seven months. A sinking fund has been accumulated to repay the full maturity of this bond issue.

Instructions

a. Using this information, prepare the current liabilities and long-term liabilities sections of a classified balance sheet at December 31, 2002.
b. Explain briefly how the information in each of the four numbered paragraphs affected your presentation of the company's liabilities.

Solution to the Demonstration Problem

a.

G & H PUMP MFG. CO.
Partial Balance Sheet
December 31, 2002

Liabilities:		
Current liabilities:		
Accounts payable and accrued expenses		$ 163,230
Income taxes payable		63,000
Accrued bond interest payable		110,000
Unearned revenue		25,300
Current portion of long-term debt		70,870
Total current liabilities		$ 432,400
Long-term liabilities:		
Note payable to Porterville Bank		$ 99,000
Mortgage note payable		169,994
Bonds payable	$2,200,000	
Add: Premium on bonds payable	1,406	2,201,406
Total long-term liabilities		$2,470,400
Total liabilities		$2,902,800

b.
1. Although the note payable to Porterville Bank is due in 30 days, it is classified as a long-term liability as it will be refinanced on a long-term basis.
2. The pending lawsuit is a loss contingency requiring disclosure, but it is not listed in the liability section of the balance sheet.
3. The $70,870 of the mortgage note that will be repaid within the next 12 months ($240,864 − $169,994) is a current liability; the remaining balance, due after December 31, 2003, is long-term debt.
4. Although the bonds payable mature in seven months, they will be repaid from a sinking fund, rather than from current assets. Therefore, these bonds retain their long-term classification.

SELF-TEST QUESTIONS

Answers to these questions appear on page 459.

1. Which of the following is characteristic of liabilities rather than of equity? (More than one answer may be correct.)
   a. The obligation matures.
   b. Interest paid to the provider of the capital is deductible in the determination of taxable income.
   c. The capital providers' claims are *residual* in the event of liquidation of the business.
   d. The capital providers normally have the right to exercise control over business operations.

2. On October 1, Dalton Corp. borrows $100,000 from National Bank, signing a six-month note payable for that amount, plus interest to be computed at a rate of 9% per annum. Indicate all correct answers.
   a. Dalton's liability at October 1 is only $100,000.
   b. The maturity value of this note is $104,500.

c. At December 31, Dalton will have a liability for accrued interest payable in the amount of $4,500.

d. Dalton's total liability for this loan at November 30 is $101,500.

3. Identify all correct statements concerning payrolls and related payroll costs.

   a. Both employers and employees pay Social Security and Medicare taxes.

   b. Workers' compensation premiums are withheld from employees' wages.

   c. An employer's total payroll costs usually exceed total wages expense by about $7\frac{1}{2}\%$.

   d. Under current law, employers are required to pay Social Security taxes on employees' earnings, but they are not required to pay for health insurance.

4. Identify the types of information that can readily be determined from an amortization table for an installment loan. (More than one answer may be correct.)

   a. Interest expense on this liability for the current year.

   b. The present value of the future payments under changing market conditions.

   c. The unpaid balance remaining after each payment.

   d. The portion of the unpaid balance that is a current liability.

5. Which of the following statements is (are) correct? (More than one statement may be correct.)

   a. A bond issue is a technique for subdividing a very large loan into many small, transferable units.

   b. Bond interest payments are contractual obligations, whereas the board of directors determines whether or not dividends will be paid.

   c. As interest rates rise, the market prices of bonds fall; as interest rates fall, bond prices tend to rise.

   d. Bond interest payments are deductible in determining income subject to income taxes, whereas dividends paid to stockholders are not deductible.

6. Identify all statements that are *consistent* with the concept of present value. (More than one answer may be correct.)

   a. The present value of a future amount always is *less* than that future amount.

   b. An amount of money available today is considered *more* valuable than the *same sum* that will not become available until a future date.

   c. A bond's issue price is equal to the present value of its future cash flows.

   d. The liability for an installment note payable is recorded at only the *principal* amount, rather than the sum of the scheduled future payments.

7. Identify those trends that are *unfavorable* from the viewpoint of a bondholder. (More than one answer may be correct.)

   a. Market interest rates are steadily rising.

   b. The issuing company's interest coverage ratio is steadily rising.

   c. The issuing company's net cash flow from operating activities is steadily declining.

   d. The issuing company's debt ratio is steadily declining.

8. A basic difference between *loss contingencies* and "real" liabilities is:

   a. Liabilities stem from past transactions; loss contingencies stem from future events.

   b. Liabilities always are recorded in the accounting records, whereas loss contingencies never are.

   c. The extent of uncertainty involved.

   d. Liabilities can be large in amount, whereas loss contingencies are immaterial.

9. Which of the following situations require recording a liability in 2002? (More than one answer may be correct.)

   a. In 2002, a company manufactures and sells stereo equipment that carries a three-year warranty.

   b. In 2002, a theater group receives payments in advance from season ticket holders for productions to be performed in 2003.

   c. A company is a defendant in a legal action. At the end of 2002, the company's attorney feels it is possible the company will lose and that the amount of the loss might be material.

d. During 2002, a Midwest agricultural cooperative is concerned about the risk of loss if inclement weather destroys the crops.

*10. Silverado maintains a fully funded pension plan. During 2002, $1 million was paid to retired workers, and workers currently employed by the company earned a portion of the right to receive pension payments expected to total $6 million *over their lifetimes.* Silverado's pension *expense* for 2002 amounts to:
   a. $1 million.
   b. $6 million.
   c. $7 million.
   d. Some other amount.

*11. Deferred income taxes result from:
   a. The fact that bond interest is deductible in the computation of taxable income.
   b. Depositing income taxes due in future years in a special fund managed by an independent trustee.
   c. Differences between certain revenue and expense items recognized in financial statements but not in income tax returns.
   d. The inability of a bankrupt company to pay its income tax liability on schedule.

ASSIGNMENT MATERIAL
DISCUSSION QUESTIONS

1. Define *liabilities*. Identify several characteristics that distinguish liabilities from owners' equity.
2. Explain the relative priority of the claims of owners and of creditors to the assets of a business. Do all creditors have equal priority? Explain.
3. Define *current liabilities* and *long-term liabilities*. Under what circumstances might a 10-year bond issue be classified as a current liability? Under what circumstances might a note payable maturing 30 days after the balance sheet date be classified as a long-term liability?
4. Jonas Company issues a 90-day, 12% note payable to replace an account payable to Smith Supply Company in the amount of $8,000. Draft the journal entries (in general journal form) to record the issuance of the note payable and the payment of the note at the maturity date.
5. Explain why an employer's "total cost" of a payroll may exceed by a substantial amount the total wages and salaries earned by employees.
6. What are workers' compensation premiums? Who pays them? Who pays Social Security and Medicare taxes?
7. Ace Garage has an unpaid mortgage loan of $63,210, payable at $1,200 per month. An amortization table indicates that $527 of the current monthly payment represents interest expense. What will be the amount of this mortgage obligation immediately *after* Ace makes this current payment?
8. A friend of yours has just purchased a house and has taken out a $50,000, 11% mortgage, payable at $476.17 per month. After making the first monthly payment, he received a receipt from the bank stating that only $17.84 of the $476.17 had been applied to reducing the principal amount of the loan. Your friend computes that at the rate of $17.84 per month, it will take over 233 years to pay off the $50,000 mortgage. Do you agree with your friend's analysis? Explain.
9. Briefly explain the income tax advantage of raising capital by issuing bonds rather than by selling capital stock.
10. Tampa Boat Company pays federal income taxes at a rate of 30% on taxable income. Compute the company's annual *after-tax* cost of borrowing on a 10%, $5 million bond issue. Express this after-tax cost as a percentage of the borrowed $5 million.
11. Why is the *present value* of a future amount always *less* than the future amount?
12. Why do bond prices vary inversely with interest rates?

Supplemental Topic: "Special Types of Liabilities."

13. Some bonds now being bought and sold by investors on organized securities exchanges were issued when interest rates were much higher than they are today. Would you expect these bonds to be trading at prices above or below their face values? Explain.

14. *The Wall Street Journal* recently quoted a market price of *102* for an issue of 8% **Nabisco** bonds. What would be the market price for $25,000 face value of these bonds (ignoring accrued interest)? Is the market rate of interest for bonds of this quality higher or lower than 8%? Explain.

15. The 6% bonds of Central Gas & Electric are selling at a market price of 72, whereas the 6% bonds of Interstate Power are selling at a price of 97. Does this mean that Interstate Power has a better credit rating than Central Gas & Electric? Explain. (Assume current long-term interest rates are in the 11% to 13% range.)

16. Does issuing bonds at a discount increase or decrease the issuing company's cost of borrowing? Explain.

17. A $200 million bond issue of NDP Corp. (a liquid company) recently matured. The entire maturity value was paid from a bond sinking fund. What effect did this transaction have on the company's current ratio? On its debt ratio? Explain.

18. As a result of issuing 20-year bonds payable, Low-Cal Foods now has an interest coverage ratio of .75 to 1. Should this ratio be of greater concern to short-term creditors or to stockholders? Explain.

19. There is an old business saying that "You shouldn't *be* in business if your company doesn't earn higher than bank rates." This means that if a company is to succeed, its return on assets should be *significantly higher* than its cost of borrowing. Why is this so important?

20. Define *estimated liabilities* and provide two examples. Are estimated liabilities recorded in accounting records?

21. What is the meaning of the term *loss contingency*? Give several examples. How are loss contingencies presented in financial statements? Explain.

22. What is the meaning of the term *commitment*? Give several examples. How are commitments usually presented in financial statements? Explain.

*23. Explain how the lessee accounts for an operating lease and a capital lease. Why is an operating lease sometimes called *off-balance-sheet financing?*

*24. Ortega Industries has a fully funded pension plan. Each year, pension expense runs in excess of $10 million. At the present time, employees are entitled to receive pension benefits with a present value of $125 million. Explain what liability, if any, Ortega Industries should include in its balance sheet as a result of this pension plan.

*25. Why do large corporations often show no liability for pensions owed to retired employees, but huge liabilities for "nonpension postretirement benefits"?

*26. When are the costs of postretirement benefits recognized as expense? When are the related cash payments made?

*27. What is meant by the term *deferred income taxes?* How is this item presented in financial statements?

EXERCISES

EXERCISE 10.1

You as a Student

LO 4

Assume that you will have a 10-year, $10,000 loan to repay to your parents when you graduate from college next month. The loan, plus 8% annual interest on the unpaid balance, is to be repaid in 10 annual installments of $1,490 each, beginning one year after you graduate. You have accepted a well-paying job and are considering an early settlement of the entire unpaid balance in just three years (immediately after making the third annual payment of $1,490).

Prepare an amortization schedule showing how much money you will need to save to pay your parents the entire unpaid balance of your loan three years after your graduation. (Round amounts to the nearest dollar.)

Supplemental Topic: "Special Types of Liabilities."

Exercises

EXERCISE 10.2
Effects of Transactions on the Accounting Equation

LO 1–6

Listed below are eight events or transactions of GemStar Corporation.

a. Made an adjusting entry to record interest on a short-term note payable.
b. Made a monthly installment payment of a fully amortizing, six-month, interest-bearing installment note payable.
c. Recorded a regular biweekly payroll, including the amounts withheld from employees, the issuance of paychecks, and payroll taxes on the employer.
d. Came within 12 months of the maturity date of a note payable originally issued for a period of 18 months.
e. Deposited employee tax withholdings with proper tax authorities.
f. Issued bonds payable at par.
g. Recognized semiannual interest expense bonds payable described in part **f** and paid bondholders the full amount.
h. Recorded the necessary adjusting entry on December 31, 2002, to accrue three months' interest on bonds payable that had been issued at a discount several years prior. The next semiannual interest payment will occur March 31, 2003.

Indicate the effects of each of these transactions on the following financial statement categories. Organize your answer in tabular form, using the illustrated column headings. Use the following code letters to indicate the effects of each transaction on the accounting element listed in the column heading: **I** for increase, **D** for decrease, and **NE** for no effect.

	Income Statement			Balance Sheet			
Transaction	Revenue − Expenses =	Net Income	Assets =	Current Liab. +	Long-Term Liab. +	Owners' Equity
a						

EXERCISE 10.3
Effects of Transactions on Various Financial Measurements

LO 1, 2, 4–6, 8

Six events relating to liabilities follow:

a. Paid the liability for interest payable accrued at the end of the last accounting period.
b. Made the current monthly payment on a 12-month installment note payable, including interest and a partial repayment of principal.
c. Issued bonds payable at 98 on March 1, 2002. The bonds pay interest March 1 and September 1.
d. Recorded September 1, 2002, interest expense and made semiannual interest payment on bonds referred to in part **c**.
e. Recorded necessary adjusting entry on December 31, 2002, for bonds referred to in part **c**.
f. Recorded estimated 6-month warranty expense on December 31, 2002.

Indicate the effects of each transaction or adjusting entry on the financial measurements in the five column headings listed below. Use the code letters **I** for increase, **D** for decrease, and **NE** for no effect.

Transaction	Current Liabilities	Long-Term Liabilities	Net Income	Net Cash Flow from Operating Activities	Net Cash Flow (from All Sources)
a					

EXERCISE 10.4
Financial Statement Presentation of Liabilities

LO 1, 5, 6, 8

Using the following information, prepare a listing of Chernin Corporation's (a) current liabilities and (b) long-term liabilities. If you do not list a particular item as a liability, explain your reasoning.

Notes payable (of which $10,000 will be repaid within the next 12 months)	$ 80,000
Interest expense that will arise from existing liabilities over the next 12 months	125,000
Lawsuit pending against the company claiming $500,000 in damages. Legal counsel can make no reasonable estimate of the company's potential liability at this time.	500,000
20-year bond issue that matures in 2 years. (The entire amount will be repaid from a bond sinking fund.)	900,000
Accrued interest payable on the 20-year bond issue as of the balance sheet date	36,000
Three-year commitment to John Higgins as chief financial officer at a salary of $250,000 per year	750,000
Note payable due in 90 days, but that will be extended for an additional 18 months	75,000
Cash deposits from customers for goods and services to be delivered over the next 9 months	300,000

EXERCISE 10.5
Employees—What Do They Really Cost?
LO 3

Magnum Plus, Inc., is a manufacturer of hunting supplies. The following is a summary of the company's annual payroll-related costs:

Wages and salaries expense (of which $2,200,000 was withheld from employees' pay and forwarded directly to tax authorities)	$7,200,000
Payroll taxes	580,000
Workers' compensation premiums	250,000
Group health insurance premiums	725,000
Contributions to employees' pension plan	450,000

a. Compute Magnum's total payroll-related costs for the year.
b. Compute the net amount of cash actually paid to employees (their take-home pay).
c. Express total payroll-related costs as a percentage of (1) total wages and salaries expense, and (2) employees' take-home pay. (Round computations to the nearest 1%.)

EXERCISE 10.6
Use of an Amortization Table
LO 4

Glen Pool Club, Inc., has a $150,000 mortgage liability. The mortgage is payable in monthly installments of $1,543, which include interest computed at an annual rate of 12% (1% monthly).

a. Prepare a partial amortization table showing the original balance of this loan, and the allocation of the first two monthly payments between interest expense and the reduction in the mortgage's unpaid balance. (Round to the nearest dollar.)
b. Prepare the journal entry to record the second monthly payment.
c. Will monthly interest increase, decrease, or stay the same over the life of the loan? Explain your answer.

EXERCISE 10.7
After-Tax Cost of Borrowing
LO 5

DuPont reports in its balance sheet $340 million of 6.2% bonds payable at par value. The company's average income tax rate is approximately 40%.

a. Compute the company's after-tax cost of borrowing on this bond issue stated as a total dollar amount.
b. Compute the company's after-tax cost of borrowing on this bond issue stated as a percentage of the amount borrowed.
c. Describe briefly the advantage of raising funds by issuing bonds as opposed to stocks.

EXERCISE 10.8
Bond Interest on Bonds Issued at Par
LO 5

On March 31, 2002, Gardner Corporation received authorization to issue $50,000 of 9%, 30-year bonds payable. The bonds pay interest on March 31 and September 30. The entire issue was dated March 31, 2002, but the bonds were not issued until April 30, 2002. They were issued at par.

a. Prepare the journal entry at April 30, 2002, to record the sale of the bonds.

b. Prepare the journal entry at September 30, 2002, to record the semiannual bond interest payment.
c. Prepare the adjusting entry at December 31, 2002, to record bond interest expense accrued since September 30, 2002. (Assume that no monthly adjusting entries to accrue interest expense had been made prior to December 31, 2002.)
d. Explain why the issuing corporation charged its bond investors for interest accrued in April 2002, prior to the issuance date (see part **b** above).

EXERCISE 10.9

Accounting for Bonds Issued at a Premium: Issuance, Interest Payments, and Retirement

LO 5, 6

Swanson Corporation issued $8 million of 20-year, 8% bonds on April 1, 2002, at 102. Interest is due on March 31 and September 30 of each year, and all of the bonds in the issue mature on March 31, 2022. Swanson's fiscal year ends on December 31. Prepare the following journal entries:
a. April 1, 2002, to record the issuance of the bonds.
b. September 30, 2002, to pay interest and to amortize the bond premium.
c. March 31, 2022, to pay interest, amortize the bond premium, and retire the bonds at maturity (make two separate entries).
d. Briefly explain the effect of amortizing the bond premium upon (1) annual net income, and (2) annual net cash flow from operating activities. (Ignore possible income tax effects.)

EXERCISE 10.10

Accounting for Bonds Issued at a Discount: Issuance, Interest Payments, and Retirement

LO 5, 6

Mellilo Corporation issued $5 million of 20-year, 9.5% bonds on July 1, 2002, at 98. Interest is due on June 30 and December 31 of each year, and all of the bonds in the issue mature on June 30, 2022. Mellilo's fiscal year ends on December 31. The company uses the straight-line method to amortize bond discounts. Prepare the following journal entries:
a. July 1, 2002, to record the issuance of the bonds.
b. December 31, 2002, to pay interest and amortize the bond discount.
c. June 30, 2022, to pay interest, amortize the bond discount, and retire the bonds at maturity (make two separate entries).
d. Briefly explain the effect of amortizing the bond discount upon (1) annual net income and (2) annual net cash flow from operating activities. (Ignore possible income tax effects.)

EXERCISE 10.11

Safety of Creditors' Claims

LO 9

Shown below are data from recent reports of two publicly owned toy makers. Dollar amounts are stated in thousands.

	Tyco Toys, Inc.	Hasbro, Inc.
Total assets	$615,132	$2,616,388
Total liabilities	349,792	1,090,776
Interest expense	28,026	37,588
Operating income	13,028	304,672

a. Compute for each company (1) the debt ratio and (2) the interest coverage ratio. (Round the debt ratio to the nearest percent and the interest coverage ratio to two decimal places.)
b. In your opinion, which of these companies would a long-term creditor probably view as the safer investment? Explain.

*EXERCISE 10.12

Accounting for Leases

LO 10

On July 1, Pine Region Dairy leased equipment from Farm America for a period of three years. The lease calls for monthly payments of $2,500 payable in advance on the first day of each month, beginning July 1.

Prepare the journal entry needed to record this lease in the accounting records of Pine Region Dairy on July 1 under each of the following independent assumptions:
a. The lease represents a simple rental arrangement.
b. At the end of three years, title to this equipment will be transferred to Pine Region Dairy at no additional cost. The present value of the 36 monthly lease payments is $76,021, of which $2,500 is paid in cash on July 1. None of the initial $2,500 is allocated to interest expense.

---

*Supplemental Topic: "Special Types of Liabilities."

c. Why is situation **a,** the operating lease, sometimes called off-balance-sheet financing?
d. Would it be acceptable for a company to account for a capital lease as an operating lease to report rent expense rather than a long-term liability?

*EXERCISE 10.13
Pension Plans
LO 10

At the end of the current year, Western Electric received the following information from its actuarial firm:

Pension expense	$2,500,000
Nonpension postretirement benefits expense	750,000

The pension plan is fully funded. Western Electric has funded only $50,000 of the nonpension postretirement benefits this year.

a. Prepare the journal entry to summarize pension expense for the entire year.
b. Prepare the journal entry to summarize the nonpension postretirement benefits expense for the entire year.
c. If the company becomes illiquid in future years, what prospects, if any, do today's employees have of receiving the pension benefits that they have earned to date?
d. Does the company have an ethical responsibility to fully fund its nonpension postretirement benefits?

*EXERCISE 10.14
Deferred Income Taxes
LO 10

The following journal entry summarizes for the current year the income taxes expense of Wilson's Software Warehouse:

Income Taxes Expense	1,500,000	
Cash		960,000
Income Taxes Payable		340,000
Deferred Income Taxes		200,000
To record income taxes expense for the current year.		

Of the deferred income taxes, only $30,000 is classified as a current liability.

a. Define the term deferred income taxes.
b. What is the amount of income taxes that the company has paid or expects to pay in conjunction with its income tax return for the current year?
c. Illustrate the allocation of the liabilities shown in the above journal entry between the classifications of current liabilities and long-term liabilities.

EXERCISE 10.15
Examining **Tootsie Roll Industries**' Capital Structure
LO 9

To answer the following questions use the annual report for **Tootsie Roll Industries, Inc.,** in Appendix A at the end of the textbook:

a. Compute the company's current ratio and quick ratio for the most recent year reported. Do these ratios provide support that **Tootsie Roll** is able to repay its current liabilities as they come due? Explain.
b. Compute the company's debt ratio. Does **Tootsie Roll** appear to have excessive debt? Explain.
c. Examine the company's statement of cash flows. Does **Tootsie Roll**'s cash flow from operating activities appear adequate to cover its current liabilities as they come due? Explain.

PROBLEMS

PROBLEM 10.1
Effects of Transactions on Financial Statements
LO 1–6, 8

Fifteen transactions or events affecting Computer Specialists, Inc., are as follows:
a. Made a year-end adjusting entry to accrue interest on a note payable.
b. A liability classified for several years as long-term becomes due within the next 12 months.

---

*Supplemental Topic: "Special Types of Liabilities."

c. Recorded the regular biweekly payroll, including payroll taxes, amounts withheld from employees, and the issuance of paychecks.
d. Earned an amount previously recorded as unearned revenue.
e. Made arrangements to extend a bank loan due in 60 days for another 18 months.
f. Made a monthly payment on a fully amortized installment note payable. (Assume this note is classified as a current liability.)
g. Called bonds payable due in seven years at a price above the carrying value of the liability in the accounting records.
h. Issued bonds payable at 97 on May 1, 2002. The bonds pay interest April 30 and October 31.
i. Recorded October 31, 2002, interest expense and made semiannual interest payment on bonds referred to in part **h**.
j. Recorded necessary adjusting entry on December 31, 2002, for bonds referred to in part **h**.
k. Issued bonds payable at 102 on August 1, 2002. The bonds pay interest July 31 and January 31.
l. Recorded necessary adjusting entry on December 31, 2002, for bonds referred to in part **k**.
m. Recorded an estimated liability for warranty claims.
n. Entered into a two-year commitment to buy all hard drives from a particular supplier at a price 10% below market.
o. Received notice that a lawsuit has been filed against the company for $7 million. The amount of the company's liability, if any, cannot be reasonably estimated at this time.

Instructions

Indicate the effects of each of these transactions upon the following elements of the company's financial statements. Organize your answer in tabular form, using the column headings shown below. Use the following code letters to indicate the effects of each transaction on the accounting element listed in the column heading: **I** for increase, **D** for decrease, and **NE** for no effect.

	Income Statement			Balance Sheet			
Transaction	Revenue − Expense =	Net Income	Assets =	Current Liab. +	Long-Term Liab. +	Owners' Equity
a							

PROBLEM 10.2
Balance Sheet Presentation of Liabilities

LO 1, 2, 4, 8

The following are selected items from the accounting records of Seattle Chocolates for the year ended December 31, 2002:

Note payable to Northwest Bank	$500,000
Income taxes payable	40,000
Accrued expenses and payroll taxes	60,000
Mortgage note payable	750,000
Accrued interest on mortgage note payable	5,000
Trade accounts payable	250,000
Unearned revenue	15,000
Potential liability in pending lawsuit	100,000

Other Information

1. The note payable to Northwest Bank is due in 60 days. Arrangements have been made to renew this note for an additional 12 months.
2. The mortgage requires payments of $6,000 per month. An amortization table shows that its balance will be paid down to $739,000 by December 31, 2003.
3. Accrued interest on the mortgage note payable is paid monthly. The next payment is due near the end of the first week in January 2003.
4. Seattle Chocolates has been sued for $100,000 in a contract dispute. It is not possible at this time, however, to make a reasonable estimate of the possible loss, if any, that the company may have sustained.

Instructions

a. Using the information provided, prepare the current and long-term liability sections of the company's balance sheet dated December 31, 2002. (Within each classification, items may be listed in any order.)

b. Explain briefly how the information in each of the four numbered paragraphs above influenced your presentation of the company's liabilities.

PROBLEM 10.3
Notes Payable: Accruing Interest
LO 2

During the fiscal year ended December 31, Swanson Corporation engaged in the following transactions involving notes payable:

Aug. 6 Borrowed $12,000 from Maple Grove Bank, signing a 45-day, 12% note payable.

Sept. 16 Purchased office equipment from Seawald Equipment. The invoice amount was $18,000, and Seawald agreed to accept, as full payment, a 10%, three-month note for the invoice amount.

Sept. 20 Paid Maple Grove Bank the note plus accrued interest.

Nov. 1 Borrowed $250,000 from Mike Swanson, a major corporate stockholder. The corporation issued Swanson a $250,000, 15%, 90-day note payable.

Dec. 1 Purchased merchandise inventory in the amount of $5,000 from Gathman Corporation. Gathman accepted a 90-day, 14% note as full settlement of the purchase. Swanson Corporation uses a perpetual inventory system.

Dec. 16 The $18,000 note payable to Seawald Equipment matured today. Swanson paid the accrued interest on this note and issued a new 30-day, 16% note payable in the amount of $18,000 to replace the note that matured.

Instructions

a. Prepare journal entries (in general journal form) to record the above transactions. Use a 360-day year in making the interest calculations.

b. Prepare the adjusting entry needed at December 31, prior to closing the accounts. Use one entry for all three notes (round to the nearest dollar.)

c. Provide a possible explanation why the new 30-day note payable to Seawald Equipment pays 16% interest instead of the 10% rate charged on the September 16 note.

PROBLEM 10.4
Preparation and Use of an Amortization Table
LO 4

On September 1, 2002, Quick Lube signed a 30-year, $1,080,000 mortgage note payable to Mifflinburg Bank and Trust in conjunction with the purchase of a building and land. The mortgage note calls for interest at an annual rate of 12% (1% per month). The note is fully amortizing over a period of 360 months.

The bank sent Quick Lube an amortization table showing the allocation of monthly payments between interest and principal over the life of the loan. A small part of this amortization table is illustrated below. (For convenience, amounts have been rounded to the nearest dollar.)

Amortization Table
(12%, 30-Year Mortgage Note Payable for $1,080,000; Payable in 360 Monthly Installments of $11,110)

Interest Period	Payment Date	Monthly Payment	Interest Expense	Principal Reduction	Unpaid Balance
Issue date	Sept. 1, 2002	—	—	—	$1,080,000
1	Oct. 1	$11,110	$10,800	$310	1,079,690
2	Nov. 1	11,110	10,797	313	1,079,377

Instructions

a. Explain whether the amounts of interest expense and the reductions in the unpaid principal are likely to change in any predictable pattern from month to month.

b. Prepare journal entries to record the first two monthly payments on this mortgage.

c. Complete this amortization table for two more monthly installments—those due on December 1, 2002, and January 1, 2003. (Round amounts to the nearest dollar.)

d. Will any amounts relating to this 30-year mortgage be classified as current liabilities in Quick Lube's December 31, 2002, balance sheet? Explain, but you need not compute any additional dollar amounts.

Problems

PROBLEM 10.5
Bond Interest (Bonds Issued at Par)
LO 5

Blue Mountain Power Company obtained authorization to issue 20-year bonds with a face value of $10 million. The bonds are dated May 1, 2002, and have a contract rate of interest of 10%. They pay interest on November 1 and May 1. The bonds were issued on August 1, 2002, at 100 plus three months' accrued interest.

Instructions
Prepare the necessary journal entries in general journal form on:
a. August 1, 2002, to record the issuance of the bonds.
b. November 1, 2002, to record the first semiannual interest payment on the bond issue.
c. December 31, 2002, to record interest expense accrued through year-end. (Round to the nearest dollar.)
d. May 1, 2003, to record the second semiannual interest payment. (Round to the nearest dollar.)
e. What was the prevailing market rate of interest on the date that the bonds were issued? Explain.

PROBLEM 10.6
Amortization of a Bond Discount and Premium
LO 5, 6

On September 1, 2002, Park Rapids Lumber Company issued $80 million in 20-year, 10% bonds payable. Interest is payable semiannually on March 1 and September 1. Bond discounts and premiums are amortized at each interest payment date and at year-end. The company's fiscal year ends at December 31.

Instructions
a. Make the necessary adjusting entries at December 31, 2002, and the journal entry to record the payment of bond interest on March 1, 2003, under each of the following assumptions:
  1. The bonds were issued at 98. (Round to the nearest dollar.)
  2. The bonds were issued at 101. (Round to the nearest dollar.)
b. Compute the net bond liability at December 31, 2003, under assumptions **1** and **2** above. (Round to the nearest dollar.)
c. Under which of the above assumptions, **1** or **2**, would the investor's effective rate of interest be higher? Explain.

*PROBLEM 10.7
Reporting Liabilities in a Balance Sheet
LO 1, 5, 6, 10

The following items were taken from the accounting records of Minnesota Satellite Telephone Corporation (MinnSat) for the year ended December 31, 2002 (dollar amounts are in thousands):

Accounts payable	$ 65,600
Accrued expenses payable (other than interest)	11,347
6¾% Bonds payable, due Feb. 1, 2003	100,000
8½% Bonds payable, due June 1, 2003	250,000
Discount on bonds payable (8½% bonds of '03)	260
11% Bonds payable, due June 1, 2012	300,000
Premium on bonds payable (11% bonds of '12)	1,700
Accrued interest payable	7,333
Bond interest expense	61,000
Other interest expense	17,000
Notes payable (short-term)	110,000
Lease payment obligations—capital leases	23,600
Pension obligation	410,000
Unfunded obligations for postretirement benefits other than pensions	72,000
Deferred income taxes	130,000
Income taxes expense	66,900
Income taxes payable	17,300
Operating income	280,800
Net income	134,700
Total assets	2,093,500

Supplemental Topic: "Special Types of Liabilities."

Other Information

1. The 6¾% bonds due in February 2003 will be refinanced in January 2003 through the issuance of $150,000 in 9%, 20-year general debentures.
2. The 8½% bonds due June 1, 2003, will be repaid entirely from a bond sinking fund.
3. MinnSat is committed to total lease payments of $14,400 in 2003. Of this amount, $7,479 is applicable to operating leases, and $6,921 to capital leases. Payments on capital leases will be applied as follows: $2,300 to interest expense and $4,621 to reduction in the capitalized lease payment obligation.
4. MinnSat's pension plan is fully funded with an independent trustee.
5. The obligation for postretirement benefits other than pensions consists of a commitment to maintain health insurance for retired workers. During 2003, MinnSat will fund $18,000 of this obligation.
6. The $17,300 in income taxes payable relates to income taxes levied in 2002 and must be paid on or before March 15, 2003. No portion of the deferred tax liability is regarded as a current liability.

Instructions

a. Using this information, prepare the current liabilities and long-term liabilities sections of a classified balance sheet as of December 31, 2002. (Within each classification, items may be listed in any order.)
b. Explain briefly how the information in each of the six numbered paragraphs affected your presentation of the company's liabilities.
c. Compute as of December 31, 2002, the company's (1) debt ratio and (2) interest coverage ratio.
d. Based solely on information stated in this problem, indicate whether this company appears to be an outstanding, medium, or poor long-term credit risk. State specific reasons for your conclusion.

CASES AND UNSTRUCTURED PROBLEMS

*CASE 10.1

The Nature of Liabilities

LO 1, 10

Listed below are eight publicly owned corporations and a liability that regularly appears in each corporation's balance sheet:

a. **Wells Fargo & Company** (banking): Deposits: interest bearing
b. **The New York Times Company**: Unexpired subscriptions
c. **The Hollywood Park Companies** (horse racing): Outstanding mutuel tickets
d. **American Greetings** (greeting cards and gift wrap products manufacturer): Sales returns
e. **Wausau Paper Mills Company**: Current maturities of long-term debt
f. **Club Med., Inc.** (resorts): Amounts received for future vacations
g. **Apple Computer, Inc.**: Accrued marketing and distribution
h. **General Motors Corporation**: Postretirement costs other than pensions

Instructions

Briefly explain what you believe to be the nature of each of these liabilities, including how the liability arose and the manner in which it is likely to be discharged.

CASE 10.2

Factors Affecting Bond Prices

LO 5, 6, 7

DuPont has two bond issues outstanding with the following characteristics:

Issue	Interest Rate	Maturity	Current Price
A	8⅛%	2004	108
B	8⅛%	2006	112

---

*Supplemental Topic: "Special Types of Liabilities."

Instructions

Answer the following questions regarding these bond issues:

a. Which issue, A or B, has the higher effective rate of interest? How can you tell?

b. Assume that the bonds of both issues have face values of $1,000 each. How much total interest does each bond from *issue A* provide investors in *12 months?* How much total interest does each bond from *issue B* provide investors in *12 months?*

c. Note that both issues are by the same company, have the same contract rate of interest, and have identical credit ratings. In view of these facts, explain the current price difference of each issue.

CASE 10.3
Loss Contingencies
LO 8

Discuss each of the following situations, indicating whether the situation is a loss contingency that should be recorded or disclosed in the financial statements of Aztec Airlines. If the situation is not a loss contingency, explain how (if at all) it should be reported in the company's financial statements. (Assume that all dollar amounts are material.)

a. Aztec estimates that $700,000 of its accounts receivable will prove to be uncollectible.

b. The company's president is in poor health and has previously suffered two heart attacks.

c. As with any airline, Aztec faces the risk that a future airplane crash could cause considerable loss.

d. Aztec is being sued for $10 million for failing to adequately provide for passengers whose reservations were cancelled as a result of the airline overbooking certain flights. This suit will not be resolved for a year or more.

BUSINESS WEEK ASSIGNMENT

*CASE 10.4
Pension Plan Expense and Income
LO 10

Accounting for postretirement benefits requires significant judgment on the part of management. Judgments related to pension benefit plans can significantly influence corporate earnings. Consider the following excerpts from David Henry's article "Why Earnings Are Too Rosy," appearing in the August 13, 2001, *Business Week*.

> Companies are inflating earnings with income from pension-plan assets, making their results look better than what's really happening with their businesses. . . . The logic behind income from well-funded plans is simple: Company accounts ought to reflect the advantage of not having to pay into the funds. For these companies, what started as pension expense has become pension income. . . . The key is expected return-on-pension assets. Under current accounting standards, companies start each year estimating the cost of pension benefits and the return that plan assets will earn. If the return exceeds the cost, the difference is booked as income. If the return is less than the cost, the difference is booked as pension expense.

Instructions

Explain how management can use discretion to make "earnings appear too rosy" as suggested by author David Henry in the *Business Week* excerpt above.

INTERNET ASSIGNMENT

INTERNET 10.1
Credit Ratings on Bonds
LO 5, 6, 9

The Internet provides a wealth of information concerning long-term liabilities, bond ratings, and credit markets. Visit the home page of **Bonds-Online** at the following Internet address:

www.bonds-online.com

Instructions

a. From the home page perform a Bond Search and select Corporate Bonds. In the Ranges section, select "Aaa/AAA" as both the minimum and maximum rating (this is the highest credit rating a company can receive). Leave all other Range selections blank. Select "no" for each item in the Apply Constraints section. In the Industry Group section, select only

---
Supplemental Topic: "Special Types of Liabilities."

"industrials" and leave all other fields blank. Select "find bonds" and identify several companies listed and the current yields of their bonds.

b. Perform a second search by selecting "B/B" as both the minimum and maximum rating (this is a relatively low credit rating). Again, leave all other Range selections blank and select "no" for each item in the Apply Constraints section. In the Industry Group section, select only "industrials" and leave all other fields blank. Select "find bonds" and identify several companies listed and the current yields of their bonds.

c. Compare the yields of the bonds from the search conducted in part **a** to those conducted in part **b**. Which search produced bonds with the highest yields? Explain why.

Internet sites are time and date sensitive. It is the purpose of these exercises to have your explore the Internet. You may need to use the Yahoo! search engine **http://www.yahoo.com** *(or another favorite search engine) to find a company's current Web address.*

OUR COMMENTS ON THE "YOUR TURN" CASES

You as a CPA for a Pawn Shop (p. 415)   Mr. Swidle needs to explain more carefully about the specific nature of the merchandise and when the merchandise will be delivered. You should question why Mr. Swidle does not want to put the check in Pawn Shop's bank account and have you record the Cash and associated Customer Deposit journal entry. The code of professional conduct requires that a professional accountant in public practice should not hold clients' monies if there is reason to believe that they were obtained from, or are to be used for, any illegal activities. You must satisfy yourself that there are good reasons for your firm to keep the money rather than recording the appropriate journal entry in Pawn Shop's records.

You as a Financial Advisor (p. 431)   The interest payments generated by a bond remain constant, regardless of fluctuations in market interest rates that occur over the bond's life. Thus, if bond issuers consistently fulfill their responsibility to make timely interest payments, the couple's annual cash flow from their investment will remain relatively stable throughout their retirement.

Fluctuations in market interest rates could adversely affect the couple should they decide to sell any of their bonds *before* the bonds mature. If interest rates are relatively high at the time the bonds are sold, their selling price may be substantially less than their redemption value at maturity.

You as a Loan Officer (p. 434)   The point that the CEO was trying to make is that $250,000 of the company's total expenses for the year were noncash expenses. As such, these expenses reduced operating income without reducing cash flow from operations. While impossible to determine from the limited information provided, the company's ability to service its debt *may be* better than the low interest coverage ratio suggests.

It is interesting to note that some credit analysts *add back* significant noncash expenses to income from operations when computing the interest coverage ratio. In this case, the addition of these two noncash items would increase the company's interest coverage ratio to 5 to 1 [($375,000 + $200,000 + $50,000) ÷ 125,000 = 5 times coverage].

You as a Public Accountant for Small Businesses (p. 439)   You should refuse the client and refer the client to a certified actuary who will have the requisite training to provide good advice. The AICPA Code of Ethics provides guidance to public accountants regarding due care in discharging professional responsibilities with competence and diligence. Article V, paragraph 3 "establishes the limitation of a member's capabilities by dictating that consultation or referral may be required when a professional engagement exceeds the personal competence of a member or a member's firm." For more information see **www.aicpa.org/about/code/comp.htm**.

ANSWERS TO SELF-TEST QUESTIONS

1. a, b 2. a, b, d 3. a, d 4. a, c, d 5. a, b, c, d 6. a, b, c, d
7. a, c 8. c 9. a, b *10. d *11. c

Supplemental Topic: "Special Types of Liabilities."

CHAPTER 11
STOCKHOLDERS' EQUITY: PAID-IN CAPITAL

Learning Objectives

After studying this chapter, you should be able to:

1. Discuss the advantages and disadvantages of organizing a business as a corporation.
2. Distinguish between publicly owned and closely held corporations.
3. Explain the rights of stockholders and the roles of corporate directors and officers.
4. Account for paid-in capital and prepare the equity section of a corporate balance sheet.
5. Contrast the features of common stock with those of preferred stock.
6. Discuss the factors affecting the market price of preferred stock and common stock.
7. Explain the significance of par value, book value, and market value of capital stock.
8. Explain the purpose and effects of a stock split.
9. Account for treasury stock transactions.

© James M. Mejuto

Sears, Roebuck & Company

Companies frequently invest large amounts of cash in the securities of other companies. These investments often earn returns in the form of interest, dividends, and capital appreciation. While it is common for businesses to purchase shares of stock in other companies, would a company ever purchase shares of its own stock on the open market?

The answer is a definite yes. Each year, for example, **Sears**, Roebuck & Company spends billions of dollars to repurchase shares of its own stock. Referred to as treasury shares, these shares of stock have been repurchased by the company, which intends to resell them in the future. One of the reasons companies such as **Sears** purchase their own shares of stock is to satisfy the requirements of stock option plans. Because these plans are an important part of employees' compensation, the company is required to have shares available to meet its commitment under these plans. **Sears** is not unique in this regard. In fact, it is difficult to find a major corporation that does not engage in treasury stock transactions on a regular basis.

• • •

In this chapter we explore numerous issues related to stockholders' equity, including treasury stock transactions, preferred stock, and stock splits. We also discuss why businesses incorporate and describe the factors that influence the price of their stock in the open market.

CORPORATIONS

The corporate form is the organization of choice for many businesses—large and small. The owners of a corporation are called **stockholders**. In many small corporations, there are only one or two stockholders. But in large corporations, such as **IBM** and **AT&T**, there are literally millions of stockholders.

A **corporation** is the only form of business organization recognized under the law as a *legal entity,* with rights and responsibilities *separate from those of its owners.* The assets of a corporation belong to the corporation *itself,* not to the stockholders. The corporation is responsible for its own debts and must pay income taxes on its earnings. As a separate legal entity, a corporation has status in court; it may enter into contracts, and it may sue and be sued as if it were a person. The major advantages and disadvantages of this form of business organization are summarized in Exhibit 11–1.

Exhibit 11–1

ADVANTAGES AND DISADVANTAGES OF THE CORPORATE FORM

LO 1 Discuss the advantages and disadvantages of organizing a business as a corporation.

Advantages	Disadvantages
1. *Stockholders are not personally liable for the debts of a corporation.* Thus the most that a stockholder can lose by investing in a corporation is the amount of his or her investment. This concept is called *limited personal liability* and often is cited as the greatest advantage of the corporate form of organization.	1. *Heavy taxation.* Corporate earnings are subject to **double taxation**. First, the corporation must pay *corporate income taxes* on its earnings. Second, stockholders must pay *personal income taxes* on any portion of these earnings that they receive as *dividends.* Together, these two levels of taxation may consume from 60% to 70% of a corporation's pretax earnings.
2. *Transferability of ownership.* Ownership of a corporation is evidenced by *transferable shares of stock,* which may be sold by one investor to another. Investment in these shares has the advantage of *liquidity,* because investors easily may convert their corporate ownership into cash by selling their shares.	2. *Greater regulation.* Corporations are affected by state and federal laws to a far greater extent than are unincorporated businesses. For example, the owners' ability to *remove business assets* from a corporation is restricted by law. A corporation must obtain authorization from government agencies to issue capital stock. Also, federal laws require publicly owned corporations to make extensive public disclosure of their financial activities.
3. *Professional management.* The stockholders own a corporation, but they do not manage it on a daily basis. To administer the affairs of the corporation, the stockholders elect a *board of directors.* The directors, in turn, hire professional managers to run the business. An individual stockholder has *no right* to participate in management unless he or she has been hired by the directors as a corporate manager.	3. *Cost of formation.* An unincorporated business can be formed at little or no cost. Forming a corporation, however, normally requires the services of an attorney.
4. *Continuity of existence.* Changes in the names and identities of stockholders do not directly affect the corporation. Therefore, the corporation may continue its operations *without disruption,* despite the retirement or death of individual stockholders. This characteristic is essential in the undertaking of most large-scale business ventures.	4. *Separation of ownership and management.* The separation of ownership and management is an advantage in many cases, but may be a disadvantage in others. If stockholders do not approve of the manner in which management runs the business, they may find it difficult to take the united action necessary to remove that management group.

Corporations

What types of businesses choose the corporate form of organization? The answer, basically, is *all kinds*. When we think of corporations, we often think of large, well-known companies such as **ExxonMobil**, **General Motors**, and **Procter & Gamble**. Indeed, almost all large businesses are organized as corporations. Limited shareholder liability, transferability of ownership, professional management, and continuity of existence make the corporation the best form of organization for pooling the resources of a great many equity investors. Not all corporations, however, are large and publicly owned. Many small businesses are organized as corporations.

Many locally owned stores, gas stations, and restaurants are organized as corporations and have a small number of stockholders—sometimes two or three members of the same family. Large, publicly held corporations, on the other hand, have many stockholders. For example, recent annual reports of **Dow Chemical** and **Aluminum Company of America (ALCOA)** indicate that they have approximately 97,200 and 95,800 stockholders, respectively.

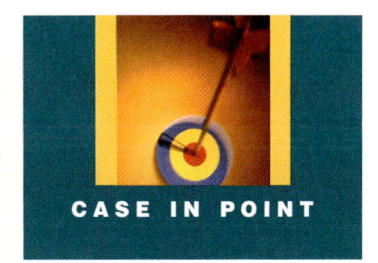

CASE IN POINT

Why Businesses Incorporate

Businesses incorporate for many reasons, but the two of greatest importance are (1) limited shareholder liability and (2) transferability of ownership.

We have previously discussed the concept of **limited personal liability**. This simply means that shareholders are not personally responsible for the debts of the corporation. Thus, if the corporation becomes illiquid, the most that a stockholder usually can lose is the amount of his or her equity investment. In this era of multimillion-dollar lawsuits, limited personal liability appeals to the owners of large and small businesses alike.

Another special feature of the corporation is the *transferability of ownership*—the idea that ownership is represented by transferable shares of **capital stock**. For a small, family-owned business, this provides a convenient means of gradually transferring ownership and control of the business from one generation to the next. For a large company, it makes ownership of the business a *highly liquid investment*, which can be purchased and sold in organized securities exchanges.[1] This liquidity is essential to a large corporation's ability to raise equity capital from thousands—perhaps millions—of individual investors.

You as a Loan Officer

GOTCHA! is a small business that manufactures board games. It is one of the many business ventures of Gayle Woods, who is very wealthy and one of your bank's most valued customers. She has done business with your bank for more than 20 years, and the balance in her personal checking, savings, and money market accounts normally exceeds $500,000. GOTCHA! is organized as a corporation, and Woods is the only stockholder.

GOTCHA! has applied for a $200,000 line of credit, which it intends to use to purchase copyrights to additional board games. Although the company is profitable, its most recent balance sheet shows total assets of only $52,000, including $47,000 in copyrights. The corporation has just under $3,000 in liabilities and over $49,000 in stockholders' equity.

Do you consider GOTCHA! a good credit risk? Would you make the loan? Under what conditions?

YOUR TURN

*Our comments appear on page 500.

---

[1] These securities exchanges include, among others, the New York Stock Exchange, the National Association of Securities Dealers' Automated Quotations (Nasdaq), the Tokyo Stock Exchange, and Mexico's Bolsa. Collectively, stock exchanges often are described simply as *the stock market*.

Publicly Owned Corporations

The capital stock of most large corporations can be bought and sold (traded) through organized securities exchanges. As these shares are available for purchase by the general public, these large corporations are said to be **publicly owned**.

Far more people have a financial interest in the shares of publicly owned companies than one might expect. If you purchase the stock of such a corporation, you become a stockholder with a *direct* ownership interest—that is, *you* are a stockholder. But mutual funds and pension funds invest heavily in the stocks of many publicly owned corporations. Thus, if you invest in a mutual fund or you are covered by a pension plan, you probably have an *indirect* financial interest in the stocks of many publicly owned corporations.

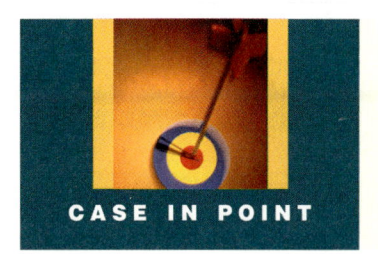

LO 2
Distinguish between publicly owned and closely held corporations.

CASE IN POINT

The stockholders in **General Motors** include more than one million men and women, as well as many pension funds, mutual investment funds, labor unions, universities, and other organizations. Almost every person covered by an employee pension plan has an indirect ownership interest in **GM**.

Corporations whose shares are *not* traded on any organized stock exchanges are said to be **closely held**. Because there is no organized market for buying and selling their shares, these corporations usually have relatively few stockholders. Often, a closely held corporation is owned by one individual or by the members of one family.

Publicly Owned Corporations Face Different Rules The government seeks to protect the interests of the public. Therefore, publicly owned corporations are subject to more regulation than those that are closely held. For example, publicly owned corporations are *required by law* to:

- Prepare and issue quarterly and annual financial statements in conformity with generally accepted accounting principles. (These statements are **public information**.)
- Have their annual financial statements audited by an independent firm of certified public accountants.
- Comply with federal securities laws, which include both criminal penalties and civil liability for deliberately or carelessly distributing misleading information to the public.
- Submit much of their financial information to the Securities and Exchange Commission for review.

Closely held corporations normally are exempt from these requirements. But our discussions will focus primarily on the accounting and reporting issues confronting *publicly owned companies*. These are the companies whose financial statements you are most likely to see—and the companies in which you are likely to invest.

FORMATION OF A CORPORATION

In the United States, a corporation is brought into existence under the laws of a particular state. The state in which the corporation is formed is called the **state of incorporation**.

The state of incorporation is not necessarily where the corporation does business. Rather, a state often is selected because of the leniency of its laws regulating corporate activities. Indeed, many corporations conduct most—sometimes all—of their business activities *outside* the state in which they are incorporated.

The first step in forming a corporation is to obtain a *corporate charter* from the state of incorporation. To obtain this charter, the organizers of the corporation submit an application called the *articles of incorporation.* Once the charter is obtained, the stockholders in the new corporation hold a meeting to elect a *board of directors* and to pass *bylaws* that will govern the corporation's activities. The directors in turn hold a meeting at which the top corporate officers and managers are appointed.

Organization Costs Forming a corporation is more costly than starting a sole proprietorship. The costs may include, for example, attorneys' fees, incorporation fees paid to the state, and other outlays necessary to bring the corporation into existence. Conceptually, organization costs are an *intangible asset* that will benefit the corporation over its entire life. As a practical matter, however, most corporations expense those costs immediately, even though they are often spread over a five-year period for income tax purposes.

Thus you will seldom see organization costs in the balance sheet of a publicly owned corporation. They have long since been recognized as an expense.

Rights of Stockholders A corporation is owned collectively by its stockholders. Each stockholder's ownership interest is determined by the number of *shares* that he or she owns.

Assume that a corporation issues 10,000 shares of capital stock. If you own 1,000 of these shares, you own *10%* of the corporation. If you acquire another 500 shares from another stockholder, you will own *15%*.

Each stockholder, or the stockholder's brokerage firm, receives from the corporation a **stock certificate** indicating the number of shares he or she owns.

The ownership of capital stock in a corporation usually carries the following basic rights:

> **LO 3**
> Explain the rights of stockholders and the roles of corporate directors and officers.

1. *To vote for directors and on certain other key issues.* A stockholder has one vote for each share owned. The issues on which stockholders may vote are specified in the corporation's bylaws.

    Any stockholder—or group of stockholders—that owns *more than 50%* of the capital stock has the power to elect the board of directors and to set basic corporate policies. Therefore, these stockholders control the corporation. Beyond their voting rights, stockholders have *no managerial authority* unless they have been appointed by the board to a management role.

2. *To participate in any dividends declared by the board of directors.* Stockholders in a corporation *may not* make withdrawals of company assets, as may the owners of unincorporated businesses. However, the directors may elect to distribute some or all of the earnings of a profitable corporation to its stockholders in the form of cash *dividends.*

    Dividends can be distributed only after they have been formally *declared* (authorized) by the board of directors. Dividends are paid to all shareholders in proportion to the number of shares owned.

3. *To share in the distribution of assets if the corporation is liquidated.* When a corporation ends its existence, the creditors must first be paid in full. Any remaining assets are divided among the shareholders—again, in proportion to the number of shares owned.

Stockholders' meetings usually are held once each year. At these meetings, stockholders may ask questions of management and vote on certain issues. In large corporations, these meetings usually are attended by relatively few people—often less than 1% of the company's stockholders. Prior to these meetings, however, the management group requests that stockholders who do not plan to attend send in *proxy statements,* granting management the voting rights associated with their shares.

Through this proxy system, management usually can secure the voting rights from enough shares to ensure its control of the corporation. In a publicly owned corporation, dissatisfied stockholders seldom are able to muster the voting power to overrule management. Therefore, dissatisfied stockholders normally sell their shares and invest in a company more to their liking.

Functions of the Board of Directors The primary functions of the **board of directors** are to set corporate policies and to protect the interests of the stockholders. Specific duties of the directors include hiring corporate officers and setting these officers' salaries, declaring dividends, and reviewing the findings of both internal auditors and independent auditors.

A closely held corporation might have only one active director—who is also the principal stockholder. But publicly owned corporations have larger boards—usually a dozen people or more.

The board of a large corporation always includes several members of top management. In recent years, increasing importance has been attached to the inclusion of "outside" directors. The term *outside directors* refers to individuals who are *not* officers of the corporation and, therefore, bring an *independent perspective* to the board.

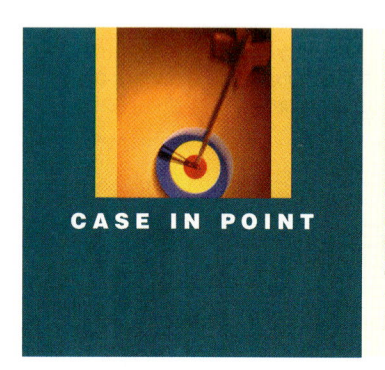

CASE IN POINT

A recent annual report of **General Mills** includes a report from the *audit committee* of the company's board of directors. The first paragraph of this report describes the committee's responsibilities:

The Audit Committee of the Board of Directors is composed of six outside directors. Its primary function is to oversee the Company's system of internal controls, financial reporting practices and audits to ensure their quality, integrity and objectivity are sufficient to protect stockholders' assets.

© Tony Freeman/PhotoEdit

Functions of the Corporate Officers The top management of a corporation is appointed (hired) by the board of directors. These individuals are called the *corporate officers,* or, more simply, "top management." Individual stockholders *do not* have the right to transact corporate business *unless they have been properly appointed to a managerial post.*

The top level of management usually includes a chief executive officer (CEO) or president, a chief financial officer (CFO) or controller, a treasurer, and a secretary. In addition, a vice president usually oversees each functional area, such as sales, personnel, and production.

The responsibilities of the CFO (controller), treasurer, and secretary are most directly related to the accounting phase of business operation. The CFO is responsible for the maintenance of adequate internal control and for the preparation of accounting records and financial statements. Such specialized activities as budgeting, tax planning, and preparation of tax returns are usually placed under the CFO's jurisdiction. The *treasurer* has custody of the company's funds and is generally responsible for planning and controlling the company's cash position. The treasurer's department also has responsibility for relations with the company's financial institutions and major creditors.

The *secretary* represents the corporation in many contractual and legal matters and maintains minutes of the meetings of directors and stockholders. Other responsibilities of the secretary are to coordinate the preparation of the annual report and to manage the investor relations department. In small corporations, one officer frequently acts as both secretary and treasurer.

The organization chart in Exhibit 11–2 indicates lines of authority extending from stockholders to the directors to the CEO and other officers.

Formation of a Corporation

Exhibit 11–2   **CORPORATE ORGANIZATION CHART**

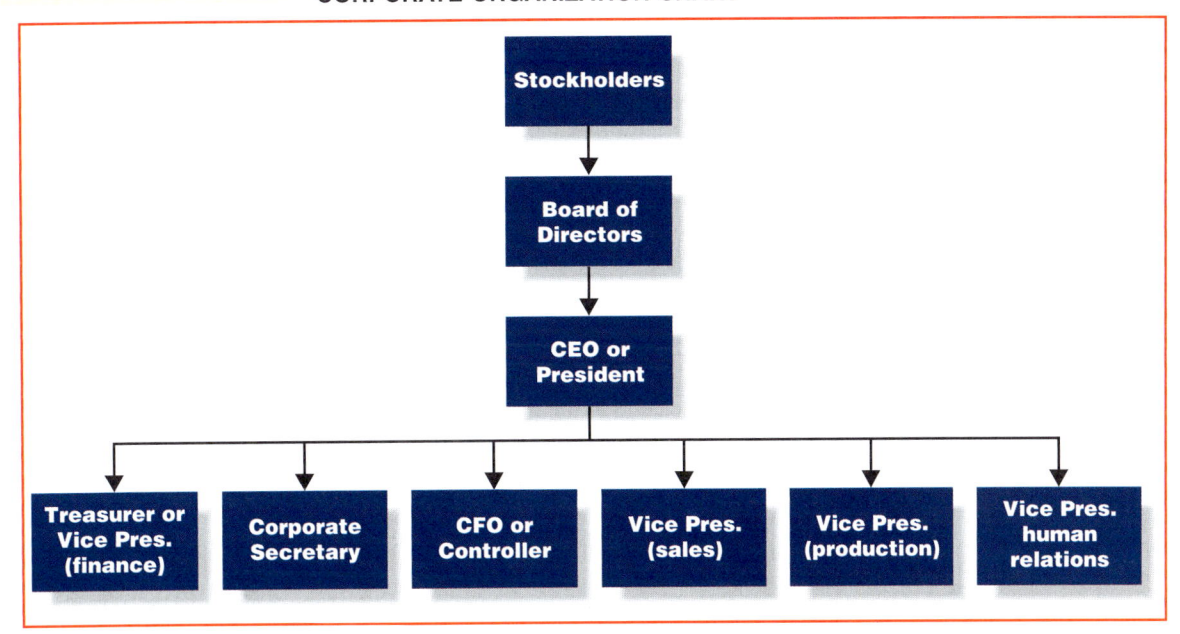

```
                    Stockholders
                         │
                         ▼
                    Board of
                    Directors
                         │
                         ▼
                    CEO or
                    President
         ┌───────┬────────┬────────┬────────┬────────┐
         ▼       ▼        ▼        ▼        ▼        ▼
    Treasurer  Corporate  CFO or   Vice     Vice     Vice Pres.
    or Vice    Secretary  Control- Pres.    Pres.    human
    Pres.                 ler      (sales)  (produc- relations
    (finance)                               tion)
```

You as the Vice President of Human Relations

Assume you have been the vice president of human relations for a large auto parts supply company for the past five years. Recently, you have been engaged in negotiation talks with the company's major union. These talks are not going well and, as a result, the union is planning to strike early in December. As part of your compensation each year, you are awarded 2,000 shares of the company's stock. You normally sell 1,000 shares each December to pay for your holiday shopping. What should you do?

*Our comments appear on page 500.

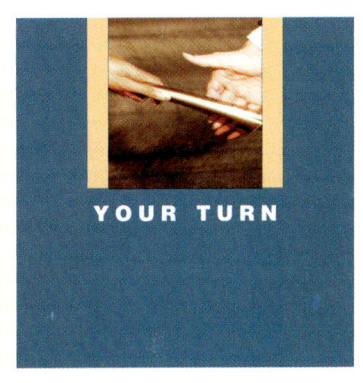

Stockholder Records in a Corporation

A large corporation with shares listed on the New York Stock Exchange usually has millions of shares outstanding and hundreds of thousands of stockholders. Each day many stockholders sell their shares; the buyers of these shares become new members of the company's family of stockholders.

A corporation must have an up-to-date record of the names and addresses of this constantly changing group of stockholders so that it can send dividend checks, financial statements, and voting forms to the right people.

There are numerous stock exchanges around the world. Europe is the second largest equity market region in the world after North America. The significant European stock exchanges are in London, Frankfurt, and Paris. Other stock exchanges around the world are more thinly traded such as the *Bolsa Mexicana de Valore* in Mexico. Each exchange has different financial reporting requirements for companies that list shares on the exchange.

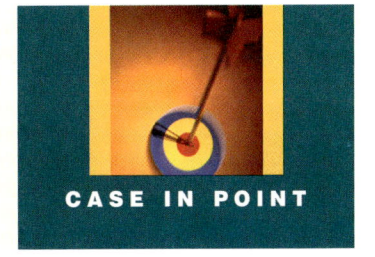

Stockholders Subsidiary Ledger   When there are numerous stockholders, it is not practical to include a separate account for each stockholder in the general ledger. Instead, a single controlling account entitled Capital Stock appears in the general ledger, and a

stockholders subsidiary ledger is maintained. This ledger contains an account for each individual stockholder. Entries in the stockholders subsidiary ledger are made in *number of shares,* rather than in dollars. Thus each stockholder's account shows the number of shares owned and the dates of acquisitions and sales. This record enables the corporation to send each stockholder a single dividend check, even though the stockholder may have acquired shares on different dates.

A corporation that has more than one type of capital stock will maintain a separate set of stockholders subsidiary records for each issue.

Stock Transfer Agent and Stock Registrar Large, publicly owned corporations use an independent **stock transfer agent** and a **stock registrar** to maintain their stockholder records and to establish strong internal control over the issuance of stock certificates. These transfer agents and registrars are usually large banks or trust companies. When stock certificates are transferred from one owner to another, the old certificates are sent to the transfer agent, who cancels them, makes the necessary entries in the stockholders subsidiary ledger, and prepares a new certificate for the new owner of the shares. This new certificate then must be registered with the stock registrar before it represents valid and transferable ownership of stock in the corporation.

Small, closely held corporations generally do not use the services of independent registrars and transfer agents. In these companies, the stockholder records usually are maintained by a corporate officer. To prevent the accidental or fraudulent issuance of an excessive number of stock certificates, the corporation should require that each certificate be signed by at least two designated corporate officers.

PAID-IN CAPITAL OF A CORPORATION

LO 4
Account for paid-in capital and prepare the equity section of a corporate balance sheet.

Stockholders' equity of a corporation is normally increased in one of two ways: (1) from contributions by investors in exchange for capital stock—called **paid-in capital** or **contributed capital**—and (2) from the retention of profits earned by the corporation over time—called **retained earnings**. As previously noted, our focus in this chapter is primarily on issues related to paid-in capital. In Chapter 12, we shift our attention to issues concerning retained earnings.

Authorization and Issuance of Capital Stock

The articles of incorporation specify the number of shares that a corporation has been authorized to issue by the state of incorporation. Issues of capital stock that will be sold to the general public must be approved by the federal Securities and Exchange Commission, as well as by state officials.

Corporations normally obtain authorization for more shares than they initially plan to issue. This way, if more capital is needed later, the corporation already has the authorization to issue additional shares.

Shares that have been *issued* and are in the hands of stockholders are called the *outstanding* shares. At any time, these outstanding shares represent 100% of the stockholders' investment in the corporation.

When a large amount of stock is to be issued, most corporations use the services of an investment banking firm, frequently referred to as an **underwriter**. The underwriter guarantees the issuing corporation a specific price for the stock and makes a profit by selling the shares to the investing public at a slightly higher price. The corporation records the issuance of the stock at the net amount received from the underwriter. The use of an underwriter assures the corporation that the entire stock issue will be sold without delay and that the entire amount of funds to be raised will be available on a specific date.

The price that a corporation will seek for a new issue of stock is based on such factors as (1) expected future earnings and dividends, (2) the financial strength of the company, and (3) the current state of the investment markets. If the corporation asks too high a price, it simply will not find an underwriter or other buyers willing to purchase the shares.

State Laws Affect the Balance Sheet Presentation of Stockholders' Equity The number of different accounts that a corporation must use in the stockholders' equity section of its balance sheet is determined largely by state laws. We have seen that corporations use separate stockholders' equity accounts to represent (1) contributed capital, or paid-in capital; and (2) earned capital, or retained earnings. Up to this point we have assumed that all paid-in capital is presented in a single account entitled Capital Stock. But this often is not the case.

Some corporations issue several *different types* (or classes) of capital stock. In these situations, a separate account is used to indicate each type of stock outstanding. A legal concept called *par value* also affects the balance sheet presentation of paid-in capital.

Par Value Par value (or stated value) represents the legal capital per share—the amount below which stockholders' equity cannot be reduced, except by losses from business operations (or by special legal action). The directors cannot declare a dividend that would cause total stockholders' equity to fall below the par value of the outstanding shares. Par value, therefore, may be regarded as a minimum cushion of equity capital existing for the protection of creditors.

Because of the legal restrictions associated with par value, state laws require corporations to show separately in the stockholders' equity section of the balance sheet the par value of shares issued. This special balance sheet presentation has led some people to believe that par value has some special significance. In many corporations, however, the par value of the shares issued is a small portion of total stockholders' equity.

A corporation may set the par value of its stock at $1 per share, $5 per share, or any other amount that it chooses. Most large corporations set the par value of their common stocks at nominal amounts, such as 1 cent per share or $1 per share. The par value of the stock is *no indication of its market value;* the par value merely indicates the amount per share to be entered in the Capital Stock account. The stocks of **Ford** and **AT&T** have par values of $1, and **Microsoft**'s stock has a par value of only one-tenth of a cent. The market value of each of these securities is far above its par value. Microsoft's stock, for example, has traded at a market value in excess of $100 per share, or more than *100,000 times* its par value.

Issuance of Par Value Stock Authorization of a stock issue does not bring an asset into existence, nor does it give the corporation any capital. The obtaining of authorization from the state for a stock issue merely affords a legal opportunity to obtain assets through the sale of stock. Additional capital is created for the company only when that stock is sold to stockholders.

When par value stock is *issued,* the Capital Stock account is credited with the par value of the shares issued, regardless of whether the issuance price is more or less than par. Assuming that 50,000 shares of $2 par value stock have been authorized and that 10,000 of these authorized shares are sold at a price of $2 each, Cash would be debited and Capital Stock would be credited for $20,000. When stock is sold for more than par value, the Capital Stock account is credited with the par value of the shares issued, and a separate account, Additional Paid-in Capital, is credited for the excess of selling price over par. If, for example, our 10,000 shares were issued at a price of $10 per share, the entry would be:

Cash	100,000	
Capital Stock		20,000
Additional Paid-in Capital		80,000
Issued 10,000 shares of $2 par value stock at a price of $10 a share.		

My Notes
Stockholders' investment in excess of par value

The additional paid-in capital does not represent a profit to the corporation. It is part of the *invested capital* and it will be added to the capital stock in the balance sheet to show the total paid-in capital. The stockholders' equity section of the balance sheet follows. (The $150,000 in retained earnings is assumed in order to have a complete illustration.)

Stockholders' equity:

Capital stock, $2 par value; authorized, 50,000 shares; issued and outstanding, 10,000 shares	$ 20,000
Additional paid-in capital	80,000
Total paid-in capital	$100,000
Retained earnings	150,000
Total stockholders' equity	$250,000

If stock is issued by a corporation for *less* than par, the account Discount on Capital Stock should be debited for the difference between the issuance price and the par value. A discount on capital stock reduces, rather than increases, the amount of stockholders' equity in the balance sheet. The issuance of stock at a discount is seldom encountered because it is illegal in many states.

No-Par Stock Some states allow corporations to issue stock without designating a par or stated value. When this "no-par" stock is issued, the *entire issue price* is credited to the Capital Stock account and is viewed as legal capital not subject to withdrawal.

Common Stocks and Preferred Stocks

The account title Capital Stock is widely used when a corporation has issued only *one type* of stock. In order to appeal to as many investors as possible, however, some corporations issue several types (or classes) of capital stock, each providing investors with different rights and opportunities.

The basic type of capital stock issued by every corporation often is called **common stock**. Common stock possesses the traditional rights of ownership—voting rights, participation in dividends, and a residual claim to assets in the event of liquidation. When the rights of stockholders are modified, the term **preferred stock** is normally used to describe the resulting type of capital stock. A few corporations issue two or more classes of preferred stock, with each class having distinctive features designed to appeal to a particular type of investor. In summary, we may say that *every* corporation has common stock and that some corporations also have one or more types of preferred stock.

The following stockholders' equity section illustrates the balance sheet presentation for a corporation having both preferred and common stock. As before, a retained earnings amount is assumed so we can provide a complete example.

LO 5
Contrast the features of common stock with those of preferred stock.

My Notes
Balance sheet presentation of common stock and of preferred stock

Stockholders' equity:

9% cumulative preferred stock, $100 par value, authorized 100,000 shares, issued 50,000 shares	$ 5,000,000
Common stock, $5 par value, authorized 3 million shares, issued 2 million shares	10,000,000
Additional paid-in capital:	
Preferred stock	200,000
Common stock	20,000,000
Total paid-in capital	$35,200,000
Retained earnings	13,500,000
Total stockholders' equity	$48,700,000

Characteristics of Preferred Stock

Most preferred stocks have the following distinctive features:

1. Preference over common stock as to dividends.
2. Cumulative dividend rights.
3. Preference over common stock as to assets in event of the liquidation of the company.
4. Callable at the option of the corporation.
5. No voting power.

Another important but less common feature of some preferred stocks is a clause permitting the *conversion* of preferred stock into common stock at the option of the holder. Preferred stocks vary widely with respect to the special rights and privileges granted. Careful study of the terms of the individual preferred stock contract is a necessary step in the evaluation of any preferred stock.

Stock Preferred as to Dividends Corporations often make periodic cash payments, called **dividends**, to stockholders.[2] Dividends normally represent a distribution of accumulated profit and therefore cannot exceed the amount of a corporation's retained earnings.

Preferred stock is said to have dividend preference because preferred stock investors are entitled to receive a specified amount each year before any dividend is paid to common stock investors. The specified dividend may be stated as a dollar amount, such as $5 per share. Some preferred stocks, however, state the specified dividend as a *percentage of par value.* For example, a share of preferred stock with a par value of $100 and a dividend preference of 9% must provide a $9 dividend each year to each share of preferred stock before any dividends can be paid on the common shares. (Preferred stocks often have par values substantially higher than common stocks. This is largely a matter of tradition and has little significance.)

> **Consolidated Edison** has two issues of preferred stock that are publicly traded on the New York Stock Exchange. The first issue is a $5 preferred stock that pays annual dividends of $5 per share and has no par value. The other issue is a 4.65% preferred with a $100 par value that pays annual dividends of $4.65 per share.
>
> Dividends on both of these issues of preferred stock must be paid in full before **Consolidated Edison** pays any dividend on its common stock.

CASE IN POINT

The holders of preferred stock have no guarantee that they will always receive the indicated dividend. A corporation is obligated to pay dividends to stockholders only when the board of directors declares a dividend. Dividends must be paid on preferred stock before anything is paid to the common stockholders, but if the corporation is not prospering, it may decide not to pay any dividends at all. For a corporation to pay dividends, profits must be earned and cash must be available. Despite this limitation, preferred stocks generally offer investors *more assurance* of regular dividend payments than do common stocks.

Cumulative Preferred Stock The dividend preference carried by most preferred stocks is a *cumulative* one. If all or any part of the regular dividend on the preferred stock is omitted in a given year, the amount omitted is said to be *in arrears* and must be paid in a subsequent year before any dividend can be paid on the common stock.

---

[2] In Chapter 12, we will discuss specific accounting issues related to cash dividends and other forms of distributions to stockholders. For the purposes of this chapter, dividends may be viewed simply as the distribution to stockholders of accumulated profits that reduce both cash and retained earnings.

Assume that a corporation was organized January 1, 2000, with 10,000 shares of $8 cumulative preferred stock and 50,000 shares of common stock. Dividends paid in 2000 were at the rate of $8 per share of preferred stock and $2 per share of common. In 2001, earnings declined sharply and the only dividend paid was $2 per share on the preferred stock. No dividends were paid in 2002. What is the status of the preferred stock at December 31, 2002?

Dividends are *in arrears* in the amount of *$14* per share ($6 omitted during 2001 and $8 omitted in 2002). On the entire issue of 10,000 shares of preferred stock, the dividends in arrears amount to *$140,000* ($14 × 10,000 shares). This amount must be paid to preferred stockholders before any future dividends can be paid to common stockholders.

Dividends in arrears are not listed among the liabilities of a corporation, because no liability exists until a dividend is declared by the board of directors. Nevertheless, the amount of any dividends in arrears on preferred stock is an important factor to investors and should always be *disclosed*. This disclosure is usually made by a note accompanying the balance sheet such as the following:

Note 6: Dividends in arrears
As of December 31, 2002, dividends on the $8 cumulative preferred stock were in arrears to the extent of $14 per share and amounted in total to $140,000.

In 2003, we shall assume that the company earned large profits, has available cash, and wished to pay dividends on both the preferred and common stocks. Before paying a dividend on the common, the corporation must pay the $140,000 in arrears on the cumulative preferred stock *plus* the regular $8 per share applicable to the current year. The preferred stockholders would, therefore, receive a total of $220,000 in dividends in 2003 ($22 per share); the board of directors would then be free to declare dividends on the common stock.

For a *noncumulative* preferred stock, any unpaid or omitted dividend is lost forever. However, few preferred stocks are noncumulative.

Stock Preferred as to Assets Most preferred stocks carry a preference as to assets in the event of liquidation of the corporation. If the business is terminated, the preferred stock is entitled to payment in full of its par value or a higher stated liquidation value before any payment is made on the common stock. This priority also includes any dividends in arrears.

Callable Preferred Stock Some preferred stocks include a *call provision*. This provision grants the issuing corporation the right to repurchase the stock from the stockholders at a stipulated *call price*. The call price is usually higher than the par value of the stock. For example, $100 par value preferred stock may be callable at $105 or $110 per share. In addition to paying the call price, a corporation that redeems its preferred stock must pay any dividends in arrears. A call provision gives a corporation flexibility to adjust its capital structure by reducing or eliminating preferred stock.

Convertible Preferred Stock To add to the attractiveness of preferred stock as an investment, corporations sometimes offer a *conversion privilege* that entitles the preferred stockholders to exchange their shares for common stock at a stipulated ratio. If the corporation prospers, its common stock will probably rise in market value, and dividends on the common stock will probably increase. The investor who buys a convertible preferred stock rather than common stock has greater assurance of regular dividends. In addition, through the conversion privilege, the investor is assured of an opportunity to share in any substantial increase in value of the company's common stock.

As an example, assume that Remington Corporation issued a 9%, $100 par, convertible preferred stock on January 1, at a price of $100 per share. Each share is convertible into four shares of the company's $10 par value common stock at any time. The common stock had a market price of $20 per share on January 1 and an annual dividend of $1 per share was being paid. During the next few years, Remington Corporation's earnings increased, the dividend on the common stock was raised to an annual rate of $3, and the market price of the common stock rose to $40 per share. At this point the preferred stock should have a market value of *at least $160,* since it could be converted at any time into four shares of common stock with a market value of $40 each. In other words, the market value of a convertible preferred stock tends to move in accordance with the price of the common.

When the dividend rate is increased on the common stock, some holders of the preferred stock may convert their holdings into common stock in order to obtain a higher cash return on their investments. If the holder of 100 shares of the preferred stock presented these shares for conversion, Remington Corporation would make the following journal entry:

9% Convertible Preferred Stock	10,000	
Common Stock		4,000
Additional Paid-in Capital: Common Stock		6,000
To record the conversion of 100 shares of preferred stock, par $100, into 400 shares of $10 par value common stock.		

My Notes

Conversion of preferred stock into common

Note that the issue price recorded for the 400 shares of common stock is based on the *carrying value of the preferred stock* in the accounting records, not on market prices at the date of conversion. (If the preferred stock originally had been issued at a price greater than par value, its carrying value would include a proportionate share of the related additional paid-in capital, as well as the par value.)

Other Features of Preferred Stock Occasionally you may encounter preferred stock with some unusual characteristics. For example, there are "participating preferreds," allowing preferred stockholders to receive dividends that are greater than the stated dollar amount or percentage. There also are "super preferreds," granting enormous voting rights—perhaps the controlling interest—to the preferred stockholders. And there are "redeemable preferreds," allowing preferred shareholders to sell their shares back to the corporation at an agreed-upon price. We will leave further discussion of such unusual features of preferred stock to more advanced courses in accounting and corporate finance.

The three primary elements of stockholders' equity for most companies are common stock, preferred stock, and retained earnings. While important, other elements that we learn about later in this chapter, as well as in Chapter 12, are typically smaller in amount than these three primary elements. The relationship of common stock, preferred stock, and retained earnings is depicted in Exhibit 11–3.

Stock Issued for Assets Other Than Cash

Corporations generally sell their capital stock for cash and use the cash to buy the various types of assets needed in the business. Sometimes, however, a corporation may issue shares of its capital stock in a direct exchange for land, buildings, or other assets. Stock may also be issued in payment for services rendered by attorneys and promoters in the formation of the corporation.

When a corporation issues capital stock in exchange for services or for assets other than cash, the transaction should be recorded at the current *market value* of the goods or services received. For some types of assets such as land or buildings, the services of a firm of professional appraisers may be useful in establishing current market value.

Often, the best evidence as to the market value of these goods or services is the *market value of the shares* issued in exchange. For example, assume that a company issues 10,000 shares of its $1 par value common stock in exchange for land. Competent

Exhibit 11–3

PRIMARY SOURCES OF CORPORATE EQUITY

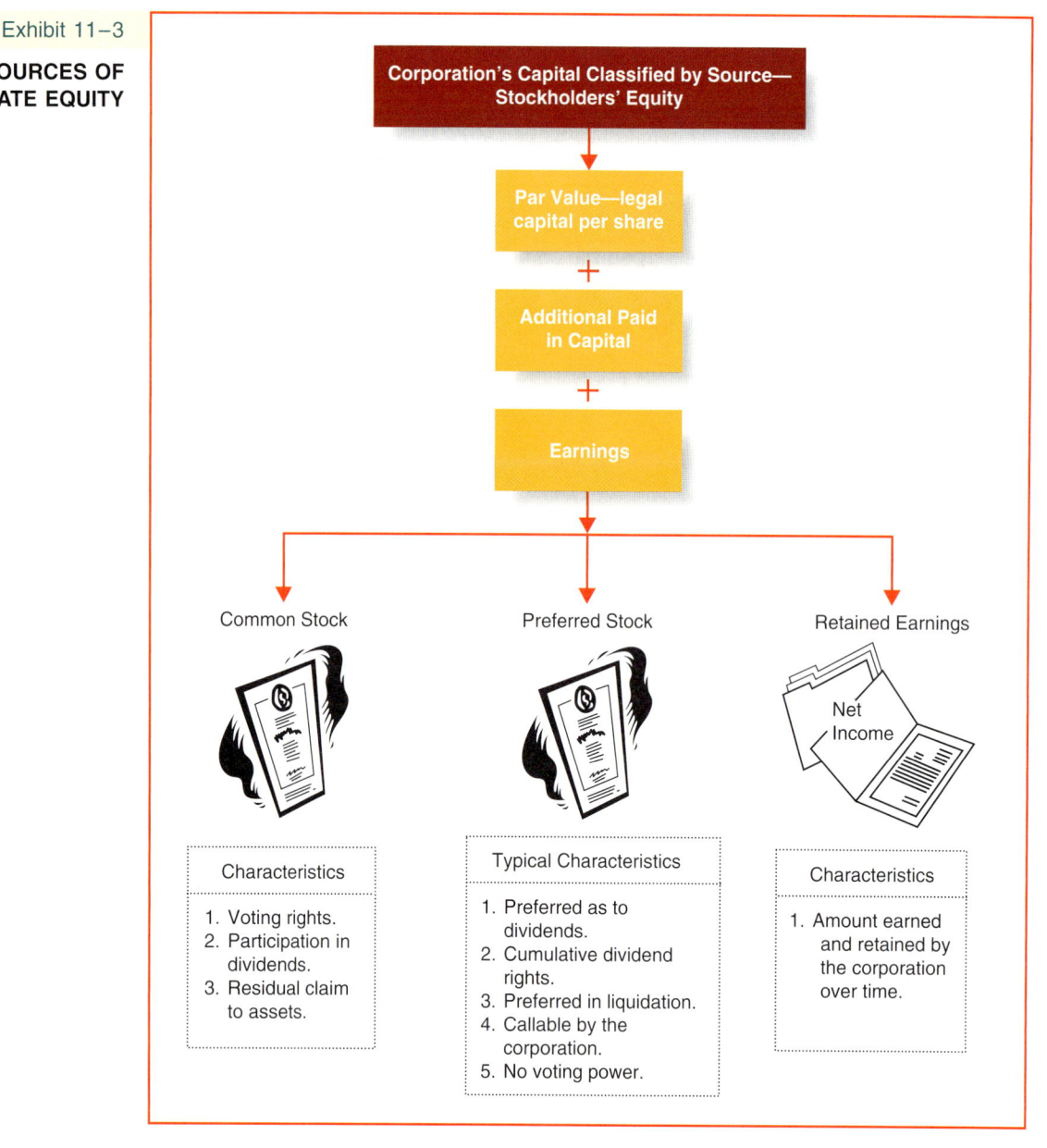

Corporation's Capital Classified by Source—Stockholders' Equity

- Par Value—legal capital per share
- **+**
- Additional Paid in Capital
- **+**
- Earnings

Common Stock

Characteristics
1. Voting rights.
2. Participation in dividends.
3. Residual claim to assets.

Preferred Stock

Typical Characteristics
1. Preferred as to dividends.
2. Cumulative dividend rights.
3. Preferred in liquidation.
4. Callable by the corporation.
5. No voting power.

Retained Earnings

Net Income

Characteristics
1. Amount earned and retained by the corporation over time.

---

appraisers may have differing opinions as to the market value of the land. But let us assume that the company's stock is currently selling on a stock exchange for $90 per share. It is logical to say that the cost of the land to the company is $900,000, the market value of the shares issued in exchange.

In summary, stock issued for assets other than cash should be recorded at the current market value of either (1) the assets received or (2) the shares issued in exchange—*whichever can be determined more objectively.*

Once the valuation has been decided, the entry to record the issuance of the stock in exchange for the land is as follows:

My Notes

Notice the use of current market values

Land	900,000	
Common Stock		10,000
Additional Paid-in Capital: Common Stock		890,000

To record the issuance of 10,000 shares of $1 par value common stock in exchange for land. Current market value of stock ($90 per share) used as basis for valuing the land.

Paid-In Capital of a Corporation

When a corporation's managers consider making a major acquisition, they must weigh the strategic implications of a change in the corporation's financial structure as it appears on the financial statements. For example, corporations can pay for an acquisition by using cash or debt financing or by issuing stock. Sometimes, agreements with existing creditors limit the amount of additional preferred stock that can be issued. Other restrictions imposed by creditors may limit the acquisition of additional debt financing. Most of these restrictions are based on numbers from audited financial statements.

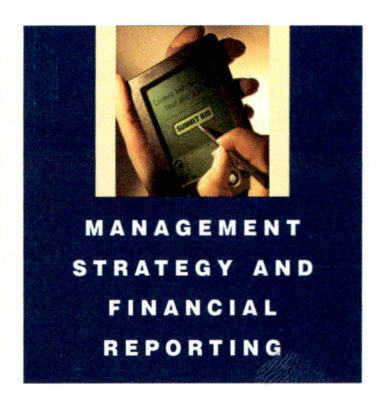

MANAGEMENT STRATEGY AND FINANCIAL REPORTING

Subscriptions to Capital Stock

Small, newly formed corporations sometimes offer investors an opportunity to "subscribe" to shares of the company's capital stock. Under a subscription plan, the investors agree to purchase specified numbers of shares at a stated price *at a future date,* often by making a series of installment payments. The stock is issued after the entire subscription price has been collected.

Selling stock through subscriptions is similar to selling merchandise on a layaway plan. One reason for this procedure is to attract small investors. Another reason is to appeal to investors who prefer not to invest cash until the corporation is ready to start business operations. Accounting for subscriptions to capital stock is explained and illustrated in more advanced accounting courses.

Donated Capital

On occasion, a corporation may receive assets as a gift. To increase local employment, for example, some cities have given corporations the land on which to build factories. When a corporation receives such a gift, both total assets and total stockholders' equity increase by the market value of the assets received. *No profit is recognized when a gift is received;* the increase in stockholders' equity is regarded as *paid-in capital.* The receipt of a gift is recorded by debiting the appropriate asset accounts and crediting an account entitled Donated Capital.

The Donated Capital account appears in the stockholders' equity section of the balance sheet, along with any Additional Paid-in Capital accounts. In addition, the *notes* accompanying the financial statements normally explain the nature of the donation.

The annual report of **Lands' End, Inc.**, includes the following note that describes the $8.4 million of donated capital on the company's balance sheet:

> Donated capital: In 1988 and 1989, a corporation owned by the principal shareholder of the company contributed $7.0 million and $1.4 million in cash, respectively, to the company in order to fund the cost of constructing an activity center in Dodgeville for use by company employees. These transactions were recorded as donated capital.

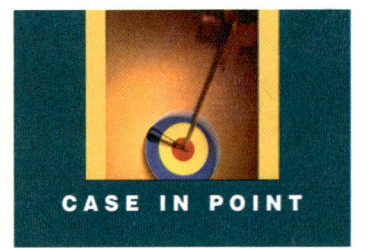

CASE IN POINT

Book Value per Share of Common Stock

Because the equity of each stockholder in a corporation is determined by the number of shares he or she owns, an accounting measurement of interest to some stockholders is book value per share of common stock. Book value per share is equal to the net assets represented by one share of stock. The term *net assets* means total assets minus total liabilities; in other words, net assets are equal to *total stockholders' equity.* Thus, in a corporation that has issued common stock only, the book value per share is computed by dividing total stockholders' equity by the number of shares outstanding (or subscribed).

For example, assume that a corporation has 4,000 shares of common stock outstanding and the stockholders' equity section of the balance sheet is as follows:

Stockholders' equity:

Common stock, $1 par value (4,000 shares outstanding)	$ 4,000
Additional paid-in capital	40,000
Retained earnings	76,000
Total stockholders' equity	$120,000

The book value per share is *$30;* it is computed by dividing the stockholders' equity of $120,000 by the 4,000 shares of outstanding stock. In computing book value, we are not concerned with the number of authorized shares but with the outstanding shares, because the total of the outstanding shares represents 100% of the stockholders' equity.

My Notes

How much is book value per share?

Book Value When a Company Has Both Preferred and Common Stock Book value is usually computed only for common stock. If a company has both preferred and common stock outstanding, the computation of book value per share of common stock requires two steps. First, the redemption value or *call price* of the entire preferred stock issue and any *dividends in arrears* are deducted from total stockholders' equity. Second, the remaining amount of stockholders' equity is divided by the number of common shares outstanding to determine book value per common share. This procedure reflects the fact that the common stockholders are the *residual owners* of the corporate entity.

To illustrate the computation of book value per share when callable preferred stock is outstanding, assume that the stockholders' equity of Hart Company at December 31 is as follows:

My Notes

Two classes of stock

Stockholders' equity:

8% preferred stock, $100 par value, callable at $110, 10,000 shares authorized and outstanding	$1,000,000
Common stock, $10 stated value, authorized 100,000 shares, issued and outstanding 50,000 shares	500,000
Additional paid-in capital: Common stock	750,000
Total paid-in capital	$2,250,000
Retained earnings	130,000
Total stockholders' equity	$2,380,000

Because of a weak cash position, Hart Company has paid no dividends during the current year. As of December 31, dividends in arrears on the cumulative preferred stock total *$80,000.*

All the equity belongs to the common stockholders, except the $1.1 million call price ($110 × 10,000 shares) applicable to the preferred stock and the $80,000 of dividends in arrears on preferred stock. The calculation of book value per share of common stock is as follows:

Total stockholders' equity		$2,380,000
Less: Equity of preferred stockholders:		
Call price of preferred stock	$1,100,000	
Dividends in arrears	80,000	1,180,000
Equity of common stockholders		$1,200,000
Number of common shares outstanding		50,000
Book value per share of common stock ($1,200,000 ÷ 50,000 shares)		$24

> **CASH EFFECTS**
>
> In a statement of cash flows, transactions with the stockholders of a corporation are classified as *financing activities*. Thus the issuance of capital stock for cash represents a *receipt* from financing activities. Distributions of cash to stockholders—including the payment of cash dividends—represent a cash *outlay*, which is also classified under financing activities.
>
> Transactions with owners do not always have an immediate effect on cash flows. Consider an exchange of the corporation's capital stock for a noncash asset, such as land. Cash is not increased or decreased by this event. These types of noncash transactions are described in a special schedule that accompanies the statement of cash flows.

MARKET VALUE   SKIP

After shares of stock have been issued, they may be sold by one investor to another. The price at which these shares change hands represents the *current market price* of the stock. This market price may differ substantially from such amounts as par value, the original issue price, and the current book value. Which is the most relevant amount? That depends on your point of view.

After shares are issued, they belong to the stockholder, not to the issuing corporation. Thus changes in the market price of these shares directly affect the financial position of the stockholder, but not that of the issuing company. This concept explains why the issuing company and stockholders apply different accounting principles to the same outstanding shares.

Accounting by the Issuer From the viewpoint of the issuing company, outstanding stock represents an amount invested in the company by its owners at a particular date. While the market value of the stockholders' investment may change, the amount of resources that they originally invested does not change.

Thus the company issuing stock records the issue price—that is, the proceeds received from issuing the stock—in its paid-in capital accounts. The balances in these accounts remain unchanged unless (1) more shares are issued or (2) outstanding shares are permanently retired (for example, preferred stock is called or stock is purchased on the open market and then retired).

Accounting by the Investor From the investor's point of view, shares owned in a publicly owned company are an asset, usually called Marketable Securities.

To the investor, the current market value of securities owned is more relevant than the original issue price—or than the securities' par values or book values. The market value indicates what the securities are worth today. Changes in market value directly affect the investor's liquidity, financial position, and net worth. For these reasons, investors show investments in marketable securities at current market value in their balance sheets.

CASE IN POINT

In a single day, the market price of **IBM**'s capital stock dropped over $31 per share, falling from $135 to $103.25. Of course, this was not a typical day. The date, October 19, 1987, will long be remembered as "Black Monday." On this day, stock prices around the world suffered the greatest one-day decline in history.

Stocks listed on the New York Stock Exchange lost about 20% of their value in less than six hours. Given that the annual dividends on these stocks averaged about 2% of their market value, this one-day market loss was approximately equal to the loss by investors of all dividend revenue for about 10 years.

How did this disastrous decline in **IBM**'s stock price affect the balance sheet of **IBM**? Actually, it didn't. **IBM**'s stock isn't owned by **IBM**—it is owned by the company's stockholders.

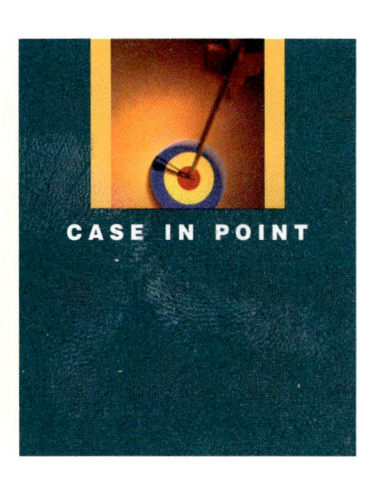

Because market prices are of such importance to investors, we will briefly discuss the factors that most affect the market prices of preferred and common stocks.

Market Price of Preferred Stock

LO 6
Discuss the factors affecting the market price of preferred stock and common stock.

Investors buy preferred stocks primarily to receive the dividends that these shares pay. Thus dividend rate is one important factor in determining the market price of a preferred stock. A second important factor is *risk*. In the long run, a company must be profitable enough to pay dividends. If there is a distinct possibility that the company will *not* operate profitably and pay dividends, the price of its preferred stock will probably decline.

A third factor greatly affecting the value of preferred stocks is the level of *interest rates*. What happens to the market price of an 8% preferred stock, originally issued at a par value of $100, if government policies and other factors cause long-term interest rates to rise to, say, 15% or 16%? If investments offering a return of 16% with the same level of risk are readily available, investors will no longer pay $100 for a share of preferred stock that provides a dividend of only $8 per year. Thus the market price of the preferred stock will fall to about half of its original issue price, or about $50 per share. At this market price, the stock offers a 16% return (called the **dividend yield**) to an investor purchasing the stock.

However, if the prevailing long-term interest rates should again decline to the 8% range, the market price of an 8% preferred stock should rise to approximately par value. In summary, the market price of preferred stock *varies inversely with interest rates*. As interest rates rise, preferred stock prices decline; as interest rates fall, preferred stock prices rise.

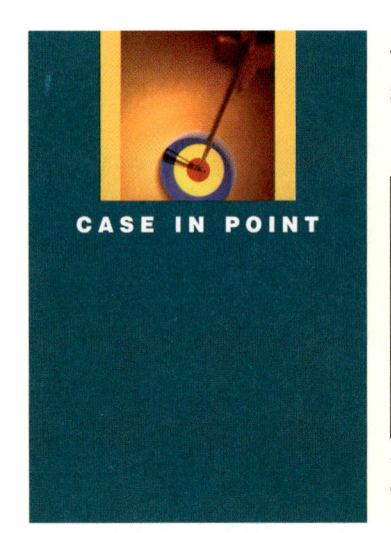

CASE IN POINT

The preceding point is illustrated by the performance of **Philadelphia Electric**'s $9^1/_2$%, $100 par value, preferred stock as interest rates have fluctuated over *four nonconsecutive years:*

	Long-Term Interest Rates*	Stock Price
Year 1	$15^1/_4$%	$ 60
Year 2	$13^1/_2$	68
Year 3	$9^1/_4$	99
Year 4	$7^1/_4$	106

*The long-term interest rates cited in this example are the market yields of federally insured 30-year, fixed-rate mortgages over a selected 13-year period.

Market Price of Common Stock

Prevailing interest rates also affect the market price of common stock. However, dividends paid to common stockholders are not fixed in amount. Both the amount of the dividend and the market price of the stock may increase dramatically if the corporation is successful. Alternatively, if the company is unsuccessful, the common stockholders may not even recover their original investment. Therefore, the most important factors in the market price of common stock are *investors' expectations* as to the future profitability of the business and the *risk* that this level of profitability may not be achieved.

Bear in mind that after shares have been issued they belong to the stockholders, not to the issuing corporation. Therefore, changes in the market price of the shares do not affect the financial statements of the corporation, and these changes are not recorded in the corporation's accounting records. The paid-in capital shown in a corporate balance

Market Value **479**

sheet represents the amount received when the stock was issued, not the current market value of shares.

You as an Investor

Assume that you are considering making a short-term investment in one of two stocks, a common stock or a preferred stock. You expect that the return on the two investments will be similar, and they have similar amounts of risk. In addition, you believe that interest rates will be increasing significantly in the next six months. Make a decision as to which stock is the better investment and support your choice.

*Our comments appear on page 500.

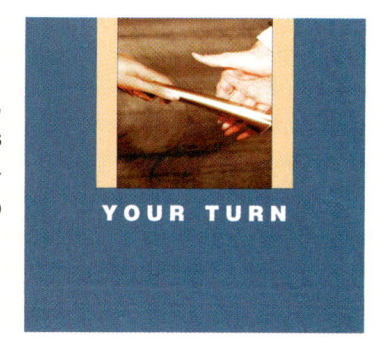

YOUR TURN

Book Value and Market Price

To some extent, *book value* is used in evaluating the reasonableness of the market price of a stock. However, it must be used with caution; the fact that a stock is selling at less than book value does not necessarily indicate a bargain.

Book value is a historical concept, representing the amounts invested by stockholders plus the amounts earned and retained by the corporation. If a stock is selling at a price *above* book value, investors believe that management has created a business worth more than the historical cost of the resources entrusted to its care. This, in essence, is the sign of a successful corporation. If the excess of market price over book value becomes great, however, investors should consider whether the company's prospects really justify a market price so much above the underlying book value of the company's resources.

On the other hand, if the market price of a stock is *less than* book value, investors believe that the company's resources are worth less than their cost while under the control of current management. Thus the relationship between book value and market price is one measure of investors' *confidence in a company's management.*

LO 7
Explain the significance of par value, book value, and market value of capital stock.

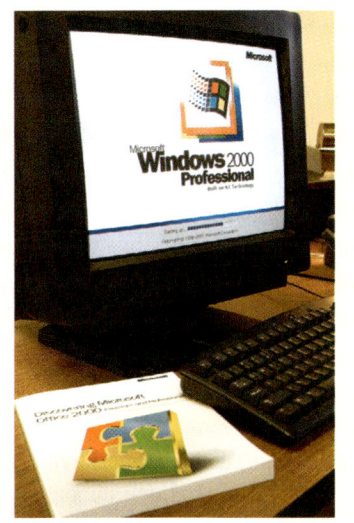

The Wild Studio, Inc.

Shortly after the introduction of its Windows software, the common stock of **Microsoft Corp.** rose to a market value of more than $100 per share, although its book value per share was only about $6.50. Investors believed that **Microsoft**'s products—and its management— made the business worth far more than the historical amounts of capital that had been invested.

In contrast, the common stock of **Tucson Electric Power** at one point sold at a market price of $5 per share, although its book value was more than $20 per share. This utility company had invested heavily in plant assets intended to generate more electrical power. Unfortunately, demand for this power did not develop, and the company found itself unable to sell its additional output. These new facilities produced very little revenue but increased operating expenses substantially. Although these new facilities had a high book value, investors did not consider them to be worth the amounts that management had invested.

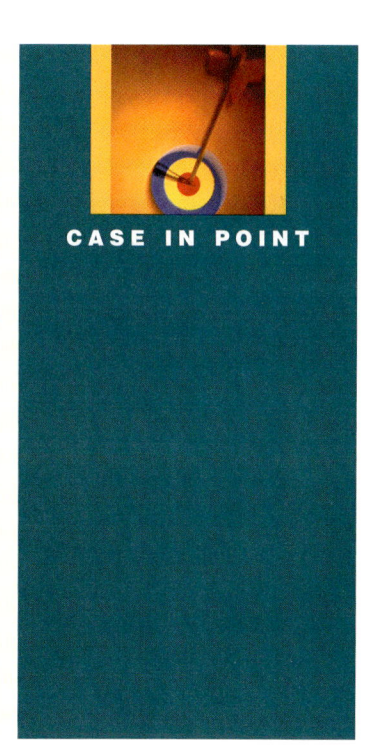

CASE IN POINT

Stock Splits

LO 8 *Explain the purpose and the effects of a stock split.*

Over time, the market price of a corporation's common stock may increase in value so much that it becomes too expensive for many investors. When this happens, a corporation may *split* its stock by increasing the number of its common shares outstanding. The purpose of a **stock split** is to reduce substantially the market price of the company's common stock, with the intent of making it more affordable to investors.

For example, assume that Felix Corporation has outstanding 1 million shares of $10 par value common stock. The market price is currently $90 per share. To make the stock more affordable, the corporation decides to increase the number of outstanding shares from 1 million to 2 million. This action is called a *2-for-1 stock split*. A stockholder who owned 100 shares of the stock before the split will own 200 shares after the split. Since the number of outstanding shares has been doubled without any change in total assets or total stockholders' equity, the market price of the stock should drop immediately from $90 to approximately $45 per share. In splitting its stock, a corporation is required to reduce the par value per share in proportion to the size of the split. As this was a 2-for-1 split, the company must reduce the par value of the stock from $10 to $5 per share. Had it been a 4-for-1 split, the par value would have been reduced from $10 to $2.50 per share and the stock price would have declined to approximately 25% of its former amount.

A stock split does not change the balance of any accounts in the balance sheet; consequently, the transaction is recorded merely by a *memorandum entry*. For Felix Corporation, this memorandum entry might read as follows:

My Notes
Memorandum entry to record a stock split

Sept. 30 Memorandum: Issued additional 1 million shares of common stock in a 2-for-1 stock split. Par value reduced from $10 per share to $5 per share.

The description of common stock also is changed in the balance sheet to reflect the lower par value and the greater number of shares outstanding.

Stock may be split in any desired ratio. Among the more common ratios are 2-for-1, 3-for-2, and 3-for-1. The determining factor is the number of shares needed to bring the price of the stock into the desired trading range. For example, assume that a $5 par value stock is selling at a price of $150 per share and that management wants to reduce the price to approximately $30 per share. This objective may be accomplished with a *5-for-1* stock split ($150 ÷ 5 = $30). Par value *after* the 5-for-1 stock split is $1 per share ($5 par value × $1/5$).

Another form of stock distribution to current stockholders is a stock dividend. While stock dividends are similar to stock splits in some respects, they are much smaller in size and have a different intent. Stock dividends usually result in an increase of 5% to 20% of outstanding stock as compared with distributions of 2:1 (100% increase) or 3:1 (200% increase) that are typical of stock splits. By distributing a stock dividend management can make a distribution to owners while preserving the company's current cash balance. Because stock dividends are important considerations in a company's dividend policy, we defer the detailed coverage of stock dividends to Chapter 12.

TREASURY STOCK

LO 9 *Account for treasury stock transactions.*

Treasury stock is defined as shares of a corporation's own capital stock that have been issued and later *reacquired by the issuing company* but that have not been canceled or permanently retired. Treasury shares may be held indefinitely or may be issued again at any time. Shares of capital stock held in the treasury are not entitled to receive dividends, to vote, or to share in assets upon dissolution of the company. In the computation of earnings per share, shares held in the treasury are not regarded as outstanding shares.

Recording Purchases of Treasury Stock

Purchases of treasury stock are usually recorded by debiting the Treasury Stock account with the cost of the stock. For example, if Riley Corporation reacquires 1,600 shares of its own $5 par stock at a price of $90 per share, the entry is as follows:

Treasury Stock	144,000	
Cash		144,000
Purchased 1,600 shares of $5 par treasury stock at $90 per share.		

Note that the Treasury Stock account is debited for the *cost* of the shares purchased, not their par value.

Treasury Stock Is Not an Asset When treasury stock is purchased, the corporation is eliminating part of its stockholders' equity by a payment to one or more stockholders. The purchase of treasury stock should be regarded as a *reduction of stockholders' equity,* not as the acquisition of an asset. For this reason, the Treasury Stock account appears in the balance sheet as a deduction in the stockholders' equity section.[3]

The presentation of treasury stock in Riley Corporation's balance sheet appears as follows, based on assumed numbers except for treasury stock:

Stockholders' equity:	
Common stock, $5 par value, authorized 250,000 shares, issued 100,000 shares (of which 1,500 are held in treasury)	$ 500,000
Additional paid-in capital: Common stock	900,000
Total paid-in capital	$1,400,000
Retained earnings	600,000
Subtotal	$2,000,000
Less: Treasury stock (1,600 shares of common, at $90 cost)	144,000
Total stockholders' equity	$1,856,000

Reissuance of Treasury Stock

When treasury shares are reissued, the Treasury Stock account is credited for the cost of the shares reissued and Additional Paid-in Capital from Treasury Stock Transactions is debited or credited for any *difference* between cost and the reissue price. To illustrate, assume that 1,000 of the treasury shares acquired by Riley Corporation at a cost of $90 per share are now reissued at a price of $115 per share. The entry to record the reissuance of these shares at a price above cost is:

Cash	115,000	
Treasury Stock		90,000
Additional Paid-in Capital: Treasury Stock Transactions		25,000
Sold 1,000 shares of treasury stock, which cost $90,000, at a price of $115 per share.		

My Notes

Treasury stock reissued at a price above cost

---

[3] Despite a lack of theoretical support, a few corporations do classify treasury stock as an asset on the grounds that the shares could be sold for cash just as readily as shares owned in another corporation. The same argument could be made for treating unissued shares as assets. Treasury shares are basically the same as unissued shares, and an unissued share of stock is definitely not an asset.

The $25,000 of additional paid-in capital resulting from the reissuance of Riley's treasury stock is reported in the stockholders' equity section of the company's balance sheet. It appears immediately after additional paid-in capital from common stock, as shown here:

Stockholders' equity:	
Common stock, $5 par value, authorized 250,000 shares, issued 100,000 shares (of which 500 are held in treasury)	$ 500,000
Additional paid-in capital:	
Common stock	900,000
Treasury stock	15,000
Total paid-in capital	$1,415,000
Retained earnings	600,000
Subtotal	$2,015,000
Less: Treasury stock (500 shares of common, at $100 cost)	50,000
Total stockholders' equity	$1,965,000

If treasury stock is reissued at a price below cost, additional paid-in capital from previous treasury stock transactions is reduced (debited) by the excess of cost over the reissue price. To illustrate, assume that Riley Corporation reissues its remaining 600 shares of treasury stock (cost $90 per share) at a price of $75 per share. The entry is:

My Notes

Reissued at a price below cost

Cash	45,000	
Additional Paid-in Capital: Treasury Stock Transactions	9,000	
Treasury Stock		54,000
Sold 600 shares of treasury stock, which cost $54,000, at a price of $75 each.		

If there is no additional paid-in capital from previous treasury stock transactions, the excess of the cost of the treasury shares over the reissue price is recorded as a debit to the Additional Paid-in Capital: Common Stock account.

No Profit or Loss on Treasury Stock Transactions Notice that *no gain or loss is recognized on treasury stock transactions,* even when the shares are reissued at a price above or below cost. A corporation earns profits by selling goods and services to outsiders, not by issuing or reissuing shares of its own capital stock. When treasury shares are reissued at a price above cost, the corporation receives from the new stockholder an amount of paid-in capital that is larger than the reduction in stockholders' equity that occurred when the corporation acquired the treasury shares. Conversely, if treasury shares are reissued at a price below cost, the corporation has less paid-in capital as a result of the purchase and reissuance of the shares. Thus any changes in stockholders' equity resulting from treasury stock transactions are regarded as changes in *paid-in capital* and are *not* included in the measurement of net income.

Restriction of Retained Earnings for Treasury Stock Owned Purchases of treasury stock, like cash dividends, are distributions of assets to the stockholders in the corporation. Many states have a legal requirement that distributions to stockholders (including purchases of treasury stock) cannot exceed the balance in the Retained Earnings account. Therefore, retained earnings usually are restricted by an amount equal to the *cost* of any shares held in the treasury.

Stock Buyback Programs

In past years, most treasury stock transactions involved relatively small dollar amounts. Hence, the topic was not of much importance to investors or other users of financial statements. Late in 1987, however, many corporations initiated buyback programs, in which they repurchased large amounts of their own common stock.[4] As a result of these programs, treasury stock has become a material item in the balance sheets of many corporations.

CASE IN POINT

Shown below is the cost of the treasury stock listed in the balance sheets of several publicly owned corporations at the end of a recent year.

	Treasury Stock	
Company	At Cost (in thousands)	As a % of Other Elements of Stockholders' Equity*
Coca-Cola	$ 5,201,194	57
ExxonMobil	16,887,000	33
Lotus	287,655	41
King World	162,054	32

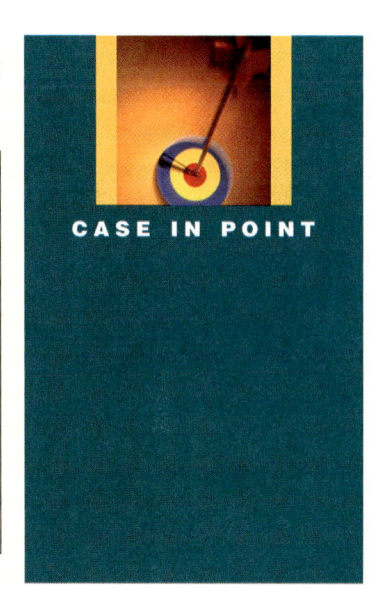

*To place these holdings in perspective, we have shown the cost of the treasury stock as a percentage of total stockholders' equity before *deducting the cost of the repurchased shares.*

Large buyback programs serve several purposes. First, by creating demand for the company's stock in the marketplace, these programs tend to increase the market value of the shares. Also, reducing the number of shares outstanding usually increases earnings per share. When stock prices are low, some companies find that they can increase earnings per share by a greater amount through repurchasing shares than through expanding business operations.

CASH EFFECTS

As noted previously, transactions between the corporation and its stockholders are classified in the statement of cash flows as *financing activities.* Accordingly, the purchase and reissuance of treasury stock result in cash flows from financing activities. When treasury stock is purchased, a financing cash *outflow* is reported in the statement of cash flows. When treasury stock is reissued, the amount of cash received is reported as a financing cash *inflow* in the statement of cash flows.

Because treasury stock transactions do not give rise to gains or losses, they have no effect on the corporation's net income. Any difference between the purchase price of the treasury stock and the cash received when it is reissued is reported as an increase or decrease in the corporation's paid-in capital.

---

[4] On October 19, 1987, a date known as "Black Monday," stocks around the world suffered a record one-day decline. Within hours of the market's close on Black Monday, many large corporations announced their intention to enter the market and spend hundreds of millions of dollars repurchasing their own shares. In the opinion of the authors, these announcements helped stabilize the investment markets and avoided a possible stock market collapse.

FINANCIAL ANALYSIS

The following information was taken from a recent annual report of **Microsoft Corporation** (in millions):

Net income	$ 9,421
Preferred stock dividends	$ 13
Average number of common shares outstanding	5,196
Average common stockholders' equity	$18,520
Average total stockholders' equity	$34,903

These frequently used measures of profitability can be derived from the above figures:

Profitability Measure	Computation	Significance
Earnings per share	$\dfrac{\text{Net income} - \text{Preferred Dividends}}{\text{Average Number of Common Shares Outstanding}}$	Net income applicable to each share of common stock
Return on common stockholders' equity	$\dfrac{\text{Net income} - \text{Preferred Dividends}}{\text{Average Common Stockholders' Equity}}$	The rate of return earned on the common stockholders' equity appropriate when company has both common and preferred stock
Return on equity	$\dfrac{\text{Net Income}}{\text{Average Total Equity}}$	The rate of return earned on the stockholders' equity in the business

Using the figures provided, **Microsoft**'s three profitability measures would be:

Earnings per share: ($9,421 − $13) ÷ 5,196 shares = $1.81

Return on common stockholders' equity: ($9,421 − $13) ÷ $18,520 = 51%

Return on equity: $9,421 ÷ $34,903 = 27%

CONCLUDING REMARKS

In this chapter, we covered the aspects of stockholders' equity that result primarily from various transactions between the company and its stockholders, including the sale and repurchase of capital stock. We explored different characteristics of stock, including the unique features of preferred stock.

Another major source of stockholders' equity is the accumulated earnings of previous years that have been retained for purposes of expansion and meeting other business objectives. This is the subject of Chapter 12, which follows. While paid-in capital and retained earnings are two distinct aspects of stockholders' equity, they are closely related and, therefore, are virtually impossible to discuss totally independently of each other. For that reason, in this chapter there are occasional references to retained earnings. Similarly, in Chapter 12 you will find references to common and preferred stock, additional paid-in capital, treasury stock, and other aspects of stockholders' equity that we covered primarily in Chapter 11. Combining the content of Chapters 11 and 12, you will have a good working knowledge of stockholders' equity and how it fits together with assets and liabilities to form the basis for a company's balance sheet.

Concluding Remarks

We began this chapter by looking at **Sears** and observing that this company, like many others, has a policy of investing in its own stock. An unusual feature of **Sears** is that the amount of treasury stock in the 2000 balance sheet is almost as great as the amount of its outstanding common stock. Combining the par value of common stock with the additional paid-in capital in excess of par value, the balance sheet includes $3,861 million of common stock issued. Treasury stock is included in the same balance sheet at $3,726 million. Does this mean that **Sears** has repurchased almost all of its outstanding stock?

The answer to this question is no, because the stock originally sold at a lower price than the price for which treasury stock has been repurchased. For example, the $3,861 million figure represents the original selling price to owners of approximately 333 million shares. This means that on average the stock originally sold for between $11 and $12 per share. During the year 2000, however, the same stock sold from a low of $25.25 to a high of $43.50. The treasury stock amount of $3,726 million represents the cost of shares purchased during 2000 and in other recent years at higher prices than the price at which the shares originally sold. Therefore, even though treasury stock in the 2000 balance sheet is nearly as large as the amount of its issued common stock, **Sears** still has outstanding a significant amount of stockholders' equity in the form of common stock that is not owned by the company.

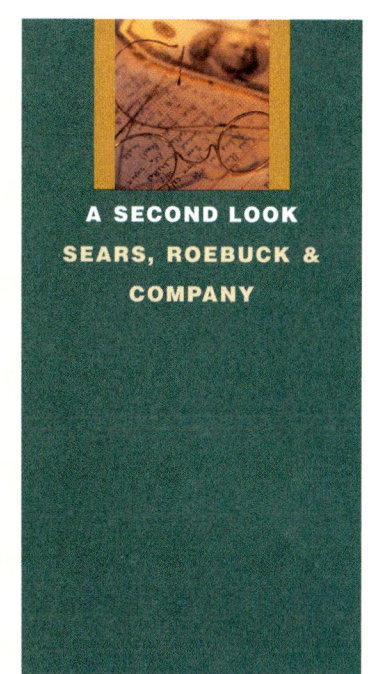

A SECOND LOOK
SEARS, ROEBUCK & COMPANY

END-OF-CHAPTER REVIEW

SUMMARY OF LEARNING OBJECTIVES

LO 1

Discuss the advantages and disadvantages of organizing a business as a corporation.
The primary advantages are no personal liability of stockholders for the debts of the business, the transferability of ownership shares, continuity of existence, ability to hire professional management, and the relative ease of accumulating large amounts of capital. The primary disadvantages are double taxation of earnings and greater governmental regulation.

LO 2

Distinguish between publicly owned and closely held corporations.
The stock of publicly owned corporations is available for purchase by the general public, usually on an organized stock exchange. Stock in a closely held corporation, in contrast, is not available to the public.

Publicly owned corporations tend to be so large that individual stockholders seldom control the corporation; in essence, most stockholders in publicly owned companies are investors, rather than owners in the traditional sense. Closely held corporations usually are quite small, and one or two stockholders often do exercise control. Publicly owned corporations are subject to more government regulation than are closely held companies, and they must disclose to the public much information about their business operations.

LO 3

Explain the rights of stockholders and the roles of corporate directors and officers.
Stockholders in a corporation normally have the right to elect the board of directors, to share in dividends declared by the directors, and to share in the distribution of assets if the corporation is liquidated.

The directors formulate company policies, review the actions of the corporate officers, and protect the interests of the company's stockholders. Corporate officers are professional managers appointed by the board of directors to manage the business on a daily basis.

LO 4

Account for paid-in capital and prepare the equity section of a corporate balance sheet.
When capital stock is issued, appropriate asset accounts are debited for cash or the market value of the goods or services received in exchange for the stock. A capital stock account (which indicates the type of stock issued) is credited for the par value of the issued shares. Any excess of the market value received over the par value of the issued shares is credited to an Additional Paid-in Capital account.

The equity section of a corporate balance sheet shows for each class of capital stock outstanding (1) the total par value (legal capital) and (2) any additional paid-in capital. Together, these amounts represent the corporation's total paid-in capital. In addition, the equity section shows separately any earned capital—that is, retained earnings.

LO 5

Contrast the features of common stock with those of preferred stock.
Common stock represents the residual ownership of a corporation. These shares have voting rights and cannot be called. Also, the common stock dividend is not fixed in dollar amount—thus it may increase or decrease based on the company's performance.

Preferred stock has preference over common stock with respect to dividends and to distributions in the event of liquidation. This preference means that preferred stockholders must be paid in full before any payments are made to holders of common stock. The dividends on preferred stock usually are fixed in amount. In addition, the stock may be callable at the option of the issuing corporation and often has no voting rights. Preferred stocks sometimes have special features, such as being convertible into shares of common stock.

LO 6

Discuss the factors affecting the market price of preferred stock and common stock.
The market price of preferred stock varies inversely with interest rates. As interest rates rise, preferred stock prices decline; as interest rates fall, preferred stock prices rise. If a company's ability to continue the preferred dividend is in doubt, this may affect preferred stock prices.

Interest rates also affect the market price of common stock. However, common stock dividends are not fixed in amount. Both the amount of the dividend and the market value of the stock may fluctuate, based on the prosperity of the company. Therefore, the principal factor in the market price of common stock is investors' expectations as to the future profitability of the company.

LO 7

Explain the significance of par value, book value, and market value of capital stock.
Par value has the least significance. It is a legal concept, representing the amount by which stockholders' equity cannot be reduced except by losses. Intended as a buffer for the protection of creditors, it usually is so low as to be of little significance.

Book value per share is the net assets per share of common stock. This value is based on amounts invested by stockholders, plus retained earnings. It often provides insight into the reasonableness of market price.

LO 8
Explain the purpose and the effects of a stock split.
When the market price of a corporation's common stock appreciates in value significantly, it may become too expensive for many investors. When this happens, the corporation may split its stock by increasing the number of its common shares outstanding. The purpose of a stock split is to reduce the market price of the company's common stock, with the intent of making it more affordable to investors. A stock split does not change the balance of any ledger account; consequently, the transaction is recorded merely by a memorandum entry.

LO 9
Account for treasury stock transactions.
Purchases of treasury stock are recorded by debiting a contra-equity account entitled Treasury Stock. No profit or loss is recorded when the treasury shares are reissued at a price above or below cost. Rather, any difference between the reissuance price and the cost of the shares is debited or credited to a paid-in capital account. While treasury stock transactions may affect cash flow, they have no effect on the net income of the corporation.

To investors, market price is the most relevant of the three values. This is the price at which they can buy or sell the stock today. Changes in market price directly affect the financial position of the stockholder, but not of the issuing company. Therefore, market values do not appear in the equity section of the issuing company's balance sheet—but they are readily available in the daily newspaper and on the Internet.

KEY TERMS INTRODUCED OR EMPHASIZED IN CHAPTER 11

Additional Paid-in Capital (p. 469) An account showing the amounts invested in a corporation by stockholders in excess of par value or stated value. In short, this account shows paid-in capital in excess of legal capital.

board of directors (p. 466) Persons elected by common stockholders to direct the affairs of a corporation.

book value per share (p. 475) The stockholders' equity represented by each share of common stock, computed by dividing common stockholders' equity by the number of common shares outstanding.

capital stock (p. 463) Transferable units of ownership in a corporation. A broad term that can refer to common stock, preferred stock, or both.

closely held corporation (p. 464) A corporation owned by a small group of stockholders. Not publicly owned.

common stock (p. 470) A type of capital stock that possesses the basic rights of ownership, including the right to vote. Represents the residual element of ownership in a corporation.

contributed capital (p. 468) The stockholders' equity that results from capital contributions by investors in exchange for shares of common or preferred stock. Also referred to as paid-in capital.

corporation (p. 462) A business organized as a legal entity separate from its owners. Chartered by the state with ownership divided into shares of transferable stock. Stockholders are not liable for debts of the corporation.

dividends (p. 471) Distribution of assets (usually cash) by a corporation to its stockholders. Normally viewed as a distribution of profits, dividends cannot exceed the amount of retained earnings. Must be formally declared by the board of directors and distributed on a per-share basis. *Note:* Stockholders *cannot* simply withdraw assets from a corporation at will.

dividend yield (p. 478) The annual dividend paid to a share of stock, expressed as a percentage of the stock's market value. Indicates the rate of return represented by the dividend.

donated capital (p. 475) An account showing capital given to a corporation for which no payment has been made and for which no capital stock has been issued in exchange. Shown in the balance sheet as an element of paid-in capital.

double taxation (p. 462) The fact that corporate income is taxed to the corporation when earned and then again taxed to the stockholders when distributed as dividends.

legal capital (p. 469) Equal to the par value or stated value of capital stock issued. This amount represents a permanent commitment of capital by the owners of a corporation and cannot be removed without special legal action. Of course, it may be eroded by losses.

limited personal liability (p. 463) The concept that the owners of a corporation are not personally liable for the debts of the business. Thus stockholders' potential financial losses are limited to the amount of their equity investment.

paid-in capital (p. 468) The amounts invested in a corporation by its stockholders (also includes donated capital).

par value (or stated value) (p. 469) The legal capital of a corporation. Represents the minimum amount per share invested in the corporation by its owners and cannot be withdrawn except by special legal action.

preferred stock (p. 470) A class of capital stock usually having preferences as to dividends and in the distribution of assets in event of liquidation.

public information (p. 464) Information that, by law, must be made available to the general public. Includes the quarterly and annual financial statements—and other financial information—about publicly owned corporations.

publicly owned corporation (p. 464) Any corporation whose shares are offered for sale to the general public.

retained earnings (p. 468) The element of owners' equity in a corporation that has accumulated through profitable business operations. Net income increases retained earnings; net losses and dividends reduce retained earnings.

state of incorporation (p. 464) The state in which the corporation is legally formed. This may or may not be the state in which the corporation conducts most or any of its business.

stock certificate (p. 465) A document issued by a corporation (or its transfer agent) as evidence of the ownership of the number of shares stated on the certificate.

stockholders (p. 462) The owners of a corporation. The name reflects the fact that their ownership is evidenced by transferable shares of capital stock.

stockholders subsidiary ledger (p. 468) A record showing the number of shares owned by each stockholder.

stock registrar (p. 468) An independent fiscal agent, such as a bank, retained by a corporation to provide assurance against overissuance of stock certificates.

stock split (p. 480) An increase in the number of shares outstanding with a corresponding decrease in par value per share. The additional shares are distributed proportionately to all common shareholders. The purpose of a stock split is to reduce market price per share and encourage wider public ownership of the company's stock. A 2-for-1 stock split will give each stockholder twice as many shares as previously owned.

stock transfer agent (p. 468) A bank or trust company retained by a corporation to maintain its records of capital stock ownership and make transfers from one investor to another.

treasury stock (p. 480) Shares of a corporation's stock that have been issued and then reacquired, but not canceled.

underwriter (p. 468) An investment banking firm that handles the sale of a corporation's stock to the public.

DEMONSTRATION PROBLEM

The stockholders' equity section of Rockhurst Corporation's balance sheet appears as follows:

Stockholders' equity:

8% preferred stock, $100 par value, callable at $102 per share, 200,000 shares authorized		$12,000,000
Common stock, $5 par value, 5,000,000 shares authorized		14,000,000
Additional paid-in capital:		
Preferred stock	$ 360,000	
Common stock	30,800,000	31,160,000
Retained earnings		2,680,000
Total stockholders' equity		$59,840,000

Instructions

On the basis of this information, answer the following questions and show any necessary supporting computations:

a. How many shares of preferred stock have been issued?
b. What is the total annual dividend requirement on the outstanding preferred stock?
c. How many shares of common stock have been issued?
d. What was the average price per share received by the corporation for its common stock?
e. What is the total amount of legal capital?
f. What is the total paid-in capital?
g. What is the book value per share of common stock? (Assume no dividends in arrears.)

Solution to the Demonstration Problem

a. 120,000 shares ($12,000,000 total par value, divided by $100 par value per share)
b. $960,000 (120,000 shares outstanding × $8 per share)
c. 2,800,000 shares ($14,000,000 total par value, divided by $5 par value per share)
d.

Par value of common shares issued	$14,000,000
Additional paid-in capital on common shares	30,800,000
Total issue price of common shares	$44,800,000
Number of common shares issued (part **c**)	2,800,000
Average issue price per share ($44,800,000 ÷ 2,800,000 shares)	$16

e. $26,000,000 ($12,000,000 preferred, $14,000,000 common)
f. $57,160,000 ($26,000,000 legal capital, plus $31,160,000 additional paid-in capital)
g.

Total stockholders' equity	$59,840,000
Less: Claims of preferred stockholders (120,000 shares × $102 call price)	12,240,000
Equity of common stockholders	$47,600,000
Number of common shares outstanding (part **c**)	2,800,000
Book value per share ($47,600,000 ÷ 2,800,000 shares)	$17

SELF-TEST QUESTIONS

Answers to these questions appear on page 500.

1. When a business is organized as a corporation, which of the following is true?
   a. Stockholders are liable for the debts of the business in proportion to their percentage ownership of capital stock.
   b. Stockholders do *not* have to pay personal income taxes on dividends received, because the corporation is subject to income taxes on its earnings.
   c. Fluctuations in the market value of outstanding shares of capital stock do *not* affect the amount of stockholders' equity shown in the balance sheet.
   d. Each stockholder has the right to bind the corporation to contracts and to make other managerial decisions.

2. Western Moving Corporation was organized with authorization to issue 100,000 shares of $1 par value common stock. Forty thousand shares were issued to Tom Morgan, the company's founder, at a price of $5 per share. No other shares have yet been issued. Which of the following statements is true?
   a. Morgan owns *40%* of the stockholders' equity of the corporation.
   b. The corporation should recognize a $160,000 gain on the issuance of these shares.
   c. If the balance sheet includes retained earnings of $50,000, total *paid-in* capital amounts to $250,000.
   d. In the balance sheet, the Additional Paid-in Capital account will have a $160,000 balance, regardless of the profits earned or losses incurred since the corporation was organized.

3. Which of the following is *not* a characteristic of the *common stock* of a large, publicly owned corporation?
   a. The shares may be transferred from one investor to another without disrupting the continuity of business operations.
   b. Voting rights in the election of the board of directors.
   c. A cumulative right to receive dividends.
   d. After issuance, the market value of the stock is unrelated to its par value.

4. Tri-State Electric is a profitable utility company that has increased its dividend to *common* stockholders every year for 42 consecutive years. Which of the following is *least* likely to affect the market price of the company's *preferred* stock by a significant amount?
   a. A decrease in long-term interest rates.
   b. An increase in long-term interest rates.
   c. The board of directors announces its intention to increase common stock dividends in the current year.
   d. Whether or not the preferred stock carries a conversion privilege.

5. The following information is taken from the balance sheet and related disclosures of Maxwell, Inc.:

Total paid-in capital	$5,400,000
Outstanding shares:	
Common stock, $5 par value	100,000 shares
6% preferred stock, $100 par value, callable at $108 per share	10,000 shares
Preferred dividends in arrears	2 years
Total stockholders' equity	$4,700,000

Which of the following statements is(are) true? (For this question, more than one answer may be correct.)

   a. The preferred dividends in arrears amount to $120,000 and should appear as a liability in the corporate balance sheet.

   b. The book value per share of common stock is $35.

   c. The stockholders' equity section of the balance sheet should indicate a deficit (negative amount in retained earnings) of $700,000.

   d. The company has paid no dividend on its *common* stock during the past two years.

6. On December 10, 2001, Smitty Corporation reacquired 2,000 shares of its own $5 par stock at a price of $60 per share. In 2002, 500 of the treasury shares are reissued at a price of $70 per share. Which of the following statements is correct?

   a. The treasury stock purchased is recorded at cost and is shown in Smitty's December 31, 2001, balance sheet as an asset.

   b. The two treasury stock transactions result in an overall net reduction in Smitty's stockholders' equity of $85,000.

   c. Smitty recognizes a gain of $10 per share on the reissuance of the 500 treasury shares in 2002.

   d. Smitty's stockholders' equity was increased by $110,000 when the treasury stock was acquired.

ASSIGNMENT MATERIAL

DISCUSSION QUESTIONS

1. Why are large corporations often said to be *publicly owned?*

2. Distinguish between corporations and sole proprietorships in terms of the following characteristics:

   a. Owners' liability for debts of the business.

   b. Transferability of ownership interest.

   c. Continuity of existence.

   d. Federal taxation on income.

3. What are the basic rights of the owner of a share of corporate stock? In what way are these basic rights commonly modified with respect to the owner of a share of preferred stock?

4. Explain the meaning of the term *double taxation* as it applies to corporate profits.

5. Distinguish between *paid-in capital* and *retained earnings* of a corporation. Why is such a distinction useful?

6. Explain the significance of *par value.* Does par value indicate the reasonable market price for a share of stock? Explain.

7. Describe the usual nature of the following features as they apply to a share of preferred stock: (a) cumulative, (b) convertible, and (c) callable.

8. Why is noncumulative preferred stock often considered an unattractive form of investment?

9. When stock is issued by a corporation in exchange for assets other than cash, accountants face the problem of determining the dollar amount at which to record the transaction. Discuss the factors to be considered and explain their significance.

10. State the classification (asset, liability, stockholders' equity, revenue, or expense) of each of the following accounts:
    a. Cash (received from the issuance of capital stock)
    b. Organization Costs
    c. Preferred Stock
    d. Retained Earnings
    e. Donated Capital
    f. Additional Paid-in Capital
    g. Income Taxes Payable
11. A professional baseball team received as a gift from the city the land on which to build a stadium. What effect, if any, will the receipt of this gift have on the baseball team's balance sheet and income statement? Explain.
12. Explain the following terms:
    a. Stock transfer agent
    b. Stockholders subsidiary ledger
    c. Underwriter
    d. Stock registrar
13. What does *book value per share* of common stock represent? Does it represent the amount common stockholders would receive in the event of liquidation of the corporation? Explain briefly.
14. How is book value per share of common stock computed when a company has both preferred and common stock outstanding?
15. What would be the effect, if any, on book value per share of common stock as a result of each of the following independent events: (a) a corporation obtains a bank loan; (b) a dividend is declared (to be paid in the next accounting period)?
16. In the stock market crash of October 19, 1987, the market price of **IBM**'s capital stock fell by over $31 per share. Explain the effects, if any, of this decline in share price on **IBM**'s balance sheet.
17. Assume that you asked your stockbroker to purchase 100 shares of **ExxonMobil Corporation** stock. How would this transaction affect the financial statements of **ExxonMobil**? Explain.
18. What is the purpose of a *stock split?*
19. What is *treasury stock?* Why do corporations purchase their own shares? Is treasury stock an asset? How should it be reported in the balance sheet?
20. In many states, the corporation law requires that retained earnings be restricted for dividend purposes to the extent of the cost of treasury shares. What is the reason for this legal rule?

EXERCISES

EXERCISE 11.1

Form of Organization

LO 1, 2, 3

Assume that you have recently obtained your scuba instructor's certification and have decided to start a scuba diving school.
a. Describe the advantages and disadvantages of organizing your scuba diving school as a:
   1. Sole proprietorship
   2. Corporation
b. State your opinion about which form of organization would be best and explain the basis for your opinion.

EXERCISE 11.2

Accounting Terminology

LO 1–9

Listed below are 12 technical accounting terms discussed in this chapter:

Par value	Board of directors	Double taxation
Book value	Paid-in capital	Dividends in arrears
Market value	Preferred stock	Closely held corporation
Retained earnings	Common stock	Publicly owned corporation

Each of the following statements may (or may not) describe one of these technical terms. For each statement, indicate the term described, or answer "None" if the statement does not correctly describe any of the terms.

a. A major *disadvantage* of the corporate form of organization.
b. From investors' point of view, the most important value associated with capital stock.
c. Cash available for distribution to the stockholders.
d. The class of capital stock that normally has the most voting power.
e. A distribution of assets that may be made in future years to the holders of common stock.
f. The group of stockholders that controls more than 50% of a corporation's voting shares.
g. A corporation whose shares are traded on an organized stock exchange.
h. Equity arising either from investments by owners or from the donation of assets to a corporation.
i. The element of stockholders' equity that is increased by net income.
j. Total assets divided by the number of common shares outstanding.
k. The class of stock whose market price normally rises as interest rates increase.

EXERCISE 11.3
Stockholders' Equity Section of a Balance Sheet
LO 4, 5

When Enviro Systems, Inc., was formed, the company was authorized to issue 5,000 shares of $100 par value, 8% cumulative preferred stock, and 100,000 shares of $2 stated value common stock. The preferred stock is callable at $106.

Half of the preferred stock was issued at a price of $103 per share, and 70,000 shares of the common stock were sold for $13 per share. At the end of the current year, Enviro Systems, Inc., has retained earnings of $382,000.

a. Prepare the stockholders' equity section of the company's balance sheet at the end of the current year.
b. Assume Enviro Systems' common stock is trading at $22 per share and its preferred stock is trading at $105 per share at the end of the current year. Would the stockholders' equity section prepared in part **a** be affected by this additional information?

EXERCISE 11.4
Dividends: Preferred and Common
LO 4, 5

A portion of the stockholders' equity section from the balance sheet of Ranchero Corporation appears as follows:

Stockholders' equity:

Preferred stock, 9% cumulative, $50 par, 40,000 shares authorized and issued	$2,000,000
Preferred stock, 12% noncumulative, $100 par, 8,000 shares authorized and issued	800,000
Common stock, $5 par, 400,000 shares authorized and issued	2,000,000
Total paid-in capital	$4,800,000

Assume that all the stock was issued on January 1 and that no dividends were paid during the first two years of operation. During the third year, Ranchero Corporation paid total cash dividends of $736,000.

a. Compute the amount of cash dividends paid during the third year to each of the three classes of stock.
b. Compute the dividends paid *per share* during the third year for each of the three classes of stock.
c. What was the average issue price of each type of preferred stock?

EXERCISE 11.5
Analyzing Stockholders' Equity

LO 4, 5, 6, 7

The year-end balance sheet of Baxter, Inc. includes the following stockholders' equity section (with certain details omitted):

Stockholders' equity:	
Capital stock:	
7% cumulative preferred stock, $100 par value, callable at $105	$ 15,000,000
Common stock, $5 par value, 5,000,000 shares authorized, 4,000,000 shares issued	20,000,000
Additional paid-in capital:	
Preferred stock	300,000
Common stock	44,000,000
Retained earnings	64,450,000
Total stockholders' equity	$143,750,000

From this information, compute answers to the following questions:

a. How many shares of preferred stock have been issued?
b. What is the total amount of the annual dividends paid to preferred stockholders?
c. What was the average issuance price per share of common stock?
d. What is the amount of legal capital and the amount of total paid-in capital?
e. What is the book value per share of common stock?
f. Is it possible to determine the fair market value per share of common stock from the stockholders' equity section above? Explain.

EXERCISE 11.6
Issuing Stock for Assets Other Than Cash

LO 2, 4

Melton Hill Development Co. issued 20,000 shares of its $2 par value common stock in exchange for 300 acres of land. The land recently had been appraised at $470,000.

a. Record this transaction under each of the following assumptions:
  1. Melton is a closely held corporation. None of its shares have changed hands in several years.
  2. Melton is a publicly owned corporation. Its stock currently is trading at $22.50 per share.
b. For each of your two journal entries, explain the reasoning behind the value that you assigned to the *land*.

EXERCISE 11.7
Reporting the Effects of Transactions

LO 4, 7

Five events pertaining to Precision Manufacturing Co. are described below.

a. Issued common stock for cash.
b. Issued common stock for land.
c. The market value of the corporation's stock increased.
d. Declared and paid a cash dividend to stockholders.
e. Received a building site as a donation from the city.

Indicate the immediate effects of the events on the financial measurements in the four columnar headings listed below. Use the code letters **I** for increase, **D** for decrease, and **NE** for no effect.

Event	Current Assets	Stockholders' Equity	Net Income	Net Cash Flow (from any source)
a				

EXERCISE 11.8
Computing Book Value

LO 4, 5, 6, 7

The following information is necessary to compute the net assets (stockholders' equity) and book value per share of common stock for Pembroke Corporation:

8% cumulative preferred stock, $100 par (callable at $110)	$200,000
Common stock, $5 par, authorized 100,000 shares, issued 60,000 shares	300,000
Additional paid-in capital	452,800
Deficit (negative amount in retained earnings)	146,800
Dividends in arrears on preferred stock, 1 full year	16,000

a. Compute the amount of net assets (stockholders' equity).
b. Compute the book value per share of common stock.
c. Is book value per share (answer to part **b**) the amount common stockholders should expect to receive if Pembroke Corporation were to cease operations and liquidate? Explain.

EXERCISE 11.9
Recording Treasury Stock Transactions

LO 9

Willingham, Inc., engaged in the following transactions involving treasury stock:

Feb. 10 Purchased for cash 14,500 shares of treasury stock at a price of $30 per share.
June 4 Reissued 6,000 shares of treasury stock at a price of $33 per share.
Dec. 22 Reissued 4,000 shares of treasury stock at a price of $28 per share.

a. Prepare general journal entries to record these transactions.
b. Compute the amount of retained earnings that should be restricted because of the treasury stock still owned at December 31.
c. Does a restriction on retained earnings affect the dollar amount of retained earnings reported in the balance sheet? Explain briefly.

EXERCISE 11.10
Effects of a Stock Split

LO 8

The common stock of Maxwell Corporation was trading at $45 per share on October 15, 2001. A year later, on October 15, 2002, it was trading at $100 per share. On this date, Maxwell's board of directors decided to split the company's common stock.

a. If the company decides on a 2-for-1 split, at what price would you expect the stock to trade immediately after the split goes into effect?
b. If the company decides on a 4-for-1 split, at what price would you expect the stock to trade immediately after the split goes into effect?
c. Why do you suppose Maxwell's board of directors decided to split the company's stock?

EXERCISE 11.11
Treasury Stock Presentation

LO 9

Vanari Company was experiencing financial difficulty late in the current year. The company's income was sluggish, and the market price of its common stock was tumbling. On December 21, the company began to buy back shares of its own stock in an attempt to boost its market price per share and to improve its earnings per share.

a. Is it unethical for a company to purchase shares of its own stock to improve measures of financial performance? Defend your answer.
b. Assume that the company classified the shares of treasury stock as short-term investments in the current asset section of its balance sheet. Is this appropriate? Explain.

EXERCISE 11.12
Authorized Stock

LO 4

The 2000 balance sheet for ConAgra Foods indicates that the company has 1,200 million shares of common stock authorized of which approximately 524 million have been issued.

a. How many additional shares of common stock could ConAgra Foods sell, not considering any treasury shares that it currently holds?
b. How are the shares that have not yet been issued included in the company's balance sheet? Do they represent an asset of the company?

EXERCISE 11.13
Tootsie Roll Industries

LO 4, 7

The annual report of **Tootsie Roll Industries, Inc.**, appears in Appendix A of this text. This report contains information describing the details of the company's stockholders' equity.

a. What are the par values of the company's two classes of common stock?
b. For the most current year shown, how many shares of each class of common stock are authorized? What is the meaning of authorized shares?
c. What is the total stockholders' equity amount for **Tootsie Roll** for the most recent year reported? Does this figure mean that the total outstanding stock is actually worth this amount? Explain your answer.

PROBLEMS

PROBLEM 11.1

Stockholders' Equity in a Balance Sheet

LO 4, 5, 6

Early in 1999, Abbottville Press was organized with authorization to issue 100,000 shares of $100 par value preferred stock and 500,000 shares of $1 par value common stock. Ten thousand shares of the preferred stock were issued at par, and 170,000 shares of common stock were sold for $15 per share. The preferred stock pays an 8% cumulative dividend and is callable at $105.

During the first four years of operations (1999 through 2002), the corporation earned a total of $1,085,000 and paid dividends of 75 cents per share in each year on its outstanding common stock.

Instructions

a. Prepare the stockholders' equity section of the balance sheet at December 31, 2002. Include a supporting schedule showing your computation of the amount of retained earnings reported. (Hint: Income increases retained earnings, whereas dividends decrease retained earnings.)

b. Are there any dividends in arrears on the company's preferred stock at December 31, 2002? Explain your answer.

c. Assume that interest rates increase steadily from 1999 through 2002. Would you expect the market price of the company's preferred stock to be higher or lower than its call price of $105 at December 21, 2002?

PROBLEM 11.2

Stockholders' Equity Section

LO 4, 5, 6

Zeller Publications was organized early in 1997 with authorization to issue 20,000 shares of $100 par value preferred stock and 1 million shares of $1 par value common stock. All of the preferred stock was issued at par, and 300,000 shares of common stock were sold for $20 per share. The preferred stock pays a 10% cumulative dividend and is callable at $105.

During the first five years of operations (1997 through 2001) the corporation earned a total of $4,460,000 and paid dividends of $1 per share each year on the common stock. In 2002, however, the corporation reported a net loss of $1,750,000 and paid no dividends.

Instructions

a. Prepare the stockholders' equity section of the balance sheet at December 31, 2002. Include a supporting schedule showing your computation of retained earnings at the balance sheet date. (Hint: Income increases retained earnings, whereas dividends and net losses decrease retained earnings.)

b. Draft a note to accompany the financial statements disclosing any dividends in arrears at the end of 2002.

c. Do the dividends in arrears appear as a liability of the corporation as of the end of 2002? Explain.

PROBLEM 11.3

Stockholders' Equity in a Balance Sheet

LO 4, 5, 6

Maria Martinez organized Manhattan Transport Company in January 1999. The corporation immediately issued at $8 per share one-half of its 200,000 authorized shares of $2 par value common stock. On January 2, 2000, the corporation sold at par value the entire 5,000 authorized shares of 8%, $100 par value, cumulative preferred stock. On January 2, 2001, the company again needed money and issued 5,000 shares of an authorized 10,000 shares of no-par, cumulative preferred stock for a total of $512,000. The no-par shares have a stated dividend of $9 per share.

The company declared no dividends in 1999 and 2000. At the end of 2000, its retained earnings were $170,000. During 2001 and 2002 combined, the company earned a total of $890,000. Dividends of 50 cents per share in 2001 and $1.60 per share in 2002 were paid on the common stock.

Instructions

a. Prepare the stockholders' equity section of the balance sheet at December 31, 2002. Include a supporting schedule showing your computation of retained earnings at the balance sheet date. (Hint: Income increases retained earnings, whereas dividends decrease retained earnings.)

b. Assume that on January 2, 2000, the corporation could have borrowed $500,000 at 8% interest on a long-term basis instead of issuing the 5,000 shares of the $100 par value cumulative preferred stock. Identify two reasons a corporation may choose to issue cumulative preferred stock rather than finance operations with long-term debt.

PROBLEM 11.4
Stockholders' Equity: A Short Comprehensive Problem

LO 4, 5

Early in the year Roger Gordon and several friends organized a corporation called Gordon Communications, Inc. The corporation was authorized to issue 50,000 shares of $100 par value, 10% cumulative preferred stock and 400,000 shares of $2 par value common stock. The following transactions (among others) occurred during the year:

- **Jan. 6** Issued for cash 20,000 shares of common stock at $14 per share. The shares were issued to Gordon and 10 other investors.
- **Jan. 7** Issued an additional 500 shares of common stock to Gordon in exchange for his services in organizing the corporation. The stockholders agreed that these services were worth $7,000.
- **Jan. 12** Issued 2,500 shares of preferred stock for cash of $250,000.
- **June 4** Acquired land as a building site in exchange for 15,000 shares of common stock. In view of the appraised value of the land and the progress of the company, the directors agreed that the common stock was to be valued for purposes of this transaction at $15 per share.
- **Nov. 15** The first annual dividend of $10 per share was declared on the preferred stock to be paid December 20. (Hint: Record the dividend by debiting Dividends and crediting Dividends Payable.)
- **Dec. 20** Paid the cash dividend declared on November 15.
- **Dec. 31** After the revenue and expenses were closed into the Income Summary account, that account indicated a net income of $147,200.

Instructions

a. Prepare journal entries in general journal form to record the above transactions. Include entries at December 31 to close the Income Summary account and the Dividends account.

b. Prepare the stockholders' equity section of the Gordon Communications, Inc., balance sheet at December 31.

PROBLEM 11.5
Analysis of an Equity Section of a Balance Sheet

LO 4, 5

The year-end balance sheet of Walker DeskTop Products includes the following stockholders' equity section (with certain details omitted):

Stockholders' equity:	
7½% cumulative preferred stock, $100 par value, callable at $105, 100,000 shares authorized	$ 2,400,000
Common stock, $2 par value, 900,000 shares authorized	900,000
Additional paid-in capital: Common stock	8,325,000
Donated capital	720,000
Retained earnings	2,595,000
Total stockholders' equity	$14,940,000

Instructions

From this information, compute answers to the following questions:

a. How many shares of preferred stock have been issued?
b. What is the total amount of the annual dividends paid to preferred stockholders?
c. How many shares of common stock are outstanding?
d. What was the average issuance price per share of common stock?
e. What is the amount of legal capital?
f. What is the total amount of paid-in capital?
g. What is the book value per share of common stock? (There are no dividends in arrears.)
h. Assume that retained earnings at the beginning of the year amounted to $717,500 and that net income for the year was $3,970,000. What was the dividend declared during the year on *each share* of common stock? (Hint: Net income increases retained earnings, whereas dividends decrease retained earnings.)

Problems

PROBLEM 11.6
Analysis of an Equity Section—More Comprehensive

LO 1–7

Quanex Corporation is a publicly owned company. The following information is excerpted from a recent balance sheet. Dollar amounts (except for per share amounts) are stated in thousands.

Stockholders' equity:	
Convertible $17.20 preferred stock, no par value, 1,000,000 shares authorized; 345,000 shares issued and outstanding; $250 per share liquidation preference (call price)	$ 86,250
Common stock, par value $0.50; 25,000,000 shares authorized	6,819
Additional paid-in capital	87,260
Retained earnings	57,263
Total stockholders' equity	$237,592

Instructions
From this information, answer the following questions:
a. How many shares of common stock have been issued?
b. What is the total amount of the annual dividends paid to preferred stockholders?
c. What is the total amount of paid-in capital?
d. What is the book value per share of common stock?
e. Briefly explain the advantages and disadvantages to **Quanex** of being publicly owned rather than operating as a closely held corporation.
f. What is meant by the term *convertible* used in the caption of the preferred stock? Is there any more information that investors need to know to evaluate this conversion feature?
g. Assume that the preferred stock currently is selling at *$248* per share. Does this provide a higher or lower dividend yield than an 8%, $50 par value preferred with a market price of $57 per share? Show computations (round to the nearest tenth of 1%). Explain why one preferred stock might yield less than another.

PROBLEM 11.7
Par, Book, and Market Values

LO 4, 7

Compuwiz Corporation is the producer of popular business software. Recently, an investment service published the following per-share amounts relating to the company's only class of stock:

Par value	$ 0.001
Book value (estimated)	6.50
Market value	$65.00

Instructions
a. Without reference to dollar amounts, explain the nature and significance of *par value, book value,* and *market value.*
b. Comment on the *relationships,* if any, among the per-share amounts shown for the company. What do these amounts imply about Compuwiz and its operations? Comment on what these amounts imply about the security of *creditors'* claims against the company.

PROBLEM 11.8
Reporting Stockholders' Equity with Treasury Stock

LO 4, 5, 7, 9

Early in 2000, Wells Corporation was formed with authorization to issue 50,000 shares of $1 par value common stock. All shares were issued at a price of $8 per share. The corporation reported net income of $82,000 in 2000, $25,000 in 2001, and $56,000 in 2002. No dividends were declared in any of these three years.

In 2001, the company purchased $35,000 of its own shares in the open market. In 2002, it reissued all of its treasury stock for $40,000.

Instructions

a. Prepare the stockholders' equity section of the balance sheet at December 31, 2002. Include a supporting schedule showing your computation of retained earnings at the balance sheet date. (Hint: Income increases retained earnings.)

b. As of December 31, compute the company's book value per share of common stock.

c. Explain how the treasury stock transactions in 2001 and 2002 were reported in the company's statement of cash flows.

PROBLEM 11.9

Reporting Stockholders' Equity with Treasury Stock and Stock Splits

LO 4, 5, 7, 8, 9

Early in 1998, Heradon Industries was formed with authorization to issue 200,000 shares of $10 par value common stock and 30,000 shares of $100 par value cumulative preferred stock. During 1998, all the preferred stock was issued at par, and 120,000 shares of common stock were sold for $16 per share. The preferred stock is entitled to a dividend equal to 10% of its par value before any dividends are paid on the common stock.

During its first five years of business (1998 through 2002), the company earned income totaling $3,700,000 and paid dividends of 50 cents per share each year on the common stock outstanding.

On January 2, 2000, the company purchased 20,000 shares of its own common stock in the open market for $400,000. On January 2, 2002, it reissued 10,000 shares of this treasury stock for $250,000. The remaining 10,000 were still held in treasury at December 31, 2002.

Instructions

a. Prepare the stockholders' equity section of the balance sheet for Heradon Industries at December 31, 2002. Include supporting schedules showing (1) your computation of any paid-in capital on treasury stock and (2) retained earnings at the balance sheet date. (Hint: Income increases retained earnings, whereas dividends reduce retained earnings. Dividends are not paid on shares of stock held in treasury.)

b. As of December 31, compute Heradon's book value per share of common stock. (Hint: Book value per share is computed only on the shares of stock outstanding.)

c. At December 31, 2002, shares of the company's common stock were trading at $30. Explain what would have happened to the market price per share had the company split its stock 2-for-1 at this date. Also explain what would have happened to the par value of the common stock and to the number of common shares outstanding.

CASES AND UNSTRUCTURED PROBLEMS

CASE 11.1

Factors Affecting the Market Prices of Preferred and Common Stocks

LO 5, 7

ADM Labs is a publicly owned company with several issues of capital stock outstanding. Over the past decade, the company has consistently earned modest profits and has increased its common stock dividend annually by 5 or 10 cents per share. Recently the company introduced several new products that you believe will cause future sales and profits to increase dramatically. You also expect a gradual increase in long-term interest rates from their present level of about 11% to, perhaps, 12% to $12\frac{1}{2}$%.

Instructions

Based on these forecasts, explain whether you would expect to see the market prices of the following issues of ADM capital stock increase or decrease. Explain your reasoning in each answer.

a. 10%, $100 par value, preferred stock (currently selling at $90 per share).

b. $5 par value common stock (currently paying an annual dividend of $2.50 and selling at $40 per share).

c. 7%, $100 par value, convertible preferred stock (currently selling at $125 per share).

CASE 11.2

Factors Affecting the Market Prices of Common Stocks

LO 7

Each of the following situations describes a recent event that affected the stock market price of a particular company.

a. The price of a common share of **McDonnell Douglas, Inc.**, increased by $5\frac{1}{8}$ dollars per share in the several days after it was announced that Saudia Airlines would order $6 billion of commercial airliners from **Boeing** and **McDonnell Douglas**.

b. **Citicorp**'s common stock price fell $3\frac{5}{8}$ per share shortly after the Federal Reserve Board increased the discount rate by $\frac{1}{4}$%. The discount rate is the rate charged to banks for short-term loans they need to meet their reserve requirements.

c. The price of a common share of **Ventitex, Inc.**, a manufacturer of medical devices, fell $10\frac{1}{4}$ (27.7%) after it was announced that representatives of the Federal Drug Administration paid a visit to the company.

Instructions

For each of the independent situations described, explain the likely underlying rationale for the change in market price of the stock.

CASE 11.3
Selecting a Form of Business Organization

LO 1, 2, 3

Interview the owners of two local small businesses. One business should be organized as a corporation and the other as either a sole proprietorship or a partnership. Inquire as to:

- *Why* this form of entity was selected.
- Have there been any unforeseen complications with this form of entity?
- Is the form of entity likely to be changed in the foreseeable future? And if so, why?

BUSINESS WEEK ASSIGNMENT

CASE 11.4
GM Acquisition and Preferred Stock

LO 5, 6

In "GM May Have Landed a Dandy Daewoo Deal," in the October 8, 2001, *Business Week*, Moon Ihlwan and David Welch explained details of the purchase agreement between **General Motors Corp.** and Korea's **Daewoo Motor Co. GM** and its partners were to put $400 million into a joint venture that took control of the **Daewoo** assets. **Daewoo**'s creditors were to receive $1.2 billion in preferred stock, paying 3.5% in the new company. Reports familiar with the deal say that **GM** had the option of buying back those preferred shares sometime after 2001. In addition, the agreement called for assuming just $830 million of **Daewoo Motors**' $17 billion debt.

Instructions

a. Define a preferred stock and identify the typical characteristics of preferred stock.
b. What are the advantages to **General Motors Corporation** of using preferred stock (rather than cash) in its acquisition of **Daewoo**? Why would the creditors of **Daewoo** desire preferred stock rather than common stock?

INTERNET ASSIGNMENT

INTERNET 11.1
Credit Ratings on Bonds

LO 4, 5, 7, 9

Visit the home page of **Staples, Inc.**, at the following Internet address:

www.staples.com

Locate the company's most current balance sheet by selecting Corporate Information.

Instructions

Answer the following questions:

a. Does the company report preferred stock in its balance sheet? If so, how many shares are currently outstanding?
b. What classifications of common stock does the company report in its balance sheet? What is the par value of each?
c. Does the company report any treasury stock? If so, what percentage of total stockholders' equity does it represent?

Internet sites are time and date sensitive. It is the purpose of these exercises to have you explore the Internet. You may need to use the Yahoo! search engine **http://www.yahoo.com** *(or another favorite search engine) to find a company's current Web address.*

OUR COMMENTS ON THE "YOUR TURN" CASES

You as a Loan Officer (p. 463) GOTCHA! does *not* appear to be a good credit risk for a $200,000 loan. The company has few liquid assets that can be used to repay a loan. Also, the proposed loan is very large in relation to the small corporation's assets and owners' equity. Because GOTCHA! is organized as a corporation, Woods is not personally responsible for the company's debts—unless she agrees to be.

Most loan officers would want to find a way to make this loan. They certainly would not want to refuse a 20-year customer of the bank a loan that amounts to less than half of the normal balance she maintains in her checking, savings, and money market accounts. But they would ask that Woods *personally guarantee* the loan, rather than depend solely on GOTCHA! for repayment. (Woods should not be offended by this requirement; in situations such as this, it is standard business practice.)

You as Vice President of Human Relations (p. 467) Do not consider selling the stock before the information about the strike becomes public. The Securities Exchange Act of 1934 precludes trading referred to as "insider trading." Specifically, insider trading occurs when a member of the board of directors, an employee of the corporation, or a major stockholder has inside information. Inside information is generally defined as any knowledge that would have a significant effect on share prices if it were to become publicly known. If the director or employee executes trades to take advantage of this private information, it is referred to as insider trading. Insider trading is unethical and prohibited by law in the United States. However, in some countries, insider trading is an accepted business practice. (For more information, visit www.sec.gov.)

You as an Investor (p. 479) While rising interest rates are not favorable for the market price on any type of stock, the market value of preferred stock is likely to be affected more so than common stock. If interest rates increase, the value of the preferred stock will fall. Because you are investing for the short term, you probably should invest in the common stock rather than the preferred stock.

ANSWERS TO SELF-TEST QUESTIONS

1. c   2. d   3. c   4. c   5. b, c, d   6. b

CHAPTER 12
INCOME AND CHANGES IN RETAINED EARNINGS

Learning Objectives

After studying this chapter, you should be able to:

1. Describe how discontinued operations, extraordinary items, and accounting changes are presented in the income statement.

2. Compute earnings per share.

3. Distinguish between basic and diluted earnings per share.

4. Account for cash dividends and stock dividends, and explain the effects of these transactions on a company's financial statements.

5. Describe and prepare a statement of retained earnings.

6. Define *prior period adjustments,* and explain how they are presented in financial statements.

7. Define *comprehensive income,* and explain how it differs from net income.

8. Describe and prepare a statement of stockholders' equity.

© James M. Mejuto

Home Depot, Inc.

A company's net income is a very important factor in evaluating its financial success or failure. Consider **Home Depot, Inc.**, for example. **Home Depot** was founded in 1978 and has rapidly become the world's largest home improvement retailer and the world's third-largest retailer overall.

One of the remarkable attributes of this very successful company is the rate of growth from year to year of its primary income statement figures—sales and net income. **Home Depot**'s financial reporting year, sometimes referred to as its fiscal period, essentially covers the period from February of one year through January of the next year. Sales grew from $30,219 million for the 1999 fiscal year (ending in January 1999) by more than 27% to $38,434 million for the 2000 fiscal year (ending in January 2000). Similarly, the next year sales grew from $38,434 million to $45,738 million, an increase of 19%. Net income followed a similar pattern. Between fiscal year 1999 and 2000, net income grew 43% from $1,614 million to $2,320 million. From 2000 to 2001, net income increased from $2,320 to $2,581 million or 11%. These figures represent large increases in these key measures of performance.

• • •

For investors seeking companies in which to place their funds, a pattern of increases in key performance figures such as sales and net income would be very attractive. In this chapter, we look more closely at the income statement and learn about the useful information available in that financial statement for making important investment and credit decisions. In addition to learning more about how an income statement is prepared, you will learn about earnings per share, dividends, and other key factors that indicate the financial success of a company.

REPORTING THE RESULTS OF OPERATIONS

The most important aspect of corporate financial reporting, in the view of many investors, is periodic income. Both the market price of common stock and the amount of cash dividends per share depend on the current and future earnings of the corporation.

Developing Predictive Information

Revenues are measures of the value of products and services that have been sold to customers. Revenue represents the increases in the company's assets that result from its profit-directed activities. Generally, revenues increase cash either at the time they are included in the income statement or at an earlier or later date. Expenses, on the other hand, are measures of the cost of producing and providing the products and services that are sold to customers. They represent decreases in the company's assets that result from its profit-directed activities. Expenses decrease cash at the time they are incurred, or at an earlier or later date. An income statement presents a company's revenues and expenses for a stated period of time, such as a quarter or year.

As this brief description of revenues and expenses indicates, the income statement provides important information for investors and creditors as they attempt to make estimates of future cash flows. Because of the importance of income reporting in making assessments about the future, events and transactions that are irregular—in that they do not recur often or are different from the company's normal, ongoing operations—require careful attention in the preparation and interpretation of an income statement. Investors, creditors, and other financial statement users have a need, as well as a right, to know those aspects of a company's income that can reasonably be expected to repeat in the future and those that are not expected to occur on a regular basis.

For information about financial performance to be of maximum usefulness to investors, creditors, and other financial statement users, the results of items that are unusual and not likely to recur should be presented separately from the results of the company's normal, recurring activities. Income from normal, recurring activities provides more useful information for predicting future earnings than income that mixes the results of normal, recurring activities with the results of unusual and nonrecurring activities.

The need to separate types of revenue and expense transactions into two major categories—normal, recurring and unusual, nonrecurring—has resulted in a multiple-section income statement that is often encountered in business today and that we discuss in the following section. Three categories of unusual, nonrecurring events that require special treatment are (1) the results of *discontinued operations,* (2) the impact of *extraordinary items,* and (3) the effects of *changes in accounting principles.* One of the challenges that has faced the accounting profession is to define these terms with sufficient clarity that users of financial statements can reliably compare the information provided by different companies.

MANAGEMENT STRATEGY AND FINANCIAL REPORTING

In the last couple of years there has been a disturbing trend among several companies to calculate earnings in their own idiosyncratic ways. These unaudited and non-GAAP earnings numbers have been included in annual reports to shareholders under a variety of names, including "pro forma," "recurring," and/or "core" earnings.

Why would management calculate a second set of earnings? Management suggests that earnings calculated by applying GAAP are inadequate for investors who want a good sense of a company's prospects. They say GAAP net income includes a lot of noncash charges and one-time expenses, but investors need information about the ongoing operations of the company. However, each company uses its own rules for these "pro forma" computations, making comparisons between companies meaningless. The SEC is considering rules to restrict use of pro forma information.

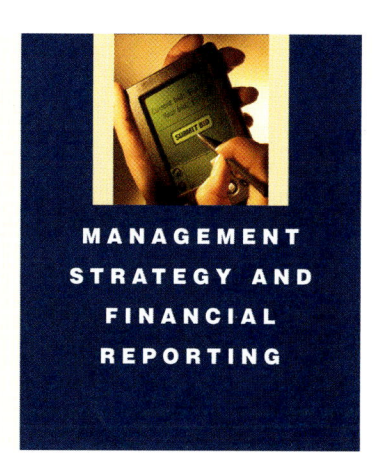

Reporting Irregular Items: An Illustration

To illustrate the presentation of irregular items in an income statement, assume that Farmer Corporation operates both a small chain of retail stores and two motels. Near the end of the current year, the company sells both motels to a national hotel chain. In addition, Farmer Corporation reports two "extraordinary items" and changes the method it uses in computing depreciation expense. An income statement illustrating the correct format for reporting these events appears in Exhibit 12–1.

Exhibit 12–1

INCOME STATEMENT WITH NONRECURRING ITEMS

FARMER CORPORATION
Income Statement
For the Year Ended December 31, 2002

Net sales		$8,000,000
Cost and expenses:		
Cost of goods sold	$4,500,000	
Selling expenses	1,500,000	
General and administrative expenses	920,000	
Loss on settlement of lawsuit	80,000	
Income taxes (on continuing operations)	300,000	7,300,000
Income from continuing operations		$ 700,000
Discontinued operations:		
Operating loss on motels (net of $90,000 income tax benefit)	$ (210,000)	
Gain on sale of motels (net of $195,000 income taxes)	455,000	245,000
Income before extraordinary items and cumulative effect of accounting change		$ 945,000
Extraordinary items:		
Gain on condemnation of land by State Highway Department (net of $45,000 income taxes)	$ 105,000	
Loss from earthquake damage to Los Angeles store (net of $75,000 income tax benefit)	(175,000)	(70,000)
Cumulative effect of change in accounting principle:		
Effect on prior years' income of change in method of computing depreciation (net of $60,000 income taxes)		140,000
Net income		$1,015,000

My Notes

Notice the order in which the irregular items are reported

Note: This income statement is designed to illustrate the presentation of various irregular items. Rarely, if ever, will all these types of events appear in the income statement of one company within a single year.

Continuing Operations

The first section of the income statement contains only the results of *continuing business activities*—that is, the retail stores. Notice that the income taxes expense shown in this section ($300,000) relates *only to continuing operations.* The income taxes relating to the irregular items are shown separately in the income statement as adjustments to the amounts of these items.

Income from Continuing Operations The subtotal *income from continuing operations* measures the profitability of the ongoing operations. This subtotal should be helpful in making predictions of the company's future earnings. For example, if we predict no significant change in the profitability of its retail stores, we would expect Farmer Corporation to earn a net income of approximately $700,000 next year.

Discontinued Operations

LO 1
Describe how discontinued operations, extraordinary items, and accounting changes are presented in the income statement.

If management enters into a formal plan to sell or discontinue a **segment of the business**, the results of that segment's operations are shown separately in the income statement. This enables users of the financial statements to better evaluate the performance of the company's ongoing (continuing) operations.

Two items are included in the **discontinued operations** section of the income statement: (1) the income or loss from *operating* the segment prior to its disposal and (2) the gain or loss on *disposal* of the segment. Notice also that the income taxes relating to the discontinued operations are *shown separately* from the income taxes expense relating to continuing business operations.

Discontinued Operations Are Not Really Unusual In recent years, a characteristic of the American economy has been the restructuring of many large corporations. As part of this restructuring, corporations often sell part of the business. Thus the presence of discontinued operations is not uncommon in the income statements of large corporations.

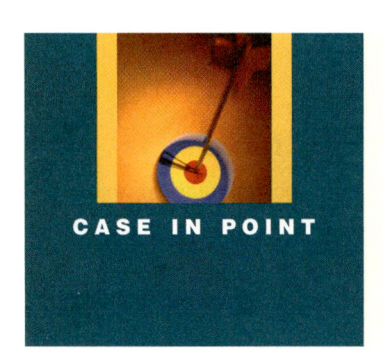

CASE IN POINT

During 1998, the **Dixie Group, Inc.**, discontinued its textile operations, which consisted of its knit fabric and apparel and the specialty yarns businesses. These operations had generally been unprofitable (approximately $16.9 million operating loss in 1996, $2.8 million operating profit in 1997, and $1.9 million operating loss in 1998). The discontinued operations resulted in a loss on disposal in the 1998 income statement. **Dixie Group**'s income from continuing operations for 1998 was $9,108,000; the loss from discontinued operations (both operations and disposal transactions) was $30,110,000, resulting in a final net loss for 1998 of $21,002,000.

Extraordinary Items

The second category of irregular events requiring disclosure in a separate section of the income statement is extraordinary items. An **extraordinary item** is a gain or loss that is (1) *unusual in nature* and (2) *not expected to recur in the foreseeable future.* By definition, extraordinary items are rare and do not appear often in the same company's income statements. An example of an extraordinary item is the loss of a company's plant due to an earthquake in a geographic location where earthquakes rarely occur.

When a gain or loss qualifies as an extraordinary item, it appears after the section on discontinued operations (if any), following the subtotal *income before extraordinary items.* Because the extraordinary item is so unusual, this subtotal is considered necessary to show investors what the net income *would have been* if the extraordinary gain or loss *had not occurred*. Extraordinary items are shown net of any related income tax effects.

Other Unusual Gains and Losses Some transactions are not typical of normal operations but also do not meet the criteria for separate presentation as extraordinary items.

> **CASE IN POINT**
>
> Extraordinary items are defined more loosely by Swedish companies than is allowed under the U.S. GAAP and may include such items as gains or losses on the sale of fixed assets, costs associated with plant closures, and foreign currency exchange gains or losses. In the Mexican GAAP, there are no specific definitions of extraordinary items. In practice, however, operations and gains or losses on fixed asset sales that are different from normal activities are considered extraordinary items.

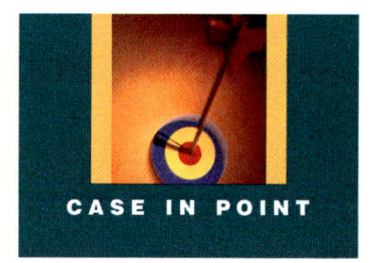

Among such events are losses incurred because of strikes and the gains or losses resulting from sales of plant assets. Such items, if material, should be individually listed as items of revenue or expense, rather than being combined with other items in broad categories such as sales revenue or general and administrative expenses.

In the income statement of Farmer Corporation (Exhibit 12–1), the $80,000 loss resulting from the settlement of a lawsuit was listed separately in the income statement but was *not* shown as an extraordinary item. This loss was important enough to bring to the attention of readers of the income statement by presenting it as a separate item, but was not considered so unusual or infrequent enough to be any extraordinary item.

Distinguishing between the Unusual and the Extraordinary In the past, some corporate managements had a tendency to classify many *losses* as extraordinary, while classifying many *gains* as a part of normal, recurring operations. This resulted in reporting higher income before extraordinary items, but the final net income figure was not affected. To counter this potentially misleading practice, the accounting profession now defines extraordinary items very carefully and intends for them to be quite rare.

There is no comprehensive list of extraordinary items. Thus the classification of a specific event is a matter of *judgment*. The table in Exhibit 12–2 is intended to provide you with general guidance on how these judgments are made.

Exhibit 12–2

ANALYSIS OF POTENTIAL EXTRAORDINARY ITEMS

Event	Analysis
Losses from a natural disaster that affects the company at *infrequent* intervals.	Not extraordinary—likely to happen again.
Losses from a natural disaster *not* likely to affect the company again.	Extraordinary—not expected to happen again.
Gains or losses from seizures of assets by a government—either through expropriation or condemnation.	Specifically called extraordinary by the FASB. For a multinational company, such losses may happen again. But for political reasons, it is better to assume that they won't.
Material loss from theft.	Extraordinary. Small theft losses, like shoplifting, are routine. But *material* theft losses are not.
Losses from inventories that have become obsolete.	Not extraordinary—a normal business risk.
Losses from an inventory made unsalable by a *newly enacted law*.	The FASB specifically identifies as extraordinary the immediate financial impact of newly enacted laws or regulations.
Receipt by a company of a large gift.	Does not appear in the income statement. Assets received as a gift are accounted for as *donated capital* (see Chapter 11).

CASE IN POINT

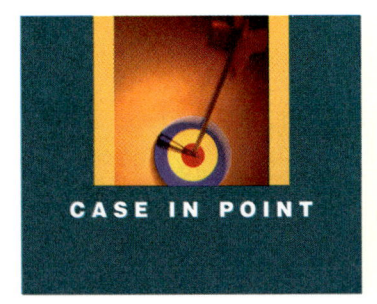

The most common type of extraordinary item is a gain or loss a company sustains when it repays its own debt. For example, **Sears, Roebuck & Company**'s 2000 annual report includes an extraordinary loss of $24 million in its 1998 income statement, presented for comparative purposes. This gain resulted from the early retirement of debt that was due in 2000 at a loss of $37 million, reducing income taxes by $13 million, for a net loss of $24 million. This extraordinary loss caused the company's 1998 net income to decline from the net income before extraordinary items of $1,072 million to $1,048 million.

Restructuring Charges One important type of unusual loss relates to restructuring of operations. As indicated previously, restructuring of operations has become a common aspect of the American economy. In fact, the 1990s were sometimes called the decade of corporate downsizing. As companies struggle to meet the competitive challenges of a global economy, they incur significant costs to close plants, reduce workforces, and consolidate operating facilities.

Restructuring charges consist of items such as losses from write-downs or sales of plant assets, severance pay for terminated workers, and expenses related to the relocation of operations and remaining personnel. In determining operating income they are presented in the company's income statement as a single item like the loss incurred in the settlement of a lawsuit in the Farmer Corporation income statement in Exhibit 12–1. If the restructuring involves discontinuing a segment of the business, the expenses related to that aspect of the restructuring are presented as discontinued operations.

CASE IN POINT

Black & Decker Corporation recently reported the following information (in millions):

Sales	$4,914.4
Cost of goods sold	3,156.6
Selling, general, and administrative expenses	1,309.6
Restructuring costs	91.3
Operating income	$ 356.9

A financial statement note explains that a major component of the $91.3 million restructuring costs was the elimination of approximately 1,500 positions and, as a result, an accrual of $74.6 million for the severance of employees. Further explanation indicates that the company plans to outsource certain products that were previously manufactured by the company and, as a result, is closing several small manufacturing facilities. This resulted in an additional $6.6 million write-down to fair value of land and building included in the restructuring charge, as were other write-downs of equipment made obsolete or redundant due to decisions to close certain facilities.

Black&Decker

Changes in Accounting Principles

The accounting principle of *consistency* refers to the fact that a business generally should continue to use the same accounting principles and methods from one period to the next.

However, this principle does not mean that a business can *never* make a change in its accounting methods. A change may be made if the need for the change can be justified and the effects of the change are *properly disclosed* in the financial statements.

The Cumulative Effect of an Accounting Change   In reporting most changes in accounting principle, the *cumulative effect* of the change on the income of *prior* years is shown in the income statement of the year in which the change is made. To compute this one-time "catch-up adjustment," we recompute the income of prior years *as if the new accounting method had always been in use*. The difference between this recomputed net income and the net income actually reported in those periods is the cumulative effect of the accounting change.

To illustrate, assume that Farmer Corporation has been using the double-declining-balance method of depreciation but decides in the current year to change to the straight-line method. The company determines that if the straight-line method had always been in use, the total net income of prior years would have been $140,000 higher than was actually reported. This $140,000 is the *cumulative effect* of the change in accounting principle and is shown as a separate item in the current year's income statement (following discontinued operations and extraordinary items, if any). Depreciation expense in the current and future years' income statements is computed by the straight-line method, just as if this method had always been in use.

Changes in Principle versus Changes in Estimate   A change in accounting principle refers to a change in the *method* used to compute financial statement amounts, rather than a change in the underlying estimates. For example, a switch from straight-line to another method of computing depreciation is regarded as a change in accounting principle. However, a change in the estimated useful life used in computing depreciation expense is a *change in estimate*. This distinction is an important one. When we change an accounting *principle* (method), the cumulative effect of the change on the income of prior years usually is reported as a one-time adjustment to income in the year of the change. Changes in *estimate,* however, affect only the current year and future years; no effort is made to recompute the income of prior years.

You as an Investor

One of the most important determinants of a company's stock price is expected future earnings. Assume that you are considering investing in Mattson Corporation and are evaluating the company's profitability in the current year. The net income of the corporation, which amounted to $4,000,000, includes the following items:

Loss on a discontinued segment of the business (net of income tax benefit)	$750,000
Extraordinary loss (net of income tax benefit)	300,000
Cumulative effect of change in accounting principle (increase in net income, net of related income taxes)	500,000

Adjust net income to develop a number that represents a good starting point for predicting the future net income of Mattson Corporation. Explain the reason for each of the adjustments. Explain how this adjusted number may help you predict future earnings for the company.

*Our comments appear on page 540.

Earnings per Share (EPS)

One of the most widely used accounting statistics is **earnings per share** of common stock. Investors who buy or sell stock in a corporation need to know the annual earnings per share. Stock market prices are quoted on a per-share basis. If you are considering investing in a company's stock at a price of $100 per share, you need to know the earnings per share and the annual dividend per share to decide whether this price is reasonable. In other words, how much earning power and how much dividend income would you be getting for each share you buy?

Computing Earnings per Share To compute earnings per share, the common stockholders' share of the company's net income is divided by the average number of common shares outstanding. The concept of earnings per share applies only to *common stock;* preferred stockholders have no claim to earnings beyond the stipulated preferred stock dividends.

Computing earnings per share is easiest when the corporation has issued only common stock, and the number of outstanding shares has not changed during the year. In this case, earnings per share is equal to net income divided by the number of shares outstanding.

What Happens If More Shares Are Issued? In many companies, the number of shares of stock outstanding changes during the year. If additional shares are sold, or if shares of common stock are retired (repurchased from the shareholders), the computation of earnings per share is based on the *weighted-average* number of shares outstanding.[1]

The weighted-average number of shares for the year is determined by multiplying the number of shares outstanding by the fraction of the year that number of shares outstanding remained unchanged. For example, assume that 100,000 shares of common stock were outstanding during the first nine months of 2002 and 140,000 shares during the last three months. The increase in shares outstanding resulted from the sale of 40,000 shares for cash. The weighted-average number of shares outstanding during 2002 is *110,000,* determined as follows:

100,000 shares × $9/12$ of a year	75,000
140,000 shares × $3/12$ of a year	35,000
Weighted-average number of common shares outstanding	110,000

This procedure gives more meaningful earnings per share data than if the total number of shares outstanding at the end of the year were used in the calculations. By using the weighted-average number of shares, we recognize that the cash received from the sale of the 40,000 additional shares was available to generate earnings only during the last three months of the year.

Preferred Dividends and Earnings per Share When a company has preferred stock outstanding, the preferred stockholders participate in net income only to the extent of the preferred stock dividends. To determine the earnings *applicable to the common stock,* we first deduct from net income the amount of current year preferred dividends. The annual dividend on *cumulative* preferred stock is *always* deducted, even if not declared by the board of directors for the current year. Noncumulative preferred dividends are deducted only if declared.

To illustrate, let us assume that Perry Corporation has 200,000 shares of common stock and 12,000 shares of $6 cumulative preferred stock outstanding throughout the year. Net income for the year totals $570,000. Earnings per share of common stock would be computed as follows:

---

[1] When the number of shares outstanding changes as a result of a stock split or a stock dividend (discussed later in this chapter), the computation of the weighted-average number of shares outstanding should be adjusted *retroactively* rather than weighted for the period the new shares were outstanding. This makes earnings per share data for prior years consistent in terms of the current capital structure.

Net income		$570,000
Less: Dividends on preferred stock (12,000 shares × $6)		72,000
Earnings applicable to common stock		$498,000
Weighted-average number of common shares outstanding		200,000
Earnings per share of common stock ($498,000 ÷ 200,000 shares)		$2.49

When there are preferred dividends in arrears, only the *current year's* cumulative preferred stock dividend is deducted in the earnings per share computation. Dividends in arrears from previous years have already been deducted in the prior years' earnings per share computations.

Presentation of Earnings per Share in the Income Statement All publicly owned corporations are *required* to present earnings per share figures in their income statements.[2] If an income statement includes subtotals for income from continuing operations, or for income before extraordinary items, per-share figures are shown for these amounts as well as for net income. These additional per-share amounts are computed by substituting the amount of the appropriate subtotal for the net income figure in the preceding calculation.

To illustrate all of the potential per-share computations, we will expand our Perry Corporation example to include income from continuing operations and income before extraordinary items. We should point out, however, that all of these figures seldom appear in the same income statement. Very few companies have discontinued operations, an extraordinary item, and an accounting change to report in the same year. The condensed income statement shown in Exhibit 12–3 is intended to illustrate the proper format for presenting earnings per share figures and to provide a review of the calculations.

My Notes

Earnings per share figures are required in the income statements of publicly owned companies

PERRY CORPORATION
Condensed Income Statement
For the Year Ended December 31, 2002

Net sales		$9,000,000
Costs and expenses (including taxes on continuing operations)		8,310,000
Income from continuing operations		$ 690,000
Loss from discontinued operations (net of income tax benefits)		(90,000)
Income before extraordinary items and cumulative effect of accounting change		$ 600,000
Extraordinary loss (net of income tax benefit)	$(120,000)	
Cumulative effect of accounting change (net of related income taxes)	90,000	(30,000)
Net income		$ 570,000
Earnings per share of common stock:		
Earnings from continuing operations		$3.09[a]
Loss from discontinued operations		(.45)
Earnings before extraordinary items and cumulative effect of accounting change		$2.64[b]
Extraordinary loss		(.60)
Cumulative effect of accounting change		.45
Net earnings		$2.49[c]

[a]($690,000 − $72,000 preferred dividends) ÷ 200,000 shares
[b]($600,000 − $72,000) ÷ 200,000 shares
[c]($570,000 − $72,000) ÷ 200,000 shares

Exhibit 12–3

EARNINGS PER SHARE PRESENTATION

---

[2] The FASB has exempted closely held corporations (those not publicly owned) from the requirement of computing and reporting earnings per share.

Interpreting the Different per-Share Amounts To informed users of financial statements, each of these figures has a different significance. Earnings per share from continuing operations represents the results of continuing and ordinary business activity. This figure is the most useful one for predicting future operating results. *Net earnings* per share, on the other hand, shows the overall operating results of the current year, including any discontinued operations or extraordinary items.

FINANCIAL ANALYSIS

The relationship between earnings per share and stock price is expressed by the **price-earnings (p/e) ratio**. This ratio is simply the current stock price divided by the earnings per share for the year (last four quarters). (A p/e ratio is *not* computed if the company has sustained a net *loss* for this period.) P/e ratios are of such interest to investors that they are published daily in the financial pages of major newspapers. Price-earnings ratios and other measures useful for evaluating financial performance are covered in Chapter 14.

Stock prices actually reflect investors' expectations of *future* earnings. The p/e ratio, however, is based on the earnings over the *past* year. Thus, if investors expect earnings to *increase* substantially from current levels, the p/e ratio will be quite high—perhaps 20, 30, or even more. But if investors expect earnings to *decline* from current levels, the p/e ratio will be quite low, say, 8 or less. A mature company with very stable earnings usually sells between 10 and 12 times earnings. Thus the p/e ratio reflects *investors' expectations* of the company's future prospects.[3]

Unfortunately, the term *earnings per share* often is used without qualification in referring to various types of per-share data. When using per-share information, it is important to know exactly *which* per-share statistic is being presented. For example, the price-earnings ratios (market price divided by earnings per share) for common stocks listed on major stock exchanges are reported daily in *The Wall Street Journal* and many other newspapers. Which earnings per share figures are used in computing these ratios? If a company reports an extraordinary gain or loss, the price-earnings ratio is computed using the per-share *earnings before the extraordinary item*. Otherwise, the ratio is based on *net earnings*.

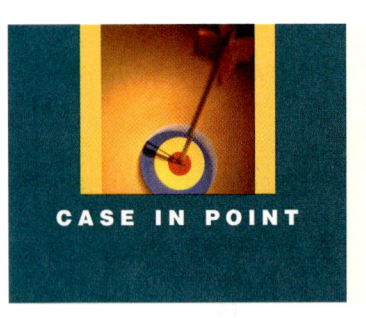

CASE IN POINT

Valuation multiples such as price-to-earnings ratios are often used to estimate a firm's value. The use of price multiples to compare firms from different countries is challenging for many reasons. One important reason is that national differences in accounting principles are a source of cross-country differences. For example, research has shown that such differences in accounting principles cause p/e ratios in Japan to be generally lower than in the United States for comparable companies with similar financial results.

Basic and Diluted Earnings per Share

LO 3
Distinguish between basic and diluted earnings per share.

Let us assume that a company has an outstanding issue of preferred stock that is convertible into shares of common stock at a rate of two shares of common stock for each share of preferred stock. The conversion of this preferred stock would increase the number of common shares outstanding and might *dilute* (reduce) earnings per share. Any common stockholder interested in the trend of earnings per share needs to know what effect the conversion of the preferred stock would have on earnings per share of common stock. Keep in mind that the decision to convert the preferred shares into common shares is made by the stockholders, not the corporation.

---

[3] A word of caution—if current earnings are *very low,* the p/e ratio tends to be quite high *regardless* of whether future earnings are expected to rise or fall. In such situations, the p/e ratio is not a meaningful measurement.

To inform investors of the potential dilution that might occur, two figures are presented for each income number from the income statement. The first figure, called **basic earnings per share**, is based on the weighted-average number of common shares *actually outstanding* during the year. This figure excludes the potential dilution represented by the convertible preferred stock. The second figure, called **diluted earnings per share**, incorporates the *impact that conversion* of the preferred stock would have on basic earnings per share.

Basic earnings per share are computed in the same manner as illustrated in our preceding example of Perry Corporation. Diluted earnings per share, on the other hand, are computed on the assumption that all the preferred stock *had been converted into common stock at the beginning of the current year.*[4] (The mechanics of computing diluted earnings per share are covered in more advanced accounting courses.)

The purpose of showing diluted earnings per share is to alert common stockholders to what *could* have happened. When the difference between basic and diluted earnings per share is significant, investors should recognize the *risk* that future earnings per share may be reduced by conversions of other securities into additional shares of common stock. When a company reports both basic and diluted earnings per share, the price-earnings ratio shown in newspapers is based on the *basic figure*.

Management's choice among the available types of stock to issue—that is, common stock, preferred stock, or another type of hybrid stock—is influenced by the firm's strategies, goals, and the type of investors that own the stock. In particular, the choice of redeemable preferred stock may be influenced by the tax code. Because financial reporting requirements differ from IRS requirements, companies sometimes create certain attributes of preferred stock that can be treated as debt for tax purposes but may appear as equity for financial reporting purposes.

MANAGEMENT STRATEGY AND FINANCIAL REPORTING

OTHER TRANSACTIONS AFFECTING RETAINED EARNINGS

Cash Dividends

Investors buy stock in a corporation with the expectation of getting their original investment back as well as a reasonable return on that investment. The return on a stock investment is a combination of two forms: (1) the increase in value of the stock (stock appreciation) and (2) **cash dividends**.

Many profitable corporations do not pay dividends. Generally, these corporations are in an early stage of development and must conserve cash for the purchase of plant and equipment or for other needs of the company. These so-called growth companies cannot obtain sufficient financing at reasonable interest rates to finance their operations, so they must rely on their earnings. Often only after a significant number of years of profitable operations does the board of directors decide that paying cash dividends is appropriate.

The preceding discussion suggests three requirements for the payment of a cash dividend. These are:

1. *Retained earnings.* Since dividends represent a distribution of earnings to stockholders, the theoretical maximum for dividends is the total undistributed net income of the company, represented by the credit balance of the Retained Earnings account.

LO 4
Account for cash dividends and stock dividends, and explain the effects of these transactions on a company's financial statement.

My Mentor

---

[4] If the preferred stock had been issued during the current year, we would assume that it was converted into common stock on the date it was issued.

As a practical matter, many corporations limit dividends to amounts significantly less than annual net income, in the belief that a major portion of the net income must be retained in the business if the company is to grow and to keep pace with its competitors.

2. *An adequate cash position.* The fact that the company reports earnings does not necessarily mean that it has a large amount of cash on hand. Cash generated from earnings may have been invested in new plant and equipment, or may have already been used to pay off debts, or to acquire a larger inventory. There is no necessary relationship between the balance in the Retained Earnings account and the balance in the Cash account. The common expression of "paying dividends out of retained earnings" is misleading. Cash dividends can be paid only out of cash.

3. *Dividend action by the board of directors.* Even though a company's net income is substantial and its cash position seemingly satisfactory, dividends are not paid automatically. A formal action by the board of directors is necessary to declare a dividend.

YOUR TURN

You as a Board Member

You are a member of the board of directors of Rollerball, Inc., a chain of outdoor sports equipment stores. Since opening eight years ago, Rollerball has grown significantly in terms of number of stores, sales, and net income.

At a recent stockholders' meeting, several stockholders complained that the board of directors unethically refused to declare and distribute cash dividends. These stockholders noted that over the last eight years the corporation retained a large amount of earnings without distributing any dividends. How would you respond to the concerns of these stockholders?

*Our comments appear on page 540.

Dividend Dates

Four significant dates are involved in the distribution of a dividend. These are:

1. *Date of declaration.* On the day on which the dividend is declared by the board of directors, a liability to make the payment comes into existence.

2. *Ex-dividend date.* The **ex-dividend date** is significant for investors in companies whose stocks trade on stock exchanges. To permit the compilation of the list of stockholders as of the record date, it is customary for the stock to go *ex-dividend* three business days before the date of record (see following discussion). A person who buys the stock before the ex-dividend date is entitled to receive the dividend that has already been declared; conversely, a stockholder who sells shares before the ex-dividend date does not receive the dividend. A stock is said to be selling ex-dividend on the day that it *loses* the right to receive the latest declared dividend.

3. *Date of record.* The **date of record** follows the date of declaration, usually by two or three weeks, and is always stated in the dividend declaration. To be eligible to receive the dividend, a person must be listed in the corporation's records as the owner of the stock on this date.

4. *Date of payment.* The declaration of a dividend always includes announcement of the date of payment as well as the date of record. Usually the date of payment comes two to four weeks after the date of record.

Journal entries are required only on the dates of declaration and of payment, as these are the only transactions affecting the corporation declaring the dividend. These entries are illustrated below:

Dec. 15	Dividends	100,000	
	Dividends Payable		100,000
	To record declaration of a cash dividend of $1 per share on the 100,000 shares of common stock outstanding. Payable Jan. 25 to stockholders of record on Jan. 10.		
Jan. 25	Dividends Payable	100,000	
	Cash		100,000
	To record payment of $1 per share dividend declared Dec. 15 to stockholders of record on Jan. 10.		

My Notes

Entries made on declaration date and . . .

on payment date

Notice that no entries are made on either the ex-dividend date or the date of record. These dates are of importance only in determining *to whom* the dividend checks should be sent. From the stockholders' point of view, it is the *ex-dividend date* that determines who receives the dividend. The date of record is of significance primarily to the stock transfer agent and the stock registrar.

Just when is the ex-dividend date in our example? It falls three *business days* before the date of record. Weekends and holidays are not counted as "business days." Thus, if January 10 is a Friday, the ex-dividend date is *January 7*. But if January 10 falls on a Monday, the ex-dividend date would be *January 5*. In this case, investors would need to purchase their shares on or before *January 4* if they are to receive this dividend.

At the end of the accounting period, a closing entry is required to transfer the debit balance of the Dividends account into the Retained Earnings account. (Some companies follow the alternative practice of debiting Retained Earnings when the dividend is declared instead of using a Dividends account. Under either method, the balance of the Retained Earnings account ultimately is reduced by all dividends declared during the period.)

Most dividends are paid in cash, but occasionally a dividend declaration calls for payment in assets *other than* cash. A large distillery once paid a dividend consisting of a bottle of whiskey for each share of stock. (This must have posed quite a storage problem to an investor owning several thousand shares.) When a corporation goes out of existence (particularly a small corporation with only a few stockholders), it may choose to distribute noncash assets to its owners rather than first converting these assets into cash.

Liquidating Dividends

A *liquidating dividend* occurs when a corporation pays a dividend that *exceeds the balance in the Retained Earnings account*. Thus the dividend returns to stockholders all or part of their paid-in capital investment. Liquidating dividends usually are paid only when a corporation is going out of existence or is making a permanent reduction in the size of its operations. Normally dividends are paid as a result of profitable operations; stockholders may assume that a dividend represents a distribution of profits unless they are notified by the corporation that the dividend is a return of invested capital.

Stock Dividends

Stock dividend is a term used to describe a distribution of *additional shares of stock* to a company's stockholders in proportion to their present holdings. In other words, the dividend is payable in *additional shares of stock* rather than in cash. Most stock dividends consist of additional shares of common stock distributed to holders of common stock. Therefore, our discussion focuses on this type of stock dividend.

An important distinction exists between a cash dividend and a stock dividend. A *cash dividend* is a distribution of cash by a corporation to its stockholders. A cash dividend reduces both assets and stockholders' equity. In a *stock dividend,* however, *no assets are distributed.* Thus a stock dividend causes *no change* in assets or in total stockholders' equity. Each stockholder receives additional shares, but his or her percentage ownership in the corporation is *no larger than before.*

To illustrate this point, assume that a corporation with 2,000 shares of stock is owned equally by James Davis and Susan Miller, each owning 1,000 shares of stock. The corporation declares a stock dividend of 10% and distributes 200 additional shares (10% of 2,000 shares), with 100 shares going to each of the two stockholders. Davis and Miller now hold 1,100 shares apiece, but each *still owns one-half of the business.* Furthermore, the corporation has not changed in size; its assets and liabilities and its total stockholders' equity are exactly the same as before the dividend.

Now let us consider the logical effect of this stock dividend on the *market price* of the company's stock. Assume that before the stock dividend, the outstanding 2,000 shares in our example had a market price of $110 per share. This price indicates a total market value for the corporation of $220,000 (2,000 shares × $110 per share). As the stock dividend does not change total assets or total stockholders' equity, the total market value of the corporation *should remain $220,000* after the stock dividend. As 2,200 shares are now outstanding, the market price of each share *should fall* to $100 ($220,000 ÷ 2,200 shares). In short, the market value of the stock *should fall in proportion* to the number of new shares issued. Whether the market price per share *will* fall in proportion to a small increase in number of outstanding shares is another matter. (In fact, market price may *rise* after the declaration of a stock dividend. Puzzling, but true.)

Entries to Record a Stock Dividend In accounting for relatively *small* stock dividends (say, less than 20%), the *market value* of the new shares is transferred from the Retained Earnings account to the paid-in capital accounts. This process sometimes is called *capitalizing* retained earnings. The overall effect is the same as if the dividend had been paid in cash, and the stockholders had immediately reinvested the cash in the business in exchange for additional shares of stock. Of course, no cash actually changes hands—the new shares of stock are sent directly to the stockholders.

To illustrate, assume that on June 1, Aspen Corporation has outstanding 100,000 shares of $5 par value common stock with a market value of $25 per share. On this date, the company declares a 10% stock dividend, distributable on July 15 to stockholders of record on June 20. The entry at June 1 to record the *declaration* of this dividend is:

My Notes

Stock dividend declared; note use of market price of stock

Retained Earnings	250,000	
Stock Dividend to Be Distributed		50,000
Additional Paid-in Capital: Stock Dividends		200,000

Declared a 10% stock dividend consisting of 10,000 shares (100,000 shares × 10%) of $5 par value common stock, market price $25 per share. Distributable July 15 to stockholders of record on June 20.

The Stock Dividend to Be Distributed account is *not a liability* because there is no obligation to distribute cash or any other asset. If a balance sheet is prepared between the date of declaration of a stock dividend and the date of distribution of the shares, this account, as well as Additional Paid-in Capital: Stock Dividends, should be presented in the stockholders' equity section of the balance sheet.

Notice that the Retained Earnings account was reduced by the *market value* of the shares to be issued (10,000 shares × $25 per share = $250,000). Notice also that *no change* occurs in the total amount of stockholders' equity. The amount removed from the Retained Earnings account was simply transferred into two other stockholders' equity accounts.

On July 15, the entry to record the *distribution* of the dividend shares is:

Stock Dividend to Be Distributed	50,000	
Common Stock		50,000
Distributed 10,000 share stock dividend declared June 1.		

My Notes

Stock dividend distributed

Reasons for Stock Dividends Although stock dividends cause *no change* in total assets, liabilities, or stockholders' equity, they are popular both with management and with stockholders. Management often finds stock dividends appealing because they allow management to distribute something of perceived value to stockholders while conserving cash, which may be needed for other purposes like expanding facilities and introducing new product lines.

Stockholders like stock dividends because they receive more shares, often the stock price does *not* fall proportionately, and the dividend is not subject to income taxes (until the shares received are sold). Also, *large* stock dividends tend to keep the stock price down in a trading range that appeals to most investors.

CASE IN POINT

An investor who purchased 100 shares of **Home Depot, Inc.**, early in 1985 would have paid about $1,700. By 2000, 15 years later, that stock was worth about $273,000!

Does this mean that each share increased in value from $17 to more than $2,730? No—in fact, this probably couldn't happen. Investors like to buy stock in lots of 100 shares. At $2,730 per share, who could afford 100 shares? Certainly not the average small investor.

Home Depot's board of directors *wanted* to attract small investors. These investors help create more demand for the company's stock—and in many cases, they also become loyal customers.

So as the price of **Home Depot**'s stock rose, the board declared numerous stock splits and stock dividends. By 2000, an investor who had purchased 100 shares in 1985 owned over *3,900* shares without ever having had to purchase additional shares. Each share had a market value of up to $70. But, most important, each of these shares was trading at a price affordable to the average investor.

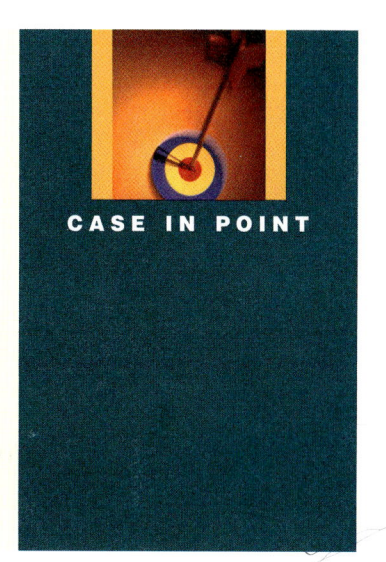

Distinction between Stock Splits and Stock Dividends What is the difference between a stock dividend and a stock split (discussed in Chapter 11)? In some respects the two are similar. Both involve the distribution of shares of a company's own stock to its present stockholders without payment by those stockholders to the company. Both stock dividends and stock splits increase the number of outstanding shares of stock in the company's stockholders' equity. The difference between a stock dividend and a stock split lies in the intent of management and the related issue of the size of the distribution. A stock dividend usually is intended to substitute for a cash dividend and is small enough that the market price of the stock is relatively unaffected. Stock dividends typically increase the number of outstanding shares by 5%, 10%, or even 20%. Stock splits, on the other hand, have the intent of reducing the market price of the stock to bring it down to a desired trading range. Stock splits typically represent much greater increases in the numbers of outstanding shares, such as 100% (2 : 1 split) or 200% (3 : 1 split).

The previous discussion focuses on the purposes and management intent of stock dividends and stock splits. Accounting for the two also varies. Stock dividends do not result in a change in the par value of the stock, and usually an amount equal to the market value of the shares issued is transferred from retained earnings to the par value and additional paid-in capital accounts. Stock splits, on the other hand, result in a pro rata reduction in the par value of the stock and no change in the actual dollar balances of the stockholders' equity accounts. Both stock dividends and stock splits are integral parts of management strategy with regard to the company's ownership and the accounting differences parallel these differences in management intent.

Statement of Retained Earnings

LO 5
Describe and prepare a statement of retained earnings.

The term *retained earnings* refers to the portion of stockholders' equity derived from profitable operations. Retained earnings is increased by earning net income and is reduced by incurring net losses and by the declaration of dividends.

In addition to a balance sheet, an income statement, and a statement of cash flows, some companies present a **statement of retained earnings**, as in Exhibit 12–4.

Exhibit 12–4
STATEMENT OF RETAINED EARNINGS FOR SALT LAKE CORPORATION

SALT LAKE CORPORATION
Statement of Retained Earnings
For the Year Ended December 31, 2002

Retained earnings, Dec. 31, 2001		$ 750,000
Net income for 2002		280,000
Subtotal		$1,030,000
Less dividends:		
Cash dividends on preferred stock ($5 per share)	$ 17,500	
Cash dividends on common stock ($2 per share)	55,300	
10% stock dividend	140,000	212,800
Retained earnings, Dec. 31, 2002		$ 817,200

Notice that the 2002 net income is added to the beginning balance of retained earnings. Earlier in this text when we studied the accounting cycle, we learned that as part of the end-of-period process of closing the books and preparing financial statements, the revenue and expense accounts are brought to a zero balance, and the net amount of these items (either net income or net loss) is added to or subtracted from owners' equity. For a corporation, net income or loss is added to or subtracted from retained earnings. The addition of net income in the statement of retained earnings is a reflection of this closing process. Notice, also, in the statement of retained earnings that the balance is reduced by the amounts of cash dividends declared during the year, as well as the amount of the stock dividend that was declared. These dividend adjustments to retained earnings are made based on their declaration, even though cash may not have been paid yet (cash dividends) or the stock may not have been issued yet (stock dividend).

Prior Period Adjustments

On occasion, a company may discover that a *material error* was made in the measurement of net income in a prior year. Because net income is closed into the Retained Earnings account, an error in reported net income will cause an error in the amount of retained earnings shown in all subsequent balance sheets. When such errors are discovered, they should be corrected. The correction, called a **prior period adjustment**, is shown in the *statement of retained earnings* as an adjustment to the balance of retained earnings at the beginning of the current year. The amount of the adjustment is shown net of any related income tax effects.

LO 6
Define *prior period adjustments*, and explain how they are presented in financial statements.

To illustrate, assume that late in 2002 Salt Lake Corporation discovers that it failed to record depreciation on certain assets in 2001. After considering the income tax effects of this error, the company finds that the net income reported in 2001 was overstated by $35,000. Thus the beginning 2002 balance of the Retained Earnings account ($750,000 at December 31, 2001) also is *overstated by $35,000*. The statement of retained earnings in *2002* must include a *correction* of the retained earnings at the beginning of the year. (See the illustration in Exhibit 12–5.)

Exhibit 12–5: STATEMENT OF RETAINED EARNINGS WITH PRIOR PERIOD ADJUSTMENT

SALT LAKE CORPORATION
Statement of Retained Earnings
For the Year Ended December 31, 2002

Retained earnings, Dec. 31, 2001		
As originally reported		$750,000
Less: Prior period adjustment for error in recording 2001 depreciation expense (net of $15,000 income taxes)		35,000
As restated		$715,000
Net income for 2002		280,000
Subtotal		$995,000
Less dividends:		
Cash dividends on preferred stock ($5 per share)	$ 17,500	
Cash dividends on common stock ($2 per share)	55,300	
10% stock dividend	140,000	212,800
Retained earnings, Dec. 31, 2002		$782,200

My Notes: Notice the adjustment to beginning retained earnings

Prior period adjustments rarely appear in the financial statements of large, publicly owned corporations. The financial statements of these corporations are audited annually by certified public accountants and are not likely to contain material errors that subsequently will require correction by prior period adjustments. Such adjustments are much more likely to appear in the financial statements of closely held corporations that are not audited on an annual basis.

Restrictions of Retained Earnings Some portion of retained earnings may be restricted because of various contractual agreements. A restriction of retained earnings prevents a company from declaring a dividend that would cause retained earnings to fall below a designated level. Most companies disclose restrictions of retained earnings in notes accompanying the financial statements. For example, a company with total retained earnings of $10 million might include the following note in its financial statements:

> **Note 7: Restriction of retained earnings**
> As of December 31, 2002, certain long-term debt agreements prohibited the declaration of cash dividends that would reduce the amount of retained earnings below $5,200,000. Retained earnings in excess of this restriction total $4,800,000.

My Notes: Note disclosure of restrictions placed on retained earnings

Comprehensive Income

The Financial Accounting Standards Board (FASB) has identified certain changes in financial position that should be recorded but should not enter into the determination of net income. One way to describe these events is that they are *recognized* (that is, recorded and become a part of the financial statements) but not *realized* (that is, not a part of the determination of the company's net income). We have studied one of these items earlier in this text—the change in market value of available-for-sale debt and equity investments.

Recall from Chapter 7 the way changes in value for various types of investments are recorded. Those investments identified as available for sale are revalued to their current market value at the end of each accounting period. These changes in value are accumulated and reported in a separate stockholders' equity account. The change in value does *not* enter into the determination of net income as it would had investments been sold. The change in market value of available-for-sale investments adds to the amount of stockholders' equity if the value has gone up; it subtracts from the amount of stockholders' equity if the value has gone down. This adjustment is described as an element of *other comprehensive income.*

Comprehensive income is a term that identifies the total of net income plus or minus the elements of other comprehensive income. Comprehensive income may be displayed to users of financial statements in any of the following ways:

LO 7 Define *comprehensive income,* and explain how it differs from net income.

- *As a second income statement.* One income statement displays the components of net income and the other displays the components of comprehensive income, one element of which is net income.
- *As a single income statement* that includes both the components of net income and the components of other comprehensive income.
- *As an element in the changes in stockholders' equity* displayed as a column in the statement of stockholders' equity (discussed later in this chapter).

In addition to the presentation of each year's changes in the elements of other comprehensive income, the accumulated amount of these changes is an element in the stockholders' equity section of the balance sheet. The components of comprehensive income are presented net of income tax, much like an extraordinary item.

Tootsie Roll Industries, Inc., whose financial statements are included in Appendix A of this text, follows the two income statement approach in presenting both net income and comprehensive income. While the title at the top of the statement is "Consolidated Statements of Earnings, Comprehensive Earnings, and Retained Earnings," it actually represents three financial statements—two income statements and a retained earnings statement. The final figure for the first 2000 income statement is called net earnings ($75,737 thousand). This figure then becomes the starting point for the second income statement, which ends with comprehensive earnings ($74,487 thousand). Notice that comprehensive earnings include net earnings, as well as two other items—gains and losses on securities and foreign currency translation adjustments. The third financial statement is a retained earnings statement in which the beginning retained earnings is increased by the amount of net earnings and reduced by the amount of dividends declared during the year. The elements of other comprehensive earnings do not increase or reduce the amount of retained earnings. The presentations of these elements of performance are presented differently across companies, but you will always find amounts for net income (or net earnings), comprehensive income (or comprehensive earnings), and beginning and ending retained earnings. If a company does not have any elements of other comprehensive income (comprehensive earnings), the information presented in **Tootsie Roll**'s second income statement is not presented.

CASH EFFECTS

Transactions between the corporation and its owners that increase or decrease cash are presented in the statement of cash flows as financing activities. Examples are the sale and repurchase of stock and the payment of cash dividends.

Stock dividends and stock splits, on the other hand, are important transactions that affect the company's stockholders' equity, but they do *not* affect the company's cash. Accordingly, they are not included in the statement of cash flows as financing activities. These transactions represent changes *within* the company's stockholders' equity, but they do not affect the total amount of stockholders' equity, nor do they affect the company's cash balances.

Statement of Stockholders' Equity

LO 8
Describe and prepare a statement of stockholders' equity.

Many corporations expand their statement of retained earnings to show the changes during the year in *all* of the stockholders' equity accounts. This expanded statement, called a **statement of stockholders' equity**, is illustrated in Exhibit 12–6 for Salt Lake Corporation.

The top line of the statement includes the beginning balance of each major category of stockholders' equity. Notice that the fourth column, Retained Earnings, is identical to the statement of retained earnings for Salt Lake Corporation that was presented in Exhibit 12–5. All events and transactions that affect retained earnings are the same as those presented in that illustration (prior period adjustment, distribution of stock dividend, net

Exhibit 12–6

STATEMENT OF STOCKHOLDERS' EQUITY

SALT LAKE CORPORATION
Statement of Stockholders' Equity
For the Year Ended December 31, 2002

	5% Convertible Preferred Stock ($100 par value)	Common Stock ($10 par value)	Additional Paid-in Capital	Retained Earnings	Treasury Stock	Total Stockholders' Equity
Balances, Dec. 31, 2001	$400,000	$200,000	$300,000	$750,000	$ –0–	$1,650,000
Prior period adjustment (net of $15,000 taxes)				(35,000)		(35,000)
Issued 5,000 common shares @ $52		50,000	210,000			260,000
Conversion of 1,000 preferred into 3,000 common shares	(100,000)	30,000	70,000			
Distributed 10% stock dividend (2,800 shares at $50; market price)		28,000	112,000	(140,000)		
Purchased 1,000 shares of common stock held in treasury at $47 a share					(47,000)	(47,000)
Net income				280,000		280,000
Cash dividends:						
Preferred ($5 a share)				(17,500)		(17,500)
Common ($2 a share)				(55,300)		(55,300)
Balances, Dec. 31, 2002	$300,000	$308,000	$692,000	$782,200	$(47,000)	$2,035,200

Note: The numbers that are not bracketed represent positive stockholders' equity amounts. The bracketed numbers represent negative stockholders' equity amounts.

income, and declaration of cash dividends on both preferred and common stock). We have added several other stock transactions to illustrate the full range of information you will typically find in a statement of stockholders' equity:

- Issuance of common stock for $260,000 (resulting in an increase in both common stock and additional paid-in capital).
- Conversion of shares of preferred stock into common stock at $100,000, resulting in a decrease in 5% convertible preferred stock and an increase in common stock and additional paid-in capital.
- Purchase of $47,000 of treasury stock, increasing the amount of treasury stock and decreasing the total of stockholders' equity (as discussed in Chapter 11).

Stockholders' Equity Section of the Balance Sheet

The stockholders' equity section of Salt Lake Corporation's balance sheet for the year ended December 31, 2002, is shown in Exhibit 12–7. Note that these figures are taken directly from the last line of the statement of stockholders' equity as illustrated in Exhibit 12–6. You should be able to explain the nature and origin of each account and disclosure printed in red as a result of having studied this chapter.

The published financial statements of leading corporations indicate that there is no one standard arrangement for the various items making up the stockholders' equity section. Variations occur in the selection of titles, in the sequence of items, and in the extent of detailed classification. Many companies, in an effort to avoid excessive detail in the balance sheet, combine several related ledger accounts into a single balance sheet item.

Exhibit 12–7

STOCKHOLDERS' EQUITY SECTION OF BALANCE SHEET

Stockholders' Equity		
Capital stock:		
5% convertible preferred, $100 par value, 3,000 shares authorized and issued		$ 300,000
Common stock, $10 par value, 100,000 shares authorized, issued 30,800 (of which 1,000 are held in treasury)		308,000
Additional paid-in capital:		
From issuance of common stock	$580,000	
From stock dividends	112,000	692,000
Total paid-in capital		$1,300,000
Retained earnings		782,200
Subtotal		$2,082,200
Less: Treasury stock (1,000 shares at $47 per share)		47,000
Total stockholders' equity		$2,035,200

CONCLUDING REMARKS

We discussed various aspects of stockholders' equity, focusing first on paid-in capital in Chapter 11 and then on earned capital in Chapter 12. These discussions complete our detailed coverage of assets, liabilities, and stockholders' equity, which began in Chapter 7 and included financial assets, inventories, plant and intangible assets, liabilities, and finally, stockholders' equity. While these chapters generally follow a balance-sheet organization, in Chapter 12 we also covered the income statement, including the presentation of irregular income items and earnings per share.

In the next chapter, we turn our attention to the statement of cash flows. Recall that companies present three primary financial statements to their stockholders, creditors, and other interested parties—a balance sheet, an income statement, and a statement of cash flows. We leave the detailed coverage of the statement of cash flows to the end because of the importance of the material we have now covered, particularly in Chapters 7–12, for a full understanding of that financial statement.

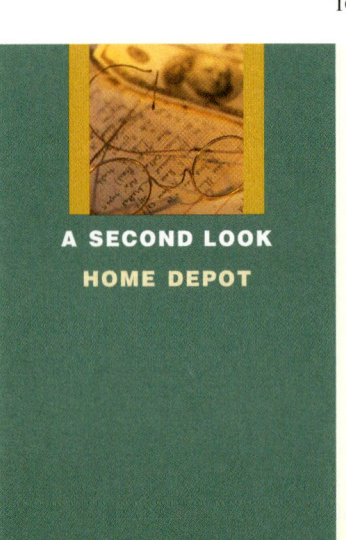

A SECOND LOOK — HOME DEPOT

Now that we have studied the income statement and other changes in retained earnings, let's take a closer look at the **Home Depot, Inc.** annual report for the year ended January 28, 2001. The income statement reveals no irregular items, such as segment disposals, extraordinary items, or changes in accounting principle. This means that for purposes of projecting future profitability, the company's net income figure is more reliable than it would otherwise be. As we would expect, basic earnings per share exceeds diluted earnings per share: $1.11 versus $1.10 for 2001, $1.03 versus $1.00 for 2000, and $.73 versus $.70 for 1999. This means that there is some risk of reduction in EPS should convertible securities actually be converted to common stock.

Home Depot presents a detailed statement of stockholders' equity and comprehensive income in its annual report. This statement discloses the impact of events such as stock purchased for compensation plans, cash dividends to stockholders, and the conversion of certain securities into common stock. Elements of other comprehensive income are presented as part of this financial statement, as opposed to the separate income statement or two income statement approaches described in the text.

As part of management's analysis and interpretation, **Home Depot** presents some interesting information about sales. For example, they disclose the number of sales transactions, average sale, average weekly sales per operating store, and an average sales per square foot of store space. This type of detailed information, while not required by generally accepted accounting principles, is very helpful to the serious analyst in better understanding the company's profitability and prospects for the future.

END-OF-CHAPTER REVIEW

SUMMARY OF LEARNING OBJECTIVES

LO 1
Describe how discontinued operations, extraordinary items, and accounting changes are presented in the income statement.
Each of these irregular items is shown in a separate section of the income statement, following income or loss from ordinary and continuing operations. Each special item is shown net of any related income tax effects.

LO 2
Compute earnings per share.
Earnings per share are computed by dividing the income applicable to the common stock by the weighted-average number of common shares outstanding. If the income statement includes subtotals for income from continuing operations, or for income before extraordinary items, per-share figures are shown for these amounts, as well as for net income.

LO 3
Distinguish between basic and diluted earnings per share.
Diluted earnings per share are computed for companies that have outstanding securities convertible into shares of common stock. In such situations, the computation of basic earnings per share is based on the number of common shares actually outstanding during the year. The computation of diluted earnings per share, however, is based on the potential number of common shares outstanding if the various securities were converted into common shares. The purpose of showing diluted earnings is to alert investors to the extent to which conversions of securities could reduce basic earnings per share.

LO 4
Account for cash dividends and stock dividends, and explain the effects of these transactions on a company's financial statements.
Cash dividends reduce retained earnings at the time the company's board of directors declares the dividends. At that time, the dividends become a liability for the company. Stock dividends generally are recorded by transferring the market value of the additional shares to be issued from retained earnings to the appropriate paid-in capital accounts. Stock dividends increase the number of shares outstanding but do not change total stockholders' equity, nor do they change the relative amount of the company owned by each individual stockholder.

LO 5
Describe and prepare a statement of retained earnings.
A statement of retained earnings shows the changes in the balance of the Retained Earnings account during the period. In its simplest form, this financial statement shows the beginning balance of retained earnings, adds the net income for the period, subtracts any dividends declared, and thus computes the ending balance of retained earnings.

LO 6
Define *prior period adjustments,* and explain how they are presented in financial statements.
A prior period adjustment corrects errors in the amount of net income reported in a *prior* year. Because the income of the prior year has already been closed into retained earnings, the error is corrected by increasing or decreasing the Retained Earnings account. Prior period adjustments appear in the statement of retained earnings as adjustments to beginning retained earnings. They are *not* reported in the income statement for the current period.

LO 7
Define *comprehensive income,* and explain how it differs from net income.
Net income is a component of comprehensive income. Comprehensive income is broad and includes the effect of certain transactions that are recognized in the financial statements but that are not included in net income because they have not yet been realized. An example is the change in market value of available-for-sale investments. Net income is presented in the income statement. Comprehensive income may be presented in a combined statement with net income, in a separate statement of comprehensive income, or as a part of the statement of stockholders' equity.

LO 8
Describe and prepare a statement of stockholders' equity.
This expanded version of the statement of retained earnings explains the changes during the year in each stockholders' equity account. It is not a required financial statement but is often prepared instead of a statement of retained earnings. The statement lists the beginning balance in each stockholders' equity account, explains the nature and the amount of each change, and computes the ending balance in each equity account.

KEY TERMS INTRODUCED OR EMPHASIZED IN CHAPTER 12

basic earnings per share (p. 513)   Net income applicable to the common stock divided by weighted-average number of common shares outstanding during the year.

cash dividend (p. 513)   A distribution of cash by a corporation to its stockholders.

comprehensive income (p. 519)   Net income plus or minus certain changes in financial position that are recorded as direct adjustments to stockholders' equity (for example, changes in the value of available-for-sale investments) rather than as elements in the determination of net income.

date of record (p. 514)   The date on which a person must be listed as a shareholder to be eligible to receive a dividend. Follows the date of declaration of a dividend by two or three weeks.

diluted earnings per share (p. 513)   Earnings per share computed under the assumption that all convertible securities had been converted into additional common shares at the beginning of the current year. The purpose of this pro forma computation is to alert common stockholders to the risk that future earnings per share might be reduced by the conversion of other securities into common stock.

discontinued operations (p. 506)   The net operating results (revenue and expenses) of a segment of a company that has been or is being sold, as well as the gain or loss on disposal.

earnings per share (p. 506)   Net income applicable to the common stock divided by the weighted-average number of common shares outstanding during the year.

ex-dividend date (p. 514)   A date three days prior to the date of record specified in a dividend declaration. A person buying a stock prior to the ex-dividend date also acquires the right to receive the dividend. The three-day interval permits the compilation of a list of stockholders as of the date of record.

extraordinary items (p. 506)   Transactions and events that are unusual in nature and occur infrequently—for example, most large earthquake losses. Such items are shown separately in the income statement after the determination of income before extraordinary items.

price-earnings (p/e) ratio (p. 512)   Market price of a share of common stock divided by annual earnings per share.

prior period adjustment (p. 518)   A correction of a material error in the earnings reported in the financial statements of a prior year. Prior period adjustments are recorded directly in the Retained Earnings account and are not included in the income statement of the current period.

restructuring charges (p. 508)   Costs related to reorganizing and downsizing the company to make the company more efficient. These costs are presented in the income statement as a single line item in determining operating income.

segment of a business (p. 506)   Those elements of a business that represent a separate and distinct line of business activity or that service a distinct category of customers.

statement of retained earnings (p. 518)   A financial statement explaining the change during the year in the amount of retained earnings. May be expanded into a statement of stockholders' equity.

statement of stockholders' equity (p. 520)   An expanded version of a statement of retained earnings. Summarizes the changes during the year in all stockholders' equity accounts. Not a required financial statement, but widely used as a substitute for the statement of retained earnings.

stock dividend (p. 515)   A distribution of additional shares to common stockholders in proportion to their holdings.

DEMONSTRATION PROBLEM

The stockholders' equity of Martinez Corporation at December 31, 2002, is shown below.

Stockholders' equity:

Common stock, $10 par, 100,000 shares authorized, 40,000 shares issued	$ 400,000
Additional paid-in capital: Common stock	200,000
Total paid-in capital	$ 600,000
Retained earnings	1,700,000
Total stockholders' equity	$2,300,000

Transactions affecting stockholders' equity during 2002 are as follows:

Mar. 31 A 5-for-4 stock split proposed by the board of directors was approved by vote of the stockholders. The 10,000 new shares were distributed to stockholders.

Apr. 1 The company purchased 2,000 shares of its common stock on the open market at $37 per share.

July 1 The company reissued 1,000 shares of treasury stock at $48 per share.

July 1 Issued for cash 20,000 shares of previously unissued $8 par value common stock at a price of $47 per share.

Dec. 1 A cash dividend of $1 per share was declared, payable on December 30, to stockholders of record at December 14.

Dec. 22 A 10% stock dividend was declared; the dividend shares are to be distributed on January 15 of the following year. The market price of the stock on December 22 was $48 per share.

Demonstration Problem

The net income for the year ended December 31, 2002, amounted to $173,000, after an extraordinary loss of $47,400 (net of related income tax benefits).

Instructions

a. Prepare journal entries (in general journal form) to record the transactions affecting stockholders' equity that took place during the year.

b. Prepare the lower section of the income statement for 2002, beginning with *income before extraordinary items* and showing the extraordinary loss and the net income. Also illustrate the presentation of earnings per share in the income statement, assuming that earnings per share are determined on the basis of the *weighted-average* number of shares outstanding during the year.

c. Prepare a statement of retained earnings for the year ending December 31, 2002.

Solution to the Demonstration Problem

a.

GENERAL JOURNAL — Page 1

Date	Account Titles and Explanations	Debit	Credit
Mar. 31	Memorandum: A 5-for-4 stock split increased the number of shares of common stock outstanding from 40,000 to 50,000 and reduced the par value from $10 to $8 per share. The 10,000 new shares were distributed.		
Apr. 1	Treasury Stock	74,000	
	Cash		74,000
	Acquired 2,000 shares of treasury stock at $37.		
July 1	Cash	48,000	
	Treasury Stock		37,000
	Additional Paid-in Capital: Treasury Stock Transactions		11,000
	Sold 1,000 shares of treasury stock at $48 per share.		
1	Cash	940,000	
	Common Stock, $8 par		160,000
	Additional Paid-in Capital: Common Stock		780,000
	Issued 20,000 shares.		
Dec. 1	Dividends	69,000	
	Dividends Payable		69,000
	To record declaration of cash dividend of $1 per share on 69,000 shares of common stock outstanding (1,000 shares in treasury are not entitled to receive dividends).		
	Note: Entry to record the payment of the cash dividend is not shown here because the action does not affect the stockholders' equity.		
Dec. 22	Retained Earnings	331,200	
	Stock Dividends to Be Distributed		55,200
	Additional Paid-in Capital: Stock Dividends		276,000
	To record declaration of 10% stock dividend consisting of 6,900 shares of $8 par value common stock to be distributed on Jan. 15 of next year.		
Dec. 31	Income Summary	173,000	
	Retained Earnings		173,000
	To close Income Summary account.		
Dec. 31	Retained Earnings	69,000	
	Dividends		69,000
	To close Dividends account.		

b.

MARTINEZ CORPORATION
Partial Income Statement
For the Year Ended December 31, 2002

Income before extraordinary items	$220,400
Extraordinary loss (net of income tax benefits)	(47,400)
Net income	$173,000
Earnings per share:*	
Income before extraordinary items	$3.73
Extraordinary loss	(0.80)
Net income	$2.93

*The 59,000 weighted-average number of shares of common stock outstanding during 2002 determined as follows:

Jan. 1–Mar. 31: (40,000 + 10,000 shares issued pursuant to a 5-for-4 split) × 1/4 of year	12,500
Apr. 1–June 30: (50,000 − 2,000 shares of treasury stock) × 1/4 of year	12,000
July 1–Dec. 31: (50,000 + 20,000 shares of new stock − 1,000 shares of treasury stock) × 1/2 of year	34,500
Weighted-average number of shares outstanding	59,000

c.

MARTINEZ CORPORATION
Statement of Retained Earnings
For the Year Ended December 31, 2002

Retained earnings, Dec. 31, 2001		$1,700,000
Net income for 2002		173,000
Subtotal		$1,873,000
Less: Cash dividends ($1 per share)	$ 69,000	
10% stock dividend	331,200	400,200
Retained earnings, Dec. 31, 2002		$1,472,800

SELF-TEST QUESTIONS

Answers to these questions appear on page 541.

1. The primary purpose of showing special types of events separately in the income statement is to:
    a. Increase earnings per share.
    b. Assist users of the income statement in evaluating the profitability of normal, ongoing operations.
    c. Minimize the income taxes paid on the results of ongoing operations.
    d. Prevent unusual losses from recurring.

2. Which of the following situations would *not* be presented in a separate section of the current year's income statement of Hamilton Corporation? During the current year:
    a. Hamilton's St. Louis headquarters are destroyed by a tornado.
    b. Hamilton sells its entire juvenile furniture operations and concentrates on its remaining children's clothing segment.
    c. Hamilton's accountant discovers that the entire price paid several years ago to purchase company offices in Texas had been charged to a Land account; consequently, no depreciation has ever been taken on these buildings.
    d. Hamilton changes from the straight-line method of depreciation to the double-declining-balance method.

3. When a corporation has outstanding both common and preferred stock:
   a. Basic and diluted earnings per share are reported only if the preferred stock is cumulative.
   b. Earnings per share are reported for each type of stock outstanding.
   c. Earnings per share are computed without regard to the amount of dividends declared on common stock.
   d. Earnings per share are computed without regard to the amount of the annual preferred dividends.
4. Which of the following is (are) *not* true about a stock dividend?
   a. Total stockholders' equity does not change when a stock dividend is declared but does change when it is distributed.
   b. Stock dividends do not change the relative portion of the company owned by individual stockholders.
   c. Between the time a stock dividend is declared and when it is distributed, the company's commitment is presented in the balance sheet as a current liability.
   d. Stock dividends have no impact on the amount of the company's assets.
5. The statement of retained earnings:
   a. Includes prior period adjustments and cash dividends, but not stock dividends.
   b. Indicates the amount of cash available for the payment of dividends.
   c. Need not be prepared if a separate statement of stockholders' equity accompanies the financial statements.
   d. Shows revenue, expenses, and dividends for the accounting period.

ASSIGNMENT MATERIAL

DISCUSSION QUESTIONS

1. What is the purpose of arranging an income statement to show subtotals for *income from continuing operations* and *income before extraordinary items?*
2. Frank's Fun Company owns 30 pizza parlors and a minor league baseball team. During the current year, the company sold three of its pizza parlors and closed another when the lease on the building expired. Should any of these events be classified as discontinued operations in the company's income statement? Explain.
3. Define *extraordinary items.* Give two examples of losses that qualify as extraordinary items and two examples of losses that would *not* be classified as extraordinary.
4. In an effort to make the company more competitive, Rytech, Inc., incurred significant expenses related to a reduction in the number of employees, consolidation of offices and facilities, and disposition of assets that are no longer productive. Explain how these costs should be presented in the financial statements of the company, and describe how an investor should view these costs in predicting future earnings of the company.
5. Both the *cumulative effect of a change in accounting principle* and a *prior period adjustment* relate to the income of past accounting periods. Distinguish between these two items and explain how each is shown in the financial statements.
6. In the current year, Stegall Products decided to switch from an accelerated method of depreciation to the straight-line method. Will the cumulative effect of this change in accounting principle increase or decrease the amount of net income reported in the current year? Explain.
7. *Earnings per share* and *book value per share* are statistics that relate to common stock. When both preferred and common stock are outstanding, explain the computation involved in determining the following:
   a. Earnings allocable to the common stockholders.
   b. Aggregate book value allocable to the common stockholders.
8. Assume a corporation has only common stock outstanding. Is the number of common shares used in the computation of earnings per share *always* the same as the number of common shares used in computing book value per share for this corporation? Is the number of common shares used in computing these two statistics *ever* the same? Explain.

9. Explain how each of the following is computed:
   a. Price-earnings ratio.
   b. Basic earnings per share.
   c. Diluted earnings per share.
10. Throughout the year, Gold Seal Company had 2 million shares of common stock and 150,000 shares of convertible preferred stock outstanding. Each share of preferred is convertible into three shares of common. What number of shares should be used in the computation of (a) basic earnings per share and (b) diluted earnings per share?
11. A financial analyst notes that Statler Corporation's earnings per share have been rising steadily for the past five years. The analyst expects the company's net income to continue to increase at the same rate as in the past. In forecasting future basic earnings per share, what special risk should the analyst consider if Statler's basic earnings are significantly larger than its diluted earnings?
12. Explain the significance of the following dates relating to cash dividends: date of declaration, date of record, date of payment, ex-dividend date.
13. What is the purpose of a *stock dividend?*
14. Distinguish between a *stock split* and a *stock dividend.* Is there any reason for the difference in accounting treatment of these two events?
15. What are *prior period adjustments?* How are they presented in financial statements?
16. Identify three items that may appear in a statement of retained earnings as changes in the amount of retained earnings.
17. If a company's total stockholders' equity is unchanged by the distribution of a stock dividend, how is it possible for a stockholder who received shares in the distribution of the dividend to benefit?
18. What is a liquidating dividend, and how does it relate to a regular (nonliquidating) dividend?
19. In discussing stock dividends and stock splits in an investments class you are taking, one of the students says, "Stock splits and stock dividends are exactly the same—both are distributions of a company's stock to existing owners without payment to the company." Do you agree? Why or why not?
20. A *statement of stockholders' equity* sometimes is described as an "expanded" statement of retained earnings. Why?

EXERCISES

EXERCISE 12.1
Stock Dividends and Stock Splits
LO 4

Assume that when you were in high school you saved $1,000 to invest for your college education. You purchased 200 shares of Wiley Incorporated, a small but profitable company. Over the three years that you have owned the stock, the corporation's board of directors took the following actions:
1. Declared a 2-for-1 stock split.
2. Declared a 20% stock dividend.
3. Declared a 3-for-1 stock split.

The current price of the stock is $12 per share.

a. Calculate the current number of shares and the market value of your investment.
b. Explain the likely reason the board of directors of the company has not declared a cash dividend.
c. State your opinion as to whether or not you would have been better off if the board of directors had declared a cash dividend instead of the stock dividend and stock splits.

EXERCISE 12.2
Accounting Terminology
LO 1, 2, 3, 4, 6, 7

The following are 10 technical accounting terms introduced or emphasized in Chapters 11 and 12:

P/e ratio	Treasury stock	Discontinued operations
Stock dividend	Extraordinary item	Prior period adjustment
Basic earnings per share	Stock subscription	Diluted earnings per share
Comprehensive income		

Exercises

Each of the following statements may (or may not) describe one of these technical terms. For each statement, indicate the term described, or answer "None" if the statement does not correctly describe any of the terms.

a. A gain or loss that is unusual in nature and not expected to recur in the foreseeable future.
b. The asset represented by shares of capital stock that have not yet been issued or subscribed.
c. A distribution of additional shares of stock that reduces retained earnings but causes no change in total stockholders' equity.
d. An agreement to purchase shares of stock at a specified price in the future.
e. An adjustment to the beginning balance of retained earnings to correct an error previously made in the measurement of net income.
f. A statistic expressing a relationship between the current market value of a share of common stock and the underlying earnings per share.
g. A separate section sometimes included in an income statement as a way to help investors evaluate the profitability of ongoing business activities.
h. A pro forma figure indicating what earnings per share would have been if all securities convertible into common stock had been converted at the beginning of the current year.
i. A broadly defined measure of financial performance that includes, but is not limited to, net income.

EXERCISE 12.3

Discontinued Operations

LO 1, 2

During the current year, SunSports, Inc., operated two business segments: a chain of surf and dive shops and a small chain of tennis shops. The tennis shops were not profitable and were sold near year-end to another corporation. SunSports' operations for the current year are summarized below. The first two captions, "Net sales" and "Costs and expenses," relate only to the company's continuing operations.

Net sales	$10,800,000
Costs and expenses (including applicable income taxes)	8,600,000
Operating loss from tennis shops (net of income tax benefit)	192,000
Loss on sale of tennis shops (net of income tax benefit)	348,000

The company had 182,000 shares of a single class of capital stock outstanding throughout the year.

a. Prepare a condensed income statement for the year. At the bottom of the statement, show any appropriate earnings per share figures. (A condensed income statement is illustrated in Exhibit 12–3.)
b. Which earnings per share figure in part **a** do you consider most useful in predicting future operating results for SunSports, Inc.? Why?

EXERCISE 12.4

Reporting an Extraordinary Item

LO 1, 2

For the year ended December 31, Global Exports had net sales of $9,000,000, costs and other expenses (including income taxes) of $6,200,000, and an extraordinary gain (net of income tax) of $420,000.

a. Prepare a condensed income statement (including earnings per share), assuming that 910,000 shares of common stock were outstanding throughout the year. (A condensed income statement is illustrated in Exhibit 12–3.)
b. Which earnings per share figure is used in computing the price-earnings ratio for Global Exports reported in financial publications such as *The Wall Street Journal*? Explain briefly.

EXERCISE 12.5

Computing Earnings per Share: Effect of Preferred Stock

LO 2

The net income of Tiny Tot Furniture, Inc., amounted to $1,850,000 for the current year.

a. Compute the amount of earnings per share assuming that the shares of capital stock outstanding throughout the year consisted of:
   1. 400,000 shares of $1 par value common stock and no preferred stock.
   2. 100,000 shares of 8%, $100 par value preferred stock and 300,000 shares of $5 par value common stock. The preferred stock has a call price of $105 per share.
b. Is the earnings per share figure computed in part **a(2)** considered to be basic or diluted? Explain.

EXERCISE 12.6
Restating Earnings per Share after a Stock Dividend
LO 2, 4

The 2002 annual report of Software City, Inc., included the following comparative summary of earnings per share over the last three years:

	2002	2001	2000
Earnings per share	$3.15	$2.41	$1.64

In 2003, Software City, Inc., declared and distributed a 100% stock dividend. Following this stock dividend, the company reported earnings per share of $1.88 for 2003.

a. Prepare a three-year schedule similar to the one above, but compare earnings per share during the years 2003, 2002, and 2001. (Hint: All per-share amounts in your schedule should be based on the number of shares outstanding *after* the stock dividend.)

b. In preparing your schedule, which figure (or figures) did you have to restate? Why? Explain the logic behind your computation.

EXERCISE 12.7
Cash Dividends, Stock Dividends, and Stock Splits
LO 4

Standard Manufacturing Company has 1,000,000 shares of $1 par value capital stock outstanding on January 1. The following equity transactions occurred during the current year:

Apr. 30 Distributed additional shares of capital stock in a 2-for-1 stock split. Market price of stock was $35 per share.
June 1 Declared a cash dividend of 60 cents per share.
July 1 Paid the 60-cent cash dividend to stockholders.
Aug. 1 Declared a 5% stock dividend. Market price of stock was $19 per share.
Sept. 10 Issued shares resulting from the 5% stock dividend declared on August 1.
Dec. 15 Declared a 50% stock dividend. Market price of stock was $23 per share.

a. Prepare journal entries to record the above transactions.
b. Compute the number of shares of capital stock outstanding at year-end.
c. What is the par value per share of Standard Manufacturing stock at the end of the year?
d. Determine the effect of each of the following on *total* stockholders' equity: stock split, declaration and payment of a cash dividend, declaration and distribution of a small stock dividend, declaration and distribution of a large stock dividend. (Your answers should be either *increase, decrease,* or *no effect.*)

EXERCISE 12.8
Effect of Stock Dividends on Stock Price
LO 4

DXY, Inc., has a total of 80,000 shares of common stock outstanding and no preferred stock. Total stockholders' equity at the end of the current year amounts to $5 million and the market value of the stock is $66 per share. At year-end, the company declares a 10% stock dividend—one share for each 10 shares held. If all parties concerned clearly recognize the nature of the stock dividend, what should you expect the market price per share of the common stock to be on the ex-dividend date?

EXERCISE 12.9
Reporting the Effects of Transactions
LO 8

Five events pertaining to Platteau Manufacturing Co. are described below.
a. Declared and paid a cash dividend.
b. Issued a 10% stock dividend.
c. Issued a 2-for-1 stock split.
d. Purchased treasury stock.
e. Reissued the treasury stock at a price greater than the purchase price.

Indicate the immediate effects of the events on the financial measurements in the four columnar headings listed below. Use the code letters **I** for increase, **D** for decrease, and **NE** for no effect.

Event	Current Assets	Stockholders' Equity	Net Income	Net Cash Flow (from any source)

Exercises

EXERCISE 12.10
Effects of Various Transactions on Earnings per Share

LO 2, 4

Explain the immediate effects, if any, of each of the following transactions on a company's earnings per share:
a. Split the common stock 4-for-1.
b. Realized a gain from the sale of a discontinued operation.
c. Switched from an accelerated method of depreciation to the straight-line method, resulting in a reduction in the Accumulated Depreciation account.
d. Declared and paid a cash dividend on common stock.
e. Declared and distributed a stock dividend on common stock.
f. Acquired several thousand shares of treasury stock.

EXERCISE 12.11
Where to Find Financial Information

LO 1, 5, 8

You have now learned about the following financial statements issued by corporations: balance sheet, income statement, statement of retained earnings, statement of stockholders' equity, and statement of cash flows. Listed below are various items frequently of interest to a corporation's owners, potential investors, and creditors, among others. You are to specify which of the above corporate financial statements, if any, reports the desired information. If the listed item is not reported in any formal financial statement issued by a corporation, indicate an appropriate source for the desired information.
a. Number of shares of stock outstanding as of year-end.
b. Total dollar amount of cash dividends declared during the current year.
c. Market value per share at balance sheet date.
d. Cumulative dollar effect of an accounting error made in a previous year.
e. Cumulative dollar effect of switching from one generally accepted accounting principle to another acceptable accounting method during the current year.
f. Detailed disclosure of why the number of shares of stock outstanding at the end of the current year is greater than the number outstanding at the end of the prior year.
g. Earnings per share of common stock.
h. Book value per share.
i. Price-earnings (p/e) ratio.
j. The total amount the corporation paid to buy back shares of its own stock, which it now holds.

EXERCISE 12.12
Comprehensive Income

LO 7

Rover, Inc., had revenues of $550,000 and expenses (other than income taxes) of $280,000 for the current year. The company is subject to a 35% income tax rate. In addition, available-for-sale investments, which were purchased for $17,500 early in the year, had a market value at the end of the year of $19,200.
a. Determine the amount of Rover's net income for the year.
b. Determine the amount of Rover's comprehensive income for the year.
c. How would your answers to parts **a** and **b** differ if the market value of Rover's investments at the end of the year had been $14,200?

EXERCISE 12.13
Analysis of Stock Information

LO 1, 8

Use the annual report of **Tootsie Roll Industries, Inc.**, in Appendix A of this text to answer these questions:
a. Study the income statements of **Tootsie Roll**. Do they include any nonrecurring items that might affect your use of the statements in predicting the future performance of the company?
b. Study the stock information included in Note 5 and respond to the following:
   1. What is the primary difference between the two classes of common stock that the company has in its capital structure?
   2. Has the company been active in issuing stock dividends and/or stock splits and, if so, what has been the impact of these distributions on the number of outstanding shares?
c. Looking at the balance sheets for 1999 and 2000:
   1. What is the total amount of paid-in capital for each year?
   2. For 1999, why is the amount of common stock only $22,815 thousand while the total stockholders' equity is much higher at $430,646 thousand?

PROBLEMS

PROBLEM 12.1
Reporting Unusual Events; Using Predictive Subtotals
LO 1, 2

Pacific Airlines operated both an airline and several motels located near airports. During the year just ended, all motel operations were discontinued and the following operating results were reported:

Continuing operations (airline):	
Net sales	$51,120,000
Costs and expenses (including income taxes on continuing operations)	43,320,000
Other data:	
Operating income from motels (net of income taxes)	864,000
Gain on sale of motels (net of income taxes)	4,956,000
Extraordinary loss (net of income tax benefit)	3,360,000

The extraordinary loss resulted from the destruction of an airliner by an earthquake.
Pacific Airlines had 1,000,000 shares of capital stock outstanding throughout the year.

Instructions

a. Prepare a condensed income statement, including proper presentation of the discontinued motel operations and the extraordinary loss. Include all appropriate earnings per share figures.

b. Assume that you expect the profitability of Pacific's airlines operations to *decline by 5%* next year, and the profitability of the motels to decline by 10%. What is your estimate of the company's net earnings per share next year?

PROBLEM 12.2
Format of an Income Statement and a Statement of Retained Earnings
LO 1, 2, 5, 6

The following data relate to the operations of Schilling Software, Inc., during 2002.

Continuing operations:	
Net sales	$19,850,000
Costs and expenses (including applicable income taxes)	16,900,000
Other data:	
Operating income during 2002 on segment of the business discontinued near year-end (net of income taxes)	140,000
Loss on disposal of discontinued segment (net of income tax benefit)	550,000
Extraordinary loss (net of income tax benefit)	900,000
Cumulative effect of change in accounting principle (increase in net income, net of related income taxes)	100,000
Prior period adjustment (increase in 2001 depreciation expense, net of income tax benefit)	350,000
Cash dividends declared	950,000

Instructions

a. Prepare a condensed income statement for 2002, including earnings per share statistics. Schilling Software, Inc., had 200,000 shares of $1 par value common stock and 80,000 shares of $6.25, $100 par value preferred stock outstanding throughout the year.

b. Prepare a statement of retained earnings for the year ended December 31, 2002. As originally reported, retained earnings at December 31, 2001, amounted to $7,285,000.

c. Compute the amount of cash dividend *per share of common stock* declared by the board of directors for 2002. Assume no dividends in arrears on the preferred stock.

d. Assume that 2003 earnings per share is a single figure and amounts to $8.00. Assume also that there are no changes in outstanding common or preferred stock in 2003. Do you consider the $8.00 earnings per share figure in 2003 to be a favorable or unfavorable statistic in comparison with 2002 performance? Explain.

PROBLEM 12.3
Reporting Unusual Events: A Comprehensive Problem

LO 1, 2, 5, 6

The income statement below was prepared by a new and inexperienced employee in the accounting department of Aspen, Inc., a business organized as a corporation.

ASPEN, INC.
Income Statement
For the Year Ended December 31, 2002

Net sales		$10,800,000
Gain on sale of treasury stock		62,000
Excess of issuance price over par value of capital stock		510,000
Prior period adjustment (net of income taxes)		60,000
Extraordinary gain (net of income taxes)		36,000
Total revenue		$11,468,000
Less:		
Cost of goods sold	$6,000,000	
Selling expenses	1,104,000	
General and administrative expenses	1,896,000	
Loss from settlement of litigation	24,000	
Income taxes on continuing operations	720,000	
Operating loss on discontinued operations (net of income tax benefit)	252,000	
Loss on disposal of discontinued operations (net of income tax benefit)	420,000	
Cumulative effect of change in accounting principle (net of income tax benefit)	84,000	
Dividends declared on capital stock	350,000	
Total costs and expenses		10,850,000
Net income		$ 618,000

Instructions

a. Prepare a corrected income statement for the year ended December 31, 2002, using the format illustrated in Exhibit 12–3. Include at the bottom of your income statement all appropriate earnings-per-share figures. Assume that throughout the year the company had outstanding a weighted average of 200,000 shares of a single class of capital stock.

b. Prepare a statement of retained earnings for 2002. (As originally reported, retained earnings at December 31, 2001, amounted to $2,175,000.)

c. What does the $62,000 "gain on sale of treasury stock" represent? How would you report this item in Aspen's financial statements at December 31, 2002?

PROBLEM 12.4
Effects of Stock Dividends, Stock Splits, and Treasury Stock Transactions

LO 4

At the beginning of the year, Travel Adventures, Inc., has total stockholders' equity of $840,000 and 40,000 outstanding shares of a single class of capital stock. During the year, the corporation completes the following transactions affecting its stockholders' equity accounts:

Jan. 10   A 5% stock dividend is declared and distributed. (Market price, $20 per share.)
Mar. 15   The corporation acquires 2,000 shares of its own capital stock at a cost of $21.00 per share.
May 30   All 2,000 shares of the treasury stock are reissued at a price of $31.50 per share.
July 31   The capital stock is split 2-for-1.
Dec. 15   The board of directors declares a cash dividend of $1.10 per share, payable on January 15.
Dec. 31   Net income of $378,000 is reported for the year ended December 31.

Instructions

Compute the amount of total stockholders' equity, the number of shares of capital stock outstanding, and the book value per share following each successive transaction. Organize your

PROBLEM 12.5
Preparing a Statement of Stockholders' Equity

LO 4, 8

solution as a three-column schedule with these separate column headings: (1) Total Stockholders' Equity, (2) Number of Shares Outstanding, and (3) Book Value per Share.

A summary of the transactions affecting the stockholders' equity of Voight Marble Corporation during the current year follows:

Prior period adjustment (net of income tax benefit)	$ (80,000)
Issuance of common stock: 10,000 shares of $10 par value capital stock at $34 per share	340,000
Declaration and distribution of 5% stock dividend (6,000 shares, market price $36 per share)	(216,000)
Purchased 1,000 shares of treasury stock at $35	(35,000)
Reissued 500 shares of treasury stock at a price of $36 per share	18,000
Net income	845,000
Cash dividends declared ($1 per share)	(142,700)

Parentheses ( ) indicate a reduction in stockholders' equity.

Instructions

a. Prepare a statement of stockholders' equity for the year. Use these column headings and beginning balances. (Notice that all additional paid-in capital accounts are combined into a single column.)

	Capital Stock ($10 par value)	Additional Paid-in Capital	Retained Earnings	Treasury Stock	Total Stockholders' Equity
Balances, Jan. 1	$1,100,000	$1,800,000	$950,000	$ –0–	$3,850,000

b. What was the overall effect on total stockholders' equity of the 5% stock dividend of 6,000 shares? What was the overall effect on total stockholders' equity of the cash dividend declared? Do these two events have the same impact on stockholders' equity? Why or why not?

PROBLEM 12.6
Recording Stock Dividends and Treasury Stock Transactions

LO 4

At the beginning of 2002, Quick Delivery Service, Inc. showed the following amounts in the stockholders' equity section of its balance sheet:

Stockholders' equity:	
Capital stock, $1 par value, 500,000 shares authorized, 382,000 issued	$ 382,000
Additional paid-in capital: Capital stock	4,202,000
Total paid-in capital	$4,584,000
Retained earnings	2,704,600
Total stockholders' equity	$7,288,600

The transactions relating to stockholders' equity during the year are as follows:

Jan. 3 Declared a dividend of $1 per share to stockholders of record on January 31, payable on February 15.

Feb. 15 Paid the cash dividend declared on January 3.

Apr. 12 The corporation purchased 6,000 shares of its own capital stock at a price of $40 per share.

May 9	Reissued 4,000 shares of the treasury stock at a price of $44 per share.
June 1	Declared a 5% stock dividend to stockholders of record at June 15, to be distributed on June 30. The market price of the stock at June 1 was $42 per share. (The 2,000 shares remaining in the treasury do not participate in the stock dividend.)
June 30	Distributed the stock dividend declared on June 1.
Aug. 4	Reissued 600 of the 2,000 remaining shares of treasury stock at a price of $37 per share.
Dec. 31	The Income Summary account, showing net income for the year of $1,928,000, was closed into the Retained Earnings account.
Dec. 31	The $382,000 balance in the Dividends account was closed into the Retained Earnings account.

Instructions

a. Prepare in general journal form the entries to record the above transactions.

b. Prepare the stockholders' equity section of the balance sheet at December 31, 2002. Use the format illustrated in Exhibit 12–7. Include a supporting schedule showing your computation of retained earnings at that date.

c. Compute the maximum cash dividend per share that legally could be declared at December 31, 2002, without impairing the paid-in capital of Quick Delivery Service. (Hint: The availability of retained earnings for dividends is restricted by the cost of treasury stock owned.)

PROBLEM 12.7

Effects of Transactions

LO 8

Tech Process, Inc., manufactures a variety of computer peripherals, such as tape drives and printers. Listed below are five events that occurred during the current year.

1. Declared a $1.00 per share cash dividend.
2. Paid the cash dividend.
3. Purchased 1,000 shares of treasury stock for $20.00 per share.
4. Reissued 500 shares of the treasury stock at a price of $18.00 per share.
5. Declared a 15 percent stock dividend.

Instructions

a. Indicate the effects of each of these events on the financial measurements in the four columnar headings listed below. Use the following code letters: **I** for increase, **D** for decrease, and **NE** for no effect.

Event	Current Assets	Stockholders' Equity	Net Income	Net Cash Flow (from any source)

b. For each event, *explain* the reasoning behind your answers. Be prepared to explain this reasoning in class.

PROBLEM 12.8

Preparing the Stockholders' Equity Section: A Challenging Case

LO 4

The Mandella family decided early in 2001 to incorporate their family-owned vineyards under the name Mandella Corporation. The corporation was authorized to issue 500,000 shares of a single class of $10 par value capital stock. Presented below is the information necessary to prepare the stockholders' equity section of the company's balance sheet at the end of 2001 and at the end of 2002.

2001. In January the corporation issued to members of the Mandella family 150,000 shares of capital stock in exchange for cash and other assets used in the operation of the vineyards. The fair market value of these assets indicated an issue price of $30 per share. In December, Joe Mandella died, and the corporation purchased 10,000 shares of its own capital stock from his estate at $34 per share. Because of the large cash outlay to acquire this treasury stock, the directors decided not to declare cash dividends in 2001 and instead declared a 10% stock dividend to be distributed in January of 2002. The stock price at the declaration date was $35 per share. (The treasury shares do not participate in the stock dividend.) Net income for 2001 was $940,000.

2002. In January the corporation distributed the stock dividend declared in 2001, and in February, the 10,000 treasury shares were sold to Maria Mandella at $39 per share. In June, the capital stock was split 2-for-1. (Approval was obtained to increase the authorized number of shares to 1 million.) On December 15, the directors declared a cash dividend of $2 per share, payable in January of 2003. Net income for 2002 was $1,080,000.

Instructions

Using the format illustrated in Exhibit 12–7, prepare the stockholders' equity section of the balance sheet at:

a. December 31, 2001.

b. December 31, 2002.

Show any necessary computations in supporting schedules.

PROBLEM 12.9
Format of an Income Statement; EPS
LO 1, 2

The following information is excerpted from the financial statements in a recent annual report of Eagle Manufacturing Corporation. (Dollar figures and shares of stock are in thousands.)

Extraordinary loss on extinguishment of debt	$ (8,490)
Loss from continuing operations	$(16,026)
Cumulative effect of change in accounting for income taxes	$(10,100)
Income from discontinued operations	$ 6,215
Preferred stock dividend requirements	$ (2,778)
Weighted-average number of shares of common stock outstanding	39,739

Instructions

a. Rearrange the items to present in good form the last portion of the income statement for Eagle Manufacturing Corporation, beginning with "Loss from continuing operations."

b. Calculate the amount of *net loss* per share for the period. (Do *not* calculate per-share amounts for subtotals, such as income from continuing operations, or loss before extraordinary items, etc. You are required to compute only a single earnings per share amount.)

CASES AND UNSTRUCTURED PROBLEMS

CASE 12.1
What's This?
LO 1

The following events were reported in the financial statements of large, publicly owned corporations:

a. **Atlantic Richfield Company (ARCO)** sold or abandoned the entire noncoal minerals segment of its operations. In the year of disposal, this segment had an operating loss. **ARCO** also incurred a loss of $514 million on disposal of its noncoal minerals segment of the business.

b. **American Airlines** increased the estimated useful life used in computing depreciation on its aircraft. If the new estimated life had always been in use, the net income reported in prior years would have been substantially higher.

c. **Union Carbide Corp.** sustained a large loss as a result of the explosion of a chemical plant.

d. **AT&T** changed the method used to depreciate certain assets. Had the new method always been in use, the net income of prior years would have been $175 million lower than was actually reported.

e. **Georgia Pacific Corporation** realized a $10 million gain as a result of condemnation proceedings in which a governmental agency purchased assets from the company in a "forced sale."

Instructions

Indicate whether each event should be classified as a discontinued operation, an extraordinary item, or the cumulative effect of an accounting change or included among the revenue and expenses of normal and recurring business operations. Briefly explain your reasons for each answer.

CASE 12.2
Is There Life without Baseball?

LO 1

Memphis Publishing, Inc. (MPI), publishes two newspapers and, until recently, owned a professional baseball team. The baseball team had been losing money for several years and was sold at the end of 2002 to a group of investors who plan to move it to a larger city. Also in 2002, MPI suffered an extraordinary loss when its Raytown printing plant was damaged by a tornado. The damage has since been repaired. A condensed income statement follows:

MEMPHIS PUBLISHING, INC.
Income Statement
For the Year Ended December 31, 2002

Net revenue		$41,000,000
Costs and expenses		36,500,000
Income from continuing operations		$ 4,500,000
Discontinued operations:		
Operating loss on baseball team	$(1,300,000)	
Gain on sale of baseball team	4,700,000	3,400,000
Income before extraordinary items		$ 7,900,000
Extraordinary loss:		
Tornado damage to Raytown printing plant		(600,000)
Net income		$ 7,300,000

Instructions

On the basis of this information, answer the following questions. Show any necessary computations and explain your reasoning.

a. What would MPI's net income have been for 2002 if it *had not* sold the baseball team?

b. Assume that for 2003 you expect a 7% increase in the profitability of MPI's newspaper business but had projected a $2,000,000 operating loss for the baseball team if MPI had continued to operate the team in 2003. What amount would you forecast as MPI's 2003 net income *if the company had continued to own and operate the baseball team*?

c. Given your assumptions in part **b,** but given that MPI *did* sell the baseball team in 2002, what would you forecast as the company's estimated net income for 2003?

d. Assume that the expenses of operating the baseball team in 2002 amounted to $32,200,000, net of any related income tax effects. What was the team's *net revenue* for the year?

CASE 12.3
Using Earnings per Share Statistics

LO 1, 2, 3

For many years New York Studios has produced television shows and operated several FM radio stations. Late in the current year, the radio stations were sold to Times Publishing, Inc. Also during the current year, New York Studios sustained an extraordinary loss when one of its camera trucks caused an accident in an international grand prix auto race. Throughout the current year, the company had 3 million shares of common stock and a large quantity of convertible preferred stock outstanding. Earnings per share reported for the current year were as follows:

	Basic	Diluted
Earnings from continuing operations	$8.20	$6.80
Earnings before extraordinary items	$6.90	$5.50
Net earnings	$3.60	$2.20

Instructions

a. Briefly explain why New York Studios reports diluted earnings per share amounts as well as basic earnings per share. What is the purpose of showing investors the diluted figures?

b. What was the total dollar amount of the extraordinary loss sustained by New York Studios during the current year?

c. Assume that the price-earnings ratio shown in the morning newspaper for New York Studios' common stock indicates that the stock is selling at a price equal to 10 times the reported earnings per share. What is the approximate market price of the stock?

d. Assume that you expect both the revenue and expenses involved in producing television shows to increase by 10% during the coming year. What would you forecast as the company's basic earnings per share for the coming year under each of the following independent assumptions? (Show your computations and explain your reasoning.)

1. *None* of the convertible preferred stock is converted into common stock during the coming year.
2. *All* of the convertible preferred stock is converted into common stock at the beginning of the coming year.

CASE 12.4

Interpreting a Statement of Stockholders' Equity

LO 8

The following information is excerpted from the Statement of Common Stockholders' Equity included in a recent annual report of **Quaker Oats Company and Subsidiaries**. (Dollar figures are in millions.)

	Common Stock		Additional Paid-in Capital	Retained Earnings	Treasury Stock	
	Shares	Amount			Shares	Amount
Balances, beginning of year	83,989,396	$420.0	$19.5	$ 998.4	4,593,664	$(132.9)
Net income				203.0		
Cash dividends declared on common stock				(95.2)		
Common stock issued for stock option plans			(1.4)		(601,383)	16.7
Repurchases of common stock					1,229,700	(68.6)
Balances, year-end	83,989,396	$420.0	$18.1	$1,106.2	5,221,981	$(184.8)

Instructions

Use the information about **Quaker Oats** to answer the following questions.

a. How many shares of common stock are outstanding at the *beginning* of the year? At the *end* of the year?

b. What was the total common stock dividend declared during the presented year? **Quaker**'s annual report disclosed that the common stock dividend during that year was $1.20 per share (30 cents per quarter). Approximately how many shares of common stock were entitled to the $1.20 per share dividend during the year? Is this answer compatible with your answers to part **a**?

c. The statement presented indicates that common stock was both issued and repurchased during the year, yet the number of common shares shown and the common stock amount (first and second columns) did not change from beginning to end of the year. Explain.

d. What was the average price per share **Quaker** paid to acquire the treasury shares held at the *beginning* of the year?

e. Was the aggregate issue price of the 601,383 treasury shares issued during the year for stock option plans higher or lower than the cost **Quaker** paid to acquire those treasury shares? (Hint: Analyze the impact on Additional Paid-in Capital.)

f. What was the average purchase price per share paid by **Quaker** to acquire treasury shares *during the current year?*

g. In its annual report, **Quaker** disclosed that the (weighted) average number of common shares outstanding during the year was 79,307,000. In part **a** above, you determined the number of common shares outstanding as of the end of the year. Which figure is used in computing *earnings per share?* Which is used in computing *book value per share?*

CASE 12.5

Classification of Unusual Items—and the Potential Financial Impact

LO 1, 2, 8

Elliot-Cole is a publicly owned international corporation, with operations in over 90 countries. Net income has been growing at approximately 15% per year, and the stock consistently trades at about 20 times earnings.

To attract and retain key management leadership, the company has developed a compensation plan in which managers receive earnings in the form of bonuses as well as opportunities to purchase shares of the company's stock at a reduced price. In general, the higher the company's net income each year, the greater the benefit to management in terms of their personal compensation.

During the current year, political unrest and economic upheaval threatened Elliot-Cole's business operations in three foreign countries. At year-end, the company's auditors insisted that management write off the company's assets in these countries, stating that these assets were "severely impaired." Said one corporate official, "We can't argue with that. Each of these countries is a real trouble spot. We might be pulling out of these places at any time, and any assets probably would just be left behind."

Management agreed that the carrying value of Elliot-Cole's assets in these three countries should be reduced to "scrap value"—which was nothing. These write-downs amounted to approximately 18% of the company's income *prior* to recognition of these losses. (These write-offs are for financial reporting purposes only; they have *no effect* on the company's income tax obligations.)

At the meeting with the auditors, one of Elliot-Cole's officers states, "There's no doubt we should write these assets off. But of course, this is an extraordinary loss. A loss of this size can't be considered a routine matter."

Instructions

a. Explain the logic behind writing down the book values of assets that are still in operation.

b. Evaluate the officer's statement concerning the classification of these losses. Do you agree that they should be classified as an extraordinary item? Explain.

c. Explain the effect that the classification of these losses—that is, as ordinary or extraordinary—will have in the current period on Elliot-Cole's:
   1. Net income.
   2. Income before extraordinary items.
   3. Income from continuing operations.
   4. Net cash flow from operating activities.

d. Explain how the classification of these losses will affect the p/e ratio reported in newspapers such as *The Wall Street Journal*.

e. Does management appear to have any self-interest in the classification of these losses? Explain.

f. Explain how (if at all) these write-offs are likely to affect the earnings of *future* periods.

g. What "ethical dilemma" confronts management in this case?

BUSINESS WEEK ASSIGNMENT

CASE 12.6

Extraordinary Items and Judgment

LO 1

Laying down rules for what companies can classify as extraordinary costs is difficult for accounting standard setters. Just how difficult became apparent when the FASB could not agree on what could be classified as extraordinary items as a result of the September 11, 2001, attack on New York's World Trade Center. As reported in David Henry's article "Commentary: Putting on a Grim New Face" in the October 15, 2001, *Business Week,* FASB standard setters could not come up with rules to cover the widespread and varied losses of the many different companies affected by the tragedy.

Instructions

Identify the difference between unusual items and extraordinary items for classification purposes on the income statement. Discuss why the FASB had difficulty identifying the costs that companies could classify as extraordinary items on their income statements as a result of the September 11, 2001, tragedy.

INTERNET ASSIGNMENT

INTERNET 12.1

Comparing Price-Earnings Ratios

LO 2

The normal price-earnings ratio of a company varies depending on expected future earnings of the company and the general price level of the stock market. On average, mature companies have lower price-earnings ratios, usually less than 20, than do emerging companies, which may be over 100. This is because of the steep growth in earnings that is characteristic of an emerging company.

Instructions

a. Visit *Fortune* magazine's Internet site and select a Fortune 500 corporation. The site's address is

www.fortune.com

b. Visit NASDAQ's home page at

www.nasdaq.com

Click on quotes at the top of the screen, then click flash quotes for NASDAQ 100 and select a small corporation.

c. Get Detailed Quotes for the companies from PCQUOTE's Internet site at

www.pcquote.com

Indicate the current price of each corporation's stock, including its high and low price for the day. (If either of the companies has a net loss for the most recent period, go back and replace it with a profitable company.)

d. Compare the price-earnings ratios (as shown on the Detailed Quote screen) of the two companies. Speculate as to why one company has a higher price-earnings ratio than the other.

Internet sites are time and date sensitive. It is the purpose of these exercises to have you explore the Internet. You may need to use the Yahoo! search engine **http://www.yahoo.com** *(or another favorite search engine) to find a company's current Web address.*

OUR COMMENTS ON THE "YOUR TURN" CASES

You as an Investor (p. 509) The best starting point for estimating the future net income of Mattson Corporation would be income from *continuing operations*. Working backwards from net income, it is calculated as $4,550,000 ($4,000,000 + $750,000 + $300,000 − $500,000). Discontinued operations, extraordinary items, and accounting changes generally would not be expected to be experienced in future years and, therefore, should be eliminated in predicting future amounts.

You as a Board Member (p. 514) You should point out to the stockholders that annual earnings do not guarantee cash available for dividends. Earnings may be invested in new stores, inventories, or any other type of asset. Since the corporation is small and growing, it is in need of capital. Profitable operations are one of the most important sources of financing for a small business.

It is not unethical to retain earnings in the business. In fact, it might be unethical and illegal to distribute cash dividends if there is significant debt outstanding to creditors. In general, creditors must be satisfied prior to distributing excessive dividends. Many long-term debt agreements prevent distribution of dividends if the result of the distribution is that retained earnings fall below a prespecified level.

To appease the stockholders, the board of directors might consider declaring a stock dividend or a stock split. This would provide the stockholders with additional shares of stock, while retaining the company's liquid assets.

ANSWERS TO SELF-TEST QUESTIONS

1. b **2.** c **3.** c **4.** a, c **5.** c

CHAPTER 13
STATEMENT OF CASH FLOWS

Learning Objectives

After studying this chapter, you should be able to:

1. Explain the purposes and uses of a statement of cash flows.
2. Describe how cash transactions are classified in a statement of cash flows.
3. Compute the major cash flows relating to operating activities.
4. Compute the cash flows relating to investing and financing activities.
5. Distinguish between the direct and indirect methods of reporting operating cash flows.
6. Explain why net income differs from net cash flows from operating activities.
7. Compute net cash flows from operating activities using the *indirect* method.
8. Discuss the likely effects of various business strategies on cash flows.
*9. Explain how a worksheet may be helpful in preparing a statement of cash flows.

Supplemental Topic, "A Worksheet for Preparing a Statement of Cash Flows."

Harrah's Entertainment, Inc.

Harrah's Entertainment, Inc.

Harrah's Entertainment, Inc., is best known for its casinos. In the company's 2000 annual report, however, **Harrah's** states that the company's people are its most important asset. The company attributes much of its success to the leadership provided by its employees and management.

Cash flow is an important aspect of any business, but particularly one like **Harrah's** whose primary line of business is entertaining people. Early in this text we introduced the idea that investors and creditors are interested in cash flow information. They want to know that they will receive a reasonable return on the money they have committed, as an investor or creditor, to a company. In addition to a return on their money, they also want the assurance that they will get their investment back at some future time. We refer to these future cash flows as cash flow prospects because they are cash flows that we expect in the future.

• • •

Historical cash flow information about a company is helpful to investors and creditors in judging future cash flows from the company to themselves. For that reason, one of the three primary financial statements is the statement of cash flows. We introduced this statement in Chapter 2, and in Chapter 13 we go into considerably more depth to help you understand how a company prepares its statement of cash flows. During 2000, **Harrah's Entertainment**'s cash increased $65,621 thousand, from $233,581 thousand to $299,202 thousand. This includes significant amounts of cash coming in and moving out of the business. For presentation purposes, **Harrah's** classified these cash flows in three categories—operating activities, investing activities, and financing activities. In this chapter, we focus on what is included in each of these categories and how they can help you better understand the financial activities of companies like **Harrah's Entertainment**.

STATEMENT OF CASH FLOWS

Purposes of the Statement

The basic purpose of a statement of cash flows is to provide information about the *cash receipts* and *cash payments* of a business entity during the accounting period. (The term **cash flows** includes both cash receipts and cash payments.) In addition, the statement is intended to provide information about the *investing* and *financing* activities of the company during the period. A statement of cash flows assists investors, creditors, and others in assessing such factors as:

- The company's ability to generate positive cash flows in future periods.
- The company's ability to meet its obligations and to pay dividends.
- The company's need for external financing.
- Reasons for differences between the amount of net income and the related net cash flows from operating activities.
- Both the cash and noncash aspects of the company's investment and financing transactions for the period.
- Causes of the change in the amount of cash and cash equivalents between the beginning and the end of the accounting period.

Stated simply, a statement of cash flows helps users of financial statements evaluate a company's ability to have sufficient cash—both on a short-run and on a long-run basis. For this reason, the statement of cash flows is useful to virtually everyone interested in the company's financial health: short- and long-term creditors, investors, management—and both current and prospective competitors.

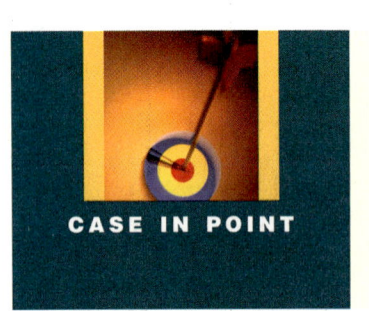

LO 1
Explain the purposes and uses of a statement of cash flows.

CASE IN POINT

The cash flow statement, while not universally mandated by governments around the world, is becoming more widely supported. The governments of France, the Netherlands, and Switzerland do not require companies to provide investors with the statement of cash flows. However, these governments recommend that companies provide it to their investors as supplemental information. In 2000, the Japanese government began mandating that publicly traded companies prepare cash flow statements for investors.

Example of a Statement of Cash Flows

An example of a statement of cash flows appears in Exhibit 13–1. Cash outflows are shown in parentheses.[1]

---

[1] In this illustration, net cash flows from operating activities are determined by the *direct method*. An alternative approach, called the *indirect method*, is illustrated later in this chapter.

ALLISON CORPORATION
Statement of Cash Flows
For the Year Ended December 31, 2002

Cash flows from operating activities:

Cash received from customers	$ 870,000	
Interest and dividends received	10,000	
Cash provided by operating activities		$880,000
Cash paid to suppliers and employees	$(764,000)	
Interest paid	(28,000)	
Income taxes paid	(38,000)	
Cash disbursed for operating activities		(830,000)
Net cash flows from operating activities		$ 50,000

Cash flows from investing activities:

Purchases of marketable securities	$ (65,000)	
Proceeds from sales of marketable securities	40,000	
Loans made to borrowers	(17,000)	
Collections on loans	12,000	
Purchases of plant assets	(160,000)	
Proceeds from sales of plant assets	75,000	
Net cash flows from investing activities		(115,000)

Cash flows from financing activities:

Proceeds from short-term borrowing	$ 45,000	
Payments to settle short-term debts	(55,000)	
Proceeds from issuing bonds payable	100,000	
Proceeds from issuing capital stock	50,000	
Dividends paid	(40,000)	
Net cash flows from financing activities		100,000
Net increase (decrease) in cash		$ 35,000
Cash and cash equivalents, Jan. 1		20,000
Cash and cash equivalents, Dec. 31		$ 55,000

Exhibit 13–1

ALLISON CORPORATION STATEMENT OF CASH FLOWS

Classification of Cash Flows

The cash flows shown in the statement are grouped into three major categories: (1) **operating activities**, (2) **investing activities**, and (3) **financing activities**.[2] We will now look briefly at the way cash flows are classified among these three categories.

LO 2
Describe how cash transactions are classified in a statement of cash flows.

Operating Activities The operating activities section shows the *cash effects* of revenue and expense transactions. Stated another way, the operating activities section of the statement of cash flows includes the cash effects of those transactions reported in the income statement. To illustrate this concept, consider the effects of credit sales. Credit sales are reported in the income statement in the period when the sales occur. But the cash effects occur later—when the receivables are collected in cash. If these events occur in different accounting periods, the income statement and the operating activities section of the statement of cash flows will differ. Similar differences may exist between the recognition of an expense and the related cash payment. Consider, for example, the expense of postretirement benefits earned by employees during the current period. If this

---

[2] A fourth classification, "effects of changes in exchange rates on cash," is used in the cash flow statements of companies with foreign currency holdings. This classification, as well as other complexities, are discussed in more advanced accounting courses.

expense is not funded with a trustee, the cash payments may not occur for many years—after today's employees have retired.

Cash flows from operating activities include:

Cash Receipts	Cash Payments
Collections from customers for sales of goods and services	Payments to suppliers of merchandise and services, including payments to employees
Interest and dividends received	Payments of interest
Other receipts from operations; for example, proceeds from settlement of litigation	Payments of income taxes
	Other expenditures relating to operations; for example, payments in settlement of litigation

Notice that receipts and payments of *interest* are classified as operating activities, not as investing or financing activities.

Investing Activities Cash flows relating to investing activities present the cash effects of transactions involving plant assets, intangible assets, and investments. They include:

Cash Receipts	Cash Payments
Cash proceeds from selling investments and plant assets	Payments to acquire investments and plant assets
Cash proceeds from collecting principal amounts on loans	Amounts advanced to borrowers

Financing Activities Cash flows classified as financing activities include the following items that result from debt and equity financing transactions:

Cash Receipts	Cash Payments
Proceeds from both short-term and long-term borrowing	Repayment of amounts borrowed (excluding interest payments)
Cash received from owners (for example, from issuing stock)	Payments to owners, such as cash dividends

Repayment of amounts borrowed refers to repayment of *loans,* not to payments made on accounts payable or accrued liabilities. Payments of accounts payable and of accrued liabilities are considered payments to suppliers of merchandise and services and are classified as cash outflows from operating activities. Also, remember that all interest payments are classified as operating activities.

Why Are Receipts and Payments of Interest Classified as Operating Activities? One might argue that interest and dividend receipts are related to investing activities, and that interest payments are related to financing activities. The FASB considered this point of view but decided instead to classify interest and dividend receipts and interest payments as operating activities. The FASB wanted net cash flows from operating activities to reflect the cash effects of the revenue and expense transactions entering into the determination of net income. Because dividend and interest revenue and interest expense enter into the determination of net income, the FASB decided to classify the related cash flows as operating activities. Payments of dividends, however,

The increase or decrease in accounts receivable is determined simply by comparing the year-end balance in the account to its balance at the beginning of the year.

In our Allison Corporation example, paragraph **1** of the additional information tells us that accounts receivable have *increased* by $30,000 during the year. The income statement shows net sales for the year of $900,000. Therefore, the amount of cash received from customers is computed as follows:

Net sales (accrual basis)	$900,000
Less: Increase in accounts receivable	30,000
Cash received from customers	$870,000

Interest and Dividends Received Our next objective is to determine the amounts of cash received during the year from dividends and interest on the company's investments. As explained in paragraph **2** of the additional information, dividend revenue is recorded on the cash basis. Therefore, the $3,000 shown in the income statement also represents the amount of cash received as dividends.

Interest revenue, on the other hand, is recognized on the accrual basis. We have already shown how to convert one type of revenue, net sales, from the accrual basis to the cash basis. We may use the same approach to convert interest revenue from the accrual basis to the **cash basis**. Our formula for converting net sales to the cash basis may be modified to convert interest revenue to the cash basis as follows:

$$\text{Interest Received} = \text{Interest Revenue} \begin{cases} + \text{ Decrease in Interest Receivable} \\ \quad\quad\quad\quad\text{or} \\ - \text{ Increase in Interest Receivable} \end{cases}$$

The income statement for Allison Corporation shows interest revenue of $6,000, and paragraph **2** states that the amount of accrued interest receivable has *decreased* by $1,000 during the year. Thus the amount of cash received as interest may be computed as follows:

Interest revenue (accrual basis)	$6,000
Add: Decrease in accrued interest receivable	1,000
Interest received (cash basis)	$7,000

The amounts of interest and dividends received in cash are combined for presentation in the statement of cash flows:

Interest received (cash basis)	$ 7,000
Dividends received (cash basis)	3,000
Interest and dividends received	$10,000

Cash Payments for Merchandise and for Expenses

The next item in the statement of cash flows, "Cash paid to suppliers and employees," includes all cash payments for purchases of merchandise and for operating expenses (excluding interest and income taxes). Payments of interest and income taxes are listed as separate items in the statement. The amounts of cash paid for purchases of merchandise and for operating expenses are computed separately.

Cash Paid for Purchases of Merchandise An accrual basis income statement reflects the *cost of goods sold* during the year, regardless of whether the merchandise was

1. If payment is made in advance, the payment creates an asset, termed a prepaid expense, or, in our formula, a "prepayment." Thus, to the extent that prepaid expenses increase over the year, cash payments *exceed* the amount recognized as expense.
2. If payment is made in the same period, the cash payment is equal to the amount of expense.
3. If payment is made in a later period, the payment reduces a liability for an accrued expense payable. Thus, to the extent that accrued expenses payable decrease over the year, cash payments exceed the amount recognized as expense.

The relationship between cash payments and accrual-basis expenses is summarized below:

$$\text{Cash Payments for Expenses} = \text{Expenses} \begin{Bmatrix} -\text{ Depreciation} \\ \text{and Other} \\ \text{Noncash} \\ \text{Expenses} \end{Bmatrix} \text{ and } \begin{Bmatrix} +\text{ Increase in} \\ \text{Related} \\ \text{Prepayments} \\ \text{or} \\ -\text{ Decrease in} \\ \text{Related} \\ \text{Prepayments} \end{Bmatrix} \text{ and } \begin{Bmatrix} +\text{ Decrease in} \\ \text{Related Accrued} \\ \text{Liabilities} \\ \text{or} \\ -\text{ Increase in} \\ \text{Related Accrued} \\ \text{Liabilities} \end{Bmatrix}$$

In a statement of cash flows, cash payments for interest and for income taxes are shown separately from cash payments for operating expenses. Using information from Allison Corporation's income statement and from paragraph **4**, we may compute the company's cash payments for operating expenses as follows:

Operating expenses (including depreciation)		$300,000
Less: Noncash expenses (depreciation)		40,000
Subtotal		$260,000
Add: Increase in short-term prepayments	$3,000	
Decrease in accrued liabilities	6,000	9,000
Cash payments for operating expenses		$269,000

Cash Paid to Suppliers and Employees The caption used in our cash flow statement, "Cash paid to suppliers and employees," includes cash payments for both purchases of merchandise and for operating expenses. This cash outflow may now be computed by combining the two previous calculations:

Cash payments for purchases of merchandise	$495,000
Cash payments for operating expenses	269,000
Cash payments to suppliers and employees	$764,000

Cash Payments for Interest and Taxes Interest expense and income taxes expense may be converted to cash payments with the same formula we used to convert operating expenses. Allison Corporation's income statement shows interest expense of $35,000, and paragraph **5** states that the liability for interest payable increased by $7,000 during the year. The fact that the liability for unpaid interest *increased* over the year means that *not all of the interest expense shown in the income statement was paid in cash* in the current year. To determine the amount of interest actually paid, we must *subtract* from total interest expense the portion that has been financed through an increase in the liability for interest payable. The computation is as follows:

LO 4
Compute the cash flows relating to investing and financing activities.

Cash Flows from Investing Activities

Paragraphs **7** through **9** in the additional information for our Allison Corporation example provide most of the information necessary to determine the cash flows from investing activities. In the following discussion, we illustrate the presentation of these cash flows and explain the sources of the information contained in the numbered paragraphs.

Much information about investing activities can be obtained simply by looking at the changes in the related asset accounts during the year. Debit entries in these accounts represent purchases of the assets, or cash outlays. Credit entries represent sales of the assets, or cash receipts. However, credit entries in asset accounts represent only the *cost* (or *book value*) of the assets sold. To determine the cash proceeds from these sales transactions, we must adjust the amount of the credit entries for any gains or losses recognized on the sales.

Purchases and Sales of Securities To illustrate, consider paragraph **7**, which summarizes the debit and credit entries to the Marketable Securities account. As explained earlier in this chapter, the $65,000 in debit entries represents purchases of marketable securities. The $44,000 in credit entries represents the *cost* of marketable securities sold during the period. However, the income statement shows that these securities were sold at a *$4,000 loss*. Thus the cash proceeds from these sales amounted to only *$40,000* ($44,000 cost, minus $4,000 loss on sale). In the statement of cash flows, these investing activities are summarized as follows:

Purchases of marketable securities	$(65,000)
Proceeds from sales of marketable securities	40,000

Loans Made and Collected Paragraph **8** provides all the information necessary to summarize the cash flows from making and collecting loans:

Loans made to borrowers	$(17,000)
Collections on loans	12,000

This information comes directly from the Notes Receivable account. Debit entries in the account represent new loans made during the year; credit entries indicate collections of the *principal* amount on outstanding notes (loans). (Interest received is credited to the Interest Revenue account and is included among the cash receipts from operating activities.)

YOUR TURN

You as a Sales Manager

Assume you are a regional sales manager for Godings Foods, Inc., a distributor of bulk food products to schools, nursing homes, hospitals, prisons, and other institutions. Recently, the purchasing agent for Baggins Preschools, Inc., tells you the company will likely have to forgo their normal monthly order because of cash flow problems. The purchasing agent tells you other companies are helping them through the cash-flow squeeze and asks if your company could loan the payment to Baggins. The purchasing agent suggests you could record the sale as revenue and increase notes receivable (rather than accounts receivable) by the same amount. Baggins is one of your largest customers and without their order, you will not meet your sales goals for the month so you are tempted to say yes. However, on reflection you wonder if it might be unethical for the company to lend its customer money to finance purchases. What should you do?

*Our comments appear on pages 598–599.

Cash Flows from Financing Activities

Cash flows from financing activities are determined by analyzing the debit and credit changes recorded during the period in the related liability and stockholders' equity accounts. Cash flows from financing activities are more easily determined than those relating to investing activities, because financing activities seldom involve gains or losses.[4] Thus the debit or credit changes in the balance sheet accounts usually are equal to the amounts of the related cash flows.

Credit changes in such accounts as Notes Payable and the accounts for long-term debt and paid-in capital usually indicate cash receipts; debit changes indicate cash payments.

Short-Term Borrowing Transactions To illustrate, consider paragraph **10**, which provides the information supporting the following cash flows:

Proceeds from short-term borrowing	$45,000
Payments to settle short-term debts	(55,000)

Notice that both the proceeds from short-term borrowing of $45,000 (a positive cash flow) and the payments to settle short-term debts of $55,000 (a negative cash flow) are presented in the statement of cash flows. Presenting both directions of the changes in cash, rather than combining the two and presenting a net amount of $10,000 ($55,000 − $45,000), is an important feature of the statement of cash flows. Presenting both positive and negative cash flows is referred to as presenting *gross* cash flows rather than presenting *net* cash flows.

Is it possible to determine the proceeds of short-term borrowing transactions throughout the year without carefully reviewing each cash receipt? The answer is yes—the proceeds from short-term borrowing are equal to the *sum of the credit entries* in the short-term *Notes Payable* account. Payments to settle short-term debts are equal to the *sum of the debit entries* in this account.

Proceeds from Issuing Bonds Payable and Capital Stock Paragraph **11** states that Allison Corporation received cash of $100,000 by issuing bonds payable. This amount was determined by summing the credit entries in the Bonds Payable account. The Bonds Payable account included no debit entries during the year; thus no bonds were retired.

Paragraph **12** states that during the year Allison Corporation issued capital stock for $50,000. The proceeds from issuing stock are equal to the sum of the credit entries made in the Capital Stock and Additional Paid-in Capital accounts ($10,000 + $40,000).

Cash Dividends Paid to Stockholders Paragraph **13** states that Allison Corporation declared and paid cash dividends of $40,000 during the year. If dividends are both declared and paid during the same year, the cash payments are equal to the related debit entries in the Retained Earnings account.

If the balance sheet includes a liability for dividends payable, the amounts debited to Retained Earnings represent dividends *declared* during the period, which may differ from the amount of dividends *paid*. To determine cash dividends paid, we must adjust the amount of dividends declared by adding any decrease (or subtracting any increase) in the Dividends Payable account over the period.

---

[4] An early retirement of debt is an example of a financing transaction that may result in a gain or a loss.

of the statement of cash flows, we have emphasized the direct method because we consider it to be the more informative and more readily understood approach. The direct method is recommended by the FASB, although companies are permitted to use either the direct or the indirect method and the majority of companies use the indirect method. In addition, when presenting cash flows from operating activities by the direct method, companies are required to disclose information that is consistent with the indirect method. Before completing our Allison Corporation illustration of preparing a statement of cash flows, we shall look more carefully at the indirect method.

Exhibit 13–4 includes a comparison of the direct and indirect methods of determining net cash provided by operating activities for Allison Corporation. The direct method is the same as discussed earlier in this chapter. The indirect method is discussed below. The two methods are more similar than it may appear at first glance. Both methods are based on the same underlying information and they result in the same net cash flow amount—in Allison Corporation's case, $50,000. Both methods convert information originally prepared on the accrual basis to information prepared on the cash basis. In Exhibit 13–4, accrual-based data appear in **blue**; cash flows are shown in **red**.

Exhibit 13–4

COMPARISON OF DIRECT AND INDIRECT METHODS

LO 5 Distinguish between the direct and indirect methods of reporting operating cash flows.

Direct Method

Cash flows from operating activities:		
Cash received from customers	$ 870,000	
Interest and dividends received	10,000	
Cash provided by operating activities		$880,000
Cash paid to suppliers and employees	$(764,000)	
Interest paid	(28,000)	
Income taxes paid	(38,000)	
Cash disbursed for operating activities		(830,000)
Net cash provided by operating activities		$ 50,000

Indirect Method

Net income		$ 65,000
Add: Depreciation expense		40,000
Decrease in accrued interest receivable		1,000
Increase in accounts payable		15,000
Increase in accrued interest liabilities		7,000
Nonoperating loss on sales of marketable securities		4,000
Subtotal		$132,000
Less: Increase in accounts receivable	$30,000	
Increase in inventory	10,000	
Increase in prepaid expenses	3,000	
Decrease in accrued operating expenses payable	6,000	
Decrease in accrued income taxes payable	2,000	
Nonoperating gain on sales of plant assets	31,000	82,000
Net cash provided by operating activities		$ 50,000

To illustrate the similarity in the computations, look briefly at the formulas for computing the cash inflows and outflows shown under the direct method (pages 551–554). Each formula begins with an income statement amount and then adds or subtracts the change during the period in related balance sheet accounts. Now look at our illustration

Changes in Accounts Receivable Receivables increase as revenue is earned and decrease as cash is collected from customers. A net increase in Accounts Receivable over the period indicates that the revenue from credit sales exceeds collections from customers. In other words, part of the revenue recognized increased receivables rather than cash. In our reconciliation of these two amounts, the net increase in Accounts Receivable is *deducted* from net income to determine cash provided by revenue transactions.

On the other hand, a net decrease in Accounts Receivable indicates cash receipts in excess of revenue from credit sales and is added to the amount of net income.

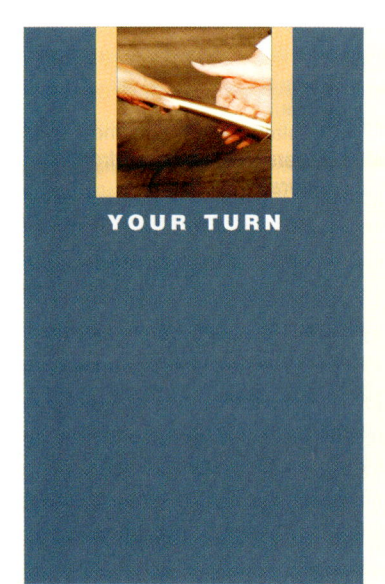

YOUR TURN

You as an Accounts Receivable Manager

Your job is to manage the accounts receivable department for a national home improvement retail chain. Each store in the chain prepares separate financial statements that are evaluated by corporate headquarters and are consolidated to prepare the year-end financial statements sent to investors. The company has a standard policy for customers of 2/10, net/30. That is, customers get a 2% discount if they pay in 10 days, but must pay the full amount within 30 days of the sale. The manager of one of the largest stores in the Northeast has complained that almost all of his store's customers take advantage of the discount. At most stores in the Southwest, however, almost none of the customers take advantage of the discount. The northeastern store manager asked you to make an exception to the standard policy for his store. This manager has requested the discount be dropped to help improve the store's cash flow statement. Will dropping the discount improve the store's cash flows? Would it be ethical for you to drop the standard policy for this store?

*Our comments appear on page 599.

Changes in Inventory The balance in the Inventory account increases as merchandise is purchased and decreases as goods are sold. A net increase in the Inventory account during the period indicates that purchases exceed the cost of goods sold. To reconcile net income with net cash flows, we deduct from net income the amount of these additional purchases (the net increase in the balance of the Inventory account).

A net decrease in the balance of the Inventory account over the period indicates that the cost of goods sold (reported in the income statement) exceeds purchases made during the period. In other words, some of the inventory sold this period was purchased in an earlier period. To the extent that the cost of goods sold consists of a decrease in inventory, cash payment is not required in the current period. Therefore, we add to net income the amount of a net decrease in Inventory.

Changes in Prepaid Expenses Prepaid Expenses appear in the balance sheet as assets. Increases in these assets result from cash payments, and decreases result from expiring amounts being recognized as expenses of the period. A net *increase* over the period in the amount of Prepaid Expenses indicates that cash payments made for these items exceeded the amounts recognized as expense. In determining net cash flows from operating activities, we deduct from net income the net increase in a company's Prepaid Expenses.

A net *decrease* in Prepaid Expenses indicates that cash outlays during the period were less than the amounts deducted as expense in the computation of net income. A net decrease in Prepaid Expenses is added back to net income.

Changes in Accounts Payable Accounts Payable are increased by purchases on account and are reduced by cash payments to suppliers. A net increase in Accounts Payable indicates that the accrual-based figure for purchases, which is included in the cost of goods sold, is greater than the cash payments made to suppliers. Therefore, in converting net income to cash flows, we add back the amount of merchandise purchases financed by a net increase in Accounts Payable.

payable. However, in the reconciliation of net income with net cash flows from operating activities, the change in the liability Deferred Income Taxes is shown separately from the net change in other accrued expenses payable. A net increase in this liability is added to net income; a net decrease is subtracted.

A Helpful Hint Based on Debits and Credits In our preceding discussion, we explained *why* increases and decreases in a number of asset and liability accounts represent differences between the net income and net cash flows for the period. We do not expect you to memorize the effects of all of these changes. Rather, we recommend that you identify the types of transactions that cause a given account balance to increase or decrease and then *evaluate the effects* of these transactions on net income and net cash flows. This type of analysis will enhance your understanding of the relationships between accrual accounting and cash transactions.

However, let us offer you a quick hint. Double-entry accounting provides a simple rule that will let you check your analysis. For those asset and liability accounts that explain timing differences between net income and net cash flows, *a net credit change in the account's balance is always added to net income; a net debit change is always subtracted*. (For practice, test this rule on the adjustments in the summary of the indirect method appearing below. It applies to every adjustment that describes an increase or decrease in a balance sheet account.)

3. *Adjusting for Nonoperating Gains and Losses*
   Nonoperating gains and losses include gains and losses from sales of investments, plant assets, and discontinued operations (which relate to investing activities); and gains and losses on early retirement of debt (which relate to financing activities).

   In a statement of cash flows, cash flows are classified as operating activities, investing activities, or financing activities. Nonoperating gains and losses, by definition, do not affect *operating activities*. However, these gains and losses do enter into the determination of net income. Therefore, in converting net income to net cash flows from operating activities, we *add back any nonoperating losses* and *deduct any nonoperating gains* included in net income. The full cash effect of the transaction is then presented as an investing activity (for example, sale of a building) or as a financing activity (for example, retirement of debt) in the statement of cash flows.

The Indirect Method: A Summary

The adjustments to net income explained in our preceding discussion are summarized as follows:

LO 7
Compute net cash flows from operating activities using the *indirect* method.

> Net income
> **Add:** Depreciation
> Decrease in accounts receivable
> Decrease in inventories
> Decrease in prepaid expenses
> Increase in accounts payable
> Increase in accrued expenses payable
> Increase in deferred income taxes payable
> Nonoperating losses deducted in computing net income
> **Deduct:** Increase in accounts receivable
> Increase in inventories
> Increase in prepaid expenses
> Decrease in accounts payable
> Decrease in accrued expenses payable
> Decrease in deferred income taxes payable
> Nonoperating gains added in computing net income
> Net cash provided by (used in) operating activities

Indirect Method May Be Required in a Supplementary Schedule

The FASB recommends use of the *direct method* in presenting net cash flows from operating activities. The majority of companies, however, elect to use the indirect method. One reason is that the FASB requires companies opting for the direct method to meet an additional reporting requirement.

Companies using the direct method are required to provide a *supplementary schedule* showing the computation of net cash flows from operating activities by the indirect method. However, no supplementary computations are required of companies that present the indirect method computations in their cash flow statements because this same information is already presented in the body of the statement under the indirect method. In the opinion of these authors, this reporting requirement undermines the FASB's efforts to encourage use of the direct method.

The Statement of Cash Flows: A Second Look

We have now completed our explanation of Allison Corporation's statement of cash flows. We have analyzed each type of cash flow by reconciling amounts included in the other two financial statements—the income statement and the balance sheet—to determine the amounts of individual operating, investing, and financing cash flows. In computing cash flows from operating activities, we began by using the direct method in which major categories of both positive and negative cash flows were determined and presented.

Subsequently we illustrated the indirect method to determine the amount of operating cash flows. Rather than adjusting each individual operating cash flow category for changes in balance sheet accounts, these same adjustments are made to net income.

Exhibit 13–5 includes an expanded statement of cash flows for Allison Corporation. This statement uses the direct method for operating activities and includes two supplemental schedules.

Supplementary Schedule A in Exhibit 13–5 illustrates the determination of net cash flows from operating activities by the *indirect method*. The purpose of this schedule is to explain the differences between the reported net income and the net cash flows from operating activities. This supplementary schedule also is required of companies that use the direct method of reporting operating cash flows.

Supplementary Schedule B in Exhibit 13–5 discloses any noncash aspects of the company's investing and financing activities. This type of supplementary schedule is

ALLISON CORPORATION
Statement of Cash Flows
For the Year Ended December 31, 2002

Exhibit 13–5

ALLISON CORPORATION (EXPANDED) STATEMENT OF CASH FLOWS

DIRECT

Cash flows from operating activities:		
Net cash provided by operating activities (see Supplementary Schedule A)		$ 50,000
Cash flows from investing activities:		
Purchases of marketable securities	$ (65,000)	
Proceeds from sales of marketable securities	40,000	
Loans made to borrowers	(17,000)	
Collections on loans	12,000	
Cash paid to acquire plant assets (see Supplementary Schedule B)	(160,000)	
Proceeds from sales of plant assets	75,000	
Net cash used in investing activities		(115,000)
Cash flows from financing activities:		
Proceeds from short-term borrowing	$ 45,000	
Payments to settle short-term debts	(55,000)	
Proceeds from issuing bonds payable	100,000	
Proceeds from issuing capital stock	50,000	
Dividends paid	(40,000)	
Net cash provided by financing activities		100,000
Net increase (decrease) in cash		$ 35,000
Cash and cash equivalents, Jan. 1		20,000
Cash and cash equivalents, Dec. 31		$ 55,000

Supplementary Schedule A: Net Cash Provided by Operating Activities

Net income		$ 65,000
Add: Depreciation expense	40,000	
Decrease in accrued interest receivable	1,000	
Increase in accounts payable	15,000	
Increase in accrued liabilities	7,000	
Nonoperating loss on sales of marketable securities	4,000	
Subtotal		$ 132,000
Less: Increase in accounts receivable	$ 30,000	
Increase in inventory	10,000	
Increase in prepaid expenses	3,000	
Decrease in accrued liabilities	8,000	
Nonoperating gain on sales of plant assets	31,000	82,000
Net cash provided by operating activities		$ 50,000

Supplementary Schedule B: Noncash Investing and Financing Activities

Purchases of plant assets	$ 200,000
Less: Portion financed through issuance of long-term debt	40,000
Cash paid to acquire plant assets	$ 160,000

My Notes

Notice this supplementary schedule illustrates the indirect method of determining cash flows from operations

---

required whenever some aspects of the company's investing and financing activities do not coincide with cash flows occurring within the current period, but still have important impacts on the company's financial position.

How would the statement of cash flows in Exhibit 13–5 differ if the indirect method were used? The information included in Supplementary Schedule A would be moved up into the "Cash flows from operating activities," section of the financial statement and would no longer be required as a supplemental disclosure. In fact, this is one reason for the popularity of the indirect method. Because it is required to be disclosed if the direct method is used, many companies simply prefer to include the reconciliation of net income to net cash from operating activities in the body of the statement of cash flows and avoid the need for the supplemental disclosure of that same information.

FINANCIAL ANALYSIS

The users of a statement of cash flows usually are particularly interested in the *net cash flows from operating activities*. Is the amount large enough to provide for necessary replacements of plant assets and maturing liabilities? And if so, is there enough left for the current dividend to look secure—or even be increased?

Consider two competitors in the import craft supplies business, Gonzalez, Inc., and Alvarez Company. These companies have approximately the same size assets, liabilities, and sales. Selected information from their most recent statements of cash flows follows:

	Beginning Cash Balance	Net Cash Flow from (in thousands)			Ending Cash Balance
		Operating Activities	Investing Activities	Financing Activities	
Gonzalez	$150	$600	$(500)	$400	$650
Alvarez	150	50	500	(50)	650

Which company is in the stronger cash flow position? Although both have the same beginning and ending cash balances ($150,000 and $650,000, respectively), Gonzalez is in the stronger position because of its strong operating cash flows of $600,000. Gonzalez has been able to invest $500,000 in operating assets, while financing only $400,000 and still have a $650,000 ending cash balance. Alvarez, on the other hand, has generated only a small amount of cash from operations ($50,000) and has sold assets to generate cash ($500,000) to support its ending cash balance. Also, Alvarez has not been able to finance its assets acquisitions and even has had to reduce its financing, possibly due to its weak operating cash flows.

Assume further that each company has current liabilities at the end of the year totaling $500,000. While both are in an equally good cash position with regard to paying these liabilities, Gonzalez followed a much more positive path to get in this position than did Alvarez. Whether Alvarez will be able to sustain its cash position over time, and therefore be able to meet its recurring obligations in the future, is questionable.

Even more important than net cash flows from operating activities in any one year is the *trend* in cash flows over a period of years—and the *consistency* of that trend from year to year. From everyone's perspective, the best results are net cash flows from operating activities that increase each year by a substantial—but also predictable—percentage.[5]

Free Cash Flow Many analysts put a company's cash flows into perspective by computing an amount called **free cash flow**. Free cash flow is intended to represent the cash flow available to management for discretionary purposes, *after* the company has met all of its basic obligations relating to business operations.

The term *free cash flow* is widely cited within the business community. Different analysts compute this measure in different ways because there is no widespread agreement as to the basic obligations relating to business operations. For example, are all expenditures for plant assets "basic obligations," or only those expenditures made to maintain the current level of productive capacity?

---

[5] Percentage change is the dollar amount of change from one year to the next, expressed as a percentage of (divided by) the amount from the *earlier* of the two years. For example, if net cash provided by operating activities was $100,000 in the first year and $120,000 in the second year, the percentage increase is 20%, computed as follows: ($120,000 − $100,000) ÷ $100,000.

Financial Analysis

One common method of computing free cash flow is to deduct from the net cash flows from operating activities any net cash used for investments in plant assets and any dividends paid. This computation follows, using information from the Allison Corporation statement of cash flows shown earlier.

Net cash flows from operating activities		$ 50,000
Less: Net cash used for acquiring plant assets ($160,000 − $75,000 proceeds)	$85,000	
Dividends paid	40,000	125,000
Free cash flow		$(75,000)

My Notes

What's left for discretionary purposes?

This computation suggests that Allison Corporation *did not* generate enough cash from operations to meet its basic obligations. Thus management had to raise cash from other sources. But, of course, an analyst always should look behind the numbers. For example, was Allison's purchase of plant assets during the year a basic obligation, or did it represent a discretionary expansion of the business?

As we have stated throughout this text, no single ratio or financial measurement ever tells the whole story.

Annotated Statement of Cash Flows: The Rowe Companies

A recent statement of cash flows of **The Rowe Companies** appears in Exhibit 13–6. We have added notations that highlight some of the concepts emphasized in this chapter.

THE ROWE COMPANIES
Consolidated Statement of Cash Flows
Years Ended January 31, 1998, 1999, 2000

(in thousands of dollars)	2000	1999	1998
Increase (Decrease) in Cash			
Cash flows from operating activities:			
Cash received from customers	$ 364,863	$ 282,710	$ 189,437
Cash paid to suppliers and employees	(340,033)	(262,017)	(180,372)
Income taxes paid, net of refunds	(6,183)	(7,726)	(6,403)
Interest paid	(5,693)	(2,686)	(694)
Interest received	288	159	337
Other receipts—net	1,156	1,684	706
Net cash and cash equivalents provided by operating activities	14,398	12,124	3,011
Cash flows from investing activities:			
Proceeds from sale of property and equipment	21	19	—
Capital expenditures	(9,155)	(8,830)	(6,951)
Payments to acquire businesses	(5,160)	(8,892)	(10,442)
Investment in Storehouse, Inc.	—	—	(2,500)
Net cash used in investing activities	(14,294)	(17,703)	(19,893)
Cash flows from financing activities:			
Net borrowings (payments) under line of credit	(164)	2,071	362
Proceeds from issuance of long-term debt	13,020	25,132	25,000
Payments to reduce long-term debt	(11,922)	(14,522)	(1,444)
Proceeds from issuance of common stock	51	460	968
Dividends paid	(1,849)	(1,714)	(1,498)
Purchase of treasury stock	(951)	(3,224)	(4,876)
Net cash provided by (used in) financing activities	(1,815)	8,203	18,512
Net increase (decrease) in cash and cash equivalents	(1,711)	2,624	1,630
Cash at beginning of year	5,104	2,480	850
Cash at end of year	$ 3,393	$ 5,104	$ 2,480

Exhibit 13–6

THE ROWE COMPANIES STATEMENT OF CASH FLOWS (DIRECT METHOD)

My Notes

Rowe uses the direct method and operations is a net source of cash

My Notes

Investing activities are net uses of cash

My Notes

Financing activities are net sources of cash in some years and net uses in other years

My Notes

The cash balance ties to the balance sheet

Exhibit 13–6

THE ROWE COMPANIES STATEMENT OF CASH FLOWS (DIRECT METHOD) (continued)

THE ROWE COMPANIES
Consolidated Statement of Cash Flows
Years Ended January 31, 1998, 1999, 2000

Reconciliation of Net Earnings to Net Cash Provided by Operating Activities

(in thousands of dollars)	2000	1999	1998
Net earnings	$ 3,544	$ 13,901	$ 11,200
Adjustments to reconcile net income to net cash provided by operating activities, net of disposition of business:			
Loss on disposition of Wexford	5,455	—	—
Depreciation and amortization	8,581	6,165	3,773
Provision for deferred compensation	816	1,083	762
Payments made for deferred compensation	(160)	(319)	(590)
Deferred income taxes	(2,099)	(472)	545
Provision for losses on accounts receivable (recoveries)	1,485	413	(1,285)
Loss on disposition of assets	29	4	—
Change in operating assets and liabilities, net of effects of acquisition and disposition of businesses:			
Decrease (increase) in accounts receivable	5,564	(9,379)	(3,963)
Decrease (increase) in inventories	(832)	(5,692)	(2,164)
Decrease (increase) in prepaid expenses and other	(887)	(795)	(468)
Decrease (increase) in other assets	472	(1,210)	378
Increase (decrease) in accounts payable	(4,750)	3,830	(2,549)
Increase (decrease) in accrued expenses	(1,715)	2,170	(2,619)
Increase (decrease) in customer deposits	(1,105)	2,425	(9)
Total adjustments	10,854	(1,777)	(8,189)
Net cash provided by operating activities	$ 14,398	$ 12,124	$ 3,011
Supplemental Disclosures of Cash Flows:			
Fair value of assets acquired other than cash		$ 37,272	$ 31,955
Liabilities assumed		(28,380)	(18,513)
Convertible debentures issued		—	(3,000)
Payments to acquire businesses		$ 8,892	$ 10,442

My Notes
Supplemental schedule uses the indirect method

My Notes
Supplemental disclosures explain noncash transactions

MANAGING CASH FLOWS

Management can do much to influence the cash flows of a particular period. In fact, it has a responsibility to manage cash flows. No business can afford to run out of cash and default on its obligations. Even being a few days late in meeting payrolls, or paying suppliers or creditors, can severely damage important business relationships. Thus one of management's most basic responsibilities is to ensure that the business has enough cash to meet its obligations as they come due.

Budgeting: The Primary Cash Management Tool

The primary tool used by management to anticipate and shape future cash flows is a *cash budget*. A **cash budget** is a *forecast* of future cash receipts and payments. This budget is *not* a financial statement and is not widely distributed to people outside of the organization. To managers, however, it is among the most useful of all accounting reports.

In many ways, a cash budget is similar to a statement of cash flows. However, the budget shows the results *expected in future periods,* rather than those achieved in the past. Also, the cash budget is more *detailed,* usually showing expected cash flows month-by-month and separately for every department within the organization.

Cash budgets serve many purposes. Among the most important are:

Managing Cash Flows

- Encouraging managers to plan and coordinate the activities of their departments in advance.
- Providing managers with advance notice of the resources at their disposal and the results they are expected to achieve.
- Providing targets useful in evaluating departmental performance.
- Providing advance warnings of potential cash shortages.

You as a Student

How is predicting future cash flows—receipts and outlays—useful in your daily life? Forecast your cash outlays in the coming month for: (1) housing, (2) food, and (3) other. Where will the cash come from to finance these outlays?

*Our comments appear on page 599.

YOUR TURN

What Priority Should Managers Give to Increasing Net Cash Flows?

Creditors and investors look to a company's cash flows to protect their investment and provide future returns. Trends in key cash flows (such as from operations and free cash flow) affect a company's credit rating, stock price, and access to additional investment capital. For these reasons, management is under constant pressure to improve the key measures of cash flow. Unfortunately, the pressure to report higher cash flows in the current period may *conflict* with managers' long-run responsibilities.

Short-Term Results versus Long-Term Growth Often, short-term operating results can be improved at the expense of long-term growth. For example, reducing expenditures for developing new products will increase earnings and net cash flows in the current period. But over time, this strategy may lessen the company's competitiveness and long-term profitability.

In contrast, the strategies most likely to promote long-term growth may *reduce* earnings and cash flows in the near term—often by large amounts.

LO 8
Discuss the likely effects of various business strategies on cash flows.

Merck & Company, Inc., the world's largest pharmaceutical company, spends as much as *$1.3 billion* each year in its efforts to develop new products. And even after **Merck** makes a "breakthrough" discovery, it takes years of testing before a new product is brought to market.

Most expenditures for research and development (R&D) are paid in cash and charged immediately to expense. Thus, in any given year, **Merck**'s R&D costs *reduce* both earnings and cash flow by more than $1 billion (before taxes). Yet **Merck**'s ongoing commitment to R&D has been a key factor in the company's success.

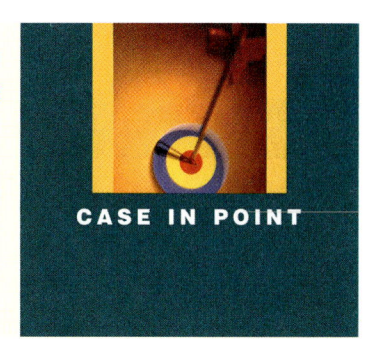

CASE IN POINT

One-Time Boosts to Cash Flows Some strategies can increase the net cash flows of the current period, but *without having much effect* on future cash flows. Such strategies include collecting receivables more quickly and reducing the size of inventory.

Assume, for example, that a company offers 60-day terms to its credit customers. Thus credit sales made in January are collected in March, and credit sales made in February are collected in April. Notice that in each month, the company is collecting about *one month's* amount of credit sales.

Now assume that on March 1, the company changes its policies to allow only *30-day* credit terms. In April, the company will collect *two months* of credit sales—those made in February (under the former 60-day terms) *and* those made in March (under the new 30-day terms).

This significantly increases the cash received from customers for the month of April. But it does not signal higher cash flows for the months ahead. In May, the company will collect only those credit sales made in April. Thus it quickly returns to the pattern of collecting about *one month's* credit sales in the current month. Shortening the collection period provided only a one-time boost in cash receipts.

A similar one-time boost may be achieved by reducing the size of inventory. This reduces the need for purchasing merchandise, *but only while inventory levels are falling.* Once the company stabilizes the size of its inventory at the new and lower level, its monthly purchases must return to approximately the quantity of goods sold during the period.

Some Strategies for Permanent Improvements in Cash Flow

Several strategies may improve cash flows in *both* the short and long term. These are *deferring income taxes, peak pricing,* and developing an *effective product mix.*

Deferring Income Taxes *Deferring* income taxes means using accounting methods for income tax purposes that legally postpone the payment of income taxes. An example is using an *accelerated depreciation method* for income tax purposes.

Deferring taxes may benefit a growing business *every year*. Thus it is an effective and popular cash management strategy.[6]

Peak Pricing Some businesses have more customers than they can handle—at least at certain times of the day or year. Examples of such businesses include popular restaurants, resort hotels, telephone companies, and providers of electricity.

Peak pricing is a strategy of using sales prices both to increase revenue and to ration goods and services when total demand exceeds supply (or capacity). A higher price is charged during the peak periods of customer demand, and a lower price during off-peak periods. Peak pricing has two related goals. First, it *increases the seller's revenue* during the periods of greatest demand. Second, it *shifts* some of the demand to off-peak periods, when the business is better able to service additional customers.

CASE IN POINT

Beach House is a popular seafood restaurant in Cardiff-by-the-Sea. A lobster dinner regularly costs $16.95. But from *4:30 to 6:00 P.M.*, it's only *$9.95*. Why? Because prior to 6:00 P.M. Beach House has lots of empty tables. Later, the restaurant becomes so crowded that it often has to turn customers away.

In many situations, peak pricing benefits the business *and the public*. Off-peak prices generally are *lower* than if peak pricing were not employed. Thus peak pricing may make goods and services available to customers who otherwise could not afford them. Also, peak pricing may prevent systems, such as cellular telephones, from becoming so overloaded that they simply cannot function.

It is important to recognize, however, that peak pricing is *not always appropriate*. For example, we would not expect hospitals or physicians to raise their prices during epidemics or natural disasters. The alternative to peak pricing is a single price all the time. In a single-price situation, demand in excess of capacity normally is handled on the basis of first-come, first-served.

---

[6] The Modified Accelerated Cost Recovery System (MACRS) is an accelerated method widely used for income tax purposes. Deferred income taxes were discussed further in Chapter 10. The reason a growing business can benefit from deferred taxes *every year* is that each year it defers a *greater amount* than comes due from the past.

Managing Cash Flows

You as a Marketing Manager

Assume you are the marketing manager for **Toys 'R' Us** (the international chain). In the 1996 Christmas season, a doll called Tickle-Me-Elmo had a suggested retail price of $29.95. The doll became overwhelmingly popular and was in short supply. Customers who bought the doll were able to resell it for *hundreds of dollars* just by running a classified ad in the newspaper.

© James M. Mejuto

Much news coverage was given to the phenomenal prices these dolls commanded. **Toys 'R' Us** easily could have sold Tickle-Me-Elmo's for $100 or more.

Would you have raised Elmo's price during this temporary period of excess demand? Explain your reasoning.

*Our comments appear on page 599.

YOUR TURN

Develop an Effective Product Mix   Another tool for increasing revenue and cash receipts is the mix of products offered for sale. The dual purposes of an effective **product mix** are to (1) increase total sales and (2) increase gross margins (that is, the excess of the selling price over the cost of the product).

Some products complement one another, meaning the customer who buys one product often may purchase the other. Common examples of **complementary products** include french fries at a hamburger stand, snacks at a movie theater, and a car wash connected to a gas station.

Some complementary products are *essential* to satisfying the customer. (Would you be happy at a sports stadium that didn't sell food?) Others increase sales by *attracting customers* who also purchase other types of merchandise.

Some complementary products appear to be only incidental to the company's main product lines. But, in reality, these incidental items may *be* the company's most important products.

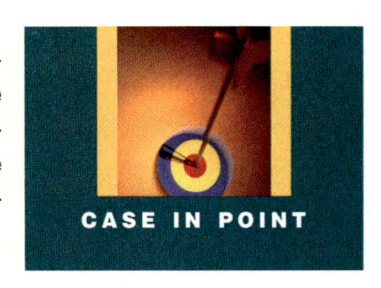

Remco Business Products, Inc., sells a variety of office products, including copy machines. Like most businesses that sell major appliances, it also sells long-term service contracts to provide maintenance and repairs at a fixed annual fee. These service contracts actually are **Remco**'s most profitable product. In fact, if you purchase a service contract, you won't need to buy a copier. **Remco** will lend you one for the life of the service contract at no additional charge.

CASE IN POINT

Whether you are an investor, a manager, or a taxpayer, you need to understand the difference between cash flows and the accrual basis of accounting. Accrual-based information is used in determining the profitability and the financial position of a business—especially a business of considerable financial strength. But in evaluating such factors as liquidity, the prospects for short-term survival, and the ability of a business to seize investment opportunities, cash flows may be more relevant than accrual-based measurements.

CASH EFFECTS

CONCLUDING REMARKS

In this chapter we have discussed the importance of the statement of cash flows in providing information for investors and creditors. We have seen how we convert accrual accounting information to cash-based information and arrange that information so that investors and creditors can better understand the cash effects of a company's operating, investing, and financing activities. In the next chapter we take a broader look at financial statement analysis, including how information from the cash flow statement is combined with information from the other financial statements, to better understand a company's financial activities.

Managers and investors alike must look beyond changes in earnings and cash flows from one period to the next. They must consider the factors that *cause* these changes and how they may affect future operations. There is more to financial statement analysis than looking at current numbers and short-term trends. The informed decision maker must *understand the company's business activities* and *anticipate the long-term effects* of its business strategies.

A SECOND LOOK
HARRAH'S ENTERTAINMENT, INC.

As we began Chapter 13, we took a quick look at **Harrah's Entertainment, Inc.**, observing that the company's cash increased by $65,621,000 during 2000. Now that we have learned more about the three primary sources of cash flows, we can better understand how **Harrah's** cash increased so much during 2000.

Following is a summary of the major categories of cash flows for **Harrah's Entertainment, Inc.**, for 2000, 1999 and 1998.

(dollars in thousands)	2000	1999	1998
Beginning cash balance	$233,581	$158,995	$116,443
Net cash from:			
Operating activities	$547,568	514,406	300,371
Investing activities	(719,582)	(184,364)	(763,238)
Financing activities	237,635	(255,456)	505,419
Ending cash balance	$299,202	$233,581	$158,995

What conclusions can you draw about **Harrah's** cash flows during this three-year period? The following items are important in assessing the company's cash position:

- Cash has consistently risen over the three-year period from $116,443 thousand at the beginning of 1998 to $299,202 thousand at the end of 2000.

- Operating activities have provided strong cash flows each year, amounting to much more than both beginning and ending cash balances each year.

- The company has consistently invested in assets over the three-year period, with cash flows from investing activities being a large negative number (i.e., cash is being paid out) each year.

- The company's use of financing for asset acquisitions has varied from year to year, providing a great deal of cash in 1998, using cash in 1999, and again providing cash in 2000.

SUPPLEMENTAL TOPIC

A WORKSHEET FOR PREPARING A STATEMENT OF CASH FLOWS

LO 9
Explain how a worksheet may be helpful in preparing a statement of cash flows.

A statement of cash flows is developed by *systematically analyzing changes in the noncash balance sheet accounts.* This process can be formalized and documented through the preparation of a specially designed worksheet. The worksheet also provides the

Supplemental Topic

accountant with visual assurance that the changes in balance sheet accounts have been fully explained.

Data for an Illustration

We will illustrate the worksheet approach using the 2002 financial data of Auto Supply Co.[1] Shown in Exhibit 13–7 are the balances in Auto's balance sheet accounts at the beginning and end of 2002. (Please notice in this illustration that the account balances at the end of the current year appear in the *right-hand* column. This format also is used in the worksheet.)

Exhibit 13–7

AUTO SUPPLY CO. BALANCE SHEETS

My Notes

Changes in the noncash accounts are the key to identifying cash flows

AUTO SUPPLY CO.
Comparative Balance Sheets

	December 31, 2001	December 31, 2002
Assets		
Cash	$ 50,000	$ 45,000
Marketable Securities	40,000	25,000
Accounts Receivable	320,000	330,000
Inventory	240,000	235,000
Plant and Equipment (net of accumulated depreciation)	600,000	640,000
Totals	$1,250,000	$1,275,000
Liabilities & Stockholders' Equity		
Accounts Payable	$ 150,000	$ 160,000
Accrued Expenses Payable	60,000	45,000
Mortgage Note Payable (long-term)	–0–	70,000
Bonds Payable (due in 2015)	500,000	350,000
Capital Stock (no par value)	160,000	160,000
Retained Earnings	380,000	490,000
Totals	$1,250,000	$1,275,000

Additional Information The following information also is used in the preparation of the worksheet. (Accrual-based measurements appear in **blue**; cash flows, in **red**.)

1. Net income for the year amounted to *$250,000*. Cash dividends of *$140,000* were declared and paid.
2. Auto's only noncash expense was depreciation, which totaled *$60,000*.
3. Marketable securities costing *$15,000* were sold for *$35,000* cash, resulting in a *$20,000* nonoperating gain.
4. The company purchased plant assets for *$100,000*, making a *$30,000* cash down payment and issuing a *$70,000* mortgage note payable for the balance of the purchase price.

The Worksheet

Auto Supply Co. reports cash flows from operating activities by the *indirect method*.[2] A worksheet for preparing a statement of cash flows appears in Exhibit 13–8.

---

[1] Our example involving Allison Corporation was quite comprehensive. Therefore, a worksheet for Allison Corporation would be too long and detailed for use as an introductory illustration of a worksheet for the statement of cash flows.

[2] If the worksheet utilizes the direct method, numerous subclassifications are required within the operating activities section. Such worksheets are illustrated in more advanced accounting courses.

To set up the worksheet, the company's balance sheet accounts are listed in the top portion of the worksheet, with the beginning balances in the first column and the year-end balances in the last (right-hand) column. (For purposes of illustration, we have shown these accounts and account balances in **black**.)

The two middle columns are used to (1) explain the changes in each balance sheet account over the year and (2) indicate how each change affected cash.

Entries in the Two Middle Columns The entries in the *top portion of the worksheet* summarize the transactions recorded in the account over the year. (Because these entries summarize transactions recorded on the accrual basis, they are shown in **blue**.)

For each summary entry in the top portion of the worksheet, we make an offsetting entry (in the opposite column) in the *bottom portion* of the worksheet indicating the *cash effects* of the transactions. These cash effects are classified as operating, investing, or financing activities and are explained with a descriptive caption. (Entries representing the *cash effects* of transactions and the related descriptive captions appear in **red**.)

Entries in the two middle columns may be made in any sequence, but we recommend the following approach:

1. Explain the change in the Retained Earnings account.
2. Account for depreciation expense (and any other noncash expenses.)
3. Account for timing differences between net income and cash flows from operating activities.
4. Explain any remaining changes in balance sheet accounts *other than Cash*. (Hint: Changes in asset accounts represent investing activities; changes in liability and equity accounts represent financing activities.)
5. Compute and record the net increase or decrease in cash.

Using this approach, the entries in our illustrated worksheet are explained next.

Entry

> **My Notes**
> Step 1: Explain the changes in retained earnings

1. Auto's net income explains a $250,000 *credit* to the Retained Earnings account. In the bottom portion of the working paper, and offsetting entry is made in the *Sources* column and is classified as an operating activity.[3]

2. Cash dividends of $140,000 caused a *debit* to the Retained Earnings account during 2002. The offsetting entry falls into the *Uses* column; payments of dividends are classified as a financing activity.

With these first two entries, we have explained how Auto's Retained Earnings account increased during 2002 from $380,000 to $490,000.

> **My Notes**
> Step 2: Account for noncash expenses

3. Auto's only noncash expense was depreciation. In the top portion of the worksheet, depreciation explains a $60,000 credit (decrease) in Plant and Equipment (which includes the Accumulated Depreciation accounts). The offsetting entry in the bottom of the worksheet is placed in the Sources column. We have explained that depreciation is not really a source of cash, but that it *is* added back to net income as a step in computing the cash flows from operating activities.

> **My Notes**
> Step 3: Account for timing differences

4–7. Fluctuations in current assets and current liabilities create *timing differences* between net income and the net cash flows from operating activities. In the top portion of the worksheet, entries (4) through (7) summarize the changes in these current asset and current liability accounts. In the bottom portion, they show how these changes affect the computation of cash flows from operating activities.

---

[3] When the *indirect method* is used, net income serves as the *starting point* for computing net cash flows from operating activities.

8. In 2002, Auto sold marketable securities with a cost of $15,000 for $35,000 cash, resulting in a $20,000 nonoperating gain. In the top portion of the worksheet, the entry explains the $15,000 credit change in the Marketable Securities account. In the bottom portion, it reports cash proceeds of $35,000. The difference? The $20,000 nonoperating gain, which is *removed from the Operating Activities section* of the worksheet and included instead within the amount reported as "Proceeds from sales of marketable securities in the investing activities category."

9. Auto purchased $100,000 in plant assets, paying $30,000 cash and issuing a $70,000 note payable. These events explain a $100,000 debit in Plant and Equipment and the $70,000 credit change in Mortgage Note Payable; they involved a cash outlay of $30,000, which is classified as an investing activity. (The $70,000 financed by issuance of a note payable is a *noncash* investing and financing activity.)

10. The $150,000 debit change in Auto's Bonds Payable account indicates that this amount of the liability has been repaid—that is, $150,000 in bonds has been retired. This is included in the financing activities category.

> **My Notes**
>
> Step 4: Explain any remaining changes in noncash accounts

At this point, we should check to determine that our entries in the two middle columns *fully explain* the differences between the beginning and ending balance of each noncash balance sheet account. If the top portion of the worksheet explains the changes in every noncash account, the bottom section should include all of the cash flows for the year.

(x) We now total the Sources (cash increases) and Uses (cash decreases) columns in the bottom portion of the worksheet. The difference between these column subtotals represents the *net increase or decrease* in cash. In our example, the Sources column totals $360,000, while the Uses column totals $365,000, indicating a *$5,000 decrease* in cash over the period. Notice that this is exactly the amount by which Cash decreased during 2002: $50,000 − $45,000 = $5,000. Our last entry, labeled *(x)*, explains the credit change in the Cash account at the top of the worksheet and brings the bottom of the worksheet into balance.

> **My Notes**
>
> Step 5: Compute and record the net change in cash

The formal statement of cash flows, reporting the cash flows from operating activities by the indirect method, can be prepared directly from the bottom portion of this worksheet. In Exhibit 13–9, amounts appearing in accrual-based accounting records are shown in blue; cash flows appear in red.

Exhibit 13-8

WORKSHEET FOR A STATEMENT OF CASH FLOWS

My Notes

Up here we summarize the changes in each noncash account

My Notes

Down here we identify and classify the related cash effects of these changes

- Cash provided by operations— $280,000
- Cash provided by investing activities— $5,000
- Cash used in financing activities— $290,000

AUTO SUPPLY CO.
Worksheet for a Statement of Cash Flows
For the Year Ended December 31, 2002

Effects of Transactions

Balance sheet effects:	Beginning Balance	Debit Changes	Credit Changes	Ending Balance
Assets				
Cash and Cash Equivalents	50,000		(x) 5,000	45,000
Marketable Securities	40,000		(8) 15,000	25,000
Accounts Receivable	320,000	(4) 10,000		330,000
Inventory	240,000		(5) 5,000	235,000
Plant and Equipment (net of accumulated depreciation)	600,000	(9) 100,000	(3) 60,000	640,000
Totals	1,250,000			1,275,000
Liabilities & Stockholders' Equity				
Accounts Payable	150,000		(6) 10,000	160,000
Accrued Expenses Payable	60,000	(7) 15,000		45,000
Mortgage Note Payable	–0–		(9) 70,000	70,000
Bonds Payable	500,000	(10) 150,000		350,000
Capital Stock	160,000			160,000
Retained Earnings	380,000	(2) 140,000	(1) 250,000	490,000
Totals	1,250,000	415,000	415,000	1,275,000

Cash effects:		Sources	Uses	
Operating activities:				
Net income		(1) 250,000		
Depreciation expense		(3) 60,000		
Increase in accounts receivable			(4) 10,000	
Decrease in inventory		(5) 5,000		
Increase in accounts payable		(6) 10,000		
Decrease in accrued expenses payable			(7) 15,000	
Gain on sales of marketable securities			(8) 20,000	
Investing activities:				
Proceeds from sales of marketable securities		(8) 35,000		
Cash paid to acquire plant assets			(9) 30,000	
Financing activities:				
Dividends paid			(2) 140,000	
Payments to retire bonds payable			(10) 150,000	
Subtotals		360,000	365,000	
Net decrease in cash		(x) 5,000		
Totals		365,000	365,000	

AUTO SUPPLY CO.
Statement of Cash Flows
For the Year Ended December 31, 2002

Cash flows from operating activities:

Net income		$250,000
Add: Depreciation expense		60,000
Decrease in inventory		5,000
Increase in accounts payable		10,000
Subtotal		$325,000
Less: Increase in accounts receivable	$ 10,000	
Decrease in accrued expenses payable	15,000	
Gain on sales of marketable securities	20,000	45,000
Net cash provided by operating activities		$280,000

Cash flows from investing activities:

Proceeds from sales of marketable securities	$ 35,000	
Cash paid to acquire plant assets (see supplementary schedule below)	(30,000)	
Net cash provided by investing activities		5,000

Cash flows from financing activities:

Dividends paid	$(140,000)	
Payments to retire bonds payable	(150,000)	
Net cash used in financing activities		(290,000)
Net decrease in cash		$ (5,000)
Cash and cash equivalents, Dec. 31, 2001		50,000
Cash and cash equivalents, Dec. 31, 2002		$ 45,000

Supplementary Schedule: Noncash Investing and Financing Activities

Purchases of plant assets	$100,000
Less: Portion financed through issuance of long-term debt	70,000
Cash paid to acquire plant assets	$ 30,000

Exhibit 13–9

AUTO SUPPLY CO. STATEMENT OF CASH FLOWS

My Notes

Compare the content of this statement with the worksheet in Exhibit 13–8

END-OF-CHAPTER REVIEW

SUMMARY OF LEARNING OBJECTIVES

LO 1
Explain the purposes and uses of a statement of cash flows.
The primary purpose of a statement of cash flows is to provide information about the cash receipts and cash payments of the entity, and how they relate to the entity's operating, investing, and financing activities. Readers of financial statements use this information to assess the liquidity of a business and to evaluate its ability to generate positive cash flows in future periods, pay dividends, and finance growth.

LO 2
Describe how cash transactions are classified in a statement of cash flows.
Cash flows are classified as (1) operating activities, (2) investing activities, or (3) financing activities. Receipts and payments of interest are classified as operating activities.

LO 3
Compute the major cash flows relating to operating activities.
The major operating cash flows are (1) cash received from customers, (2) cash paid to suppliers and employees, (3) interest and dividends received, (4) interest paid, and (5) income taxes paid. These cash flows are computed by converting the income statement amounts for revenue, cost of goods sold, and expenses from the accrual basis to the cash basis. This is done by adjusting the income statement amounts for changes occurring over the period in related balance sheet accounts.

LO 4
Compute the cash flows relating to investing and financing activities.
Cash flows from investing and financing activities are determined by examining the entries in the related asset and liability accounts, along with any related gains or losses shown in the income statement. Debit entries in asset accounts represent purchases of assets (an investing activity). Credit entries in asset accounts represent the cost of assets sold. The amount of these credit entries must be adjusted by any gains or losses recognized on these sales transactions.

Debit entries to liability accounts represent repayment of debt, while credit entries represent borrowing. Both types of transactions are classified as financing activities. Other financing activities include the issuance of stock (indicated by credits to the paid-in capital accounts) and payment of dividends (indicated by a debit change in the Retained Earnings account).

LO 5
Distinguish between the direct and indirect methods of reporting operating cash flows.
The direct and indirect methods are alternative formats for reporting net cash flows from operating activities. The *direct* method shows the specific cash inflows and outflows comprising the operating activities of the business. By the *indirect* method, the computation begins with accrual-based net income and then makes adjustments necessary to arrive at net cash flows from operating activities. Both methods result in the same dollar amount of net cash flows from operating activities.

LO 6
Explain why net income differs from net cash flows from operating activities.
Net income differs from net operating cash flows for several reasons. One reason is noncash expenses, such as depreciation and the amortization of intangible assets. These expenses, which require no cash outlays when they are recognized, reduce net income but do not require cash payments. Another reason is the many timing differences existing between the recognition of revenue and expense and the occurrence of the underlying cash flows. Finally, nonoperating gains and losses enter into the determination of net income, but the related cash flows are classified as investing or financing activities, not operating activities.

LO 7
Compute net cash flows from operating activities using the *indirect* method.
The indirect method uses net income (as reported in the income statement) as the starting point in the computation of net cash flows from operating activities. Adjustments to net income necessary to arrive at net cash flows from operating activities are described in three categories: noncash expenses, timing differences, and nonoperating gains and losses. Adjustments reconcile net income (accrual basis) to net cash flows from operating activities. Specific adjustments from each category are illustrated in the summary analysis of the indirect method on page 564.

LO 8
Discuss the likely effects of various business strategies on cash flows.
It is difficult to predict the *extent* to which a business strategy will affect cash flows. However, an informed decision maker should understand the *direction* in which a strategy is likely to affect cash flows—both in the short term and over a longer term.

Demonstration Problem

*LO 9
Explain how a worksheet may be helpful in preparing a statement of cash flows.
A worksheet can be used to analyze the changes in balance sheet accounts other than Cash and, thereby, determine the related cash flows. In the top portion of the worksheet, entries are made summarizing the changes in each noncash account. In the bottom half, offsetting entries are made to represent the cash effects of the transactions summarized in the top portion. The entries in the bottom half of the worksheet are classified into the same categories as in a statement of cash flows—operating, investing, and financing. The statement of cash flows then is prepared from the data in the bottom portion of the worksheet.

KEY TERMS INTRODUCED OR EMPHASIZED IN CHAPTER 13

accrual basis (p. 547) A method of summarizing operating results in terms of revenue earned and expenses incurred, rather than cash receipts or cash payments.

cash basis (p. 552) The practice of summarizing operating results in terms of cash receipts and cash payments, rather than revenue earned or expenses incurred.

cash budget (p. 568) A detailed forecast of expected future cash receipts, usually organized department by department and month by month for the coming year.

cash equivalents (p. 547) Highly liquid short-term investments, such as Treasury bills, money market funds, and commercial paper. For purposes of preparing a statement of cash flows, money held in cash equivalents is considered the same as cash. Thus transfers between a bank account and cash equivalents are not considered receipts or disbursements of cash.

cash flows (p. 544) A term describing both cash receipts (inflows) and cash payments (outflows).

complementary products (p. 571) Products that "fit together"—that tie in with a company's other products. As a result, customers attracted to one product may also purchase others.

financing activities (pp. 545–546) Transactions such as borrowing, repaying borrowed amounts, raising equity capital, or making distributions to owners. The cash effects of these transactions are reported in the financing activities section of the statement of cash flows. Noncash aspects of these transactions are disclosed in a supplementary schedule.

free cash flow (p. 566) The portion of the annual net cash flows from operating activities that remains available for discretionary purposes after the basic obligations of the business have been met. Can be computed in several different ways.

investing activities (pp. 545–546) Transactions involving acquisitions or sales of investments or plant assets and making or collecting loans. The cash aspects of these transactions are shown in the investing activities section of the statement of cash flows. Noncash aspects of these transactions are disclosed in a supplementary schedule to this financial statement.

operating activities (p. 545) Transactions entering into the determination of net income, with the exception of gains and losses relating to financing or investing activities. The category includes such transactions as selling goods or services, earning investment income, and incurring costs and expenses, such as payments to suppliers and employees, interest and income taxes. The cash effects of these transactions are reflected in the operating activities section of the statement of cash flows.

peak pricing (p. 570) The strategy of charging a higher price during periods of high demand, and a lower price during periods of slack demand. Intended to both maximize revenue and shift excess demand to periods in which it can be more easily accommodated.

product mix (p. 571) The variety and relative quantities of goods and services that a company offers for sale.

DEMONSTRATION PROBLEM

You are the chief accountant for Modern Consumer Products, Inc. Your assistant has prepared an income statement for the current year and has developed the following additional information by analyzing changes in the company's balance sheet accounts.

---

*Supplemental Topic, "A Worksheet for Preparing a Statement of Cash Flows."

MODERN CONSUMER PRODUCTS, INC.
Income Statement
For the Year Ended December 31, 2002

Revenue:		
Net sales		$9,500,000
Interest income		320,000
Gain on sales of marketable securities		70,000
Total revenue and gains		$9,890,000
Costs and expenses:		
Cost of goods sold	$4,860,000	
Operating expenses (including depreciation of $700,000)	3,740,000	
Interest expense	270,000	
Income taxes	300,000	
Loss on sales of plant assets	90,000	
Total costs, expenses, and losses		9,260,000
Net income		$ 630,000

Changes in the company's balance sheet accounts over the year are summarized as follows:

1. Accounts Receivable decreased by $85,000.
2. Accrued Interest Receivable increased by $15,000.
3. Inventory decreased by $280,000, and Accounts Payable to suppliers of merchandise decreased by $240,000.
4. Short-term prepayments of operating expenses decreased by $18,000, and accrued liabilities for operating expenses increased by $35,000.
5. The liability for Accrued Interest Payable decreased by $16,000 during the year.
6. The liability for Accrued Income Taxes Payable increased by $25,000 during the year.
7. The following schedule summarizes the total debit and credit entries during the year in other balance sheet accounts:

	Debit Entries	Credit Entries
Marketable Securities	$ 120,000	$ 210,000
Notes Receivable (cash loans made to others)	250,000	190,000
Plant Assets (see paragraph **8**)	3,800,000	360,000
Notes Payable (short-term borrowing)	620,000	740,000
Bonds Payable		1,100,000
Capital Stock		50,000
Additional Paid-in Capital (from issuance of stock)		840,000
Retained Earnings (see paragraph **9**)	320,000	630,000

8. The $360,000 in credit entries to the plant asset accounts is net of any debits to accumulated depreciation when plant assets were retired. Thus the $360,000 in credit entries represents the *book value* of all plant assets sold or retired during the year.
9. The $320,000 debit to retained earnings represents dividends declared and paid during the year. The $630,000 credit entry represents the net income for the year.
10. All investing and financing activities were cash transactions.
11. Cash and cash equivalents amounted to $448,000 at the beginning of the year and to $330,000 at year-end.

Instructions

You are to prepare a statement of cash flows for the current year, following the format illustrated in Exhibit 13–1. Cash flows from operating activities are to be determined by the *direct method*. Place brackets around dollar amounts representing cash outlays. Show separately your computations of the following amounts:

a. Cash received from customers
b. Interest received
c. Cash paid to suppliers and employees
d. Interest paid
e. Income taxes paid
f. Proceeds from sales of marketable securities
g. Proceeds from sales of plant assets
h. Proceeds from issuing capital stock

Solution to the Demonstration Problem

MODERN CONSUMER PRODUCTS, INC.
Statement of Cash Flows
For the Year Ended December 31, 2002

Cash flows from operating activities:		
Cash received from customers (a)	$ 9,585,000	
Interest received (b)	305,000	
Cash provided by operating activities		$9,890,000
Cash paid to suppliers and employees (c)	$(7,807,000)	
Interest paid (d)	(286,000)	
Income taxes paid (e)	(275,000)	
Cash disbursed for operating activities		(8,368,000)
Net cash provided by operating activities		$1,522,000
Cash flows from investing activities:		
Purchases of marketable securities	$ (120,000)	
Proceeds from sales of marketable securities (f)	280,000	
Loans made to borrowers	(250,000)	
Collections on loans	190,000	
Cash paid to acquire plant assets	(3,800,000)	
Proceeds from sales of plant assets (g)	270,000	
Net cash used in investing activities		(3,430,000)
Cash flows from financing activities:		
Proceeds from short-term borrowing	$ 740,000	
Payments to settle short-term debts	(620,000)	
Proceeds from issuing bonds payable	1,100,000	
Proceeds from issuing capital stock (h)	890,000	
Dividends paid	(320,000)	
Net cash provided by financing activities		1,790,000
Net increase (decrease) in cash		$ (118,000)
Cash and cash equivalents, Jan. 1		448,000
Cash and cash equivalents, Dec. 31		$ 330,000

MODERN CONSUMER PRODUCTS, INC. (continued)
Statement of Cash Flows
For the Year Ended December 31, 2002

Supporting computations:

a. Cash received from customers:

Net sales		$9,500,000
Add: Decrease in accounts receivable		85,000
Cash received from customers		$9,585,000

b. Interest received:

Interest income		$ 320,000
Less: Increase in accrued interest receivable		15,000
Interest received		$ 305,000

c. Cash paid to suppliers and employees:

Cash paid for purchases of merchandise:

Cost of goods sold		$4,860,000
Less: Decrease in inventory		280,000
Net purchases		$4,580,000
Add: Decrease in accounts payable to suppliers		240,000
Cash paid for purchases of merchandise		$4,820,000

Cash paid for operating expenses:

Operating expenses		$3,740,000
Less: Depreciation (a "noncash" expense)	$700,000	
Decrease in prepayments	18,000	
Increase in accrued liabilities for operating expenses	35,000	753,000
Cash paid for operating expenses		$2,987,000

Cash paid to suppliers and employees
($4,820,000 + $2,987,000) $7,807,000

d. Interest paid:

Interest expense		$ 270,000
Add: Decrease in accrued interest payable		16,000
Interest paid		$ 286,000

e. Income taxes paid:

Income taxes expense		$ 300,000
Less: Increase in accrued income taxes payable		25,000
Income taxes paid		$ 275,000

f. Proceeds from sales of marketable securities:

Cost of marketable securities sold (credit entries to the Marketable Securities account)		$ 210,000
Add: Gain reported on sales of marketable securities		70,000
Proceeds from sales of marketable securities		$ 280,000

g. Proceeds from sales of plant assets:

Book value of plant assets sold (paragraph **8**)		$ 360,000
Less: Loss reported on sales of plant assets		90,000
Proceeds from sales of plant assets		$ 270,000

h. Proceeds from issuing capital stock:

Amounts credited to the Capital Stock account		$ 50,000
Add: Amounts credited to Additional Paid-in Capital account		840,000
Proceeds from issuing capital stock		$ 890,000

SELF-TEST QUESTIONS

Answers to these questions appear on page 599.

1. The statement of cash flows is designed to assist users in assessing each of the following, *except:*
   a. The ability of a company to remain liquid.
   b. The company's profitability.
   c. The major sources of cash receipts during the period.
   d. The reasons why net cash flows from operating activities differ from net income.

2. Which of the following is *not* included in the statement of cash flows, or in a supplementary schedule accompanying the statement of cash flows?
   a. Disclosure of the amount of cash invested in money market funds during the accounting period.
   b. A reconciliation of net income to net cash flows from operating activities.
   c. Disclosure of investing or financing activities that did not involve cash.
   d. The amount of cash and cash equivalents owned by the business at the end of the accounting period.

3. Cash flows are grouped in the statement of cash flows into the following major categories:
   a. Operating activities, investing activities, and financing activities.
   b. Cash receipts, cash disbursements, and noncash activities.
   c. Direct cash flows and indirect cash flows.
   d. Operating activities, investing activities, and collecting activities.

4. The following is a list of various cash payments and cash receipts:

Cash paid to suppliers and employees	$400,000
Dividends paid	18,000
Interest paid	12,000
Purchases of plant assets	45,000
Interest and dividends received	17,000
Payments to settle short-term debt	29,000
Income taxes paid	23,000
Cash received from customers	601,000

   Based only on the above items, net cash flows from operating activities are:
   a. $138,000   b. $91,000   c. $183,000   d. $120,000

5. During the current year, two transactions were recorded in the Land account of Pollard Industries. One involved a debit of $320,000 to the Land account; the second was a $210,000 credit to the Land account. Pollard's income statement for the year reported a loss on sale of land in the amount of $25,000. All transactions involving the Land account were cash transactions. These transactions would be shown in the statement of cash flows as:
   a. $320,000 cash provided by investing activities, and $210,000 cash disbursed for investing activities.
   b. $210,000 cash provided by investing activities, and $320,000 cash disbursed for investing activities.
   c. $235,000 cash provided by investing activities, and $320,000 cash disbursed for investing activities.
   d. $185,000 cash provided by investing activities, and $320,000 cash disbursed for investing activities.

6. Which of the following business strategies is *most likely* to increase the net cash flows of a software developer in the short run but *reduce* them over a longer term?
   a. Develop software that is more costly to create but easier to update and improve.
   b. Lower the price of existing versions of products as customer demand begins to fall.

c. Purchase the building in which the business operates (assume the company currently rents this location).
d. Reduce expenditures for the purpose of developing new products.

ASSIGNMENT MATERIAL

DISCUSSION QUESTIONS

1. Briefly state the purposes of a statement of cash flows.
2. Does a statement of cash flows or an income statement best measure the profitability of a financially sound business? Explain.
3. Two supplementary schedules frequently accompany a statement of cash flows prepared by the direct method. Briefly explain the content of these schedules.
4. Give two examples of cash receipts and two examples of cash payments that fit into each of the following classifications:
   a. Operating activities
   b. Investing activities
   c. Financing activities
5. Why are payments and receipts of interest classified as operating activities rather than as financing or investing activities?
6. Define *cash equivalents* and list three examples.
7. During the current year, Morgan Corporation transferred $300,000 from its bank account into a money market fund. Will this transaction appear in a statement of cash flows? If so, in which section? Explain.
8. In the long run, is it more important for a business to have positive cash flows from its operating activities, investing activities, or financing activities? Why?
9. Of the three types of business activities summarized in a statement of cash flows, which type is *least* likely to show positive net cash flows in a successful, growing business? Explain your reasoning.
10. The items and amounts listed in a balance sheet and an income statement correspond to specific accounts in a company's ledger. Is the same true about the items and amounts in a statement of cash flows? Explain.
11. Lewis, Inc., had net sales for the year of $870,000. Accounts receivable increased from $90,000 at the beginning of the year to $162,000 at year-end. Compute the amount of cash collected during the year from customers.
12. Describe the types of cash payments summarized by the caption "Cash paid to suppliers and employees."
13. Identify three factors that may cause net income to differ from net cash flows from operating activities.
14. Briefly explain the difference between the *direct* and *indirect methods* of computing net cash flows from operating activities. Which method results in higher net cash flows?
15. Are cash payments of accounts payable viewed as operating activities or financing activities? Referring to the statement of cash flows illustrated in Exhibit 13-1, state the caption that includes amounts paid on accounts payable.
16. Checkmore, Inc., acquired land by issuing $500,000 of capital stock. No cash changed hands in this transaction. Will the transaction be disclosed in the company's statement of cash flows? Explain.
17. The only transaction recorded in the plant asset accounts of Dalton Company in the current year was a $170,000 credit to the Land account. Assuming that this credit resulted from a cash transaction, does this entry indicate a cash receipt or a cash payment? Should this $170,000 appear in the statement of cash flows, or is some adjustment necessary?
18. During the current year, the following credit entries were posted to the paid-in capital accounts of Crawford Shipyards:

Capital Stock	$10,000,000
Additional Paid-in Capital	78,500,000

Explain the type of cash transaction that probably caused these credit changes, and illustrate the presentation of this transaction in a statement of cash flows.

19. At the beginning of the current year, Cimino Corporation had dividends payable of $1,500,000. During the current year, the company declared cash dividends of $3,800,000, of which $800,000 appeared as a liability at year-end. Determine the amount of cash dividends *paid* during this year.
20. Define the term *free cash flow*. Explain the significance of this measurement to (1) short-term creditors, (2) long-term creditors, (3) stockholders, and (4) management.
21. Describe a *cash budget* and explain its usefulness to management.
22. Explain the concept of *peak pricing* and provide an example from your own experience.
23. From management's perspective, identify some of the characteristics of an effective product mix.
24. Explain why speeding up the collection of accounts receivable provides only a one-time increase in cash receipts.

EXERCISES

EXERCISE 13.1

Using a Statement of Cash Flows

LO 1, 2

The statement of cash flows for Auto Supply Co. appears in Exhibit 13–9. Assume that with respect to routine business operations, this was a *typical year*. Use this cash flow statement to evaluate the company's ability to maintain the current level of dividend payments over the foreseeable future. Explain your reasoning.

EXERCISE 13.2

Using a Statement of Cash Flows

LO 1, 2, 6

The Rowe Companies' 2000 statement of cash flows appears in Exhibit 13–6. Study the statement and respond to the following questions:

a. What was the company's free cash flow in 2000?
b. What were the major sources and uses of cash from financing activities during 2000? Did the net effect of financing activities result in an increase or a decrease in cash during the year?
c. What happened to the total amount of cash and cash equivalents during the year? Assuming 2000 was a typical year for The Rowe Companies, is the firm in a position to continue its dividend payments in the future? Explain.
d. Look at the reconciliation of net income to net cash provided by operating activities and explain the following:
   1. Loss on the disposition of Wexford.
   2. Decrease in accounts receivable.

EXERCISE 13.3

Computing Cash Flows

LO 4

An analysis of the Marketable Securities controlling account of Rubright Products, Inc., shows the following entries during the year:

Balance, Jan. 1	$ 290,000
Debit entries	125,000
Credit entries	(140,000)
Balance, Dec. 31	$ 275,000

In addition, the company's income statement includes a $35,000 loss on sales of marketable securities. None of the company's marketable securities is considered a cash equivalent.

Compute the amounts that should appear in the statement of cash flows as:
a. Purchases of marketable securities.
b. Proceeds from sales of marketable securities.

EXERCISE 13.4
Comparing Net Sales and Cash Receipts
LO 3, 6

During the current year, Donahue, Inc., made cash sales of $285,000 and credit sales of $460,000. During the year, accounts receivable decreased by $32,000.
a. Compute for the current year the amounts of:
1. Net sales reported as revenue in the income statement.
2. Cash received from collecting accounts receivable.
3. Cash received from customers.
b. Write a brief statement explaining *why* cash received from customers differs from the amount of net sales.

EXERCISE 13.5
Computing Cash Paid for Purchases of Merchandise
LO 3

The general ledger of Protech provides the following information relating to purchases of merchandise:

	End of Year	Beginning of Year
Inventory	$820,000	$780,000
Accounts payable to merchandise suppliers	430,000	500,000

The company's cost of goods sold during the year was $3,850,000. Compute the amount of cash payments made during the year to suppliers of merchandise.

EXERCISE 13.6
Reporting Lending Activities and Interest Revenue
LO 3, 4

During the current year, New Hampshire Savings and Loan Association made new loans of $14 million. In addition, the company collected $36 million from borrowers, of which $30 million was interest revenue. Explain how these cash flows will appear in the company's statement of cash flows, indicating the classification and the dollar amount of each cash flow.

EXERCISE 13.7
Format of a Statement of Cash Flows
LO 2

The accounting staff of Dakota Outfitters, Inc., has assembled the following information for the year ended December 31, 2002:

Cash and cash equivalents, Jan. 1	$ 21,800
Cash and cash equivalents, Dec. 31	60,800
Cash paid to acquire plant assets	21,000
Proceeds from short-term borrowing	10,000
Loans made to borrowers	5,000
Collections on loans (excluding interest)	4,000
Interest and dividends received	27,000
Cash received from customers	795,000
Proceeds from sales of plant assets	9,000
Dividends paid	55,000
Cash paid to suppliers and employees	635,000
Interest paid	19,000
Income taxes paid	71,000

Using this information, prepare a statement of cash flows. Include a proper heading for the financial statement, and classify the given information into the categories of operating activities, investing activities, and financing activities. Determine net cash flows from operating activities by the direct method. Place brackets around the dollar amounts of all cash disbursements.

EXERCISE 13.8
Effects of Business Strategies
LO 8

Indicate how you would expect the following strategies to affect the company's net cash flows from *operating activities* (1) in the near future and (2) in later periods (after the strategy's long-term effects have "taken hold"). *Fully explain your reasoning.*

a. A successful pharmaceutical company substantially reduces its expenditures for research and development.
b. A restaurant that previously sold only for cash adopts a policy of accepting bank credit cards, such as Visa and MasterCard.
c. A manufacturing company reduces by 50% the size of its inventories of raw materials (assume no change in inventory storage costs).
d. Through tax planning, a rapidly growing real estate developer is able to defer significant amounts of income taxes.
e. A rapidly growing software company announces that it will stop paying cash dividends for the foreseeable future and will instead distribute stock dividends.

EXERCISE 13.9
An Analysis of Possible Reconciling Items
LO 6, 7

An analysis of the annual financial statements of Mariner Corporation reveals the following:

a. The company had a $5 million extraordinary loss from the early retirement of bonds payable.
b. Depreciation for the year amounted to $8 million.
c. During the year, $2 million in cash was transferred from the company's checking account into a money market fund.
d. Accounts receivable from customers increased by $4 million over the year.
e. Cash received from customers during the year amounted to $167 million.
f. Prepaid expenses decreased by $1 million over the year.
g. Dividends declared during the year, $7 million; dividends paid during the year, $6 million.
h. Accounts payable (to suppliers of merchandise) increased by $2.5 million during the year.
i. The liability for accrued income taxes payable amounted to $5 million at the beginning of the year and $3 million at year-end.

In the computation of net cash flows from operating activities by the *indirect method,* explain whether each of the above items should be *added to net income, deducted from net income,* or *omitted from the computation.* Briefly explain your reasons for each answer.

EXERCISE 13.10
Computation of Net Cash Flows from Operating Activities—Indirect Method
LO 7

The following data are taken from the income statement and balance sheet of Harmon Machinery, Inc.:

	Dec. 31 2002	Jan. 1 2002
Income statement:		
Net Income	$427,000	
Depreciation Expense	125,000	
Amortization of Intangible Assets	40,000	
Gain on Sale of Plant Assets	90,000	
Loss on Sale of Investments	35,000	
Balance sheet:		
Accounts Receivable	$335,000	$380,000
Inventory	503,000	575,000
Prepaid Expenses	22,000	10,000
Accounts Payable (to merchandise suppliers)	379,000	410,000
Accrued Expenses Payable	180,000	155,000

Using this information, prepare a partial statement of cash flows for the year ended December 31, 2002, showing the computation of net cash flows from operating activities by the *indirect* method.

588 Chapter 13 Statement of Cash Flows

EXERCISE 13.11

Tootsie Roll Industries: Using a Statement of Cash Flows

LO 1, 2, 4

Statements of cash flows for **Tootsie Roll Industries, Inc.**, for 1998, 1999, and 2000 appear in Appendix A.

a. Focus on the statement of cash flows for the year ended December 31, 1998, and respond to the following:
   1. Describe the major reasons why the company's cash and cash equivalents increased by $20,311,000 during the year.
   2. Assuming that the company had not purchased shares of its own stock during 1998, calculate the amount of:
      —Cash flows for the year from financing activities.
      —Cash and cash equivalents at the end of the year.
   3. Calculate the amount of the company's free cash flow.
   4. At the end of 1997, **Tootsie Roll** had a cash balance of $60,433,000. During that year, cash increased $68,176 thousand from operations, decreased $31,698 from investing activities, and decreased $21,704 thousand from financing activities. From a cash flow perspective do you believe the company's performance was better in the year ended December 31, 1998, than in the prior year? Justify your answer.

b. Comparing 1999 and 1998, what were the primary changes in cash flows that occurred? Is the company's cash position stronger or weaker at the end of 1999 than 1998?

PROBLEMS

PROBLEM 13.1

Classifying Cash Flows

LO 2

Among the transactions of Vandergriff, Inc. were the following:

a. Made payments on accounts payable to merchandise suppliers.
b. Paid the principal amount of a note payable to First Bank.
c. Paid interest charges relating to a note payable to First Bank.
d. Issued bonds payable for cash; management plans to use this cash in the near future to expand manufacturing and warehouse capabilities.
e. Paid salaries to employees in the finance department.
f. Collected an account receivable from a customer.
g. Transferred cash from the general bank account into a money market fund.
h. Used the cash received in **d,** above, to purchase land and a building suitable for a manufacturing facility.
i. Made a year-end adjusting entry to recognize depreciation expense.
j. At year-end, purchased for cash an insurance policy covering the next 12 months.
k. Paid the quarterly dividend on preferred stock.
l. Paid the semiannual interest on bonds payable.
m. Received a quarterly dividend from an investment in the preferred stock of another corporation.
n. Sold for cash an investment in the preferred stock of another corporation.
o. Received cash upon the maturity of an investment in cash equivalents. (Ignore interest.)

Instructions

Most of the preceding transactions should be included among the activities summarized in a statement of cash flows. For each transaction that should be included in this statement, indicate whether the transaction should be classified as an operating activity, an investing activity, or a financing activity. If the transaction *should not be included* in the current year's statement of cash flows, briefly explain why not. (Assume that net cash flows from operating activities are determined by the *direct method*.)

PROBLEM 13.2

Format of a Statement of Cash Flows

LO 2, 3, 4

The accounting staff of Reizenstein Company has assembled the following information for the year ended December 31, 2002:

Cash sales	$ 800,000
Credit sales	2,500,000
Collections on accounts receivable	2,200,000
Cash transferred from the money market fund to the general bank account	250,000
Interest and dividends received	100,000
Purchases (all on account)	1,800,000
Payments on accounts payable to merchandise suppliers	1,500,000
Cash payments for operating expenses	1,050,000
Interest paid	180,000
Income taxes paid	95,000
Loans made to borrowers	500,000
Collections on loans (excluding receipts of interest)	260,000
Cash paid to acquire plant assets	3,100,000
Book value of plant assets sold	660,000
Loss on sales of plant assets	80,000
Proceeds from issuing bonds payable	2,500,000
Dividends paid	120,000
Cash and cash equivalents, Jan. 1	517,000

Instructions

Prepare a statement of cash flows in the format illustrated in Exhibit 13–1. Place brackets around amounts representing cash outflows. Use the *direct method* of reporting cash flows from operating activities.

Some of the items above will be listed in your statement without change. However, you will have to combine certain given information to compute the amounts of (1) collections from customers, (2) cash paid to suppliers and employees, and (3) proceeds from sales of plant assets. (Hint: Not every item listed is used in preparing a statement of cash flows.)

PROBLEM 13.3
Reporting Investing Activities

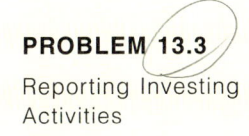

LO 4

An analysis of the income statement and the balance sheet accounts of Fowler Fashions at December 31, 2002, provides the following information:

Income statement items:	
Gain on Sale of Marketable Securities	$ 42,000
Loss on Sales of Plant Assets	33,000
Analysis of balance sheet accounts:	
Marketable Securities account:	
Debit entries	$ 75,000
Credit entries	90,000
Notes Receivable account:	
Debit entries	210,000
Credit entries	162,000
Plant and Equipment accounts:	
Debit entries to plant asset accounts	196,000
Credit entries to plant asset accounts	120,000
Debit entries to accumulated depreciation accounts	75,000

Additional Information

1. Except as noted in **4,** payments and proceeds relating to investing transactions were made in cash.
2. The marketable securities are not cash equivalents.

3. All notes receivable relate to cash loans made to borrowers, not to receivables from customers.
4. Purchases of new equipment during the year ($196,000) were financed by paying $60,000 in cash and issuing a long-term note payable for $136,000.
5. Debits to the accumulated depreciation accounts are made whenever depreciable plant assets are retired. Thus the book value of plant assets retired during the year was $45,000 ($120,000 − $75,000).

Instructions

a. Prepare the investing activities section of a statement of cash flows. Show supporting computations for the amounts of (1) proceeds from sales of marketable securities and (2) proceeds from sales of plant assets. Place brackets around numbers representing cash outflows.
b. Prepare the supporting schedule that should accompany the statement of cash flows in order to disclose the noncash aspects of the company's investing and financing activities.
c. Assume that Fowler Fashions' management expects approximately the same amount of cash to be used for investing activities next year. In general terms, explain how the company might generate cash for this purpose.

PROBLEM 13.4
Reporting Investing Activities
LO 4

An analysis of the income statement and the balance sheet accounts of Ranger Imports at December 31, 2002, provides the following information:

Income statement items:
Gain on Sale of Plant Assets	$ 12,000
Loss on Sales of Marketable Securities	16,000

Analysis of balance sheet accounts:

Marketable Securities account:
Debit entries	$ 78,000
Credit entries	62,000

Notes Receivable account:
Debit entries	55,000
Credit entries	60,000

Plant and Equipment accounts:
Debit entries to plant asset accounts	150,000
Credit entries to plant asset accounts	140,000
Debit entries to accumulated depreciation accounts	100,000

Additional Information

1. Except as noted in **4** below, payments and proceeds relating to investing transactions were made in cash.
2. The marketable securities are not cash equivalents.
3. All notes receivable relate to cash loans made to borrowers, not to receivables from customers.
4. Purchases of new equipment during the year ($150,000) were financed by paying $50,000 in cash and issuing a long-term note payable for $100,000.
5. Debits to the accumulated depreciation accounts are made whenever depreciable plant assets are sold or retired. Thus the book value of plant assets sold or retired during the year was $40,000 ($140,000 − $100,000).

Instructions

a. Prepare the investing activities section of a statement of cash flows. Show supporting computations for the amounts of (1) proceeds from sales of marketable securities and (2) proceeds from sales of plant assets. Place brackets around amounts representing cash outflows.
b. Prepare the supplementary schedule that should accompany the statement of cash flows in order to disclose the noncash aspects of the company's investing and financing activities.
c. Does management have *more* control or *less* control over the timing and amount of cash outlays for investing activities than for operating activities? Explain.

PROBLEM 13.5

Reporting Operating Cash Flows by the Direct Method

LO 3

The following income statement and selected balance sheet account data are available for Hernandez, Inc., at December 31, 2002:

HERNANDEZ, INC.
Income Statement
For the Year Ended December 31, 2002

Revenue:		
Net sales		$2,850,000
Dividend income		104,000
Interest income		70,000
Gain on sales of marketable securities		4,000
Total revenue and gains		$3,028,000
Costs and expenses:		
Cost of goods sold	$1,550,000	
Operating expenses	980,000	
Interest expense	185,000	
Income taxes	110,000	
Total costs and expenses		2,825,000
Net income		$ 203,000

	End of Year	Beginning of Year
Selected account balances:		
Accounts receivable	$ 650,000	$ 720,000
Accrued interest receivable	9,000	6,000
Inventories	800,000	765,000
Short-term prepayments	20,000	15,000
Accounts payable (merchandise suppliers)	570,000	562,000
Accrued operating expenses payable	65,000	94,000
Accrued interest payable	21,000	12,000
Accrued income taxes payable	22,000	35,000

Additional Information

1. Dividend revenue is recognized on the cash basis. All other income statement amounts are recognized on the accrual basis.
2. Operating expenses include depreciation expense of $115,000.

Instructions

a. Prepare a partial statement of cash flows, including only the *operating activities* section of the statement and using the *direct method*. Place brackets around numbers representing cash payments. Show supporting computations for the following:
   1. Cash received from customers
   2. Interest and dividends received
   3. Cash paid to suppliers and employees
   4. Interest paid
   5. Income taxes paid
b. Management of Hernandez, Inc., is exploring ways to increase the cash flows from operations. One way that cash flows could be increased is through more aggressive collection of receivables. Assuming that management has already taken all the steps possible to increase revenues and reduce expenses, describe two other ways that cash flows from operations could be increased.

PROBLEM 13.6
Reporting Operating Cash Flows by the Indirect Method

LO 6, 7

Using the information presented in Problem **13.5**, prepare a partial statement of cash flows for the current year, showing the computation of net cash flows from operating activities by the *indirect method*. Explain why the decline in accounts receivable over the year was *added* to net income in computing the cash flows from operating activities.

PROBLEM 13.7
Preparing a Statement of Cash Flows: A Comprehensive Problem without a Worksheet

LO 2, 3, 4, 6, 8

You are the controller for 21st Century Technologies. Your staff has prepared an income statement for the current year and has developed the following additional information by analyzing changes in the company's balance sheet accounts.

21st CENTURY TECHNOLOGIES
Income Statement
For the Year Ended December 31, 2002

Revenue:

Net sales		$3,200,000
Interest revenue		40,000
Gain on sales of marketable securities		34,000
Total revenue and gains		$3,274,000

Costs and expenses:

Cost of goods sold	$1,620,000	
Operating expenses (including depreciation of $150,000)	1,240,000	
Interest expense	42,000	
Income taxes	100,000	
Loss on sales of plant assets	12,000	
Total costs, expenses, and losses		3,014,000
Net income		$ 260,000

Additional Information

1. Accounts receivable increased by $60,000.
2. Accrued interest receivable decreased by $2,000.
3. Inventory decreased by $60,000, and accounts payable to suppliers of merchandise decreased by $16,000.
4. Short-term prepayments of operating expenses increased by $6,000, and accrued liabilities for operating expenses decreased by $8,000.
5. The liability for accrued interest payable increased by $4,000 during the year.
6. The liability for accrued income taxes payable decreased by $14,000 during the year.
7. The following schedule summarizes the total debit and credit entries during the year in other balance sheet accounts:

	Debit Entries	Credit Entries
Marketable Securities	$ 60,000	$ 38,000
Notes Receivable (cash loans made to borrowers)	44,000	28,000
Plant Assets (see paragraph **8**)	500,000	36,000
Notes Payable (short-term borrowing)	92,000	82,000
Capital Stock		20,000
Additional Paid-in Capital—Capital Stock		160,000
Retained Earnings (see paragraph **9**)	120,000	260,000

8. The $36,000 in credit entries to the Plant Assets account is net of any debits to Accumulated Depreciation when plant assets were retired. Thus the $36,000 in credit entries represents the book value of all plant assets sold or retired during the year.
9. The $120,000 debit to retained earnings represents dividends declared and paid during the year. The $260,000 credit entry represents the net income shown in the income statement.
10. All investing and financing activities were cash transactions.
11. Cash and cash equivalents amounted to $244,000 at the beginning of the year and to $164,000 at year-end.

Instructions

a. Prepare a statement of cash flows for the current year. Use the *direct method* of reporting cash flows from operating activities. Place brackets around dollar amounts representing cash outflows. Show separately your computations of the following amounts:
   1. Cash received from customers.
   2. Interest received.
   3. Cash paid to suppliers and employees.
   4. Interest paid.
   5. Income taxes paid.
   6. Proceeds from sales of marketable securities.
   7. Proceeds from sales of plant assets.
   8. Proceeds from issuing capital stock.

b. Explain the *primary reason* why:
   1. The amount of cash provided by operating activities was substantially greater than the company's net income.
   2. There was a net decrease in cash over the year, despite the substantial amount of cash provided by operating activities.

c. 21st Century's controller thinks that through more efficient cash management, the company could have held the increase in accounts receivable for the year to $10,000, without affecting net income. Explain how holding down the growth in receivables affects cash. Compute the effect that limiting the growth in receivables to $10,000 would have had on the company's net increase or decrease in cash (and cash equivalents) for the year.

*PROBLEM 13.8

Prepare and Analyze a Statement of Cash Flows with a Worksheet

LO 1-9

SPACENET 2010 was founded in 2001 to apply a new technology for efficiently transmitting closed-circuit (cable) television signals without the need for an in-ground cable. The company earned a profit of $115,000 in 2001, its first year of operations, even though it was serving only a small test market. In 2002, the company began dramatically expanding its customer base. Management expects both sales and net income to more than triple in each of the next five years.

Comparative balance sheets at the ends of 2001 and 2002, the company's first two years of operations, follow. (Notice that the balances at the end of the current year appear in the right-hand column.)

Additional Information

The following information regarding the company's operations in 2002 is available in either the company's income statement or its accounting records:

1. Net income for the year was $440,000. The company has never paid a dividend.
2. Depreciation for the year amounted to $147,000.
3. During the year the company purchased plant assets costing $2,200,000, for which it paid $1,850,000 in cash and financed $350,000 by issuing a long-term note payable. (Much of the cash used in these purchases was provided by short-term borrowing, as described below.)
4. In 2002, SPACENET 2010 borrowed $1,450,000 against a $5 million line of credit with a local bank. In its balance sheet, the resulting obligations are reported as notes payable (short-term).
5. Additional shares of capital stock (no par value) were issued to investors for $500,000 cash.

---

*Supplemental Topic, "A Worksheet for Preparing a Statement of Cash Flows."

SPACENET 2010
Comparative Balance Sheets

	December 31, 2001	December 31, 2002
Assets		
Cash and cash equivalents	$ 80,000	$ 37,000
Accounts receivable	100,000	850,000
Plant and equipment (net of accumulated depreciation)	600,000	2,653,000
Totals	$780,000	$3,540,000
Liabilities & Stockholders' Equity		
Notes payable (short-term)	$ –0–	$1,450,000
Accounts payable	30,000	63,000
Accrued expenses payable	45,000	32,000
Notes payable (long-term)	390,000	740,000
Capital stock (no par value)	200,000	700,000
Retained earnings	115,000	555,000
Totals	$780,000	$3,540,000

Instructions

a. Prepare a worksheet for a statement of cash flows, following the general format illustrated in Exhibit 13–8. (*Note:* If this problem is completed as a group assignment, each member of the group should be prepared to explain in class all entries in the worksheet, as well as the group's conclusions in parts **c** and **d**.)

b. Prepare a formal statement of cash flows for 2002, including a supplementary schedule of noncash investing and financing activities. (Follow the format illustrated in Exhibit 13–9. Cash provided by operating activities is to be presented by the *indirect method*.)

c. Briefly explain how operating activities can be a net *use* of cash when the company is operating so profitably.

d. Because of the expected rapid growth, management forecasts that operating activities will be an even greater use of cash in the year 2003 than in 2002. If this forecast is correct, does SPACENET 2010 appear to be heading toward illiquidity? Explain.

---

*PROBLEM 13.9
Prepare and Analyze a Statement of Cash Flows; Involves Preparation of a Worksheet

LO 1–9

Marvel Tool, Inc., sells a single product (a combination screwdriver, plier, hammer, and crescent wrench) exclusively through television advertising. The comparative income statements and balance sheets are for the past two years.

Additional Information

The following information regarding the company's operations in 2002 is available from the company's accounting records:

1. Early in the year the company declared and paid a $4,000 cash dividend.
2. During the year marketable securities costing $15,000 were sold for $14,000 cash, resulting in a $1,000 nonoperating loss.
3. The company purchased plant assets for $20,000, paying $2,000 in cash and issuing a note payable for the $18,000 balance.
4. During the year the company repaid a $10,000 note payable, but incurred an additional $18,000 in long-term debt as described in **3**.
5. The owners invested $15,000 cash in the business as a condition of the new loans described in paragraph **4**.

---

*Supplemental Topic, "A Worksheet for Preparing a Statement of Cash Flows."

MARVEL TOOL, INC.
Comparative Income Statement
For the Years Ended December 31, 2001 and 2002

	2001	2002
Sales	$500,000	$350,000
Less: cost of goods sold	200,000	140,000
Gross profit on sales	$300,000	$210,000
Less: operating expenses (including depreciation of $34,000 in 2001 and $35,000 in 2002)	260,000	243,000
Loss on sale of marketable securities	–0–	1,000
Net income (loss)	$ 40,000	($ 34,000)

MARVEL TOOL, INC.
Comparative Balance Sheets

	December 31, 2001	December 31, 2002
Assets		
Cash and cash equivalents	$ 10,000	$ 60,000
Marketable securities	20,000	5,000
Accounts receivable	40,000	23,000
Inventory	120,000	122,000
Plant and equipment (net of accumulated depreciation)	300,000	285,000
Totals	$490,000	$495,000
Liabilities & Stockholders' Equity		
Accounts payable	$ 50,000	$ 73,000
Accrued expenses payable	17,000	14,000
Note payable	245,000	253,000
Capital stock (no par value)	120,000	135,000
Retained earnings	58,000	20,000
Totals	$490,000	$495,000

Instructions

a. Prepare a worksheet for a statement of cash flows, following the general format illustrated in Exhibit 13–8. (*Note:* If this problem is completed as a group assignment, each member of the group should be prepared to explain in class all entries in the worksheet, as well as the group's conclusions in parts **c, d,** and **e.**)

b. Prepare a formal statement of cash flows for 2002, including a supplementary schedule of noncash investing and financing activities. (Use the format illustrated in Exhibit 13–9. Cash provided by operating activities is to be presented by the *indirect method.*)

c. Explain how Marvel Tool, Inc., achieved positive cash flows from operating activities, despite incurring a net loss for the year.

d. Does the company's financial position appear to be improving or deteriorating? Explain.

e. Does Marvel Tool, Inc., appear to be a company whose operations are growing or contracting? Explain.

f. Assume that management *agrees* with your conclusions in parts **c, d,** and **e.** What decisions should be made and what actions (if any) should be taken? Explain.

CASES AND UNSTRUCTURED PROBLEMS

CASE 13.1

Another Look at Allison Corporation

LO 1

This case is based on the statement of cash flows for Allison Corporation, illustrated in Exhibit 13–1. Use this statement to evaluate the company's ability to continue paying the current level of dividends—$40,000 per year. The following information also is available:

1. The net cash flows from operating activities shown in the statement are relatively normal for Allison Corporation. Net cash flows from operating activities have not varied by more than a few thousand dollars in any of the past three years.
2. The net outflow for investing activities was unusually high, because the company modernized its production facilities during the year. The normal investing cash outflow is about $45,000 per year, the amount required to replace existing plant assets as they are retired. Over the long run, marketable securities transactions and lending transactions have a very small impact on Allison's net cash flows from investing activities.
3. The net cash flows from financing activities were unusually large in the current year because of the issuance of bonds payable and capital stock. These securities were issued to finance the modernization of the production facilities. In a typical year, financing activities include only short-term borrowing transactions and payments of dividends.

Instructions

a. Based solely on the company's past performance, do you believe that the $40,000 annual dividend payments are secure? That is, does the company appear able to pay this amount in dividends every year without straining its cash position? Do you think it more likely that Allison Corporation will increase or decrease the amount of dividends that it pays? Explain fully.

b. Should any of the unusual events appearing in the statement of cash flows for the current year affect your analysis of the company's ability to pay future dividends? Explain.

CASE 13.2

Cash Budgeting for You as a Student

LO 1, 8

Individuals generally do not prepare statements of cash flows concerning their personal activities. But they do engage in cash budgeting—if not on paper, then at least in their heads.

Assume, for example, it is December 29—a Monday. In two days your rent for January, $200, will be due. You now have $140 in the bank; every Friday you receive a paycheck for $100. You probably see the problem. And it probably doesn't look too serious; you can find a way to deal with it. That's what *budgeting* is all about.

Let's take this example a step further. In addition to the facts given above, your weekly cash payments include meals, $30; entertainment, $20; and gasoline, $10.

Instructions

a. Using the following cash budget, compute your cash balance at the end of weeks 2, 3, and 4.

	Week 1	Week 2	Week 3	Week 4
Beginning cash balance	$ 140	$(20)	$?	$?
Expected cash receipts	100	100	100	100
Less: Expected cash outlays:				
Monthly rent	(200)			
Meals	(30)			
Entertainment	(20)			
Gasoline	(10)			
Ending cash balance	$ (20)	$?	$?	$?

b. Evaluate your financial situation.

CASE 13.3

Lookin' Good?

LO 1, 4, 8

It is late summer and Public Motors, an auto manufacturer, is facing a financial crisis. A large issue of bonds payable will mature next March, and the company must issue stock or new bonds to raise the money to retire this debt. Unfortunately, profits and cash flows have been declining over recent years. Management fears that if cash flows and profits do not improve in the current year, the company will not be able to raise the capital needed to replace the maturing bonds. Therefore, members of management have made the following proposals to improve the cash flows and profitability that will be reported in the financial statements dated this coming December 31.

1. Switch from the LIFO method to the FIFO method of valuing inventories. Management estimates that the FIFO method will result in a lower cost of goods sold but in higher income taxes for the current year. However, the additional income taxes will not actually be paid until early next year.
2. Switch from the 150% declining-balance method of depreciation to the straight-line method and lengthen the useful lives over which assets are depreciated. (These changes would be made only for financial reporting purposes, not for income tax purposes.)
3. Pressure dealers to increase their inventories—in short, to buy more cars. (The dealerships are independently owned; thus dealers are the customers to whom Public Motors sells automobiles.) Management estimates that this strategy could increase sales for the current year by 5%. However, any additional sales in the current year would be almost entirely offset by fewer sales in the following year.
4. Require dealers to pay for purchases more quickly. Currently, dealers must pay for purchases of autos within 60 days. Management is considering reducing this period to 30 days.
5. Pass up cash discounts offered for prompt payment (that is, 2/10, n/30), and do not pay any bills until the final due date.
6. Borrow at current short-term interest rates (about 10%) and use the proceeds to pay off long-term debt bearing an interest rate of 13%.
7. Substitute stock dividends for the cash dividends currently paid on capital stock.

Instructions

a. Prepare a schedule with four columns. The first column is to be headed "Proposals" and is to contain the paragraph numbers of the seven proposals listed above. The next three columns are to be headed with the following financial statement captions: (1) "Net Income," (2) "Net Cash Flows from Operating Activities," and (3) "Cash."

For each of the seven proposals in the left column, indicate whether you expect the proposal to "Increase," "Decrease," or have "No Effect" in the current year on each of the financial statement captions listed in the next three columns. (*Note:* Only a few months remain in the current year. Therefore, you are to determine the *short-term* effects of these proposals.)

b. For each of the seven proposals, write a short paragraph explaining the reasoning behind your answers to part a.

CASE 13.4

Peak Pricing

LO 8

"Peak pricing is unfair. It makes goods and services available only to the wealthy and prices the average person out of the market."

Instructions

a. Comment on the extent to which you agree or disagree with the preceding statement.
b. What is the alternative to peak pricing?
c. Explain how peak pricing might be applied by:
   1. A hotel in Palm Springs, California. (Palm Springs is a winter resort in southern California with wonderful golf facilities. In the summer months, however, temperatures are well over 100 degrees and the tourist business slows dramatically.)
   2. Movie theaters.
d. Both in general terms and using specific examples, describe the conditions (if any) under which you might regard peak pricing as *unethical*.

BUSINESS WEEK ASSIGNMENT

CASE 13.5

Texas Instruments Inc.'s Cash Position

LO 6, 8

Texas Instruments Inc. (TI) didn't get to be 71 years old without knowing how to ride out hard times. In "Up a Creek—with Lots of Cash," from the November 12, 2001, edition of *Business Week,* Peter Coy reports about the impact of the tech-led downturn on **Texas Instruments**. **TI**'s net sales fell more than 40% in the third quarter of 2001 as compared to a year earlier and it lost nearly $120 million in the third quarter compared to profits of $680 million the previous year.

TI is hardly up against the wall, however. With a stockpile of $3 billion in cash and marketable securities, **TI** continues payment of $150 million in dividends per year and **TI** continues to buy back its own shares to cover exercise of employee stock options. Peter Coy comments:

> As always in an economic slump, cash is once again king, and companies are going all out to make sure they have enough of it. . . . Businesses are taking steps to keep cash from going out the door and they are bringing in fresh money.

Instructions

a. Explain how it is possible to have cash increasing and net income decreasing.
b. Name at least three strategies that **TI**'s management can undertake to "keep cash from going out the door."
c. Name at least three strategies that **TI**'s management can undertake to "bring in fresh money."

INTERNET ASSIGNMENT

INTERNET 13.1

Comparing Cash Flow Information from Two Companies

LO 2, 3, 4

In the long run, a company must generate positive net cash flows from operating activities to survive. A business that has negative cash flows from operations will not be able to raise cash indefinitely from other sources and will eventually cease existing. Many creditors and stockholders are reluctant to invest in companies that do not generate positive cash flows from operations. However, some investors will invest in companies with negative cash flows from operations due to an optimistic future outlook for the company. Thus, investors have invested millions of dollars into Internet companies that have negative cash flows from operations.

Instructions

a. Visit **Coca-Cola**'s Internet site (**www.coke.com**) and select Investor Relations. Under Financial Information, select the most recent annual report. In the annual report, view the Consolidated Statements of Cash Flows.
b. Visit **Amazon.com**'s Internet site (**www.amazon.com**) and select About Amazon.com. Then select Investor Relations and click SEC Filings. Select the most recent 10-K filing and view the Cash Flow Statement.
c. Compare the Net Cash Provided by Operating Activities for each company. Which company has higher Net Cash Provided by Operating Activities? Speculate why one company has much higher Net Cash Provided by Operating Activities than the other company.
d. What type of company may have Negative Net Cash Provided by Operating Activities?
e. What type of company may have large Positive Net Cash Provided by Operating Activities?

Internet sites are time and date sensitive. It is the purpose of these exercises to have you explore the Internet. You may need to use the Yahoo! search engine **http://www.yahoo.com** *(or another favorite search engine) to find a company's current Web address.*

OUR COMMENTS ON THE "YOUR TURN" CASES

You as a Sales Manager (p. 556) It is ethical for companies to make loans to their customers so that their customers can place orders for their products. This is called vendor financing and it is a useful selling technique *in moderation.* However, Godings Foods, Inc., must be careful so that it doesn't end up buying its own product. The problem is, the sale may not be real revenue, it might be a bad note receivable. For this reason, many companies have policies against vendor financing.

As a sales manager, your responsibility is to check the corporate policy about vendor financing before you respond to the Baggins' request. Corporate policies of this nature are determined by top headquarters management such as the president, vice president of marketing, and/or the CEO.

You as an Accounts Receivable Manager (p. 562) The actual cash flows from sales are reduced for those customers who take advantage of the discount allowed in the standard policy. Thus, on average, the cash flows from sales of comparable merchandise will be lower for the store in the Northeast, where customers have traditionally taken the discount, than for stores in the Southwest, where customers have decided not to use the available discount. However, eliminating the discount for the northeastern store may cause customers to purchase products elsewhere and significantly reduce cash flows from sales. In addition, it will most certainly delay the receipt of cash because customers will delay cash payment from 10 to 30 days. If corporate management compares the cash flow statements of stores without recognizing the differences in customer attitudes toward the discount, the manager of the northeastern store may be at a disadvantage.

It would be unethical to make an exception to the corporate customer discount policy as requested by the manager of the northeastern store. Corporate policies of this nature are determined by top headquarters management such as the president, vice president of marketing, and/or the CEO. The individuals in the organization who are responsible for determining those policies must approve exceptions or changes to standard policies.

You as a Student (p. 569) Predicting future cash flows can help you plan and manage your financial affairs, begin saving for major cash outlays, and avoid financial crises.

Forecasting your own cash flows for the coming month will vary with your lifestyle and the time of year. For example, your housing costs may be based on rent or on the costs of home ownership. Don't forget utilities.

Your projected food costs will depend on what and where you eat. Other expenditures include such things as clothing, entertainment, transportation (including auto insurance and car repairs), and school expenses.

Where will the cash come from? Good question. Do *you* know?

You as a Marketing Manager (p. 571) We would advise you *not* to raise Elmo's price (and Toys 'R' Us didn't). The additional revenue that Toys 'R' Us might receive from raising the price of a single product is probably immaterial. On the other hand, raising the price of a popular and highly publicized toy right before Christmas might lead to charges of price gouging and other bad publicity.

In fact, an alternative to consider would be to cut Elmo's price, not raise it. You might publicize the reduced sales price and promise to continue it for at least a month after Christmas. In the long term, the chance to enhance customer relations is far more important than a short-term increase in revenue.

ANSWERS TO SELF-TEST QUESTIONS

1. b **2.** a **3.** a **4.** c **5.** d **6.** d

CHAPTER 14
FINANCIAL STATEMENT ANALYSIS

Learning Objectives

After studying this chapter, you should be able to:

1. Explain the uses of dollar and percentage changes, trend percentages, component percentages, and ratios.

2. Discuss the quality of a company's earnings, assets, and working capital.

3. Explain the nature and purpose of classifications in financial statements.

4. Prepare a classified balance sheet and compute widely used measures of liquidity and credit risk.

5. Prepare a multiple-step and a single-step income statement and compute widely used measures of profitability.

6. Put a company's net income into perspective by relating it to sales, assets, and stockholders' equity.

7. Compute the ratios widely used in financial statement analysis and explain the significance of each.

8. Analyze financial statements from the viewpoints of common stockholders, creditors, and others.

Courtesy of Johnson & Johnson

Johnson & Johnson

Johnson & Johnson is the world's most comprehensive and broadly based manufacturer of health care products and related services. In 2000 it had over $29 billion in sales. Other measures of **Johnson & Johnson**'s size include the facts that it employs 97,800 people, has 190 operating companies in 51 countries throughout the world, and sells products in more than 175 countries.

How does one get a handle on the financial performance of a huge company such as **Johnson & Johnson**? Financial statements, including the balance sheet, income statement, and statement of cash flows, provide a wealth of information that is helpful in performing this significant task. Financial statement analysis involves taking key items from these financial statements and gleaning as much useful information as possible from them. For example, we might determine that the amount of **Johnson & Johnson**'s 2000 net income ($4,800 million) represented a return in excess of 15% on the total assets used to generate that income ($31,321 million). Is a return on assets of 15% satisfactory or unsatisfactory? This is a difficult question to answer. To make this judgment we would need more information than we have at this point. For example, we would like to know the trend in various financial measures for **Johnson & Johnson** for several years. We would also like to know information about other companies with similar operating characteristics (i.e., in the same industry). We will study all of this and more in this chapter as we look at the interesting and challenging subject of financial statement analysis.

• • •

Financial measures are used often to evaluate corporate performance. As a result, the Securities and Exchange Commission, the Financial Accounting Standards Board, the financial press, and the accounting profession are committed to high-quality financial reporting. Throughout this text, we have emphasized the importance of integrity in financial reporting as a means of protecting the interests of investors and creditors. This chapter explores in-depth financial statement analysis, building on the introductory sections of this important subject in preceding chapters.

Our discussion of financial statement analysis is divided into three sections. First, we consider general tools of analysis that emphasize comparing information about enterprises with relevant benchmarks. Second, we consider measures of liquidity and credit risk, followed by a consideration of profitability. Third, we present and discuss a comprehensive illustration in which we analyze a company's financial statements from the perspective of three important users of information—common stockholders, long-term creditors, and short-term creditors. Throughout this chapter, we draw on information that was covered in earlier chapters and we use new information that is presented here for the first time.

Financial Statements Are Designed for Analysis

In today's global economy, investment capital is always on the move. Through organized capital markets such as the New York Stock Exchange, investors each day shift billions of investment dollars among different companies, industries, and nations. Capital flows to those areas in which investors expect to earn the greatest returns with the least risk. How do investors forecast risk and potential returns? One of the most important ways is by analyzing accounting information for a specific company in the context of its unique industry setting.

The goal of accounting information is to provide economic decision makers with useful information. The financial statements generated through the accounting process are designed to assist users in identifying key relationships and trends. The financial statements of most publicly owned companies are classified and are presented in comparative form. Often, the word *consolidated* appears in the headings of the statements. Users of financial statements should have a clear understanding of these terms.

Most business organizations prepare **classified financial statements**, meaning that items with certain characteristics are placed together in a group, or classification. The purpose of these classifications is to *develop useful subtotals* that will assist users of the statements in their analyses. These classifications and subtotals are standardized throughout most of American business, a practice that assists decision makers in comparing the financial statements of different companies. An example of a classified financial statement is a balance sheet that separates assets and liabilities into current and noncurrent categories.

In **comparative financial statements**, the financial statement amounts *for several time periods* appear side by side in vertical columns. This assists investors in identifying and evaluating significant changes and trends.

Most large corporations own other companies through which they conduct some of their business activities. A corporation that owns other businesses is the **parent company**, and the owned companies are called **subsidiaries**. For example, **PepsiCo.**, which makes Pepsi Cola, also owns and operates **Tropicana** and **Frito-Lay**. In essence, these subsidiaries are part of the organization generally known as PepsiCo. **Consolidated financial statements** present the financial position and operating results of the parent company and its subsidiaries *as if they were a single business organization.*

For Example . . . At this point, take a brief look at the financial statements of **Tootsie Roll Industries, Inc.**, which appear in Appendix A at the end of the text. These financial statements illustrate all of the concepts discussed; they are classified and presented in comparative form, and they describe a consolidated business entity. These financial statements also have been *audited* by **PricewaterhouseCoopers LLP**, an international public accounting firm.

Two issues confront accountants analyzing international companies. First, there is great variation in accounting measurement, disclosure, and audit quality across countries. Second, obtaining the information necessary to conduct cross-border accounting analyses is frequently difficult and sometimes not possible. Financial reporting in China is a case in point. Until recent years China did not have active stock markets requiring financial reporting. In addition, there was no external auditing in forms that would be familiar to Westerners.

CASE IN POINT

TOOLS OF ANALYSIS

Significant changes in financial data are easier to see when financial statement amounts for two or more years are placed side by side in adjacent columns. Such a statement is called a *comparative financial statement*. The amounts for the most recent year are usually placed in the left-hand money column, closest to the words that describe the item. The balance sheet, income statement, and statement of cash flows are often prepared in the form of comparative statements. A highly condensed comparative income statement covering three years is shown in Exhibit 14–1.

Exhibit 14–1
COMPARATIVE INCOME STATEMENT

BENSON CORPORATION
Comparative Income Statement
For the Years Ended December 31, 2002, 2001, 2000
(in thousands of dollars)

	2002	2001	2000
Net sales	$600	$500	$400
Cost of goods sold	370	300	235
Gross profit	$230	$200	$165
Expenses	194	160	115
Net income	$ 36	$ 40	$ 50

Comparative statements place important financial information in a context that is useful for gaining better understanding. For example, knowing that Benson Corporation had sales of $600,000 in 2002 after years in which sales were $500,000 (2001) and $400,000 (2000) is helpful in understanding Benson's sales trend.

Few figures in a financial statement are highly significant in and of themselves. It is their relationship to other quantities or the amount and direction of change that is important. Analysis is largely a matter of establishing significant relationships and identifying changes and trends. Four widely used analytical techniques are (1) dollar and percentage changes, (2) trend percentages, (3) component percentages, and (4) ratios.

Dollar and Percentage Changes

The dollar amount of change from year to year is significant, and expressing the change in percentage terms adds perspective. For example, if sales this year have increased by $100,000, the fact that this is an increase of 10% over last year's sales of $1 million puts it in a different perspective than if it represented a 1% increase over sales of $10 million for the prior year.

The dollar amount of any change is the difference between the amount for a *comparison* year and the amount for a *base* year. The percentage change is computed by dividing the amount of the dollar change between years by the amount for the base year.

LO 1
Explain the uses of dollar and percentage changes, trend percentages, component percentages, and ratios.

My Notes

Dollar and percentage changes

	In Thousands			Increase or (Decrease)			
	Year 2002	Year 2001	Year 2000	2002 over 2001		2001 over 2000	
				Amount	%	Amount	%
Net sales	$600	$500	$400	$100	20%	$100	25%
Net income	36	40	50	(4)	(10)	(10)	(20)

Although net sales increased $100,000 in both 2001 and 2002, the percentage change differs because of the change in the base from 2000 to 2001. These calculations present no problems when the figures for the base year are positive amounts. If a negative amount or a zero amount appears in the base year, however, a percentage change cannot be computed. Thus if Benson Corporation had incurred a net loss in 2001, the percentage change in net income from 2001 to 2002 could not have been calculated.

Evaluating Percentage Changes in Sales and Earnings Computing the percentage changes in sales, gross profit, and net income from one year to the next gives insight into a company's rate of growth. If a company is experiencing growth in its economic activities, sales and earnings should increase at *more than the rate of inflation*. Assume, for example, that a company's sales increase by 6% while the general price level rises by 10%. The entire increase in the dollar amount of sales may be explained by inflation, rather than by an increase in sales volume (the number of units sold). In fact, the company may well have sold *fewer* goods than in the preceding year.

In measuring the dollar or percentage change in *quarterly* sales or earnings, it is customary to compare the results of the current quarter with those of the *same quarter in the preceding year*. Use of the same quarter of the preceding year as the base period prevents our analysis from being distorted by seasonal fluctuations in business activity.

Percentages Become Misleading When the Base Is Small Percentage changes may create a misleading impression when the dollar amount used as a base is unusually small. Occasionally we hear a television newscaster say that a company's profits have increased by a very large percentage, such as 900%. The initial impression created by such a statement is that the company's profits must now be excessively large. But assume, for example, that a company had net income of $100,000 in its first year, that in the second year net income drops to $10,000, and that in the third year net income returns to the $100,000 level. In this third year, net income has increased by $90,000, representing a 900% increase over the profits of the second year. What needs to be added is that this 900% increase in profits in the third year follows a very small profit in the second year and *exactly offsets* the 90% decline in profits in the second year.

Trend Percentages

The changes in financial statement items from a base year to following years are often expressed as *trend percentages* to show the extent and direction of change. Two steps are necessary to compute trend percentages. First, a base year is selected and each item in the financial statements for the base year is given a weight of 100%. The second step is to express each item in the financial statements for following years as a percentage of its base-year amount. This computation consists of dividing an item such as sales in the years after the base year by the amount of sales in the base year.

For example, assume that 1997 is selected as the base year and that sales in the base year amounted to $300,000 as shown in the following table. The trend percentages for sales are computed by dividing the sales amount of each following year by $300,000.

Also shown in the illustration are the yearly amounts of net income. The trend percentages for net income are computed by dividing the net income amount for each following year by the base-year amount of $15,000.

Dollar Amounts	2002	2001	2000	1999	1998	1997
Sales	$450,000	$360,000	$330,000	$321,000	$312,000	$300,000
Net income	22,950	14,550	21,450	19,200	15,600	15,000
Trend Percentages	**2002**	**2001**	**2000**	**1999**	**1998**	**1997**
Sales	150%	120%	110%	107%	104%	100%
Net income	153	97	143	128	104	100

These trend percentages indicate a modest growth in sales in the early years and accelerated growth in 2001 and 2002. Net income also shows an increasing growth trend with the exception of the year 2001, when net income declined despite a solid increase in sales. The problem was overcome in 2002 with a sharp rise in net income. Overall the trend percentages give a picture of a profitable, growing enterprise.

CASE IN POINT

During the first six months of 1999, **Fruit of the Loom, Inc.**, reported operating income of $28.1 million, compared to $160.7 million reported for the first six months of 1998. These figures represent an 83% decline in operating performance, computed as follows:

Decline in operating income ($160.7 − $28.1)	$132.6
Base period operating income (first 6 months of 1998)	$160.7
Percentage decrease ($132.6 ÷ $160.7)	83%

How much of an increase in operating income would be required in the first six months of 2000 to return to the 1998 level? The correct answer is an astounding 472%, computed as follows:

Required increase to reach 2000 operating level (from $28.1 to $160.7)	$132.6
Base period operating income (first 6 months of 1999)	$ 28.1
Required percentage increase ($132.6 ÷ $28.1)	472%

Unfortunately, **Fruit of the Loom, Inc.**, did not increase its operating income anywhere near the required 472% during the first six months of 2000.

© David Young-Wolff/PhotoEdit

Component Percentages

Component percentages indicate the *relative size* of each item included in a total. For example, each item in a balance sheet could be expressed as a percentage of total assets. This shows quickly the relative importance of each type of asset as well as the relative amount of financing obtained from current creditors, long-term creditors, and stockholders. By computing component percentages for several successive balance sheets, we can see which items are increasing in importance and which are becoming less significant.

Another application of component percentages is to express all items in an income statement as a percentage of net sales. Such a statement is called a *common size income statement*. See the condensed income statement in dollars and in common size form in Exhibit 14–2.

Exhibit 14–2

COMPONENT PERCENTAGES

My Notes

Are the year-to-date changes favorable?

	Income Statement			
	Dollars		Component Percentages	
	2002	2001	2002	2001
Net sales	$1,000,000	$600,000	100.0%	100.0%
Cost of goods sold	700,000	360,000	70.0	60.0
Expenses (including income taxes)	250,000	180,000	25.0	30.0
Net income	$ 50,000	$ 60,000	5.0%	10.0%

Looking only at the component percentages, we see that the increase in cost of goods sold (60% to 70%) was only partially offset by the decrease in expenses as a percentage of net sales, causing net income to decrease from 10% to 5% of net sales.

Ratios

A ratio is a simple mathematical expression of the relationship of one item to another. Every percentage may be viewed as a ratio—that is, one number expressed as a percentage of another.

Ratios may be stated in several ways. To illustrate, let us consider the current ratio, which expresses the relationship between a company's most liquid assets (current) and its liabilities that require payment soon (current). If current assets are $100,000 and current liabilities are $50,000, we may say either that the current ratio is 2 to 1 (which is written as 2 : 1) or that current assets are 200% of current liabilities. Either statement correctly summarizes the relationship—that is, that current assets are twice as large as current liabilities.

Ratios are particularly important in understanding financial statements because they permit us to compare information from one financial statement with information from another financial statement. For example, we might compare net income (taken from the income statement) with total assets (taken from the balance sheet) to see how effectively management is using available resources to earn a profit. For a ratio to be useful, however, the two amounts being compared must be logically related. In subsequent sections of this chapter, we will make extensive use of ratios to better demonstrate important dimensions of an enterprise's financial activities.

Standards of Comparison

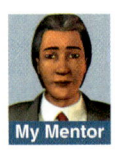

In using dollar and percentage changes, trend percentages, component percentages, and ratios, financial analysts constantly search for some standard of comparison against which to judge whether the relationships they have found are favorable or unfavorable. Two such standards are (1) the past performance of the company and (2) the performance of other companies in the same industry. For internal management purposes, another important comparison is with expected or budgeted numbers.

Past Performance of the Company Comparing financial information for a current period with similar information for prior years affords some basis for judging whether the condition of the business is improving or worsening. This comparison of data over time is sometimes called *horizontal* analysis, to express the idea of reviewing data for a number of consecutive periods. It is distinguished from *vertical,* or *static,* analysis, which refers to the review of the financial information within a single accounting period.

In addition to determining whether the situation is improving or becoming worse, horizontal analysis may aid in making estimates of future prospects. Because changes may reverse their direction at any time, however, projecting past trends into the future always involves risk.

A weakness of horizontal analysis is that comparison with the past does not afford any basis for evaluation in absolute terms. The fact that net income was 2% of sales last year and is 3% of sales this year indicates improvement, but if there is evidence that net income *should be* 7% of sales, the record for both years is unfavorable.

Industry Standards The limitations of horizontal analysis may be overcome to some extent by finding appropriate benchmarks against which to measure a particular company's performance. The benchmarks used by most analysts are the performance of comparable companies and the average performance of several companies in the same industry.[1]

Assume, for example, that the revenue of Alpha Airlines drops by 5% during the current year. If the revenue for the airlines industry had dropped an average of 15% during this year, Alpha's 5% decline might be viewed as a *favorable* performance. As another example, assume that Omega Co. earns a net income equal to 3% of net sales. This would be substandard if Omega were a manufacturer of commercial aircraft, but it would be satisfactory performance if it were a retail grocery chain because of the difference in earnings expected in the two industries.

When we compare a given company with its competitors or with industry averages, our conclusions are valid only if the companies in question are reasonably comparable. Because of the large number of diversified companies formed in recent years, the term *industry* is difficult to define, and even companies that fall roughly within the same industry may not be comparable in many respects. For example, one company may engage only in the marketing of oil products; another may be a fully integrated producer from the well to the gas pump; yet both are said to be in the oil industry.

Quality of Earnings

Profits are the lifeblood of a business entity. No entity can survive for long and accomplish its other goals unless it is profitable. Continuous losses drain assets from the business, consume owners' equity, and leave the company at the mercy of creditors. In assessing the prospects of a company, we are interested not only in the total *amount* of earnings but also in the *rate* of earnings on sales, on total assets, and on owners' equity. In addition, we must look at the *stability* and *source* of earnings. An erratic earnings performance over a period of years, for example, is less desirable than a steady level of earnings. A history of increasing earnings is preferable to a flat earnings record.

LO 2
Discuss the quality of a company's earnings, assets, and working capital.

A breakdown of sales and earnings by *major product lines* may be useful in evaluating the future performance of a company. Publicly owned companies include with their financial statements supplementary schedules showing sales and profits by product line and by geographical area. These schedules assist financial analysts in forecasting the effect on the company of changes in consumer demand for particular types of products.

Financial analysts often express the opinion that the earnings of one company are of higher quality than earnings of other similar companies. This concept of *quality of earnings* arises because each company's management can choose from a variety of accounting principles and methods, all of which are considered generally acceptable. A company's management often is under heavy pressure to report rising earnings, and accounting policies may be tailored toward this objective. We have already pointed out the impact on current reported earnings of the choice between the LIFO and FIFO methods

---

[1] Industry data are available from a number of sources. For example, Robert Morris Associates publishes *Annual Statement Studies,* which includes data from many thousands of annual reports, grouped into several hundred industry classifications. Industry classifications are subdivided further by company size. Dun & Bradstreet, Inc., annually publishes *Key Business Ratios* for more than 800 lines of business.

of inventory valuation and the choice of depreciation policies. In judging the quality of earnings, the financial analyst should consider whether the accounting principles and methods selected by management lead to a conservative measurement of earnings (high quality) or tend to inflate reported earnings (low quality).

MANAGEMENT STRATEGY AND FINANCIAL REPORTING

The quality of earnings are much more difficult to judge when considering international companies because financial reporting requirements differ around the globe. However, as business becomes more global, managers have a need to raise capital from investors and creditors in many global markets. As a result, companies must adapt strategies to report their financial condition as transparently as possible to a large set of diverse creditors and investors. One strategy used by many U.S. companies and many other large foreign companies is to issue additional financial statement disclosures to comply with overseas stock exchanges and regulatory requirements. For example, many companies publish financial statements based on both U.S. GAAP and International Accounting Standards.

Quality of Assets and the Relative Amount of Debt

Although a satisfactory level of earnings may be a good indication of the company's long-run ability to pay its debts and dividends, we must also look at the composition of assets, their condition and liquidity, the timing of repayment of liabilities, and the total amount of debt outstanding. A company may be profitable and yet be unable to pay its liabilities on time; sales and earnings may appear satisfactory, but plant and equipment may be deteriorating because of poor maintenance policies; valuable patents may be expiring; substantial losses may be imminent due to slow-moving inventories and past-due receivables. Companies with large amounts of debt often are vulnerable to increases in interest rates and to even temporary reductions in cash inflows.

MEASURES OF LIQUIDITY AND CREDIT RISK

Liquidity refers to a company's ability to meet its continuing obligations as they arise. For example, a company may have borrowed money and must make quarterly interest and principal payments to a financial institution. A company may purchase its inventory and other necessities on credit and pay the seller within 30 days of the purchase date. Transactions like these require a company to maintain a close watch on its liquidity.

We emphasize throughout this text the importance to investors, creditors, and other users of financial statements of information that permits them to assess the amount, timing, and uncertainty of future cash flows from the enterprise to them. As a result, analyzing an enterprise's liquidity and its credit risk is very important and is a natural place for us to start our study of analyzing financial statements.

In this section we learn about ways to assess liquidity, starting with the classified balance sheet and then looking at a number of ratios commonly used to glean information about liquidity from the financial statements.

A Classified Balance Sheet

LO 3
Explain the nature and purpose of classifications in financial statements.

In a classified balance sheet, assets usually are presented in three groups: (1) current assets, (2) plant and equipment, and (3) other assets. Liabilities are classified into two categories: (1) current liabilities and (2) long-term or noncurrent liabilities. A classified balance sheet for Computer City appears in Exhibit 14–3.

The classifications *current assets* and *current liabilities* are especially useful in evaluating the liquidity of the business entity.

Measures of Liquidity and Credit Risk

Exhibit 14–3
COMPUTER CITY CLASSIFIED BALANCE SHEET

COMPUTER CITY
Balance Sheet
December 31, 2002

Assets

Current assets:			
Cash			$ 30,000
Marketable Securities			11,000
Notes Receivable			5,000
Accounts Receivable			60,000
Inventory			70,000
Prepaid Expenses			4,000
Total current assets			$180,000
Plant and equipment:			
Land			$151,000
Building	$120,000		
Less: Accumulated Depreciation	9,000	111,000	
Sales Fixtures and Equipment	$ 45,000		
Less: Accumulated Depreciation	27,000	18,000	
Total plant and equipment			280,000
Other assets:			
Land Held as a Future Building Site			170,000
Total assets			$630,000

Liabilities & Stockholders' Equity

Current liabilities:		
Notes Payable (due in 6 months)		$ 10,000
Accounts Payable		62,000
Income Taxes Payable		13,000
Sales Taxes Payable		3,000
Accrued Expenses Payable		8,000
Unearned Revenue and Customer Deposits		4,000
Total current liabilities		$100,000
Long-term liabilities:		
Mortgage Payable (due in 10 years)		110,000
Total liabilities		$210,000
Stockholders' equity:		
Capital Stock (15,000 shares issued and outstanding)	$150,000	
Retained Earnings	270,000	
Total stockholders' equity		420,000
Total liabilities & stockholders' equity		$630,000

LO 4
Prepare a classified balance sheet and compute widely used measures of liquidity and credit risk.

Current Assets Current assets are relatively liquid resources. This category includes cash, investments in marketable securities, receivables, inventories, and prepaid expenses. To qualify as a current asset, an asset must already be cash or must be capable of *being converted into cash* or used up within a relatively short period of time, without interfering with normal business operations.

Current assets are tied to an enterprise's operating cycle. Most companies have several operating cycles within a year. This means that they take cash and purchase inventory, sell the inventory, and collect the receivable in cash several times within a year. For these companies, the time period used to identify current assets is one year, so any asset that is expected to be converted into cash within one year is classified as a current asset in the enterprise's balance sheet. Some enterprises, however, have relatively long operating cycles. For example, a company that constructs very large items (for example, airplanes or ships) may have a production period that extends well beyond one year. In these cases, the length of the company's operating cycle is used to define those assets that are classified as current. While most current assets are expected to be converted into cash, we also include as current assets those that will be used up or consumed during the year or operating cycle, if longer. For example, prepaid expenses are classified as current assets on the basis that their having been paid in advance preserves cash that otherwise would have to be paid in the current period. Combining these ideas, current assets can be defined as assets that are already cash, or are expected to be converted into cash or used up within the next year or operating cycle, whichever is longer.

In a balance sheet, current assets are listed in order of liquidity. (The closer an asset is to becoming cash, the greater its liquidity.) Thus cash always is listed first among the current assets, usually followed by investments in marketable securities, receivables, inventory, and prepaid expenses, in that order.

Current Liabilities   Current liabilities are *existing debts* that are expected to be paid by using the enterprise's current assets. Among the most common current liabilities are notes payable (due within one year), accounts payable, unearned revenue, and accrued expenses, such as income taxes payable, salaries payable, or interest payable. In the balance sheet, notes payable usually are listed first, followed by accounts payable; other types of current liabilities may be listed in any sequence.

The *relationship* between current assets and current liabilities is as important as the total dollar amount in either category. Current liabilities must be paid in the near future, and the cash to pay these liabilities is expected to come from current assets. Thus decision makers evaluating the liquidity of a business often compare the relative amounts of current assets and current liabilities, whereas an evaluation of *long-term* credit risk requires a comparison of total assets to total liabilities.

We will now use Computer City's classified balance sheet to examine some widely applied measures of short-term liquidity and long-term credit risk.

Working Capital

Working capital is a measurement sometimes used to express the relationship between current assets and current liabilities. Working capital is the *excess* of current assets over current liabilities. Computer City's working capital is *$80,000,* computed as follows:

My Notes

Working capital varies by industry and company size

Current assets	$180,000
Less: Current liabilities	100,000
Working capital	$ 80,000

Recall that current assets are expected to convert into cash (or be used up) within a relatively short period of time, and that current liabilities require a prompt cash payment. Thus working capital measures a company's potential excess *sources* of cash over its upcoming *uses* of cash.

The amount of working capital that a company needs to satisfy its liabilities as they come due varies with the size of the organization and the nature of its business activities.[2] An analyst familiar with the nature of a company's operations usually can

---

[2] A company with current liabilities in excess of its current assets has a *negative* amount of working capital. Negative working capital does not necessarily mean that a company is at risk of going bankrupt. As explained in the next Case in Point, telephone companies may fall into this category.

determine from the amount of working capital whether the company is in a sound financial position or is heading for financial difficulties.

Current Ratio

A widely used measure of short-term debt-paying ability is the **current ratio**. This ratio is computed by *dividing* total current assets by total current liabilities.

In the illustrated balance sheet of Computer City, current assets amount to $180,000 and current liabilities total $100,000. Therefore, Computer City's current ratio is *1.8 to 1,* computed as follows:

Current assets	$180,000
Current liabilities	$100,000
Current ratio ($180,000 ÷ $100,000)	1.8 to 1

My Notes
A widely used measure of liquidity

A current ratio of 1.8 to 1 means that the company's current assets are 1.8 times as large as its current liabilities.

The *higher* the current ratio, the more liquid the company appears to be. Historically, some bankers and other short-term creditors have believed that a company should have a current ratio of 2 to 1 or higher to qualify as a good credit risk. Such rules of thumb should be used carefully, however, because many successful businesses have current ratios of less than 2 to 1 because their receivables and inventory convert into cash quickly relative to the amount and timing of their payables. Likewise, it is possible for financially weak businesses to have high current ratios as a result of slow turnover in receivables and inventory. In other words, care must be taken in interpreting all ratios, including the current ratio, to ensure that inappropriate conclusions are not reached as a result of superficial analysis. Confirming the information communicated via one ratio by looking at other financial measures is often a good way to help ensure a valid interpretation.

Quick Ratio

Inventory and prepaid expenses are the *least liquid* of the current assets. In a business with a long operating cycle, it may take several months to convert inventory into cash. Therefore, some short-term creditors prefer the **quick ratio** (sometimes called the acid-test ratio) to the current ratio as a measure of short-term liquidity.

The quick ratio compares only the *most liquid* current assets—called **quick assets**—with current liabilities. Quick assets include cash, marketable securities, and receivables—the current assets that can be converted most quickly into cash. Computer City's quick ratio is *1.06 to 1,* computed as follows:

Quick assets (cash, marketable securities, and receivables)	$106,000
Current liabilities	$100,000
Quick ratio ($106,000 ÷ $100,000)	1.06 to 1

Quick ratios are especially useful in evaluating the liquidity of companies that have inventories of slow-moving merchandise (such as real estate), or inventories that have become excessive in size.

My Notes
A more demanding measure of liquidity

Debt Ratio

If a business fails and must be liquidated, the claims of creditors take priority over those of the owners. But if the business has a great deal of debt, there may not be enough assets even to make full payment to all creditors.

A basic measure of the safety of creditors' claims is the **debt ratio**, which states total liabilities as a *percentage* of total assets. A company's debt ratio is computed by dividing total liabilities by total assets, as shown below for Computer City:

Total liabilities	$210,000
Total assets	$630,000
Debt ratio ($210,000 ÷ $630,000)	33$\frac{1}{3}$%

The debt ratio is not a measure of short-term liquidity. Rather, it is a measure of creditors' *long-term* risk. The smaller the portion of total assets financed by creditors, the smaller the risk that the business may become unable to pay its debts. From the creditors' point of view, the *lower* the debt ratio, the *safer* their position.

Many financially sound American companies traditionally have maintained debt ratios under 50%. But again, the financial analyst must be familiar with industry characteristics. Banks, for example, may have very high debt ratios—often over 90%.

Evaluating Financial Ratios

We caution users of financial statements *against* placing much confidence in rules of thumb, such as *a current ratio should be at least 2 to 1, a quick ratio should be at least 1 to 1,* or *a debt ratio should be under 50%*. To interpret any financial ratio properly, the decision maker must first understand the characteristics of the company and the industry in which it operates.

Retailers, for example, tend to have higher current ratios than do wholesalers or manufacturing companies. Service-type businesses—which have no inventory—generally have lower current ratios than merchandising or manufacturing companies. Large businesses with good credit ratings and reliable sources of cash receipts are able to operate with lower current ratios than are small companies whose continuous inflow of cash may be less predictable.

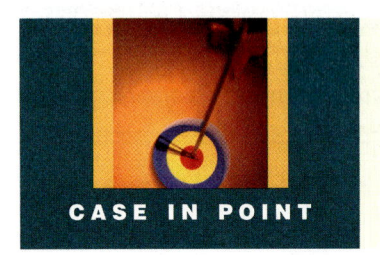

CASE IN POINT

Large telephone companies are regarded within the business community as pillars of financial strength. Yet these companies do not have high current ratios. Such financially sound companies as **Bell Atlantic**, **BellSouth NYNEX**, and **Pacific Telesis** often operate with current ratios of less than 1 to 1.

Although a high current ratio is one indication of strong debt-paying ability, an extremely high ratio—say, 4 or 5 to 1—may indicate that *too much* of the company's resources are tied up in current assets. In maintaining such a highly liquid position, the company may be using its financial resources inefficiently and not earning the return that could be earned if the assets were invested in a more productive way.

Standards for Comparison Financial analysts generally use two criteria in evaluating the reasonableness of a financial ratio. One criterion is the *trend* in the ratio over a period of years. By reviewing this trend, analysts are able to determine whether a company's performance or financial position is improving or deteriorating. Second, analysts often compare a company's financial ratios with those of *similar companies* and with *industrywide averages*. These comparisons assist analysts in evaluating a particular ratio in light of the company's current business environment.

Annual Reports Publicly owned corporations issue **annual reports** that provide a great deal of information about the company. For example, annual reports include

Measures of Liquidity and Credit Risk

comparative financial statements that have been audited by a firm of independent public accountants. They also include five- or ten-year *summaries* of key financial data, and **management's discussion and analysis** of the company's operating results, liquidity, and financial position. This is where management identifies and discusses favorable and unfavorable trends and events that may affect the company in the future. (For example, in Appendix A, find the management discussion in the **Tootsie Roll Industries, Inc.**, annual report.)

Annual reports are mailed directly to all stockholders of the corporation. They are also available to the public either through the Internet, in libraries, or by writing or calling the stockholder relations department of the corporation.

Industry Information Financial information about *entire industries* is available through financial publications (such as Dun & Bradstreet, Inc.), and through on-line databases (such as Media General Financial Services). Such information allows investors and creditors to compare the financial health of an individual company with the industry in which that company operates.

CASE IN POINT

Media General Financial Services continuously updates financial ratios for individual companies and provides norms for entire industries. As an example of industry norm data, the average current ratios of several industry groupings are shown below for a recent year:

Industry Group	Average Current Ratio
Air transportation (major carriers)	.9 to 1
Retail (general merchandise)	1.9 to 1
Retail (apparel)	2.3 to 1
Wholesale (grocery)	1.2 to 1
Manufacturing (computers)	1.6 to 1
Telephone (regional)	.8 to 1

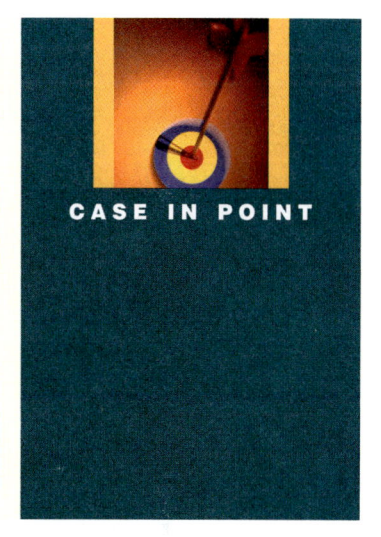

Usefulness and Limitations of Financial Ratios A financial ratio expresses the relationship of one amount to another. Most users of financial statements find that certain ratios assist them in quickly evaluating the financial position, profitability, and future prospects of a business. A comparison of key ratios for several successive years usually indicates whether the business is becoming stronger or weaker. Ratios also provide a way to compare quickly the financial strength and profitability of different companies.

Users of financial statements should recognize, however, that ratios have several limitations. For example, management may enter into year-end transactions that temporarily improve key ratios—a process called **window dressing**.

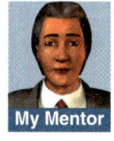

To illustrate, the balance sheet of Computer City (Exhibit 14–3) includes current assets of $180,000 and current liabilities of $100,000, indicating a current ratio of *1.8 to 1*. What would happen if shortly before year-end, management used $20,000 of the company's cash to pay accounts payable that are not due until January of 2003? This transaction would reduce current assets to $160,000 ($180,000 − $20,000) and current liabilities to $80,000 ($100,000 − $20,000), resulting in an increase in the current ratio to a more impressive 2 to 1 ($160,000 ÷ $80,000). Is the company really better off as a result of having simply paid $20,000 of liabilities a few days early? The answer is probably no, although looking only at the current ratio one might think it is stronger after paying the $20,000 than before. Such steps to window dress the financial statements are common and, within reason, are a natural part of financial reporting. The astute reader of financial statements needs to be aware of this and should look for instances where there is evidence that steps have been taken to artificially improve a company's appearance. Usually this can be done by looking at multiple financial measures rather than focusing on a single financial measure.

Financial statement ratios contain the same limitations as do the dollar amounts used in financial statements. For example, many assets are reported at historical cost rather than current market value. Also, financial statement ratios express only *financial* relationships. They give no indication of a company's progress in achieving nonfinancial goals, such as improving customer satisfaction or worker productivity. A thorough analysis of investment opportunities involves more than merely computing and comparing financial ratios.

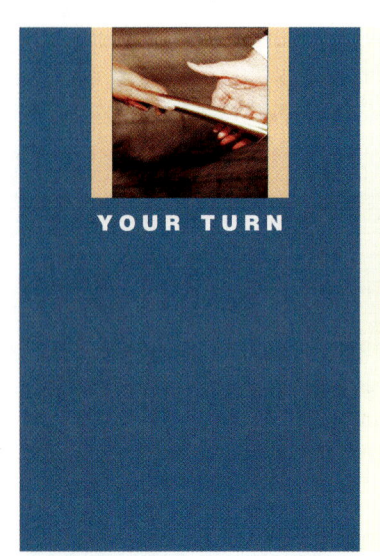

YOUR TURN

You as a Potential Investor

Assume that you have several thousand dollars to invest in the stock market. Given that "people will always have to eat," you have decided to explore the possibility of investing in **Wendy's** and **McDonald's**. Your analysis of each company's financial statements reveals that both have negative working capital and both have current and quick ratios of less than 1 to 1.

Based on your findings, should you be concerned about the short-term liquidity of these two companies? Explain.

*Our comments appear on page 663.

Liquidity, Credit Risk, and the Law

Accountants view a business entity as separate from the other economic activities of its owners, regardless of how the business is organized. The law, however, draws an important distinction between *corporations* and *unincorporated* business organizations. Users of financial statements should understand this legal distinction, as it may affect both creditors and owners.

Under the law, the owners of unincorporated businesses (sole proprietorships and partnerships) are *personally liable* for any and all debts of the business organization. Therefore, creditors of unincorporated businesses often base their lending decisions on the financial position of the *owners,* rather than the financial strength of the business entity.[3]

If a business is organized as a corporation, however, the owners (stockholders) are *not* personally responsible for the liabilities of the business. Creditors may look *only to the business entity* in seeking payment of their claims. Therefore, the liquidity of the business entity becomes much more important if the business is organized as a corporation.

Small Corporations and Loan Guarantees Small corporations often do not have sufficient financial resources to qualify for the credit they need. In such cases, creditors may require that one or more of the company's stockholders personally guarantee (or cosign) specific debts of the business entity. By cosigning debts of the corporation, the

---

[3] In a *limited* partnership, only the *general partners* are personally responsible for the debts of the business. Every limited partnership must have one or more general partners.

individual stockholders *do* become personally liable for the debt if the corporation fails to make payment.

CASE IN POINT

Two brothers, Bob and Jack, each decided to form small businesses. Bob started a small appliance store that was organized as a sole proprietorship. Jack started a car wash that was organized as a corporation, with himself as the primary stockholder. As the businesses grew, each needed additional capital for expansion purposes. The bank was willing to loan additional funds to Bob's appliance store because Bob had considerable personal assets, and the bank knew that if necessary, it could access those assets for repayment. Jack's business, on the other hand, had a more difficult time getting the additional funding it required because of the limited liability feature of his corporation. Jack, too, had significant personal resources, and he agreed to cosign a note with the company so that he could obtain the required bank financing. While the two businesses were initially organized as different legal forms, they became similar when Jack committed his personal assets to the company to obtain the bank financing.

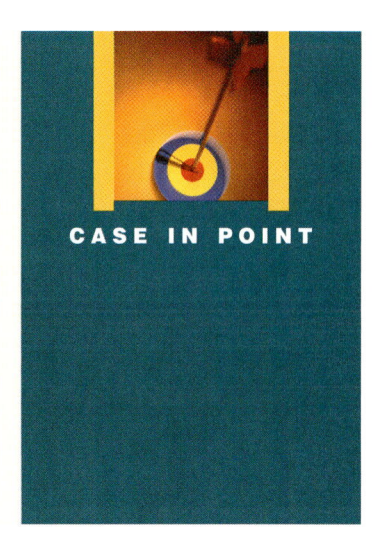

MEASURES OF PROFITABILITY

Measures of a company's *profitability* are of interest to equity investors and management, and are drawn primarily from the income statement. The measures that we discuss in this chapter include percentage changes in key measurements, gross profit rates, operating income, net income as a percentage of sales, earnings per share, return on assets, and return on equity.

Public opinion polls show that many people believe that most businesses earn a profit equal to 30% or more of the sales price of their merchandise. Actually, this is far from true. Most successful companies earn a net income of between 5% and, perhaps, 15% of sales revenue.

CASE IN POINT

In **Target Corporation**'s 2000 income statement, revenues are reported at $36,362 million and net income at $1,264 million. While both numbers are large in absolute terms, net income was only 3.5% of sales ($1,264/$36,362). Of every dollar of sales revenue, the company's costs exceeded 96 cents. While this does not sound like a particularly strong level of performance, it actually represents an improvement over each of the two previous years. It is also consistent with the profitability of other large retail establishments.

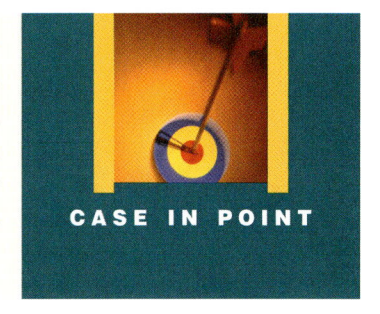

Classifications in the Income Statement

An income statement may be prepared in either the *multiple-step* or the *single-step* format. The multiple-step income statement is more useful in illustrating accounting concepts because it provides more detailed information than the single-step format. A multiple-step income statement for Computer City is shown in Exhibit 14–4.

A knowledge of accounting does not enable you to say what the level of corporate earnings *should be;* however, it does enable you to read audited financial statements that show what corporate earnings *actually are*. Moreover, you are aware that the information in published financial statements of corporations has been audited by CPA firms and has been reviewed in detail by government agencies, such as the Securities and Exchange Commission (SEC). Consequently, you know that the profits reported in these published

Exhibit 14–4

COMPUTER CITY INCOME STATEMENT (MULTIPLE-STEP)

COMPUTER CITY
Income Statement
For the Year Ended December 31, 2002

Net sales		$900,000
Less: Cost of goods sold (including transportation-in)		540,000
Gross profit		$360,000
Less: Operating expenses:		
Selling expenses:		
Sales Salaries and Commissions	$64,800	
Advertising	42,000	
Delivery Service	14,200	
Depreciation: Store Equipment	9,000	
Other Selling Expenses	6,000	
Total selling expenses		$136,000
General and Administrative Expenses:		
Administrative and Office Salaries	$93,000	
Utilities	3,100	
Depreciation: Building	3,000	
Other General and Administrative Expenses	4,900	
Total general and administrative expenses		104,000
Total operating expenses		240,000
Operating income		$120,000
Less (add): Nonoperating items:		
Interest Expense	$12,000	
Purchase Discounts Lost	1,200	
Interest Revenue	(3,200)	
Income before income taxes		10,000
		$110,000
Income Taxes Expense		38,000
Net income		$ 72,000
Earnings per share		$4.80

financial statements are reasonably reliable; they have been determined in accordance with generally accepted accounting principles and verified by independent experts.

Some Specific Examples of Corporate Earnings and Losses

Not all leading corporations earn a profit every year. For the 10 years from 1981 through 1990, **Pan American Airways** reported a net loss each year. Late in 1991, Pan Am—at one time America's "flagship" airline—ceased operations. Many American corporations had some bad years in the early 1990s. Each of America's Big Three automakers reported huge losses. So did most of the nation's major airlines. Even **IBM** sustained a net loss—the first in the company's 80-year history.

The oil companies have been particularly subject to criticism for so-called excessive profits, so let us briefly look at the profits of **ExxonMobil**, the world's largest oil company. Recent financial statements (audited by **PricewaterhouseCoopers LLP**) show that 2000 profits amounted to $17.7 billion. Standing alone, that figure seems enormous—but we need to look a little farther. The total revenue was over $228 billion, so net income amounted to slightly less than 7.8% of sales. On the other hand, income taxes, excise taxes, and other taxes and duties levied on **Exxon** amounted to more than $55 billion, or about three times as much as the company's profit. Thus taxation represents a far greater portion of the cost of a gallon of gasoline than does the oil company's profit. In previous years, these relationships were even more pronounced. In 1999, for example, taxes represented about seven times as much as ExxonMobil's net income.

You as a Member of the House of Representatives

Assume you are a member of the U.S. House of Representatives. Because of the recent global financial crises and the spectacular crash of the technology stocks, your constituents have been pushing you to mandate more regulation of stock exchanges. These constituents claim that unfettered global capital markets have become a free-for-all and that there is a need for more oversight, tighter regulation, and higher ethical standards. They state that the accounting and corporate-governance requirements for the companies listed on U.S. exchanges are not meeting the public's expectations. How would you respond?

*Our comments appear on page 664.

Multiple-Step Income Statements

A multiple-step income statement draws its name from the *series of steps* in which costs and expenses are deducted from revenue. As a first step, the cost of goods sold is deducted from net sales to determine the subtotal *gross profit*. As a second step, operating expenses are deducted to obtain a subtotal called **operating income** (or income from operations). As a final step, income taxes expense and other nonoperating items are taken into consideration to arrive at *net income*.

Notice that the income statement is divided into four major sections: (1) revenue, (2) cost of goods sold, (3) operating expenses, and (4) nonoperating items. Multiple-step income statements are noted for their numerous sections and the development of significant subtotals.

LO 5
Prepare a multiple-step and a single-step income statement and compute widely used measures of profitability.

The Revenue Section In a merchandising company, the revenue section of the income statement usually contains only one line, entitled *net sales*. (Other types of revenue, if any, appear in the final section of the statement.)

Investors and managers are vitally interested in the *trend* in net sales. As one means of evaluating this trend, they often compute the percentage change in net sales from year to year. A **percentage change** is the dollar amount of the *change* in a financial measurement, expressed as a percentage. It is computed by dividing the dollar amount of increase or decrease by the dollar amount of the measurement *before* the change occurred. (Dollar changes *cannot* be expressed as percentages if the financial statement amount in the earlier period is zero or has changed from a negative amount to a positive amount.)

In our economy, most prices increase over time. The average increase in prices during the year is called the *rate of inflation*. Because of inflation, a company's net sales may increase slightly from year to year even if the company is not selling greater amounts of merchandise. If a company's physical sales volume is increasing, net sales usually will grow faster than the rate of inflation.

If a company's sales grow faster than the *industry average,* the company increases its **market share**—that is, its share of total industry sales.

Publicly owned corporations include in their annual reports schedules summarizing operating data—such as net sales—for a period of 5 or 10 years. This information is also readily available through several on-line databases.

The Cost of Goods Sold Section The second section of a merchandising company's income statement shows cost of goods sold for the period. Cost of goods sold usually appears as a single dollar amount, which includes such incidental items as freight costs and normal shrinkage losses.

Gross Profit: A Key Subtotal In a multiple-step income statement, gross profit appears as a subtotal. This makes it easy for users of the income statement to compute the company's *gross profit rate* (or profit margin).

CASE IN POINT

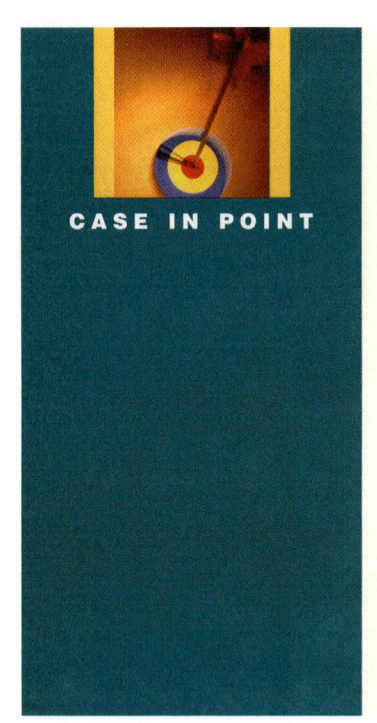

Procter & Gamble is a major consumer products company that manufactures and sells a wide variety of well-known brands, including Folgers coffee, Cover Girl beauty care, Bounty paper towels, and Pampers diapers. Sales (in millions) for the five-year period ending in 2001 were as follows:

	2001	2000	1999	1998	1997
Sales	$39,244	$39,951	$38,125	$37,154	$35,764
Percentage increase (decrease)	(1.8%)	4.8%	2.6%	3.9%	1.4%

Sales grew during the first four years of the five-year period and then declined in the fifth year. The highest rate of growth was in 2000 (4.8%), and the decline in 2001 was 1.8%. Each year's percentage is computed by taking the difference from the previous year and dividing that amount by the previous year's total. For example, the rate of growth in sales for 1999 over 1998 is computed as follows: [($38,125 − $37,154)/$37,154 = 2.6%]. The following interpretation of the 1999 growth percentage is presented in the company's 1999 annual report: "Net sales grew to a record $38.1 billion, up 3% versus last year. While this growth rate was below our expectations, we are encouraged by the increased percentage of sales in products that leverage our technology advantages."

The gross profit rate is gross profit expressed as a *percentage of net sales*. In 2002, Computer City earned an average gross profit rate of *40%*, computed as follows:

Dollar amount of gross profit	$360,000
Net sales	$900,000
Gross profit rate ($360,000 ÷ $900,000)	40%

In evaluating the gross profit rate of a particular company, the analyst should consider the rates earned in prior periods, as well as the rates earned by *other companies* in the same industry. For most merchandising companies, gross profit rates usually lie between 20% and 50%, depending on the types of products they sell. These rates usually are lowest on fast-moving merchandise, such as groceries, and highest on specialty and novelty products.

Under normal circumstances, a company's gross profit rate tends to remain *reasonably stable* from one period to the next. Significant changes in this rate may provide investors with an early indication of changing consumer demand for the company's products.

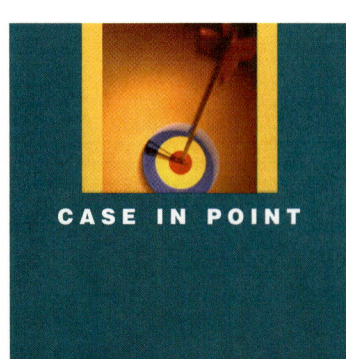

CASE IN POINT

The gross profit percentage of most companies remains relatively constant over time. For example, the following are the gross profit rates of four major U.S. corporations for the years 1998, 1999, and 2000:

	2000	1999	1998
3M	47%	48%	47%
Microsoft	87	86	84
Alcoa	24	23	22
Sears	26	27	27

While the percentages vary considerably from one industry to another, for each company the rates are relatively constant for all three years.

The Operating Expense Section Operating expenses are incurred for the purpose of *producing revenue*. These expenses often are subdivided into the classifications of *selling expenses* and *general and administrative expenses*. Subdividing operating expenses into functional classifications aids management and other users of the statements in separately evaluating different aspects of the company's operations. For example, selling expenses often rise and fall in concert with changes in net sales. Administrative expenses, on the other hand, usually remain more constant from one period to the next.

Operating Income: Another Key Subtotal Some of the revenues and expenses of a business result from activities other than the company's basic business operations. Common examples include interest earned on investments and income taxes expense.

Operating income (or income from operations) shows the relationship between revenue earned from customers and expenses incurred in producing this revenue. In effect, operating income measures the profitability of a company's *basic or core business operations* and leaves out other types of revenue and expenses.

Nonoperating Items Revenue and expenses that are not directly related to the company's primary business activities are listed in a final section of the income statement following operating income.

Two significant nonoperating items are interest expense and income taxes expense. Interest expense results from the manner in which assets are *financed*, not the manner in which these assets are used in business operations. Income taxes expense is not included among the operating expenses because paying income taxes *does not help to produce revenue*. Nonoperating revenues, such as interest and dividends earned on investments, also are listed in this final section of the income statement.

Net Income Many equity investors consider net income (or net loss) to be the most important figure in a company's financial statements. This amount usually represents the overall increase (or decrease) in owners' equity resulting from all profit-directed activities during the period.

Financial analysts often compute net income as a *percentage of net sales* (net income divided by net sales). This measurement provides an indication of management's *ability to control expenses* and to retain a reasonable portion of its revenue as profit.

The normal ratio of net income to net sales varies greatly by industry. In some industries, companies may be successful by earning a net income equal to only 2% or 3% of net sales. In other industries, net income may be much higher. In 2002, Computer City's net income amounts to 8% of net sales, which is very good for a computer retailer.

Net income	$ 72,000
Net sales	$900,000
Net income as a percentage of net sales ($72,000 ÷ $900,000)	8%

LO 6
Put a company's net income into perspective by relating it to sales, assets, and stockholders' equity.

Earnings per Share

Ownership of a corporation is evidenced by *shares* of capital stock. What does the net income of a corporation mean to someone who owns, say, 100 shares of a corporation's capital stock? To assist individual stockholders in relating the corporation's net income to *their ownership shares*, large corporations compute **earnings per share** and show these amounts at the bottom of their income statements.[4]

---

[4] Only publicly held corporations are *required* to report earnings on a per share basis. For small businesses such as Computer City, the reporting of earnings per share is optional.

In the simplest case, earnings per share is net income, expressed on a per-share basis. For example, the balance sheet in Exhibit 14–3 indicates that Computer City has 15,000 shares of capital stock outstanding.[5] Assuming these shares had been outstanding all year, earnings per share amounts to *$4.80:*

Net income	$72,000
Shares of capital stock outstanding	15,000
Earnings per share ($72,000 ÷ 15,000 shares)	$4.80

Earnings per share is one of the most widely used of all accounting ratios. The *trend* in earnings per share—and the expected earnings in future periods—are *major factors* affecting the market value of a company's shares.

Price-Earnings Ratio

LO 7
Compute the ratios widely used in financial statement analysis and explain the significance of each.

Financial analysts express the relationship between the market price of a company's stock and the underlying earnings per share as a **price-earnings (p/e) ratio**. This ratio is computed by dividing the current market price per share of the company's stock by annual earnings per share. (A p/e ratio cannot be computed for a period in which the company incurs a net loss.)

To illustrate, assume that at the end of 2002, Computer City's capital stock is trading among investors at a market price of *$96* per share. The p/e ratio of the company's stock is computed as follows:

Current market price per share of stock	$96
Earnings per share (for the last 12 months)	$4.80
Price-earnings ratio ($96 ÷ $4.80)	20

Technically, this ratio is 20 to 1. But it is common practice to omit the "to 1" and merely to describe a p/e ratio by the first number. The p/e ratios of many publicly owned corporations are quoted daily in the financial pages of many newspapers.

The p/e ratio reflects *investors' expectations* concerning the company's *future performance*. The more optimistic these expectations, the higher the p/e ratio is likely to be. Traditionally, stocks of financially sound companies with stable earnings usually sell at between 12 and 15 times earnings. If investors anticipate rapid earnings growth, p/e ratios rise into the twenties, thirties, or even higher.

A p/e ratio of 10 or less often indicates that investors expect earnings to *decline* from the current level. It could also mean, however, that the stock is *undervalued*. Likewise, a stock with a p/e ratio of 30 or more usually means that investors expect earnings to *increase* from the current level. However, it may also signal that the stock is *overvalued*.

One word of caution. If earnings decline to *very low levels*, the price of the stock usually does not follow the earnings all the way down. Therefore, a company with *very low earnings* is likely to have a *high p/e ratio* even if investors are not optimistic about future earnings.

Single-Step Income Statements

In their annual reports, many publicly owned corporations present their financial statements in a highly condensed format. For this reason, the *single-step* income statement

---

[5] Assume that all 15,000 shares have been outstanding throughout the year. Computation of earnings per share in more complex situations is addressed in Chapter 12.

is widely used in annual reports. The 2002 income statement of Computer City appears in Exhibit 14–5 in a single-step format.

Exhibit 14–5

COMPUTER CITY INCOME STATEMENT (SINGLE STEP)

COMPUTER CITY
Income Statement
For the Year Ended December 31, 2002

Revenue:		
Net sales		$900,000
Interest earned		3,200
Total revenue		$903,200
Less: Costs and expenses:		
Cost of goods sold	$540,000	
Selling expenses	136,000	
General and administrative expenses	104,000	
Interest expense	12,000	
Purchase discounts lost	1,200	
Income taxes expense	38,000	
Total costs and expenses		831,200
Net income		$ 72,000
Earnings per share		$4.80

The single-step form of income statement takes its name from the fact that all costs and expenses are deducted from total revenue in a single step. No subtotals are shown for gross profit or for operating income, although the statement provides investors with enough information to compute these subtotals on their own.

Evaluating the Adequacy of Net Income

How much net income must a business earn to be considered successful? Obviously, the dollar amount of net income that investors consider adequate depends on the *size of the business*. An annual net income of $1 million might seem impressive for an automobile dealership but would represent very poor performance for a company the size of **General Motors**, **Ford**, or **DaimlerChrysler**.

Investors usually consider two factors in evaluating a company's profitability: (1) the trend in earnings and (2) the amount of current earnings in relation to the amount of the resources needed to produce the earnings.

Some investors regard the *trend* in earnings from year to year as more important than the amount of net income in the current period. Equity investors stand to benefit from the company's performance over the long run. Years of steadily increasing earnings may increase the value of the stockholders' investment manyfold.

In evaluating the current level of earnings, many investors use *return on investment* analysis.

Return on Investment (ROI)

We have emphasized throughout this text that a basic purpose of accounting is to assist decision makers in efficiently allocating and using economic resources. In deciding where to invest their money, equity investors want to know how efficiently companies utilize resources. A common method of evaluating the efficiency with which financial resources are employed is to compute the rate of return earned on these resources. This rate of return is called the *return on investment,* or *ROI*.

Mathematically, computing return on investment is simple: the annual return (or profit) generated by the investment is stated as a *percentage* of the average amount invested throughout the year. The basic idea is illustrated by the following formula:

$$\text{Return on Investment (ROI)} = \frac{\text{Return}}{\text{Average Amount Invested}}$$

My Notes
ROI general formula

The return is earned throughout the period. Therefore, it is logical to express this return as a percentage of the *average* amount invested during the period, rather than the investment at year-end. The average amount invested usually is computed by adding the amounts invested as of the beginning and end of the year, and dividing this total by 2.

The concept of ROI is applied in many different situations, such as evaluating the profitability of a business, a branch location, or a specific investment opportunity. As a result, a number of variations in the basic ROI ratio have been developed, each suited to a particular type of analysis. These ratios differ in the manner in which return and average amount invested are defined. We will discuss two common applications of the ROI concept: *return on assets* and *return on equity*.

Return on Assets (ROA) This ratio is used in evaluating whether management has earned a reasonable return with the assets under its control. In this computation, return usually is defined as *operating income,* since interest expense and income taxes are determined by factors other than the manner in which assets are used. The **return on assets** is computed as follows:

$$\text{Return on Assets (ROA)} = \frac{\text{Operating Income}}{\text{Average Total Assets}}$$

My Notes
The return on total assets is operating income

Let us now determine the return on assets earned by the management of Computer City in 2002. Operating income, as shown in the income statement in Exhibit 14–4, amounts to *$120,000*. Assume that Computer City's assets at the beginning of 2002 totaled $570,000. The illustrated balance sheet in Exhibit 14–3 shows total assets of $630,000 at year-end. Therefore, the company's *average* total assets during the year amounted to *$600,000* [($570,000 + $630,000) ÷ 2]. The return on assets in 2002 is *20%*, determined as follows:

$$\frac{\text{Operating Income}}{\text{Average Total Assets}} = \frac{\$120,000}{\$600,000} = 20\%$$

Most successful businesses earn a return on average total assets of, perhaps, 15% or more. At this writing, businesses must pay interest rates of between 6% and 12% to borrow money. If a business is well managed and has good future prospects, management should be able to earn a return on assets that is higher than the company's cost of borrowing.

Return on Equity (ROE) The return on assets that we calculated above measures the efficiency with which management has utilized the assets under its control, regardless of whether these assets were financed with debt or equity capital. The **return on equity** ratio, in contrast, looks only at the return earned by management on the stockholders' investment—that is, on *owners' equity*.

The return to stockholders is *net income,* which represents the return from all sources, both operating and nonoperating. Thus return on equity is computed as follows:

$$\text{Return on Equity (ROE)} = \frac{\text{Net Income}}{\text{Average Total Stockholders' Equity}}$$

My Notes

The return on equity is net income

To illustrate, let us again turn to the 2002 financial statements of Computer City. The company earned net income of *$72,000*. The year-end balance sheet (Exhibit 14–3) shows total stockholders' equity of $420,000. To enable us to complete our computation, we will assume that the stockholders' equity at the *beginning* of the year amounted to $380,000. Therefore, the *average* stockholders' equity for the year amounts to *$400,000* [($380,000 + $420,000) ÷ 2]. The return on stockholders' equity in 2002 is *18%*, computed as follows:

$$\frac{\text{Net Income}}{\text{Average Total Stockholders' Equity}} = \frac{\$72,000}{\$400,000} = 18\%$$

Traditionally, stockholders have expected to earn an average annual return of 12% or more from equity investments in large, financially strong companies. Annual returns on equity of 30% or more are not uncommon, especially in rapidly growing companies with new or highly successful products.

The return on equity may be higher or lower than the overall return on assets, depending on how the company has financed its assets and on the amounts of its nonoperating revenue and expenses. A company that suffers a net loss provides its stockholders with a *negative* return on stockholders' equity.

CASE IN POINT

Four well-known corporations earned these returns on assets and on equity in 2000:

	Return on Assets	Return on Equity
Procter & Gamble	11%	34%
Alcoa	6%	17%
Federal Express	6%	15%
ConAgra	3%	14%

Many companies earn approximately the same rates of return year after year. In others, the annual rates of return fluctuate greatly, particularly when net income significantly changes.

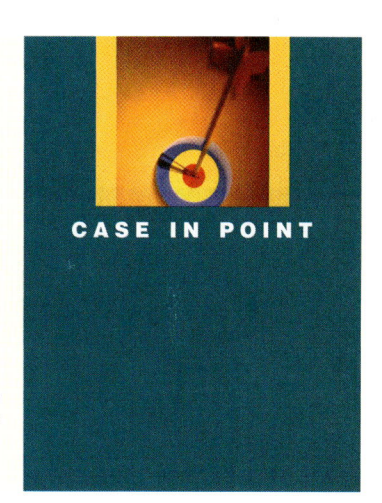

COMPREHENSIVE ILLUSTRATION: SEACLIFF COMPANY

Now that we have presented techniques that are useful in better understanding an enterprise's financial statements, we will show the comprehensive analysis of a company. This illustration draws from material presented in this chapter as well as from information presented earlier in the text. We take a comprehensive look at the analysis of financial statements from the perspectives of three important groups: common stockholders, long-term creditors, and short-term creditors.

The basic information for our analysis is contained in a set of condensed two-year comparative financial statements for Seacliff Company shown in Exhibits 14–6 through 14–10. Summarized statement data, together with computations of dollar increases and decreases, and component percentages where applicable, have been compiled. For convenience in this illustration, relatively small dollar amounts have been used in the Seacliff Company financial statements.

Exhibit 14–6 SEACLIFF INCOME STATEMENTS

SEACLIFF COMPANY
Comparative Income Statement
For the Years Ended December 31, 2002, and December 31, 2001

	2002	2001	Increase or (Decrease) Dollars	%	Percentage of Net Sales 2002	2001
Net sales	$900,000	$750,000	$150,000	20.0	100.0	100.0
Cost of goods sold	530,000	420,000	110,000	26.2	58.9	56.0
Gross profit on sales	$370,000	$330,000	$ 40,000	12.1	41.1	44.0
Operating expenses:						
Selling expenses	$117,000	$ 75,000	$ 42,000	56.0	13.0	10.0
General and administrative expenses	126,000	95,000	31,000	32.6	14.0	12.7
Total operating expenses	$243,000	$170,000	$ 73,000	42.9	27.0	22.7
Operating income	$127,000	$160,000	$ (33,000)	(20.6)	14.1	21.3
Interest expense	24,000	30,000	(6,000)	(20.0)	2.7	4.0
Income before income taxes	$103,000	$130,000	$ (27,000)	(20.8)	11.4	17.3
Income taxes	28,000	40,000	(12,000)	(30.0)	3.1	5.3
Net income	$ 75,000	$ 90,000	$ (15,000)	(16.7)	8.3	12.0
Earnings per share of common stock	$ 13.20	$ 20.25	$ (7.05)	(34.8)		

Exhibit 14–7 SEACLIFF STATEMENTS OF RETAINED EARNINGS

SEACLIFF COMPANY
Statement of Retained Earnings
For the Years Ended December 31, 2002, and December 31, 2001

	2002	2001	Increase or (Decrease) Dollars	%
Retained earnings, beginning of year	$176,000	$115,000	$ 61,000	53.0
Net income	75,000	90,000	(15,000)	(16.7)
	$251,000	$205,000	$ 46,000	22.4
Less: Dividends on common stock ($5.00 per share in 2001, $4.80 per share in 2002)	$ 24,000	$ 20,000	$ 4,000	20.0
Dividends on preferred stock ($9 per share)	9,000	9,000		
	$ 33,000	$ 29,000	$ 4,000	13.8
Retained earnings, end of year	$218,000	$176,000	$ 42,000	23.9

Comprehensive Illustration: Seacliff Company

Exhibit 14–8

SEACLIFF BALANCE SHEETS

SEACLIFF COMPANY
Condensed Comparative Balance Sheet*
December 31, 2002, and December 31, 2001

			Increase or (Decrease)		Percentage of Total Assets	
Assets	**2002**	**2001**	**Dollars**	**%**	**2002**	**2001**
Current assets	$390,000	$288,000	$102,000	35.4	41.1	33.5
Plant and equipment (net)	500,000	467,000	33,000	7.1	52.6	54.3
Other assets (loans to officers)	60,000	105,000	(45,000)	(42.9)	6.3	12.2
Total assets	$950,000	$860,000	$ 90,000	10.5	100.0	100.0
Liabilities & Stockholders' Equity						
Liabilities:						
Current liabilities	$112,000	$ 94,000	$ 18,000	19.1	11.8	10.9
12% long-term note payable (due in 7 years)	200,000	250,000	(50,000)	(20.0)	21.1	29.1
Total liabilities	$312,000	$344,000	$ (32,000)	(9.3)	32.9	40.0
Stockholders' equity:						
9% preferred stock, $100 par, callable at 105	$100,000	$100,000	—	—	10.5	11.6
Common stock, $50 par	250,000	200,000	$ 50,000	25.0	26.3	23.2
Additional paid-in capital	70,000	40,000	30,000	75.0	7.4	4.7
Retained earnings	218,000	176,000	42,000	23.9	22.9	20.5
Total stockholders' equity	$638,000	$516,000	$122,000	23.6	67.1	60.0
Total liabilities & stockholders' equity	$950,000	$860,000	$ 90,000	10.5	100.0	100.0

*In order to focus attention on important subtotals, this statement is highly condensed and does not show individual asset and liability items. These details will be introduced as needed in the next discussion. For example, a list of Seacliff Company's current assets and current liabilities appears in Exhibit 14–19.

Exhibit 14–9

SEACLIFF STATEMENT OF CASH FLOWS

SEACLIFF COMPANY
Condensed Comparative Statement of Cash Flows
For the Years Ended December 31, 2002, and December 31, 2001

	2002	2001	Increase or (Decrease) Dollars	%
Cash flows from operating activities:				
Net cash flows from operating activities	$ 19,000	$ 95,000	$(76,000)	(80.0)
Cash flows from investing activities:				
Purchases of plant assets	(63,000)	(28,000)	(35,000)	125.0
Collections of loans from officers	45,000	(35,000)	80,000	N/A*
Net cash used by investing activities	$(18,000)	$(63,000)	$ 45,000	(71.4)
Cash flows from financing activities:				
Dividends paid	$(33,000)	$(29,000)	$ (4,000)	13.8
Repayment of long-term debt	(50,000)	–0–	(50,000)	N/A*
Proceeds from issuing capital stock	80,000	–0–	80,000	N/A*
Net cash used by financing activities	$ (3,000)	$(29,000)	$ 26,000	(89.7)
Net increase (decrease) in cash and cash equivalents	$ (2,000)	$ 3,000	$ (5,000)	N/A*
Cash and cash equivalents, beginning of the year	40,000	37,000	3,000	8.1
Cash and cash equivalents, end of the year	$ 38,000	$ 40,000	$ (2,000)	(5.0)

*N/A indicates that computation of the percentage change is not appropriate. Percentage changes cannot be determined if the base year is zero or if a negative amount (cash outflow) changes to a positive amount (cash inflow).

Exhibit 14–10

SEACLIFF NOTES TO FINANCIAL STATEMENTS

SEACLIFF COMPANY
Notes to Financial Statements
For the Years Ended December 31, 2002, and December 31, 2001

Note 1—Accounting Policies

Inventories Inventories are determined by the LIFO method.

Depreciation Depreciation is computed by the straight-line method. Buildings are depreciated over 40 years, and equipment and fixtures over periods of 5 or 10 years.

Note 2—Unused Lines of Credit

The company has a confirmed line of credit in the amount of $35,000. None was in use at December 31, 2002.

Note 3—Contingencies and Commitments

As of December 31, 2002, the company has no material commitments or noncancellable obligations. There currently are no loss contingencies known to management.

Note 4—Current Values of Financial Instruments

All financial instruments appear in the financial statements at dollar amounts that closely approximate their current values.

Note 5—Concentrations of Credit Risk

The company engages in retail sales to the general public from a single location in Seattle, Washington. No individual customer accounts for more than 2% of the company's total sales or accounts receivable. Accounts receivable are unsecured.

Analysis by Common Stockholders

Common stockholders and potential investors in common stock look first at a company's earnings record. Their investment is in shares of stock, so *earnings per share* and *dividends per share* are of particular interest.

Earnings per Share of Common Stock As indicated in Chapter 12, earnings per share of common stock are computed by dividing the income applicable to the common stock by the weighted-average number of shares of common stock outstanding during the year. Any preferred dividend requirements must be subtracted from net income to determine income applicable to common stock, as shown in the computations for Seacliff Company in Exhibit 14–11.

		2002	2001
Net income		$75,000	$90,000
Less: Preferred dividend requirements		9,000	9,000
Income applicable to common stock	(a)	$66,000	$81,000
Shares of common stock outstanding, during the year	(b)	5,000	4,000
Earnings per share of common stock (a ÷ b)		$ 13.20	$ 20.25

Exhibit 14–11

EARNINGS PER SHARE OF COMMON STOCK

My Notes

Earnings related to number of common shares outstanding

Notice that earnings per share have decreased by *$7.05* in 2002, representing a decline of nearly *35%* from their level in 2001 ($7.05 ÷ $20.25 = 34.8%). Common stockholders consider a decline in earnings per share to be an unfavorable development. A decline in earnings per share generally represents a decline in the profitability of the company and creates uncertainty as to the company's prospects for future growth.

With such a significant decline in earnings per share, we should expect to see a decline in the market value of Seacliff's common stock during 2002. [For purposes of our illustration, we assume the common stock had a market value of *$160* at December 31, 2001, and of *$132* at the end of 2002. This drop of $28 per share represents a *17½%* decline in the market value of every common stockholder's investment ($28 decline ÷ $160 = 17.5%).]

Price-Earnings Ratio As we mentioned earlier in this chapter, the relationship between the market price of common stock and earnings per share is widely recognized and is expressed as a ratio, called the *price-earnings ratio* (or *p/e ratio*). The p/e ratio is determined by dividing the market price per share by the annual earnings per share.

The average p/e ratio of the 30 stocks included in the Dow Jones Industrial Average has varied widely in recent years, ranging from a low of about 10 to a high of about 18. The outlook for future earnings is the major factor influencing a company's p/e ratio. Companies with track records of rapid growth may sell at p/e ratios of perhaps 20 to 1, or even higher. Companies with "flat" earnings or earnings expected to decline in future years often sell at price-earnings ratios below 10 to 1.

At the end of 2001, Seacliff's p/e ratio was approximately *8 to 1* ($160 ÷ $20.25 = 7.9), suggesting that investors *were expecting* earnings to decline in 2002. At December 31, 2002, the price-earnings ratio was *10 to 1* ($132 ÷ $13.20 = 10.0). A p/e ratio in this range suggests that investors expect future earnings to stabilize around the current level.

Dividend Yield Dividends are of prime importance to some stockholders, but a secondary factor to others. Some stockholders invest primarily to receive regular cash income, while others invest in stocks principally with the expectation of rising market prices. If a corporation is profitable and retains its earnings for expansion of the business, the expanded operations should produce an increase in the net income of the company and thus tend to make each share of stock more valuable.

In comparing the merits of alternative investment opportunities, we should relate earnings and dividends per share to the *market value* of the stock. Dividends per share divided by market price per share determine the *yield* rate of a company's stock. Dividend yield is especially important to those investors whose objective is to maximize the dividend revenue from their investments. For Seacliff, the dividend yield on its common stock was 3.1% in 2001 ($5/$160) and 3.6% in 2002 ($4.80/$132).

Summary of Earnings and Dividend Data for Seacliff The relationships of Seacliff's per-share earnings and dividends to its year-end stock prices are summarized in Exhibit 14–12.

Exhibit 14–12

EARNINGS AND DIVIDENDS PER SHARE OF COMMON STOCK

My Notes

Earnings and dividends related to market price of common stock

Date	Market Value per Share	Earnings per Share	Price-Earnings Ratio	Dividends per Share	Dividend Yield, %
Dec. 31, 2001	$160	$20.25	8	$5.00	3.1
Dec. 31, 2002	132	13.20	10	4.80	3.6

The decline in market value during 2002 presumably reflects the decreases in both earnings and dividends per share. Investors appraising this stock at December 31, 2002, should consider whether a price-earnings ratio of 10 and a dividend yield of 3.6% meet their expectations in light of alternative investment opportunities. These investors will also place considerable weight on estimates of the company's prospective future earnings and the probable effect of such estimated earnings on the market price of the stock and on dividend payments.

Revenue and Expense Analysis The trend of earnings of Seacliff Company is unfavorable, and stockholders will want to know the reasons for the decline in net income. The comparative income statements in Exhibit 14–6 show that despite a 20% increase in net sales, net income fell from $90,000 in 2001 to $75,000 in 2002, a decline of 16.7%. As a percentage of net sales, net income fell from 12% to only 8.3%. The primary causes of this decline were the increases in selling expenses (56.0%), in general and administrative expenses (32.6%), and in the cost of goods sold (26.2%), all of which exceeded the 20% increase in net sales.

Let us assume that further investigation reveals Seacliff Company decided in 2002 to reduce its sales prices in an effort to generate greater sales volume. This would explain the decrease in gross profit rate from 44% to 41.1% of net sales. Since the dollar amount of gross profit increased $40,000 in 2002, the strategy of reducing sales prices to increase volume would have been successful if there had been little or no increase in operating expenses. However, operating expenses rose by $73,000, resulting in a $33,000 decrease in operating income.

The next step is to find which expenses increased and why. An investor may be limited here, because detailed operating expenses are not usually shown in published financial statements. Some conclusions, however, can be reached on the basis of even the condensed information available in the comparative income statements for Seacliff Company shown in Exhibit 14–6.

The substantial increase in selling expenses presumably reflects greater selling effort during 2002 in an attempt to improve sales volume. However, the fact that selling expenses increased $42,000 while gross profit increased only $40,000 indicates that the cost of this increased sales effort was not justified in terms of results. Even more bothersome is the increase in general and administrative expenses. Some growth in administrative expenses might be expected to accompany increased sales volume, but because some of the expenses are fixed, the growth generally should be *less than proportional* to any increase in sales. The increase in general and administrative expenses from 12.7% to 14% of sales should be of concern to informed investors.

Management generally has greater control over operating expenses than over revenue. The *operating expense ratio* is often used as a measure of management's ability to control its operating expenses. We show the unfavorable trend in this ratio for Seacliff Company in Exhibit 14–13.

	2002	2001
Operating expenses	(a) $243,000	$170,000
Net sales	(b) $900,000	$750,000
Operating expense ratio (a ÷ b)	27.0%	22.7%

Exhibit 14–13

OPERATING EXPENSE RATIO

My Notes

Does a higher operating expense ratio indicate higher net income?

If management were able to increase the sales volume while at the same time increasing the gross profit rate and decreasing the operating expense ratio, the effect on net income could be dramatic. For example, if in the year 2003 Seacliff Company can increase its sales by 11% to $1,000,000, increase its gross profit rate from 41.1 to 44%, and reduce the operating expense ratio from 27 to 24%, its operating income will increase from $127,000 to $200,000 ($1,000,000 − $560,000 − $240,000), an increase of over 57%.

Return on Investment (ROI)

The rate of return on investment (often called ROI) is a measure of management's efficiency in using available resources. Regardless of the size of the organization, capital is a scarce resource and must be used efficiently. In judging the performance of branch managers or of companywide management, it is reasonable to raise the question: What rate of return have you earned on the resources under your control?

Return on Assets An important test of management's ability to earn a return on funds supplied from all sources is the rate of return on total assets.

As noted previously, the income figure used in computing this ratio should be *operating income,* since interest expense and income taxes are determined by factors other than the efficient use of resources. Operating income is earned throughout the year and therefore should be related to the *average* investment in assets during the year. In Exhibit 14–14, the computation of this ratio of Seacliff Company assumes total assets at the beginning of 2001 were $820,000.

	2002	2001
Operating income	(a) $127,000	$160,000
Total assets, beginning of year	(b) $860,000	$820,000
Total assets, end of year	(c) $950,000	$860,000
Average investment in assets [(b + c) ÷ 2]	(d) $905,000	$840,000
Return on assets (a ÷ d)	14%	19%

Exhibit 14–14

PERCENTAGE RETURN ON ASSETS

My Notes

Earnings related to investment in assets

This ratio shows that the rate of return earned on the company's assets fell in 2002. Before drawing conclusions as to the effectiveness of Seacliff's management, however, we should consider the trend in the return on assets earned by other companies of similar kind and size.

Return on Common Stockholders' Equity We introduced the concept of return on equity using a company that had only one class of capital stock. Therefore, the return on equity was simply net income divided by average stockholders' equity. But Seacliff has issued both preferred stock *and* common stock. The preferred stock does not participate fully in the company's earnings; rather, the return to preferred stockholders is limited to their dividend. Thus, we must adjust the return on equity computation to reflect the return on *common* stockholders' equity.

The return to common stockholders is equal to net income *less* any preferred dividends. Thus the return on common stockholders' equity, assuming common stockholders' equity at the beginning of 2001 was $355,000, is computed in Exhibit 14–15.

Exhibit 14–15

RETURN ON COMMON STOCKHOLDERS' EQUITY

My Notes

Does the use of leverage benefit common stockholders?

		2002	2001
Net income		$ 75,000	$ 90,000
Less: Preferred dividend requirements		9,000	9,000
Net income applicable to common stock	(a)	$ 66,000	$ 81,000
Common stockholders' equity, beginning of year	(b)	$416,000	$355,000
Common stockholders' equity, end of year	(c)	$538,000	$416,000
Average common stockholders' equity [(b + c) ÷ 2]	(d)	$477,000	$385,500
Return on common stockholders' equity (a ÷ d)		13.8%	21.0%

In both years, the rate of return on common stockholders' equity was higher than the 12% rate of interest paid to long-term creditors or the 9% dividend rate paid to preferred stockholders. This result was achieved through the favorable use of leverage.

Leverage

Applying leverage means using borrowed money to earn a return *greater* than the cost of borrowing, increasing net income and the return on common stockholders' equity. In other words, if you can borrow money at 12% and use it to earn 20%, you will benefit by doing so. However, leverage can act as a double-edged sword; the effects may be favorable or unfavorable to the holders of common stock.

If the rate of return on total assets should fall *below* the average rate of interest on borrowed capital, leverage will *reduce* the return on common stockholders' equity. In this situation, paying off the loans that carry high interest rates would appear to be a logical move. However, many companies do not have enough cash to retire long-term debt on short notice. Therefore, the common stockholders may become locked in to the unfavorable effects of leverage.

In deciding how much leverage is appropriate, the common stockholders should consider the *stability* of the company's return on assets as well as the relationship of this return to the average cost of borrowed capital. If a business incurs so much debt that it becomes unable to meet the required interest and principal payments, the creditors may force liquidation or reorganization of the business.

MANAGEMENT STRATEGY AND FINANCIAL REPORTING

Management determines the financial structure of the company. The financial (or capital) structure is the proportion of debt and equity capital and the particular forms of debt (e.g., long versus short) and equity (e.g., common versus preferred) chosen to finance the assets of the firm. Management maximizes the firm's value by minimizing the firm's cost of financing its assets.

When determining the financial structure, management must consider the impact of changes in the structure of its financial reports because creditors frequently use financial ratios in debt agreements with firms. These agreements (called debt covenants) frequently require the firm to repay the debt if the firm's financial ratios fall outside of predetermined ranges identified in the agreement. Thus managers must be aware of these pre-existing agreements and the associated accounting ratios when considering a change to their capital structure via additional borrowing or issuing of additional equity.

Comprehensive Illustration: Seacliff Company

Debt Ratio One indicator of the amount of leverage used by a business is the debt ratio. This ratio measures the proportion of the total assets financed by creditors, as distinguished from stockholders. It is computed by dividing total liabilities by total assets. A *high* debt ratio indicates an extensive use of leverage, that is, a large proportion of financing provided by creditors. A low debt ratio, on the other hand, indicates that the business is making little use of leverage.

The debt ratio at year-end for Seacliff is determined as shown in Exhibit 14–16.

	2002	2001
Total liabilities	(a) $312,000	$344,000
Total assets (or total liabilities & stockholders' equity)	(b) $950,000	$860,000
Debt ratio (a ÷ b)	32.8%	40.0%

Exhibit 14–16
DEBT RATIO

My Notes
Proportion of assets financed by creditors

Seacliff Company has a lower debt ratio in 2002 than in 2001. Is this favorable or unfavorable?

From the viewpoint of the common stockholder, a high debt ratio will produce maximum benefits if management is able to earn a rate of return on assets greater than the rate of interest paid to creditors. However, a high debt ratio can be *unfavorable* if the return on assets falls *below* the rate of interest paid to creditors. Since the return on total assets earned by Seacliff Company has declined from 19% in 2001 to a relatively low 14% in 2002, the common stockholders probably would *not* want to risk a high debt ratio. The action by management in 2002 of retiring $50,000 in long-term liabilities will help to protect the common stockholders from the unfavorable effects of leverage if the rate of return on assets continues to decline.

Analysis by Long-Term Creditors

Bondholders and other long-term creditors are primarily interested in three factors: (1) the rate of return on their investment, (2) the firm's ability to meet its interest requirements, and (3) the firm's ability to repay the principal of the debt when it falls due.

Yield Rate on Bonds The yield rate on bonds or other long-term indebtedness cannot be computed in the same manner as the yield rate on shares of stock, because bonds, unlike stocks, have a definite maturity date and amount. The ownership of a 12%, 10-year, $1,000 bond represents the right to receive $120 each year for 10 years plus the right to receive $1,000 at the end of 10 years. If the market price of this bond is $950, the yield rate on an investment in the bond is the rate of interest that will make the *present value* of these two contractual rights equal to the $950 market price.

When bonds sell at maturity value, the yield rate is equal to the bond interest rate. *The yield rate varies inversely with changes in the market price of the bond.* If interest rates rise, the market price of existing bonds will fall; if interest rates decline, the price of bonds will rise. If the price of a bond is above maturity value, the yield rate is less than the bond interest rate; if the price of a bond is below maturity value, the yield rate is higher than the bond interest rate.

Interest Coverage Ratio Bondholders feel that their investments are relatively safe if the issuing company earns enough income to cover its annual interest obligations by a comfortable margin.

A common measure of creditors' safety is the ratio of operating income available for the payment of interest to the annual interest expense, called the *interest coverage ratio* or *times interest earned*. See this computation for Seacliff Company in Exhibit 14–17.

Exhibit 14–17

INTEREST COVERAGE RATIO

My Notes

Long-term creditors watch this ratio

	2002	2001
Operating income (before interest and income taxes)	(a) $127,000	$160,000
Annual interest expense	(b) $ 24,000	$ 30,000
Interest coverage (a ÷ b)	5.3 times	5.3 times

The ratio remained unchanged at a satisfactory level during 2002. A ratio of 5.3 times interest earned would be considered strong in many industries. In the electric utilities industry, for example, the interest coverage ratio for the leading companies presently averages about 3, with the ratios of individual companies varying from 2 to 6.

Debt Ratio Long-term creditors are interested in the percentage of total assets financed by debt, as distinguished from the percentage financed by stockholders. The percentage of total assets financed by debt is measured by the debt ratio, which was computed in Exhibit 14–16.

From a creditor's viewpoint, the lower the debt ratio the better, since this means that stockholders have contributed a higher percentage of the funds to the business, and therefore the margin of protection to creditors against a shrinkage of the assets is high.

As shown in Exhibit 14–18, the debt ratio, or the percentage of assets financed by debt, decreased from 2001 to 2002 from 40% to 32.8%. This would generally be considered by long-term creditors to be a favorable change because the debt burden, including required interest payments, is less in 2002 than in 2001, thereby making the claim of each creditor more secure.

Exhibit 14–18

DEBT RATIO

	2002	2001
Total liabilities	(a) $312,000	$344,000
Total assets	(b) $950,000	$860,000
Debt ratio (a ÷ b)	32.8%	40%

Secured Claims Sometimes the claims of long-term creditors are secured with specific collateral, such as the land and buildings owned by the borrower. In these situations, the secured creditors may look primarily to the *value of the collateral* in assessing the safety of their claims.

Assets pledged as collateral to secure specific liabilities are disclosed in notes to the financial statements. As Seacliff makes no such disclosures, we may assume that none of its assets has been pledged as collateral to secure specific liabilities.

Analysis by Short-Term Creditors

Bankers and other short-term creditors share the interest of stockholders and bondholders in the profitability and long-run stability of a business. Their primary interest, however, is in the current position of the company—its ability to generate sufficient funds (working capital) to meet current operating needs and to pay current debts promptly. Thus the analysis of financial statements by a banker considering a short-term loan, or by a trade creditor investigating the credit status of a customer, is likely to center on the working capital position of the prospective debtor.

Amount of Working Capital Working capital is the excess of current assets over current liabilities. It represents the cash and near-cash assets that provide a "cushion" of liquidity over the amount expected to be needed in the near future to satisfy maturing obligations. The details of the working capital of Seacliff Company are shown in Exhibit 14–19.

Comprehensive Illustration: Seacliff Company

Exhibit 14–19 — SEACLIFF SCHEDULE OF WORKING CAPITAL

SEACLIFF COMPANY
Comparative Schedule of Working Capital
As of December 31, 2002, and December 31, 2001

	2002	2001	Increase or (Decrease) Dollars	%	Percentage of Total Current Items 2002	2001
Current assets:						
Cash	$ 38,000	$ 40,000	$ (2,000)	(5.0)	9.7	13.9
Receivables (net)	117,000	86,000	31,000	36.0	30.0	29.9
Inventories	180,000	120,000	60,000	50.0	46.2	41.6*
Prepaid expenses	55,000	42,000	13,000	31.0	14.1	14.6
Total current assets	$390,000	$288,000	$102,000	35.4	100.0	100.0
Current liabilities:						
Notes payable to creditors	$ 14,600	$ 10,000	$ 4,600	46.0	13.1*	10.7*
Accounts payable	66,000	30,000	36,000	120.0	58.9	31.9
Accrued liabilities	31,400	54,000	(22,600)	(41.9)	28.0	57.4
Total current liabilities	$112,000	$ 94,000	$ 18,000	19.1	100.0	100.0
Working capital	$278,000	$194,000	$ 84,000	43.3		

*Amounts adjusted so that totals equal 100.0.

This schedule shows that current assets increased $102,000, while current liabilities rose by only $18,000, with the result that working capital increased $84,000.

Quality of Working Capital In evaluating the debt-paying ability of a business, short-term creditors should consider the quality of working capital as well as the total dollar amount. The principal factors affecting the quality of working capital are (1) the nature of the current assets and (2) the length of time required to convert these assets into cash.

The schedule in Exhibit 14–19 shows an unfavorable shift in the composition of Seacliff Company's working capital during 2002: cash decreased from 13.9% to 9.7% of current assets, while inventory rose from 41.6% to 46.2%. Inventory is a less liquid resource than cash. Therefore, the quality of working capital is not as liquid as in 2001. *Turnover rates* (or *ratios*) may be used to assist short-term creditors in estimating the time required to turn assets such as receivables and inventory into cash.

Accounts Receivable Turnover Rate As explained in Chapter 7, the accounts receivable turnover rate indicates how quickly a company converts its accounts receivable into cash. The accounts receivable turnover *rate* is determined by dividing net sales by the average balance of accounts receivable.[6] The number of *days* required (on average) to collect accounts receivable then may be determined by dividing the number of days in a year (365) by the turnover rate. The computations in Exhibit 14–20 use the data in our Seacliff example, assuming accounts receivable at the beginning of 2001 were $80,000.

---

[6] Ideally, the accounts receivable turnover is computed by dividing net *credit* sales by the *monthly* average of receivables. Such detailed information, however, generally is not provided in annual financial statements.

Exhibit 14–20

ACCOUNTS RECEIVABLE TURNOVER

My Notes

Are customers paying promptly?

	2002	2001
Net sales	(a) $900,000	$750,000
Receivables, beginning of year	$ 86,000	$ 80,000
Receivables, end of year	$117,000	$ 86,000
Average receivables	(b) $101,500	$ 83,000
Receivable turnover per year (a ÷ b)	8.9 times	9.0 times
Average number of days to collect receivables (divide 365 days by receivable turnover)	41 days	41 days

There has been no change in the average time required to collect receivables. The interpretation of the average age of receivables depends upon the company's credit terms and the seasonal activity immediately before year-end. For example, if the company grants 30-day credit terms to its customers, the analysis in Exhibit 14–20 indicates that accounts receivable collections are lagging. If the terms are for 60 days, however, collections are being made ahead of schedule.

Inventory Turnover Rate The inventory turnover rate indicates how many times during the year the company is able to sell a quantity of goods equal to its average inventory. Mechanically, this rate is determined by dividing the cost of goods sold for the year by the average amount of inventory on hand during the year. The number of days required to sell this amount of inventory may be determined by dividing 365 days by the turnover rate. These computations were explained in Chapter 8 and are demonstrated in Exhibit 14–21 using the data of Seacliff Company, assuming inventory at the beginning of 2001 was $100,000. The trend indicated by this analysis is unfavorable, since the length of time required for Seacliff to turn over (sell) its inventory is increasing.

Exhibit 14–21

INVENTORY TURNOVER

	2002	2001
Cost of goods sold	(a) $530,000	$420,000
Inventory, beginning of year	$120,000	$100,000
Inventory, end of year	$180,000	$120,000
Average inventory	(b) $150,000	$110,000
Average inventory turnover per year (a ÷ b)	3.5 times	3.8 times
Average number of days to sell inventory (divide 365 days by inventory turnover)	104 days	96 days

Companies that have low gross profit rates often need high inventory turnover rates in order to operate profitably. This is another way of saying that if the gross profit rate is low, a high volume of transactions is necessary to produce a satisfactory amount of profits. Companies that sell high markup items, such as jewelry stores and art galleries, can operate successfully with much lower inventory turnover rates.

Operating Cycle The inventory turnover rate indicates how quickly inventory *sells*, but not how quickly this asset converts into *cash*. Short-term creditors, of course, are interested primarily in the company's ability to generate cash.

The period of time required for a merchandising company to convert its inventory into cash is called the *operating cycle*. The illustration appeared in Chapter 6 and is repeated in Exhibit 14–22 for your convenience.

Comprehensive Illustration: Seacliff Company

Exhibit 14–22

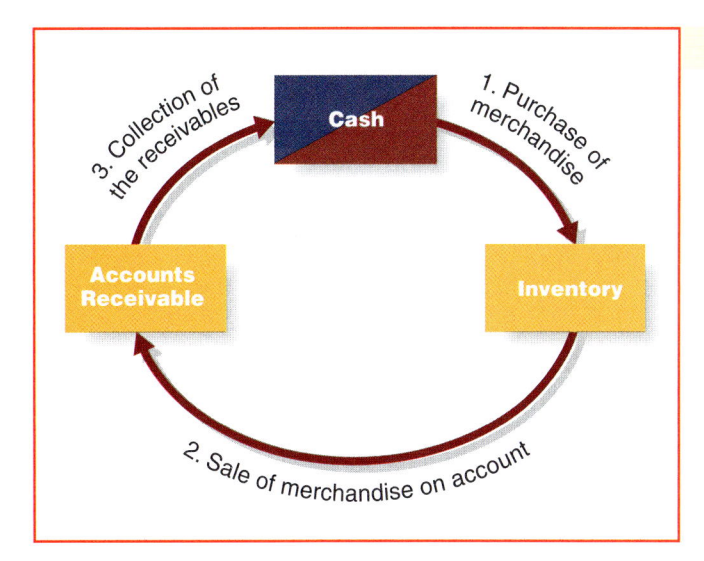

OPERATING CYCLE

My Notes

The operating cycle repeats continuously

Seacliff's operating cycle in 2002 was approximately 145 days, computed by adding the 104 days required to turn over inventory and the average 41 days required to collect receivables. This compares to an operating cycle of only 137 days in 2001, computed as 96 days to dispose of the inventory plus 41 days to collect the resulting receivables. From the viewpoint of short-term creditors, the *shorter* the operating cycle, the *higher the quality* of the borrower's working capital. Therefore, these creditors would regard the lengthening of Seacliff Company's operating cycle as an unfavorable trend.

Current Ratio The current ratio expresses the relationship between current assets and current liabilities. A strong current ratio provides considerable evidence that a company will be able to meet its obligations coming due in the near future. The current ratio for Seacliff Company is computed in Exhibit 14–23.

	2002	2001
Total current assets	(a) $390,000	$288,000
Total current liabilities	(b) $112,000	$ 94,000
Current ratio (a ÷ b)	3.5	3.1

Exhibit 14–23

CURRENT RATIO

My Notes

Does this indicate satisfactory debt-paying ability?

Quick Ratio Because inventories and prepaid expenses are further removed from conversion into cash than other current assets, the *quick ratio* is sometimes computed as a supplement to the current ratio. The quick ratio compares the most liquid current assets (cash, marketable securities, and receivables) with current liabilities. Seacliff Company has no marketable securities; its quick ratio is computed in Exhibit 14–24.

	2002	2001
Quick assets (cash and receivables)	(a) $155,000	$126,000
Current liabilities	(b) $112,000	$ 94,000
Quick ratio (a ÷ b)	1.4	1.3

Exhibit 14–24

QUICK RATIO

My Notes

A measure of liquidity

Here again the analysis reveals a favorable trend and a strong position. If the credit periods extended to customers and granted by creditors are roughly equal, a quick ratio of 1.0 or better is considered satisfactory.

Unused Lines of Credit From the viewpoint of a short-term creditor, a company's unused lines of credit represent a resource almost as liquid as cash. An unused line of credit means that a bank has agreed in advance to lend the company any amount, up to the specified limit. As long as this line of credit remains available, creditors know that the business can borrow cash quickly and easily for any purpose, including payments of creditors' claims.

Existing unused lines of credit are *disclosed* in notes accompanying the financial statements. See (Note 2 to the financial statements) in Exhibit 14–10. Short-term creditors would view Seacliff's $35,000 line of credit as enhancing the company's liquidity.

Cash Flow Analysis

We often have stressed the importance of a company being able to generate sufficient cash flows from its operations. In 2001, Seacliff generated net cash flows of $95,000 from its operating activities—a relatively "normal" amount, considering that net income for the year was $90,000. This $95,000 remained *after* payment of interest to creditors and amounted to more than three times the dividends paid to stockholders. Thus in 2001 the net cash flows from operating activities appeared quite sufficient to ensure that Seacliff could pay its interest obligations and also pay dividends.

In 2002, however, net cash flows from operating activities declined to $19,000, an amount far below the company's $75,000 net income and only approximately 58% of the amount of dividends paid. Stockholders and creditors would view this dramatic decline in cash flows as a negative and potentially dangerous development.

A reconciliation of Seacliff's net income in 2002 with its net cash flows from operating activities is shown in Exhibit 14–25.

Exhibit 14–25

SEACLIFF RECONCILIATION OF NET INCOME TO NET CASH FROM OPERATING ACTIVITIES

Net income		$ 75,000
Add:		
Depreciation expense	$30,000	
Increase in notes payable to suppliers	4,600	
Increase in accounts payable	36,000	70,600
		$145,600
Less:		
Increase in accounts receivable	$31,000	
Increase in inventories	60,000	
Increase in prepaid expenses	13,000	
Decrease in accrued liabilities	22,600	126,600
Net cash flows from operating activities		$ 19,000

(As explained in Chapter 13, the FASB requires companies to provide this reconciliation either in the body of the statement of cash flows or in a supplemental schedule.)

The primary reasons for Seacliff's low net operating cash flows appear to be the growth in uncollected accounts receivable and inventories, combined with the substantial reduction in accrued liabilities. Given the significant increase in sales during 2002, the increase in accounts receivable is to be expected. The large reduction in accrued liabilities may be a one-time event that will not necessarily recur next year. The large increase in inventory, however, may have reduced Seacliff's liquidity unnecessarily.

Seacliff's financial position, particularly its short-term liquidity, would appear considerably stronger if its increased sales volume were supported by a higher *inventory turnover rate,* instead of a larger inventory.

Cash Flows from Operations to Current Liabilities An additional measure of liquidity that is sometimes computed, based in part on information from the statement of cash flows, is the ratio of cash flows from operations to current liabilities. This measure provides evidence of the company's ability to cover its currently maturing liabilities from normal operations. For 2001 and 2002, the ratio is computed for Seacliff Corporation in Exhibit 14–26.

	2002	2001
Cash flows from operations	(a) $ 19,000	$95,000
Current liabilities	(b) $112,000	$94,000
Cash flows from operations to current liabilities (a ÷ b)	.17	1.01

Exhibit 14–26

CASH FLOWS FROM OPERATIONS TO CURRENT LIABILITIES

As you can see from this measure, Seacliff was much stronger in 2001 than in 2002. In 2001, operating cash flows were slightly more than current liabilities at year-end, indicating an ability to cover current obligations from normal operations without regard to the amount of existing current assets. In 2002, however, operations provided only 17% as much cash as is needed to meet current obligations, implying a need to rely more heavily on existing current assets than in 2001.

Usefulness of Notes to Financial Statements

A set of financial statements normally is accompanied by several *notes,* disclosing information useful in *interpreting* the statements. Users should view these notes as an *integral part* of the financial statements.

In preceding chapters we have identified many items that are disclosed in notes accompanying the financial statements. Among the most useful are the following:

- Accounting policies and methods.
- Unused lines of credit.
- Significant commitments and loss contingencies.
- Current values of financial instruments (if different from the carrying values shown in the statements).
- Dividends in arrears.
- Concentrations of credit risk.
- Assets pledged to secure specific liabilities.

In Exhibit 14–10 the notes accompanying Seacliff's financial statements are quite clean—that is, they contain no surprises or cause for concern. Of course, the unused line of credit disclosed in Note 2 would be of interest to anyone evaluating the company's short-term debt-paying ability.

You as a Financial Analyst

Assume that you are a financial analyst and that two of your clients are requesting your advice on certain companies as potential investments. Both clients are interested in purchasing common stock. One is primarily interested in the dividends to be received from the investment. The second is primarily interested in the growth of the market value of the stock. What information would you advise your clients to focus on in their respective analyses?

*Our comments appear on page 664.

YOUR TURN

Summary of Analytical Measurements

The financial ratios and other measurements introduced throughout this textbook, including this chapter—and their significance—are summarized in Exhibit 14–27.

Exhibit 14–27

SUMMARY OF ANALYTICAL MEASURES

Ratios or Other Measurements	Method of Computation	Significance
Measures of short-term liquidity		
Current ratio	$\dfrac{\text{Current Assets}}{\text{Current Liabilities}}$	A measure of short-term debt-paying ability
Quick ratio	$\dfrac{\text{Quick Assets}}{\text{Current Liabilities}}$	A measure of short-term debt-paying ability
Working capital	Current Assets − Current Liabilities	A measure of short-term debt-paying ability
Net cash provided by operating activities	Appears in the statement of cash flows	Indicates the cash generated by operations after allowing for cash payment of expenses and operating liabilities
Cash flow from operations to current liabilities	$\dfrac{\text{Cash Flows from Operating Activities}}{\text{Current Liabilities}}$	Indicates ability to cover currently maturing obligations from recurring operations
Receivables turnover rate	$\dfrac{\text{Net Sales}}{\text{Average Accounts Receivable}}$	Indicates how quickly receivables are collected
Days to collect average accounts receivable	$\dfrac{365 \text{ days}}{\text{Receivables Turnover Rate}}$	Indicates in days how quickly receivables are collected
Inventory turnover rate	$\dfrac{\text{Cost of Goods Sold}}{\text{Average Inventory}}$	Indicates how quickly inventory sells
Days to sell the average inventory	$\dfrac{365 \text{ days}}{\text{Inventory Turnover Rate}}$	Indicates in days how quickly inventory sells
Operating cycle	Days to Sell Inventory + Days to Collect Receivables	Indicates in days how quickly cash invested in inventory converts back into cash
Free cash flow	Net Cash from Operating Activities − Cash Used for Investing Activities and Dividends	Excess of operating cash flow over basic needs
Measures of long-term credit risk		
Debt ratio	$\dfrac{\text{Total Liabilities}}{\text{Total Assets}}$	Percentage of assets financed by creditors; indicates relative size of the equity position
Trend in net cash provided by operating activities	Appears in comparative statements of cash flows	Indicator of a company's ability to generate the cash necessary to meet its obligations
Interest coverage ratio	$\dfrac{\text{Operating Income}}{\text{Annual Interest Expense}}$	Indicator of a company's ability to meet its interest payment obligations
Measures of profitability		
Percentage changes; that is, in net sales and net income	$\dfrac{\text{Dollar Amount of Change}}{\text{Financial Statement Amount in the Earlier Year}}$	The rate at which a key measure is increasing or decreasing; the "growth rate"
Gross profit rate	$\dfrac{\text{Gross Profit}}{\text{Net Sales}}$	A measure of the profitability of the company's products
Operating expense ratio	$\dfrac{\text{Operating Expenses}}{\text{Net Sales}}$	A measure of management's ability to control expenses
Operating income	Gross Profit − Operating Expenses	The profitability of a company's basic business activities
Net income as a percentage of net sales	$\dfrac{\text{Net Income}}{\text{Net Sales}}$	An indicator of management's ability to control costs
Earnings per share	$\dfrac{\text{Net Income − Preferred Dividends}}{\text{Average Number of Common Shares Outstanding}}$	Net income applicable to each share of common stock

(continued on next page)

Ratios or Other Measurements	Method of Computation	Significance
Return on assets	$\dfrac{\text{Operating Income}}{\text{Average Total Assets}}$	A measure of the productivity of assets, regardless of how the assets are financed
Return on equity	$\dfrac{\text{Net Income}}{\text{Average Total Equity}}$	The rate of return earned on the stockholders' equity in the business
Return on common stockholders' equity	$\dfrac{\text{Net Income} - \text{Preferred Dividends}}{\text{Average Common Stockholders' Equity}}$	The rate of return earned on the common stockholders' equity appropriate when company has both common and preferred stock
Measures for evaluating the current market price of common stock		
Market value of financial instruments	Quoted in financial press or disclosed in financial statements	Reflects both investors' expectations and current market conditions
Price-earnings ratio	$\dfrac{\text{Current Stock Price}}{\text{Earnings per Share}}$	A measure of investors' expectations about the company's future prospects
Dividend yield	$\dfrac{\text{Annual Dividend}}{\text{Current Stock Price}}$	Dividends expressed as a rate of return on the market price of the stock
Book value per share	$\dfrac{\text{Common Stockholders' Equity}}{\text{Shares of Common Stock Outstanding}}$	The recorded value of net assets underlying each share of common stock

CONCLUDING REMARKS

For the most part, our discussion in this chapter has been limited to the kinds of analysis that can be performed by external users who do not have access to the company's accounting records. Investors and creditors must rely to a considerable extent on the financial statements published in annual and quarterly reports. In the case of publicly owned corporations, additional information is filed with the Securities and Exchange Commission (SEC) and is available to the public in hard copy, as well as on the Internet. In fact, the Internet is the fastest growing source of *free* information available to decision makers in this information age.

Many financial analysts who evaluate the financial statements and future prospects of publicly owned companies sell their conclusions and investment recommendations for a fee. For example, detailed financial analyses of most large companies are available from **Standard & Poor's**, **Moody's Investors Service**, and **The Value Line Investment Survey**. Anyone may subscribe to these investment services.

Bankers and major creditors usually are able to obtain detailed financial information from borrowers simply by requesting it as a condition for granting a loan. Suppliers and other trade creditors may obtain some financial information about almost any business from credit-rating agencies, such as **Dun & Bradstreet**.

Stock prices, like p/e ratios, are a *measure of investors' expectations*. A company may be highly profitable and growing fast. But if investors had expected even better performance, the market price of its stock may decline. Similarly, if a troubled company's losses are smaller than expected, the price of its stock may rise.

In financial circles, evaluating stock price by looking at the underlying profitability of the company is termed **fundamental analysis**. This approach to investing works better in the long run than in the short run. In the short run, stock prices can be significantly affected by many factors, including short-term interest rates, current events, political events, fads, and rumors. But in the long run, good companies increase in value.

In summary, successful investing requires more than an understanding of accounting concepts. It requires experience, judgment, patience, and the ability to absorb some losses. But a knowledge of accounting concepts is invaluable to the long-term investor—and it reduces the risk of "getting burned."

Up to this point, we have focused on the preparation and use of financial information in the United States. In Chapter 15 we discuss international business and accounting because business activities between countries are increasing daily. This globalization of business is one of the most dramatic changes that has ever occurred. It will continue to significantly impact business activity for many years to come.

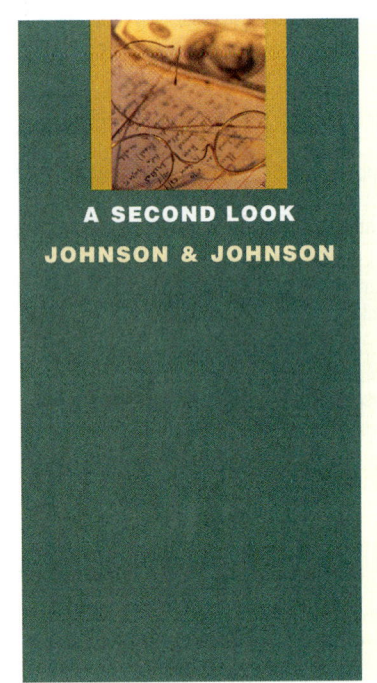

A SECOND LOOK
JOHNSON & JOHNSON

As we opened Chapter 14, we took a quick look at a key ratio from **Johnson & Johnson**'s financial statements, the return on assets (15%). We raised the issue of needing comparative information for this ratio to be meaningful, including information about **Johnson & Johnson** over several time periods and industry information that would allow comparisons with other similar companies.

Like many companies, **Johnson & Johnson**, includes multiyear summaries of key financial data from the company's financial statements in its annual reports. While these summaries do not include all of the information found in the individual financial statements for each year, they provide valuable comparative information of key financial figures for up to 10 years in a convenient and comparative framework.

Companies have a great deal of latitude in preparing the multiyear summaries included in their annual reports. Some companies, such as **Johnson & Johnson**, present more dollar amounts and relatively few ratios. Others emphasize ratios that have been computed based on information in the financial statements in a manner similar to that illustrated in this chapter. A multiyear summary, combined with the more detailed information presented in the full financial statements that typically include the three most recent years can be very helpful in gaining a long-term understanding of the financial success (or failure) of a company.

END-OF-CHAPTER REVIEW

SUMMARY OF LEARNING OBJECTIVES

LO 1
Explain the uses of dollar and percentage changes, trend percentages, component percentages, and ratios.
An important aspect of financial statement analysis is determining relevant relationships among specific items of information. Companies typically present financial information for more than one time period, which permits users of the information to make comparisons that help them understand changes over time. Dollar and percentage changes and trend percentages are tools for comparing information from successive time periods. Component percentages and ratios, on the other hand, are tools for establishing relationships and making comparisons within an accounting period. Both types of comparisons are important in understanding an enterprise's financial position, results of operations, and cash flows.

LO 2
Discuss the quality of a company's earnings, assets, and working capital.
Assessing the quality of information is an important aspect of financial statement analysis. Enterprises have significant latitude in the selection of financial reporting methods within generally accepted accounting principles. Assessing the quality of a company's earnings, assets, and working capital is done by evaluating the accounting methods selected for use in preparing financial statements. Management's choice of accounting principles and methods that are in the best long-term interests of the company, even though they may currently result in lower net income, reported total assets, or working capital, leads to a conclusion of high quality in reported accounting information.

LO 3
Explain the nature and purpose of classifications in financial statements.
In classified financial statements, items with certain common characteristics are placed together in a group, or classification. The purpose of these classifications is to develop subtotals that will assist users in analyzing the financial statements.

LO 4
Prepare a classified balance sheet and compute widely used measures of liquidity and credit risk.
In a classified balance sheet, assets are subdivided into the categories of current assets, plant and equipment, and other assets. Liabilities are classified either as current or long-term.

The liquidity measures derived from the balance sheet are as follows:

Working capital. Current assets minus current liabilities.

Current ratio. Current assets divided by current liabilities.

Quick ratio. Quick assets divided by current liabilities.

A measure of long-term credit risk is the debt ratio, which is total liabilities expressed as a percentage of (divided by) total assets.

LO 5
Prepare a multiple-step and a single-step income statement and compute widely used measures of profitability.
In a multiple-step income statement, the cost of goods sold is deducted from net sales to provide the subtotal, gross profit. Operating expenses then are deducted to arrive at income from operations. As a final step, nonoperating items are added together and subtracted from income from operations to arrive at net income. In a single-step income statement, all revenue items are listed first, and then all expenses are combined and deducted from total revenue.

The profitability measures discussed in this chapter are as follows:

Percentage change. The dollar amount of change in a financial statement item from one period to the next, expressed as a percentage of (divided by) the item value in the earlier of the two periods being compared.

Gross profit rate. Dollar amount of gross profit divided by net sales. A measure of the profitability of a company's products.

Net income as a percentage of sales. Net income divided by net sales. A measure of management's ability to control expenses.

Earnings per share. In the simplest case, net income divided by shares of capital stock outstanding. Indicates the earnings applicable to each share of stock.

Price-earnings ratio. Market price of the stock, divided by earnings per share. A measure of investors' expectations regarding future profitability.

Return on assets. Operating income divided by average total assets. Measures the return generated by assets, regardless of how the assets are financed.

Return on equity. Net income divided by average total equity. Indicates the rate of return earned on owners' equity.

LO 6
Put a company's net income into perspective by relating it to sales, assets, and stockholders' equity.
Financial accounting information is most useful if viewed in comparison with other relevant information. Net income is an important measure of the financial success of an enterprise. To make the amount of net income even more useful than if it were viewed simply in isolation, it is often compared with the sales from which net income results, the assets used to generate the income, and the amount of stockholders' equity invested by owners to earn the net income.

LO 7
Compute the ratios widely used in financial statement analysis and explain the significance of each.
Ratios are mathematical calculations that compare one financial statement item with another financial statement item. The two items may come from the same financial statement, such as the current ratio, which compares the amount of current assets with the amount of current liabilities, both of which appear in the statement of financial position (balance sheet). On the other hand, the items may come from two different financial statements, such as the return on stockholders' equity, which compares net income from the income statement with the amount of stockholders' equity from the statement of financial position (balance sheet). Accountants and financial analysts have developed many ratios that place information from a company's financial statements in a context to permit better understanding to support decision making.

LO 8
Analyze financial statements from the viewpoints of common stockholders, creditors, and others.
Different groups of users of financial statements are interested in different aspects of a company's financial activities. Short-term creditors are interested primarily in the company's ability to make cash payments in the short term; they focus their attention on operating cash flows and current assets and liabilities. Long-term creditors, on the other hand, are more interested in the company's long-term ability to pay interest and principal and would not limit their analysis to the company's ability to make cash payments in the immediate future. The focus of common stockholders can vary from one investor to another, but generally stockholders are interested in the company's ability to pay dividends and increase the market value of the stock of the company. Each group may focus on different information in the financial statements to meet its unique objectives.

KEY TERMS INTRODUCED OR EMPHASIZED IN CHAPTER 14

annual report (p. 612) A document issued annually by publicly owned companies to their stockholders. Includes audited comparative financial statements, management's discussion and analysis of performance and liquidity, and other information about the company.

classified financial statements (p. 602) Financial statements in which similar items are arranged in groups, and subtotals are shown to assist users in analyzing the statements.

comparative financial statements (p. 602) Financial statements of one company for two or more years presented in a side-by-side format to facilitate comparison.

consolidated financial statements (p. 602) Financial statements that show the combined activities of a parent company and its subsidiaries.

current assets (p. 609) Cash and other assets that can be converted into cash or used up within one year or the operating cycle (whichever is longer) without interfering with normal business operations.

current liabilities (p. 610) Existing liabilities that are expected to be satisfied by using the enterprise's current assets.

current ratio (p. 611) Current assets divided by current liabilities. A measure of short-term debt-paying ability.

debt ratio (p. 612) Total liabilities divided by total assets. Represents the portion of total assets financed by debt, rather than by equity capital.

earnings per share (p. 619) Net income expressed on a per-share basis.

fundamental analysis (p. 639) Evaluating the reasonableness of a company's stock price by evaluating the performance and financial strength of the company.

management's discussion and analysis (p. 613) A discussion by management of the company's performance during the current year and its financial position at year-end. These discussions are included in the annual reports of publicly owned companies.

market share (p. 617) A company's percentage share of total dollar sales within its industry.

operating cycle (p. 609) The time required to invest cash in inventory, sell the inventory, and collect the receivable, resulting in an increase in cash.

operating income (p. 617) A subtotal in a multiple-step income statement representing the income resulting from the company's principal business activities.

parent company (p. 602) A corporation that does portions of its business through other companies that it owns (termed *subsidiaries*).

percentage change (p. 617) The change in a dollar amount between two accounting periods, expressed as a percentage of the amount in an earlier period. Used in evaluating rates of growth (or decline).

price-earnings (p/e) ratio (p. 620) The current market price of a company's capital stock, expressed as a multiple of earnings per share. Reflects investors' expectations regarding future earnings.

quick assets (p. 611) The most liquid current assets. Include only cash, marketable securities, and receivables.

quick ratio (p. 611) Quick assets (cash, marketable securities, and receivables) divided by current liabilities. A measure of short-term debt-paying ability. (Sometimes referred to as the acid-test ratio.)

return on assets (p. 622) Operating income expressed as a percentage of average total assets. A measure of the efficiency with which management utilizes the assets of a business.

return on equity (p. 622) Net income expressed as a percentage of average total stockholders' equity. A measure of the rate of return earned on the stockholders' equity in the business.

subsidiary (p. 602) A company that is owned and operated by a parent company. In essence, the subsidiary is a part of the parent organization.

window dressing (p. 613) Measures taken by management to make a business look as strong as possible at the balance sheet date.

working capital (p. 610) Current assets less current liabilities. A measure of short-term debt-paying ability.

DEMONSTRATION PROBLEM

The following data are adapted from a recent annual report of **Walgreen Drug Stores** (dollar amounts are stated in millions):

	2001	2000
Balance sheet data:		
Quick assets	$ 815.2	$ 627.3
Current assets	4,393.9	3,550.1
Current liabilities	3,011.6	2,303.7
Stockholders' equity	5,207.2	4,234.0
Total assets	8,833.8	7,103.7
Income statement data:		
Net sales	$24,623.0	$21,206.9
Gross profit	6,574.1	5,741.0
Operating income	1,398.3	1,224.1
Net income	885.6	776.9

Instructions

a. Compute the following for 2001 and 2000. (Round to one decimal place.)
   1. Working capital
   2. Current ratio
   3. Quick ratio
b. Comment on the trends in the liquidity measures and state whether **Walgreens** appears to be able to satisfy its liabilities at the end of 2001.
c. Compute the percentage changes for 2001 in the amounts of net sales and net income. (Round to one-tenth of 1%.)
d. Compute the following for 2001 and 2000. (Round to one-tenth of 1%. For items **3** and **4**, use the year-end amounts stated above as substitutes for average assets and average stockholders' equity.)
   1. Gross profit rate
   2. Net income as a percentage of sales
   3. Return on assets
   4. Return on stockholders' equity
e. Comment on the trends in the profitability measures computed in parts **c** and **d**.

Solution to the Demonstration Problem

a.

		2001	2000
1.	**Working capital:**		
	$4,393.9 − $3,011.6	$1,382.3	
	$3,550.1 − $2,303.7		$1,246.4
2.	**Current ratio:**		
	$4,393.9 ÷ $3,011.6	1.46 to 1	
	$3,550.1 ÷ $2,303.7		1.54 to 1
3.	**Quick ratio:**		
	$815.2 ÷ $3,011.6	.27 to 1	
	$627.3 ÷ $2,303.7		.27 to 1

b. Working capital at the end of 2001 has increased relative to 2000, whereas the current ratio has declined and the quick ratio has stayed essentially the same. The relatively low current and quick ratios may be of some concern in terms of the company's ability to satisfy its future obligations.

c. Percentage change from 2000:

	2001
Net sales: [($24,623.0 − $21,206.9) ÷ $21,206.9]	+16.1%
Net income: [($885.6 − $776.9) ÷ $776.9]	+14.0%

d.

		2001	2000
1.	**Gross profit rate:**		
	$6,574.1 ÷ $24,623.0	26.7%	
	$5,741.0 ÷ $21,206.9		27.1%
2.	**Net income as a percentage of sales:**		
	$885.6 ÷ $24,623.0	3.6%	
	$776.9 ÷ $21,206.9		3.7%
3.	**Return on assets:**		
	$1,398.3 ÷ $8,833.8	15.8%	
	$1,224.1 ÷ $7,103.7		17.2%
4.	**Return on equity:**		
	$885.6 ÷ $5,207.2	17.0%	
	$776.9 ÷ $4,234.0		18.3%

e. The trends in the profitability measures are negative. Net sales are increasing, but the gross profit percentage declined slightly, indicating that costs are rising more rapidly than sales. Income as a percentage of sales is also down slightly, as are return on assets and return on equity. The company remains profitable and appears to be in a relatively strong position, but the negative trends in these measures of profitability may signal issues of concern if they continue over time.

SELF-TEST QUESTIONS

Answers to these questions appear on page 664.

1. Which of the following usually is *least* important as a measure of short-term liquidity?
   a. Quick ratio.
   b. Current ratio.
   c. Debt ratio.
   d. Cash flows from operating activities.

2. In each of the past five years, the net sales of Beta Co. have increased at about half the rate of inflation, but net income has increased at approximately *twice* the rate of inflation. During this period, the company's total assets, liabilities, and equity have remained almost unchanged; dividends are approximately equal to net income. These relationships suggest (indicate all correct answers):
   a. Management is successfully controlling costs and expenses.
   b. The company is selling more merchandise every year.
   c. The annual return on assets has been increasing.
   d. Financing activities are likely to result in a net use of cash.

3. From the viewpoint of a stockholder, which of the following relationships do you consider of *least* significance?

a. The return on assets consistently is higher than the industry average.
b. The return on equity has increased in each of the past five years.
c. Net income is greater than the amount of working capital.
d. The return on assets is greater than the rate of interest being paid to creditors.

4. The following data are available from the annual report of Foxall Motors:

Current assets	$ 480,000	Current liabilities	$300,000
Average total assets	2,000,000	Operating income	240,000
Average total equity	800,000	Net income	80,000

Which of the following statements are correct? (More than one statement may be correct.)
a. The return on equity exceeds the return on assets.
b. The current ratio is .625 to 1.
c. Working capital is $1,200,000.
d. None of the above answers is correct.

5. Spinx Corporation's net income was $400,000 in 2001 and $160,000 in 2002. What percentage increase in net income must Spinx achieve in 2003 to offset the decline in profits in 2002?
   a. 60%   b. 150%   c. 600%   d. 67%

6. If a company's current ratio declined in a year during which its quick ratio improved, which of the following is the most likely explanation?
a. Inventory is increasing.
b. Inventory is declining.
c. Receivables are being collected more rapidly than in the past.
d. Receivables are being collected more slowly than in the past.

7. In financial statement analysis, the most difficult of the following items to predict is whether:
a. The company's market share is increasing or declining.
b. The company will be liquid in six months.
c. Profits will increase in the coming year.
d. The market price of capital stock will rise or fall over the next two months.

ASSIGNMENT MATERIAL

DISCUSSION QUESTIONS

1. In financial statement analysis, what is the basic objective of observing trends in data and ratios? Suggest some other standards of comparison.
2. In financial statement analysis, what information is produced by computing a ratio that is not available in a simple observation of the underlying data?
3. Distinguish between *trend percentages* and *component percentages*. Which would be better suited for analyzing the change in sales over a term of several years?
4. Differentiate between *horizontal* and *vertical* analysis.
5. Assume that Femco Corporation is engaged in the manufacture and distribution of a variety of chemicals. In analyzing the financial statements of this corporation, why would you want to refer to the ratios and other measurements of companies in the chemical industry? In comparing the financial results of Femco Corporation with another chemical company, why would you be interested in the accounting principles used by the two companies?
6. Explain how the following accounting practices tend to raise or lower the quality of a company's earnings. (Assume the continuance of inflation.)
   a. Adoption of an accelerated depreciation method rather than straight-line depreciation.
   b. Adoption of FIFO rather than LIFO for the valuation of inventories.
   c. Adoption of a 7-year life rather than a 10-year life for the depreciation of equipment.

7. What is the basic purpose of *classifications* in financial statements? Identify the classifications widely used in a balance sheet, a multiple-step income statement, and a statement of cash flows.

8. Distinguish between the terms *classified, comparative,* and *consolidated* as they apply to financial statements. May a given set of financial statements have more than one of these characteristics?

9. Identify three liquidity measures. Explain briefly how each is computed.

10. What is the characteristic common to all *current assets?* Many retail stores regularly sell merchandise on installment plans, calling for payments over a period of 24 or 36 months. Do such receivables qualify as current assets? Explain.

11. What is the *quick ratio?* Under what circumstances are short-term creditors most likely to regard a company's quick ratio as more meaningful than its current ratio?

12. The current assets of Rockmore Corporation are cash, $80,000; accounts receivable, $340,000; and inventory, $120,000. Current liabilities amount to $320,000. Compute the current ratio, quick ratio, and the amount of working capital.

13. How is the debt ratio computed? Is this ratio a measure of short-term liquidity, or something else?

14. Distinguish between a multiple-step and a single-step income statement. Which format results in the higher amount of net income?

15. Identify four ratios or other analytical tools used to evaluate profitability. Explain briefly how each is computed.

16. Assume that the net sales of a large department store have grown annually at a rate of 5% over each of the past several years. Do you think that the store is selling 5% more merchandise each year? Explain.

17. How does income taxes expense differ from normal operating expenses such as advertising and salaries? How is income taxes expense presented in a multiple-step income statement?

18. Distinguish between *operating income* and *net income*.

19. Net sales of the Maryville General Store have been increasing at a reasonable rate, but net income has been declining steadily as a percentage of these sales. What appears to be the problem?

20. Why might earnings per share be more significant to a stockholder in a large corporation than the total amount of net income?

21. Assume that Congress announces its intention to limit the prices and profits of pharmaceutical companies as part of an effort to control health care costs. What effect would you expect this announcement to have on the p/e ratios and stock prices of pharmaceutical companies such as **Merck** and **Bristol-Myers/Squibb**? Explain.

22. Under what circumstances might a company have a high p/e ratio even when investors are *not* optimistic about the company's future prospects?

23. Walker Company earned a 16% return on its total assets. Current liabilities are 10% of total assets. Long-term bonds carrying an 11% coupon rate are equal to 30% of total assets. There is no preferred stock. Is this application of leverage favorable or unfavorable from the viewpoint of Walker Company's stockholders?

24. Ahi Co. has a current ratio of 3 to 1. Ono Corp. has a current ratio of 2 to 1. Does this mean that Ahi's operating cycle is longer than Ono's? Why?

25. An investor states, "I bought this stock for $50 several years ago and it now sells for $100. It paid $5 per share in dividends last year so I'm earning 10% on my investment." Evaluate this statement.

26. Ramson Products experiences a considerable seasonal variation in its business. The high point in the year's activity comes in November, the low point in July. During which month would you expect the company's current ratio to be higher? If the company were choosing a fiscal year for accounting purposes, what advice would you give?

27. Under what circumstances would you consider a corporate net income of $1 million for the year as being unreasonably low? Under what circumstances would you consider a corporate profit of $1 million as being unreasonably high?

EXERCISES

EXERCISE 14.1

Percentage Changes

LO 1

Selected information taken from financial statements of Marshall Company for two successive years follows. You are to compute the percentage change from 2001 to 2002 whenever possible. Round all calculations to the nearest whole percentage.

		2002	2001
a.	Accounts receivable	$126,000	$160,000
b.	Marketable securities	–0–	250,000
c.	Retained earnings	80,000	(80,000)
d.	Notes receivable	120,000	–0–
e.	Notes payable	870,000	800,000
f.	Cash	84,000	80,000
g.	Sales	970,000	900,000

EXERCISE 14.2

Trend Percentages

LO 1

Compute *trend percentages* for the following items taken from the financial statements of Lopez Plumbing over a five-year period. Treat 1998 as the base year. State whether the trends are favorable or unfavorable. (Dollar amounts are stated in thousands.)

	2002	2001	2000	1999	1998
Sales	$81,400	$74,000	$61,500	$59,000	$50,000
Cost of goods sold	58,500	48,000	40,500	37,000	30,000

EXERCISE 14.3

Common Size Income Statements

LO 1

Prepare *common size* income statements for Messer Company, a sole proprietorship, for the two years shown below by converting the dollar amounts into percentages. For each year, sales will appear as 100% and other items will be expressed as a percentage of sales. (Income taxes are not involved as the business is not incorporated.) Comment on whether the changes from 2001 to 2002 are favorable or unfavorable.

	2002	2001
Sales	$500,000	$400,000
Cost of goods sold	330,000	268,000
Gross profit	$170,000	$132,000
Operating expenses	130,000	116,000
Net income	$ 40,000	$ 16,000

EXERCISE 14.4

Accounting Terminology

LO 1–7

The following are 12 technical accounting terms introduced or emphasized in this chapter:

P/e ratio	Market share	Current ratio
Debt ratio	Earnings per share	Operating income
Quick ratio	Operating activities	Return on equity
Subsidiary	Comparative financial statements	Parent company

Each of the following statements may (or may not) describe one of these technical terms. For each statement, indicate the term described, or answer "None" if the statement does not correctly describe any of the terms.

a. A ratio that relates the total net income of a corporation to the holdings of individual stockholders.

b. The classification in a statement of cash flows from which it is most important to generate positive cash flows.

c. A measure of the long-term safety of creditors' positions.
d. A measure of investors' expectations of the future profitability of a business.
e. An ROI measure of the effectiveness with which management utilizes a company's resources, regardless of how those resources are financed.
f. A company that does business through other companies that it owns.
g. A measure of the profitability of a company's *primary* business activities.
h. The most widely used measure of short-term debt-paying ability.
i. A form of business organization in which the owners are *personally* liable for the debts of the business organization.
j. Financial statements in which similar items are grouped in a manner that develops useful subtotals.

EXERCISE 14.5
Measures of Liquidity
LO 3, 4

Kids Toys is a manufacturer of toys and children's products. The following are selected items appearing in a recent balance sheet (dollar amounts are in millions):

Cash and short-term investments	$ 47.3
Receivables	159.7
Inventories	72.3
Prepaid expenses and other current assets	32.0
Total current liabilities	130.1
Total liabilities	279.4
Total stockholders' equity	344.0

a. Using the information above, compute the amounts of Kids Toys (1) quick assets and (2) total current assets.
b. Compute for Kids Toys the (1) quick ratio, (2) current ratio, and (3) dollar amount of working capital. (Round ratios to one decimal place.)
c. Discuss whether Kids Toys appears liquid from the viewpoint of a short-term creditor.

EXERCISE 14.6
Multiple-Step Income Statements
LO 5

SYMONDS, INC.
Statement of Earnings
For the Year Ended December 31, 2002

Net sales	$4,395,253
Costs and expenses:	
Cost of goods sold	(2,821,455)
Operating expenses	(1,004,396)
Interest revenue	15,797
Earnings before income taxes	$ 585,199
Income taxes	(231,160)
Net earnings	$ 354,039
Earnings per share	$1.58

Comparative balance sheets report average total assets for the year of *$2,450,000* and average total equity of *$1,825,000* (dollar amounts in thousands, except earnings per share).

a. Prepare an income statement for the year in a multiple-step format.
b. Compute the (1) gross profit rate, (2) net income as a percentage of net sales, (3) return on assets, and (4) return on equity for the year. (Round computations to the nearest one-tenth of 1%.)
c. Explain why interest revenue is not included in the company's gross profit computation.

Exercises

EXERCISE 14.7

Comparative Analysis

LO 6

Parker Hannifin Corporation reported the following basic earnings per share figures for the 11 years ending in 2000:

1990	$1.00	1993	1.60	1996	2.15	1999	2.85
1991	.54	1994	.48	1997	2.46	2000	3.34
1992	.58	1995	1.97	1998	2.91		

Throughout this period, the average number of shares of common stock outstanding remained relatively constant, ranging from a low of 108,632,000 in 1991 to a high of 110,331,000 in 2000. Diluted earnings per share averaged between $.01 and $.02 per share lower than basic earnings per share throughout the 1990–2000 period.

a. Compute the percentage change in basic earnings per share for each year from 1991 through 2000. What conclusions can you reach about the pattern of basic earnings per share over this period of time?

b. What does the information provided above about the average number of outstanding shares of common stock and basic earnings per share allow you to conclude about the company's net income over this period of time?

c. Should the risk of conversion of other securities into common stock be of particular risk to the common stockholders of **Parker Hannifin Corporation**?

EXERCISE 14.8

ROI

LO 6

Shown below are selected data from a recent annual report of **Sprint Corporation**, a large telecommunications provider. (Dollar amounts are in millions.)

	Beginning of the Year	End of the Year
Total assets	$14,548	$15,196
Total stockholders' equity	4,562	4,674
Operating income		2,422
Net income		349

a. Compute for the year **Sprint**'s return on average total assets. (Round computations to the nearest one-tenth of 1%.)

b. Compute for the year **Sprint**'s return on average total stockholders' equity. (Round computations to the nearest one-tenth of 1%.)

c. Could the increase in **Sprint**'s total stockholders' equity for the year be the result of an increase in *market value* of the company's stock? Explain.

EXERCISE 14.9

Computing and Interpreting Rates of Change

LO 1, 6

Selected information from the financial statements of Montes Hardware includes the following:

	2002	2001
Net sales	$2,200,000	$2,000,000
Total expenses	1,998,000	1,800,000

a. Compute the percentage change in 2002 for the amounts of (1) net sales and (2) total expenses.

b. Using the information developed in part **a**, express your opinion as to whether the company's *net income* for 2002:

1. Increased at a greater or lower percentage rate than did net sales.
2. Represented a larger or smaller percentage of net sales revenue than in 2001. For each answer, explain your reasoning *without* making any computations or references to dollar amounts.

EXERCISE 14.10
Research Problem
LO 6

Obtain from your library (or other source) the most recent annual report of a publicly owned company.

a. Using the annual report data, compute the basic measures of liquidity, long-term credit risk, and profitability summarized in Exhibit 14–27. Compare these measures to the appropriate industry norms available in your library. Briefly comment on your findings.

b. Using the financial pages of a daily newspaper (such as *The Wall Street Journal*), determine (1) the current market price of your company's common stock, (2) its 52-week high and low market prices, and (3) its p/e ratio. Briefly comment on your findings.

c. Based on your analysis in parts **a** and **b**, make a recommendation as to whether investors should buy shares of the stock, hold the shares they currently own, or sell the shares they currently own. Defend your position.

EXERCISE 14.11
Tootsie Roll Industries, Inc., Management Discussion and Analysis
LO 3, 4, 6

The annual report of a publicly owned corporation includes *management's discussion and analysis* of the company's operations, financial condition, and liquidity. The annual report of **Tootsie Roll Industries, Inc.**, including the discussion and analysis by management, appears in Appendix A at the end of this textbook.

Read management's discussion and analysis. Identify at least five items that should be of interest to investors in understanding the financial results of the year 2000, but which investors would *not* be able to determine for themselves from the financial statements. Briefly discuss the *usefulness* of each disclosure to investors. Be prepared to explain your findings in class, including references to the appropriate pages and paragraphs in the illustrated discussion.

EXERCISE 14.12
Evaluating Employment Opportunities
LO 4, 6

Assume that you will soon graduate from college and that you have job offers with two pharmaceutical firms. The first offer is with Alpha Research, a relatively new and aggressive company. The second is with Omega Scientific, a very well-established and conservative company.

Financial information pertaining to each firm, and to the pharmaceutical industry as a whole, is as follows:

Financial Measure	Alpha	Omega	Industry Average
Current ratio	2.2 to 1	4.5 to 1	2.5 to 1
Quick ratio	1.2 to 1	2.8 to 1	1.5 to 1
Return on assets	17%	8%	10%
Return on equity	28%	14%	16%
P/e ratio	20 to 1	10 to 1	12 to 1

The Omega offer is for $36,000 per year. The Alpha offer is for $32,000. However, unlike Omega, Alpha awards its employees a stock option bonus based on profitability for the year. Each option enables the employee to purchase shares of Alpha's common stock at a significantly reduced price. The more profitable this company is, the more stock each employee can buy at a discount.

Show how the above information may help you justify accepting the Alpha Research offer, even though the starting salary is $4,000 lower than the Omega Scientific offer.

EXERCISE 14.13
Ratios for a Retail Store
LO 7

Selected financial data for BargainCo., a retail store, appear as follows:

	2002	2001
Sales (all on account)	$750,000	$610,000
Cost of goods sold	495,000	408,000
Average inventory during the year	110,000	102,000
Average receivables during the year	150,000	100,000

a. Compute the following for both years:
   1. Gross profit percentage
   2. Inventory turnover
   3. Accounts receivable turnover
b. Comment on favorable and unfavorable trends.

EXERCISE 14.14

Computing Ratios

LO 7

A condensed balance sheet for Stensaker Corporation prepared at the end of the year appears as follows:

Assets		Liabilities & Stockholders' Equity	
Cash	$ 65,000	Notes payable (due in 6 months)	$ 40,000
Accounts receivable	155,000	Accounts payable	110,000
Inventory	270,000	Long-term liabilities	330,000
Prepaid expenses	60,000	Capital stock, $5 par	300,000
Plant & equipment (net)	570,000	Retained earnings	430,000
Other assets	90,000		
Total	$1,210,000	Total	$1,210,000

During the year the company earned a gross profit of $1,116,000 on sales of $2,950,000. Accounts receivable, inventory, and plant assets remained almost constant in amount throughout the year.

Compute the following:
a. Current ratio
b. Quick ratio
c. Working capital
d. Debt ratio
e. Accounts receivable turnover (all sales were on credit)
f. Inventory turnover
g. Book value per share of capital stock

EXERCISE 14.15

Current Ratio, Debt Ratio, and Earnings per Share

LO 7

Selected items from successive annual reports of Modico, Inc., appear as follows:

	2002	2001
Total assets (40% of which are current)	$400,000	$325,000
Current liabilities	$ 80,000	$100,000
Bonds payable, 12%	100,000	50,000
Capital stock, $5 par value	100,000	100,000
Retained earnings	120,000	75,000
Total liabilities & stockholders' equity	$400,000	$325,000

Dividends of $16,000 were declared and paid in 2002.

Compute the following:
a. Current ratio for 2002 and 2001
b. Debt ratio for 2002 and 2001
c. Earnings per share for 2002

EXERCISE 14.16
Ratio Analysis for Two Similar Companies

LO 7

Selected data from the financial statements of Italian Marble Co. and Brazil Stone Products for the year just ended follow. Assume that for both companies dividends declared were equal in amount to net earnings during the year and therefore stockholders' equity did not change. The two companies are in the same line of business.

	Italian Marble Co.	Brazil Stone Products
Total liabilities	$ 200,000	$ 100,000
Total assets	800,000	400,000
Sales (all on credit)	1,800,000	1,200,000
Average inventory	240,000	140,000
Average receivables	200,000	100,000
Gross profit as a percentage of sales	40%	30%
Operating expenses as a percentage of sales	36%	25%
Net income as a percentage of sales	3%	5%

Compute the following for each company and state a brief conclusion about which company is in the stronger financial position.
a. Net income
b. Net income as a percentage of stockholders' equity
c. Accounts receivable turnover
d. Inventory turnover

PROBLEMS

PROBLEM 14.1
Comparing Operating Results with Average Performance in the Industry

LO 1, 5

Outdoors, Inc., manufactures camping equipment. Shown below for the current year are the income statement for the company and a common size summary for the industry in which the company operates. (Notice that the percentages in the right-hand column are *not* for Outdoors, Inc., but are average percentages for the industry.)

	Outdoors, Inc.	Industry Average
Sales (net)	$20,000,000	100%
Cost of goods sold	9,800,000	57
Gross profit on sales	$10,200,000	43%
Operating expenses:		
Selling	$ 4,200,000	16%
General and administrative	3,400,000	20
Total operating expenses	$ 7,600,000	36%
Operating income	$ 2,600,000	7%
Income taxes	1,200,000	3
Net income	$ 1,400,000	4%
Return on assets	23%	14%

Instructions

a. Prepare a two-column common size income statement. The first column should show for Outdoors, Inc., all items expressed as a percentage of net sales. The second column should show the equivalent industry average for the data given in the problem. The purpose of this common size statement is to compare the operating results of Outdoors, Inc., with the average for the industry.

PROBLEM 14.2
Analysis to Identify Favorable and Unfavorable Trends
LO 3, 5

b. Comment specifically on differences between Outdoors, Inc., and the industry average with respect to gross profit on sales, selling expenses, general and administrative expenses, operating income, net income, and return on assets. Suggest possible reasons for the more important disparities.

The following information was developed from the financial statements of Custom Logos, Inc. At the beginning of 2002, the company's former supplier went bankrupt, and the company began buying merchandise from another supplier.

	2002	2001
Gross profit on sales	$1,008,000	$1,134,000
Income before income taxes	230,400	252,000
Net income	172,800	189,000
Net income as a percentage of net sales	6.0%	7.5%

Instructions
a. Compute the net sales for each year.
b. Compute the cost of goods sold in dollars and as a percentage of net sales for each year.
c. Compute operating expenses in dollars and as a percentage of net sales for each year. (Income taxes expense is not an operating expense.)
d. Prepare a condensed comparative income statement for 2001 and 2002. Include the following items: net sales, cost of goods sold, gross profit, operating expenses, income before income taxes, income taxes expense, and net income. Omit earnings per share statistics.
e. Identify the significant favorable and unfavorable trends in the performance of Custom Logos, Inc. Comment on any unusual changes.

PROBLEM 14.3
Measures of Liquidity
LO 3, 4

Some of the accounts appearing in the year-end financial statements of Zero Degree Frozen Dinners appear below. This list includes all of the company's current assets and current liabilities.

Sales	$1,980,000
Accumulated depreciation: equipment	370,000
Notes payable (due in 90 days)	70,000
Retained earnings	241,320
Cash	67,600
Capital stock	150,000
Marketable securities	175,040
Accounts payable	125,430
Mortgage payable (due in 15 years)	320,000
Salaries payable	7,570
Dividends	25,000
Income taxes payable	14,600
Accounts receivable	230,540
Inventory	179,600
Unearned revenue	10,000
Unexpired insurance	4,500

Instructions
a. Prepare a schedule of the company's current assets and current liabilities. Select the appropriate items from the preceding list.
b. Compute the current ratio and the amount of working capital. Explain how each of these measurements is computed. State, with reasons, whether you consider the company to be in a strong or weak current position.

PROBLEM 14.4
Liquidity of Safeway
LO 3, 4, 7

Safeway, Inc., is one of the world's largest supermarket chains. These selected items were adapted from a recent Safeway balance sheet. (Dollar amounts are in millions.)

Cash	$ 74.8
Receivables	152.7
Merchandise inventories	1,191.8
Prepaid expenses	95.5
Fixtures and equipment	2,592.9
Retained earnings	284.4
Total current liabilities	1,939.0

Instructions
a. Using the information above, compute the amounts of Safeway's total current assets and total quick assets.
b. Compute the company's (1) current ratio, (2) quick ratio, and (3) working capital. (Round to one decimal place.)
c. From these computations, are you able to conclude whether Safeway is a good credit risk for short-term creditors or on the brink of bankruptcy? Explain.
d. Is there anything unusual about the operating cycle of supermarkets that would make you think that they normally would have lower current ratios than, say, large department stores?
e. What *other types of information* could you utilize in performing a more complete analysis of Safeway's liquidity?

PROBLEM 14.5
Balance Sheet Measures of Liquidity and Credit Risk
LO 3, 4, 7

A recent balance sheet of SweetCo., Inc., included the following items, among others. (Dollar amounts are stated in thousands.)

Cash	$ 49,625
Marketable securities (short-term)	55,926
Accounts receivable	23,553
Inventories	32,210
Prepaid expenses	5,736
Retained earnings	121,477
Notes payable to banks (due within one year)	20,000
Accounts payable	5,912
Dividends payable	1,424
Accrued liabilities (short-term)	21,532
Income taxes payable	6,438

The company also reported total assets of $353,816 thousand, total liabilities of $81,630 thousand, and a return on total assets of *18.1%*.

Instructions
a. Compute SweetCo's (1) quick assets, (2) current assets, and (3) current liabilities.
b. Compute SweetCo's (1) quick ratio, (2) current ratio, (3) working capital, and (4) debt ratio. (Round to one decimal place.)
c. Discuss the company's liquidity from the viewpoints of (1) short-term creditors, (2) long-term creditors, and (3) stockholders.

PROBLEM 14.6
Financial Statement Analysis

LO 4, 5

Shown below are selected data from the financial statements of Duncan & Sons, a retail furniture store.

From the balance sheet:

Cash	$ 30,000
Accounts receivable	150,000
Inventory	200,000
Plant assets (net of accumulated depreciation)	500,000
Current liabilities	150,000
Total stockholders' equity	300,000
Total assets	1,000,000

From the income statement:

Net sales	$1,500,000
Cost of goods sold	1,080,000
Operating expenses	315,000
Interest expense	84,000
Income taxes expense	6,000
Net income	15,000

From the statement of cash flows:

Net cash provided by operating activities (including interest paid of $79,000)		$ 40,000
Net cash used in investing activities		(46,000)
Financing activities:		
Amounts borrowed	$ 50,000	
Repayment of amounts borrowed	(14,000)	
Dividends paid	(20,000)	
Net cash provided by financing activities		16,000
Net increase in cash during the year		$ 10,000

Instructions

a. Explain how the interest expense shown in the income statement could be $84,000, when the interest payment appearing in the statement of cash flows is only $79,000.

b. Compute the following (round to one decimal place):
  1. Current ratio
  2. Quick ratio
  3. Working capital
  4. Debt ratio

c. Comment on these measurements and evaluate Duncan & Sons's short-term debt-paying ability.

d. Compute the following ratios (assume that the year-end amounts of total assets and total stockholders' equity also represent the average amounts throughout the year):
  1. Return on assets
  2. Return on equity

e. Comment on the company's performance under these measurements. Explain *why* the return on assets and return on equity are so different.

f. Discuss (1) the apparent safety of long-term creditors' claims and (2) the prospects for Duncan & Sons continuing its dividend payments at the present level.

PROBLEM 14.7
Evaluating Short-Term Debt-Paying Ability

LO 4, 7

Listed below is the working capital information for Nogacho Products, Inc., at the beginning of the year.

Cash	$425,000
Temporary investments in marketable securities	216,000
Notes receivable—current	324,000
Accounts receivable	540,000
Allowance for doubtful accounts	27,000
Inventory	432,000
Prepaid expenses	64,000
Notes payable within one year	165,000
Accounts payable	445,500
Accrued liabilities	42,500

The following transactions are completed during the year:

0. Sold on account inventory costing $72,000 at a "reduced for quick sale" price of $65,000.
1. Issued additional shares of capital stock for cash, $800,000.
2. Sold temporary investments costing $60,000 for $54,000 cash.
3. Acquired temporary investments, $105,000. Paid cash.
4. Wrote off uncollectible accounts, $18,000.
5. Sold on account inventory costing $75,000 for $90,000.
6. Acquired plant and equipment for cash, $480,000.
7. Declared a cash dividend, $240,000.
8. Declared a 10% stock dividend.
9. Paid accounts payable, $120,000.
10. Purchased goods on account, $90,000.
11. Collected cash on accounts receivable, $180,000.
12. Borrowed cash from a bank by issuing a short-term note, $250,000.

Instructions

a. Compute the amount of quick assets, current assets, and current liabilities at the beginning of the year as shown by the above account balances.
b. Use the data compiled in part **a** to compute: (1) current ratio, (2) quick ratio, and (3) working capital.
c. Indicate the effect (Increase, Decrease, or No Effect) of each independent transaction listed above on the current ratio, quick ratio, working capital, and net cash flows from operating activities. Use the following format (item **0** is given as an example):

Effect on

Item	Current Ratio	Quick Ratio	Working Capital	Net Cash Flows from Operating Activities
0	D	I	D	NE

PROBLEM 14.8
Classified Financial Statements; Ratio Analysis

LO 4, 5, 7

Velasco Department Store has advertised for an accounting student to work in its accounting department during the summer, and you have applied for the job. To determine whether you are familiar with the content of classified financial statements, use the following data provided by the controller of Velasco. The data are derived from the store's operations in the year ended December 31, 2002.

Available information (dollar amounts in thousands):

Problems

Net sales	$10,000
Net income	?
Current liabilities	2,000
Selling expenses	1,000
Long-term liabilities	1,600
Total assets (and total liabilities & stockholders' equity)	6,800
Stockholders' equity	?
Gross profit	?
Cost of goods sold	7,000
Current assets	4,000
Income taxes expense and other nonoperating items	220
Operating income	?
General and administrative expenses	980
Plant and equipment	2,600
Other assets	?

Instructions

a. Using the supplied data, prepare for Velasco Department Store a condensed:
  1. Classified balance sheet at December 31, 2002.
  2. Multiple-step income statement for the year ended December 31, 2002. Show supporting computations used in determining any missing amounts. (*Note:* Your financial statements should include only as much detail as these captions permit. For example, the first asset listed in your balance sheet will be "Current assets . . . $4,000.")

b. Compute at year-end the company's:
  1. Current ratio.
  2. Working capital.

c. Compute the company's 2002:
  1. Gross profit rate.
  2. Return on total assets. (Round to the nearest percent.)
  3. Return on total stockholders' equity.

Note: In the last two computations, use the amounts of total assets and stockholders' equity from your classified balance sheet as a substitute for the average amounts during the year.)

d. Assume that you get the summer job with Velasco Department Store. Your first project is to compute the store's working capital and current ratio as of June 1, 2003. You notice that both measures differ significantly from the December 31, 2002, amounts computed in part **b**. Explain why these measures may have changed so dramatically in just five months.

PROBLEM 14.9

Basic Ratio Analysis

LO 4, 5, 7

Blockbuster Entertainment Corporation operates under the name **Blockbuster Video** and is engaged primarily in the business of renting videotapes. The following selected data are from a recent annual report. (Dollar amounts are stated in thousands.)

	Beginning of the Year	End of the Year
Total current assets	$ 54,130	$ 92,592
Total current liabilities	63,481	83,357
Total assets	234,698	417,413
Total stockholders' equity	124,058	208,189
Operating income		76,141
Net income		44,152

The company has long-term liabilities that bear interest at annual rates ranging from 11% to 16%.

Instructions

a. Compute the company's current ratio at (1) the *beginning* of the year and (2) the *end* of the year. (Carry to two decimal places.)

b. Compute the company's working capital at (1) the beginning of the year and (2) the end of the year. (Express dollar amounts in thousands.)

c. Is the company's short-term debt-paying ability improving or deteriorating? As a short-term creditor, would you consider the company to be as good a credit risk as, say, **BellSouth**—a regional telephone company with a current ratio of .9 to 1? Explain.

d. Compute the company's (1) return on average total assets and (2) return on average stockholders' equity. (Round average assets and average equity to the nearest dollar and final computations to the nearest 1%.)

e. As an equity investor, do you think that **Blockbuster**'s management is utilizing the company's resources in a reasonably efficient manner? Explain.

PROBLEM 14.10

Ratios; Consider Advisability of Incurring Long-Term Debt

LO 5, 7

At the end of the year, the following information was obtained from the accounting records of Petock Products:

Sales (all on credit)	$2,750,000
Cost of goods sold	1,755,000
Average inventory	351,000
Average accounts receivable	300,000
Interest expense	45,000
Income taxes	84,000
Net income	159,000
Average investment in assets	1,800,000
Average stockholders' equity	895,000

Instructions

a. From the information given, compute the following:
  1. Inventory turnover
  2. Accounts receivable turnover
  3. Total operating expenses
  4. Gross profit percentage
  5. Return on average stockholders' equity
  6. Return on average assets

b. Petock has an opportunity to obtain a long-term loan at an annual interest rate of 12% and could use this additional capital at the same rate of profitability as indicated by the given data. Would obtaining the loan be desirable from the viewpoint of the stockholders? Explain.

PROBLEM 14.11

Ratios: Evaluation of Two Companies

LO 5, 7, 8

Shown below are selected financial data for Another World and Imports, Inc., at the end of the current year:

	Another World	Imports, Inc.
Net credit sales	$675,000	$560,000
Cost of goods sold	504,000	480,000
Cash	51,000	20,000
Accounts receivable (net)	75,000	70,000
Inventory	84,000	160,000
Current liabilities	105,000	100,000

Assume that the year-end balances shown for accounts receivable and for inventory approximate the average balances of these items throughout the year.

Instructions

a. For each of the two companies, compute the following:
   1. Working capital
   2. Current ratio
   3. Quick ratio
   4. Number of times inventory turned over during the year and the average number of days required to turn over inventory (round computation to the nearest day)
   5. Number of times accounts receivable turned over during the year and the average number of days required to collect accounts receivable (round computation to the nearest day)
   6. Operating cycle

b. From the viewpoint of a short-term creditor, comment on the *quality* of each company's working capital. To which company would you prefer to sell $20,000 in merchandise on a 30-day open account?

PROBLEM 14.12

Ratios; **Goodyear** versus **B.F. Goodrich**

LO 4, 5, 7

Goodyear Tire and Rubber and **B.F. Goodrich** are two of the world's largest publicly owned manufacturers of tire products. Shown below are data from the companies' recent annual reports. (Dollar amounts are stated in thousands.)

	Goodyear	Goodrich
Total current assets	$3,841,600	$ 950,000
Total current liabilities	2,736,300	600,700
Total quick assets	1,883,300	459,300
Average total assets	9,789,600	2,489,600
Average stockholders' equity	3,281,700	1,000,800
Operating income	1,135,400	242,900
Net income	611,000	118,000

Instructions

a. Compute the following for each company (round computations to one decimal place):
   1. Current ratio
   2. Quick ratio
   3. Working capital
   4. Return on average total assets
   5. Return on average total stockholders' equity

b. From the viewpoint of a short-term creditor, which of these companies appears to have the greater short-term debt-paying ability? Explain.

c. In which company does management appear to be using the resources under its control most efficiently? Explain the reasons for your answer.

PROBLEM 14.13

Effects of Transactions on Various Ratios

LO 7

Listed in the left-hand column is a series of 12 business transactions and events relating to the activities of Hardeman Industries. Opposite each transaction is listed a particular ratio used in financial analysis.

	Transaction	Ratio
(1)	Purchased inventory on open account	Quick ratio
(2)	A larger physical volume of goods was sold at smaller unit prices	Gross profit percentage
(3)	Corporation declared a cash dividend	Current ratio (assume ratio is greater than 1:1)
(4)	An uncollectible account receivable was written off against the allowance account	Current ratio (assume ratio is greater than 1:1)
(5)	Issued additional shares of common stock and used proceeds to retire long-term debt	Debt ratio
(6)	Paid stock dividend on common stock, in common stock	Earnings per share
(7)	Conversion of a portion of bonds payable into common stock (ignore income taxes)	Interest coverage ratio
(8)	Appropriated retained earnings	Rate of return on stockholders' equity
(9)	During period of rising prices, company changed from FIFO to LIFO method of inventory pricing	Inventory turnover
(10)	Paid a previously declared cash dividend	Debt ratio
(11)	Purchased factory supplies on open account	Current ratio (assume ratio is greater than 1:1)
(12)	Issued shares of capital stock in exchange for patents	Debt ratio

Instructions

What effect would each transaction or event have on the ratio listed opposite to it? That is, as a result of this event would the ratio increase, decrease, or remain unchanged? Your answer for each of the 12 transactions should include a brief explanation.

CASES AND UNSTRUCTURED PROBLEMS

CASE 14.1

Season's Greetings

LO 1

Holiday Greeting Cards is a local company organized late in July of 2001. The company's net income for each of its first six calendar quarters of operations is summarized below. (Amounts are stated in thousands of dollars.)

	2002	2001
First quarter (Jan. through Mar.)	$ 253	–0–
Second quarter (Apr. through June)	308	–0–
Third quarter (July through Sept.)	100	$ 50
Fourth quarter (Oct. through Dec.)	450	500
Total for the calendar year	$1,111	$550

Glen Wallace reports the business and economic news for a local radio station. On the day that Holiday Greeting Cards released the above financial information, you heard Wallace make the following statement during his broadcast: "Holiday Greeting Cards enjoyed a 350% increase in its profits for the fourth quarter, and profits for the entire year were up by over 100%."

Instructions

a. Show the computations that Wallace probably made in arriving at his statistics. (Hint: Wallace did not make his computations in the manner recommended in this chapter. His figures, however, can be developed from this financial data.)

b. Do you believe that Wallace's percentage changes present a realistic impression of Holiday Greeting Cards' rate of growth in 2002? Explain.

c. What figure would you use to express the percentage change in Holiday's fourth-quarter profits in 2002? Explain why you would compute the change in this manner.

CASE 14.2
Evaluating Debt-Paying Ability

LO 3, 4, 5

You are a loan officer with First Texas Bank. Dan Scott owns two successful restaurants, each of which has applied to your bank for a $250,000 one-year loan for the purpose of opening a second location. Condensed balance sheets for the two business entities are shown below.

TEXAS STEAK RANCH
Balance Sheet
December 31, 2002

Assets		Liabilities & Stockholders' Equity	
Current assets	$ 75,000	Current liabilities	$ 30,000
Plant and equipment	300,000	Long-term liabilities	200,000
		Capital stock	100,000
		Retained earnings	45,000
Total assets	$375,000	Total liabilities & stockholders' equity	$375,000

THE STOCKYARDS
Balance Sheet
December 31, 2002

Assets		Liabilities & Owners' Equity	
Current assets	$ 24,000	Current liabilities	$ 30,000
Plant and equipment	301,000	Long-term liabilities	200,000
		Capital, Dan Scott	95,000
Total assets	$325,000	Total liabilities & owners' equity	$325,000

Both restaurants are popular and have been successful over the past several years. Texas Steak Ranch has been slightly more profitable, but the operating results for the two businesses have been quite similar. You think that either restaurant's second location should be successful. On the other hand, you know that restaurants are a very "faddish" type of business and that their popularity and profitability can change very quickly.

Dan Scott is one of the wealthiest people in Texas. He made a fortune—estimated at more than $2 billion—as the founder of Micro Time, a highly successful manufacturer of computer software. Scott now is retired and spends most of his time at Second Life, his 50,000-acre cattle ranch. Both of his restaurants are run by experienced professional managers.

Instructions

a. Compute the current ratio and working capital of each business entity.

b. Based on the information provided in this case, which of these businesses do you consider to be the better credit risk? Explain fully.

c. What simple measure might you insist upon that would make the other business as good a credit risk as the one you identified in part **b**? Explain.

CASE 14.3
Strategies to Improve the Current Ratio
LO 4

Jenkins Improvement Centers owns a chain of nine retail stores that sell building materials, hardware, and garden supplies. In early October, the company's current ratio is 1.7 to 1. This is about normal for the company, but it is lower than the current ratios of several large competitors. Management feels that to qualify for the best credit terms from its suppliers, the company's year-end balance sheet should indicate a current ratio of at least 2 to 1.

Instructions
a. Indicate whether taking each of the following actions would increase or decrease the company's current ratio. Explain your reasoning.
  1. Pay some of the company's current liabilities
  2. Purchase large amounts of inventory on account
  3. Offer credit customers a special discount if they pay their account balance prior to year-end
b. Propose several other ethical steps that management might take to increase the company's current ratio prior to year-end.

CASE 14.4
Limit on Dividends
LO 8

During each of the past 10 years, Loomis, Inc. has increased the common stock dividend per share by about 10%. Total dividends now amount to $9 million per year, consisting of $2 million paid to preferred stockholders and $7 million paid to common stockholders. The preferred stock is cumulative but not convertible. Annual net income had been rising steadily until two years ago, when it peaked at $44 million. Last year, increased competition caused net income to decline to $37 million. Management expects income to stabilize around this level for several years. This year, Loomis, Inc. issued bonds payable. The contract with bondholders requires the company to limit total dividends to not more than 25% of net income.

Instructions
Evaluate this situation from the perspective of:
a. Common stockholders.
b. Preferred stockholders.

CASE 14.5
Improving Cash Flow
LO 8

Kelsay MicroLabs develops and manufactures pharmaceutical products. The company has been growing rapidly during the past 10 years, due primarily to having discovered, patented, and successfully marketed dozens of new products. Profits have increased annually by 30% or more. The company pays no dividend but has a very high price-earnings ratio. Due to its rapid growth and large expenditures for research and development, the company has experienced occasional cash shortages. To solve this problem, Kelsay has decided to improve its cash position by (1) requiring customers to pay for products purchased on account from the company in 30 days instead of 60 days and (2) reducing expenditures for research and development by 25%.

Instructions
Evaluate this situation from the perspective of:
a. Short-term creditors.
b. Common stockholders.

CASE 14.6
Declining Interest Rate
LO 8

Metro Utilities has outstanding 16 issues of bonds payable, with interest rates ranging from $5\frac{1}{2}$% to 14%. These bonds were sold over several years during which interest rates varied dramatically. The company's rate of return on assets consistently averages 12%. Almost every year, the company issues additional bonds to finance growth, to pay maturing bonds, or to call outstanding bonds when advantageous. During the current year, long-term interest rates have fallen dramatically. At the beginning of the year, these rates were between 12% and 13%; now, however, they are down to between 8% and 9%. Management currently is planning a large 8% bond issue.

Instructions
Evaluate this situation from the perspective of:
a. Holders of $5\frac{1}{2}$% bonds, maturing in 11 years but callable now at 103.
b. Holders of 14% bonds, maturing in 23 years but callable now at 103.
c. Common stockholders.

BUSINESS WEEK ASSIGNMENT

CASE 14.7

Financial Analysis and the Quality of Earnings at **Amazon.com**

LO 1, 2

In "Making Bad News Pay," *Business Week,* September 3, 2001, Pallavi Gogoi described David W. Tice, a professional stock-market bear. Tice sells scathing research reports to institutional investors describing why the stock prices of some companies could be headed down. Tice finds his targets by going over balance sheets, income statements, and cash flow statements with a fine-tooth comb. He looks for misleading numbers of bogus information that, once uncovered, results in an abrupt decline in the stock price.

For example, Tice has focused on **Amazon.com**. According to the *Business Week* article, Tice is convinced that **Amazon**'s business is flawed because of the difficulty of translating rising sales into profits. Tice also suggests that **Amazon**'s growth in its core business of books, music, and videos has slowed to a crawl, and that it now emphasizes its faster-growing consumer electronics business. He calls it a classic case of "Don't look over here, look over there."

Instructions

a. Identify and describe at least four tools of analysis that Tice is likely to use in his search for companies to include in his research reports.

b. Describe how the tools you identified in part **a** would help Tice come to the conclusions discussed in the *Business Week* article about **Amazon.com**.

INTERNET ASSIGNMENT

INTERNET 14.1

Evaluating Liquidity and Profitability

LO 7, 8

Use the Internet search engine of your choice and do a general search on the name of a company of interest to you (e.g., **General Motors**, **Johnson & Johnson**, **Coke**, etc.). Explore the web site of the company you chose and locate the most recent financial statements of the company of your choice. You may need to look under a category that provides general information about the company and/or investor information.

Instructions

a. Find and read the description of the company, including the type of business it is in. Why is gaining an understanding the industry and type of business an important starting point for financial statement analysis?

b. Locate the company's primary financial statements. Find the summary table of ratios in this chapter in Exhibit 14-27. Calculate three of the listed ratios under each of the following categories: "Measures of short-term liquidity," and "Measures of Profitability." Show your work in calculating these ratios. Write a brief statement describing what you have learned about your company's liquidity and profitability.

c. Why do you think the Internet has become such a widely used source of financial information by investors and creditors?

Internet sites are time and date sensitive. It is the purpose of these exercises to have you explore the Internet. You may need to use the Yahoo! search engine **http://www.yahoo.com** *(or another favorite search engine) to find a company's current Web address.*

OUR COMMENTS ON THE "YOUR TURN" CASES

You as a Potential Investor (p. 614) It is common for fast-food restaurants (such as **Wendy's** and **McDonald's**) to report seemingly low measures of short-term liquidity. This does not mean, however, that these companies will have difficulty paying their current liabilities as they become due. In fact, both **Wendy's** and **McDonald's** are extremely *liquid* companies. The reason the financial measures of their liquidity appear insufficient is that (1) all their sales are cash sales and, therefore, they have no accounts receivable, and (2) their inventory converts into cash at a faster rate than their current liabilities come due.

664 Chapter 14 Financial Statement Analysis

You as a Member of the House of Representatives (p. 617) There is no correct answer to the question of whether the stock exchanges should be more highly regulated. Supporters of free-market capitalism would suggest that normal market forces guide investors to the stock exchanges that have the "right" amount of regulation. That is, if the U.S. exchange requirements are too liberal, investors will purchase stocks on other exchanges where the requirements to be listed meet their expectations. One could argue, for example, that because the New York Stock Exchange (NYSE) has maintained its market share of 83% to 85% in the trading volumes of the companies it has listed over the last five years, its regulation level should be considered appropriate.

Alternatively, others argue that financial crises such as the 1987 stock-market crash, the 1998 Asian financial crisis, or the September 11 attack on the World Trade Center show that U.S. exchanges (particularly the NYSE) are at the heart of global markets. It is clear that these markets are vulnerable to disruptions and wild market swings and that regulation might prevent these swings.

You could explain to your constituents that the NYSE currently has more than one-third of its employees involved in self-regulatory functions. The Securities and Exchange Commission provides oversight for all U.S. securities exchanges and must answer to the U.S. Congress. The House of Representatives maintains its vigilance of the SEC and the capital markets through the Committee of Financial Services. These checks and balances are important and help maintain the integrity of U.S. securities markets.

You as a Financial Analyst (p. 637) For your client who is primarily interested in the dividends that will be received, you might advise him to evaluate much as a short-term creditor would. This would focus attention on liquidity—the current and quick ratios and the extent to which operating activities are generating positive cash flows. Also, you should suggest that he look at the company's dividend policy and the consistency with which dividends have been paid in the past. For the investor that is more interested in the market value of the stock, you should suggest that she look at a broader set of information that focuses on the long-term potential for successful operations of the companies being considered—net income, growth over time in sales, and return on assets and stockholders' equity. You should also suggest that she look at the pattern of changes in the value of the stock of the companies. For both investors, information in management's discussion and analysis may be helpful in identifying companies that are consistent with the specific investment objectives of each client.

ANSWERS TO SELF-TEST QUESTIONS

1. c   **2.** a, c, d   **3.** c   **4.** d (see below)   **5.** b (see below)   **6.** b   **7.** d

Why answers a, b, and c in question **4** are incorrect:

a. The return on assets, 12% ($240,000 ÷ $2,000,000), exceeds the return on equity, which is 10% ($80,000 ÷ $800,000).

b. The current ratio is 1.6 to 1 ($480,000 ÷ $300,000).

c. Working capital amounts to $180,000 ($480,000 − $300,000).

Increase in net income required in question **5**: ($400,000 − $160,000) ÷ $160,000 = 150%

COMPREHENSIVE PROBLEM 3

Tootsie Roll Industries, Inc.

ANALYSIS OF THE FINANCIAL STATEMENTS OF A PUBLICLY OWNED CORPORATION

The purpose of this Comprehensive Problem is to acquaint you with the content of an annual report. It is based upon the 2000 annual report of **Tootsie Roll Industries, Inc.**, reproduced in Appendix A of this textbook. The problem contains three major parts, which are independent of one another. *Part I* is designed to familiarize you with the content of an annual report; *Part II* involves analysis of the company's liquidity; and *Part III* analyzes the trend in its profitability.

If you work this problem as a group assignment, each group member should be prepared to discuss the group's findings and conclusions in class.

A good starting point for understanding the financial statements of a company such as **Tootsie Roll Industries, Inc.**, is to understand the accounting policies used in preparing those statements. The first note accompanying the financial statements provides a brief description of the major accounting policies the company used. Most of the areas discussed in this note have been covered in this text.

Part I

Annual reports include not only comparative financial statements but also the following sources of information:

- Multiyear summary of financial highlights, a summary of key statistics for the past 5 or 10 years.
- A letter from management addressed *To Our Stockholders*.
- A discussion by management of the results of operations and the company's financial condition.
- Several pages of *Notes* that accompany the financial statements.
- Reports by management and by the independent auditors in which they express their respective responsibilities for the financial statements.

Instructions

Answer each of the following questions and briefly explain *where* in the statements, notes, or other sections of the annual report you located the information used in your answer.

a. How many years are covered in each of the primary comparative financial statements? Were all of these statements audited? Name the auditors. What were the auditors' conclusions concerning these statements?

b. **Tootsie Roll Industries, Inc.**, combines its statement of retained earnings with another financial statement. Where are details about changes in the amount of retained earnings found?

c. Over the three years presented, have the company's annual net cash flows been positive or negative from (1) operating activities, (2) investing activities, and (3) financing activities? Has the company's cash balance increased or decreased during each of these three years?

d. What was the amount of net sales during the *fourth quarter* of the fiscal year ended December 31, 2000? What was the percentage change in this fourth quarter's net sales relative to sales in the fourth quarter of the prior year? Comment on the pattern of quarterly sales *within* the year, and offer your own explanation for this pattern.

e. What does management conclude about the company's general financial conditions? What are the primary indicators of the company's financial strength in the eyes of management?

f. What is management's assessment of the impact of international operations in 2000?

Part II

Assume that you are the credit manager of a medium-size supplier of ingredients used to manufacture candy. **Tootsie Roll Industries** wants to make credit purchases from your company, with payment due in 60 days.

Instructions

a. As general background, read the section *Management's Discussion and Analysis of Financial Condition and Results of Operations.* Next compute the following for the fiscal years ending December 31, 2000, and December 31, 1999 (round percentages to the nearest tenth of one percent, and other computations to one decimal place):

   1. Current ratio.
   2. Quick ratio.
   3. Amount of working capital.
   4. Percentage change in working capital from the prior year.
   5. Percentage change in cash and cash equivalents from the prior year.

b. Based upon your analysis in part **a**, does the company's liquidity appear to have *increased* or *decreased* during the most recent fiscal year? Explain.

c. Comment on the company's liquidity.

d. Other than the ability of **Tootsie Roll** to pay for its purchases, do you see any major considerations that should enter into your company's decision? Explain.

e. Your company assigns each customer one of the four credit ratings listed below. Assign a credit rating to **Tootsie Roll Industries** and write a memorandum explaining your decision. (In your memorandum, you may refer to any of your computations or observations in parts **a** through **c**, and to any information contained in the annual report.)

Possible Credit Ratings

A Outstanding Little or no risk of inability to pay. For customers in this category, we fill any reasonable order without imposing a credit limit. The customer's credit is reevaluated annually.

B Good Customer has good debt-paying ability but is assigned a credit limit that is reviewed every 90 days. Orders above the credit limit are accepted only on a cash basis.

C Marginal Customer appears sound, but credit should be extended only on a 30-day basis and with a relatively low credit limit. Creditworthiness and credit limit are reevaluated every 90 days.

D Unacceptable Customer does not qualify for credit.

Part III

As general background, read the *Five-Year Summary of Earnings and Financial Highlights,* the letter addressed *To Our Stockholders,* and *Management's Discussion and Analysis of Financial Condition and Results of Operations.*

Instructions

a. Compute the following for the fiscal years ending December 31, 2000, and December 31, 1999 (round percentages to the nearest tenth of one percent):

1. Percentage change in net sales (relative to the prior year).
2. Percentage change in net earnings.
3. Gross profit rate.
4. Net income as a percentage of sales.
5. Return on average total assets.
6. Return on average total equity.

b. Write a statement that describes your conclusion(s) concerning trends in **Tootsie Roll**'s profitability during the period covered in your analysis in part **a** above. Justify your conclusion(s).

CHAPTER 15
GLOBAL BUSINESS AND ACCOUNTING

Learning Objectives

After studying this chapter, you should be able to:

1. Define four mechanisms companies use to globalize their business activities.

2. Identify how global environmental forces—(a) political and legal systems, (b) economic systems, (c) culture, and (d) technology and infrastructure—affect financial reporting practices.

3. Explain why there is demand for harmonization of global financial reporting standards.

4. Demonstrate how to convert an amount of money from one currency to another.

5. Compute gains or losses on receivables or payables that are stated in a foreign currency when exchange rates fluctuate.

6. Describe several techniques for "hedging" against losses from fluctuations in exchange rates.

7. Discuss how global sourcing increases product cost complexity.

8. Explain the importance of the Foreign Corrupt Practices Act.

© James M. Mejuto

The Carrefour Group and Wal-Mart Inc.

Retailing on a global scale is not for the meek. Designing stores and delivering products that will be appreciated in a diverse set of countries with diverse populations is a significant challenge. Several large retailers aspire to be global. The one that comes closest is France's **Carrefour Group**, with stores in 31 countries. A visit to **Carrefour**'s website provides a clear indication of their international orientation. Visitors can access the site in five languages.

Another global retailer is **Wal-Mart**. **Wal-Mart** currently has stores in nine countries after creating its first store outside of the United States only a decade ago. Visitors can access the **Wal-Mart** website only in English. **Wal-Mart** executives have established a challenging goal to have international operations contribute one-third of **Wal-Mart**'s profits within the next five years.

Both **Carrefour** and **Wal-Mart** face financial reporting issues associated with their global reach. Because **Carrefour** is listed on the Paris Stock Exchange, their financial reports to investors comply with France's generally accepted accounting principles. Alternatively, **Wal-Mart**, listed on the New York Stock Exchange, prepares financial statements according to U.S. GAAP. What limitations do the restrictions associated with different financial reporting requirements place on companies like **Carrefour** and **Wal-Mart**? Do they encounter difficulties accessing global capital? Are international acquisitions difficult because financial reports differ around the globe?

• • •

The London-based International Accounting Standards Board began a mission in 1993 to develop financial reporting rules that all countries could use. The board has made significant progress. In this chapter we provide you with a foundation for understanding the richness and complexity of international financial reporting issues.

Accounting rules, procedures, and standards in almost any chosen country are different from those in the United States and different from those in other countries. Although some developing countries are adopting the international accounting standards discussed in the opening story, developed countries such as the United Kingdom, Japan, and Germany have established their own accounting rules, procedures, and standards. The goal of the International Accounting Standards Board is to identify a set of accounting standards that will be acceptable to all governments and their related securities markets. This is a very ambitious goal because accounting rules, procedures, and standards are affected by the political, legal, economic, and cultural systems in which they are embedded. Thus, the variations in these systems from country to country have a significant impact on how investors and creditors understand and use financial statement information.

The objective of this chapter is to introduce you to the complexity of global business and to explore some of the accounting issues associated with global business. This is only a brief introduction. As your business education progresses, additional details will be added to the ideas introduced here.

GLOBALIZATION

Globalization occurs as managers become aware of and engage in cross-border trade and operations. Think of globalization as a continuous process where at the most basic level a purely domestic company's managers become aware that changes in foreign exchange rates, international technological advances, cultural diversity, or international political and economic issues will have an impact on their ability to compete. An example of a higher level of globalization is a multinational enterprise that begins with raw material extraction and ends with final product assembly and sales in multiple foreign locations. **Carrefour** and **Wal-Mart**, both global Fortune 500 companies, provide examples of firms with explicit global goals but different levels of globalization. In Exhibit 15–1 we show the global reach of **Carrefour** and **Wal-Mart**. Notice that **Carrefour**, as compared to **Wal-Mart**, has both a larger portion of sales revenue and a larger percentage of store locations in international settings.

Exhibit 15–1

GLOBALIZATION OF CARREFOUR AND WAL-MART IN 2000

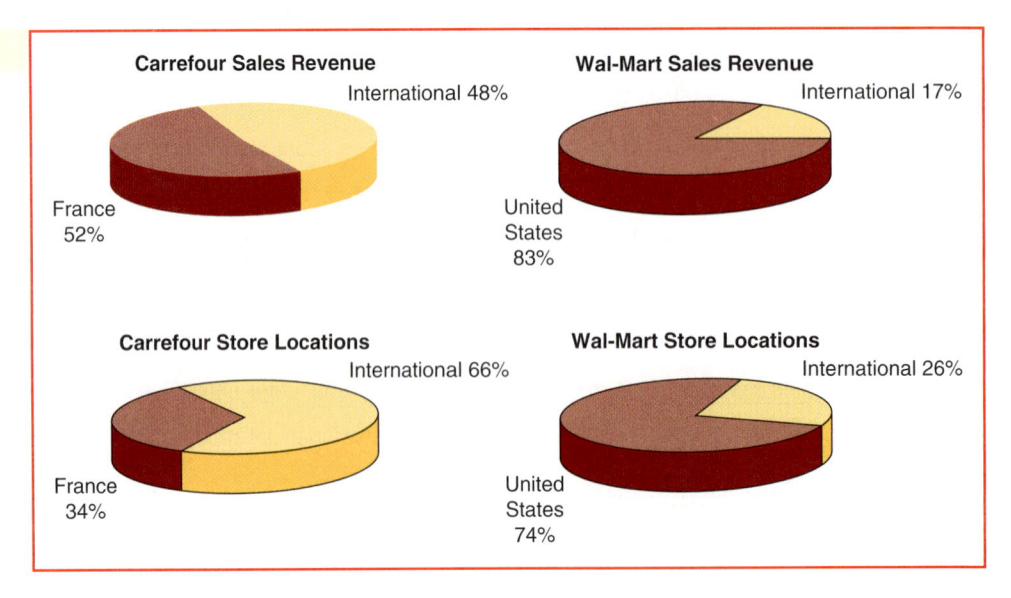

Carrefour Sales Revenue: France 52%, International 48%
Wal-Mart Sales Revenue: United States 83%, International 17%
Carrefour Store Locations: France 34%, International 66%
Wal-Mart Store Locations: United States 74%, International 26%

Globalization typically progresses through a series of stages that include exporting, licensing, joint ventures, wholly owned subsidiaries, and, finally, global sourcing. **Exporting** is, at the simplest level, selling a good or service to a foreign customer. While *exporting* maintains control over product creation, *licensing* gives up some control for a monetary return. **International licensing** is a contractual agreement between a company and a foreign party allowing the use of trademarks, patents, technology, designs, processes, intellectual property, or other proprietary advantage. Most major multinational food manufacturing companies are involved in some form of international product licensing. An **international joint venture** is a company owned by two or more companies from different countries. A **wholly owned international subsidiary** is created when a company uses its own funds to construct or purchase 100% equity control of a foreign subsidiary. Finally, **global sourcing** is the close coordination of R&D, manufacturing, and marketing across national boundaries and typically includes exporting, licensing, joint ventures, and wholly owned subsidiaries in cross-border operations.

As shown in Exhibit 15–2, companies typically engage in globalization through an outward growth path. Those companies wishing to globalize typically progress through the following stages: (1) exporting domestically produced products, (2) establishing licensing and joint venture arrangements, (3) creating wholly owned subsidiaries, and (4) full-scale global sourcing. In practice, there are many subcategories that are not shown in the exhibit, and companies may pursue multiple globalization processes simultaneously.

LO 1
Define four mechanisms companies use to globalize their business activities.

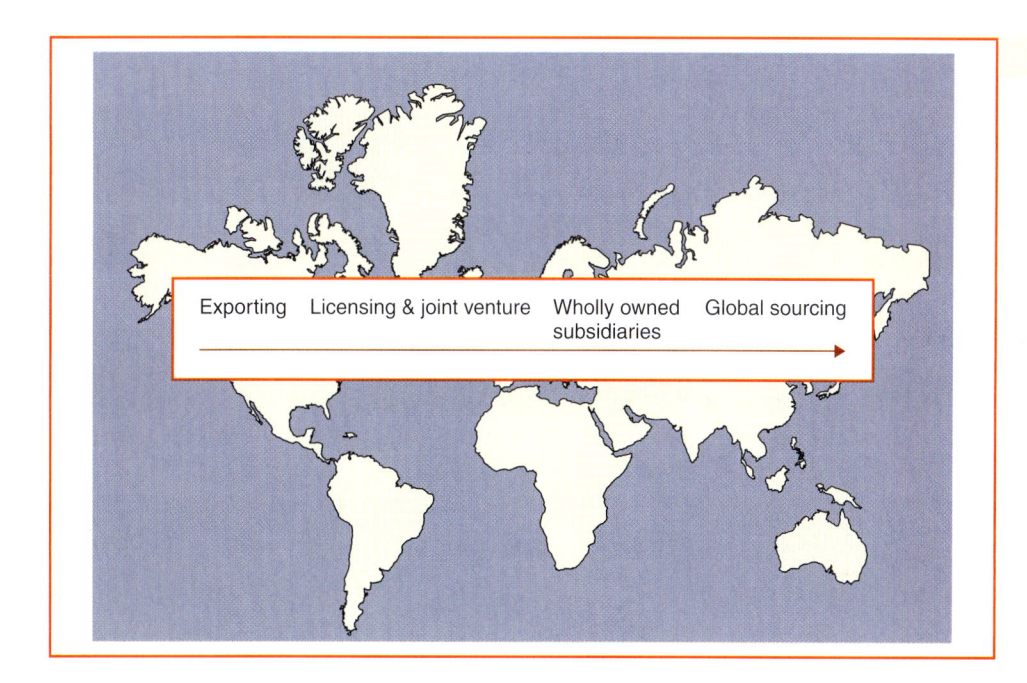

Exhibit 15–2

PROCESSES FOR INCREASING GLOBALIZATION

Exporting → Licensing & joint venture → Wholly owned subsidiaries → Global sourcing

Globalization has implications for the type of accounting information gathered, created, and reported. U.S. GAAP requirements for exporting, licensing, joint ventures, and wholly owned subsidiaries are very different. In addition, differences in currency exchange rates create financial reporting issues. For instance, when payments are made in U.S. dollars, exports are treated identically to a domestic sale. However, when the sales revenue is denominated in a foreign currency, exports create additional financial accounting issues that are discussed in more detail later in this chapter. Choosing to enter into a licensing agreement creates an intangible that also can be complicated by foreign exchange issues. An international joint venture inevitably raises foreign currency exchange and level of control issues. Finally, international wholly owned subsidiaries must be consolidated with the U.S. parent's financial reports. Management decisions about how to globalize clearly impact their financial statements.

CASE IN POINT

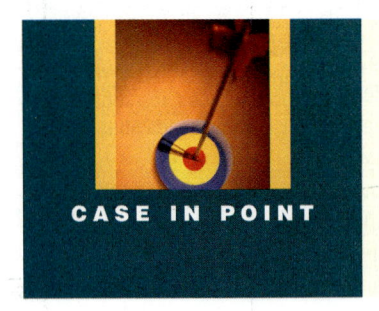

General Mills provides an excellent example of the globalization process. Exporting of flour began shortly after the creation of the company in 1928. Today, **General Mills** exports 650 items to 100 markets. Its first international business, **General Mills Canada**, was started in 1954. Joint ventures and licensing agreements with Nestlé in Europe (1989), Maizena in Latin America (1994), and, more recently, Want Want Holdings Ltd. in China have made **General Mills** a multinational company.

ENVIRONMENTAL FORCES SHAPING GLOBALIZATION

LO 2
Identify how global environmental forces—(a) political and legal systems, (b) economic systems, (c) culture, and (d) technology and infrastructure—affect financial reporting practices.

To help you understand how international environmental forces affect the accounting information measured, reported, and created, we consider environmental forces in four categories: (1) political and legal systems, (2) economic systems, (3) culture, and (4) technology and infrastructure.

These categories are not independent. A country's economy and culture have an influence on its political and legal structures. Culture affects and is affected by economics. As illustrated in Exhibit 15–3, the technological position of a country is dependent on political, demographic, and cultural issues.

Exhibit 15–3
ENVIRONMENTAL FORCES IMPACTING GLOBALIZATION

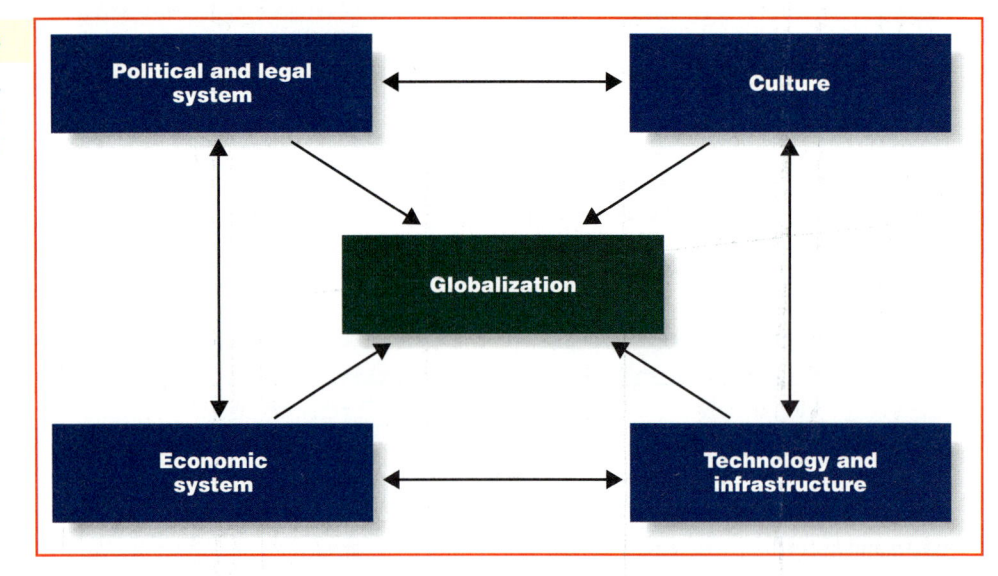

[Diagram showing four boxes — Political and legal system, Culture, Economic system, Technology and infrastructure — all connected by arrows to a central Globalization box.]

Political and Legal Systems

LO 2a
Identify how political and legal systems affect financial reporting practices.

Managers operating in or planning operations in foreign settings must monitor political risks associated with that foreign country. Political risk occurs because governments have the ability to shift asset ownership from the company to the government or because the company may be asked to relinquish command over operations due to government intervention. For example, when Iran nationalized its oil industry in the late 1970s, many companies lost ownership of the assets they had invested in oil exploration, drilling, and oil delivery. United States GAAP requires companies to include in their financial reports discussions about political risk that may significantly impair assets or profits.

Laws enacted by foreign governments often have an impact on the net profits earned from international activities. Taxes, tariffs, and licensing fees vary substantially from country to country. Laws restricting the flow of currency can affect the amounts of foreign-earned profits that can be transferred out and used elsewhere. Ownership requirements are a common form of governmental control. For example, governments

Environmental Forces Shaping Globalization

in China and India have ownership restrictions on subsidiaries in their countries. Joint ventures in China typically result in Chinese companies (or citizens) owning at least 51% of the joint venture company.

Other types of political intervention include content or value-added requirements and sourcing requirements. Trade agreements often specify the source of raw materials or labor content to allow preferential treatment in tariffs and customs for products or services that are produced in the regions covered by the agreement. For example, NAFTA (the North American Free Trade Agreement) specifies **regional value content** conditions to qualify for favorable tariff and customs duty treatment. Regional value content requirements come into play when a good is manufactured partially in countries that are members of the free trade agreement and partially in countries that are not. These rules can be very complex and dictate the amount of total cost or the percentage of the sales price that must be added in those countries that have signed the free trade agreement.

Governments create tariffs, duties, and special trade zones that affect the cost associated with producing and selling goods and services in global markets. For example, the U.S. government has identified several **foreign trade zones** within the United States. Goods imported into these zones are duty-free until they leave the zone. Companies that import raw materials frequently set up their factories in these trade zones. These companies are not required to pay duty on the imported raw materials until the finished product is shipped out of the zone. Using foreign trade zones can have an impact on revenue recognition and the cost of goods sold. In addition, a delay in paying the duty enlarges the company's working capital as discussed in Chapter 14.

CASE IN POINT

Mexico has created special laws for a **maquiladora**, which is a joint venture manufacturing plant typically located in northern Mexico. These companies enjoy exemptions from Mexican laws governing foreign companies. In addition, the United States grants exemptions from, or reductions in, customs duties on re-exported goods (that is, raw materials sent from the United States to Mexico for assembly and exported back into the United States for insertion into the finished product). Companies that create maquiladoras benefit from high-quality labor at low wages.

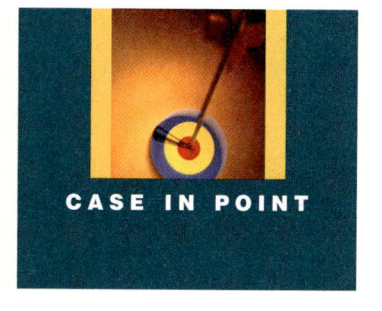

The costs added by the governments where a company is operating or planning to operate must be considered when resource allocation decisions are made. A manager practicing global sourcing will need information on taxes, tariffs, local content laws, and so on to make effective, competitive resource decisions.

Legal reporting requirements vary significantly from country to country. Differences in accounting practices are a reflection of the legal environment in which the business operates and the primary providers of capital for the business. For example, in the United Kingdom and the United States, reporting requirements are based primarily on the need to provide useful information for investors and creditors. These are countries where companies raise capital primarily by selling their securities in well-developed capital markets. In Europe and Japan, on the other hand, banks provide much of the capital for business. In those countries, accounting requirements are more legalistic and are intended to satisfy governmental reporting requirements, including income tax reporting. In South America, financial reporting is oriented toward the needs of governmental planning and follows practices dictated by the government.

As countries change and grow, governments try to manage that growth through political and legal means. For example, in addition to creating legal reporting requirements for companies wishing to raise capital in equity markets, governments also use tax incentives that encourage or discourage ownership of stocks. Policies also affect the level of individual savings, which impacts the availability of capital. Educational policies impact the literacy rate, extent of formal education and training, and the number of accounting professionals. The political and legal structures of each country provide the framework for their economic structures. Although the political, legal, and economic structures are discussed here as separate ideas, you should think of these structures as highly related. These structures evolve and change over time, affecting the flow of capital and goods across borders.

Economic Systems

LO 2b Identify how economic systems affect financial reporting practices.

The economic systems under which businesses operate significantly affect the form and availability of accounting information. In a **planned economy**, the government uses central planning to allocate resources and determine output among various segments of the economy. Land and production facilities are government owned and controlled. The former Soviet Union and Soviet Eastern Bloc countries used central planning and had planned economies. China continues to use central planning extensively. In **market economies**, ownership of land and the means of production are private, and markets dictate the allocation of resources and the output among segments of the economy.

Companies formerly operating in a planned economy can encounter significant difficulties when attempting to operate in a market economy. The reverse can also be true. Many companies from market economies have been unsuccessful when attempting to do business in foreign locations that are primarily planned economies.

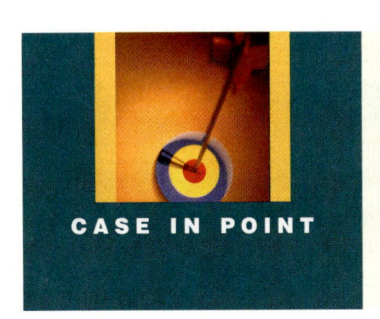

CASE IN POINT

In 2000, **Amoco Corporation** abandoned a joint venture in Russia because of bureaucratic and technological difficulties. The number of failed and abandoned joint ventures in Russia is a reminder that expertise in one economic system may not transfer to other locations.

Obtaining capital and creating international business partnerships require an understanding of international differences in how capital is acquired and how businesses are organized. Although the United States has a strong capital market where companies can acquire capital by issuing equity shares in the company, many other countries have either no capital market or a very restricted, low-volume market. In those countries, banks or governments are the dominant providers of capital. Islamic governments, such as Iran and Sudan, do not allow banks to make interest payments to depositors. Instead, individual depositors share in the bank's profits. Commercial borrowers pay the bank and its depositors a share of their profits instead of interest. Government restrictions on the availability of capital significantly influence how accounting information is created and reported.

In some countries businesses arrange themselves into **industrial organizations** as one method of raising capital. In South Korea and Japan, companies group themselves into conglomerates representing different industries. South Korean conglomerates, called *chaebol,* and Japanese conglomerates, called *keiretsu,* consist of companies that are grouped as customers and suppliers, and they usually contain a bank. Within these cartels of companies, suppliers receive loans, investment capital, technology, and long-term supply agreements from customers higher up on the pyramid. Suppliers integrate their operations with other suppliers and with their customers. Transactions between suppliers and customers are not arm's-length as in most U.S. transactions. In the United States, antitrust and price-fixing laws preclude the type of organized business groups found in Japan and South Korea.

Culture

LO 2c Identify how culture affects financial reporting practices.

Think of culture as the mental mindset that affects the way individuals in a society act and perceive each other's actions.[1] U.S. cultural practices have significant effects on the way foreign companies conduct business in the United States. Likewise, certain forms

---

[1] For a more detailed discussion of the information in this section, see G. Hofstede, *Cultures and Organizations: Software of the Mind* (Berkshire, England: McGraw-Hill, 1991).

of advertising, methods of acquiring business, and hierarchical organizational structures, which are common practices in the United States, would not be acceptable in some international settings. Cultural differences mandate that companies wishing to do business in diverse cultural settings invest in training for their current employees, hire new employees with cultural expertise, or, more often, both. Ignoring cultural variables can create significant business problems.

> In fiscal 2001, **Wal-Mart** reported a .13% decrease in the international segment's operating income as a percent of segment sales. Management said one cause of the decrease was in the company's Germany units. Some business writers have suggested that **Wal-Mart**'s overseas problems were avoidable and the result of exporting its culture wholesale rather than adapting to local markets.*
>
> *See "Wal-Mart: Wal Around the World," *The Economist,* December 8, 2001, page 55.

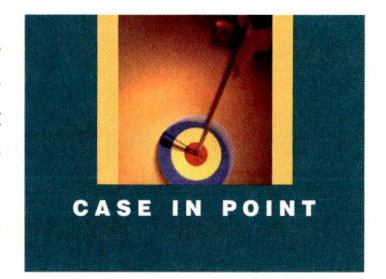

CASE IN POINT

Experts have identified four cultural mindsets that significantly differ among international locations.

- *Individualism versus collectivism.* The degree of interdependence that a society maintains among individuals, where high interdependence connotes collectivism. Citizens of Asian countries typically score higher on collectivism than those in the United States.
- *Uncertainty avoidance.* The extent to which members of a society feel uncomfortable or threatened by unknown or uncertain situations. Citizens of South American countries score high on uncertainty avoidance.
- *Short-term versus long-term orientation.* With a long-term orientation, perseverance, thriftiness, maintaining order, and lasting relationships are highly valued. A short-term orientation focuses on the past and the present, ignores the future, and values personal stability.
- *Large versus small power distance.* Large power distance cultures accept unequally distributed power within and across institutions and organizations. The idea that everyone is created equal or should have an equal voice is more highly valued in small power distance societies.

Exhibit 15–4 provides a rough measure of the relative differences between selected countries.

Exhibit 15–4

CULTURAL MINDSETS

Country	Individualism	Uncertainty Avoidance	Long-Term Orientation	High Power Distance
Japan	L	H	H	M
South Korea	L	H	H	H
Brazil	L	H	M	H
Italy	M	H	*	M
Germany	M	M	L	L
United States	H	M	L	M
Great Britain	H	L	L	L
Sweden	M	L	L	L

H = High, M = Medium, L = Low.
*Not available.

We can use Exhibit 15–4 to understand how cultural variables can affect both the type of accounting information that is produced and how that information is used. Studies have shown that in South Korea and Japan, where collectivism is high, less emphasis is placed on the transparency of financial statements for investors and the professionalism of accountants is low. The needs of creditors are given preference over the needs of investors, and the government—in particular the tax authority—has significant influence over financial reporting requirements. Thus, because financing for companies comes primarily from a bank in the keiretsu or chaebol, most financial accounting information is kept within the collectivist group. In addition, because of the strict government control of accounting regulations, the accounting profession in Asian countries has been slow to develop. The relative number of independent accountants is small, but increasing in many Asian countries.

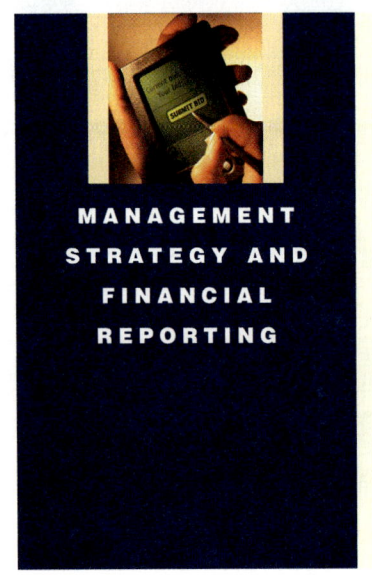

MANAGEMENT STRATEGY AND FINANCIAL REPORTING

The Japanese government is creating amendments to the Japanese securities law that will radically change the way companies in Japan report financial statement information. Business leaders in Japan are calling it Japan's accounting "Big Bang." As the Japanese Finance Ministry phases in tougher accounting standards over the next several years, managers of several Japanese companies will be changing their business strategies.

For example, until recently, parent companies in Japan only counted operations as subsidiaries if they had more than 50% ownership. However, because of keiretsu structures, big companies often control their smaller suppliers and sometimes shift unwanted losses from the parent's books to these affiliates. Thus, investors have difficulty figuring out the profitability of the big company. Under the Big Bang rules, if the parent exercises de facto control by financing the affiliate's debt or picking its board, the parent must consolidate the affiliate as a 100% owned subsidiary. It is expected that under the new rules, Japan's **Mazda Motor Corp.** must consolidate 88 more dealers and parts suppliers (many of them unprofitable) into its financial statements. Under the new rules of the Big Bang, Japanese companies will re-examine the strategies that link them to their affiliates.

Technology and Infrastructure

LO 2d
Identify how technology and infrastructure affect financial reporting practices.

Other cross-border differences create global business challenges because of variations in infrastructure and educational level. The ability to transfer information and knowledge between and among various geographic locations and peoples can be difficult. Frequently companies that create joint ventures or start wholly owned operations in some foreign locations find few employees with the education and technical training available in the U.S. workforce.

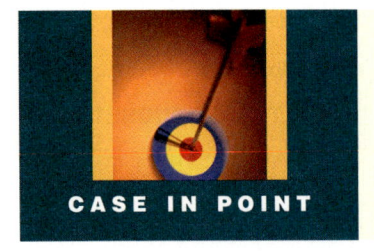

CASE IN POINT

Western-style management training is a very recent development in many countries. Budapest has one of the oldest graduate management programs in Eastern Europe, and it was founded in 1988. Thus, Eastern Europe is more than 80 years behind when compared to the Harvard Business School, founded in 1908.

More specifically, because companies in formerly planned economies used centrally determined accounts and procedures, accounting as a profession did not exist in Eastern Europe prior to 1988. Thus companies establishing business operations in Eastern European locations have difficulty locating trained accounting personnel. In addition prior business records are unreliable. Before the early 1990s, there were no independent auditors, public accountants, or management accountants in most Eastern European countries.

Differences in internal accounting systems can also create problems in international business dealings, particularly when one organization acquires or creates a joint venture with another. Internal accounting information is critical for understanding how a business operates, and how to value that business, which is one of the main functions of accountants. Cultural, educational, language, and software differences hinder the free flow of information. Potential benefits from acquired international operations are sometimes lost because of the inability to transfer valuable information within and between international companies.

> **CASE IN POINT**
>
> When **Upjohn** (a U.S. pharmaceutical company) merged with **Pharmecia** (a Swiss-based pharmaceutical company) the new company faced serious infrastructure hurdles related to merging their accounting systems to create their annual financial reports. Prior to the merger each company had its own accounting system software and hardware. Each company used a different set of accounting requirements for financial reporting purposes. Because the cost of merging the accounting systems was underestimated, the merger did not attain all of its potential benefits.

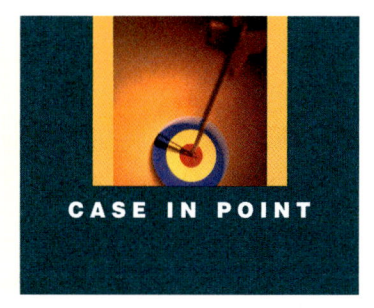

Infrastructure impediments also pose problems for globalization. Poor access to communication equipment (for example, telephones, faxes, and computers), necessary R&D facilities (for example, specialized laboratory equipment, computer-aided design or manufacturing), and fluctuating or unreliable power sources create significant hurdles to establishing international business in some locations. Manufacturing plants in many developing countries are not heated or cooled, which can create adverse operating environments for equipment that relies on lubricants and coolants. Inadequate transportation systems can slow the transfer of goods in and out of an international location. When estimating costs for inventory balance sheet items or cost of goods sold, accountants need to incorporate these unexpected costs into their computations to properly compute the cost of exported products.

HARMONIZATION OF FINANCIAL REPORTING STANDARDS

Cross-border differences in accounting practices create problems in trying to analyze and compare accounting information. For example, financial reporting in the United States is based primarily on the principle of historical cost without adjustment for changes in general price levels. South and Central American countries such as Brazil or Mexico, on the other hand, have experienced such high rates of inflation that inflation-adjusted information is required. Similarly, differences exist in the financial reporting requirements in the United States and Mexico in such important areas as earnings per share, consolidation of financial statements, and reporting for retiree medical and insurance benefits. These differences cause the financial statements of a U.S. company and a Mexican company to be very different and difficult to compare.

LO 3
Explain why there is demand for harmonization of global financial reporting standards.

As long as an enterprise operates solely within its own borders, differences in financial reporting practices between countries are not as significant a problem as they are if business activity extends across borders. When a company buys or sells products in another country, the lack of comparability of accounting information becomes a greater problem. Similarly, cross-border financing, in which a company sells its securities in the capital markets of another country, has become increasingly popular. Business activities that cross borders create the need for more comparable information between companies that reside in different countries.

The need for comparable information has led to an interest in the harmonization of accounting standards, a term used to describe the standardization of accounting methods and principles used in different countries throughout the world. The International Accounting Standards Board (IASB) is particularly interested in harmonization and is charged with the responsibility of establishing and gaining acceptance of international accounting standards (IAS). This committee represents 120 professional organizations from 91 countries and over 1 million accounting professionals worldwide. While IASB has no regulatory authority in any country, it uses its influence to move the reporting standards of all countries closer together in hopes of better harmonizing those standards. For countries that do not have well-developed capital markets, the IASB standards provide a model that often has a significant influence on their early attempts to develop standardized accounting practices.

Exhibit 15–5 provides a flavor of the differences that currently exist among financial reporting requirements around the world. The first column shows that the number of available auditors in any particular country varies significantly. This variation is a direct result of the environmental variables discussed earlier. The United States and the United Kingdom have the most highly developed capital markets in the world and the related auditing demands are evident in the table. Column two shows that asset revaluations are more likely to be allowed in countries like Brazil that have experienced long periods of high inflation. Variations in inventory valuation and depreciation practices are illustrated in columns four and five. The final column in Exhibit 15–5 displays differences in segment disclosure. Segment information has been in demand from investors in recent years. Countries such as Germany and Brazil, where capital is typically provided by banks, require lower levels of segment disclosure. These banks usually have access to inside information from their borrowers. Thus, demand for segment information to be included on required external financial reports is much lower in these countries.

Exhibit 15–5

GLOBAL VARIATION IN ACCOUNTING PRACTICES

Country/Standards	Auditors per 100,000	Asset Valuation Method	LIFO Used	Depreciation Basis	Segment Disclosure Required
IAS		Revaluation allowed	Used	Economic based	Yes
United States	168	Historic cost	Used	Economic based	Yes
United Kingdom	352	Revaluation allowed	Not used	Economic based	Yes
Germany	26	Historic cost	Not used	Tax based	Limited
Brazil	1	Revaluation allowed	Not used	Economic based	No
Japan	10	Historic cost	Used	Tax based	Yes

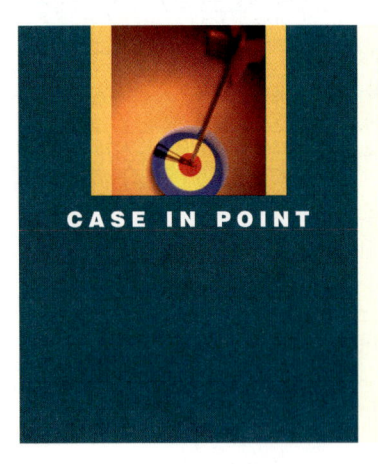

CASE IN POINT

In 1993 the IASB and the International Organization of Securities Commissions (IOSCO) reached a very significant agreement on a comprehensive list of forty core standards. The agreement asserts that on completion of the core standards acceptable to IOSCO, it will endorse the international accounting standards and recommend them for cross-border capital raising and listing purposes in all global markets. The U.S. Securities and Exchange Commission (SEC) is a member of IOSCO.

In May 1999 after IASC completed work on the key components of the forty standards, the Technical Committee of IOSCO assessed the IASC's core standards. In 2000 IOSCO decided to recommend that members permit foreign issuers to use IAS in addition to national standards for cross-border offering and listing purposes. For current information on this process see: www.IASB.org.uk.

FOREIGN CURRENCIES AND EXCHANGE RATES

In addition to the environmental characteristics just discussed, companies with international business dealings encounter financial measurements and problems from multiple currencies. Consider, for example, a Japanese company that sells merchandise to a U.S. corporation. The Japanese company will want to be paid in Japanese currency—yen—but the U.S. company's bank account contains U.S. dollars. Thus one currency must be converted into another.

Foreign Currencies and Exchange Rates

Most banks participate in an international currency exchange that enables them to buy foreign currencies at the prevailing *exchange rate*. Thus a U.S. corporation can pay a liability to a Japanese company through the international banking system. The U.S. company will pay its bank in dollars. The bank will then use these dollars to purchase the required amount of yen on the international currency exchange and will arrange for delivery of the yen to the Japanese company's bank.[2]

Exchange Rates

A currency **exchange rate** is the amount it costs to purchase one unit of currency with another currency. Thus the exchange rate may be viewed as the "price" of buying one unit of a foreign currency, stated in terms of the domestic currency (which for our purpose is U.S. dollars). Exchange rates fluctuate daily, based on the worldwide supply and demand for particular currencies. The current exchange rate between the dollar and most major currencies is published daily in the financial press. For example, a few of the exchange rates recently listed in *The Wall Street Journal* are shown in Exhibit 15–6.

PhotoDisc

Exhibit 15–6

U.S. DOLLAR EQUIVALENTS FOR FIVE FOREIGN CURRENCIES

Country/Region	Currency	Exchange Rate (in dollars)	Exchange Rate (in foreign currency)
Britain	Pound (£)	$1.4450	0.692
Europe*	Euro (€)	0.8949	1.117
Japan	Yen (¥)	0.00764	130.9
Mexico	Peso ($)	0.10946	9.136
India	Rupee (Rs)	0.02045	48.889

* In 2002, Austria, Belgium, Finland, France, Germany, Greece, Ireland, Italy, Luxembourg, the Netherlands, Portugal, and Spain began using the euro.

Exchange rates may be used to determine how much of one currency is equivalent to a given amount of another currency. Assume that a U.S. company owes a Japanese company 1 million yen (expressed ¥1,000,000). How many dollars are needed to settle this obligation, assuming that the current exchange rate is $0.00764 per yen? To restate an amount of foreign currency in terms of the equivalent amount of U.S. dollars, we multiply the foreign currency amount by the exchange rate, as follows:[3]

LO 4
Demonstrate how to convert an amount of money from one currency to another.

Amount Stated in Foreign Currency	×	Exchange Rate (in dollars)	=	Equivalent Number of U.S. Dollars
¥1,000,000	×	$0.00764 per yen	=	$7,640

This process of restating an amount of foreign currency in terms of the equivalent number of dollars is called *translating* the foreign currency.

Exchange Rate Jargon   In the financial press, currencies are often described as "strong" or "weak," or as rising or falling against one another. For example, an evening newscaster

My Mentor

---

[2] Alternatively, the U.S. company may send the Japanese company a check (or a bank draft) stated in dollars. The Japanese company can then arrange to have the dollars converted into yen through its bank in Japan.

[3] To convert an amount of dollars into the equivalent amount of a foreign currency, we would *divide* the dollar amount by the exchange rate. For example, $7,640 ÷ $0.00764 per yen = ¥1,000,000.

might say, "A strong dollar rose sharply against the weakening British pound, but fell slightly against the Japanese yen and the Swiss franc." What does this tell us about exchange rates?

To understand such terminology, we must remember that an exchange rate is simply the price of one currency *stated in terms of another currency*. Throughout this chapter, we refer to the prices of various foreign currencies stated in terms of *U.S. dollars*. In other countries, however, the U.S. dollar is a foreign currency, and its price is stated in terms of the local (domestic) currency.

To illustrate, consider the last column in our table from *The Wall Street Journal*. Exhibit 15–6 shows the exchange rate for the Japanese yen to be $0.00764. At this exchange rate, $1 is equivalent to ¥130.9 (¥130.9 × $0.00764 per yen = $1). Thus, while we would say that the exchange rate for the Japanese yen is *$0.00764,* the Japanese would say that the exchange rate for the U.S. dollar is *¥130.9*.

Now let us assume that the exchange rate for the yen (stated in dollars) rises to $0.0109. At this exchange rate, $1 is equivalent to only ¥92 (¥92 × $0.0109 = $1). In the United States, we would say that the exchange rate for the yen has *risen* from $0.00764 to $0.0109. In Japan, however, they would say that the exchange rate for the dollar has *fallen* from ¥130.9 to ¥92. In the financial press, it might be said that "the yen has risen against the dollar" or that "the dollar has fallen against the yen." The two statements mean the same thing—that the yen has become more valuable relative to the dollar.

Now let us return to our original phrase, "A strong dollar rose sharply against the weakening British pound, but fell slightly against the Japanese yen and the Swiss franc." When exchange rates are stated in terms of U.S. dollars, this statement means that the price (exchange rate) of the British pound fell sharply, but the prices of the Japanese yen and the Swiss franc rose slightly. A currency is described as "strong" when its exchange rate is rising relative to most other currencies and as "weak" when its exchange rate is falling. Exchange rates fluctuate because of changes in the environmental forces discussed earlier in this chapter.

Accounting for Transactions with Foreign Companies

LO 5
Compute gains or losses on receivables or payables that are stated in a foreign currency when exchange rates fluctuate.

When a U.S. company buys or sells merchandise in a transaction with a foreign company, the transaction price may be stipulated either in U.S. dollars or in units of the foreign currency. If the price is stated in *dollars,* the U.S. company encounters no special accounting problems. The transaction may be recorded in the same manner as are similar transactions with domestic suppliers or customers.

If the transaction price is stated in terms of the *foreign currency,* the company encounters two accounting problems. First, as the U.S. company's accounting records are maintained in dollars, the transaction price must be *translated* into dollars before the transaction can be recorded. The second problem arises when (1) the purchase or sale is made *on account* and (2) the exchange rate *changes* between the date of the transaction and the date that the account is paid. This fluctuation in the exchange rate will cause the U.S. company to experience either a *gain* or a *loss* in the settlement of the transaction.

Credit Purchases with Prices Stated in a Foreign Currency Assume that on August 1 a U.S. company buys merchandise from a British company at a price of 10,000 British pounds (£10,000), with payment due in 60 days. The exchange rate on August 1 is *$1.63* per British pound. The entry on August 1 to record this purchase (assuming use of a perpetual inventory system) would be:

My Notes
The amount of a foreign currency credit purchase is determined by using the exchange rate on the date it is journalized

Inventory	16,300	
Accounts Payable		16,300

To record the purchase of merchandise from a British company for £10,000 when the exchange rate is $1.63 per pound (£10,000 × $1.63 = $16,300).

Let us now assume that by September 30, when the £10,000 account payable must be paid, the exchange rate has fallen to *$1.61* per British pound. If the U.S. company had paid for the merchandise on August 1, the cost would have been $16,300. On September 30, however, only *$16,100* is needed to pay the £10,000 liability (£10,000 × $1.61 = $16,100). Thus *the decline in the exchange rate has saved the company $200.* This savings is recorded in the accounting records as a *Gain on Fluctuations in Foreign Exchange Rates.* The entry on September 30 to record payment of the liability and recognition of this gain would be:

Accounts Payable	16,300	
Cash		16,100
Gain on Fluctuations in Foreign Exchange Rates		200
To record payment of £10,000 liability to British company and to recognize gain from decline in exchange rate:		
Original liability (£10,000 × $1.63)	$16,300	
Amount paid (£10,000 × $1.61)	16,100	
Gain from decline in exchange rate	$ 200	

My Notes

The foreign exchange rate gain for the credit purchase is determined by using the exchange rate on the payment date

Now let us assume that instead of declining, the exchange rate had *increased* from $1.63 on August 1 to *$1.66* on September 30. Under this assumption, the U.S. company would have to pay *$16,600* to pay off the £10,000 liability on September 30. Thus the company would be paying *$300 more* than if the liability had been paid on August 1. This additional $300 cost was caused by the increase in the exchange rate and should be recorded as a loss. The entry on September 30 would be:

Accounts Payable	16,300	
Loss on Fluctuations in Foreign Exchange Rates	300	
Cash		16,600
To record payment of £10,000 liability to British company and to recognize loss from increase in exchange rate:		
Original liability (£10,000 × $1.63)	$16,300	
Amount paid (£10,000 × $1.66)	16,600	
Loss from increase in exchange rate	$ 300	

My Notes

A foreign exchange rate loss occurs if the exchange rate increases between the credit purchase date and the payment date

In summary, having a liability that is fixed in terms of a foreign currency results in a gain for the debtor if the exchange rate declines between the date of the transaction and the date of payment. The gain results because fewer dollars will be needed to repay the debt than had originally been owed. An increase in the exchange rate, on the other hand, causes the debtor to incur a loss. In this case, the debtor will have to spend more dollars than had originally been owed in order to purchase the foreign currency needed to pay the debt.

Credit Sales with Prices Stated in a Foreign Currency A company that makes credit *sales* at prices stated in a foreign currency also will experience gains or losses from fluctuations in the exchange rate. To illustrate, let us change our preceding example to assume that the U.S. company *sells* merchandise on August 1 to the British company at a price of £10,000. We shall again assume that the exchange rate on August 1 is $1.63 per British pound and that payment is due in 60 days. The entry on August 1 to record this sale would be:

Accounts Receivable	16,300	
Sales		16,300
To record sale to British company with sales price set at £10,000 (£10,000 × $1.63) = $16,300. To be collected in 60 days.		

In 60 days (September 30), the U.S. company will collect from the British company the U.S. dollar equivalent of £10,000. If the exchange rate on September 30 has fallen to $1.61 per pound, the U.S. company will collect only $16,100 (£10,000 × $1.61 = $16,100) in full settlement of its account receivable. Since the receivable had originally been equivalent to $16,300, the decline in the exchange rate has caused a loss of $200 to the U.S. company. The entry to be made on September 30 would be:

My Notes
A foreign exchange rate loss occurs when the exchange rate decreases between the credit sales date and the payment date

Cash	16,100	
Loss on Fluctuations in Foreign Exchange Rates	200	
Accounts Receivable		16,300
To record collection of £10,000 receivable from British company and to recognize loss from fall in exchange rate since date of sale:		
Original sales price (£10,000 × $1.63)	$16,300	
Amount received (£10,000 × $1.61)	16,100	
Loss from decline in exchange rate	$ 200	

Now consider the alternative case, in which the exchange rate rises from $1.63 at August 1 to $1.66 at September 30. In this case, the British company's payment of £10,000 will convert into $16,600, creating a gain for the U.S. company. The entry on September 30 would then be:

Cash	16,600	
Accounts Receivable		16,300
Gain on Fluctuations in Foreign Exchange Rates		300
To record collection of £10,000 receivable from British company and to recognize gain from increase in exchange rate:		
Original sales price (£10,000 × $1.63)	$16,300	
Amount received (£10,000 × $1.66)	16,600	
Gain from incease in exchange rate	$ 300	

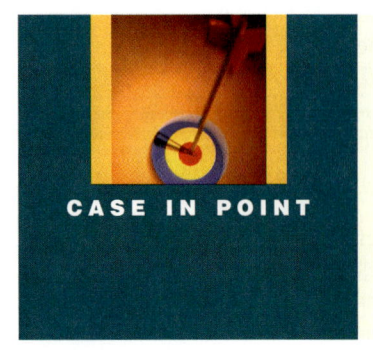

CASE IN POINT

Companies reporting under U.S. GAAP requirements typically mention the impact of foreign exchange rate fluctuations on their annual report outcomes in the Management's Discussion and Analysis section of the annual report. For example, in **Wal-Mart**'s 2001 annual report the following comment was included:

> In fiscal 2001, the foreign currency translation adjustment increased from the fiscal 2000 level by $229 million to $684 million, primarily due to the dollar strengthening against the British pound and the German mark.*

*See Wal-Mart's 2001 annual report at www.wal-mart.com.

Adjustment of Foreign Receivables and Payables at the Balance Sheet Date We have seen that fluctuations in exchange rates may cause gains or losses for companies with accounts payable or receivable in foreign currencies. Exchange rates fluctuate on a daily basis. For convenience, however, the company usually waits until the account is paid or collected before recording the related gain or loss. An exception to this convenient practice occurs at the end of the accounting period. An *adjusting entry* is made to recognize any gains or losses that have accumulated on any foreign payables or receivables through the balance sheet date.

To illustrate, assume that on November 10 a U.S. company buys equipment from a Japanese company at a price of 10 million yen (¥10,000,000), payable on January 10 of the following year. If the exchange rate is $0.0100 per yen on November 10, the entry to record the purchase would be:

Equipment	100,000	
Accounts Payable		100,000
To record purchase of equipment from Japanese company at a price of ¥10,000,000, payable January 10 (¥10,000,000 × $0.0100 = $100,000).		

My Notes

Assets purchased on account must be recorded in dollars using the exchange rate on the date of purchase

Now assume that on December 31, the exchange rate has fallen to $0.0097 per yen. At this exchange rate, the U.S. company's account payable is equivalent to only $97,000 (¥10,000,000 × $0.0097). Gains and losses from changes in exchange rates are recognized in the period *in which the change occurs*. Therefore, the American company should make an adjusting entry to restate its liability at the current dollar-equivalent and to recognize any related gain or loss. This entry, dated December 31, would be:

Accounts Payable	3,000	
Gain on Fluctuations in Foreign Exchange Rates		3,000
To adjust balance of ¥10,000,000 account payable to amount indicated by year-end exchange rate:		
Original account balance	$100,000	
Adjusted balance (¥10,000,000 × $0.0097)	97,000	
Required adjustment	$ 3,000	

My Notes

The foreign exchange rate gain on accounts payable is included in year-end statements

Similar adjustments should be made for any other accounts payable or receivable at year-end that are fixed in terms of a foreign currency.

If the exchange rate changes again between the date of this adjusting entry and the date that the U.S. company pays the liability, an additional gain or loss must be recognized. Assume, for example, that on January 10 the exchange rate has risen to $0.0099 per yen. The U.S. company must now spend $99,000 to buy the ¥10,000,000 needed to pay its liability to the Japanese company. Thus, the rise in the exchange rate has caused the U.S. company a $2,000 loss since year-end. The entry to record payment of the account on January 10 would be:

Accounts Payable	97,000	
Loss on Fluctuations in Foreign Exchange Rates	2,000	
Cash		99,000
To record payment of ¥10,000,000 payable to Japanese company and to recognize loss from rise in exchange rate since year-end:		
Account payable, December 31	$97,000	
Amount paid, January 10	99,000	
Loss from increase in exchange rate	$ 2,000	

Notice the *overall effect* of entering into this credit transaction stated in yen was a $1,000 gain due to fluctuations in the exchange rate for the yen between November 10 and the date of payment (January 10). The U.S. company recognized a $3,000 gain on fluctuations in the exchange rate from November 10 through the balance sheet date (December 31). This was partially offset in the next fiscal year by a $2,000 loss on fluctuations in the exchange rate between December 31 and January 10. The overall effect can be computed directly by multiplying the amount of the foreign currency times the *change* in exchange rates between the transaction date and the payment date (¥10,000,000 × [$0.0100 − $0.0099] = $1,000 gain).

CASH EFFECTS Notice that the cash effects from foreign exchange rate fluctuations for associated transactions do not occur until the transaction is completed and the payment is made. That is, foreign exchange rate gains or losses recorded for receivables or payables do not involve cash flows (excluding tax effects). As we have demonstrated, the cash flow effect of the exchange rate fluctuation associated with the credit transaction for the purchase of equipment occurs on the date of payment, January 10 (expected cash outflow = $100,000; actual cash outflow = $99,000). The $3,000 gain recorded at the balance sheet date and the $2,000 loss recorded at the date of payment have no associated cash flow effects.

Gains and losses from fluctuations in exchange rates on transactions carried out in a foreign currency should be included in the income statement. They typically follow income from operations and are presented in a manner much like interest expense and gains and losses on the sale of plant assets.

Currency Fluctuations—Who Wins and Who Loses?

Gains and losses from fluctuations in exchange rates are sustained by companies (or individuals) that have either payables or receivables that are *fixed in terms of a foreign currency*. United States companies that import foreign products usually have large foreign liabilities. Companies that export U.S. products to other countries are likely to have large receivables stated in foreign currencies.

As foreign exchange rates (stated in dollars) *fall,* U.S.-based importers will gain and exporters will lose. When a foreign exchange rate falls, the foreign currency becomes *less expensive.* Therefore, importers will have to spend fewer dollars to pay their foreign liabilities. Exporters, on the other hand, will have to watch their foreign receivables become worth fewer and fewer dollars.

When foreign exchange rates *rise,* this situation reverses. Importers will lose, because more dollars are required to pay the foreign debts. Exporters will gain, because their foreign receivables become equivalent to an increasing number of dollars.

Strategies to Avoid Losses from Rate Fluctuations There are two basic approaches to avoiding losses from fluctuations in foreign exchange rates. One approach is to insist that receivables and payables be settled at specified amounts of domestic currency. The other approach is called *hedging* and can be accomplished in a number of ways.

To illustrate the first approach, assume that a U.S. company makes large credit sales to companies in Mexico, but anticipates that the exchange rate for the Mexican peso will gradually decline. The U.S. company can avoid losses by setting its *sales prices in dollars.* Then, if the exchange rate does decline, the Mexican companies will have to spend more pesos to pay for their purchases, but the U.S. company will not receive fewer dollars. On the other hand, the U.S. company will benefit from making credit *purchases* from Mexican companies at *prices stated in pesos,* because a decline in the exchange rate will reduce the number of dollars needed to pay for these purchases.

The interests of the Mexican companies, however, are exactly the opposite of those of the U.S. company. If the Mexican companies anticipate an increase in the exchange rate for the U.S. dollar, they will want to buy at prices stated in pesos and sell at prices stated in dollars. Ultimately, the manner in which the transactions will be priced simply depends on which company is in the better bargaining position.

Hedging Hedging refers to the strategy of "sitting on both sides of the fence"—that is, of taking offsetting positions so that your gains and losses tend to offset one another. To illustrate the concept, assume that you make a large bet on a football game. Later you have second thoughts about the bet, and you want to eliminate your risk of incurring a loss. You could "hedge" your original bet by making a similar bet on the other team. In this way, you will lose one bet, but you will win the other—your loss will be offset by a corresponding gain.

LO 6
Describe several techniques for hedging against losses from fluctuations in exchange rates.

A company that has similar amounts of accounts receivable and accounts payable in the same foreign currency automatically has a hedged position. A decrease in the foreign exchange rate will cause losses on the foreign receivables and gains on the foreign payables. If the exchange rate rises, the gains on the foreign receivables will be offset by losses on the foreign payables.

Most companies, of course, do *not* have similar amounts of receivables and payables in the same foreign currency. However, they may create this situation by buying or selling foreign currency **future contracts**. These contracts, commonly called *futures,* are the right to receive a specified quantity of foreign currency at a future date. In short, they are accounts receivable in foreign currency. Thus a company that has only foreign accounts payable may hedge its position by purchasing a similar dollar amount of foreign currency future contracts. Then, if the exchange rate rises, any losses on the foreign payables will be offset by a gain in the value of the future contracts.

A company with only foreign receivables may hedge its position by *selling* future contracts, thus receiving dollars today and *creating a liability* payable in foreign currency.

Some companies devote significant resources to hedging instruments while others rely on natural hedges and thus do not report hedging activity on their financial statements. For example, **Smartdisk Corp.**, a manufacturer of computer peripherals, states in their 2000 annual report that they do not engage in hedging activities. On the other hand, according to **Carrefour**'s 2000 annual report, management clearly has adopted a hedging strategy to minimize exposure to foreign exchange risk. There is great diversity of opinion among managers about the wisdom of trying to hedge foreign exchange risk with hedging instruments.

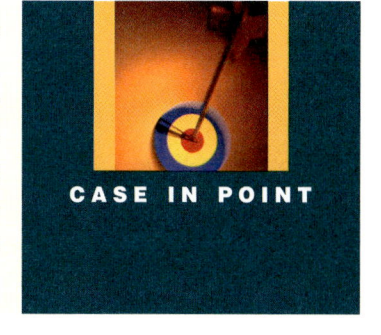

CASE IN POINT

Exchange Rates and Competitive Prices Up to this point, we have discussed only the gains and losses incurred by companies that have receivables or payables stated in a foreign currency. However, fluctuations in exchange rates change the *relative prices* of goods produced in different countries. Exchange rate fluctuations may make the prices of a country's products more or less competitive both at home and to customers throughout the world. Even a small store with no foreign accounts receivable or payable may find its business operations greatly affected by fluctuations in foreign exchange rates.

Consider, for example, a small store in Kansas that sells a U.S.-made brand of television sets. If foreign exchange rates fall, which happens when the dollar is strong, the price of foreign-made television sets will decline. Thus, the store selling U.S.-made television sets may have to compete with stores selling imported television sets at lower prices. Also, a strong dollar makes U.S. goods *more expensive to customers in foreign countries*. Thus a U.S. television manufacturer will find it more difficult to sell its products abroad.

The situation reverses when the dollar is weak—that is, when foreign exchange rates are relatively high. A weak dollar makes foreign imports more expensive to U.S. consumers. Also, a weak dollar makes U.S. products less expensive to customers in foreign countries.

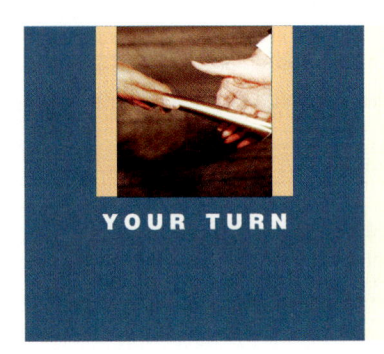

YOUR TURN

You as a Consumer

Assume you are in the market for a new racing bicycle. You are considering buying an Italian, British, or U.S. racing bicycle. You have recently heard that the dollar is strengthening against the euro and is falling against the British pound. These trends are expected to continue for another month. How would this news affect your assessment of choices among racing bicycles?

*Our comments appear on page 704.

In summary, we may say that a strong U.S. dollar *helps companies that sell foreign-made goods in the U.S. market*. A weak dollar, on the other hand, *gives a competitive advantage to companies that sell U.S. products both at home and abroad*.

Consolidated Financial Statements That Include Foreign Subsidiaries

In Chapter 14, we discussed the concept of *consolidated* financial statements. These statements view the operations of the parent company and its subsidiaries as if the affiliated companies were a single business entity. Several special accounting problems arise in preparing consolidated financial statements when subsidiaries operate in foreign countries. First, the accounting records of the foreign subsidiaries must be translated into U.S. dollars. Second, the accounting principles in use in the foreign countries may differ significantly from U.S. generally accepted accounting principles.

These problems pose interesting challenges to professional accountants and will be addressed in later accounting courses. Readers of the financial statements of U.S.-based corporations, however, should know that the consolidated financial statements of these companies are expressed in U.S. dollars and conform to U.S. generally accepted accounting principles.

GLOBAL SOURCING

LO 7
Discuss how global sourcing increases product cost complexity.

Differences in exchange rates can create significant complexities for firms practicing global sourcing. An article in the *Los Angeles Times* illustrated the additional problems associated with determining the cost of producing a doll using inputs from several countries. Exhibit 15–7 traces the multicountry path of a Barbie™ doll from its raw materials source in a Saudi Arabian oil field to U.S. toy stores. After the oil is refined to produce ethylene, Taiwan uses the ethylene to produce vinyl pellets that are shipped to Dongguan in China's Guangdong province. At the Chinese joint-venture

Global Sourcing

factory, 5,500 workers, paid between $30 and $40 per month, make the plastic doll and her clothes. However, most of the machinery and tools, including the plastic mold injection machines, are imported from the United States, Europe, and Japan. The molds themselves come directly from the United States. Japan contributes Barbie's nylon hair. Hong Kong manages the entire process, arranging banking and insurance, supervising exporting and importing, and overseeing transportation back to the United States. Finally, U.S. domestic packaging, trucking, advertising, and other functions that employ thousands of U.S. workers result in a $10.00 Barbie™ at your local toy store. **Mattel Inc.** has indicated that the typical profit from the sale of a Barbie™ is about $1.00.

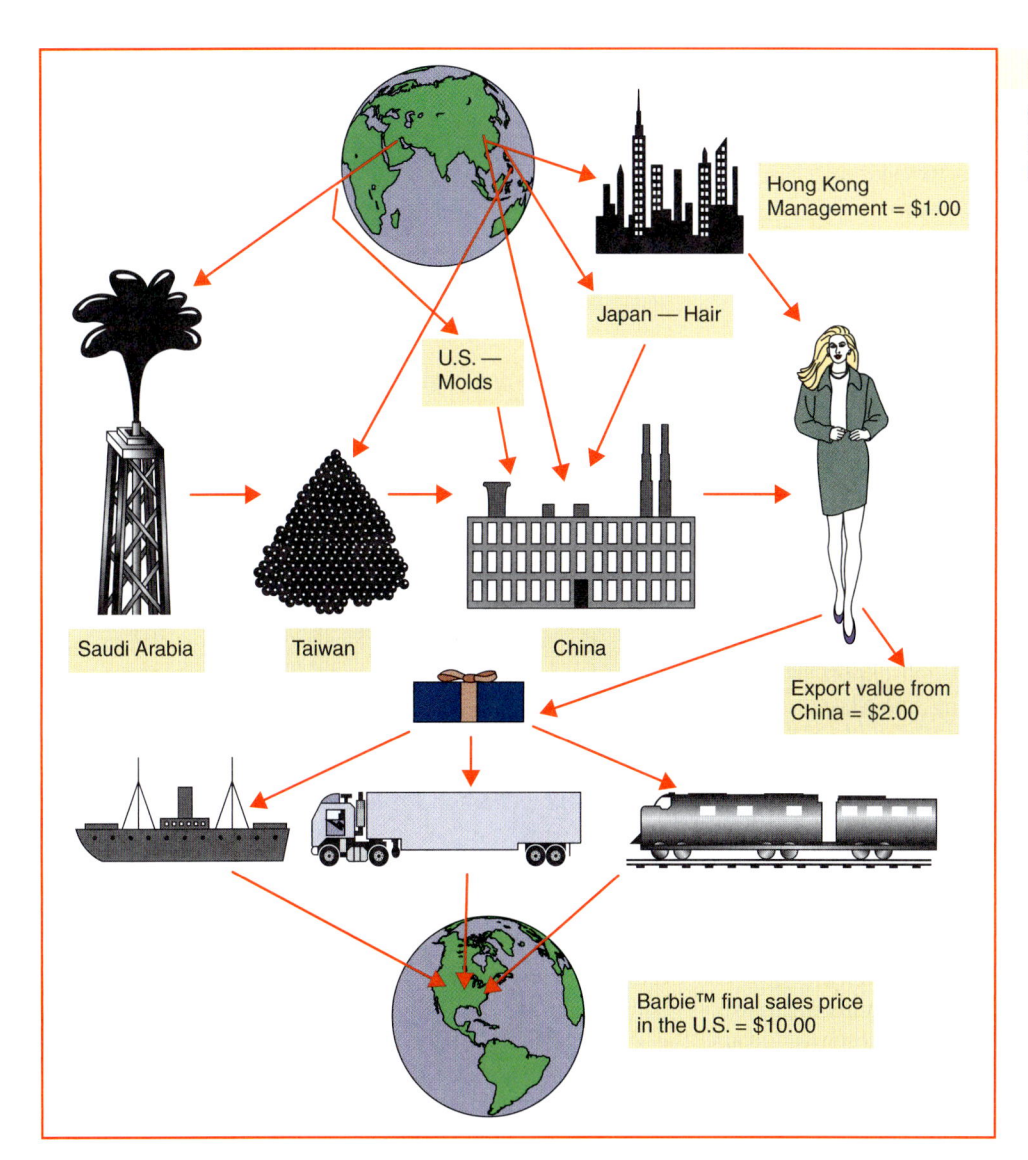

Exhibit 15–7

GLOBAL SOURCING FOR MATTEL INC.'S BARBIE™ DOLL

Hong Kong Management = $1.00

Japan — Hair

U.S. — Molds

Saudi Arabia

Taiwan

China

Export value from China = $2.00

Barbie™ final sales price in the U.S. = $10.00

Exhibit 15–8 illustrates the costs and exchange rate issues involved in the production of a Barbie™ doll. Panel A below provides the currency exchange rates for the countries involved in global sourcing for the Barbie™ doll. Panel B includes estimated product export costs for the **Mattel Inc.** Barbie™ made at the Meitai factory in Dongguan, China. The estimated costs in the exhibit are based on a single day's reported exchange rates. Companies must choose a representative exchange rate to compute the cost buildup in their domestic currency.

Exhibit 15–8

EXCHANGE RATES AND ESTIMATED PRODUCT COST FOR BARBIE DOLLS

Estimated Product Cost for Barbie™*

Panel A: Exchange Rates[†]

Country	Currency	U.S. $ Equivalent
Saudi Arabia	Riyal	.2667
Taiwan	Taiwanese dollar	.0326
Hong Kong	Hong Kong dollar	.1286
Japan	Yen	.0095
China	Renminbi	.1225

Panel B: Estimated Product Cost Buildup

Input	Foreign Currency Value	U.S. $ Equivalent
Raw materials:		
Saudi Arabia	0.6374 riyal	$0.17
Taiwan	4.908 Taiwanese dollars	0.16
Japan	22.11 yen	0.21
China	0.898 renminbi	0.11
Direct labor:		
China	2.857 renminbi	0.35
Overhead:		
Hong Kong	7.776 Hong Kong dollars	1.00
Total export cost		$2.00

*Estimates based on information provided in R. Tempest, "Barbie and the World Economy," *Los Angeles Times*, September 22, 1996, p. 1.
[†]Based on exchange rates from www.xe.com/ucc.

The information in the exhibits do not provide details about customs duties, import and export fees, multicountry tax laws, and tax treaties. These are also costs of doing business in a global environment. Many companies underestimate the cost of globalizing their business operations because they are not familiar with the environmental characteristics discussed at the beginning of this chapter. Making accurate estimates of costs for global sourcing is a challenge for companies wishing to become more global.

Foreign Corrupt Practices Act

In many countries, product costs also include expenses incurred to expedite official paperwork. Kenyan business executives refer to *kitu kidogo* ("something small"), the Chinese pay *huilu,* Russians shell out *vzyatka,* and Middle Easterners pay *baksheesh.* In dozens of countries around the world, bribery is part of doing business. In many countries, this officially sanctioned corruption is not viewed as wrong or unethical. However, U.S.-based businesses are prohibited from influence peddling. The **Foreign Corrupt Practices Act** (FCPA), passed in 1977 and amended in 1986 by the U.S. Congress, prescribes fines and jail time for American managers violating its rules. Over the past 20 years, some U.S. companies have complained about the advantage experienced by international competitors who are not bound by the FCPA.

Experiences in the past 5 to 10 years have changed international attitudes about the impact of corrupt practices on economic viability. In particular, the 1997–1998 Asian crisis was blamed partly on graft and influence peddling. According to some estimates, corruption associated with doing business in China can add 5 percent to operating costs. Corruption can be so rampant that companies refuse to operate in some foreign locations, causing countries to lose valuable direct foreign investment.

The International Monetary Fund and the World Bank instituted policies in the late 1990s to cut off funding to countries ignoring corrupt practices. In 1997, $292 million in loans to Kenya were suspended until policies and procedures to prevent corruption were instituted. Many of the recommended policies and procedures are modeled after the FCPA. The scope of the FCPA is very broad. Under FCPA rules, it is illegal for all U.S. companies, their affiliates, and their agents to bribe a government official. Criminal and civil prosecution can lead to fines of up to $2 million for the company and $100,000 for executives involved, with prison terms of up to five years.

You as Head of International Acquisitions

Assume you are the head of international acquisitions for a large multinational toy company traded on the New York Stock Exchange. You have been involved for several months in a deal to acquire a large facility in a midsize city in central China. This building will be remodeled by your company to produce a range of toy products for the Chinese market. For a variety of reasons, progress has been extremely slow on completing the acquisition. In particular, city administrators have continually delayed issuing the necessary paperwork. You decide to fly to China to meet with the city's top three officials. During your meeting it becomes clear that the three city officials would guarantee processing the associated paperwork much faster if your company would provide a significant payment to each of them to help expedite the necessary work. These administrators pointed out that a German company that acquired a facility in the city the previous year was willing to pay extra to expedite paperwork.

Your CEO has made it clear to you that the China project is very important and expediting it is critical for its long-run success. What should you do?

*Our comments appear on page 704.

The FCPA has implications for accounting in two specific areas: record keeping and internal control procedures. The act requires that all payments, including improper payments, be recorded and disclosed. Further, the act requires an adequate system of internal controls that maintains the integrity of the company's assets, allowing only authorized personnel to have access to them. The 1986 amendment to the FCPA distinguished between *influence peddling,* to motivate the awarding of business that would not otherwise have been awarded, and *facilitating payments,* to motivate officials to undertake actions more rapidly than they might otherwise. A facilitating payment might be given to a customs official to expedite imported merchandise through customs. This latter type of payment is not illegal under the act. Companies engaging in globalization must ensure that their cross-border employees comply with the FCPA.

LO 8
Explain the importance of the Foreign Corrupt Practices Act.

CONCLUDING REMARKS

In this chapter we have established a framework to help you understand international financial reporting issues. You have learned how global environmental differences create demand for different types of financial information. However, other global forces, particularly global securities markets and large international firms, are pushing for a uniform set of international accounting standards for financial reporting. What do the development of international accounting standards foreshadow? We believe that although significant progress toward harmonization is occurring, there will not be uniform global reporting requirements in widespread use in the near future. Users of international financial statements should expect wide variation in disclosure levels and financial reporting practices for several years to come.

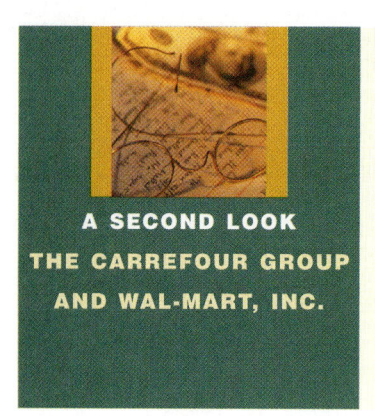

A SECOND LOOK
THE CARREFOUR GROUP AND WAL-MART, INC.

Wal-Mart and **Carrefour** are learning from their global retailing experiences. **Wal-Mart**, the world's largest retailer, made a successful large acquisition of ASDA in the United Kingdom in 2000 and **Carrefour** merged with **Promodès** in 2001 to become the world's second largest retailer. Retail sites in multiple countries create issues, including exchange rate fluctuations, that complicate the ability to manage and prepare financial reports. Accounting information is a very important component of the information used by **Carrefour** and **Wal-Mart** to help them operate in their global environment. Accounting information is critical for making global financing, acquisition, and operating decisions. In other accounting courses, you will learn more about how companies like **Carrefour** and **Wal-Mart** use accounting information to report on and manage their global operations.

END-OF-CHAPTER REVIEW

SUMMARY OF LEARNING OBJECTIVES

LO 1
Define four mechanisms companies use to globalize their business activities.
Companies globalize their business activities through exporting, licensing, joint ventures, and wholly owned subsidiaries. Multinational companies use a global sourcing approach.

LO 2
Identify how global environmental forces—(a) political and legal systems, (b) economic systems, (c) culture, and (d) technology and infrastructure—affect financial reporting practices.
Countries use their political and legal systems to transfer and control business assets. Market versus centrally planned economic systems create different demands for financial reporting. Culture influences business relationships through beliefs and expectations of customers and business associates. The technology and infrastructure of each global location will affect the type and costs of business activities and related financial accounting reports.

LO 3
Explain why there is demand for harmonization of global financial reporting requirements.
Cross-border differences in accounting and reporting create analysis and comparability problems between and among companies. The need for comparable information has led to the demand for harmonization.

LO 4
Demonstrate how to convert an amount of money from one currency to another.
To convert a foreign currency to an equivalent dollar amount, multiply the foreign currency by the foreign exchange rate. To convert a dollar amount into an equivalent amount of foreign currency, divide the dollar amount by the exchange rate.

LO 5
Compute gains or losses on receivables or payables that are stated in a foreign currency when exchange rates fluctuate.
The receivable or payable is recorded on the date the transaction is agreed to using the prevailing exchange rate. When exchanging cash completes the transaction, the exchange rate at the completion date is used to record the cash flow; the difference between the cash exchanged and the receivable or payable is recorded as a foreign exchange gain or loss.

LO 6
Describe several techniques for hedging against losses from fluctuations in exchange rates.
Hedging is offsetting the potential for losses from foreign exchange rate fluctuations. It can be accomplished by having offsetting receivables and payables in the foreign currency or by buying or selling foreign currency future contracts.

LO 7
Discuss how global sourcing increases product cost complexity.
When some of the activities of designing, developing, producing, marketing, and servicing a product or service occur in more than one country, then global considerations affect product costs. These considerations include foreign exchange gains and losses, taxes, import and export duties, trade agreements, foreign trade zones, and limitations on currency flows.

LO 8
Explain the importance of the Foreign Corrupt Practices Act.
The FCPA prohibits influence peddling through bribery in international locations. The act requires companies engaged in global business activities to maintain good record keeping and adequate internal controls to safeguard company assets.

KEY TERMS INTRODUCED OR EMPHASIZED IN CHAPTER 15

cross-border financing (p. 677) Occurs when a company sells its securities in the capital markets of another country.

exchange rate (p. 679) The amount it costs to purchase one unit of currency with another currency.

exporting (p. 671) Selling a good or service to a foreign customer in a foreign country.

Foreign Corrupt Practices Act (p. 688) Passed in 1977 and amended in 1986 by the U.S. Congress, prescribes fines and jail time for American managers violating its rules. It distinguishes between illegal influence peddling to motivate awarding of business that would not otherwise have been awarded and legal facilitating payments made to motivate officials to undertake actions more rapidly than they might otherwise.

foreign trade zones (p. 673) Goods imported into these designated U.S. areas are duty free until they leave the zone.

future contracts (p. 685) A contract giving the right to receive a specified quantity of foreign currency at a future date.

globalization (p. 670) Occurs as managers become aware of and engage in cross-border trade and operations.

global sourcing (p. 671) The close coordination of R&D, manufacturing, and marketing across national boundaries.

harmonization of accounting standards (p. 677) The standardization of accounting methods and principles used in different countries throughout the world.

hedging (p. 685) The practice of minimizing or eliminating risk of loss associated with foreign currency fluctuations.

industrial organizations (p. 674) Exist when companies group themselves into conglomerates representing different industries. South Korean conglomerates, called *chaebol,* and Japanese conglomerates, called *keiretsu,* consist of companies that are grouped as customers and suppliers and usually contain a bank.

infrastructure (p. 677) Access to communication, transportation, and utilities provided to businesses in each global location.

International Accounting Standards Board (p. 677) Charged with the responsibility of creating and promulgating international standards.

international joint venture (p. 671) A company owned by two or more companies from different countries.

international licensing (p. 671) A contractual agreement between a company and a foreign party allowing the use of trademarks, patents, technology, designs, processes, intellectual property, or other proprietary advantage.

maquiladora (p. 673) A joint venture manufacturing plant located in Mexico that enjoys exceptions from Mexican laws governing foreign companies. The United States allows exemptions from, or reductions in, customs duties on re-exported goods from maquiladoras.

market economies (p. 674) Exist when ownership of land and the means of production are private and markets dictate the allocation of resources and the output among segments of the economy.

planned economy (p. 674) Exists when the government uses central planning to allocate resources and determine output among various segments of the economy. Government ownership of land and the means of production characterize planned economies.

regional value content (p. 673) Rules that dictate the amount of total cost that must be added in those countries that have signed a free trade agreement. Products that satisfy these rules receive favorable tariffs and custom duty.

wholly owned international subsidiary (p. 671) Created through a company's foreign direct investment; using domestically generated funds in another country to purchase 100% equity control of a foreign subsidiary.

DEMONSTRATION PROBLEM

IronMan, Inc., is a U.S. company that manufactures exercise machines and distributes several lines of imported bicycles. Selected transactions of the company were as follows in 2001:

Oct. 4 Purchased manufacturing equipment from Rhine Mfg. Co., a German company. The purchase price was €400,000, due in 60 days. Current exchange rate, $0.7020 per euro. (Debit the Equipment account.)

Oct. 18 Purchased 2,500 racing bicycles from Ninja Cycles, a Japanese company, at a price of ¥60,000,000. Payment is due in 90 days; the current exchange rate is $0.0110 per yen. (IronMan uses the perpetual inventory system.)

Nov. 15 Purchased 1,000 touring bicycles from Royal Lion Ltd., a British corporation. The purchase price was £192,500, payable in 30 days. Current exchange rate, $1.65 per British pound.

Dec. 3 Issued a check to First Bank for the U.S. dollar-equivalent of €400,000 in payment of the account payable to Rhine Mfg. Co. Current exchange rate, $0.7110 per euro.

Dec. 15 Issued a check to First Bank for dollar-equivalent of £192,500 in payment of the account payable to Royal Lion Ltd. Current exchange rate, $1.60 per British pound.

Instructions

a. Prepare entries in general journal form to record the preceding transactions.

b. Prepare the December 31 adjusting entry relating to the account payable to Ninja Cycles. The year-end exchange rate is $0.0113 per Japanese yen.

c. Identify some methods that IronMan, Inc., could use to decrease its exposure to foreign exchange rate fluctuations.

d. Discuss environmental characteristics of Japan, Germany, and the United Kingdom that influence their exchange rate fluctuations.

Solution to the Demonstration Problem

a. The general journal entries to record the transactions are as follows:

Demonstration Problem

GENERAL JOURNAL

Date	Account Titles and Explanation	Debit	Credit
Oct. 4	Equipment	280,800	
	Accounts Payable (Rhine Mfg. Co.)		280,800
	To record purchase of equipment from Rhine Mfg. Co. for €400,000, exchange rate $0.7020 per euro (€400,000 × $0.7020 = $280,800).		
Oct. 18	Inventory	660,000	
	Accounts Payable (Ninja Cycles)		660,000
	Purchase 2,500 bicycles from Ninja Cycles for ¥60,000,000, exchange rate $0.0110 (¥60,000,000 × $0.0110 = $660,000).		
Nov. 15	Inventory	317,625	
	Accounts Payable (Royal Lion Ltd.)		317,625
	Purchased 1,000 bicycles from Royal Lion Ltd. for £192,500, due in 30 days. Exchange rate $1.65 per pound (£192,500 × $1.65 = $317,625).		
Dec. 3	Accounts Payable (Rhine Mfg. Co.)	280,800	
	Loss on Fluctuations of Foreign Exchange Rates	3,600	
	Cash		284,400
	Paid €400,000 liability to Rhine Mfg. Co. (Original balance less amount paid equals loss: $280,800 − (€400,000 × $0.7110) = −$3,600).		
Dec. 15	Accounts Payable (Royal Lion Ltd.)	317,625	
	Gain on Fluctuations of Foreign Exchange Rates		9,625
	Cash		308,000
	Paid £192,500 liability to Royal Lion Ltd. (Original balance less amount paid equals gain: $317,625 − (£192,500 × $1.60) = $9,625).		

b. The December 31 adjusting entry for the account payable to Ninja Cycles:

GENERAL JOURNAL

Date	Account Titles and Explanation	Debit	Credit
Dec. 31	Loss on Fluctuations in Foreign Exchange Rates	18,000	
	Accounts Payable (Ninja Cycles)		18,000
	To adjust balance of ¥60,000,000 liability to amount indicated by year-end exchange rate: (Original balance less adjusted balance equals loss: $660,000 − (¥60,000,000 × $0.0113) = −$18,000).		

c. IronMan could use offsetting payables and receivables to control potential foreign exchange rate losses. For example, if IronMan could export its exercise equipment to Japan, then it would have a receivable to offset its payable. IronMan could also purchase future contracts maturing at the same time the liabilities were due. Gains and losses on the future contracts would offset gains and losses resulting from foreign currency fluctuations.

d. Germany has a lower volume and smaller capitalized equities market. Banks are the major providers of capital to businesses in Germany. Japan has *keiretsu* organizations for many of its industrial groups. These organizations include manufacturers, distributors, wholesalers, retailers, and suppliers who work together and share resources. The accounting profession is much weaker in both Germany and Japan than in the United States. The United Kingdom is most like the United States with active equity markets, a strong accounting profession, and similar accounting rules.

SELF-TEST QUESTIONS

Answers to these questions appear on page 704.

1. Which of the following statements are *true* about globalization methods? (Identify all correct answers.)
   a. International licensing involves the creation of a new company that is owned by two or more firms from different countries.
   b. Exporting involves contracts that allow a foreign company to use a domestic company's trademarks, patents, processes, or technology.
   c. Global sourcing involves the close coordination of research and development, purchasing, marketing, and manufacturing across national boundaries.
   d. A wholly owned international subsidiary is created when a foreign government owns 100% of the equity in a U.S.-based firm.

2. Which of the following environmental factors can affect the cost of doing business in a foreign country?
   a. The educational level of the workforce.
   b. Laws regulating the transfer of profits out of a country.
   c. Tax and tariff regulations.
   d. Restricted access to communication and transportation networks.

3. A country whose citizens are highly group oriented and who accept unequal power distributions between and within organizations would be considered:
   a. Individualistic and low power distance.
   b. Collectivist and high power distance.
   c. Individualistic and high power distance.
   d. Collectivist and low power distance.

4. On March 1, Laton Products (a U.S. firm) purchased manufacturing inputs from a Mexican supplier for 20,000 pesos, payable on June 1. The exchange rate for pesos on March 1 was $0.17. If the exchange rate increases to $0.19 on June 1, what amount of gain or loss would be reported by Laton related to the currency exchange?
   a. $400 gain.
   b. $200 loss.
   c. $400 loss.
   d. $200 gain.

5. On January 1, 2001, a German company purchased merchandise from a U.S. firm for $50,000, payable on March 1. The exchange rate for euro on January 1 was $0.70. If the exchange rate increases to $0.72 on March 1, what amount of gain or loss would the U.S. firm report related to currency fluctuations?
   a. $1,000 gain.
   b. $1,000 loss.
   c. $500 gain.
   d. No gain or loss would be reported.

ASSIGNMENT MATERIAL
DISCUSSION QUESTIONS

1. In general terms, identify several factors that prompt different countries to develop different accounting principles.
2. What is the International Accounting Standards Board? Why has the board been unable to obtain global application of its standards?

Discussion Questions

3. Translate the following amounts of foreign currency into an equivalent number of U.S. dollars using the exchange rates in Exhibit 15–6.
   a. £800,000
   b. ¥350,000
   c. €50,000

4. Assume that a U.S. company makes a purchase from a British company and agrees to pay a price of £2 million.
   a. How will the U.S. company determine the cost of this purchase for the purpose of recording it in the accounting records?
   b. Briefly explain how a U.S. company can arrange the payment of pounds to a British company.

5. A recent newspaper shows the exchange rate for the British pound at $1.63 and for the yen at $0.0106. Does this indicate that the pound is a stronger currency than the yen? Explain.

6. Explain how an increase in a foreign exchange rate will affect a U.S. company that makes:
   a. Credit sales to a foreign company at prices stated in the foreign currency.
   b. Credit purchases from a foreign company at prices stated in the foreign currency.
   c. Credit sales to a foreign company at prices stated in U.S. dollars.

7. You are the purchasing agent for a U.S. business that purchases merchandise on account from companies in Mexico. The exchange rate for the Mexican peso has been falling against the dollar and the trend is expected to continue for at least several months. Would you prefer that the prices for purchases from the Mexican companies be specified in U.S. dollars or in Mexican pesos? Explain.

8. CompuTech is a U.S.-based multinational corporation. Foreign sales are made at prices set in U.S. dollars, but foreign purchases are often made at prices stated in foreign currencies. If the exchange rate for the U.S. dollar has risen against most foreign currencies throughout the year, would CompuTech have recognized primarily gains or losses as a result of exchange rate fluctuations? Explain.

9. Explain two ways in which a company that makes purchases on account from foreign companies can protect itself against the losses that would arise from a sudden increase in the foreign exchange rate.

10. What does the *globalization* of business mean? Think of two companies with which you are familiar. How would you describe their level of globalization?

11. Why is it important for a company and its accountants to understand its level of globalization?

12. You've just read in *The Wall Street Journal* that the U.S. dollar has weakened relative to the euro. All else equal, what would you expect to happen to the quantity of Italian leather jackets sold in the United States? Why?

13. A U.S. company purchased a shipment of fabrics from Bahrain for 3,500,000 dinars. At current exchange rates, what is the value of this contract in U.S. dollars?

14. What is the difference between an international licensing agreement and an international joint venture?

15. Visit the IASB website at www.iasb.org.uk. Identify the current board members and the countries they represent. Speculate about why Indonesia is not represented.

16. To maintain a high level of control over production operations and final product quality, what types of globalization activities could a company engage in?

17. How might the required financial reports differ between countries that are individualistic and collectivist?

18. What do the phrases *high power distance* and *low power distance* mean? How would the organizational structures of companies operating in high and low power distance countries differ?

19. A French furniture maker agrees to purchase wood stain from a U.S. paint manufacturer. If all payments are to be made in U.S. dollars, which company bears the risk of exchange rate gains and losses?

20. In the United States, what is a foreign trade zone? What is the advantage of operating in one?

21. What is meant by the phrase *natural hedging against exchange rate risk?*

EXERCISES

EXERCISE 15.1
Global Business Terminology

LO 1–8

The following are nine global business terms used in this chapter:

- hedging
- Foreign Corrupt Practices Act
- globalization
- foreign exchange risk
- planned economy
- international licensing
- International Accounting Standards Board
- harmonization
- exporting

Each of the following statements may describe one of these terms. For each statement, indicate the global business term described, or answer "None" if the statement does not correctly describe any of the terms.

a. The amount it costs to purchase one unit of currency with another currency.
b. Selling a good or service to a foreign customer.
c. A cross-border contractual agreement allowing one company to use trademarks, patents, or technology of another company.
d. Distinguishes between illegal influence peddling and legal facilitating payments.
e. The practice of minimizing or eliminating risk of loss associated with foreign currency fluctuations.
f. Markets dictate the allocation of resources and output among segments of the economy.
g. The group charged with the responsibility of creating and encouraging the use of international accounting standards.

EXERCISE 15.2
External Financial Reports and Globalization

LO 1, 2

With a group of two or three students, choose a publicly traded global company that you think you might want to invest in some time in the future. Use the Internet or annual report data to answer the following questions.

a. In which geographical regions does the company operate?
b. What is the proportion of total sales represented by foreign sales? How has this changed over the past 5 years?
c. What efforts has the company recently undertaken to increase/decrease globalization (for example, joint ventures, licensing agreements, etc.)?
d. What are the company's hedging practices/policies?
e. Have any overseas activities been unsuccessful, discontinued, or resulted in asset losses? If so, what happened?
f. Overall, how aggressively do you feel this company is pursuing globalization?

EXERCISE 15.3
NAFTA and Regional Value Content

LO 2, 7

To qualify for favorable tariff and customs duty treatment under NAFTA, a product or service must meet regional value content requirements. The regional value content is defined as the final selling price of the good or service less costs incurred outside the United States, Canada, or Mexico. The regional value content must be (1) greater than or equal to 60% of the selling price of the finished good or (2) greater than or equal to 50% of the cost of the finished good.

Larron Products manufactures an electronic sensor that it markets and sells in the United States. Components from Germany and Japan are shipped to Mexico, where they are assembled into the final product and shipped to the United States. The current sales price per unit is $1,600 and 10,000 units are expected to be sold during the coming year. Per-unit costs of producing the sensor are as follows:

German components	$100
Japanese components	500
Mexican labor and materials	400

Perform the computations to determine if this sensor qualifies for favorable treatment under either of the NAFTA content requirements (60% of the selling price or 50% of the cost).

Exercises

EXERCISE 15.4

Locating International Business Information

LO 2, 7, 8

The Central Intelligence Agency (CIA) of the U.S. government maintains an Internet site containing information on various countries (www.odci.gov). The site includes a database known as the "World Fact Book." Use the CIA data or other publicly available data to answer the following questions about Indonesia.

a. What are the country's main exports and imports?
b. What is the educational and job classification composition of the labor force?
c. How would you describe the infrastructure and technology base of the country?
d. What are the political and legal risks of doing business there?
e. If you were advising a U.S. company that wanted to locate a wholly owned subsidiary in Indonesia, what aspects of the country would you stress that management take into account when deciding whether to invest there and how to organize the subsidiary's manufacturing process?

EXERCISE 15.5

Currency Fluctuations: Who Wins and Who Loses?

LO 2, 5

Indicate whether each of the companies or individuals in the following independent cases would benefit more from a strong U.S. dollar (relatively low foreign exchange rates) or a weak U.S. dollar (relatively high foreign exchange rates). Provide a brief explanation of your reasoning.

a. **Boeing** (a U.S. aircraft manufacturer that sells many planes to foreign customers)
b. A **Nikon** camera store in Beverly Hills, California (Nikon cameras are made in Japan)
c. **Toyota** (made by the Japanese auto manufacturer in Japan)
d. The Mexico City dealer for **Caterpillar** tractors (made in the United States)
e. A U.S. tourist visiting England
f. A small store that sells U.S.-made video recorders in Toledo, Ohio (the store has no foreign accounts receivable or payable)

EXERCISE 15.6

Foreign Currency Transactions

LO 4, 5

The following table summarizes the facts of five independent cases (labeled **a** through **e**) of U.S. companies engaging in credit transactions with foreign corporations while the foreign exchange rate is fluctuating:

	Column			
Case	Type of Credit Transaction 1	Currency Used in Contract 2	Exchange Rate Direction 3	Effect on Income 4
a	Sales	Foreign currency	Falling	_____
b	Purchases	U.S. dollars	Rising	_____
c	_____	Foreign currency	Rising	Loss
d	Sales	_____	Falling	No effect
e	Purchases	Foreign currency	_____	Gain

You are to fill in each blank space after evaluating the information about the case provided in the other three columns. The content of each column and the word or words that you should enter in the blank spaces are described as follows:

Column 1 indicates the type of credit transaction in which the U.S. company engaged with the foreign corporations. The answer entered in this column should be either *Sales* or *Purchases*.

Column 2 indicates the currency in which the invoice price is stated. The answer may be either *U.S. dollars* or *Foreign currency*.

Column 3 indicates the direction in which the foreign currency exchange rate has moved between the date of the credit transaction and the date of settlement. The answer entered in this column may be either *Rising* or *Falling*.

Column 4 indicates the effect of the exchange rate fluctuation on the income of the American company. The answers entered in this column are to be selected from the following: *Gain, Loss,* or *No effect.*

EXERCISE 15.7
Harmonization around the World
LO 3

With another student of your choosing (or assigned to you by your instructor) visit the IASB website at www.iasb.org.uk and prepare a one-page report in which you:

a. Name three governments that have agreed to let companies that prepare their financial reports *only* in accordance with IAS list their stocks on the country's securities markets.

b. Name three governments that have not agreed to let companies that prepare their financial reports *only* in accordance with IAS list their stocks on the country's securities markets.

c. Investigate and report on the plans of the European Commission regarding the use of IAS for companies wanting to list on European stock exchanges.

EXERCISE 15.8
Foreign Corrupt Practices Act
LO 8

Company A, a U.S. company, has a subsidiary located in Country Z, where various forms of bribery are accepted and expected. To oversee the operations of the subsidiary, A sent one of its top U.S. managers to Country Z. Manager M engaged in the following activities while in Country Z during recent months of operation:

a. Paid the equivalent of $200 to a government inspector to reschedule the inspection date of a new manufacturing facility from April 15 to February 15.

b. Paid an average of $50 each to four local police officers who are in charge of patrolling the area around the new manufacturing facility. The officers have agreed to increase the number of times they check the area.

c. Company N, a domestic company, is in competition with Company A for a government contract. Company A has learned that N has given approximately $5,000 to the official who will make the final contract decision. To remain in the running, Manager M authorized Company A to pay an equal amount to the official.

d. The electric utilities are government owned and operated. Due to the frequency of severe storms, there are often power outages due to downed lines. Manager M has paid the official in charge of coordinating repair crews $200 to ensure that the manufacturing plant's power is one of the first restored.

Under the Foreign Corrupt Practices Act, as amended, which of the above activities do you think would be considered illegal? From an operations standpoint, which of the above activities would be considered bad management practice? Are there solutions other than bribery?

PROBLEMS

PROBLEM 15.1
Exchange Rates and Export Decision
LO 4, 5

The Cramer Cookie Company is a relatively new company and so far has sold its products only in its home country, Denmark. In December, Cramer determined that it had excess capacity to produce more of its special Christmas cookies. It is trying to decide whether to use that capacity to ship a batch of cookies overseas. The marketing department has determined that the United States and Great Britain are the two most viable markets. Cramer has enough excess capacity to produce only one batch, which can be shipped to either country. The materials and labor cost to produce the batch amount to 8,500 kroner. The marketing department, which located a shipping company that could deliver to either location, also provided the following information:

	United States	Great Britain
Shipping cost	3,000 U.S. dollars	2,000 U.S. dollars
Duties/customs charges and miscellaneous selling expenses	400 U.S. dollars	480 British pounds
Total sales revenue	5,200 U.S. dollars	2,800 British pounds
Exchange rate data	1 krone = 0.147 U.S. dollars	1 krone = 0.088 British pounds

Instructions

a. If Cramer exports the batch to the United States, what is its estimated profit/loss in Danish kroner?

b. If Cramer exports the batch to Great Britain, what is its estimated profit/loss in Danish kroner?

c. If the British pound has exhibited rather large fluctuations relative to the Danish kroner recently, how might this impact Cramer's decision on which country to ship to?

PROBLEM 15.2

Gains and Losses from Exchange Rate Fluctuations

LO 1, 4–6

Europa-West is a U.S. corporation that purchases automobiles from European manufacturers for distribution in the United States. A recent purchase involved the following events:

Nov. 12 Purchased automobiles from Stockholm Motors in Swedish Kroner for Sk20,000,000, payable in 60 days. Current exchange rate, $0.07025 per krona (Europa-West uses the perpetual inventory system.)

Dec. 31 Made year-end adjusting entry relating to the Sk20,000,000 account payable to Stockholm Motors. Current exchange rate, $0.07147 per krona.

Jan. 11 Issued a check to World Bank for $1,421,400 in full payment of the account payable to Stockholm Motors.

Instructions

a. Prepare in general journal form the entries necessary to record the preceding events.

b. Compute the exchange rate (price) of the krona in U.S. dollars on January 11.

c. Explain a hedging technique that Europa-West might have used to protect itself from the possibility of losses resulting from a significant increase in the exchange rate for the krona.

PROBLEM 15.3

Exchange Rates and Income Effects

LO 4–7

Wallerton, Inc., is a U.S. company that conducts some business in Canada. The pro forma income statement for next year follows. Wallerton wants to know the impact of three possible exchange rate scenarios for the Canadian dollar on its pro forma income statement: Assume one Canadian dollar is equivalent to either $.75, $.80, or $.85 in U.S. dollars.

WALLERTON, INC.
Pro Forma Income Statement
For the Period Ending December 31, 2003

	U.S. Business	Canadian Business
Sales	$304.00	C$ 4
Cost of Goods Sold	50.00	200
Gross Profit	**$254.00**	**C$(196)**
Operating Expenses:		
Fixed	30.00	–0–
Variable	30.72	–0–
Total	$ 60.72	–0–
Operating Earnings	$193.28	C$(196)
Interest Expenses	3.00	10
Earnings before Tax	**$190.28**	**C$(206)**

Additional information

Possible Exchange Rate	Projected U.S. Sales
$.75	$300
.80	304
.85	307

Instructions

a. Complete the chart in the working papers related to the following pro forma income statements in U.S. dollars:

	C$ = $.75	C$ = $.80	C$ = $.85
Sales:			
(1) U.S.			
(2) Canadian			
(3) Total			
Cost of Goods Sold			
(4) U.S.			
(5) Canadian			
(6) Total			
(7) Gross Profit		$97.20	
Operating Expenses:			
(8) U.S. Fixed			
(9) U.S. Variable			
10% of Sales			
(10) Total			
Operating Earnings			$29.36
Interest Expenses:			
(12) U.S.			
(13) Canadian			
(14) Total			
Earnings before Tax	$32.20		

b. Explain the impact of a stronger Canadian dollar on Earnings before Tax.

PROBLEM 15.4

Exchange Rates and Production Decisions

LO 3, 4

The Ulsa Company has manufacturing subsidiaries in Malaysia and Malta. It is considering shipping the subcomponents of Product Y to one or the other of these countries for final assembly. The final product will be sold in the country where it is assembled. Other information is as follows:

	Malaysia	Malta
Average exchange rate	$1 = 4.30 ringgit	$1 = 0.40 lira
Import duty	5%	15%
Income tax rate	20%	10%
Unit selling price of Product Y	645 ringgit	70 lira
Price of subcomponent	215 ringgit	20 lira
Final assembly costs	200 ringgit	25 lira
Number of units to be sold	12,000 units	8,000 units

In both countries, the import duties are based on the value of the incoming goods in the receiving country's currency.

Instructions

a. For each country, prepare an income statement on a per-unit basis denominated in that country's currency.
b. In which country would the highest profit per unit (in dollars) be earned?
c. In which country would the highest total profit (in dollars) be earned?

PROBLEM 15.5

Global Trade Agreements

LO 2, 7

Form a group of students and research a trade agreement (other than NAFTA) involving a group of countries. (Examples include the General Agreement on Tariffs and Trade [GATT] and Mercosur's Common External Tariff [CET]—Latin America.) How do the requirements for the researched trade agreement differ from or remain the same as those listed for NAFTA?

PROBLEM 15.6

A Comprehensive Problem on Exchange Rate Fluctuations

LO 1, 4–6

Wolfe Computer is a U.S. company that manufactures portable personal computers. Many of the components for the computer are purchased abroad, and the finished product is sold in foreign countries as well as in the United States. Among the recent transactions of Wolfe are the following:

Oct. 28 Purchased from Mitsutonka, a Japanese company, 20,000 disk drives. The purchase price was ¥180,000,000, payable in 30 days. Current exchange rate, $0.0105 per yen. (Wolfe uses the perpetual inventory method; debit the Inventory of Raw Materials account.)

Nov. 9 Sold 700 personal computers to the Bank of England for £604,500 due in 30 days. The cost of the computers, to be debited to the Cost of Goods Sold account, was $518,000. Current exchange rate, $1.65 per British pound. (Use one compound journal entry to record the sale and the cost of goods sold. In recording the cost of goods sold, credit Inventory of Finished Goods.)

Nov. 27 Issued a check to Inland Bank for $1,836,000 in *full payment* of account payable to Mitsutonka.

Dec. 2 Purchased 10,000 gray-scale monitors from German Optical for €1,200,000, payable in 60 days. Current exchange rate, $0.7030 per euro. (Debit Inventory of Raw Materials.)

Dec. 9 Collected dollar-equivalent of £604,500 from the Bank of England. Current exchange rate, $1.63 per British pound.

Dec. 11 Sold 10,000 personal computers to Computique, a Swiss retail chain, for SwF23,750,000, due in 30 days. Current exchange rate, $0.6000 per franc. The cost of the computers, to be debited to Cost of Goods Sold and credited to Inventory of Finished Goods, is $7,400,000.

Instructions

a. Prepare in general journal form the entries necessary to record the preceding transactions.
b. Prepare the adjusting entries needed at December 31 for the €1,200,000 account payable to German Optical and the SwF23,750,000 account receivable from Computique. Year-end exchange rates, $0.7000 per euro and $0.5980 per Swiss franc. (Use a separate journal entry to adjust each account balance.)
c. Compute (to the nearest dollar) the unit sales price of computers in U.S. dollars in either the November 9 or December 11 sales transaction. (The sales price is the same in each transaction.)
d. Compute the exchange rate for the yen, stated in U.S. dollars, on November 27.
e. Explain how Wolfe Computer could have hedged its position to reduce the risk of loss from exchange rate fluctuations on (1) its foreign payables and (2) its foreign receivables.

PROBLEM 15.7

Tootsie Roll's Globalization

LO 1, 2, 6, 7

Consider the annual report of **Tootsie Roll Industries, Inc.**, that appears in Appendix A at the end of this textbook. Use this report to assess the globalization of **Tootsie Roll** by answering the following questions:

a. What are the locations of **Tootsie Roll**'s international subsidiaries? What other global operations does **Tootsie Roll** undertake?
b. Refer to note 12. What percentages of net assets, sales revenue, and earnings were obtained from international operations in 2000? in 1999?

c. What explanation does management provide in their operating report for the trend in international sales and earnings between 1999 and 2000?
d. Refer to the income statement. How did foreign currency translation adjustments impact earnings? Is there any evidence that management undertakes any formal hedging to attempt to reduce the impact of currency exchange risk on earnings?
e. Refer to note 4: What percentage of current taxes was paid to foreign countries?
f. Do you believe **Tootsie Roll Industries, Inc.**, is a multinational company? Why or why not?

CASES AND UNSTRUCTURED PROBLEMS

CASE 15.1

Decisions to Globalize Are Complex

LO 1, 2

Bristow Inc. is interested in establishing a presence in Country Y. Bristow is expecting demand for several of its products to increase in that country because a major customer, Kale Enterprises, is building a large manufacturing plant in Y. Bristow has been supplying Kale's other foreign manufacturing operations mainly through exporting. However, shipping costs and long delivery times have been somewhat troublesome to both companies in the past. Bristow has also identified several other companies native to Country Y as potential customers.

Bristow currently has operations only in the United States. Kale Enterprises is a successful global company with operations in over 20 countries. Bristow's managers have identified the following possible options:

a. Simply export to Country Y.
b. A company in Y has expressed an interest in licensing Bristow's technology and has the capability and capacity to produce the products used by Kale.
c. A joint venture with Kale may be possible, but managers for Kale would be willing to enter into an agreement only if substantial control for Bristow's operations is given to Kale managers.
d. Bristow's managers have located a company that could be purchased and operated as a subsidiary. The company currently produces products similar to Bristow, but it is using outdated technology.

Instructions

Discuss what factors should be considered when choosing among the above options. Develop a list of additional information you believe would be useful in making the decision.

CASE 15.2

Disclosure Requirements

LO 2, 3, 5

The International Organization of Securities Commissions (IOSCO) is a group of top securities administrators from about 50 countries. The Securities and Exchange Commission (SEC) is a member of IOSCO. IOSCO is a primary supporter of the internationalization of accounting standards through the International Accounting Standards Board (IASB). At a recent meeting a discussion of the pros and cons of internationalizing accounting standards included the following arguments:

Pro:

Having the same accounting standards for external reporting for all securities markets will reduce misunderstandings and create comparable information. For example, investors will be able to compare the financial reports of similar companies located in, say, the United States with those located in China and decide where best to allocate their investments. One set of accounting standards will also save corporations money because they will not need multiple sets of books to track their international operations.

Con:

Requiring companies that list on all global securities exchanges to use the same external reporting requirements will mislead investors. For example, in countries where the majority of investment funds come from banks in the form of long-term borrowing, debt to equity ratios will look very different than those of comparable U.S. firms. Accounting information must reflect its environment. Besides, as all business becomes global, reporting requirements will naturally evolve to what investors demand.

Instructions

Write a one-page summary reflecting your opinion about the value of harmonizing accounting standards for global equity markets. Support your opinions by referencing comparable cross-country companies you have located on the Internet.

BUSINESS WEEK ASSIGNMENT

CASE 15.3

LO 2, 3

Inside Japan

Finding an auditor in Japan can be challenging. Chester Dawson in an August 13, 2001, *Business Week* article, "Bean-Counting American-Style," states that demand for U.S.-trained CPAs has really taken off as more Japanese companies go global and more foreign firms enter Japan. A significant revision in reporting requirements over the past few years has increased demand for qualified accountants. Dawson reports that

> Until 1999, the country's publicly traded companies were not required to include subsidiaries in mid-year earnings reports, leaving plenty of room for balance-sheet shell games. Another sweeping change is the requirement that companies carry securities on their books at current values and not the purchase price. "Japanese accounting standards are shifting to U.S. accounting standards," says Jeffrey Alfano, an audit senior manager at **Deloitte Touche Tohmatsu** in Tokyo.

Instructions

a. Identify two other students to form a group (or your instructor will identify these students). With your group members prepare a one-page typed paper identifying some political, legal, economic, cultural, and/or technological/infrastructure issues that you think are affecting Japan's accounting profession.

b. Discuss among your group members what you think the last sentence in the quotation from *Business Week* means. In particular, include in your group paper one paragraph giving the group consensus about whether you think Japanese standards are shifting to U.S. standards and whether you believe it will be good for their capital markets and their investors. Provide supporting evidence.

INTERNET ASSIGNMENT

INTERNET 15.1

U.S. Foreign Trade Zones

LO 1, 2, 7

The National Association of Foreign Trade Zones (FTZs) maintains an Internet site containing information on U.S. foreign trade zones. Locate the site by searching under "foreign trade zone," or go to:

www.naftz.org

Instructions

a. How many general-purpose foreign trade zones are there in the United States?
b. What is the difference between a zone and a subzone?
c. In your state, how many foreign trade zones are there and where are they located? What types of businesses use them?
d. Other information is available at the site. Use that information to answer the following:
   1. How are FTZs created?
   2. What businesses utilize FTZs?
   3. What benefits can firms obtain from operating in FTZs?

Internet sites are time and date sensitive. It is the purpose of these exercises to have you explore the Internet. You may need to use the Yahoo! search engine **http://www.yahoo.com** *(or any other favorite search engine) to find a company's current Web address.*

OUR COMMENTS ON THE "YOUR TURN" CASES

You as a Consumer (p. 686) If the U.S. dollar strengthens against the euro over the coming month, then goods imported from Italy should cost U.S. customers less. Goods imported from the United Kingdom should cost more as the dollar weakens against the pound. As the dollar strengthens, you can purchase more euros with each dollar; therefore, you should investigate the prices of racing bicycles imported from Italy. If you believe the dollar will continue to strengthen over the coming month, you should delay your shopping to get the greatest benefit from the exchange rate fluctuations toward the end of the month.

You as Head of International Acquisitions (p. 689) It is true that in many countries there are no laws that prohibit businesses from paying government officials from other countries a bribe. In Germany businesses that make bribery payments to government officials *inside* of Germany are engaging in unethical and illegal activities. But these same activities are considered ethical and legal for business dealings with government officials *outside* of Germany. In the United States, these bribery payments are illegal; it is considered unethical to make payments to government officials within the United States or in other countries.

Unless the payments suggested by the three city officials are small enough and meet the guidelines of facilitating payments, the payments would be illegal under the Foreign Corrupt Practices Act. However, before directly telling the Chinese officials that you are unwilling to make payments to expedite the paperwork, other alternatives could be considered. Given the nature of the products made by the company (toys) and the plan to sell the product to Chinese customers, a potential solution is to make a charitable donation to the city to create a park or play area for Chinese children. By taking this approach, instead of the direct payment to the city officials, the company gets the benefit of avoiding the illegal bribe and creating some goodwill with the citizens of the city. In addition, the city officials can take credit for the negotiation that created the new park.

ANSWERS TO SELF-TEST QUESTIONS

1. c 2. a, b, c, d 3. b 4. c $(.17 - .19) \times 20,000$
5. d (the transaction was denominated in dollars)

APPENDIX A

A NEW GENERATION
Tootsie Roll Annual Report*

*Reprinted with permission

Corporate Profile

Tootsie Roll Industries, Inc. has been engaged in the manufacture and sale of candy for 104 years. Our products are primarily sold under the familiar brand names, Tootsie Roll, Tootsie Roll Pops, Caramel Apple Pops, Child's Play, Charms, Blow Pop, Blue Razz, Cella's, Mason Dots, Mason Crows, Junior Mints, Charleston Chew, Sugar Daddy, Sugar Babies, Andes and Fluffy Stuff.

Corporate Principles

We believe that the differences among companies are attributable to the caliber of their people, and therefore we strive to attract and retain superior people for each job.

We believe that an open family atmosphere at work combined with professional management fosters cooperation and enables each individual to maximize his or her contribution to the company and realize the corresponding rewards.

We do not jeopardize long-term growth for immediate, short-term results.

We maintain a conservative financial posture in the deployment and management of our assets.

We run a trim operation and continually strive to eliminate waste, minimize cost and implement performance improvements.

We invest in the latest and most productive equipment to deliver the best quality product to our customers at the lowest cost.

We seek to outsource functions where appropriate and to vertically integrate operations where it is financially advantageous to do so.

We view our well known brands as prized assets to be aggressively advertised and promoted to each new generation of consumers.

Melvin J. Gordon, Chairman and Chief Executive Officer and Ellen R. Gordon, President and Chief Operating Officer.

To Our Shareholders

We are pleased to report that Tootsie Roll Industries once again posted record operating results in 2000.

Sales reached $427 million, a record high for the twenty-fourth consecutive year and an 8% increase over 1999 sales of $397 million. Sales growth is attributed to a strong Halloween selling season and successful promotional programs, as well as additional sales from businesses that were acquired during the year.

Earnings per share reached $1.53, an increase of 9% over 1999 earnings per share of $1.41. Net earnings reached $76 million, an increase of 6% over 1999 net earnings of $71 million. This was the nineteenth consecutive year of record earnings. Earnings per share increased by a higher percentage than net earnings due to the lower number of average shares outstanding in 2000.

The financial resources we have carefully cultivated through the years enabled us to take several key actions in 2000:

- Cash dividends were paid for the fifty-eighth consecutive year, and the quarterly rate was increased by 15%.
- Our thirty sixth consecutive stock dividend was distributed.
- 957,450 of the company's common shares were repurchased in the open market.
- Significant capital was invested in plant and equipment to improve efficiency and to support future sales growth.
- Two branded candy businesses were acquired.

While we anticipate that the investments we undertook this year will contribute to our operations in years to come, our financial position remains strong, giving us the flexibility to react to new investment opportunities, including acquisitions, which may arise in the future.

Sales and Marketing

Record sales levels reached in 2000 were largely the result of acquisitions and continued execution of sales and marketing programs that have proven successful in recent years. These efforts and the acquired product lines helped us gain access to new distribution opportunities for our product lines. They also helped us to sustain the traditionally high sell-through that makes our products appealing to retailers and distributors alike across all trade classes.

A significant portion of our sales and marketing effort was again directed at Halloween, which has long been our most significant selling period, and remained so this year. Our bagged goods, including variety packs comprised of popular product assortments offered at value oriented price points, continued to move well through supermarket, mass merchandise, drug and warehouse club channels.

In the area of merchandising, we expanded our use of display ready cases at Halloween and throughout the year. These cases are printed in vivid colors and feature convenient, removable side panels that improve product visibility and brand recognition at the retail level. We also expanded distribution of freestanding floor displays, both with mixed assortments and with straight goods. Specialized, retailer-oriented merchandising adaptations such as these ensure that our venerable brands retain their place in the contemporary retail environment.

Another way we have worked to retain a contemporary market for

Financial Highlights

	December 31, 2000	1999
	(in thousands except per share data)	
Net Sales	$427,054	$396,750
Net Earnings	75,737	71,310
Working Capital	145,765	168,423
Net Property, Plant and Equipment	131,118	95,897
Shareholders' Equity	458,696	430,646
Average Shares Outstanding*	49,434	50,412
Per Share Items*		
Net Earnings	$1.53	$1.41
Shareholders' Equity	9.36	8.62
Cash Dividends Paid	.27	.23

*Based on average shares outstanding adjusted for stock dividends.

our products is through product extensions. This year we introduced Wild Berry Dots, a new flavor profile in the Dots line that features tart berry flavors sprinkled with super-sour flavor crystals.

We also extended the Charleston Chew brand with the expansion of Mini Charleston Chews, a bite-sized version that consumers can share with friends or save for later in the convenient, recloseable box.

We have further grown our business through seasonal offerings of bagged goods at Valentine's Day, Easter and Christmas. Festive graphics and attractive price points increasingly make these holidays occasions for consumers to bring home Tootsie Roll products. Additionally, sales in our seasonal line came from our 2000 Christmas tin, the latest in a collectable series. Collectable tins help to create an important and nostalgic impression of our brands.

Lastly, sales growth in 2000 was positively impacted by two acquisitions completed during the first half of the year.

Acquisitions

Both children and adults have long enjoyed cotton candy at special events such as fairs, carnivals and the circus. In February we acquired the assets of a small manufacturer that, after many years of research and development, perfected a way to mass produce commercial quantities of this melt-in-your-mouth treat in attractive, shelf-stable packages. Sold under the brand name Charms Fluffy Stuff, we hope to expand distribution of this unique confection to the range of outlets and trade classes where our other products are sold, and make Fluffy Stuff a special treat that is available every day. This acquisition included a production facility in Maryland.

In May we acquired Andes Candies, a more familiar, but equally unique confection, along with its production facility located in Wisconsin. Andes products are easily recognizable for their attractive foil wrappers and distinctive rectangular shape. The most popular flavor in the Andes line is Cream de Menthe, a 50 year old confection. It consists of a thin layer of refreshing green mint, sandwiched between two layers of chocolaty goodness and is wrapped in green foil.

During the last half of the year we successfully absorbed both the Fluffy Stuff and the Andes businesses into our own. Our sales and marketing organizations quickly integrated both product lines and we are well along in the task of developing appropriate promotional strategies for these new items.

Advertising and Public Relations

We continued to utilize television to bring our advertising message to children and adults during 2000. Network, spot and cable T. V. carried a variety of targeted themes including the classic "How Many Licks?" featuring Tootsie Pops, along with "That's a Blow Pop" and several other commercials that were run on prominent cartoon, game and adventure shows.

Tootsie Rolls have been included in military rations for many years, and in 2000 we were honored to participate in a reunion marking the 50th anniversary of the Korean War Battle of the Chosin Reservoir. This battle was noteworthy both because our 15,000 Marine and Army troops were outnumbered by 120,000 Chinese enemy troops and because of the harsh, 36 degree below zero temperatures our men had to endure. Time and again we heard poignant stories from Marine veterans who survived for days on Tootsie Rolls and Charms squares because their regular food rations were frozen solid. It was gratifying to participate in the events honoring the "Chosin Few" brave survivors of one of the most famous military battles ever fought by the U.S. armed forces.

Numerous articles and stories appeared during the year in recognition of the company and its accomplishments. Most notably, our Chairman and Chief Executive Officer was ranked as the top performing executive in the food/beverage category by Chief Executive magazine, and our President and Chief Operating Officer shared her management insights in a number of publications including Fortune and Executive Excellence magazines. Tootsie Roll was also honored as one of the "100 Best Corporate Citizens" by Business Ethics magazine.

Capital Expenditures

Our capital expenditure program continues to focus on initiatives that increase capacity, improve product quality, or reduce cost. Capital expenditures in 2000 were $16 million, encompassing a variety of projects including enhanced environmental air control, additional kitchen capacity and state of the art inspection systems to keep up with increased throughput.

Also during 2000 we completed our first headquarters expansion and renovation in 14 years and commenced construction to increase the size of our Tennessee distribution center. Both of these projects provide infrastructure needed to support the integration of recent acquisitions as well as general growth in our business.

Information Technology

With the Year 2000 software issue behind us, we focused on two key initiatives this year. First was the successful integration of the two acquisitions into our business systems. Secondly, we commenced projects involving several critical business applications. Although these do not impact our general operating system, these subsystems must evolve in order to take full advantage of current technologies and to keep pace with the ever-changing environment in which we do business.

Methodologies that were quite acceptable even a few years ago can quickly become outdated. We are committed to deploying leading edge practices and technologies in every aspect of our operations and view our information technologies as a prime strategic tool for future growth.

Purchasing

Prices for key raw materials were generally favorable during the year, although savings in this category were partially offset by increased costs for packaging materials. Management tools such as our commodity hedging program and competitive bidding process help to ensure that the company's purchases are sourced as economically as possible.

Also during 2000 we successfully incorporated the purchasing of ingredients and packaging for Andes and Fluffy Stuff into our centralized purchasing systems.

International

Sales grew in our Mexican operation as a result of marketing improvements, successful promotions and strong second half seasonal sales. Profits increased by an even greater percentage as a result of intensified cost control measures.

Canadian sales were steady, with continued strength in bagged items at Halloween. Export sales grew due to the foreign sales of the companies acquired and accelerated sales and marketing efforts in selected markets for our existing core brands. We hope to build upon this base and develop synergies across product lines to further improve international distribution.

In Appreciation...

We wish to thank the many loyal employees, customers, suppliers, sales brokers and foreign distributors with whom we work, as well as our shareholders who have been supportive through the years. While we are pleased with the record results achieved in 2000, we are committed to build upon them for the future.

Melvin J Gordon

Melvin J Gordon
Chairman of the Board and
Chief Executive Officer

Ellen R Gordon

Ellen R. Gordon
President and
Chief Operating Officer

Management's Discussion and Analysis of Financial Condition and Results of Operations

(in thousands except per share, percentage and ratio figures)

NET SALES
Millions of dollars
96: $341
97: $376
98: $389
99: $397
00: $427

NET EARNINGS
Millions of dollars
96: $47.2
97: $60.7
98: $67.5
99: $71.3
00: $75.7

FINANCIAL REVIEW

This financial review discusses the company's financial condition, results of operations, liquidity and capital resources. It should be read in conjunction with the Consolidated Financial Statements and related footnotes that follow this discussion.

FINANCIAL CONDITION

Our financial condition remained strong in 2000, bolstered by another year of record profits. Net earnings rose from $71,310 in 1999 to $75,737 in 2000. Shareholders' equity increased by 6.5% from $430,646 in 1999 to $458,696 in 2000, due principally to the addition of these earnings, partially offset by stock repurchases of $32,945 and cash dividends declared of $13,350.

The company has paid cash dividends for fifty-eight consecutive years. Shareholders also received a 3% stock dividend in 2000, the thirty-sixth consecutive year that one has been distributed.

The company responded to several investment opportunities during the year. In February we acquired substantially all of the assets of a small manufacturer of shelf stable cotton candy. This product is sold under the brand name Charms Fluffy Stuff and is suitable for national distribution.

In May we acquired substantially all of the assets of Andes Candies. Andes is best known as the maker of Andes Creme de Menthe Thins, a three layered, chocolaty rectangular mint sold nationally through a variety of outlets including supermarkets, drug chains and mass merchandisers.

The combined $74,293 purchase price for these acquisitions was financed by a combination of cash and short term borrowings, which were paid off prior to year end. In addition, cash outflows during the year related to capital expenditures were $16,189. The company continues to be financed principally by funds generated from operations rather than with borrowed funds.

The investments made in 2000 are reflected in the following ratios: current ratio declined from 4.0 to 1 to 3.5 to 1; quick ratio declined from 3.2 to 1 to 2.7 to 1; current liabilities to net worth declined from 13.0% to 12.5% and debt to equity remained negligible at 1.6% compared to 1.7% a year ago.

The company retains a conservative financial posture and sufficient capital to respond to future investment opportunities. Accordingly, we continue to seek appropriate acquisitions to complement our existing business.

RESULTS OF OPERATIONS

2000 vs. 1999

Net sales increased in 2000 to $427,054, a record level for the twenty-fourth consecutive year and a 7.6% increase over 1999 sales of $396,750. Sales remained at the highest level in the third quarter, due to successful Halloween and Back to School promotions.

Other factors contributing to sales increases during the year were growth across many of our core brands, gains in our seasonal lines, incremental business from product line extensions, increases in certain international markets and sales from acquired brands.

Comparing quarterly sales in 2000 to those of 1999, increases were seen in each quarter. The third quarter showed the largest increase in dollar terms due to Halloween, and the fourth quarter showed the greatest growth in percentage terms due to $14,457 in sales from acquired brands. In the fourth quarter we experienced both increased competitive pressures and general softness throughout the segment of the industry in which we principally operate.

Cost of goods sold as a percentage of sales remained consistent at 48.5% in 2000 versus 48.5% in 1999. Raw material prices were generally favorable during the year but were offset by higher packaging costs and product mix variations, some of which are related to the acquired brands. The company continues to focus on cost control throughout all levels of its operations.

Gross margin grew by 7.7% to $219,954 due to increased sales. As a percentage of sales, gross margin remained constant at 51.5% in 2000 versus 51.5% in 1999. Gross margins in the third and fourth quarters continue to be somewhat lower due to the seasonal nature of our business and the product mix sold in those quarters.

Operating expenses, comprised of marketing, selling, advertising, physical distribution, general and administrative expenses, as a percentage of sales, increased slightly from 24.4% to 24.8%. Amortization of intangible assets increased from $2,706 to $3,420 reflecting the partial year impact of two acquisitions. Earnings from operations increased from $104,519 to $110,729, a 5.9% increase.

Other income, consisting primarily of interest and dividend income net of interest expense was, $7,079 versus $6,928 last year.

The effective tax rate of 35.7% was comparable to the prior year rate of 36.0%.

Consolidated net earnings rose 6.2% to a new company record of $75,737. Our net earnings were 17.7% of sales in 2000 and 18.0% of sales in 1999. Earnings per share increased by 8.5% to a record $1.53 from the previous record of $1.41 reached in 1999. Earnings per share increased by a greater percentage than net earnings due to lower average shares outstanding during 2000 as a result of share repurchases made during the year.

2000 was the nineteenth year of record earnings achievement for the company.

1999 vs. 1998

1999 was our twenty-third consecutive year of record sales achievement. Sales of $396,750 were up 2.1% over 1998 sales of $388,659. The third quarter, driven by Halloween sales, continued to be our largest selling period and surpassed levels attained in previous years. Also in 1999, the timing of certain Halloween shipments had a favorable effect on the third quarter and a corresponding unfavorable impact on the fourth quarter as compared to the prior year.

Throughout the year, sales were attributable to successful promotional programs as we continued to broaden distribution in mass merchandisers and other select trade classes with our core product offerings. Line extensions, new products and seasonal packs all contributed to added sales.

Sales growth occurred in our two most significant foreign operations as well. In Mexico, stabilizing local conditions and aggressive new marketing and promotional programs complemented the already strong business we have developed for the Christmas holiday season in that market.

Sales growth in our Canadian operation was attributable to another strong Halloween season coupled with further distribution gains in the mass merchandiser and grocery trade classes. Also, the new Way 2 Sour Blow Pop was successfully introduced in this market.

Cost of goods sold, as a percentage of sales, remained steady at 48.5% versus 48.3%. This reflected generally stable cost levels for packaging and minor ingredients, although certain of our raw material costs did increase somewhat. These increases were largely offset by higher production efficiencies associated with increased volumes in relation to fixed costs.

Gross margin dollars grew by 1.6% to $204,189, and remained steady as a percent of sales at 51.5% versus 51.7% in 1998, due to the factors cited above.

Operating expenses as a percentage of sales, declined slightly from 25.7% to 25.1%. This improvement was due to effective expense control programs aimed at holding down costs. Earnings from operations increased by 3.2% to $104,519, or 26.3% of sales, as a result of favorable gross margins and operating expenses.

Other income increased by $2,130 to $6,928, primarily reflecting significantly lower foreign exchange losses in Mexico where local economic conditions improved. Also, interest expense was lower and interest income was higher due to lower average borrowings and increased investments in marketable securities, respectively, during 1999. Interest income was also higher in 1999 due to higher interest rates. The effective tax rate was 36.0% in 1999 versus 36.3% in 1998.

Consolidated net earnings rose 5.6% to a new company record of $71,310. Earnings per share increased by 6.0% to $1.41 from the previous record of $1.33 reached in 1998. Earnings per share increased by a greater percent than net earnings due to lower average shares outstanding during 1999 as a result of share repurchases made during the year.

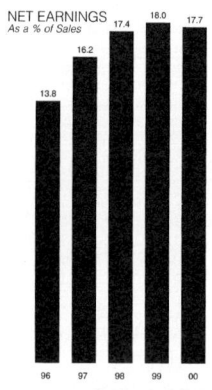

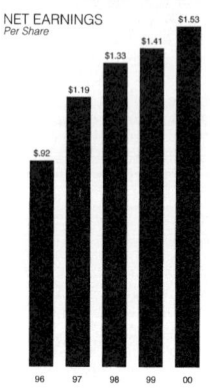

Our net earnings as a percent of sales increased to 18.0% from 17.4%. 1999 was the eighteenth consecutive year of record earnings achievement for the company.

LIQUIDITY AND CAPITAL RESOURCES

Cash flows from operating activities increased to $84,881 in 2000 from $72,935 in 1999 and $77,735 in 1998. The increase in 2000 was principally attributable to higher net earnings, and the additional depreciation and amortization related to the acquired businesses.

In 1999, the decrease in cash flows from operating activities was principally attributable to increases in other receivables and prepaid expenses and other assets. Also, depreciation expense was lower in 1999 due to foreign currency translation.

Cash flows from investing activities in 2000 reflect $74,293 for the purchase of Fluffy Stuff and Andes Candies, capital expenditures of $16,189 and a net decrease in marketable securities of $24,015 which was used to help finance those expenditures.

In 1999 capital expenditures were $20,283 and there was a net increase in marketable securities of $6,710. In 1998, capital expenditures were $14,878 and there was a net increase in marketable securities of $19,951.

Cash flows from financing activities reflect share repurchases of $32,945, $26,869 and $13,445 in 2000, 1999 and 1998, respectively. Short term borrowings in 2000 were primarily related to the Andes acquisition which were subsequently repaid. In 1998 there was also a short term borrowing which was subsequently repaid during that same year.

Cash dividends of $13,091, $11,313 and $9,150 were paid in 2000, 1999 and 1998, respectively. The increase in 2000 was 15.7% over 1999 and 2000 represented the fifty-eighth consecutive year in which we have paid cash dividends.

QUANTITATIVE AND QUALITATIVE DISCLOSURE OF MARKET RISK AND OTHER MATTERS

The company is exposed to various market risks, including fluctuations in sugar, corn, edible oils, cocoa and packaging costs. The company also invests in securities with maturities of up to three years, the majority of which are held to maturity, which limits the company's exposure to interest rate fluctuations. There has been no material change in the company's market risks during 2000.

In June 1998, the Financial Accounting Standards Board issued Statement of Financial Accounting Standards No. 133, Accounting for Derivative Instruments and Hedging Activities (SFAS No. 133). SFAS No. 133 establishes accounting and reporting standards requiring that every derivative instrument be recorded in the balance sheet as either an asset or liability measured at its fair value. The company has concluded that adoption of SFAS No. 133 will not have a material impact on the company's results of operations.

The results of our operations and our financial condition are expressed in the following financial statements.

Appendix A

CONSOLIDATED STATEMENT OF
Earnings, Comprehensive Earnings and Retained Earnings

TOOTSIE ROLL INDUSTRIES, INC. AND SUBSIDIARIES (in thousands except per share data)

For the year ended December 31,

	2000	1999	1998
Net sales	$427,054	$396,750	$388,659
Cost of goods sold	207,100	192,561	187,617
Gross margin	219,954	204,189	201,042
Selling, marketing and administrative expenses	105,805	96,964	97,071
Amortization of intangible assets	3,420	2,706	2,706
Earnings from operations	110,729	104,519	101,265
Other income, net	7,079	6,928	4,798
Earnings before income taxes	117,808	111,447	106,063
Provision for income taxes	42,071	40,137	38,537
Net earnings	$ 75,737	$ 71,310	$ 67,526
Net earnings	$ 75,737	$ 71,310	$ 67,526
Other comprehensive earnings (loss), net of tax			
Unrealized gains (losses) on securities	(856)	930	976
Foreign currency translation adjustments	(394)	653	(30)
Other comprehensive earnings (loss)	(1,250)	1,583	946
Comprehensive earnings	$ 74,487	$ 72,893	$ 68,472
Retained earnings at beginning of year	$158,619	$164,652	$159,124
Net earnings	75,737	71,310	67,526
Cash dividends ($.27, $.23 and $.19 per share)	(13,350)	(11,654)	(9,484)
Stock dividends	(40,883)	(65,689)	(52,514)
Retained earnings at end of year	$180,123	$158,619	$164,652
Earnings per share	$ 1.53	$ 1.41	$ 1.33
Average common and class B common shares outstanding	49,434	50,412	50,920

(The accompanying notes are an integral part of these statements.)

CONSOLIDATED STATEMENT OF
Financial Position
TOOTSIE ROLL INDUSTRIES, INC. AND SUBSIDIARIES (in thousands)

Assets

	December 31, 2000	December 31, 1999
CURRENT ASSETS:		
Cash and cash equivalents	$ 60,882	$ 88,504
Investments	71,605	71,002
Accounts receivable trade, less allowances of $2,147 and $2,032	23,568	19,032
Other receivables	1,230	5,716
Inventories:		
Finished goods and work-in-process	24,984	20,689
Raw materials and supplies	16,906	14,396
Prepaid expenses	2,685	3,124
Deferred income taxes	1,351	2,069
Total current assets	203,211	224,532
PROPERTY, PLANT AND EQUIPMENT, at cost:		
Land	8,327	7,981
Buildings	36,937	30,330
Machinery and equipment	183,858	145,789
	229,122	184,100
Less—Accumulated depreciation	98,004	88,203
	131,118	95,897
OTHER ASSETS:		
Intangible assets, net of accumulated amortization of $26,917 and $23,497	121,263	85,137
Investments	62,548	87,167
Cash surrender value of life insurance and other assets	44,302	36,683
	228,113	208,987
	$562,442	$529,416

(The accompanying notes are an integral part of these statements.)

Liabilities and Shareholders' Equity

(in thousands except per share data)

	December 31, 2000	December 31, 1999
CURRENT LIABILITIES:		
Accounts payable	$ 10,296	$ 12,845
Dividends payable	3,436	3,035
Accrued liabilities	33,336	31,945
Income taxes payable	10,378	8,284
Total current liabilities	57,446	56,109
NONCURRENT LIABILITIES:		
Deferred income taxes	12,422	9,520
Postretirement health care and life insurance benefits	6,956	6,557
Industrial development bonds	7,500	7,500
Deferred compensation and other liabilities	19,422	19,084
Total noncurrent liabilities	46,300	42,661
SHAREHOLDERS' EQUITY:		
Common stock, $.69-4/9 par value—120,000 and 120,000 shares authorized—32,986 and 32,854, respectively, issued	22,907	22,815
Class B common stock, $.69-4/9 par value—40,000 and 40,000 shares authorized—16,056 and 15,707, respectively, issued	11,150	10,908
Capital in excess of par value	256,698	249,236
Retained earnings, per accompanying statement	180,123	158,619
Accumulated other comprehensive earnings (loss)	(10,190)	(8,940)
Treasury stock (at cost)—52 shares and 50 shares, respectively	(1,992)	(1,992)
	458,696	430,646
	$562,442	$529,416

CONSOLIDATED STATEMENT OF
Cash Flows

TOOTSIE ROLL INDUSTRIES, INC. AND SUBSIDIARIES   (in thousands)

	For the year ended December 31,		
	2000	1999	1998
CASH FLOWS FROM OPERATING ACTIVITIES:			
Net earnings	$75,737	$71,310	$67,526
Adjustments to reconcile net earnings to net cash provided by operating activities:			
Depreciation and amortization	13,314	9,979	12,807
(Gain) loss on retirement of fixed assets	(46)	(43)	118
Changes in operating assets and liabilities, excluding acquisitions:			
Accounts receivable	(4,460)	400	(915)
Other receivables	4,486	(2,392)	1,358
Inventories	(768)	1,592	(106)
Prepaid expenses and other assets	(7,903)	(15,672)	(7,723)
Accounts payable and accrued liabilities	(1,717)	968	(596)
Income taxes payable and deferred	5,691	2,232	(625)
Postretirement health care and life insurance benefits	399	412	241
Deferred compensation and other liabilities	337	4,162	5,004
Other	(189)	(13)	646
Net cash provided by operating activities	84,881	72,935	77,735
CASH FLOWS FROM INVESTING ACTIVITIES:			
Acquisitions of businesses, net of cash acquired	(74,293)	—	—
Capital expenditures	(16,189)	(20,283)	(14,878)
Purchase of held to maturity securities	(156,322)	(238,949)	(259,112)
Maturity of held to maturity securities	176,576	235,973	240,195
Purchase of available for sale securities	(78,993)	(117,694)	(217,799)
Sale and maturity of available for sale securities	82,754	113,960	216,765
Net cash used in investing activities	(66,467)	(26,993)	(34,829)
CASH FLOWS FROM FINANCING ACTIVITIES:			
Issuance of notes payable	43,625	—	7,000
Repayments of notes payable	(43,625)	—	(7,000)
Treasury stock purchases	—	(1,019)	(973)
Shares repurchased and retired	(32,945)	(25,850)	(12,472)
Dividends paid in cash	(13,091)	(11,313)	(9,150)
Net cash used in financing activities	(46,036)	(38,182)	(22,595)
Increase (decrease) in cash and cash equivalents	(27,622)	7,760	20,311
Cash and cash equivalents at beginning of year	88,504	80,744	60,433
Cash and cash equivalents at end of year	$60,882	$88,504	$80,744
Supplemental cash flow information:			
Income taxes paid	$35,750	$38,827	$40,000
Interest paid	$ 1,067	$ 453	$ 803

(The accompanying notes are an integral part of these statements.)

Notes to Consolidated Financial Statements ($ in thousands except per share data)

TOOTSIE ROLL INDUSTRIES, INC. AND SUBSIDIARIES

NOTE 1—SIGNIFICANT ACCOUNTING POLICIES:

Basis of consolidation:

The consolidated financial statements include the accounts of Tootsie Roll Industries, Inc. and its wholly-owned subsidiaries (the company), which are primarily engaged in the manufacture and sale of candy products. All significant intercompany transactions have been eliminated.

The preparation of financial statements in conformity with generally accepted accounting principles requires management to make estimates and assumptions that affect the reported amounts of assets and liabilities and disclosure of contingent assets and liabilities at the date of the financial statements and the reported amounts of revenues and expenses during the reporting period. Actual results could differ from those estimates.

Revenue recognition and other accounting pronouncements:

Revenues are recognized when products are shipped and delivered to customers. Shipping and handling costs of $26,661, $24,260 and $24,342 in 2000, 1999, 1998, respectively, are included in selling, marketing and administrative expenses. Accounts receivable are unsecured. The Company adopted Securities and Exchange Commission Staff Accounting Bulletin No. 101, which clarifies the existing guidance on the recognition, presentation and disclosure of revenue in the financial statements, during the fourth quarter of 2000 with no material effect on its financial position or results of operations.

As of January 1, 2001, the Company adopted Statement of Financial Accounting Standards No. 133, "Accounting for Derivative Instruments and Hedging Activities" (SFAS No. 133), which was issued by the Financial Accounting Standards Board in 1998. The adoption of SFAS No. 133 will not have a material effect on the Company's results of operations or financial position.

Cash and cash equivalents:

The company considers temporary cash investments with an original maturity of three months or less to be cash equivalents.

Investments:

Investments consist of various marketable securities with maturities of generally less than one year. In accordance with Statement of Financial Accounting Standards (SFAS) No. 115, "Accounting For Certain Investments in Debt and Equity Securities," the company's debt and equity securities are considered as either held to maturity, available for sale or trading. Held to maturity securities represent those securities that the company has both the positive intent and ability to hold to maturity and are carried at amortized cost. Available for sale securities represent those securities that do not meet the classification of held to maturity, are not actively traded and are carried at fair value. Unrealized gains and losses on these securities are excluded from earnings and are reported as a separate component of shareholders' equity, net of applicable taxes, until realized. Trading securities relate to deferred compensation arrangements and are carried at fair value.

Inventories:

Inventories are stated at cost, not in excess of market. The cost of domestic inventories ($37,505 and $29,111 at December 31, 2000 and 1999, respectively) has been determined by the last-in, first-out (LIFO) method. The excess of current cost over LIFO cost of inventories approximates $2,993 and $5,008 at December 31, 2000 and 1999, respectively. The cost of foreign inventories ($4,385 and $5,974 at December 31, 2000 and 1999, respectively) has been determined by the first-in, first-out (FIFO) method.

From time to time, the company enters into commodity futures and option contracts in order to fix the future price of certain key ingredients which may be subject to price volatility (primarily sugar and corn syrup). Gains or losses, if any, resulting from these contracts are considered as a component of the cost of the ingredients being hedged. At December 31, 2000 the company had open contracts to purchase most of its expected 2001 sugar usage.

Property, plant and equipment:

Depreciation is computed for financial reporting purposes by use of both the straight-line and accelerated methods based on useful lives of 20 to 35 years for buildings and 12 to 20 years for machinery and equipment. For income tax purposes the company uses accelerated methods on all properties. Depreciation expense was $10,069, $7,663 and $10,101 in 2000, 1999 and 1998, respectively.

Carrying value of long-lived assets:

In the event that facts and circumstances indicate that the company's long-lived assets may be impaired, an evaluation of recoverability would be performed. Such an evaluation entails comparing the estimated future undiscounted cash flows associated with the asset to the asset's carrying amount to determine if a write down to market value or discounted cash flow value is required. The company considers that no circumstances exist that would require such an evaluation.

Postretirement health care and life insurance benefits:

The company provides certain postretirement health care and life insurance benefits. The cost of these postretirement benefits is accrued during employees' working careers.

Income taxes:

The company uses the liability method of computing deferred income taxes.

Intangible assets:

Intangible assets represent the excess of cost over the acquired net tangible assets of operating companies and is amortized on a straight-line basis over a 15 to 40 year period. The company assesses the recoverability of its intangible assets using undiscounted future cash flows.

Foreign currency translation:

During 1997, management determined that the Mexican economy was hyper-inflationary. Accordingly, the US dollar was used as the functional currency for the company's Mexican operations, and translation gains and losses were included in the determination of 1998 earnings. Effective January 1, 1999, management determined that the Mexican economy was no longer hyper-inflationary and designated the local currency as the functional currency. Accordingly, the net effect of translating the Mexican operations' financial statements was reported in a separate component of shareholders' equity beginning on January 1, 1999.

Comprehensive earnings:

Comprehensive earnings includes net earnings, foreign currency translation adjustments and unrealized gains/losses on marketable securities.

Earnings per share:

A dual presentation of basic and diluted earnings per share is not required due to the lack of potentially dilutive securities under the company's simple capital structure. Therefore, all earnings per share amounts represent basic earnings per share.

NOTE 2—ACQUISITIONS:

During 2000, the company acquired the assets of two confectionery companies for $74,293 in cash, which was funded through existing cash and $38,800 of short term borrowings. The acquisition cost has been allocated to the assets acquired and liabilities assumed based on their respective appraised values as follows:

Current assets	$ 6,304
Property, plant and equipment	29,400
Intangible assets, primarily trademarks	39,546
Liabilities	(957)
Total purchase price	$ 74,293

The acquisitions were accounted for by the purchase method. Accordingly, the operating results of the acquired businesses have been included in the consolidated financial statements since the date of acquisition. The operating results of the acquired businesses did not have a material effect on the company's financial statements.

NOTE 3—ACCRUED LIABILITIES:

Accrued liabilities are comprised of the following:

	December 31,	
	2000	1999
Compensation	$10,069	$ 8,993
Other employee benefits	4,107	4,067
Taxes, other than income	2,174	2,248
Advertising and promotions	9,038	8,508
Other	7,948	8,129
	$33,336	$31,945

NOTE 4—INCOME TAXES:

The domestic and foreign components of pretax income are as follows:

	2000	1999	1998
Domestic	$115,823	$110,052	$106,667
Foreign	1,985	1,395	(604)
	$117,808	$111,447	$106,063

The provision for income taxes is comprised of the following:

	2000	1999	1998
Current:			
Federal	$33,908	$34,290	$34,373
Foreign	426	783	618
State	3,613	4,294	4,286
	37,947	39,367	39,277
Deferred:			
Federal	3,500	1,039	(250)
Foreign	346	(388)	(479)
State	278	119	(11)
	4,124	770	(740)
	$42,071	$40,137	$38,537

Deferred income taxes are comprised of the following:

	December 31,	
	2000	1999
Workers' compensation	$ 405	$ 396
Reserve for uncollectible accounts	455	467
Other accrued expenses	1,397	1,214
VEBA funding	(370)	(347)
Other, net	(536)	339
Net current deferred income tax asset	$ 1,351	$ 2,069

	December 31,	
	2000	1999
Depreciation	$12,076	$10,563
Postretirement benefits	(2,345)	(2,220)
Deductible goodwill	7,855	5,647
Deferred compensation	(6,174)	(4,947)
Accrued commissions	2,232	2,011
Foreign subsidiary tax loss carryforward	(521)	(1,898)
Other, net	(701)	364
Net long-term deferred income tax liability	$12,422	$ 9,520

At December 31, 2000, gross deferred tax assets and gross deferred tax liabilities were $14,876 and $25,947, respectively.

The effective income tax rate differs from the statutory rate as follows:

	2000	1999	1998
U.S. statutory rate	35.0%	35.0%	35.0%
State income taxes, net	2.2	2.6	2.6
Amortization of intangible assets	0.4	0.4	0.4
Other, net	(1.9)	(2.0)	(1.7)
Effective income tax rate	35.7%	36.0%	36.3%

The company has not provided for U.S. federal or foreign withholding taxes on $5,864 of foreign subsidiaries' undistributed earnings as of December 31, 2000 because such earnings are considered to be permanently reinvested. When excess cash has accumulated in the company's foreign subsidiaries and it is advantageous for tax or foreign exchange reasons, subsidiary earnings may be remitted, and income taxes will be provided on such amounts. It is not practicable to determine the amount of income taxes that would be payable upon remittance of the undistributed earnings.

NOTE 5—SHARE CAPITAL AND CAPITAL IN EXCESS OF PAR VALUE:

	Common Stock		Class B Common Stock		Treasury Stock		Capital in excess of par value
	Shares (000's)	Amount	Shares (000's)	Amount	Shares (000's)	Amount	
Balance at January 1, 1998	15,851	$11,008	7,547	$ 5,241	—	$ —	$187,259
Issuance of 3% stock dividend	473	329	225	156	—	—	51,780
Purchase of shares for the treasury	—	—	—	—	(20)	(973)	—
Issuance of 2-for-1 stock split	16,305	11,323	7,748	5,381	(5)	—	(16,704)
Conversion of Class B common shares to common shares	98	68	(98)	(68)	—	—	—
Purchase and retirement of common shares	(288)	(201)	—	—	—	—	(12,271)
Balance at December 31, 1998	32,439	22,527	15,422	10,710	(25)	(973)	210,064
Issuance of 3% stock dividend	971	674	461	320	(1)	—	64,514
Purchase of shares for the treasury	—	—	—	—	(24)	(1,019)	—
Conversion of Class B common shares to common shares	176	122	(176)	(122)	—	—	—
Purchase and retirement of common shares	(732)	(508)	—	—	—	—	(25,342)
Balance at December 31, 1999	32,854	22,815	15,707	10,908	(50)	(1,992)	249,236
Issuance of 3% stock dividend	969	673	470	326	(2)	—	39,742
Conversion of Class B common shares to common shares	121	84	(121)	(84)	—	—	—
Purchase and retirement of common shares	(958)	(665)	—	—	—	—	(32,280)
Balance at December 31, 2000	32,986	$22,907	16,056	$11,150	(52)	$(1,992)	$256,698

The Class B Common Stock has essentially the same rights as Common Stock, except that each share of Class B Common Stock has ten votes per share (compared to one vote per share of Common Stock), is not traded on any exchange, is restricted as to transfer and is convertible on a share-for-share basis, at any time and at no cost to the holders, into shares of Common Stock which are traded on the New York Stock Exchange.

Average shares outstanding and all per share amounts included in the financial statements and notes thereto have been adjusted retroactively to reflect annual three percent stock dividends and the two-for-one stock split distributed in 1998.

NOTE 6—INDUSTRIAL DEVELOPMENT BONDS:

Interest on industrial development bonds is payable at various times during the year based upon the interest calculation option (fixed, variable or floating) selected by the company. As of December 31, 2000 and 1999, interest was calculated under the floating option (4.7% in each of these years) which requires monthly payments of interest. Principal on the bonds is due in its entirety in the year 2027.

In connection with the issuance of the bonds, the company entered into a letter of credit agreement with a bank for the amount of principal outstanding plus 48 days' accrued interest. The

Appendix A

letter of credit, which expires in January 2002, carries an annual fee of 32 1/2 basis points on the outstanding principal amount of the bonds.

NOTE 7—EMPLOYEE BENEFIT PLANS:

Pension plans:

The company sponsors defined contribution pension plans covering certain nonunion employees with over one year of credited service. The company's policy is to fund pension costs accrued based on compensation levels. Total pension expense for 2000, 1999 and 1998 approximated $2,535, $2,062 and $1,951, respectively. The company also maintains certain profit sharing and savings-investment plans. Company contributions in 2000, 1999 and 1998 to these plans were $754, $616 and $582, respectively.

The company also contributes to multi-employer defined benefit pension plans for its union employees. Such contributions aggregated $787, $713 and $680 in 2000, 1999 and 1998, respectively. The relative position of each employer associated with the multi-employer plans with respect to the actuarial present value of benefits and net plan assets is not determinable by the company.

Postretirement health care and life insurance benefit plans:

The company provides certain postretirement health care and life insurance benefits for corporate office and management employees. Employees become eligible for these benefits if they meet minimum age and service requirements and if they agree to contribute a portion of the cost. The company has the right to modify or terminate these benefits. The company does not fund postretirement health care and life insurance benefits in advance of payments for benefit claims.

The changes in the accumulated postretirement benefit obligation at December 31, 2000 and 1999 consist of the following:

	December 31,	
	2000	1999
Benefit obligation, beginning of year	$6,557	$6,163
Net periodic postretirement benefit cost	518	531
Benefits paid	(119)	(137)
Benefit obligation, end of year	$6,956	$6,557

Net periodic postretirement benefit cost included the following components:

	2000	1999	1998
Service cost—benefits attributed to service during the period	$286	$306	$258
Interest cost on the accumulated postretirement benefit obligation	341	302	279
Amortization of unrecognized net gain	(109)	(77)	(99)
Net periodic postretirement benefit cost	$518	$531	$438

For measurement purposes, an 7.5% annual rate of increase in the per capita cost of covered health care benefits was assumed for 2000; the rate was assumed to decrease gradually to 5.5% for 2004 and remain at that level thereafter. The health care cost trend rate assumption has a significant effect on the amounts reported. The weighted-average discount rate used in determining the accumulated postretirement benefit obligation was 7.25% at December 31, 2000 and 1999.

Increasing or decreasing the health care trend rates by one percentage point in each year would have the following effect:

	1% Increase	1% Decrease
Effect on postretirement benefit obligation	$800	$(657)
Effect on total of service and interest cost components	$109	$ (87)

NOTE 8—OTHER INCOME, NET:

Other income (expense) is comprised of the following:

	2000	1999	1998
Interest income	$7,636	$7,449	$6,934
Interest expense	(866)	(453)	(756)
Dividend income	421	611	822
Foreign exchange losses	(42)	(126)	(2,140)
Royalty income	225	263	155
Miscellaneous, net	(295)	(816)	(217)
	$7,079	$6,928	$4,798

NOTE 9—COMMITMENTS:

Rental expense aggregated $580, $457 and $432 in 2000, 1999 and 1998, respectively. Future operating lease commitments are not significant.

NOTE 10—COMPREHENSIVE INCOME:

Components of accumulated other comprehensive earnings (loss) are shown as follows:

	Foreign Currency Items	Unrealized Gains (Losses) on Securities	Accumulated Other Comprehensive Earnings/(Loss)
Balance at January 1, 1998	$(11,052)	$ (417)	$(11,469)
Change during period	(30)	976	946
Balance at December 31, 1998	(11,082)	559	(10,523)
Change during period	653	930	1,583
Balance at December 31, 1999	(10,429)	1,489	(8,940)
Change during period	(394)	(856)	(1,250)
Balance at December 31, 2000	$(10,823)	$ 633	$(10,190)

The individual tax effects of each component of other comprehensive earnings (loss) for the year ended December 31, 2000 are shown as follows:

	Before Tax Amount	Tax (Expense) Benefit	Net-of-Tax Amount
Foreign currency translation adjustment	$ (394)	$ —	$ (394)
Unrealized gains (losses) on securities:			
Unrealized holding gains (losses) arising during 2000	(914)	339	(575)
Less: reclassification adjustment for gains (losses) realized in earnings	446	(165)	281
Net unrealized gains	(1,360)	504	(856)
Other comprehensive earnings	$(1,754)	$ 504	$(1,250)

NOTE 11—DISCLOSURES ABOUT THE FAIR VALUE OF FINANCIAL INSTRUMENTS:

Carrying amount and fair value:

The carrying amount approximates fair value of cash and cash equivalents because of the short maturity of those instruments. The fair values of investments are estimated based on quoted market prices. The fair value of the company's industrial development bonds approximates their carrying value because they have a floating interest rate. The carrying amount and estimated fair values of the company's financial instruments are as follows:

	2000		1999	
	Carrying Amount	Fair Value	Carrying Amount	Fair Value
Cash and cash equivalents	$ 60,882	$ 60,882	$ 88,504	$ 88,504
Investments held to maturity	98,164	100,127	110,245	111,151
Investments available for sale	22,565	22,565	37,390	37,390
Investments in trading securities	13,424	13,424	10,534	10,534
Industrial development bonds	7,500	7,500	7,500	7,500

A summary of the aggregate fair value, gross unrealized gains, gross unrealized losses and amortized cost basis of the company's investment portfolio by major security type is as follows:

	December 31, 2000				December 31, 1999			
	Amortized Cost	Fair Value	Unrealized Gains	Unrealized Losses	Amortized Cost	Fair Value	Unrealized Gains	Unrealized Losses
Held to Maturity:								
Unit investment trusts of preferred stocks	$ 1,462	$ 3,381	$1,919	$ —	$ 2,592	$ 4,618	$ 2,026	$ —
Municipal bonds	97,744	97,807	63	—	109,256	108,160	—	(1,096)
Unit investment trusts of municipal bonds	941	932	—	(9)	959	935	—	(24)
Private export funding securities	4,115	4,104	—	(11)	4,933	4,933	—	—
	$104,262	$106,224	$1,982	$ (20)	$117,740	$118,646	$ 2,026	$(1,120)
Available for Sale:								
Municipal bonds	$ 32,487	$ 32,221	$ —	$ (266)	$ 40,930	$ 40,603	$ —	$ (327)
Mutual funds	2,454	3,724	1,270	—	3,007	5,698	2,691	—
	$ 34,941	$ 35,945	$1,270	$ (266)	$ 43,937	$ 46,301	$ 2,691	$ (327)

Held to maturity securities of $6,097 and $7,495 and available for sale securities of $13,380 and $8,911 were included in cash and cash equivalents at December 31, 2000 and 1999, respectively. There were no securities with maturities greater than three years and gross realized gains and losses on the sale of available for sale securities in 2000 and 1999 were not significant.

NOTE 12—GEOGRAPHIC AREA AND SALES INFORMATION:
Summary of sales, net earnings and assets by geographic area

	2000			1999			1998		
	United States	Mexico and Canada	Consolidated	United States	Mexico and Canada	Consolidated	United States	Mexico and Canada	Consolidated
Sales to unaffiliated customers	$394,545	$32,509	$427,054	$365,975	$30,775	$396,750	$363,569	$25,090	$388,659
Sales between geographic areas	3,626	3,343		3,787	1,794		2,805	4,374	
	$398,171	$35,852		$369,762	$32,569		$366,374	$29,464	
Net earnings	$ 73,929	$ 1,808	$ 75,737	$ 69,917	$ 1,393	$ 71,310	$ 68,521	$ (995)	$ 67,526
Total assets	$540,697	$21,745	$562,442	$505,152	$24,264	$529,416	$467,265	$20,158	$487,423
Net assets	$439,685	$19,011	$458,696	$409,160	$21,486	$430,646	$378,892	$17,565	$396,457

Total assets are those assets associated with or used directly in the respective geographic area, excluding intercompany advances and investments.

Major customer
Revenues from a major customer aggregated approximately 17.8%, 17.9% and 17.2% of total net sales during the years ended December 31, 2000, 1999 and 1998, respectively.

Report of Independent Accountants

To the Board of Directors and Shareholders of Tootsie Roll Industries, Inc.

In our opinion, the accompanying consolidated statement of financial position and the related consolidated statements of earnings, comprehensive earnings and retained earnings and of cash flows present fairly, in all material respects, the financial position of Tootsie Roll Industries, Inc. and its subsidiaries at December 31, 2000 and 1999, and the results of their operations and their cash flows for each of the three years in the period ended December 31, 2000 in conformity with accounting principles generally accepted in the United States of America. These financial statements are the responsibility of the Company's management; our responsibility is to express an opinion on these financial statements based on our audits. We conducted our audits of these statements in accordance with auditing standards generally accepted in the United States of America, which require that we plan and perform the audit to obtain reasonable assurance about whether the financial statements are free of material misstatement. An audit includes examining, on a test basis, evidence supporting the amounts and disclosures in the financial statements, assessing the accounting principles used and significant estimates made by management, and evaluating the overall financial statement presentation. We believe that our audits provide a reasonable basis for our opinion expressed above.

PricewaterhouseCoopers LLP

Chicago, Illinois
February 12, 2001

Appendix A

Quarterly Financial Data (Unaudited)

TOOTSIE ROLL INDUSTRIES, INC. AND SUBSIDIARIES

(Thousands of dollars except per share data)

2000	First	Second	Third	Fourth	Total
Net sales	$78,015	$90,376	$165,873	$92,790	$427,054
Gross margin	41,067	48,209	83,225	47,453	219,954
Net earnings	13,063	15,652	31,514	15,508	75,737
Net earnings per share	.26	.32	.64	.31	1.53

1999	First	Second	Third	Fourth	Total
Net sales	$74,200	$88,265	$152,667	$81,618	$396,750
Gross margin	38,815	45,902	77,651	41,821	204,189
Net earnings	12,325	14,751	29,283	14,951	71,310
Net earnings per share	.24	.29	.58	.30	1.41

1998	First	Second	Third	Fourth	Total
Net sales	$69,701	$85,931	$144,230	$88,797	$388,659
Gross margin	36,966	45,133	73,251	45,692	201,042
Net earnings	11,217	13,910	27,216	15,183	67,526
Net earnings per share	.22	.28	.53	.30	1.33

Net earnings per share is based upon average outstanding shares as adjusted for 3% stock dividends issued during the second quarter of each year.

2000-1999 QUARTERLY SUMMARY OF TOOTSIE ROLL INDUSTRIES, INC. STOCK PRICE AND DIVIDENDS PER SHARE

STOCK PRICES*

	2000 High	2000 Low	1999 High	1999 Low
1st Qtr	32-7/8	28-5/16	46-15/16	39-3/4
2nd Qtr	38	30-3/8	46-3/4	38-1/8
3rd Qtr	42-7/16	34-7/8	39-7/16	30
4th Qtr	47-13/16	35-5/8	33-7/16	29-13/16

*NYSE — Composite Quotations

Estimated Number of shareholders at December 31, 2000 9,500

DIVIDENDS

	2000	1999
1st Qtr	$.0608	$.0495
2nd Qtr	$.0700	$.0607
3rd Qtr	$.0700	$.0608
4th Qtr	$.0700	$.0608

NOTE: In addition to the above cash dividends, a 3% stock dividend was issued on April 19, 2000 and April 21, 1999. Cash dividends are restated to reflect 3% stock dividends.

Five Year Summary of Earnings and Financial Highlights

TOOTSIE ROLL INDUSTRIES, INC. AND SUBSIDIARIES

(Thousands of dollars except per share, percentage and ratio figures)

(See Management's Comments starting on page 5)	2000	1999	1998	1997	1996
Sales and Earnings Data					
Net sales	$427,054	$396,750	$388,659	$375,594	$340,909
Gross margin	219,954	204,189	201,042	187,281	162,420
Interest expense	866	453	756	483	1,498
Provision for income taxes	42,071	40,137	38,537	34,679	27,891
Net earnings	75,737	71,310	67,526	60,682	47,207
% of sales	17.7%	18.0%	17.4%	16.2%	13.8%
% of shareholders' equity	16.5%	16.6%	17.0%	17.3%	15.1%
Per Common Share Data (1)					
Net sales	$ 8.64	$ 7.87	$ 7.63	$ 7.34	$ 6.64
Net earnings	1.53	1.41	1.33	1.19	.92
Shareholders' equity	9.36	8.62	7.82	6.88	6.10
Cash dividends declared	.27	.23	.19	.15	.12
Stock dividends	3%	3%	3%	3%	3%
Additional Financial Data					
Working capital	$145,765	$168,423	$175,155	$153,355	$153,329
Net cash provided by operating activities	84,881	72,935	77,735	68,176	76,710
Net cash used in investing activities	66,467	26,993	34,829	31,698	52,364
Net cash used in financing activities	46,036	38,182	22,595	21,704	26,211
Property, plant & equipment additions	16,189	20,283	14,878	8,611	9,791
Net property, plant & equipment	131,118	95,897	83,024	78,364	81,687
Total assets	562,442	529,416	487,423	436,742	391,456
Long term debt	7,500	7,500	7,500	7,500	7,500
Shareholders' equity	458,696	430,646	396,457	351,163	312,881
Average shares outstanding (1)	49,434	50,412	50,920	51,163	51,310

(1) Adjusted for annual 3% stock dividends and the 2-for-1 stock split effective July 13, 1998.

Appendix A

Board of Directors

Melvin J. Gordon[1]	Chairman of the Board and Chief Executive Officer
Ellen R. Gordon[1]	President and Chief Operating Officer
Charles W. Seibert[2][3]	Retired Banker
Lana Jane Lewis-Brent[2][3]	President, Paul Brent Designer, Inc.
Richard P. Bergeman[2][3]	Retired Senior Vice President, Bestfoods

[1] Member of the Executive Committee
[2] Member of the Audit Committee
[3] Member of the Compensation Committee

Officers

Melvin J. Gordon	Chairman of the Board and Chief Executive Officer
Ellen R. Gordon	President and Chief Operating Officer
G. Howard Ember, Jr.	Vice President, Finance & Asst. Secy.
John W. Newlin, Jr.	Vice President, Manufacturing
Thomas E. Corr	Vice President, Marketing & Sales
James M. Hunt	Vice President, Physical Distribution
Barry P. Bowen	Treasurer & Asst. Secy.
Daniel P. Drechney	Controller

Offices, Plants

Executive Offices	7401 S. Cicero Ave. Chicago, Illinois 60629 www.tootsie.com
Plants	Illinois Tennessee Massachusetts Wisconsin Maryland New York Mexico City
Foreign Sales Offices	Mexico City, Mexico Mississauga, Ontario

Subsidiaries

Andes Candies L.P.
Andes Manufacturing LLC
Andes Services LLC
C.C. L.P., Inc.
C.G.C. Corporation
C.G.P., Inc.
Cambridge Brands, Inc.
Cambridge Brands Mfg., Inc.
Cambridge Brands Services, Inc.
Cella's Confections, Inc.
Charms Company
Charms L.P.
Charms Marketing Company
Henry Eisen Advertising Agency, Inc.
J.T. Company, Inc.
O'Tec Industries, Inc.
Tootsie Roll of Canada Ltd.
Tootsie Roll Central Europe Ltd.
The Tootsie Roll Company, Inc.
Tootsie Roll Management, Inc.
Tootsie Roll Mfg., Inc.
Tootsie Rolls—Latin America, Inc.
Tootsie Roll Worldwide Ltd.
The Sweets Mix Company, Inc.
TRI de Latino America S.A. de C.V.
TRI Finance, Inc.
TRI International Co.
TRI-Mass., Inc.
TRI Sales Co.
Tutsi S.A. de C.V.
World Trade & Marketing Ltd.

Other Information

Stock Exchange	New York Stock Exchange, Inc. (Since 1922)
Stock Identification	Ticker Symbol: TR CUSIP No. 890516 10-7
Stock Transfer Agent and Stock Registrar	Mellon Investor Services LLC Overpeck Centre 85 Challenger Road Ridgefield Park, NJ 07660 1-800-851-9677 www.mellon-investor.com
Independent Accountants	PricewaterhouseCoopers LLP 200 East Randolph Drive Chicago, IL 60601
General Counsel	Becker Ross Stone DeStefano & Klein 317 Madison Avenue New York, NY 10017
Annual Meeting	May 7, 2001 Mutual Building, Room 1200 909 East Main Street Richmond, VA 23219

TR Listed NYSE

Printed on recycled paper.

APPENDIX B

THE TIME VALUE OF MONEY: FUTURE AMOUNTS AND PRESENT VALUES

Learning Objectives

After studying this appendix, you should be able to:

1. Explain what is meant by the *time value of money*.
2. Describe the relationships between *present values* and *future amounts*.
3. Explain three basic ways in which decision makers apply the time value of money.
4. Compute future amounts and the investments necessary to accumulate future amounts.
5. Compute the present values of future cash flows.
6. Discuss accounting applications of the concept of present value.

LO 1
Explain what is meant by the *time value* of money.

LO 2
Describe the relationships between *present values* and *future amounts*.

THE CONCEPT

One of the most basic—and important—concepts of investing is the *time value* of *money*. This concept is based on the idea that an amount of money available today can be safely invested to accumulate to a larger amount in the future. As a result, an amount of money available today is considered to be equivalent in value to a *larger sum* available at a future date.

In our discussions, we will refer to an amount of money available today as a *present value*. In contrast, an amount receivable or payable at a future date will be described as a *future amount*.

To illustrate, assume that you place $500 in a savings account that earns interest at the rate of 8% per year. The balance of your account at the end of each of the next four years is illustrated in Exhibit B–1.

These balances represent different time values of your $500 investment. When you first open the account, your investment has a *present value* of only $500. As time passes, the value of your investment increases to the *future amounts* illustrated in the graph. (Throughout this appendix, present values will be illustrated in **red**, and future amounts will be shown in **blue**.)

Relationships between Present Values and Future Amounts

The difference between a present value and any future amount is the *interest* that is included in the future amount. We have seen that interest accrues over time. Therefore, the difference between the present value and a future amount depends on *two factors:* (1) the *rate of interest* at which the present value increases and (2) the *length of time* over which interest accumulates. (Notice in our graph, the farther away the future date, the larger the future amount.)

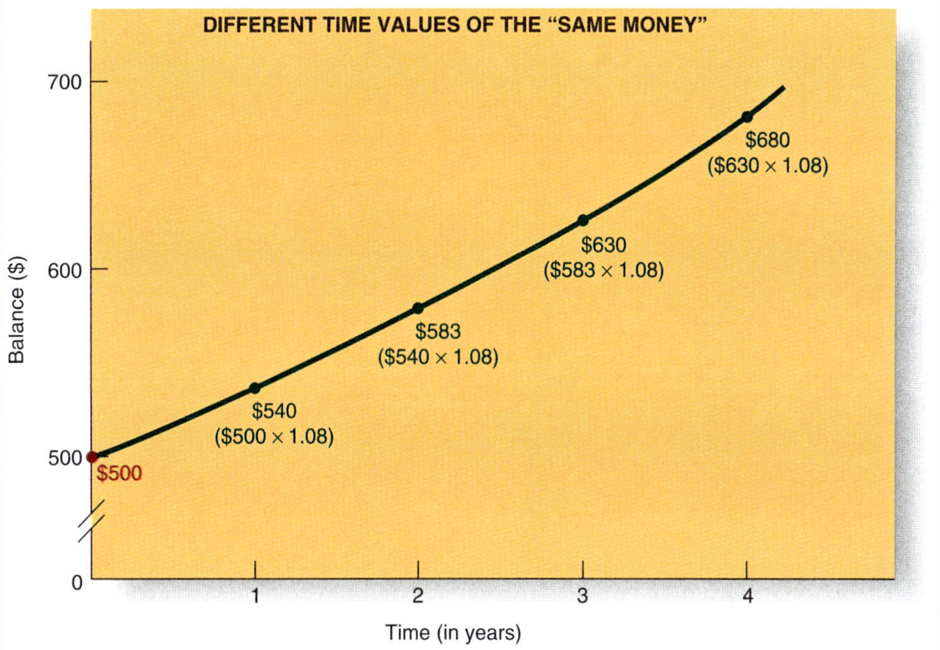
DIFFERENT TIME VALUES OF THE "SAME MONEY"
Balance ($)
700
600
500
0
$500
$540
($500 × 1.08)
$583
($540 × 1.08)
$630
($583 × 1.08)
$680
($630 × 1.08)
1
2
3
4
Time (in years)

Exhibit B–1

THE VALUES OF MONEY OVER TIME

My Notes

Future values are bigger, but are they worth more? This is the real issue.

Present Values Change over Time The present value of an investment gradually increases toward the future amount. In fact, when a future date *arrives,* what once was a future amount becomes the present value of the investment. For example, at the end of the first year, $540 will no longer be a future amount—it will be the present value of your savings account.

The Basic Concept (Stated Several Different Ways) Notice that the present value of our savings account is *always less than its future amounts.* This is the basic idea underlying the time value of money. But this idea often is expressed in different ways, including the following:

- A present value is always *less than* a future amount.
- A future amount is always *greater than* a present value.
- A dollar available today is always worth *more* than a dollar that does not become available until a future date.
- A dollar available at a future date is always worth *less* than a dollar that is available today.

Read these statements carefully. All four reflect the idea that a present value is the "equivalent" of a larger number of dollars at a future date. This is what is meant by the time value of money.

Compound Interest

The relationships between present values and future amounts assume that the interest earned on the investment is *reinvested,* rather than withdrawn. This concept often is called *compounding the interest.* Compounding has an interesting effect. Reinvesting the interest causes the amount invested to increase each period. This, in turn, causes more interest to be earned in each successive period. Over a long period of time, an investment in which interest is compounded continuously will increase to surprisingly large amounts.

CASE IN POINT

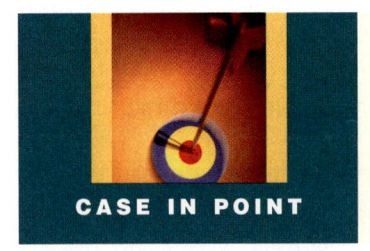

In 1626, Peter Minuit is said to have purchased Manhattan Island from a group of Indians for $24 worth of "beads, cloth, and trinkets." This episode often is portrayed as an incredible bargain—even a steal. But if the Indians had invested this $24 to earn interest at a compound interest rate of 8%, they would have more than enough money today to buy the island back—along with everything on it.

Applications of the Time Value of Money Concept

LO 3
Explain three basic ways in which decision makers apply the time value of money.

Investors, accountants, and other decision makers apply the time value of money in three basic ways. These applications are summarized below, along with a typical example.

1. The amount to which an investment will accumulate over time. *Example:* If we invest $5,000 each year and earn an annual rate of return of 10%, how much will be accumulated after 10 years?
2. The amount that must be invested every period to accumulate a required future amount. *Example:* We must accumulate a $200 million bond sinking fund over the next 20 years. How much must we deposit into this fund each year, assuming that the fund's assets will be invested to earn an annual rate of return of 8%?
3. The present value of cash flows expected to occur in the future. *Example:* Assuming that we require a 15% return on our investments, how much can we afford to pay for new machinery that is expected to reduce production costs by $20,000 per year for the next 10 years?

We will now introduce a framework for answering such questions.

FUTURE AMOUNTS

A future amount is simply the dollar amount to which a present value *will accumulate* over time. As we have stated, the difference between a present value and a related future amount depends on (1) the interest rate and (2) the period of time over which the present value accumulates.

Starting with the present value, we may compute future amounts through a series of multiplications, as illustrated in our graph in Exhibit B–1. But there are faster and easier ways. For example, many financial calculators are programmed to compute future amounts; you merely enter the present value, the interest rate, and the number of periods. Or you may use a *table of future amounts,* such as **Table FA–1** in Exhibit B–2.

The Tables Approach

LO 4
Compute future amounts and the investments necessary to accumulate future amounts.

A table of future amounts shows the future amount to which *$1* will accumulate over a given number of periods, assuming that it has been invested to earn any of the illustrated interest rates. We will refer to the amounts shown in the body of this table as *factors,* rather than as dollar amounts.

To find the future amount of a present value *greater* than $1, simply multiply the present value by the factor obtained from the table. The formula for using the table in this manner is:

Future Amount = Present Value × Factor (from Table FA–1)

Future Amounts

Exhibit B–2

THE FUTURE VALUE OF $1

Table FA-1
Future Value of $1 After *n* Periods

Number of Periods (*n*)	1%	1½%	5%	6%	8%	10%	12%	15%	20%
1	1.010	1.015	1.050	1.060	1.080	1.100	1.120	1.150	1.200
2	1.020	1.030	1.103	1.124	1.166	1.210	1.254	1.323	1.440
3	1.030	1.046	1.158	1.191	1.260	1.331	1.405	1.521	1.728
4	1.041	1.061	1.216	1.262	1.360	1.464	1.574	1.749	2.074
5	1.051	1.077	1.276	1.338	1.469	1.611	1.762	2.011	2.488
6	1.062	1.093	1.340	1.419	1.587	1.772	1.974	2.313	2.986
7	1.072	1.110	1.407	1.504	1.714	1.949	2.211	2.660	3.583
8	1.083	1.126	1.477	1.594	1.851	2.144	2.476	3.059	4.300
9	1.094	1.143	1.551	1.689	1.999	2.358	2.773	3.518	5.160
10	1.105	1.161	1.629	1.791	2.159	2.594	3.106	4.046	6.192
20	1.220	1.347	2.653	3.207	4.661	6.727	9.646	16.367	38.338
24	1.270	1.430	3.225	4.049	6.341	9.850	15.179	28.625	79.497
36	1.431	1.709	5.792	8.147	15.968	30.913	59.136	153.152	708.802

My Notes
Approach to computing future amount

Let us demonstrate this approach using the data for our savings account, illustrated in Exhibit B–1. The account started with a present value of $500, invested at an annual interest rate of 8%. Thus the future values of the account in each of the next four years can be computed as follows (rounded to the nearest dollar):

My Notes
Using the table to compute the amounts in our graph

Year	Future Amount	Computation (Using Table FA-1)
1	$540	$500 × 1.080 = $540
2	$583	$500 × 1.166 = $583
3	$630	$500 × 1.260 = $630
4	$680	$500 × 1.360 = $680

Computing a future amount is relatively easy. The more interesting question is: How much must we *invest today* to accumulate a required future amount?

Computing the Required Investment At the end of 2002, Metro Recycling agrees to create a fully funded pension plan for its employees by December 31, 2007 (in five years). It is estimated that $5 million will be required to fully fund the pension plan at December 31, 2007. How much must Metro invest in this plan *today* (December 31, 2002) to accumulate the promised $5 million by the end of 2007, assuming that payments to the fund will be invested to earn an annual return of 8%?

Let us repeat our original formula for computing future amounts using Table FA-1:

My Notes
Our original formula . . .

Future Amount = Present Value × Factor (from Table FA-1)

In this situation, we *know* the future amount—$5 million. We are looking for the *present value* which, when invested at an interest rate of 8%, will accumulate to $5 million in five years. To determine the *present value,* the formula shown above may be restated as follows:

restated to find the present value

$$\text{Present Value} = \frac{\text{Future Amount}}{\text{Factor (from Table FA-1)}}$$

Referring to Table FA–1, we get a factor of *1.469* at the intersection of five periods and 8% interest. Thus, the amount of the required investment at the end of 2002 is $3,403,676 ($5 million ÷ 1.469). Invested at 8%, this amount will accumulate to the required $5 million at the end of five years as illustrated in Exhibit B–3.

Exhibit B–3

THE FUTURE AMOUNT OF A SINGLE INVESTMENT

Future amount $5,000,000

Year 1　Year 2　Year 3　Year 4　Year 5

Present value $3,403,676

The Future Amount of an Annuity

In many situations, an investor is to make a *series* of investment payments rather than a single payment. As an example, assume that you plan to invest $500 into your savings account at the end of each of the next five years. If the account pays annual interest of 8%, what will be the balance in your savings account at the end of the fifth year? Tables, such as Table FA–2 in Exhibit B–4, may be used to answer this question. Table FA–2 presents the future amount of an *ordinary annuity of $1,* which is a series of payments of $1 made at the *end* of each of a specified number of periods.

Exhibit B–4

FUTURE VALUE OF AN ORDINARY ANNUITY

Table FA–2
Future Amount of $1 Paid Periodically for *n* Periods

Number of Periods (n)	1%	1½%	5%	6%	8%	10%	12%	15%	20%
1	1.000	1.000	1.000	1.000	1.000	1.000	1.000	1.000	1.000
2	2.010	2.015	2.050	2.060	2.080	2.100	2.120	2.150	2.200
3	3.030	3.045	3.153	3.184	3.246	3.310	3.374	3.473	3.640
4	4.060	4.091	4.310	4.375	4.506	4.641	4.779	4.993	5.368
5	5.101	5.152	5.526	5.637	5.867	6.105	6.353	6.742	7.442
6	6.152	6.230	6.802	6.975	7.336	7.716	8.115	8.754	9.930
7	7.214	7.323	8.142	8.394	8.923	9.487	10.089	11.067	12.916
8	8.286	8.433	9.549	9.897	10.637	11.436	12.300	13.727	16.499
9	9.369	9.559	11.027	11.491	12.488	13.579	14.776	16.786	20.799
10	10.462	10.703	12.578	13.181	14.487	15.937	17.549	20.304	25.959
20	22.019	23.124	33.066	36.786	45.762	57.275	72.052	102.444	186.688
24	26.974	28.634	44.502	50.816	66.765	88.497	118.155	184.168	392.484
36	43.079	47.276	95.836	119.121	187.102	299.127	484.463	1014.346	3539.009

To find the future amount of an ordinary annuity of payments greater than $1, we simply multiply the amount of the periodic payment by the factor appearing in the table, as shown here:

$$\frac{\text{Future Amount}}{\text{of an Annuity}} = \text{Periodic Payment} \times \text{Factor (from Table FA–2)}$$

My Notes

Approach to computing the future amount of an annuity

In our example, a factor of 5.867 is obtained from the table at the intersection of five periods and 8% interest. If this factor is multiplied by the periodic payment of $500, we find that your savings account will accumulate to a balance of $2,934 ($500 × 5.867) at the end of five years. Therefore, if you invest $500 at the end of each of the next five years in the savings account, you will accumulate $2,934 at the end of the 5-year period.

While computing the future amount of an investment is sometimes necessary, many business and accounting problems require us to determine the *amount of the periodic payments* that must be made to accumulate the required future amount.

Computing the Required Periodic Payments Assume that Ultra Tech Company is required to accumulate $10 million in a *bond sinking fund* to retire bonds payable five years from now. The *bond indenture* requires Ultra Tech to make equal payments to the fund at the end of each of the next five years. What is the amount of required periodic payment, assuming that the fund will earn 10% annual interest? To answer this question, we simply rearrange the following formula for computing the future amount of an annuity:

$$\frac{\text{Future Amount}}{\text{of an Annuity}} = \text{Periodic Payment} \times \text{Factor (from Table FA–2)}$$

My Notes

Our original formula . . .

In our example, we know that Ultra Tech is required to accumulate a future amount of $10 million. However, we need to know the amount of the periodic payments that, when invested at 10% annual interest, will accumulate to that future amount. To make this calculation, the formula may be stated as follows:

$$\text{Periodic Payment} = \frac{\text{Future Amount of an Annuity}}{\text{Factor (from Table FA–2)}}$$

restated to find the amount of the periodic payments

The amount of each required payment, therefore, is $1,638,000 ($10 million ÷ **6.105**). If payments of $1,638,000 are made at the end of each of the next five years to a bond sinking fund that earns 10% annual interest, the fund will accumulate to $10 million, as shown in Exhibit B–5.

Exhibit B–5

FUTURE AMOUNT OF A SERIES OF INVESTMENTS

Interest Periods of Less Than One Year

In our computations of future amounts, we have assumed that interest is paid (compounded) or payments are made annually. Therefore, in using the tables, we used *annual* periods and an *annual* interest rate. Investment payments or interest payments may be made on a more frequent basis, such as monthly, quarterly, or semiannually. Tables FA–1 and FA–2 may be used with any of these payment periods, *but the rate of interest must represent the interest rate for that period.*

As an example, assume that 24 monthly payments are to be made to an investment fund that pays a 12% annual interest rate. To determine the future amount of this investment, we would multiply the amount of the monthly payments by the factor from Table FA–2 for 24 periods, using a *monthly* interest rate of 1%—the 12% annual rate divided by 12 months.

PRESENT VALUES

LO 5
Compute the present values of future cash flows.

As indicated previously, the present value is *today's* value of funds to be received in the future. While present value has many applications in business and accounting, it is most easily explained in the context of evaluating investment opportunities. In this context, the present value is the amount that a knowledgeable investor would pay *today* for the right to receive an expected future amount of cash. The present value is always *less* than the future amount, because the investor will expect to earn a return on the investment. The amount by which the future cash receipt exceeds its present value represents the investor's profit.

The amount of the profit on a particular investment depends on two factors: (1) the rate of return (called the *discount rate*) required by the investor and (2) the length of time until the future amount will be received. The process of determining the present value of a future cash receipt is called *discounting* the future amount.

To illustrate the computation of present value, assume that an investment is expected to result in a $1,000 cash receipt at the end of one year and that an investor requires a 10% return on this investment. We know from our discussion of present and future values that the difference between a present value and a future amount is the return (interest) on the investment. In our example, the future amount would be equal to 110% of the original investment, because the investor expects 100% of the investment back plus a 10% return on the investment. Thus the investor would be willing to pay *$909* ($1,000 ÷ 1.10) for this investment. This computation may be verified as follows (amounts rounded to the nearest dollar):

Amount to be invested (present value)	$ 909
Required return on investment ($909 × 10%)	91
Amount to be received in one year (future value)	$1,000

As illustrated in Exhibit B–6, if the $1,000 is to be received *two years* in the future, the investor would pay only *$826* for the investment today [($1,000 ÷ 1.10) ÷ 1.10]. This computation may be verified as follows (amounts rounded to the nearest dollar):

Amount to be invested (present value)	$ 826
Required return on investment in first year ($826 × 10%)	83
Amount invested after one year	$ 909
Required return on investment in second year ($909 × 10%)	91
Amount to be received in two years (future value)	$1,000

The amount that our investor would pay today, $826, is the present value of $1,000 to be received two years from now, discounted at an annual rate of 10%. The $174 difference between the $826 present value and the $1,000 future amount is the return (interest revenue) to be earned by the investor over the two-year period.

Present Values

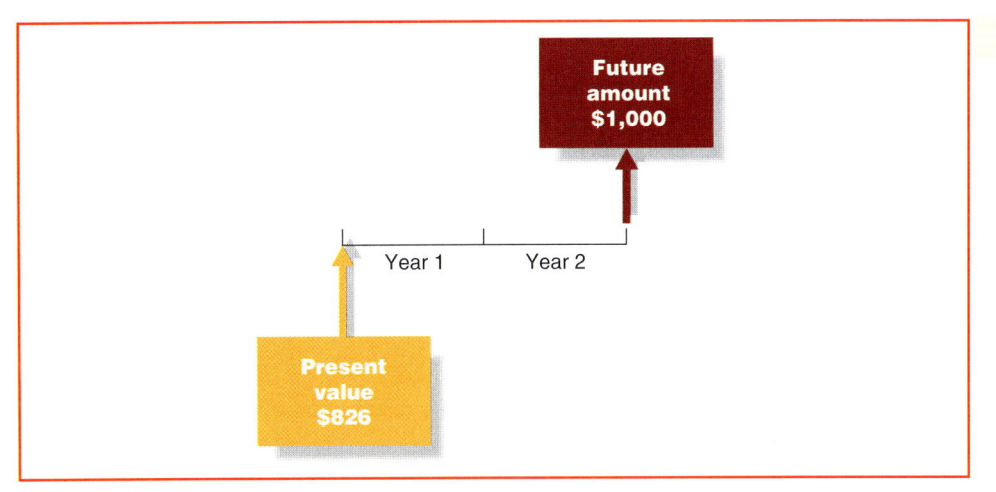

Exhibit B–6

PRESENT VALUE OF $1,000 TO BE RECEIVED IN A SINGLE SUM IN TWO YEARS

Using Present Value Tables

Although we can compute the present value of future amounts by a series of divisions, tables are available that simplify the calculations. We can use a table of present values to find the present value of $1 at a specified discount rate and then multiply that value by the future amount as illustrated in the following formula:

Present Value = Future Amount × Factor (from Table PV–1)

Referring to **Table PV–1** in Exhibit B–7, we find a factor of **.826** at the intersection of two periods and 10% interest. If we multiply this factor by the expected future cash receipt of $1,000, we get a present value of *$826* ($1,000 × .826), the same amount computed previously.

My Notes

Formula for finding present value

Table PV–1
Present Values of $1 Due in *n* Periods

Number of Periods (*n*)	1%	1½%	5%	6%	8%	10%	12%	15%	20%
1	.990	.985	.952	.943	.926	.909	.893	.870	.833
2	.980	.971	.907	.890	.857	.826	.797	.756	.694
3	.971	.956	.864	.840	.794	.751	.712	.658	.579
4	.961	.942	.823	.792	.735	.683	.636	.572	.482
5	.951	.928	.784	.747	.681	.621	.567	.497	.402
6	.942	.915	.746	.705	.630	.564	.507	.432	.335
7	.933	.901	.711	.665	.583	.513	.452	.376	.279
8	.923	.888	.677	.627	.540	.467	.404	.327	.233
9	.914	.875	.645	.592	.500	.424	.361	.284	.194
10	.905	.862	.614	.558	.463	.386	.322	.247	.162
20	.820	.742	.377	.312	.215	.149	.104	.061	.026
24	.788	.700	.310	.247	.158	.102	.066	.035	.013
36	.699	.585	.173	.123	.063	.032	.017	.007	.001

Exhibit B–7

PRESENT VALUE OF $1

What Is the Appropriate Discount Rate?

As explained earlier, the *discount rate* may be viewed as the investor's required rate of return. All investments involve some degree of risk that actual future cash flows may turn out to be less than expected. Investors will require a rate of return that justifies taking this risk. In today's market conditions, investors require annual returns of between 5% and 8% on low-risk investments, such as government bonds and certificates of deposit. For relatively high-risk investments, such as the introduction of a new product line, investors may expect to earn an annual return of perhaps 15% or more. When a higher discount rate is used, the present value of the investment will be lower. In other words, as the risk of an investment increases, its value to investors decreases.

The Present Value of an Annuity

Many investment opportunities are expected to produce annual cash flows for a number of years, instead of one single future cash flow. Let us assume that Camino Company is evaluating an investment that is expected to produce *annual net cash flows of* $10,000 in *each of the next three years*.[1] If Camino Company expects a 12% return on this type of investment, it may compute the present value of these cash flows as follows:

Year	Expected New Cash Flows	×	Present Value of $1 Discounted at 12%	=	Present Value of Net Cash Flows
1	$10,000		.893		$ 8,930
2	10,000		.797		7,970
3	10,000		.712		7,120
Total present value of the investment					$24,020

This analysis indicates that the present value of the expected net cash flows from the investment, discounted at an annual rate of 12%, amounts to $24,020. This is the maximum amount that Camino Company could afford to pay for this investment and still expect to earn the 12% required rate of return, as shown in Exhibit B–8.

Exhibit B–8

PRESENT VALUE OF THREE $10,000 CASH FLOWS DISCOUNTED AT 12%

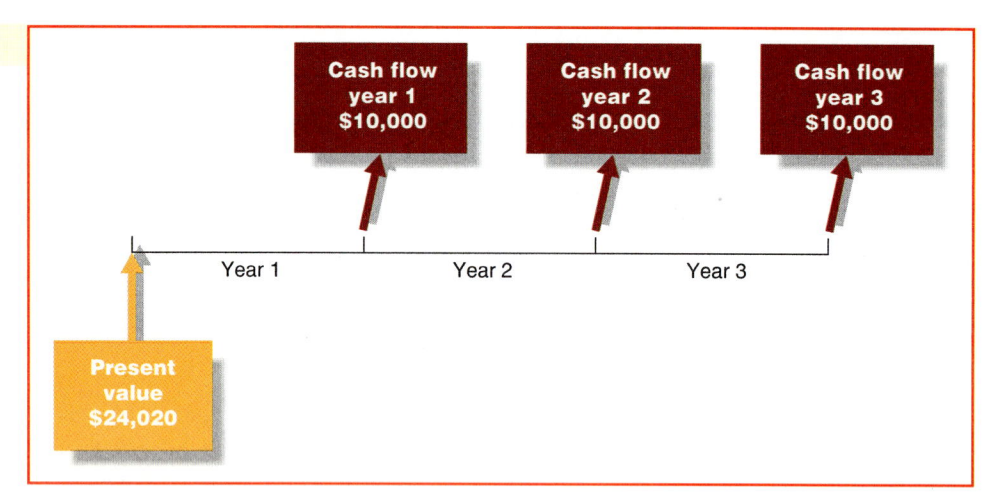

Cash flow year 1 $10,000 | Cash flow year 2 $10,000 | Cash flow year 3 $10,000

Year 1 — Year 2 — Year 3

Present value $24,020

In the preceding analysis, we computed the present value of the investment by separately discounting each period's cash flows, using the appropriate factors from **Table PV–1**. Separately discounting each period's cash flows is necessary only when the cash flows vary in amount from period to period. Since the annual cash flows in our example are *uniform in amount*, there are easier ways to compute the total present value.

---

[1] "Annual net cash flows" normally are the net result of a series of cash receipts and cash payments occurring throughout the year. For convenience, we follow the common practice of assuming that the entire net cash flows for each year occur at *year-end*. This assumption causes relatively little distortion and greatly simplifies computations.

Many financial calculators are programmed to compute the present value of an investment, after the interest rate, the future cash flows, and the number of periods have been entered. Another approach is to refer to a *present value annuity table,* which shows the present value of *$1 to be received each period for a specified number of periods.* An annuity table labeled **Table PV–2** appears in Exhibit B–9.[2]

To illustrate the use of **Table PV–2**, let's return to the example of the investment by Camino Company. That investment was expected to return $10,000 per year for the next three years, and the company's required rate of return was 12% per year. Using **Table PV–2**, we can compute the present value of the investment with the following formula:

Present Value of an Annuity = Periodic Cash Flows × Factor (from Table PV–2)

As illustrated in **Table PV–2**, the present value of $1 to be received at the end of the next three years, discounted at an annual rate of 12%, is **2.402**. If we multiply 2.402 by the expected future annual cash receipt of $10,000, we get a present value of $24,020, which is the same amount produced by the series of calculations made earlier.

My Notes

Formula to find the present value of a series of cash flows

Table PV–2
Present Values of $1 to Be Received Periodically for *n* Periods

Number of Periods (*n*)	1%	1½%	5%	6%	8%	10%	12%	15%	20%
1	0.990	0.985	0.952	0.943	0.926	0.909	0.893	0.870	0.833
2	1.970	1.956	1.859	1.833	1.783	1.736	1.690	1.626	1.528
3	2.941	2.912	2.723	2.673	2.577	2.487	2.402	2.283	2.106
4	3.902	3.854	3.546	3.465	3.312	3.170	3.037	2.855	2.589
5	4.853	4.783	4.329	4.212	3.993	3.791	3.605	3.352	2.991
6	5.795	5.697	5.076	4.917	4.623	4.355	4.111	3.784	3.326
7	6.728	6.598	5.786	5.582	5.206	4.868	4.564	4.160	3.605
8	7.652	7.486	6.463	6.210	5.747	5.335	4.968	4.487	3.837
9	8.566	8.361	7.108	6.802	6.247	5.759	5.328	4.772	4.031
10	9.471	9.222	7.722	7.360	6.710	6.145	5.650	5.019	4.192
20	18.046	17.169	12.462	11.470	9.818	8.514	7.469	6.259	4.870
24	21.243	20.030	13.799	12.550	10.529	8.985	7.784	6.434	4.937
36	30.108	27.661	16.547	14.621	11.717	9.677	8.192	6.623	4.993

Exhibit B–9

PRESENT VALUE OF AN ORDINARY ANNUITY

Discount Periods of Less Than One Year

The interval between regular periodic cash flows is called the *discount period.* In our preceding examples, we have assumed cash flows once a year. Often cash flows occur on a more frequent basis, such as monthly, quarterly, or semiannually. The present value tables can be used with discount periods of any length, *but the discount rate must be for that length of time.* For example, if we use **Table PV–2** to find the present value of a series of *quarterly* cash payments, the discount rate must be the *quarterly* rate.

There are many applications of the present value concept in accounting. In the next several pages, we will discuss some of the most important of these applications.

VALUATION OF FINANCIAL INSTRUMENTS

Accountants use the phrase *financial instruments* to describe cash, equity investments in another business, and any contracts that call for receipts or payments of cash. (Notice

LO 6

Discuss accounting applications of the concept of present value.

---

[2] This table is for an *ordinary* annuity, which assumes that the periodic cash flows occur at the *end* of each period.

that this phrase applies to all financial assets, as well as most liabilities. In fact, the only common liabilities *not* considered financial instruments are unearned revenue and deferred income taxes.)

Whenever the present value of a financial instrument *differs significantly* from the sum of the expected future cash flows, the instrument is recorded in the accounting records at its *present value*—not at the expected amount of the future cash receipts or payments.

Let us illustrate with a few common examples. Cash appears in the balance sheet at its face amount. This face value *is* a present value—that is, the value of the cash today.

Marketable securities appear in the balance sheet at their *current market values*. These too are present values—representing the amount of cash into which the security can be converted *today*.

Accounts receivable and accounts payable normally appear in the balance sheet at the amounts expected to be collected or paid in the near future. Technically, these are *future amounts,* not present values. But they usually are received or paid within 30 or 60 days. Considering the short periods of time involved, the differences between these future amounts and their present values simply are *not material*.

Interest-Bearing Receivables and Payables

When a financial instrument calls for the receipt or payment of interest, the difference between present value and the future amounts *does* become material. Thus interest-bearing receivables and payables initially are recorded in accounting records at the *present value* of the future cash flows—also called the "principal amount" of the obligation. This present value often is *substantially less* than the sum of the expected future amounts.

Consider, for example, $100 million in 30-year, 9% bonds payable issued at par. At the issuance date, the present value of this bond issue is $100 million—the amount of cash received. But the future payments to bondholders are expected to total *$370* million, computed as follows:

Future interest payments ($100 million × 9% × 30 years)	$270,000,000
Maturity value of the bonds (due in 30 years)	100,000,000
Sum of the future cash payments	$370,000,000

Thus the $100 million issuance price represents the present value of $370 million in future cash payments to be made over a period of 30 years.

In essence, interest-bearing financial instruments are "automatically" recorded at their present values simply because we do not include future interest charges in the original valuation of the receivable or the liability.

"Non-Interest-Bearing" Notes

On occasion, companies may issue or accept notes that make no mention of interest, or in which the stated interest rates are unreasonably low. If the difference between the present value of such a note and its face amount is *material,* the note initially is recorded at its present value.

To illustrate, assume that on January 1, 2002, Elron Corporation purchases land from U.S. Development Co. As full payment for this land, Elron issues a $300,000 installment note payable, due in three annual installments of $100,000, beginning on December 31, 2002. This note makes *no mention* of interest charges.

Clearly, three annual installments of $100,000 are not the equivalent of $300,000 available today. Elron should use the *present value* of this note—not the face amount—in determining the cost of the land and reporting its liability.

Assume that a realistic interest rate for financing land over a three-year period currently is 10% per annum. The present value of Elron's installment note, discounted at 10%, is *$248,700* [$100,000, 3-year annuity × **2.487** (from **Table PV–2**) in Exhibit B–9]. Elron

Valuation of Financial Instruments

should view this $248,700 as the "principal amount" of this installment note payable. The remaining $51,300 ($300,000 − $248,700) represents interest charges included in the installment payments.

Elron should record the purchase of the land and the issuance of this note as follows:[3]

Land	248,700	
Notes Payable		248,700
Purchased land, issuing a 3-year installment note payable with a present value of $248,700.		

(U.S. Development Co. should make similar computations in determining the sales price of the land and the valuation of its note receivable.)

Elron also should prepare an *amortization table* to allocate the amount of each installment payment between interest expense and reduction in the principal amount of this obligation. This table, based on an original unpaid balance of $248,700, three annual payments of $100,000, and an annual interest rate of 10%, is illustrated in Exhibit B–10.

AMORTIZATION TABLE
(3-Year, $300,000 Installment Note Payable, Discounted at 10% per Annum)

Interest Period	Payment Date	Annual Payment	Interest Expense (10% of the Last Unpaid Balance)	Reduction in Unpaid Balance	Unpaid Balance
Issue date	Jan. 1, 2002				$248,700
1	Dec. 31, 2002	$100,000	$24,870	$75,130	173,570
2	Dec. 31, 2003	100,000	17,357	82,643	90,927
3	Dec. 31, 2004	100,000	9,073*	90,927	–0–

*In the last period, interest expense is equal to the amount of the final payment minus the remaining unpaid balance. This compensates for the use of a present value table with factors carried to only three decimal places.

Exhibit B–10

AMORTIZATION TABLE FOR A DISCOUNTED NOTE PAYABLE

The entry at December 31, 2002, to record the first installment payment will be as follows:

Interest Expense	24,870	
Notes Payable	75,130	
Cash		100,000
Made annual payment on installment note payable to U.S. Development Co.		

Market Prices of Bonds

The market price of bonds may be regarded as the *present value* to bondholders of the future principal and interest payments. To illustrate, assume that a corporation issues $1,000,000 face value of 10-year, 9% bonds when the going market rate of interest is

---

[3] There is an alternative recording technique that makes use of an account entitled Discount on Notes Payable. This alternative approach produces the same results and will be explained in later accounting courses.

10%. Since bond interest is paid semiannually, we must use 20 *semiannual* periods as the life of the bond issue and a 5% *semiannual* market rate of interest in our present value calculations. The expected issuance price of this bond issue may be computed as follows: Note that because the market rate of interest exceeds the bond's coupon rate, the bonds are issued at a $62,210 discount.

Present value of future principal payments:	
$1,000,000 due after 20 semiannual periods, discounted at 5%:	
$1,000,000 × .377 (from Table PV–1)	$377,000
Present value of future interest payments:	
$45,000 per period ($1,000,000 × 9% × 1/2) for 20 semiannual periods, discounted at 5%: $45,000 × 12.462 (from Table PV–2)	560,790
Expected issuance price of bond issue	$937,790

Capital Leases

We briefly discuss capital leases as a Supplemental Topic in Chapter 10, but do not illustrate the accounting for these instruments. This appendix gives us an opportunity to explore this topic in greater detail.

A capital lease is regarded as a sale of the leased asset by the lessor to the lessee. At the date of this sale, the lessor recognizes sales revenue equal to the *present value* of the future lease payments receivable, discounted at a realistic rate of interest. The lessee also uses the present value of the future payments to determine the cost of the leased asset and the valuation of the related liability.

To illustrate, assume that on December 1, Pace Tractor uses a *capital lease* to finance the sale of a tractor to Kelly Grading Co. The tractor was carried in Pace Tractor's perpetual inventory records at a cost of $15,000. Terms of the lease call for Kelly Grading Co. to make *24* monthly payments of *$1,000* each, beginning on December 31. These lease payments include an interest charge of *1%* per month. At the end of the 24-month lease, title to the tractor will pass to Kelly Grading Co. at no additional cost.

Accounting by the Lessor (Pace Tractor) Table PV–2 shows that the present value of $1 to be received monthly for 24 months, discounted at 1% per month, is **21.243**. Therefore, the present value of the 24 future lease payments is $1,000 × **21.243**, or *$21,243*. Pace Tractor should record this capital lease as a sale of the tractor at a price equal to the present value of the lease payments, as follows:

Lease Payment Receivable (net)	21,243	
Sales		21,243
Financed sale of a tractor to Kelly Grading Co. using a capital lease requiring 24 monthly payments of $1,000.		
Payments include a 1% monthly interest charge.		
Cost of Goods Sold	15,000	
Inventory		15,000
To record cost of tractor sold under capital lease.		

Notice that the sales price of the tractor is only $21,243, even though the gross amount to be collected from Kelly Grading Co. amounts to $24,000 ($1,000 × 24 payments). The difference between these two amounts, $2,757, will be recognized by Pace Tractor as interest revenue over the term of the lease.

To illustrate the recognition of interest revenue, the entry on December 31 to record collection of the first monthly lease payment (rounded to the nearest dollar) will be:

Valuation of Financial Instruments

Cash	1,000	
Interest Revenue		212
Lease Payments Receivable (net)		788
Received first lease payment from Kelly Grading Co.: $1,000 lease payment received, less $212 interest revenue ($21,243 × 1%), equals $788 reduction in lease payments receivable.		

After this first monthly payment is collected, the present value of the lease payments receivable is reduced to $20,455 ($21,243 original balance, less $788). Therefore, the interest revenue earned during the *second* month of the lease (rounded to the nearest dollar) will be *$205* ($20,455 × 1%).[4]

Accounting by the Lessee (Kelly Grading Co.) Kelly Grading Co. also should use the present value of the lease payments to determine the cost of the tractor and the amount of the related liability, as follows:

Leased Equipment	21,243	
Lease Payment Obligation		21,243
To record acquisition of a tractor through a capital lease from Pace Tractor. Terms call for 24 monthly payments of $1,000, which include a 1% monthly interest charge.		

The entry on December 31 to record the first monthly lease payment (rounded to the nearest dollar) will be:

Interest Expense	212	
Lease Payment Obligation	788	
Cash		1,000
To record first monthly lease payment to Pace Tractor: $1,000 lease payment, less $212 interest expense ($21,243 × 1%), equals $788 reduction in lease payment obligation.		

Obligations for Postretirement Benefits

As we explain in the Supplemental Topic in Chapter 10, any unfunded obligation for postretirement benefits appears in the balance sheet at the *present value* of the expected future cash outlays to retired employees. The computation of this present value is so complex that it is performed by a professional actuary. But the present value of this obligation normally is far less than the expected future payments, as the cash payments will take place many years in the future.

Each year, the present value of an unfunded obligation for postretirement benefits will increase—as the future payment dates become closer. This steady growth in the present value of the unfunded obligation is recognized annually as part of the company's current postretirement benefits expense. (One might argue that the growth in this

---

[4] Both Pace Tractor and Kelly Grading Co. would prepare *amortization tables* showing the allocation of each lease payment between interest and the principal amount due.

liability actually represents interest expense. Nonetheless, the present value of the liability increases as the payment dates draw closer.)

Disclosure of Up-to-Date Present Value Information

Financial instruments originally are recorded in accounting records at (or near) their present values. But present values represent future cash flows discounted at *current* interest rates. Thus, as interest rates change, so do the present values of many financial instruments. (For the remainder of this discussion, we refer to present value determined under *current* market conditions as *current value*.)

Cash, investments in marketable securities, and postretirement obligations appear in the financial statements at current values. For most short-term instruments, current values remain quite close to the original carrying values. But for long-term financial instruments, such as bonds payable, current values may differ substantially from the amounts originally recorded.

The FASB requires companies to disclose the current values of financial instruments whenever these values *differ significantly* from the recorded amounts. These disclosures are most likely to affect long-term notes receivable and payable (including bonds payable) and long-term lease obligations.

In computing current value, current interest rates serve as the discount rate. Thus, as interest rates *rise,* current values *fall;* as interest rates *fall,* current values *rise*. The amount of change is greatest on long-term financial instruments for which the future cash flows are fixed—that is, not adjustable to reflect changes in interest rates.

The disclosure of current values can shed light on a company's past investing and financing activities. Assume, for example, that a company's long-term debt has a current value well *below* its carrying value in the company's balance sheet. This means that interest rates have *increased* since the company arranged this debt. Thus the company apparently arranged its long-term financing in a period of low interest rates—a good move.

Deferred Income Taxes

The only long-term liability *not* shown at the present value of the expected future payments is the obligation for deferred income taxes. Deferred taxes are treated differently because they do not involve a "contract" for future payments. Future payments of deferred taxes, if any, depend on the company's taxable income in future periods and also the corporate income tax laws in future years.

Many accountants believe that deferred income taxes *should* be shown at the estimated present value of the future outlays. This is not likely to happen, however, as the computations would be overwhelmingly complex.

In conclusion, the obligation for deferred income taxes is the only long-term liability that is *not* reported at its present value. Hence, one might argue that these obligations are overstated in terms of an equivalent number of today's dollars.

CAPITAL BUDGETING: ANOTHER APPLICATION OF PRESENT VALUE

Capital budgeting is the process of planning and evaluating proposals for capital expenditures, such as the acquisition of plant assets or the introduction of a new product line. Perhaps the most widely used approach in the evaluation of proposed capital expenditures is *discounting* the expected future cash flows to their *present value*.

Assume that Globe Mfg. Co. is considering a proposal to purchase new equipment in order to produce a new product. The equipment costs $400,000, has an estimated 10-year service life, and an estimated salvage value of $50,000. Globe estimates that production and sale of the new product will increase the company's annual net cash flows by $100,000 per year for the next 10 years. If Globe requires a 15% annual rate of return on investments of this nature, the present value of these cash flows may be computed as follows:

Present value of expected annual net cash inflows of $100,000 for 10 years, discounted at 15% per year: $100,000 × 5.019 (from Table PV–2)	$501,900
Present value of estimated salvage value to be received at the end of the tenth year: $50,000 × .247 (from Table PV–1)	12,350
Present value of estimated future cash inflows	$514,250
Less: Amount to be invested (already a present value)	400,000
Net present value of proposal	$114,250

My Notes

Is this project worth a $400,000 investment?

This analysis indicates that the present value of the expected net cash flows from this investment, discounted at an annual rate of 15%, amounts to $514,250. This is the maximum amount Globe could afford to invest in this project and still expect to earn the required 15% annual rate of return. As the cost of this investment is only $400,000, Globe can expect to earn more than its required 15% return.

The *net present value* of a proposal is the *difference* between the total present value of the future net cash flows and the cost of the investment. When the net present value is equal to zero, the investment provides a rate of return exactly equal to the rate used in discounting the cash flows. A *positive* net present value means that the investment provides a rate of return *greater* than the discount rate; a *negative* net present value means that the investment yields a return of *less* than the discount rate.

Since the discount rate usually is the minimum rate of return required by the investor, proposals with a positive net present value are considered acceptable, and those with a negative net present value are viewed as unacceptable.

ASSIGNMENT MATERIAL

DISCUSSION QUESTIONS

1. Explain what is meant by the phrase the *time value of money*.
2. Explain why the present value of a future amount is always *less* than the future amount.
3. Identify the two factors that determine the difference between the present value and the future amount of an investment.
4. Describe three basic investment applications of the concept of the time value of money.
5. Briefly explain the relationships between present value and (a) the length of time until the future cash flow occurs, and (b) the discount rate used in determining present value.
6. Define *financial instruments*. Explain the valuation concept used in initially recording financial instruments in financial statements.
7. Are normal accounts receivable and accounts payable financial instruments? Are these items shown in the balance sheet at their present values? Explain.
8. Identify three financial instruments shown in financial statements at present values that may *differ significantly* from the sum of the expected future payments or receipts.
9. What is the only long-term liability that is *not* recorded at its present value? What are the implications in terms of today's dollars?
10. Assuming no change in the expected amount of future cash flows, what factors may cause the present value of a financial instrument to change? Explain fully.
11. Define *capital budgeting*. Explain briefly how the present value concept relates to capital budgeting decisions.

PROBLEMS

PROBLEM B.1
Using Future Amount Tables
LO 1, 2, 4

Use Table FA–1 (in Exhibit B–2) and Table FA–2 (in Exhibit B–4) to determine the future amounts of the following investments:
a. $20,000 is invested for 10 years, at 6% interest, compounded annually.
b. $100,000 is to be received five years from today, at 10% annual interest.
c. $10,000 is invested in a fund at the end of each of the next 10 years, at 8% interest, compounded annually.
d. $50,000 is invested initially, plus $5,000 is invested annually at the end of each of the next three years, at 12% interest, compounded annually.

PROBLEM B.2
Bond Sinking Fund
LO 3, 4

Tilman Company is required by a bond indenture to make equal annual payments to a bond sinking fund at the end of each of the next 20 years. The sinking fund will earn 8% interest and must accumulate to a total of $500,000 at the end of the 20-year period.

Instructions
a. Calculate the amount of the annual payments.
b. Calculate the total amount of interest that will be earned by the fund over the 20-year period.
c. Make the general journal entry to record redemption of the bond issue at the end of the 20-year period, assuming that the sinking fund is recorded on Tilman's accounting records at $500,000 and bonds payable are recorded at the same amount.
d. What would be the effect of an increase in the rate of return on the required annual payment? Explain.

PROBLEM B.3
Using Present Value Tables
LO 1, 2, 5

Use Table PV–1 (in Exhibit B–7) and Table PV–2 (in Exhibit B–9) to determine the present value of the following cash flows:
a. $15,000 to be paid annually for 10 years, discounted at an annual rate of 6%. Payments are to occur at the end of each year.
b. $9,200 to be received today, assuming that the money will be invested in a 2-year certificate of deposit earning 8% annually.
c. $300 to be paid monthly for 36 months, with an additional "balloon payment" of $12,000 due at the end of the thirty-sixth month, discounted at a monthly interest rate of $1\frac{1}{2}\%$. The first payment is to be one month from today.
d. $25,000 to be received annually for the first three years, followed by $15,000 to be received annually for the next two years (total of five years in which collections are received), discounted at an annual rate of 8%. Assume collections occur at year-end.

PROBLEM B.4
Present Value and Bond Prices
LO 3, 5, 6

On June 30 of the current year, Rural Gas & Electric Co. issued $50,000,000 face value, 9%, 10-year bonds payable, with interest dates of December 31 and June 30. The bonds were issued at a discount, resulting in an effective *semiannual* interest rate of 5%.

Instructions
a. Compute the issue price for the bond that results in an effective semiannual interest rate of 5%. (*Hint:* Discount both the interest payments and the maturity value over 20 semiannual periods.)
b. Prepare a journal entry to record the issuance of the bonds at the sales price you computed in part a.
c. Explain why the bonds were issued at a discount.

PROBLEM B.5
Valuation of a Note Payable
LO 3, 5, 6

On December 1, Showcase Interiors purchased a shipment of furniture from Colonial House by paying $10,500 cash and issuing an installment note payable in the face amount of $28,800. The note is to be paid in 24 monthly installments of $1,200 each. Although the note makes no mention of an interest charge, the rate of interest usually charged to Showcase Interiors in such transactions is $1\frac{1}{2}\%$ per month.

Problems

Instructions

a. Compute the present value of the note payable, using a discount rate of $1\frac{1}{2}\%$ per month.

b. Prepare the journal entries in the accounts of Showcase Interiors on:
   1. December 1, to record the purchase of the furniture (debit Inventory).
   2. December 31, to record the first $1,200 monthly payment on the note and to recognize interest expense for one month by the effective interest method. (Round interest expense to the nearest dollar.)

c. Show how the liability for this note would appear in the balance sheet at December 31. (Assume that the note is classified as a current liability.)

PROBLEM B.6

Capital Leases: A Comprehensive Problem

LO 3, 5, 6

Custom Truck Builders frequently uses long-term lease contracts to finance the sale of its trucks. On November 1, 2002, Custom Truck Builders leased to Interstate Van Lines a truck carried in the perpetual inventory records at $33,520. The terms of the lease call for Interstate Van Lines to make 36 monthly payments of $1,400 each, beginning on November 30, 2002. The present value of these payments, after considering a built-in interest charge of 1% per month, is equal to the regular $42,150 sales price of the truck. At the end of the 36-month lease, title to the truck will transfer to Interstate Van Lines.

Instructions

a. Prepare journal entries for 2002 in the accounts of Custom Truck Builders on:
   1. November 1, to record the sale financed by the lease and the related cost of goods sold. (Debit Lease Payments Receivable for the $42,150 present value of the future lease payments.)
   2. November 30, to record receipt of the first $1,400 monthly payment. (Prepare a compound journal entry that allocates the cash receipt between interest revenue and reduction of Lease Payments Receivable. The portion of each monthly payment recognized as interest revenue is equal to 1% of the balance of the account Lease Payments Receivable, at the beginning of that month. Round all interest computations to the nearest dollar.)
   3. December 31, to record receipt of the second monthly payment.

b. Prepare journal entries for 2002 in the accounts of Interstate Van Lines on:
   1. November 1, to record acquisition of the leased truck.
   2. November 30, to record the first monthly lease payment. (Determine the portion of the payment representing interest expense in a manner parallel to that described in part **a**.)
   3. December 31, to record the second monthly lease payment.
   4. December 31, to recognize depreciation on the leased truck through year-end. Compute depreciation expense by the straight-line method, using a 10-year service life and an estimated salvage value of $6,150.

c. Compute the net carrying value of the leased truck in the balance sheet of Interstate Van Lines at December 31, 2002.

d. Compute the amount of Interstate Van Lines' lease payment obligation at December 31, 2002.

PROBLEM B.7

Valuation of a Note Receivable with an Unrealistic Interest Rate

LO 5, 6

On December 31, Richland Farms sold a tract of land, which had cost $930,000, to Skyline Developers in exchange for $150,000 cash and a five-year, 4% note receivable for $900,000. Interest on the note is payable annually, and the principal amount is due in five years. The accountant for Richland Farms did not notice the unrealistically low interest rate on the note and made the following entry on December 31 to record this sale.

Cash	150,000	
Notes Receivable	900,000	
Land		930,000
Gain on Sale of Land		120,000
Sold land to Skyline Developers in exchange for cash and five-year note with interest due annually.		

Instructions

a. Compute the present value of the note receivable from Skyline Developers at the date of sale, assuming that a realistic rate of interest for this transaction is 12%. (*Hint:* Consider both the annual interest payments and the maturity value of the note.)

b. Prepare the journal entry on December 31 to record the sale of the land correctly. Show supporting computations for the gain or loss on the sale.

c. Explain what effects the error made by Richland Farms' accountant will have on (1) the net income in the year of the sale and (2) the combined net income of the next five years. Ignore income taxes.

NAME INDEX

Abercrombie & Fitch, 260
Ace Hardware Stores, 235
Adolph Coors, 308
Albertsons, 307
Aluminum Company of America (Alcoa), 273, 463, 618, 623
Amazon.com, 598, 663
America Online (AOL), 3, 12, 25
American Airlines, 72, 164, 273, 536
American Cancer Society, 16, 17
American Express, 284, 285
American Greetings, 456
Amoco Corporation, 674
AOL, 3, 12, 25
Apple Computer, 126, 132, 276, 304, 339, 456
ARCO, 536
AT&T, 462, 469, 536, 751
Atlantic Richfield Company (ARCO), 536
Avis Rent-a-Car, 172

B.F. Goodrich, 659
Barbie, 687, 688
Beach House, 570
Bell Atlantic, 612
BellSouth NYNEX, 612
Benckiser, Inc., 759
Black & Decker, 508
Blockbuster Entertainment Corporation, 657
Blockbuster Video, 657
Bloomberg, 316
Boeing, 34, 222, 329, 498, 697
Bolsa Mexicana de Valore, 274, 467
Bonds-Online, 457
Boston Celtics, 747
Bounty, 618
Bridgestone/Firestone, 18
Bristol-Myers/Squibb, 646

California Public Employees Retirement System, 34
Campbell Soup Company, 100
Carnival Corporation, 58, 135, 156, 164
Carrefour, 669, 670, 685, 690
Carte Blanche, 285
Caterpillar, 697
Central Hudson Gas & Electric Corporation, 266
Central Intelligence Agency (CIA), 697
China Airlines, 34
Chrysler, 37, 373, 380
Circuit City, 175, 192, 214
Cisco Systems, 41
Citicorp, 295, 498
Club Med., Inc., 456
Coca-Cola, 289, 290, 386, 387, 598
Comp USA, 354
ConAgra, 623
Consolidated Edison, 471
Consolidated Freightlines, 381
Coopers & Lybrand, 746
Cover Girl, 618

Critical Path Inc., 133
CSFB Direct, 274
CVS, 223

Dac-Easy, 192
Daewoo Motor Co., 499
DaimlerChrysler, 621
Dawson, Chester, 703
Dell Computer, 273, 276, 329
Dixie Group, 506
Dow Chemical, 381, 463
Dun & Bradstreet, 434, 607n, 613, 639
DuPont, 409, 433, 436

E. I. duPont de Nemours & Co., 409, 433, 436
EDGAR, 84, 361
Elgin, Ben, 133
Enron, 360
Excel, 192
ExxonMobil, 463, 616

Famous San Diego Chicken, 751
Federal Express (FedEx), 53, 367, 390, 623
Federal Trade Commission, 9
Fleming, 339
Folgers, 618
Food Lion, 400
Foodtown, 235
Ford Motor Company, 215, 342, 343, 353, 354, 381, 469, 621
Fortune, 540
Frito-Lay, 602
Fruit of the Loom, 605

Gap, Inc., 259
Gateway, 276, 354
General Electric, 153
General Mills, 466, 672
General Mills Canada, 672
General Motors, 102, 222, 273, 299, 300, 440, 456, 463, 464, 499, 621, 751
Georgia Pacific, 536
Getty, J. Paul, 101
Giannoulas, Ted, 751
Gogoi, Pallavi, 663
Goodyear Tire and Rubber, 659
Gravity Syndicate, 744
Gross, Neil, 405
Guess, Inc., 331

H. J. Heinz, 53, 399, 547
Harrah's Entertainment, 543, 544, 572
Henry, David, 3, 173, 216, 457
Hershey's, 172
Hofstede, G., 674n
Hollywood Park Companies, 456
Home Depot, 503, 517, 522
Huffy Corporation, 307

IBM, 222, 430, 462, 477, 616, 751
Intel, 10, 41, 65, 75
International Aerospace Machinists, 34

J.C. Penney, 102, 273, 339, 340
Johnson & Johnson, 601, 640

KG Instruments International, 223
Kmart, 102

Lands' End, 475
Limited Too, 260
Litton Industries, 559

Maizena, 672
MasterCard, 284, 285
Mattel, 687
Mazda Motor Corp., 676
McDonald's, 84, 386, 614, 663
McDonnell Douglas, 498
McKesson HBOC, 173
Media General Financial Services, 613
Merck, 299, 300, 569, 646
Merrill Lynch, 274
Microsoft, 41, 56, 263, 273, 288, 306, 469, 479, 484, 618, 757
Minnesota Power, 286
Minuit, Peter, 726
Moody's Investors Service, 639

NASDAQ, 540
National Association of Foreign Trade Zones, 703
Neiman-Marcus, 102
Nestlé, 672
New York Bond Exchange, 419
New York Stock Exchange, 274
New York Times Company, 456
Nikon, 697
Nordstrom, 102

Occidental Petroleum, 456
Oshkosh B' Gosh, 342

Pacific Bell (PacBell), 418
Pacific Telesis, 612
Pampers, 618
Pan American Airways, 616
Papa John's Pizza, 273
Parker Hannifin, 649
PCQUOTE, 540
Peachtree, 192
Pennsylvania Power Company, 307
PepsiCo, 89, 116, 602
Pfizer, 273
Pharmecia, 677
Philadelphia Electric, 478
Pre-Paid Legal Services, 173
Price, Samuel, 746
Price Waterhouse, 746

743

PricewaterhouseCoopers, 21, 602, 616, 746
Procter & Gamble, 16, 56, 463, 555, 618, 623, 759
Promodès, 690

Quaker Oats, 353, 538
Quanex Corporation, 497

Remco Business Products, 571
Renault, 441
Rite Aid, 221, 222, 244
Robert Morris Associates, 607n
Rowe Companies, 567, 585
Rutgers University, 37

Safeway, 319, 341, 354, 361, 410, 654
Salomon Smith Barney, 274
Schwartz, Bill, 429n
Sears, Roebuck & Co., 223, 293, 339, 419, 461, 485, 508, 618
Smartdisk Corp., 685
Sony, 5, 21, 386, 754

Sprint, 649
Standard & Poor's, 434, 639
Staples, 361, 499
Stockmaster, 663

Target Corporation, 615
Teléfonos de México, 45
Texas Instruments, 598
3M, 286, 618
Thrifty Rent-A-Car, 380
Tice, David W., 663
Tickle-Me-Elmo, 571
Tokyo Stock Exchange, 274
Tootsie Roll Industries, 36, 75, 76, 176, 180, 182, 254, 309, 355, 401, 452, 494, 520, 531, 588, 602, 613, 650, 665–667, 701–702, 705–723
Toyota, 697
Toys 'R' Us, 571, 599
Tropicana, 602
Trump, Donald, 420
TRW, 745
Tucson Electric Power, 479

U.S. Steel, 381
UAL Corporation, 145
Union Carbide, 536
United Airlines, 145
Upjohn, 677

Value Line Investment, 639
Ventitex Inc., 499
Visa, 284, 285

Wal-Mart, 102, 223, 234, 339, 669, 670, 675, 682, 690
Walt Disney Company, 102
Want Want Holdings, 672
Waterhouse, Edwin, 746
Wausau Paper Mills, 456
Wells Fargo, 456
Wendy's, 614, 663
Westinghouse Electric, 305

Yahoo!, 216, 386

SUBJECT INDEX

AAA, 22
Accelerated depreciation, 373
Accommodation endorsement, 433n
Account, 91
Accountability, 90
Accounting
  careers, 25–28
  language of business, as, 4
  stepping stone, as, 28
  user's perspective, 4
Accounting careers, 25–28
Accounting changes, 508–509
Accounting cycle, 88–219
  adjusted trial balance, 155
  adjusting entries; *see* Adjusting entries
  after-closing trial balance, 188
  closing entries, 182–187
  posting, 96–99
  preparing financial statements, 176–180
  recording transactions, 93–96
  steps in process, 191–192
  trial balance, 115–116
Accounting education, 27
Accounting equation, 48, 54, 55
Accounting information, 4–6
  external users, 8–9
  financial, 8–10
  integrity of, 19–25
  internal, 15–19
  internal users, 15
  timeliness, 17–18
  types, 5–6
Accounting period, 101
Accounting principles, 19, 45–46
Accounting process, 5
Accounting records, 90
Accounting system, 6–8
Accounts payable, 411
Accounts receivable, 275–285
  allowance for doubtful accounts, 277–278
  confirmation process, 287
  credit card sales, 284–285
  direct write-off method, 282–283
  estimating, 278
  estimating credit losses, 279–282
  factoring, 284
  financial analysis, 286–287
  income tax regulations, 283
  internal controls, 283
  management of, 283–284
  recovery of receivable previously written off, 279
  uncollectible accounts, 276–277
  valuation, 282
  writing off uncollectible accounts, 278–279
Accounts receivable aging schedule, 280
Accounts receivable ledger, 225
Accounts receivable turnover rate, 286, 633–634
Accrual basis of accounting, 104, 547
Accrual of interest, 295

Accrue, 147
Accrued liabilities, 413
Accumulated depletion, 389
Accumulated depreciation, 144, 372
Acid-test ratio, 611
Actuary, 438
Additional paid-in capital, 469
Adequate disclosure, 63–64, 180–182, 738
Adjusted trial balance, 155
Adjusting entries, 134–173
  accruing income taxes expense, 150–151
  accruing uncollected revenue, 149
  accruing unpaid expenses, 148–149
  characteristics, 137–139
  converting assets to expenses, 140–145
  converting liabilities to revenue, 145–147
  effects of, 153–155
  matching principle, 152
  materiality, 152–153
  need for, 136
  realization principle, 151
  types, 136–137
Advance collections, 146
After-closing trial balance, 188
Aging the accounts receivable, 280
AICPA, 21–22
AICPA code of professional conduct, 24
Allowance for doubtful accounts, 277–278
American Accounting Association (AAA), 22
American Institute of CPAs (AICPA), 21–22
Amortization, 383, 389
Amortization table, 416–418, 735
Analytical measurements; *see* Financial analysis; Ratio analysis
Annual financial statements, 11
Annual report, 612–613, 705–723
Annual Statement Studies, 607n
Articles of incorporation, 465
Articulation, 43, 59
Audit, 21
Average-cost method, 322–323, 326, 328, 334
Average number of days to sell inventory, 340

Bad debts, 276–282
Baksheesh, 688
Balance sheet, 180
  assets, 44–47
  classified, 608–610
  liabilities, 47
  owner's equity, 47–48
  report form, 180
  statement of cash lows, 559
  stockholders' equity, 469, 521–522
Balance sheet approach, 280–281
Bank credit cards, 285
Bank service charges, 270
Bank statement, 268–269
Bankruptcy, 434
Bar coded merchandise, 234
Basic earnings per share, 513

Bearer bonds, 419n
Big Bang rules, 676
Black Monday, 483n
Board of directors, 466
Bond discount, 423–426
Bond premium, 426–429
Bonds, 418–432, 631
  after issuance, 430
  defined, 418
  discount/premium, 423
  early retirement, 431
  interest rates, and, 430, 431n
  issuance, 419
  issued between interest dates, 422
  market price, 735–736
  present value, 429–430
  quoted market prices, 419
  tax advantages, 420
  transferability, 419
  types, 419–420
  volatility, 430
Book value, 144, 372, 479
Book value per share, 475–476, 639
Bookkeeping, 27–28
Bribery, 688
Budgeting, 568–569
Buildings, 369
Business entity, 44
Buyback programs, 483

Call price, 419, 472
Call provision, 472
Callable bond, 419
Callable preferred stock, 472
Capital budgeting, 738–739
Capital expenditures, 370–371
Capital lease, 437, 438, 736–737
Capital stock, 63, 463
Capitalize, 370
Careers in accounting, 25–28
Carrying value, 144, 372
Cash
  balance sheet treatment, 265–266
  bank reconciliation, 269–272
  bank statements, 268–269
  budget, 273
  disbursements, 268
  internal control, 267–268
  management of, 266–267
  petty cash, 273
  statement of cash flows, 266
Cash and cash equivalents, 265
Cash basis accounting, 104, 552
Cash budget, 273, 568–569
Cash disbursements, 268
Cash discount, 237
Cash dividends, 513–515
Cash equivalents, 265, 547
Cash flow analysis, 636–637
Cash flow management, 568–571

745

Subject Index

Cash flow prospects, 9
Cash flow statement; *see* Statement of cash flows
Cash management, 266–267
Certificate in financial management (CFM), 22
Certificate of internal auditing (CIA), 23
Certificate of Management Accounting (CMA), 23
Certified public accountants (CPAs), 23
CFM, 22
CFO, 26, 466
Chaebol, 674
Changes in accounting principles, 508–509
Changes in estimates, 509
Check authorization, 268
Check register, 236
Chief financial officer (CFO), 26, 466
CIA, 23
Classified balance sheet, 608–610
Classified financial statements, 602
Closely held corporations, 464
Closing entries, 182–187
   closing process, summarized, 187
   dividends account, 186
   expense accounts, 184–185
   income summary account, 185–186
   periodic inventory system, 232–233
   perpetual inventory system, 230
   revenue accounts, 183–184
CMA, 23
Code of professional conduct, 24
Collateral, 410
Collectivism, 675
Commitments, 433
Common size income statement, 606
Common stock, 470, 478
Comparable store sales, 242
Comparative financial statements, 602, 603
Compensating balance, 265
Competence, 22, 23, 24
Complementary products, 571
Complete physical count, 230
Component percentages, 605–606
Compound interest, 725
Comprehensive income, 519–520
Concentration of credit risk, 287
Conceptual framework, 20
Confidentiality, 24
Confirmation process, 287
Conservatism, 104, 282
Consistency
   depreciation, 379–380
   inventory valuation, 328
Consolidated financial statements, 602
Contingencies, 432–433
Contra-asset account, 144
Contra-liability account, 424
Contra-revenue account, 240, 241
Contributed capital, 468
Control; *see* Internal control
Controller, 26, 466
Controlling accounts, 225, 246
Conversion privilege, 472
Convertible preferred stock, 472–473
Copyright, 387
Corporate charter, 465
Corporate officers, 466
Corporate organization chart, 467
Corporations, 42, 61–62, 460–500, 749–759
   accounting (investor/issuer), 477
   advantages/disadvantages, 462
   authorization/issuance of stock, 468–470
   board of directors, 466
   book value per share, 475–476
   closely held, 464
   common stock, 470, 478
   donated capital, 475
   double taxation, 757
   financial analysis, 484
   formation, 464–465
   income tax, 751–753
   incorporating established business, 758–759
   market value, 477–479
   officers, 466
   organization chart, 467
   paid-in capital, 468–477
   preferred stock, 470–473, 478
   publicly owned, 464
   S, 758
   sources of equity, 474
   stock buyback programs, 483
   stock issued for assets other than cash, 473–474
   stock split, 480
   stockholder records, 467–468
   stockholders' rights, 465–466
   subscriptions to capital stock, 475
   treasury stock, 480–483
   why incorporate, 463
Corrupt practices, 688–689
Cost accounting, 27
Cost flow assumptions, 322–328
Cost layer, 321
Cost of goods sold, 223, 320, 332, 337–338; *see also* Inventory
Cost of producing accounting information, 7
Cost principle, 45
Cost ratio, 337
Coupon bonds, 419n
CPAs, 23
Credit, 91
Credit balance, 91–92
Credit card draft, 284
Credit card sales, 284–285
Credit losses, 279–282
Credit rating, 434
Credit risk, 287, 614
Credit terms, 236–237
Creditors, 47, 410
Creditors' claims, 410, 434
Creditworthiness, 434–436
Cross-border financing, 677
Cultural mindsets, 675
Culture, 674–676
Cumulative preferred stock, 471–472
Currency fluctuations, 684–685
Current assets, 180, 609–610
Current liabilities, 180, 411–414, 610
   accounts payable, 411
   accrued liabilities, 413
   current portion of long-term debt, 413
   notes payable, 411–411
   payroll liabilities, 413–414
   unearned revenue, 414
Current portion of long-term debt, 413, 418
Current ratio, 190, 436, 611, 635, 638
Custodian (petty cash), 273
Customer ledger, 225
Cutoff of transactions, 331

Date of declaration, 514
Date of record, 514
Debenture bond, 419
Debit, 91
Debit balance, 91–92
Debit-credit rules, 92, 105
Debt, 410, 435
Debt-paying ability, 436
Debt ratio, 436, 611–612, 631, 632, 638
Debt service, 416
Decelerated depreciation methods, 392
Declining-balance method, 376–378
Deferred charges, 387
Deferred income taxes, 440–441, 738
Deferred revenue, 145–146
Deflation, 46
Delivery expenses, 241
Demand liabilities, 410n
Departmental profit margin, 243
Depletion, 389
Deposits in transit, 270
Depreciable assets, 142
Depreciation, 142–145, 371–380, 389
   causes, 372
   consistency, 379–380
   decelerated methods, 392
   declining-balance method, 376–378
   double-declining-balance method, 376–377
   financial statement disclosure, 379–380
   fractional periods, 375–376
   half-year convention, 375–376
   MACRS, 391
   150%-declining-balance method, 377
   revision of estimated useful lives, 380
   straight-line method, 374–376
   SYD, 391
   unit-of-output, 391
   usage of, by businesses, 378, 392
Depreciation process, 143, 371
Depreciation rate, 375
Diluted earnings per share, 513
Direct method, 548–561
Direct write-off method, 282–283
Disclosure, 63–64, 180–182, 738
Discontinued operations, 506
Discount period, 237
Discount rate, 429, 731
Discounting, 295, 730
Dividend dates, 514–515
Dividend yield, 478, 627, 639
Dividends, 105, 179, 754–755
   cash, 513–515
   dates, 514–515
   liquidity, 515
   stock, 515–518
Dividends in arrears, 472
Dollar/percentage changes, 603–604
Donated capital, 475
Double-declining balance, 376–377
Double-entry accounting, 93

Subject Index

Double taxation, 462, 757
Drawing account, 745

Earnings per share (EPS), 484, 509–513, 619–620, 638
Earnings statement; *see* Income statement
Earnings, quality of, 607
Economic systems, 674
Effective interest rate, 429
Employee withholdings, 414
EPS, 484, 509–513, 619–620, 638
Equipment, 369
Estimated liabilities, 432
Estimated useful life, 143
Ethical conduct, 24
Exchange rates, 679–680, 685–686
Ex-dividend date, 514
Expanded accounting equation, 54, 55
Expenses, 55, 103
Exporting, 671
External financial reporting, 9–10
External users, 8–9
Externally reported information, 13–15
Extraordinary items, 506–507

F.O.B. destination, 332
F.O.B. shipping point, 332
Facilitating payments, 689
Factor, 284
Factoring, 284
FASB, 20
FCPA, 688–689
FIFO, 323–324, 326, 328, 334
Film rights, 387
Financial accounting, 5
Financial accounting information, 8–10
Financial Accounting Standards Board (FASB), 20
Financial analysis, 60–61, 190, 600–667
  accounting methods, 341
  accounts receivable, 286–287
  component percentages, 605–606
  corporations, 484
  debt, 608
  dollar/percentage changes, 603–604
  earnings per share, 512
  financial assets, 285–287
  financial statements, 602
  illustration, 623–637
  inventory, 339–341
  liabilities, 435–436
  merchandising companies, 242–243
  quality of assets, 608
  quality of earnings, 607–608
  R&D costs, 388
  ratios, 606; *see also* Ratio analysis
  standards of comparison, 606–607
  statement of cash flows, 566–567
  trend percentages, 604–605
Financial assets, 262–317
  accounts receivable, 275–285; *see also* Accounts receivable
  cash, 265–273; *see also* Cash
  defined, 264
  financial analysis, 285–287
  marketable securities; *see* Short-term investments

Financial assets—*Cont.*
  notes receivable, 292–296
  valuation, 264–265
Financial forecast, 26
Financial instruments, 733
Financial ratios, 610–614
Financial statement articulation, 59
Financial statements, 11–13, 40–86
  annual, 11
  balance sheet; *see* Balance sheet
  cash flow statement; *see* Statement of cash flows
  classified, 602
  comparative, 602, 603
  consolidated, 603
  defined, 11
  income statement; *see* Income statement
  interim, 11, 191
  management, and, 64–65
  outsiders, and, 63–64
  preparing, 177–180
  relationship among, 58–60, 180–182
  year-to-date, 190
Financing activities, 546, 551, 558–559
Financing lease, 437
First-in, first-out (FIFO), 323–324, 326, 328, 334
Fiscal year, 101
Fixed-percentage-of-declining-balance depreciation, 376
Flow assumption, 321–328
Foreign Corrupt Practices Act (FCPA), 688–689
Foreign currencies/companies, 680–684
Foreign trade zones, 673
Formulas, 387
Franchises, 386–387
Free cash flow, 566–567, 638
Fundamental analysis, 639
Future amount, 726–730
Future amount of annuity, 728–729
Future contracts, 685
Future value tables, 727

GAAP, 19
Gain, 290
General Accounting Office (GAO), 27
General credit obligations, 410
General journal, 96
General ledger software, 194
General partner, 747
General partnership, 747
General-purpose information, 14
Generally accepted accounting principles (GAAP), 19
Global business and accounting, 668–704
  consolidated financial statements, 686
  culture, 674–676
  currency fluctuations, 684–685
  economic systems, 674
  exchange rates, 679–680, 685–686
  FCPA, 688–689
  foreign currency/companies, 680–684
  global sourcing, 686–688
  globalization, 670–671
  hedging, 685
  political/legal systems, 672–674
  standards, 677–678
  technology/infrastructure, 676–677

Global sourcing, 686–688
Globalization, 670–671
Going-concern assumption, 45
Goods in transit, 332
Goodwill, 383–386
Government accounting, 27
Gross profit, 223
Gross profit margin, 242–244
Gross profit method, 337–338
Gross profit rate, 242, 617–618, 638

Half-year convention, 375, 376
Harmonization of accounting standards, 677
Hedging, 685
Huilu, 688

IASB, 677
IIA, 22
IMA, 22
Immaterial, 152
Income statement, 55–56, 100–103, 177–179
  accounting periods, 101
  classifications, 615–616
  common size, 600
  earnings per share, 511
  expenses, 103
  financial assets, 288
  inventory valuation, 335–336
  limitations, 179
  merchandising company, 223
  multiple-step, 617–620
  net income/loss, 99, 100
  partnerships, 761–762
  revenue, 102
  single-step, 620–621
Income statement approach, 281–282
Income summary, 183–186
Income tax; *see* Taxes
Indenture contract, 410
Indirect method, 559–566
Individualism, 675
Industrial organizations, 674
Industry information, 607n, 613
Industry standards, 607
Inflation, 46, 617
Influence peddling, 689
Information needs, 7
Infrastructure, 677
Installment notes payable, 416–418
Institute of Internal Auditors (IIA), 22
Institute of Management Accountants (IMA), 22
Insurance policies, 141
Intangible assets, 383–388
  amortization, 383
  copyright, 387
  franchises, 386–387
  goodwill, 383–386
  operating expenses, 383
  other assets, 387
  patents, 386
  R&D costs, 388
  trademarks/trade names, 386
Integrity, 19, 23, 24
Interest accrual, 295
Interest-bearing receivable/payables, 734
Interest coverage ratio, 434, 436, 631–632, 638
Interest expense, 148

Subject Index

Interim financial statements, 12, 191
Internal auditing, 27
Internal control
 cash, 267–268
 receivables, 283
Internal control structure, 21
Internal Revenue Service (IRS), 27
Internal users, 15
International Accounting Standards Board (IASB), 677
International business; see Global business and accounting
International joint venture, 671
International licensing, 671
International Organization of Securities Commissions (IOSCO), 678, 702
Inventory, 222; see also Periodic inventory system; Perpetual inventory system
 average-cost method, 322–323, 326, 328, 334
 consistency, 328
 cost flow assumptions, 322–328
 defined, 320
 errors, 335–337
 estimating ending, 337–338
 FIFO, 323–324, 326, 328, 334
 financial analysis, 339–341
 income statement, 335–336
 JIT systems, 328–329
 LCM rule, 331
 LIFO, 324–325, 328, 334–335
 overstatement/understatement, 336–337
 physical, 330
 shrinkage losses, 330
 specific identification, 322, 325–326, 328, 333
 write down, 330–331
Inventory errors, 335–337
Inventory shrinkage, 230, 329, 330
Inventory subsidiary ledger, 229
Inventory turnover rate, 339–340, 634, 638
Investing activities, 546, 549, 556–557
Invoice approval form, 268
IOSCO, 678, 702
Irregular items, 505–508
IRS, 27
Issued shares, 468

JIT inventory system, 328–329
Jobs (accounting), 25–28
Journal, 96
Judgment, 22, 23
Junk bonds, 420
Just-in-time (JIT) inventory system, 328–329

Keiretsu, 674
Key Business Ratios, 607n
Kitu kidogo, 688

Land, 369
Land improvements, 369
Last-in, first-out (LIFO), 324–325, 328, 334–335
LCM rule, 331
Lease, 437
Lease payment obligations, 437–438, 736–737
Ledger, 90–91
Ledger account, 91
Legal capital, 469

Lessee, 437
Lessor, 437
Leverage, 435, 630
Liabilities, 47, 408–459
 bonds, 418–432; see also Bonds
 commitments, 433
 current, 411–414; see also Current liabilities
 deferred income taxes, 440–441
 estimated, 432
 financial analysis, 435–436
 installment notes payable, 416–418
 lease payment obligations, 437–438
 long-term, 415–432
 loss contingency, 432–433
 nature of, 410–411
 pensions, 438–439
 postretirement benefits, 438–439
LIFO, 324, 328, 334–335
LIFO reserve, 342–343
Limited liability, 61
Limited liability partnership, 748
Limited partner, 747
Limited partnership, 614n, 747
Limited personal liability, 463
Line of credit, 266, 636
Liquidating dividend, 515
Liquidation of LIFO reserve, 342
Liquidity, 63, 189, 608, 614
Loan guarantee, 433n, 757, 614–615
Long-term liabilities, 415–432
Long-term orientation, 675
Loss, 290
Loss contingencies, 432–433
Lower-of-cost-or-market (LCM) rule, 331

MACRS, 376n, 391
Maker, 292
Management accounting, 5, 26
Management strategy (earnings numbers), 505
Management's discussion and analysis, 613
Manufacturers, 222
Maquiladora, 673
Mark-to-market, 274–275, 290–292
Market economy, 674
Market share, 617
Marketable securities, 298; see also Short-term investments
Matching principle, 103, 152
Materiality, 152–153
Maturity date, 293, 410
Maturity value, 293
Medicare taxes, 414n
Merchandising companies, 220–260
 accounting information needs, 223–224
 evaluation of, 242–243
 general ledger accounts, 224
 income statement, 223
 manufacturing companies, compared, 222
 periodic inventory system, 231–233; see also Periodic inventory system
 perpetual inventory system, 227–230; see also Perpetual inventory system
 purchases, 236–239
 retailers, 222–223
 sales, 239–249
 subsidiary ledger accounts, 224–226
 wholesalers, 223

Modified accelerated cost recovery system (MACRS), 376n, 391
Mortgage bond, 419
Moving average method, 322
Moving costs, 387
Multiple-step income statement, 617–620
Mutual agency, 747

n/30, 237
Name lists, 387
Natural resources, 388–389
Negative amortization, 416n
Negative cash flows, 43
Negative income tax, 151
Negative working capital, 610n
Net identifiable assets, 384
Net income, 55, 99, 619, 620, 756
Net income as percentage of sales, 638
Net income percentage, 190
Net loss, 55, 100
Net present value, 739
Net realizable value, 265
Net sales, 242
net 30 days, 237
No-par stock, 470
Non-GAAP earnings numbers, 505
Non-interest-bearing note, 734–735
Noncash charge or expense, 394
Noncash investing and financing transactions, 57
Noncumulative preferred stock, 472
Notes (accompanying financial statements), 180–181, 637
Notes payable, 411–413
Notes receivable, 292–296
NSF check, 270

Objective evidence, 104
Objectivity, 24, 104
Objectivity principle, 45–46
Obsolescence, 372
Off-balance-sheet financing, 437
Off-peak prices, 570
150% declining-balance method, 376, 377
Operating activities, 545–546, 549, 551–555
Operating cycle, 222, 340, 436, 634–635, 638
Operating expense ratio, 638
Operating income, 619, 638
Operating lease, 437, 438
Organization chart, 16
Organization costs, 465
Other comprehensive income, 519–520
Outside directors, 466
Outstanding checks, 270
Outstanding shares, 468
Over/understatement, 336–337
Owners' equity, 47–48, 62

p/e ratio, 512, 620, 627, 639
Paid-in capital, 468
Par value, 469
Parent company, 602
Participating preferreds, 473
Partners' equity, 62
Partnership contract, 749
Partnerships, 61, 62, 746–749, 760–766
 accounting practices, 748–749, 760–766
 allocating net return, 762–766

Partnerships—*Cont.*
  contract, 749
  evaluating financial statements, 749
  general, 747
  income statement, 761–762
  limited, 747–748
  limited liability, 748
  new, 760–761
  overview, 750
  statement of partners' equity, 762
Patent, 386
Payee, 292
Payroll liabilities, 413–414
Payroll taxes, 414
Peak pricing, 570
Pension fund, 438–439
Percentage changes, 604, 617
Periodic inventory system, 231–233, 332–335
  average cost, 334
  cost of goods sold, 231–232
  FIFO, 334
  LIFO, 334
  perpetual system, compared, 233
  purchases, 231
  selection criteria, 235
  specific identification, 333
  who uses them, 234
Perpetual inventory system, 227–230
  closing entries, 230
  collection of accounts receivable, 228–229
  inventory subsidiary ledger, 229
  modification, 339
  payment of accounts receivable, 228
  periodic system, compared, 233
  purchases, 227–228
  sales, 228
  selection criteria, 235
  taking a physical inventory, 229–230
  who uses them, 234
Petty cash, 273
Physical count, 229–230
Physical deterioration, 372
Physical inventory, 229–230, 330
Planned economy, 674
Plant assets, 368–382
  acquisition, 368–371
  building, 369
  capital vs. revenue expenditures, 370–371
  defined, 368
  depreciation, 371–380; *see also* Depreciation
  disposal, 380–382
  equipment, 369
  impairment, 380
  land, 369
  land improvements, 369
  lump-sum purchase, 369–370
  trade-ins, 382
Plant rearrangement costs, 387
Point-of-sale (POS) terminal, 236
POS terminal, 236
Positive cash flows, 43
Post-closing trial balance, 188
Posting, 96–99
Postretirement benefits, 438–439, 737
Power distance, 675
Predictive information, 504
Preferred stock, 470–473, 478

Prepaid expenses, 140
Present value, 384, 429, 730–733
Present value of annuity, 732–733
Present value tables, 731
Price-earnings (p/e) ratio, 512, 620, 627, 639
Principal amount, 411
Prior period adjustment, 518–519
Pro forma information, 505
Processes, 387
Product mix, 571
Professional competence, 22, 23, 24
Professional judgment, 22, 23
Professional organizations, 21–22
Profit and loss statement; *see* Income statement
Profit margin, 243–244
Profitability, 63, 188–189
Promissory note, 292
Provision for income taxes, 752
Proxy statements, 465
Proxy system, 466
Public accounting, 26
Public information, 464, 745
Publicly owned corporations, 464
Purchase discount, 237
Purchase discounts lost, 237
Purchase discounts taken, 238
Purchases
  credit terms/cash discounts, 236–238
  gross invoice price, 238
  purchase discounts taken, 238
  returns of unsatisfactory merchandise, 238–239
  transportation costs, 239

Quality of earnings, 607
Quarterly statements, 101
Quick assets, 611
Quick ratio, 436, 611, 635, 638

R&D costs, 388
Rate of inflation, 617
Ratio analysis, 606; *see also* Financial analysis
  financial ratios, 610–614
  long-term credit risk, 638
  market price of common stock, 639
  profitability, 621–623, 638–639
  short-term liquidity, 638
Realization principle, 102
Receivables; *see* Accounts receivable; Notes receivable
Receivables turnover rate, 638
Recording transactions
  ledger accounts, 93–96
  revenues/expenses, 105–115
Redeemable preferreds, 473
Regional value content, 673
Registered bonds, 419n
Report form, 180
Research and development (R&D) costs, 388
Residual value, 374
Restricted cash, 265
Restriction on retained earnings, 519
Restructuring charges, 508
Retail method, 338
Retailers, 222–223
Retained earnings, 63, 100, 179, 518–519, 754
Retirement pensions, 438

Return of investment, 9
Return on assets (ROA), 435n, 622, 629, 639
Return on common stockholders' equity, 484, 629–630, 639
Return on equity (ROE), 190, 435n, 484, 622–623, 639
Return on investment (ROI), 9, 621–622, 629
Revenue, 55, 102
Revenue expenditures, 370–371
ROA, 622
ROE, 622–623
ROI, 621–622, 629
Running balance, 97

S corporation, 758
Salaries expense, 147
Sales, 239–242
  delivery expenses, 241
  sales discounts, 240–241
  sales returns and allowances, 240
  sales taxes, 241–242
Sales discount, 237, 240–241
Sales per square foot of selling space, 242
Sales returns and allowances, 240
Sales taxes, 241–242
Salvage value, 374
Same-store sales, 242
SEC, 20
Secretary, 466
Secured claims, 632
Securities and Exchange Commission (SEC), 20
Segment of the business, 506
Shareholders, 462
Shareholders' rights, 465–466
Shop supplies, 140–141
Short-term investments, 273–275, 289–292
  financial statements, 292
  mark-to-market, 274–275, 290–292
  purchases, 289
  recognition of income, 289
  sales, 290
Short-term liquidity, 63
Short-term orientation, 675
Shrinkage losses, 230, 329, 330
Single-step income statement, 620–621
Sinking fund, 420
Social Security taxes, 414n
Sole proprietorship, 61, 62, 743–745, 750
Special journal, 236
Specific identification, 322, 325–326, 328, 333
Spreadsheet software, 194
Stable-dollar assumption, 46
Standard-setting bodies, 19–20
Standards for Professional Practice of Internal Auditing, 22
State of incorporation, 464
Stated value, 469
Statement of cash flows, 56–57, 542–599
  balance sheet, and, 559
  cash, 266
  cash/cash equivalents, 547, 551
  direct method, 548–561
  financial analysis, 566–567
  financial assets, 288
  financing activities, 546, 551, 558–559
  free cash flow, 566–567
  illustration, 548–559

Subject Index

Statement of cash flows—*Cont.*
   indirect method, 559–566
   investing activities, 546, 549, 556–557
   operating activities, 545–546, 549, 551–555
   plant transactions, 390
   sample statement, 565, 567–568
   supplementary schedules, 565–566
   worksheet, 572–577
Statement of financial position; *see* Balance sheet
Statement of operations; *see* Income statement
Statement of partners' equity, 748, 762
Statement of retained earnings, 179, 518–519
Statement of stockholders' equity, 520–521
Statements of Financial Accounting Standards, 20
Stock buyback programs, 483
Stock certificate, 465
Stock dividend, 515–518
Stock exchanges, 463n
Stock market, 463n
Stock registrar, 468
Stock split, 480, 517
Stock transfer agent, 468
Stockholders, 61, 462
Stockholders subsidiary ledger, 467–468
Stockholders' equity, 62, 469, 521–522
Stockholders' meetings, 465
Stockholders' rights, 465–566
Straight-line method of depreciation, 143, 374–376
Strong currency, 680
Subscriptions to capital stock, 475
Subsidiary, 602
Subsidiary ledger, 224–226
Subsidiary ledger accounts, 224
Substance over form, 415
Sum-of-the-years' digits (SYD), 391
Super preferreds, 473
Supplies expense, 140–141
SYD, 391

T account, 91
Take-home pay, 414
Taking a physical inventory, 229–230, 330
Tangible plant assets, 368
Tax accounting, 6
Tax planning, 757
Tax refunds, 151
Taxable income, 752
Taxes
   accounts receivable, 283
   accruing income tax expense, 150–151
   bond financing, 420
   corporations, 751–753
   deferred, 440–441, 570
   double taxation, 757
   mark-to-market, 292
   unprofitable periods, 151
10 eom, 237
Time period principle, 101
Time value of money, 724–742
   capital budgeting, 738–739
   disclosure, 738
   financial instruments, 733
   future amount, 726–730
   present value, 730–733
Timeliness, 17–18
Times interest earned (interest coverage ratio), 434, 436, 631–632, 638
Timing differences, 155; *see also* Adjusting entries
Trade accounts payable, 411
Trade names, 386
Trademarks, 386
Transferability of ownership, 61, 462
Translating the foreign currency, 679
Transportation in, 239
Treasurer, 466
Treasury stock, 480–483
Trend percentages, 604–605
Trial balance, 115–116

Turnover rates, 436, 633
2-for-1 stock split, 480
2/10, n/30, 237
200% declining-balance method, 376–377

Unaudited earnings numbers, 505
Uncertainty avoidance, 675
Uncollected revenue, 149
Uncollectible accounts, 276–277
Under/overstatement, 336–337
Underwriter, 419, 468
Unearned revenue, 145–146, 414
Units-of-output method of depreciation, 391
Unlimited liability, 61
Unpaid expenses, 147
Unrealized holding gain (loss) on investments, 274
Unusual gains/losses, 507
Useful life, 142

Vice-president, 466
Voucher, 268
Voucher system, 268
Vzyatka, 688

Wages expense, 147, 413
Weak currency, 680
What-if analysis, 196
Wholesalers, 223
Wholly owned international subsidiary, 671
Window dressing, 64, 613
Workers' compensation, 414
Working capital, 190, 436, 610, 632–633, 638
Worksheet, 192–196
Write-down, 330–331
Writing off uncollectible accounts, 278–279

Year-to-date financial statements, 190

Zero-coupon bonds, 429n

CHECK FIGURES FOR PROBLEMS

CHAPTER 1

No check figures required. Problem material is qualitative in nature.

CHAPTER 2

2.1 Total assets = $1,020,300; Total liabilities = $720,300
2.2 For part d—paid $14,500 of accounts payable.
2.3 Ending cash balance = $41,250
2.4 Ending cash balance = $42,600
2.5 Total assets = $553,080; Total liabilities = $215,850
2.6 Total assets = $1,001,470; Total liabilities = $622,050
2.7 Total assets (8/3) = $236,700; Total liabilities (8/3) = $91,000
2.8 Total assets (10/6) = $173,590; Cash balance (10/6) = $29,400
2.9 Total assets = $51,500; Total liabilities = $23,100
2.10 Total assets = $114,735; Total liabilities = $106,200

CHAPTER 3

3.1 Liabilities (Accounts Payable) increased (credited) $8,000 on 2/18.
3.2 Debit Accounts Payable $100 on 8/5.
3.3 Debit Advertising Expense $165 on 9/14.
3.4 Total stockholders equity (6/30) = $63,990
3.5 Total assets (5/31) = $579,400

CHAPTER 4

4.1 Adjusting entry (4): Debit Depreciation Expense: Carts, $1,000
4.2 Adjusting entry (7): Debit Unearned Camper Revenue, $900
4.3 Adjusting entry (3): Credit Unexpired Insurance, $500
4.4 Adjusting entry (1): Credit Prepaid Film Rental, $15,200
4.5 Net Income for the year ended 12/31/02 = $29,400
4.6 Owners' Equity is understated as a result of transaction g.

COMPREHENSIVE PROBLEM 1

Part d: Net Income on 9/30 = $9,000

CHAPTER 5

5.1 Retained earnings on 12/31/02 = $21,000
5.2 Total assets on 12/31/02 = $113,400
5.3 Net loss for the year ended 12/31/02 = $(31,240)
5.4 Net income for the quarter ended 9/30 = $54,800
5.5 Total assets on 12/31/02 = $139,770
5.6 Total debit column of balance sheet figures = $184,400
5.7 Total debit column of balance sheet figures = $377,250
5.8 Year-end current ratio = 2.21 to1

CHAPTER 6

6.1 Gross profit for year ended 12/31 = $327,968
6.2 Eight units on hand at 5/24 = $2,400
6.3 Change in net sales during 2001–2002 = 6%
6.4 Debit Cost of Goods Sold $294 on 6/15 (part 1)
6.5 Debit Cost of Goods Sold $6,000 on 2/9 (part a)
6.6 Cost of Goods Sold on 1/6 = $6,100

CHAPTER 7

7.1 Adjusted cash balance on 7/31 = $129,714
7.2 Adjusted cash balance on 11/30 = $15,745
7.3 Debit Uncollectible Accounts Expense $25,500 on 12/31
7.4 Debit Uncollectible Accounts Expense $160,000 on 12/31
7.5 Debit Loss on Sale of Investments $6,060 on 8/7 (part b)
7.6 Credit Interest Revenue $3,125 on 6/1 (part a)

COMPREHENSIVE PROBLEM 2

Part k: Net Income 12/31/2002 = $90,825

CHAPTER 8

8.1 Debit Cost of Goods Sold $30,200 on 1/15 (part 3)
8.2 Inventory balance on 9/30 (LIFO method) = $20,250
8.3 Inventory balance (FIFO method) = $20,300
8.4 Debit Cost of Goods Sold $1,208 (part a, average cost method)

- 8.5 Inventory balance (FIFO method) = $6,710
- 8.6 Gross profit percentage in 2002 = 36%
- 8.7 Estimated ending inventory (part a) = $52,800
- 8.8 Inventory turnover rate (part b) = 7.18 times

CHAPTER 9

- 9.1 Debit Depreciation Expense: Computing Equipment $27,100 (part d)
- 9.2 Depreciation Expense, 2007 = $10,000 (straight-line)
- 9.3 Depreciation Expense, 2005 = $1,231 (200% declining-balance)
- 9.4 Credit Gain on Sale of Plant Assets on 4/1, $550,000
- 9.5 No check figures given
- 9.6 Estimated goodwill of Phil's Garage = $1,362,500

CHAPTER 10

- 10.1 Income statement, transaction d: increase revenues, increase net income
- 10.2 Total current liabilities = $381,000
- 10.3 Debit Interest Expense on 12/31, $6,428
- 10.4 Debit Interest Expense on 11/1, $10,797
- 10.5 Debit Bond Interest Expense on 12/31, $166,667
- 10.6 Debit Bond Interest Expense on 12/31, $2,653,334 (part 2)
- 10.7 Total liabilities = $1,088,620 (part a)

CHAPTER 11

- 11.1 Total stockholders' equity on 12/31 = $3,805,000
- 11.2 Total stockholders' equity on 12/31 = $8,360,000
- 11.3 Total stockholders' equity on 12/31 = $2,452,000
- 11.4 Debit Organization Costs $7,000 on 1/7
- 11.5 Dividends per share of common stock (part h) = $4.25
- 11.6 Total paid-in capital (part c) = $180,329
- 11.7 No check figures given
- 11.8 Total stockholders' equity = $568,000
- 11.9 Total stockholders' equity = $6,695,000

CHAPTER 12

- 12.1 Net income = $10,260,000
- 12.2 Net income = $1,740,000
- 12.3 Net income = $336,000
- 12.4 Total stockholders' equity at 12/31 = $1,146,600
- 12.5 Total stockholders' equity at 12/31 = $4,795,300
- 12.6 Total stockholders' equity at 12/31 = $8,792,800
- 12.7 Event 4: increase current assets, stockholders' equity, and cash
- 12.8 Total stockholders' equity at 12/31/02 = $5,914,000
- 12.9 Net loss = $(28,401)

CHAPTER 13

- 13.1 Event "c" is an operating activity
- 13.2 Cash and cash equivalents at year-end = $412,000
- 13.3 Net cash used in investing activities = $(39,000)
- 13.4 Net cash used in investing activities = $(25,000)
- 13.5 Net cash flow from operating activities = $316,000
- 13.6 Net cash flow from operating activities = $316,000
- 13.7 Cash and cash equivalents, end of year = $164,000
- 13.8 Net decrease in cash for the year = $43,000
- 13.9 Net increase in cash for the year = $50,000

CHAPTER 14

- 14.1 Industry average net income as a percentage of sales = 4%
- 14.2 Net income for 2002 = $172,800
- 14.3 Total current liabilities = $227,600
- 14.4 Current ratio = 0.8 to 1
- 14.5 Current ratio = 3 to 1
- 14.6 Return on assets = 10.5%
- 14.7 Quick ratio = 2.26 to 1
- 14.8 Net income = $800
- 14.9 Return on average total assets = 23%
- 14.10 Accounts receivable turnover = 9.2 times
- 14.11 Operating cycle, Another World = 102 days
- 14.12 Goodyear's quick ratio = .7 to 1
- 14.13 part 9, increase in inventory turnover

COMPREHENSIVE PROBLEM 3

Part II Percentage change in working capital, Dec. 31, 2000 = −13.5%

CHAPTER 15

- 15.1 Profit if sold in U.S. = 3,740 kroner
- 15.2 January 11, gain from decline in exchange rate = $8,000
- 15.3 Earnings before tax = $32.20 (when C$ = $.75)
- 15.4 Profit per unit stated in Maltese Lira = 19.80
- 15.5 No check figures given.
- 15.6 December 31, exchange rate gain on Accounts Payable = $3,600
- 15.7 Percentage of foreign net assets in 2000 = 4.15%